The Handbook of Commodity Investing

The Frank J. Fabozzi Series

Fixed Income Securities, Second Edition by Frank J. Fabozzi
Focus on Value: A Corporate and Investor Guide to Wealth Creation by James L. Grant and James A. Abate
Handbook of Global Fixed Income Calculations by Dragomir Krgin
Managing a Corporate Bond Portfolio by Leland E. Crabbe and Frank J. Fabozzi
Real Options and Option-Embedded Securities by William T. Moore
Capital Budgeting: Theory and Practice by Pamela P. Peterson and Frank J. Fabozzi
The Exchange-Traded Funds Manual by Gary L. Gastineau
Professional Perspectives on Fixed Income Portfolio Management, Volume 3 edited by Frank J. Fabozzi
Investing in Emerging Fixed Income Markets edited by Frank J. Fabozzi and Efstathia Pilarinu
Handbook of Alternative Assets by Mark J. P. Anson
The Global Money Markets by Frank J. Fabozzi, Steven V. Mann, and Moorad Choudhry
The Handbook of Financial Instruments edited by Frank J. Fabozzi
Collateralized Debt Obligations: Structures and Analysis by Laurie S. Goodman and Frank J. Fabozzi
Interest Rate, Term Structure, and Valuation Modeling edited by Frank J. Fabozzi
Investment Performance Measurement by Bruce J. Feibel
The Handbook of Equity Style Management edited by T. Daniel Coggin and Frank J. Fabozzi
The Theory and Practice of Investment Management edited by Frank J. Fabozzi and Harry M. Markowitz
Foundations of Economic Value Added: Second Edition by James L. Grant
Financial Management and Analysis: Second Edition by Frank J. Fabozzi and Pamela P. Peterson
Measuring and Controlling Interest Rate and Credit Risk: Second Edition by Frank J. Fabozzi, Steven V. Mann, and Moorad Choudhry
Professional Perspectives on Fixed Income Portfolio Management, Volume 4 edited by Frank J. Fabozzi
The Handbook of European Fixed Income Securities edited by Frank J. Fabozzi and Moorad Choudhry
The Handbook of European Structured Financial Products edited by Frank J. Fabozzi and Moorad Choudhry
The Mathematics of Financial Modeling and Investment Management by Sergio M. Focardi and Frank J. Fabozzi
Short Selling: Strategies, Risks, and Rewards edited by Frank J. Fabozzi
The Real Estate Investment Handbook by G. Timothy Haight and Daniel Singer
Market Neutral Strategies edited by Bruce I. Jacobs and Kenneth N. Levy
Securities Finance: Securities Lending and Repurchase Agreements edited by Frank J. Fabozzi and Steven V. Mann
Fat-Tailed and Skewed Asset Return Distributions by Svetlozar T. Rachev, Christian Menn, and Frank J. Fabozzi
Financial Modeling of the Equity Market: From CAPM to Cointegration by Frank J. Fabozzi, Sergio M. Focardi, and Petter N. Kolm
Advanced Bond Portfolio Management: Best Practices in Modeling and Strategies edited by Frank J. Fabozzi, Lionel Martellini, and Philippe Priaulet
Analysis of Financial Statements, Second Edition by Pamela P. Peterson and Frank J. Fabozzi
Collateralized Debt Obligations: Structures and Analysis, Second Edition by Douglas J. Lucas, Laurie S. Goodman, and Frank J. Fabozzi
Handbook of Alternative Assets, Second Edition by Mark J. P. Anson
Introduction to Structured Finance by Frank J. Fabozzi, Henry A. Davis, and Moorad Choudhry
Financial Econometrics by Svetlozar T. Rachev, Stefan Mittnik, Frank J. Fabozzi, Sergio M. Focardi, and Teo Jasic

The Handbook of Commodity Investing

FRANK J. FABOZZI
ROLAND FÜSS
DIETER G. KAISER

John Wiley & Sons, Inc.

Published by John Wiley & Sons, Inc., Hoboken, New Jersey.
Published simultaneously in Canada.

For general information on our other products and services or for technical support, please contact our Customer Care Department within the United States at (800) 762–2974, outside the United States at (317) 572–3993 or fax (317) 572–4002.

Wiley also publishes its books in a variety of electronic formats. Some content that appears in print may not be available in electronic formats. For more information about Wiley products, visit our Web site at www.wiley.com.

ISBN-13 978-0-470-11764-4

Printed in the United States of America.

10 9 8 7 6 5 4 3 2 1

Contents

Foreword

"*Those who cannot remember the past are condemned to repeat it.*"—So wrote the philosopher and poet George Santayana about a hundred years ago. He was not writing about commodities, of course, but doubtless he would recognize the conundrum present in today's capital markets. Powerful commodity cycles of significant duration—such as the one we are in—are extremely rare events, separated by such long interludes of weak performance. When they do occur, there are few people around with the specialized knowledge necessary to understand them properly. In other words, each generation of fund managers and asset allocators has to learn afresh about the market characteristics of commodities. This lack of knowledge, together with the opaque nature of many terminal markets, gives commodities an aura of mystery, with the news media often portraying the exchanges as little more than casinos and labeling the market participants as "speculators" rather than "investors."

By trivializing and demonizing investment in commodities, the news media is to some degree responsible for deterring fund managers from making appropriate and profitable asset allocation decisions. For example, at the bottom of the last commodity cycle, the *Financial Times* reduced its commodities coverage to an eighth of one page—tantamount to a news blackout. Small wonder then that many institutions forgot how to trade commodities altogether and had zero asset allocations to commodities. Armed with this handbook—which brings together views from experts in many different fields engaged with the commodities markets—market professionals can gain new illumination as well as confidence in this complex investment process. The chapters in this book allow readers to take a "knowledge shortcut," and, perhaps, avoid some of the pitfalls that lie in wait for the unwary.

Of course, there are many ways of approaching commodity investment. A good starting point is to formulate a top-down view and then calibrate the time horizons over which the chosen strategy plays out. For instance, in the "softs" and "agricultural" markets, traders often focus on short-term, "high-frequency," seasonal cycles that relate, say, to weather patterns in crop-producing areas. So a long-term view in agricultural commodities would be 12 to 24 months—equating to one or two planting and harvesting cycles. Agricultural trading remains dominated by producers and consumers: Financial market investors are relative newcomers to this arena, perhaps put off until now by the sharp swings in the futures curves that are seen from time to time. In the metals markets, on the other hand, trends of shortages and surpluses can persist for years on end, as the supply-side response to high or low prices can be very extended. Building a new copper mine in response to a high copper price might take five years or more. In this case, a long-term view might be measured in years rather than months. As a result, there is usually more depth to the futures markets for metals and plenty of opportunities for investors to take a fundamental view. For strategic commodities such as gold, investors, governments, and central banks might be focusing on cycles of supply and demand measured in decades. Such commodities have efficient and deep futures markets that can sometimes be dominated by financial participants rather than producers and consumers.

A common reason that investors give for seeking commodity exposure—irrespective of their time horizon—is to gain exposure to the so-called "super cycle." Great changes are under way in the world economy, with the urbanization of China and, to a lesser extent, India, driving a massive surge in infrastructure spending. For the first time in history, more people live in cities than in the countryside and their material needs have led to an acceleration in demand-trend growth rates for metals, energy, and food. The supply side has been slow to react fully to this change for many reasons: skills shortages, environmental factors, infrastructure constraints, and political interference. Many commodities have reached "tipping points," flipping from surpluses into shortages.

These changes are proving to be persistent. The shift in the balance of economic growth from the developed world to the developing world shows no sign of reversal. Industries that once existed mainly to serve the developed world now have to reconfigure to feed the new world too—and that takes vast quantities of money and a long period of time. In a nutshell, it is likely that the current period of elevated commodity prices will be prolonged, with the prices of commodities rationing demand rather than supply.

It is the curse of markets that while there is much hard data to analyze about the past, there is no such data about the future. This means that analysts are typically biased toward previous commodity prices when predicting future commodity price behavior. As a consequence, market commentators have been consistently underestimating the price of many commodities. In the 1980s and 1990s, the view that commodity prices always fall in real terms in the long run became deeply entrenched. The slow realization that changes in the structure of the world economy will likely lead to permanent upwards shift in the real cost of raw materials for industry has been hard for many people to accept.

There are, of course, as many ways to gain exposure to the commodity markets as there are reasons for doing so. Some investors, especially pension funds, are looking for diversification. Commodities bring to a larger portfolio returns that are correlated with inflation but are uncorrelated with equities and bonds. This type of investor is usually allocating only a small portion of their asset base to the theme, and has thus far focused predominantly on passive commodity futures strategies. Other investors are focusing more on the long-term returns that are available from procyclical exposure. These strategies can be implemented using either actively managed commodity related equities, or commodity futures. The returns from either of these approaches can be truly spectacular, albeit volatile. The clear trend over time however, is for more assets to be allocated into commodity exposure of various types.

Whatever your motivation for investment in commodities, this book will help to increase your understanding, hence reducing risk and—hopefully—enhancing returns.

Graham Birch, Ph.D.
Managing Director
Head of Global Natural Resources
BlackRock Investment Management (U.K.) Limited

Preface

The Handbook of Commodity Investing provides an overview of the basics and foundations of commodity investing, as well as recent theory and empirical evidence on the commodity markets. The chapters are written by leading practitioners and academics, and explain the complexities of commodity investments, their associated risks, and how investors can optimize their portfolios by including different types of commodity investments. Each chapter contains valuable information relevant to both practitioners, who are currently using or contemplating using commodities as part of their asset allocation, and academics, who are analyzing the commodity markets theoretically or empirically.

The book is divided into six parts. Part One covers the mechanics of the commodity markets. Chapter 1, by Frank Fabozzi, Roland Füss, and Dieter Kaiser, is a primer on the basics of commodity investing. The authors provide insight into the market participants, commodity sectors, commodity exchanges, return components of commodity futures, and the risk and performance characteristics of the sectors. The chapter concludes that, based on a Markowitz mean-variance analysis, commodity futures can yield diversification benefits in a traditional investor portfolio consisting of U.S. and global equities, bonds, and a riskless asset. In Chapter 2, Mark Anson discusses the pricing and economics of commodity futures. Chapter 3, by Joshua Woodard, provides a review of commodity investments in the context of a diversified portfolio in several tactical and strategic dimensions. Chapter 4, by Zeno Adams, Roland Füss, and Dieter Kaiser, explores the macroeconomic determinants of commodity futures returns, and finds that most commodities exhibit an inflation hedge property when compared with U.S. inflation. In Chapter 5, Viola Markert and Heinz Zimmermann discuss the relationship between risk premiums and convenience yield models. They demonstrate, both theoretically and empirically, that the futures term structure, convenience yields, and roll returns largely anticipate subsequent spot price changes. Chapter 6 is a survey by Fritz Helmedag of the different approaches to calculating the optimal rotation period for renewable sources such as the timber sector.

Part Two is devoted to the performance measurement of commodity investments. In Chapter 7, Roland Füss, Christian Hoppe, and Dieter Kaiser provide an overview of commodity futures indexes, and shed new light on the problems arising from the heterogeneity of these benchmarks. Claude Erb, Campbell Harvey, and Christian Kempe highlight in Chapter 8 the problems of determining the strategic value of commodities. In Chapter 9, Reinhold Hafner and Maria Heiden provide a statistical analysis of commodity futures returns using the Dow Jones-AIG commodity index. Bernd Scherer and Li He use the mean-variance spanning test in Chapter 10 to determine whether commodities should be considered an asset class of their own. Chapter 11, by Thomas Schneeweis, Raj Gupta, and Jason Remillard, gives a theoretical overview of the construction of indexes that try to capture the performance of commodity trading advisors (CTAs). The chapter is also an empirical study of the relative performance benefits of CTA strategies.

Part Three covers the important topic of risk management for commodity investments. In Chapter 12, Jeffrey Christian provides an introduction to risk management from a practitioner's perspective. In Chapter 13, Moazzam Khoja offers his seven golden principles for effective risk management of commodity futures portfolios. Chapter 14, by Ted Kury, presents a model of forward prices with time-varying volatility and time-varying correlation. The model can be used to quantify cross-commodity risk in portfolios of futures contracts. In Chapter 15, Chakriya Bowman and Aasim Husain show how futures can be incorporated into commodity price forecasts. Their empirical results suggest that futures prices can provide reasonable guidance about likely spot price developments over the longer term.

Part Four comprises seven chapters that explore how commodity products can be implemented within an investor's asset allocation. In Chapter 16, François-Serge Lhabitant provides an overview of the tools CTAs use to run their futures portfolios, and illustrates how they differ from other commodity investments. Hilary Till and Joseph Eagleeye demonstrate in Chapter 17 how to efficiently design a commodity futures trading program. In Chapter 18, Markus Mezger distinguishes between the different sources of return in commodity investing, showing how investment managers can extract alpha from commodity investing. Juliane Proelss and Denis Schweizer in Chapter 19 demonstrate how to reach the efficient frontier of commodity investments. They stress the importance of analyzing the return distribution characteristics of single commodities before considering them as portfolio diversifiers. In Chapter 20, R. McFall Lamm discusses whether CTAs and hedge funds can be suitable choices for investors seeking active commodity investments. Mark Shore, in Chapter 21, shows how the introduction of commodities, hedge funds, and CTAs can change the risk and performance metrics of a traditional portfolio. He also compares the impacts of these different forms of alternative investments. In Chapter 22, Theo Nijman and

Laurens Swinkels clarify the benefits of commodity investing for investors with a liability structure sensitive to the nominal or real interest rate and inflation.

Part Five presents the various commodity products currently available to investors. In Chapter 23, Lynne Engelke and Jack Yuen provide an overview of the different types of commodity investments. In Chapter 24, Carol Alexander and Aanand Venkatramanan discuss the valuation principles of commodity options. In Chapter 25, Matthias Muck and Markus Rudolf illustrate, both theoretically and empirically, that the nonarbitrage approach cannot be used effectively for pricing nonstorable goods such as electricity forwards. Paul Ali, in Chapter 26, explores the securitization of commodity price risk, explaining how collateralized commodity obligations can be used for financial institutions to hedge credit risk or for investors to obtain exposure to commodity prices in the form of a debt instrument. Chapter 27, by Martin Eling, uses the CISDM CTA indexes to review historical CTA performance using several performance measures. Greg Gregoriou and Fabrice Rouah, in Chapter 28, investigate the performance and the survival of micro CTAs. Their findings suggest that micro CTAs are at high risk of failure, but can nonetheless be attractive investments because of their potential to produce future stars. In Chapter 29, Oliver Engelen and Dieter Kaiser give an overview and statistical analysis of hedge funds investing in energy markets.

The final section, Part Six, covers some of the more important commodity sectors. In Chapter 30, Roland Eller and Christian Sagerer provide a classification scheme for commodities, as well as an overview of all commodity sectors. Charlie Cai, Iain Clacher, Robert Faff, and David Hillier provide a practical guide to gold as an investment asset in Chapter 31. In Chapter 32, Thomas Heidorn and Nadeshda Demidova-Menzel show that gold may be considered a hedge against the U.S. dollar exchange rate for "soft" currencies, but not for the euro. Chapter 33, by Jeffrey Christian, is a fundamental analysis of the world silver market. He shows how silver can be an interesting investment, both on its own and as part of a diversified investment portfolio. Chapter 34, by Michael Killick, is a primer on base metals investing covering an overview of the industry, its market structure, and investment strategies associated with this commodity. Stefan Ulreich, in Chapter 35, covers electricity trading in the European Union, a market where prices are influenced by fuel market movements, weather incidents, political decisions, and the general economy. In Chapter 36, Chris Harris provides an overview of the natural gas market in Great Britain, particularly the relationship of natural gas to other commodities such as oil, electricity, coal, and carbon dioxide. Stefan Ulreich, in Chapter 37, covers emissions trading in the European Union. He concludes that by linking schemes of other countries to the European Union's emissions trading scheme, the market has the potential to become global. Chapter 38 is an overview of commodity market fundamentals for grain, cattle, and hogs by Ronald Spurga, who shows that the driving forces of agricultural commodity prices are characterized by supply, demand, seasonality, carry-over, and the stocks-to-use ratio. Rohit Savant, in Chapter 39, provides a fundamental analysis of the world sugar market, and highlights arbitrage opportunities between futures and options on sugar traded on the Intercontinental Exchange (ICE), Nybot, and the London International Financial Futures and Options Exchange (LIFFE).

We wish to express our deepest gratitude to the contributors to this book. We are delighted by the efforts every single author put into their chapters, despite their already overwhelming workloads, to create what we believe to be a landmark commodity investing book. We are also very grateful to Graham Birch for providing the foreword. Finally, we would like to thank our families for continued understanding and support of this book project.

Frank J. Fabozzi
Roland Füss
Dieter G. Kaiser

About the Editors

Frank J. Fabozzi is Professor in the Practice of Finance and Becton Fellow in the School of Management at Yale University. Prior to joining the Yale faculty, he was a Visiting Professor of Finance in the Sloan School at MIT. Professor Fabozzi is a Fellow of the International Center for Finance at Yale University and on the Advisory Council for the Department of Operations Research and Financial Engineering at Princeton University. He is the editor of the *Journal of Portfolio Management.* He earned a doctorate in economics from the City University of New York in 1972. In 2002, Professor Fabozzi was inducted into the Fixed Income Analysts Society's Hall of Fame and is the 2007 recipient of the C. Stewart Sheppard Award given by the CFA Institute. He earned the designation of Chartered Financial Analyst and Certified Public Accountant. He has authored and edited numerous books about finance.

Dieter G. Kaiser is a Director, Alternative Investments, in the hedge fund portfolio management team at Feri Institutional Advisors GmbH in Bad Homburg, Germany, where he also runs a fund of commodity hedge funds. From 2003 to 2007, he was responsible for institutional research at Benchmark Alternative Strategies GmbH in Frankfurt, Germany. He has written several articles on alternative investments (hedge funds, venture capital, and commodities) that have been published in renowned academic and professional journals. He is also the author and editor of seven books. Dieter Kaiser holds a Diploma in Business Administration from the University of Applied Sciences Offenburg, a Master of Arts in Banking and Finance from the Frankfurt School of Finance and Management, and a Ph.D. in Finance from the Chemnitz University of Technology. On the academic side, he is a Research Fellow at the Centre of Practical Quantitative Finance at the Frankfurt School of Finance and Management.

Roland Füss is a full professor in the Department of Finance, Accounting and Real Estate at the European Business School (EBS), International University Schloss Reichartshausen in Oestrich-Winkel, Germany. He holds a diploma in Business Administration from the University of Applied Science in Lörrach, and a diploma in Economics from the University of Freiburg, Germany, where he also obtained his Ph.D. and his Habilitation.

From 2000 to 2007, he worked at the University of Freiburg as research assistant and lecturer in the Department of Applied Econometrics, and assistant professor in the Department of Finance and Banking. His research focuses on alternative investments, politics and financial markets, risk management, and applied econometrics. Professor Füss has authored numerous articles in finance journals as well as book chapters. He is a member of the Verein für Socialpolitik, the German Finance Association, and the German Academic Association for Business Research.

Contributing Authors

Zeno Adams	University of Freiburg
Commerzbank Ag	Frankfurt School of Finance and Management
Carol Alexander	University of Reading
Paul U. Ali	Melbourne University Law School
Mark J. P. Anson	Hermes Pensions Management Ltd.
Chakriya Bowman	Australian National University
Charlie X. Cai	The University of Leeds
Jeffrey M. Christian	CPM Group
lain Clacher	The University of Leeds
Nadeshda Demidova-Menzel	Equinet AG (ESN)
Joseph Eagleeye	Premia Capital Management, LLC
Martin Eling	University of St. Gallen
Roland Eller	Roland Eller Consulting GmbH
Oliver Engelen	Benchmark Capital Management GmbH
Lynne Engelke	Citi Alternative Investments
Claude Erb	Managing Director TCW
Frank J. Fabozzi	Yale University
Robert Faff	The University of Leeds
Roland Füss	University of Freiburg
Greg N. Gregoriou	State University of New York (Plattsburgh)
Raj Gupta	University of Massachusetts
Reinhold Hafner	Risklab Germany GmbH
Chris Harris	Networks and Agreements RWE npower
Campbell R. Harvey	Duke University
Li He	QS Research Center, Deutsche Asset Management, New York
Maria Heiden	Risklab Germany GmbH
Thomas Heidorn	Frankfurt School of Finance and Management
David Hillier	The University of Leeds
Fritz Helmedag	Chemnitz University of Technology
Christian Hoppe	Senior Specialist Securitization and Credit Derivatives
Aasim M. Husain	International Monetary Fund

Dieter G. Kaiser	Frankfurt School of Finance and Management
Christian Kempe	Berlin & Co
Moazzam Khoja	Sungard Kiodex
Michael Killick	Lincoln Vale Group
Ted Kury	The Energy Authority®
François-Serge Lhabitant	HEC Lausanne and EDHEC Business School
Viola Markert	CYD Research GmbH
R. McFallLamm, Jr.	Global Investment Management Deutsche Bank
Markus Mezger	Tiberius Asset Management
Matthias Muck	University of Bamberg
Theo E. Nijman	Tilburg University
Juliane Proelss	European Business School, International University
Jason Remillard	University of Massachusetts
Fabrice Douglas Rouah	State Street Corporation
Markus Rudolf	WHU–Otto Beisheim School of Management
Christian Sagerer	JPMorgan Chase Bank
Rohit Savant	CPM Group
Bernd Scherer	Morgan Stanley Investment Management
Thomas Schneeweis	University of Massachusetts
Denis Schweizer	European Business School, International University
Mark S. Shore	Alternative Investment Consultant
Ronald C. Spurga	ABN AMRO Bank
Laurens A. P. Swinkels	Erasmus University Rotterdam
Hilary Till	Premia Capital Management, LLC
Stefan Ulreich	E.ON Energie AG
Aanand Venkatramanan	University of Reading
Joshua D. Woodard	University of Illinois
Jack C. Yuen	Citi Alternative Investments
Heinz Zimmermann	University of Basel

PART One

Mechanics of the Commodity Market

CHAPTER 1

A Primer on Commodity Investing

Frank J. Fabozzi, Ph.D., CFA
Professor in the Practice of Finance
School of Management
Yale University

Roland Füss, Ph.D.
Professor of Finance
Endowed Chair of Asset Management
European Business School (EBS)
International University Schloss Reichartshausen

Dieter G. Kaiser, Ph.D.
Director Alternative Investments
Feri Institutional Advisors GmbH
Research Fellow
Centre for Practical Quantitative Finance
Frankfurt School of Finance and Management

Commodities are currently enjoying a renaissance due to institutional investors such as pension funds and traditional portfolio managers. Many market participants attribute the recent dramatic price increases in commodities to increased demand for consumer goods, particularly from the populous countries of India and China. Demand from Brazil and Russia, two of the fastest-growing economies currently, has undoubtedly also played a part. (Collectively, these four countries are referred to as the *BRIC countries*.)

Globalization and economic and political convergence have been behind the stimulated growth in these economies to a large extent. Besides increased investment on an enterprise level, increasing state investment in infrastructure in China has also led to enormous demand for commodities. This has caused a shock to the worldwide supply and demand dynamics, leading to at least short-term price increases.

Such dramatic increases in commodity prices are often explained by the *commodity super cycle theory*. According to Heap, a *super cycle* is a lasting boom in real commodity prices, usually brought on by urbanization and industrialization in a major economy.[1] Hence, super cycles are driven by demand caused by an expansion of material-based production due to intense economic activity. The economic situation in China is of crucial importance to the commodity markets. China has greatly increased its share of global commodity consumption over the past few years, and is seen as the major driver of the current commodity boom.

For example, between 2001 and 2005, China's demand for copper, aluminum, and iron increased by 78%, 85%, and 92%, respectively. This clearly shows China's considerable influence on commodity pricing. This super cycle, however, is not characterized by a continuous growth phase, as the events of May 2006 show. Many commodities were under pressure during that time, and actually lost about one-fourth of their value.

Under market conditions like these, the question inevitably arises as to whether this is a temporary price correction or a general trend change. Following the super cycle theory, a long-lasting upward trend in commodities in the future is likely, as most remain far below their historic highs when adjusted for inflation.

Compared to foreign exchange or equity markets, there is almost no way to intervene in commodity markets. Because the production side reacts very sluggishly to market distortions, short-term supply and demand shocks are compensated for only by price movements.[2] These inherent asset class volatilities are the main reason many investors have refrained from investing in commodities, despite the fact they can provide valuable diversification

---

[1]Alan Heap, "China—The Engine of Commodities Super Cycle," *Citigroup Global Equity Research* (March 2005). The past 200 years have seen several such upswings, lasting from between 15 and 25 years. For example, in the late nineteenth century, industrialization in the United States triggered such a boom. The postwar period of 1945 to 1975, when enormous resources were needed to rebuild Europe, can also be characterized as a super cycle.

[2]In contrast, central banks possess a variety of money market instruments to maintain the value and stability of their currency. At the same time, central banks can control—at least to some extent—the economic development of an economy through changes in interest rates to avoid inflationary or deflationary tendencies.

benefits to traditional security portfolios because of their low correlation with bonds and stocks.[3]

This chapter first discusses the basics of commodity markets by describing the market participants, the commodity subsectors, and the different kinds of commodity investment vehicles available to investors. Subsequently, we illustrate the return components of index-based, that is, passive long-only, commodity futures investments in the context of the price discovery process, and we investigate the risk/return characteristics of commodity futures indexes. Following this, we provide an empirical analysis of portfolio allocation of traditional security portfolios, explicitly taking commodity futures into account.

MARKET PARTICIPANTS

Futures market participants are normally classified into hedgers, speculators (traders), and arbitrageurs. Commodity producers pass on the price risk that results from highly volatile and difficult to forecast commodity futures markets to speculators, and therefore pay a premium. Commodity producers have a distinct interest in hedging the price of their product in advance (a short hedge).

For example, consider the situation in the classic agricultural market. Farmers face a weather-dependent, volatile supply that is met by a relatively stable demand. Contrary to the maintenance cost for cattle breeding or the purchase cost of seed, the selling price generally is known only upon completion.

We see the opposite in the manufacturing industry: As the manufacturing industry hedges increasing commodity prices (a long hedge), the contrarian position to the commodity producers' short positions is taken. Airline companies, for example, often appear as long hedgers to guard against increasing fuel prices, the underlying in which the airline companies are short. If an existing or expected cash position is compensated for via an opposite future, the market participant is classified as a *hedger*. Hence, for the commodity producer, there is a fixed net profit; for the commodity manufacturer, there is a fixed purchase price.

Speculators represent the largest group in the futures markets. Their main task is to provide liquidity on the one hand, while balancing the long and short hedges on the other hand. Contrary to the commodity producers or the manufacturing industry, which try to avoid susceptibility to

[3]Kenneth A. Froot, "Hedging Portfolios with Real Assets," *Journal of Portfolio Management* (Summer 1995), pp. 60–77.

unfavorable price developments, the intention of speculators is to take a distinct market position and speculate for a price change. To make a profit, speculators deliberately take on risk by betting on rising or falling prices. As opposed to hedging, speculation is subject to both huge gains and huge losses, since speculators do not hold compensating cash positions.

The third and smallest group of market participants is the *arbitrageurs*, who try to take advantage of time- or location-based price differences in commodity futures markets, or between spot and futures markets, in order to generate riskless profits. Clearly, this group also intends to make profits, but their trading activity does not involve taking risky positions. Moreover, they use economic and financial data to detect existing price differences with respect to time and location. If these price differences exceed interlocal or intertemporal transfer costs such as shipping, interest rates, warehouse costs, or insurance costs, riskless profits can be realized. Consequently, price differences among the markets are adjusted, price relationships among the markets are restored, and arbitrageurs guarantee market balancing.

In the case of cash and carry arbitrage, the resale price of today's leveraged spot position is simultaneously set by selling the commodity futures. This short futures position implies an unconditional commitment to purchase the underlying at maturity. At maturity of the futures, the specified commodities are tendered against the maturing short futures. If the profit from the spot trade of the physical commodity exceeds the value of the futures plus the cost of debt financing, the arbitrageur will realize a profit from what is known as a *basis trade*.

COMMODITY SECTORS

Investments in international commodity markets differ greatly from other investments in several important ways. First, commodities are real assets—primarily consumption and not investment goods. They have an intrinsic value, and provide utility by use in industrial manufacturing or in consumption. Furthermore, supply is limited because in any given period, commodities have only a limited availability. For example, renewable commodities like grains can be produced virtually without limitation. However, their yearly harvest is strictly limited. In addition, the supply of certain commodities shows a strong seasonal component. While metals can be mined almost all year, agricultural commodities like soybeans depend on the harvesting cycle.

Another important aspect of commodities as an asset class is heterogeneity. The quality of commodities is not standardized; every commodity has its own specific properties. A common way to classify them is to distinguish between soft and hard commodities. *Hard commodities* are products from the energy, precious metals, and industrial metals sectors. *Soft commodities* are usually weather-dependent, perishable commodities for consumption from the agricultural sector, such as grains, soybeans, or livestock, such as cattle or hogs. Exhibit 1.1 show the classification of commodity sectors.

Storability and availability (or renewability) are also important features of commodities. However, because storability plays a decisive role in pricing, we distinguish between storable and nonstorable commodities. A commodity is said to have a high degree of storability if it is not perishable and the cost of storage remains low with respect to its total value. Industrial metals such as aluminum or copper are prime examples: They fulfill both criteria to a high degree. In contrast, livestock is storable to only a limited degree, as it must be continuously fed and housed at current costs, and is only profitable in a specific phase of its life cycle.

Commodities such as silver, gold, crude oil, and aluminum are nonrenewable. The supply of nonrenewable commodities depends on the ability of producers to mine raw material in both sufficient quantity and sufficient quality.

The availability of commodity manufacturing capacities also influences supply. For some metals (excluding precious metals) and crude oil, the discovery and exploration of new reserves of raw materials is still an important issue. The price of nonrenewable resources depends strongly on current investor demand, while the price of renewable resources depends more on estimated future production costs.[4] The monetary benefit from holding a commodity physically instead of being long the respective futures is called the *convenience yield*. The convenience yield reflects market participants' expectations regarding a possible future scarcity of a short-term nonrenewable commodity.

COMMODITIES AS AN ASSET CLASS OF THEIR OWN

There is a broad consensus among academics and practitioners that commodities compared to other alternative assets can be considered—in a portfolio context—as an asset class of their own.[5] By definition, an asset class consists of similar assets that show a homogeneous risk-return profile (a

[4]The events following Hurricane Katrina in 2005 clearly illustrated the insufficiency of the refinery capacities for crude oil and natural gas. Declining investment in this sector over the years has led to a bottleneck. The absence of investment in the industrial metals sector is also an issue for the supply side.

[5]In reality, most alternative investments such as hedge funds or private equity are not an asset class in their own, but are considered alternative investment strategies within an existing asset class.

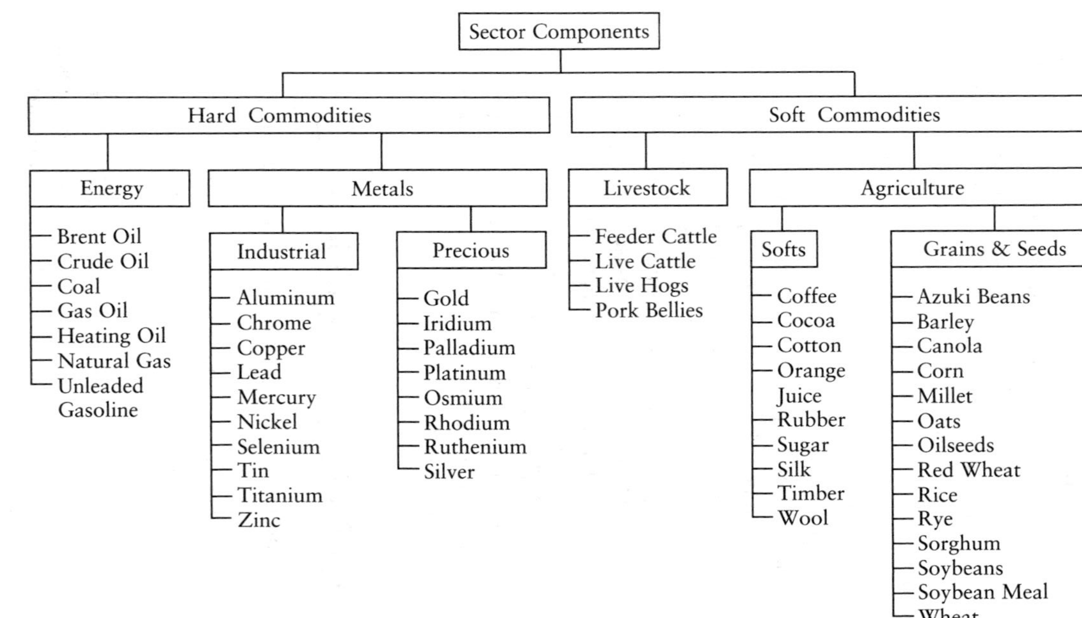

EXHIBIT 1.1 Classification of Commodity Sectors

high internal correlation), and a heterogeneous risk-return profile toward other asset classes (a low external correlation). The key properties are common value drivers, and not necessarily common price patterns. This is based on the idea that a separate asset class contains a unique risk premium that cannot be replicated by combining other asset classes.[6] Furthermore, it is generally required that the long-term returns and liquidity from an asset class are significant to justify an allocation.

To describe existing asset classes, Greer explains the decomposition into so-called super classes: *capital assets, store of value assets*, and *consumable or transferable assets*.[7] Continuous performance is a characteristic of capital assets. Equity capital like stocks provides a continuous stream of dividend payments, while fixed income guarantees regular interest payments in the absence of the default of the obligor. Redemption of invested loan capital can then be allocated among other investments.

Common to all capital assets is that their valuation follows the net present value method by discounting expected future cash flows. In contrast, real estate as an asset class has a hybrid classification. On the one hand, real estate can be classified as a capital asset because it promises a continuous rental stream and has market value. On the other hand, some features of real estate assets can justify their classification as store of value assets (for example, if the real estate is used for the owner's own purpose). Such store of value assets cannot be consumed, nor do they generate income; classic examples are foreign exchange, art, and antiquities.

Commodities belong to the third super class—*consumable or transferable* (C/T) assets. In contrast to stocks and bonds, C/T assets, physical commodities like energy, grains, or livestock, do not generate continuous cash flows, but rather have an economic value. Grains, for example, can be consumed or used as input goods; crude oil is manufactured into a variety of products. This difference is what makes commodities a unique asset class.

Hence, it is obvious that commodity prices cannot be determined by the net present value method or by discounting future cash flows. Thus, interest rates have only a minor influence on the value of commodities. Moreover, commodity prices are the result of the interaction between supply and demand on specific markets.[8] In this context, it is not surprising that the

---

[6]Bernd Scherer, "Commodities as an Asset Class: Testing for Mean Variance Spanning under Arbitrary Constraints," *Deutsche Bank—An Investors' Guide to Commodities* (April 2005), pp. 35–42.

[7]Robert J. Greer, "What is an Asset Class, Anyway?" *Journal of Portfolio Management* (Winter 1997), pp. 86–91.

[8]James H. Scott, "Managing Asset Classes," *Financial Analysts Journal* (January–February 1994), pp. 62–69.

capital asset pricing model (CAPM) cannot adequately explain commodity futures returns. As we have noted, commodities are not capital assets.[9]

The line between the super classes is blurred in the case of gold. On the one hand, gold as a commodity is used in such things as electrical circuitry because of its excellent conductivity. On the other hand, gold as a store of value asset is a precious metal and is used for investment, similarly to currencies. The rising demand of commodities since the stock market downturn in 2002 clearly demonstrates this characteristic. Because gold can be leased, Anson has even classified it as a capital asset.[10]

Another specific criterion that differentiates commodities from capital assets is that commodities are denominated worldwide in U.S. dollars, while the value of a specific commodity is determined through global rather than regional supply and demand. In comparison, equity markets reflect the respective economic development within a country or a region.

Prospects for Commodity Market Participation

In general, there are several ways to participate in commodity markets via a number of different kinds of financial instruments. The most important are (1) direct investment in the physical good; (2) indirect investment in stocks of natural resource companies or (3) commodity mutual funds; (4) an investment in commodity futures, or (5) an investment in structured products on commodity futures indexes.

---

[9]The two components of risk, systematic (market) and unsystematic (company-specific), are considered within the CAPM framework. Since unsystematic risk is eliminated in a broadly diversified portfolio, investors are only compensated for systematic risk. The risk premium is then the product of systematic risk (beta) multiplied by the market price of risk, defined as the difference between the expected return of the market portfolio and the riskless interest rate. In the CAPM, the market portfolio is composed only of stocks and bonds, so commodity returns cannot be represented by financial market returns. Thus, it is not possible to distinguish between systematic and unsystematic risk. Finally, commodity prices depend on global supply and demand and not on the perception of the market regarding an adequate risk premium for a specific asset class. See Claude Erb and Campbell R. Harvey, "The Tactical and Strategic Value of Commodity Futures," *Financial Analysts Journal* (April/May 2006), pp. 69–97; and Zvi Bodie and Victor I. Rosansky, "Risk and Return in Commodity Futures," *Financial Analysts Journal* (May/June 1980), pp. 27–39.

[10]Precious metals such as gold, silver, or platinum can generate a lucrative stream of income by being leased at market leasing rates. See Mark J. P. Anson, *The Handbook of Alternative Assets*, 2nd ed. (Hoboken, NJ: John Wiley & Sons, 2006).

Buying the Physical Good

First, it seems obvious to invest directly in commodities by purchasing the physical goods at the spot market. However, immediate or within-two-days delivery is frequently not practical for investors. According to Geman, precious metals such as gold, silver, or platinum are an exception, as they do not have high current costs and do not require storage capacity.[11] However, a portfolio consisting solely of precious metals would not be a sufficiently diversified portfolio for investors to hold.

Commodity Stocks

An investment in commodity stocks (*natural resource companies*), which generate a majority of their profits by buying and selling physical commodities, may conceivably be considered an alternative investment strategy. In general, the term "commodity stock" cannot be clearly differentiated. It consists of listed companies that are related to commodities (i.e., those that explore, mine, refine, manufacture, trade, or supply commodities to other companies). Such an indirect investment in commodities (e.g., the purchase of petrochemical stocks) is only an insufficient substitute for a direct investment. By investing in such stocks, investors do not receive direct exposure to commodities because listed natural resource companies all have their own characteristics and inherent risks.

Georgiev shows that these sector-specific stocks are only slightly correlated with commodity prices, and hence prices of commodity stocks do not completely reflect the performance of the underlying market.[12] This is because stocks reflect other price-relevant factors such as the strategic position of the company, management quality, capital structure (the debt/equity ratio), the expectations and ratings of company and profit growth, risk sensitivity, as well as information transparency and information credibility.[13]

Stock markets also show quick and more sensible reactions to expected developments that can impact company value. Hence, other causes of independent price discovery exist that differ from a pure commodity investment. Moreover, there may be temporary market disequilibriums, especially for stocks with low free float, where few buy and sell transactions can already cause major price reactions. Finally, natural resource companies are subject to operational risk caused by human or technical failure, internal

[11]Hélyette Geman, *Commodities and Commodity Derivatives: Modeling and Pricing for Agriculturals, Metals and Energy* (Chichester: John Wiley & Sons, 2005).
[12]Georgi Georgiev, Benefits of Commodity Investment, Working Paper, 2005.
[13]For example, consider the poor information policy of Shell in the matter of the Brent Spar oil platform in 1995, which led to a massive stock price decline.

regulations, or external events. This means that when investing in a company listed on the stock exchange, both the associated market risk as well as any idiosyncratic risk must be considered carefully.[14]

However, the risk of commodity stocks is not completely reflected in the price volatility. First, particularly in the energy and metal sectors, there is the paradox that companies threaten their own business fundamentals by extracting exhaustible resources. On the one hand, long-term decreasing total reserves mean rising prices and a positive prospective for investors and commodity producers. On the other hand, commodity producers suffer when resources are depleted.

Second, there is always the risk of a total loss if prices decrease below total production costs and the extraction of a commodity is stopped. By constructing an index consisting of commodity stocks, Gorton and Rouwenhorst show empirically that observed return correlations with commodity futures are even lower than those with the S&P 500.[15] Furthermore, the commodity stock index exhibits lower historical returns than a direct commodity investment.[16]

Commodity Funds

Finally, in contrast to an investment in commodity stocks, one can actively invest in commodity funds, realizing an adequate diversification benefit with moderate transaction costs. Commodity funds differ in terms of management style, allocation strategy, geographic, and temporal investment horizon in the denominated currency, and investment behavior. It is also important for investors to distinguish between active and passive funds (i.e., index tracking funds). Commodity stock indexes (e.g., the MSCI World Materials, the FTSE World Mining, the HSBC Global Mining, the Morgan Stanley Commodity Related Index, the FTSE World Oil, and Gas, or the FTSE Goldmines) and commodity futures indexes can be used to benchmark actively managed commodity funds. *Commodity trading advisors* (CTAs) also present an alternative to actively managed investment products. Today, there are also about 450 hedge funds with energy- and commodity-related trading strategies.

---

[14]Note that the majority of large oil and energy companies hedge the risk associated with buying and selling oil products in order to smooth yearly profits.

[15]Gary Gorton and K. Geert Rouwenhorst, "Facts and Fantasies about Commodity Futures," *Financial Analysts Journal* (April–May 2006), pp. 47–68.

[16]For example, the returns of European oil companies covary strongly with EuroStoxx, but less with oil price returns. Exceptions are gold and silver stocks, whose beta to the domestic stock index is smaller than the beta to the gold and silver price.

Commodity Futures Indexes

Nowadays, investors can choose from an increasing number of investible commodity futures indexes as a *passive* form of investing in commodities (see Exhibit 1.2). Commodities have an exceptional position among alternative investments because they provide investible indexes for a broad universe of commodity sectors. According to Doyle, Hill, and Jack, between U.S. $55 billion and $60 billion were invested in the Goldman Sachs Commodity Index (GSCI) in March 2007, and another U.S. $15 billion was linked to the Dow Jones-AIG Commodity Index.[17] Estimates for December 2006 state that about U.S. $90 billion of invested capital from pension and mutual funds are invested in commodity-based indexes or products.[18]

For the majority of investors, an index-oriented investment represents the most reasonable way to obtain exposure to commodities or an individual commodity sector. Such an investment can be done cost-effectively using the following two types of financial products:

- Exchange-traded funds (ETFs) on commodity indexes.
- Commodity index certificates closely tied to commodity indexes.

Index funds have the advantage of being relatively easy to trade and reasonably priced. Another advantage of funds over certificates is the nonexisting credit risk of the issuer. Because ETFs represent special assets, investor deposits are safe even if the investment company goes bankrupt.

Certificates constitute legal obligations that can be quickly and fairly cheaply issued by banks. In the case of commodity index certificates, the issuing institution invests in futures markets and rolls the futures contracts for a fee. The term of a certificate is normally restricted to a fixed date (e.g., rainbow certificates, whose underlyings are different subindexes or asset classes, or discount and bonus certificates). But there are also open-end certificates.

However, because the indexes, like the commodities themselves, are denominated in U.S. dollars, investors are exposed to currency risk. Quanto certificates, discount certificates with a currency hedge, can be used to mitigate this risk.

[17]Emmet Doyle, Jonathan Hill, and Ian Jack, Growth in Commodity Investment: Risks and Challenges for Commodity Market Participants, Financial Services Authority, Working Paper, 2007.

[18]In 2001, the total invested capital in the GSCI was between $4 billion and $5 billion. At the beginning of 2007, Standard & Poor's acquired the GSCI Commodity Index, which was subsequently renamed the S&P GSCI Commodity Index.

EXHIBIT 1.2 Commodity Futures Indexes

	Reuters/Jefferies Commodity Research Bureau (RJ/CRB)	Goldman Sachs Commodity Index (GSCI)	DowJones/AIG Commodity Index (DJ-AIGCI)
Introduced in	2005	1991	1998
Historical data available since	1982	1970	1991
Number of commodities	19	24	19
Weighting scheme	Within a graduated system of four groups, based on liquidity and economic relevance	Rolling five-year average of world production	Liquidity data, in conjunction with dollar-weighted production from the past five years
Rebalancing frequency	Monthly	Yearly	Yearly
Allocation restrictions	None	None	33% maximum per sector; 2% market minimum per commodity
Relevant futures price on which the index calculation is based	Next futures contract/delivery month	Next month with sufficient liquidity	Next futures contract/delivery month
Roll period	4 Days	5 Days	5 Days
Calculation method	Arithmetic	Arithmetic	Arithmetic

The main disadvantage of index certificates is that they often use excess return indexes as the underlying instrument. These indexes do not consider all the return components, in contrast to total return indexes, which may lead to lower returns during periods of high interest rates. Investing in a low performance excess return index compared to a total return index can nevertheless be an advantage because the latter bears little or no initial costs and no yearly management fees. Hence, for investors with short-term investment horizons, certificates on excess return indexes with lower returns can be a smart choice during periods of low interest rates.

Another disadvantage of index-based commodity investments is that due to their construction, they can only consider short-term futures contracts. Commodity funds not linked to commodity indexes, however, can freely determine their optimal term by investing directly in commodity futures contracts. And similarly to purchasing rainbow certificates on different asset classes, there is also the possibility of purchasing commodity funds that do not invest exclusively in commodity indexes, but also include commodity stocks to a certain extent.

Commodity Futures

In addition to options and other derivatives, commodity products are based primarily on futures contracts. A futures contract is a mutual binding agreement between two parties to deliver or accept and pay (or undertake a cash settlement): (1) a qualitative explicitly determined underlying (in this case commodities); (2) in a certain quantity; (3) at a fixed date; and (4) at a fixed, already at conclusion of the contract determined price. Futures can be described as mutually binding, exchange-traded "unconditional" forward contracts, since the conclusion of a futures contract leads to a legally binding accomplishment in the future if there is no compensating contrary transaction.[19]

Contract sizes in the commodity market are standardized. The smallest tradable unit represents a contract, and the smallest possible price change of a futures is called a *tick*. The value of the minimum price change is the U.S. dollar and cent-denominated tick, multiplied by the contract size (also known as the *point value*) of the commodity. It is common practice to deposit a margin for every futures contract. The amount is determined by the exchange, but it is usually between 2% and 10% of the contract.[20]

[19]In contrast, in the case of conditional forward contracts such as options, the option holder has no obligation to exercise his option right, and can thus abandon the option at maturity.

[20]However, futures commission merchants may charge higher margins than the exchanges.

However, the margin changes according to the price and volatility of the contract.

In this context, we also distinguish between the initial margin, the minimum deposit required to invest in a futures contract, and the maintenance margin, the minimum deposit required to be on account at the exchange as long as the futures position is held. If the capital deposit on the account falls to or below the value of the maintenance margin due to price variations, the broker issues a margin call to recoup the initial value of the clients' capital. If an investor does not want to increase the margin, he can also close part of or the entire position, and accept a loss. For collateral in terms of the initial margin, investors in futures receive interest income from money market interest.

Generally, for commodity futures, there are two forms of settlement: delivery of the commodity at maturity, which happens in about 2% of the cases, and closing the futures position (i.e., buying or selling the same amount of contracts before maturity). Daily price limits are a specific characteristic of commodity futures markets. They were established to allow the market to stabilize during times of extreme movements (e.g., a cooling-off phase).[21] Hence, daily price limits, again determined by the exchange, represent the maximum possible increase or decrease of a commodity price from the settlement price of the preceding trading day. In the case of limit up (limit down), the sellers (buyers) are outnumbered by buyers (sellers) who are willing to buy (sell) at the upper (lower) price limit. At this price limit, there may still be trading activity, but it may not exceed (limit up) or fall short of (limit down) the price limit.

The following are the contract specifications published regularly by the futures exchanges:

- *The type and quality of the futures underlying.* The type of commodity, abbreviation, and futures exchange.
- *The contract size.* The amount and units of the underlying asset per futures contract.
- *Price determination.* The formal notation of futures prices at the futures exchange.
- *Trading hours.*
- *The tick.* The minimum permissible price fluctuation.
- *The currency* in which the futures contract is quoted.
- *The daily price limit.*

[21]Franklin R. Edwards and Salah Neftci, "Extreme Price Movements and Margin Levels in Futures Markets," *Journal of Futures Markets* (December 1998), pp. 639–655.

- *The last trading date.*
- *Delivery regulations* (e.g., delivery month, type of settlement).

Investors in commodity futures can profit from price movements of the underlying commodity without having to fulfill the logistical or storage requirements connected with a direct purchase. However, this is only possible if the position is closed before maturity. The advantages of futures investments lie especially in the tremendous flexibility and leveraged nature of the futures position due to the low capital requirements. Thus, a shift of an existing futures position is possible at any time, even in the short term. By holding long or short positions, investors can profit from rising and falling markets. Furthermore, the futures markets are characterized by a high degree of liquidity and low transaction costs.

Despite the numerous advantages of an active investment in commodity futures, it is not always advisable for a private investor to take futures positions in such volatile commodities. Even if diversification by a large number of different futures contracts were guaranteed, the investor would still face the problem of maintaining an exposure to commodity prices without the liability of physical delivery of the underlying contract. This requires continuously closing existing futures positions and reestablishing new positions by opening more futures contracts. This is referred to as *rolling of futures contracts*, and it may be quite costly depending on the forward curve of the futures market.[22] In addition, falling futures prices may constantly trigger margin calls (although margins can be withdrawn if the futures prices increase). Overall, however, compared to traditional assets, managing futures positions requires a great deal of time and effort.[23]

COMMODITY EXCHANGES

The trading of commodity futures takes place at specialized exchanges that function as public marketplaces, where commodities are purchased and sold at a fixed price for a fixed delivery date. Commodity futures exchanges are mostly structured as membership associations, and operate for the benefit of

[22]An active, indirect investment in commodities can be achieved by purchasing futures contracts and closing them prior to maturity. In order to keep an exposure to commodities, investors must buy another futures contract with a later maturity date (this is called *rolling*, and must be repeated before each maturity date).

[23]It is also possible to invest in commodity swaps and forwards. These instruments, however, are of minor liquidity since they are tailor-made for individual investors. Furthermore, these derivatives are not traded at the exchange, and commodity investment strategies of individual investors cannot be publicly observed.

their members. Transactions must be made as standardized futures contracts by a broker who is also a member of the exchange. Only members are allowed to trade.[24] The main task of a commodity exchange is to provide an organized marketplace with uniform rules and standardized contracts.

The first commodity exchange was founded by Japanese farmers trading rice futures contracts in Osaka. In the United States, the Chicago Board of Trade, founded in 1848, was the first institution. Even today, most commodities are still traded there.[25] The British London Metal Exchange was founded in 1877.

Energy futures trading, however, only began with the foundation of the International Petroleum Exchange (IPE) in London in 1980.[26] Trading of WTI crude oil at the New York Mercantile Exchange (NYMEX) began in 1983; trading of Brent crude oil began in 1988. In terms of traded volume, the Chicago Mercantile Exchange (CME), founded in 1998, is the world's most important futures exchange. There are about 30 commodity exchanges worldwide; the most important are listed in Exhibit 1.3. Based on traded volume, the majority of commodity futures trading takes place in the United States, United Kingdom, Japan, and China.

PRICES AT THE COMMODITY FUTURES EXCHANGES

Backwardation and Contango

One of the primary questions regarding commodity futures is the existence of risk premiums in commodity markets.[27] In this context, we refer to the price discovery and the related term structure of commodity futures markets. Assuming that the spot futures arbitrage relationship holds, the valid futures price of a commodity at time t and the remaining time to maturity T, $F(t,T)$ equals the cash price $S(t)$, multiplied by the continuously compounded riskless interest rate r (storage cost is neglected here):

$$F_0 = S_0 e^{rT} \tag{1.1}$$

---

[24]Membership in commodity exchanges is restricted to individuals who often act in the name of investment banks, brokers, or producers.

[25]According to Geman, in the United States most futures exchanges still function as open outcry trading systems, although many exchanges around the world operate on an electronic platform. See Geman, *Commodities and Commodity Derivatives: Modeling and Pricing for Agriculturals, Metals and Energy*, p. 11.

[26]Since 2005, the IPE operates under the name ICE Futures.

[27]See Kat and Oomen, "What Every Investor Should Know About Commodities: Part I."

EXHIBIT 1.3 Major Commodity Exchanges

Exchange Name	Abbreviation	Country	Traded Futures	Web Site
Chicago Board of Trade	CBOT	U.S.	Agricultural products and oil	cbot.com
Chicago Mercantile Exchange	CME	U.S.	Agricultural products and livestock	cme.com
New York Mercantile Exchange	NYMEX	U.S.	Energy and metals	nymex.com
Intercontinental Exchange	ICE	U.K.	Energy	theice.com
London Metal Exchange	LME	U.K.	Metals	lme.co.uk
Winnipeg Commodity Exchange	WCE	Canada	Agricultural products	wce.ca
Tokyo Commodity Exchange	TOCOM	Japan	Energy and metals	tocom.or.jp
Shanghai Metal Exchange	SHME	China	Metals	shme.com
Dalian Commodity Exchange	DCE	China	Agricultural products and oil	dce.com.cn
Brazilian Mercantile and Futures Exchange	BM&F	Brazil	Agricultural products	bmf.com.br
Risk Management Exchange	RMX	Germany	Agricultural products and livestock	wtb-hannover.de
National Commodity and Derivatives Exchange	NCDEX	India	Agricultural products and metals	ncdex.com

In contrast to financial securities, commodities, however, do involve storage costs. Let U_t denote the cash value of storage costs, which are assumed to be proportional to the commodities' price and can thus be interpreted as a negative return:

$$F_0 = S_0 e^{(r+U)T} \tag{1.2}$$

However, the aforementioned arbitrage relationship does not hold for commodities. Note that the spot futures parity varies from the future parity, which states that the futures price observed today is an undistorted estimate of the cash price $E_t[S(T)]$ at maturity. If we consider the forward curve of a specific commodity displaying the future price at different maturity dates of the contract, we observe two different trends: In the case of *backwardation*, the term structure curve has a negative trend (i.e., futures prices with longer time to maturity are lower than current spot prices, $F_{t,T} < S_t$ for increasing T). Hence, the investment return lies on average above the forward premium (i.e., an investor can generate profits by holding long positions in the respective futures contracts). In the case of *contango*, however, the opposite holds, based on the assumption of rational expectations. In a *contangoed* situation, the futures price lies above the actual spot price—hence the forward curve displays a positive slope.

In the literature, there are numerous explanations for this, but each sheds light on only a fraction of the complex "futures puzzle."[28] Lewis attributes the varying term structures between commodity sectors to the *theory of storage cost*, and to the existence of a *convenience yield* (Y).[29] Considering the futures price of consumption goods, we must adjust equation 1.2 for the physical ownership of a scarce commodity:

$$P_0 = S_0 e^{(r+U-Y)T} \tag{1.3}$$

[28]For a review of the different approaches, see Claude Erb and Campbell R. Harvey, "The Tactical and Strategic Value of Commodity Futures," *Financial Analysts Journal* (April–May 2006), pp. 69–97; and Barry Feldman and Hilary Till, "Separating the Wheat from the Chaff: Backwardation as the Long-Term Driver of Commodity Futures Performance; Evidence from Soy, Corn and Wheat Futures from 1950 to 2004," Working Paper, 2007.

[29]According to Kaldor's theory of storage, the convenience yield reflects the utility of holding the physical commodity, in contrast to a pure contractual agreement about the delivery of the specific commodity. The utility results from the prevention of costs associated with disruptions in the production process. See Hélyette Geman, "Energy Commodity Prices: Is Mean-Reversion Dead?" *Journal of Alternative Investments* (Fall 2005), pp. 31–45; and Nicolas Kaldor, "Speculation and Economic Stability," *Review of Economic Studies* (October 1939), pp. 1–27.

The convenience yield varies over time (e.g., in the case of an unexpected increase or decrease in commodity supply). Commodities exposed to strong stock price variations from sudden supply or demand shocks are likely to exhibit a change or even a reversion in the term structure. The slope of the term structure curve thus indicates the stock of a commodity, and reflects market expectations for its availability in the future.[30]

Backwardation and contango depend strongly on the respective supply and demand situation of global commodity markets. Anson distinguishes between markets that offer price risk hedges for producers on the one hand, and hedges for commodity consumers on the other.[31] According to the theory of normal backwardation, the demand for short hedges greatly exceeds that for long hedges—hence, speculators have incentives to take these excessive positions. In order to compensate speculators, the short hedgers provide a risk premium that constitutes a deduction from the expected spot price. A contangoed market may arise when buyers depend on delivery schedules (e.g., in the manufacturing industry). Thus, there may be a surplus of long hedgers, which may lead to a falling term structure curve.

The theory of backwardation is confirmed by the empirical evidence that the slope of the term structure curve is determined by the storability of the individual commodity (the *storage hypothesis*). Eagleeye and Till conclude that the key to a successful long-term investment lies in choosing an index that gives more weight to sectors with low storage capacity. They refer to the GSCI due to its high proportion of energy (74.57% as of January 2006).[32]

---

[30]The theory of *normal backwardation*, which dates to Keynes, is closely linked to the theory of convenience yield. Normal backwardation states that the futures price is lower than the expected spot price in the future, $F(t,T) < E[S(T)]$. Keynes argued that in commodity markets, backwardation does not describe an abnormal market situation, but is due to the fact that commodity producers hedge their price risk more frequently than commodity consumers. See John M. Keynes, *A Treatise on Money* (London: Macmillan, 1930). This argument has set off an academic discussion lasting until today. See, for example, Colin A. Carter, Gordon C. Rausser, and Andrew Schmitz, "Efficient Asset Portfolios and the Theory of Normal Backwardation," *Journal of Political Economy* (April 1983), pp. 319–331; Lester Telser, "Futures Trading and the Storage of Cotton and Wheat," *Journal of Political Economy* (June 1958), pp. 233–255; and Paul Cootner, "Returns to Speculators: Telser versus Keynes," *Journal of Political Economy* (August 1960), pp. 398–404.

[31]Anson, *The Handbook of Alternative Assets.*

[32]Joseph Eagleeye and Hilary Till, "Commodities—Active Strategies for Enhanced Return," in *The Handbook of Inflation Hedging Investments*, edited by Robert J. Greer (Hoboken, NJ: John Wiley & Sons, 2005), pp. 127–158.

EXHIBIT 1.4 Backwardation in Commodities

		Number of Observations (in months)			
Sector	Observation Period	Total	In Calculation	In Back-wardation	Percentage of Backwardation
Agricultural	1970–2006	444	281	69	15.54%
Energy	1983–2006	288	275	140	48.61%
Industrial Metals	1977–2006	360	236	66	18.33%
Livestock	1970–2006	444	275	150	33.78%
Precious Metals	1973–2006	408	264	14	3.43%

To verify the storage hypothesis, we analyze the individual subindexes of the GSCI. We thus determine the monthly share in percent of backwardation and contango over our observation period (January 1970–December 2006) for the agricultural, energy, industrial metals, livestock, and precious metals sectors.[33] We choose the GSCI because of its availability and its long data history. Its subindexes are available in all three index versions (total return, excess return, and spot return), and it provides the longest actually calculated index series since 1992.

As Exhibit 1.4 shows, backwardation is no temporary phenomenon. The energy sector and the livestock sector, which contain the majority of nonstorable commodities, are characterized by a high percentage of backwardation. The precious metals sector, on the other hand, has been almost exclusively in contango due to its low storage costs.

Return Components of Commodity Futures Investments

To compare the long-term performance of commodities and other asset classes, we assume a fully collateralized commodity futures investment. Such diversified long-term passive commodity portfolios are characterized by long-only positions in commodity futures. In comparison to futures investments, which may require a margin depending on capital invested, the futures position is fully collateralized with cash. This means that, for such an unleveraged total return index, the initial and maintenance margins, as well as the entire outstanding cash, are invested at the riskless interest rate. Hence, the return of such an investible index can be decomposed into the

[33]For this purpose, we compare the monthly returns of the spot and the excess return indexes. If the excess return exceeds the spot return, the market is backwardated, and vice versa; months with a spread of less than 0.1% are not considered.

following three return components:[34] the spot return, the roll return (generated by switching from the maturing futures contract into the next closest futures contract), and the collateral return (the interest payment on the cash position). If we consider a commodity futures portfolio instead of an individual futures contract, an additional component may exist, the so-called rebalancing (diversification) return:

$$\text{Total return} = \text{Spot return} + \text{Roll return} + \text{Collateral return} + \text{Rebalancing return} \tag{1.4}$$

The majority of investors focus on an increase in physical commodity prices, that is, the *spot return*, R_S, defined as the percentage change of the spot price S_t of the respective commodity:

$$R_S = \frac{S_t - S_{t-1}}{S_{t-1}} \tag{1.5}$$

The spot price is influenced by fundamental factors like changes in supply, global demand variations, or unexpected price changes.[35] These price changes at the spot market are immediately reflected at the futures market.

Theoretically, the spot return is the component of the commodity futures return that is most strongly correlated with unexpected inflation.[36]

Forecasting spot prices is difficult because their factors are unpredictable. The prices of the respective commodities can vary greatly due to differences in commodity type, extraction method, production, and use. Industrial metals, for example, are used in manufacturing. Thus, their demand depends strongly on worldwide economic development. In contrast, the supply of agricultural products is determined mainly by the harvest,[37] which in turn depends on other factors (similarly to the energy sector). Extreme drought, frost, or thunderstorms can reduce the harvest or even destroy it entirely. In

[34]For example, Ernest M. Ankrim and Chris R. Hensel, "Commodities in Asset Allocation: Real-Asset Alternative to Real Estate?" *Financial Analysts Journal*, (May/June 1993), pp. 20–29; Erb and Harvey, "The Tactical and Strategic Value of Commodity Futures," and Robert J. Greer, "The Nature of Commodity Index Returns," *Journal of Alternative Investments* (Summer 2000), pp. 45–52.

[35]Adam De Chiara and Daniel M. Raab, "The Benefits of Real Asset Portfolio Diversification," *Euromoney International Commodities Review* (2002), pp. 3–10.

[36]Ankrim and Hensel, "Commodities in Asset Allocation: Real-Asset Alternative to Real Estate?"

[37]Supply exhibits a strong seasonal component. Agricultural commodities can only be produced at specific times, and in amounts that may fluctuate.

addition, all commodities are dependent on political factors. Besides numerous market barriers, which are known ex ante, other factors like political instability or war can lead to volatility in commodity prices.

The *roll return* R_r results from the extension of the futures contract and the shape of the term structure curve. The roll return reflects the profit from the convergence of the futures price toward the spot price over time, and the subsequent rolling of the maturing futures into the next nearest month's futures contract. If the commodity market is in backwardation (contango), the rolling from the maturing to the next shortest futures contract generates positive (negative) income.[38] Given that the futures price $F_{t-1,t}$ and the spot price S_t are equal at contract maturity, the selling price of the near month futures contracts prior to expiration varies from the new futures contract, $F_{t,T}$, by the amount of backwardation (contango) (see Exhibit 1.5). This means we can express the roll return at time t as:

$$R_r = \frac{F_{t,T} - F_{t-1,t}}{F_{t-1,t}} = \frac{F_{t,T} - S_t}{S_t} \tag{1.6}$$

where a negative (positive) value corresponds to a positive (negative) roll return and thus to backwardation (contango).

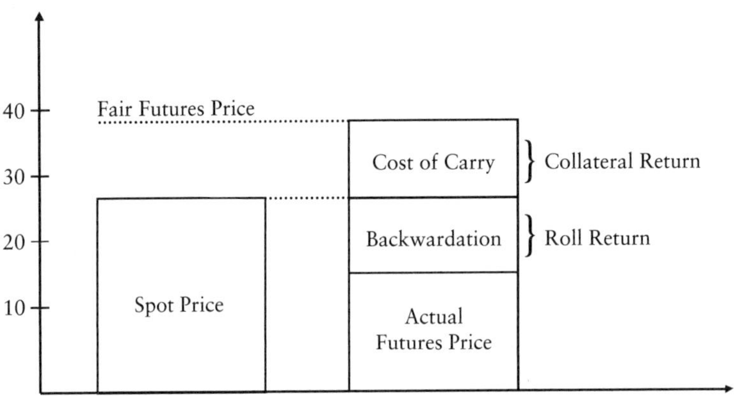

EXHIBIT 1.5 Return Components of Commodity Futures

[38]Note that the futures contract is rolled before maturity. Thus the roll return results from selling the maturing future and investing the returns into the next nearest futures contract. The roll return is positive when the market is in backwardation, and negative when it is in contango. In a contangoed situation, the spot price to which the initial futures contract converges is lower than the price of the new futures contract.

Generally, when investing in a futures contract, it is only necessary to deposit a margin payment (a fixed percentage of the underlying capital), and not the total position. In contrast, a collateral return is based on the assumption that the whole futures position is collateralized by cash. Interest is thus paid on this capital at the U.S. Treasury bill rate, which is explicitly considered in the total return index.

Booth and Fama introduced the *rebalancing return* as a fourth return component by stating that a significant return portion of a value-weighted commodity index stems from the reallocation of the sectors or commodities in the index.[39] This is because the individual commodities are only marginally correlated, or not correlated at all.[40] If the price movements follow a random walk or in contrast return to their long-term average level—that is, production costs (mean reversion)—the construction of a value-weighted commodity index can generate a surplus in this asset class.[41] As a result of spot price volatility, there is a regular shift in index composition. If a commodity in the portfolio shows continuous appreciation, this commodity's share of total portfolio value will increase as well.

According to their construction principles, the commodity indexes we describe here constitute a fixed weight for all commodities with respect to relative index value. Thus they must be rebalanced on a regular basis: Futures that have increased in value are sold; those that have decreased in value are purchased.

Unlike a pure buy-and-hold strategy, where the value of the portfolio increases linearly with market value, such a dynamic asset allocation strategy enables investors to participate strongly in booming markets.[42] Thus, a "free lunch" may be obtained via the lower systematic risk achieved by reducing the standard deviation of the portfolio, without any effect on arithmetic return.[43] According to this, the rebalancing approach[44] mentioned

---

[39]The rebalancing return is often called the diversification return. See, for example, David G. Booth and Eugene F. Fama, "Diversification Returns and Asset Contributions," *Financial Analysts Journal* (January/February 1992), pp. 26–32.

[40]Based on a comparison between the Dow Jones-AIG Commodity Index and a self-constructed index with constant weights, Chiara and Raab show that a yearly rebalanced index leads to higher returns as long as the underlying commodities are not perfectly correlated. See Chiara and Raab, "The Benefits of Real Asset Portfolio Diversification."

[41]Greer, "The Nature of Commodity Index Returns."

[42]André F. Perold and William F. Sharpe, "Dynamic Strategies for Asset Allocation," *Financial Analysts Journal* (January/February 1988), pp. 16–27.

[43]John Y. Campbell, "Diversification: A Bigger Free Lunch," *Canadian Investment Review* (Winter 2000), pp. 14–15.

[44]The literature often mentions a constant-mix strategy in the context of fixed portions relative to the total portfolio.

above leads to significantly higher returns, especially in volatile, trendless markets like the commodity market.

Exhibit 1.6 decomposes the annualized monthly total returns of the sector indexes into their individual return components and corresponding standard deviations. Over our entire sample period, all subindexes show positive total returns.[45] The industrial metals, precious metals, and agricultural sectors show on average negative roll returns, while energy and livestock commodities generate positive returns from the roll procedure. This coincides with the *theory of storage*.

Exhibit 1.6 also clearly shows that the *collateral yield*, at about 6%, constitutes a relatively large part of the total return, thus explaining the tremendous difference between the returns of the total and excess return indexes. Furthermore, the average spot return, which is highly volatile, is of special interest and is positive for all individual sectors. Hence, the majority of total return variation is based on the spot price. This result concurs significantly with the studies of Ankrim and Hensel[46] as well as Erb and Harvey.[47]

The following section takes a closer look at the different types of futures indexes that can be used for performance measurement. These indexes are closely linked with the sources of futures return. The total return index as a performance index results from the actual futures return plus the

EXHIBIT 1.6 Return Components of the Goldman Sachs Subindexes

	Spot Return		Roll Return		Collateral Return		Total Return	
Sector	μ(%)	σ(%)	μ(%)	σ(%)	μ(%)	σ(%)	μ(%)	σ(%)
Agricultural	4.60	19.68	−3.86	5.60	6.15	0.87	6.89	19.44
Energy	7.87	31.14	2.55	7.64	5.26	2.03	15.68	31.54
Industrial metals	7.52	22.62	−1.07	6.31	6.21	0.93	12.65	23.74
Livestock	4.02	19.41	1.20	8.26	6.17	0.95	11.38	18.30
Precious metals	8.96	23.13	−6.22	2.49	6.24	0.91	8.98	23.15

[45]The periods under consideration for the individual subindexes follow those in Exhibit 1.4.

[46]Ankrim and Hensel, "Commodities in Asset Allocation: Real-Asset Alternative to Real Estate?"

[47]Erb and Harvey, "The Tactical and Strategic Value of Commodity Futures."

interest rate payment on the collateral. The futures return itself is composed of the spot and roll return, and is called the excess return:

$$\begin{aligned}\text{Total return} &= \text{Collateral return} + \text{Futures return} \\ &= \text{Collateral return} + \text{Spot return} + \text{Roll return} \qquad (1.7)\end{aligned}$$

$$\text{Excess return} = \text{Spot return} + \text{Roll return} = \text{Futures return} \qquad (1.8)$$

A *spot return index* does not represent the prices at the spot market, but rather measures the price movements at the futures market, since reliable prices are not immediately available for all commodities. Hence, we can calculate the spot return index by using the *near-month contract* or *spot month contract* as a proxy for the spot price of each individual commodity.[48] Just before maturity, the calculation is related to the next contract. The replacement is done without considering any discrepancies in value between the shortest and the second-shortest future.[49] Thus, the spot return index is a general indicator of existing price trends in commodity markets, and cannot be used as a performance measure or for comparison with other financial asset returns.

In the case of the *excess return index*, by switching from a maturing to a new contract (which is actually done from the fifth to the ninth working day of the month), a futures contract is rolled. The roll performance is captured in the index, so that the performance of the excess return index is composed of the spot return on the one hand, and the roll performance on the other (e.g., see the GSCI Energy Index in Exhibit 1.7). Because investors might hold and roll the underlying commodity futures themselves, the index is theoretically replicable, and can thus serve as a basis for financial instruments. According to its construction, the underlying of the excess return index is assumed to be an *un*collateralized futures instrument (i.e., a leveraged spot position).

In contrast to the excess return indexes, the total return index is based on a fully cash-collateralized commodity investment. Hence, in the long run, tremendous return differences can arise between the total and the

[48]Viola Markert, Commodities as Assets and Consumption Goods: Implications for the Valuation of Commodity Futures, Doctoral Dissertation, University of St. Gallen and Basel (2005); and Gorton and Rouwenhorst, "Facts and Fantasies about Commodity Futures."

[49]As a result of the roll procedure, there is an increase or decrease in the index depending on the forward curve of the underlying commodity.

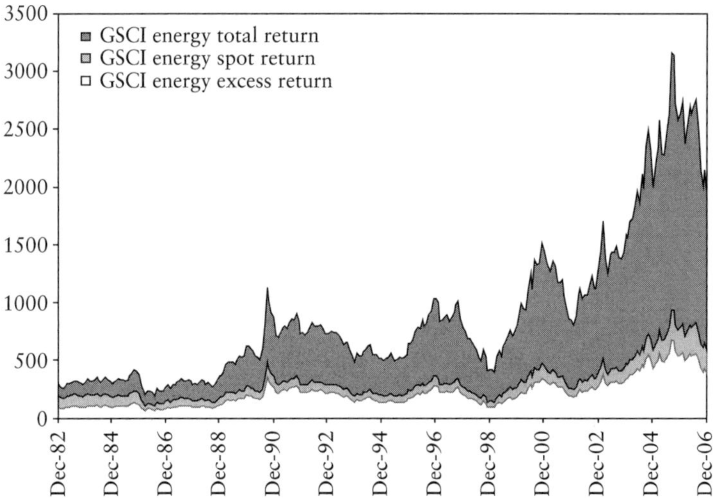

EXHIBIT 1.7 Excess Return of Commodity Futures

excess return indexes.[50] However, we cannot compare the excess return index directly with the total return index; that is, the excess return plus Treasury bill rate does not equal the total return. We must consider the influence of the reinvestment of the Treasury bill collateral income into commodity futures, as well as the deposit of the profits (withdrawal of losses) from the futures contracts into (out of) the Treasury bills.

MODELS OF EXPECTED RETURNS

The literature contains several models that can be used to arrive at commodity futures returns expectations. In this context, Erb and Harvey mention four:[51]

- The capital asset pricing model (CAPM)
- The insurance perspective

[50]It can be advisable to invest in, for example, a certificate on a total return index in comparison to an underperforming excess return index, because there are no initial up-front payments and no yearly management fees. Thus, it may be sensible to purchase certificates on the seemingly worse excess return index during times of low interest rates. Note also that there are opportunity costs from investing in total return indexes, since the entire capital must be invested in Treasury bills and cannot be allocated more efficiently.

[51]Erb and Harvey, "The Tactical and Strategic Value of Commodity Futures."

- The hedging pressure hypothesis
- The theory of storage

Under the CAPM framework, the market beta drives the prospective capital asset returns. However, as we discussed earlier, commodity futures are not considered capital assets. Thus, application of the CAPM model is of limited use.

The insurance perspective argues that risk premiums are available if hedgers use commodity futures to avoid commodity price risk. Hedgers (producers) hold commodities in stock, and therefore must have a short position in commodity futures. To attract speculators, hedgers must offer an insurance premium. Therefore, the futures price for a commodity is less than the expected spot price in the future ("normal backwardation").[52] Unfortunately, expected futures spot prices are unobservable. This theory suggests that all long positions in commodity futures have a positive expected excess return, which consequently justifies "long-only" investments. But this model implicitly assumes that hedgers hold commodities in stocks, and seek to mitigate price risk by selling commodity futures.

We can consider the hedging pressure hypothesis as a continuation of the insurance perspective. It also highlights the fact that consumers who demand commodities may want to hedge their risk. Anson uses the example of Boeing as a consumer of aluminum.[53] The airplane producer is short in aluminum because it does not own any aluminum mining interests and can therefore eliminate the risk of higher futures prices by taking a long position in aluminum futures. This causes the futures price to be higher than the expected spot price in the future. Under these circumstances, investors seeking to earn an insurance premium will choose to short the commodity futures. The hedging pressure hypothesis argues that investors will receive a risk premium that is a positive excess return for going short in a "normal contangoed" commodity futures market.

The theory of storage emphasizes the role of inventories, and conceptually links inventories with commodity futures prices. The difference between futures prices and spot prices can be explained by storage costs and the so-called *convenience yield* of holding specific commodities in inventory. The underlying idea is that the holder of a storable commodity has a consumption option that is implicitly embedded in a convenience yield. Inventories act as a damper on price volatility because they provide an additional way to balance supply and demand. This theory predicts an inverse relationship between the level of inventories and the convenience yield—the

[52]John M. Keynes, *A Treatise on Money* (London: Macmillan, 1930).
[53]Anson, *The Handbook of Alternative Assets*.

lower the inventories, the higher the convenience yield. Difficult-to-store commodities should therefore have lower inventory levels and higher convenience yields than easy-to-store commodities. According to Till, examples of difficult-to-store commodities include heating oil, live cattle, and live hogs.[54]

RISK AND PERFORMANCE CHARACTERISTICS

Based on their historical return, risk, and correlation performance, commodity investments have an advantage over traditional assets, but they exhibit some similarities to stocks. Kaplan and Lummer, for example, conclude in their empirical investigation that commodities show an equity-like performance over the long run.[55] This finding is also supported by many other studies such as Greer, who concludes that the performance of unleveraged commodity indexes from 1970 to 1999 was on average positive, and comparable to equities with regard to return and volatility.[56]

Bodie and Rosansky[57] analyze an equally weighted commodity futures portfolio between 1949 and 1976, and Gorton and Rouwenhorst[58] between 1959 and 2004. Both studies confirm equity-like returns for commodities. In addition, during the high inflation period of the 1970s, commodities had the highest real returns by far of all the asset classes. Gorton and Rouwenhorst found differences with traditional assets. They show that commodity returns exhibit positive skewness, in contrast to stocks, which have negative skewness and thus include higher downside risk.[59]

Exhibit 1.8 shows the performance of both traditional and alternative assets starting with a reference basis of 100 in December 1993. After consolidating in 2006, the GSCI, which is heavily invested in energy, currently shows very strong performance, along with indirect real estate and hedge funds. In contrast, equity investments in emerging markets show the smallest price increases.

---

[54]Hilary Till, "Two Types of Systematic Return Available in the Futures Markets," *Commodities Now* (September 2000), pp. 1–5.

[55]Paul D. Kaplan and Scott L. Lummer, GSCI Collateralized Futures as a Hedging and Diversification Tool for Institutional Portfolios: An Update, Working Paper, 1997.

[56]Greer, "The Nature of Commodity Index Returns."

[57]Bodie and Rosansky, "Risk and Return in Commodity Futures."

[58]Gorton and Rouwenhorst, "Facts and Fantasies about Commodity Futures."

[59]Gorton and Rouwenhorst, "Facts and Fantasies about Commodity Futures."

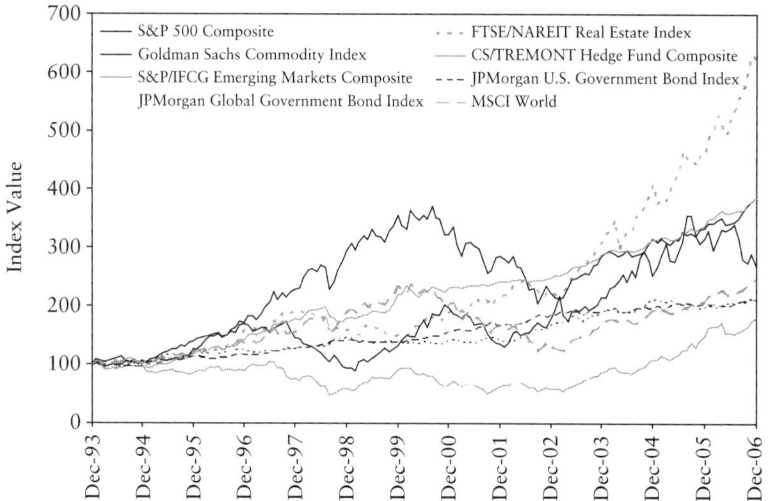

EXHIBIT 1.8 Performance of the Goldman Sachs Commodity Index Compared to Other Financial Assets

During the January 1994–December 2006 period, commodities had an annualized return of 9.64%, with a volatility of 20.25% (see Exhibit 1.9).[60] Thus, compared to other observed asset classes, commodities have a high average volatility. However, note that the downside risk of the S&P 500 Composite, the S&P/IFCG Emerging Markets, and the FTSE/NAREIT Real Estate Index are higher because of their negative skewness; commodities possess positive skewness.

The most beneficial investment in terms of the Sharpe ratio is the CS/Tremont Hedge Fund Index. However, hedge fund investors also face high excess kurtosis. When considering only return and volatility, an indirect investment in real estate also seems less favorable due to negative skewness and positive excess kurtosis. Furthermore, the poor performance of emerging market equities seen in Exhibit 1.8 is also confirmed by the descriptive statistics, especially considering the exorbitant volatility.

As mentioned above, commodities serve an important diversification function in asset allocation due to their long-term low correlation with stocks, bonds, real estate, hedge funds, and, to a lesser extent, their absolute performance characteristics. According to Greer, commodity indexes have a

[60]The high variability can be explained by the GSCI's large share in energy. The energy sector currently represents over 70% of the total index (as at end 2006), and is itself composed of 40% crude oil, which has experienced extreme volatility over the last few years.

EXHIBIT 1.9 Annualized Average Monthly Return and Volatility (January 1994–December 2006)

	r_{ann}	σ_{ann}	r_{Min}	r_{Max}	Skewness	Excess Kurtosis	Sharpe Ratio
GSCI Composite	9.64%	20.25%	−14.41%	16.88%	0.063	0.024	0.281
S&P 500 Composite	11.43%	14.27%	−14.46%	9.78%	−0.622	0.838	0.524
MSCI World	7.91%	13.43%	−13.45%	8.91%	−0.658	0.890	0.294
Emerging Markets	6.76%	20.62%	−25.56%	12.37%	−0.765	1.877	0.136
Hedge Funds Composite	10.71%	7.66%	−7.55%	8.53%	0.099	2.465	0.882
Real Estate Index	14.99%	13.04%	−14.58%	10.39%	−0.510	1.472	0.846
JPMorgan U.S. Govt. Bonds	5.91%	4.65%	−4.68%	3.71%	−0.509	1.084	0.421
JPMorgan Global Bonds	5.98%	6.23%	−4.30%	5.65%	0.320	0.336	0.325
T-bill rate	3.96%	0.49%	0.07%	0.53%	−0.644	−1.049	—

negative correlation with stocks and bonds and a positive correlation with the inflation rate, especially unexpected changes in inflation. There are, however, significant differences among the individual commodity sectors: Energy, metals, livestock, and sugar show the best inflation hedging potential. Greer also finds very high correlation coefficients among different kinds of commodity sectors.[61]

According to Kat and Oomen, commodity futures and traditional assets like stocks and bonds are uncorrelated.[62] In specific phases, the correlation admittedly increases—therefore not all commodities are useful for portfolio diversification in every market phase. However, even in down markets, commodities as a group do not lose their diversification potential. According to Anson, there are three reasons for low or negative correlations between commodities and stocks/bonds.[63] First, inflation has a positive effect on commodity prices, but a negative effect on equity and bond markets. Second, investor expectations in commodity markets are different from those in equity and bond markets. Finally, a trade-off between capital return and commodity return exists in industrial production.

Exhibit 1.10 shows the return correlation structure between the total return indexes of various asset classes. As can be seen, correlation is only significant at the 5% level between commodities and hedge funds, which turn out to be relatively low at 0.167. This can be traced back to the commodity trading advisors and managed futures funds included in the CS/Tremont Hedge Fund Composite Index.

On the other hand, the return correlation between the money market and the commodity market is negative. Hence, the results of several academic studies[64] are confirmed for our sample period: Commodities show a high diversification potential in traditional *and* alternative security portfolios. Chong and Miffre support the findings that the conditional correlations between commodity futures and the S&P 500 decrease during times of down markets, that is, exactly when market risk increases and

[61]Greer, "The Nature of Commodity Index Returns."
[62]Harry M. Kat and Roel C. A. Oomen, "What Every Investor Should Know About Commodities, Part II: Multivariate Return Analysis," *Journal of Investment Management* (Third Quarter 2007).
[63]Anson, *The Handbook of Alternative Assets.*
[64]See, for example, Kat and Oomen, "What Every Investor Should Know About Commodities: Part I"; Hilary Till, "Taking Full Advantage of the Statistical Properties of Commodity Investments," *Journal of Alternative Investments* (Summer 2001), pp. 63–66; Evert B. Vrugt, Rob Bauer, Roderick Molenaar, and Tom Molenaar, Dynamic Commodity Timing Strategies, Working Paper, 2004; and Gorton and Rouwenhorst, "Facts and Fantasies about Commodity Futures."

EXHIBIT 1.10 Correlation Matrix

	GSCI Commodity Index	S&P 500 Composite	MSCI World	S&P/IFCG Emerging Markets	CS/Tremont Hedge Fund Comp.	FTSE/NAREIT Real Estate	JPMorgan U.S. Govt. Bonds	JPMorgan Global Govt. Bonds	U.S. Treasury Bill Rate
GSCI Commodity Index	1								
S&P 500 Composite	0.003	1							
MSCI World	0.068	0.937[b]	1						
S&P/IFCG Emerging Markets	0.136	0.643[b]	0.724[b]	1					
CS/Tremont Hedge Fund Comp.	0.167[a]	0.487[b]	0.493[b]	0.503[b]	1				
FTSE/NAREIT Real Estate	0.005	0.299[b]	0.314[b]	0.350[b]	0.223[b]	1			
JPMorgan U.S. Govt. Bonds	0.079	−0.098	−0.159[a]	−0.216[b]	0.098	0.032	1		
JPMorgan Global Govt. Bonds	0.156	−0.016	0.064	−0.069	−0.050	0.118	0.597[b]	1	
U.S. Treasury bill rate	−0.063	0.084	0.008	−0.180[a]	0.102	−0.066	0.105	−0.084	1

[a,b] Denote significance of the correlation coefficient at the 95% and 99% confidence levels, respectively.

diversification is strongly needed.[65] The conditional correlations between commodities and fixed income, on the other hand, increase during times of increased bond volatility.

PORTFOLIO OPTIMIZATION WITH COMMODITIES

In this section, we analyze whether an allocation in commodities yields any diversification benefits for a portfolio consisting of U.S. and global stocks, fixed income, and a riskless asset represented by the Treasury bill rate (i.e., whether the efficient frontier shifts into the upperleft corner in the expected return-standard deviation diagram). According to Markowitz,[66] these portfolios are considered from the set of all efficient portfolios (efficient in the sense that no others exhibit a superior risk-return combination). These efficient portfolios are located on the borderline formed by the set of all portfolios between the *minimum variance portfolio* (MVP) and the *maximum return portfolio* (MaxEP).

Exhibit 1.11 shows how portfolio efficiency can be improved by including commodities in a traditional portfolio, thus rotating the efficient frontier counterclockwise around the MVP (the Treasury bill rate). The

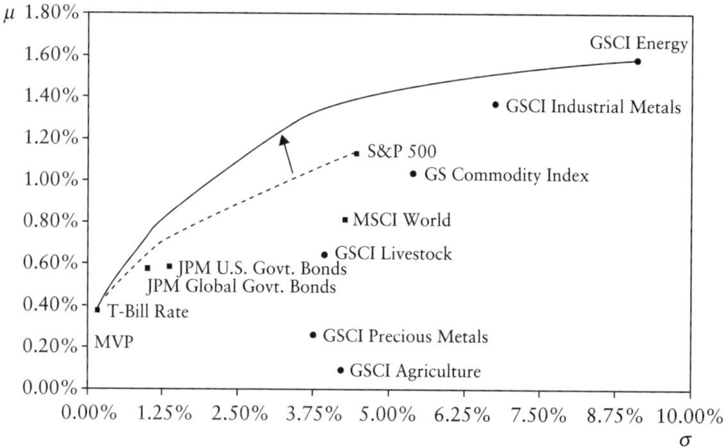

EXHIBIT 1.11 Expected Return-Standard Deivation ($\mu - \sigma$) Portfolio Optimization (monthly returns in percent)

[65]James Chong and Joelle Miffre, Conditional Risk Premia and Correlations in Commodity Futures Markets, Working Paper, 2006.

[66]Harry M. Markowitz, "Portfolio Selection," *Journal of Finance* (March 1952), pp. 77–91.

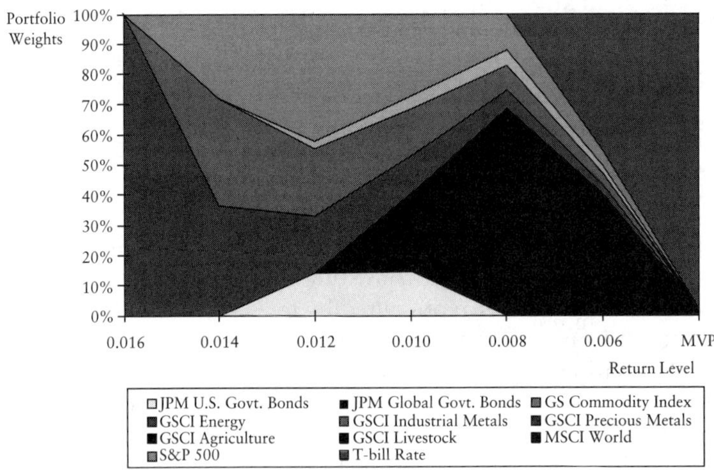

EXHIBIT 1.12 μ-σ-Portfolio Allocation (monthly returns in percent)

upward shift of the efficient frontier also provides higher risk-adjusted returns. The efficient frontier of the traditional portfolio is limited by a 98% investment in Treasury bills for the MVP, and 100% in the S&P 500 for the MaxEP.

Starting from the MVP and incorporating individual commodity sectors, the share of global bonds initially increases to 69% (see Exhibit 1.12). Subsequently, the proportions of the energy and industrial metals sectors increase continuously, together with the share of U.S. stocks. At a monthly return level of about 1%, livestock is represented with a share of about 4% to 5%. However, agricultural and precious metals are excluded entirely from the allocation. At a monthly return level of about 1.4%, the portfolio only consists of an allocation in the S&P 500 (28%), the energy sector (37%), and the industrial metals sector (35%).

Thus, with an increasing return level, the proportion of commodities in the portfolio expands as the allocation in U.S. stocks increases. It is remarkable that the GSCI Composite is not included in any allocations. It seems advisable to invest directly in the respective individual subsectors.

CONCLUSION

In an environment of historically low interest rates, markedly reduced upward potential, and continuously decreasing risk premiums for traditional asset classes, there is growing demand from institutional and private investors for alternative investments. An allocation to commodities offers not only a hedge against inflation, but also effective diversification because of its low correlation with traditional asset classes.

In the long run, commodity investments show equity-like returns, but are accompanied by lower volatility and shortfall risk. The advantages hold for passive investment in commodity futures indexes, which are considered indicators of commodity market price movements. However, the futures indexes of individual providers differ with regard to sector weights, index construction, and calculation method—hence there are tremendous variations in risk-return characteristics.

In a total and excess return index, an important return component results from the risk premium connected with the roll yield. This results from rolling commodity futures positions with a backwardated term structure. A direct investment in commodities generates positive roll returns in certain backwardated markets. Investors in passive commodity futures indexes must take into account that, independent from the term structure curve, only long positions can be held. According to Akey, one solution may be to use an active and tactical benchmark in the form of a commodity trading advisor index (a CTA index).[67]

In view of current global market demand, we assume that the growth of commodity consumption, particularly in the BRIC countries (Brazil, India, Russia, and China) will continue to generate high demand for commodities in all sectors. But because low commodity prices over the last two decades did not lead to sufficient investment in increased production capacity, we expect that pricing pressure on the commodity markets will intensify. In addition, we expect to see short-run scarcity in the commodity supply due to increasing inventories. In light of this tremendous development and according to the commodity super cycle theory, we predict a lasting boom in the commodity markets in the near future.

---

[67]Rian P. Akey, "Commodities: A Case for Active Management," *Journal of Alternative Investments* (Fall 2005), pp. 8–30.

CHAPTER 2

The Pricing and Economics of Commodity Futures

Mark J. P. Anson, Ph.D., JD, CFA, CAIA, CPA
President and Executive Director of Investment Services
Nuveen Investments, Inc.

Capital assets such as stocks and bonds can be valued on the basis of the net present value of expected future cash flows. Expected cash flows and discount rates are a prime ingredient to determine the value of capital assets. Conversely, commodities do not provide a claim on an ongoing stream of revenue in the same fashion as stocks and bonds, with the exception of precious metals such as gold, silver, and platinum which can be lent out at a market lease rate. Consequently, they cannot be valued on the basis of net present value, and interest rates have only a small impact on their value.

Another distinction between capital assets and commodities is the global nature of commodity markets. Worldwide, commodities are denominated in U.S. dollars. Furthermore, the value of a particular commodity is dependent upon global supply and demand imbalances rather than regional imbalances. Thus, commodity prices are determined globally rather than regionally. This is very different from bond and equity markets, which mainly reflect the economic developments within their own countries and regions.

Finally, commodities do not conform to traditional asset pricing models such as the *capital asset pricing model* (CAPM). Under the CAPM, there are two components of risk: market or systematic risk and company specific or unsystematic. Since unsystematic can be diversified away in a portfolio, investors will only be compensated for systematic risk, known as *beta*. Thereby, financial markets compensate for market risk by assigning a market risk premium above the risk-free rate. Bodie and Rosanksy[1] and Dusak[2] find that commodity beta values are not consistent with the CAPM. The reason is twofold. First, under the CAPM, the market portfolio is typically defined as a portfolio of financial assets such as stocks and bonds, and commodity returns map poorly onto financial market returns. Consequently, distinctions between market/systematic risk and unsystematic risk cannot be made. Second, commodity prices are dependent upon global supply and demand factors, not what the market perceives to be an adequate risk premium for this asset class.

Therefore, commodities can be seen as a separate asset class from stocks, bonds, and real estate. However, like stocks and bonds, there are different investment strategies within this asset class. In this chapter, we provide an overview of the pricing and underlying economics of the physical commodities markets.

THE RELATIONSHIP BETWEEN FUTURES PRICES AND SPOT PRICES

The easiest way to gain exposure to commodities is through commodity futures contracts. These contracts are transparent, are denominated in standard units, are exchange traded, have daily liquidity, and depend upon the spot prices of the underlying commodity. The last point, the relationship between spot and futures prices, must be developed to understand the dynamics of the commodity futures markets.

A futures contract obligates the seller of the futures contract to deliver the underlying asset at a set price at a specified time. Conversely, the buyer of a futures contract agrees to purchase the underlying asset at the set price and at a specified time. If the seller of the futures contract does not wish to deliver the underlying asset, she must close out her short futures position by purchasing an offsetting futures contract. Similarly, if the buyer of the futures contract does not wish to take delivery of the underlying asset, he must close out his long futures position by selling an offsetting futures contract. Only a very small percentage of futures contracts (usually less than 1%) result in delivery of the underlying asset.

There are three general types of futures contracts regulated by the Commodity Futures Trading Commission: financial futures, currency futures,

[1]Zvi Bodie and Victor Rosansky, "Risk and Return in Commodity Futures," *Financial Analysts Journal* (May/June 1980), pp. 27–39.

[2]Katherine Dusak, "Futures Trading and Investor Returns: An Investigation of Commodity Market Risk Premiums," *Journal of Political Economy* (November-December 1973), pp. 1387–1406.

and commodity futures. Commodity trading advisors and commodity pool operators invest in all three types of futures contracts. Additionally, many hedge fund managers apply arbitrage strategies with respect to financial and currency futures. The following examples demonstrate these arbitrage opportunities. We begin with financial futures.

Financial Futures

Financial futures include U.S. Treasury bond futures, agency futures, Eurodollar CD futures, and stock index futures. In the United States, these contracts are traded on the Chicago Board of Trade, the Chicago Mercantile Exchange, and the FINEX division of the New York Board of Trade. Consider the example of a financial asset that pays no income.

In the simplest case, if the underlying asset pays no income, then the relationship between the futures contract and the spot price is

$$F = Se^{r(T-t)} \tag{2.1}$$

where F = the price of the futures contract.
S = the spot price of the underlying asset.
e = the exponential operator, used to calculate continuous compounding.
r = the risk-free rate.
$T - t$ = the time until maturity of the futures contract.

In other words, the price of the futures contract depends upon the current price of the underlying financial asset, the risk-free rate, and the time until maturity of the futures contract. Notice that the price of the futures contract depends upon the risk-free rate and not the required rate of return for the financial asset. The reason that this is the case is because of arbitrage opportunities that exist for speculators such as hedge funds.

Consider the situation where $F > Se^{r(T-t)}$. A hedge fund manager could make a profit by applying the following strategy:

1. Borrow cash at the risk-free rate, r, and purchase the underlying asset at current price S.
2. Sell the underlying asset for delivery at time T and at the futures price F.
3. At maturity, deliver the underlying asset, pay the interest and principal on the cash borrowed, and collect the futures price F.

Exhibit 2.1 demonstrates this arbitrage strategy.

EXHIBIT 2.1 Financial Asset Arbitrage when $F > Se^{r(T-t)}$

Time	Cash Inflow	Cash Outflow	Net Cash
t (initiate the arbitrage)	S (cash borrowed)	S (to purchase the asset)	$S - S = 0$
T (maturity of the futures contract)	F (price for future delivery of the asset)	$Se^{r(T-t)}$ (pay back principal and interest)	$F - Se^{r(T-t)}$

Two points about Exhibit 2.1 must be noted. First, to initiate the arbitrage strategy, no net cash is required. The cash outflow matches the cash inflow. This is one reason why arbitrage strategies are so popular.

Second, at maturity (time T), the hedge fund manager receives a positive net cash payout of $F - Se^{r(T-t)}$. How do we know that the net payout is positive? Simple, we know that at the initiation of the arbitrage strategy that $F > Se^{r(T-t)}$. Therefore, $F - Se^{r(T-t)}$ must be positive.

If the reverse situation were true at time t, $F < Se^{r(T-t)}$, then a reverse arbitrage strategy would make the same amount of profit: Buy the futures contract and sell short the underlying asset. This is demonstrated in Exhibit 2.2.

Exhibit 2.2 demonstrates the arbitrage profit $Se^{r(T-t)} - F$. How do we know this is a profit? Because we started with the condition that $Se^{r(T-t)} > F$. At maturity of the futures contract, the hedge fund manager will take delivery of the underlying asset at price F and use the delivery of the asset to cover her short position.

In general, futures contracts on financial assets are settled in cash, not by physical delivery of the underlying security.[3] However, this does not change the arbitrage dynamics demonstrated above. The hedge fund manager will simply close out her short asset position and long futures position

EXHIBIT 2.2 Financial Asset Arbitrage when $F < Se^{r(T-t)}$

Time	Cash Inflow	Cash Outflow	Net Cash
t (initiate the arbitrage)	S (the asset is sold short)	S (invested at interest rate r)	$S - S = 0$
T (maturity of the futures contract)	$Se^{r(T-t)}$ (receive principal and interest)	F (the price paid for the asset at maturity of the futures contract)	$Se^{r(T-t)} - F$

[3]However, certain futures exchanges allow for a procedure known as *exchange for physicals*, where a holder of a financial asset can exchange the financial asset at maturity of the futures contract instead of settling in cash.

at the same time and net the gains and losses. The profit will be the same as that demonstrated in Exhibit 2.2.

Most financial assets pay some form of income. Consider stock index futures contracts. A stock index tracks the changes in the value of a portfolio of stocks. The percentage change in the value of a stock index over time is usually defined so that it equals the percentage change in the total value of all stocks comprising the index portfolio. However, stock indexes are usually not adjusted for dividends. In other words, any cash dividends received by an investor actually holding the stocks is not reflected in measuring the change in value of the stock index.

There are futures contracts on the S&P 500, the Nikkei 225 Stock Index, the NASDAQ 100 Index, the Russell 1000 Index, and the Dow Jones Industrials Stock Index. By far, the most popular contract is the S&P 500 futures contract (SPX) traded on the Chicago Mercantile Exchange.

Consider the S&P 500 futures contract. The pricing relationship as shown in equation (2.1) applies. However, equation (2.1) must be adjusted for the fact that the holder of the underlying stocks receives cash dividends, while the holder of the futures contract does not.

In Exhibit 2.2 we demonstrated how an arbitrage strategy may be accomplished by borrowing cash at the risk-free rate to purchase the underlying financial asset. With respect to stocks, the hedge fund manager receives the benefit of cash dividends from purchasing the stocks. The cash dividends received reduce the borrowing cost of the hedge fund manager. This must be factored into the futures pricing equation. We can express this relation as

$$F = Se^{(r-q)(T-t)} \tag{2.2}$$

where the terms are the same as before, and q is equal to the dividend yield on the basket of stocks.

The dividend rate, q, is subtracted from the borrowing cost, r, to reflect the reduction in carrying costs from owning the basket of stocks. Consider the example of a three-month futures contract on the S&P 500. Assume that the index is currently at 1,200, that the risk-free rate is 6%, and that the current dividend yield on the S&P 500 is 2%. Using equation (2.2), the fair price for a three-month futures contract on the S&P 500 is

$$F = 1{,}200e^{(0.06-0.02)(0.25)} = 1{,}212$$

Notice again that the futures price on stock index futures does not depend upon the expected return on stocks. Instead, it depends on the risk-free rate and the dividend yield. Expected asset returns do not affect the pricing relationship between the current asset price and the future asset price because any expected return that the underlying asset should earn will also be reflected in the futures price. Therefore, the difference between the futures price and the spot price should reflect only the time value of money, adjusted for any income earned by the financial asset over the term of the futures contract.

Suppose that instead of a price of 1,212, the three-month futures contract for the S&P 500 was priced at 1,215. Then a hedge fund could establish the following arbitrage: borrow cash at an interest rate of 6% and purchase a basket of S&P 500 stocks worth \$300,000 (\$250 × 1,200, where each point of the S&P 500 is worth \$250 in the underlying futures contract), and sell the S&P 500 futures at a price of 1,215. At the end of three months, the hedge fund would earn the following arbitrage profit:

$$\text{Futures price received for the S\&P 500 stocks} = 1{,}215 \times \$250 = \$303{,}750$$

$$\text{Plus dividend yield on stocks} = \$300{,}000 \times \left(e^{(0.02)\times(0.25)} - 1\right) = \$1{,}504$$

$$\text{Less repayment of the loan plus interest}$$

$$= \$300{,}000 \times e^{(0.06)\times(0.25)} = \$304{,}534$$

$$\text{Equals arbitrage profits} \qquad \$704$$

Exhibit 2.3 demonstrates the stock index arbitrage flow chart. A reverse arbitrage similar to Exhibit 2.2 can be implemented when $F < Se^{(r-q)(T-t)}$. That is, short the stocks, invest the cash at the risk-free rate, and buy the futures contract.

Currencies

A foreign currency may be considered an income producing asset. The reason is that the holder of the foreign currency can earn interest at the risk-free rate prevailing in the foreign country. We define this foreign risk-free

EXHIBIT 2.3 Stock Index Arbitrage when $F > Se^{(r-q)(T-t)}$

Time	Cash Inflow	Cash Outflow	Net Cash
t (initiate the arbitrage)	S (cash borrowed)	S (to purchase S&P 500 stocks)	$S - S = 0$
T (maturity of the futures contract)	F (price for future delivery of S&P 500 stocks)	$Se^{(r-q)(T-t)}$ (pay back principal and interest less dividends received)	$F - Se^{(r-q)(T-t)}$

rate as f. Considered in this context, the relationship between a futures contract on a foreign currency and the current spot exchange rate can be expressed as

$$F = Se^{(r-f)(T-t)} \tag{2.3}$$

where the terms are defined as before, and f is the risk-free interest rate in the foreign country.

Equation (2.3) is similar to equation (2.2) because a foreign currency may be considered analogous to an income producing asset or a dividend paying stock. Equation (2.3) also expresses the well-known *interest rate parity theorem*. This theorem states that the exchange rate between two currencies will be dependent upon the differences in their interest rates.

Consider the exchange rate between the U.S. dollar and the Japanese yen. Assume that the current U.S. risk-free rate is 6% while that for the yen is approximately 1%. Also, assume that the current spot rate for yen to dollars is 120 yen per U.S. dollar, or 0.00833 dollars per yen. A three-month futures contract on the yen/dollar exchange rate would be

$$F = 0.00833e^{(0.06-0.01)(0.25)} = 0.0084382$$

The futures price on Japanese yen for three months is 0.0084382 dollars per yen, or 118.51 yen per dollar.

To demonstrate a currency arbitrage when $F > Se^{(r-f)(T-t)}$ consider a hedge fund manager who can borrow 12,000 yen for three months at a rate of 1%. In three months, she will have to repay $12{,}000e^{(0.01\times0.25)} = 12{,}030$ yen. The manager converts the yen into dollars at the spot exchange rate of 120 yen/\$1 = \$100. This \$100 can then be invested at the U.S. risk-free rate of interest for three months to earn $\$100e^{(0.060\times0.25)} = \$101.50$. If the three-month currency futures price on Japanese yen were the same as the spot exchange rate of 120 yen/\$l, the hedge fund manager would need to sell 12,030/120 = \$100.25 dollars to repay the yen loan. Since the manager receives \$101.50 back from her three-month investment in the United States, she will pocket the difference of \$101.50 − \$100.25 = \$1.25 in arbitrage profits.

Exhibit 2.4 demonstrates that 150 yen of arbitrage profits may be earned if the futures contract price does not take into account the differences in the interest rates between the foreign and domestic currencies. The 150 yen of arbitrage profit may be converted back to dollars: 150 yen/120 = \$1.25. Therefore, to prevent arbitrage, the currency futures price for Japanese yen must be 118.51 yen per U.S. dollar. Then the amount of cash inflow received will be exactly equal to the cash outflow necessary to pay back the Japanese yen loan: \$101.50 × 118.51 yen/USD = 12,030 yen.

EXHIBIT 2.4 Currency Arbitrage when $F > Se^{(r-f)(T-t)}$

Time	Cash Inflow	Cash Outflow	Net Cash
t (initiate the futures contract)	12,000 yen borrowed at 1%	12,000 yen/120 = \$100 invested at 6%	0
T (maturity of the futures contract)	\$101.50 from U.S. interest bearing account	12,030 yen to repay loan plus interest	(\$101.50 × 120)− 12,030 yen = 150 yen

In practice, arbitrage opportunities do not occur as obviously as our example. Currency prices may be out of balance for only a short period of time. It is the nimble hedge fund manager that can take advantage of pricing discrepancies. Furthermore, more famous hedge fund managers engage in currency speculation as opposed to currency arbitrage. In currency speculation, the hedge fund manager takes an unhedged position on one side of the market. Cash is committed to establish the position. The best example of this is George Soros's bet against the British pound sterling in 1992.

Commodity Futures

Commodities are not financial assets. Nonetheless, the pricing dynamics between spot prices and futures prices are similar to those for financial assets. However, there are important distinctions that will affect the pricing relationship.

First, there are storage costs associated with physical commodities. These storage costs must be factored into the pricing equation. Storage costs can be considered as negative income. In other words, there is a cash outflow associated with holding the physical commodity. This is in contrast to financial assets discussed above. With financial assets, we demonstrated that income earned on the underlying asset will defray the cost of purchasing that asset. With physical commodities, however, there is both the cost of financing the purchase of the physical commodity and the storage cost associated with its ownership. This relationship may be expressed as

$$F = Se^{(r+c)(T-t)} \tag{2.4}$$

where the terms are as defined before, and c is the storage cost associated with ownership of the commodity.

In equation (2.4), the cost of storage, c, is added the cost of financing the purchase of the commodity. For example, consider a one-year futures contract on crude oil. Assume that (1) it costs 2% of the price of crude oil to store a barrel of oil and the payment is made at the end of the year; (2) the current price of oil is \$50; and (3) the risk-free rate of interest is 6%.[4] Then the future value of a one-year crude oil futures contract is

$$F = \$50e^{(0.06+0.02)(1)} = \$54.16$$

A second difference between commodity futures and financial futures is the *convenience yield*. Consumers of physical commodities feel that there are benefits from the ownership of the commodity that are not obtained by owning a futures contract; that it is convenient to own the physical commodity. This benefit might be the ability to profit from temporary or local supply and demand imbalances, or the ability to keep a production line in process. Alternatively, the convenience yield for certain metals can be measured in terms of *lease rates*. Gold, silver, and platinum can be leased (loaned) to jewelry and electronic manufacturers with the obligation to repay the precious metal at a later date.

Taking both the cost of storage and the convenience yield into account, the price of a futures contract may be stated as

$$F = Se^{(r+c-y)(T-t)} \tag{2.5}$$

where the terms are defined as before and y is the convenience yield.

Notice that the convenience yield is subtracted from the risk-free rate, r, and the storage cost, c. Similar to financial assets, the convenience yield, y, reduces the cost of ownership of the asset.

Consider the following example. The current price of an ounce of gold is \$400, the risk-free rate is 6%, the cost of storage is 2% of the purchase price, and the lease rate to lend gold is 1%. A six-month futures contract on gold will be

$$F = \$400e^{(0.06+0.02-0.01)(0.5)} = \$429$$

[4]If the storage costs are expressed as a dollar amount, then the appropriate equation is $F = (S + C)e^{r(T-t)}$ where C represents the present value of all storage costs incurred during the life of the futures contract.

EXHIBIT 2.5 Commodity Futures Arbitrage when $F > Se^{(r+c-y)(T-t)}$

Time	Cash Inflow	Cash Outflow	Net Cash
t (initiate the arbitrage)	S (cash borrowed)	S (to purchase the asset)	$S - S = 0$
T (maturity of the futures contract)	F (price for future delivery of the commodity)	$Se^{(r+c-y)(T-t)}$ (pay back principal and interest on loan plus storage costs less income from lease revenue)	$F - Se^{(r+c-y)(T-t)}$

Assume that $F > Se^{(r+c-y)(T-t)}$. Then an investor can earn an arbitrage profit by borrowing S to purchase the underlying commodity and selling the futures contract, F. This arbitrage is detailed in Exhibit 2.5.[5]

Exhibit 2.5 demonstrates the payment received from the arbitrage. At maturity of the futures contract, the investor receives a positive cash flow of $F - Se^{(r+c-y)(T-t)}$ where $Se^{(r+c-y)(T-t)}$ represents the cash that must be paid back for the loan, interest on the loan, and storage costs less any value received from the gold lease rate.

This arbitrage cannot work in reverse if the investor does not already own the commodity. Except for precious metals, commodities are difficult to borrow. Consequently, they cannot be shorted in the same fashion as financial assets. Furthermore, companies that own the underlying commodity do so for its consumption value rather than its investment value.

ECONOMICS OF THE COMMODITY MARKETS: NORMAL BACKWARDATION VERSUS CONTANGO

With this pricing framework in place, we turn to the economics of commodity consumption, production, and hedging. Commodity futures contracts exhibit a term structure similar to that of interest rates. This curve can be downward sloping or upward sloping. The reasons for the different curves will be determined by the actions of hedgers and speculators.

[5]In practice, storage costs may be quoted in dollar terms rather than as a percentage of the commodity's value, while convenience yields are quoted as a percentage of the commodity's value. Consider the case where C is equal to the present value of the storage costs that must be paid over the life of the futures contract. Then equation (2.5) can be expressed as

$$F = Se^{(r-y)(T-t)} + Ce^{r(T-t)}$$

EXHIBIT 2.6 Beta Coefficients and Correlation Coefficients of Four Large Petroleum Companies

	Stock Market Beta	Stock Market Correlation Coefficient	Crude Oil Beta	CrudeOil Correlation Coefficient
ExxonMobile	0.67	0.86	−0.04	−0.14
Chevron/Texaco	0.67	0.60	−0.08	−0.22
Royal Dutch Shell	0.85	0.78	0.38	0.02
BP Amoco	0.71	0.55	0.12	0.26

Consider a petroleum producer such as ExxonMobil. Through its exploration, developing, refining, and marketing operations, this company is naturally long crude oil exposure. This puts Exxon at risk to declining crude oil prices. To reduce this exposure, Exxon will sell crude oil futures contracts.[6]

From Exxon's perspective, by selling crude oil futures contracts it can separate its commodity price risk from its business risk (i.e., the ability to find crude oil, refine it, and market it to consumers). By hedging, Exxon can better apply its capital to its business risks rather than holding a reserve of capital to protect against fluctuating crude oil prices. Simply stated, hedging allows for the more efficient use of ExxonMobil's invested capital. ExxonMobil's stock price has virtually no economic link to fluctuating oil prices. This can be seen in Exhibit 2.6 which reports the correlation coefficients and the betas associated with the stock returns for Exxon, as well as three other large petroleum companies compared to the S&P 500. Also reported in the exhibit is the correlation coefficients and betas for the stock returns of the four oil companies compared to the price of crude oil. However, there must be someone on the other side of the trade to bear the price risk associated with buying the futures contract. This is the speculator.

If Exxon transfers its risk to the speculator, the speculator must be compensated for this risk. The speculator is compensated by purchasing the futures contract from the petroleum producer at less than the expected future spot price of crude oil. That is, the price established in the commodity futures contract will be below the expected future spot price of crude oil. The speculator will be compensated by the difference between the futures price and the expected spot price. This may be expressed as

$$E(S_T) > F_T \tag{2.6}$$

[6]Oil producers have energy trading desks to hedge their long crude oil exposure. Another way that Exxon hedges this risk is through long-term delivery contracts where the price of crude oil is fixed in the contract.

where $E(S_T)$ = the expected spot price of the underlying commodity at time T (the maturity of the futures contract)

F_T = the agreed upon price in the futures contract to be paid at time T

If the inequality of equation (2.6) remains true at the maturity of the futures contract, the speculator will earn a profit of $S_T - F_T$. However, nothing is certain, commodity prices can fluctuate. It might turn out that the price agreed upon in the futures contract exceeds the spot price at time T. Then the speculator will lose an amount equal to $F_T - S_T$.

This is the risk that the petroleum producer transferred from its income statement to that of the speculator's. Therefore, to ensure the speculator is compensated more often than not for bearing the commodity price risk, it must be the case that agreed upon futures price F_T is sufficiently discounted compared to the expected future spot price S_T. This condition of the futures markets is referred to as *normal backwardation*, or simply, *backwardation*.

The term *backwardation* comes from John Maynard Keynes. Keynes was the first to theorize that commodity producers were the natural hedgers in the commodity markets and therefore would need to offer a risk premium to speculators in order to induce them to bear the risk of fluctuating commodity prices. This risk premium is represented by the difference of $E(S_T) - F_T$. Conversely, hedgers, because they are reducing their risks, are willing to enter into contracts where the expected payoff is slightly negative.[7]

Backwardated commodity markets have downward sloping futures curves. The longer dated the futures contract the greater must be the discount compared to the expected future spot price to compensate the speculator for assuming the price risk of the underlying commodity for a longer period of time. Therefore, longer dated futures contracts are priced cheaper than shorter-term futures contracts.

The reverse situation of a backwardated commodity market is a *contango market*. In a contango market, the inequality sign in equation (2.6) is reversed—the expected future spot price, S_T, is less than the current futures price, F_T.

---

[7]Although the term *backwardation* is used to describe generally the condition where futures prices are lower than the current spot price, the term *normal backwardation* refers to the precise condition where the expected future spot price is greater than the current futures price. I am indebted to Ray Venner, Ph.D., of the CalPERS Investment Staff for this important distinction.

A contango situation will occur when the most likely hedger of the commodity is naturally short the underlying commodity. Consider the aircraft manufacturer, Boeing. The single largest raw material input in the construction of any jet aircraft is aluminum for the superstructure of the plane. Boeing is a major consumer of aluminum, but it does not own any aluminum mining interests. Therefore, it is naturally short aluminum and must cover this short exposure by purchasing aluminum to meet its manufacturing needs.

This puts Boeing at risk to rising aluminum prices. To hedge this risk, Boeing can purchase aluminum futures contracts.[8] However, a speculator must be lured to the market to sell the futures contract to Boeing and to take on commodity price risk. To entice the speculator, Boeing must be willing to purchase the futures contract at a price F_T that is greater than the expected future spot price:

$$F_T > E(S_T) \tag{2.7}$$

Boeing is willing to purchase the futures contract at an expected loss in return for eliminating the uncertainty over aluminum prices. The speculator will sell the futures contract and expect to earn a profit of $F_T - E(S_T)$. Of course, the speculator might earn more or less (or even lose money) depending upon the actual spot price of aluminum at maturity of the futures contract. If the inequality in equation (2.7) remains true at maturity of the aluminum futures contract, then the speculator will earn $F_T - S_T$.

The reader might ask why the speculator is necessary. Why doesn't Boeing negotiate directly with aluminum producers in fixed price contracts to lock in the price of aluminum and eliminate its commodity price exposure? To the extent it can, Boeing does. In fact, to the extent that commodity producers and commodity consumers can negotiate directly with one another, price risk can be eliminated without the need for speculators. However, the manufacture of aluminum does not always match Boeing's production cycle, and Boeing will have short-term demands for aluminum that will expose it to price risk. Speculators fill this gap.

Similarly, ExxonMobil has a nondiversified exposure to crude oil. It can reduce the price risk associated with oil by selling its production forward. Yet, in many cases there may not be a willing consumer to purchase the forward production of crude oil. Therefore, ExxonMobil must sell its

[8] This is but one way that Boeing hedges its short exposure to aluminum. It can enter into long-term contracts to purchase aluminum at fixed prices. These are essentially custom-tailored futures contracts, or forward contracts.

future production at a discount to entice the speculator/investor into the market.

Contango futures markets have an upward sloping price curve. That is, the longer dated the futures contract, the greater must be the futures price that the speculator receives from selling the futures contract to the hedger. Higher prices reflect the additional risk that the speculator accepts over the longer period of time.

Backwardated versus contango markets also depend upon global supply and demand of the underlying commodity. Consider the case of crude oil. In early 1999, the market was awash in crude oil. Additional production from Iraq, a slowdown in Asian economies from the Asian Contagion in 1998, and lack of agreement (read cheating) by OPEC members led to a glut of crude oil. As a result, crude oil futures contracts reflected a contango market.

However, backwardated versus contango markets can also reflect who bears the most risk of commodity price changes at any given time. For example, in December 2005, most consumers of crude oil had experienced a significant period of prolonged crude oil price increases. The cost of a gallon of gasoline in the United States peaked at $3.25 a gallon in the late autumn of 2005. In addition, ongoing concern over the stability of Iraq—the second largest producer of oil in OPEC—led to instability of crude oil prices. Then the devastating impact of Hurricane Katrina (remember the complete evacuation of New Orleans) and other tropical storms in autumn 2005 disrupted oil supplies throughout the United States.

As a result, in late 2005, the risk of commodity price changes was felt squarely by oil consumers and not oil producers. Oil consumers are naturally short crude oil and they bore greater risk regarding the future price of crude oil than the oil producers because of all of the adverse supply shocks in the oil market during 2005. To hedge this risk, they purchased crude oil futures contracts to lock in with certainty the price of their oil consumption. The result is demonstrated by the contango crude oil market displayed in Exhibit 2.7. Consumers of oil were literally shocked by all of the price shocks associated with crude oil over the prior 18 months and naturally became cautious and risk averse concerning the direction of oil prices in the near future. As a result, the primary hedger of oil prices in late 2005 was not the oil producers but oil consumers. The result was a contango market where oil consumers had to compensate speculators by purchasing crude oil futures contracts at a futures price that was greater than the expected future spot price (see equation (2.7)).

In contrast, consider Exhibit 2.8. This is the futures market for crude oil in April 2008. This market clearly demonstrates a back-wardated crude oil price curve.

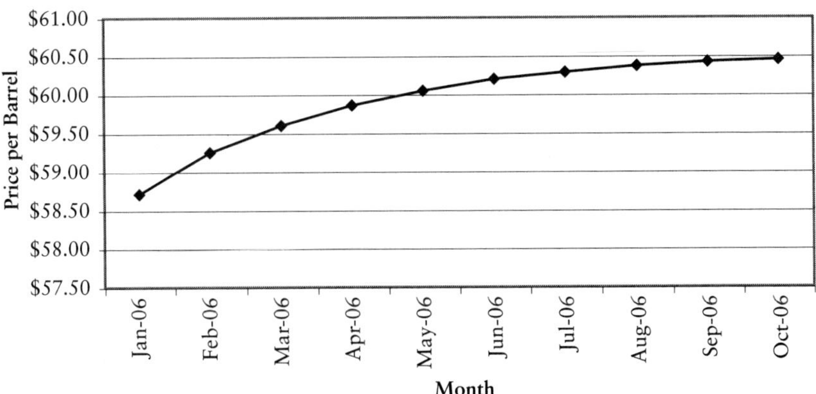

EXHIBIT 2.7 Contango Market for Crude Oil Futures, December 2005

Why the difference? In 2008, the crude oil market was functioning normally. There were no excessive price shocks, no drastic weather, and Iraq had been liberated from the oppressive regime of Sadaam Hussein. At this time, the price risk of crude oil rested upon the shoulders of crude oil producers. In order to hedge their risk, they had to entice speculators into the market by offering a futures price that was sufficiently less than the expected future spot price. The result is the backwardated curve in Exhibit 2.8.

Commodity markets are backwardated most of the time. In fact, the crude oil market is in backwardation approximately 70% of the time. The reason is that backwardated markets encourage commodity producers to

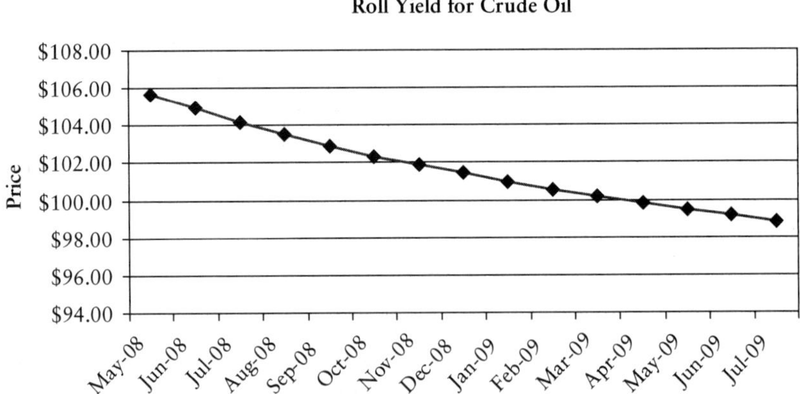

EXHIBIT 2.8 Backwardated Market for Crude Oil Futures, April 2008

produce. Consider Exhibit 2.8. ExxonMobil has a choice: It can produce crude oil immediately and sell it at a price of $106.00 per barrel or it can wait 12 months and sell it at an expected price of $98.00. The choice is easy: ExxonMobil would prefer to produce today and sell crude oil at a higher price rather than produce tomorrow and sell it at a lower price. Therefore, backwardation is a necessary condition to encourage current production of the underlying commodity.

However, sometimes supply and demand become unbalanced as was the case with crude oil in 2005. When this occurs, commodity futures markets can reverse their natural course and flip between backwardation and contango. In addition, a contango market can develop when the risk bearing shifts from commodity producers to commodity consumers. This happened in December 2005. After several price shocks over the prior two years, commodity crude oil consumers became extremely risk averse. Their increased level of risk aversion led to a shift in the risk bearing for crude oil prices, and they became the dominant hedger in the crude oil market. This resulted in the contango market documented in Exhibit 2.7.

Exhibits 2.7 and 2.8 also highlight another useful point: the role of the speculator. The speculator does not care whether the commodity markets are in backwardation or contango; she is agnostic. All the speculator cares about is receiving an appropriate premium for the price risk she will bear. If the market is backwardated, the speculator is willing to purchase the futures contract from the hedger, but only at a discount. If the commodities market is in contango, the speculator will sell the futures contract, but only at a premium.

One last important point must be made regarding Exhibits 2.7 and 2.8. The speculator/investor in commodity futures can earn a profit no matter which way the commodity markets are acting. The conclusion is that the expected long-term returns to commodity investing are independent of the long-term commodity price trends. As we just demonstrated, the speculator is agnostic with respect to the current price trend of crude oil. Investment profits can be earned whether the market is in backwardation or contango. Therefore, profits in the commodity markets are determined by the supply and demand for risk capital, not the long-term pricing trends of the commodity markets.

COMMODITY PRICES COMPARED TO FINANCIAL ASSET PRICES

In this section, we compare commodity prices to financial asset prices. Financial asset prices reflect the long-term discounted value of a stream of expected future revenues. In the case of stock prices, this future revenue stream may be eternal. In the case of a bond, the time is finite but can be very long, 10 to 20 years of expected cash flows. Investors in financial assets are compensated for the risk of fluctuating cash flows, and this risk is reflected in the interest rate used to discount those cash flows.

Thus, long-term expectations and interest rates are critical for pricing financial assets. Conversely, speculators and investors in commodities earn returns for bearing short-term commodity price risk. By bearing the price risk for commodity producers and commodity consumers, commodity investors and speculators receive exposure to the hedger's short-term earnings instead of its long-term cash flows. This point is all the more illuminated by how quickly the commodity markets can flip-flop between a contango market and a backwardated market. Exhibits 2.7 and 2.8 demonstrate that the nature of risk bearing can shift dramatically from producers to consumers of commodities.

This short-term exposure to a hedger's earnings illustrates that commodities will be priced very differently from financial assets. Long-term expectations and interest rates have only a minimal impact on commodity prices. Therefore, commodity prices can react very differently from financial asset prices when short-term expectations and long-term expectations diverge. This divergence occurs naturally as part of the course of the business cycle.

For instance, at the bottom of a recession, the short-term expectation of the economy's growth is negative. Commodity prices will decline to reflect this lower demand for raw inputs. However, it is at the bottom of a recession when discount rates are low and when long-term earnings expectations are revised upwards that stocks and bonds begin to perform well. The converse is true at the peak of an expansion. Commodity prices are high, but long-term earnings expectations decline.

The different reactions to different parts of the business cycle indicate that commodities tend to move in the opposite direction of stocks and bonds. This has important portfolio implications. Suffice for now to understand that commodity prices follow different pricing dynamics than that of financial assets.

CONCLUSION

Commodity futures contracts are important tools not only for hedgers but also for speculators. Many institutional investors nowadays make use of the futures markets to earn risk premiums. This chapter laid the groundwork in terms of pricing dynamics and discussed the economics of commodity futures markets. Starting with a demonstration of arbitrage strategies to financial and currency futures markets, the pricing dynamics between commodity spot and futures prices as well as important distinctions to the former markets that will affect this pricing relationship were highlighted. These are the storage costs associated with physical commodities and the convenience yield which both have to be factored into the pricing equation. In the next step, this pricing framework allowed us to turn to the economics of commodity consumption, production, and hedging. Thereby, the term structure of commodity futures contracts are determined by the actions of hedgers and speculators on the commodities markets. Backwardated commodity markets exhibit downward sloping futures curves whereas the reverse situation with an upward sloping price curve is referred to as contango markets. Consequently, speculators/investors in commodity futures can earn a profit no matter which way the commodity markets are acting. The conclusion is that the expected long-term returns to commodity investing are independent of the long-term commodity price trends. Therefore, profits in the commodity markets are determined by the supply and demand for risk capital, and not by the long-term pricing trends of the commodity markets.

CHAPTER 3

Commodity Futures Investments: A Review of Strategic Motivations and Tactical Opportunities

Joshua D. Woodard
Ph.D. Candidate
Office for Futures and Options Research (OFOR)
University of Illinois at Urbana-Champaign

The motivation for investing in commodity futures dates back to at least the 1930s when John Maynard Keynes[1] proposed the theory of normal backwardation. The theory of normal backwardation posits that futures markets are essentially insurance markets. Under the assumption that hedgers were primarily producers of commodities, Keynes reasoned that long speculators should earn a risk premium for taking on the spot price risk hedgers wished to shed. This view was debated extensively throughout the next four decades but was almost always addressed in an isolated, individual market context.[2] The advent of Markowitz's mean-variance model and the development of Sharpe's *capital asset pricing model* (CAPM), however,

The author would like to thank the editors, as well as Philip Garcia, Jason Franken, and Thorsten Egelkraut, for helpful comments and suggestions on earlier drafts.

[1]John M. Keynes, *A Treatise on Money,* vol. 2 (London: Macmillan, 1930).

[2]See, for example, Paul H. Cootner, "Returns to Speculators: Telser versus Keynes," *Journal of Political Economy* 68, no. 4 (1960), pp. 396–404; and Lester G. Telser, "Futures Trading and the Storage of Cotton and Wheat," *Journal of Political Economy* 66, no. 3 (1958), pp. 233–255.

prompted new thinking on the nature of speculative returns in commodity futures markets.

In 1973, Dusak[3] challenged the conventional notion of risk premiums by applying the CAPM framework to commodity futures returns. She argued that in principle futures markets are no different than any other market for risky assets. Specifically, the portfolio approach makes no presumption as to whether absolute returns are positive, negative, or zero, but rather that the returns on any risky asset are determined by that asset's contribution to the risk-return of a large diversified portfolio. Dusak's empirical analysis revealed risk premiums which were very close to zero and had virtually no systematic risk. Alone, these findings implied that commodity futures may only have trivial implications for the investment portfolio. Dusak's data, which only covered corn, wheat, and soybeans, were limited in scope, however, and her results were not generated with a specific view toward evaluating the investment performance of commodities in a diversified portfolio.

In the late 1970s, researchers began considering that commodity futures might be attractive portfolio components. In the first article on the subject, Greer[4] highlighted the investment potential of commodity futures by demonstrating that unlevered futures investments were less risky than stocks and provided an inflation hedge. Bodie and Rosansky,[5] using a more extensive data set than that employed by Dusak, found that an equally weighted portfolio of commodity futures had risk-adjusted excess returns which were similar to the S&P 500 yet still had a negative stock market beta. These findings did not conform well to the CAPM as Dusak had reported but did provide further support for considering commodity futures as part of a broader investment strategy.

The findings of these early studies opened the door to a relatively long line of literature investigating the potential investment benefits of commodity futures. The appeal of a natural hedge against the business cycle, as well as the recent run-up in commodity prices, has provoked renewed interest in commodity futures. The purpose of this chapter is to provide a review of research relevant to commodity futures investment. We synthesize the findings of several previous studies and examine their consistency with results for the period July 1996 to June 2006 using stocks, bonds, and commodity

---

[3]Katherine Dusak, "Futures Trading and Investor Returns: An Investigation of Commodity Market Risk Premiums," *Journal of Political Economy* 81, no. 6 (1973), pp. 1387–1406.

[4]Robert J. Greer, "Conservative Commodities: A Key Inflation Hedge," *Journal of Portfolio Management* 4, no. 4 (1978), pp. 26–29.

[5]Zvi Bodie and Victor I. Rosansky, "Risk and Return in Commodity Futures," *Financial Analysts Journal* 36, no. 3 (1980), pp. 27–39.

futures.[6] The data period considered here is relatively short compared to earlier studies, which increases the potential for idiosyncratic effects. Nonetheless, the results may provide insightful information regarding the stability and robustness of earlier findings.

The literature has traditionally dichotomized commodity futures investments as either strategic or tactical. Strategic investments, which are addressed in the next section, are usually viewed in a static context where long-only investments are considered. Strategic allocations seek to exploit the long-run characteristics among different asset classes through passive investment. Tactical opportunities, which are addressed in the following section, take advantage of the possibility that futures returns may vary in response to structural factors, such as inflation, and imply that dynamic trading schemes can be formulated in response to macroeconomic conditions and short-term aberrations.

STRATEGIC MOTIVATION FOR COMMODITY INVESTMENTS

There are numerous strategic motivations for holding passive long-only commodity futures in a portfolio of stocks and bonds.[7] These include the possibility of earning risk premiums,[8] the low correlation of commodities with stocks and bonds, and protection against inflation and business cycles.

---

[6]There is also a branch of the literature on commodity investments that focuses on managed futures and commodity funds. See, for example, Scott H. Irwin, Terry R. Krukemyer, and Carl R. Zulauf, "Investment Performance of Public Commodity Pools: 1979–1990," *Journal of Futures Markets* 13, no. 7 (1993), pp. 799–820; Franklin R. Edwards and Mustafa Onur Caglayan, "Hedge Fund and Commodity Fund Investments in Bull and Bear Markets," *Journal of Portfolio Management* 27, no. 4 (2001), pp. 97–108; and Edwin J. Elton, Martin J. Gruber, and Joel C. Rentzler, "Professionally Managed, Publicly Traded Commodity Funds," *Journal of Business* 60, no. 2 (1987), pp. 175–199. We do not address these here since they introduce an extra dimension to the problem, namely manager skill.

[7]Analysis of short positions is beyond the scope of this chapter. While considering the possibility of short sales complicates estimation somewhat, the issues explored in this chapter can easily be generalized to allow for short positions.

[8]Alternative views of basis behavior, such as the convenience yield hypothesis, are not discussed here. See Holbrook Working, "Theory of the Inverse Carrying Charge in Futures Markets," *Journal of Farm Economics* 30, no. 1 (1948), pp. 1–28; Holbrook Working, "The Theory of Price of Storage," *American Economic Review* 39,

Empirical Evidence of Risk Premiums

Historically, empirical confirmation of risk premiums has been somewhat contentious.[9] As pointed out by Garcia and Leuthold,[10] the detection of significant risk premiums seems to be sensitive to the assumptions and methods used in the estimation. In addition, the results across studies appear to be influenced heavily by the sample period. This is particularly true for individual commodity futures, which have high idiosyncratic risk. Portfolios of commodity futures, however, generally exhibit significant long-only risk premiums similar to those found for equities.[11] This effect is largely because portfolios are less risky than their constituents.

As noted, Dusak[12] did not find any evidence of risk premiums in her sample. Bodie and Rosansky[13] found positive excess returns for 22 of the

---

no. 6 (1949), pp. 1254–1262; Colin A. Carter, "Commodity Futures Markets: A Survey," *Australian Journal of Agricultural and Resource Economics* 43, no. 2 (1999), pp. 209–247; Martin Benirschka and James K. Binkley, "Optimal Storage and Marketing over Space and Time," *American Journal of Agricultural Economics* 77, no. 3 (1995), pp. 512–524; and Eugene F. Fama and Kenneth R. French, "Commodity Futures Prices: Some Evidence of Forecast Power, Premiums, and the Theory of Storage," *Journal of Business* 60, no. 1 (1987), pp. 55–73.

[9]See, for example, Cootner, "Returns to Speculators: Telser versus Keynes," Dusak, "Futures Trading and Investor Returns: An Investigation of Commodity Market Risk Premiums"; Eugene F. Fama and Kenneth R. French, "Commodity Futures Prices: Some Evidence of Forecast Power, Premiums, and the Theory of Storage," *Journal of Business* 60, no. 1 (1987), pp. 55–73; Telser, "Futures Trading and the Storage of Cotton and Wheat"; Colin A. Carter, Gordon C. Rausser, and Andrew Schmitz, "Efficient Asset Portfolios and the Theory of Normal Backwardation," *Journal of Political Economy* 91, no. 2 (1983), pp. 319–331; and Bruce Bjornson and Colin A. Carter, "New Evidence on Agricultural Commodity Return Performance under Time-Varying Risk," *American Journal of Agricultural Economics* 79, no. 3 (1997), pp. 918–930.

[10]Philip Garcia and Raymond Leuthold, "A Selected Review of Agricultural Commodity Futures and Options Markets," *European Review of Agricultural Economics* 31, no. 3 (2004), pp. 235–272.

[11]See, for example, Bodie and Rosansky, "Risk and Return in Commodity Futures"; Zvi Bodie, "Commodity Futures as a Hedge against Inflation," *Journal of Portfolio Management* 9, no. 3 (1983), pp. 12–17; Claude B. Erb and Campbell R. Harvey, "The Tactical and Strategic Value of Commodity Futures," *Financial Analysts Journal* 62, no. 2 (2006), pp. 69–97; and Gary Gorton and K. Geert Rouwenhorst, "Facts and Fantasies about Commodity Futures," *Financial Analysts Journal 62,* no. 2 (2006), pp. 47–68.

[12]Dusak, "Futures Trading and Investor Returns: An Investigation of Commodity Market Risk Premiums."

[13]Bodie and Rosansky, "Risk and Return in Commodity Futures."

23 individual commodities evaluated, but only marginal evidence of statistical significance. Samuelson[14] argued that futures prices should not have any upward or downward drift on average.[15] Carter, Rausser, and Schmitz,[16] using a respecification of Dusak's model which used a market portfolio that included commodities and allowed speculative positions to be net short or long depending on hedging pressure, found evidence of time-varying seasonal risk premiums. In another study, Chang[17] used nonparametric procedures to investigate wheat, corn, and soybean returns from 1951 to 1980. He found empirical evidence of significant risk premiums, but noted that the magnitudes varied through time.

Fama and French[18] investigated the normal backwardation issue by analyzing 21 agricultural, wood, livestock, and metal commodities. They found evidence of time-varying risk premiums for 7 of the 21 commodities. However, their particular test was only designed to detect variation in expected premiums. Thus, failure to find evidence of premiums using their test did not preclude the possibility of positive expected premiums.

To investigate the issue further, Fama and French conducted *t*-tests on simple average returns to test whether returns were significantly different from zero for each commodity as well as for an equally weighted portfolio of all commodities. They reported that only 5 of 21 commodities provided statistically significant positive returns. On the other hand, they found an average return of 0.54% a month with a *t*-statistic of 1.87 for the equally weighted portfolio of all commodities, indicating "marginally reliable normal backwardation that is also nontrivial in magnitude." Thus, while individual markets did not appear to provide consistent risk premiums, a portfolio of futures did appear to provide significant premiums. One explanation for this finding is that diversification across commodities reduces portfolio risk without reducing return. Bodie and Rosansky[19] revealed similar findings with respect to a portfolio of commodity futures.

---

[14]Paul Samuelson, "Proof that Properly Anticipated Prices Fluctuate Randomly." *Industrial Management Review* 6, no. 2 (1965), pp. 41–49.

[15]See also, Telser, "Futures Trading and the Storage of Cotton and Wheat."

[16]Carter, Rausser, and Schmitz, "Efficient Asset Portfolios and the Theory of Normal Backwardation."

[17]Eric C. Chang, "Returns to Speculators and the Theory of Normal Backwardation," *Journal of Finance* 40, no. 1 (1985), pp. 193–208.

[18]Eugene F. Fama and Kenneth R. French, "Commodity Futures Prices: Some Evidence of Forecast Power, Premiums, and the Theory of Storage," *Journal of Business* 60, no. 1 (1987), pp. 55–73.

[19]Bodie and Rosansky, "Risk and Return in Commodity Futures."

In a more recent study, Gorton and Rouwenhorst[20] constructed an equally weighted index of 36 commodity futures for the period July 1959 to December 2004 and came to similar conclusions. Their portfolio had an average return and *t*-statistic of 5.23% and 2.92. For individual commodities, however, the presence of positive risk premiums varied. Erb and Harvey[21] reported similar findings for a wide variety of commodity futures and commodity future subindexes for the period 1982 to 2004.[22]

We investigate the risk premium issue here in a manner similar to Gorton and Rouwenhorst using simple *t*-tests on arithmetic returns.[23] The individual commodities chosen for the analysis, crude oil, copper, silver, gold, wheat, soybeans, corn, lean hogs, and live cattle, are among the most heavily traded contracts in each of the main commodity subclasses, energy, industrial metals, precious metals, agricultural, and livestock. The futures contract for the Goldman Sachs Commodity Index[24] (GSCI) is included as a measure of aggregate commodity performance.

Exhibit 3.1 presents descriptive statistics for selected fully collateralized commodity futures returns for the 10-year period from July 1996 to June 2006. Seven of the 10 commodities have positive returns for the sample period while corn, wheat, and hogs have negative returns. Four contracts, crude oil, copper, cattle, and the GSCI, all have significant positive returns as estimated by a simple *t*-statistic. Corn and wheat exhibit significant negative returns. The findings for this sample are consistent with those of earlier studies in that the returns on individual commodities vary substantially,

---

[20]Gary Gorton and K. Geert Rouwenhorst, "Facts and Fantasies about Commodity Futures," *Financial Analysts Journal* 62, no. 2 (2006), pp. 47–68.

[21]Claude Erb and Campbell Harvey, "The Strategic and Tactical Value of Commodity Futures," *Financial Analyst Journal* 62, no. 2 (2006), pp. 69–97.

[22]This discussion is by no means exhaustive. For further discussion see, for example, Garcia and Leuthold, "A Selected Review of Agricultural Commodity Futures and Options Markets"; Colin A. Carter, "Commodity Futures Markets: A Survey," *Australian Journal of Agricultural and Resource Economics* 43, no. 2 (1999), pp. 209–247; and Hendrik Bessembinder, "Systematic Risk, Hedging Pressure, and Risk Premiums in Futures Markets," *Review of Financial Studies* 5, no. 4 (1992), pp. 637–667.

[23]Our analysis employs arithmetic returns. Alternatively, log returns or geometric returns could have been used; however, it is highly unlikely that the choice would affect the qualitative implications of our results.

[24]The GSCI is an economic-production-weighted index published by Goldman Sachs. The contract weights are determined according to world production and thus the GSCI is currently heavily weighted toward energy exposures. A futures contract on the index trades on the Chicago Mercantile Exchange (CME). Our analysis is based on the futures contract, not the underlying index.

EXHIBIT 3.1 Descriptive Statistics: Monthly Arithmetic Returns, July 1996 to June 2006

	Average	Standard Error	t-Statistic	Median	Standard Deviation	Skewness	Kurtosis	Range	Minimum	Maximum
Stocks	0.0064	0.0041	1.5446	0.0087	0.0451	−0.4814	0.3350	0.2425	−0.1458	0.0967
Bonds	0.0057	0.0011	5.3652	0.0066	0.0117	−0.5527	0.9007	0.0681	−0.0368	0.0313
T-bills	0.0030	0.0001	22.7571	0.0035	0.0015	−0.3038	−1.4070	0.0048	0.0007	0.0055
Corn	−0.0112	0.0059	−1.8798	−0.0193	0.0652	0.0536	−0.0535	0.3259	−0.1715	0.1545
Soybeans	0.0070	0.0065	1.0729	−0.0015	0.0711	−0.0364	0.8091	0.4193	−0.2097	0.2096
Wheat	−0.0105	0.0060	−1.7495	−0.0174	0.0660	0.2733	−0.3778	0.3261	−0.1648	0.1612
Crude oil	0.0225	0.0087	2.5855	0.0208	0.0951	0.1671	0.3605	0.5777	−0.2205	0.3573
Silver	0.0091	0.0067	1.3623	0.0016	0.0731	−0.0932	0.6225	0.4208	−0.2349	0.1858
Gold	0.0050	0.0038	1.3230	−0.0006	0.0417	0.7701	1.1927	0.2587	−0.0947	0.1640
Copper	0.0171	0.0070	2.4418	0.0069	0.0768	1.1049	2.5822	0.4918	−0.1327	0.3592
Hogs	−0.0008	0.0077	−0.1066	−0.0011	0.0842	−0.1089	1.4314	0.5184	−0.2587	0.2597
Cattle	0.0085	0.0040	2.1224	0.0057	0.0440	−1.2621	6.5614	0.3522	−0.2301	0.1221
GSCI	0.0131	0.0054	2.4465	0.0119	0.0587	0.1462	−0.3506	0.2752	−0.1121	0.1631

while the return on the aggregate index, the GSCI, provides strong evidence of positive returns with a statistically significant monthly average return of 1.31%. One departure is the fact that crude oil has both higher average returns and a higher statistical significance than GSCI, which is mostly attributable to the run-up in energy prices for the period.

Commodities Futures as an Asset Class

While some research has questioned the notion of positive expected risk premiums in the Keynesian sense, numerous studies have documented the benefits of holding commodity futures in a diversified portfolio. Given that commodity futures portfolios tend to have positive expected returns, at least on average, it is natural to ask how they compare to more traditional assets. Bodie and Rosansky[25] found that an equally weighted index of futures had statistically significant returns that were comparable to stocks for the period 1950 to 1976. Using 1970 to 1997 data, Kaplan and Lummer[26] found that a collateralized investment in the GSCI had returns which were slightly greater than those for stocks and slightly riskier. Gorton and Rouwenhorst[27] found that an equally weighted portfolio of 36 commodity futures had a return that was comparable to stocks for the period 1959 to 2004. During that period, the average excess return and standard deviations of stocks (bonds) was 5.65% (2.22%) and 14.85% (8.47%), while commodities had an average excess return and standard deviation of 5.23% and 12.10%. Furthermore, the futures portfolio had a higher Sharpe ratio than both stocks and bonds. Last, they reported that stocks and bonds were relatively uncorrelated with commodities.

The high return of commodities and the low degree of systematic risk suggests that commodities might be valuable portfolio additions. Bodie and Rosanky[28] found that an allocation of 40% to commodity futures significantly decreased portfolio risk while increasing expected return relative to a portfolio of stocks only. Kaplan and Lummer found that adding the GSCI to a diversified portfolio of stocks and bonds increased expected returns while decreasing risk. Jaffe[29] reported that the addition of gold futures

[25]Bodie and Rosansky, "Risk and Return in Commodity Futures."

[26]Paul D. Kaplan and Scott L. Lummer, GSCI Collateralized Futures as a Hedging and Diversification Tool for Institutional Portfolios: an Update, Working Paper, Ibbotson Associates, 1997.

[27]Gorton and Rouwenhorst, "Facts and Fantasies about Commodity Futures."

[28]Bodie and Rosansky, "Risk and Return in Commodity Futures."

[29]Jeffrey F. Jaffe, "Gold and Gold Stocks as Investments for Institutional Portfolios," *Financial Analysts Journal* 45, no. 2 (1989), pp. 53–60.

increased the return and decreased the risk of a diversified portfolio for the period 1971 to 1987. Analyzing data for the period January 1994 to June 2006, Woodard, Egelkraut, Garcia, and Pennings[30] found that the addition of the GSCI, as well as certain individual commodity futures significantly increased the Sharpe ratio when added to a portfolio of stocks and bonds.

Anson[31] found that commodity futures outperformed stocks and bonds in terms of overall returns for the period 1970 to 2000, but that commodities exhibited marginally greater volatility. He also separately generates "efficient frontiers" of stock and bond portfolios with and without 10% allocations to several different commodity futures indexes. In all cases, he showed that the addition of futures significantly shifted the frontiers up for almost all risk levels. In another study, Fortenbery and Hauser[32] analyzed the investment benefits of corn, soybeans, live cattle, and hog futures. Their study, which used data for July 1976 to December 1985, found that while the addition of futures rarely increased portfolio return, they did provide risk reduction benefits through their ability to diversify nonsystematic risk.

Analysis of the recent period confirms the findings of earlier studies. Referring to Exhibit 3.1, which contains descriptive statistics for the S&P 500 Total Return Index (stocks), the Lehman Brothers U.S. Aggregate Bond Total Return Index (bonds), and commodity futures, the GSCI has significantly higher returns than both stocks and bonds (1.31%, 0.64%, and 0.57%) but also greater standard deviation (5.87%, 4.51%, and 1.17%). Stocks (bonds) have a t-statistic of 1.55 (5.37). Surprisingly, four futures contracts, crude oil, copper, cattle, and the GSCI, have t-statistics greater than that for stocks, indicating the presence of positive long-only risk premiums for these commodities.

Exhibit 3.2 presents correlations of monthly returns for stocks, bonds, and commodities as well as for changes in inflation measured by the Consumer Price Index (CPI). Similar to previous studies, we find low correlations between the GSCI and stocks and bonds. Overall, commodities are relatively uncorrelated across commodity classes. Within commodity classes, however, some significant correlations arise. Silver, gold, and copper are all highly correlated, with correlations ranging between 0.33 and

[30]Joshua D. Woodard, Thorsten M. Egelkraut, Philip Garcia, and Joost M. E. Pennings, Portfolio Diversification with Commodity Futures: Properties of Levered Futures, Working Paper, August 2006.

[31]Mark J. P. Anson, *Handbook of Alternative Investments,* 2nd ed. (Hoboken, NJ: John Wiley & Sons, 2006).

[32]T. Randall Fortenbery and Robert J. Hauser, "Investment Potential of Agricultural Futures Contracts," *American Journal of Agricultural Economics* 72, no. 3 (1990), pp. 721–727.

EXHIBIT 3.2 Monthly Arithmetic Return Correlations, July 1996 to June 2006

	Stocks	Bonds	T-bills	Corn	Soybeans	Wheat	Crude Oil	Silver	Gold	Copper	Hogs	Cattle	GSCI	CPI
Stocks	1.0000													
Bonds	−0.0550	1.0000												
T-bills	0.0439	0.1102	1.0000											
Corn	0.1246	0.0033	−0.0487	1.0000										
Soybeans	0.1716	0.0728	−0.1187	0.6681	1.0000									
Wheat	0.0770	−0.0296	−0.0859	0.5923	0.4214	1.0000								
Crude oil	−0.0262	0.0214	−0.0394	−0.0123	−0.0377	0.1447	1.0000							
Silver	0.1689	−0.0781	−0.0954	0.0310	−0.0478	−0.0254	0.1154	1.0000						
Gold	−0.0346	0.1241	−0.1709	0.0173	0.0186	0.0796	0.1973	0.5694	1.0000					
Copper	0.2937	−0.1716	−0.0840	0.1117	0.0963	0.1042	0.1781	0.3463	0.3296	1.0000				
Hogs	−0.0584	0.0493	0.0193	−0.0362	0.0285	−0.0085	0.0884	−0.0215	0.0420	0.0357	1.0000			
Cattle	0.0013	−0.2024	−0.1201	0.1549	0.0466	0.2244	−0.0140	−0.1247	−0.0431	0.0344	0.3143	1.0000		
GSCI	0.0054	0.0308	−0.0768	0.1200	0.0824	0.2883	0.8969	0.1033	0.2534	0.2739	0.0964	0.0168	1.0000	
CPI	−0.0993	−0.0877	0.0315	−0.0466	0.0051	0.0169	0.1492	0.0468	0.1370	0.1160	0.0597	0.0840	0.1954	1.0000

0.57. Crude oil is moderately correlated with wheat, silver, gold, and copper. The correlation between the GSCI and crude oil is 0.89, which is not surprising given the heavy weight of energy in the GSCI. Wheat, crude oil, silver, gold, and copper are all positively correlated with current inflation while stocks and bonds are negatively correlated with inflation. Hogs are relatively uncorrelated with all other assets as well as inflation. In fact, hogs are the least correlated of the commodities with the GSCI. Last, the agricultural grains are all highly correlated, with correlations for those commodities ranging between 0.421 and 0.668.

To investigate the role of commodities within a diversified portfolio of stocks and bonds, we turn attention to estimating optimal portfolios. In what follows, we estimate several portfolios which are partitioned according to various conditioning criteria. Three portfolios are estimated for each conditioning criterion. Portfolios in each section are designated as follows: portfolio I consists of stocks and bonds only; portfolio II includes stocks, bonds, and the GSCI; and portfolio III allows for investment in stocks, bonds, and individual commodities. Portfolio III is estimated in an effort to identify the sources of commodity benefits.

Each individual commodity futures return is approximated by a long-only, fully collateralized index. Optimal weights are estimated by maximizing the Sharpe ratio, calculated as the ratio of excess returns to standard deviation. Excess returns are calculated by subtracting the average T-bill return from the average portfolio return. The scope of what follows is relatively broad. Thus, while the Sharpe ratio criterion is admittedly simple, it is selected for its simplicity and transparency. The estimation assumes monthly rebalancing. The analyses are conducted ex post and are thus a backward-looking estimate of the best-case scenarios.

Exhibit 3.3 presents portfolio estimates for the full sample, July 1996 to June 2006. The full sample portfolios serve as the baseline to portfolios estimated in subsequent sections. Full sample portfolio I consists of an allocation of 91.3% to bonds and 8.7% to stocks. The Sharpe ratio is 0.246, and the mean monthly arithmetic return and standard deviation are 0.58% and 1.12%. The optimal allocation to stocks is exceedingly small as there is considerable uncertainty about their growth for the period. Adding the GSCI significantly increases overall performance, increasing the Sharpe ratio of portfolio II to 0.296. The benefits of the GSCI are primarily driven by energy futures which are heavily weighted in the GSCI and perform well during the period. Two other commodities, copper and cattle, enter the portfolio even more importantly than crude oil if judged by their weights. This is a reflection of the strong positive returns and negative correlations these commodities demonstrate with other components of the portfolio, particularly bonds. Portfolio III, which

EXHIBIT 3.3 Maximum Sharpe Ratio Portfolio Weights, July 1996 to June 2006

Full Sample	I	II	III
Stocks	0.0870	0.0780	0.0210
Bonds	0.9130	0.8070	0.7230
GSCI	—	0.1150	0.0000
Corn	—	—	0.0000
Soybeans	—	—	0.0040
Wheat	—	—	0.0000
Crude oil	—	—	0.0490
Silver	—	—	0.0180
Gold	—	—	0.0000
Copper	—	—	0.0640
Hogs	—	—	0.0000
Cattle	—	—	0.1200
Sharpe ratio	0.2460	0.2960	0.4050
T-bill average	0.0030	0.0030	0.0030
Average return	0.0058	0.0066	0.0077
Standard deviation	0.0112	0.0122	0.0115

includes individual commodities, has a Sharpe ratio of 0.405. Portfolios II and III have significantly greater returns than portfolio I, but only marginally greater risk.

Not all individual commodities are part of the optimal portfolio. Corn, wheat, gold, and hogs all have optimal weights of 0.0%, and soybeans constitute less than 0.5%. This indicates that while some commodities may provide significant benefits over extended periods, not all commodities have reliable long-only returns.[33]

Commodities and Inflation

Commodities have long been viewed as a hedge against inflation. Following Greer,[34] Bodie, and Rosansky[35] examined the response of stocks, bonds,

[33] Although we do not address the issue of short selling here, this does not preclude the possibility that some commodities may have significant benefits in short positions. For example, corn has significant negative returns. Also, Erb and Harvey found that strategies employing short positions based on term structure indicators performed significantly better than long-only positions. Erb and Harvey, "The Tactical and Strategic Value of Commodity Futures."

[34] Greer, "Conservative Commodities: A Key Inflation Hedge."

[35] Bodie and Rosansky, "Risk and Return in Commodity Futures."

and commodities to inflation acceleration for the period 1950 to 1976. They found that annual excess returns of commodities were positively correlated with changes in inflation, 0.52, while stocks and bonds were negatively correlated with changes in inflation, −0.48 and −0.20, and that commodities provided an effective inflation hedge during the highest inflationary periods. Stocks and bonds, on the other hand, performed poorly during those periods.

Becker and Finnerty[36] came to similar conclusions for the period 1970 to 1990. They found that both equally weighted and production-weighted indexes of commodities were valuable portfolio components. Commodities were more beneficial in the 1970s than in the 1980s, a finding they attributed to their inflation hedging ability. Gay and Manaster[37] also suggested that commodity futures may provide effective hedges against inflation.

Ankrim and Hensel[38] found that commodity spot prices reacted positively to changes in unexpected inflation while financial assets reacted negatively. Kaplan and Lummer[39] also supported the notion that commodities performed better during inflationary periods while stocks and bonds performed poorly. Gorton and Rouwenhorst[40] examined the correlation of stocks, bonds, and commodities to inflation at horizons ranging from one month to five years. They reported that commodities (stocks and bonds) were positively (negatively) correlated with inflation at all horizons. Finally, Kat and Oomen[41] found that commodities performed well in the face of unexpected inflation, but that this varied significantly over individual commodities for the period January 1965 to February 2005. Energy, metals, cattle, and sugar offered the best hedging potential while grains, oil seeds,

---

[36]Kent G. Becker and Joseph E. Finnerty, "Indexed Commodity Futures and the Risk and Return of Institutional Portfolios," in *Advances in Investment Management and Portfolio Analysis, Vol. 4,* edited by Cheng-Few Lee (Greenwich: JAI Press, 1997), pp. 1–14.

[37]Gerald D. Gay and Steven Manaster, "Hedging against Commodity Price Inflation: Stocks and Bills as Substitutes for Futures Contracts," *Journal of Business* 55, no. 3 (1982), pp. 317–343.

[38]Ernest M. Ankrim and Chris R. Hensel, "Commodities in Asset Allocation: A Real-Asset Alternative to Real Estate," *Financial Analysts Journal* 49, no. 3 (1993), pp. 20–29.

[39]Kaplan and Lummer, GSCI Collateralized Futures as a Hedging and Diversification Tool for Institutional Portfolios: An Update.

[40]Gorton and Rouwenhorst, "Facts and Fantasies about Commodity Futures."

[41]Harry M. Kat and Roel C. A. Oomen, "What Every Investor Should Know about Commodities, Part II: Multivariate Return Analysis," *Journal of Management* (forthcoming 2007).

softs, pork, and palladium were mostly uncorrelated with unexpected inflation.

Overall, the findings of previous studies support the notion that futures, on average, are positively correlated with inflation and provide a reasonable inflation hedge for traditional assets, although this varies across individual commodities. There are a few reasons we might expect these findings. First, commodities are a component of inflation. They also affect input prices of finished goods. Further, stocks and bonds represent a claim on future earnings and the value of those earnings can be eroded by inflation and high input costs.

Bjornson and Carter,[42] by exception, came to a slightly different conclusion. They developed a single-beta conditional equilibrium asset pricing model to describe commodity returns and found evidence of time-varying risk premiums that differed predictably based on information about interest rates and economic conditions. Interestingly, they concluded that expected commodity returns were inversely related to interest rates, economic growth, and inflation.[43]

Exhibit 3.2 presents the correlations of assets with monthly changes in inflation. Consistent with previous studies, 9 of 10 commodities are positively correlated with inflation. The aggregate index, the GSCI, is highly correlated with inflation, 0.195. The strength of this relationship with inflation varies for individual commodities. Grains are not highly correlated with inflation overall, and corn is negatively correlated with inflation. Crude oil, gold, and copper, however, are highly correlated with inflation. Consistent with Gorton and Rouwenhorst,[44] both stocks and bonds have strong negative correlations with inflation.

Next, we turn to the analysis of optimal commodity investments during high and low inflationary environments. The data are partitioned according to whether the monthly change in the CPI was above the 75th percentile (high), or below the 25th percentile (low) to evaluate the effects of extreme inflation on optimal asset allocations. Exhibit 3.4 displays optimal Sharpe ratio allocations for high and low inflation portfolios.

Portfolios I and II perform better during low inflation months relative to high inflation months. Stocks have a significantly greater allocation during periods of low inflation, 24.76%, than what is reported for the full

---

[42]Bruce Bjornson and Colin A. Carter, "New Evidence on Agricultural Commodity Return Performance under Time-Varying Risk," *American Journal of Agricultural Economics* 79, no. 3 (1997), pp. 918–930.

[43]See Bjornson and Carter for additional discussion of asset pricing model applications to commodities.

[44]Gorton and Rouwenhorst, "Facts and Fantasies about Commodity Futures."

EXHIBIT 3.4 Optimal Portfolio Weights: High and Low Inflation, July 1996 to June 2006

	Low Inflation			High Inflation		
	I	II	III	I	II	III
Stocks	0.2476	0.2495	0.2294	0.0000	0.0000	0.0000
Bonds	0.7524	0.7328	0.6604	1.0000	0.7877	0.6779
GSCI	—	0.0177	0.0000	—	0.2123	0.0916
Corn	—	—	0.0000	—	—	0.0000
Soybeans	—	—	0.0000	—	—	0.0000
Wheat	—	—	0.0000	—	—	0.0000
Crude oil	—	—	0.0127	—	—	0.0119
Silver	—	—	0.0647	—	—	0.0853
Gold	—	—	0.0000	—	—	0.0000
Copper	—	—	0.0000	—	—	0.0286
Hogs	—	—	0.0000	—	—	0.0000
Cattle	—	—	0.0329	—	—	0.1048
Sharpe ratio	0.7343	0.7378	0.8406	0.2361	0.6212	0.9310
T-bill average	0.0027	0.0027	0.0027	0.0028	0.0028	0.0028
Average return	0.0108	0.0108	0.0114	0.0053	0.0110	0.0126
Standard deviation	0.0110	0.0110	0.0104	0.0106	0.0132	0.0106

sample portfolios (i.e., the baseline), 8.7%. This is consistent with earlier studies which have identified a negative relationship between equities and inflation. The GSCI has a marginal share, 1.77%, in portfolio II. Further, the performance of low inflation portfolios I and II are virtually identical. Crude oil, silver, and cattle have allocations in low inflation portfolio III, but affect performance only slightly.

While commodities have virtually no role in the low inflation portfolios, they significantly improve the performance of high inflation portfolios. For example, including the GSCI nearly triples the Sharpe ratio. The GSCI allocation is 21.23% in high inflation portfolio II whereas the allocation of stocks is 0.0%. Silver and cattle both have greater allocations in the high inflation (8.53% and 10.48%) than in the low inflation portfolio (6.47% and 3.29%). The same is true for crude oil, with the GSCI acting as a surrogate to crude oil in the high-inflation portfolio.[45] This is consistent with the findings of Kat and Oomen[46] regarding the performance of individual commodities.

---

[45]Replication of that portfolio excluding the GSCI resulted in a crude oil allocation of 7.62%.

[46]Kat and Oomen, "What Every Investor Should Know about Commodities, Part II: Multivariate Return Analysis."

Interestingly, both sets of portfolios exhibit below average Treasury bill returns. T-bills are often used as a proxy for expected inflation. Thus, this suggests that most of the variation in the results is due to unexpected inflation. This is consistent with the findings of Gorton and Rouwenhorst[47] who concluded that stock, bond, and commodity returns were more sensitive to unexpected inflation. Still, these findings are not surprising. As noted, commodities are a component of inflation. Also, the detrimental effect of inflation on equities is well accepted, at least for unexpected inflation. Overall, analysis of the recent period corroborates the findings of earlier portfolio studies. Namely, stocks and bonds tend to be negatively impacted by inflation, particularly unexpected inflation, while commodities respond positively.

Commodity Returns, Business Cycles, and Economic Growth

Bjornson and Carter[48] suggested that commodities may act as a hedge against business cycles, as commodities and capital assets are affected differently by macroeconomic factors. Part of the reason is that stocks and bonds are affected by long-term expectations of future cash flows whereas commodities are influenced primarily by short-term shocks. Therefore, we would expect commodities and capital assets to perform much differently at different points in the business cycle. Additionally, we may expect some commodities to exhibit positive demand effects in response to economic growth.

The effects of macroeconomic factors on the interactions among commodities, stocks, and bonds are not perfectly understood though. In particular, individual commodities may be influenced differently by economic growth and the conditions associated with such growth. For example, Bjornson and Carter predicted an inverse relationship between agricultural commodity returns and the business cycle, while Fama and French[49] found that metals exhibited significant business cycle exposure. Gorton and Rouwenhorst[50] found that stocks and commodities, on average, tended to do better during expansion, bonds had superior performance during recessions,

[47]Gorton and Rouwenhorst, "Facts and Fantasies about Commodity Futures."

[48]Bjornson and Carter, "New Evidence on Agricultural Commodity Return Performance under Time-Varying Risk."

[49]Eugene F. Fama and Kenneth R. French, "Business Cycles and the Behavior of Metals Prices," *Journal of Finance* 43, no. 5 (1988), pp. 1075–1093.

[50]Gorton and Rouwenhorst, "Facts and Fantasies about Commodity Futures."

and commodities usually performed worst during late recession when their demand was lowest. Kat and Oomen[51] found that energy was a good diversifier during recessions and that metals, livestock, and softs performed better at the end of expansions.

Exhibit 3.5 displays quarterly asset return correlations with changes in real seasonally adjusted GDP. Seasonally adjusted GDP is used so that any seasonal effects are filtered out of the results (seasonality is addressed later). As a group, futures returns tend to be positively correlated with GDP. Stocks are also highly correlated with GDP while bonds, on the other hand, are negatively correlated. Since stocks and commodities are positively correlated with real economic growth we expect them to perform well during those periods.

Exhibit 3.6 contains portfolio optimizations for the highest and lowest half of GDP growth. To simplify the analysis, we do not condition on the particular phase of the business cycle but rather only consider the magnitude of economic growth. Bonds outperform stocks and commodities during low GDP growth periods. The converse is true during high growth periods. Portfolio II has optimal allocations of 43.21% and 32.83% for stocks and the GSCI when GDP growth is high, and for both asset classes 0% when it is low. Furthermore, the high-growth portfolios outperform their counterparts as they have both higher returns and Sharpe ratios.

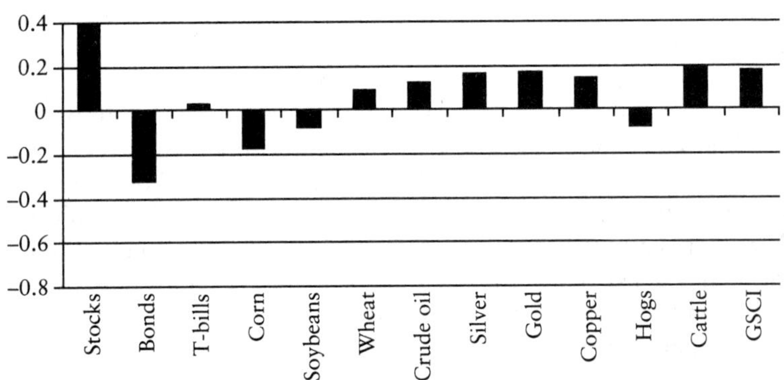

EXHIBIT 3.5 Correlation with Changes in GDP: Quarterly Returns, July 1996 to June 2006

[51]Kat and Oomen, "What Every Investor Should Know about Commodities, Part II: Multivariate Return Analysis."

EXHIBIT 3.6 Optimal Portfolio Weights: GDP Growth, July 1996 to June 2006

	Low GDP Growth			High GDP Growth		
	I	II	III	I	II	III
Stocks	0.0000	0.0000	0.0000	0.6131	0.4321	0.2934
Bonds	1.0000	1.0000	0.8072	0.3869	0.2396	0.3183
GSCI	—	0.0000	0.0000	—	0.3283	0.0000
Corn	—	—	0.0000	—	—	0.0000
Soybeans	—	—	0.0817	—	—	0.0000
Wheat	—	—	0.0000	—	—	0.0000
Crude oil	—	—	0.0000	—	—	0.1391
Silver	—	—	0.0130	—	—	0.0324
Gold	—	—	0.0000	—	—	0.0000
Copper	—	—	0.0448	—	—	0.0210
Hogs	—	—	0.0000	—	—	0.0000
Cattle	—	—	0.0535	—	—	0.1958
Sharpe ratio	0.3853	0.3853	0.6286	0.3078	0.4421	0.5004
Average return	0.0069	0.0069	0.0082	0.0112	0.0149	0.0140
Standard deviation	0.0101	0.0101	0.0082	0.0264	0.0268	0.0219
T-bill average	0.0030	0.0030	0.0030	0.0031	0.0031	0.0031

The results suggest that high economic growth may increase commodity demand, subsequently pushing up prices on average. Consistent with Gorton and Rouwenhorst,[52] we find that during growth phases, stocks and commodities tend to do well while bonds perform poorly. This is in contrast with Bjornson and Carter's suggestion that expected commodity returns tend to be higher when there is low economic growth and low inflation.[53] One reason for this discrepancy may be that we do not differentiate between accelerating and decelerating growth periods. As Anson[54] pointed out, commodity prices tend to decline at the bottom of a recession to reflect the low demand for raw inputs. Long-run expectations for capital assets on the other hand are revised upward and subsequently begin to perform well at this point in the business cycle. Thus, accounting for whether the economy is heating up or cooling down may permit different findings. Also, our analysis of business cycles does not address the question of growth and

[52]Gorton and Rouwenhorst, "Facts and Fantasies about Commodity Futures."

[53]Bjornson and Carter, "New Evidence on Agricultural Commodity Return Performance under Time-Varying Risk."

[54]Mark J. P. Anson, *Handbook of Alternative Investments,* 2nd ed. (Hoboken, NJ: John Wiley & Sons, 2006).

inflation jointly as Bjornson and Carter. Last, their study addressed agricultural commodities. However, we find significant heterogeneity among commodities, particularly for the agricultural commodities. For example, the correlations of corn, soybeans, and hogs with economic growth are negative, while the correlations for all other commodities are positive.

TACTICAL OPPORTUNITIES IN COMMODITY INVESTMENTS

While there are numerous strategic motivations for investing in commodity futures, the fact remains that consistent positive risk premiums have not been observed historically for all commodities. One explanation for these findings is the notion of time-varying risk premiums. The presence of time-varying risk premiums suggests that even in rational and efficient markets it may be optimal to hold futures in some periods and not in others. For example, in a recent study, Vrugt, Bauer, Molenaar, and Steenkamp[55] found evidence that predictability in futures returns was great enough to be exploited by dynamic trading strategies. Along these lines, several tactical trading opportunities present themselves. These include tactical trading schemes based on the monetary environment, seasonal criteria, the term structure, and momentum. The portfolio results presented in the tactical section are ex post optimizations which are based on ex ante criteria. This approach is similar to that employed in previous studies.[56]

Monetary Policy Environment and Interest Rates

Interest rates are a pervasive factor for the macroeconomy and commodity markets alike. Yet their role on commodity investment performance is not well understood. Frankel[57] argued that real interest rates should be inversely related to real commodity prices because interest rates have a negative relationship with the desire to carry commodity inventories. As such, interest rates are an important determinant of consumption and inventory demand, and thus prices. Following this logic, expansive

[55]Evert B. Vrugt, Rob Bauer, Roderick Molenaar, and Tom Steenkamp, Dynamic Commodity Timing Strategies, Working Paper, July 2004.

[56]See, for example, Gerald R. Jensen, Robert R. Johnson, and Jeffrey M. Mercer, "Efficient Use of Commodity Futures in Diversified Portfolios," *Journal of Futures Markets* 20, no. 5 (2000), pp. 489–506.

[57]Jeffrey A. Frankel The Effect of Monetary Policy on Real Commodity Prices, NBER Working Paper Series, December 2006.

monetary policy, which lowers the real interest rate, should lead to an increase in real commodity prices, and vice versa for restrictive monetary policy.[58] Bjornson and Carter's results, which suggested that commodity futures returns were higher during times of low interest rates, support this notion.[59]

In contrast, Jensen, Johnson, and Mercer[60] found that commodity investments performed better during periods of restrictive monetary policy. They employed an ex ante measure of Fed policy, namely whether the last change in the discount rate was positive (restrictive) or negative (expansive), to determine monetary stringency. During expansive monetary environments, both managed and unmanaged futures provided virtually no benefits. They also showed that metal, energy, and agricultural grain futures performed better during restrictive periods. Livestock performed better during expansive periods, but poorly during restrictive periods. They also found that the performance of a portfolio which took short positions in unmanaged futures during expansive periods, and long positions during restrictive periods, outperformed a simple buy and hold approach.

Exhibit 3.7 presents results for the monetary policy analysis for the recent period. We classify the data as either expansive or restrictive and estimate optimal portfolios.[61] The period is classified as restrictive (expansive) if the last change in the Fed funds rate was positive (negative).[62] Fifty-eight months were characterized by expansive monetary policy while 62 were restrictive.

Our analysis suggests that commodities perform relatively better, as measured by their optimal allocations, during expansive monetary periods, but only marginally so. In both cases, however, commodities improve overall portfolio performance. Referring to portfolio II, the GSCI has a slightly

---

[58]Interestingly, to the extent that lower real interest rates stimulate the macroeconomy, this proposition would be consistent with our findings above concerning commodity performance over the business cycle.

[59]Bjornson and Carter, "New Evidence on Agricultural Commodity Return Performance under Time-Varying Risk."

[60]Jensen, Johnson, and Mercer, "Efficient Use of Commodity Futures in Diversified Portfolios."

[61]Others have suggested that the term structure of interest rates, which is not addressed here, may also have implications for commodity futures price dynamics. See, for example, Bjornson, Carter, and Vrugt, et al. for investigation of this dimension.

[62]This is similar to the measure employed by Jensen, Johnson, and Mercer except we use the Fed funds instead of the discount rate. Jensen, Johnson, and Mercer, "Efficient Use of Commodity Futures in Diversified Portfolios."

EXHIBIT 3.7 Optimal Portfolio Weights, Monetary Policy, July 1996 to June 2006

	Expansive			Restrictive		
	I	II	III	I	II	III
Stocks	0.0999	0.0840	0.0434	0.0573	0.0556	0.0000
Bonds	0.9001	0.7882	0.6055	0.9427	0.8472	0.8649
GSCI	—	0.1278	0.0000	—	0.0972	0.0000
Corn	—	—	0.0000	—	—	0.0000
Soybeans	—	—	0.0773	—	—	0.0000
Wheat	—	—	0.0000	—	—	0.0000
Crude oil	—	—	0.0618	—	—	0.0252
Silver	—	—	0.0353	—	—	0.0102
Gold	—	—	0.0000	—	—	0.0000
Copper	—	—	0.0000	—	—	0.0997
Hogs	—	—	0.0000	—	—	0.0000
Cattle	—	—	0.1768	—	—	0.0000
Sharpe ratio	0.2005	0.2394	0.4326	0.3016	0.3614	0.5063
Average return	0.0047	0.0054	0.0081	0.0068	0.0077	0.0089
Standard deviation	0.0121	0.0133	0.0136	0.0100	0.0107	0.0101
T-bill average	0.0022	0.0022	0.0022	0.0038	0.0038	0.0038

higher allocation during expansive periods versus restrictive. Stocks also have a higher allocation during expansive periods. Overall, superior portfolio performance is observed during restrictive periods. In all cases, the restrictive portfolios have higher return and lower risk than expansive portfolios. This is due to the strong performance of bonds during high interest rate environments.

Evaluation of portfolio III reveals that four commodities, soybeans, crude oil, silver, and cattle, perform better in the expansive portfolio. Cattle futures have the strongest response. Their allocation is 0.0% during restrictive periods and 17.68% during expansive. Alternatively, copper performs better in restrictive policy environments. Overall though, commodities tend to perform better during expansive monetary environments.

The results generated here do not conform well to those of Jensen, Johnson, and Mercer. There are numerous possibilities for this. First, while there are strong theoretical reasons and empirical support for expecting commodities to perform better during expansive monetary regimes, Jensen, Johnson, and Mercer did employ a much larger data period of 27 years. Thus, their results may be more robust in a statistical sense. The question arises, however, that if the tactic did not work for the last ten years, then how many years would one have to pursue it before it came to fruition? Also, it is likely that significant structural change has occurred in the last

10 years and thus the systematic relationships reflected in their results may have changed. Also, over their data period, interest rates showed significant volatility. In contrast, over the recent period interest rates were relatively low and changed only modestly.

More importantly, Jensen, Johnson, and Mercer used the discount rate while we use the Fed funds rate. Though these rates tend to be closely related, it is possible that significant differences may arise depending on if the analysis is conducted using one or the other. Investigation of this issue revealed that using the Fed funds rate as opposed to the discount rate causes a classification change for one period within the recent data period. The Fed funds rate increased 0.25% on March 25, 1997 while the discount rate was unchanged. The monetary environment is classified as expansive for both measures prior to March 1997. Thus, the period April 1997 to September 1998 is classified as restrictive when using the Fed funds criteria as opposed to the discount rate.

It seems reasonable to interpret the March 25, 1997 Fed funds increase as an indication of restrictive monetary policy. Indeed, there was a significant decline in commodities during this period. Using the discount rate as the criterion during this period would have caused this large decline to be incorrectly classified as expansive. Thus, the restrictive estimates would have been biased toward finding strong commodity performance during restrictive periods. There were numerous instances during the sample period of Jensen, Johnson, and Mercer that the Fed funds rate was changed prior to the discount rate. This fact may partially explain their findings. Clearly though, this is an area in need of further research.

The use of an ex ante monetary policy indicator implies that commodities should have a marginally higher allocation during expansionary monetary environments. Not only is this effect the opposite of what Jensen, Johnson, and Mercer found, it is also sensitive. This highlights that although tactical schemes based on anticipating systematic macro relationships can be fruitful they are also somewhat weak, unstable, and uncertain.

Term Structure

The hedging pressure theory[63] was developed to explain the apparent contradiction between the normal backwardation hypothesis and the fact that not all commodities historically provided positive long-only risk premiums. Keynes' original notion assumed that hedgers were net short, and thus speculators were net long. The hedging pressure theory relaxed this assumption

[63]See, for example, Bessembinder, "Systematic Risk, Hedging Pressure, and Risk Premiums in Futures Markets."

by positing that net hedging pressure (whether short or long) could have a significant impact on the magnitude and direction of risk premiums. This implied that speculators should not be concerned with which direction the market is going since they can earn risk premiums whether the market is in backwardation (by going long) or in contango (by going short).

As Erb and Harvey[64] pointed out, one goal of tactical asset allocation should be to identify reliable sources of return. Along these lines, the term structure of a commodity may provide valuable information as to expected futures returns. Erb and Harvey noted that when the term structure of a commodity is in backwardation an investor can expect that the long-only excess return will be positive on average and vice versa when it is in contango. They found from July 1992 to May 2004 that the average annualized excess return of the GSCI was 11.2% when the term structure was in backwardation and −5.0% when it was in contango. They found similar results for individual futures over the period December 1982 to May 2004. Using a portfolio of 12 commodities, they constructed an equally weighted, monthly rebalancing long-short portfolio that went long (short) the six commodities, which were the most backwardated (contangoed) as measured by the ratio of the nearby and next-nearby futures price. The return on the long-short portfolio had an average excess return more than three times greater than a long-only portfolio. Further, the Sharpe ratio was approximately five times greater suggesting that the term structure of a commodity may be a good indicator of risk premiums. Chong and Miffre[65] reported similar findings regarding the term structure and expected risk premiums. In addition, they found that risk premiums changed from positive to negative over time.

Exhibit 3.8 presents results of the term structure analysis for the period July 1996 to June 2006. The sample is split into two parts depending on whether crude oil is in backwardation or contango previous to the first day of the month. We use crude oil's term structure as the conditioning criteria because energy's total production value relative to other commodities worldwide is extremely high. The fact that energy is a major input in the production of other commodities further motivates its use. The optimal long-only Sharpe ratio portfolios are estimated for each group.[66]

[64]Erb and Harvey, "The Tactical and Strategic Value of Commodity Futures."

[65]James Chong and Joëlle Miffre, Conditional Risk Premia, Volatilities and Correlations in Commodity Futures Markets, Working Paper, April 2006.

[66]To simplify the analysis, we do not consider short positions. While the analysis could be extended to allow for short positions this would not affect the nature of the results. Regardless of whether short positions are allowed, we would expect the portfolio to be more net long, relatively speaking, when the term structure is backwardated, and vice versa when it is contangoed.

EXHIBIT 3.8 Optimal Portfolio Weights, Term Structure, July 1996 to June 2006

	Backwardation			Contango		
	I	II	III	I	II	III
Stocks	0.0139	0.0154	0.0000	0.2028	0.1914	0.1110
Bonds	0.9861	0.7991	0.6944	0.7972	0.7736	0.7784
GSCI	—	0.1855	0.0000	—	0.0351	0.0000
Corn	—	—	0.0000	—	—	0.0000
Soybeans	—	—	0.0048	—	—	0.0000
Wheat	—	—	0.0000	—	—	0.0000
Crude oil	—	—	0.0599	—	—	0.0033
Silver	—	—	0.0000	—	—	0.0293
Gold	—	—	0.0000	—	—	0.0000
Copper	—	—	0.0524	—	—	0.0780
Hogs	—	—	0.0070	—	—	0.0000
Cattle	—	—	0.1816	—	—	0.0000
Sharpe ratio	0.2720	0.3717	0.5929	0.2512	0.2564	0.3358
Average return	0.0061	0.0084	0.0100	0.0062	0.0062	0.0068
Standard deviation	0.0121	0.0149	0.0121	0.0114	0.0111	0.0104
T-bill average	0.0028	0.0028	0.0028	0.0033	0.0033	0.0033

Crude oil term structure has significant power in predicting positive returns for commodities. Stocks have only a marginal role in the optimal portfolio when crude oil is in backwardation. Backwardation portfolio I has an allocation of 1.3% to stocks versus 20.28% for the contango portfolio. This is consistent across portfolios I, II, and III. Referring to backwardation portfolio II, including the GSCI increases the Sharpe ratio by more than 35%. The GSCI has an above average allocation under backwardation, 18.55%, and only a marginal share, 3.51%, under contango. This is consistent with the fact that crude oil tends to drive the returns of the GSCI and that greater long-only returns are expected when the term structure is in backwardation.

The results for portfolio III reveal similar predictive power. Four commodities, soybeans, crude oil, copper, and cattle, all comprise significant shares when crude oil is in backwardation. Only one of those commodities, copper, is given a significant allocation when crude oil is in contango. Crude oil has a marginal share of 0.33%, and silver has a share of 2.93% under contango. In terms of overall performance, the addition of commodities greatly increases portfolio performance for the backwardation portfolios while their inclusion only has slight impacts on contango portfolios. The results suggest that tactical trading strategies based on the term structure may have significant ramifications for asset allocation.

Seasonality

Gorton and Rouwenhorst[67] argued that seasonality in commodity spot prices will not likely influence futures returns because seasonal variation is expected, and thus should already be embedded in the futures prices. However, Fama and French[68] noted that the seasonal nature in the supply and demand of some commodities implies they will contain seasonality in the basis and thus the term structure. For example, Carter, Rausser, and Schmitz[69] found evidence of seasonality in risk premiums, and Grauer[70] found evidence of seasonality in commodity betas.

Fama and French[71] investigated the seasonal hypothesis for agricultural, wood, livestock, and metal futures. They did not find evidence of seasonality in the basis for metals. However, they did find strong seasonality for many agricultural commodities including corn, soybeans, and wheat. Livestock products had the strongest evidence of seasonality. They attributed this finding to the fact that livestock are essentially nonstorable and storage costs for other agricultural commodities are higher relative to their value than in the case for metals. Thus, nominal interest rates can only explain a small fraction of livestock basis variation, and hence, much of the basis variation can be attributed to seasonality.

Following this line of reasoning, we posit that optimal portfolio allocations may display seasonality. This is investigated by partitioning the data according to four seasons, winter (December to February), spring (March to May), summer (June to August), and fall (September to November) and conducting portfolio optimizations. Exhibit 3.9 presents results for the seasonal analysis.

Portfolio I indicates that stocks outperform bonds during spring months. Adding the GSCI significantly improves portfolio performance. Spring portfolio II has optimal weights of 47%, 0%, and 53% for stocks, bonds, and the GSCI. Spring portfolio III indicates risk-adjusted returns in the spring are primarily generated by soybeans, crude oil, copper, and cattle; these commodities have optimal weights of 15.77%, 19.83%, 16.75%, and 37.26%.

During the summer months, stocks reverse their performance, as do bonds and commodities. Bond allocations dominate the portfolio in

---

[67]Gorton and Rouwenhorst, "Facts and Fantasies about Commodity Futures."

[68]Fama and French, "Commodity Future Prices: Some Evidence of Forecast Power, Premiums, and the Theory of Storage."

[69]Carter, Rausser, and Schmitz, "Efficient Asset Portfolios and the Theory of Normal Backwardation."

[70]Frederick L. A. Grauer, Equilibrium in Commodity Futures Markets: Theory and Tests, PhD. Dissertation (1977).

[71]Fama and French, "Business Cycles and the Behavior of Metals Prices."

EXHIBIT 3.9 Optimal Portfolio Weights: Seasonal Portfolios, July 1996 to June 2006

	Spring			Summer			Fall			Winter		
	I	II	III	I	II	III	I	II	III	I	II	III
Stocks	1.0000	0.4700	0.1040	0.0000	0.0000	0.0000	0.1716	0.1716	0.0602	0.0441	0.0838	0.0000
Bonds	0.0000	0.0000	0.0000	1.0000	0.8216	0.7591	0.8284	0.8284	0.6729	0.9559	0.8106	0.7431
GSCI	—	0.5300	0.0000	—	0.1784	0.0000	—	0.0000	0.0000	—	0.1056	0.0000
Corn	—	—	0.0000	—	—	0.0000	—	—	0.0000	—	—	0.0435
Soybeans	—	—	0.1577	—	—	0.0000	—	—	0.0000	—	—	0.0000
Wheat	—	—	0.0000	—	—	0.0000	—	—	0.0000	—	—	0.0000
Crude oil	—	—	0.1983	—	—	0.1145	—	—	0.0000	—	—	0.0397
Silver	—	—	0.0000	—	—	0.0000	—	—	0.0334	—	—	0.1454
Gold	—	—	0.0000	—	—	0.0000	—	—	0.0000	—	—	0.0000
Copper	—	—	0.1675	—	—	0.0000	—	—	0.0370	—	—	0.0095
Hogs	—	—	0.0000	—	—	0.0000	—	—	0.0027	—	—	0.0000
Cattle	—	—	0.3726	—	—	0.1264	—	—	0.1937	—	—	0.0188
Sharpe ratio	0.1632	0.2588	0.3650	0.2967	0.4058	0.5252	0.5444	0.5444	0.9145	0.2966	0.3566	0.6423
Average return	0.0099	0.0138	0.0150	0.0070	0.0092	0.0105	0.0092	0.0092	0.0112	0.0058	0.0066	0.0106
Standard deviation	0.0420	0.0415	0.0327	0.0131	0.0150	0.0140	0.0113	0.0113	0.0090	0.0093	0.0101	0.0119
T-bill average	0.0030	0.0030	0.0030	0.0031	0.0031	0.0031	0.0030	0.0030	0.0030	0.0030	0.0030	0.0030

summer portfolio I (100%), II (82.16%), and III (75.91%). The GSCI comprises a significant portion of summer portfolio II, 17.84%, but not as much as during the spring months, 53%. The summer portfolios also exhibit lower risk and returns than the spring portfolios but higher Sharpe ratios. Last, individual commodities display strong summer seasonality as evidenced by their low allocations. Only crude oil and cattle enter summer portfolio III, but with much smaller shares, 11.45% and 12.64%, than in the spring.

Overall, the fall portfolios perform better than those for any other season as they have the highest Sharpe ratios. Traditional assets dominate the fall allocations. Stocks have above average allocations in fall portfolios I and II, 17.16% and 17.16%, relative to the full sample, 8.70% and 7.80%. The GSCI has no allocation in the fall portfolios. Of the individual commodities, silver, copper, and hogs comprise only marginal shares, while cattle enter with a 20% allocation. The addition of individual commodity futures does significantly improve overall portfolio performance though, increasing the Sharpe ratio by about 0.37. Furthermore, the benefits from adding commodities come both in the form of significant risk reduction and return enhancement.

The winter portfolios have the lowest risk but also the lowest return. Winter portfolio II has optimal portfolio weights that are comparable to those for the full sample analysis. The analysis of individual commodities, however, generates some interesting results. Surprisingly, corn has a 4.35% allocation in winter portfolio III, whereas it has an optimal weight of 0.0% for the full sample. Silver and cattle also show strong seasonality during the winter months with allocations of 14.54% and 1.88%.

Overall, the addition of the GSCI to stocks and bonds increases the Sharpe ratio significantly during three of four seasons and the inclusion of individual commodities nearly doubles the Sharpe ratio in all cases. Further, the results indicate the presence of strong seasonal performance for most commodities. Oil performs best in a portfolio sense during the spring and summer. Cattle futures also display strong seasonality with optimal weights ranging from 37.26% in the spring to 1.88% in the winter. Corn, soybeans, copper, and silver also display strong seasonality. Finally, three commodities, hogs, gold, and wheat, perform poorly in all seasons.

The results support that optimal portfolio allocations can vary significantly throughout the year. This is consistent with earlier research which has documented seasonality in the basis. While Gorton and Rouwenhorst[72] were correct in that the market will embed seasonal information into the futures price because seasons are expected, they may not be correct in asserting that it will not affect futures risk premiums. One explanation is that

[72]Gorton and Rouwenhorst, "Facts and Fantasies about Commodity Futures."

although the market "expects" the changing seasons, the degree and direction of hedging pressure can vary throughout the year for different commodities. The results suggest that the market rewards speculators differently for the different risks they assume across seasons.

Momentum in Commodity Returns

Recent research has suggested the presence of momentum in commodity returns.[73] There are numerous explanations for this phenomenon. The hedging pressure hypothesis implies that long risk premiums are more likely after the market has experienced large gains and vice versa for short positions when the market has recently experienced losses. This may result in momentum effects if hedging pressure increases as a result of market adjustments after broad moves. Other, perhaps interrelated, explanations include the presence of behavioral biases such as overreaction.[74]

Miffre and Rallis[75] found that market volatility is positively related to momentum returns. Interestingly, they were also able to link the presence of momentum to the term structure. Market volatility was found to be positively related to the propensity for the term structure to be in contango or backwardation, and further that successful momentum strategies bought (sold) high volatility futures which were in backwardation (contango) and ignored low volatility contracts. For 31 commodities over the period January 1979 to September 2004, momentum strategies had average annual returns of 9.38%, outperforming an equally weighted long-only approach, which lost 2.64%. The momentum returns were further found to be uncorrelated with the returns of traditional asset classes.

Georgiev[76] examined the performance of four short-run momentum based strategies for crude oil, natural gas, unleaded gas, and heating oil for the period 1993 to 2004. He found that in all cases the actively traded portfolios performed better than passive buy-and-hold portfolios, and that the addition of active strategies to diversified portfolios significantly reduced

---

[73]See, for example, Jolle Miffre and Georgios Rallis, Momentum Strategies in Commodity Futures Markets, Cass Business School Research Paper, August 2006; Craig Pirrong, Momentum in Futures Markets, EFA 2005 Moscow Meetings Paper, February 2005, and Erb and Harvey, "The Tactical and Strategic Value of Commodity Futures."

[74]See, for example, N. Barberis, A. Shleifer, and R. Vishny, "A Model of Investor Sentiment," *Journal of Financial Economics* 49, no. 3 (1998), pp. 307–343.

[75]Miffre and Rallis, Momentum Strategies in Commodity Futures Markets.

[76] Georgi Georgiev, "Active Long-Only Investment in Energy Futures," *Journal of Alternative Investments* 7, no. 2 (2004), pp. 32–43.

risk and increased expected return. Anson[77] found that a 10% investment in the Mount Lucas Management Index (MLMI), which mimics a simple 12-month trend following strategy, increased risk-adjusted returns when added to a portfolio of stocks and bonds. Erb and Harvey[78] also investigated the returns to momentum strategies by constructing long-short portfolios based on whether the previous annual return was positive or negative. They reported that a simple equally weighted portfolio of 12 diversified commodities had a higher return and Sharpe ratio (6.54% and 0.85) than a long-only GSCI (4.39% and 0.25).

We investigate the impacts of intermediate-term momentum by estimating optimal weights for portfolios which are stratified by whether or not the previous return to crude oil is positive or negative. Crude oil returns tend to drive the GSCI, and hence, momentum in crude oil will likely precipitate momentum in the GSCI. Energy is also a major input for the production of many other commodities and could be expected to be a leading indicator of other commodity prices or at the very least a factor of their contemporaneous price. Further, previous research has identified the existence of comovement and "herding" behavior in commodity prices.[79]

Exhibit 3.10 presents results for the momentum portfolios. The results strongly suggest the presence of momentum for the portfolios analyzed. When the lag crude oil return is positive, the allocation to the GSCI (portfolio II) is 26.11%, whereas it is 0% when the return is negative. Further, the individual commodities are heavily weighted (portfolio III) following positive crude oil returns, about 40%, whereas they are smaller following negative crude oil returns, about 9%.

Stocks respond negatively to lag crude oil returns. This is not surprising given that energy is such a large portion of input costs for many firms. Stocks do not enter the optimal portfolios (I, II, or III) when the previous crude oil return is positive and have above average weightings when the previous crude oil return is negative. As noted, the GSCI displays strong momentum effects to lag crude oil changes as well. The optimal GSCI

---

[77]Anson, Handbook of Alternative Investments, 2nd ed.

[78] Erb and Harvey, "The Tactical and Strategic Value of Commodity Futures."

[79]See, for example, Robert S. Pindyck and Julio J. Rotemberg, "The Excess Co-Movement of Commodity Prices," *Economic Journal* 100, no. 403 (1990), pp. 1173–1189. Others, however, have questioned the presence of excess comovement in commodity prices. See, for example, Kat and Oomen, "What Every Investor Should Know about Commodities, Part II: Multivariate Return Analysis," and Chunrong Ai, Arjun Chatrath, and Frank Song, "On the Comovement of Commodity Prices," *American Journal of Agricultural Economics* 88, no. 3 (2006), pp. 574–588.

EXHIBIT 3.10 Optimal Portfolio Weights, Momentum, July 1996 to June 2006

	Positive Lag Crude Oil Return			Negative Lag Crude Oil Return		
	I	II	III	I	II	III
Stocks	0.0000	0.0000	0.0000	0.1682	0.1682	0.0952
Bonds	1.0000	0.7389	0.6050	0.8318	0.8318	0.8147
GSCI	—	0.2611	0.1226	—	0.0000	0.0000
Corn	—	—	0.0000	—	—	0.0000
Soybeans	—	—	0.0165	—	—	0.0000
Wheat	—	—	0.0000	—	—	0.0000
Crude oil	—	—	0.0051	—	—	0.0147
Silver	—	—	0.0446	—	—	0.0000
Gold	—	—	0.0000	—	—	0.0000
Copper	—	—	0.0196	—	—	0.0754
Hogs	—	—	0.0000	—	—	0.0000
Cattle	—	—	0.1866	—	—	0.0000
Sharpe ratio	0.1764	0.3278	0.4857	0.4384	0.4384	0.5101
Average return	0.0050	0.0083	0.0088	0.0086	0.0086	0.0091
Standard deviation	0.0127	0.0169	0.0123	0.0119	0.0119	0.0112
T-bill average	0.0028	0.0028	0.0028	0.0034	0.0034	0.0034

allocation is higher when the previous change in crude oil is positive and lower when it is negative (portfolio II). The results for individual commodities are consistent with this finding. For example, cattle (silver and GSCI) have a weight of 18.86% (4.46% and 12.26%) when the lag change is positive and 0% (0% and 0%) when it is negative.[80]

The results support the findings of earlier studies on the positive performance of momentum strategies. In addition, we also establish a link between commodity returns and subsequent stock market performance in the context of the diversified portfolio. Namely, equities tend to perform poorly following positive crude oil returns, whereas commodities are inclined to manifest momentum. The results suggest that crude oil may have pervasive implications for portfolio allocation decisions.

[80]Crude oil does not enter the portfolio strongly because the GSCI substitutes for most of its exposure. We replicated the analysis for portfolio III excluding the GSCI and found a weight of 7.5%. This is consistent with positive crude oil momentum.

CONCLUSION

The purpose of this chapter was to provide a review of commodity investments in the context of the diversified portfolio. We explored several strategic and tactical dimensions of the futures investment problem and investigated their implications for portfolio performance during the recent period July 1996 to June 2006. Four main themes arose out of the results of past and current work.

First, while the existence of risk premiums in commodity futures markets has been a point of contention, historically, long portfolios of futures have displayed positive risk premiums. Consistent long-only risk premiums for individual commodities are doubtful, however, as their risk-adjusted returns entail a high degree of idiosyncratic risk.

Second, commodity index investments have historically exhibited risk-adjusted returns similar to stocks. Further, the correlations of commodities with stocks, bonds, inflation, and the business cycle render them attractive portfolio components in a strategic sense.

Third, previous studies have documented that commodities appear to exhibit time-varying, and oftentimes negative, risk premiums. The market can transmit important information in this respect via the term structure by indicating whether commodity futures should be included in the portfolio as well as whether risk premiums are likely to be earned as a result of going short or long.

Finally, commodity futures returns may vary systematically and predictably to economic, monetary, inflationary, and seasonal factors and may also exhibit momentum. Consideration of these factors can have significant implications for optimal investment behavior. However, detecting meaningful signals from economic, inflationary, and monetary variables ex ante can be challenging. Furthermore, the variation of commodities to monetary conditions is unstable at best, at least in a portfolio context.

The bulk of our analysis consisted of estimating "optimal" portfolios in a simple mean-variance framework when conditioning on various ex post and ex ante criteria. As our review and analysis noted, the performance of futures investments can vary significantly through time, across commodities, and even with respect to structural factors. Consequently, the dynamic nature of commodity price behavior reinforces the importance of understanding the fundamental nature of inter-asset relations when making portfolio allocation decisions.

CHAPTER 4

Macroeconomic Determinants of Commodity Futures Returns

Zeno Adams
Research Assistant
Endowed Chair of Asset Management
European Business School (EBS)
International University Schloss Reichartshausen

Roland Füss, Ph.D.
Professor of Finance
Endowed Chair of Asset Management
European Business School (EBS)
International University Schloss Reichartshausen

Dieter G. Kaiser, Ph.D.
Director Alternative Investments
Feri Institutional Advisors GmbH
Research Fellow
Centre for Practical Quantitative Finance
Frankfurt School of Finance and Management

Commodities have enjoyed a renewed high interest and increasing attention from both investors and academics within the last years. After oil prices were in discussion during the oil price shocks in the 1970s, a period of declining commodity prices followed for the next 20 years, which went along with little attention from the academic side. As of the third quarter 2007, prices of most commodities are at a record high in nominal terms and at a still very high level in real terms, and futures prices suggest that the high prices are expected to stay high for some time.

Most of the literature on commodities concentrates on long-term passive investments in commodity futures. However, a pure buy-and-hold strategy may lead to higher risk positions and further disadvantages for the investor. On the one hand, investors have no influence on the timing and the weights of the constituents of the portfolio and thus cannot react to market changes. On the other hand, Akey shows that active management gives the investor the opportunity to minimize risk and take advantage of the market circumstances.[1] In order to be successful, the investor needs a sound understanding of the determinants of commodity prices and the interdependencies between them and traditional assets. Commodities are a very heterogeneous asset class and daily price changes are mainly driven by a variety of commodity specific factors. However, commodity prices are also subject to macroeconomic changes that are common to all commodities. Pindyck and Rotemberg find comovements between largely unrelated commodities that are affected by common macroeconomic shocks.[2] Hence, current and expected values of macroeconomic factors such as inflation, interest rates, and industrial production affect the supply and demand for commodities and thus their current and expected prices. They show that the demand for commodities can be determined directly, such as through an increase in world industrial production, which will raise the demand for energy as well as for industrial and precious metals, or it can also be influenced indirectly through storage costs. For storable commodities, the demand for holding storage and hence current prices are driven by the opportunity costs of holding storage. For instance, higher interest rates can directly lower commodity prices because of its negative effect on economic conditions in general and the demand for commodities in particular. At the same time, commodity prices can also decline because of an increase in the opportunity costs for holding storage. Accordingly, the aim of this chapter is to show the relationship between commodities and the macroeconomy.[3]

COMMODITIES AS AN INFLATION HEDGE

According to Greer, one important property of commodity investments, besides being implemented as an instrument for diversification, is that

[1]Rian P. Akey, "Commodities: A Case for Active Management," *Journal of Alternative Investments* (Fall 2005), pp. 8–29.

[2]Robert S. Pindyck and Julio J. Rotemberg, "The Excess Co-Movement of Commodity Prices," *The Economic Journal* (December 1990), pp. 1173–1189.

[3]For empirical evidence that commodities are on average affected by the same macroeconomic determinants that also affect stock and bond markets see Warren Bailey and K. C. Chan, "Macroeconomic Influences and the Variability of the Commodity Futures Basis," *Journal of Finance* (June 1993), pp. 555–573.

commodities can be used as a hedge against inflation.[4] The value of nominally denominated assets such as bonds and stocks decreases when inflation and unexpected inflation increases. In theory, stocks represent claims against real assets but as companies have nominally fixed contracts with suppliers, workers, and capital, stocks do not react directly to an increase in inflation. Stocks represent company ownership and a share in the payout of dividends. Bonds represent a claim on debt repayment and, in contrast to stocks, the bondholder receives a predefined stream of cash flows. The present value of the future cash flows depends on the size and timing of the cash flow and the assumed interest rate. Commodity futures in contrast represent the expected spot price in the future and therefore futures prices increase when expected inflation increases. In fact, the increase of commodity prices itself causes inflation as commodities are part of the basket of goods from which the aggregated inflation of an economy is calculated. Furthermore, futures represent short-term contracts and can react to changes in unexpected inflation as the new information is taken into account when rolling into the next future. Previous studies show empirically that annual returns of commodity futures are positively correlated with changes in inflation and that commodities provide an effective inflation hedge during periods of high inflation.[5] Gorton and Rouwenhorst show for the time period 1959 to 2004 that commodities can be used as a hedge against inflation, so that a positive correlation between the total return indexes and the U.S. CPI (Consumer Price Index) ranging from 0.01 for monthly futures to 0.45 for five-year averages of monthly futures exists.[6] In contrast, the correlation coefficients between stocks, bonds, and inflation range between −0.12 and −0.32 depending on the time period under consideration.

For our empirical analysis we use the excess return indexes of the Goldman Sachs Commodity Index (GSCI) for energy, industrial metals, precious metals, agriculture, and livestock to construct an equally weighted

[4]Robert J. Greer, "Conservative Commodities: A Key Inflation Hedge," *Journal of Portfolio Management* (Summer 1978), pp. 26–29.

[5]See, for example, Zvi Bodie and Victor I. Rosansky, "Risk and Return in Commodity Futures," *Financial Analysts Journal* (May–June 1980), pp. 3–14; Ernest M. Ankrim and Chris R. Hensel, "Commodities in Asset Allocation: A Real-Asset Alternative to Real Estate," *Financial Analysts Journal* (May–June 1993), pp. 20–29; and Kenneth A. Froot, "Hedging Portfolios with Real Assets," *Journal of Portfolio Management* (Summer 1995), pp. 60–77.

[6]Gary Gorton and Geert K. Rouwenhorst, "Facts and Fantasies about Commodities Futures," *Financial Analysts Journal* (April 2006), pp. 47–68.

composite index.[7] The excess return index does not include the return of the collateral and thus provides a better exposure to commodities than, say, the total return index which is heavily influenced by the return of the risk-free rate of the collateral. All subindexes are normalized to 100 in 1983Q1. After this date the composite index was not rebalanced as this would amount in an active trading strategy of selling the subindex with increasing returns and buying the subindex with decreasing returns. This approach ensures pure development of commodity prices; that is, we try to avoid performance influences which arise from portfolio rebalancing. For a measure of inflation we use the U.S. CPI as well as the CPI for Europe and Asia. Normally, in literature on commodities only the U.S. CPI is considered, which seems to be too narrow of a perspective.[8] Investors are concerned about inflation in their respective home country and not necessarily about U.S. inflation. For instance, European or Asian investors shift money into commodities when inflation in Europe or Asia rises. However, including Asian and European inflation can solve this problem but also raises others. First, inflation measures in those regions are averages of different countries, which might bias the estimated correlation, and second, European or Asian investors also have to consider exchange rate movements when investing in dollar denominated commodities, so that the effects of exchange rate movements have to be taken into account as well. Exhibit 4.1 shows the correlation coefficients between inflation in the different regions and the commodity index returns for the time period 1983Q1 to 2007Q1.[9] As can be seen, the commodity composite index is positively correlated with U.S. inflation but the correlation can be almost completely attributed to the energy index.

World stocks and bonds are negatively correlated with U.S. inflation as the nominally denominated value of those assets decreases when inflation increases. Thus, higher inflation means lower returns for stocks and bonds. European inflation is positively and significantly correlated with energy but again uncorrelated with the other commodity indexes. Asian inflation is

---

[7]The composite index offered by Goldman Sachs is a production-weighted index with energy having a weight of around 70%. Our equally weighted index has the advantage of not being dominated by the energy sector. However, as mentioned above, the index is not rebalanced so that the weights in this passive index can vary according to the magnitude of price changes in the individual commodity sectors over time.

[8]See, for example, Claude B. Erb and Campbell R. Harvey, "The Strategic and Tactical Value of Commodity Futures," *Financial Analysts Journal* (March–April 2006), pp. 69–97.

[9]We also compared European inflation with the commodity indexes denominated in euros instead of U.S. dollars. The results (not shown here) did not change significantly.

EXHIBIT 4.1 Correlations between Monthly Inflation of Different Countries and Commodity Returns, January 1983 to January 2007

Variable	U.S. Inflation	EU Inflation	Asian Inflation
Composite	0.3131[a]	0.1022	−0.0619
Agriculture	−0.0148	0.0008	0.0301
Energy	0.3405[a]	0.2141[a]	−0.1251[b]
Industrial metals	0.0735	−0.0578	0.0890
Livestock	0.0400	−0.0159	−0.0183
Precious metals	0.0735	−0.0844	−0.0245
MSCI World	−0.0301	−0.0994	0.1044
JPM Global Bond Index	−0.0750	−0.0049	−0.0833

[a], [b], and [c] denotes significance at the 1%, 5%, and 10% level, respectively.

negatively correlated with energy returns which seems puzzling. However, the correlation coefficients may be biased due to exchange rate movements and the problem of averaging inflation over different countries with different levels of economic development. Furthermore, there are short-term market fluctuations which are inherent to monthly data.

Those short-term price fluctuations could obscure the correlation relationship, so that averages over longer periods of time can give a better picture of the underlying relationships. If the investment horizon expands to one, three, and five years, the correlation with EU and Asian inflation shows a more heterogeneous picture. Exhibit 4.2 displays the correlation of U.S., EU, and Asian inflation with commodity returns averaged and rolled over different time horizons. As can be seen, most commodities are now positively and significantly correlated with inflation in the United States, Europe, and Asia. Furthermore, correlations become stronger over a longer period of time, which suggests that short-run correlations are heavily influenced by short-term market fluctuations. In the United States, correlations are particularly high for energy over the one-year period and for industrial and livestock for averages of three and five years. Correlation between the agriculture index and inflation is much stronger in Asia and in Europe than in the United States and increases with the investment horizon. The European and Asian markets have to be read again with caution. The coherency with the agriculture index seems to be strong, especially in Asia. However, other indexes are significantly negative. Particularly the precious metals index is negatively correlated with inflation, also to a weaker extent for the United States. Accordingly, for the European and Asian markets the composite commodity index cannot be used as an inflation protector, but particular constituents of the index do exhibit the inflation hedge property, which becomes more efficient over longer investment horizons.

EXHIBIT 4.2 Correlations of Rolling Average Means for Different Time Horizons

	U.S. Inflation			EU Inflation			Asian Inflation		
Index	1 year	3 years	5 years	1 year	3 years	5 years	1 year	3 years	5 years
Composite	0.532[a]	0.568[a]	0.658[a]	−0.269[a]	−0.323[a]	−0.188[a]	−0.118	−0.025	−0.026
Agriculture	0.058	0.216[a]	0.426[a]	0.114	0.283[a]	0.520[a]	0.407[a]	0.672[a]	0.786[a]
Energy	0.550[a]	0.467[a]	0.332[a]	−0.064	−0.255[a]	−0.406[a]	−0.255[a]	−0.324[a]	−0.461[a]
Industrial Metals	0.367[a]	0.586[a]	0.743[a]	−0.224[a]	−0.184[a]	0.018	0.108	0.172[a]	0.191[a]
Livestock	0.402[a]	0.694[a]	0.907[a]	−0.051	0.087	0.322[a]	−0.015	0.274[a]	0.394[a]
Precious Metals	−0.312[a]	−0.380[a]	−0.404[a]	−0.706[a]	−0.770[a]	−0.792[a]	−0.272[a]	−0.334[a]	−0.511[a]

[a], [b], and [c] denotes significance at the 1%, 5%, and 10% level, respectively.

The drawback of computing correlations between averages is that time periods of highly positive or negative returns and inflation cannot be taken into account as the averages smooth the time series. Those periods, however, are of particular interest as the inflation hedge property becomes especially valuable during periods of high inflation. Additionally, it would be interesting to know if the correlations remain stable over time. For this reason one-year and five-year rolling correlation coefficients have been computed for the U.S. CPI and the commodity indexes in order to show the time varying behavior. Exhibit 4.3 shows the rolling correlation coefficients for the different time periods.[10]

Common to all commodity indexes is the fact that the one-year correlation coefficients fluctuate strongly from year to year and range between +0.8 and −0.8 as in the case of industrial metals and the composite index.[11] For this reason it can be concluded that over short periods of time commodities do not offer an efficient inflation protection. Over longer time periods of five years, the correlations are more stable but generally of small magnitude, ranging between zero for agriculture and around 0.4 for the energy index.

Therefore, the inflation hedge property often claimed in the literature[12] can be strong but also negative during short time periods, but generally remains unclear when European or Asian inflation is considered. Denson shows for the U.S. inflation that the rolling correlations fluctuate strongly in the short run, but are more stable and on average positive when considered over more than three years. Thus, in the long run a positive relationship between U.S. inflation and commodities exists.[13] In order to test the inflation hedge property in more detail, the inflation is decomposed into expected inflation and unexpected inflation. The reason is that to some extent expected inflation may be already incorporated in stocks and bonds, so that

[10]Exhibit 4.2 shows the correlations of returns averaged over one, three, and five years whereas Exhibit 4.3 shows the monthly rolling correlation coefficients over observation periods of one and five years.

[11]However, it should be noted that the coefficients are in part biased due to the autocorrelation that is generated by the rolling window. In addition, only linear interdependence under the assumption of normality is captured with this measure. Furthermore, the correlation coefficients are only meaningful if the multivariate distribution is elliptic. Since most monthly commodity index returns have a positive skewness and/or an excess kurtosis, the joint distribution is far from being elliptic, and thus the correlation coefficient does not exhaust the full interval $[-1, +1]$.

[12]See, for example, Robert J. Greer, "The Nature of Commodity Index Returns," *Journal of Alternative Investments* (Summer 2000), pp. 45–52.

[13]Edwin Denson, "Should Passive Commodities Investments Play a Role in Your Portfolio?" *Investment Viewpoints*, UBS Global Asset Management (2006).

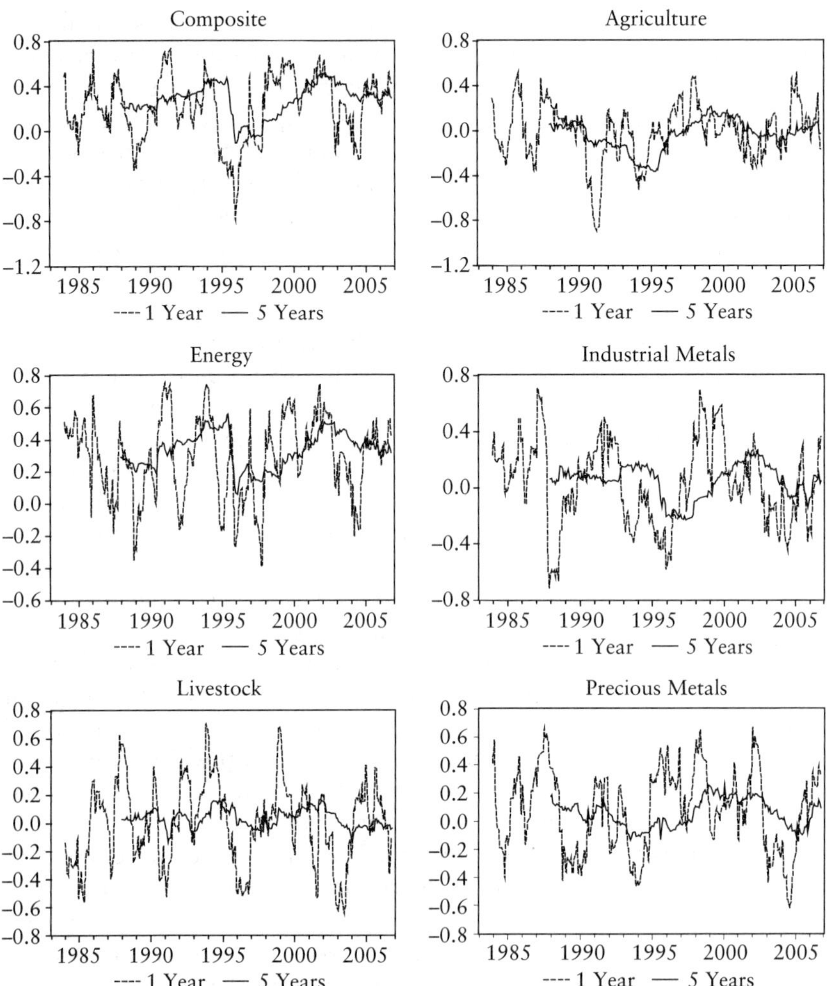

EXHIBIT 4.3 Rolling Correlation Coefficients for Different Investment Horizons

the inflation hedge property becomes especially valuable in the case of unexpected changes to inflation. Thus, the commodity returns are regressed on the two components of inflation according to the following equation:

$$R_t = \beta_0 + \beta_1 E(\pi_t) + \beta_2(\pi - E(\pi_t)) + e_t \qquad (4.1)$$

R_t is the return of the respective GSCI commodity excess return index, β_0 is a constant, the term $\beta_1 E(\pi_t)$ is expected inflation, whereas $\beta_2(\pi - E(\pi_t))$ is the remaining unexpected inflation and e_t is an error term. The coefficients β_1 and β_2 measure the effectiveness of the hedge in the case of expected and unexpected inflation, respectively. A common approximation for the market's expectation of inflation is the short-term interest rate, that is, the unexpected inflation is inflation minus the short-term interest rate. Under the assumption of a constant real interest rate r_t, the Fisher equation $i_t = r_t + E(\pi)$ shows that expected inflation can be expressed by the short-term nominal interest rate. Another possible proxy for unexpected inflation, which will be used here, is the change in inflation, $\Delta\pi_t$. Based on the random walk hypothesis, the best expectation of this year's inflation is the inflation of last year.[14] Monthly inflation is computed as the percentage change in CPI and unexpected inflation is computed as the change in inflation:

$$\pi_t = (\log CPI_t - \log CPI_{t-1}) \cdot 100 \tag{4.2}$$

$$\pi_t^{\text{unexpected}} = \pi_t - \pi_{t-1} \tag{4.3}$$

Exhibit 4.4 shows the estimated coefficients and *t*-statistics in brackets for the monthly commodity indexes. As can be seen, a positive relationship between expected and unexpected U.S. inflation and the composite as well as the energy index exists. For both commodity indexes, the effect of unexpected inflation is much larger than for expected inflation, so that the hedging property is much higher when inflation is unexpected. In the case of European inflation, the inflation hedge property actually holds only for unexpected inflation. While expected inflation should also be included in the pricing of nominally denominated assets, such as stocks and bonds, it is the hedge against unexpected inflation that makes the commodity investments especially valuable. Erb and Harvey conclude that commodities which are only storable to a limited extent, such as copper, heating oil, and livestock, provide a better hedge against unexpected inflation than commodities which are suitable for storage.[15] One reason for this could be that an increase in demand for the former type of commodities increases prices directly while in the latter case prices are only affected after the storages have been depleted.

To a lesser extent, unexpected inflation in the United States also plays a role for the industrial and precious metals indexes where the effects are

[14]Harry M. Kat and Roel C. Oomen, "What Every Investor Needs to Know About Commodities, Part II: Multivariate Return Analysis," *Journal of Investment Management* (3rd Quarter 2007), pp. 1–25.

[15]Erb and Harvey, "The Strategic and Tactical Value of Commodity Futures."

EXHIBIT 4.4 Regression Results for the Inflation Hedge Property

	U.S. Inflation			EU Inflation			Asian Inflation		
Index	β_0	β_1	β_2	β_0	β_1	β_2	β_0	β_1	β_2
Composite	−0.439	2.859[a]	5.532[a]	0.295	−0.021	2.535[c]	0.353	−0.137	−0.321
	[−1.307]	[2.833]	[6.329]	[0.569]	[−0.022]	[2.805]	[1.183]	[−0.373]	[0.257]
Agriculture	−0.063	−1.103	0.198	−0.785	0.903	−0.718	−0.601[c]	0.479	0.095
	[−0.156]	[−0.901]	[0.186]	[−1.310]	[0.816]	[−0.688]	[−1.770]	[1.151]	[0.296]
Energy	−1.393[c]	7.601[a]	12.699[a]	−0.977	3.114	9.249[a]	1.105[c]	−1.141	−1.303[b]
	[−1.909]	[3.469]	[6.691]	[−0.881]	[1.520]	[4.879]	[1.701]	[−1.431]	[−2.119]
Industrial Metals	0.490	0.236	2.274[c]	1.469[c]	−1.896	−0.641	0.122	0.852	0.556
	[0.945]	[0.151]	[1.686]	[1.918]	[−1.341]	[−0.481]	[0.281]	[1.604]	[1.356]
Livestock	−0.311	1.637	0.104	0.133	−0.057	−0.365	0.198	−0.164	−0.075
	[−0.832]	[1.460]	[0.107]	[0.810]	[0.955]	[−0.380]	[0.633]	[−0.426]	[−0.254]
Precious Metals	−0.248	−0.276	2.033[c]	0.783	−2.271[b]	−0.679	−0.294	−0.096	−0.143
	[−0.615]	[−0.228]	[1.933]	[1.312]	[−2.060]	[−0.654]	[0.339]	[−0.230]	[−0.446]

[a], [b], and [c] denotes significance at the 1%, 5%, and 10% level, respectively.

significant at the 10% level. In the case of Asian inflation, it does not come as a surprise that almost none of the t-statistics are significant since the correlation coefficients were not significant on a monthly basis.[16] An attempt to explain the inverse relationship between stocks and commodities and inflation is provided by Akey.[17] If it is reasonable to assume sticky output prices, an increase in inflation due to increasing commodity prices raises the costs for firms who buy commodities as inputs for production. Higher costs reduce the profits of firms and thus put downward pressure on stock prices. Over time, higher commodity prices lead to the entry of new commodity producing firms in the market.[18] This raises the supply of commodities while at the same time firms reduce their demand for commodities due to the higher costs. Both effects decrease commodity prices and, as the central bank reduces inflation to more normal levels, profits of firms and, thus, stock prices increase again.

Another, possibly more relevant explanation is proposed by Greer.[19] When inflation increases, the central bank is expected to raise interest rates, which reduce the present value of future cash flows and thus lower stock and bond prices. Commodity prices, however, already incorporate the new inflation rate, so that investors have incentives to move out of stocks and bonds and into commodities.

DYNAMIC LINKAGES OF MONETARY POLICY AND COMMODITY RETURNS: A VECTOR AUTOREGRESSIVE ANALYSIS

The inflation target of the Federal Reserve Bank is the core inflation which excludes the very volatile energy and agriculture indexes, so that changes in those commodities at first do not affect the inflation target. When commodity prices increase to very high levels, however, the effects start to show in the core inflation which in turn induces a reaction from the central bank in order to keep inflation under control. This is why this section describes the existence of interdependencies between monetary policy and commodity prices. The effect of a contractive monetary policy can be

[16]One exception is the energy index where the correlations as well as the OLS regression coefficients are negative.

[17]Akey, "Commodities: A Case for Active Management."

[18]Some commodity producing firms such as oil companies have considerable sunk costs so that supply may be very inelastic even in the long run.

[19]Greer, "The Nature of Commodity Index Returns."

thought of as a continuation of the inflation effect. As discussed in the previous section, an increase in inflation increases commodity prices as investors take advantage of the inflation hedge property and increase their demand for commodities. Higher inflation then induces the central bank to increase interest rates in order to decrease inflation. The following period of disinflation reduces the demand for commodities so that their prices return to their long-run levels. Armesto and Gavin find evidence that commodity futures markets respond positively to an unexpected increase in the federal funds rate target by raising the inflation rate expected by the market participants for the next three to nine months.[20] Jensen, Johnson, and Mercer[21] analyze the effects of monetary policy in the United States by distinguishing between subperiods of expansive and contractive monetary policy.[22] For the time period 1973 to 1999, the authors find significantly higher returns during periods of restrictive monetary policy and relatively low returns during an expansive period. This seems to be especially the case for energy and industrial metals, whereas livestock exhibits inverse but insignificant coefficients. Similar effects have been found by Kat and Oomen who consider single commodities instead of aggregated indexes.[23]

Frankel proposes an arbitrage model in the style of the overshooting exchange rate model of Dornbusch in order to explain the inverse relationship between the real interest rate and commodity prices.[24] The main arguments are that high real interest rates increase the opportunity costs of investors who hold commodities in storage, which leads to a temporary

[20]Michelle T. Armesto and William T. Gavin, "Monetary Policy and Commodity Futures," *Federal Reserve Bank of St. Louis Review* (2005).

[21]Gerald R. Jensen, Robert R. Johnson, and Jeffery M. Mercer, "Tactical Asset Allocation and Commodity Futures," *Journal of Portfolio Management* (Summer 2002), pp. 100–111.

[22]A change in monetary policy is observed if the Federal Reserve Bank changes the direction of interest rate movements after a prolonged period of interest changes of the same direction. For example, a contractive monetary policy is observed if the Fed increases the interest rate after a foregoing period of decreasing interest rates.

[23]Harry M. Kat and Roel C. Oomen, "What Every Investor Needs to Know About Commodities, Part I: Univariate Return Analysis," *Journal of Investment Management* (First Quarter 2007).

[24]Jeffrey Frankel, Commodity Prices, Monetary Policy, and Currency Regimes, NBER Working Paper No. C0011 (May 2006). See also Rüdiger Dornbusch, "Expectations and Exchanges Rate Dynamics," *Journal of Political Economy* (December 1976), pp. 1161–1176.

reduction in the demand for storable commodities.[25] Furthermore, speculators now have higher incentives to move out of commodities and invest in fixed income assets such as bonds. Both effects reduce the demand for commodities and thus decrease commodity prices. In the theoretical model, a monetary contraction increases nominal interest rates i and often at the same time decreases expected inflation, so that the ex ante real interest rate $r = i - \pi^e$ increases. For the reasons described, commodity prices decline. The decline continues until commodities are generally considered undervalued and it is expected that commodity prices will appreciate by more than the costs of holding commodities in storage. Accordingly, investors are now willing to hold commodities in storage and demand for commodities increases again. In the long run, the contractive monetary policy also reduces inflation and the increase in real money growth, whereas the real interest rate and commodity prices remain unchanged. The theoretical justification for the overshooting effect is that commodity prices are flexible and adjust rapidly while most other prices are sticky in the short run. Denoting s as the log-nominal price of commodities and p as the log-overall price level so that $q = (s - p)$ denotes real commodity prices, the expected change in the real price level can be expressed as

$$E[\Delta(s - p)] = E[\Delta(q)] = -\theta(q - \overline{q}) \tag{4.4}$$

$$E[\Delta(s)] = -\theta(q - \overline{q}) + E[\Delta p] \tag{4.5}$$

If real commodity prices are higher than the long-run expected price level $\overline{q}$, commodity prices are expected to decrease at a rate θ so that there is a tendency to revert back to a long-run equilibrium. Furthermore, an arbitrage consideration equates the expected appreciation of commodity prices $E[\Delta(s)]$ plus the convenience yield adjusted for costs with the nominal interest rate i:

$$E[\Delta(s)] + c = i \quad \text{where} \quad c \equiv cy - sc - rp \tag{4.6}$$

cy denotes the convenience yield from holding the stock, which can be interpreted as the insurance value of having an assured supply in the case of a negative supply shock. The storage costs, sc, are the costs for the rent and

[25]On the one hand, holding commodities in storage gives the investor the return of an appreciation of the commodities in the future as well as a convenience yield which is the assurance of having a critical supply in case of a negative supply shock. On the other hand, the investor has to pay the opportunity costs, that is, the real interest rates as well as storage costs, and a risk premium for the uncertainty of future price changes.

the security firm, and the risk premium, rp, is the premium for buying and storing the commodities today in spite of the uncertainty of future commodity prices.

Substituting $E[\Delta(s)]$ from equation 4.5 in 4.6 and rearranging results in

$$-\theta(q - \overline{q}) + E[\Delta p] = i - c \tag{4.7}$$

and

$$q - \overline{q} = -\left(\frac{1}{\theta}\right)(i - E[\Delta p] - c) \tag{4.8}$$

with $i - E[\Delta p] \equiv i - \pi^e = r$. Equation (4.8) states that if the real interest rate is higher than the convenience yield minus storage costs and the risk premium, then investors will find it more profitable to invest in fixed income and to reduce their demand for commodities, which leads to a lower real price of commodities relative to their long-run level, $\overline{q}$. This could in part explain why commodity prices were low during the period of high interest rates in the 1980s and were high in the last years when real interest rate have been low. In order to test empirically for this negative relationship, an OLS regression can be applied. Frankel uses annual data of spot prices and finds a significant negative relationship between three major composite indexes and the real interest rate for the time period 1950 to 2005.[26]

Using monthly futures excess return indexes we apply a Vector Autoregressive (VAR) model which is a simultaneous equation model that also considers the time dimension by including lagged variables. The reasons are that applying OLS regression with real commodity prices in levels would result in an estimation bias, since the commodity indexes are nonstationary. Furthermore, it is unlikely that a change in the real interest rate affects commodity prices in the same month so that one would like to take lags into account. The real commodity indexes are computed as

$$\text{index}_{\text{real}} = \log\left(\frac{\text{index}_{\text{nominal}}}{CPI} \cdot 100\right)$$

In order to have stationary variables, the real indexes are then differenced:[27]

$$\Delta\text{index}_{\text{real}} = \text{index}_{\text{real},t} - \text{index}_{\text{real},t-1}$$

[26] Frankel, Commodity Prices, Monetary Policy, and Currency Regimes.

[27] The stationarity of the differenced variables was tested using the unit root test from Peter C. B. Phillips and Pierre Perron, "Testing for a Unit Root in Time Series Regression," *Biometrika* (1988), pp. 335–346.

The real interest rate is already stationary in levels and is computed by subtracting the inflation rate from the one-year U.S. Treasury Bond. The VAR model for the case of the two variables with n lags can be expressed as:

$$\begin{aligned}\Delta p_t = \mu_1 + \alpha_1 \Delta p_{t-1} + \alpha_2 \Delta p_{t-2} + \ldots + \alpha_n \Delta p_{t-n} \\ + \beta_1 r_{t-1} + \beta_2 r_{t-2} + \ldots + \beta_n r_{t-n} + \varepsilon_{1,t}\end{aligned} \tag{4.9a}$$

$$\begin{aligned}r_t = \mu_2 + \gamma_1 \Delta p_{t-1} + \gamma_2 \Delta p_{t-2} + \ldots + \gamma_n \Delta p_{t-n} \\ + \lambda_1 r_{t-1} + \lambda_2 r_{t-2} + \ldots + \lambda_n r_{t-n} + \varepsilon_{2,t}\end{aligned} \tag{4.9b}$$

where Δp_t is the change in the real commodity index at time t, r_t is the real interest rate, μ_i are constants, and $\varepsilon_{i,t}$ are error terms. As can be seen from the first equation, real commodity prices depend on their own realizations from the previous n periods as well as on lagged real interest rates. The real interest rate in the second equation depends on the same variables, so that the two variables have a dynamic interdependent relationship. In contrast to OLS regression the estimated parameters α_i, β_i, γ_i, and λ_i cannot be interpreted as elasticities, since a shock to the first equation, $\Delta\varepsilon_{1,t}$, increases Δp_t in the same period but also increases r_{t+1} by $\gamma_1 \Delta\varepsilon_{1,t}$ in the next period which in turn has an effect on real commodity prices via the parameter β_1 in period $t+2$ and so on. If the model is correctly specified, the error terms $\varepsilon_{1,t}$ and $\varepsilon_{2,t}$ have a mean of zero. Furthermore, correlation, but no autocorrelation should exist between the two error terms. Otherwise, the goodness of fit of the model can be raised by including more variables or more lags. However, including more lags or variables raises the data requirements. Furthermore, too many parameters reduce the number of degrees of freedom which can result in an estimation bias of the parameters. The number of optimal lags can be determined with the Akaike criterion which takes the trade-off between too many and too few lagged variables into account:

$$AIC = \ln\left|\widehat{\Omega}\right| + \frac{2p^d}{T} \tag{4.10}$$

where $\left|\widehat{\Omega}\right|$ is the determinant of the estimated covariance matrix of residuals, p the number of lags, d the number of equations, and T is the number of observations. For the VAR model the Akaike criterion suggests using lags between 5 and 8, depending on the respective commodity index.[28] Exhibit 4.5 shows

[28]For an introduction into VAR models and their applications see Walter Enders, *Applied Economic Time Series* (Hoboken, NJ: John Wiley & Sons, 2004), pp. 264–272. The coefficients of lagged commodity prices and of equation (4.9b) are not reported to conserve space.

EXHIBIT 4.5 The Effects of an Increase in the Real Interest Rate on Commodity Prices*

	Composite	Agriculture	Energy	Industrial Metals	Livestock	Precious Metals
β_1	0.001 [0.127]	0.009 [0.893]	−0.004 [−0.173]	0.008 [0.671]	−0.013 [−1.347]	0.020 [2.143]
β_2	−0.006 [−0.563]	0.002 [0.162]	−0.010 [−0.439]	−0.004 [−0.295]	0.010 [0.929]	−0.001 [−0.126]
β_3	−0.020 [−1.989]	−0.023 [−1.941]	−0.035 [−1.468]	−0.023 [−1.556]	−0.006 [−0.604]	−0.021 [−2.002]
β_4	0.045 [4.546]	0.041 [3.390]	0.069 [3.060]	0.036 [2.451]	0.005 [0.479]	0.051 [4.694]
β_5	−0.026 [−2.955]	−0.027 [−2.244]	−0.038 [−1.951]	−0.027 [−2.137]	0.004 [0.405]	−0.017 [−1.544]
β_6	—	0.023 [1.905]	—	—	−0.007 [−0.681]	−0.019 [−1.730]
β_7	—	−0.010 [−0.974]	—	—	−0.005 [−0.524]	0.016 [1.454]
β_8	—	—	—	—	—	−0.024 [−2.418]
R^2	0.110	0.061	0.064	0.077	0.056	0.185

**t*-statistics in brackets. Lag length criteria: AIC; based on 289 monthly observations from January 1983 to January 2007.

the coefficients of the VAR model as well as the *t*-statistics in brackets for all 8 lags. As expected, changes in the real interest rate do not show any influences in the first month but rather affect the real commodity prices significantly starting from lag 4. Furthermore, for almost all commodity indexes it seems to be the case that the effects are not always negative but rather have an alternating sign.

However, it is not possible to see the overall impact of the real interest rate and its propagation mechanism over time by looking only at the estimated coefficients. Impulse response functions show the dynamic development of the commodity prices in response to an increase in the interest rate over time. The impulse response functions can be compactly written in matrix notation as:

$$y_t = \sum_{k=0}^{\infty} C_k \varepsilon_{t-k} \tag{4.11}$$

with C_0 as the unit matrix. This is the Vector Moving Average (VMA) description of the VAR model, which explains the development of the matrix of variables y_t by weighted past shocks ε_{t-k}. The impulse response functions show the values of y_t over time with a shock relative to y_t without a shock.[29] This, however, implicitly assumes the error terms $\varepsilon_{i,t}$ between the two equations to be uncorrelated. Since this is rarely the case, "orthogonalized impulse response functions" have to be estimated. This is done by transforming the parameter matrix C_k in equation 4.11 so that the residuals are uncorrelated and can be expressed as $\tilde{C}_k = C_k \cdot T$, where T is the transformation matrix with the property $T^{-1}\widehat{\Omega} \cdot T^{-1} = I$. The modified residuals are now $V_{t-k} = T^{-1} \cdot \varepsilon_{t-k}$ which leads to an orthogonal and thus uncorrelated covariance matrix Ω. The idea of this transformation is to attribute a shock which effects the whole system to one specific variable. This also means that the impulse response functions react sensitively to changes of the variable to which the shock is attributed to if high correlation between the equations exists. For the impulse response functions presented below, this change in the Cholesky ordering has been performed to test the robustness of the results. Exhibit 4.6 shows the residual correlation matrix for the real commodity prices and the real interest rate.

As can be seen, the correlations between the residuals of the real interest rate and the change in commodity prices are low with 0.089 between interest rate and industrial metals as the highest correlation. Thus, the impulse response functions are robust with respect to the Cholesky ordering. Under the assumption of shocks to the real interest rate affecting commodity prices, however, the Cholesky ordering has been set in the order real interest rate-commodity index. Exhibit 4.7 shows the impulse response functions for the increase in the real interest rate in the order of two standard deviations.

As can be seen most clearly for precious metals, the real interest rate first has the expected negative sign but then changes to a positive effect before turning negative again. Except for livestock this occurrence seems to be the case for all the commodity indexes but is probably only due to market fluctuations. An increase in the real interest rate leads to a decrease in the demand for commodities that reduces their real price. The lower price in turn may lead some market participants to increase their commodity holdings, increasing the price again. In conclusion, the negative relationship

EXHIBIT 4.6 Residual Correlation Matrix

Variable	Δp_t, Composite	Δp_t, Agriculture	Δp_t, Energy	Δp_t, Industrial	Δp_t, Precious Metals	Δp_t, Livestock
r_t	0.060	0.081	0.047	0.089	−0.001	−0.011

[29]The shocks are usually in the order of one or two standard deviations.

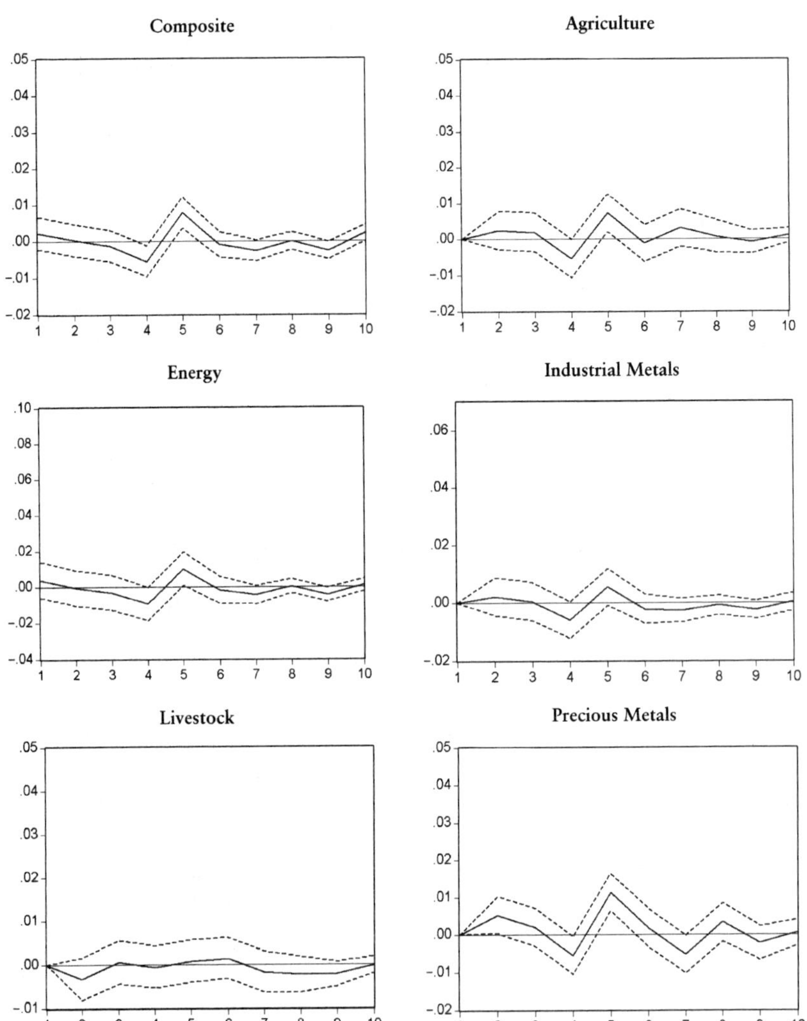

EXHIBIT 4.7 Impulse Response Function for an Increase in the Real Interest Rate

between the real interest rate and commodity prices is significant but not very strong and confirms the previous theoretical derivations as well as the results found in many other studies.[30]

[30]See, for example, Frankel, "Commodity Prices, Monetary Policy, and Currency Regimes." Frankel furthermore investigates the effects on inventories and small economies.

COMMODITIES AND EXCHANGE RATES

Commodities account for a quarter of merchandise trade, which again accounts for a quarter in world GDP. Since many developing countries depend on the export of only a few commodities, it is important to understand the effects of exchange rate deviations on commodity prices. Many commodities are denominated in U.S. dollars so that exchange rate movements vis-à-vis the dollar affect the prices for exporters and importers of commodities. Thus, in addition to the market risk, investors also face an exchange rate risk.

However, the effects of a volatile exchange rate go beyond the investors' risk. A general depreciation of the dollar for example increases the dollar-denominated commodity prices, as commodity exporters from other countries demand a higher price in return for the exchange rate loss and vice versa.[31] Exchange rate movements of single currencies can have substantial effects on the profits of commodity producing firms as well as on supply changes.[32] One prominent example is the case of South Africa in 2001 where the Rand depreciated against the dollar by 35% while at the same time the gold price in dollars actually decreased by 2.9%. This raised profits of South African gold companies which in turn expanded production in the following period. However, it should be noticed that the commodity supply of nonstorable commodities is fixed in the short run since investment in commodity infrastructure can take years, so that price movements can be either caused by changes in the U.S. dollar or by changes in demand. Only in the long run do further investments in commodity production lead to an increase in supply. The short-run supply of storable commodities is somewhat more elastic as long as commodity producing firms still have inventories. The relationship between supply and demand is shown in Exhibit 4.8, which displays a falling demand curve, D, in reaction to higher prices and fixed short-run supply curves, $S^s(ns)$ and $S^s(s)$. If demand increases, the supply of nonstorable commodities, $S^s(ns)$, is fixed in the short run or increases marginally in the case of storable commodities, $S^s(s)$, so that mainly prices increase. Over time, the long-run supply, S^l, responds to changes in the price level resulting in an increase in output and a slight decrease in prices.

This makes it difficult to predict commodity price movements in the future. If world demand remains high in the coming years, if new

[31]See Robert Keyfitz, Currencies and Commodities: Modelling the Impact of Exchange Rates on Commodity Prices in the World Market, Development Prospect Group, World Bank, 2004.

[32]Exchange rate movements may come into effect with a lag since in practice this kind of risk is often hedged for the near future.

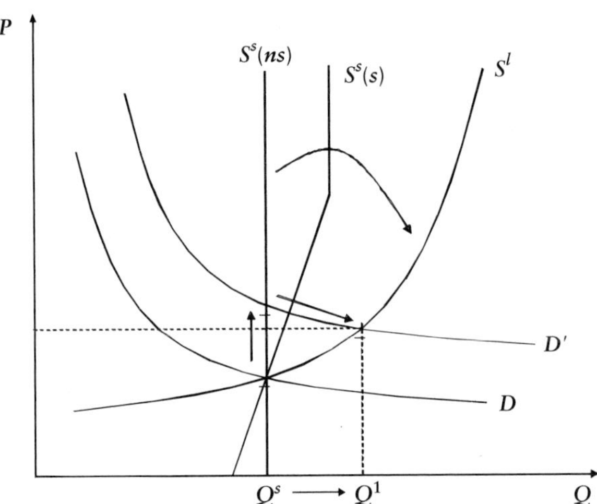

EXHIBIT 4.8 Short-Run and Long-Run Responses to Changes in Demand

investments in commodities are not yet completed, and if the U.S. dollar continues to depreciate, commodity prices will remain high or will even further increase in the near future. On the other hand, an appreciating U.S. dollar and a higher supply would tend to mean-revert commodity prices to the long-term real price level, which in theory is the cost of production. The relationship between the dollar and the commodity composite index can be seen in Exhibit 4.9 where the dollar exchange rate index is a weighted average of the foreign exchange value of the dollar against a subset of broad index currencies. The weights are computed as an average of U.S. bilateral import shares from and export shares to the issuing country.[33] In order to illustrate the negative relationship more clearly, the exchange rate index is measured on the left axis in inverted scale and the commodity index is measured on the right axis.

As can be seen, the negative relationship holds for most of the observed period with deviations during the mid-1980s but also during the past few years where the commodity index strongly increased while the exchange rate remained relatively stable. In the face of high growth in emerging markets, especially in India and China, this suggests that the latest increase in commodity prices is due to higher world demand rather than movements in the exchange rate. Exhibit 4.10 shows the monthly correlation coefficients

[33]The index is provided by the Federal Reserve Bank, see http://www.federalreserve.gov/pubs/bulletin/2005/winter05_index.pdf.

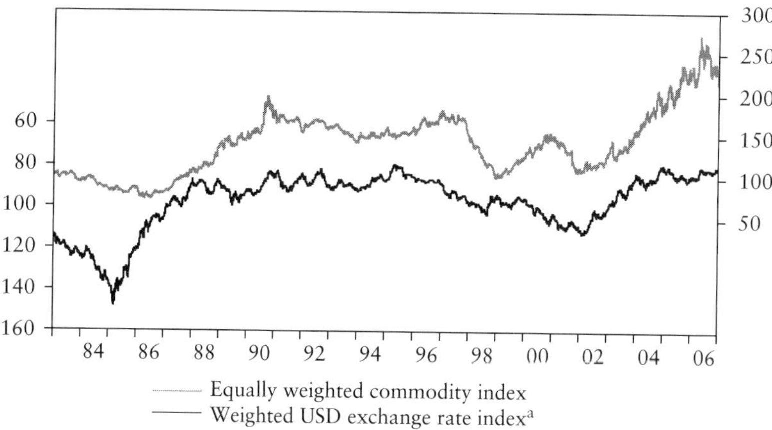

EXHIBIT 4.9 The Relationship between the Weighted Dollar Exchange Rate and Commodity Prices
[a]Exchange rate measured in inverted scale on the left axis and the commodity index on the right axis; based on 289 monthly observations from January 1983 to January 2007.

between the weighted exchange rate index and the individual commodity index returns.

As can be seen, most correlation coefficients have the expected negative sign but are only significantly negative in the case of industrial and precious metals. This supports the argument that an increase in the exchange rate—which corresponds to an appreciation of the dollar—decreases commodity prices and vice versa, albeit not all commodities are affected by the same magnitude.

COMMODITIES AND THE BUSINESS CYCLE

The effects of inflation and the real interest rate discussed in the previous sections imply cyclical behavior of commodities. In a period of strong expansion, consumer demand is high, unemployment low, and wages increase

EXHIBIT 4.10 Correlations between Commodities and the Exchange Rate (January 1983 to January 2007)

Variable	Composite	Agriculture	Energy	Industrial Metals	Livestock	Precious Metals
ΔExchange Rate Index	−0.122	0.058	−0.084	−0.339[a]	0.026	−0.384[b]

[a], [b], and [c] denotes significance at the 1%, and 5%, level, respectively.

more than under normal circumstances. This increases inflation, which, in turn, raises commodity prices if commodities exhibit the inflation hedge property. In addition, high economic activity also means an increase in the demand for commodities as most commodities are required as input to firms' production. The increase in inflation induces the central bank to raise the real interest rate in order to prevent the economy from overheating. When the increase in the real interest rate takes place, the expansion reaches its peak before growth slows, since investments decline due to higher financing costs. With a lag of several months the higher real interest rate reduces the demand for commodities which in turn leads to a decrease of commodity prices. During recessions commodity prices are expected to behave analogous: at the beginning of a recession, the demand for commodities is low, which reduces commodity prices. When the real interest rate is cut by the central bank, commodity prices are expected to increase again.[34]

An empirical examination of the business cycle behavior is complicated by the fact that the change in the real interest rate does not always take place at the same point in the business cycle; that is, the lag for which changes in the real interest rate affect the demand for commodities can vary and other factors like exchange rate movements which are not strongly related to the business cycle might obscure the relationship.[35] Exhibit 4.11 shows the quarterly changes in world industrial production for the time period 1983Q1 to 2007Q1.[36] On the one hand, industrial production is not perfectly correlated with the business cycle. An increase in economic activity leads firms to reduce their storages before increasing production and a recession fills storages up before firms reduce production. However, the advantage is its closer relation with commodity demand, especially for energy and industrial metals which is the reason for choosing world industrial production instead of world GDP, where the linkage to commodity demand may not be as direct.

[34]For further literature on the relationship between commodity prices and the business cycle see, for example, Bruce Bjornson and Colin A. Carter, "New Evidence on Agricultural Commodity Return Performance under Time-Varying Risk," *American Journal of Agricultural Economics* (August 1997), pp. 918–930; and Eugene F. Fama and Kenneth R. French, "Business Cycles and the Behavior of Metals Prices," *Journal of Finance* (December 1988), pp. 1075–1093, among others.

[35]Furthermore, business cycles are far from recurrent regular patterns. In fact, many economists believe business cycles to be only stochastic fluctuations of the market. See, for example, Robert G. King, Charles I. Plosser, James H. Stock, and Mark W. Watson, "Stochastic Trends and Economic Fluctuations," *American Economic Review* (September 1991), pp. 819–840.

[36]Our proxy for world industrial production includes all OECD countries plus Brazil, Mexico, India, and China. China is included in the index from 1990Q1 on.

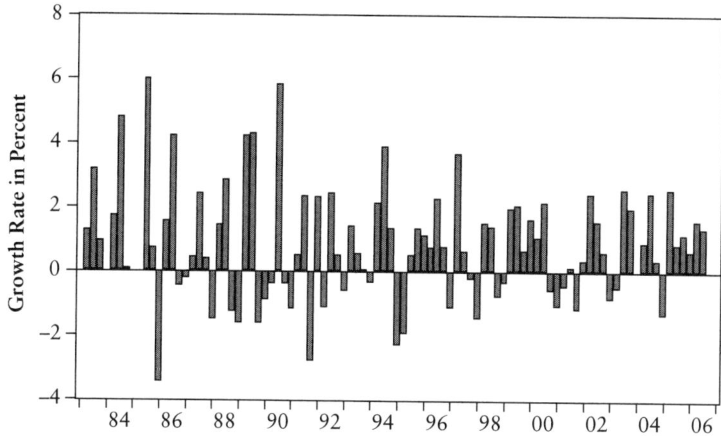

EXHIBIT 4.11 Quarterly Changes in World Industrial Production

The quarterly changes in industrial production are now divided into subperiods: strong expansion, weak expansion, strong recession, and weak recession. We define a strong expansion as a period in which growth is positive and increasing for at least two quarters. A weak expansion corresponds to the same time period with positive but decreasing growth. A strong recession occurs when growth becomes increasingly negative for at least two quarters, and a weak recession corresponds to two consecutive quarters of negative but increasing growth. Exhibit 4.12 displays the four phases of the business cycle.

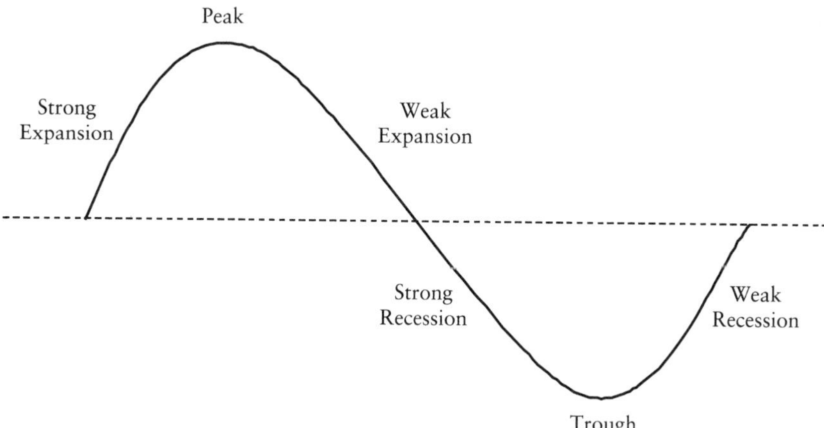

EXHIBIT 4.12 Business Cycle Phases

EXHIBIT 4.13 Return Properties During Different Phases of the Business Cycle

Index	Strong Expansion (#18)	Weak Expansion (#23)	Strong Recession (#4)	Weak Recession (#8)
Composite	7.09	2.62	−3.52	−9.99
Agriculture	−5.81	−6.43	−1.76	−12.76
Energy	37.37	10.03	−7.45	−4.89
Industrial metals	4.12	−4.39	−5.73 (22.14)	−6.30
Livestock	−4.03	5.79	−1.06	−9.76
Precious metals	−1.79	1.21	−13.87	−13.77
JPM Bonds	7.77	7.58	−4.74	5.04
MSCI World	15.86	6.17	6.37	2.69

For the time period 1983Q1 to 2007Q1, the most phases detected were strong and weak expansions as industrial production follows a positive long-term growth path. Accordingly, only four and eight periods were observed for the strong and weak recession, respectively, while a strong or weak expansion occurred 18 and 23 times. Exhibit 4.13 shows the average returns of the individual commodity index as well as the average returns for stocks and bonds under the respective phase of the business cycle. The clearest result can be seen for the energy index which is probably most strongly affected by changes in industrial production. In a strong expansion, energy demand is especially high, driving up energy prices while prices decrease during recession periods. The other index which is expected to show a strong reaction to the business cycle is industrial metals. Returns are positive during a strong expansion and decrease otherwise except for the strong recession. The return of 22.14% seems to be puzzling but is the result of only one outlier of 39.32% in 1989Q1. If this outlier is removed, the return becomes a more reasonable −5.73%. It is worth noticing that the returns for the energy and industrial metals index are much lower during weak expansions than during strong ones. On the one hand, this may be due to lower demand during these phases. However, it might be also by reason of increased interest rates which lower commodity prices as well. In fact, if a strong expansion precedes a weak expansion, the weak expansion may be because of increased real interest rates. The agricultural and precious metals index show negative returns for almost all periods as those indexes generally declined during the period under consideration. For the precious metals index, however the returns are more negative during recession periods than during expansive periods.

Many commodity indexes such as agriculture, industrial metals, and livestock show less negative returns during strong recessions than during weak recessions. This could be because of the effect of a lower real interest rate during recession periods. During strong recession periods, the bond index for example exhibits negative returns and the lower real interest rate in general might induce investors to shift part of their capital into commodities, so that the lower demand during those periods is partly compensated by the gain in relative attractiveness of commodities.

Combining the demand effects from the business cycle and the exchange rate effects discussed above, an estimation equation can be expressed by the following regression:

$$R_t = \alpha + \beta_1 \cdot \Delta IPW_{t-1} + \beta_2 \cdot \Delta EXC_t + \varepsilon_t \tag{4.12}$$

where R_t denotes the quarterly return of the individual commodity index, ΔIPW_{t-1} is the percentage change in world industrial production from the previous quarter, and ΔEXC_t is the percentage change in the weighted exchange rate index. The lag in world industrial production takes into account that most commodities are storable to some degree, so that higher demand for commodities does not increase commodity prices until the following quarter. Exchange rate movements in contrast affect commodity prices directly and enter equation (4.12) in the current period. Exhibit 4.14 displays the regression results for the time period 1983Q1 to 2007Q1. The coefficient β_1 in the case of the composite index shows that an increase in world demand for commodities by 1% increases commodity prices with a lag of one quarter on average by 0.6%. However, the effect is only significant for the energy index but insignificant for the other indexes.

A general appreciation of the U.S. dollar by 1% decreases commodity prices by around 0.6% in the case of precious metals and by around 1% for

EXHIBIT 4.14 The Effects of World Demand and the Exchange Rate on Commodity Returns, (1983Q1 to 2007Q1)

Variable	Composite	Agriculture	Energy	Industrial Metals	Livestock	Precious Metals
α	−0.106	−0.577	−1.059	1.023	0.296	-1.234^{c}
	[−0.162]	[−0.655]	[−0.583]	[0.799]	[0.334]	[−1.871]
β_1	0.600^{c}	-0.750^{c}	3.060^{a}	0.312	0.102	0.265
	[1.816]	[−1.681]	[3.325]	[0.481]	[0.227]	[0.795]
β_2	−0.182	0.080	−0.324	-1.048^{a}	0.041	-0.603^{a}
	[−1.182]	[0.386]	[−0.755]	[−3.478]	[0.195]	[−3.882]

[a], [b], and [c] denotes significance at the 1%, 5%, and 10% level, respectively; based on quarterly data (96 observations).

industrial metals. Thus, a higher value of the dollar has a negative effect on commodity prices.

CONCLUSION

This chapter presented an overview of macroeconomic influences on commodity prices and provided empirical evidence for the relationship between commodity prices and inflation, monetary policy, exchange rate movements, and the business cycle. Commodities are a very heterogeneous asset class but some effects apply to all indexes: Most commodities exhibit an inflation hedge property when compared with U.S. inflation. For European and Asian inflation and when considering different time horizons, the inflation hedge property becomes more ambiguous, so that the general effect is unclear. Closely linked to inflation are the changes in the real interest rate. An increase in the real interest rate decreases real commodity prices with a lag of two or more quarters as investors react to increasing opportunity costs and shift part of their financial capital out of commodities. Exchange rate movements can have considerable effects on the supply and demand for commodities since most commodities are denominated in U.S. dollars. A general depreciation of the dollar increases commodity prices as export countries demand higher prices in order to compensate the exchange rate loss. Changes in the return patterns of commodities over time are reflected in different phases of the business cycle. In a period of economic expansion the demand for commodities increases. At the same time, the central bank is likely to raise real interest rates which decreases the demand for commodities. While the former increases commodity prices, the latter decreases them, so that a decomposition of the effects would be necessary and remains to further research. The overall picture, however, is that commodity returns are higher during expansive periods and lower or negative during recessions, which means that the demand effect is stronger compared to the real interest rate effect.

CHAPTER 5

The Relationship Between Risk Premium and Convenience Yield Models

Viola Markert, Ph.D.
Managing Director
CYD Research GmBH

Heinz Zimmermann, Ph.D.
Professor of Finance
Wirtschaftswissenschaftliches Zentrum WWZ
University of Basel

The valuation of commodity futures contracts is typically regarded to be more complex than the valuation of financial assets and their derivatives. The reason is the hybrid character of the underlying commodity: On one hand, commodities serve as consumption and processing goods. On the other hand, they also share certain characteristics of financial assets in the sense that they have a unique equilibrium market price, and that they are subject to speculative storage. In short, commodity spot prices are a mixture of prices for consumption goods, reflecting the current scarcity of the good, and of asset prices, reflecting the expectation of future spot prices and an expected risk premium. Depending on either view, commodity futures are:

- Derivatives written on asset-like underlying securities and should be valued using arbitrage-based techniques, or alternatively
- Derivatives written on nontradable state variables or spot commodity prices and should be valued with equilibrium asset pricing techniques

As a result of that hybrid character, two broad classes of valuation models are used for commodity futures: *risk premium models* (RPM) and *convenience yield models* (CYM). Risk premium models value commodity futures with respect to the expected commodity spot price discounted by an appropriate risk premium. They derive the risk premium from specific equilibrium conditions and fundamental factors such as aggregate wealth, real consumption, or the hedging pressure.

Convenience yield models, in turn, are arbitrage-based valuation concepts. They value commodity futures with respect to the current commodity spot price and an appropriate convenience yield. Convenience yields depend on inventories and reflect expectations about the availability of commodities, sometimes called the "immediacy" of a market. If inventories are low, the convenience yield is high, and vice versa.[1]

Resulting from the hybrid role of commodities as assets and consumption goods, there is a large variety of valuation models for commodity futures. For hardly any other type of derivative security, both arbitrage-related and equilibrium asset pricing concepts have been applied so naturally alongside each other for such a long time—starting from the early literature in the 1930s until today. Keynes' (1930) theory of "normal backwardation"[2] is one of the first equilibrium asset pricing models for commodity futures. The works of Kaldor (1939) and Working (1948, 1949) introduce the first arbitrage-related concepts.[3] Examples from the more recent literature are the risk premium model of DeRoon, Nijman, and Veld (2000) and the convenience yield model of Cassus and Collin-Dufresne (2005).[4]

In this chapter, the risk premium model and the convenience yield model in commodity futures valuation are highlighted, and the way they can be related. It is shown that these models are mutually consistent, and how they can be used to explain the term structure of commodity futures prices, and

[1]The concept was developed by Kaldor as a theoretical explanation of Keynes' normal backwardation in commodities markets; Nicholas Kaldor, "Speculation and Economic Stability," *Review of Economic Studies* 26, no. 1 (1939), pp. 1–27.

[2]The practical usage of "backwardation" refers to markets in which futures prices are below *current* spot prices. Keynes' "normal backwardation" refers to futures prices below *expected* spot prices at expiration. See John M. Keynes, *A Treatise on Money, Vol. 2: The Applied Theory of Money* (London: Macmillan, 1930), pp. 142–147.

[3]Holbrook Working, "Theory of the Inverse Carrying Charge in Futures Markets," *Journal of Farm Economics* 30, no. 1 (1948) pp. 1–28; and Holbrook Working, "The Theory of Price of Storage," *American Economic Review* 39, no. 6 (1949), pp. 1254–1262.

[4]Frans A. De Roon, Theo E. Nijman, and Chris Veld, "Hedging Pressure Effects in Futures Markets," *Journal of Finance* 55, no. 3 (2000), pp. 1437–1456; and Jaime Casassus and Pierre Collin-Dufresne, "Stochastic Convenience Yield Implied from Commodity Futures and Interest Rates," *Journal of Finance* 60, no. 5 (2005), pp. 2283–2331.

the return components of futures contracts. For example, the decomposition of futures returns into a "roll" and "spot" yield is common among practitioners, but the relation to economic pricing models remains often obscure. We highlight these basic relations with empirical characteristics of commodity futures returns.

LIMITATION OF RISK NEUTRAL PRICING

It is well-known from general finance textbooks that arbitrage pricing can typically not be applied to commodity futures contracts due to the value of commodities as consumption and processing goods. The underlying of financial futures contracts are financial assets (stocks, bonds, or other derivatives) that are, by definition, in strictly positive supply, always available, and fully tradable. Therefore, it is always possible to construct a portfolio that replicates the payoff of the futures contract. In order to exclude arbitrage opportunities, the futures price satisfies

$$F_{t,T} = S_t \; e^{[r-\delta](T-t)}$$

which means that after adjusting for time (interest, r) and payoffs (dividends, coupons, δ), the futures price is fully determined by the current spot price of the underlying asset, S. In practitioner wording, the equation states that the futures price corresponds to the *cost of carry*, which consists of the spot price, the risk-free rate, and the dividend yield of the underlying, and refers to the costs associated with carrying (maintaining) a spot position over the life of a futures (or general: a derivatives) contract.

Commodities differ in several important aspects from financial assets. First, they do not pay a financial yield like dividends or coupons to the owner, but entail storage costs. If they are expressed as a constant proportion of the value of the underlying they can be treated as negative dividend yields. Then, the cost of carry for commodity futures comprises the commodity spot price, the risk-free rate, and the storage costs, m. The previous equation becomes

$$F_{t,T} = S_t \; e^{[r+m](T-t)} \tag{5.1}$$

representing the cost-of-carry formula for commodity futures.

Second, and more important, unlike financial assets, the main purpose of commodities is consumption and processing. By definition, commodities are not designed to be carried from one period to the next and the commodity supply is not stable over time. Therefore, no replicating portfolio can be constructed, and equation (5.1) cannot be expected to hold in general.

To illustrate the effect of consumption and processing for the feasibility of the replication trading strategy, assume there are two types of inventories of the commodity:

- *Speculative inventories* of excess supplies of the commodity, which are not needed for consumption or processing over the life of the futures contract.
- *Consumption inventories* of the commodity, which are needed for consumption or processing in the nearer future.

If the commodity futures price exceeds the cost-of-carry price in equation (5.1),

$$F_{t,T} > S_t \, e^{[r+m](T-t)}$$

arbitrage implies to short the futures contract and to invest in the replicating portfolio. For the replicating portfolio, the arbitrageur has to borrow the amount of $S_t \, e^{m(T-t)}$ to buy the commodity in the cash market and to cover the instantaneous storage costs m. Through this trading strategy, arbitrageurs increase speculative inventories of the commodity, drive down the futures price and drive up the commodity spot price until equation (5.1) is restored. Consequently, the futures price cannot exceed the cost-of-carry price in equation (5.1) in the absence of arbitrage.[5]

The distinctive nature of commodity futures becomes important when the futures price falls short of the price in equation (5.1), that is,

$$F_{t,T} < S_t \, e^{[r+m](T-t)}$$

In this case, arbitrage would imply to go short in the replicating portfolio and long in the futures contract: Take a long position in the futures

[5]It should be noted that this mechanism only works if the underlying is storable over the life of the futures contract. The storability and feasibility of the trading strategy depend on the type of the commodity. Some commodities, like electricity, cannot be stored and have to be consumed immediately. Others, like meat or grains, are perishable and can only be stored for a limited time period. For agricultural goods, moreover, the quality varies from harvest to harvest, and the stored commodity of last year's harvest might be a different good from this year's harvest. For these commodities it is possible that $F_{t,T} > S_t \, e^{(r+m)(T-t)}$; that is, the futures price can exceed the cost of carry.

contract, (short) sell the commodity to save the storage costs m and invest the proceeds at the riskless rate r.

(Short) selling of the physical commodity is possible as long as there are positive supplies of speculative inventories. If the commodity becomes scarce and these inventories are driven down to zero, the futures price can fall short of equation (5.1), or the spot price can rise above the (discounted) futures price in equation (5.1), respectively. Owners of consumption inventories cannot (short) sell their inventories if they need the physical commodity for consumption or processing. In other words, for the owner of consumption inventories the commodity is a different good from the commodity futures contract, which is useless for production and consumption. Consequently, consumption inventories of the commodity cannot be used to build a replicating portfolio for the commodity futures contract, and the futures contract cannot be used to replace inventories of the physical commodity in consumption or processing.

Arbitrage and the replicating portfolio work in one way, but not in the other. This mechanism establishes an arbitrage (upper) bound for commodity futures rather than an arbitrage price,

$$F_{t,T} \leq S_t \, e^{[r+m](T-t)} \tag{5.2}$$

In fact, it is not even necessary that speculative inventories are driven down to zero. It is sufficient that there is a positive probability of zero inventories over the life of the futures contract to drive the spot price above the discounted futures value, $F_{t,T} \, e^{-(r+m)(T-t)} \leq S_t$. If there is a possibility that stockouts occur, the ownership of the physical commodity is more valuable than the ownership of the commodity future because only the holder of the physical commodity can benefit from potential temporary shortages of the commodity.

Several authors show that the payoff from holding commodity inventories is equal to an option payoff.[6] If there is a positive probability that inventories are driven to zero over the life of the futures contract,

---

[6]Robert H. Litzenberger and Nir Rabinowitz, "Backwardation in Oil Futures Markets: Theory and Empirical Evidence," *Journal of Finance* 50, no. 5 (1995), pp. 1517–1545; Nikolaos T. Milonas and Stavros B. Thomadakis, "Convenience Yield and the Option to Liquidate for Commodities with a Crop Cycle," *European Review of Agricultural Economics* 24, no. 2 (1997), pp. 267–283; Nikolaos T. Milonas and Stavros B. Thomadakis, "Convenience Yields as Call Options: An Empirical Analysis," *Journal of Futures Markets* 17, no. 1 (1998), pp. 1–15; and Richard Heaney, "Approximation for Convenience Yield in Commodity Futures Pricing," *Journal of Futures Markets* 22, no. 10 (2002), pp. 1005–1017.

this option has a strictly positive value. Consequently, the spot price of the commodity will always exceed the discounted futures price by the value of this option, and equation (5.2) becomes a strict inequality, $F_{t,T} < S_t \, e^{(r+m)(T-t)}$.

If speculative inventories of the commodity are empty, it is not possible to construct a replicating portfolio or to value commodity futures based on a replicating portfolio as the previous section has shown. Risk-neutral valuation concepts fail for the same reason: If inventories are empty there will still be a market price for the commodity. But this price only reflects the current scarcity of the commodity and its consumption value, not its asset value. If inventories are zero, "any information about the future supply and demand of the underlying commodity cannot influence the corresponding cash price" as Neftci notes.[7] From a financial point of view, the underlying is not a tradable asset anymore and the commodity spot price is detached from price expectations.

If standard arbitrage arguments cannot be applied to price commodity futures, one has to look for alternatives. Two well-established models, the convenience yield model (CYM) and the risk premium model (RPM), are presented in the next section, and their relationship is examined.

TWO BASIC MODELS

The first part of this section addresses the general functional form of risk premium models for commodity futures based on the notion that commodity futures are pure assets and can be valued by equilibrium asset pricing. The second part derives the general functional form of convenience yield models from the fact that the physical commodity is not a pure asset as opposed to the futures contract. The last part of this section combines the two models in one equation. In the rest of the chapter, it is shown how the two models help in interpreting the term structure of commodity futures and the (actual and expected) returns on futures contracts (see Exhibit 5.1).

Risk Premium Models

The physical commodity is not a pure asset due to its additional value as a production and consumption good. In order to make this difference explicit,

[7]Sahli N. Neftci, *An Introduction in the Mathematics of Financial Derivatives*, 2nd ed. (Orlando, FL: Academic Press, 2000).

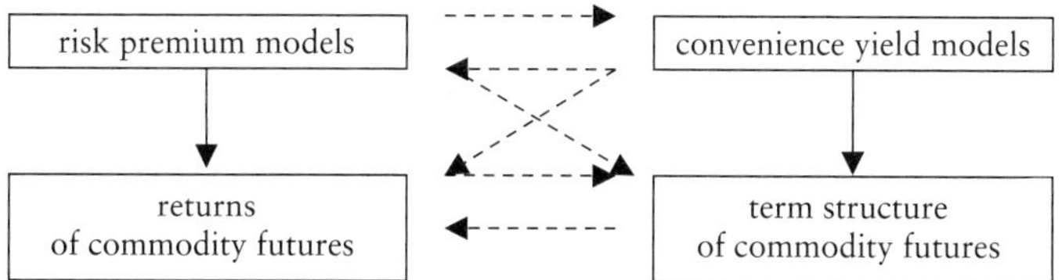

EXHIBIT 5.1 Relationship between Risk Premium and Convenience Yield Models
Source: Viola Market, Commodities as Assets and Consumption Goods: Implications for the Valuation of Commodity Futures (Doctoral Dissertation, University of St. Gallen and Basel, 2005).

we denote the spot price of the physical commodity by S_t^C, and the spot price of an asset by S_t^A.

A general form to express asset values is[8]

$$S_t^A = e^{-[r+rp+m](T-t)} E_t\left[S_T^A\right] \tag{5.3}$$

where S_T^A depicts the price for the asset at time $T \geq t$; r is the risk-free rate and rp the asset specific risk premium using continuous compounding. m denotes a known yield which can be either interpreted as the proportional storage cost of commodities or the (negative) dividend yield of stocks, $m = -\delta$.

For a commodity, we can define a hypothetical or *quasi-asset value* of the commodity as the risk-adjusted present value of the expected commodity spot price of time T.

$$S_t^A = e^{-[r+rp+m](T-t)} \ E_t\left[S_T^C\right] \tag{5.4}$$

Notice that due to the additional consumption of the physical commodity, the actual spot price is above the quasi-asset value, $S_t^C \geq S_t^A$, but the magnitude of the deviation cannot be determined in the context of this model.

[8]Asset values can be more generally expressed as $S_t^A = E_t[\Lambda_{t,T} X_T]$, where $\Lambda_{t,T}$ is a stochastic deflator and X_T denotes the payoff for the asset of time I.

The relationship of the commodity futures price $F_{t,T}$ to the quasi-asset value follows from the cost-of-carry formula (5.1)[9],

$$F_{t,T} = e^{[r+m](T-t)} S_t^A \tag{5.5}$$

and is given by arbitrage. In contrast, the commodity futures price cannot be directly related to the current spot price in the context of this model, but replacing (5.4) in equation (5.5) leads to

$$F_{t,T} = e^{-rp(T-t)} E_t \left[S_T^C \right] \tag{5.6}$$

This equation is the general risk premium model for commodity futures stating that the commodity futures price equals the expected commodity spot price, discounted by a risk premium or excess return to compensate for the price risk of the commodity. Since futures contracts have a zero value at initiation, they do not bind any capital and do not pay a risk-free rate.

Convenience Yield Models

The risk premium model does not provide a relationship between the "quasi-asset price" (given by equation (5.4)) and the actual spot price of commodities. In general the two prices cannot be expected to coincide.[10] Specifically, we claim that $S_t^C \geq S_t^A$ because of the additional consumption value of the physical commodity and the nonnegativity constraints of inventories. Convenience yield models determine the difference between S_t^A and S_t^C. The various models differ in the way they motivate the convenience yield, and in the functional form of the relationship. We chose a particularly simple form, namely

$$\frac{S_t^C}{S_t^A} = [1 + CY]^{(T-t)} = e^{cy(T-t)} \tag{5.7}$$

[9]In the stochastic deflator setting, we have $0 = E_t[\Lambda_{t,T}(S_t^C - F_{t,T})]$ which can be expressed as $F_{t,T}E_t[\Lambda_{t,T}] = E_t[\Lambda_{t,T}S_t^C]$. Recognizing $E_t[\Lambda_{t,T}] = e^{-(r+m)(T-t)}$ and $S_t^A = E_t[\Lambda_{t,T}S_t^C]$, equations (5.5) and (5.6) are straightforward.

[10]See Kenneth R. French, "A Comparison of Futures and Forward Prices," *Journal of Financial Economics* 12, no. 3 (1983), pp. 311–342, in which he notes "a present value of the maturity spot price is not observable for most commodities" (p. 314).

where CY (cy) denotes the convenience yield in terms of simple (continuously compounded) returns. It can be interpreted as the proportion of the commodity spot price which is not attributable to its value as an asset but to other benefits of the commodity, particularly its consumption value.[11] Often, the convenience yield is compared to the dividend yield which accrues to the holder of common stock. Similar to dividend yields, the convenience yield captures the (nonmonetary) benefit which accrues to the owner of the physical commodity.

Replacing S_t^A in equation (5.5) by equation (5.7), the futures price of commodities can now be directly related to the spot price of the commodity, namely

$$F_{t,T} = e^{[r+m](T-t)} S_t^A \equiv e^{[r+m](T-t)} \frac{S_t^C}{e^{cy(T-t)}} = e^{[r+m-cy](T-t)} S_t^C \tag{5.8}$$

It is apparent that the convenience yield captures the deviation of the futures price from the cost-of-carry formula in equation (5.1). Since CY is assumed to be positive, the futures price falls short of the cost-of-carry formula.

Synthesis

Comparing equations (5.6) and (5.8) provides a synthesis of the two models:

$$F_{t,T} = e^{-rp(T-t)} E_t\left[S_T^C\right] = e^{[r+m-cy](T-t)} S_t^C \tag{5.9}$$

The commodity futures price equals the expected spot price of the commodity discounted by an appropriate risk premium. To the extent that the physical commodity is storable, the commodity spot price behaves like an asset and contains information about this expectation and the expected risk premium. The convenience yield measures how valuable the informational content of the spot price is. The higher inventories are, the lower is the convenience yield; that is, the more the spot price behaves like an asset and reflects spot price expectations and expected risk premiums. As inventories decrease, the link between current commodity spot prices and price expectations weakens, which is reflected in a higher convenience yield.

[11]Please note that for nonstorable commodities, like electricity, the commodity spot price only reflects the current demand and supply condition and is completely detached from spot price expectations or the "quasi-asset price." For these commodities it is also possible that $S^C < S^A$ or $CY < 0$ and $cy < 0$.

Our derivation clarifies two points:

- Convenience yield models can be "derived" from risk premium models for commodity futures; that is, the two valuation approaches are mutually consistent.
- It seems to be more appropriate to view convenience yields as a residual in the asset pricing formula for commodity spot prices (equation (5.4)) rather than in the cost-of-carry formula for commodity futures prices (equation (5.1)). After all, it is the commodity spot price and not the commodity futures price, which does not obey the laws of asset pricing.

This idea is implicitly accounted for by many convenience yield models, but there are only few articles which provide a direct comparison and application of both types of models. Fama and French emphasize that the "two popular views of commodity futures prices" are "alternative but not competing views" and (implicitly) combine risk premium and convenience yield models in one equation.[12] Bessembinder et al. equate the risk premium with the convenience yield formula to estimate the expected mean reversion in commodity spot prices from current spot- and futures prices of the commodity.[13] Both articles use risk premium models and convenience yield models in a common application but they do not discuss the economic relationship between them.

TERM STRUCTURE OF COMMODITY PRICES

In this section, we investigate the interpretation of the term structure of commodity futures prices under the two models discussed before.

TS Under the Risk Premium Model

We examine two futures contracts with maturities T_1 and T_2 and take the natural log of equation (5.6). The logarithmic futures prices become

$$\ln F_{t,T_1} = -rp(T_1 - t) + \ln E_t\left[S_{T_1}^C\right]$$

[12]Eugene F. Fama and Kenneth R. French, "Commodity Futures Pricing: Some Evidence on Forecast Power, Premiums, and the Theory of Storage," *Journal of Business* 60, no. 1 (1987), pp. 55–73.

[13]Hendrik Bessembinder, Jay F. Coughenour, Paul J. Seguin, and Margaret Monroe Smoller, "Mean Reversion in Equilibrium Asset Prices: Evidence from the Futures Term Structure," *Journal of Finance* 50, no. 1 (1995), pp. 361–375.

and

$$\ln F_{t,T_2} = -rp(T_2 - t) + \ln E_t\left[S^C_{T_2}\right]$$

Representing the slope of the relevant segment of the term structure by $\ln\frac{F_{t,T_2}}{F_{t,T_1}}$, we get

$$\ln\frac{F_{t,T_2}}{F_{t,T_1}} = \ln E_t\left[S^C_{T_2}\right] - \ln E_t\left[S^C_{T_1}\right] - rp(T_2 - t - T_1 + t)$$

The first two terms denote the expected growth rate of the spot price between T_1 and T_2, as perceived from t; this will be denoted by

$$\hat{\alpha}^C_S(t, T_1, T_2) \equiv \ln E_t\left[S^C_{T_2}\right] - \ln E_t\left[S^C_{T_1}\right]$$

implying

$$\ln\frac{F_{t,T_2}}{F_{t,T_1}} = \hat{\alpha}^C_S(t, T_1, T_2) - rp(T_2 - T_1) \tag{5.10}$$

Thus, after adjusting for the risk premium, the term structure reflects current expectations about future spot price changes. A downward sloping term structure (backwardation) is either explained by a substantial risk premium, or anticipated decreases of the spot price, or both.

For financial futures, this expression looks different. Here, the asset price satisfies equation (5.4); substituting S^C by S^A, solving for the expected spot price and taking logs gives

$$\ln E_t\left[S^A_{T_1}\right] = \ln S^A_t + [r + rp + m](T_1 - t)$$

which implies

$$\begin{aligned}\ln\frac{F_{t,T_2}}{F_{t,T_1}} &= \ln\frac{E_t\left[S^A_{T_2}\right]}{E_t\left[S^A_{T_1}\right]} - rp(T_2 - T_1)\\ &= \ln E_t\left[S^A_{T_2}\right] - \ln E_t\left[S^A_{T_1}\right] - rp(T_2 - T_1)\\ &= [r + rp + m](T_2 - T_1) - rp(T_2 - T_1)\end{aligned}$$

and

$$\ln\frac{F_{t,T_2}}{F_{t,T_1}} = [r + m](T_2 - T_1) \tag{5.11}$$

Thus, for financial futures, the slope of the term structure just reflects the risk-free rate adjusted by the yield, $\delta = -m$.

Equation (5.10) is the most specific expression that we can get for the term structure of commodity futures. Unlike the term structure of financial futures prices, equation (5.11), the term structure of commodity futures can assume almost any shape—upward sloping, downward sloping, hump shaped—depending on the expected change in spot prices. Similar to forward curves for interest rates, it reflects the points on the path that investors expect the commodity spot price will take. Based on this, Bessembinder et al. use the term structure of futures prices to detect the expected mean reversion in commodity spot prices. They find significant evidence for expected mean reversion of prices for agricultural goods and metals, but no evidence for expected mean reversion of prices for financial assets.[14]

TS Under the Convenience Yield Model

Under the convenience yield model, the natural logarithm of the commodity futures price using equation (5.8) is

$$\ln F_{t,T} = [r + m - cy](T - t) + \ln S_t^C$$

and the slope of the term structure becomes

$$\ln \frac{F_{t,T_2}}{F_{t,T_1}} = [r + m - cy](T_2 - T_1) \tag{5.12}$$

In convenience yield models, the term structure of commodity futures reflects the risk-free rate, storage costs, and the convenience yield factor. A decreasing term structure (backwardation) is explained by high convenience yields compared to interest and storage costs, which occurs if the supply of the commodity in current spot markets is scarce, and inventory levels are low. If there is a substantial risk of zero speculative inventories, the convenience yield can be substantial and pressures the curve further down.[15]

Notice that we have assumed for simplicity that the risk-free rate and the convenience yield are constant and, moreover, do not depend on the time horizon $T - t$ of the contract. This implies that the log-term structure is linear in the time horizon (T_1, T_2). However, in reality, both the risk-free rate and the convenience yield are time-varying (possibly stochastic), and

[14]Bessembinder et al., "Mean Reversion in Equilibrium Asset Prices: Evidence from the Futures Term Structure."

[15]As explained in previous footnotes, if a commodity cannot be stored, the convenience yield can be positive or negative, reflecting the positive or negative deviation of the current commodity spot price from its quasi-asset price.

depend on the time to maturity, r_t^T and cy_t^T. In this case, the term structure of commodity prices reflects both the term structure of interest rates and the term structure of convenience yields.

Relationship

Now, the relationship between the two models is easily established. For equations (5.10) and (5.12) to be mutually consistent, the following must hold:

$$\hat{\alpha}_S^C(t, T_1, T_2) - rp(T_2 - T_1) = [r + m - cy](T_2 - T_1)$$

which implies[16]

$$\hat{\alpha}_S^C(t, T_1, T_2) = [r + rp + m - cy](T_2 - T_1) \tag{5.13}$$

For financial assets, where $cy = 0$ and $m = -\delta$, this equation states that the spot price is expected to grow by the risk-free rate, the risk premium minus the dividend yield—which is the well-known asset pricing relationship.

For commodities, the spot price is also expected to grow at the risk-free rate, the risk premium, and storage costs. However, today's spot price, S_t^C, can overshoot the discounted expected spot price.[17] The convenience yield, $cy(T_2 - T_1)$, captures this deviation and thereby reflects the expected decline of commodity spot prices.

Empirical Example

To illustrate the preceding discussion, we display in Exhibit 5.2 the term structure for four commodities as of January 2007: gold, crude oil, coffee, and natural gas. The term structure of oil futures prices is interesting because it displays backwardation and contango at the same time. The term structure of gold follows a straight line. The curve for natural gas exhibits strong cyclical components, while the term structure for coffee is increasing but somehow concave. The interpretation of these structures follows directly from our preceding discussion, and is delivered in Exhibit 5.3.

For a commodity that is close to a financial asset, gold, the slope of the curve simply represents the risk-free rate of interest plus storage costs (equation (5.11)). The term structure of oil looks different: After adjusting for a risk premium, the term structure reflects expectations about rising spot

[16]See also equation (4) in Kenneth R. French, "Detecting Spot Price Forecasts in Futures Prices," *Journal of Business* 59, no. 2 (1986), pp. 39–54.

[17]For nonstorable commodities, the spot price can also undershoot the discounted expected spot price.

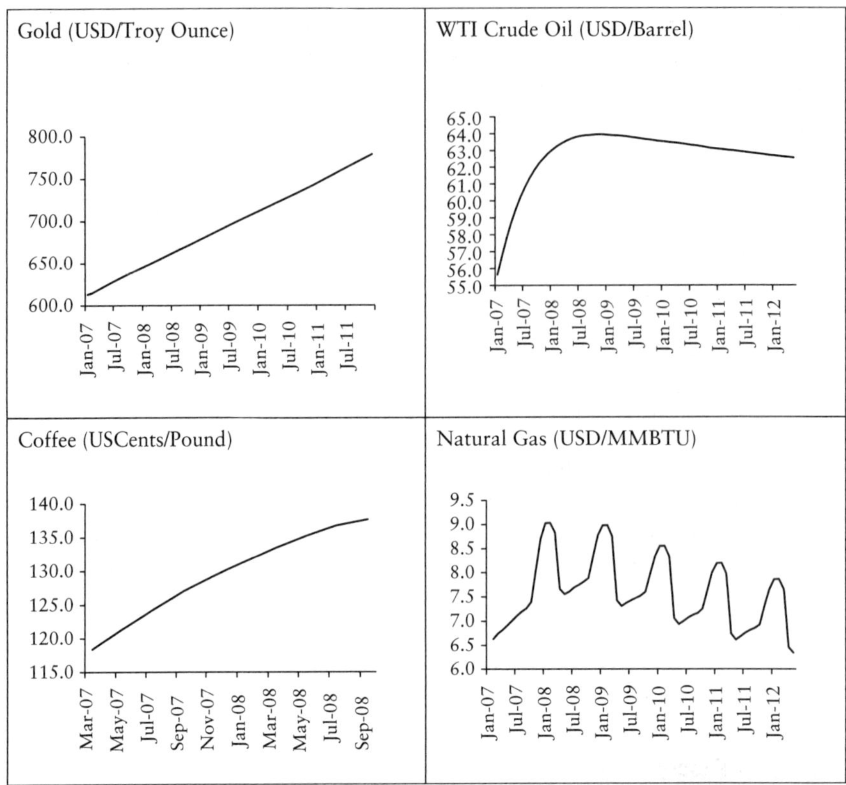

EXHIBIT 5.2 Term Structures for Different Commodities, January 9, 2007
Source: Exhibit created from data obtained from Datastream.

prices until June 2008, and gradually decreasing prices thereafter (equation (5.10)). The rising term structure at the short end is generally interpreted as a consequence of the substantial amount of money flowing to the commodities markets in the past months, particularly into the commodity indexes where oil represents a large fraction. Rolling the futures contracts pushes nearby prices below those of contracts for later delivery. In real terms, contango can be seen as a signal of temporary surplus in the physical oil market, where high inventories are accumulated driving down the convenience yield on the physical commodity to discourage further storage. At longer time horizons, the picture is reversed; if worries about the security of future supplies dominate and inventories are reduced, the link between current spot prices and price expectations weakens, which is reflected in higher convenience yields (backwardation).

EXHIBIT 5.3 Interpretation of Term Structures in Exhibit 5.2

	Risk Premium Model	Convenience Yield Model
	Expected change in spot prices − Risk premium $\hat{\alpha}_S^C(t, T_1, T_2) - rp(T_2, T_1)$	Risk free rate + Storage cost − Convenience yield (= temporary scarcity) $(r + m - cy)(T_2 - T_1)$
Crude oil	Net of the risk premium—the oil price is expected to rise until June 2008 and then to decrease gradually	Strong supply of oil and negative cost of carry discourage additional storage
Gold	Net of the risk premium—the gold price is expected to rise by the cost-of-carry (risk-free rate and storage cost)	Risk-free rate and storage cost
Natural gas	Net of the risk premium—the gas price is expected to be high in winter times (when natural gas is scarce and valuable) and to be low in summer times, January 2007 (warm winter, no scarcity) is an exception of this rule	Strong supply in summer times (and warm Winter 2007); first expected shortage in future winter times
Coffee	Net of the risk premium—the coffee price is expected to increase	Strong supply of coffee, negative cost-of-carry

Contango is also the picture for coffee futures across the whole maturity spectrum and can be interpreted, after adjusting for a risk premium, as reflecting expectations about increasing spot prices. In real terms, the negative cost-of-carry is caused by low current spot prices and high inventories. A recent market commentary on the coffee market illustrates this point:

> *The bulls are pointing to 2007's expected 31.5 million bag Brazilian crop as reason enough to buy coffee now. After all, it is a substantial decrease from 2006's massive 43 million bag harvest and some analysts expect Brazilian coffee exports to drop as much as 10% in 2007 as a result. While this may be true, this viewpoint does not take into account the massive supplies in storage left over*

> *from the 2006 harvest. The South American coffee harvest typically wraps up in October. Most of this coffee is still sitting in Brazilian warehouses looking for a home. But Brazil is becoming much more active in exporting at current price levels. In December, coffee exports from Brazil were up 26.4% over last year at the same time.*[18]

The term structure for natural gas is more complex and is driven, net of the risk premium, by high spot price expectations in the winter (when natural gas is scarce and valuable) and low price expectations in summer times. Notice that the typical pattern is violated in our example for the next-to-expire January 2007 contract because of high winter temperatures and no scarcity in the supply. Of course, storability of this commodity is limited, so that convenience yields can have either sign, and constitute a substantial portion of the cost-of-carry.

FUTURES RETURNS

In this section, we investigate the interpretation of futures returns, based on the risk premium and convenience yield model.

Returns Under the Risk Premium Model

Under the risk premium model as given in equation (5.6), the natural logarithm of a futures price in t of a contract with maturity T is given by

$$\ln F_{t,T} = -rp(T-t) + \ln E_t\left[S_T^C\right]$$

and one period later, the respective expression is

$$\ln F_{t+1,T} = -rp(T-t-1) + \ln E_{t+1}\left[S_T^C\right]$$

The continuously compounded futures return over $[t,\ t+1]$ then becomes

$$\begin{aligned}
\tilde{r}_{F,t,t+1,T} &= \ln \tilde{F}_{t+1,T} - \ln F_{t,T} \\
&= -rp(T-t-1) + \ln \tilde{E}_{t+1}\left[S_T^C\right] - \left(-rp(T-t) + \ln E_t\left[S_T^C\right]\right) \\
&= -rp(-1) + \ln \tilde{E}_{t+1}\left[S_T^C\right] - \ln E_t\left[S_T^C\right] \\
&= rp + \ln \tilde{E}_{t+1}\left[S_T^C\right] - \ln E_t\left[S_T^C\right]
\end{aligned}$$

[18] James Cordier and Michael Gross, Liberty Trading Group, Tampa, FL.

Defining $\tilde{\Delta}\ln E_{t,t+1,T} \equiv \ln \tilde{E}_{t+1}\left[S_T^C\right] - \ln E_t\left[S_T^C\right]$, which is the *change of conditional expectations* of the spot price in T from t to $t+1$, we have

$$\tilde{r}_{F,t,t+1,T} = rp + \tilde{\Delta}\ln E_{t,t+1,T} \tag{5.14}$$

Thus according to the risk premium model, the change in futures prices is the sum of a risk premium and the change in spot price expectations. Notice that $\tilde{\Delta}\ln E_{t,t+1,T}$ should not be confused with $\hat{\alpha}_S^C(t, T_1, T_2)$ in the term structure equation (5.10) which was, loosely speaking, the expected "change" (specifically: growth rate) of the spot price between T_1 and T_2 as perceived in t. The relationship between the "change of expectations" (which is a random variable in t) and "expected change" (which is not random in t) will be discussed later and in this chapter's appendix.

Returns Under the Convenience Yield Model

The futures price under the convenience yield model is given by equation (5.8), and its natural logarithm in t and $t+1$ is, respectively, given by

$$\ln F_{t,T} = [r + m - cy](T - t) + \ln S_t^C$$

$$\ln F_{t+1,T} = [r + m - cy](T - t - 1) + \ln S_{t+1}^C$$

where we assume, for a moment, a constant convenience yield. Futures returns can then be expressed as

$$\begin{aligned}
\tilde{r}_{F,t,t+1,T} &= \ln \tilde{F}_{t+1,T} - \ln F_{t,T} \\
&= [r + m - cy](T - t - 1) + \ln \tilde{S}_{t+1}^C \\
&\quad - \left([r + m - cy](T - t) + \ln S_t^C\right) \\
&= [r + m - cy](-1) + \ln\left[\tilde{S}_{t+1}^C\right] - \ln\left[S_t^C\right]
\end{aligned}$$

respectively

$$\tilde{r}_{F,\,t,\,t+1,\,T} \equiv -\,[r + m - cy] + \tilde{r}_{S,\,t,\,t+1}^C \tag{5.15}$$

where $\tilde{r}_{S,\,t,\,t+1}^C$ denotes the log price change of the spot commodity price over the time interval $[t,\, t+1]$. According to this expression, the futures return has two components: the first corresponds to the slope of the observed term structure over the respective time horizon (here: $[t, t+1]$). Based on our assumption that r, m and cy are constant, this component is nonstochastic. The second component is the stochastic spot return of the commodity.

In general, however, the interest rate and the convenience yield are not constant. If we admit a time-varying convenience yield, the above expression can be generalized to

$$\begin{aligned}
\tilde{r}_{F,t,t+1} &= \ln \tilde{F}_{t+1,T} - \ln F_{t,T} \\
&= [r+m](T-t-1) - c\tilde{y}_{t+1}(T-t-1) + \ln \tilde{S}^C_{t+1} \\
&\quad - \left([r+m](T-t) - cy_t(T-t) + \ln S^C_t\right) \\
&= [r+m](-1) - \left[\underbrace{c\tilde{y}_{t+1}(T-t-1) - cy_t(T-t)}_{+cy_t - (c\tilde{y}_{t+1} - cy_t)(T-t-1)}\right] + \ln\left[\tilde{S}^C_{t+1}\right] - \ln\left[S^C_t\right]
\end{aligned}$$

and consequently

$$\tilde{r}_{F,t,t+1} = -[r+m] + \left[cy_t - \Delta c\tilde{y}_{t,t+1}(T-t-1)\right] + \tilde{r}^C_{S,t,t+1} \tag{5.16}$$

Therefore, according to the convenience yield model, the change in futures prices can be formally represented by the sum of the cost of carry and convenience yield over the time period, the actual change in spot prices over that time period and the change in convenience yields for the remaining time to maturity. A final warning: Equations (5.15) and (5.16) show how futures returns, spot returns, and convenience yields are analytically related under the CYM—but they do not postulate a causal relationship in the sense that the convenience yield (or its change) is causing futures prices to fluctuate. This point will be further discussed next.

Relationship

Relating the futures return under the RPM as given by equation (5.14) and the CYM given by equation (5.15) implies

$$\tilde{\Delta} \ln E_{t,t+1,T} = -[r + rp + m - cy] + \tilde{r}^C_{S,t,t+1} \tag{5.17}$$

or taking expectations yields

$$E_t\left[\tilde{\Delta} \ln E_{t,t+1,T}\right] = -[r + rp + m - cy] + E_t\left[\tilde{r}^C_{S,t,t+1}\right] \tag{5.18}$$

In the chapter's appendix, it is shown in equation (A5.4) that if the distribution of the spot price follows a log-normal distribution, then the expected value of the change in conditional expectations is given by

$$E_t\left[\tilde{\Delta}\ln E_{t,t+1,T}\right] = -\frac{1}{2}\sigma^2 \tag{5.19}$$

which is "small," but not zero as one would be tempted to expect (i.e., based on the law of iterated expectations). Of course, log-normality may be a strong assumption for spot prices, and therefore, this relationship holds as a first approximation, at best.

The expected log spot return of the commodity, measured over a unitary time interval, should therefore satisfy

$$E_t\left[\tilde{r}^C_{S,t,t+1}\right] = [r + rp + m - cy] - \frac{1}{2}\sigma^2 \tag{5.20}$$

if both models, RPM and CYM, are valid.

Synthesis with the Term Structure

Notice that the condition by equation (5.20) is closely related to the term structure condition given by equation (5.13):

$$\hat{\alpha}^C_S(t, T_1, T_2) = [r + rp + m - cy](T_2 - T_1)$$

where the left hand side represents the expected growth rate of the spot price between T_1 and T_2 perceived in t. In order to compare the two expressions, we set $T_1 = t + 1$ and $T_2 = T$, and the equation becomes

$$\hat{\alpha}^C_S(t, t+1, T) = [r + rp + m - cy](T - t - 1)$$

which implies, together with equation (5.20),[19]

$$\hat{\alpha}^C_S(t, t+1, T) = \left(E_t\left[\tilde{r}^C_{S,t,t+1}\right] + \frac{1}{2}\sigma^2\right)(T - t - 1) \tag{5.21}$$

This is verified in the appendix, by inserting (A5.5), $E_t\left[\tilde{r}^C_{S,t,t+1}\right] = \mu$, into (A5.6).

The Treatment of Causality

Although the aim of the last two sections is to provide a unified view of RPM and CYM—that is, to relate convenience yields, risk premiums, price

[19]At this stage, the notation may appear somehow confusing. Equation (5.21) can also be expressed as $\hat{\alpha}^C_S(t, t+1, T) = E_t\left[\tilde{r}^C_{S,t+1,T}\right] + \frac{1}{2}\sigma^2(T - t - 1)$.

expectations, and other variables—it is important to treat causality issues separately. For instance, equation (5.13) could be written as

$$cy(T_2 - T_1) = [r + rp + m](T_2 - T_1) - \hat{\alpha}_S^C(t, T_1, T_2) \qquad (5.22)$$

and thereby generating the impression that convenience yields are *caused* by risk premia. This interpretation is fallacious because convenience yields do not contain information about the expected risk premium. They only capture by how much the expected change in the commodity spot price differs from the change of the asset value—as defined in equation (5.7), or more precisely: convenience yields reflect the proportion of the expected change in commodity spot prices which is not attributable to the risk premium and the risk-free rate.

This is apparent when we compare the expected spot price change in equation (5.4) of a financial asset as underlying

$$\hat{\alpha}_S^A(t, T_1, T_2) \equiv \ln E_t\left[S_{T_2}^A\right] - \ln E_t\left[S_{T_1}^A\right] \equiv [r + rp - \delta](T_2 - T_1)$$

(with $m = -\delta$) with the respective expression in equation (5.13), where a commodity is the underlying,

$$\hat{\alpha}_S^C(t, T_1, T_2) \equiv \ln E_t\left[S_{T_2}^C\right] - \ln E_t\left[S_{T_1}^C\right] \equiv [r + rp + m - cy](T_2 - T_1)$$

The convenience yield only captures the additional value of the commodity as a consumption good, $\ln S_t^C - \ln S_t^A$. The risk premium, in turn, compensates for price risk and influences the value of the commodity as a traded asset, $\ln S_t^A$. Unless the additional consumption value and the risk premium are correlated, the convenience yield or the term structure should not contain any information about the expected risk premium. A pure change in the risk premium will affect $\ln S_t^A$, $\ln S_t^C$, and $\ln F_{t,T_1}$, $\ln F_{t,T_2}$, but leave the convenience yield, $\ln S_t^C - \ln S_t^A$, unaffected.

A simplified case of equation (5.22) is illustrated in Exhibit 5.4, which is adapted and slightly extended from Figure 1 in Gorton and Rouwenhorst.[20] We set $T_1 = t$ and $T_2 = t$, so that $\ln E_t(S_{T_1}^C) \equiv \ln S_t^C$

$$\begin{aligned} cy(T - t) &\equiv [r + rp + m](T - t) - \hat{\alpha}_S^C(t, t, T) \\ &= [r + rp + m](T - t) + \left(\ln S_t^C - \ln E_t\left(S_T^C\right)\right) \end{aligned}$$

which highlights the previous discussion.

[20]Figure 1 in Gorton and Rouwenhorst is similar to part of Exhibit 5.4 but focuses only on the risk premium. Convenience yield is not shown in their Figure 1. Exhibit 5.4 integrates the convenience yield and the "quasi-asset value." Gorton and Rouwenhorst, "Facts and Fantasies about Commodity Futures."

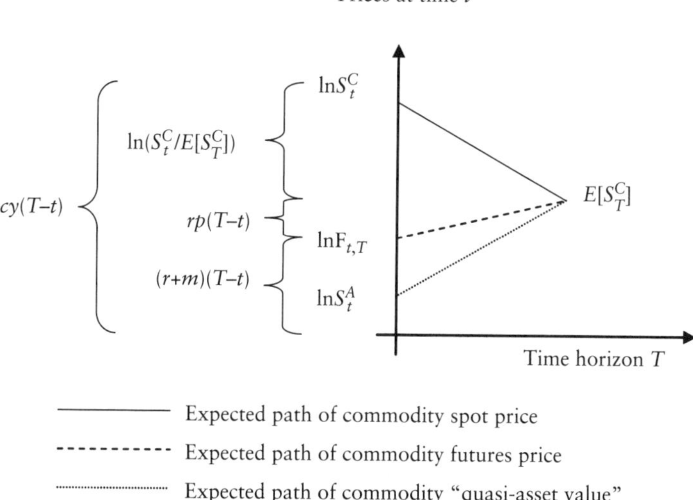

EXHIBIT 5.4 Graphical Relationship between Risk Premium- and Convenience Yield Models

A COMMON DECOMPOSITION OF FUTURES RETURNS

Under the RPM, equation (5.14), futures returns can be understood as the sum of a risk premium and the change of conditional spot price expectations. The practical problem in the identification of these components is that neither risk premia nor changes in expectations can be directly observed. Alternatively, one could use the decomposition derived from the CYM as given by equation (5.15) where at least the second term on the right-hand side of that equation can be easily observed, but the economic rationale for the first term does not seem to be straightforward.[21] However, it can be easily substituted by an expression known from the CYM-version of the term-structure as given by equation (5.12).

[21]It may even appear fallacious to practitioners because they use convenience yields to explain the term structure of commodity prices, but not to express futures returns. Specifically, it could create the impression that the convenience yield (or its change) is causing futures prices to fluctuate. This would be an unusual and economically doubtful interpretation because convenience yields represent no actual "yield" in the sense of a return component. We have rather characterized it as an extra value component of a consumption good not captured by a standard asset pricing perspective.

Spot Plus Roll Yield

Considering two futures contracts with expiration $T_1 = t + 1$ (the nearby future[22]) and $T_2 = T$ (the next-to-expire futures contract) in equation (5.12),

$$\ln \frac{F_{t,T}}{F_{t,t+1}} = [r + m - cy](T - t - 1) \qquad (5.23)$$

we are able to substitute $[r + m - cy]$ with equation (5.15) to get

$$\tilde{r}_{F,t,t+1,T} = -\frac{\ln \frac{F_{t,T}}{F_{t,t+1}}}{T - t - 1} + \tilde{r}^C_{S,t,t+1} = \underbrace{\frac{\ln \frac{F_{t,t+1}}{F_{t,T}}}{T - t - 1}}_{roll\ y} + \underbrace{\tilde{r}^C_{S,t,t+1}}_{spot\ y} \qquad (5.24)$$

The term $\frac{\ln \frac{F_{t,t+1}}{F_{t,T}}}{T-t-1}$ is called *roll yield* by investment practitioners.[23] In contrast to maintaining a spot position over time, futures contracts expire and hence, a futures position must be periodically "rolled" over time: the expiring futures contract must be sold and the next-to-expire contract must be bought. In backwardation, where the futures price curve is downward sloping, an investor sells a higher priced expiring contract and buys a lower priced next nearby-futures contract—the roll return is positive. Obviously, the shape of the term structure of futures prices at the short end determines the sign and the magnitude of the roll yield.

A word of caution: Sometimes, practitioners associate the roll yield with the risk premium. This is an oversimplified and dangerous interpretation. Taking expectations of the futures returns in equation (5.14) gives

$$E_t\left[\tilde{r}_{F,t,t+1,T}\right] = \underbrace{E_t\left[\tilde{\Delta}\ln E_{t,t+1,T}\right]}_{=-\frac{1}{2}\sigma^2} + rp = \underbrace{-[r + m - cy]}_{roll\,y} + E_t\left[\tilde{r}^C_{S,t,t+1}\right]$$

[22]The use of the nearest-to-maturity futures price is often used as proxy for the spot price in the empirical literature. It ensures that both futures and spot prices refer to the same quality of the commodity and avoids the problem of nonsynchronous observations of spot and futures prices. See Fama and French, "Commodity Futures Pricing: Some Evidence on Forecast Power, Premiums, and the Theory of Storage."

[23]Notice that in equation (5.15) the convenience yield is assumed to be constant. The generalization in (5.16) with a time-dependent yield would make the roll-yield component slightly more complex.

implying

$$\underbrace{-[r+m-cy]}_{roll\,y} = rp - \left(E_t\left[\tilde{r}^C_{S,t,t+1}\right] + \frac{1}{2}\sigma^2\right) \tag{5.25}$$

and together with equation (5.21)

$$\underbrace{-[r+m-cy]}_{roll\,y} = rp - \frac{\hat{\alpha}^C_S(t, t+1, T)}{(T-t-1)}$$

Naturally, the roll yield is only equal to the risk premium, rp, if the expected growth rate of the spot price, $\hat{\alpha}^C_S$, is zero. However, this does not hold in general. Rather, equation (5.25) shows that the (average[24]) roll yield reflects the expected deviation of the expected spot price change from the risk premium. The roll yield is the return component which comes from the economic fact that the expected spot returns of commodities have different determinants than expected returns on financial assets. For those, the expected log-spot price change (asset return) is equal to the risk-free rate plus the risk premium (minus dividend yield; equation (5.4)), so that the roll yield is equal to the risk-free rate (minus dividend yield).

The common interpretation by practitioners to associate roll yields with risk premiums is therefore strongly simplified and not valid in general. It is, after all, the same interpretation as for convenience yields in the context of equation (5.22): Convenience yields reflect the proportion of the expected change in commodity spot prices which is not attributable to the risk premium and the risk-free rate. The relationship between roll yield and convenience yields is directly derived from equation (5.23) and is clarified next.

Approximating the Convenience Yield

In practice, it is not possible to observe convenience yields directly. We can rearrange (5.23) to receive

$$\frac{\ln \dfrac{F_{t,T}}{F_{t,t+1}}}{T-t-1} = -r + [cy - m]$$

[24]We have assumed constant parameters, including the convenience yield, in this formulation; in reality, this assumption does not hold, so that our remark should be about "average" roll yields.

However, the storage costs cannot be directly observed. It is therefore convenient to measure convenience yields *net of storage costs*, denoted by $\hat{cy}$:

$$\hat{cy} \equiv cy - m = r + \underbrace{\frac{\ln \frac{F_{t,T}}{F_{t,t+1}}}{T - t - 1}}_{roll\,y} \tag{5.26}$$

This is just the roll yield plus the risk-free interest rate. This approximation is useful in empirical applications.

Data

For the empirical illustrations in Exhibits 5.5 and 5.6, we have selected 23 commodities futures contracts traded at various exchanges across the world. The analysis is based on daily settlement prices of the second-to-expire contract, starting (mostly) in January 1986 and ending in December 2006. For the return calculation it is also ensured that the rollover of the futures positions takes place before the delivery period starts; that is, returns represent replicable trading strategies.

Empirical Results

Exhibit 5.5 shows the average spot, roll, and futures returns for the various commodities. About half of the commodities have negative futures returns (column 5). If the average futures return reflects a risk premium, a negative value indicates that a positive risk premium is earned on a short futures position. Substantial short premiums are observed for corn, soybean oil, wheat, cocoa, coffee, and natural gas. For most other commodities, average futures returns are positive.

A comparison of spot returns (column 4) with futures returns reveals that, in the long run, there is no strong relationship between commodity futures returns and commodity spot price changes. For many commodities with negative futures returns (short premiums), the spot return is even positive such as for corn, soybean oil, wheat, and natural gas. For energy commodities with positive futures returns (long premiums), the spot return is also positive but can only explain around 30% to 50% of the futures return (see WTI crude oil, Brent crude oil, or Gas oil). A univariate regression of futures returns on spot returns shows that only 19.7% of the cross-sectional variance of futures returns is explained by spot returns (see last row of Exhibit 5.5). Contrary to the marketing story of many commodity investment vehicles, it should

Commodity	Annualized ConvYield	Annualized Log Returns			Annualized Volatility			
		Roll	Spot	Futures	ConvYield	Roll	Spot	Futures
Corn	−6.3%	−11.1%	2.2%	−8.9%	19.8%	8.0%	22.7%	20.7%
Soybean meal	8.6%	4.1%	1.3%	5.5%	16.7%	6.8%	23.4%	22.2%
Soybean oil	−1.5%	−6.7%	1.5%	−5.2%	9.6%	4.1%	23.3%	22.8%
Soybeans	0.3%	−1.5%	1.2%	−0.3%	13.0%	8.3%	22.5%	20.8%
Wheat	−2.9%	−8.2%	1.8%	−6.4%	22.2%	8.7%	24.2%	22.5%
Feeder cattle	6.9%	2.2%	1.9%	4.0%	10.7%	4.6%	13.3%	12.5%
Live cattle	5.7%	1.6%	2.0%	3.5%	22.4%	8.9%	16.4%	13.8%
Lean hogs	−1.2%	−3.4%	1.3%	−2.1%	45.5%	21.5%	30.7%	22.5%
Cocoa	−5.7%	−9.9%	−1.6%	−11.5%	10.3%	4.5%	29.4%	28.8%
Coffee	−3.7%	−7.7%	−3.1%	−10.8%	21.1%	9.2%	39.0%	37.6%
Cotton	−0.3%	−1.2%	−0.5%	−1.7%	26.0%	18.7%	29.2%	22.8%
Sugar	5.4%	−0.3%	3.5%	3.2%	20.6%	10.1%	34.7%	33.1%
Lumber	1.4%	−2.7%	2.9%	0.2%	25.4%	10.0%	27.0%	25.1%
Orange juice	−1.3%	−5.5%	2.9%	−2.5%	17.4%	6.9%	27.6%	26.6%
Copper[a]	5.7%	3.1%	5.8%	8.9%	7.1%	4.2%	23.6%	23.1%
Palladium	4.1%	0.0%	6.0%	6.1%	6.9%	2.9%	29.6%	29.4%
Platinum	4.7%	0.5%	5.7%	6.2%	4.9%	2.5%	21.0%	20.8%
WTI crude oil	8.2%	4.0%	4.0%	8.0%	24.7%	7.0%	35.7%	35.2%
Brent crude oil[a]	5.5%	3.8%	6.8%	10.6%	9.8%	5.5%	31.9%	31.5%
Natural gas[b]	−20.4%	−24.4%	7.3%	−17.1%	63.3%	18.2%	52.6%	48.7%
Gasoline	9.8%	5.6%	4.0%	9.6%	40.1%	11.6%	35.1%	33.3%
Heating oil	5.3%	1.0%	3.5%	4.5%	32.9%	9.4%	34.9%	33.9%
Gas oil	6.1%	3.5%	3.8%	7.3%	14.6%	8.0%	32.8%	32.0%
Ø	1.5%	−2.3%	2.8%	0.5%				
R-squared for univariate regressions of futures returns on convenience yields, spot, and roll returns								
	85.7%	88.6%	19.7%					

[a]December 29, 1989 to December 29, 2006.

[b]December 31, 1990 to December 29, 2006.

Source: Exhibit created from data obtained from Datastream.

Note: Data from daily observations on December 31, 1985 to December 29 2006.

not be possible for an investor in commodity futures or commodity indexes (calculated from commodity futures) to benefit from the market-wide expectation of increasing commodity spot prices: According to the risk premium model in equation (5.6) the expected spot price is already reflected in the commodity futures price or, in terms of equation (5.7), the expected spot price growth is already reflected in the futures term structure.

According to the return decomposition in equation (5.24), the difference between the futures return and the spot return is the roll return (shown in column 3). The roll return captures the slope of the term structure of futures prices and can be positive (negative slope, backwardation) or negative (positive slope, contango). We observe positive roll returns for soybean meal, feeder and live cattle, copper, crude oil, and gasoline contracts, but small or negative average roll returns on most other commodities. Interestingly, there is a close association between futures and roll returns for many commodities. The negative futures returns for most agricultural commodities and for natural gas can be mostly attributed to the large negative roll returns, the positive futures return for the energy contracts is also driven by the positive roll return. The R^2 in a regression of futures returns on roll returns is 88.6%.[25]

The empirical relationship between futures returns and roll returns suggests two interpretations: (1) futures returns are driven by roll returns and (2) roll returns reflect risk premiums. This would contradict our interpretation of equations (5.16), (5.22), and (5.25). A different picture emerges, however, if the decomposition of futures returns is conditioned on the sign of the roll return (i.e., backwardation and contango). This is shown in the Exhibit 5.6.

Based on equation (5.25), positive roll returns indicate the expectation of declining spot prices (and a long risk premium), and negative roll returns are an indicator for expected rising spot prices (and a short risk premium). This is reflected in the figures displayed in Exhibit 5.6. In backwardated markets, spot prices decline for most commodities, while in contango markets, spot prices increase. In fact, the observed roll return is largely compensated by subsequent spot price changes. On average, the 20.3% (minus 15.9%) roll return in the backwardation (contango) market is offset by the subsequent 17.1% spot price decrease (14.4% increase). This suggests that (1) roll returns are largely offset by subsequent spot price changes; and (2) roll returns largely reflect expected changes of commodity spot prices.

[25]Erb and Harvey have earlier investigated this relationship for a similar data set; see Claude B. Erb and Campbell R. Harvey, "The Tactical and Strategic Value of Commodity Futures," *Financial Analysts Journal* 62, no. 2 (2006), pp. 69–97.

EXHIBIT 5.6 Roll, Spot, and Futures Returns Conditioned on the Roll Return

	Backwardation Times				Contango Times				
		Annualized Log Returns				Annualized Log Returns			
Commodity	Percent of time	Roll	Spot	Futures	Percent of time	Roll	Spot	Futures	Conditioned Annualized Log Returns
Corn	10.3%	28.7%	−67.5%	−38.8%	89.7%	−15.6%	10.2%	−5.5%	0.9%
Soybean meal	54.8%	14.4%	−13.6%	0.8%	45.2%	−8.4%	19.5%	11.1%	−4.6%
Soybean oil	19.1%	8.9%	0.4%	9.3%	80.9%	−10.4%	1.8%	−8.6%	8.8%
Soybeans	23.8%	19.0%	−18.9%	0.1%	76.2%	−7.9%	7.4%	−0.5%	0.4%
Wheat	20.0%	23.1%	−19.0%	4.1%	80.0%	−16.0%	7.0%	−9.0%	8.0%
Feeder cattle	55.5%	10.6%	−2.9%	7.7%	44.5%	−8.4%	7.9%	−0.6%	4.5%
Live cattle	46.3%	21.5%	−17.0%	4.5%	53.7%	−15.6%	18.3%	2.7%	0.6%
Lean hogs	49.8%	40.1%	−42.6%	−2.5%	50.2%	−46.6%	44.9%	−1.7%	−0.4%
Cocoa	12.3%	9.9%	−17.0%	−7.0%	87.7%	−12.7%	0.5%	−12.2%	9.8%
Coffee	19.4%	27.4%	−24.3%	3.1%	80.6%	−16.2%	2.0%	−14.1%	12.0%
Cotton	30.6%	26.3%	−22.2%	4.0%	69.4%	−13.3%	9.1%	−4.2%	4.2%
Sugar	47.7%	15.3%	−20.1%	−4.7%	52.3%	−14.5%	25.0%	10.5%	−7.7%
Lumber	43.6%	20.1%	−29.1%	−9.1%	56.4%	−20.3%	27.7%	7.3%	−8.1%
Orange juice	35.2%	13.0%	−16.2%	−3.2%	64.8%	−15.5%	13.3%	−2.1%	0.3%
Copper[a]	51.3%	10.1%	6.7%	16.8%	48.7%	−4.3%	5.8%	1.5%	7.8%
Palladium	46.4%	4.2%	22.0%	26.3%	53.6%	−3.6%	−7.8%	−11.4%	18.3%
Platinum	46.4%	4.7%	5.7%	10.4%	53.6%	−3.2%	5.7%	2.5%	3.5%
WTI crude oil	55.7%	20.5%	−4.5%	16.0%	44.3%	−16.8%	14.7%	−2.1%	9.9%
Brent crude oil[a]	56.5%	16.6%	−3.0%	13.6%	43.5%	−12.8%	19.5%	6.7%	4.8%
Natural gas[b]	22.7%	44.3%	−47.4%	−3.1%	77.3%	−44.6%	23.4%	−21.2%	15.7%

(Continued)

EXHIBIT 5.6 (Continued)

	Backwardation Times				Contango Times				
		Annualized Log Returns				Annualized Log Returns			
Commodity	Percent of time	Roll	Spot	Futures	Percent of time	Roll	Spot	Futures	Conditioned Annualized Log Returns
Gasoline	55.9%	31.6%	−20.6%	11.0%	44.1%	−27.4%	35.2%	7.8%	2.7%
Heating oil	34.9%	34.9%	−30.3%	4.7%	65.1%	−17.2%	21.6%	4.4%	−1.2%
Gas oil	48.5%	22.6%	−13.0%	9.6%	51.5%	−14.4%	19.5%	5.1%	2.0%
Ø	38.6%	20.3%	−17.1%	3.2%	61.4%	−15.9%	14.4%	−1.5%	4.0%
R-squared for univariate regressions of futures returns on spot- and roll returns									
		12.50%	72.32%			5.39%	23.49%		

Source: Exhibit created from data obtained from Datastream.
Note: Data from daily observations on December 31, 1985 to December 29, 2006.
[a]December 29, 1989 to December 29, 2006.
[b]December 31, 1990 to December 29, 2006.

However, the figures also suggest that the roll return overshoots the expected spot price changes: We observe, on average, a positive (negative) net futures return in times of backwardation (contango). If average futures returns reflect risk premiums, this observation would suggest that a small portion of the roll return does reflect a risk premium. This is contrary to our interpretation of equation (5.25), which relies on the assumption of an unconditional, constant risk premium. If this assumption is relaxed, results in Exhibit 5.6 provide evidence for a time varying risk premium of commodities conditional on convenience yields or the expected spot price change.

CONCLUSION

Arbitrage pricing cannot be applied to commodity futures because the physical commodity does not represent a pure asset: Since consumption and processing of the commodity can drive down inventories to zero, it is not always possible to construct a replicating portfolio for the futures contract, and commodity spot prices do not (fully) reflect price expectations and risk premiums.

The two alternative valuation principles for commodity futures are *risk premium model* (RPM) and *convenience yield model* (CYM). Risk premium models derive futures prices from expected commodity spot prices at maturity, and convenience yield models derive futures prices from the current commodity spot price.

The chapter shows that the two valuation principles are mutually consistent if convenience yields are regarded as the deviation of the commodity spot price from its asset value (the present value of the expected commodity spot price at maturity). By combining risk premium models and convenience yield models, it can be shown that convenience yields reflect the proportion of the expected change in commodity spot prices which is not attributable to the risk premium and the risk-free rate (i.e., to the quasi-asset value of the commodity). All relationships are summarized in Exhibit 5.7.

The relationship between futures returns and convenience yields, or the term structure respectively, is of particular interest. Can futures returns be predicted based on the term structure or convenience yields? At first sight, equations (5.15) and (5.16) seem to suggest such a relationship. But it has been shown that convenience yields only reflect the temporary "consumption value" of the commodity and are, in general, independent from the expected risk premium. Again, convenience yields reflect the expected change in commodity spot prices which is not driven by the risk premium or the cost of carry. The same interpretation should be applied to roll returns,

EXHIBIT 5.7 Summary of Relationships

	Term Structure	Futures Returns
	$\ln \frac{F_{t,T_2}}{F_{t,T_1}}$	$\tilde{r}_{F,t,t+1,T}$
Risk premium model	$\hat{\alpha}_S^C(t, T_1, T_2) - rp(T_2, T_1)$	$rp + \tilde{\Delta} \ln E_{t,t+1,T}$
Convenience yield model	$(r + m - cy)(T_2 - T_1)$	$\underbrace{-[r + m - cy]}_{roll\,y} + \tilde{r}^C_{S,t,t+1}$
Relationship	$\hat{\alpha}_S^C(t, T_1, T_2) = [r + rp + m - cy](T_2, T_1)$	$\tilde{\Delta} \ln E_{t,t+1,T} = -[r + rp + m - cy] + \tilde{r}^C_{S,t,t+1}$ $E_t\left[\tilde{\Delta} \ln E_{t,t+1,T}\right] = -[r + rp + m - cy] + E_t\left(\tilde{r}^C_{S,t,t+1}\right) = -\frac{1}{2}\sigma^2$

For $T_1 = t + 1, T_2 = T$:

$$\hat{\alpha}_S^C(t, t+1, T) = \left(E_t\left[\tilde{r}^C_{S,t,t+1}\right] + \frac{1}{2}\sigma^2\right)(T - t - 1)$$

because they differ from (storage cost adjusted) convenience yields by the risk-free rate. Therefore, average roll yields reflect the expected deviation of the spot price change from the risk premium.

Our empirical illustrations confirm this view: The futures term structure, convenience yields, and roll returns largely anticipate subsequent spot price changes. However, a small portion of roll returns is not compensated by subsequent spot price changes and could be explained as time-varying risk premiums that are conditional on roll returns and expected spot price changes. This requires more detailed analysis.

APPENDIX

We show that unlike intuition would suggest, $E_t\left[\tilde{\Delta}\ln E_{t,t+1,T}\right]$ is not equal to zero. Notice that the expression is defined by

$$E_t\left[\tilde{\Delta}\ln E_{t,t+1,T}\right] \equiv E_t\left(\ln \tilde{E}_{t+1}\left[S_T^C\right]\right) - \ln E_t\left[S_T^C\right] \qquad \text{(A5.1)}$$

The first expression on the right hand side is the expected value of the natural log of $\tilde{E}_{t+1}\left[S_T^C\right]$ which is a random variable, conditional on the information in t. We assume for expositional reasons that the spot price follows a geometric Wiener-process; that is, the natural log of the spot price is normally distributed with mean μ and variance σ^2 both proportional to the time interval over which the price change is measured. The conditional expectation is therefore given by

$$\tilde{E}_{t+1}\left[S_T^C\right] = \tilde{S}_{t+1}^C e^{(\mu+0.5\sigma^2)(T-t-1)}$$

which is an approximation using Ito's lemma. Hence, the natural log, $\ln \tilde{E}_{t+1}\left[S_T^C\right]$, is normally distributed with expectation

$$E_t\left(\ln \tilde{E}_{t+1}\left[S_T^C\right]\right) = E_t\left(\ln \tilde{S}_{t+1}^C\right) + (\mu + 0.5\sigma^2)(T-t-1),$$

and substituting $E_t\left(\ln \tilde{S}_{t+1}^C\right) = \ln S_t^C + \mu$ yields

$$E_t\left(\ln \tilde{E}_{t+1}\left[S_T^C\right]\right) = \ln S_t^C + \mu + (\mu + 0.5\sigma^2)(T-t-1) \qquad \text{(A5.2)}$$

The second expression on the right hand side of (A5.1) is

$$\ln E_t\left[S_T^C\right] = \left(\ln S_t^C\right) + (\mu + 0.5\sigma^2)(T-t) \qquad \text{(A5.3)}$$

Inserting (A5.2) and (A5.3) in (A5.1) gives

$$\begin{aligned} E_t\left[\tilde{\Delta}\ln E_{t,t+1,T}\right] &= E_t\left(\ln \tilde{E}_{t+1}\left[S_T^C\right]\right) - \ln E_t\left(S_T^C\right) \\ &= \ln S_t^C + \mu + (\mu + 0.5\sigma^2)(T-t-1) \\ &\quad - \left[\ln S_t^C + (\mu + 0.5\sigma^2)(T-t)\right] \end{aligned}$$

respectively,

$$E_t\left[\tilde{\Delta}\ln E_{t,t+1,T}\right] = -0.5\,\sigma^2 \qquad \text{(A5.4)}$$

This should be contrasted to the expected spot return over a (unit) time interval

$$E_t\left(\tilde{r}^C_{S,t,t+1}\right) = E_t\left(\ln\left[\tilde{S}^C_{t+1}\right] - \ln\left[S^C_t\right]\right) = \mu \tag{A5.5}$$

or the expected "change" (growth rate) of the spot price between T_1 and T_2 as perceived in t, given by

$$\begin{aligned}\hat{\alpha}^C_S(t, T_1, T_2) &\equiv \ln E_t\left\lfloor S^C_{T_2}\right\rfloor - \ln E_t\left\lfloor S^C_{T_1}\right\rfloor \\ &= \left\{\ln S^C_t + (\mu + 0.5\sigma^2)(T_2 - t)\right\} \\ &\quad - \left\{\ln S^C_t + (\mu + 0.5\sigma^2)(T - t)\right\}\end{aligned}$$

which is

$$\hat{\alpha}^C_S(t, T_1, T_2) = (\mu + 0.5\sigma^2)(T_2 - T_1) \tag{A5.6}$$

The simplifying assumption regarding the Wiener-process of the underlying spot price can be easily generalized, as shown in Ross.[26] For a mean-reverting process

$$dS^C_t = \kappa\left(\alpha - S^C_t\right)dt + \sigma\left(S^C_t\right)^\gamma dz_t$$

where α is the long-run average to which the price reverts, κ is the speed at which the price is pulled to its long-run average, and γ is the sensitivity of the price volatility to price levels, the expected spot price is

$$E_t\left[S^C_T\right] = e^{-\kappa(T-t)}\left[S^C_t - \alpha(1 - e^{\kappa(T-t)})\right]$$

and the futures price is

$$F_{t,T} = e^{-[\kappa + rp](T-t)}\left[S^C_t - \alpha\left(1 - e^{\kappa(T-t)}\right)\right]$$

Based on this, the preceding analysis can be generalized accordingly.

[26] Stephen A. Ross, "Hedging Long-Run Commitments: Exercises in Incomplete Market Pricing," Chapter 19 in *Corporate Hedging in Theory and Practice: Lessons from Metallgesellschaft*, edited by Christopher L. Culp and Merton H. Miller (London: Risk Books, 1999), pp. 269–288.

CHAPTER 6

The Optimal Rotation Period of Renewable Resources: Theoretical Evidence from the Timber Sector

Dr. Fritz Helmedag
Professor of Economics
Chemnitz University of Technology

Wood has always been and still is one of the most important natural substances. It can be used for light and warmth, as a raw material for furniture, and the construction of buildings and boats. Trees cover approximately one third of the earth's surface. About 2 billion tons of timber are harvested per annum, which is more than the yearly output of steel and cement taken together. These figures alone suffice to justify that the economics of forestry is put on the agenda. In the face of discussions on climate change and the vital role of renewable resources, the optimal cutting strategy deserves special attention. For about two centuries, however, this issue has been under investigation. Actually, the answer to the question when to log a tree depends on the specific goal of the decision maker. This fact has not always been stated precisely. The chapter provides a survey of the different approaches and clarifies the conditions for their application.

PRODUCTION AS A TIME CONSUMING PROCESS

The production of a good is a process of varying length. Nevertheless, in the majority of cases, it can be organized in a way that there is a continuous flow of more or less finished products, some just being started and others completed. Besides that, in special branches, a certain period of time has to elapse in order to allow products to mature. The difference becomes obvious if the production process in an automobile factory is compared to the one in the timber sector.

In industry, the period to which quantities like profit or costs refer is open. The figures are related to the chosen time span that can be a day, a week, a month or a year. Likewise, in a timber company, cultivation will usually be shaped as woodland with a mixed age structure. Trees are cut when they have reached a designated size. Thus, the planning of such a synchronized stock depends on the knowledge when harvesting is most lucrative: Forestry management requires clarity about how long a single tree should grow. This problem of the so-called "optimal rotation period" arises with all renewable resources, not only in tilling the soil, but also in animal farming such as pig fattening.[1]

However, it is astounding that, for the "simple problem" of optimal forestry, several wrong analyses are encountered.[2] As Johansson and Löfgren point out: "Some of the greatest economists have solved the problem incorrectly."[3] It may seem convenient to rely on a widely accepted solution, yet, it is rewarding to look at alternatives carefully to see which specific questions they answer.[4] When we investigate the chosen example, it will become apparent how the determination of the optimal cultivation cycle in forestry serves as a demonstration object to compare different economic calculations. Especially, the investors' maxim can be distinguished from the entrepreneurs' objective.

Consider the following situation. We assume that wood is growing on a piece of land. During harvest, cutting and transport costs are proportional

[1]Occasionally, the expression *reproducible resources* is used when the regeneration cycle is less than one year; rice or corn cultivation comes to mind. When considering such production processes, labor input is to be optimized and not the production cycle discussed here.

[2]See, for example, Holger Wacker and Jürgen-E. Blank, *Ressourcenökonomik, Band I: Einführung in die Theorie regenerativer natürlicher Ressourcen* (München/Wien: Oldenbourg 1998), p. 105; and Ulrich Hampicke, *Ökologische Ökonomie, Individuum und Natur in der Neoklassik, Natur in der Ökonomischen Theorie*, Teil 4 (Opladen: Westdeutscher Verlag 1992), p. 76.

[3]Per-Olov Johansson and Karl-Gustaf. Löfgren, *The Economics of Forestry and Natural Resources* (Oxford: Blackwell, 1985), p. 74.

[4]See, for instance, Paul A. Samuelson, "Economics of Forestry in an Evolving Society," *Economic Enquiry* 14, no. 4 (1976), pp. 466–492; and Ulrich van Suntum, "Johann Heinrich von Thünen als Kapitaltheoretiker," in *Studien zur Entwicklung der Ökonomischen Theorie XIV, Johann Heinrich von Thünen als Wirtschaftstheoretiker*, edited by Heinz Rieter (Berlin: Dunker & Humblot 1995), pp. 87–113.

to the proceeds. Hence, the net price based on units of quantity (weight or volume) is given and therefore can be used as a numéraire. Due to these assumptions, the physical output is equivalent to its monetary valuation. The revenue of a hectare of trees of age t is specified as follows:

$$f(t) = \frac{1}{30}t^4(15 - t) \tag{6.1}$$

The time t is interpreted as number of years. Exhibit 6.1 depicts the production result depending on the growth period.

The productivity of time is calculated via:

$$f'(t) = \frac{4}{30}t^3(15 - t) - \frac{1}{30}t^4 = \frac{1}{6}t^3(12 - t) \tag{6.2}$$

Setting this equal to zero, the first derivative yields the output maximum at $t_m = 12$. The average output per interval is:

$$\frac{f(t)}{t} = \frac{1}{30}t^3(15 - t) \tag{6.3}$$

For an extremum, it is necessary that:

$$\left(\frac{f(t)}{t}\right)' = \frac{1}{10}t^2(15 - t) - \frac{1}{30}t^3 = \frac{1}{30}t^2(45 - 4t) = 0 \tag{6.4}$$

The average periodical output is maximized at $t_d = 11.25$. Exhibit 6.2 illustrates equations (6.2) and (6.3).

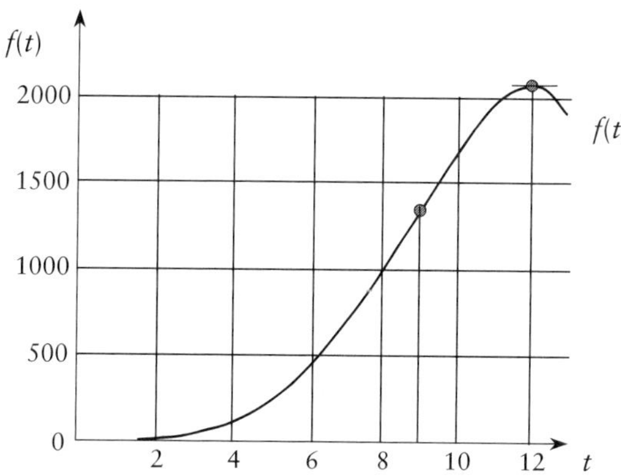

EXHIBIT 6.1 The Production Function
Source: Author.

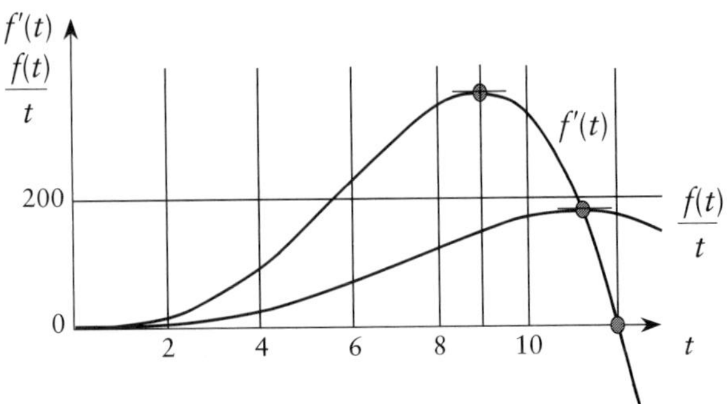

EXHIBIT 6.2 Productivity and Average Output
Source: Author.

To emphasize the underlying objective is what will matter most in analyzing the different alternatives. First, we turn to profit maximization: Which kind of woodland cultivation fulfils this goal? In order to answer this question correctly, one has to take into account the actual situation in which a concrete decision is required.

NET PROCEEDS VERSUS COST RETURN

The Maximum Future Profit

The first scenario considers a cultivator of fallow woodland who borrows the money for planting costs per hectare (L). For simplicity's sake, the bank loan is supposed to be bearing a continuous compounding at an interest rate i and is paid back completely when the stand is cut. The surplus per hectare at time t, also referred to as *profit* from this point on, is positive if the interest on the planting costs is not too high:

$$G(t) = f(t) - Le^{it} > 0 \quad \text{for } 0 \leq L < f(t) \quad \text{and} \quad 0 \leq i < i_{\max} \qquad (6.5)$$

Maximizing the income[5] leads to:

$$G'(t) = f'(t) - iLe^{it} = 0 \qquad (6.6)$$

From equation (6.6) follows:

$$it = \ln\left(\frac{f'(t)}{iL}\right) \qquad (6.7)$$

[5]We do not state sufficient conditions here and later. Also, we only give solutions that are relevant from an economic point of view.

Hence, we derive the production period:

$$t_G = \frac{1}{i} \cdot \ln\left(\frac{f'(t_G)}{iL}\right) > 0 \quad \text{for } f'(t_G) > iL \tag{6.8}$$

Setting $i = 10\%$ and $L = 100$, we calculate $t_G = 11.883$.

At this point in time, the profit per hectare amounts to $G(t_G) = 1743.517$. But the cultivator has to wait t_G years for this event to occur. However, it is possible to accomplish a backward distribution of the future value. In general, the annuity z which is equivalent to a prospective payoff $E(T)$ at time T can be obtained with:

$$E(T) = \int_0^T z \cdot e^{i(T-t)}\, dt = \int_0^T z \cdot e^{it}\, dt = \left[\frac{z}{i} e^{it}\right]_0^T = \frac{z}{i}\left(e^{iT} - 1\right) \tag{6.9}$$

And, therefore:

$$z = \frac{iE(T)}{e^{iT} - 1} \tag{6.10}$$

Inserting $G(t_G)$ and the other data into equation (6.10) yields:

$$z_G = \frac{1743.517 \cdot 0.1}{e^{0.1 \cdot 11.883} - 1} = 76.424$$

The annuity z_G is equivalent to the present value of the profit accruing in t_G years. Thus, this rent is also suited to characterize the respective lucrativeness.[6]

An Upper Limit to the Interest Rate

While the optimization of future profit plays no role in the literature, the determination of the optimal span of time to invest a sum of money can be found. In this approach, which is often connected with the names Knut Wicksell (1851–1926) and Kenneth E. Boulding (1910–1993), for example, the question arises how long (newly) bought wine is to be kept in the cellar if the development of prices as a function of time is known.[7] Using continuously compounding interest, Wicksell's terminology deals with the

---

[6]Alternative projects of different lengths are assumed to be executed several times; the minimum time period for comparison is the smallest common multiple of the individual cultivation cycles.

[7]See Knut Wicksell, *Vorlesungen über Nationalökonomie auf Grundlage des Marginalprinzips*, vol. 1 (Jena: Gustav Fischer, 1913), p. 238; and Kenneth E. Boulding, *Economic Analysis*, vol. 2, 4th ed. (New York: Harper and Row, 1966), p. 672.

maximization of the *interest generating energy* r of the capital advanced, subject to the condition that the revenue covers the initial investment including interest:

$$r \rightarrow \text{Max! s.t. } Le^{rt} = f(t) \tag{6.11}$$

Exhibit 6.3 illustrates the graphical solution to the problem: A curve representing a continuously compounded investment progresses in such a way that the production function is just touched upon.

To calculate the t-value in question, the constraint in equation (6.11) is logarithmized and solved for r:

$$r = \frac{\ln\left(\frac{f(t)}{L}\right)}{t} \tag{6.12}$$

The first derivative with respect to time reads:

$$\frac{dr}{dt} = \frac{\left(\frac{f'(t)}{f(t)}\right)t - \ln\left(\frac{f(t)}{L}\right)}{t^2} \tag{6.13}$$

We obtain the investment interval t_W by setting the nominator equal to zero:

$$t_W = \frac{f(t_W) \cdot \ln\left(\frac{f(t_W)}{L}\right)}{f'(t_W)} \tag{6.14}$$

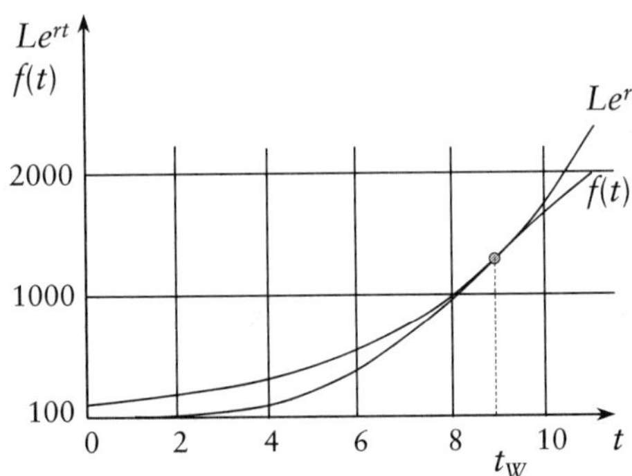

EXHIBIT 6.3 An Upper Limit to the Interest Rate
Source: Author.

In our example, equation (6.14) yields a growth period $t_W = 8.893$. With this (minimum) duration corresponds the highest rate of interest r^* this project is able to yield. At the same time, the critical market interest rate $i_{\max}$ is determined. It must not be exceeded if the investment is to be profitable. The maximum rate of return on the advanced costs amounts to:

$$r^* = \frac{f'(t_W)}{f(t_W)} = i_{\max} = 0.286 \tag{6.15}$$

The future profit is computed with:

$$f(t_W) = Le^{r^* t_W} = 1273.038$$

Calculating the equivalent profit flow over time according to (6.10), one has to take into account that the costs bear an interest rate of $i = 0.1 < r^*$:

$$z_W = \frac{\left(1273.038 - 100 \cdot e^{0.1 \cdot 8.893}\right) \cdot 0.1}{e^{0.1 \cdot 8.893} - 1} = 71.835$$

This annuity is smaller than the one in the previous case. Therefore, the Wicksell-Boulding solution or the maximization of the profit rate alias the return on costs respectively has to be judged as suboptimal.

CAPITAL MANAGEMENT IN FORESTRY

The Stumpage Value

We began our study with a cultivator who borrowed the planting cost L at the interest rate i. It would be interesting to know the limit of a bank loan if the stand is used as a collateral and the profit for repayment. Then, the problem is to find today's top price that a current cultivation could fetch in the future market. We are looking for the maximum capital value of wood (KW_H):

$$KW_H = f(t)e^{-it} - L = \frac{f(t) - Le^{it}}{e^{it}} = \frac{G(t)}{e^{it}} \rightarrow \text{Max!} \tag{6.16}$$

Optimization leads to:

$$\frac{dKW_H}{dt} = f'(t)e^{-it} - f(t)i \cdot e^{-it} = 0 \tag{6.17}$$

Therefore:

$$i = \frac{f'(t)}{f(t)} \tag{6.18}$$

William St. Jevons' (1835–1882) and Irving Fisher's (1867–1947) respective rules enunciate an optimal maturity time of a singular project.[8] If the growth rate of wood drops down to the level of the interest rate, the value of the timber stock reaches its maximum. Thus, increasing the interest rate reduces the rotation period. Equation (6.15), which corresponds to equation (6.18) for $t_W = t$, provides the previously mentioned maximum interest rate $i_{\max}$. For a given market interest rate $i = 10\%$, we obtain as cultivation cycle and capital value: $t_H = 11.140$ and $KW_H = 550.433$.

For comparison purposes, the corresponding cash flow is of interest. Since this time we have a forward distribution of a present value into the future ("capital regain"), we start with:

$$\begin{aligned} KW(0) &= \int_0^T v \cdot \mathrm{e}^{-it} dt = \left[\frac{v}{-i} \mathrm{e}^{-it} \right]_0^T \\ &= -\frac{v}{i} \left(\mathrm{e}^{-iT} - 1 \right) = \frac{v}{i} \left(1 - \mathrm{e}^{-iT} \right) \end{aligned} \tag{6.19}$$

Solving for the annuity v gives:

$$v = \frac{KW(0) \cdot i}{1 - \mathrm{e}^{-iT}} \tag{6.20}$$

The concrete result attains the highest value so far:

$$v_H = \frac{550.433 \cdot 0.1}{1 - \mathrm{e}^{-0.1 \cdot 11.140}} = 81.939$$

Thus, the Jevons-Fisher formula seems to deserve priority. After all, the outcome exceeds the maximization of the return on an investment in the Wicksell-Boulding vein. However, the optimal use of forest soil is not a problem of a single investment, but of a continuous silviculture.

The Productive Powers of Woodland

The previous maximization of a capital value referred to trees of the same age. Besides, the question arises which profit potential a piece of fallow land

[8] See William St. Jevons, *The Theory of Political Economy*, 2nd ed. (London: Macmillan, 1879), p. 266; and Irving Fisher, *The Theory of Interest* (New York: Macmillan, 1930), p. 164.

has, whose sole possible exploitation is forestry. Consequently, the capital value of the entire future timber and, therefore, the right price of the plot has to be calculated. This approach was taken by forester Martin Faustmann (1822–1876) in the 19th century: "What is the pure money return bare woodland will continuously yield every year in the same amount from now on?"[9]

The value of real estate (KW_F) reflects a sequence of infinite successions of the same project, taking compound interest rate effects into account. By this, Faustmann was hoping to gain "necessary insight into forest destruction by fire, insects, man."[10] The productive value of the soil—and not the value of wood destroyed—according to Faustmann amounts to:

$$KW_F = -L + (f(t) - L)\mathrm{e}^{-it} + (f(t) - L)\mathrm{e}^{-2it} + \cdots \tag{6.21}$$

Rearranging yields:

$$KW_F = \left(f(t)\mathrm{e}^{-it} - L\right) + \left(f(t)\mathrm{e}^{-it} - L\right)\mathrm{e}^{-it} + \left(f(t)\mathrm{e}^{-it} - L\right)\mathrm{e}^{-2it} + \cdots \tag{6.22}$$

Now it is possible to apply the formula for the infinite geometric series:

$$KW_F = \frac{f(t)\mathrm{e}^{-it} - L}{1 - \mathrm{e}^{-it}} = \frac{KW_H}{1 - \mathrm{e}^{-it}} = \frac{G(t)}{\mathrm{e}^{it} - 1} \tag{6.23}$$

Of course, the Faustmann capital value—like all profitable investments with infinite lifetime—grows beyond all limits for an interest rate converging to zero. This phenomenon is independent of the future profit $G(t)$. In such a situation, one has to look for a different method with which a precise rotation period can be found. Furthermore, the interest rate must not exceed $i_{\max}$ because otherwise profits $G(t)$ are actually losses and the capital value becomes negative too. Within the admissible range, the latter moves in the opposite direction of changes in the interest rate.

---

[9] Martin Faustmann, "Berechnung des Werthes, welchen Waldboden, sowie noch nicht haubare Holzbestände für die Waldwirthschaft besitzen," *Allgemeine Forst- und Jagd-Zeitung* (December 1849), pp. 441–455, p. 442. *Note:* Unless otherwise stated, all translations are the author's.

[10] Faustmann, "Berechnung des Werthes, welchen Waldboden, sowie noch nicht haubare Holzbestände für die Waldwirthschaft besitzen," p. 441. Obviously, the definitive uselessness of soil for forestry purposes is meant; this raises the problem of an adequate compensation.

The necessary condition for the maximization of the Faustmann value reads:

$$\frac{dKW_F}{dt} = \frac{\left[f'(t)e^{-it} + f(t)\left(-ie^{-it}\right)\right]\left(1 - e^{-it}\right) - \left(f(t)e^{-it} - L\right)\left(ie^{-it}\right)}{\left(1 - e^{-it}\right)^2} = 0 \tag{6.24}$$

Therefore:

$$f'(t)\left(1 - e^{-it}\right) = i\left(f(t)\left(1 - e^{-it}\right) + f(t)e^{-it} - L\right) \tag{6.25}$$

And respectively:

$$f'(t) = \frac{i(f(t) - L)}{1 - e^{-it}} \tag{6.26}$$

From this, t can be deduced if the interest rate as well as the explicit production function is known. In our example we obtain $t_F = 10.666$ and $KW_F = 828.745$. If this capital value can be realized by selling the land (or leasing it), then the following perpetuity is generated:[11]

$$Z_F = i \cdot KW_F = 0.1 \cdot 828.745 = 82.8745$$

A backward distribution of $G(t_F)$ according to (6.10) entails the same result.[12] Before checking whether the plot actually gets the Faustmann value, we consider a completely different model in the next section.

REVENUES FINANCE EXPENDITURES

Thünen: Over the Top

Up until now, we envisaged to cultivate on our woodland a cohort of trees of the same age that were jointly cut down. In reality, there is an ongoing process of cultivating and harvesting. In our example, this means that

[11]The formula follows from equation (6.20) for $T \to \infty$.

[12]An alternative way of deriving the Faustmann rotation is to insert the future profit $G(t) = f(t) - Le^{it}$ into equation (6.10) and to optimize z with respect to t. This concurs with the search for a maximum annuity of the hypothetical process chain.

depending on the rotation period t, the t-th portion of a hectare is logged and subsequently reforested.

The topic of a *sustained* instead of *suspended* enterprise is found in the works of Johann Heinrich von Thünen (1783–1850).[13] In contrast to Faustmann, Thünen does not just mention the distinction, but actually applies it by aiming at an income accruing in each time interval. The procedures discussed earlier treated the task as a problem of an investment decision. Thünen however focuses on the *periodical profit* (PG) of the forester. By doing so, he deducts from the proceeds the planting costs L as well as the (forgone) interest on the monetary value of the timber stand. In the continuous case, stumpage equals the integral $F(t)$ over the production function $f(t)$. Thus, Thünen's maximand is:[14]

$$PG_T = \frac{f(t) - if(t) - L}{T} \tag{6.27}$$

The advantage of this approach is to point the objective function right from the outset toward a continuous surplus that therefore directly leads to a synchronized cultivation. The revenues of such a subdivided forest finance the planting costs of new trees that, as a result, cannot give rise to any interest demands. In the Thünen approach, the necessary condition reads:

$$\frac{dPG_T}{dt} = \frac{(f'(t) - if(t))t - f(t) + iF(t) + L}{t^2} = 0 \tag{6.28}$$

According to this procedure, a single tree will reach an age of:

$$t_T = \frac{f(t_T) - iF(t_T) - L}{f'(t_T) - if(t_T)} \tag{6.29}$$

This yields $t_T = 10.453$ and $PG_T = 113.488$.

---

[13]See Johann H. v. Thünen, *Der isolierte Staat in Beziehung auf Landwirtschaft und Nationalökonomie, Dritter Theil, Grundsätze zur Bestimmung der Bodenrente, der vorteilhaftesten Umtriebszeit und des Werths der Holzbestände von verschiedenem Alter für Kieferwaldungen* (1863), 3rd edition, edited by H. Schumacher-Zarchlin (Berlin: Wiegant, Hempel & Parey, 1875).

[14]See Ulrich van Suntum, "Johann Heinrich von Thünen als Kapitaltheoretiker," p. 108. For the discrete case see Peter Manz, "Forestry economics in the steady state: the contribution of J. H. von Thünen," *History of Political Economy* 18, no. 2 (1986), pp. 281–290.

The higher surplus of the synchronized production represents an incentive to focus on the maximization of the periodical profit caused by a staggered silviculture as compared to the successive methods treated earlier. But, from an economic point of view, it is questionable to allow the opportunity costs to enter the objective function. Rather, the subsequent comparison with an alternative use of the stumpage serves as a criterion whether the forestry should be continued or not. Because of this, Thünen's thoughts fail to convince.

Back to the Roots: 1788

Nonetheless, there is another cut-down rule which has been discussed among forest economists for some time. According to this guideline, the difference between revenues und planting costs per unit of time (and area)(PG_J) is decisive:

$$PG_J = \frac{f(t) - L}{t} \tag{6.30}$$

Actually, in 1788 such an instruction was decreed by the Royal and Imperial Austrian government during the reign of Emperor Joseph II.[15] This directive equals Thünen's formula for $i = 0$. The optimization requires:

$$\frac{dPG_J}{dt} = \frac{f'(t)t - (f(t) - L)}{t^2} = 0 \tag{6.31}$$

Solving for t leads to:

$$t_J = \frac{f(t_J) - L}{f'(t_J)} \tag{6.32}$$

Interestingly, with interest tending to zero, the Faustmann solution converges to equation (6.32) as well. This follows from applying l'Hospital's rule to (6.26):

$$f'(t) = \lim_{i \to 0} \frac{i(f(t) - L)}{te^{-it}} = \frac{f(t) - L}{t} \tag{6.33}$$

Substituting our revenue function in (6.32) and (6.30) gives $t_J = 11.296$ and $PG_J = 169.108$.

[15]See F. C. Osmaston, *The Management of Forests* (London: George Allen and Unwin, 1968), p. 188.

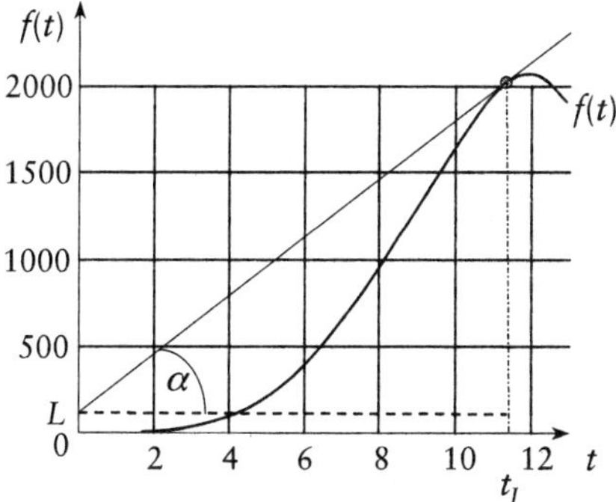

EXHIBIT 6.4 The Maximum Land Rent
Source: Author.

In this case, the optimal rotation period can be easily extracted from a graphic (see Exhibit 6.4).

A tangent from the planting costs towards $f(t)$ is drawn, determining the angle α, which represents the maximum surplus per hectare over time. This is the highest attainable profit stream.

Hence, it becomes clear under which circumstances forestry is no longer worthwhile. When an alternative turns out to be lucrative, stumpage and soil are sold in order to capitalize the sales proceeds (U). Then, the following condition holds:

$$U \cdot i > PG_J \tag{6.34}$$

Putting It to the Test

In an often cited paper, Samuelson discusses the just described maximization of the sustained net yield.[16] According to him, the *Austrian cameral valuation method* is incorrect since it does not take interest rate effects into account.[17] Therefore, the difference per year between timber yield and planting costs appears to him not all that important:

> *This is so absurd as to be almost believable to the layman—up to the moment when the economist breaks the news to the farmer . . . that he can mine the forest by cutting it down without replanting and sell the land, thereafter putting the proceeds into the bank . . . and subsequently earn interest forever.*[18]

[16]Samuelson, "Economics of Forestry in an Evolving Society," p. 477.
[17]Samuelson, "Economics of Forestry in an Evolving Society," p. 489.
[18]Samuelson, "Economics of Forestry in an Evolving Society," p. 474.

With the insights obtained so far, we are able to appreciate Samuelson's criticism. Suppose a forester owning one hectare of Joseph II synchronized wood follows the recommendation and cuts down the stock, sells the timber and even finds afterward a buyer for the land paying Faustmann's value. In total, our ex-forester receives:

$$U = \int_0^{t_J} \frac{1}{t_J} f(t)\, dt + KW_F = 606.401 + 828.745 = 1435.146$$

On the other hand, the periodic profit PG_J computed earlier (interpreted as a perpetuity) represents a present value of:

$$\frac{PG_J}{i} = \frac{169.108}{0.1} = 1691.08$$

Obviously, when seeking advice from Samuelson one takes a loss: The (maximum) company value U is smaller than the amount we calculate for our illustration! Indeed, a basic principle of economic behavior states that the continuous surplus of an enterprise should exceed the interest on the capitalization of the firms' assets. This is not the case here since the clear-cutting condition (6.34) is violated. Therefore, running the business based on the "rule of thumb"[19] from 1788 yields better results than the proposed logging instruction in the given situation.

However, it needs to be taken into account that the direct comparison between the theories is improper: Faustmann is (yet) located on empty land and looks for its value, whereas Joseph II continuously wants to make as much profit as possible out of his already existing trees.[20] This discrepancy is also of importance to the modern forester. Furthermore, institutional changes need to be taken into account.

[19]See Philip A. Neher, "Forests," in *The New Palgrave*, vol. 2 (London, New York, and Tokyo: Macmillan/Stockton Press/Maruzen, 1994), pp. 412–414.

[20]In science, there has been a long-term conflict between these opposing schools. For the history of this quarrel, see Cristof Wagner, *Lehrbuch der theoretischen Forsteinrichtung* (Berlin: Parey, 1928), who summarizes: "Hence, we have sustainability against profitability, Prussia versus Saxony" (p. 199). However, this confrontation misses the point. A sustainable production is also possible with the Faustmann rotation period, but leads to suboptimal earnings. Inserting in equation (6.30) t_F from our illustration, we gain: $PG_F = 165.920 < PG_J = 169.108$.

FROM FEUDALISM TO CAPITALISM

The Accumulation Phase

In what follows, an entrepreneur seeking to maximize his profit is introduced as an idealized economic agent. This person is not constrained by the capital he is able to invest in a project, but by the demand side. His main task is to supply goods at prices no less than unit costs. For analytical reasons, we assume that the entrepreneur does not resort to own money—his reputation or a convincing business concept will grant him a loan. From this standpoint, rates on return—figures providing a relationship of surplus to capital advanced—are not suitable as an indication for economic success. The limits of woodland prices and forest values first and foremost reflect the concerns of investors, not those of entrepreneurs striving for profit maximization.

In our model world, at least one of the entrepreneur's problems is not that difficult. The revenues of wood production are known; sales do not pose a problem. Once all costs including the use of forest soil have to be incurred, which rotation period proves to be optimal?

In a first step, the woodland shall only be available for purchase by foresters accumulating land piece by piece at the Faustmann value. Period after period, depending on a given growth phase T, an additional part $1/T$ of a hectare is acquired. Additionally, there are planting costs. Hence, the following debt has amassed until the (yet unknown) optimal rotation period T is reached:

$$D_{\text{Buy}}(T) = \int_0^T \frac{1}{T}(KW_F + L)e^{i(T-t)}dt = (KW_F + L)\left(\frac{e^{iT} - 1}{iT}\right) \qquad (6.35)$$

Substituting in this expression the Faustmann rotation t_F as well as the other data, we get:

$$D_{\text{Buy}}(t_F) = (828.745 + 100)\left(\frac{e^{0.1 \cdot 10.666} - 1}{0.1 \cdot 10.666}\right) = 1659.20$$

The interest accumulated with this debt during the construction of the silviculture just equals the periodic surplus from the synchronized cultivation:

$$PG_F = \frac{f(t_F) - L}{t_F} = i \cdot D_{\text{Buy}}(t_F) = 165.920$$

This equation characterizes the nature of Faustmann's woodland value from a buyer's point of view: It represents the maximum amount of money an entrepreneur without means is able to pay for additional land in order to create a staggered forest while time elapses.[21] If the purchaser wants to make profit, the actual price for the additional woodland bought year after year must be *lower* than the Faustmann value. It is therefore a constraint for forestry business just as the maximum interest rate $i_{\max}$ is.

In order to prepare for the next section, let us now take a short look at the alternative to woodland acquisition: The entrepreneur disburses a rent R per period and hectare. While the necessary expenses for the planting still sum up until the desired ages of the trees are reached, the formula for the accumulated debt from rent payments looks different. The total loan at time T amounts to

$$\begin{aligned} D_{\text{Rent}}(T) &= \int_0^T t\frac{1}{T}\text{R}e^{i(T-t)}\,dt + \int_0^T \frac{1}{T}\text{L}e^{i(T-t)}dt \\ &= \frac{R\left(e^{iT} - iT - 1\right) + Li\left(e^{iT} - 1\right)}{i^2 T} \end{aligned} \tag{6.36}$$

For the entrepreneur's profits after completion of the synchronized silviculture, we obtain:

$$PG(T) = \frac{f(T) - L}{T} - R - i \cdot D_{\text{Rent}}(T) \tag{6.37}$$

With a given rent R, our model forester chooses the appropriate T. Depending on the assumptions about the variables and data, he can pay off his debt sooner or later. Hence, provided the undertaking is crowned with success, there will be no more borrowing costs one fine day—the same situation as with the purchase of forest soil. Then, the following equation holds:

$$PG(t) = \frac{f(t) - L}{t} - R \tag{6.38}$$

Let us take a closer look at the long run and the determination of the rent.

[21]"Herr Faustmann must have reasoned along lines somewhat as follows: If I were to start planning a forest from scratch, how much could I afford to pay for bare land?" G. Robinson Gregory, *Forest Resource Economics* (New York: John Wiley & Sons, 1972), pp. 286. In Appendix A of this chapter, it is proven that the accumulated debt from the purchase of land at the Faustmann price and the subsequent planting of the whole area cannot be made up by revenues since they merely suffice to pay for interest.

Land Rent in Competition

From a modern stance, the 1788 regulation has one disadvantage. It served as a maxim in feudalism: Forestry was performed by the proprietor himself, who at times possessed giant estates. He acted in personal union as a landowner as well as a timber producer without consideration of rent payments. Furthermore, Nature herself took care of the first cultivation free of charge. Under these circumstances, the landowner was geared to the entire continuous stream of income from his property.

In modern capitalism, separation serves the purpose of realizing something important: The function of an entrepreneur and a resource provider has to be distinguished. Otherwise, the income categories *profit of wood production* and *rent for land lease* cannot be isolated. In the following, we consider the long-term situation where investment expenses to create a synchronized production structure has already been paid off. Let us assume that the use of a hectare requires payment of rent $R \geq 0$. Moreover, in every period there is one hectare ready for harvesting. Equation (6.38) provides the hectare profit (HG):

$$HG = t \cdot PG(t) = f(t) - L - R \cdot t \tag{6.39}$$

The last term on the right side of equation (6.39) states the total rent due. Differentiating yields:

$$HG' = f'(t) - R \tag{6.40}$$

Thus, the necessary condition for an optimum reads:

$$f'(t) = R \tag{6.41}$$

This result makes sense from an economic point of view: In equilibrium, productivity of time equals rent. If land is available at no costs, harvesting occurs at the maximum return $f(t_m)$ independent of the interest rate and planting costs. As expected, the earnings per hectare are smaller than those under the 1788 regime:

$$\frac{HG_m}{t_m} = \frac{f(t_m) - L}{t_m} - R = \frac{2073.6 - 100}{12} - 0 = 164.466$$

Nevertheless, total profit is higher since more soil is cultivated for free:

$$HG_m = 164.466 \cdot 12 = 1973.6 > PG_J \cdot t_J = 169.108 \cdot 11.296 = 1910.24$$

In such a situation, consumption of land does not need to be taken into account. Rather, it seems now reasonable to choose the same amount of costs L which also may be a wage bill as a reference point for a comparison between different logging strategies. Equation (6.41) informs us when to terminate the trees' growth. Minimizing the costs per unit of timber then proves to be the crucial criterion for the choice of technique in forestry.

If rent has to be paid, then the life cycle of the trees is shortened compared to their maximum size. To boot, if profits vanish in consequence of the competition for scarce plots of the same fertility, HG in equation (6.39) will tend to zero. Consequently, the landowner can pocket the maximum profit per hectare in the form of rent:

$$R_{\max} = \frac{f(t) - L}{t} \tag{6.42}$$

This is equivalent to the Joseph II case: There are no entrepreneurial foresters, but only proprietors who maximize their income per area unit; the economy shows signs of feudalism.[22] For modern times, David Ricardo's (1772–1823) exploration of capitalism is appropriate. He considered an expanding economy where land of decreasing quality is taken under the plough. Then, the farmers do not pay any rent for the least cultivated plot. Nevertheless, the superior ground receives a premium depending on its fertility.

LOOKING BACK AND AROUND

Initially, there was a forester who sought advice from an economist but received inadequate counsel. And this happened in a field where established knowledge is supposed to be solid: The analysis of a clearly structured microeconomic decision situation.

The question arises why the academic tenet led to wrong conclusions. The answer is that different problem-solving approaches were mixed up. Computing the maximum interest rate on the costs advanced or the determination of (interest rate dependent) capital values of timber or land respectively may be significant within the investment calculus, but this does not provide an optimal cut-down strategy from an entrepreneurial point of view in long-term forestry.

[22]In Appendix B of this chapter it is demonstrated, what the owner of a plot of soil must do to realize a synchronized planting.

Moreover, the widely accepted Faustmann approach suffers from a discrepancy between theory and practice which has to be explained. Without doubt, the choice of the interest rate used in calculations is more or less arbitrary. Remarkably, however, often unrealistically low interest rates are chosen for the purpose of obtaining desired results. Many years ago, a silviculture interest rate of 3.5% had been proposed.[23] But convincing arguments for such conventions are still lacking.[24] In fact, the use of a forestry interest rate makes the Faustmann formula compatible to real behavior. Thus, the observable forest management reconciles something that is felt to be right with a supposedly correct course of action, which unfortunately does not quite fit the plan. Consequently, demands from scientists for an allegedly necessary deforestation policy are ignored.[25]

When a forester pays a rent for someone's land, he compensates differences in fertility—and who has nothing special to offer will earn nothing in return. The choice of the profit maximizing rotation period depends on these rent rates. Harvesting takes place when the increase in the value of wood has decreased toward the payment for a part of the earth's surface. If land is free of charge, trees grow up until the maximum return $f(t_m)$, which is equivalent to the minimization of cultivation costs. Production efficiency on fertile land, on the other hand, includes a compensation for Nature's extra powers. The optimal time for logging can be observed between t_J—Joseph II's interval maximizing rent per hectare—and t_m, the span of time until tree growth has peaked.

The deliberations above reveal why fallow field generally is quite cheap: The price of soil as a capitalized rent merely reflects differences in fertility. Against this background, the significance of the Faustmann formula fades away, even when its proper purpose is considered, namely the determination of pure land value. The productive power of soil merely provides an extreme solution never attained in practice.

Demand dictates the price of real estate when supply cannot be increased. Contrary to timber, the available ground and its quality is a fixed

[23]See Max Robert Pressler, *Der Rationelle Waldwirth und sein Waldbau des höchsten Ertrages, Zweites (selbstständiges) Buch, Die forstliche Finanzrechnung mit Anwendung auf Wald-Werthschätzung und -Wirthschaftsbetrieb* (Dresden: Tuerk, 1859), p. 10.

[24]See the reflections of Wolfgang Sagl, *Bewertung in Forstbetrieben* (Berlin and Wien: Blackwell Wissenschafts-Verlag, 1995), p. 59.

[25]Swiss foresters have to deal with the following instruction: "The cultivation cycle within Switzerland needs to be reduced by one third . . . and the average wood supply is to be reduced to 50 per cent of today's value." Peter Manz, *Die Kapitalintensität der schweizerischen Holzproduktion, Eine theoretische und empirische Untersuchung* (Bern: Paul Haupt, 1987), p. 189.

quantity. Hence, the rent requested for its use reflects scarcity. In capitalism, these circumstances determine the value of landed property.

Yet, forestry comes up with another peculiarity: In Central Europe, there is almost no stock of trees currently available for rent. The rather long gestation periods require contracts with a legal force over several generations. According to § 594 b BGB, German law provides that rent contracts signed for more than thirty years have a period of notice of just one year after this time. The only alternative would be to sign the contract for the lifetime of the renter or the landowner which also does not guarantee the necessary long-term planning certainty. Hence, forestry is performed almost exclusively by the landowner.

CONCLUSION

In closing, we will point out the capital theoretic implications of the preceding analysis. Provided that the forests possess a perfectly adjusted age spectrum, the interest rate is of no special significance. Though the return of a single tree depends on its maturity, there is a quasi-physically determined way of generating the maximum surplus. It is the task of the accumulation process to install the optimal production structure efficiently.

Just as with the continuous and circular production in the industrial sector, one has to free oneself from the concrete product and the time until its completion in order to consider the flows as a whole. In any case, it is misleading to interpret the interest on the costs during a production period as profit, instead of paying attention to the difference between revenue and costs.[26] The production process in general is not organized successively but synchronized. Hence, the result of this investigation fits into a uniform and elementary theory of the choice of technique, which offers more explanatory power than other endeavors to treat the subject.

APPENDIX A

In footnote 21, it has been remarked that the accumulated debt from the purchase of land at a price equal to the Faustmann value (6.23) and the

[26]See in detail Fritz Helmedag, "Warenproduktion mittels Arbeit oder die Neueröffnung der Debatte," in *Nach der Wertdiskussion*, edited by Kai Eicker-Wolf, Torsten Niechoj, and Dorothee Wolf (Forschungsgruppe Politische Ökonomie: Marburg, 1999), pp. 67–91.

subsequent planting of the whole area cannot be retired out of revenues. The share of interest in total debt amounts to

$$\left(\frac{f(t)e^{-it} - L}{1 - e^{-it}} + L\right)(e^{it} - 1) = f(t) - L \tag{A6.1}$$

Thus, net revenues are just enough to pay interest.

If land is purchased successively, production also covers merely interest. During the gestation period of the staggered silviculture, the entrepreneur has to buy additional plots step by step. Substituting in the formula for the debts from the gradual acquisition of land (6.35) the Faustmann value (6.23), leads to the interest charge at time t:

$$i \cdot D_{\text{Buy}} = i(KW_F + L)\left(\frac{e^{it} - 1}{it}\right) = i\left(\frac{f(t)e^{-it} - L}{1 - e^{-it}} + L\right)\left(\frac{e^{it} - 1}{it}\right) \tag{A6.2}$$

This expression boils down to:

$$i \cdot D_{\text{Buy}} = \frac{f(t) - L}{t} \tag{A6.3}$$

Obviously, the successive sale of soil at the Faustmann value entails a synchronized production. This is the only way to pay the burden of interest with the proceeds. Redemption, let alone profit, is out of the question. Actually, the Faustmann capital value sets an upper limit to the price of a piece of land.

APPENDIX B

Now we fulfil the promise given in footnote 22, namely to illustrate in some detail how the planting of a synchronized forest comes about. Consider a forester who owns a plot of soil. Investments are financed by loans. It is to clarify whether the agent will be free from the "fetters of interest" at the end of the construction period. Then, he can continuously pocket profits according to the Joseph II rule.

One might think that—notwithstanding the intention to create finally a staggered forest—the whole area is planted in the first instance. In the years to come $(1/t)$-th of the stock is sold and replanted respectively. This procedure, however, has the disadvantage that trees are cut which do not refund their compounded planting costs during the start-up period. Such loss-making deals must be excluded. The critical minimum growth time t_K results from:

$$f(t_K) = Le^{it_K} \tag{B6.1}$$

Inserting the data of the example gives:

$$t_K = 4.63 \tag{B6.2}$$

At the beginning of the project the open space in percent is:

$$\frac{1}{t_J} \cdot t_K = 40.99\% \tag{B6.3}$$

Thus, initially the forester cultivates approximately 60% of the soil. Let us first calculate the cumulated costs up to the minimum age t_K. The first planting amounts to:

$$FP = 0.5901 \cdot 100 \cdot \mathrm{e}^{0.1 \cdot 4.63} = 93.757 \tag{B6.4}$$

Besides, the costs of the succeeding seedlings have to be taken into account:

$$SP = \int_0^{4.63} \frac{1}{t_J} \cdot 100 \cdot \mathrm{e}^{0.1(4.63-t)} dt = 52.127 \tag{B6.5}$$

After 4.63 years, the forester faces a totally wooded area and a mountain of debt to the tune of:

$$\mathrm{D}(\mathrm{t_K}) = FP + SP = 93.757 + 52.127 = 145.884 \tag{B6.6}$$

Short of knowing how the repayment is stipulated, we charge interest until t_J:

$$D(t_J) = 145.884 \cdot \mathrm{e}^{0.1(t_J - 4.63)} = 284.124 \tag{B6.7}$$

But from t_K onwards there are net revenues that are brought to a bank in order to yield interest:

$$\mathrm{N}(t_J) = \int_{4.63}^{t_J} \frac{1}{t_J}(f(t) - 100)\mathrm{e}^{0.1(t_J - t)} dt = 665.408 \tag{B6.8}$$

Balancing gives:

$$V(t_J) = \mathrm{N}(t_J) - D(t_J) = 665.408 - 284.124 = 381.284 \tag{B6.9}$$

Apparently, once the forester has created a synchronized silviculture, he possesses not only a fortune of $V(t_J) = 381.284$ but he also receives the maximum profit $PG_J = 169.108$ per hectare and year from this time on.

PART Two

Performance Measurement

CHAPTER 7

Review of Commodity Futures Performance Benchmarks

Roland Füss, Ph.D.
Professor of Finance
Endowed Chair of Asset Management
European Business School (EBS)
International University Schloss Reichartshausen

Christian Hoppe
Senior Specialist Securitization and Credit Derivatives
Commerzbank AG

Dieter G. Kaiser, Ph.D.
Director Alternative Investments
Feri Institutional Advisors GmbH
Research Fellow
Centre for Practical Quantitative Finance
Frankfurt School of Finance and Management

Along with growing investor interest in commodity investments has come a dramatic increase in the number of commodity indexes being published worldwide. These indexes are widely used as price indicators for economists and investors. However, they are also rapidly assuming the role of comparison benchmarks in portfolio management, as well as acting as underlying instruments for certain derivative structures.

Recent empirical studies have focused mainly on single commodity indexes or a group of subindexes of the same provider, using a comparison analysis to contrast the risk and return of these indexes versus traditional asset classes. This approach, however, neglects the questions of validity and reliability that arise from using commodity indexes from various providers. An effective empirical approach would focus on the heterogeneity of commodity indexes by comparing the risk-return behavior of single commodity subindexes in order to detect significant shifts among individual benchmark portfolios.

This chapter will examine for the first time the entire universe of commodity indexes for three index types: spot, excess, and total return. Our data come from nine index providers and cover the period January 2001 to September 2006. We examine the heterogeneity of performance results with the help of different statistical variables, and distinguish between both, published aggregated indexes (composite indexes), which include all commodity sectors according to different weighting schemes, and sector-specific indexes (sector indexes). According to the literature, one solution to the problem of a representative benchmark; that is, in the case of heterogeneous risk-return characteristics of financial benchmark portfolios, is to equally weight the respective indexes. Due to the fact that equal weighting does not completely eliminate distortions in the benchmark, we advise using an unbiased procedure such as principal components analysis.

In general, enormous differences in the risk-return characteristics exist *within* the various sector indexes as well as *between* the same commodity sectors of various index providers we study here. Some overlapping index performance differences are to be expected per se due to the heterogeneity of the commodity sectors and their various factors of influence. However, we find considerably divergent results even within, for example, the industrials group.[1] Furthermore, due to differences in index construction, we find enormous performance deviations among the total and excess return indexes.

This chapter is organized as follows. The next section contains a summary of the various commodity indexes and their respective construction features. We then describe our data basis and compare statistical properties. The crucial question here is: To what extent does the choice of a specific index family lead to distortions and/or divergent results in performance evaluation? The subsequent section provides a possible solution to the heterogeneity problem by using principal components analysis to construct an implicit index that represents an aggregation of competing indexes. We conclude with a summary of the main results, and discuss the recommended course of action for investors.

---

[1]The largest observed difference in annualized returns is in the industrial metals—total return indexes (Commodity Research Bureau versus Rogers International Commodity Index (RICI)). If we adjust the RICI by removing indexes with a history of less than one year, the maximum difference is reduced to 13.45%, which clearly dilutes the statement about degree of heterogeneity.

SUMMARY OF COMMODITY INDEXES

Choosing a benchmark should be the first step when investing in a particular asset class. It constitutes the operationalization of investors' preferences and serves as a reference point within the performance measurement. According to Sharpe, a suitable benchmark must be a cost-effective investment alternative that is available for purchase in the market and subject to the same restrictions as the actively (or passively) managed portfolio.[2] It should be difficult to beat on a risk-adjusted basis and be chosen prior to managing the actual portfolio. For active and passive investment strategies, a well-established index is often chosen as a neutral reference point. And in traditional markets, indexes of reputable providers are already established as reference portfolios. However, in the commodity universe, choosing a benchmark is a much more complex task.

Erb and Harvey discuss how to define a representative commodity futures benchmark.[3] They note that the concept of market capitalization in an aggregated equity or fixed income index is not transferable to a commodity futures index because the outstanding buy and sell positions will cancel each other out in futures contracts. Hence, there are no uniform restrictions on the design of commodity futures indexes, and they may vary greatly in composition, weighting scheme, or rebalancing frequency, all of which may result in tremendous divergences in the risk-return characteristics. Therefore, Erb and Harvey propose considering individual commodity indexes as different portfolio strategies.[4]

Since the universe of commodity futures has grown continuously, it is possible to conduct a historical time series analysis. CRB/Reuters and the Goldman Sachs Commodity Index (GSCI) have the longest histories; the latter has the largest open interest. The GSCI was introduced in 1991 and backfilled to 1970.[5] Furthermore, the performance of the Rogers International Commodity Index and the Deutsche Bank Liquid Commodity Index (DBLCI) are hypothetically traced back to the base year 1984 (RICI) and 1988 (DBLCI) in the year of introduction 1998 and 2003, respectively. Thus, when a benchmark is introduced, the best practice is ideally to backfill performance

[2]William F. Sharpe, "Asset Allocation: Management Style and Performance Measurement," *Journal of Portfolio Management* 18, no. 2 (1992), pp. 7–19.

[3]Claude B. Erb and Campbell R. Harvey, "The Tactical and Strategic Value of Commodity Futures," *Financial Analysts Journal* 62, no. 2 (2006), pp. 69–97.

[4]Erb and Harvey, "The Tactical and Strategic Value of Commodity Futures."

[5]In 1970, the composite index was composed of only cattle, corn, soybeans, and wheat. Currently, these make up only 12.3% of the index and are therefore significantly less important than crude oil, currently the largest constituent with 34.4% (as of March 23, 2007). Nowadays, a classification typically includes energy, agriculture with soft commodities and grains and seeds, industrials, precious metals, livestock, and others (e.g., rubber and wood).

for a certain number of years.[6] Among the latest commodity index providers are Lehman Brothers (LBCI) and Deutsche Börse (CXCI), which were both released in 2006. The weights of commodity futures are derived from production quantities as (1) lagged rolling five-year averages (e.g., the GSCI); (2) liquidity (e.g., the DJAIG); (3) production volume (e.g., the DJAIG); (4) open interest (e.g., the CXCI); or (5) equally weighted (the CRB)). Depending on the weighting scheme, significant shifts through time may result. Thus, as Exhibit 7.1 for the GSCI shows, long-term historical comparison is limited.

In general, the market is determined by the commodity indexes shown in Exhibit 7.2. The scope of the individual indexes varies among providers. For example, Dow Jones-American International Group (DJAIG) calculates 84 commodity indexes for different subsectors and individual commodities; Mount Lucas Management (MLM), on the other hand, restricts itself to just one.[7] Most providers, however, have indexes for several sectors, such as energy, metal, or agriculture. Only Standard & Poor's (S&P)

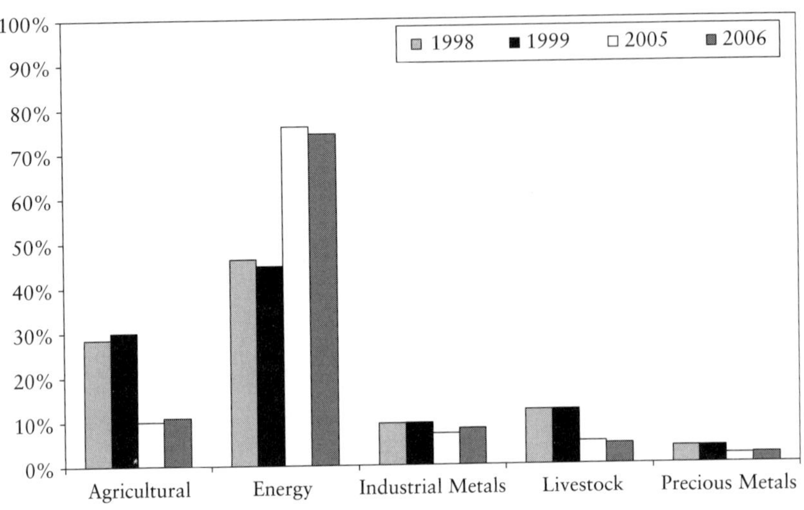

EXHIBIT 7.1 GSCI Index Weighting over Time
Source: Exhibit created from data obtained from Bloomberg.

[6] For example, the GSCI indexes were backfilled to 1970.

[7] The MLM index differentiates itself by also containing fixed income and FX futures. Its composition is inspected and adjusted by a committee once a year. Furthermore, the rules for weighting and rolling follow those for trend-following strategies: They are subject to yearly changes, but are not touched during the rest of the year. In this way, MLM is still classified as a passive index. It is distinctly different from the other indexes shown in Exhibit 7.2.

EXHIBIT 7.2 Summary of Index Providers

Criterion	CRB/Reuters	DJAIG	RICI	GSCI	S&P	LBCI	MCCI	DBLCI	CXCI	MLM
Number of indexes	20	84	31	43	5	69	6	60	36	1
Subsectors	8	23	n.a.	7	None	4	n.a.	4	5	3
Index types	SR, TR	SR, TR, ER	TR, ER	SR, TR, ER	SR, TR	SR, TR, ER	TR, ER	TR, ER	SR, TR, ER	TR
Release date	January 1957	January 1999	January 1998	January 1991	October 2001	July 2006	January 2000	March 2003	November 2006	January 1988
Index basis date	January 1967	January 1991	January 1984	January 1970	December 1997	January 2000	January 2000	December 1988	November 2006	January 1988
Backfilled since	January 1957	January 1991	January 1984	January 1970	January 1988	January 2000	January 2000	December 1988	November 2006	January 2000
Exists since max	January 1947	January 1991	January 1984	January 1970	January 1970	January 2000	January 2000	December 1988	November 2006	January 2000
Investible since	January 1986	July 1998	July 1998	January 1994	August 2001	January 2000	January 2000	March 2003	November 2006	January 1988
Number of commodities	17	19	36	24	17	20	n.a.	6	21	Approx. 25
Selection criterion	Diversification	Liquidity and diversification	Worldwide demand	Economically important portfolio	Commercial open interest	Trading volume in USD	n.a.	Six commodities, representing one sector each	Open interest	Volume and open interest
Futures selection	AM from two to five futures contracts with a maturity of up to six months	Nearby futures contract	Nearby futures contract	Nearby futures contract	Average of two nearby futures contracts	Future with highest liquidity	n.a.	(Liquid) future with highest roll return	Future with highest open interest	Trend-following
Futures source	International	International	International	International	U.S. futures only	International	n.a.	International	International	International

(*Continued*)

EXHIBIT 7.2 (Continued)

Criterion	CRB/Reuters	DJAIG	RICI	GSCI	S&P	LBCI	MCCI	DBLCI	CXCI	MLM
Diversification	No limits	Per Sector: Max 33%; Per Commodity: Min 2%, Max 15%	No limits	No limits	No limits	No limits	n.a.	No limits	No limits	No limits
Index weighting	Equally weighted[a]	Four-year average liquidity and production volume	Production volume	Five-year average of world production	Two-year average of commercial open interest (in USD) and liquidity	Rolling two-year USD trading volume	n.a.	Trading volume	Open interest	Equally weighted
Index calculation	GA	AA	AA	AA	AA and GA	n.a.	n.a.	AA	AA	AA
Release	Daily	Daily	Daily	Daily	Daily	Daily	n.a.	Daily	Daily	Daily
Rolling frequency	Monthly	n.a.	Monthly	Monthly	Six times a year	Monthly	n.a.	Monthly	Dynamic	Depends on strategy
Rebalancing	Permanently	Yearly	Yearly	Yearly	Yearly	Yearly	n.a.	Yearly	Yearly	Yearly

Note: AA = arithmetic averaging; GA = geometric averaging; n.a. = not available.

[a]Since the CRB/Reuters composite index consists of 17 equally-weighted subindexes, there appears deviations from the sector weightings depending on the number of commodities. For example, crude oil, heating oil, and natural gas have a share of 17.65% in the energy index, whereas industrial metals only include copper and cotton with a share of 11.76% (see also Exhibit 7.3).

Source: Authors.

offers composite indexes. Note that total return indexes are generally computed by all providers, while spot and excess return indexes are not offered on a regular basis.[8]

The amount of subsectors or commodity types, respectively, in each (composite) index depends on the individual selection criteria of the index provider. Popular criteria are liquidity (DJAIG, S&P, LBCI, CXCI), economic or industrial importance (RICI, GSCI), and the mapping of a sufficiently large commodity universe (CRB). The Liquid Commodities Index (DBLCI) from Deutsche Bank is constructed from six subsectors or commodities that are themselves a large part of their sector.[9] With 36 commodities, the Rogers International Commodity Index (RICI) provides the largest number of subsectors, as well as the most exotic. The indexes we study here generally differ with respect to the number of commodities covered and their broadness, and they range from 6 to 36 different commodities.

All index providers must rebalance the individual sectors and change their index composition on a yearly basis, except for CRB, which is permanently rebalanced due to equal weighting, and CXCI, which rebalances quarterly. The DJAIG is the only index that sets fixed constraints for individual sectors (a maximum of 33%) and commodities (between 2% and 15%).

Most of the futures found in the indexes are international (originating usually in the United States or Great Britain). An exception is the S&P, which contains only U.S.-based futures. Japanese, Canadian, or Australian futures are only very seldom considered (e.g., RICI).

Most index providers perform a monthly rollover, which, in commodity indexes, usually occurs onto the nearby future (e.g., DJAIG, RICI, GSCI; in comparison to the average from two nearby futures in the case of S&P). In general, this rollover method is called *continuous nearby*. Only CXCI, in order to always have the futures with the highest liquidity, rolls the futures as soon as the open interest of the new futures exceeds that of the old one. Alternatively, DBLCI chooses the futures with the highest anticipated rollover return.

CRB uses a different approach called *forward averaging:* A choice and subsequent average (arithmetic mean) is made, and calculated from two to five futures with a maturity of up to six months.

Index calculation and weighting follow the rules of commodity selection. Two popular methods are using the arithmetic averaging of production (DJAIG, RICI, GSCI), and using liquidity data (S&P, LBCI, DBLCI,

---

[8]DJAIG is the only provider of indexes on forwards of composite indexes.

[9]Examples are West Texas intermediate crude oil for energy, and aluminum for industrial metals.

EXHIBIT 7.3 Commodity Sector Weights as of January 2007

	CRB	DJAIG	RICI[a]	GSCI
Energy	17.65%	32.98%	48.00%	67.58%
Grains and seeds	17.65%	20.91%	16.52%	8.64%
Industrial metals	11.76%	21.62%	10.30%	12.29%
Livestock and meats	11.76%	9.15%	3.00%	5.30%
Precious metals	17.65%	9.11%	6.80%	2.53%
Soft commodities	23.53%	6.16%	15.38%	3.66%
Total (rounded)	100.00%	100.00%	100.00%	100.00%

Source: Exhibit created from data obtained from Commodity Research Bureau, Dow Jones, Beeland Management Company, and Goldman Sachs.
[a]As of the end of 2005.

CXCI). CRB uses the geometric averaging and equal weights the index components. This procedure shields CRB from the extreme changes common to important commodity (classes) like oil or energy, but it also allows less important commodities to receive higher weights.

This approach, however, denies higher exposures to rallying commodities, while simultaneously increasing exposure to commodities with decreasing value. As a result, we believe the arithmetic mean is the best choice, as it better reflects market trends by allocating exposure evenly to individual commodity components. However, the S&P index is an exception—here, arithmetically and geometrically computed indexes are provided. The stability and consistency of the index weights is maintained by monthly rebalancing.

Exhibit 7.3 compares the weights of the individual commodity sectors in the composite indexes of the most important commodity index providers.[10]

EMPIRICAL ANALYSIS OF THE COMMODITY BENCHMARK PROBLEM

This section compares the data series for nine different commodity index providers based on the CRB sector classification. Our calculations are based on continuously compounded daily and monthly returns for January 2001

[10]The individual sectors are aggregated on the basis of CRB's classification as follows: energy (crude oil, heating oil, natural gas), grains and seeds (corn, soybeans, wheat), industrials (aluminum, copper, cotton, nickel, zinc), livestock (live cattle, lean hogs), precious metals (gold, platinum, silver), and soft commodities (cocoa, coffee, orange juice, sugar).

to September 2006.[11] We investigate the three index types as available for the composite index: *total return* (TR), *excess return* (ER), and *spot return* (SR). We also examine the six sector indexes: energy, grains and seeds, industrials, livestock and meats, precious metals, and soft commodities. Exhibit 7.4 summarizes index provider availability.

EXHIBIT 7.4 Commodity Index Components of the Database

Sector/Index		CRB	DJAIG	RICI	GSCI	SPCX	LBCI	MCCI	DBLCI	MLM
Composite	TR		X	X	X	X	X	X	X	X[c]
	ER			X	X		X	X	X	
	SR	X	X		X		X			
Energy	TR	X	X	11/2004	X		X	X	X	
	ER			11/2004	X		X	X	X	
	SR		X		X		X			
Grains and seeds	TR	X	X		X		X		X[a]	
	ER			01/2006[a]	X		X		X[a]	
	SR		X		X		X			
Industrial metals	TR	X	X	01/2006	X		X	X[b]	X	
	ER			01/2006	X		X	X	X	
	SR	X	X		X		X			
Livestock and meats	TR	X	X		X		X		X[a]	
	ER				X		X		X[a]	
	SR	X	X		X		X			
Precious metals	TR	X	X	01/2006	X		X		X	
	ER			01/2006	X		X		X	
	SR		X		X		X			
Softs	TR	X	X	11/2004	X		X	X	X[a]	
	ER			11/2004	X		X		X[a]	
	SR		X		X		X			

[a]Index construction is equally weighted, contrary to Exhibit 7.2.
[b]Data available only on a weekly basis.
[c]Data available only on a monthly basis.
Source: Exhibit created from data obtained from Bloomberg.

[11]Our observation period results from the index with the shortest data history, the Lehman Brothers total return composite index, whose data tracking began on December 29, 2000.

In order to determine whether there is any heterogeneity among the indexes, we use one- and two-dimensional quantitative measures and their extreme values and differences (range), which can be interpreted as the maximum possible bias between two commodity indexes. In practice, this suggests that the extent of the spread or the respective choice of a specific index can influence and/or distort an investment decision compared with indexes of other providers.

Return and Volatility

If we consider the historical development of the total return composite indexes in Exhibit 7.5 since January 2001, we note that all indexes except MLM follow an overall trend of varying intensity. As discussed earlier, this may be attributable to differences in index construction, selection criteria, and weighting schemes (see Exhibit 7.2).

In order to quantify the diverging values of the commodity indexes, we next compare the generated annualized returns. Exhibit 7.6 shows significant divergences within the respective sectors, which can either increase or decrease depending on the chosen index version. Among the total return indexes, the maximum return differences are most significant within industrials (44.9%), energy (28.5%), and softs (17.6%). The maximum return difference within industrials is between CRB and RICI. However, note that data for the latter exists only since January 2006. Adjusting

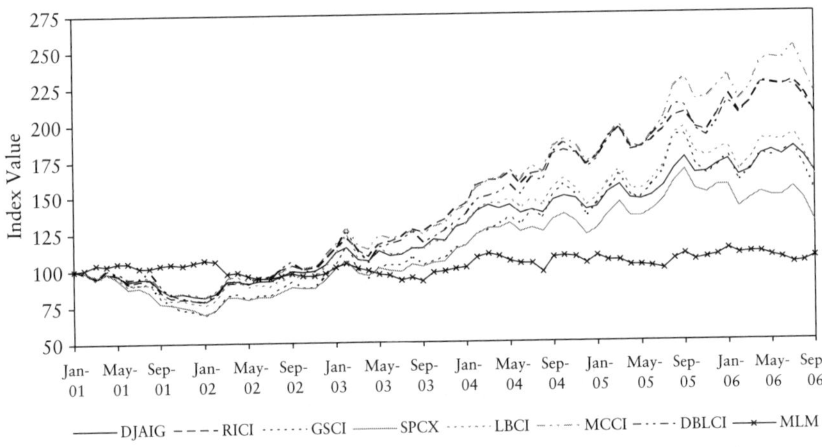

EXHIBIT 7.5 Historical Performance of the Composite Indexes (monthly data time series, indexed to 100)
Source: Exhibit created from data obtained from Bloomberg.

EXHIBIT 7.6 Annualized Returns, January 2001 to September 2006

Sector Indexes	Min	Max	Range	Mean	Friedman Test
		Total Return Index			
Composite	1.67%	16.34%	14.67%	10.72%	11.691
Energy	3.03%	31.49%	28.46%	15.09%	33.513[a]
Grains and seeds	-2.45%	7.11%	9.56%	2.71%	18.553[a]
Industrial metals	14.63%	59.53%	44.90%	29.14%	10.782[c]
Livestock and meats	2.04%	11.10%	9.06%	4.43%	8.859[c]
Precious metals	15.70%	17.16%	1.46%	16.44%	2.788
Softs	-5.97%	11.66%	17.63%	1.59%	12.259[b]
		Excess Return Index			
Composite	7.43%	13.79%	6.36%	10.86%	7.212
Energy	-0.24%	28.35%	28.59%	12.40%	36.335[a]
Grains and seeds	-26.46%	2.43%	28.89%	−7.24%	3.176
Industrial metals	21.04%	52.99%	31.95%	29.11%	6.653[c]
Livestock and meats	0.12%	8.43%	8.31%	3.06%	6.382[b]
Precious metals	10.93%	14.35%	3.42%	13.09%	1.971
Softs	-6.09%	8.98%	15.07%	−0.35%	3.294
		Spot Return Index			
Composite	8.18%	25.36%	17.17%	15.62%	12.053[a]
Energy	18.43%	25.91%	7.48%	21.05%	2.735
Grains and seeds	7.89%	8.87%	0.97%	8.30%	1.059
Industrial metals	9.37%	25.82%	16.45%	19.93%	6.265[c]
Livestock and meats	3.80%	9.25%	5.46%	5.76%	3.335
Precious metals	16.43%	17.75%	1.32%	17.15%	2.735
Softs	6.08%	14.05%	7.97%	10.32%	1.853

Source: Exhibit created from data obtained from Bloomberg.
Note: The calculations for the Friedman test are based on N = 68 monthly return observations. Indexes with shorter life spans are not considered.
[a], [b], and [c] denote significance at confidence levels of 99%, 95%, and 90%, respectively.

for this very short history leads to a maximum difference of 13.5% (CRB versus LBCI).

The explanation for the difference in energy indexes is similar. However, the maximum difference is reduced by 6.8% to 21.7% (DBLCI 31.5% versus LBCI 9.8%). The highest degree of homogeneity can be found in the precious metal total return indexes, with a maximum difference of below 1.5%. Only the grains and seeds spot return indexes remain under this value, with a difference of less than 1%.

In general, these significant differences suggest that heterogeneity is present. To verify whether the calculated index returns differ significantly, we apply the nonparametric Friedman test for dependent samples in Exhibit 7.6. The Friedman rank variance analysis simultaneously checks for l dependent sample differences with respect to the central tendency. The decision to use a nonparametric test under the assumption of dependent samples is justified by the fact that returns of commodity futures indexes are generally not normally distributed. Additionally, the different index providers refer partially to the same futures contracts, hence this leads us to the assumption of combined samples. The hypotheses are:[12]

H_0. Several dependent samples stem from the same population, or from all l samples follow the same return levels.

H_1. Several dependent samples stem from different populations, or at least from one of the l samples follow a diverging return.

Hence, investigating the null hypothesis involves verifying whether the populations, from which the l samples stem, coincide with regard to the central tendency. Considering that the rank sum $\sum_{j=1}^{l} R_{ij}$ for each of the n units equals $[l \cdot (l+1)]/2$ with $i = 1, \ldots, n$, and with n units the total sum of possible rank values is $[n \cdot l \cdot (l+1)]/2$, the test statistic can be deducted from the deviations of sample rank values from their respective expected values.

To avoid having the deviations cancel each other out, we use squared differences according to the variance calculation. Due to sample error, we must consider the possible variance of the rank values of l samples and n units, as well as the correction factor $[(l-1)]/l$ for finite populations. We thus obtain the following test statistic:

$$F = \frac{l-1}{l} \sum_{j=1}^{l} \frac{\left[R_j - \frac{n \cdot (l+1)}{2}\right]^2}{\frac{n \cdot (l^2 - 1)}{12}} = \frac{12}{n \cdot l \cdot (l+1)} \sum_{j=1}^{l} R_j^2 - 3n \cdot (l+1) \tag{7.1}$$

which, for large samples ($n \geq 10$ and $l \geq 4$), is approximately χ^2 distributed with $v = l - 1$ degrees of freedom.[13]

---

[12] Myles Hollander and Douglas A. Wolfe, *Nonparametric Statistical Methods*, (New York: John Wiley & Sons, 1999).

[13] Peter Sprent and Nigel C. Smeeton, *Applied Nonparametric Statistical Methods* (Boca Raton, FL: Chapman and Hall/CRC, 2007); Myles Hollander and Douglas A. Wolfe, *Nonparametric Statistical Methods* (New York: John Wiley & Sons, 1999). This approximated test is more conservative in most cases.

Significant differences occur primarily within the total return indexes. We note a highly significant deviation at the 1% significance level for grains and seeds as well as energy. The significant differences in return levels for the energy sector also remain when referring to excess return indexes. Major deviations are most obvious in the total return indexes because of differing construction methodologies; their influence in spot return indexes is only minor. However, note that the Friedman test for ordinally scaled variables considers the rank sequence and not the absolute return differences.

Exhibit 7.7 provides further investigation into the return properties by comparing the respective (minimal, maximal, and average percentage) periods with positive returns as fraction of the total period among the different index providers. On an average daily basis, only eight of the 21 indexes have more than 50% positive daily returns (industrials and precious metals for the spot and total return composite). On an average monthly basis, however, all indexes—with the exception of grains and seeds and softs for the excess and total return indexes—have more than 50% of all months a positive return.

On a disaggregated level, this number increases the most for LBCI, going from 49.6% to 66.2%. The smoothing effect evident from using monthly data, however, implies that the respective reference numbers diverge even more. For example, the maximum difference in the spot composite indexes increases from 1.5% to 8.8%; for industrials total return index, it goes from 7.8% to 22.1%.

Exhibit 7.8 subsequently calculates the percentage of average gain and loss on a daily and monthly basis resulting from the periods of positive and negative returns. The results show that the energy sector earned the largest average daily and monthly gain over all index variations. We assume the energy sector is highly volatile as it also shows the largest average losses per period.

In comparison, the industrials, precious metals, and soft commodities sectors show the worst average values on a daily basis. On a monthly basis, the lowest performers are the composite total return index with 4.12%, the composite spot return index with 4.05%, and the livestock and meats excess return index with 3.49%. In general, for the majority of indexes, the average return increase dominates the loss in value over a period. This ratio is negative only for livestock and meats and precious metals.

Another decision criterion which determines the success of an investment is implied risk, here expressed as the return volatility (the annualized standard deviation). Although RICI's missing data history distorts the statements at first, even after adjusting for it, significant differences between the

EXHIBIT 7.7 Periods with Positive Returns, January 2001 to September 2006

Daily Returns—Number of Days with Positive Returns

	Total Return Index				Excess Return Index				Spot Return Index			
Sector Indexes	Min	Max	Range	Mean	Min	Max	Range	Mean	Min	Max	Range	Mean
Composite	48.6%	52.5%	3.8%	50.9%	48.4%	52.0%	3.6%	49.9%	49.6%	51.1%	1.5%	50.1%
Energy	47.3%	53.0%	5.7%	49.0%	46.8%	51.6%	4.8%	49.2%	47.4%	48.5%	1.1%	47.9%
Grains and seeds	46.0%	50.7%	4.7%	47.5%	45.3%	47.6%	2.4%	46.5%	47.2%	48.3%	1.1%	47.6%
Industrial metals	48.6%	56.4%	7.8%	52.4%	48.8%	55.2%	6.4%	51.7%	49.5%	51.7%	2.2%	50.3%
Livestock and meats	48.4%	54.4%	6.0%	49.9%	47.8%	50.0%	2.2%	48.8%	48.0%	48.4%	0.4%	48.2%
Precious metals	51.6%	56.0%	4.4%	53.0%	50.5%	53.6%	3.1%	51.8%	51.7%	52.2%	0.5%	52.0%
Softs	43.8%	53.7%	9.9%	47.9%	43.6%	48.8%	5.2%	46.4%	47.0%	49.2%	2.2%	48.4%

Monthly Returns—Number of Months with Positive Returns

	Total Return Index				Excess Return Index				Spot Return Index			
Sector Indexes	Min	Max	Range	Mean	Min	Max	Range	Mean	Min	Max	Range	Mean
Composite	52.9%	61.8%	8.8%	57.9%	54.4%	60.3%	5.9%	57.6%	57.4%	66.2%	8.8%	62.1%
Energy	48.5%	61.8%	13.2%	54.7%	50.0%	60.3%	10.3%	55.3%	52.9%	57.4%	4.4%	55.9%
Grains and seeds	45.6%	54.4%	8.8%	49.1%	41.2%	50.0%	8.8%	45.6%	54.4%	55.9%	1.5%	55.4%
Industrial metals	52.9%	75.0%	22.1%	61.1%	57.4%	75.0%	17.6%	61.8%	58.8%	64.7%	5.9%	61.4%
Livestock and meats	50.0%	63.2%	13.2%	55.9%	52.9%	63.2%	10.3%	56.9%	48.5%	54.4%	5.9%	51.8%
Precious metals	50.0%	63.2%	13.2%	58.1%	50.0%	58.8%	8.8%	55.9%	57.4%	60.3%	2.9%	58.8%
Softs	40.9%	57.4%	16.4%	47.3%	40.9%	55.9%	15.0%	45.5%	52.9%	54.4%	1.5%	53.9%

Source: Exhibit created from data obtained from Bloomberg.

EXHIBIT 7.8 Average Gain and Loss, January 2001 to September 2006

		Daily Returns											
		Total Return Index				Excess Return Index				Spot Return Index			
Sector Indexes		Min	Max	Range	Mean	Min	Max	Range	Mean	Min	Max	Range	Mean
Composite	Gain	0.77%	1.14%	0.37%	0.92%	0.83%	1.14%	0.32%	0.98%	0.32%	1.15%	0.83%	0.82%
	Loss	−1.13%	−0.74%	0.39%	−0.90%	−1.13%	−0.81%	0.32%	−0.94%	−1.12%	−0.30%	0.83%	−0.77%
Energy	Gain	1.28%	1.75%	0.47%	1.57%	1.31%	1.76%	0.46%	1.53%	1.62%	1.81%	0.19%	1.73%
	Loss	−1.65%	−1.23%	0.42%	−1.51%	−1.66%	−1.24%	0.42%	−1.49%	−1.61%	−1.53%	0.08%	−1.58%
Grains and seeds	Gain	0.82%	1.05%	0.23%	0.98%	0.75%	0.99%	0.24%	0.86%	1.01%	1.06%	0.05%	1.03%
	Loss	−0.96%	−0.82%	0.14%	−0.92%	−0.97%	−0.70%	0.26%	−0.82%	−0.97%	−0.95%	0.02%	−0.96%
Industrial metals	Gain	0.87%	1.54%	0.67%	1.06%	0.78%	1.83%	1.05%	1.11%	0.30%	1.00%	0.70%	0.83%
	Loss	−1.65%	−0.85%	0.81%	−1.04%	−1.90%	−0.75%	1.15%	−1.07%	−0.94%	−0.29%	0.65%	−0.77%
Livestock and meats	Gain	0.54%	0.76%	0.22%	0.69%	0.58%	0.73%	0.15%	0.68%	0.73%	0.82%	0.10%	0.77%
	Loss	−0.78%	−0.57%	0.21%	−0.71%	−0.74%	−0.57%	0.17%	−0.68%	−0.82%	−0.69%	0.12%	−0.75%
Precious metals	Gain	0.74%	1.34%	0.60%	0.88%	0.79%	1.27%	0.48%	0.92%	0.79%	0.83%	0.04%	0.81%
	Loss	−1.61%	−0.79%	0.83%	−0.96%	−1.53%	−0.80%	0.73%	−1.00%	−0.85%	−0.80%	0.06%	−0.83%
Softs	Gain	0.72%	0.98%	0.26%	0.88%	0.71%	1.06%	0.35%	0.87%	0.87%	1.02%	0.15%	0.95%
	Loss	−1.05%	−0.59%	0.46%	−0.86%	−1.05%	−0.60%	0.45%	−0.83%	−0.98%	−0.78%	0.20%	−0.90%

(Continued)

EXHIBIT 7.8 (Continued)

		Monthly Returns											
		Total Return Index				Excess Return Index				Spot Return Index			
Sector Indexes		Min	Max	Range	Mean	Min	Max	Range	Mean	Min	Max	Range	Mean
Composite	Gain	2.20%	5.02%	2.82%	4.12%	3.81%	5.09%	1.28%	4.57%	1.98%	5.53%	3.56%	4.05%
	Loss	−5.61%	−2.32%	3.28%	−3.70%	−5.43%	−3.37%	2.07%	−4.16%	−4.77%	−1.61%	3.16%	−3.40%
Energy	Gain	6.45%	9.14%	2.69%	7.81%	6.19%	8.57%	2.39%	7.42%	7.59%	8.85%	1.26%	8.38%
	Loss	−8.71%	−4.78%	3.93%	−6.75%	−8.98%	−4.82%	4.16%	−6.97%	−7.14%	−6.88%	0.26%	−6.97%
Grains and	Gain	4.10%	4.88%	0.78%	4.47%	3.73%	5.01%	1.28%	4.21%	4.49%	4.91%	0.42%	4.72%
seeds	Loss	−4.18%	−3.50%	0.68%	−3.88%	−3.83%	−2.53%	1.30%	−3.39%	−4.61%	−4.22%	0.39%	−4.36%
Industrial	Gain	4.16%	6.48%	2.32%	5.70%	4.57%	6.10%	1.53%	5.46%	2.11%	5.64%	3.53%	4.54%
metals	Loss	−4.69%	−2.67%	2.02%	−3.46%	−3.87%	−2.76%	1.11%	−3.35%	−3.77%	−1.74%	2.03%	−3.18%
Livestock	Gain	2.97%	3.88%	0.91%	3.49%	2.76%	3.45%	0.69%	3.18%	4.06%	5.26%	1.20%	4.58%
and meats	Loss	−4.08%	−2.71%	1.37%	−3.57%	−3.96%	−2.90%	1.06%	−3.54%	−4.34%	−3.71%	0.62%	−3.95%
Precious	Gain	4.09%	6.67%	2.58%	4.68%	4.13%	6.30%	2.17%	4.68%	4.25%	4.44%	0.19%	4.34%
metals	Loss	−4.23%	−2.97%	1.25%	−3.33%	−4.57%	−2.87%	1.70%	−3.48%	−3.10%	−2.73%	0.37%	−2.98%
Softs	Gain	2.88%	5.44%	2.57%	4.35%	2.61%	5.39%	2.77%	4.06%	3.88%	6.19%	2.31%	5.05%
	Loss	−5.16%	−2.12%	3.04%	−3.80%	−5.19%	−2.39%	2.80%	−3.67%	−4.62%	−3.55%	1.07%	−4.11%

Source: Exhibit created from data obtained from Bloomberg.

indexes remain. Hence, the assumption of heterogeneity of indexes in regard to volatility expressed as return variation around the mean again prevails.

The lowest risk is found in the spot return composite index, for example, the CRB (6.3%); the highest is found in the GSCI (23.3%) (see Exhibit 7.9). Volatility is identical within the grains and seeds spot return (a maximum difference of 0.1%), and precious metals spot return indexes (a maximum difference of 0.8%).

The use of monthly data can lead to a stronger reduction in minimum values than maximum values, which are partially increasing. As a result, the difference (range) among the extreme values can increase when compared to daily data. Hence, the volatility of the RICI total return index decreased from 13.2% to 11.9%.

On the other hand, the annualized standard deviation of the Deutsche Bank indexes increased from 21.8% to 23.3%. These descriptive results strongly illustrate the diverging implications for investors when making investment decisions or conducting performance evaluation. So, within our sample period, we find average sector-specific volatilities of between 13.95% and 34.02%. For all sectors and index types, we find an average of 20.25%.

Correlations

Another clue when investigating diverging commodity index performance can be found by analyzing intrasector correlation structures among indexes of different providers. On a daily basis, the maximum difference of correlation coefficients among the indexes of a sector ranges from 0.021 (precious metals excess return) to 0.924 (livestock and meats spot return). For monthly data, the numbers range from 0.021 (precious metals spot return) to 0.728 (composite total return), as can be seen in Exhibit 7.10.

Without including the MLM composite indexes, the maximum difference in total return index variants is 0.130. Considering the extreme values, it is obvious that no negative correlations exist. This means that the individual indexes develop at most independently, but not contrarily.

The highest degree of homogeneity exists among the precious metals spot return indexes, with an average correlation coefficient of 0.987. The smallest average correlation coefficient is found in livestock and meats spot return, with 0.461. Furthermore, note that only 15 of the 42 minimum values fall below 0.500; only four fall between 0 and 0.250. Hence, when

EXHIBIT 7.9 Volatility, January 2001 to September 2006

Daily Returns

Sector Indexes	Total Return Index				Excess Return Index				Spot Return Index			
	Min	Max	Range	Mean	Min	Max	Range	Mean	Min	Max	Range	Mean
Composite	15.42%	23.25%	7.83%	18.90%	16.94%	23.26%	6.32%	19.78%	6.34%	23.30%	16.95%	16.31%
Energy	26.36%	35.05%	8.68%	31.73%	26.37%	35.06%	8.69%	31.26%	32.57%	35.11%	2.54%	34.02%
Grains and seeds	17.62%	20.91%	3.29%	19.97%	13.82%	20.53%	6.71%	17.43%	20.75%	20.87%	0.12%	20.82%
Industrial metals	19.75%	33.12%	13.37%	22.83%	17.58%	55.86%	38.29%	27.12%	6.50%	21.23%	14.72%	17.49%
Livestock and meats	12.03%	15.62%	3.59%	14.50%	12.03%	15.06%	3.03%	13.95%	15.22%	18.36%	3.14%	16.34%
Precious metals	17.04%	32.32%	15.28%	20.27%	17.66%	29.62%	11.96%	20.75%	17.66%	18.41%	0.75%	17.97%
Softs	13.22%	21.84%	8.62%	18.06%	13.24%	21.84%	8.61%	17.70%	18.16%	20.41%	2.25%	19.13%

Monthly Returns

Sector Indexes	Total Return Index				Excess Return Index				Spot Return Index			
	Min	Max	Range	Mean	Min	Max	Range	Mean	Min	Max	Range	Mean
Composite	10.35%	22.30%	11.95%	16.68%	15.10%	22.34%	7.24%	18.49%	8.14%	22.09%	13.95%	16.05%
Energy	24.32%	35.28%	10.96%	31.13%	24.35%	35.29%	10.95%	30.59%	31.08%	35.07%	3.99%	33.26%
Grains and seeds	15.89%	21.03%	5.14%	18.87%	9.65%	21.05%	11.41%	15.46%	19.85%	22.85%	3.00%	21.19%
Industrial metals	15.84%	24.59%	8.75%	20.75%	16.17%	24.56%	8.38%	20.08%	8.59%	21.11%	12.52%	17.42%
Livestock and meats	11.99%	16.18%	4.19%	15.08%	11.96%	15.87%	3.91%	14.48%	16.90%	20.26%	3.37%	18.37%
Precious metals	15.52%	23.77%	8.26%	17.50%	15.13%	23.74%	8.61%	17.78%	15.24%	16.65%	1.42%	16.06%
Softs	11.88%	23.32%	11.44%	17.92%	11.94%	23.30%	11.37%	17.23%	16.42%	22.83%	6.41%	19.96%

Source: Exhibit created from data obtained from Bloomberg.

EXHIBIT 7.10 Correlations and the Heterogeneity Index of Commodity Futures Indexes, January 2001 to September 2006

Daily Data															
	Total Return Index					Excess Return Index					Spot Return Index				
	Min	Max	Range	Mean	HI	Min	Max	Range	Mean	HI	Min	Max	Range	Mean	HI
Composite	0.840	0.965	0.125	0.923	7.7%	0.875	0.956	0.081	0.932	6.8%	0.266	0.959	0.693	0.619	38.1%
Energy	0.882	0.989	0.107	0.937	6.3%	0.885	0.981	0.096	0.945	5.5%	0.947	0.977	0.030	0.964	3.6%
Grains and seeds	0.835	0.966	0.131	0.903	9.7%	0.233	0.835	0.601	0.571	42.9%	0.850	0.956	0.106	0.910	9.0%
Industrial metals	0.120	0.986	0.866	0.647	35.3%	0.450	0.987	0.537	0.750	25.0%	0.363	0.958	0.595	0.656	34.4%
Livestock and meats	0.792	0.979	0.187	0.881	11.9%	0.866	0.972	0.107	0.905	9.5%	0.021	0.945	0.924	0.461	53.9%
Precious metals	0.855	0.998	0.144	0.911	8.9%	0.974	0.995	0.021	0.986	1.4%	0.939	0.997	0.058	0.960	4.0%
Softs	0.297	0.940	0.642	0.579	42.1%	0.244	0.965	0.721	0.606	39.4%	0.398	0.926	0.528	0.578	42.2%

Monthly Data															
	Total Return Index					Excess Return Index					Spot Return Index				
	Min	Max	Range	Mean	HI	Min	Max	Range	Mean	HI	Min	Max	Range	Mean	HI
Composite	0.252	0.980	0.728	0.776	22.4%	0.903	0.982	0.079	0.951	4.9%	0.250	0.957	0.706	0.683	31.7%
Energy	0.913	0.990	0.077	0.956	4.4%	0.932	0.990	0.058	0.971	2.9%	0.938	0.989	0.051	0.957	4.3%
Grains and seeds	0.831	0.971	0.140	0.921	7.9%	0.837	0.889	0.051	0.870	13.0%	0.862	0.974	0.111	0.925	7.5%
Industrial metals	0.671	0.990	0.319	0.885	11.5%	0.905	0.990	0.085	0.960	4.0%	0.650	0.997	0.346	0.826	17.4%
Livestock and meats	0.830	0.997	0.166	0.901	9.9%	0.843	0.997	0.153	0.902	9.8%	0.321	0.981	0.660	0.636	36.4%
Precious metals	0.878	0.998	0.120	0.970	3.0%	0.964	0.998	0.033	0.983	1.7%	0.977	0.998	0.021	0.987	1.3%
Softs	0.289	0.966	0.677	0.605	39.5%	0.338	0.966	0.629	0.635	36.8%	0.445	0.934	0.489	0.619	38.1%

Source: Exhibit created from data obtained from Bloomberg.

considering correlation analysis, the commodity index universe presents more likely a homogeneous picture.[14]

In addition to the preceding correlation analysis, we also derive a simple reference number for determining heterogeneity in the indexes of different index providers:

$$HI = 1 - \text{average correlation}. \quad (7.2)$$

Hence a heterogeneity indicator (HI) of 1 represents a perfectly heterogeneous situation. With values around 40%, the strongest heterogeneity seems to be in the soft commodity sector, independent from the return frequency. At the same time, daily calculated index returns have a tendency toward stronger heterogeneity, especially for the industrials indexes. It is obvious that the heterogeneity indicator for the composite, industrials, livestock and meats, and soft commodities spot return indexes shows higher values.

Skew and Kurtosis

In order to further verify the quality of commodity index returns, we must investigate skew and kurtosis in more detail, since those qualities

[14]The average correlations between individual commodity futures and specific commodity sectors are generally low. Erb and Harvey study 12 commodity futures and show that the average correlation coefficient between them and the GSCI composite index is a mere 0.20 for the time period December 1982 to May 2005. For individual commodity futures, they find an average correlation coefficient of only 0.09. In light of the extraordinary heterogeneity of commodity futures returns, the authors conclude that the average commodity investment does not exist, but that commodities are "a market of individual dissimilar assets." These results are confirmed by Gorton and Rouwenhorst for the period July 1959 to December 2004 with their construction of a commodity futures index. They found a correlation of 0.0975 among individual commodity futures. The existence of lower correlations between individual commodity markets allows for the construction of diversified commodity portfolios with correspondingly low risks. These commodity portfolios further serve to reduce the total risk of portfolios composed primarily of financial asset classes. See Erb and Harvey, "The Tactical and Strategic Value of Commodity Futures"; and Gary Gorton and K. Geert Rouwenhorst, "Facts and Fantasies about Commodity Futures," *Financial Analysts Journal* 62, no. 2 (2006), pp. 47–68.

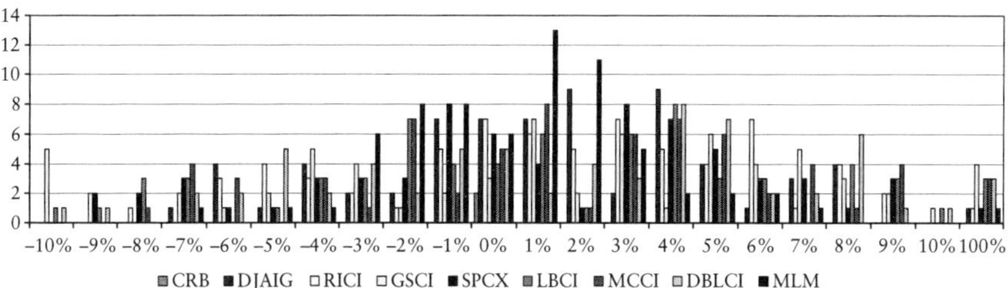

EXHIBIT 7.11 Frequency Distribution of the Monthly Returns of the Composite Indexes
Source: Exhibit created from data obtained from Bloomberg.

allow us to draw conclusions about future return probabilities. The monthly returns of the total return composite indexes in Exhibit 7.11 exhibit exemplary frequency distributions. Nevertheless, they do not have a uniform distribution pattern. We also do not see low return variations around a positive mean as well as no contemporaneously prevention of extreme values (fat tails), which are both return characteristics investors find desirable.

In order to quantify the assumption of nonnormality in Exhibit 7.11, we calculate the normalized third central distributional moment called skewness, defined by an asymmetric, unimodal frequency distribution. We distinguish between left skewed, right skewed, and normally distributed return distributions. If the result of the relative skewness parameter is smaller than zero (left skewed), there is a higher probability of high negative monthly returns when compared to the normal distribution.

The results in Exhibit 7.12 show rather small deviations among individual skewness values. The largest difference of 2.201 is found for the industrials excess return indexes (RICI versus MCCI), and is due to the fact that RICI tracking started in 2006, a good year for commodity investing. Leaving out the RICI, however, decreases the maximum difference to a negligible skewness of 0.260. The high percentage of left-skewed indexes on the one hand and their reduction by switching to monthly data on the other hand is, however, remarkable. The strongest shift is observed within the industrials total return indexes. Based on the average skewness parameters, the number of sectors with left-skewed distributions is reduced by 25% when monthly index data are considered. For risk-averse investors, the monthly return distribution in the industrials excess return index is most advantageous, with an average skew of

EXHIBIT 7.12 Skewness, Excess Kurtosis, and Normal Distribution, January 2001 to September 2006

		Daily Returns											
		Total Return Index				Excess Return Index				Spot Return Index			
Sector Indexes		Min	Max	Range	Mean	Min	Max	Range	Mean	Min	Max	Range	Mean
Composite	Skewness	–0.162	0.093	0.255	–0.039	–0.163	0.088	0.252	–0.078	–0.096	0.175	0.271	0.046
	Ex. Kurtosis	0.508	1.478	0.970	1.134	1.184	1.467	0.283	1.303	0.971	1.812	0.840	1.326
	J.B. Test	16.5	142.9	126.3	88.5	90.0	141.3	51.3	110.7	60.5	206.3	145.8	119.4
	#NV/#nNV		0/7				0/5				0/4		
Energy	Skewness	–0.164	0.097	0.261	–0.046	–0.170	0.100	0.269	–0.064	–0.166	0.023	0.189	–0.060
	Ex. Kurtosis	0.687	3.645	2.958	1.682	0.680	3.645	2.965	1.790	1.689	1.889	0.201	1.781
	J.B. Test	10.3	838.3	828.0	229.2	10.2	838.3	828.2	265.5	179.3	231.2	51.9	202.2
	#NV/#nNV		0/7				0/5				0/3		
Grains and seeds	Skewness	0.139	0.520	0.381	0.349	0.137	0.550	0.413	0.303	0.065	0.398	0.333	0.234
	Ex. Kurtosis	1.796	2.948	1.151	2.203	0.695	8.234	7.539	3.326	1.782	2.036	0.254	1.882
	J.B. Test	226.1	613.5	387.4	351.3	3.7	4,265.1	4,261.4	1,228.4	224.4	261.3	36.9	241.6
	#NV/#nNV		0/5						1/3		0/3		
Industrial metals	Skewness	–0.346	0.297	0.643	–0.136	–0.391	1.811	2.201	0.161	–0.366	0.113	0.479	–0.158
	Ex. Kurtosis	0.738	6.188	5.450	4.229	4.968	39.401	34.433	12.373	4.231	6.388	2.157	5.268
	J.B. Test	5.0	2,408.4	2,403.3	1,355.9	1,561.4	11,806.8	10,245.4	3,971.0	1,127.1	2,567.3	1,440.2	1,793.8
	#NV/#nNV		1/5				0/5				0/4		
Livestock and meats	Skewness	–0.257	–0.130	0.127	–0.179	–0.194	–0.142	0.052	–0.169	–0.085	0.590	0.675	0.194
	Ex. Kurtosis	0.564	1.871	1.307	1.071	0.743	1.218	0.474	0.981	0.975	27.449	26.473	9.469
	J.B. Test	24.2	236.3	212.1	93.8	42.1	102.5	60.4	70.1	61.5	47,329.0	47,267.4	12,947.5
	#NV/#nNV		0/5				0/3				0/4		
Precious metals	Skewness	–0.692	–0.454	0.238	–0.576	–0.879	–0.286	0.593	–0.599	–0.658	–0.274	0.383	–0.516
	Ex. Kurtosis	3.363	5.662	2.298	4.848	2.258	7.065	4.807	4.877	4.730	7.971	3.241	5.914
	J.B. Test	93.0	2,095.7	2,002.7	1,478.2	61.8	3,155.1	3,093.3	1,666.1	1,500.4	4,008.6	2,508.2	2,404.6
	#NV/#nNV		0/6				0/4				0/3		
Softs	Skewness	–0.154	0.373	0.527	0.112	–0.157	0.364	0.522	0.128	–0.150	0.251	0.401	0.043
	Ex. Kurtosis	0.572	8.222	7.649	2.312	1.287	8.234	6.947	3.214	0.594	13.993	13.399	5.290
	J.B. Test	20.6	4,251.0	4,230.4	773.3	44.3	4,265.1	4,220.8	1,167.8	22.4	12,300.1	12,277.7	4,147.2
	#NV/#nNV		0/6						0/4		0/3		

Sector Indexes		Total Return Index				Excess Return Index				Spot Return Index			
		Min	Max	Range	Mean	Min	Max	Range	Mean	Min	Max	Range	Mean
Composite	**Skewness**	−0.188	0.470	0.659	−0.034	−0.188	−0.041	0.147	−0.114	−0.404	0.030	0.434	−0.160
	Ex. Kurtosis	−0.653	1.483	2.136	−0.157	−0.672	−0.054	0.618	−0.428	−0.327	1.154	1.481	0.227
	J.B. Test	0.02	8.87	8.84	1.73	0.03	1.47	1.44	0.83	0.09	5.71	5.62	1.63
	#NV/#nNV	7/1				5/0				3/0			
Energy	Skewness	−0.217	0.254	0.471	0.081	−0.208	0.256	0.464	0.049	0.037	0.241	0.203	0.166
	Ex. Kurtosis	−0.981	0.120	1.101	−0.317	−0.985	0.110	1.095	−0.428	−0.141	0.283	0.424	0.059
	J.B. Test	0.32	1.10	0.79	0.66	0.52	1.10	0.57	0.78	0.07	0.90	0.82	0.51
	#NV/#nNV	6/0				5/0				3/0			
Grains	**Skewness**	−0.056	0.205	0.261	0.101	0.107	0.210	0.103	0.150	−0.067	0.000	0.067	−0.038
	Ex. Kurtosis	−0.222	1.252	1.474	0.554	−0.228	1.216	1.444	0.325	0.140	1.036	0.895	0.727
	J.B. Test	0.25	4.65	4.41	2.15	0.13	4.45	4.32	1.75	0.06	3.11	3.05	2.04
	#NV/#nNV	4/0				3/0				3/0			
Industrial metals	Skewness	0.528	1.269	0.741	0.761	0.568	1.285	0.717	0.817	0.297	0.863	0.567	0.648
	Ex. Kurtosis	−0.016	2.616	2.632	1.137	−0.069	2.654	2.723	1.229	0.072	1.431	1.360	0.733
	J.B. Test	3.94	17.11	13.17	8.39	3.72	13.75	10.03	8.22	1.03	14.46	13.43	7.60
	#NV/#nNV	2/4				2/3				3/0			
Livestock and meats	**Skewness**	−0.809	−0.088	0.721	−0.554	−0.798	−0.639	0.159	−0.744	−0.421	−0.099	0.322	−0.238
	Ex. Kurtosis	−0.497	1.134	1.631	0.386	0.375	1.063	0.688	0.800	0.062	0.876	0.814	0.327
	J.B. Test	0.80	11.22	10.42	6.01	5.09	10.55	5.46	8.54	0.12	4.24	4.12	1.43
	#NV/#nNV	2/2				1/2				3/0			
Precious metals	Skewness	−0.428	0.400	0.828	−0.027	−0.046	0.411	0.457	0.104	−0.110	0.048	0.158	−0.013
	Ex. Kurtosis	−0.460	1.179	1.638	0.450	−0.438	0.568	1.007	0.162	0.172	0.734	0.562	0.463
	J.B. Test	0.04	6.10	6.06	1.66	0.07	0.95	0.88	0.46	0.11	1.69	1.58	0.82
	#NV/#nNV	5/0				4/0				3/0			
Softs	**Skewness**	0.105	1.155	1.050	0.482	0.107	1.186	1.079	0.442	−0.020	0.553	0.573	0.245
	Ex. Kurtosis	−0.349	2.599	2.948	0.491	−0.014	2.700	2.714	0.917	−0.498	1.149	1.647	0.311
	J.B. Test	0.13	11.59	11.46	4.06	0.13	12.38	12.24	4.02	0.23	7.31	7.08	2.91
	#NV/#nNV	3/2				3/1				2/1			

Source: Exhibit created from data obtained from Bloomberg.

Notes: The J.B. test statistic is asymptotically χ^2-distributed with two degrees of freedom. The normal distribution can be rejected when the test statistic exceeds the critical values of 9.21, 5.99, and 4.61 for significance levels of 1%, 5%, and 10%, respectively. #NV = number of normally distributed indexes; #nNV = number of nonnormally distributed indexes.

0.817. Livestock and meats excess return index has the worst, with −0.744.[15]

The measure of the strength of concentration of a distribution around its expected value is called kurtosis. It is calculated as the normalized fourth central moment. The results of the kurtosis analysis are also summarized in Exhibit 7.12, where a relative kurtosis value of 3 or an excess kurtosis value of 0 defines the existence of a normal distribution. Having thick distribution ends ("fat tails") is referred to as having positive excess kurtosis; having thinner tails when compared to the normal distribution indicates negative excess kurtosis.

Risk-averse investors prefer negative excess kurtosis or in comparison to normal distribution lower probability of extreme values. Negative skewness and positive excess kurtosis are distribution properties, which investors do not appreciate, because they imply more overall large returns (positive and negative) compared to the normal distribution. The larger negative returns are generally not compensated for by larger positive returns.

We see from Exhibit 7.12 that the kurtosis values tend to be approximately homogeneous. Only three sector indexes have larger maximum differences:

The industrials excess return index on a daily data basis has a 34.4 difference in excess kurtosis. However, adjusting for the RICI with an excess kurtosis of 39.40 decreases the difference to 1.21.

The livestock and meats spot return index on a daily data basis has a 26.5 difference – DJAIG (27.45) versus LBCI (0.98).

The soft commodities spot return index on a daily data basis has a 13.4 difference in excess kurtosis – DJAIG (0.59) versus GSCI (13.99).

The kurtosis of the livestock and meats – DJAIG index is influenced heavily by two extreme daily return values: 12.83% (on February 10, 2006), and +14.28% (on January 13, 2006). Adjusting for these values decreases the average excess kurtosis to 1.91. The comparable daily returns for the soft commodities – GSCI Index are −11.76% (June 7, 2004), and +10.34% (June 8, 2004). The adjusted kurtosis is 2.64. The fact that the

[15]According to Kat and Oomen, the return distributions of daily commodity indexes have very few skew properties. This, however, is contrary to the results of Anson and Gorton and Rouwenhorst. Using monthly data, these authors verified empirically that commodity futures prices follow a return distribution with right skew due to the supply shock vulnerability of commodities. Harry M. Kat and Roel C. A. Oomen, "What Every Investor Should Know About Commodities, Part I," *Journal of Investment Management* 5, no. 1 (2007), pp. 1–25; Mark J. P. Anson, *The Handbook of Alternative Assets* (Hoboken, NJ: John Wiley & Sons, 2006); and Gorton and Rouwenhorst, "Facts and Fantasies about Commodity Futures."

extreme values occurred on consecutive days suggests that problems in the index calculation dominate the true return deviations.

The kurtosis effects from daily data indicate a leptokurtic distribution for almost all indexes. This for risk-averse investors unfavorable distribution feature is especially apparent within industrials and precious metals.[16] Similarly to equity returns, Exhibit 7.12 substantiates a shift from a leptokurtic to a platykurtic or mesokurtic distribution when moving to monthly data.

Taking the empirical distribution moment results skewness S and kurtosis K as a basis, the normal distribution assumption can be statistically verified using Jarque-Bera test. The null hypothesis H_0: "The returns follow a normal distribution," is tested against the alternative hypothesis H_1: "The returns do not follow a normal distribution." The respective Jarque-Bera test statistic is

$$JB = \frac{n}{6} \cdot \left[S^2 + \frac{1}{4} \cdot (K - 3)^2 \right] \tag{7.3}$$

In the case of normal distribution, skewness and excess kurtosis $(K - 3)$ take a value of 0 (or 3 for kurtosis, respectively), which also yields a value of 0 for the test statistic. High values for the test statistic in Exhibit 7.12, however, suggest rejection of the normal distribution assumption. The Jarque-Bera values based on monthly data indicate a generally more homogeneous picture than those based on daily data.

The largest Jarque-Bera values on a monthly basis are in the index variants of industrials—LBCI and MCCI (Total return = 14.62 and 17.11; Excess return = 13.75 and 11.27; Spot return = 14.46 and n.a.). Exhibit 7.12 summarizes the frequency of *occurrence of normally* (#NV) and *nonnormally distributed* (#nNV) indexes (see the last lines). For monthly data, 19 of 42 strategy indexes, or 45%, indicate nonnormally distributed return distributions. Based on average Jarque-Bera values, the null hypothesis is rejected for only five strategy indexes—industrials and livestock and meats—according to the critical value of the null hypothesis (existence of normality). However, the extent to which the values for the test statistic exceed the critical values needed to accept the null hypothesis (the existence of a normal distribution) is not excessively high.

[16]This coincides with the empirical results of Kat and Oomen, who verified excess kurtosis or fat tails for all commodities except cattle, hogs, cacao, azuki beans, rubber, silk, wood, and eggs. See Kat and Oomen, "What Every Investor Should Know About Commodities, Part I."

To conclude, note that the monthly results for the commodity indexes studied here tend to follow a normal distribution for the sample period. This suggests a homogeneous picture because of the only minor differences among the individual sector groups.

The Sharpe and Sortino Ratios

Following up on the preceding daily and monthly return analysis, we now use two-dimensional performance measures to examine discrepancies among the indexes. These measures offer the advantage of simultaneously combining return and risk into a single performance number. The Sharpe ratio relates the realized excess return, defined as the difference between portfolio return and the risk-free interest rate, to the risk taken, and can be interpreted as the risk premium per unit of total risk.[17] Thus, the higher the compensation for risk taken, the higher the Sharpe ratio.

On average, the most attractive risk-adjusted returns are found in the industrials index variants (see Exhibit 7.13). The results based on daily data, however, are overshadowed by those based on monthly data. In addition to industrials, all index variants of precious metals show a positive Sharpe ratio, that is, a positive risk premium.

The least attractive sectors are grains and seeds and soft commodities (total return and excess return indexes), and livestock and meats (all index variants). All have a negative average Sharpe ratio or risk premium on average. At the index provider level, the RICI industrials index (total return and excess return indexes) yields the highest Sharpe ratios due to its short history characterized by a positive environment. The grains and seeds excess return index of RICI is the worst performer, with a Sharpe ratio of −3.18 since inception.

Independent from the adjustment for such extreme values, the results in Exhibit 7.13 confirm a rather homogeneous character. The maximum monthly differences range from a negligible 0.03 for grains and seeds spot return indexes (DJAIG versus GSCI), to 1.78 for industrials total return indexes (CRB versus RICI), or to 0.88 when not including RICI (CRB versus MCCI).

The Deutsche Bank index family (DBLCI) has the largest number of risk-return-dominating indexes, with seven "maximum" Sharpe ratios, followed by CRB and DJAIG with four each. On the other hand, the Goldman Sachs index family has eight "minimum" Sharpe ratios. This number would be even worse if the list were adjusted for the RICI indexes (six minimum

[17]William F. Sharpe, "Mutual Fund Performance," *Journal of Business* 39, no. 1 (1966), pp. 119–129. In this study, we use a risk-free interest rate of 4%.

EXHIBIT 7.13 Sharpe and Sortino Ratios, January 2001 to September 2006

Daily Returns

		Total Return Index				Excess Return Index				Spot Return Index			
Sector Indexes		Min	Max	Range	Mean	Min	Max	Range	Mean	Min	Max	Range	Mean
Composite	Sharpe	−0.03	0.57	0.60	0.30	−0.04	0.42	0.46	0.23	0.25	0.84	0.59	0.57
	Sortino	−0.01	0.15	0.16	0.08	−0.01	0.11	0.13	0.06	0.06	0.26	0.20	0.14
Energy	Sharpe	−0.28	0.86	1.14	0.13	−0.38	0.74	1.12	0.06	0.19	0.36	0.17	0.26
	Sortino	−0.12	0.33	0.45	0.05	−0.16	0.29	0.45	0.02	0.09	0.17	0.09	0.12
Grains and seeds	Sharpe	−0.35	0.08	0.43	−0.15	−0.60	0.05	0.65	−0.26	0.08	0.13	0.05	0.10
	Sortino	−0.11	0.02	0.13	−0.04	−0.16	0.01	0.17	−0.07	0.03	0.04	0.02	0.03
Industrial metals	Sharpe	0.32	1.71	1.39	1.00	0.73	0.97	0.24	0.88	0.70	0.93	0.23	0.80
	Sortino	0.10	0.81	0.72	0.36	0.23	0.65	0.42	0.34	0.07	0.30	0.23	0.21
Livestock and meats	Sharpe	−0.27	0.47	0.74	−0.08	−0.39	0.25	0.64	−0.17	−0.16	0.12	0.28	−0.05
	Sortino	−0.06	0.09	0.15	−0.02	−0.09	0.05	0.13	−0.04	−0.04	0.03	0.07	−0.01
Precious metals	Sharpe	0.06	0.58	0.52	0.47	−0.09	0.42	0.51	0.27	0.55	0.63	0.08	0.58
	Sortino	0.03	0.16	0.13	0.13	−0.04	0.11	0.15	0.07	0.15	0.17	0.02	0.16
Softs	Sharpe	−0.62	0.29	0.91	−0.21	−0.60	0.07	0.67	−0.34	0.05	0.31	0.25	0.20
	Sortino	−0.19	0.07	0.26	−0.05	−0.16	0.02	0.18	−0.08	0.01	0.09	0.08	0.06

(Continued)

EXHIBIT 7.13 (Continued)

		Monthly Returns											
		Total Return Index				Excess Return Index				Spot Return Index			
Sector Indexes		Min	Max	Range	Mean	Min	Max	Range	Mean	Min	Max	Range	Mean
Composite	Sharpe	−0.28	0.63	0.91	0.29	0.04	0.48	0.44	0.29	0.36	0.95	0.59	0.61
	Sortino	−0.17	0.59	0.76	0.28	0.04	0.44	0.40	0.26	0.27	1.02	0.75	0.56
Energy	Sharpe	−0.18	0.98	1.16	0.22	−0.28	0.85	1.14	0.15	0.25	0.42	0.17	0.32
	Sortino	−0.18	1.15	1.33	0.25	−0.28	0.98	1.26	0.18	0.30	0.52	0.22	0.39
Grains and seeds	Sharpe	−0.44	0.06	0.50	−0.16	−3.18	−0.18	3.00	−1.09	0.08	0.11	0.03	0.09
	Sortino	−0.36	0.06	0.41	−0.14	−1.30	−0.17	1.13	−0.55	0.07	0.10	0.02	0.09
Industrial metals	Sharpe	0.32	2.11	1.78	1.08	0.75	1.85	1.10	1.09	0.58	0.95	0.37	0.77
	Sortino	0.35	3.81	3.46	1.42	0.82	3.17	2.35	1.42	0.36	1.10	0.75	0.80
Livestock and meats	Sharpe	−0.20	0.53	0.73	−0.02	−0.32	0.31	0.63	−0.10	−0.10	0.15	0.25	−0.01
	Sortino	−0.16	0.40	0.56	−0.02	−0.25	0.22	0.47	−0.08	−0.08	0.14	0.22	0.00
Precious metals	Sharpe	0.38	0.73	0.35	0.63	0.18	0.56	0.38	0.45	0.70	0.75	0.05	0.73
	Sortino	0.42	0.69	0.26	0.60	0.19	0.51	0.31	0.41	0.67	0.72	0.05	0.68
Softs	Sharpe	−0.58	0.26	0.84	−0.25	−0.73	0.09	0.82	−0.42	0.04	0.32	0.27	0.19
	Sortino	−0.49	0.23	0.71	−0.18	−0.52	0.09	0.62	−0.29	0.04	0.33	0.29	0.20

Source: Exhibit created from data obtained from Bloomberg.

values)—the number of inferior commodity futures indexes would increase by two. The number of sector indexes with a negative Sharpe ratio is largest within the excess return indexes, with 43% (daily data) and 37% (monthly data). The number is lowest within the spot return indexes, with 13% (daily data) and 8% (monthly data), respectively.

By replacing standard deviation in the Sharpe ratio with the downside deviation measure, we can obtain the Sortino ratio, a default variance-based performance measure that measures excess return over a minimum return per unit of downside deviation. This downside risk measure allows us to modify the risk concept so that only negative shifts of the return from a predetermined minimum return (target return) are perceived as risk. Hence, we implicitly consider the skewness of the distribution by including downside risk while neglecting the right side of the probability distribution.

Compared to the Sharpe ratio, the sector indexes with left-skewed return distributions appear less attractive. The positive implications for the maximum values range between 0.0 and 0.80 (industrials total return index on a daily basis, RICI with 1.51 versus 2.50). The extreme values within industrials again result from RICI's short history.

Strategies with higher Sharpe ratios also tend to have higher Sortino ratios. Hence, we see that the industrials total return indexes on a daily basis (including RICI) have 1.46, and the softs excess return indexes on a daily basis have −0.49. These are the highest and lowest average Sortino ratios, respectively. At the index provider level, the industrials—total return index on a daily basis from RICI has 2.50, followed by DBLCI with 1.65 (the highest Sortino ratio), and the softs total return index on a daily basis from GSCI has −0.86 (the lowest). Divergence among index providers is similarly compared with the Sharpe ratio.

A SOLUTION FOR HETEROGENEOUS INDEXES

In light of the existing heterogeneity and missing representation of commodity indexes, this section attempts to construct a more representative and stable benchmark. We follow Amenc and Martellini's methodology, and refer to this benchmark as an *index of indexes*.[18] The idea here is to combine the individual competing indexes so that their common inherent information is used effectively. In this case, the literature often suggests constructing an equally weighted portfolio composed of the individual indexes in order to obtain a one-dimensional overview of contrasting return

[18]Noel Amenc and Lionel Martellini, The Brave New World of Hedge Fund Indices, Working Paper, Edhec Business School, Lille, 2002.

information. Because the individual index providers consider different futures contracts with respect to choice and size, such an equally weighted index seems to represent performance more completely.

However, in following this approach, distortions may occur if the performance of an index (or a small group of indexes) differs distinctly from the majority being studied. To avoid such a bias in the information and to guarantee a high degree of representativity, we use factor analysis, which explicitly neglects the assumption of equal weights. In a statistical-econometrical sense, the best possible one-dimensional extraction of relevant information within the commodity futures sector coincides with the largest share of explained variance, that is, the largest possible share of information contained in the index provider data. With respect to factor analysis, this means the first component generated by *principal components* (PC) analysis represents the "pure" composite or sector index, because it comprises the largest share of variation among the indexes under consideration.

During the procedure of this multivariate method, the correlation structures of the individual indexes are first analyzed to reveal their interdependencies. The goal is to select a handful of factors out of the huge amount of observable variables that reproduce the data structure to a high degree, and to explain the variance in these variables with implicit factors. Mathematically speaking, M correlated variables are transformed into a reduced number of orthogonal factors F in such a way that every implicit factor can be represented as a linear combination of the initial variables.

Starting from the definition of a return matrix R:[19]

$$R = (R_{tm})_{1 \leq t \leq T,\, 1 \leq m \leq M} \tag{7.4}$$

with M variables or respective individual indexes of a sector and $T = 68$ monthly return observations, we obtain the factor notation:

$$R_{tm} = \sum_{i=1}^{m} \sqrt{\lambda_i U_{im} V_{ti}} \tag{7.5}$$

with: $(U) = (U_{im})_{1 \leq i,\, m \leq M}$ the matrix of the μ eigenvectors of $R'R$,
$(U^T) = (U_{mi})_{1 \leq i,\, m \leq M}$ the transposition of U, and
$V = (V_{ti})_{1 \leq t \leq T, 1 \leq m \leq M}$ the matrix of the eigenvectors RR'.

[19]The notation occurs primarily in accordance to Amenc and Martellini. See Amenc and Martellini, "The Brave New World of Hedge Fund Indices."

Defining $S_{im} = \sqrt{\lambda_i} U_{im}$ as the factor sensitivity of the m-th variable with respect to the i-th factor, Equation (7.5) can be written as:

$$R_{tm} = \sum_{i=1}^{1} \sqrt{\lambda_i} U_{im} V_{ti} + \varepsilon_{tm} = \sum_{i=1}^{1} S_{im} F_{ti} + \varepsilon_{tm} \tag{7.6}$$

with $i = 1 \ldots M$ factors F_t representing a set of orthogonal variables. The choice of the factors is conducted according to the Kaiser criterion. The first I factors explain an as large as possible share of the return variance of the commodity indexes, while the unexplained part is interpreted as white noise, that is, the residuals ε_{tm} are uncorrelated. The share of explained variance for the first I factors is then given by $\sum_{i=1}^{I} \lambda_i / \sum_{i=1}^{M} \lambda_i$.

In order to achieve "the best one-dimensional summary" of a set of competing indexes, we set $I = 1$ in equation (7.6). Hence, we consider only the first factor with the largest share of explained variance.

Exhibit 7.14 shows the implicit pure composite and sector indexes extracted from the PC analysis using the total return indexes as an example. Only one factor was generated in all cases, so one-dimensionality is assured and Varimax rotation to generate ordinary structure can be neglected.

The explained variance for the composite index is 83.79%. For the sector indexes, it is 96.37% for energy; 93.69% for grains and seeds; 89.13%

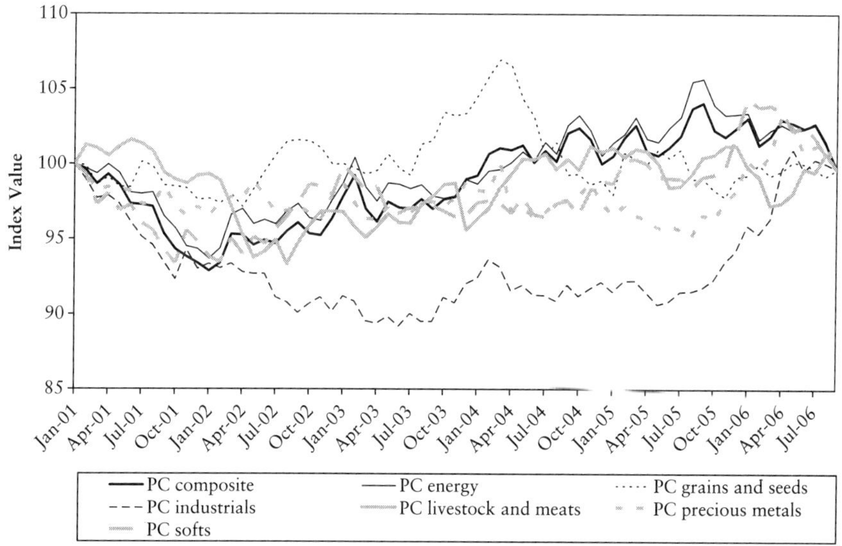

EXHIBIT 7.14 Total Return Indexes after Principal Components Analysis
Source: Exhibit created from data obtained from Bloomberg.

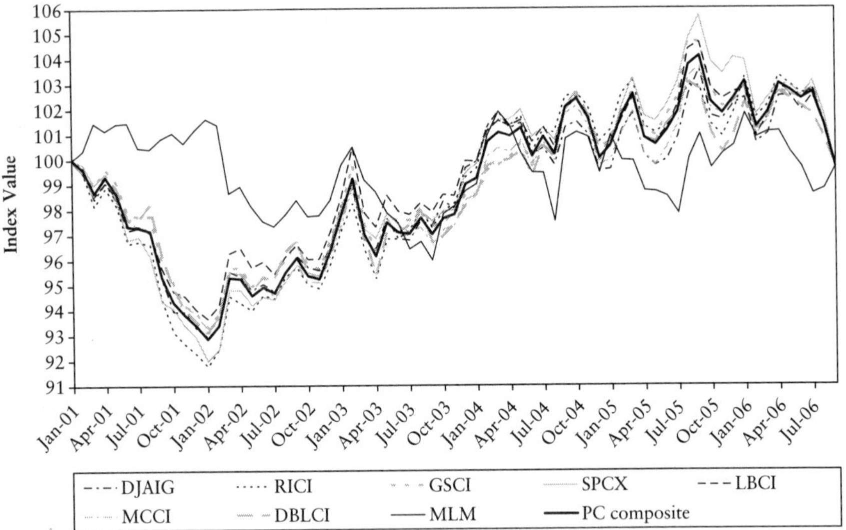

EXHIBIT 7.15 Comparison of the Initial Total Return Composite Indexes with the Implicit Total Return Composite Index
Source: Exhibit created from data obtained from Bloomberg.

for industrials; 92.14% for livestock and meats; 96.48% for precious metals; and 68.93% for soft commodities. For the sake of simplicity, we refrain from transforming the standardized factor values onto the initial variable levels when representing performance, even though the return time series are standardized before subjected to principal component analysis.

We compare the original time series of the total return composite indexes based on standardized returns with the implicit "pure" composite index after PC analysis. Exhibit 7.15 shows clearly that there are fewer distortions after the factor analysis when compared to equal weights. This is because we do not include the contrarian development of the MLM composite index in the construction of the index of indexes.[20]

CONCLUSION

A commodity futures index offers broad exposure to individual commodity sectors via the futures market. Because these, based on technical rules,

[20]The strong deviation in the development of the MLM index is motivated by the index composition, which includes commodity futures as well as financial and interest rate futures.

passive, long-only indexes represent an investible and replicable investment alternative, they can be used for benchmark purpose on one hand, and as an underlying for numerous derivative financial instruments on the other. Almost a dozen of these indexes exist, but they differ dramatically in composition and in construction, and hence exhibit divergent performance attributes.

This study analyzes the published composite and sector commodity indexes of nine chosen providers for the total return, excess return, and spot return index types. The index providers differ with regard to the number of sectors included, their selection criteria, and their index weights. Our empirical results show a potentially strong performance divergence among the individual strategies depending on which statistical ratios are chosen. On a daily basis, we observe differences for our sample period among the individual total return sector indexes with regard to annualized return performance of up to 44.90%, a Sharpe ratio of up to 1.39, a Sortino ratio of up to 2.03, correlation coefficients of up to 0.866, and volatility of up to 15.28%.

The industrials and energy sectors, as well as the composite indexes, exhibit the highest degree of heterogeneity with regard to annualized performance among all indexes. We find the highest degree of homogeneity in the grains and seeds—spot return indexes, with a difference of less than 1%. Generally speaking, the observed differences in annualized return performance are highest for the total return indexes and lowest for the spot return indexes.

Our results also display a more homogeneous picture of commodity indexes generated from daily data than from monthly data. Independent of the return frequency, the soft commodities sector shows the highest degree of heterogeneity, according to the heterogeneity indicator. As for the higher moments of the return distribution of commodity futures indexes, we can conclude that the considered commodity indexes follow a normal distribution on monthly basis, and hence are more likely to show a homogeneous picture. Also with regard to two-dimensional performance measures, such as the Sharpe or Sortino ratios, commodity futures appear to be a rather homogeneous asset class. Independent of the extent of heterogeneity observed, investors should always consider several variables when making investment decisions. Optimization on the basis of an isolated variable or index is not informative and thus not advisable.

Despite the partial homogeneity, interested investors can also judge possible investments via arithmetic means and the extreme values in the context of commodity investments instead of comparing them with a single index. Thus the realized results can serve as a kind of benchmark in the sense of an index on one hand, and as a range of statistical values on the other hand.

Alternatively, an index of indexes can be considered for comparison purposes as shown, for example, on the basis of principal components analysis. We could also verify that the factor analysis approach is connected with less distortions than an equally weighted index of indexes, and should thus be preferred by investors.

When judging our results and the conclusions reached about the partially low degree of heterogeneity within the sector indexes, note that most currently available index providers were initially founded with the boom of the commodities market, and that the available data was produced from backfilling. Hence, it is possible that the index values calculated afterward oriented themselves to the actual values of established indexes, and were therefore responsible for part of the homogeneity. To be most effective, these "new" indexes must first prove themselves with their own real history. For the interested investor, this implies that the homogeneity we find here may just be preliminary. Great care should be taken in choosing a suitable benchmark for all future investment decisions.

CHAPTER 8

Performance Characteristics of Commodity Futures

Claude Erb, CFA
Managing Director
TCW

Campbell R. Harvey, Ph.D.
J. Paul Sticht Professor of International Business
Fuqua School of Business
Duke University

Christian Kempe, CFA
Portfolio Manager
FOCAM AG

In the early years of this century, investors shunned commodity investments. This was due to their only moderate returns having been achieved in the 1980s and 1990s, their perceived high-risk profile, and because research was lacking. Little knowledge was available about this asset class. In the very-recent past, however, many investors have been moving funds into commodities since this asset class has generated remarkably good returns over the five-year period ending in 2006. Prominent institutional investors, including Harvard University, PGGM (Dutch health and welfare sector fund), and the Ontario Teachers' Pension Plan, have allocated some portion of their assets to commodities. According to Layard-Liesching, institutional investors have invested $120 billion in long-only commodity strategies, while an estimated $50 billion of this amount is invested in the Goldman Sachs Commodity Index (GSCI).[1] Akey estimates that assets linked to passive commodity indexes surged to $84 billion at the end of the first quarter of 2006, which represents a nearly doubling from the year-earlier estimate of $40 billion.[2] CalPERS estimates that open interest in commodity futures were $350 billion at the end of 2005.[3] The investment and academic communities are now showing a renewed interest in commodities. Commodities have emerged from their former obscurity and made their way to the front pages of mainstream investment magazines. This chapter purports to provide an introduction on the performance characteristics of commodity futures and provide an overview of the relevant literature.

Financial assets are held for investment purposes, whereas the ultimate use for commodities is in the production of final goods. Financial assets have an active market for borrowing and lending, which is not true for commodities. "Storing" of financial assets is cheap in comparison to commodities where storage costs can, in some cases, be prohibitively high. An inherent feature of commodities is that supply and demand will be often not in balance leading to occasional volatile price swings. The major reason for this is the long lead-time between making a production decision involving the commodity in question and its actual availability.

There are a number of options available to investors seeking commodity exposure. The most feasible approach, though, is holding a long position in collateralized commodity futures. Futures are agreements to buy or sell a commodity at a future date but at a price that is agreed upon today. Except for collateral requirements used as margin to take a position, futures do not require a cash outlay for either buyers or sellers.

HISTORICAL RETURNS

To investigate the long-term risk and return properties of commodities, Gorton and Rouwenhorst constructed a commodity futures index covering

[1]Ronald G. Layard-Liesching, "Investing in Commodities," in *Global Perspectives on Investment Management: Learning from the Leaders*, edited by Rodney N. Sullivan (Charlottesville: CFA Institute, 2006).

[2]Rian P. Akey, "Alpha, Beta and Commodities: Can a Commodities Investment Be Both a High Risk-Adjusted Return Source, and a Portfolio Hedge?" *Journal of Wealth Management* (Fall 2006), pp. 63–84.

[3]CalPERS, Investments in Commodity Futures, Presentation (March 2006).

the time period July 1959 through December 2004.[4] The index is fully collateralized by a position in 30-day U.S. Treasury bills, and contracts are rebalanced to equal weights on a monthly basis.[5] The rebalancing procedure is equivalent to a trading strategy that buys losers and sells winners at the end of each month. Temporary price fluctuations that partially revert during the next month can, thus, cause the equally weighted index to outperform the buy-and-hold index.

Gorton and Rouwenhorst compare the inflation-adjusted average annualized returns of their index under different assumptions about rebalancing with an equally weighted portfolio of spot commodity prices.[6] Their results indicate that over the whole sample period the returns for an investment in commodity futures have exceeded both the return to a holder of spot commodities and inflation. The negligible buy-and-hold spot return of 3.47% was lower than the average inflation of 4.13%, consistent with the notion that over the studied period, from 1959 to 2004, commodity prices did not keep pace with inflation. Furthermore, they find that the historical performance of the monthly rebalanced futures index is lower than that of an index that is rebalanced less frequently.

Furthermore Gorton and Rouwenhorst show that the historical risk premium for annualized monthly returns of commodity futures was about 5.23% a year, which is about equal to the risk premium of stocks, 5.65% a year, as measured by the S&P 500. At the same time, commodity futures returns exhibited lower risk than stocks; the standard deviation was 12.10% and 14.85%, respectively. With regard to a measure incorporating both return and risk, they present the Sharpe ratio, defined as the average excess return divided by its standard deviation. In this context, commodity futures returns provided a superior Sharpe ratio of 0.43 versus 0.38 and 0.26 for stocks and bonds, respectively.

In contrast, Erb and Harvey stress the obstacles involved in finding an objective representative of the asset class commodity futures and discuss

---

[4]This index initially consisted of nine commodity futures, which has gradually increased to 36. They claim that using a broad index to investigate commodity futures helps to "reduce the noise inherent in individual commodity data." See Gary Gorton and K. Geert Rouwenhorst, "Facts and Fantasies about Commodity Futures," *Financial Analyst Journal* (March–April 2006), pp. 47–68.

[5]Popular collateralized commodity futures indexes such as the Goldman Sachs Commodity Index and the Dow Jones-AIG Commodity Index are not equally weighted and weighting schemes are based on production levels for the former and liquidity measures on the latter. The Reuters/Jefferies CRB Futures Price Index was historically a geometrically averaged and equally weighted index, but after changes in its weighting methodology it is now fairly similar to the DJ-AIGCI.

[6]Gorton and Rouwenhorst, "Facts and Fantasies about Commodity Futures."

some of the challenges in determining a return figure.[7] For instance, the concept of market capitalization to determine the composition of an aggregate market, as it is applied in stock and bond markets, is irrelevant with commodity futures because the outstanding value of long and short futures contracts is exactly offsetting. Consequently, there is not an agreed-upon composition in the commodity futures market. The three most widely known commodity futures indexes (GSCI, Dow Jones-AIG Commodity Index, Reuters/Jefferies CRB Index) differ in their constituents, weighting schemes, and rebalancing rules and, thus, offer varying return and risk characteristics.[8] Erb and Harvey, therefore, propose that investors should view the different commodity indexes as different commodity portfolio strategies.

With the passage of time, the universe of commodity futures increases. When conducting a historical time series analysis, there will always be a trade-off between simultaneously providing a sufficiently long enough time period for analysis and identifying a broad representative cross-section of individual commodity futures. The GSCI offers the longest history of available commodity futures indexes. It was created in 1991 with a backfilled history that begins on January 2, 1970. The weights of the commodity futures are determined on delayed rolling five-year averages of production quantities. In 1970, the index included only four commodity futures: cattle, corn, soybeans, and wheat. As of February 2007, these original constituents make up only 13.4% of the entire index, which is, significantly smaller than the two most important components at present; that is, crude oil and Brent crude oil, which represent 48.3% of the index. The index's changing composition makes long-term historical comparisons difficult at best.

For their analysis, Erb and Harvey considered the 12 individual constituents of the GSCI that have been available since December 1982. At that time, heating oil entered the GSCI as the first energy component. Exhibit 8.1 provides a detailed review of the historical risk premiums for the individual commodity futures, the six GSCI sectors, the GSCI (Composite), and U.S. bonds and stocks. Erb and Harvey demonstrate that only four (copper, heating oil, live cattle, and cotton) of the 12 individual commodity futures provided positive excess returns. Hence, it is fair to say that the average

---

[7]Claude Erb and Campbell Harvey, "The Strategic and Tactical Value of Commodity Futures," *Financial Analyst Journal* (March–April 2006), pp. 69–97.

[8]In general, commodity return indexes can be split into three categories. Spot indexes, which measure the return stemming from changes in commodity prices. *Excess return* (ER) indexes, which measure the return of investing in commodity futures by taking both spot return and roll yield into account. Finally, *total return* (TR) indexes also incorporate the collateral yield.

EXHIBIT 8.1 Historical Excess Returns (December 1982–December 2004)

Index/Sector/Commodity Futures/Portfolio	Geometric Mean (%)	Standard Deviation (%)	Sharpe Ratio
GSCI	4.49	16.97	0.26
Sectors			
Nonenergy	−0.12	9.87	−0.01
Energy	7.06	31.23	0.23
Livestock	2.45	14.51	0.17
Agriculture	−3.13	14.35	−0.22
Industrial metals	4.00	22.82	0.18
Precious metals	−5.42	14.88	−0.36
Commodity futures			
Heating oil	5.53	32.55	0.17
Live cattle	5.07	13.98	0.36
Live hogs	−2.75	24.21	−0.11
Wheat	−5.39	21.05	−0.26
Corn	−5.63	22.65	−0.25
Soybeans	−0.35	21.49	−0.02
Sugar	−3.12	38.65	−0.08
Coffee	−6.36	39.69	−0.16
Cotton	0.10	22.64	0.00
Gold	−5.68	14.36	−0.40
Silver	−8.09	25.03	−0.32
Copper	6.17	25.69	0.24
Portfolios			
Initially EW; buy-and-hold	0.70	10.61	0.07
EW rebalanced	1.01	10.05	0.10
Average of 12 commodity futures	−1.71	25.16	−0.07
Bonds (Lehman Aggregate)	3.45	4.65	0.74
Stocks (S&P 500)	7.35	15.30	0.48

Source: Erb and Harvey, "The Strategic and Tactical Value of Commodity Futures," p. 74.

annualized excess return of the average individual commodity futures has been approximately zero. Exhibit 8.1 gives further information for the excess returns of an initially *equally weighted* (EW) buy-and-hold portfolio, of an EW portfolio rebalanced monthly, and of the average of the 12 commodity futures. The EW portfolio, rebalanced monthly, had an excess return of 1.01% in a year, which appears much smaller than the excess return of the GSCI of 4.49%.[9]

In another study, Kat and Oomen investigated 42 different commodity futures covering the period January 1965 to February 2005, using daily settlement prices (where available). They conclude that most commodity futures did not offer a risk premium. Kat and Oomen cautiously remind investors "how dangerous it is to draw general conclusions about the risk premium in commodity futures by only looking at the returns on one specific index."[10]

Gorton and Rouwenhorst empirically investigated the distribution of monthly returns of commodity futures, stocks, and bonds. Over the 1959 to 2004 time period, they find that commodity futures monthly returns had a standard deviation of 3.47, compared to 4.27 for stocks and 2.45 for bonds. The authors further investigate the return patterns and, therefore, state both skewness and kurtosis. They furthermore provide evidence that all three asset classes cannot be fully described by a normal distribution. The skewness of stock returns equaled −0.34; that is, investors faced a distribution that is characterized by many small gains, however, by a higher probability of extreme losses in comparison to normal distribution. This introduces undesirable additional risk to stock investors. Contrarily, there were substantial positive price outliers with commodity futures; the skewness was 0.71. Commodity futures returns had a positive kurtosis of 4.53, indicating a distribution that is more peaked and has more realizations in the tails than would be warranted by a normal distribution.[11]

Commodity markets are regularly faced with a constellation of supply/demand disequilibrium. In the short run, new supplies of commodities cannot be instantly drilled, grown, or mined. In the absence of immediate new supplies, there are only two variables that can adjust to equilibrate supply and demand: a change in inventory and/or a change in price. In a first scenario, consider an unexpected surge in demand for oil, which could have been caused by particularly cold weather or military actions. In times of adequate inventories, reserve stockpiles will decrease and the price will possibly go up slightly or might even stay constant. However, if there are not

---

[9]Erb and Harvey, "The Strategic and Tactical Value of Commodity Futures."

[10]Harry M. Kat and Roel C. A. Oomen, "What Every Investor Should Know about Commodities, Part I: Univariate Return Analysis," *Journal of Investment Management* 5, no. 1 (2007), pp. 1–25.

[11]Gorton and Rouwenhorst, "Facts and Fantasies about Commodity Futures."

sufficient inventories, only the price can respond, hence it will move up sharply within days. In a second, opposing scenario, the market might be confronted with an ample supply, for example, one caused by a recent rise in OPEC output quotas. Under these circumstances, the oil market has two ways to react: a build-up in inventories and a price decrease. This asymmetrical pattern is the reason behind the returns' positive skewness.[12]

RETURN DECOMPOSITION AND DIVERSIFICATION RETURN

While it is surely important to calculate and know historical returns, investors must formulate forward-looking expectations for future returns. This issue is addressed by decomposing the return into building blocks.

Erb and Harvey suggest that the return of a cash-collateralized portfolio of commodity futures can be decomposed into three components:[13]

- Cash return = Collateral return
- Excess return = Spot return + Roll return
- Diversification return[14]

Regarding the first component, in a collateralized commodity futures index investment for every desired US$1 in commodity futures exposure, the investor sets aside US$1 in collateral such as Treasury bills or similar cash equivalents. The position is, thus, not leveraged but fully collateralized. The cash return depends on the type of collateral used. Assuming the investor uses Treasury bills as collateral, the cash return (collateral return) will be equal to the Treasury bill rate.

The second building block comprises the excess return as the sum of spot return and roll return. The spot return is the change in the commodity price in the spot market and the most straightforward component for investors to understand. This is the directional exposure to commodities most investors require when their investment decision is based on a bullish outlook for commodities. Occasionally investors do delve into the

[12]Hilary Till, "Risk Management Lessons in Leveraged Commodity Futures Trading," *Commodities* (September 2002), pp. 1–4.
[13]Erb and Harvey, "The Strategic and Tactical Value of Commodity Futures."
[14]The term *diversification return* was coined by Booth and Fama. See David Booth and Eugene Fama, "Diversification Return and Asset Contributions," *Financial Analysts Journal* (May–June 1992), pp. 26–32.

question of which commodities offer the highest expected future returns. It may come as a surprise to some of these investors that spot prices have not been a meaningful driver of historical total returns. In this context, Beenen writes, "Over the long term price movements have contributed little to the return, as commodities tend to mean revert to inflation/cost of production."[15] Futures investors almost never intend to take delivery of a commodity. Instead, they wish to maintain a commodity futures position. This is done by continuously "rolling over" market exposure, that is selling an expiring futures contract and buying a yet-to-expire contract. The roll return stems from this procedure. Technically speaking, the roll return depends on the return from "rolling" up or down the futures curve, depending on the shape of the curve. There are two distinct term structures: backwardation and contango. With backwardation, futures prices decline with time to maturity (futures price is at a discount to spot price and "rolls up" to the spot price as the delivery date approaches). Earning a roll yield when a futures curve is backwardated is analogous to the returns a long-term bond investor earns from rolling down a steeply sloped yield curve. With contango, futures prices rise with time to maturity (futures price is at a premium to spot price and "rolls down" to the spot price as the delivery date approaches). It is important to note that the roll yield is not related to direct exposure to actual commodities. The spot price can stay constant (spot return equals zero), but an investor will still be able to earn a roll return if a backwardated future was purchased. With a contango future and a constant spot price, the reverse occurs. Under these circumstances the investor will face a loss from the futures contract converging to a lower spot price. This is known as negative roll return. In summary, only when the future spot price deviates from the futures price there will be a roll yield. Obviously, the future spot price is unknown at inception of a future agreement. The roll yield can be considered to be a risk premium priced into the future contract to compensate the holder for bearing the commodity price risk. In Exhibit 8.2, Erb and Harvey illustrate how important roll returns have been in explaining commodity futures' excess returns from December 1982 through May 2004. The adjusted coefficient of determination (R^2) indicates that roll returns described 91.6% of the variation of individual commodity futures returns. It is worth

[15]Jelle Beenen, "Commodity Investing: A Pension Fund Perspective," *Futures Industry* (September–October 2005), pp. 18–22.

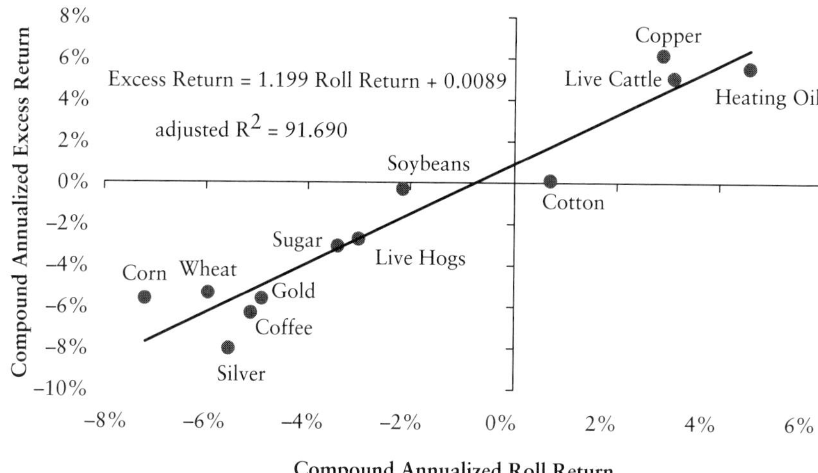

EXHIBIT 8.2 Commodity Excess Returns and Roll Returns, December 1982 to May 2004
Source: Erb and Harvey, "The Strategic and Tactical Value of Commodity Futures," p. 80. Copyright 2006 CFA Institute. Reproduced and republished from the *Financial Analysts Journal* with permission from CFA Institute. All rights reserved.

noting that, in a historical perspective, roll returns have thus been the dominant driver of commodity futures' performance.[16]

As a third building block, Erb and Harvey refer to the diversification return stemming from constructing portfolios by combing different assets. Due to different price behavior of the portfolio holdings, the better performing constituents gain in relative weight versus the worse performing constituents. Rebalancing occurs when the weights of the different portfolio constituents need to be adjusted back to index weights. The return for an equally weighted portfolio can exceed the average returns for its constituents. Erb and Harvey dubbed this the *rebalancing effect* or, metaphorically, "turning water into wine." The so-called "diversification return" is defined

[16]A number of other studies have also shown that, over long time frames, roll yields are the main, reliable source of return for commodity futures investors, typically accounting for the majority of a long commodity futures investment. Please refer to, for example, Kat and Oomen, "What Every Investor Should Know about Commodities, Part I: Univariate Return Analysis"; Daniel J. Nash, "Long-Term Investing in Commodities," *Global Pensions Quarterly* (January 2001), pp. 25–31; and Hilary Till and Joseph Eagleeye, "Timing is Everything, Especially with a Commodity Index," *Futures Magazine* (August 2003).

as the difference between a rebalanced portfolio's geometric return and the weighted average geometric return of the portfolio's constituents. Erb and Harvey coined diversification return as "the one free lunch that can raise a portfolio's geometric return."[17] Exhibit 8.3 describes the mechanics of the portfolio diversification return for an equally weighted portfolio using historical annual excess returns for the GSCI heating oil index and the S&P 500 over the 1994 to 2003 period. Heating oil had a geometric annual excess return of 8.21%; the S&P 500 had a geometric annual excess return of 6.76%; and the equally weighted average of these two returns was 7.49%. If an investor had invested in an equally weighted portfolio with annual rebalancing toward equal weights, the geometric excess return would have been 10.95%. This return is significantly larger than the return of either of

EXHIBIT 8.3 Mechanics of the Diversification Return: S&P 500 and Heating Oil, 1994–2003

	Heating Oil Excess Return	S&P 500 Excess Return	Equal-Weighted Excess Return
1994	19.96%	−2.92%	8.52%
1995	7.73%	31.82%	19.78%
1996	67.37%	17.71%	42.54%
1997	−35.06%	28.11%	−3.48%
1998	−50.51%	23.51%	−13.50%
1999	73.92%	16.30%	45.11%
2000	66.71%	−15.06%	25.82%
2001	−36.62%	−15.97%	−26.30%
2002	41.40%	−23.80%	8.80%
2003	21.90%	27.62%	24.76%
Geometric return	8.21%	6.76%	10.95%
Standard deviation	43.51%	19.85%	21.26%
Weighted average Geometric mean			7.49%
Diversification return			3.46%

Source: Erb and Harvey, "The Strategic and Tactical Value of Commodity Futures," p. 85. Copyright 2006 CFA Institute. Reproduced and republished from the *Financial Analysts Journal* with permission from CFA Institute. All rights reserved.

[17]Campbell calls portfolio diversification the one "free lunch" in finance because it allows an investor to reduce a portfolio's standard deviation of return without reducing the portfolio's arithmetic return. See John Y. Campbell, "Diversification: A Bigger Free Lunch," *Canadian Investment Review* (Winter 2000), pp. 14–15.

the two portfolio constituents. The diversification return is simply the difference between 10.95% and 7.49%, or 3.46%.[18]

Erb and Harvey illustrate in Exhibit 8.4 that a higher average standard deviation for all individual portfolio constituents and a lower correlation of returns between each constituent lead to a higher diversification return.[19]

Erb and Harvey criticize Gorton and Rouwenhorst for mistaking a diversification return for a risk premium. Gorton and Rouwenhorst report a 4.52% excess return for their equally weighted and rebalanced portfolio.[20]

EXHIBIT 8.4 Diversification Return Drivers

		Diversification Return Number of Securities in Portfolio				
Average Correlation	Average Standard Deviation	10	15	20	25	30
0.0	10%	0.45%	0.47%	0.48%	0.48%	0.48%
0.1	10%	0.41%	0.42%	0.43%	0.43%	0.44%
0.2	10%	0.36%	0.37%	0.38%	0.38%	0.38%
0.3	10%	0.32%	0.33%	0.33%	0.34%	0.34%
0.0	20%	1.80%	1.87%	1.90%	1.92%	1.93%
0.1	20%	1.62%	1.68%	1.71%	1.73%	1.74%
0.2	20%	1.44%	1.49%	1.52%	1.54%	1.55%
0.3	20%	1.26%	1.31%	1.33%	1.34%	1.35%
0.0	30%	4.05%	4.20%	4.28%	4.32%	4.35%
0.1	30%	3.65%	3.78%	3.85%	3.89%	3.92%
0.2	30%	3.24%	3.36%	3.42%	3.46%	3.48%
0.3	30%	2.84%	2.94%	2.99%	3.02%	3.05%
0.0	40%	7.20%	7.47%	7.60%	7.68%	7.73%
0.1	40%	6.48%	6.72%	6.84%	6.91%	6.96%
0.2	40%	5.76%	5.97%	6.08%	6.14%	6.19%
0.3	40%	5.04%	5.23%	5.32%	5.38%	5.41%

Source: Erb and Harvey, "The Strategic and Tactical Value of Commodity Futures," p. 86. Copyright 2006 CFA Institute. Reproduced and republished from the *Financial Analysts Journal* with permission from CFA Institute. All rights reserved.

[18]Erb and Harvey, "The Strategic and Tactical Value of Commodity Futures."

[19]On page 86 of their article, Erb and Harvey also present a formula for the diversification return: $½(1 - 1/K)\sigma^2(1 - \sigma)$ where K = number of securities, σ^2 = average variance of all portfolio constituents, and σ = average correlation of portfolio constituents.

[20]Gorton and Rouwenhorst, "Facts and Fantasies about Commodity Futures."

Erb and Harvey approximate a diversification return for the index Gorton and Rouwenhorst used in the range of 3.0% through 4.5%. This comprises almost all of the excess return. This complicates the argument for a risk premium. In response to Erb and Harvey, Gorton and Rouwenhorst published a note which draws the conclusion that "diversification returns are a mathematical property of geometric averages . . . It is not common to subtract this difference from the risk premium estimate."[21]

CORRELATIONS

Allocating funds to an asset that exhibits a negative correlation to a given portfolio can improve the return and risk characteristics of that portfolio even if the newly allocated asset is characterized by a substantially higher stand-alone risk. Gorton and Rouwenhorst reveal that commodity futures returns have been negatively correlated with returns of stocks and bonds at quarterly, annual, and five-year horizons. They find that at a five-year horizon commodity future returns had negative correlation coefficients of −0.42 and −0.25 with stocks and bonds, respectively. Their numbers further indicate that correlation patterns increase with the holding period and they conclude that diversification benefits are greatest when measured over longer time horizons.

Thus, the question arises, why are correlations negative? Or, asked differently, why does commodity price behavior deviate from patterns observed in prices of financial assets such as stocks and bonds? There are several reasons for this, the most important one being a positive reaction to inflation and different investment behavior over the business cycle. Commodity markets are characterized by unique idiosyncrasies. For example, such events as droughts, frosts, extreme weather conditions, strikes and current economic conditions have the potential to severely impact commodity prices, while at the same time such events have only a very limited effect on stocks and bonds.

In adverse market circumstances, stocks and bonds often fall in tandem. During unfavorable periods, noncorrelation, or better, negative correlation, appears to be especially valuable to investors. For this reason, Gorton and Rouwenhorst isolated the 5% and 1% worst-equity market months during 1959 and 2004. They observe that diversification benefits from investments in commodity futures persist. Gorton and Rouwenhorst show that, during the 1% of months with lowest stock returns when stocks fell, on average,

[21]For a more complete discussion, see G. Gorton and K. Geert Rouwenhorst, A Note on Erb and Harvey, Yale ICF Working Paper No. 06–02, January 2006.

13.87% a month, commodity futures returned an average of 2.38%. In another study, Idzorek analyzes annual data between 1970 and 2004 finding eight years that U.S. stocks had negative total returns. During these eight years, while U.S. stocks suffered a −12.28% average arithmetic annual return, commodities offered a high average arithmetic annual return of 19.02%.[22] These empirical findings provide evidence that commodity futures have historically performed significantly better when stocks and bonds falter most.

While Gorton and Rouwenhorst examined the correlation properties of their broad commodity futures index, Erb and Harvey pursued an extensive study to obtain correlation patterns in individual commodity futures and specific commodity futures sectors. Exhibit 8.5 illustrates that average correlations are low. The average correlation of the 12 commodity futures with the GSCI is 0.20 and the average cross-correlation of individual commodity futures is only 0.09 providing evidence that they are driven by somewhat unrelated fundamentals. Agriculture and livestock commodities, for example, are more likely to be affected by seasonal weather and harvest productivity patterns whereas energy and industrial metals mostly depend on the current state of world economic growth. Amid this high degree of heterogeneity in commodity futures returns, the "average commodity" does not appear to exist. Erb and Harvey suggest that commodity futures represent "a market of individual dissimilar assets." In practice it is, therefore, possible to be in a general uptrend or downtrend market for commodities, while at the same time an individual commodity exhibits an entirely opposite price move.

INFLATION

The ultimate objective of investors is to preserve the real purchasing power of their assets. For that reason, inflation must be considered. Ideally, portfolio assets exhibit a positive relationship to inflation. Unfortunately, many traditional asset classes are vulnerable to high inflation and represent a poor inflation hedge. Analyzing the hedging properties of commodity futures

[22]Thomas M. Idzorek, "Strategic Asset Allocation and Commodities," Chapter 6 in *Intelligent Commodity Investing*, edited by Hilary Till and Joseph Eagleeye (London: Risk Books, 2007). To analyze the return properties of commodity futures, Idzorek formed an equally weighted composite of four total return commodity indexes: Goldman Sachs Commodities Index (GSCI), Dow Jones-AIG Commodity Index (DJ-AIG), Reuters/Jefferies CRB Index (RJ-CRB), and Gorton and Rouwenhorst Commodity Index (GRCI).

EXHIBIT 8.5 Excess Return Correlations, December 1982 to May 2004 (monthly observations)

A. Correlation of sectors and commodities

	GSCI	Nonenergy	Energy	Livestock	Agriculture	Industrial Metals	Precious Metals
Sector							
Nonenergy	0.36						
Energy	0.91	0.06					
Livestock	0.20	0.63	0.01				
Agriculture	0.24	0.78	0.01	0.12			
Industrial metals	0.13	0.31	0.03	−0.02	0.17		
Precious metals	0.19	0.20	0.14	0.03	0.08	0.20	
Commodity							
Heating oil	0.87	0.08	0.94	0.04	0.00	0.05	0.13
Cattle	0.12	0.50	−0.03	0.84	0.07	0.03	0.01
Hogs	0.21	0.52	0.06	0.81	0.13	−0.06	0.05
Wheat	0.25	0.66	0.06	0.18	0.79	0.05	0.06
Corn	0.14	0.58	−0.03	0.10	0.78	0.12	−0.01
Soybeans	0.20	0.58	0.02	0.11	0.72	0.18	0.14
Sugar	0.03	0.21	−0.06	−0.05	0.35	0.14	0.05
Coffee	−0.01	0.15	−0.04	−0.07	0.23	0.07	0.01
Cotton	0.11	0.25	0.06	0.00	0.27	0.17	0.04
Gold	0.20	0.16	0.16	0.01	0.07	0.18	0.97
Silver	0.08	0.19	0.02	0.02	0.10	0.19	0.77
Copper	0.15	0.36	0.04	0.01	0.22	0.94	0.20

B. Correlation of commodities											
	Heating Oil	Cattle	Hogs	Wheat	Corn	Soybeans	Sugar	Coffee	Cotton	Gold	Silver
Heating oil											
Cattle	0.00										
Hogs	0.06	0.37									
Wheat	0.06	0.12	0.17								
Corn	−0.04	0.05	0.11	0.52							
Soybeans	0.05	0.03	0.14	0.43	0.70						
Sugar	−0.04	0.02	−0.10	0.11	0.12	0.09					
Coffee	−0.07	−0.06	−0.06	0.00	0.03	0.07	−0.01				
Cotton	0.05	−0.06	0.06	0.05	0.11	0.18	−0.02	−0.01			
Gold	0.15	−0.02	0.04	0.07	−0.01	0.14	0.02	0.00	0.03		
Silver	0.02	−0.01	0.05	0.03	0.09	0.13	0.07	0.04	0.04	0.66	
Copper	0.07	0.03	−0.02	0.08	0.16	0.23	0.14	0.11	0.19	0.18	0.21

Source: Erb and Harvey, "The Strategic and Tactical Value of Commodity Futures," p. 75.

Note: Average correlation: GSCI with commodity sectors, 0.34; GSCI with individual commodities, 0.20; heating oil with other commodities, 0.03; and individual commodities, 0.09.

appears complicated, as Akey points out, that "we have not experienced an inflationary environment of any magnitude in the last quarter-century and we do not have the luxury of backfilling our active data set to include information from the 1970s."[23]

Gorton and Rouwenhorst show for the time period from July 1959 to December 2004, that on a one-year horizon, stocks and bonds had correlation coefficients of −0.19 and −0.32, respectively. These numbers imply that traditional asset classes such as stocks and bonds usually suffer in periods of high inflation. Why do these conventional asset classes provide a poor inflation hedge? Bonds are nominally denominated assets providing a predetermined stream of cash flows in the future. The problem the bond investor could face is that inflation will be higher than it will be expected. In this adverse situation, the real purchasing power of a bond's cash flow will fall short of expectations. Considering an investment in stocks, rising inflation usually increases supply costs to companies and, assuming sticky output prices, higher costs squeeze margins resulting in lower profits and deflated stock prices. One could also argue that, when applying a dividend discount model, inflation decreases the present value of future dividends through a greater nominal interest rate.

In contrast, commodity futures' prices offer opposing inflation hedging properties, that is, they are positively correlated with inflation. Kat and Oomen show based on daily settlement prices on 142 different commodity futures contracts for the time period from January 1965 to February 2005 that commodity futures returns are positively correlated with unexpected inflation.[24] Considering a one-year horizon, Gorton and Rouwenhorst show that the correlation coefficient between commodity futures and inflation between July 1959 and December 2004 was 0.29. One explanation that Erb and Harvey provide for positive correlations with inflation is that commodities are, to a certain extent, linked to inflation because they represent about a 40% weight in the U.S. Consumer Price Index (CPI).

Erb and Harvey, additionally, investigated the inflation sensitivity of individual commodity futures. They provide evidence that not all commodity futures can be considered as a good inflation hedge. The authors demonstrate that commodity futures with the highest historical roll return had the highest correlation with inflation as can be viewed in Exhibit 8.6. In the past, commodities that were difficult-to-store, such as heating oil, copper,

[23]Akey, "Alpha, Beta and Commodities: Can a Commodities Investment Be Both a High Risk-Adjusted Return Source, and a Portfolio Hedge?"

[24]Harry M. Kat and Roel C. A. Oomen, "What Every Investor Should Know about Commodities, Part II: Multivariate Return Analysis," *Journal of Investment Management* 5, no. 3 (2007).

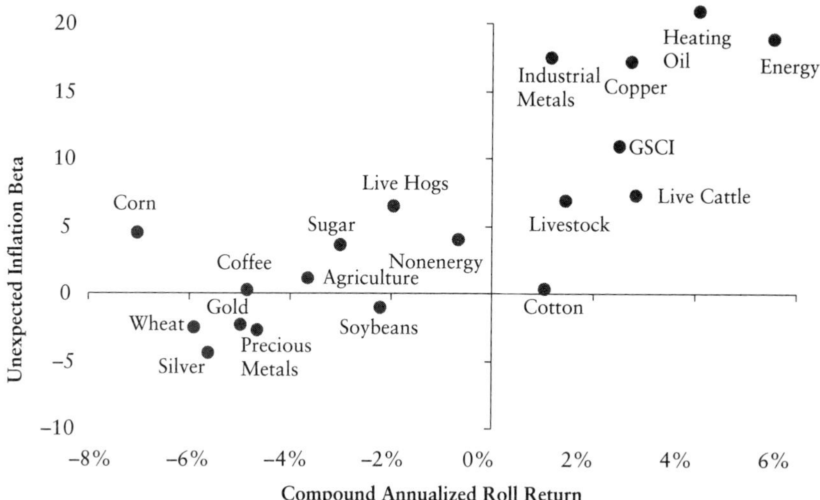

EXHIBIT 8.6 Unexpected Inflation Betas and Roll Returns, December 1982 to December 2003

Source: Erb and Harvey, "The Strategic and Tactical Value of Commodity Futures," p. 83. Copyright 2006 CFA Institute. Reproduced and republished from the *Financial Analysts Journal* with permission from CFA Institute. All rights reserved.

and live cattle had both high roll yields and positive inflation betas. Erb and Harvey give the following conclusions regarding inflation exposure:

- Individual commodity futures have experienced varying exposures to inflation.
- The commodity futures' magnitude of hedging has been correlated with its roll yield.
- The ability of a commodity futures portfolio to serve as an inflation hedge is driven by the composition of the portfolio.
- A portfolio that historically maximized the ability to hedge inflation focused on commodity futures that are difficult to store.

RETURNS OVER THE BUSINESS CYCLE

It was already demonstrated that commodity futures exhibit negative correlation with both stocks and bonds. One of the reasons for this phenomenon is their opposite reaction to inflation, as shown in the previous section.

Another reason is the different behavior they have shown over the business cycle. Obviously, asset returns do vary with the stage of the business cycle. However, what is the reasoning behind this? A good starting point in answering this question is to ponder what commodity futures, stocks, and bonds conceptually represent. A commodity futures' long-position is a claim on an unanticipated commodity price change where there are no cash flows involved. In contrast, stocks represent company ownership and a share in residual cash flows. Bonds represent a claim on debt repayment and, in contrast to stocks, the bondholder receives a stream of cash flows. The present value of future cash flows depends on the size and timing of the cash flow and the interest rate assumed. Because the future is uncertain, it is expectation, or more precisely the change in expectations, that drives the performance of stocks and bonds. In this context, current business conditions play only a minor role. Generally, both stocks and bonds tend to perform best when economic conditions are at their worst and the potential for improvement is highest. On the other hand, when the economy is strong and the potential for negative surprises is great, stocks and bonds tend to perform worst. In contrast, commodities are more directly tied to current economic conditions. In summary, commodities tend to generate their best returns in periods of high economic activity and their worst returns in periods of low activity.

Gorton and Rouwenhorst identified seven complete business cycles during the measurement period 1959 through 2004. They show that commodity futures offered a positive average return of 3.74% in an early stage of a recession, while stocks and bonds lost on average 18.64% and 3.88%, respectively. The returns reversed in a late stage of a recession: stocks and bonds yielded high positive performance, while commodity futures had negative returns. Gorton and Rouwenhorst caution that these results are *ex post facto* and purely descriptive as business cycles can only be dated "after the fact." These findings, however, demonstrate that investments in commodity futures have the capability to add diversity to a traditional portfolio consisting of stocks and bonds.

TACTICAL ASSET ALLOCATION

Gorton and Rouwenhorst suggest that a diversified investment in commodity futures is capable of earning a risk premium equivalent to a stock investment. The authors depict no active strategy approaches.

Contrarily, Erb and Harvey describe four tactical approaches which will now be examined. These four strategies are based on two primary ideas: pursuing a momentum strategy, and using the information content of

EXHIBIT 8.7 GSCI Momentum Returns, December 1969 to May 2004

Trailing Annual Excess Return	12/1969–5/2004	12/1969–12/1982	12/1982–5/2004
Greater than 0	13.47%	17.49%	11.34%
Less than 0	−5.49%	−9.89%	−4.07%

Source: Erb and Harvey, "The Strategic and Tactical Value of Commodity Futures," p. 91.

the term structure. Some of these strategies go beyond conventional long-only investments and may also encompass going short particular commodity futures. The first two strategies aim to profit from return momentum. The underlying assumption is that movements in asset prices over a particular period of time, for example 6 or 12 months, tend to predict future movements in the same direction.

First, Erb and Harvey exploit a strategy on the GSCI, which goes long the index for one month if the previous one-year's excess return was positive, and going short the index if the prior one-year's excess return was negative. Exhibit 8.7 portrays the results of this strategy. The momentum effect is evident over different time intervals, although it appears strongest in the first 13 years of the sample period, with returns of 17.49% if the GSCI had positive momentum versus −9.89% if the GSCI had negative momentum.

Subsequently, a momentum strategy on individual commodity futures is presented. In this approach, an equally weighted portfolio of the four commodity futures having the highest prior 12-month returns (winner portfolio), a portfolio of the four worst-performing commodity futures (loser portfolio), and a long-short portfolio are created. The long-short portfolio achieved the highest excess return of 10.8%. The results are reproduced in Exhibit 8.8. Exhibit 8.9 shows the development of an investment according to the different strategies.

Alternatively, a momentum strategy could apply the principle of going long those individual commodity futures that had positive returns over the past 12 months and going short those that had negative returns. In the event that all individual commodity futures had negative past returns, all portfolio positions would be short. The opposite constellation would be true if all commodity futures had positive past returns, all portfolio positions would then be long. Exhibit 8.10 displays the growth of $1 invested in this trend-following strategy (rebalanced monthly) in comparison to an equally weighted portfolio of the 12 components of the GSCI and the GSCI itself. The trend-following portfolio had the highest return of 6.54% versus

EXHIBIT 8.8 Momentum Portfolios (December 1982–May 2004)

Portfolio	Excess Return
Winner	7.0%
Loser	−3.4%
Long-Short	10.8%

Source: Erb and Harvey, "The Strategic and Tactical Value of Commodity Futures," p. 92. Copyright 2006 CFA Institute. Reproduced and republished from the *Financial Analysts Journal* with permission from CFA Institute. All rights reserved.

4.39% for the long-only GSCI and only 1.01% for the equally weighted portfolio.[25]

The third and fourth strategies employ the information content of the term structure of future prices, which can be considered the most useful information for identifying prospective performance. The GSCI futures

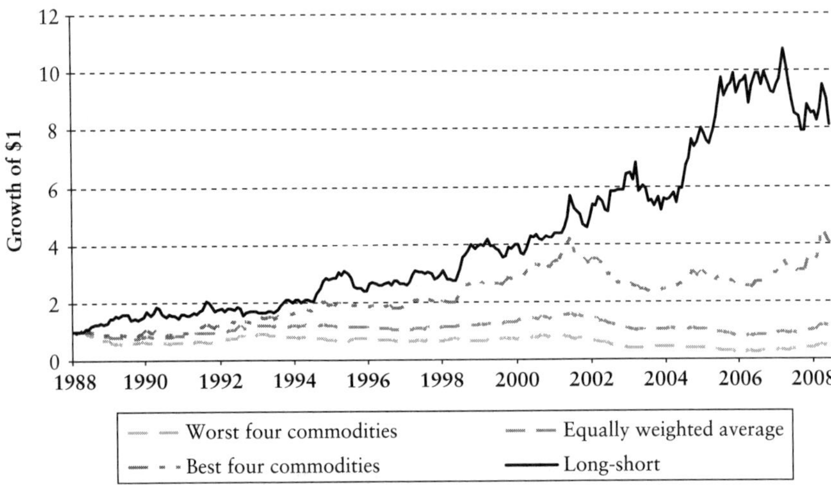

EXHIBIT 8.9 Momentum Portfolios, December 1982 to May 2004
Source: Erb and Harvey, "The Strategic and Tactical Value of Commodity Futures," p. 92 retained. Copyright 2006 CFA Institute. Reproduced and republished from the *Financial Analysts Journal* with permission from CFA Institute. All rights reserved.

[25] Erb and Harvey, "The Strategic and Tactical Value of Commodity Futures."

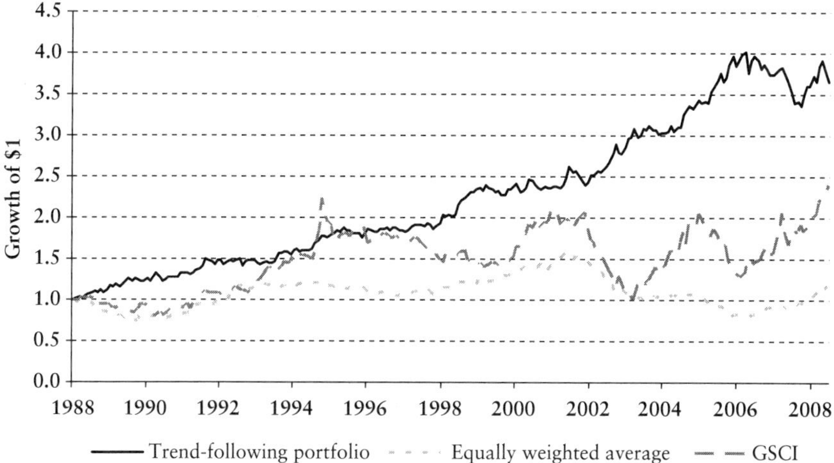

EXHIBIT 8.10 Individual Commodity Momentum Portfolio, December 1982 to May 2004

Source: Erb and Harvey, "The Strategic and Tactical Value of Commodity Futures," p. 93.

contract has been in backwardation about 50% of the time since its inception in 1992.

In a third strategy, Erb and Harvey present a relatively straightforward approach in using the information content in the term structure of the GSCI. They suggest a strategy which goes long the GSCI when it is backwardated and short when it is contangoed. As Exhibit 8.11 illustrates, for

EXHIBIT 8.11 GSCI Term Structure Strategy (July 1992–May 2004)

Strategy	Compound Annualized Excess Return	Annualized Standard Deviation	Sharpe Ratio
Long if GSCI backwardated	11.25%	18.71%	0.60
Long if GSCI contangoed	−5.01%	17.57%	−0.29
Long if GSCI backwardated; short if GSCI contangoed	8.18%	18.12%	0.45

Source: Erb and Harvey, "The Strategic and Tactical Value of Commodity Futures," p. 93.

the time period 1992 until 2004 the annualized excess return of this long-short strategy was 8.18%. The results for being long, when the GSCI was backwardated produced an annual excess return of 11.25%. On the contrary, an investor who would have been long if the term structure had been contangoed experienced a negative annualized excess return of −5.01%. These are impressive results, and they provide investors with an important yardstick. Historically, the payoff to timing, based on the term structure, has been a successful strategy. Assuming that the same factors will prevail in the future, pursuing the same, or some similar, strategy appears an appropriate one for a prudent investor.

Erb and Harvey present a fourth strategy: the investor goes long the six commodities that each month had the highest ratio of nearby futures price to next-nearby futures price and short the six commodities with the lowest ratio of nearby futures price to next-nearby futures price. From the results in Exhibit 8.12, it is evident that commodity futures price term structures have given investors a valuable tactical allocation framework for allocations among individual commodity futures. A long-only GSCI investment yielded the best annualized excess return of 4.49%. However, also taking risk into consideration, the long-short portfolio offered a Sharpe ratio that is almost twice as high as the Sharpe ratio for the long-only GSCI and more than four times higher than the ratio for the equally weighted portfolio. Erb and Harvey conclude: "Historically, the term structure seems to have been an effective tactical indicator of when to go long or go short a broadly diversified commodity futures portfolio."

EXHIBIT 8.12 Term Structure Strategy on Individual Commodities' Term Structures, December 1982 to May 2004

Strategy	Compound Annualized Excess Return	Annualized Standard Deviation	Sharpe Ratio
Long backwardated commodities and short contangoed commodities	3.65%	7.79%	0.47
Long EW portfolio	1.01%	10.05%	0.10
Long GSCI	4.49%	16.97%	0.26

Source: Erb and Harvey, "The Strategic and Tactical Value of Commodity Futures," p. 93.

CONCLUSION

In this chapter, we provided an overview of the performance characteristics of commodity futures. Based on the cited studies we can show that commodity futures have low correlations to stocks and bonds, are a hedge against inflation, and thus provide diversification benefits to a traditional portfolio. Historically, individual commodity futures exhibited unique characteristics complicating the argument that the universe of all commodity futures represents an asset class. The intrinsic characteristics of commodity futures and the high degree of heterogeneity argue for active investing instead of a purely passive investment. Added value can be achieved through skillful management, such as applying, for example, momentum-based strategies and approaches based on term structures of future prices. Some authors claim that return prospects from commodity futures may be lower than history suggests.[26] It is conceivable that with commodity investors, versus commodity commercials, taking up an ever increasing share of the commodity futures markets that future roll returns could diminish.[27] Many commodity futures term structures today imply lower, or even negative, future roll returns.[28] Therefore, potential commodity investors must pursue a diligent and careful analysis over the entire universe of commodity futures.

Although prudent investors might assume much lower future returns from investments in commodity futures than historical returns suggest, such positive characteristics as commodities' uncorrelated nature to bonds and

---

[26]Wilshire currently forecasts a 5.5% annual return for commodity futures, which consists of 2.5% inflation plus 3.0% for the combined roll and rebalancing returns. See Steven Foresti and Thomas Toth, Commodity Futures Investing: Is All That Glitters Gold? Presentation, Wilshire Associates, Inc. (March 2005); Barclays' research comes up with a conservative return forecast of 6.0% annual return for commodity futures, which consists of 2.0% real spot return plus a 3.25% risk-free rate estimate plus a 0.75% roll yield estimate. See David W. Burkart, *Commodities and Real-Return Strategies in the Investment Mix* (Charlottesville: CFA Institute, 2006).

[27]See also Kat and Oomen, "What Every Investor Should Know about Commodities, Part I: Univariate Return Analysis."

[28]Akey notes that, "While many attribute the move from backwardation to contango as a fund-driven phenomenon (i.e., the long-biased investor money flowing into the asset class through index-linked products have disrupted a balance in the term structure), others find such analysis ignores the backwardation in many other commodity markets." See Akey, "Alpha, Beta and Commodities: Can a Commodities Investment Be Both a High Risk-Adjusted Return Source, and a Portfolio Hedge?"

stocks, and their inflation hedging properties, presumably will continue to exist in the future although there is no guarantee.[29] Therefore, the impetus behind a strategic allocation must not necessarily be to seek high investment returns but, alternatively, to achieve an increase in portfolio diversification while reducing the overall portfolio risk.

[29]Kat and Oomen even argue "a zero or even negative risk premium is not necessarily a reason to refrain from allocating to a particular asset class. It very much depends on what the remainder of the return distribution looks like. As long as the lack of expected return is compensated by significant positive skewness and/or low or even negative correlation with other asset classes, it may still make sense to invest in it, despite the low expected return." See Kat and Oomen, "What Every Investor Should Know about Commodities, Part I: Univariate Return Analysis."

CHAPTER 9

Statistical Analysis of Commodity Futures Returns

Reinhold Hafner, Ph.D.
Managing Director
risklab germany GmbH

Maria Heiden
Analyst
Varengold Wertpapierhandelsbank AG

Commodity investments have become increasingly popular among investors over the last couple of years. Initially reserved for high-net-worth individuals, commodities progressively drew the attention of private and institutional investors. There seem to be two main reasons for the attractiveness of commodities. First, commodities tend to offer diversification benefits with respect to other investment opportunities such as stocks and bonds. Second, commodities have shown up remarkable performance in recent years, with the total return index of the Dow Jones-AIG Commodity Index family returning in excess of 16% each year from 2002 to 2006.

In a low interest rate environment, the strong performance of commodity investments was the main driver behind their success. The recent price surge in commodities is the result of strong demand shocks across all sectors, supply shocks in some sectors (e.g., crude oil), and structural money flows into all sectors from different investor types (private investors, institutional investors, banks, and hedge funds). In particular, the strong economic growth of rapidly developing countries like China, India, and Brazil and the accompanying need for energy and industrial metals led to a structural excess demand on commodity markets.

Investors usually obtain commodity exposure via futures contracts. Commodity futures do not represent direct exposure to actual commodities.

In fact, commodity futures represent bets on the expected future spot price. Inventory decisions, storage cost, and interest rates link the expected future spot price to the current spot price. Unlike equities, which entitle the holder to a continuing stake in a company, commodity futures contracts specify a delivery date for the underlying physical commodity. In order to avoid delivery and maintain a long futures position, maturing contracts are sold and contracts that have not yet reached the delivery period are purchased. This process is known as *rolling* a futures position. The return associated with this process—the *roll return* (or *roll yield*)—is an important component of the total return of a commodity investment.[1]

Though the statistical properties of financial asset returns have been studied extensively, few studies have been done on the price fluctuations of commodities. Except of Gorton and Rouwenhorst,[2] Erb and Harvey,[3] and Kat and Oomen,[4] an in-depth analysis of commodity futures as an asset class has been lacking. In this chapter, we investigate the empirical properties of a diversified basket of commodity futures represented by the Dow Jones-AIG Commodity Index. This index is constructed as a *rolling index* without a prespecified maturity. It serves itself as an underlying for derivatives and passive investment products (e.g., exchange-traded funds). In our analysis, we derive some stylized facts about commodity futures and address some commonly raised questions by investors:

- What is the risk-return profile of commodities?
- What is the contribution of the different return components (spot, roll, and collateral return) to the total return of a commodity investment?
- Are commodity returns normally distributed or do they exhibit skewness and/or excess kurtosis?
- Do commodity returns show serial correlation?
- Do commodities offer diversification benefits to a portfolio of traditional asset classes?
- Do commodities offer an inflation hedge?

---

[1]When we speak of commodities or commodity indexes, we actually mean commodity futures and commodity futures indexes.

[2]Gary Gorton and K. Geert Rouwenhorst, "Facts and Fantasies about Commodity Futures," *Financial Analysts Journal* 62, no. 2 (2006), pp. 47–68.

[3]Claude Erb and Campbell R. Harvey, "The Tactical and Strategic Value of Commodity Futures." *Financial Analysts Journal* 6, no. 2 (2006), pp. 69–97.

[4]Harry M. Kat and Roel C. A. Oomen, "What Every Investor Should Know About Commodities Part I" *Journal of Investment Management* 5, no. 1 (2007), pp. 1–25; and Harry M. Kat and Roel C. A. Oomen, "What Every Investor Should Know About Commodities, Part II: Multivariate Analysis," *Journal of Investment Management* 5, no. 3 (2007), pp. 1–25.

SOURCES OF RETURN: AN ILLUSTRATION

To ensure comparability between the performance of an investment in commodity futures and other asset classes, we need to control for leverage when calculating futures returns. We make the common assumption that futures positions will be fully collateralized. Given this assumption, the total return of a commodity futures investment is[5]

$$\text{Total return} = \text{Futures return} + \text{Collateral return} \tag{9.1}$$

The *collateral return* is the interest earned on the cash value of the investment, that is, the fully collateralized commodity futures position. The *futures return* or *excess return* is the percentage change in price of the relevant futures contract. It can be decomposed in a spot and roll return component:

$$\text{Futures return} = \text{Spot return} + \text{Roll return} \tag{9.2}$$

The *spot return* is the percentage change in the spot price of the underlying commodity. Because "good" spot price data are not available for most commodities, the price of the *near-month contract* (also called *spot-month contract*) is taken to approximate the spot price.[6] The *roll return* is implicitly defined by equation (9.2). It is the return one would obtain if at maturity of the futures contract the spot price was unchanged, that is, the return from "rolling" up or down the term structure of futures prices. When the market is in backwardation the roll return is positive; when it is in contango the roll return is negative.

Combining equations (9.1) and (9.2), we obtain the decomposition of the total return of a collateralized commodity futures investment:

$$\text{Total return} = \text{Spot return} + \text{Roll return} + \text{Collateral return}. \tag{9.3}$$

To illustrate the return decomposition of futures or excess returns into spot and roll returns, let us consider the situation in the crude oil market over the period December 2005 to June 2006. The prices of the crude oil

---

[5]See Harry M. Kat and Roel C. A. Omen, "What Every Investor Should Know About Commodities Part I.

[6]See Viola Markert, Commodities as Assets and Consumption Goods: Implications for the Valuation of Commodity Futures, Ph.D. thesis, University St. Gallen (2005); and Gary Gorton and K. Geert Rouwenhorst, "Facts and Fantasies about Commodity Futures," *Financial Analysts Journal* 62, no. 2 (2006), pp. 47–68.

futures contracts are shown in Exhibit 9.1 for the different maturities. For each monthly observation date (in rows), the table shows the futures curve up to the maturity July 2006 (in columns). The price of the spot-month futures contract (printed in bold letters) is taken as a proxy for the spot price.

We start by computing the futures return time series. At the end of December 2005 ("roll-over date"), the investor opens a long position in the February contract for a price of 61.04. Before the January contract expires, the investor closes his position in the February contract for a price of 68.35. Simultaneously, he opens a new position in the March contract for a price of 67.92. The (simple) futures return for January can then be calculated as

$$\text{Futures return } (Jan) = \frac{68.35}{61.04} - 1 = 11.98\%$$

Analogously, the February futures return is computed as

$$\text{Futures return } (Feb) = \frac{61.10}{67.92} - 1 = 10.04\%$$

The complete futures return or excess return series is shown in the "Futures Return" column in Exhibit 9.2.

In a second step, we compute the corresponding spot return series. The spot return for January is given by

$$\text{Spot return } (Jan) = \frac{68.35}{57.98} - 1 = 17.89\%$$

In the same way, we obtain the spot return for February:

$$\text{Spot return } (Feb) = \frac{61.10}{68.35} - 1 = -10.61\%$$

EXHIBIT 9.1 Futures Prices for Crude Oil

Crude Oil (USD)	Jan 06	Feb 06	Mar 06	Apr 06	May 06	Jun 06	Jul 06
30 Dec 05	**57.98**	*61.04*	62.09	62.35	62.70	63.00	63.25
31 Jan 06		**68.35**	*67.92*	68.74	69.28	69.70	70.01
28 Feb 06			**61.10**	*61.41*	63.01	64.06	64.83
31 Mar 06				**60.57**	*66.63*	67.93	68.67
28 Apr 06					**71.95**	*71.88*	73.50
31 May 06						**69.23**	*71.29*
30 Jun 06							**68.94**

Source: Exhibit created from data obtained from Bloomberg.

EXHIBIT 9.2 Futures, Spot, and Roll Returns for Crude Oil

	Futures Return	Spot Return	Roll Return
Jan 06	11.98%	17.89%	−5.91%
Feb 06	−10.04%	−10.61%	0.57%
Mar 06	−1.37%	−0.87%	−0.50%
Apr 06	7.98%	18.79%	−10.80%
May 06	−3.69%	−3.78%	0.09%
Jun 06	−3.30%	−0.42%	−2.88%

Source: Exhibit created from data obtained from Bloomberg.

The complete series of spot returns is shown in the column "Spot Return" in Exhibit 9.2. The roll return is the difference between the futures return and the spot return. It is shown in the last column of Exhibit 9.2. Obviously, although the spot price of crude oil went up in the sample period, the roll returns were mostly negative. This is due to the contango situation, which characterized the crude oil market for most of the years 2005 and 2006.[7]

UNIVARIATE ANALYSIS

The aim of this section and the next is to characterize the commodity futures asset class. We use publicly available index data from Dow Jones Indexes and AIG International Inc. to identify the main (statistical) properties of commodity futures (index) returns. This section provides a univariate analysis of commodity returns, whereas the next section examines their multivariate characteristics.

Data

The Dow Jones-AIG Commodity Index (DJ-AIGCI) is a rolling, highly liquid, well diversified and investable commodity futures index.[8] It mimics the performance of a broad basket of futures contracts traded at U.S.

[7]Over the last two decades, the NYMEX WTI crude oil market was approximately 60% in backwardation and 40% in contango.

[8]The CBOT introduced futures contracts on the DJ-AIGCI in November 16, 2001. In addition, there exist a number of exchange traded funds, structured products, certificates, etc. that provide easy exposure to the DJ-AIGCI.

exchanges and the LME on 19 physical commodities from the energy, industrials and metals, and agriculture sector.[9]

Our sample comprises monthly index data of the DJ-AIGCI total return, excess return, and spot return index over the period January 1991 to July 2006. To study the relationship of commodities with traditional asset classes, our sample also includes monthly time series of the Standard & Poor's 500 total return index (S&P 500) and the JPMorgan Government Bond U.S. total return index (JPM U.S. Bond). To study if commodities serve as an inflation hedge, our sample also includes monthly data of the OECD U.S. Consumer Price Index (CPI).

Risk and Return Characteristics

Exhibit 9.3 compares the total return index of the DJ-AIGCI with the excess and spot return index between January 1991 and July 2006. Apparently,

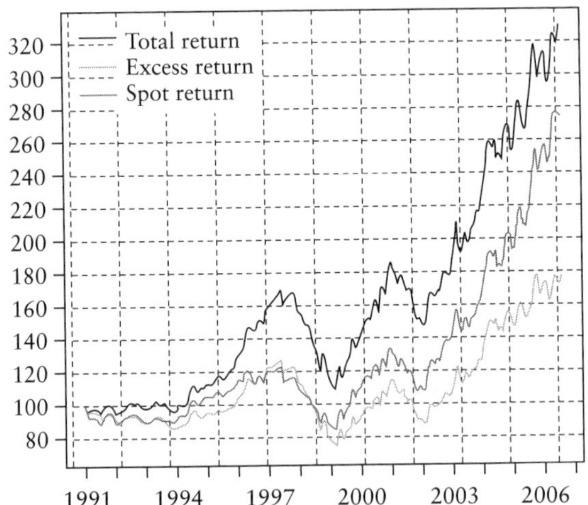

EXHIBIT 9.3 Performance of the DJ-AIGCI Spot, Excess and Total Return Index, January 1991 to July 2006
Source: Exhibit created from data obtained from Bloomberg.

---

[9]The weighting scheme of the DJ-AIGCI relies primarily on liquidity data and, to a lesser extent, on dollar-adjusted production data. To help insure diversified exposure, the index relies on several diversification rules. For example, no single commodity may constitute more than 15% or less than 2% of the index. The index is rebalanced annually by an Oversight Committee.

there are large differences between the historical performance of the spot, excess, and total return index. The total return index has outperformed the spot and excess return index. Because the majority of commodities were trading in contango in the sample period, the spot return index was better performing than the excess return index.

Exhibit 9.4 reports an average annual (arithmetic) roll yield of −2.76%. This means that an investor has lost on average −2.76% p.a. from rolling futures forward to the next maturity. Approximately 50% of the total return, or roughly 4% p.a., can be attributed to the interest rate component—the collateral return. The collateral return overcompensates for the negative roll return such that an investor in commodity futures could fully benefit from the attractive spot return of commodities in the period 1991 to 2006.

Exhibit 9.5 compares the performance of the DJ-AIGCI total return index ("Commodities"), the S&P 500 total return index ("Stocks"), and the JPM U.S. Bond total return index ("Bonds") for the period January 1991 to July 2006. Three observations can be made from this exhibit:

1. Stocks outperformed commodities in the sample period; both asset classes outperformed bonds.
2. Stocks and commodities have experienced higher volatility than bonds.
3. Since 1999, commodities are in a bull market.

Exhibit 9.6 summarizes the risk-return characteristics of the three asset classes. It reports the annualized geometric and arithmetic mean, the annualized volatility or standard deviation, the risk premium (over the average implied collateral return), the t-statistic for a risk premium of zero, and the Sharpe ratio for the three asset classes. The values for the t-statistic indicate a statistically significant positive risk premium for all three asset classes. While commodities exhibit a similar volatility than stocks in the sample period, their average return is significantly lower. This results in a lower Sharpe ratio for commodities than for stocks.

EXHIBIT 9.4 Average Annualized Spot, Roll, Collateral, and Total Return of the DJ-AIGCI, January 1991 to July 2006

	Total Return	Spot Return	Roll Return	Collateral Return
Geometric mean	7.95%	6.69%	−2.74%	4.02%
Arithmetic mean	8.73%	7.45%	−2.76%	4.04%

Source: Exhibit created from data obtained from Bloomberg.

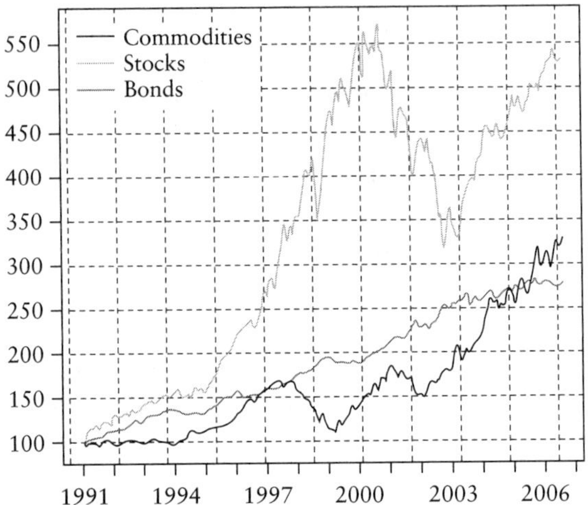

EXHIBIT 9.5 Performance of Commodities (DJ-AIGCI total return), Stocks (S&P 500), and Bonds (JPM U.S. Bond), January 1991 to July 2006
Source: Exhibit created from data obtained from Bloomberg.

EXHIBIT 9.6 Annual Risk-Return Characteristics of Commodities (DJ-AIGCI total return), Stocks (S&P 500), and Bonds (JPM U.S. Bond), January 1991 to July 2006

	Commodities	Stocks	Bonds
Geometric mean	7.95%	11.31%	6.79%
Arithmetic mean	8.73%	12.36%	6.90%
Volatility	12.14%	13.81%	4.53%
Risk premium	4.69%	8.32%	2.86%
t-Statistic	5.28	8.24	8.63
Sharpe ratio	0.39	0.60	0.63

Source: Exhibit created from data obtained from Bloomberg.

Distributional Characteristics

Exhibit 9.7 presents descriptive statistics on the distribution of monthly total returns of commodities, stocks, and bonds. The distribution of commodity returns appears to be close to a normal distribution, as the skewness and excess kurtosis values are around zero and the median closely

EXHIBIT 9.7 Summary Statistics for Monthly Total Returns of Commodities, Stocks, and Bonds

	Commodities	Stocks	Bonds
Minimum	−7.54%	−14.46%	−4.68%
25% quantile	−1.23%	−1.62%	−0.23%
Mean	0.70%	0.98%	0.56%
Median	0.72%	1.24%	0.57%
75% quantile	2.54%	3.74%	1.44%
Maximum	10.23%	11.44%	3.72%
Skewness	0.10	−0.48	−0.51
Excess kurtosis	0.05	0.90	0.98

Source: Exhibit created from data obtained from Bloomberg.

matches the mean.[10] To check more rigorously, we perform Jarque-Bera and Anderson-Darling normality tests.[11] The null hypothesis of a normal distribution cannot be rejected at the 5% level in both tests, thus supporting the hypothesis of normally distributed commodity returns. Exhibit 9.8 illustrates these findings graphically. The empirical density is computed as a smoothed function of the histogram using a normal kernel.[12] Superimposed on the empirical density is a normal distribution having the same mean and the same variance as that estimated from the sample. In contrast to commodities, the Gaussian assumption is rejected for stocks and bonds at all relevant significance levels.

Serial Correlation

To test whether monthly commodity returns are independent, we plot the *sample autocorrelation function* (ACF) in Exhibit 9.9. Although some autocorrelations (e.g., at lag 3) are statistically different from zero at the 5% level, there is no systematic pattern of autocorrelations. To investigate this further, we compute the Ljung-Box test statistic of the joint null hypothesis that all of the first 10 autocorrelations are zero. The p-value of 0.11 indicates no significant autocorrelation for commodity returns up to lag 10.

[10]The normal distribution exhibits a skewness and excess kurtosis (defined as kurtosis minus 3) of 0.

[11]For a detailed description of these tests and other statistical concepts used in this chapter, see, for example, Ruey S. Tsay, *Analysis of Financial Time Series* (Hoboken, NJ: John Wiley & Sons, 2005).

[12]See Bernard W. Silverman, *Density Estimation for Statistics and Data Analysis* (London: Chapman and Hall, 1986).

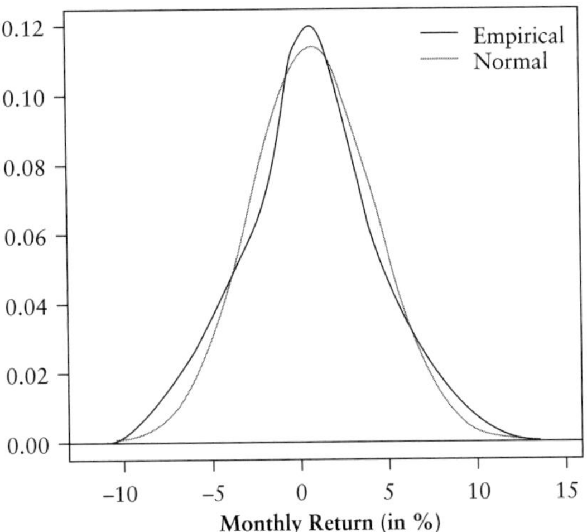

EXHIBIT 9.8 Empirical and Normal Density of Monthly Commodity Returns as Represented by the DJ-AIGCI Total Return Index, January 1991 to July 2006
Source: Exhibit created from data obtained from Bloomberg.

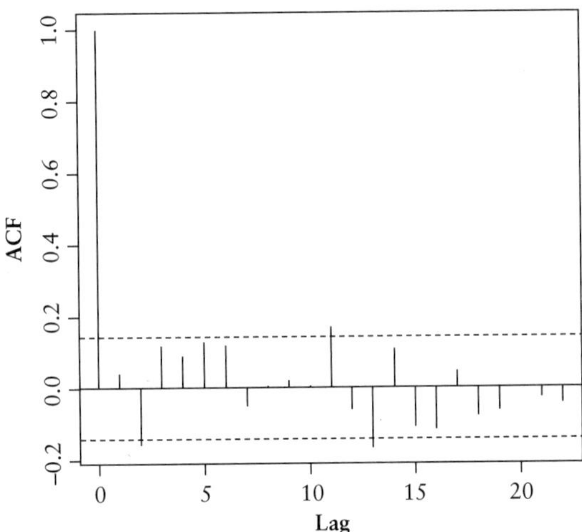

EXHIBIT 9.9 Sample Autocorrelation Function (ACF) of Monthly Commodity Returns Over the Time Period January 1991 to July 2006
Source: Exhibit created from data obtained from Bloomberg.
Note: The parallel lines indicate the 95% confidence interval.

For the stock and bond market indexes, we find also little evidence of statistically significant autocorrelation. This is consistent with informationally efficient markets, where price changes must be unpredictable if they are properly anticipated by market participants.

MULTIVARIATE ANALYSIS

Dependence Structure with Stocks and Bonds

Exhibit 9.10 shows the (linear) correlations between commodities, stocks, and bonds. As was already documented by Gorton and Rouwenhorst,[13] the correlation of commodities with stocks and bonds is close to zero. This makes commodities effective in diversifying equity and bond portfolios.

However, from an asset allocation perspective it is not so much the average correlation that matters, but more the correlation in negative market environments, particularly in crash situations. It is thus important to analyze whether the zero correlation between commodities and stocks holds up when stock returns are negative—a time when diversification is needed most. Exhibit 9.11 shows a scatter plot of commodity and stock returns, where data points with a positive (negative) stock return are marked with a cross (circle). The pattern of data points indicates a zero correlation between commodity and stock returns for both positive and negative stock returns. In fact, when stock returns are positive (negative) the sample correlation is 0.03 (0.07). During the months of negative equity performance, when stocks fell on average by 3.13% per month, commodities experienced a positive average return of 0.20% per month. It thus seems that the diversification benefits of commodities work well in poor equity market environments.

The analysis has shown that commodities show little correlation with stocks and bonds. This leads to the conclusion that commodities are actually an asset class in its own right.

EXHIBIT 9.10 Correlations between Monthly Returns of Commodities, Stocks, and Bonds, January 1991 to July 2006

	Commodities	Stocks	Bonds
Commodities	1.00	0.08	0.01
Stocks	0.08	1.00	−0.04
Bonds	0.01	−0.04	1.00

Source: Exhibit created from data obtained from Bloomberg.

[13]See Gorton and Rouwenhorst, "Facts and Fantasies about Commodity Futures."

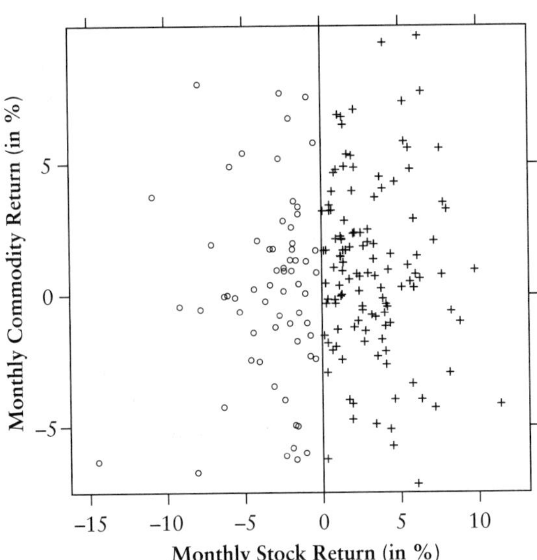

EXHIBIT 9.11 Stock Returns versus Commodity Returns
Source: Exhibit created from data obtained from Bloomberg.
Note: Positive (negative) stock returns are marked with a cross (circle).

Commodity Returns and Inflation

Bottom line, investors care about real returns; that is, they want to outperform inflation. It is very well known that traditional asset classes often exhibit a negative correlation to inflation. The reasoning is as follows: In times of economic growth, prices and interest rates tend to rise. Higher prices and higher interest rates reduce the growth potential and the profits of a company. This reduces the present value of future cash flows and thus stock and bond prices. For commodities the opposite is true. In situations of economic growth, inventories are falling and commodity prices tend to rise. From this point of view, higher inflation is likely to come along with negative stock and bond returns, but positive commodity returns. Since expected future inflation will already be incorporated in asset prices, asset prices may also be sensitive to unexpected inflation. Unexpected inflation is not easy to measure. Following Kat and Oomen,[14] we use the change of inflation as a proxy for unexpected inflation.

[14]See Kat and Oomen, "What Every Investor Should Know About Commodities Part II: Multivariate Return Analysis."

EXHIBIT 9.12 Correlations between Monthly Returns of Commodities, Stocks, and Bonds with Different Components of Inflation, January 1991 to July 2006

	Inflation	Unexpected Inflation
Commodities	0.14[a]	0.28[a]
Stocks	−0.10	−0.05
Bonds	−0.06	0.04

Source: Exhibit created from data obtained from Bloomberg.
[a]Indicates the correlation is significant at the 5% level.

Exhibit 9.12 shows the correlations between monthly returns of commodities, stocks, and bonds with inflation—defined as the one month relative change of CPI—and unexpected inflation. The latter is defined as the change of inflation. As suggested by economic theory, stocks and bonds are negatively correlated with inflation, while the correlation of commodities with inflation is positive. Only the correlation of commodities with inflation is statistically different from zero at the 5% level. Commodity returns are even more positively correlated to unexpected inflation. Again, the correlation coefficient is statistically significant at the 5% level. Unlike stocks and bonds, commodities therefore tend to provide investors with a hedge against inflation.

CONCLUSION

Using monthly data from Dow Jones-AIG over the time period January 1991 to July 2006, our analysis led to the following observations on commodity (futures) index returns:[15]

- The total return from an unleveraged commodity index investment is positive, on average, and comparable in magnitude and volatility to equity returns.
- The average spot and collateral return is positive, while the average roll return is negative. This means that, on average, the market was in contango.
- Commodity index returns are almost normally distributed. Skewness and excess kurtosis is minimal and largely insignificant.
- Commodity index returns exhibit only little serial correlation.

[15]Note that these results partially depend on the sample period and observation frequency.

- Commodity index returns are uncorrelated with stock and bond returns. This holds also true in negative equity market environments when diversification is needed most.
- Commodity index returns are positively correlated with inflation. They are even more positively correlated with unexpected inflation—defined as the change in the rate of inflation.

Our analyses suggest that commodities are an asset class which is attractive to diversify traditional portfolios of stocks and bonds.

CHAPTER 10

The Diversification Benefits of Commodity Futures Indexes: A Mean-Variance Spanning Test

Bernd Scherer, Ph.D.
Managing Director
Global Head of Quantitative Structured Products
Morgan Stanley Investment Management

Li He, Ph.D.
Quantitative Research Analyst
Deutsche Asset Management

It is well known that commodity investment provides diversification benefits to a portfolio. (See, for example, Abanomey and Mathur[1]; Anson[2]; Gorton and Rouwenhorst[3]; Jensen, Johnson, and Mercer[4]; and the CISDM

[1]Walid S. Abanomey and Ike Mathur, "The Hedging Benefits of Commodity Futures in International Portfolio Diversification," *Journal of Alternative Investments* (Winter 1999), pp. 51–62.
[2]Mark J. P. Anson, "Maximizing Utility with Commodity Futures Diversification," *Journal of Portfolio Management* 25, no. 4 (1999), pp. 86–94.
[3]Gary Gorton and Geert K. Rouwenhorst, "Facts and Fantasies about Commodity Futures," *Financial Analysts Journal* 62, no. 2 (2006), pp. 47–68.
[4]Gerald R. Jensen, Robert R. Johnson, and Jeffrey M. Mercer, "Tactical Asset Allocation and Commodity Futures," *Journal of Portfolio Management* 58, no. 2 (2002), pp. 100–111.

Research Department.[5] Commodity futures tend to have equity-like returns, and are negatively correlated with stocks and bonds. When the returns on bonds or equities are low, the returns on commodity futures might be high. Thus, adding commodities in the investment universe makes it possible to achieve higher returns of the whole portfolio without increasing risks. Furthermore, commodities might help investors hedge against inflation since commodities tend to have higher returns when inflation rises, while bonds and equities tend to perform worse with rising inflation. Investors are therefore getting more interested in the statistical and economic foundations of commodity investing. In this chapter, we investigate whether commodities extend the investment universe for U.S.-based investors. In other words, does the inclusion of commodities into portfolios lead to *statistically significant* improvements in the efficiency (best risk-return trade-off) of an investor's portfolio?[6]

The outline of this chapter is as follows. First, we review the term asset class from a financial economist's perspective. We argue that the gist of an asset class is that it can provide a risk premium (additional return over the risk free rate) that cannot be explained by existing asset classes. Next we apply standard statistical tests to find out whether commodities indeed expose investors to asset class specific returns. That is, are investors better off adding commodities to a given portfolio?[7] Finally, we review the logic for the existence of an unconditional risk premium in commodity investing and elaborate on the practical difficulties of capturing asset class specific returns by unconditional long-only investing in commodity indexes.

---

[5]CISDM Research Department, "The Benefits of Commodity Investment: 2006 Update," Center for International Securities and Derivatives Markets, Isenberg School of Management, University of Massachusetts, Amherst, Massachusetts (2006), http://cisdm.som.umass.edu/research/pdffiles/benefitsofcommodities.pdf.

[6]For the more formally minded reader, we need to test whether adding commodities to the investment opportunity set (U.S. equities and U.S. bonds) significantly improves the utility of mean-variance investors.

[7]We look at the asset allocation problem from the perspective of an asset only investor (i.e., an investor with an implicit cash benchmark). For an investor with fixed income-like pension liabilities many arguments made in this chapter do not hold. For example: While commodities reduce risk due to their low correlation with other assets for an asset only investor they actually increase risk for a liability driven investor. A low correlation with the local discount factor (bonds) here means that assets and liabilities are likely to drift apart, which makes commodities not a diversifying but a risk-increasing investment.

HOW FINANCIAL ECONOMISTS VIEW ASSET CLASSES

In practical investment management an asset class is a group of assets that investors regard as homogeneous enough (high internal correlation) as well as unique enough (low external correlation) to consider separate strategic allocations worthwhile. Equities and government bonds are an example of asset classes that offer distinctly different economic characteristics. While equities participate in economic growth, government bonds offer a recession hedge that secures an investor's nominal wealth. Both assets offer distinct features that cannot be replicated by the other asset. There is no redundancy here.

Why do investors care about the notion of an asset class? That is, why do investors have a desire to group assets together into categories? First, it is easier to make top-down investment decisions across assets that react to different economic forces. Asset classes as such should reflect economically meaningful categories, that is, they should differ in their economic sensitivities.[8] Second, asset classes make it easier for the analyst to employ quantitative portfolio construction (asset allocation) techniques. Mean-variance optimizers tend to magnify the impact of the estimation error on portfolio weights. For example, if assets A and B have similar features (i.e., high correlation and similar risk), and asset A has a slightly higher return due to estimation error, the portfolio optimizer will put most (or all) of its weights on asset A even though assets A and B are quite similar. Both assets are seen as close substitutes, while asset classes by definition are not. Finally, there is a continuing search in the financial industry to uncover new asset classes. After all, finding a new asset class promises larger risk diversification for clients and asset managers find a new product offering. For these reasons asset classes are normally used to split up the investment universe into buckets that are used for asset allocation as well as manager search purposes. Also asset managers tend to have organized their firms across asset classes for very much the same reasons.

Now that we know the potential benefits from defining (and finding) new asset classes we need to answer an important question: How can we reliably test for asset classes? Practitioners often focus on low (external) correlation as indication whether a group of assets form an asset class. This however can prove fallacious. Low correlation is not enough. After all, lottery tickets have (by definition) zero correlation with equities and bonds. Their negative expected return will stop us from investing any fraction of

[8]From this it is easy to see why hedge funds cannot be an asset class. They do not share unique economic exposures as they are rather a form of unconstrained investing.

our wealth into those assets. What is the correct (statistical) interpretation of an asset class?[9] It is defined in the following section.

REMOVE THE BORDER

Any suspected asset class i with returns (R_i) earning a risk premium above cash (c) that cannot be explained by other $j = 1, \ldots, J$ already existing asset classes with risk premium $(R_j - c)$ can be regarded as an asset class in its own right.

What does this mean? Suppose equities and bonds earn a risk premium of 5% and 2% each. Their volatilities are 15% and 5%. Assume further zero correlation between both asset classes. Let us engineer a new asset that implicitly consists of 25% equities, 25% bonds, and 50% asset-class-specific risk with 30% volatility and zero expected return. The correlation of this new asset with equities turns out to be

$$\rho = \frac{Cov(0.25 \cdot R_e + 0.25 \cdot R_b + 0.5 \cdot R_a, R_e)}{\sqrt{Var(0.25 \cdot R_e + 0.25 \cdot R_b + 0.5 \cdot R_a)}\sqrt{Var(R_e)}}$$
$$= \frac{0.25 \cdot \text{Var}(R_e)}{\sqrt{0.25^2 \text{Var}(R_e) + 0.25^2 \text{Var}(R_b) + 0.5^2 \text{Var}(R_a)}\sqrt{\text{Var}(R_e)}} = 0.24 \tag{10.1}$$

This asset enjoys low correlation, but it offers no extra return relative to an investment of 25% equity, 25% bonds, and 50% cash. Even worse it exposes the investor to too much risk as a return matching investment in 25% equity, 25% bonds, and 50% cash would also carry substantially lower risk. We see that low correlation and the existence of a risk premium is not enough to conclude that we have found an asset class. Any portfolio optimization exercise would find that investment opportunities are already spanned by existing assets and that the new asset would only expose investors to additional risk. The mean-variance optimizer would not invest into this asset, and the efficient frontier would not shift to the upper left. What distinguishes an asset class from a redundant asset is a return on its asset specific risk. What happens if the expected return on our asset specific risk is positive? In this case we suspect we have found a new asset class, but we must make sure it is not only

[9]See Robert J. Greer, "What is an Asset Class, Anyway?" *Journal of Portfolio Management* 23, no. 2 (1997), pp. 86–91.

positive but also statistically significant. What this means is that a shift in the frontier to the upper left is not enough either. It needs to be a statistically significant shift.

How can we test for a statistically meaningful improvement of our investment universe? We first need to find a portfolio of existing asset classes that tracks any suspected asset class as closely as possible. In other words, we try to replicate returns of a potentially new asset class with what we already got. After we have found this portfolio we can then measure the differential (asset class specific) returns and test whether they are statistically significant. Rather than this two step procedure we run a regression between the excess returns of a candidate asset class and other established asset classes.[10]

$$(R_i - c) = \alpha + \sum_{j=1}^{J} \beta_j (R_j - c) + \varepsilon \tag{10.2}$$

If the constant term in this regression (α) is significantly different from zero, we can consider it as an asset class. The regression coefficients β_j can be interpreted as the portfolio weights in a tracking portfolio of "old" assets that try to replicate a "new" asset class. This is the basic idea behind all tests for what academics call mean-variance spanning. Only if asset-class-specific returns are statistically different from zero have we found a new asset class. We notice that correlation plays only an indirect roll. What matters is whether part of the risk premium is not explained by other asset classes. Obviously, the higher the correlation, the more systematic exposures and hence explained risk premium exists. But high correlation is not necessarily enough to justify a negative judgment. Neither is low correlation enough to prove uniqueness. After all, coin flipping is very diversifying. In fact, we test whether a given asset class extends the mean-variance frontier (shifts it to the upper left) in a statistically significant way.

---

[10]Most formal tests on mean-variance spanning use total returns (not risk premia). These tests also need the sum of exposures (betas) to existing assets to add up to one. However, as we use excess returns over cash, betas (effectively weights of a replicating portfolio) do not need to add to one. The missing allocation can always be filled up with cash (negative cash in case of leverage) to create portfolios that add up (to one). For a review on mean-variance spanning tests, see Frans A. DeRoon and Theo E. Nijman, "Testing for Mean Variance Spanning: A Survey," *Journal of Empirical Finance* 8, no. 2 (2001), pp. 111–155.

RISK, RETURN, AND DIVERSIFICATION

In this section, we look at an investor that currently holds U.S. Equity (proxied by the value-weighted returns on all NYSE, AMEX, and Nasdaq stocks[11]) and U.S. bonds (proxied by Lehman Brothers U.S. Aggregate Bond Index). We investigate five commodity indexes for their diversifying properties. Four of them are commodity indexes in the usual sense, that is, they represent a portfolio of cash collateralized commodity futures:[12] the Goldman Sachs Commodity Index (GSCI), the Deutsche Bank Liquid Commodity Index (DBLCI), the Deutsche Bank Liquid Commodity Index—Mean Reversion (DBLCI-MR), and the Deutsche Bank Liquid Commodity Index—Optimum Yield (DBLCI-OY). The fifth one is an index for commodity stocks (CSI). The CSI is a 50/50 mix of MSCI world energy and world material. The data range is from January 1989 to June 2006. We calculate monthly excess returns (over one-month Treasury bill rate) in dollars.[13] Exhibit 10.1 surveys the different index concepts.[14] Both the GSCI and DBLCI are passive indexes that attempt to capture an unconditional risk premium. Contrary to that philosophy are the DBLCI-MR and the DBLCI-OY. Here both indexes reflect active strategies (overweight relative cheap commodities, and underweight relative expensive commodities or roll into futures contracts to optimize roll yield).

Exhibit created from data obtained from Goldman Sachs, Deutsche Bank, and MSCI Barra.

---

[11]The data source is the Data Library of Dr. Kenneth R. French's web site, http://mba.tuck.dartmouth.edu/pages/faculty/ken.french/data_library.html.

[12]A commodity futures contract is an agreement to buy or sell a quantity of the underlying commodity at a date in the future at a specified price. The specified price is the futures price, which is agreed on when the counterparties of the commodity futures contract enter the contract. Contracts are available for energy, livestock, agriculture, industrial, and precious metals. Commodity indices in turn have exposure to these sectors according to their specific index construction rules.

[13]When we talk about commodity investments we mean cash collateralized investments in commodity futures to put the returns at par with unleveraged investments. With cash collateralization we mean that a futures contract with 200,000 U.S. dollar value is backed by a 200,000 U.S. dollar cash deposit. This is equivalent to a margin account that requires us to deposit the total contract value.

[14]The source for GSCI information is Goldman Sachs web site, http://www2.goldmansachs.com/gsci/. The sources for information about Deutsche Bank commodity indexes are "A User Guide To Commodities," Deutsche Bank (July 2006), http://dbfunds.db.com/Pdfs/dbuserguidetocomm.pdf; and e-mail communications with Michael Lewis of Deutsche Bank. The information in Exhibit 10.1 for CSI is for its components: the MSCI world energy and world materials. The sources are http://www.mscibarra.com/ and e-mail communications with client service of MSCI. The data source for CSI is FactSet.

EXHIBIT 10.1 Alternative Index Construction Rules

Characteristic	GSCI	DBLCI	DBLCI-MR	DBLCI-OY	CSI
Launch date	1991	2003	2003	2006	1999
Index philosophy	Weights are determined by the world production averages	Exposure to most liquid commodities in the respective sectors	Exploit the mean reverting tendency of commodity prices	Exploit the commodity term structure dynamics	Market cap weighted exposure to commodity stocks
Reweighting	Annual rebalancing	Annual, monthly for sweet light crude oil (WTI) and heating oil	Annual	Annual	Quarterly
Current universe	24 commodities	6 commodities	6 commodities	6 commodities	50:50 mix of MSCI world energy and world material
History	Backfilled to 1969	Backfilled to 1969	Backfilled to 1969	Backfilled to 1969	Backfilled to 1994

EXHIBIT 10.2 Unconditional Historic Correlation and Annualized Volatility (main diagonal) for the Investment Opportunity Set (based on monthly excess returns), January 1989 to June 2006

	GSCI	DBLCI	DBLCI-MR	DBLCI-OY	CSI	U.S. Bonds	U.S. Equity
GSCI	0.19	0.93	0.79	0.89	0.24	−0.01	−0.04
DBLCI	0.93	0.20	0.89	0.95	0.20	−0.06	−0.04
DBLCI-MR	0.79	0.89	0.17	0.87	0.22	−0.07	−0.03
DBLCI-OY	0.89	0.95	0.87	0.15	0.26	−0.09	0.00
CSI	0.24	0.20	0.22	0.26	0.15	0.04	0.63
U.S. Bonds	−0.01	−0.06	−0.07	−0.09	0.04	0.04	0.12
U.S. Equity	−0.04	−0.04	−0.03	0.00	0.63	0.12	0.14

Source: Exhibit created from data obtained from Bloomberg, FactSet, Datastream, and Kenneth French's website http://mba.tuck.dartmouth.edu/pages/faculty/ken.french/data_library.html.

Exhibit 10.2 presents the correlations and annualized volatilities for the investment opportunity set. We multiply the monthly volatility by $\sqrt{12}$ to get the annualized volatility. The four commodity indexes for futures are fairly similar in terms of volatility and correlation. Note that even though the DBLCI-OY shows the lowest volatility (15%), this volatility is still higher than U.S. equities for the same time period. The index for commodity stocks (CSI) is different from the commodity future indexes using correlation as a measure of similarity. First, the four commodity future indexes are highly correlated among themselves, while the correlations of CSI with the four commodity future indexes are relatively low. For example, the correlation of DBLCI and DBLCI-OY is 0.95, while the correlation of CSI and DBLCI-OY is only 0.26. Second, the four commodity future indexes are negatively correlated with U.S. bonds and equity, while the CSI is positively correlated with U.S. bonds and equity. For example, the correlation of CSI and U.S. equity is 0.63, which is intuitive since the CSI is a portfolio of commodity stocks.

Exhibit 10.3 presents the monthly risk premium, standard deviation, and respective *t*-value for the investment opportunity set. Each of the three DB commodity future indexes (DBLCI, DBLCI-MR, and DBLCI-OY) has a high monthly risk premium (over 80 basis points) with a *t*-value larger than 2. The DBLCI-OY has the largest *t*-value[15] ($2.76 = \frac{0.0084}{0.0438}\sqrt{210}$). This is not

[15]The *t*-value (significance of monthly average returns) is calculated by multiplying the ratio of risk premium to standard deviation with the square root of the number of observations. Note that the returns need to be normal for the t-test to be valid. Otherwise, a nonparametric test such as the Wilcoxon test needs to be applied.

EXHIBIT 10.3 Monthly Risk Premium, Standard Deviation, and Respective *t*-value (210 observations) for the Investment Opportunity Set (based on monthly excess returns), January 1989 to June 2006

	GSCI	DBLCI	DBLCI-MR	DBLCI-OY	CSI	U.S. Bonds	U.S. Equity
Risk premium	0.57%	0.85%	0.80%	0.84%	0.59%	0.22%	0.64%
Standard deviation	5.56%	5.70%	5.04%	4.38%	4.42%	1.09%	4.13%
t-value	1.50	2.16	2.31	2.76	1.93	2.93	2.24

Source: Exhibit created from data obtained from Bloomberg, FactSet, Datastream, and Kenneth French's website http://mba.tuck.dartmouth.edu/pages/faculty/ken.french/data_library.html.

entirely surprising since the DBLCI-OY takes into consideration the commodity term structure dynamics. The CSI has a relatively high monthly risk premium (59 basis points) with a *t*-value of 1.93. However this does not necessarily qualify commodity investments as an asset class.

We see that commodity investments provide diversification benefits to the portfolio due to their low correlation with existing asset classes. However, as we have seen in our previous discussion that this is not a sufficient condition to qualify for an asset class.[16] All commodity indexes also provide a substantial risk premium that has the same level of magnitude of the equity risk premium or above. Again this is strong circumstantial evidence but no proof to make commodities an asset class in its own. What will really matter is the significance of the asset class specific risk premium, not the significance of the total risk premium.

EMPIRICAL RESULTS

Investors with Equity and Bond Universe

This section applies the regression based mean-variance spanning tests to a U.S.-based investor. To formally test whether commodities extend the investment opportunity set, we need to remove that part of the risk premium that is already explained by existing asset classes (here equities and bonds)

[16] See Gorton and Rouwenhorst, "Facts and Fantasies about Commodity Futures."

and test whatever is left (α) for significance. We apply the regression based tests for mean-variance spanning to our commodity indexes.[17] Specifically, we regress the five commodity indexes on the U.S. equity and bond index.[18] In other words, we start with looking at a U.S.-based investor that used to invest in U.S. equities and U.S. bonds to see whether an investment into commodities will improve her risk return trade-off. We present the regression coefficients and the corresponding p-values. The p-values calculate the likelihood that a given statistic has been produced by chance (i.e., purely accidental). A p-value of 5% indicates significance at the 5% level; that is, only in 5% of all random samples would we see a value of the test statistic that is that high. It also means that the null hypothesis is rejected at the 5% significance level. For robustness, we report the usual p-values, the p-values of White adjustment, and the p-values of Newey-West adjustment. The latter two (White and Newey-West adjusted p-values) are robust to deviations from the classical regression assumptions.[19]

Exhibit 10.4 shows the regression coefficients together with their respective p-values. While we cannot reject the null hypothesis (at the 5% level), that commodities are not a unique asset class for the GSCI and CSI, we can do so for the DBLCI, DBLCI-MR as well as the DBLCI-OY. Investing into the DBLCI, DBLCI-MR, or DBLCI-OY would have significantly extended the investment universe over this time period. The main reason for this is that the risk premia for the GSCI and CSI indexes have not been significant for the respective time period in the first place.

The only exception is the CSI. Not only does it show the most pronounced and most significant equity beta, but also the lowest and most insignificant alpha. This confirms the intuition of many practitioners that commodity stocks trade more like stocks and much less so than commodities.

[17]More sophisticated statistical procedures, which account for missing data and account for the covariance structure between commodities and time series that have a longer history, implicitly assume mean-variance spanning. This makes them of little appeal.

[18]See this chapter's appendix for an implementation in Microsoft Excel.

[19]The classical regression models assume that the regression residuals are spherical; that is, the residuals have constant variances and are not correlated. The White adjustment is robust when the regression residuals do not have constant variances, and the Newey-West adjustment is robust when the regression residuals are serially correlated and/or do not have constant variances. See William H. Greene, *Econometric Analysis* (Upper Saddle River, NJ: Prentice Hall, 2003) for details.

EXHIBIT 10.4 Estimated Parameters and the Corresponding *p*-values from Linear Regression of Commodity Excess Returns versus Equity and Bond Market Excess Returns (based on monthly excess returns), January 1989 to June 2006

		Regression Estimate	*p*-value	White Adjustment *p*-value	Newey-West Adjustment *p*-value
GSCI	α	0.01	0.13	0.14	0.16
	$\beta_{US\ Bonds}$	−0.02	0.96	0.96	0.96
	$\beta_{US\ Equity}$	−0.05	0.59	0.66	0.70
DBLCI	α	0.01	0.02	0.02	0.03
	$\beta_{US\ Bonds}$	−0.31	0.39	0.34	0.35
	$\beta_{US\ Equity}$	−0.05	0.62	0.69	0.73
DBLCI-MR	α	0.01	0.01	0.02	0.03
	$\beta_{US\ Bonds}$	−0.33	0.31	0.28	0.29
	$\beta_{US\ Equity}$	−0.03	0.76	0.79	0.82
DBLCI-OY	α	0.01	0.00	0.00	0.01
	$\beta_{US\ Bonds}$	−0.36	0.20	0.15	0.15
	$\beta_{US\ Equity}$	0.01	0.93	0.94	0.95
CSI	α	0.00	0.45	0.44	0.43
	$\beta_{US\ Bonds}$	−0.14	0.52	0.43	0.42
	$\beta_{US\ Equity}$	0.68	0.00	0.00	0.00

Source: Exhibit created from data obtained from Bloomberg, FactSet, Datastream, and Kenneth French's website http://mba.tuck.dartmouth.edu/pages/faculty/ken.french/data_library.html.

Extending the Universe: The Inclusion of Inflation-Linked Bonds

Interest in commodities has also grown as inflation hedging benefits have been highlighted by investors and commodity index providers. Commodities tend to have higher returns when inflation rises, while stocks and bonds tend to perform worse with rising inflation. Commodities, particularly energy, are an important input factor. An increase in commodity prices is therefore likely to feed through to broader CPI (consumer price inflation) measures. However, if the correlation between inflation-linked bonds—*Treasury inflation protected securities* (TIPS)[20]—and commodity indexes is

[20]TIPS are inflation-protected securities issued by the U.S. Treasury. The principal is linked to the Consumer Price Index (CPI). Interest is paid semiannually, with a fixed coupon rate of the inflation adjusted principal. For details about TIPS, see http://www.treasurydirect.gov/indiv/research/indepth/tips/res_tips_rates.htm.

substantial, or more precisely if part of the risk premium earned by commodities is already explained by inflation-linked bonds, the case for commodities is weakened.[21]

In our framework, we can investigate this by running a linear regression of commodity returns against bond, equity, and inflation-linked bond returns. In other words, we add inflation-linked bonds to an investor's core universe and test whether adding on commodities will help to significantly improve the risk return efficiency of portfolios. For inflation-linked bonds we use monthly returns for U.S. TIPS by Merrill Lynch (Merrill Lynch U.S. Treasury Inflation-linked, available since September 2000[22]). In the rest of this section, we first show the summary statistics. Then we present the regression coefficients and the corresponding *p*-values.

Exhibits 10.5 and 10.6 present the summary statistics of the commodity, equity, and bond indexes. Note that the risk premium for U.S. equities is negative (−12 basis points) for this time period. The negative risk premium is not statistically significant though. The risk premium for CSI is positive (105 basis points) with a *t*-statistics of 1.84. The correlation between CSI and U.S. equity is 0.70.

EXHIBIT 10.5 Unconditional Historic Correlation and Annualized Volatility (main diagonal) for the Investment Opportunity Set (based on monthly excess returns), September 2000 to June 2006

	GSCI	DBLCI	DBLCI-MR	DBLCI-OY	CSI	U.S. Bonds	U.S. Equity	TIPS
GSCI	0.22	0.93	0.69	0.88	0.34	0.02	−0.02	0.21
DBLCI	0.93	0.18	0.80	0.93	0.33	0.01	0.02	0.23
DBLCI-MR	0.69	0.80	0.13	0.77	0.29	0.04	0.08	0.22
DBLCI-OY	0.88	0.93	0.77	0.15	0.43	−0.06	0.14	0.14
CSI	0.34	0.33	0.29	0.43	0.17	−0.21	0.70	−0.12
U.S. Bonds	0.02	0.01	0.04	−0.06	−0.21	0.04	−0.34	0.85
U.S. Equity	−0.02	0.02	0.08	0.14	0.70	−0.34	0.15	−0.24
TIPS	0.21	0.23	0.22	0.14	−0.12	0.85	−0.24	0.06

Source: Exhibit created from data obtained from Bloomberg, FactSet, Datastream, and Kenneth French's website http://mba.tuck.dartmouth.edu/pages/faculty/ken.french/data_library.html.

[21]Given the high volatility of commodity investments, the inflation hedging argument is already weak as this kind of "hedge" would expose investors at the same time to considerable (noninflation-related) noise. It is further weakened by the existence of an asset that can pinpoint inflation risks.

[22]The results are similar if we use Lehman Brothers TIPS, available from March 2000.

EXHIBIT 10.6 Monthly Risk Premium, Standard Deviation, and Respective *t*-value (210 observations) for the Investment Opportunity Set (based on monthly excess returns) January 1989 to June 2006

	GSCI	DBLCI	DBLCI-MR	DBLCI-OY	CSI	U.S. Bonds	U.S. Equity	TIPS
Risk premium	0.81%	1.06%	0.96%	1.49%	1.05%	0.20%	−0.12%	0.44%
Standard deviation	6.27%	5.32%	3.86%	4.32%	4.77%	1.06%	4.45%	1.75%
t-value	1.07	1.66	2.08	2.88	1.84	1.60	−0.22	2.12

Source: Exhibit created from data obtained from Bloomberg, FactSet, Datastream, and Kenneth French's website http://mba.tuck.dartmouth.edu/pages/faculty/ken.french/data_library.html.

Exhibit 10.5 also confirms our intuition that commodity indexes and inflation-linked bonds should show positive correlation. U.S. equity and CSI instead show negative correlation with TIPS. Some part of the risk premium for commodities can surely be attributed to TIPS. How will this change our results? Will commodities still look like an asset class of its own?

Exhibit 10.7 presents the regression estimates and the corresponding *p*-values, where again White *p*-value stands for *p*-value with White adjustment and NW *p*-value stands for *p*-value with Newey-West adjustment. The left panel shows the regression results including TIPS, and the right panel shows the regression results excluding TIPS. We need to run two separate regressions for comparative purposes. Due to the data availability for TIPS, we can only look at a shorter time horizon.

Interestingly, we see a material shift in sign and size of bond beta (and its significance) when TIPS are included. This indicates that commodity returns are correlated with inflation as the regression builds a leveraged long or short portfolio of nominal and real bonds in order to isolate the effect of inflation. Including TIPS, all alpha values drop (due to the return explained by existing inflation-linked assets) and all *p*-values rise, thus weakening the case for commodities as an asset class. At the 10% confidence level, only the DBLCI-OY and the CSI remain significant. The significance of the CSI is surprising. However this is due to significant exposures to value and size that are not captured by simple market returns. Introducing these factors would leave its alpha largely insignificant.[23]

[23]The *p*-values of alpha for CSI are 0.49, 0.45 (with White correction), 0.24 (with Newey-West correction) if we include the value and size factors in the right hand side of the regressions. DBLCI-OY remains significant at the 10% significance level with the value and size factors. The data source for the value and size factors is Dr. Kenneth French's Data Library at http://mba.tuck.dartmouth.edu/pages/faculty/ken.french/data_library.html.

EXHIBIT 10.7 Asset Class Regressions (based on monthly excess returns), September 2000 to June 2006

		Regression Including TIPS				Regression Excluding TIPS			
		Estimate	*p*-value	White *p*-value	NW *p*-value	Estimate	*p*-value	White *p*-value	NW *p*-value
GSCI	α	0.00	0.60	0.61	0.56	0.01	0.32	0.32	0.26
	$\beta_{US\ Bonds}$	−3.59	0.01	0.00	0.00	0.12	0.87	0.86	0.87
	$\beta_{US\ Equity}$	−0.07	0.68	0.65	0.63	−0.01	0.94	0.94	0.93
	$\beta_{US\ TIPS}$	2.58	0.00	0.00	0.00				
DBLCI	α	0.01	0.28	0.29	0.24	0.01	0.12	0.11	0.07
	$\beta_{US\ Bonds}$	−3.33	0.00	0.00	0.00	0.12	0.86	0.86	0.86
	$\beta_{US\ Equity}$	−0.02	0.88	0.88	0.87	0.03	0.83	0.84	0.82
	$\beta_{US\ TIPS}$	2.39	0.00	0.00	0.00				
DBLCI-MR	α	0.01	0.13	0.13	0.11	0.01	0.06	0.05	0.04
	$\beta_{US\ Bonds}$	−1.79	0.04	0.02	0.06	0.29	0.54	0.57	0.56
	$\beta_{US\ Equity}$	0.06	0.58	0.55	0.53	0.09	0.42	0.43	0.38
	$\beta_{US\ TIPS}$	1.44	0.00	0.00	0.02				
DBLCI-OY	α	0.01	0.02	0.02	0.01	0.02	0.01	0.01	0.00
	$\beta_{US\ Bonds}$	−2.45	0.01	0.01	0.01	−0.06	0.91	0.91	0.90
	$\beta_{US\ Equity}$	0.09	0.43	0.35	0.33	0.13	0.30	0.28	0.20
	$\beta_{US\ TIPS}$	1.66	0.00	0.00	0.00				
CSI	α	0.01	0.01	0.01	0.00	0.01	0.01	0.01	0.00
	$\beta_{US\ Bonds}$	−0.24	0.76	0.74	0.67	0.11	0.79	0.73	0.65
	$\beta_{US\ Equity}$	0.75	0.00	0.00	0.00	0.76	0.00	0.00	0.00
	$\beta_{US\ TIPS}$	0.25	0.60	0.50	0.46				

Source: Exhibit created from data obtained from Bloomberg, FactSet, Datastream, and Kenneth French's website http://mba.tuck.dartmouth.edu/pages/faculty/ken.french/data_library.html.

The fact that the DBLCI-OY comes out as the index with the best asset specific risk return relation has nothing to do with the authors' affiliation. There are more likely more subtle things at work. Note that all indexes follow different construction rules. They are essentially constructed by applying a given construction rule to the history of known futures returns. At the date of their first release they represent perfectly in sample optimized baskets, unless you believe that an index provider would launch an index with inferior risk return characteristics than its competitors. As times goes by, the performance becomes more out of sample and the significance of the risk premium usually drops. In this light, it is not surprising that the GSCI that was launched in 1991 by now exhibits not quite so strong performance. The GSCI returned 15.3% against 11.6% for the S&P 500 for the time period up to 1992 (i.e., with backfilled data) but returned less than half of its original return (7%) versus an almost unchanged return of 10.4% for the S&P 500 between 1992 and 2004.[24]

The evidence on commodities as an asset class is less clear than what is commonly believed. Commodities prove to be highly useful for a traditional investor focusing on bonds and equities, but much less so for an investor that is willing to include inflation-linked bonds. Having said that, the documented results still show economic significance (i.e., they are economically meaningful) and might be sample specific. After all, even a p-value of 0.24 indicates a test statistic that still leans more towards the existence of commodities as an asset class than not.

So far we implicitly assumed that commodity indexes reflect asset class returns, the same way a capitalization-weighted stock index reflected the return of equities as an asset class. Whether commodity indexes are representative of an asset class and as such reflect a passive form of investment is subject to some debate. We will argue in the next section that commodity indexes are more active strategies rather than passive investments due to the lack of an objective market weighting.[25]

POTENTIAL PITFALLS OF COMMODITY INDEX PERFORMANCE

Normal Backwardation Is Not Normal

To answer the question whether commodities are an asset class of their own, we should answer the question whether there is an unconditional risk premium for commodity investments. An unconditional risk premium

[24]See Claude B. Erb and Campbell R. Harvey, "The Tactical and Strategic Value of Commodity Futures," *Financial Analysts Journal* 62, no. 2 (2006), pp. 69–97.
[25]See Erb and Harvey for an extensive treat of this idea. Erb and Harvey, "The Tactical and Strategic Value of Commodity Futures."

can be collected by a buy-and-hold investor over time as compensation for taking on commodity risk. This contrasts with a conditional risk premium that only materializes conditional on a particular economic environment. The strategic buy-and-hold investor in commodities will not be able to collect a conditional risk premium. The question we want to ask here is: How much theoretical support is there for the existence of an unconditional risk premium?[26]

The support for the existence of an unconditional risk premium for investors who strategically long commodity futures is Keynes' theory of normal backwardation.[27] Normal backwardation postulates that today's futures price is lower than the expected future spot price. The idea here is that producers of commodities would sell commodity futures to provide insurance against fluctuations in the commodity prices. For example, a corn producer will sell corn futures to hedge the risk that the corn price might be low in the future. Investors who buy corn futures essentially provide insurance for the corn producer. Hence, they would require a futures price lower

---

[26]The most commonly used framework for the existence of a structural risk premium is the *capital asset pricing model* (CAPM). According to the CAPM, the expected rate of return of a given security is the risk free rate plus the market risk premium times the beta of the security, where the market risk premium is the excess return of the market over the risk-free rate, and the beta of the security measures the sensitivity of the security to the market (or measures the systematic risk). The market is the whole stock market. A usual proxy for the market is a value-weighted stock market index, such as S&P 500. In the CAPM, the market risk-adjusted excess returns of the commodity futures should be proportional to its market beta. The empirical literature shows little support for a CAPM-motivated risk premium. Dusak documents low expected returns and low stock market betas for wheat, corn, and soybeans for the time period 1952 to 1967. Katherine Dusak, "Futures Trading and Investor Returns: An Investigation of Commodity Market Risk Premiums," *Journal of Political Economy* 81, no. 6 (1973), pp. 1387–1406.

More recently, Erb and Harvey report insignificant betas for a variety of risk indexes such as the market, value-minus-growth, small-minus-large stocks as well as bond market risk. These findings are consistent with our own data that suggest very low correlations between futures-based commodity indexes and stock returns (e.g., zero correlation between U.S. equities and DBLCI-OY). Given the theoretical and empirical problems attached to the CAPM, we should not be overly concerned. We will ignore the CAPM here because, after all, it is difficult to see how we can apply the CAPM to commodities, if commodities themselves are not part of the market portfolio. Claude B. Erb and Campbell R. Harvey, The Tactical and Strategic Value of Commodity Futures, Working Paper, Unabridged Version (January 2006).

[27]John M. Keynes, *A Treatise on Money*, vol. 2 (London: Macmillan, 1930).

than the expected future spot price. A long position in the corn futures will receive an unconditional risk premium from corn producers for taking the future spot price fluctuation risk. In essence, the theory of normal backwardation implies that there is an insurance risk premium for risk-averse investors to induce them to hold the commodity futures. The theory can only be tested indirectly as normal backwardation is not observable. After all, the expected future spot price is not observable. If, however, we could instead find positive excess returns for all commodity futures we might use this as ex post evidence for the existence of normal backwardation (i.e., an unconditional risk premium).

The empirical findings about normal backwardation are negative. For example, Bodie and Rosansky,[28] Kolb,[29] and Gorton and Rouwenhorst[30] document the excess returns of individual commodity futures and find that the theory of normal backwardation is rejected for average individual commodity futures. In Exhibit 10.8 we plot annualized excess returns versus annualized roll returns. The roll return is the return from the passage of time (carry) assuming the term structure of futures contract does not change. If a market is in backwardation (longer term futures contracts sell at lower prices, i.e. downward sloping term structure of futures prices) the return from rolling up the curve (i.e., selling a 3-month futures after 1 month as a 2-month futures, the expected roll return) is positive, while it is negative if markets are in contango (upwards sloping term structure). The greater the slope of the term structure, the more pronounced these effects are.

Only 3 out of 12 commodity futures had positive excess returns over cash and only three commodity futures had a significant positive roll return. The theory of normal backwardation is inconsistent with these observations or, as Kolb phrased it, normal backwardation is not normal. This sharply contrasts with Keynes theory of normal backwardation that applies (if it were correct) also to markets that are in contango (where the futures price is higher than the current spot price as it usually is with financial markets).[31]

[28]Zvi Bodie and Victor Rosansky, "Risk and Return in Commodity Futures," *Financial Analysts Journal* 36, no. 3 (1980), pp. 27–39.
[29]Robert W. Kolb, "Is Normal Backwardation Normal?" *Journal of Futures Markets* 12, no. 1 (1992), pp. 75–91.
[30]Gorton andRouvenhorst, "Facts and Fantasies about Commodity Futures."
[31]Note that the theory of normal backwardation is different from backwardation. Backwardation is a phenomenon that the futures prices decrease as the time to maturity of the futures increases; that is, futures with short maturities are traded at higher prices. We can view backwardation as a positive carry on a commodity futures contract but this does not guarantee positive excess returns.

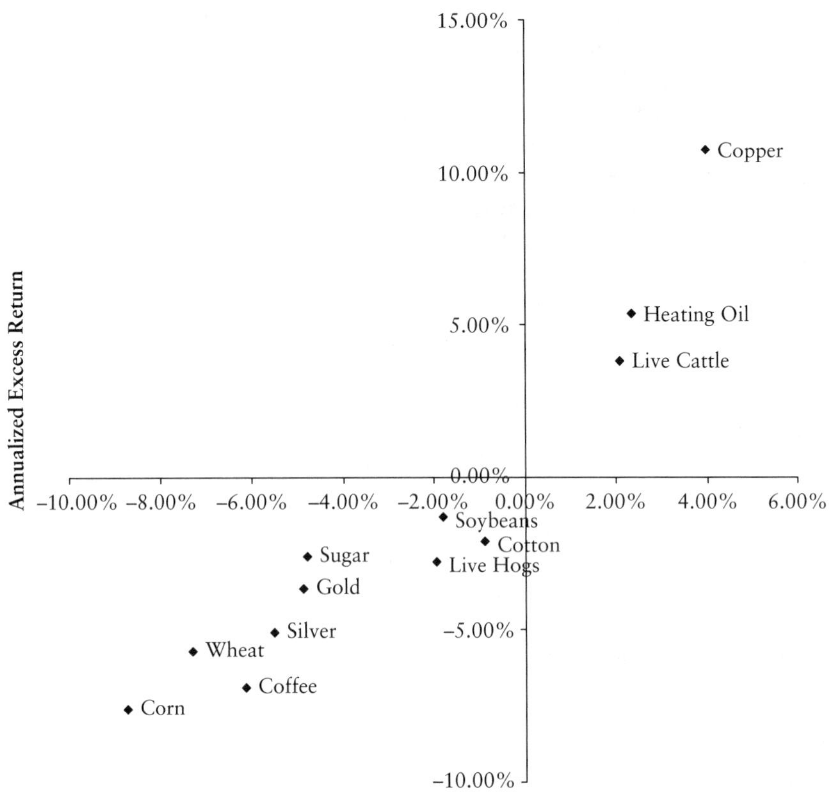

EXHIBIT 10.8 Excess Return versus Roll Return for Various Commodity Futures (based on monthly data), December 1982 to October 2006
Source: Exhibit created from data obtained from Datastream.

More modern theories argue for a conditional risk premium. The hedging pressure hypothesis[32] is the most prominent among those. While Keynes normal backwardation assumes that commodity suppliers always need to pay a risk premium to induce speculators to hold commodities, that hedging pressure hypothesis works both ways. If the demand side needs to get hold of commodities in order to avoid disruption or bottlenecks in production

[32]The hedging pressure hypothesis is due to the following: Paul H. Cootner, "Returns to Speculators: Telser versus Keynes," *Journal of Political Economy* 68, no. 4 (1960), pp. 396–404; and Richard Deaves and Itzhak Krinsky, "Do Futures Prices for Commodities Embody Risk Premiums?" *Journal of Futures Markets* 15, no. 6 (1995), pp. 637–648.

and therefore has to hedge against uncertain supplies, he will be required to pay a risk premium to those who are normally short the futures contract. Several studies find empirical evidence to support the hedging pressure hypothesis.[33] This form of risk premium is here for an investor that engages in tactical asset allocation, but not for the strategic buy and hold investor. Hedging pressure however can not be used to argue that commodity index returns will provide a structural risk premium.

To summarize, normal backwardation does not exist. Not surprisingly commodity indexes (that are ex post optimized up to the date they are released) are heavily geared toward those commodity futures that have been showing the best excess returns (energy in particular oil). Even worse, hedging pressure can and will change and, as such, there is no theoretical support for an unconditional risk premium. This leads index providers to move to the other extreme. The DBLCI-OY explicitly tries to capture the conditional nature of excess returns. While this is more in line with theoretical considerations as well as empirical evidence, it is nevertheless an active strategy.

Risk Premium or Diversification Return?

We can view a commodity index as a portfolio of individual commodity returns. Hence its return critically depends on the weighting scheme as well as individual future returns.[34] While individual commodity futures show an ambiguous picture of excess returns (time varying risk premium that is not even clear to be ex ante positive), the opposite is true for returns on commodity indexes. Bodie and Rosansky as well as Gorton and Rouwenhorst document statistically significant returns for an equally weighted portfolio, that is, a portfolio without a particular bias to future contracts with positive

---

[33]The *weather risk premium* is the most obvious form of a time varying risk premium that is due to seasonal hedging pressure. Here the demand side is willing to place a premium on the futures price to secure supply and avoid disruptions. Examples include a fear of frost in Brazil will induce the demand side (Starbucks) to pay up for production certainty. However, note that this is a conditional, that is, a time-varying risk premium. Empirical evidence is provided in Hendrik Bessembinder, "Systematic Risk, Hedging Pressure and Risk Premiums in Futures Markets," *Review of Financial Studies* 5, no. 4 (1992), pp. 637–667; and Frans DeRoon, Theo E. Nijman, and Chris Veld, "Hedging Pressure Effects in Futures Markets," *Journal of Finance* 55, no. 3 (2000), pp. 1437–1456.

[34]The *rebalancing bonus* (also called *volatility pumping*) is described in Robert Fernholz and Brian Shay, "Stochastic Portfolio Theory and Stock Market Equilibrium," *Journal of Finance* 37, no. 2 (1982), pp. 615–624; and David G. Luenberger, *Investment Science* (New York: Oxford University Press, 1998).

excess returns. Where does this contradiction come from? Why do commodity indexes provide positive excess returns, even though their constituents on average do not?

Erb and Harvey[35] argue that a commodity futures index is not necessarily a good measure of the aggregate commodity market performance because part of the excess returns is due to a rebalancing effect. In the absence of market weightings for commodity index constituents,[36] future positions will be reweighed to some initial weight. We can indirectly infer the effect of a rebalancing bonus from Exhibit 10.8. Equal weighting all 12 commodity futures returns leads to an annualized excess return of −1.88%. This differs strongly from the empirical evidence on commodity returns with the GSCI returning a whopping 3.97% excess return over the same period or with the excess return of an equally weighted portfolio over the same time period of 1.21%. Heuristically, the rebalancing bonus works in the following way. We know that the geometric return is a negative function of variance. Reducing this variance drag will increase the geometric return of a portfolio. As a result the geometric return of a rebalanced portfolio tends to exceed the weighted average return of its components. We can approximate the rebalancing return as one half times the difference between the average variance of $i = 1, \ldots, n$ portfolio components, σ_i^2, and the portfolio variance, σ_{ew}^2 of an equally weighted portfolio:[37]

$$\mathit{diversification} - \mathit{return} \approx \tfrac{1}{2}\left(n^{-1} \sum_{i=1}^{n} \sigma_i^2 - \sigma_{ew}^2 \right)$$

Commodities are an ideal environment for this strategy as they exhibit high individual volatility as well as low internal correlation. As such the diversification benefits of holding an equally weighted portfolio and maintaining the minimum risk by rebalancing are largest (reducing the variance drag).

[35] Erb and Harvey, "The Tactical and Strategic Value of Commodity Futures."

[36] By the very definition of a futures contract for every long (positioned) investor there must be an equivalent short (positioned) investor in the same contract. As such the outstanding value of long and short futures contracts must exactly offset each other. As a result there is no commodity futures market capitalization. Philosophically all commodity indices therefore present active strategies as the natural passive position is impossible to define.

[37] Erb and Harvey derive several approximations for the diversification return. See Erb and Harvey "The Tactical and Strategic Value of Commodity Futures."

Note that this essentially is a concave strategy[38] that will only fail if there are long pronounced trends in a given commodity contract. In this case, we continuously cut back on winning commodities and reinvest in losing commodities (here a convex strategy would perform best). In the previous case, the diversification return was 2.96%. This is not a risk premium but the return of an active strategy.

CONCLUSION

As interests in commodity investing grow, investors gradually view commodities as an asset class in addition to equities and bonds. We first reviewed the concept of an asset class arguing that it is the significance of an asset class specific risk premium that matters, not the significance of a risk premium per se.

Adding commodities to a portfolio of U.S. bonds and equities improves the risk return trade-off materially for all periods under consideration. This effect is very strong, both economically as well as statistically, and forms the conventional wisdom about the strategic value of commodities.

The traditional case for commodities, however, comes with three pinches of salt. First, the historic return of commodity indexes is essentially a mixture of an in sample optimized (with hindsight constructed) basket of commodity futures up to its launch date and true out-of-sample performance thereafter. Second, given that individual futures contracts do not generally provide a risk premium, the size (and sign) of an index risk premium is not a given without a view on the underlying commodity returns. Finally, commodity index returns benefit (to varying degrees) from the rebalancing bonus which does not reflect a risk premium, but rather an active strategy. The case for an unconditional long position in commodities is weakened after we allow inflation-linked bonds into an investor's universe. After all, commodities have been motivated via their inflation hedging properties. Thus, it seems important to introduce a pure inflation hedge into the investment opportunities. Not surprisingly, we find our statistical evidence to weaken, even though the economic significance remains strong.

Our thoughts in this chapter suggest that unlike with equity or bond investments, where the uninformed investor naively buys an index fund to gain exposure to a structural risk premium, more care must be taken in the commodity space. Informed active strategies will prove to be crucial to reap the rewards from taking commodity risks.

---

[38]Andre F. Perold and William F. Sharpe, "Dynamic Strategies for Asset Allocation," *Financial Analysts Journal* (January/February, 1995), pp. 149–160.

APPENDIX

Asset Spanning Regression in Microsoft Excel

This appendix gives an example of asset spanning regression in Microsoft Excel. Exhibit 10A.1 shows the monthly excess returns of DBLCI-OY, U.S. bonds and U.S. equities from January 1989 to September 1990 in an Excel worksheet.[39] To test whether the DBLCI-OY earns a risk premium that cannot be explained by U.S. bonds and U.S. equities, we regress the monthly

EXHIBIT 10A.1 Monthly Excess Returns of DBLCI-OY, U.S. Bonds, and U.S. Equities, January 1989 to September 1990

	A	B	C	D
1	Date	DBLCI-OY	U.S. Bonds	U.S. Equity
2	1/31/1989	0.0023	0.0093	0.0606
3	2/28/1989	0.0378	−0.0133	−0.0225
4	3/31/1989	0.0586	−0.0040	0.0148
5	4/28/1989	0.0297	0.0142	0.0415
6	5/31/1989	−0.0225	0.0169	0.0314
7	6/30/1989	0.0336	0.0233	−0.012
8	7/31/1989	−0.0459	0.0114	0.0701
9	8/31/1989	0.0380	−0.0219	0.0147
10	9/29/1989	0.0467	−0.0014	−0.008
11	10/31/1989	0.0018	0.0179	−0.0361
12	11/30/1989	0.0158	0.0026	0.0109
13	12/29/1989	0.0484	−0.0034	0.0122
14	1/31/1990	−0.0145	−0.0222	−0.0758
15	2/28/1990	0.0023	−0.0025	0.0092
16	3/30/1990	−0.0191	−0.0057	0.0177
17	4/30/1990	−0.0139	−0.0161	−0.0352
18	5/31/1990	−0.0369	0.0219	0.0821
19	6/29/1990	−0.0237	0.0098	−0.0105
20	7/31/1990	0.0729	0.0075	−0.0162
21	8/31/1990	0.1344	−0.0201	−0.0985
22	9/28/1990	0.1474	0.0023	−0.0598

Source: Exhibit created from data obtained from Bloomberg, Thomson Financial DataStream, and Kenneth French's website http://mba.tuck.dartmouth.edu/pages/faculty/ken.french/data_library.html.

[39]Note that the regression example here has only 21 observations due to the limited space. The sample sizes for the regressions in the main text are larger.

excess returns of DBLCI-OY on the monthly excess returns of U.S. bonds and equities. We use the Linear Regression Tool of Excel to do the regression. For example, on the menu bar, we click Tools, Data Analysis, then choose Regression from the Analysis Tools, and then click OK. In the pop-up window, we enter $B$2:$B$22 in "Input Y Range", and enter $C$2:$D$22 in "Input X Range", then click ok. Exhibit 10A.2 shows the regression outputs. We notice that the regression coefficients for the regression intercept, U.S. bonds and U.S. equity are 0.02, 0.08, and -0.65, respectively. The corresponding *p*-values are 0.03, 0.92, and 0.02. The small *p*-value for the regression intercept (0.03) means that the DBLCI-OY is not spanned by the U.S. bonds and U.S. equities at the 3% significance level.

Additional Regression Statistics

In order to make meaningful interpretations for the regression coefficients, we need to check whether the implied assumptions of OLS regressions are satisfied. Thus we check the regression diagnostics.

Exhibit 10A.3 presents the regression diagnostics for the regressions in Exhibit 10.4. We test whether the regression residuals are uncorrelated and normal. The second column "DW statistics" shows the Durbin-Watson statistic for the serial correlation tests. If the Durbin-Watson statistic is 2, it means that there are no serial correlations in the residuals. If the Durbin-Watson statistic is greater (smaller) than 2, it means that there are negative (positive) serial correlations in the residuals. The third column shows the *p*-values of the correlation test (the Ljung-Box test). The null hypothesis is that there is no correlation. The fourth column shows the *p*-values of the normality test (the Jarque-Bera test). The null hypothesis is that the residuals are normal. We notice from Exhibit 10A.3 that the *p*-values for the GSCI, DBLCI, DBLCI-MR, and DBLCI-OY are small, which means that the null hypothesis of zero correlation and normality are rejected for those indexes.

Exhibit 10A.4 presents the regression diagnostics for the regressions in Exhibit 10.7. The *p*-values for the normality tests are large for all the regressions, which means that the null hypothesis of normality is not rejected. The *p*-values for the correlation tests are large except for DBLCI-OY, so the White and Newey-West *p*-values would be more accurate than the *p*-values without adjustments.

EXHIBIT 10A.2 Regression Output of the Monthly Excess Returns of DBLCI-OY on the Monthly Excess Returns of U.S. Bonds and U.S. Equity, January 1989 to September 1990

Summary Output

Regression Statistics	
Multiple *R*	0.570891396
R-square	0.325916986
Adjusted *R*-square	0.251018874
Standard error	0.044099412
Observations	21

ANOVA

	df	*SS*	*MS*	*F*	Significance *F*
Regression	2	0.016925119	0.008462559	4.351471287	0.028735612
Residual	18	0.035005647	0.001944758		
Total	20	0.051930766			

	Coefficients	Standard Error	*t*-Stat	*p*-value	Lower 95%	Upper 95%
Intercept	0.02309118	0.00968636	2.38388582	0.02834815	0.00274087	0.04344149
X variable 1	0.08212403	0.82220385	0.09988281	0.92154142	−1.64526350	1.80951156
X variable 2	−0.64988523	0.25623885	−2.53624787	0.02068561	−1.18822349	−0.11154697

Source: Exhibit created from data obtained from Bloomberg, Thomson Financial DataStream, and Kenneth French's website http://mba.tuck.dartmouth.edu/pages/faculty/ken.french/data_library.html.

EXHIBIT 10A.3 Regression Diagnostics (based on monthly excess returns from January 1989 to June 2006)

	DW Statistics	*p*-value (correlation test)	*p*-value (normality test)
GSCI	1.83	0.00	0.00
DBLCI	1.89	0.00	0.00
DBLCI-MR	1.80	0.00	0.00
DBLCI-OY	1.77	0.03	0.00
CSI	1.93	0.84	0.07

Source: Exhibit created from data obtained from Bloomberg, FactSet, Datastream, and Kenneth French's website http://mba.tuck.dartmouth.edu/pages/faculty/ken.french/data_library.html.

EXHIBIT 10A.4 Spanning Regression Diagnostics (based on monthly excess returns from September 2000 to June 2006)

Panel A: Regression Including TIPS			
	DW Statistics	*p*-value (correlation test)	*p*-value (normality test)
GSCI	1.85	0.15	0.56
DBLCI	1.74	0.12	0.29
DBLCI-MR	1.80	0.51	0.22
DBLCI-OY	1.66	0.00	0.36
CSI	2.30	0.15	0.68
Panel B: Regression Excluding TIPS			
	DW Statistics	*p*-value (correlation test)	*p*-value (normality test)
GSCI	1.90	0.15	0.81
DBLCI	1.88	0.11	0.39
DBLCI-MR	1.94	0.22	0.29
DBLCI-OY	1.74	0.01	0.37
CSI	2.31	0.20	0.69

Source: Exhibit created from data obtained from Bloomberg, FactSet, Datastream, and Kenneth French's website http://mba.tuck.dartmouth.edu/pages/faculty/ken.french/data_library.html.

CHAPTER 11

CTA/Managed Futures Strategy Benchmarks

Performance and Review

Thomas Schneeweis, Ph.D.
Director
Center for International Securities and Derivatives Markets
Isenberg School of Management
University of Massachusetts

Raj Gupta, Ph.D.
Director of Research
Center for International Securities and Derivatives Markets
Isenberg School of Management, University of Massachusetts

Jason Remillard
Quantitative Analyst
Minerva Alternate Strategies, Inc.

The term *managed futures* represents an industry comprised of professional money managers known as *commodity trading advisors* (CTAs)[1] or *commodity pool operators* (CPOs)[2] who manage client assets on a

[1]The Commodity Futures Trading Commission (CFTC) defines *commodity trading advisor* (CTA) as any person, who, for compensation or profit, directly or indirectly advises others as to the advisability of buying or selling commodity futures or option contracts.
[2]CFTC defines *commodity pool operator* (CPO) as any individual or firm that operates a commodity pool. (For example: If a pool is organized as a limited partnership,

discretionary basis using global forward, futures, and options markets as the primary investment medium. Managed futures provide direct exposure to international financial and nonfinancial asset sectors while offering (through their ability to take both long and short investment positions) a means to gain exposure to risk-return patterns not easily accessible with investment in traditional long-only stock and bond portfolios as well as in many alternative investments such as real estate, private equity, or commodities. Previous research has shown that managed futures often provide (1) a reduction in the volatility of stock and bond portfolios as the result of managed futures low or negative return correlation with stock and bond markets; and (2) enhanced returns to stock, bond, and stock and bond portfolios during economic environments in which traditional stock and bond investments often offer limited return opportunities.[3]

While academic research has centered primarily on the benefits and risks of managed futures, less work exists on determining the relative performance benefits of individual CTAs or individual CTA strategies. One reason for the lack of research in this area is that traditional multifactor benchmark models, which are used to describe the market factors driving traditional stock and bonds as well as many hedge fund strategies, have little use in describing the return behavior of CTAs. This is mainly due to the underlying strategy focus of CTAs, which results in investment holdings which do not traditionally track long-only stock and bond indexes. In fact, managed futures have been described principally as absolute return strategies since their goal was to obtain positive returns across a variety of market environments. This approach has often led to a low exposure to traditional equity benchmarks (e.g., zero beta) and as a result, relative performance has often been measured in comparison to the risk-free rate. Today, it is well understood that managed futures require a broader understanding of the underlying risk structure of the strategy and that a range of benchmarking alternatives may be used to provide an understanding of the underlying returns to a CTA strategy and its performance relative to similar strategies.

It is not possible in this analysis to convey all the details related to the benchmarking of managed futures. In this chapter we provide (1) a brief

---

its general partner typically is its CPO.) A commodity pool is an investment trust, syndicate, or similar form of enterprise operated for the purpose of trading commodity futures or option contracts.

[3]Thomas Schneeweis and Jason Remillard, Benefits of Managed Futures, CISDM Working Paper Series, 2006.

synopsis of the benefits of managed futures investment; (2) a short review of manager-based CTA benchmark construction; and (3) an empirical analysis on the relative performance of various CTA benchmarks (noninvestible manager-based indexes, investible manager-based indexes, and passive-security-based indexes). In this analysis the various CTA indexes are compared on a zero risk (e.g., Treasury bill), total risk (Sharpe ratio), market factor risk (e.g., S&P 500), strategy risk (e.g., passive futures-based CTA index) and peer group basis (investible and noninvestible manager-based indexes). Lastly, for a selected set of CTAs with full data over the period of analysis an example of excess return determination on a zero risk, total risk, market risk, strategy (passive futures-based CTA index) and peer group basis is provided.

GROWTH AND BENEFIT OF MANAGED FUTURES

Futures and options have been used for centuries both as a risk management tool and as a return enhancement vehicle. Managed futures, as an investment alternative, has been available primarily since the 1970s and has experienced significant growth over the past several decades. Credit Agricole Structured Asset Management (CASAM) and the Center of International Securities and Derivatives Markets (CISDM) currently manage a database that consists of both live and dead CTA fund managers. As shown in Exhibit 11.1, the assets under management in the CASAM/CISDM CTA database have grown from approximately $10 billion in 1990 to about $162 billion at the end of September 2006.

The growth in investor demand for managed futures products indicates increased investor appreciation of the potential benefits of managed futures. Such benefits include reduced portfolio risk, potential for enhanced portfolio returns, ability to profit in different economic environments, and the ease of global diversification.[4] Furthermore, managed futures benefits from the special opportunities that futures/options traders have in lower transaction costs, lower market impact costs, use of leverage, and trading in liquid markets.

[4]An often overlooked benefit to U.S. investors is that actual investment in overseas futures contracts to a U.S. investor may only expose the investor to exchange rate risk on the change in the value of the futures contract and the required margin requirement of the foreign futures exchange.

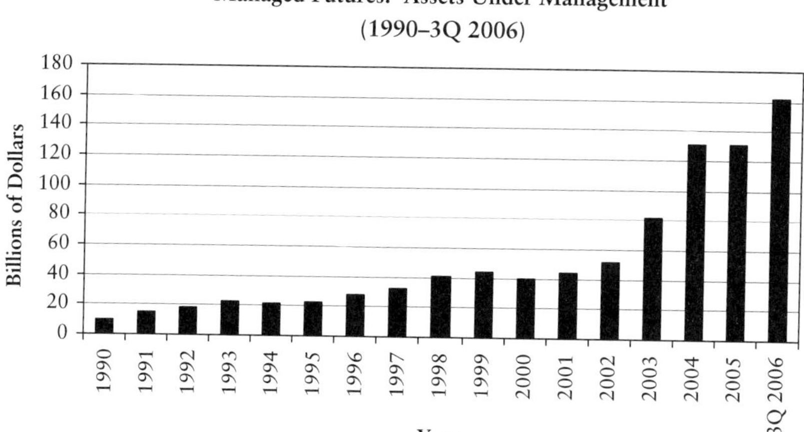

EXHIBIT 11.1 Managed Futures Assets Under Management
Source: Exhibit created from data obtained from CASAM/CISDM, BarclayHedge, Credit Suisse, Calyon Financial, FTSE, MLM, and S&P web sites.

GENERAL DESCRIPTION OF MANAGED FUTURES

Managed futures have long been regarded as skill-based investment strategies. Skill-based strategies obtain returns from the unique skill or strategy of the trader. Given that these strategy returns are based on managers attempting to maximize returns within the parameters of their trading strategy and are not managed to track a particular stock or bond index, CTAs are frequently referred to as *absolute return strategies*. Because managed futures are actively managed, trader skill is important. However, the lack of direct stock or bond index tracking by CTAs does not mean that managers do not have similar sensitivities to traditional market factors or that a CTA index of like managers with a common basis of return movement cannot be created. For instance, it has been shown that specific managed futures returns are also driven by systematic movement in market factors (such as price momentum) that can be replicated using similar traded securities (futures).[5] In fact, a significant majority of CTAs apply momentum-based strategies.

It is important to note that many managed futures strategies trade primarily in futures markets, which can be considered a net zero sum game. If

[5]Richard Spurgin, Thomas Schneeweis, and Georgi Georgiev, Benchmarking Commodity Trading Advisor Performance with a Passive Futures-Based Index, CISDM Working Paper Series, 2003.

CTAs were only trading against other CTAs then one may conclude that managed futures returns were based solely on manager skills. However, academics[6] and practitioners[7] have shown that some spot market players are willing to sell or hedge positions even if they expect spot positions to rise or fall in their favor (e.g., currency and interest rate futures may be traded profitably as traders act in full knowledge of government policy to smooth price movements).[8] In brief, one may think of managed futures returns as a combination of manager skill and an underlying return to the strategy itself.

CTA INDEX CONSTRUCTION

CTA Index Design

In the traditional asset area, a wide set of manager-based (e.g., Morningstar, Lipper) and systematic passive stock and bond indexes (e.g., S&P 500, Russell 2000) exist. Each differs in performance, selection, and classification. Similarly, in the CTA area, a number of manager-based, peer-group-based indexes as well as systematic investible passive-security-(futures-) based CTA indexes exist. Investors should note that each CTA manager-based and/or security-based index series has its own approach to performance presentation, manager selection, and investment style classification; however, each generally attempts to meet a series of attributes. While there is no final agreement as to the criteria for creating such an index, for CTA indexes to reflect the investment practices and index characteristics common to traditional stock and bond indexes, indexes should consider the following attributes:

- *Unambiguous.* CTAs included in an index and the weight assigned to each fund should be fully disclosed and readily obtainable. The factors or market strategy the index is designed to track should be explicitly

[6]For the arguments on the sources of return to managed futures see Richard Spurgin, Some Thoughts on the Source of Return to Managed Futures, CISDM Working Paper Series, 2005.

[7]For the discussion on optimal currency hedging policy with biased forward rates, see Mark Kritzman, "The Optimal Currency Hedging Policy with Biased Forward Rates," *Journal of Portfolio Management* 19, no. 4 (1993), pp. 94–100.

[8]Other examples of individuals willing to pay to reduce risk are those who buy insurances. Insurance firms obtain a positive return to risk investment from individuals wishing to hedge various risks.

defined. Guidelines for altering the components and weights should be specified in advance.

- *Investibility.* While the individual "style" indexes themselves may not be directly investible, it is expected that investors will be able to earn the returns associated with the indexes with minimal tracking error and at relatively low cost.
- *Measurability.* Investors will have access to the prices or returns used to compute the indexes so that individual index returns can be independently verified.
- *Appropriateness.* The indexes will exclude funds that a typical investor would not hold, and will employ commonsense weighting schemes and rebalancing approaches.
- *Accountability.* Changes in the indexes' components and computation will be made by a committee whose membership is public, and will be based on established and explicitly articulated procedures.

Major CTA Indexes

Manager Based Publicly available manager-based CTA indexes can be broadly classified into two categories: Noninvestible manager-based (active) indexes and Investible manager-based (active) indexes. The noninvestible manager-based indexes are generally constructed by major database providers from managers reporting to their respective databases. It is important to point out that none of these noninvestible manager-based CTA indexes completely represent the universe of CTAs and that while the various databases may contain similar managers some managers only report to a single database as illustrated in Exhibit 11.2. In contrast, investible manager-based indexes are generally constructed from a smaller set of managers who report directly to the index provider and are often based on managed accounts in contrast to pooled investment vehicles. In fact, the criteria used by various database providers to create noninvestible indexes or by investible CTA platform providers to construct these indexes may vary widely and can be summarized as follows:

- *Selection criteria.* Decision rules that determine which CTAs are included in the index. Examples of selection criteria include length of track record, assets under management, and restrictions on new investment.
- *Style classification.* How each CTA is assigned to a style-specific index, and whether or not a fund that fails to satisfy the style classification methodology is excluded from the index.

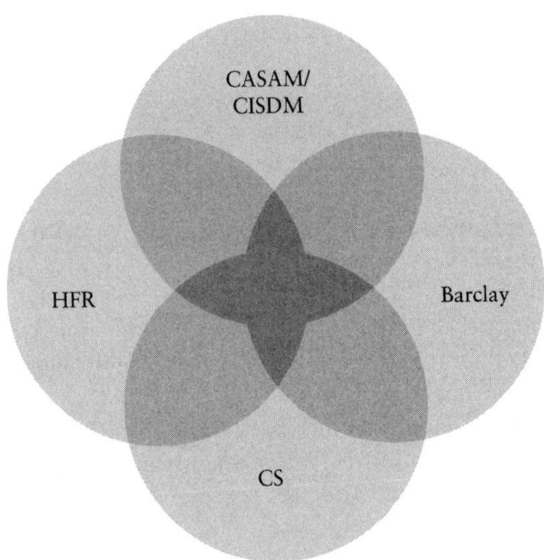

EXHIBIT 11.2 Representation of Universe of Managers of Public Databases
Source: Authors.

- *Weighting scheme.* The weight a particular fund's return is given in the index. Common weighting schemes are equally weighted and dollar-weighted-based on assets under management.
- *Investibility.* Whether the index is directly or indirectly investible.

For some in the CTA industry, concerns over the previously mentioned index criteria are understandable. If one uses the aforementioned standards for CTA strategy-based (e.g., peer group) indexes then none of the noninvestible and few currently available investible manager-based peer group indexes are true indexes, such that perhaps the term benchmarks may be a better descriptor. Exhibit 11.3 provides a brief comparison of both investible and noninvestible manager-based CTA indexes as well as passive security-based CTA indexes that are currently in existence.

Investible Passive-Security- (Futures-) Based CTA Indexes For a number of CTA strategies there exists investible passive-security- (futures-) based indexes. These indexes have been created to have return characteristics reflective of the corresponding noninvestible and/or investible manager-based CTA indexes. Given that these investible indexes are designed to

EXHIBIT 11.3 Comparison of Existing CTA Indexes

	Major Noninvestible and Investible Active-Manager and Passive-Security-Based CTA Indexes										
	Noninvestible CTA Indexes						Investible CTA Indexes			Passive CTA Indexes	
	CASAM/CISDM		Barclay Trader Index CTA	CS/ Tremont	Calyon Financial Barclay	BTOP50	S&P Managed Futures	CSFB/ Tremont INVX	FTSE CTA/ Managed Futures	MLM	MSFB
Weighting	Equal	Asset	Equal	Asset	Equal	Equal	Equal	Asset	Multiple Criteria	Multiple Criteria	Multiple Criteria
Data Availability	2001	1992	1987	2003	2000	2003	2002	2003	2004	1988	2003
Strategy Classifications	7	7	6	None	None	None	None	None	None	3	3
Updates	Monthly	Monthly	Monthly	Monthly	Daily	Monthly	Daily	Monthly	Daily	Monthly	Daily
Constituency Disclosed	No	No	No	No	Yes	Yes	Yes	Yes	Yes	Security Based	Security Based

Source: Exhibit created from data obtained from CASAM/CISDM, BarclayHedge, Credit Suisse, Calyon Financial, FTSE, MLM, and S&P web sites.

reflect the performance of manager-based CTA strategies, investible security-based CTA indexes are generally trend following because discretionary CTAs are by their very nature difficult to track in a systematic manner.

CTA Strategy Indexes

The term *managed futures* is broad in that it encompasses a variety of different CTA strategies. CTAs are generally grouped within two primary types of trading strategies: discretionary or systematic. Within each of the generic forms of trading, managers may trade particular market segments such as currency, financial, physical commodity, and equity.

Trading Strategy Focus

- *Discretionary.* Trade financial, currency, and commodity futures/options-based on a wide variety of trading models including those based on fundamental economic data and/or individual trader's beliefs.
- *Systematic.* Trade primarily in the context of a predetermined systematic trading model. Most systematic CTAs follow a trend-following program although some trade countertrend. In addition, trend-following CTAs may concentrate on short-, mid-, or long-term trends or a combination thereof.

Futures Markets Traded

Currency. Trade currency futures/options and forward contracts.

Diversified. Trade financial futures/options, currency futures/options and forward contracts as well as commodity futures/options.

Financial. Trade financial futures/options as well as currency futures/options and forward contracts.

Physical. Trade OTC and exchange-traded futures and/or options in energy, agricultural, and metals markets.

Equity. Trade OTC and exchange-traded futures and/or options in equity-related markets.

Noninvestible Active Manager-Based CTA Indexes Noninvestible indexes form the largest set of CTA indexes. Principal CTA noninvestible manager-based indexes include the Barclay BTOP 50 Index, CASAM/CISDM CTA

Indexes, Barclay CTA Index, CS/Tremont Managed Futures Index, and Calyon Financial Barclay Index. Characteristics of each of the indexes differ as follows:

- *CASAM/CISDM.* The CASAM/CISDM Indexes are a set of asset-weighted and equally weighted indexes. These indexes span various market segments such as currencies, financials, and diversified as well as trading strategies such as systematic or discretionary. The CASAM/CISDM Hedge Fund/CTA Database is used to select managers for the various indexes. The indexes are updated monthly with historical index values dating back to 1979.
- *Barclay Group.* The Barclay Group Indexes are a set of equally weighted indexes. Indexes span various market segments such as currencies, financials, and diversified as well as trading strategies such as systematic or discretionary. The Barclay Group CTA Database is used to select managers for the various indexes. The indexes are updated monthly with historical index values dating back to 1987. In addition to CTA indexes derived from the Barclay CTA database, Barclay also provides two additional indexes that represent returns to the overall CTA Universe.
- *Calyon Financial/Barclay Index.* The Calyon Financial Barclay Index provides daily returns from a collection of major CTAs that are open to new investment. Selection of the pool of qualified CTAs used in construction of the Index is conducted annually, with rebalancing on January 1 of each year. The index is equal weighted and updated daily. The index was launched in 2000 and is updated monthly.
- *Barclay BTOP 50 Index.* The BTOP50 Index attempts to replicate the overall composition of the managed futures industry in terms of both trading style and overall market exposure. The BTOP50 employs a top-down approach in selecting its constituent CTAs. The largest investible trading advisor programs, as measured by assets under management, are selected for inclusion in the index. Selected trading advisor programs represent, in aggregate, no less than 50% of the investible assets of the Barclay CTA Universe each year. The index was launched in 2003 and is updated monthly.
- *Credit Suisse/Tremont Managed Futures Index.* The Credit Suisse/Tremont Managed Futures Index is an asset-weighted index based on funds reporting to the TASS database. Unlike CISDM or the Barclay Group, Credit Suisse/Tremont does not provide indexes for various market segments or strategies. The TASS Database is used to select managers for this index. The indexes are updated monthly with historical index values dating back to 1994.

Manager-Based Investible CTA Indexes In addition to manager-based noninvestible CTA indexes manager-based investible CTA indexes are also available. The principal manager-based investible indexes include the S&P Managed Futures Index, the CS/Tremont INVX, and the FTSE Hedge CTA/Managed Futures index. Characteristics of each index are as follows:

- *S&P Managed Futures Index (S&P MFI).* The S&P MFI is an equally weighted investible index designed to be representative of investments in managed futures/CTAs programs. Specifically, the index aims to track systematic managers employing mainly technical trend-following and pattern-recognition trading methodologies. The index is updated daily and was launched in 2002. Currently, the S&P Managed Futures Index is not offered as an investment product.
- *Credit Suisse/Tremont Managed Futures INVX Index.* The Credit Suisse/Tremont Managed Futures INVX Index is an asset-weighted index based on eligible investible funds reporting to the TASS database. The TASS Database is used to select managers for this index. Eligible funds must have a minimum of $50 million in assets under management with a track record greater than 12 months. The index is reviewed and rebalanced semi-annually. The index was launched in 2004.
- *Other Manager-Based CTA Indexes.* There are several other investible manager-based CTA indexes such as the FTSE Hedge CTA/Managed Futures Index. Each of these indexes differs as to selection methodology, weighting scheme, and style classification.[9]

Investible Passive CTA Indexes

Like other security-based investible indexes (e.g., S&P 500), CTA passive security-based indexes are based on a systematic approach index creation and reflect a particular approach to futures/option trading with the goal of replicating the underlying return stream to the particular CTA trading strategy. For instance, the MLM Index™ is based on a particular trend-following model of futures prices for a basket of actively traded futures contracts consisting of commodities, global bonds, and currencies. Other passive investible CTA indexes such as the MFSB provide CTA indexes and also attempt to generate returns similar to certain types of trend-based strategies.[10]

[9]We have not included the MSCI systematic CTA indexes in this study due to its more heterogeneous nature which includes more global macro players.

[10]Spurgin, Schneeweis, and Georgiev. "Benchmarking Commodity Trading Advisor Performance with a Passive Futures-Based Index." The MFSB Indices are based on the methodology presented in this article.

Issues in CTA Benchmark Design

Since each benchmark index differs to some extent in the methodology in which they are constructed, it is important to understand some of the potential problems and limitations that can become a factor in the design of an appropriate CTA benchmark. These potential problems are discussed next.

Data Issues If one uses a current database to construct one's own index, that index may contain selection, backfill, or survivorship bias. When a public database is used as a basis for index calculation, the public index return data before the index inception date may also contain backfill and survivorship bias.

- *Selection Bias.* This type of bias exists in most indexes. It arises from the selection methodologies used by the index provider to select funds in the index. Selection bias can exist in various forms (e.g., if funds are asset weighted, the index is impacted by larger funds whereas if funds are equal weighted the index is impacted by funds with higher volatilities).
- *Backfill Bias.* Since managers typically voluntarily report their results to benchmark index providers this can present issues that impact the performance of such benchmarks and can potentially provide a misleading representation of the true performance of the industry or strategy being presented. A manager may elect to begin submitting his or her returns to an index only when their results appear favorable. Most of the major CTA indexes only have limited backfill bias since many have been in existence since the early 1990s and only in the initial month of reporting are new managers part of the index. In practice, backfill bias is difficult to estimate since certain managers may start reporting to newer databases at any point in time.
- *New Manager Bias.* New managers often have fewer assets under management and may trade more concentrated portfolios. As a result their performance may not reflect larger mature managers. To eliminate the upward bias resulting from potential new manager bias, index providers typically discard the first 12 to 24 months of reported returns in calculating their indexes or require a particular amount of assets under management.
- *Survivorship Bias.* This bias exists when one creates a CTA index from a current database that includes only those managers who have survived over time. This leads to an upward bias in benchmark index reporting since it does not take into account those managers who performed poorly and have ceased operating or reporting. Most of the major CTA indexes have no survivorship bias since they have been in

existence since the early 1990s in that they do not restate their historical index return data when managers stop reporting.

Weighting The methodology in which an index is weighted can have a significant impact on the interpretation of the performance of an underlying index.

- *Asset versus Equal Weighting.* Asset-weighted indexes place proportionately greater emphasis on the returns on larger CTAs when computing their index performance. This can be an issue in benchmark design since an asset-weighted index suggests the performance of those CTAs in the index with the highest assets under management better represents the performance of the given benchmark. This methodology is more firm specific than industry specific. Equally weighted indexes do not present any size-related bias since each fund is given equally proportional weighting in the calculation of the benchmark index.

Manager Selection Constructing a CTA index entails selecting a set of managers that are intended to be representative of a larger universe of CTAs. Determining the process for choosing managers, ensuring those managers reflect the intended composite or strategy index being constructed, and deciding the appropriate number of managers for inclusion into the index all present issues in index construction.

- *Fund Composite/Strategy Listing.* Defining the CTA universe is a difficult exercise. There is no general agreement regarding which investment strategies should be presented or the weights that should be used in determining the performance of such a composite index. As a result, most investible indexes are constructed at the strategy level, such that the historical pattern of returns may be expected to reflect future performance characteristics.
- *Number of Funds/Managers.* There is no single number of managers required for an index to represent a particular strategy. However, academic research has shown that approximately four to six CTAs are required to represent a particular CTA strategy. One issue of importance however is the degree to which the managers in the index are equal or asset weighted. A strictly asset-weighted approach may weigh the index toward a single group of managers such that diversification within the strategy may be reduced. In addition, if the managers within the index have dramatically different volatilities, the manager with the highest volatility will dominate the return movement of the index.

- *Manager Selection Process.* Most indexes rely on a set of published quantitative measures as well as a qualitative oversight approach to manager selection. The quantitative approaches may differ across strategies, however, they are used to create a set of managers, which generally trade in similar areas and are sensitive to similar economic factors.

EMPIRICAL ANALYSIS

Data and Methodology

For any particular investor, the fundamental basis for using a particular CTA index or benchmark is that it should have similar trading and market factor characteristics to the corresponding CTA or CTA strategy under consideration. In this analysis we provide information on the various trading and market factor characteristics of a wide range of alternative CTA noninvestible manager-based, investible manager-based, and investible passive-security- (futures-) based indexes. It is important to point out, the CTA indexes reflect the performance of a portfolio of CTAs. Therefore, similar to stock indexes and individual stocks, while the returns of a CTA index may be reflective of the expected returns of a specific CTA, in a particular strategy the risk estimate for an index will generally be less than any individual CTA.

Our analysis consists of using monthly return data for investible and noninvestible active manager-based CTA indexes as well as investible passive security-based CTA strategy indexes for the period January 2001 through September 2006. It is important to note that several of the noninvestible and investible manager indexes used in this study were created post January 2001. To the degree that survivorship bias and/or selection bias exists in these indexes prior to their date of creation those returns may be upwardly biased. For the purposes of our study, the indexes created from the major databases, CISDM, Barclay, and CS are not affected by survivorship or backfill bias. However, the BTOP50, S&P, FTSE, and CS investible manager-based indexes were created post January 2001 and may contain a degree of manager selection or backfill bias in their returns between January 2001 and their date of creation. Similarly, the MSFB index was relaunched in 2001 and to the degree that the passive systematic trend-following model was based on data in 2001, the returns from the period of testing may result in upward bias returns for that period.[11]

[11]Spurgin, Schneeweis, and Georgiev, "Benchmarking Commodity Trading Advisor Performance with a Passive Futures-Based Index."

Lastly, there has been considerable discussion as to the alternative means of determining a CTA's alpha. As previously discussed, CTAs have been described as skill-based investment strategies. Academic research has demonstrated CTA returns are in part driven systematically by market factors such as price momentum, rather than exclusively by individual manager's alpha.[12] In brief, one can think of CTA returns as a combination of manager skill and an underlying return to the CTA strategy or investment style itself. Therefore, in order to claim alpha, one should be able to depict a return in excess of an equally risky and equally investible CTA investment strategy. The use of the risk-free rate, or an S&P 500 based CAPM while investible does not reflect similar risk to a CTA. As such, a CTA's excess return based on them should not be considered an example of manager skill. Similarly, the use of return based on an assumed Sharpe ratio or non-investible multifactor model should not be considered an example of a manager's alpha, but only his or her excess return relative to that individual risk measure.[13]

In short, while many CTAs continue to compare themselves with Treasury bill returns, the S&P 500, or even returns based on an expected Sharpe ratio, the actual excess return of a CTA after considering a wider range of comparable risky assets is often close to zero (see Exhibit 11.4). This is not to say that CTAs do not provide value, only that the returns to CTAs are commensurate with the underlying risks to which they are exposed. For instance, the source of CTA returns may be due to risks from a variety of market factors (e.g., trading processes) which provide an example of a multifactor benchmark model for a CTA strategy (see Exhibit 11.5). A similar sensitivity by certain CTA strategies to stock and bond markets or to common trading processes would reflect their sensitivities to common market factors. In brief, the sensitivity of various CTA strategies to various return factors is based on their similar risk exposure.

In this analysis we also use several investible security (futures) CTA strategy-based measures of return estimation. To the degree that the

---

[12]Schneeweis and Remillard, "Benefits of Managed Futures."

[13]In fact, one can use a number of performance measures to test the relative return performance of CTAs. See Simon Taylor, "A Brief History of Performance Ratios," Hedgequest, Searching for the Perfect Risk-Adjusted Performance Measure, pp. 4–8, Summer 2005). As discussed previously, for instance, CTAs were once described as absolute return vehicles since their return was supposedly uncorrelated with any traditional index. If a CTA's equity beta was close to zero, then the comparison benchmark return was the risk-free rate. Current academic research has shown, however, that such simple "CAPM"-based measures of return performance often underspecify the CTA's expected risk and therefore the CTA's expected return.

EXHIBIT 11.4 Excess Return/Alpha Determination Based on Single- and Multifactor Benchmarks

Benchmark Comparisons			
Excess Return Alpha Determination			
Market Based:	Benchmark	Computation	Calculation
	T-bill	$Ri - Rf$	5.00%
	CAPM	$Ri - (Rf + (Rm - Rf) \times Bi)$	4.50%
	Expected Sharpe Ratio (variance)	(Historical return − Expected return from Sharpe ratio = .66)	2.00%
	Multifactor	$Ri -$ (B1 × R1(S&P 500) + ··· + BN RN(Lehman High Yield) + ···)	4.50%
Security (Futures) Based:	Strategy Replication (passive)	$Ri -$ (passive-futures-based replicating strategy)	0.50%
Relative Performance Determination			
Manager Based:	Benchmark	Computation	Calculation
	Indexes	$Ri -$ (Investible + Noninvestible Index Ri)	2.00%
	Peer Group	$Ri -$ (Strategy-Based Peer Group Ri)	1.00%

Source: Authors.

Note: The various measures of excess return described in this exhibit do not consider the required return to increase the Sharpe ratio of a stand alone portfolio. In general to achieve enhanced risk-adjusted performance (Sharpe ratio) by adding an asset to a portfolio one should examine the correlation of that asset to the existing portfolio. Given the low equity and bond betas for most CTAs, the results using this approach would be similar to the results using a CAPM or Jensen measure.

$$R_i = \alpha_i + \beta_{i,1} F_1 + \ldots \beta_{i,K} F_K + e_i$$

where

R_i = Return on fund i

α_i = Abnormal return (or alpha) for portfolio i

$\beta_{i,K}$ = Beta coefficient of fund i for market factor K or trading factor K

F_K = Return on market factor K

e_i = Statistical noise of fund i

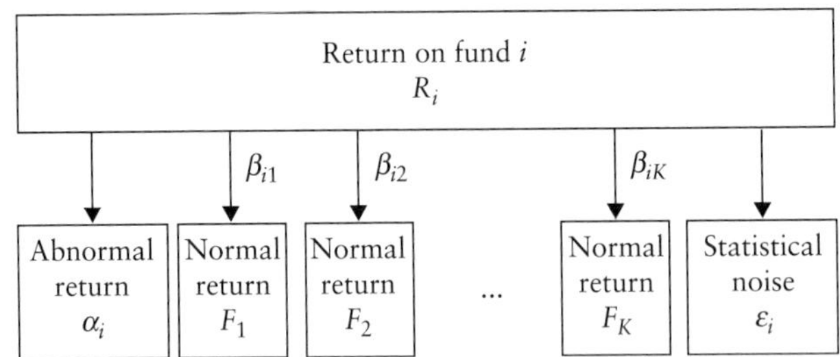

EXHIBIT 11.5 Multifactor Regression Format
Source: Authors.

measures fully represent comparable investible returns, such tradable alternatives provide a means to measure manager alpha. Additionally, a set of noninvestible and investible manager-based CTA indexes are used to offer a means of relative peer return comparisons. However, peer-group-based relative return estimates are not measures of absolute manager skill but only relative manager skill.

In order to focus on the impact of various potential benchmarks, we also estimate the benchmark-based excess return comparison detailed in Exhibit 11.4 to 77 CTAs within the CASAM/CISDM database with full monthly return data from January 2001 to September 2006. These CTAs are grouped based on the CASAM/CISDM investment strategy/market classifications (discretionary, systematic, currency, diversified, and financial). The CTAs are also classified into short, medium, long, and multiple time frames based on the time period used in their trading decision model (e.g., systematic trend-following CTAs). By categorizing CTAs into these trading time classifications, we then compare the average performance of these CTAs to determine the impact of alternative trading time classifications on the use of current CTA manager-based benchmarks on measuring excess returns. In this analysis, we focus on the impact of using short, medium, long, and multiple trading time frames on diversified and financial CTAs, where our sample of funds was large enough to break out into smaller subgroups.

Lastly, since the 77 CTAs were determined for the December 2006 CASAM/CISDM database, the managers selected contain both survivorship and backfill bias and the reported return level is expected to be above indexes based on all CTAs existing over the period used for analysis.

Empirical Results on Industry Level

Here we review the historical performance, market factor characteristics, and relative return comparisons of the CTA indexes. We first analyze the performance of both investible and noninvestible active manager-based CTA strategy indexes as well as investible passive-security-based CTA strategy. Secondly, we review the correlation of the various CTA benchmarks on a range of market factors and compare noninvestible manager-based indexes, investible manager-based indexes, and investible passive-security-based indexes. Lastly, we analyze the relative performance of various manager-based CTA indexes and sample CTAs across a range of previously discussed CTA benchmarks.

Noninvestible CTA Indexes Exhibit 11.6 depicts the return performance, market factor correlations, and benchmark comparisons of noninvestible CTA indexes for the period January 2001 through September 2006. During this time, all of the major industry level noninvestible CTA indexes reported a range of annualized returns and volatility levels. For instance, the CS/Tremont Managed Futures index has both the highest return (6.74%) and the highest standard deviation (12.49%), while the Barclay Traders index had the lowest return (4.70%) and the lowest standard deviation (7.92%). This wide deviation in return and risk is indicative of differences in index construction (e.g., the CS is asset-weighted and the Barclay index is equal weighted) that may lead to wide differences in return for seemingly similar index representations.

A comparison of noninvestible CTA indexes to major market factors shows these indexes to consistently have a negative correlation with both equity and high yield debt markets; however, a weak positive correlation is found to exist between the CTA indexes and the Lehman U.S. Government Credit Index. These CTA indexes are highly correlated with both investible and noninvestible manager-based indexes as evidenced by their correlations to the CASAM/CISDM and S&P indexes. With correlations of approximately 0.70 to the MFSB Composite Index and approximately 0.50 to the MLM Composite Index, noninvestible CTA indexes are moderately correlated to strategy-based CTA indexes. In brief, little difference in relative return movement or market factor sensitivity seems to exist among the major providers of industry level manager benchmarks.

EXHIBIT 11.6 Performance and Benchmark Comparisons of Noninvestible CTA Indexes

2001–9/2006	Annualized Return	Annualized Standard Deviation	Sharpe Ratio	Maximum Drawdown	Skewness	Kurtosis
CASAM/CISDM CTA Asset Weighted Index	6.53%	7.98%	0.50	–8.25%	–0.03	–0.37
CASAM/CISDM CTA Equal Weighted Index	6.40%	8.51%	0.46	–8.75%	0.20	–0.32
CS/Tremont Managed Futures	6.74%	12.49%	0.34	–13.92%	–0.09	–0.33
Barclay Trader Indexes CTA	4.70%	7.92%	0.28	–7.74%	0.12	0.03
Calyon Financial/Barclay Index	6.12%	9.39%	0.39	–10.30%	–0.15	0.54
BTOP 50	6.20%	9.78%	0.38	–10.92%	–0.05	0.13
S&P 500 Total Return Index	1.91%	14.10%	–0.04	–38.87%	–0.45	0.49
Lehman U.S. Government/Credit	5.78%	4.64%	0.71	–4.58%	–0.76	1.50
Lehman U.S. Corporate High Yield	8.99%	8.25%	0.79	–12.04%	–0.64	3.16

	Correlations						
2001–9/2006	S&P 500 Total Return Index	Lehman U.S. Government/ Credit	Lehman U.S. Corporate High Yield	MLM Composite Index	MFSB Composite Index	CASAM/ CISDM CTA Asset Weighted Index	S&P Managed Futures Investible Index
CASAM/CISDM CTA Asset Weighted Index	–0.17	0.34	–0.10	0.52	0.71	1.00	0.93
CASAM/CISDM CTA Equal Weighted Index	–0.24	0.33	–0.16	0.49	0.74	0.95	0.94
CS/Tremont Managed Futures	–0.25	0.34	–0.16	0.52	0.69	0.97	0.95

Barclay Trader Indexes CTA	−0.24	0.35	−0.18	0.49	0.74	0.95	0.95
Calyon Financial/Barclay Index	−0.24	0.31	−0.16	0.49	0.72	0.96	0.93
BTOP 50	−0.27	0.35	−0.17	0.50	0.72	0.96	0.95
S&P 500 Total Return Index	1.00	−0.31	0.52	−0.19	−0.23	−0.17	−0.32
Lehman U.S. Government/Credit	−0.31	1.00	0.13	0.26	0.21	0.34	0.35
Lehman U.S. Corporate High Yield	0.52	0.13	1.00	−0.04	−0.21	−0.10	−0.21

Benchmark (Excess Return) Comparison of Noninvestible CTA Indexes: 2001–9/2006

	Absolute Return Based	Total Risk Based	Market Factor Based	Security (Futures) Based	Security (Futures) Based	Manager-Based Noninvestible	Manager-Based Investible
Index	**T-bill**	**Sharpe Ratio**	**CAPM**	**MLM Composite Index**	**MFSB Composite Index**	**CASAM/ CISDM CTA Asset Weighted Index**	**S&P Managed Futures Investible Index**
CASAM/CISDM CTA Asset Weighted Index	4.03%	−1.24%	2.12%	4.33%	1.03%	0.00%	2.10%
CASAM/CISDM CTA Equal Weighted Index	3.89%	−1.72%	1.98%	4.19%	0.90%	−0.13%	1.97%
CS/Tremont Managed Futures Index	4.23%	−4.01%	2.32%	4.53%	1.23%	0.20%	2.31%
Barclay Trader Indexes CTA Index	2.19%	−3.04%	0.28%	2.49%	−0.81%	−1.84%	0.27%
Calyon Financial/Barclay Index	3.62%	−2.58%	1.71%	3.92%	0.62%	−0.41%	1.70%
BTOP 50 Index	3.69%	−2.76%	1.78%	3.99%	0.70%	−0.33%	1.77%

Source: Exhibit created from data obtained from CASAM/CISDM, BarclayHedge, Credit Suisse, Calyon Financial, FTSE, MLM, and S&P web sites.

Exhibit 11.6 also shows how benchmark excess return estimates differ for noninvestible CTA indexes. As expected, the T-bill benchmark results in the highest excess returns for all CTA indexes when compared to other benchmarks. Given the low betas that exist for CTAs, the results for using the T-bill benchmark are similar to that of the CAPM. However, when total risk is considered with an assumed required Sharpe ratio of 0.66, all the various indexes indicated a negative excess return performance.[14]

Exhibit 11.6 depicts the difference in excess return estimates that are obtained using both market and manager/futures-based benchmarks. Compared to Sharpe-based differential excess return, the greater market-based excess return is indicative of the benefits of CTAs when considered as a diversification tool in contrast to stand-alone investment vehicles. However, the lower excess return (and high correlation), which results from the use of passive futures-based indexes relative to a market-based excess return estimate, also indicates that simple market-based models of return estimate may underspecify the true strategy return process of the underlying CTA strategies. In brief, results show that the excess return or peer group estimates can be significantly impacted by the benchmark by which they are calculated.

Most of the major CTA benchmark indexes are not directly investible. As such, they fail to reflect the actual performance of investible alternatives. Exhibit 11.7 depicts the return performance, market factor correlations, and benchmark comparisons of investible manager and security-based CTA indexes for the period January 2001 through September 2006. Over the period of analysis, S&P Managed Futures index return/standard deviation (4.43%/15.63%) was lower than comparable investible manager-based CTA indexes; FTSE CTA/Managed Futures (7.73%/14.64%), CS/Tremont (6.98%/12.82%). The higher returns for the FTSE and CS returns may be in part due to the later date of their creation. As such their historical return may contain a degree of backfill and survivor bias that results in their upward return bias relative to the S&P CTA index. Comparing the performance of noninvestible manager-based CTA indexes, and investible manager-based CTA indexes (S&P managed futures), the excess peer returns were higher when the investible manager index was used. This is due in part to the relatively low returns of the S&P managed futures index compared to other investible CTA alternatives.

Exhibit 11.7 depicts the return performance and market factor correlations of investible passive-security-based CTA indexes. Of the two representative security-based CTA indexes (MLM and MFSB), both indexes had similar risk sensitivity and market factor correlations as the investible

[14]A Sharpe ratio of 0.66 was combined with the asset standard deviation and relevant risk-free rate to determine the required rate of return of the asset.

EXHIBIT 11.7 Performance and Benchmark Comparisons of Investible CTA Indexes

2001–9/2006	Annualized Return	Annualized Standard Deviation	Sharpe Ratio	Maximum Drawdown	Skewness	Kurtosis
Active Manager Based						
S&P Managed Futures Investible Index	4.43%	15.63%	0.12	−17.84%	−0.07	−0.41
FTSE CTA/Managed Futures	7.73%	14.64%	0.36	−16.67%	0.33	−0.29
CS/Tremont INVX Managed Futures	6.49%	13.27%	0.30	−16.53%	−0.16	−0.25
CS/Tremont SECT Managed Futures	6.98%	12.82%	0.35	−15.62%	−0.01	−0.12
MSCI Hedge Invest Systematic Trading Index	3.94%	6.97%	0.21	−10.92%	0.03	0.06
Security Based						
MLMCITR Index	2.21%	6.35%	−0.05	−8.94%	0.33	2.41
MFSB Composite	5.50%	10.65%	0.28	−15.00%	0.07	1.37
S&P 500 Total Return Index	1.91%	14.10%	−0.04	−38.87%	−0.45	0.49
Lehman U.S. Government/Credit	5.78%	4.64%	0.71	−4.58%	−0.76	1.50
Lehman U.S. Corporate High Yield	8.99%	8.25%	0.79	−12.04%	−0.64	3.16

	Correlations						
2001–9/2006	S&P 500 Total Return Index	Lehman U.S. Government/ Credit	Lehman U.S. Corporate High Yield	MLM Composite Index	MFSB Composite Index	CASAM/CISDM CTA Asset Weighted Index	S&P Managed Futures Investible Index
Active Manager Based							
S&P Managed Futures Investible Index	−0.32	0.35	−0.21	0.53	0.71	0.93	1.00
FTSE CTA/Managed Futures	−0.24	0.32	−0.14	0.52	0.69	0.91	0.91
CS/Tremont INVX Managed Futures	−0.28	0.31	−0.18	0.52	0.67	0.94	0.93
CS/Tremont SECT Managed Futures	−0.32	0.32	−0.20	0.49	0.72	0.95	0.95

(Continued)

EXHIBIT 11.7 (Continued)

	Correlations						
2001–9/2006	S&P 500 Total Return Index	Lehman U.S. Government/Credit	Lehman U.S. Corporate High Yield	MLM Composite Index	MFSB Composite Index	CASAM/CISDM CTA Asset Weighted Index	S&P Managed Futures Investible Index
Security Based							
MLMCITR Index	−0.19	0.26	−0.04	1.00	0.12	0.52	0.53
MFSB Composite	−0.23	0.21	−0.21	0.12	1.00	0.71	0.71
S&P 500 Total Return Index	1.00	−0.31	0.52	−0.19	−0.23	−0.17	−0.32
Lehman U.S. Government/Credit	−0.31	1.00	0.13	0.26	0.21	0.34	0.35
Lehman U.S. Corporate High Yield	0.52	0.13	1.00	−0.04	−0.21	−0.10	−0.21

	Benchmark (Excess Return) Comparison of Investible CTA Indexes: 2001–9/2006						
	Absolute Return Based	Total Risk Based	Market Factor Based	Security (Futures) Based	Security (Futures) Based	Manager-Based Noninvestible	Manager-Based Investible
Index	T-bill	Sharpe Ratio	CAPM	MLM Composite Index	MFSB Composite Index	CASAM/ CISDM CTA Asset Weighted Index	S&P Managed Futures Investible Index
S&P Managed Futures Investible Index	1.92%	−8.39%	0.01%	2.22%	−1.08%	−2.10%	0.00%
FTSE CTA/Managed Futures Index	5.22%	−4.44%	3.31%	5.52%	2.22%	1.20%	3.30%
CS/Tremont INVX Managed Futures Index	3.98%	−4.78%	2.07%	4.28%	0.98%	−0.05%	2.06%
CS/Tremont SECT Managed Futures Index	4.47%	−3.99%	2.56%	4.77%	1.47%	0.44%	2.55%

Source: Exhibit created from data obtained from CASAM/CISDM, BarclayHedge, Credit Suisse, Calyon Financial, FTSE, MLM, and S&P web sites.

manager-based CTA indexes. Moreover, for the period of analysis, the MFSB index has similar return and risk characteristics as well as peer group correlations to the investible manager-based indexes.[15]

Exhibit 11.7 also shows how benchmark excess return estimates differ for investible CTA indexes. When total risk is considered, with an assumed required Sharpe ratio of 0.66, all the various indexes indicated a negative excess return performance. As previously noted, given the low S&P-based betas that exist for CTAs, the results for using the market-factor-based excess returns (CAPM) are similar to the T-bill benchmark. As shown for noninvestible manager-based CTA indexes, comparing the performance of investible CTA indexes to other noninvestible manager-based indexes, investible manager-based CTA indexes, and investible passive-security-based indexes results in excess return estimates that vary by index provider. Investible CTA indexes had higher excess returns relative to the MLM Composite strategy-based index given its considerably lower returns compared to the MFSB Composite index. One reason for the different returns of the two representative passive investible CTA indexes is that the MFSB index uses a range of moving average time frames in determining its trading whereas the MLM is primarily long term in nature. Thus the two security-based benchmarks used in this analysis differ in benchmark construction. Excess returns of investible CTA indexes or the MFSB Composite Index as well as comparable investible and noninvestible manager-based indexes are generally less than those obtained when using absolute return-based (T-bill) and market-factor-based (CAPM) benchmarks. Again, these results show that the excess return estimates can be significantly impacted by the index in which they are calculated.

Empirical Results on Strategy Index Level

While the previous subsection reviewed benchmark performance at the overall index level, individual CTAs should be analyzed within their relative strategy grouping. In this section, we review some of the performance characteristics, market factor correlations, and benchmark return comparisons for a range of CTA strategies (e.g., currency, financial, and diversified).

Currency CTAs Exhibit 11.8 shows the return performance, correlations, and benchmark comparisons of noninvestible manager-based and investible

[15]The MFSB program is not currently offered in a publicly available form. The return estimates, however, are all out of sample and reflect both internal trading costs and a 50 basis point management fee. For purposes of disclosure, one of the authors of this paper has a direct investible interest in the MFSB program.

EXHIBIT 11.8 Performance and Benchmark Comparisons of Currency CTA Indexes

2001–9/2006	Annualized Return	Annualized Standard Deviation	Sharpe Ratio	Maximum Drawdown	Skewness	Kurtosis
Manager (noninvestible)						
CASAM/CISDM CTA Asset Weighted Currency Index	2.66%	6.36%	0.03	–9.74%	0.12	–0.32
CASAM/CISDM CTA Equal Weighted Currency Index	5.29%	6.11%	0.45	–7.37%	0.96	0.85
Barclay Trader Indexes Currency	3.22%	6.22%	0.11	–6.61%	1.13	1.47
Manager (investible)	NA	NA	NA	NA	NA	NA
Security (investible)						
MLMCFXTR Index	5.14%	5.83%	0.45	–5.06%	0.30	0.49
MFSB Currency	0.96%	22.27%	–0.07	–35.33%	1.03	0.71
S&P 500 Total Return Index	1.91%	14.10%	–0.04	–38.87%	–0.45	0.49
Lehman U.S. Government/Credit	5.78%	4.64%	0.71	–4.58%	–0.76	1.50
Lehman U.S. Corporate High Yield	8.99%	8.25%	0.79	–12.04%	–0.64	3.16

	Correlations					
2001–9/2006	S&P 500 Total Return Index	Lehman U.S. Government/ Credit	Lehman U.S. Corporate High Yield	MLMCFXTR Index	MFSB Currency Index	CASAM/CISDM CTA Asset Weighted Currency Index
Manager (noninvestible)						
CASAM/CISDM CTA Asset Weighted Currency Index	0.26	0.13	0.28	0.56	0.55	1.00
CASAM/CISDM CTA Equal Weighted Currency Index	–0.10	0.14	–0.09	0.62	0.79	0.60
Barclay Trader Indexes Currency	–0.04	0.21	–0.06	0.72	0.82	0.64
Manager (investible)	NA	NA	NA	NA	NA	NA
Security (investible)						
MLMCFXTR Index	0.04	0.22	0.03	1.00	0.58	0.56

MFSB Currency	−0.03	0.06	−0.06	0.58	1.00	0.55
S&P 500 Total Return Index	1.00	−0.31	0.52	0.04	−0.03	0.26
Lehman U.S. Government/Credit	−0.31	1.00	0.13	0.22	0.06	0.13
Lehman U.S. Corporate High Yield	0.52	0.13	1.00	0.03	−0.06	0.28

	Benchmark (Excess Return) Comparison of Currency CTA Indexes: 2001–9/2006					
	Absolute Return	Total Risk Based	Market Factor Based	Security (Futures) Based	Security (Futures) Based	Manager-Based Noninvestible
Index	Based T-bill	Sharpe Ratio	CAPM	MLMCFXTR Index	MFSB Currency Index	CASAM/CISDM CTA Asset Weighted Currency Index
CASAM/CISDM CTA Asset Weighted Currency Index	0.16%	−4.04%	−1.75%	−2.48%	1.70%	0.00%
CASAM/CISDM CTA Equal Weighted Currency Index	2.78%	−1.25%	0.87%	0.14%	4.32%	2.62%
Barclay Trader Indexes Currency	0.71%	−3.39%	−1.20%	−1.92%	2.25%	0.55%

Source: Exhibit created from data obtained from BarclayHedge, MLM, and S&P web sites and Datastream.

security-based currency CTA indexes. There exists little public information on investible manager-based benchmarks at the CTA Currency strategy level. The various noninvestible currency CTA indexes performed similarly during the period with annualized returns ranging between 2.66% and 5.29% and standard deviations ranging between 6.11% and 6.36%, respectively. Conversely, while the investible security-based MLM Currency Index had a risk/return profile similar to that of noninvestible currency CTA indexes, the MFSB Currency CTA Index posted a significantly lower annualized return of only 0.96% with a much higher standard deviation of 22.27%.

With the exception of the CASAM/CISDM CTA Asset Weighted Currency Index, both noninvestible and security-based investible CTA indexes had little or no market factor correlation with the S&P 500 and Lehman High Yield indexes, but had weak positive correlations with the Lehman U.S. Government/Credit index. Currency CTA indexes are shown to have higher correlations when compared relative to strategy and market-based indexes. This is expected given that security and market-based indexes are constructed using strategies or funds which trade commodity-based financial instruments, and as such, are more comparable than when comparing such CTAs to indexes that are composed of traditional stock and bond asset classes.

Excess return estimates for currency CTA indexes reflect results that vary based on the benchmark used. As in previous analysis, the excess return declines as one moves from an absolute return-based benchmark (T-bill), to a market-factor-based performance measure (CAPM), to a total risk-based measure (Sharpe ratio). In this analysis, the excess returns for the noninvestible indexes decreases as one moves from the noninvestible CTA currency index to the security-based MLM Currency Index, and increases slightly as one moves from noninvestible CTA currency indexes to the security-based MFSB Currency Index. Excess returns of noninvestible currency CTA indexes are found to be comparable to the absolute return and market-factor-based returns when compared relative to the manager-based noninvestible CASAM/CISDM index. These indexes provide evidence that index design can have a clear impact of benchmark comparison measurements.

Financial CTAs Exhibit 11.9 shows the return performance, correlations, and benchmark comparisons of both investible and noninvestible financial CTA indexes. Noninvestible financial CTA indexes incurred higher zero and risk adjusted returns over the period in comparison to investible financial CTA indexes as well as the S&P 500. Financial CTAs showed some variability in terms of risk between indexes with annualized standard deviations ranging between 6.57% and 13.43%. Security-based financial CTA indexes are also found to have incurred larger maximum drawdowns

EXHIBIT 11.9 Performance and Benchmark Comparisons of Financial CTA Indexes

2001–9/2006	Annualized Return	Annualized Standard Deviation	Sharpe Ratio	Maximum Drawdown	Skewness	Kurtosis
Manager (noninvestible)						
CASAM/CISDM CTA Asset Weighted Financial Index	10.32%	10.05%	0.78	−10.25%	0.07	0.35
CASAM/CISDM CTA Equal Weighted Financial Index	6.17%	8.69%	0.42	−8.69%	0.14	−0.21
Barclay Trader Indexes Financial & Metals	5.12%	6.57%	0.40	−6.04%	0.43	0.74
Manager (investible)	NA	NA	NA	NA	NA	NA
Security (investible)						
MLMCFITR Index	2.27%	6.89%	−0.03	−14.05%	−0.66	1.14
MFSB Financial	6.02%	13.43%	0.26	−21.01%	−0.02	2.36
S&P 500 Total Return Index	1.91%	14.10%	−0.04	−38.87%	−0.45	0.49
Lehman U.S. Government/Credit	5.78%	4.64%	0.71	−4.58%	−0.76	1.50
Lehman U.S. Corporate High Yield	8.99%	8.25%	0.79	−12.04%	−0.64	3.16

	Correlations					
2001–9/2006	S&P 500 Total Return Index	Lehman U.S. Government/ Credit	Lehman U.S. Corporate High Yield	MLMCFITR Index	MFSB Financial Index	CASAM/CISDM CTA Asset Weighted Financial Index
Manager (noninvestible)						
CASAM/CISDM CTA Asset Weighted Financial Index	−0.22	0.33	−0.17	0.52	0.56	1.00
CASAM/CISDM CTA Equal Weighted Financial Index	−0.30	0.41	−0.21	0.58	0.60	0.86
Barclay Trader Indexes Financial & Metals	−0.34	0.47	−0.16	0.58	0.53	0.85
Manager (investible)	NA	NA	NA	NA	NA	NA

(Continued)

EXHIBIT 11.8 (Continued)

	Correlations					
2001–9/2006	S&P 500 Total Return Index	Lehman U.S. Government/ Credit	Lehman U.S. Corporate High Yield	MLMCFITR Index	MFSB Financial Index	CASAM/CISDM CTA Asset Weighted Financial Index
Security (investible)						
MLMCFITR Index	−0.32	0.67	−0.14	1.00	0.37	0.52
MFSB Financial	−0.22	0.21	−0.18	0.37	1.00	0.56
S&P 500 Total Return Index	1.00	−0.31	0.52	−0.32	−0.22	−0.22
Lehman U.S. Government/Credit	−0.31	1.00	0.13	0.67	0.21	0.33
Lehman U.S. Corporate High Yield	0.52	0.13	1.00	−0.14	−0.18	−0.17

	Benchmark (Excess Return) Comparison of Financial CTA Indexes: 2001–9/2006					
	Absolute Return Based	Total Risk Based	Market Factor Based	Security (Futures) Based	Security (Futures) Based	Manager-Based Noninvestible
Index	T-bill	Sharpe Ratio	CAPM	MLMCFITR Index	MFSB Financial Index	CASAM/CISDM CTA Asset Weighted Financial Index
CASAM/CISDM CTA Asset Weighted Financial Index	7.82%	1.18%	5.90%	8.05%	4.30%	0.00%
CASAM/CISDM CTA Equal Weighted Financial Index	3.66%	−2.07%	1.75%	3.89%	0.15%	−4.15%
Barclay Trader Indexes Financial & Metals Index	2.62%	−1.72%	0.71%	2.85%	−0.90%	−5.20%

Source: Exhibit created from data obtained from BarclayHedge, MLM, and S&P web sites and Datastream.

over the period in comparison to noninvestible manager-based financial CTA indexes. All financial CTA indexes were found to have negative market factor correlations with the S&P 500 and Lehman U.S. Corporate High Yield Index and were positively correlated with the Lehman U.S. Government/Credit Index. Surprisingly, the MLM Financial CTA index had a considerable higher positive correlation to the Lehman Government/Credit Index (0.67) when compared to other financial CTA indexes.

Positive correlations are found between all financial CTA indexes and strategy and market-based indexes. Financial CTA indexes on average tend to be moderately correlated with the strategy-based MLM and MFSB Financial indexes with correlations of approximately 0.55. Such CTAs on average tend to have even higher correlations with the manager-based CASAM/CISDM Financial index. Again, the results indicate the relative differences that exist between industry and market factor correlations among the various investible and noninvestible indexes. Excess return estimates for financial CTA indexes fluctuate considerably across various benchmarks. However, what is significant is that with the exception of the MLM Financial Index which considerably underperformed relative to comparable financial CTA indexes, the manager- and security–based passive indexes often result in lower excess return estimates than the market-based estimates.

Diversified CTAs Exhibit 11.10 shows the return performance, correlations, and benchmark comparisons of investible composite and noninvestible diversified CTA indexes. During the period, noninvestible diversified CTA indexes considerably outperformed the MLM Composite index while performing in line with the MFSB Composite index. Risk-adjusted returns of both investible composite and noninvestible diversified CTA indexes underperformed major traditional asset class indexes except for the S&P 500. Consistent with previous findings, market factor correlations of diversified CTA indexes with the S&P 500 and Lehman U.S. Corporate High Yield Index are negative and positive with the Lehman U.S Government Credit Index. Diversified CTA indexes are found to be moderately correlated with strategy-based MLM and MFSB Composite indexes and have an even higher correlation with the manager-based noninvestible CASAM/CISDM CTA Asset Weighted Diversified Index.

Lastly, excess returns for some diversified CTA indexes are found to fluctuate considerably but follow similar patterns shown in previous strategy examples. Using market-factor-based benchmarks, the excess return declines as one moves from an absolute-based return (T-bill) to a market-based performance measure (CAPM), to a total risk measure (Sharpe ratio). As expected, excess returns shrink when diversified CTA indexes are

EXHIBIT 11.10 Performance and Benchmark Comparisons of Diversified CTA Indexes

2001–9/2006	Annualized Return	Annualized Standard Deviation	Sharpe Ratio	Maximum Drawdown	Skewness	Kurtosis
Manager (noninvestible)						
CASAM/CISDM CTA Asset Weighted Diversified Index	5.69%	9.19%	0.35	−11.36%	−0.06	−0.70
CASAM/CISDM CTA Equal Weighted Diversified Index	7.18%	10.76%	0.44	−11.37%	0.06	−0.40
Barclay Trader Indexes Diversified	5.32%	11.40%	0.25	−11.96%	0.01	−0.17
Manager (investible)	NA	NA	NA	NA	NA	NA
Security (investible)						
MLMCITR Index	2.21%	6.35%	−0.05	−8.94%	0.33	2.41
MFSB Composite	5.50%	10.65%	0.28	−15.00%	0.07	1.37
S&P 500 Total Return Index	1.91%	14.10%	−0.04	−38.87%	−0.45	0.49
Lehman U.S. Government/Credit	5.78%	4.64%	0.71	−4.58%	−0.76	1.50
Lehman U.S. Corporate High Yield	8.99%	8.25%	0.79	−12.04%	−0.64	3.16

	Correlations					
2001–9/2006	S&P 500 Total Return Index	Lehman U.S. Government/ Credit	Lehman U.S. Corporate High Yield	MLMCITR Index	MFSB Composite Index	CASAM/CISDM CTA Asset Weighted Diversified Index
Manager (noninvestible)						
CASAM/CISDM CTA Asset Weighted Diversified Index	−0.18	0.30	−0.11	0.54	0.67	1.00

CASAM/CISDM CTA Equal Weighted Diversified Index	−0.24	0.33	−0.14	0.50	0.71	0.96
Barclay Trader Indexes Diversified	−0.25	0.33	−0.18	0.50	0.72	0.96
Manager (investible)	NA	NA	NA	NA	NA	NA
Security (investible)						
MLMCITR Index	−0.19	0.26	−0.04	1.00	0.12	0.54
MFSB Composite	−0.23	0.21	−0.21	0.12	1.00	0.67
S&P 500 Total Return Index	1.00	−0.31	0.52	−0.19	−0.23	−0.18
Lehman U.S. Government/Credit	−0.31	1.00	0.13	0.26	0.21	0.30
Lehman U.S. Corporate High Yield	0.52	0.13	1.00	−0.04	−0.21	−0.11

Benchmark (Excess Return) Comparison of Diversified CTA Indexes: 2001–9/2006

	Absolute Return Based	Total Risk Based	Market Factor Based	Security (Futures) Based	Security (Futures) Based	Manager-Based Noninvestible
Index	**T-bill**	**Sharpe Ratio**	**CAPM**	**MLMCITR Index**	**MFSB Composite Index**	**CASAM/CISDM CTA Asset Weighted Diversified Index**
CASAM/CISDM CTA Asset Weighted Diversified Index	3.18%	−2.88%	1.27%	3.48%	0.18%	0.00%
CASAM/CISDM CTA Equal Weighted Diversified Index	4.68%	−2.42%	2.77%	4.98%	1.68%	1.50%
Barclay Trader Indexes Diversified	2.81%	−4.71%	0.90%	3.11%	−0.18%	−0.37%

Source: Exhibit created from data obtained from BarclayHedge, MLM, and S&P web sites and Datastream.

compared relative to the peer group, noninvestible CASAM/CISDM CTA Asset Weighted Diversified Index.

Discretionary CTAs Exhibit 11.11 shows the return performance, correlations, and benchmark comparisons of noninvestible discretionary and investible composite CTA indexes. Discretionary CTA indexes are by the very nature of their construction difficult to benchmark. As indicated in Exhibit 11.8, there is a relatively lower correlation between the CASAM/CISDM index and other noninvestible discretionary indexes. This is consistent with the lack of homogeneity within the discretionary trading strategy area. Given their relatively low standard deviations compared to other CTA strategies, the relative differences between absolute return-based (T-bill), market-factor-based (CAPM), and total risk-based (Sharpe ratio) benchmark metrics are less than that exhibited among other CTA indexes. As expected, the manager-based noninvestible discretionary CTA indexes may provide a reasonable peer group alternative. In this case of discretionary CTAs, no investible futures-based index currently exists.

Systematic CTAs Exhibit 11.12 shows the return performance, correlations, and benchmark comparisons of noninvestible systematic CTA indexes and investible composite CTA indexes. Noninvestible systematic CTA indexes considerably outperformed the MLM Composite CTA index with higher returns, lower volatility, and smaller maximum drawdowns. In contrast, the MFSB Composite index had higher absolute returns, but similar risk-adjusted returns when relative to noninvestible systematic indexes.

All systematic CTA indexes were found to have negative market factor correlations with the S&P 500 and Lehman U.S. Corporate High Yield Index and were positively correlated with the Lehman U.S. Government/Credit Index. Positive correlations are found between all systematic CTA indexes and strategy- and market-based indexes. Systematic CTA indexes on average tend to be moderately correlated with the strategy-based MLM and MFSB Composite indexes with correlations of approximately 0.48 and 0.75, respectively. Such CTAs on average tend to have even higher correlations with the manager-based CASAM/CISDM CTA Asset Weighted Systematic Index. Again, the results indicate the relative differences that exist between industry and market factor correlations among the various investible and noninvestible indexes.

Given the low correlation with the S&P 500, absolute return-based (T-bill) and market-factor-based (CAPM) excess returns metrics for noninvestible systematic CTA indexes are found to be somewhat similar. As in previous examples, using their corresponding expected Sharpe ratios as a

EXHIBIT 11.11 Performance and Benchmark Comparisons of Discretionary CTA Indexes

2001–9/2006	Annualized Return	Annualized Standard Deviation	Sharpe Ratio	Maximum Drawdown	Skewness	Kurtosis
Manager (noninvestible)						
CASAM/CISDM CTA Asset Weighted Discretionary Index	9.56%	5.82%	1.21	–3.82%	1.43	3.25
CASAM/CISDM CTA Equal Weighted Discretionary Index	9.85%	4.24%	1.73	–2.41%	0.24	–0.64
Barclay Trader Indexes Discretionary	5.95%	3.66%	0.94	–3.29%	0.22	1.38
Manager (**investible**)	NA	NA	NA	NA	NA	NA
Security (**investible**)						
MLMCITR Index	NA	NA	NA	NA	NA	NA
MFSB Composite	NA	NA	NA	NA	NA	NA
S&P 500 Total Return Index	1.91%	14.10%	–0.04	–38.87%	–0.45	0.49
Lehman U.S. Government/Credit	5.78%	4.64%	0.71	–4.58%	–0.76	1.50
Lehman U.S. Corporate High Yield	8.99%	8.25%	0.79	–12.04%	–0.64	3.16

	Correlations					
2001–9/2006	S&P 500 Total Return Index	Lehman U.S. Government/ Credit	Lehman U.S. Corporate High Yield	MLMCITR Index	MFSB Composite Index	CASAM/CISDM CTA Asset Weighted Discretionary Index
Manager (noninvestible)						
CASAM/CISDM CTA Asset Weighted Discretionary Index	0.08	0.13	0.05	0.34	0.28	1.00
CASAM/CISDM CTA Equal Weighted Discretionary Index	0.14	0.27	0.13	0.32	0.20	0.59
Barclay Trader Indexes Discretionary	0.27	–0.01	–0.02	0.07	0.16	0.34
Manager (**investible**)	NA	NA	NA	NA	NA	NA

(Continued)

EXHIBIT 11.11 (Continued)

2001–9/2006	Correlations: S&P 500 Total Return Index	Lehman U.S. Government/ Credit	Lehman U.S. Corporate High Yield	MLMCITR Index	MFSB Composite Index	CASAM/CISDM CTA Asset Weighted Discretionary Index
Security (investible)						
MLMCITR Index	NA	NA	NA	NA	NA	NA
MFSB Composite	NA	NA	NA	NA	NA	NA
S&P 500 Total Return Index	1.00	–0.31	0.52	–0.19	–0.23	0.08
Lehman U.S. Government/Credit	–0.31	1.00	0.13	0.26	0.21	0.13
Lehman U.S. Corporate High Yield	0.52	0.13	1.00	–0.04	–0.21	0.05

	Benchmark (Excess Return) Comparison of Discretionary CTA Indexes: 2001–9/2006					
	Absolute Return Based	Total Risk Based	Market Factor Based	Security (Futures) Based	Security (Futures) Based	Manager-Based Noninvestible
Index	T-bill	Sharpe Ratio	CAPM	MLMCITR Index	MFSB Composite Index	CASAM/CISDM CTA Asset Weighted Discretionary Index
CASAM/CISDM CTA Asset Weighted Discretionary Index	7.06%	3.22%	5.15%	NA	NA	0.00%
CASAM/CISDM CTA Equal Weighted Discretionary Index	7.34%	4.54%	5.43%	NA	NA	0.28%
Barclay Trader Indexes Discretionary	3.45%	1.03%	1.53%	NA	NA	–3.62%

Source: Exhibit created from data obtained from BarclayHedge, MLM, and S&P web sites and Datastream.

EXHIBIT 11.12 Performance and Benchmark Comparisons of Systematic CTA Indexes

2001–9/2006	Annualized Return	Annualized Standard Deviation	Sharpe Ratio	Maximum Drawdown	Skewness	Kurtosis
Manager (noninvestible)						
CASAM/CISDM CTA Asset Weighted Systematic Index	5.34%	7.10%	0.40	−5.88%	0.01	−0.05
CASAM/CISDM CTA Equal Weighted Systematic Index	5.99%	9.05%	0.39	−9.91%	0.18	−0.37
Barclay Trader Indexes Systematic						
Manager (investible)	4.27%	9.66%	0.18	−10.13%	0.10	−0.07
Security (investible)	NA	NA	NA	NA	NA	NA
MLMCITR Index	2.21%	6.35%	−0.05	−8.94%	0.33	2.41
MFSB Composite	5.50%	10.65%	0.28	−15.00%	0.07	1.37
S&P 500 Total Return Index	1.91%	14.10%	−0.04	−38.87%	−0.45	0.49
Lehman U.S. Government/Credit	5.78%	4.64%	0.71	−4.58%	−0.76	1.50
Lehman U.S. Corporate High Yield	8.99%	8.25%	0.79	−12.04%	−0.64	3.16

	Correlations					
2001–9/2006	S&P 500 Total Return Index	Lehman U.S. Government/ Credit	Lehman U.S. Corporate High Yield	MLMCITR Index	MFSB Composite Index	CASAM/CISDM CTA Asset Weighted Systematic Index
Manager (noninvestible)						
CASAM/CISDM CTA Asset Weighted Systematic Index	−0.12	0.36	−0.07	0.47	0.73	1.00
CASAM/CISDM CTA Equal Weighted Systematic Index	−0.26	0.33	−0.16	0.48	0.74	0.91
Barclay Trader Indexes Systematic	−0.28	0.36	−0.18	0.48	0.75	0.92
Manager (investible)	NA	NA	NA	NA	NA	NA

(Continued)

EXHIBIT 11.12 (Continued)

	Correlations					
2001–9/2006	S&P 500 Total Return Index	Lehman U.S. Government/ Credit	Lehman U.S. Corporate High Yield	MLMCITR Index	MFSB Composite Index	CASAM/CISDM CTA Asset Weighted Systematic Index
Security (investible)						
MLMCITR Index	–0.19	0.26	–0.04	1.00	0.12	0.47
MFSB Composite	–0.23	0.21	–0.21	0.12	1.00	0.73
S&P 500 Total Return Index	1.00	–0.31	0.52	–0.19	–0.23	–0.12
Lehman U.S. Government/Credit	–0.31	1.00	0.13	0.26	0.21	0.36
Lehman U.S. Corporate High Yield	0.52	0.13	1.00	–0.04	–0.21	–0.07

	Benchmark (Excess Return) Comparison of Systematic CTA Indexes: 2001–9/2006					
	Absolute Return Based	Total Risk Based	Market Factor Based	Security (Futures) Based	Security (Futures) Based	Manager-Based Noninvestible
Index	T-bill	Sharpe Ratio	CAPM	MLMCITR Index	MFSB Composite Index	CASAM/CISDM CTA Asset Weighted Systematic Index
CASAM/CISDM CTA Asset Weighted Systematic Index	2.84%	–1.85%	0.93%	3.14%	–0.16%	0.00%
CASAM/CISDM CTA Equal Weighted Systematic Index	3.49%	–2.49%	1.57%	3.78%	0.49%	–0.41%
Barclay Trader Indexes Systematic	1.77%	–4.61%	–0.15%	2.06%	–1.23%	–2.13%

Source: Exhibit created from data obtained from BarclayHedge, MLM, and S&P web sites and Datastream.

benchmark, the excess returns were negative. Compared to manager-based benchmark metrics, each of the noninvestible systematic CTA indexes incurred negative excess return estimates.

Empirical Results on Average Manager Level

The previous section used existing CTA benchmarks as surrogates for CTA strategy-based portfolios. In this section, a set of CTAs with full data over the period January 2001 to September 2006 are used. The performance, market correlations, and relative benchmark performance of each CTA is determined. Financial and diversified CTAs are used as a basis for reviewing the average performance, average market factor correlations, and average relative benchmark performance of the CTAs. As important, many CTAs use a variety of momentum models in determining trading strategies. Most current CTA benchmarks are not broken down into subsamples based on the length of the period used in determining buy and sell recommendations. For instance, many CTAs' momentum models may be short term (e.g., seven days), midterm (e.g., 15 days), or longer term in nature (e.g., 30+ days). In the following exhibits we also depict the average performance of CTAs sampled categorized by their respective trading time frames. Lastly, both CASAM/CISDM indexes and indexes based on a portfolio of similar CTAs are created to provide a basis for a peer group benchmark. Note that in this analysis, a peer group benchmark is based on current CTAs reporting to the database, and as a result, contains considerable backfill bias. As such, the constructed CTA benchmark return estimates are upward biased. For more accurate peer group analysis, one should ensure that managers are reviewed that do not contain significant backfill bias.

Average Manager Level Comparison: Financial CTAs Exhibit 11.13 shows the average performance of portfolio financial CTAs sampled categorized by their respective trading time frames. In this example, financial CTAs with short trading time periods on average had considerably lower returns and less volatility than financial CTAs with long trading time periods. These short trading time period CTAs also, on average, had lower correlations with traditional financial CTA indexes which are often used to represent their return. This indicates that for financial CTAs in general (as well as in other CTA strategies) that for peer group and other comparisons, the underlying trading-time-frame focus of the strategy must be considered to provide a better basis for CTA comparison.

EXHIBIT 11.13 Average Performance Portfolio Level Comparison: Financial CTAs

	Average Performance of Financial CTAs: 2001–9/2006					
Time Period	Average Annualized Return	Average Annualized Standard Deviation	Average Sharpe Ratio	Average Maximum Drawdown	Average Skewness	Average Kurtosis
All	4.58%	21.80%	0.12	–28.54%	0.27	0.54
Short	4.05%	11.81%	0.08	–17.65%	0.40	1.33
Multiple	3.99%	19.72%	0.08	–25.21%	–0.14	0.44
Medium	2.47%	33.80%	0.00	–41.30%	0.10	–0.12
Long	5.33%	23.81%	0.16	–31.01%	0.33	0.38

	Average Correlations of Financial CTAs: 2001–9/2006						
Time Period	S&P 500 Total Return Index	Lehman U.S. Government/ Credit	Lehman U.S. Corporate High Yield	CASAM/CISDM CTA Asset Weighted Index	S&P Managed Futures Investible Index	CASAM/CISDM CTA Asset Weighted Financial Index	MFSB Financial Index
All	–0.30	0.28	–0.20	0.73	0.72	0.71	0.46
Short	–0.28	0.17	–0.21	0.41	0.38	0.46	0.37
Multiple	–0.35	0.30	–0.26	0.85	0.89	0.77	0.42
Medium	–0.43	0.36	–0.23	0.79	0.83	0.80	0.68
Long	–0.27	0.31	–0.18	0.82	0.80	0.79	0.46

	Benchmark (Excess Return) Comparison of Financial CTAs: 2001–9/2006						
Time Period	T-bill	CAPM	Sharpe Ratio	CASAM/CISDM CTA Asset Weighted Index	S&P Managed Futures Investible Index	CASAM/CISDM CTA Asset Weighted Financial Index	MFSB Financial Index
All	2.07%	0.16%	–0.12	–1.96%	0.15%	–5.74%	–1.44%
Short	1.54%	–0.37%	–0.06	–2.48%	–0.38%	–6.27%	–1.97%
Multiple	1.49%	–0.42%	–0.12	–2.54%	–0.43%	–6.33%	–2.03%
Medium	–0.03%	–1.95%	–0.22	–4.06%	–1.96%	–7.85%	–3.55%
Long	2.82%	0.91%	–0.13	–1.21%	0.90%	–4.99%	–0.69%

Source: Exhibit created from data obtained from S&P web site and Datastream.

Average Manager Level Comparison: Diversified CTAs In the previous section we concentrated on examining the characteristics of a portfolio of CTAs by trading time. Exhibit 11.14 shows the average performance of diversified CTAs sampled categorized by their respective trading time frames. As shown previously, diversified CTAs with short trading time periods on average had considerably lower returns and less volatility. Moreover, CTAs with short trading time periods had lower correlations with most market factors, as well as CTA indexes with managers whose strategy was more longer term in nature. However, risk-adjusted returns were greater for CTAs with long time frames. Diversified CTAs also had similarly negative correlations with U.S. equity and high yield debt indexes regardless of their time periods.

Exhibit 11.14 also shows the comparison of diversified CTAs sampled measured against various benchmark metrics when such CTAs are separated based on their time periods. The excess return estimates of diversified CTAs for each time period varies depending on the benchmark used. In this case however, while the short trading period CTAs have the lowest zero risk excess return and CAPM return, their Sharpe-based return comparisons are similar to other managers. This is consistent with their overall lower volatility. Likewise their average peer group and futures-based index comparisons returns are less than their comparable longer trading time managers. As discussed previously, comparing managers with different trading focuses can lead investors to improper comparisons.

ISSUES IN PERFORMANCE MEASUREMENT

The results in the previous sections provide a "half full" or "half empty" view of CTA benchmark creation and performance measurement. Historically, CTA returns have often been compared to T-bill returns since CTAs have been shown to have a low correlation to equity markets (low beta). Therefore, on a CAPM basis, the risk-free rate may be regarded as a CAPM-based return alternative. For others, since futures require only margin, the investible alternative is often Treasury bills. To the degree that CTAs offer a positive "traders" return, that return would be in excess of the Treasury bill return.

Modern asset theory, however, now views required asset return as a function of a wider range of potential return to risk tradeoffs. Risk is often described as either total risk (as expressed by standard deviation and the traditional Sharpe ratio) or market risk (as described by the CAPM). However, Treasury bill, beta adjusted, or total risk-based return comparisons fail to provide an estimate of the true *alpha*. Measurement of alpha requires that the comparison asset be investible and reflect the underlying strategy and risks of the comparison asset. As such, passive-security- (futures-) based

EXHIBIT 11.14 Average Performance and Benchmark Comparison of Diversified CTAs

	Average Performance of Diversified CTAs: 2001–9/2006					
Time Period	Average Annualized Return	Average Annualized Standard Deviation	Average Sharpe Ratio	Average Maximum Drawdown	Average Skewness	Average Kurtosis
All	9.52%	20.31%	0.36	−23.87%	0.21	0.51
Short	3.66%	7.95%	0.26	−11.75%	0.30	1.63
Multiple	9.35%	17.74%	0.40	−20.30%	0.27	0.25
Medium	8.55%	21.21%	0.32	−25.29%	0.17	0.45
Long	12.62%	26.19%	0.40	−30.31%	0.22	0.51

	Average Correlations of Diversified CTAs: 2001–9/2006						
Time Period	S&P 500 Total Return Index	Lehman U.S. Government/ Credit	Lehman U.S. Corporate High Yield	CASAM/CISDM CTA Asset Weighted Index	S&P Managed Futures Investible Index	CASAM/CISDM CTA Asset Weighted Diversified Index	MFSB Composite Index
All	−0.20	0.23	−0.14	0.67	0.69	0.69	0.52
Short	−0.19	0.13	−0.18	0.38	0.41	0.39	0.49
Multiple	−0.20	0.31	−0.11	0.71	0.73	0.73	0.58
Medium	−0.15	0.15	−0.11	0.65	0.66	0.67	0.48
Long	−0.26	0.27	−0.17	0.74	0.75	0.77	0.52

(Continued)

EXHIBIT 11.14 (Continued)

	Benchmark (Excess Return) Comparison of Diversified CTAs: 2001–9/2006						
Time Period	T-bill	CAPM	Sharpe Ratio	CASAM/CISDM CTA Asset Weighted Index	S&P Managed Futures Investible Index	CASAM/CISDM CTA Asset Weighted Diversified Index	MFSB Composite Index
All	7.01%	5.10%	−0.06	2.99%	5.09%	3.83%	4.01%
Short	1.15%	−0.76%	−0.04	−2.88%	−0.77%	−2.03%	−1.85%
Multiple	6.85%	4.93%	−0.05%	−2.82%	4.92%	−3.67%	−3.85%
Medium	6.05%	4.13%	−0.08	2.02%	4.12%	2.86%	3.05%
Long	10.12%	8.20%	−0.07	6.09%	8.19%	6.94%	7.12%

Source: Exhibit created from data obtained from S&P web site and Datastream.

strategy replicates may be one means of measuring manager-based skill above the returns inherent in the underlying strategy and the resultant *manager alpha*. Given the issues involved in absolute, market or passive index performance comparison, peer group comparison remains at the heart of CTA analysis although it fails to provide an estimate of absolute manager skill. Even in this case, most peer group comparisons often fail to provide adequate comparisons. To be truly comparable, the peer CTAs must use similar trading-time decision rules to the comparison CTA managers.

In this short synopsis, it is impossible to detail all the research related to CTA benchmark performance comparison. Issues of concern not directly addressed in this analysis include the problems of survivorship and backfilling bias when one creates comparison, in-house peer group benchmarks from current databases. Unless one has a set of historical data basis from which to create similar size, age, and other manager characteristic-based portfolios, new-listed managers and peer groups based off of them will have a return advantage over older managers who have remained in data bases over a number of years. Lastly, research has shown that uses of commonly available indexes differ in a number of design areas. Some indexes are asset weighted, or equal weighted. Some indexes rebalanced monthly, others annually. These differences can result in major differences in seemingly similar strategy indexes. Unless rebalanced relatively often, an index may become overweighted to certain CTAs or CTA groups. Moreover, some CTAs have higher volatility than other CTAs in the same strategy grouping. Regardless of the number of managers in an index, the most volatile managers will have a relatively greater impact on the return process. Few if any CTAs indexes volatility adjust among representative managers.

It is obvious that while problems related to CTA benchmark performance exist, few if any existing benchmarks or indexes have attempted to correct these problems. However, with greater competition among index providers as well as consultants, one may anticipate that a number of additional methodologies will be proposed that provide adequate peer analysis and manager skill appraisal.

CONCLUSION

While academic research has centered primarily on the benefits of managed futures, less work exists on determining the relative performance benefits of individual CTAs or CTA strategies. One reason for the lack of research in this area is that traditional multifactor benchmark models which are used to describe the market factors driving traditional stock and bond as well as many hedge fund strategies have little use in describing the return behavior of CTAs. This is mainly due to the underlying strategy focus of CTAs results in investment holdings which do not traditionally benchmark long-only stock and bond indexes. In fact, managed futures were once described principally as absolute return strategies since their goal was to obtain positive returns across a variety of markets. This approach often led to a low exposure to traditional equity benchmarks (zero beta) and, as a result, relative performance was often measured in comparison to the risk-free rate. Today, it is well understood that managed futures require a broader understanding of the underlying risk structure of the strategy and that a range of benchmarking alternatives may be used to provide an understanding of the underlying returns to a CTA strategy and its performance relative to similar strategies. Our empirical results show that the various manager- and security-based indexes have similar exposure to market factors as well as moderate intrastrategy correlations. However, results also indicate differences in benchmark return among the various investible and noninvestible indexes as well as between various risk-based measures of expected return. In short, results indicate both the potential use of various benchmarks to capture underlying return process yet the necessity of understanding the structure and return process embedded in each benchmarking approach.

PART Three

Risk Management

CHAPTER 12

Some Thoughts on Risk Management for Commodity Portfolios

Jeffrey M. Christian
Managing Director
CPM Group

Commodities have been an integral part of the portfolios of many investors for centuries. Some investors have focused heavily on commodities, while others have used commodities as a subsector of a broader portfolio in which they allocate varying percentages of assets. Others have neglected or ignored commodities entirely.

Since the middle of the present decade, investment managers have focused increased attention on commodities as a part of a diversified portfolio. Others have rolled out investment funds specifically targeting investments. In some instances, these have been funds that only participate in futures, forwards, and options; in essence, these are variations of the commodity pools and commodity funds that have operated for decades in the futures markets, primarily in the United States. Other funds have taken a broader approach toward defining commodities investments, including, for example, equities of companies that produce commodities and options on such equities. Some funds have been created that are long-only commodities funds, in many ways similar to the natural resource equity mutual funds that also have been around since the 1970s.

The issue of managing risk in commodities portfolios depends in many ways on how one defines such commodities portfolios and their components. The risk management issues related to a long-only commodities futures and options fund will be quite distinct from the risk management issues related to a commodities subaccount or allocation within a larger diversified portfolio.

Furthermore, the approach to managing such risk will depend heavily on many other aspects of the portfolio, from maturity exposures to tenure, and will include the investment objectives of the portfolio manager(s).

The focus of this chapter is on the concepts related primarily to a diversified commodities portfolio that includes physicals, futures, forwards, exchange-traded options, over-the-counter options, commodities-related equities, equity options, and cash components. This is a classic commodities-oriented hedge fund, trading both long and short positions across a basket of assets. A portion of such a fund would be in cash and cash equivalents, while another portion of the fund may well be in equities and other securities that are not related to commodities in any direct way. Such a portion of a portfolio would be a hedge against the commodities exposure of the bulk of the fund.

The management of risk in portfolios is an issue of key importance to the overall performance of portfolios on a long-term basis. While risk management receives a great deal of lip service, the construction, execution, and maintenance of risk management programs falls far short of ideals for most funds. This is true not only of commodities-oriented funds and portfolios, but of most types of investment portfolios, from hedge funds to more staid and ostensibly conservatively managed funds.

IDEALS AND REALITIES

The application of risk management techniques, strategies, tactics, and instruments varies widely among commodities-oriented portfolios. In truth, most commodities-oriented portfolios use very rudimentary and quantitative risk management techniques and approaches. If there are more than 6,000 commodity trading advisors, commodity pool operators, and commodities-oriented hedge funds in operation, the vast majority of these use rudimentary spreadsheets on desktop computers to manage their portfolios, including calculating and monitoring risk. Only the largest funds have the financial and managerial wherewithal to install and use sophisticated risk management programs.

Related to the software involved is the management structure of the fund, and whether there is a sufficient division, separation, and segregation between the portfolio management staff and the risk management supervisors or auditors. In most funds, there does not appear a wide enough separation between these functions. Many funds in fact are run by a handful of people and do not have the staffing required to develop a sufficiently separated risk monitoring program. Again, in this way, commodities portfolio managers in fact are not that different from the majority of equity portfolio managers. In both groups, a great deal of service is paid to the virtues and advantages of a quantitatively driven and adamantly adhered to risk management program, but in both groups oftentimes practices fall far short of the desired levels of risk management.

A large part of the reason for this is a lack of financial resources. Good quality risk management programs often are priced in a range of $150,000 or more per year to manage and utilize. This is out of the financial reach of most of the smaller funds. Larger funds will utilize these services, but oftentimes they do not fully use the services available to them. Like the home electronics consumer who uses only the most simple functions on his latest electronic gadget, many larger funds have elected to employ expensive and sophisticated risk management programs and services, but only use them to generate the most simple metrics, ignoring more complex and possibly more telling risk metrics available from the programs.

A survey of hedge funds by the consulting company Mercer Oliver Wyman, encompassing not only commodities-oriented funds but all hedge funds that responded to the survey, in 2006 concluded that the largest and most prominent hedge funds have employed extremely sophisticated risk management programs and systems, and have developed detailed and sophisticated comprehension of their risk profiles. Most funds, however, have not achieved this level of risk management.

These gaps in risk analysis and management are dangerous in the commodities markets, in which many sectors are extremely thinly traded and often do not have accurate and reliable statistics on the depth and breadth of their liquidity. Additionally, funds will purchase over-the-counter exotic derivatives that only can be resold to the issuing bank or brokerage company, and often lack the understanding of the illiquidity inherent in such investment instruments.

There are many people in the fund management community who react harshly to criticism that risk management is woefully inadequate. Many will argue that there are no generally accepted quantitative methodologies for accurately measuring risks, both portfolio-wide and related to individual assets and positions, and, therefore, the concept of compelling managers to adopt risk management programs should be seen as inappropriate intrusions. These arguments often sound more like justifications for lax controls than empirically defensible positions. The lack of consensus on which risk metrics are best for identifying the true risks inherent in portfolios is no defense for not using some management techniques to pay attention to the potential risks in a portfolio. That said, a shockingly high proportion of commodities and other fund managers appear to "manage" their risk exposures in nonquantified, nonquantitative, "intuitive" ways.

VARIOUS APPROACHES

There are a variety of approaches to risk management. As the occasional financial disaster at various funds illustrates, not all funds adopt and maintain tight risk controls on their portfolios, positions, and investment managers. The most common approach may be tracking the value at risk across the portfolio. Other fund managers will pay more attention to the risks inherent in independent positions.

In order to adequately understand the risks a portfolio faces, a myriad of measurements ought to be taken. A deep understanding of the types of risks a fund manager faces needs to be present in management as well. A fund faces risk across its portfolio, as well as risks on individual positions. Oftentimes the risks inherent in individual positions relate to those of other positions, so that their effects on the total portfolio might be masked in some risk metric calculations. There are operational risks, liquidity risks, systemic risks, regulatory risks, and other forms of risks.

Most risks can be quantified. Once a quantitative approach toward a given risk has been chosen, the way that risk is measured needs to be addressed. Some funds will use standard deviations, maximum drawdowns or Sharpe ratios as their only or major risk measurement. Others will look at value at risk or other metrics. The most sophisticated risk managers will use a variety of measurement techniques to examine risk from differing perspectives.

They also will run stress tests to examine the effects on individual positions and the overall portfolio of major economic or financial market shifts and price shocks to a portfolio. Funds will manage their risks by assessing not only the value at risk in individual investments but across the portfolio in a number of economic and financial market scenarios. Preferably before a position is initiated and added to a portfolio, the effects of various financial market developments on that asset's value will be tested: What happens to the value of that asset under various price, currency, interest rate, and other scenarios. Additionally, the effect of adding that asset to an existing portfolio will be studied, to see how the asset's value interacts with the other portfolio components, not only initially but under various scenarios.

THE INFRASTRUCTURE

A solid, independent computer system, either in-house, externally managed, or, ideally both, is required to properly manage risk. Risk metrics should be undertaken internally on an intraday basis by a risk manager. They also should be run on an end-of-day basis by an external risk management program and service, to check and verify the internal management program.

Software to manage these programs is rare and expensive. Again, this is a problem for all fund management companies, and not just those focusing on commodities investments. It is particularly problematic for commodities portfolios, however, since most of the programs, software, services, and vendors that provide services to the fund management industry do not cover all of the markets and types of instruments that are utilized by commodities funds. Most prime brokers are woefully unprepared to provide good risk management services related to over-the-counter commodities options, for example, which are among the most useful and interesting commodities instruments for a portfolio manager. The same is true for more exotic commodities assets.

Just as the software and services are rare, finding personnel to manage these positions is equally daunting. Given the fact that commodities were deemed uninteresting for much of the period from the middle of the 1980s through the middle of the 2000s, there are few skilled professionals with modern sophisticated quantitative understandings of market risk management that are well versed in commodities. Most of the people in this rare breed are well attended by their employers, and are not available to others in the industry either as potential hires or as advisors and consultants.

PORTFOLIO GUIDELINES AND LIMITS

Various funds place a wide range of limits on the positions that they will hold, and on other aspects of their funds' managements. These limits are arbitrarily determined by the fund management committee, preferably before the fund initiates trading and preferably based on a body of knowledge and experience on the part of the fund managers. It is not clear whether there are any such things as typical limits and guidelines. Limiting the amount of an investment in any single position or asset (e.g., to no more than 15% of assets under management) is often found in the guidelines of many commodity funds. This limit will be calculated before the position is established, and should be tracked daily.

How exposure is measured and calculated is also very important. We define exposure in two ways. One is as a percentage of assets under management. A more important measure is in terms of the maximum gains and losses that could be generated by a given position as a percentage of the assets under management at any given time.

It is also advisable to run iteratives to calculate the potential gains and losses of particular strategies under varying price scenarios, and compare these to the potential risks and returns of alternate strategies, before putting positions in place. This allows the portfolio manager to examine whether a given strategy is more or less attractive as a way to buy exposure to a given commodity, compared to alternative approaches to the same investment.

In precious metals funds, the part of the portfolio that can be invested in any given market—gold, silver, platinum, palladium—are widespread (e.g., to no more than 35% of the assets under management). In diversified hedge funds these limits tend to be lower (e.g., 20% of the assets under management).

It is also useful to measure the size of positions relative to the overall liquidity, measured or estimated, in individual markets, limiting the exposure to any given market as a percentage of the liquidity in that market. As with every measure of risk, defining the yardsticks is critical. Portfolio managers should look at individual futures or options contracts, such as the July 2008 Comex silver futures contract, or the April 2008 $675 call option contract. Recent trading problems at other fund management companies have highlighted the importance of paying attention to the size of one's position relative to the narrowly defined market for that asset.

A major, related problem for commodities investments is the illiquidity of over-the-counter markets. Many investors have sought palladium options, for example. There are no exchange traded options for palladium, so that any investment fund interested in buying palladium options must use a metals dealer that is willing to write such options. This limits the fund to reselling these options to the original writer. It is not uncommon that liquidity problems sharply reduce the value of such options, so that while the price change in the underlying asset may show an attractive return, the value placed on the dealer options written against that underlying commodity has a radically different return.

Some funds will have measurements of liquidity problems that trigger liquidation of positions should they be crossed. Other funds will use similar measurements, but will choose to manage illiquid positions in other ways and not liquidate them merely because they have become more vulnerable to larger losses.

At the extreme level, there are performance restrictions and limits. It is common for a fund to have a provision that if it loses 25% or more of its net asset value from its most recent high watermark, it is required to liquidate its positions and notify shareholders before determining its next actions, based on the guidance the fund managers receive from a majority of the shareholders.

TECHNIQUES

There are an infinite variety of investment management strategies that can be employed to avoid losses, capitalize gains, and minimize adverse risks as the values of positions change. This is true for positions that are both gaining value and losing value.

A fund might lighten up on positions as they gain in value, or lock in profits by taking offsetting positions. For example, if an asset rises a given percentage or to a level at which the portfolio manager expects the price increase to pause, stop, or reverse, the manager might sell all or a portion of the position and use perhaps 10% of the net proceeds to purchase out of the money calls in the asset or a comparable. In this way, the manager has capitalized a gain but preserves some upward price exposure should the asset continue to appreciate in price. An alternative approach to this would be for the manager to buy out of the money puts and maintain the position. The manager might sell a portion of the long underlying position to pay for the puts, or it may deploy fresh capital to purchase the puts. If the asset stops rising in value and falls back, the puts will gain in value, offsetting some of the loss in the value of the underlying position while maintaining the overall long exposure. The fund may resell the puts, at a profit, while maintaining its long position. It also might reposition the puts, selling them back but purchasing lower cost new puts with lower strike prices to maintain protection against further weakness in prices while simultaneously maintaining the underlying long position and capitalizing some of the profits it has generated on its original puts.

Which of these strategies is most useful depends on the manager's perspective of future price moves, among other things. If the manager feels that prices are likely to rise further later, but that the price appreciation has gone too fast, the latter strategy makes more sense. If the portfolio manager feels the bulk of the longer term upward move is behind the market, the former strategy makes more sense. The manager's price expectation is only one factor determining the relative value of the alternative strategies. Depending on market conditions, the prices of the puts or calls available to the manager to effect one or the other strategy may make one or the other technique unattractive. As mentioned above, a variety of strategies should be compared and contrasted to see which ones have the preferable risk-reward profiles before any one is executed. With both strategies, it is imperative that the manager is careful not to hedge the gains away entirely.

The same practice can be used with assets the value of which have been declining. If a portfolio manager is short an asset that has fallen in value, he or she might buy the position back if prices fall sharply, using a portion of the proceeds to purchase a put below the sales price level. Or the portfolio manager might buy some calls to hedge against a rebound in prices, while maintaining the overall short position in the underlying asset. Similar techniques can be employed for positions that are experiencing losses, both on the short and long sides of the market.

A variety of options spreads also can be employed in any number of scenarios to reduce the risk of an overall position while maintaining the basic posture toward the market, long or short. The mechanics are the mirror image of those discussed above. Additionally, there are other strategies involving put and call spreads, butterfly spreads, and other options patterns that allow for varying exposures to rising or falling prices.

It is probably apparent from all of the proceeding that the author has a proclivity toward using options. This is true. In fact, while most commodities fund managers will primarily focus on futures, using options to hedge the underlying futures position, one can also use options to establish the basic position it decides to take, and later use futures or forwards to hedge the underlying options position. This provides increased flexibility in repositioning the positions as the price of the basic commodity changes.

RISK MANAGEMENT ANALYSIS REQUIREMENTS FOR TRADING OPTIONS

Utilizing options creates a requirement for advanced options risk analysis tools that will measure and report the risk of an actively managed investment portfolio that combines options and futures on commodities. The major risk measurements related to options often are called "the Greeks" because of the use of Greek letters (and similar words) to label them. *Delta* (Δ) measures the sensitivity of an option price to changes in the price of the underlying commodity. For each option purchased and held in a portfolio, it is important to calculate the current delta and the forward delta to a predetermined future date, as well as to track the delta for each trade over time. *Gamma* measures how fast the delta of a given option changes given a unit change in the price of the underlying asset. *Vega* is the change in the price of an option that results from a 1% change in volatility. (Vega is not a Greek letter.) *Theta* is the change in the option premium for a given change in the period to expiry of the options. Theta measures the time decay factor for the options under different time scenarios.

Measuring and monitoring the Greeks of options is critical not only for each position but also on an aggregate basis for each asset class, to measure these risks on a portfolio basis. At the end of each day, the implied volatility surface (based on the closing exchange options prices) should be used to calculate that day's delta and all of the other Greeks described above. This provides a volatility curve or grid. At-the-money options have different volatilities than out-of-the-money options. For over the counter options, a volatility grid also should be reviewed on a daily basis or even throughout the trading day.

CONCLUSION

Managing the myriad risks attendant to holding a diversified portfolio of commodities-oriented assets is a very important task. Unfortunately, it seems to be overlooked or handled in qualitative or sloppy fashion at many funds. Partly this reflects a lack of financial resources, and perhaps some shortage of statistical sophistication, on the part of many fund management operations. Even at firms with sufficient supplies of both financial resources and sophistication, risk management often turns sloppy and falls short of what quantitatively oriented managers and observers would like to see.

The nature of such risk management programs will vary widely, depending on the nature of the fund and the assets it deploys. Funds that focus primarily on futures and exchange-traded options will be able to manage a risk monitoring program that focuses on these assets. More diverse funds which invest in more exotic compound options programs purchased in the over-the-counter market, or equities and equity options, as well as futures, forwards, and exchange-traded options will find much more complex intraportfolio correlation and need to invest in more complex and sophisticated risk monitoring programs.

CHAPTER 13

Effective Risk Management Strategies for Commodity Portfolios

Moazzam Khoja, CFA
Senior Vice President-Strategy
Sungard Kiodex

There is a lot of recent excitement around the commodity markets, particularly energy, as evidenced by the amount of press and editorials while oil prices reached record highs, leading many industry experts to predict that energy trading will become an integral part of broader financial markets in the near future. Number of banks, futures commission, merchants, and hedge funds that are entering, or considering entering, the potentially lucrative commodity market continues to increase.

There are, however, some fundamental differences between commodity markets and other markets such as stock, money, interest rate, and exchange market. This chapter will highlight those differences by outlining seven operational guidelines that should be part of a firm's best practices when trading commodities as well as things an investor should know before investing in commodity trading firms.

The data and conclusions presented in this chapter are drawn from the author's experience advising commodity trading firms and builds upon a case study surveying best practices among three top commodity trading firms.

MEAN REVERSION BEHAVIOR OF COMMODITY RETURNS

In the current market, absolute mean reversion, defined as the tendency of the commodity's spot prices (front month contract) to revert to a long term average price, is a myth. The historical price for West Texas Instruments (WTI) in Exhibit 13.1 shows from 2002 to 2005, the front month contract

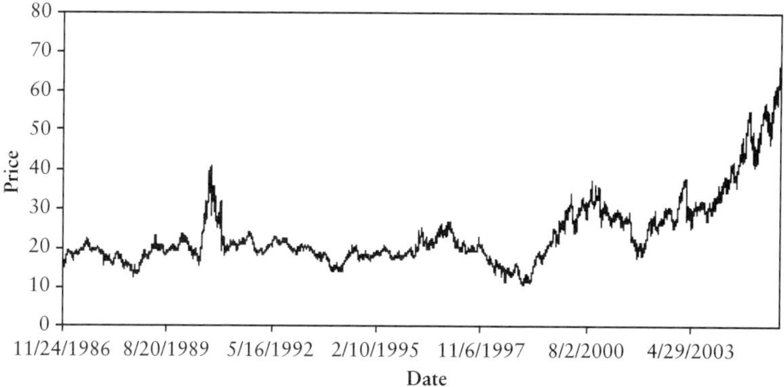

EXHIBIT 13.1 NYMEX WTI Spot Price (1986–2005)
Source: Data from NYMEX.

on the New York Mercantile Exchange (NYMEX) WTI has not reverted to a long-term average.

While absolute mean reversion is not something that exists in commodity markets, prices do, however, revert to an average level—a phenomenon called *relative mean reversion*. Exhibit 13.2 illustrates the difference, in relative terms, between the prices of the front month contract and a long dated NYMEX contract expressed in relative terms (to be specific, natural log). The black line in the exhibit represents change between the front month and the 10th month contract while the gray line simply represents the relative change between the front month contract and the 30th month contract.

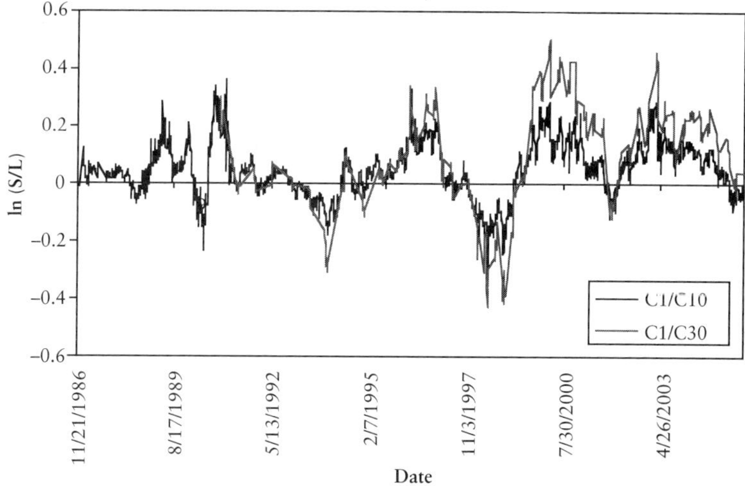

EXHIBIT 13.2 Relative Mean Reversion on NYMEX WTI
Source: Data from NYMEX.

As seen in the Exhibit 13.2, the front month contract does not revert to an absolute level of a long-term average price, but the movement of the curve is not unrestrained either. Therefore, the price of the commodity, in this case WTI, is constrained by its relative position to the long dated contract on the same commodity. As a conclusion to this section, a risk management system that does not value and compute risk for trades using a relative mean reversion model, runs the risk of misrepresenting the firm's risk and producing incorrect value at risk reports.

MARKING THE NET ASSET VALUE

Since the majority of commodity trades are *over-the-counter* (OTC) contracts traded through a network of brokers and dealers, commodity markets are notoriously opaque. Consequently, since OTC data is not available through exchanges, it is difficult if not impossible to accurately mark your book and know precisely what the market is trading at any given time. Even if OTC contracts are cleared through an exchange such as NYMEX ClearPort, derivatives are often valued using forward curves that are often not traded on exchanges. As such, the value of these derivatives depends on the OTC forward prices of these contracts. In order to independently value positions, it is imperative as a risk manager and investor to have access to accurate and independent forward curves. Using exchange-traded contracts or NYMEX cleared prices as a proxy to the OTC market can lull investors and risk managers into a false sense of security believing that they have the market data to price OTC derivatives and obtain an accurate net asset value.

To illustrate the danger of not incorporating appropriate market data into your risk management practices, note the differences in Exhibit 13.3

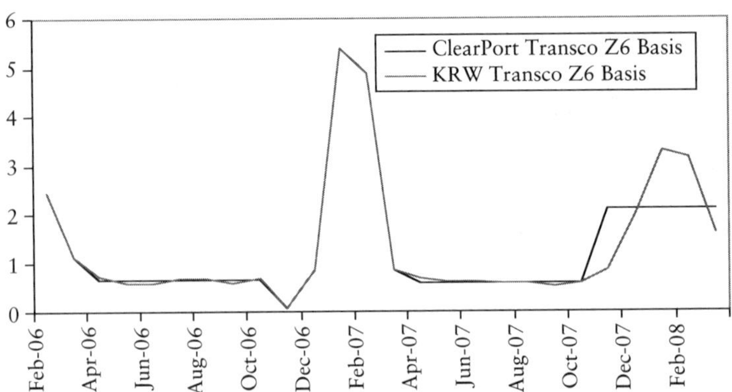

EXHIBIT 13.3 Exchange versus Independent Market Data: Transco Z6 Basis Forward Curve
Source: NYMEX ClearPort and Kiodex Global Market Data.

EXHIBIT 13.4 Difference in Net Asset Value given Hypothetical MMBTU[1]

	Position in MMBTU	Net Asset Value Clearport Prices	Net Asset Value Kiodex Market Data
Nov-07	300,000	$ 630,000	$ 254,752
Dec-07	620,000	$1,302,000	$1,202,796
Jan-08	620,000	$1,303,000	$2,041,658
Feb-08	280,000	$ 588,000	$ 881,944
Mar-08	310,000	$ 651,000	$ 496,579
	Total	$4,473,000	$4,877,729

[1]MMBTU is the unit of natural gas contract that trades as the unit of energy produced by the given heat content of that natural gas.

between exchange data and an independent source. The forward prices shown are for IF Transco Z6 (exchange data) versus OTC broker data on the same natural gas location. The discrepancy between the curves is due to the fact that the exchange data does not provide seasonal variations in winter 2007 (November 2007 to March 2008). Even if you assume a similar average price for a winter strip coming from the exchange and broker data, but with different seasonal shaping from the curve of OTC broker data, the firm taking unequally weighted positions in winter months would cause a different net asset value. A volume weighted average price in a shaped curve will differ from a flat curve when trade quantities are uneven.

Exhibit 13.4 shows the difference in the net asset value that would be reported using hypothetical volume positions contrasting exchange prices with independent market data.

Getting the right data is paramount to ensure an accurate net asset value. A firm may underreport its net asset value if it were long winter spreads at Transco Z6 with uneven volumes as shown above. Without high-quality independent market data, a commodity trading firm will not accurately know its net asset value and may be over or understating its risk.

MEASURING EVENT RISKS

Event risk, denned as a catastrophic unforeseen event, often leads to unusual market anomalies. One of these anomalies, seen during hurricane Katrina, was the breakdown of intercommodity correlations. Basic economic relationships between commodities, that is, crude oil prices and refined oil prices (crude is a major input to the refinery process), ensure that certain commodity markets generally correlate with each other. Similarly, one would expect power and natural gas to be closely correlated since natural gas fuels power plants. But after hurricane Katrina moved through the

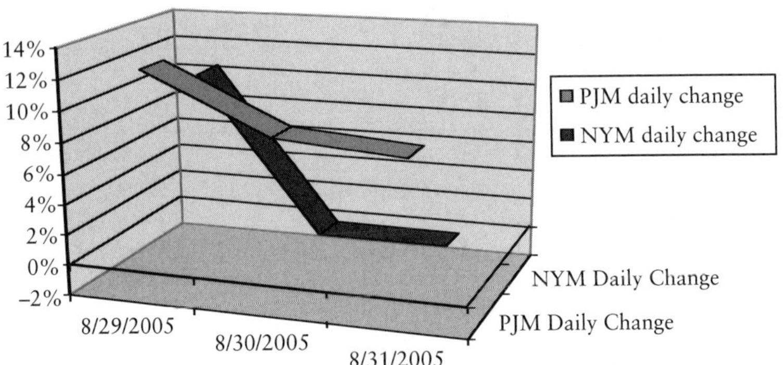

EXHIBIT 13.5 NYMEX and PJM Daily Movement, August 29, 2005 to August 31, 2005

Gulf in August 2005, power and natural gas prices, which usually move in tandem, became "unhitched."

The effect of this type of event is illustrated in the following example. Assume that a fund had a short position on 500 MW/Hour spark spreads between PJM Western Hub and NYMEX HH on August 26, 2005 (three days before hurricane Katrina hit the Gulf) and this position with a $13 million notional would require 10% margin or economic capital, which is $1.3 million of cash investments. Katrina caused an unusual breakdown in the NYM natural gas and PJM power price correlation for a few days around August 29, 2005. Exhibit 13.5 shows that the daily movement of PJM prices was not matched by corresponding movement in NYMEX natural gas prices causing the spread position to take an unusual level of stress.

The change in *profit and loss* (P&L) shown in Exhibit 13.6 amounts to a net loss of around $2.8 million within three days to the fund. This caused more than double the loss of total capital invested in the endeavor.

It is impossible to predict event risk, but it is possible to measure the impact of an event on a portfolio. By measuring the impact on the portfolio, a firm can keep track of its liquidity situation should an event occur. The next section will detail how to test the effects of events on the portfolio.

STRESS TESTING USING VALUE AT RISK

Many risk managers consider running *value-at-risk* (VaR) the sole measure for managing a commodity firm's risk. This is a mistake. Although necessary, VaR cannot identify unforeseen catastrophic events like hurricane Katrina. VaR quantifies the amount of "risk capital" needed to support a fund. As an application to the credit management process, it is used to identify the maximum potential credit exposure due to a commodity derivatives

EXHIBIT 13.6 Loss as a Percent of Capital Calculation

		Notional	$(13,023,920)			
		Capital	$1,302,392			
Date	PJM	IF Tran Z6	MTM	P&L Change	PJM Daily Change	NYM Daily Change
8/26/2005	$ 77.52	$10.3210	$ (47)	$—		
8/29/2005	$ 87.20	$11.4120	$ (256,166)	$ (256,119)	12.48%	10.57%
8/30/2005	$ 94.76	$11.4120	$(1,522,560)	$(1,266,393)	8.68%	0.00%
8/31/2005	$102.41	$11.4095	$(2,806,972)	$(1,284,412)	8.07%	–0.02%
		Loss as percent of capital		–215.52%		

operation. VaR can also be used as a way to allocate risk capital via limits to different traders within a firm.

Commodity markets are more exposed to the effects of "events" than other asset classes. The VaR approach that identifies the 5% worst-case scenario to a firm's risk does not account for events when historical correlation patterns break down. The only way to address such issues is to conduct stress tests. There are three ways to stress test a portfolio. First, shift forward curves arbitrarily and see the resulting change in the net asset value. Second, simulate price movements to mimic a historical event like a hurricane. Third, use the *front-month equivalents* (FME) of each commodity and create a matrix of price movements with different correlations.

FME is a statistical measure that defines the entire position of a commodity in an equivalent front month contract. It uses relative prices, correlations, and standard deviation to value the FME. The FME equivalent distills all the positions in different months into an equivalent position in the front-month contract. It can then be shocked with different assumptions of intercommodity correlations. For example, consider the FME of NYMEX Heating Oil and NYMEX Unleaded Gasoline shown in Exhibit 13.7.

The FME of long heating oil 11,813 BBL equivalents and FME UNL is short 11,882 BBL can be shocked in a matrix as illustrated in Exhibit 13.8 to see the resulting changes in the net asset value.

In Exhibit 13.8, assuming a large $3.00 per gallon change in price for both heating oil and unleaded gasoline, one can see the resulting change in the net asset value of the firm using the two different correlation assumptions. A correlation of −1 is highly unlikely; it assumes that the price of heating oil and unleaded gas will move in opposite directions. But if such an event occurred one could see the impact on the value of the portfolio and measure liquidity constraints, if any. Therefore, conducting stress tests should be considered best practices for any risk management process in order to identify the potential impact of a catastrophic event to the portfolio. This should be done with a view to identify a firm's liquidity needs in such a scenario.

MEASURING LIQUIDITY RISKS

Can your fund survive sudden liquidation of positions? Does your manager have concentrated positions which are difficult to liquidate? Inability to liquidate positions caused Long Term Capital Management crises in 1998 and it is widely believed to be the major cause of Amaranth's and MotherRock's debacle in 2006. When a trader has large concentrated position it incurs "market impact cost" to unwind.

EXHIBIT 13.7 Basis Report

Energy basis: Volume	Volume						
		report description:		external id:	all	inco terms:	all
report id:	20905733	trade type:	all	external id2:	all	MOT:	all
report name:	Basis	market:	all	counterparty ext id:	all	transport:	all
portfolio:	WP(USD)	commodity:	all	group id:	all	physical M2M:	all
data source:	Official	counterparty:	all	trade id:		loading location:	all
run by:	moazzam.khoja@kiodex.com	run on:	01/12/06 2:19 PM	trader:	all	discharge location:	all
as of date:	12/02/05			trade date:	. . .	event type:	
granularity:	Monthly			term date:	. . .	event date:	

	NYMEX WTI		NYMEX HO		NYMEX UNL		Total	Total
month	delta (bbl)	position (bbl)	delta (bbl)	position (bbl)	delta (bbl)	position (bbl)	delta (bbl)	position (bbl)
Total	366,507	500,000	11,813	11,905	(11,813)	(11,905)	366,507	500,000
FME	366,507	—	11,813	—	(11,882)	—	366,438	—
Jan—06	366,507	500,000	11,813	11,905	0	(11,905)	378,320	500,000
Feb—06	0	—	0	—	(11,813)	—	(11,813)	—

Source: Data from Kiodex Risk Workbench.

EXHIBIT 13.8 Price Changes Affecting Net Asset Value

	$3.00		
Price Change Scenario	FME	Correlation 1	Correlation −1
NYMEX heating oil	11,813	35,439	(35,439)
NYMEX unleaded gasoline	(11,882)	(35,646)	(35,646)
Change in the net asset value		$(207)	$(71,085)

Market Impact cost is the percentage loss to the portfolio in order to unwind large position. Using 5-minute interval data, the analysis in Exhibit 13.9 calculates the coefficient of price change for unusually large volumes (two standard deviation volume movement) on NYMEX Henry Hub Natural Gas Prompt contract. The author estimated a regression on five minute interval price and volume data to show that if one brings a large order, denned as the order size equal to two times the standard deviation of usual volume in each five minute interval, then there could be 0.00025% impact cost. Assume your fund has a 5,000 open contract position. To unwind this position would cost $5 million. Risk managers should calculate impact costs for each contract. Next, they should set maximum open position limits using the impact cost and their tolerance. A firm will be able to survive liquidation event if the manager forces a *maximum open position* limit.

$$\text{Total MMBTU} = \text{Number of contracts} \times 10000 \text{ (NYM HH)}$$

$$\text{Impact cost per MMBTU} = \text{Total MMBTU} \times \text{Coefficient for change in price}$$

$$\text{Possible impact cost} = \text{Impact cost per MMBTU} \times \text{Price per MMBTU} \times \text{Total MMBTU}$$

Liquidity cost is often overlooked by many managers when managing commodities fund. It can have dangerous consequences. A fund manager

EXHIBIT 13.9 Impact Cost Calculation

Number of contracts	5,000
Total MMBTU	50,000,000
Coefficient for chg. price	0.00025%
Impact cost per MMBTU	1.2449%
Price per MMBTU	$8.00
Possible Impact Cost	$(4,979,406)

Source: Data from GLOBEX.

must measure liquidity cost and impose maximum open position limits on traders to ensure that the fund can sustain such a catastrophic liquidity event.

PERFORMANCE ATTRIBUTION

Is your P&L a function of strategy or chance? Exhibit 13.10 illustrates how different strategies can produce a P&L attribution based on changes in forward curves, volatilities, time, interest rates, and foreign exchange. A risk manager must be able to attribute the P&L into its components. It is important to know which strategy made money and whether the firm made money adhering to their strategy or if there was a strategy "drift."

Assume a fund invests in three strategies: outright speculation, speculation on spreads, and speculation on implied volatility. Hypothetical positions in each of the strategies for January 2006 contracts are shown in Exhibit 13.11. For each of the strategies, the change in MTM for different days is calculated. For the volatility strategy, the change in MTM is further broken down between changes in the forward curves and changes in the implied volatilities. The returns are calculated on capital invested (the margin required) to take these positions on NYMEX.

A few interesting insights are drawn from Exhibit 13.11. The volatility strategy that should have shown P&L due to the volatility changes is, in fact, showing most of its profits due to the changes in the forward curves. Although, it is a very good return on investment, investors and risk managers should be wary of this performance since the return was due to the change in the forward curves and not volatility.

The spread and outright strategy also shows interesting dynamics. Although the spread strategy lost money in the period, its standard deviation was very low. If the investor wanted to allocate a portion of the fund in a less volatile strategy, it indeed achieved the objective. Return per unit of standard deviation is a good measure to show a strategy's efficiency post facto.

You need to be able to explain your P&L. If you do not know how your firm is making or losing money, you do not know if your strategy is working. If you can explain your P&L, you can take corrective measures to ensure that you are allocating resources to the winning strategies.

MITIGATING OPERATIONAL RISKS

Many firms that have lost money attribute the losses to lax operational controls. One area that is particularly prone to operations mistakes is the

EXHIBIT 13.10 Mark-to-Market Report

Portfolio	Total quantity	Trade id	Underlying	Total P & I	Forwards	Fx	Volatility	Time	Interest rates
WP	n/a	—	—	(916,171)	(893,599)	0	4,131	(17,596)	(1)
WP Outright	500,000	—	—	(339,833)	(339,994)	0	0	203	(2)
WP Spread	500,000	—	—	(10,779)	(10,774)	0	0	(4)	0
WP Vol Strategy	500,000	—	—	(565,559)	(542,832)	0	4,131	(17,795)	0
Total:	n/a	—	—	—	—	—	—	—	—
CONFIGURE REPORT									
VIEW MARKET DATA SOURCES									

Source: Data from Kiodex Risk Workbench.

EXHIBIT 13.11 Forward and Volatility Strategies

	Changes Due to Forwards		Changes Due to Forwards and Volatilities	
Date	Outright	Spread	Option Forward	Option Volatilities
11/29/2005	50,780	1,587	(202,446)	13,782
11/30/2005	423,697	(14,776)	192,070	871
12/1/2005	219,334	(3,576)	335,869	(9,365)
12/2/2005	450,427	(2,036)	291,891	(21,653)
12/3/2005	—	—	—	—
12/4/2005	—	—	—	—
12/5/2005	(135,004)	12,651	227,057	(19,636)
12/6/2005	(85,197)	(7,542)	12,173	(333)
12/7/2005	105,138	(12,754)	(288,079)	(14,633)
12/8/2005	644,860	(7,544)	605,416	(1,900)
12/9/2005	(339,833)	(10,779)	(542,832)	4,131
12/10/2005	—	—	—	—
12/11/2005	—	—	—	—
12/12/2005	263,751	(943)	879,378	23,937
12/13/2005	267,772	32,329	34,152	2,480
12/14/2005	(348,594)	11,473	(256,211)	3,976
12/15/2005	(447,890)	(14,057)	(424,184)	—
Total P&L	1,069,241	–15,967	864,254	–18,343
STDEV	36.48%	7.98%	41.52%	
Capital	$810,000	$145,238	$847,500	
Return on Capital	132.01%	–10.99%	99.81%	
Return on STDEV	3.62	(1.38)	2.40	

Source: Data from Kiodex Global Market Data and Multifactor Model.

accurate setting of energy commodity attributes. There are thousands of energy commodities (denned by product or location) and most of them have unique settlement mechanisms, holiday calendars, and OTC averaging conventions. Due to the sheer number of variables at play, the risk of a transaction risk materially increases. To mitigate this risk, the firm needs an auditable process of trade recording. This process should include reconciliation with the primary broker and OTC confirmations. Trade recording and confirmations or reconciliations should also be done by different people within your organization to ensure objectivity and to serve a gate keeping function. All amendments to trades must also be recorded and documented. Therefore, Microsoft Excel is not an adequate risk management system. A risk management process needs to include an auditable risk management reporting system into which all trades are entered. The separation of trade entry and confirmation process may cause the firm to misreport its risk and net asset values to its stakeholders.

CONCLUSIONS

Commodity markets provide a unique opportunity for investors. It provides better returns to investors and it reduces portfolio risk due to its lower return correlation with stocks. When an investor ensures due diligence, investing in commodities trading fund can be highly lucrative. This chapter provides seven golden principals on due diligence:

1. A commodity trading fund should measure risk using commodity specific models that incorporate relative mean reversion.
2. They should use independent source of market data to calculate their net asset value. Measuring through independent source would also reduce chances of fraud and misrepresentation.
3. Events such as hurricane Katrina have shown that it is the biggest threat to a commodity trading firm. Nobody can stop events but a firm can measure the impact of a catastrophic event on a firms's viability.
4. Just relying on value at risk in a commodity trading firm that is prone to huge shocks and where traders can take highly leveraged position is a recipe for disaster. At any given moment, a firm's inability to liquidate out of position can cause undesirable consequences. Long Term Capital Management and Amaranth disasters are attributed to their inability to liquidate out of undesirable positions.
5. Funds should have mechanism to measure market impact cost to liquidate position. Concentration limits should ensure that firm will have the wherewithal to pay up liquidation costs.
6. A good fund not only measures the profitability but also keenly measures its performance attributes. It knows how they are making money, what strategy is working and what strategy is not.
7. None of the above guidelines work until a firm has proper controls and it records and reports its transactions.

There is no guarantee that a fund will not meltdown or blow up. But, if one adheres to the above guidelines, the chances of such an occurrence reduce considerably.

CHAPTER 14

Quantifying Cross-Commodity Risk in Portfolios of Futures Contracts

Ted Kury
Senior Structuring and Pricing Analyst
The Energy Authority®

Forward price models can be a critical component of the risk management framework. Despite the utility of forward price models, models of spot prices are far more prevalent in the energy industry. Yet, for most questions involving changes in portfolio value, only a model of forward prices provides meaningful results. In this chapter, a tractable model of forward prices with time-varying volatility is presented. Rather than attempt to fit volatility parameters for an entire forward curve, the model recognizes that each forward contract may exhibit unique volatility characteristics and error structure. Further, the model incorporates the interrelationship between contracts of the same commodity and across commodities and allows for temporal changes to these interrelationships.

RISK MANAGEMENT OF COMMODITY FUTURES PORTFOLIOS

Assessing the Risk of Forward Price Movements

The risk management process varies greatly from organization to organization, but regardless of whether it is simple or complex, the crucial first step is always the same. Before risk can be managed, risk must be quantified. Many different types of entities may buy or sell commodities futures contracts in order to hedge risk. An oil producer may sell a portion of its expected future production today to be delivered at some point in time. By selling at a known price for the product, the producer has protected future cash flow from volatile prices for a portion of its sales. However, the hedger has not eliminated risk, it has simply exchanged spot price risk for forward price risk. Now, if the hedger intends to hold the futures contract to expiration, then forward price risk may not be important. However, there may be external factors that make it critical. First, if the futures contracts are sold on the NYMEX, there are margin requirements associated with the forward position. If forward prices rise, collateral may be required to maintain the position. Further, the risk policy of the producer's firm may maintain value at risk or stop loss limits associated with forward positions. The inability to maintain the forward position in the face of collateral calls or internal risk limits will result in the positions being liquidated, generally at a loss. The hedger is then subject to the same cash flow risk that it faced before the forward sale, but with the additional cost of the forward position. Therefore, properly assessing the risk of forward price movements is critical in the risk management process.

Modeling Spot and Forward Prices

Before we begin, it is critical to differentiate between the modeling of spot prices and the modeling of forward prices. While the spot and futures products share many of the same characteristics, they are distinct. The spot price of a commodity is the price paid for a unit of that commodity, generally the day before or the hour before it is delivered. The futures price of a commodity is an agreement to pay a particular price for a unit of the commodity, to be delivered at some point in the future. In most cases, this is for an equal amount of the commodity on each day of a particular month. Pricing models for both spot and futures prices each have their uses, but the models cannot be substituted for one another, as they have different temporal characteristics.

The behavior of spot commodity prices has been studied at length, and a number of different models, such as the single and multifactor mean reverting models of Pindyck[1] and Schwartz,[2] the mean reverting with jump diffusion models of Clewlow and Strickland[3] and Clewlow, Strickland,

---

[1]Robert Pindyck, "The Long Run Evolution of Energy Prices," *The Energy Journal* 20, no. 2 (April 1999), pp. 1–27.
[2]Eduardo Schwartz, "The Stochastic Behavior of Commodity Prices: Implications for Valuation and Hedging," *Journal of Finance* 52, no. 3 (July 1997), pp. 923–973.
[3]Les Clewlow and Chris Strickland, *Energy Derivatives: Pricing and Risk Management* (London: Lacima Publications, 2000).

Kaminski,[4] the price spike models of Kholodnyi[5] and regime switching models derived from Hamilton[6] have emerged. These models can help to quantify the expected distribution of prices at the point when the spot day or spot hour occurs, but they provide no insight into the distribution of the price of any product other than the spot commodity at the time of delivery. For example, if you are interested in the distribution of natural gas prices on May 14, 2008, these price models may help you. If, however, you are interested in the distribution of prices for the May 2008 natural gas futures contract five days from now, they are useless.

Along with the temporal characteristics of the underlying product, the term structure of volatility is different in the different markets. Under the assumption of normally distributed shocks, the uncertainty in spot prices grows proportionally with the square root of time. Volatility in futures prices, however, behaves a bit differently. The contracts that are closer to expiration, also known as the *front months of the forward curve*, tend to be much more volatile than the contracts that are further from expiration, also known as the back months. In general, forward price volatility increases as time to expiry decreases. This behavior is a consequence of any mean reverting behavior of the spot price,[7] and a model of forward prices should incorporate this market behavior.

In addition to the term structure of the forward price volatility, it is also important to capture the relationship between futures contracts of the same commodity and across commodities. Like volatility, this relationship is not uniform. Contracts in consecutive months show a greater tendency to move together than contracts that are separated by years. Contracts in a particular winter or summer season may show a greater tendency to move together than contracts in different seasons. Across commodities, the forward curves for commodities that are close substitutes may move differently than the forward curve for commodities that are not. Finally, the correlation between the next contract to expire on the forward curve, also known as the prompt month contract, and the remainder of the forward curve may change as that contract gets closer to expiry. This behavior should be reflected in the model. Kury[8]

---

[4]Les Clewlow, Chris Strickland, and Vince Kaminski, "Extending Mean-Reversion Jump Diffusion," *Energy Power Risk Management* (February 2001).

[5]Valery Kholodnyi, The Stochastic Process for Power Prices with Spikes and Valuation of European Contingent Claims on Power, TXU Preprint, 2000.

[6]James Hamilton, *Time Series Analysis* (Princeton: Princeton University Press, 1994).

[7]Les Clewlow and Chris Strickland, "Simulating Spots," *Energy Risk* (May 2004), pp. 48–51.

[8]Ted Kury, "A Model of Time-Varying Volatilities in Futures Contracts," *Energy Risk* (June 2006), pp. 66–70.

introduced such a model, but acknowledged several limitations. In this chapter, the treatment of that model is expanded and a new methodology for modeling any excess kurtosis in forward price returns is proposed.

A TIME VARYING MODEL OF FORWARD VOLATILITY

The Model of Forward Prices

The derivation of a model for forward prices requires some assumptions about the behavior of the spot price of the commodity. For our purposes, we are going to use the single-factor mean-reverting framework of Pindyck.[9] This framework is flexible, powerful, and intuitive. The seminal asset pricing models of Black and Scholes[10] assumed that asset prices followed a geometric Brownian motion. Pindyck tested the prices of crude oil, natural gas, and coal and showed a tendency for them to revert to a long-term price. This conclusion also makes intuitive sense to anyone who has looked at the price of a commodity after a supply or demand shock has occurred and concluded that it is just "too high," and should eventually come down. Perhaps most importantly, the possibility that price follows a geometric Brownian motion is not eliminated in the single-factor mean-reverting model. This assumption still exists as the special case where $\alpha = 0$. The spot price (S), then, of the commodity is assumed to show the following form:

$$\ln S_t = \ln S_{t-1} + \alpha(\mu - \ln S_{t-1}) + \varepsilon_t \tag{14.1}$$

where $\varepsilon_t \sim N(0, \sigma^2)$, α is the mean reversion rate, and μ is the log of the long run equilibrium price.

From this model, Clewlow and Strickland[11] and Lucia and Schwartz[12] have shown that the volatility of the forward price can be expressed as:

$$\sigma_t = \frac{\sigma}{2\alpha t}\cdot(1 - e^{-2\alpha t}) \tag{14.2}$$

[9]Robert Pindyck, "The Long Run Evolution of Energy Prices," *The Energy Journal* 20, no. 2 (April 1999), pp. 1–27.

[10]Fischer Black and Myron Scholes, "The Pricing of Options and Corporate Liabilities," *Journal of Political Economy* 81, no. 3 (July 1973), pp. 637–654.

[11]Les Clewlow and Chris Strickland, Valuing Energy Options in a One Factor Model Fitted to Forward Prices, Working Paper, University of Technology, Sydney, 1999.

[12]Julio Lucia and Eduardo Schwartz, Electricity Prices and Power Derivatives: Evidence from the Nordic Power Exchange, Working Paper, UCLA, 2001.

That is, that forward volatility at any time t is inversely proportional to both the mean reversion rate of the commodity and the time to expiry of the futures contract, and directly proportional to the theoretical volatility at expiration. We can use the graphs of the partial derivatives of (14.2) with respect to σ and α to illustrate these relationships. As shown in Exhibit 14.1, a change in σ, holding α constant, results in a level shift of the volatility curve and a slight increase in the slope. In Exhibit 14.2, a change in α, holding σ constant, results in a change in the slope.

In this model, the futures prices themselves are assumed to follow a random walk. Pindyck[13] and Alexander,[14] for example, have worked to fit GARCH models to futures prices, but their results have not been conclusive. The assumption of weak-form efficiency in the natural gas markets has been tested,[15] and the random walk model of futures prices is supported

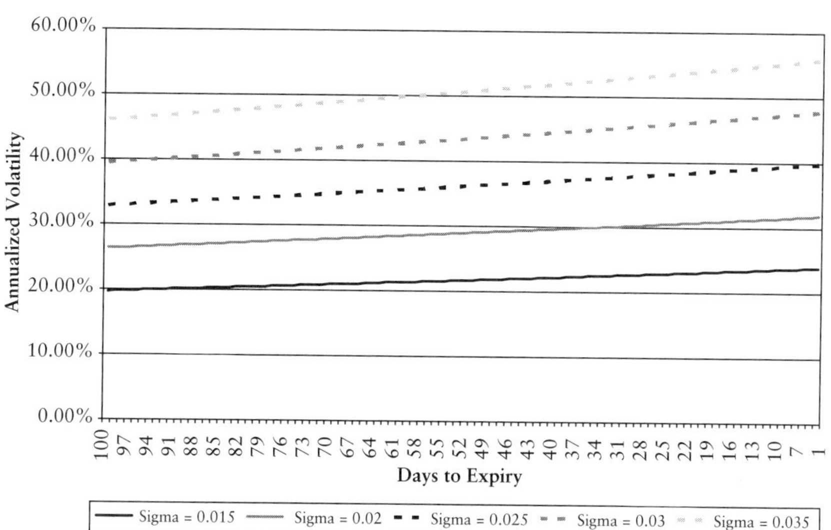

EXHIBIT 14.1 Sample Volatility Curves with Constant Mean Reversion Rates, Alpha = 0.002

[13]Robert Pindyck, Volatility in Natural Gas and Oil Markets, Working Paper, MIT, 2004.

[14]Carol Alexander, "Correlation in Crude Oil and Natural Gas Markets," in *Managing Energy Price Risk*, 3rd ed., edited by Vincent Kaminski (London: Risk Books, 2004).

[15]Ted Kury and John Lehman, Testing the Efficiency of the Natural Gas Futures Market, Working Paper, The Energy Authority, 2006.

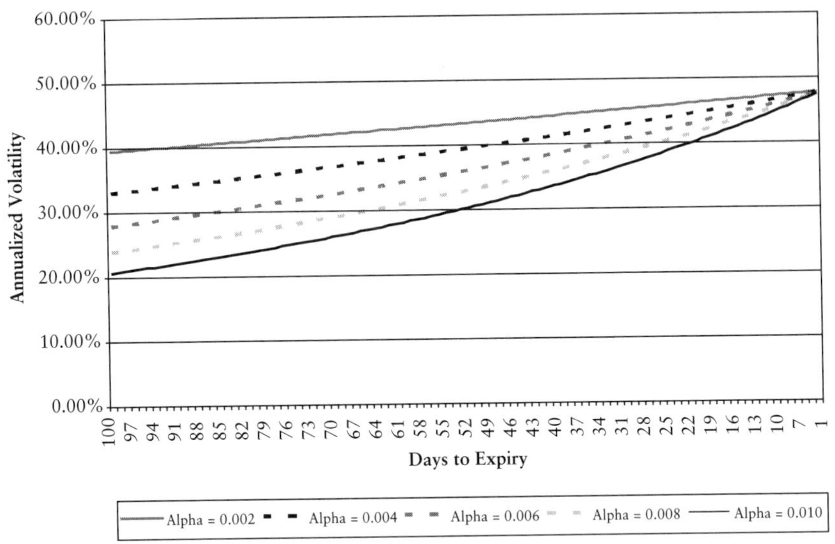

EXHIBIT 14.2 Sample Volatility Curves with Constant Terminal Volatilities, Sigma = 0.03

empirically. Futures price returns do exhibit conditional heteroscedasticity, however, and we will see that the condition is time to expiration.

Volatility Curves Exhibit Distinct Characteristics

It is important to stress that these volatility curves exist distinctly for each forward contract, as each contract may exhibit its own volatility structure. For example, the spot price of electricity tends to revert to the mean more quickly than the price of natural gas, and thus its futures contracts will exhibit a steeper volatility curve. Spot natural gas prices may revert more quickly than spot oil prices in some months, but not in others. Further, summer electricity prices tend to be more volatile—and thus their futures contracts tend to be more volatile—than other months. Winter natural gas prices may exhibit similar behavior. Thus, allowing each contract to follow its own term structure of volatility leads to a more robust model.

In order to illustrate the unique volatility characteristics of natural gas contracts of different months, we can show, in Exhibit 14.3, the historical volatility of NYMEX natural gas futures contracts, with the three most volatile contracts in each year highlighted in gray. Note that there is little pattern as to which contracts are most volatile. Frequently, they are the winter contracts, as we would expect, but some spring, summer, and fall contracts

EXHIBIT 14.3 Historical Volatilities of NYMEX Natural Gas Contracts

	Annualized Volatilities						
	2000	2001	2002	2003	2004	2005	2006
Jan	20.03%	28.27%	32.73%	31.90%	31.68%	25.88%	24.86%
Feb	19.21%	32.69%	33.41%	33.33%	32.98%	26.40%	25.68%
Mar	18.76%	33.67%	33.50%	38.68%	31.87%	25.55%	27.03%
Apr	17.41%	28.76%	33.90%	38.29%	27.28%	21.76%	23.61%
May	16.18%	25.55%	34.54%	35.44%	26.44%	21.43%	23.65%
Jun	16.82%	26.41%	34.61%	34.42%	26.45%	21.24%	24.24%
Jul	20.35%	27.80%	34.83%	33.60%	25.59%	21.41%	25.11%
Aug	20.93%	29.06%	34.79%	32.25%	24.85%	21.70%	26.01%
Sep	21.30%	31.59%	35.90%	32.43%	24.93%	22.85%	27.79%
Oct	20.97%	32.59%	37.13%	32.27%	25.61%	24.63%	28.17%
Nov	21.54%	33.09%	34.39%	30.97%	25.52%	23.55%	26.05%
Dec	22.77%	32.50%	32.42%	29.92%	25.44%	22.92%	23.05%

are more volatile than winter contracts in certain years. The threat, or absence, of hurricanes in the Gulf Coast, to cite one example, can affect the volatility of the fall natural gas contracts.

Nonlinear Optimization of Volatility Functions

The absolute value of the daily log price returns of each futures contract can be fit to this volatility function using nonlinear optimization techniques. The volatility function is continuous and twice differentiable, and because there are only two free parameters, the matrix of second derivatives will not be unwieldy. Therefore, we can use one of the hill-climbing methodologies such as Newton-Raphson[16]; Gauss-Newton[17]; Goldfeld, Quandt, and Trotter[18]; Broyden, Fletcher, Goldfarb, Shanno (BFGS)[19]; and Berndt, Hall,

[16]William Press, Saul Teukolsky, William Vetterling, and Brian Flannery, *Numerical Recipes in C: The Art of Scientific Computing* (Cambridge: Cambridge University Press, 1992).

[17]Estima, *RATS Version 6 User's Guide* (Evanston: Estima, 2004).

[18]Stephen Goldfeld, Richard Quandt, and Hale Trotter, "Maximization by Quadratic Hill Climbing," *Econometrica* 34 (July 1966), pp. 541–551.

[19]William Press, Saul Teukolsky, William Vetterling, and Brian Flannery, *Numerical Recipes in C: The Art of Scientific Computing* (Cambridge: Cambridge University Press, 1992).

Hall, and Hausman (BHHH)[20] to perform the nonlinear optimization. The benefit of these hill-climbing algorithms is that they are straightforward to implement. However, they are also local search algorithms, so it may be necessary to perform the optimization with a range of initial values to ensure that the solution converges to a global, rather than local, maximum. A more efficient alternative may be to start the optimization with a small number of iterations of a global search algorithm such as the simplex algorithm[21] of Dantzig, and then switch to one of the hill-climbing algorithms. Once the proper area of the volatility surface in which to search has been determined, repeating this optimization daily while adding additional data points should not change the surface significantly. That is, the initial fitting methodology does not need to be repeated daily. However, it is still prudent to repeat it periodically.

Nonlinear optimization can often fail to converge to a solution. This tendency to fail can be exacerbated in more complex models, so it is best to be as parsimonious with the parameters as possible. We have tested a number of variables to see if the fit of the volatility function can be improved, such as seasonal parameters for all commodities in the form of Fourier series, dummy variables for Mondays (as the first trading day after two nontrading days) and Thursdays (the day that the Department of Energy's Energy Information Administration publishes the volume of natural gas in United States storage facilities), and none improve the fit sufficiently for the added computational complexity.

The volatility curves and absolute value of the daily log price returns of the April 2007 and November 2007 NYMEX natural gas contracts as of January 2007, are shown in Exhibit 14.4 and Exhibit 14.5, respectively. As expected, the volatility curve for the product nearer to expiration is much steeper.

For the April contract, approximately 40% of the volatilities fall above the best-fit line, 6% fall above twice the best-fit line, and 1% fall above three times the best-fit line. For the November contract, approximately 52% of the volatilities fall above the best-fit line, 16% fall above twice the best-fit line, and 5% fall above three times the best-fit line. This is more than we would expect from normally distributed errors, and suggests that there

---

[20]Ernst K. Berndt, Bronwyn H. Hall, Robert E. Hall, and Jerry A. Hausman, "Estimation and Inference in Nonlinear Structural Models," *Annals of Economic and Social Measurement* 3/4 (October 1974), pp. 653–665.

[21]William Press, Saul Teukolsky, William Vetterling, and Brian Flannery, *Numerical Recipes in C: The Art of Scientific Computing* (Cambridge: Cambridge University Press, 1992).

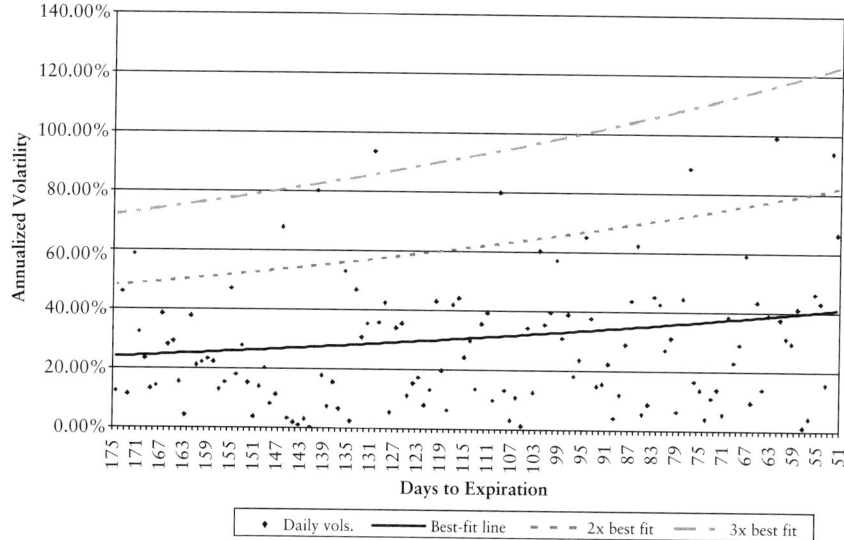

EXHIBIT 14.4 Volatility Curve for the April 2007 NYMEX Natural Gas Contract

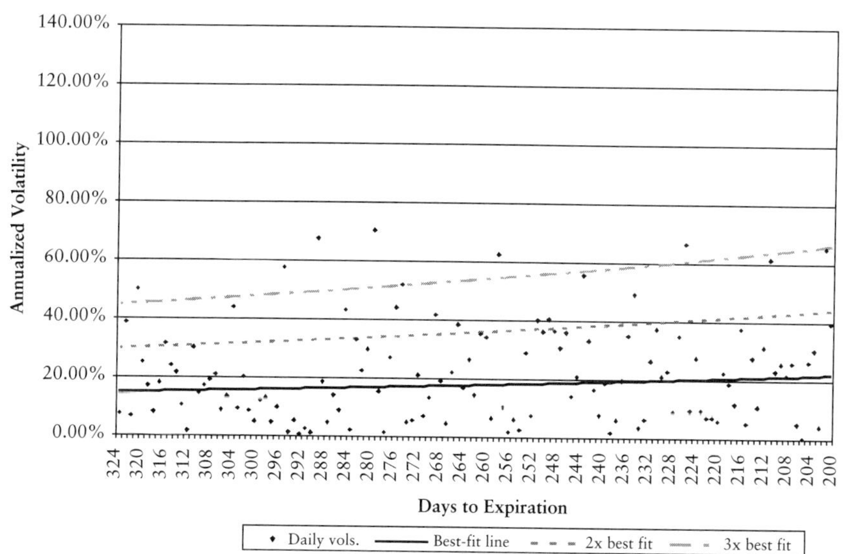

EXHIBIT 14.5 Volatility Curve for the November 2007 NYMEX Natural Gas Contract

may be excess kurtosis in the error distribution. When the volatility curves in Exhibit 14.4 and Exhibit 14.5 are multiplied by standard normal random variables generated within the Monte Carlo simulation,[22] there is a danger of underrepresenting the tails of the volatility distribution if there is excess kurtosis in the price returns.

Modeling Excess Kurtosis in the Volatility Function

We can reflect any excess kurtosis in the price return distribution by fitting the volatility curve assuming Student-*t* distributed errors, instead of normally distributed ones. In addition to a parameter for standard deviation, the Student-*t* distribution utilizes a parameter for degrees of freedom. With infinite degrees of freedom, the Student-*t* distribution collapses to the normal distribution. However, as the degrees of freedom decrease, the kurtosis of the Student-*t* distribution increases. An advantage of utilizing the Student-*t* distribution is that it does not force us to abandon our assumption of normally distributed errors. The normal distribution still exists as a special case. Therefore, if the value of the degrees of freedom parameter is very large, there will be little difference in the simulations. If, however, the degrees of freedom are small, the simulations will better reflect any excess kurtosis in the return distribution.

We can illustrate the difference that this modeling change makes by refitting the April 2007 contract shown in Exhibit 14.4. When we perform the optimization assuming that the errors follow the Student-*t* distribution, we find that the degrees of freedom parameter is 6. This is very low and tells us that there is considerable excess kurtosis in the price returns of this contract. The revised volatility curve reflecting this assumption is shown in Exhibit 14.6.

Now, approximately 33% of the daily volatilities fall above the best-fit line, 3% fall above twice the best-fit line, and none fall above three times the best-fit line. This is much closer to what we would expect. Multiplying this volatility curve by the standard normal random variables in the Monte Carlo simulation, results in a much better representation of the volatility distribution.

---

[22]Monte Carlo simulation is an estimation technique that relies on a series of random draws, or iterations, from a given distribution to generate a range of possible outcomes. With sufficient draws, the law of large numbers implies that the average of the iterations should approximate the true value. See, for example, Bruno Dupire (ed.), *Monte Carlo: Methodologies and Applications for Pricing and Risk Management* (London: Risk Books, 1998).

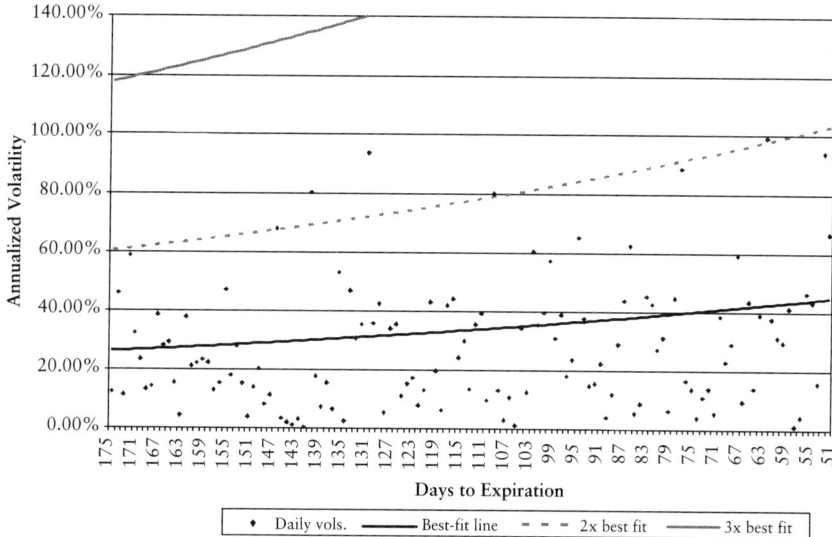

EXHIBIT 14.6 Refit Volatility Curve for the April 2007 NYMEX Natural Gas Contract

Effects on Modeling Volatility with Simple Standard Deviation

Some applications of forward curve models choose to represent forward volatility as the standard deviation of the forward price returns over some historical time period, and assume that this volatility will persist into the future. This assumption violates two characteristics of forward price volatility that are reflected in our model. First, since volatility increases as time to expiration decreases, the expected volatility for today is always greater than yesterday, and less than the volatility for tomorrow. Therefore, estimating today's volatility with volatility derived from historical prices will understate today's volatility. Second, tomorrow's volatility is expected to be greater than today's, and so using that estimate to project volatility going forward understates future volatility. A magnification of Exhibit 14.6, as Exhibit 14.7, may be used to illustrate the difference between a methodology based on historical prices and our methodology of time-varying volatility. The dashed line is the expected forward volatility used in simulations of our model, and the gray line is the standard deviation of the previous 30 days' price returns.

It may not appear that the difference between the two methodologies is significant, but consider that just a 10% difference in assumed volatility will change the value at risk calculation of a $20 million portfolio by approximately

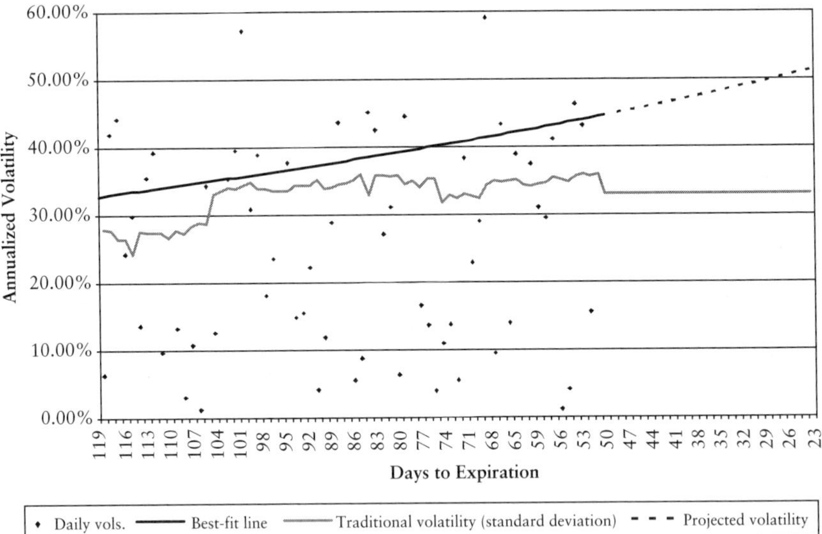

EXHIBIT 14.7 Historical and Projected Volatility Curve for April 2007 NYMEX NG Contract

$3 million, or 15% of the total portfolio value, at the 95th percentile. That is, the 95th percentile value at risk will be understated by 15% of the total portfolio value with the less rigorous model of forward volatility.

A MODEL OF CONTRACT INTERRELATIONSHIPS

The Decomposition of the Correlation Matrix

Once the volatility term structure for each contract has been parameterized, attention turns to modeling the interrelationships of the forward contracts. In doing so, we are not only trying to capture the relationships between contracts of the same commodity as efficiently as possible, but between other commodities as well. Because the evolution of a nonlinear system of forward prices is modeled through time, there is no closed form solution to our problem. We will have to use simulation to model our system of forward curves.

One general methodology involves the decomposition of the correlation matrix of the daily log price returns. However, by this methodology, future correlations between contracts will simply mirror historical ones. In reality, the correlation between the prompt month contract and the remainder of the forward curve may change, as the prompt month contract gets closer to expiration. Our methodology involves decomposition of the matrix of normalized shocks. We construct the correlation matrix of the daily price returns divided by the expected volatility, from our volatility model, for that particular contract on that particular day. The normalized shocks will then be distributed identically to the standard normal random variables that will generate in our simulations of the forward prices. In this way, we will not overestimate the correlation between the prompt month contract and the rest of the forward price curve.

One method for generating correlated random numbers involves the complete decomposition of the correlation matrix. Cholesky decomposition[23] can be used for this purpose. Given a correlation matrix **C** with dimension $N \times N$, we find the triangular matrix **A** such that $\mathbf{C} = \mathbf{AA}'$. Then, we can generate vector **B** of N independent standard normal random variables. The vector $\mathbf{D} = \mathbf{AB}$ is then a vector of standard normal random variables with the proper cross-correlations.

Data in the energy industry can be difficult to acquire. Further, any pricing data gathered may not be the best representation of a market price for a product because it does not represent the interactions between many buyers and sellers. The NYMEX is a liquid market and the pricing of contracts is transparent. However, many energy products are only traded "over the counter," and the pricing may be influenced by the liquidity and transparency of the market at the time the product is traded. Therefore, there may be internal inconsistencies in the relationships between the prices of different products. Further, the data set of prices may include data series with different time frames, and the cross-commodity relationships may not be consistent through time. As a result, the correlation matrix derived from this data may not be positive semidefinite. If the correlation matrix is not at least positive semidefinite, then the matrix **A** will have complex elements, and be useless for simulations. Cholesky decomposition also captures all of the contract interrelationships, some of which may not be meaningful, that is, in the noise.

An alternative to Cholesky decomposition is eigen decomposition.[24] Given the same correlation matrix **C** with dimension $N \times N$, we can derive a vector λ, of eigenvalues, and an $N \times N$ matrix **X** of eigenvectors such that $\mathbf{CX} = \lambda\mathbf{X}$. The rows of **X** describe an interaction between the different contracts on the forward curve, and the magnitude of their corresponding value in λ describes their relative importance in explaining the system. In general, the percent of the total variation explained by the ith eigenvector is the ith eigenvalue over N. Eigen decomposition enjoys several advantages over Cholesky decomposition. First, eigen decomposition is absolutely foolproof

[23]William Greene, *Econometric Analysis* (New York: Macmillan, 1990).
[24]William Greene, *Econometric Analysis* (New York: Macmillan, 1990).

for any symmetric—like a correlation—matrix. This makes it a reliable component of any automated system. Second, using the eigenvectors, or principal components of the correlation matrix allows us to explain the relationships in a large matrix with a relatively small number of equations and to model as much of the interrelationship as necessary. As such, we can choose successive eigenvectors to explain 95%, 99%, or even 100% of the variation in the correlation matrix. If the correlation matrix is not positive semidefinite, the result of the eigen decomposition will be one or more small, negative eigenvalues which can be ignored.

The Principal Components of the Forward Curve for Crude Oil

In Exhibit 14.8, we can see the first three principal components of the crude oil forward curve. These explain over 99% of the relationships in the correlation matrix.

We can gain some insight into the relative importance of these principal components by weighting them with the square root of their respective eigenvalues, shown in Exhibit 14.9.

The first principal component is the level component, and reflects the tendency of the crude oil forward contracts to move up or down together. Note how the weighted eigenvectors are nearly equal for all of the contracts.

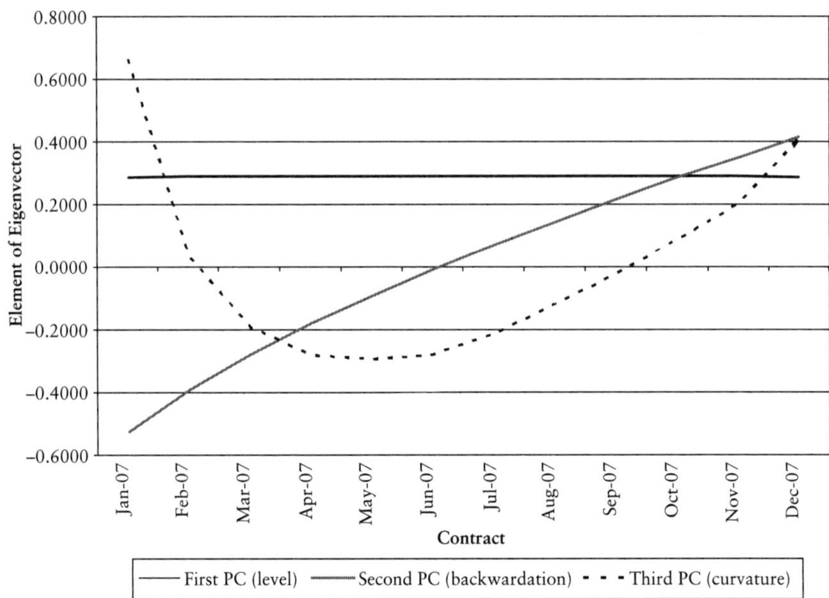

EXHIBIT 14.8 First Three Principal Components of the NYMEX CL Forward Curve

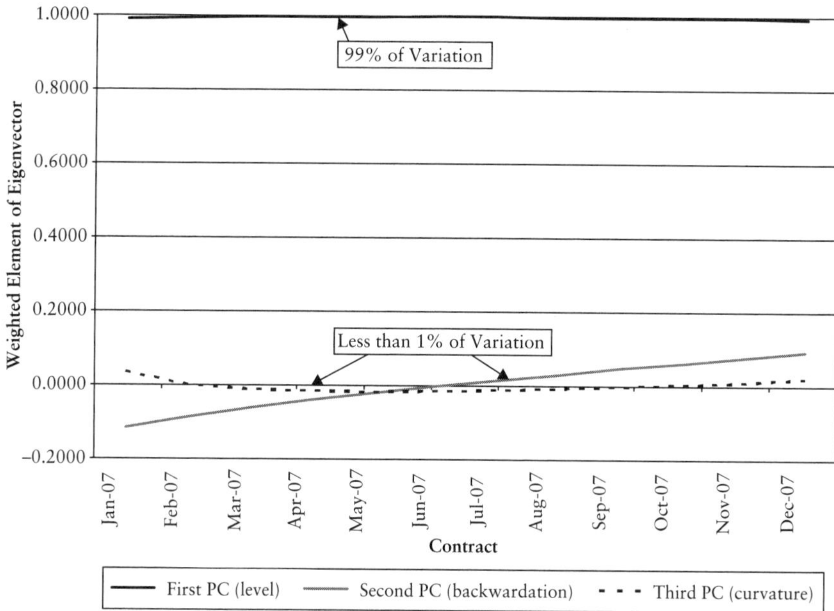

EXHIBIT 14.9 Weighted Principal Components of the NYMEX CL Forward Curve

That means that the first random number generated will have nearly the same effect on each contract. This eigenvector alone explains 99% of the daily variation in the first 12 months of the crude oil forward curve. The second principal component reflects the tendency of the curve to change its tilt. If the second random number is positive, the January contract will fall while the December contract will rise. That is, the degree of backwardation in the forward curve will decrease. If the second random number is negative, then the January contract will rise and the December contract will fall, increasing the degree of backwardation in the forward curve. This eigenvector explains less than 1% of the variation in the forward curve. Finally, the third principal component reflects the tendency of the forward curve to change curvature. When the January and December contracts are rising, the May, June, and July curves will be falling. This eigenvector also explains less than 1% of the variation in the forward curve.

The Principal Components of the Forward Curve for Natural Gas

In Exhibit 14.10, we can see the first four principal components of the natural gas forward curve. These explain 99% of the relationship in that

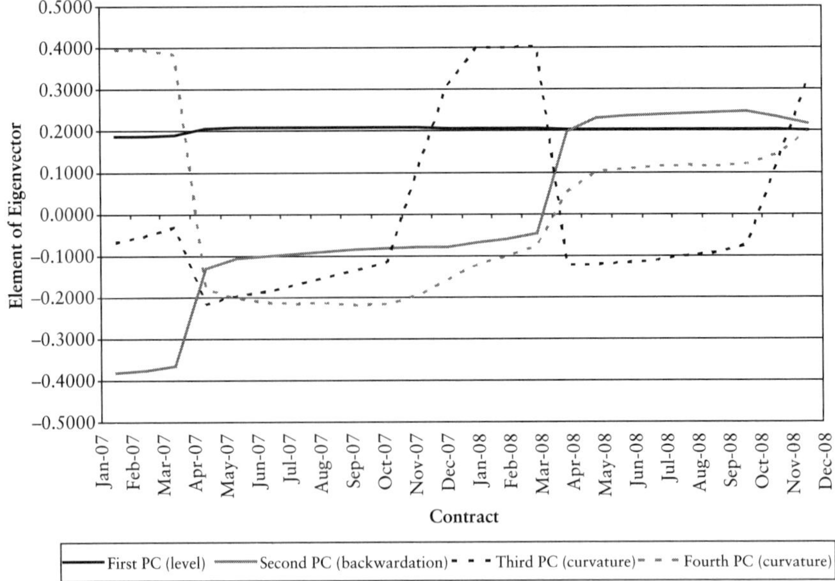

EXHIBIT 14.10 First Four Principal Components of the NYMEX NG Forward Curve

correlation matrix. Again, we can gain insight into their relative importance by weighting them, in Exhibit 14.11.

As with crude oil, the first principal component is the level component. This component is not nearly as flat as it was for crude oil. There is less of a tendency for natural gas contracts to move up or down together, and this principal component only explains 92% of the variation in the natural gas forward curve. If we used only the first principal component of the crude oil correlation matrix, we would still capture almost all of the variation in the correlation matrix. For natural gas, however, one principal component would be insufficient. The second principal component again reflects the tendency of the curve to change its tilt, but notice that instead of a relatively straight line, as in the case of crude oil, the natural gas curve has jumps from each March-to-April contract. This second principal component explains 5% of the variation, and is much more significant in natural gas than crude oil. The third and fourth principal components reflect the tendency to change curvature. The third principal component captures the changes in the relationship between winter and summer contracts, and explains roughly 2% of the variation. The fourth component shows the tendency of the April 2007 through March 2008

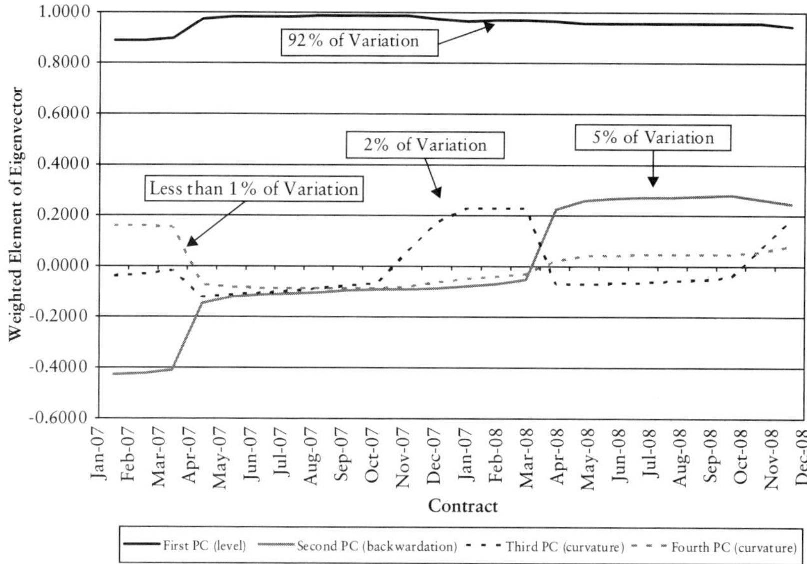

EXHIBIT 14.11 Weighted Principal Components of the NYMEX NG Forward Curve

strip to move counter to the rest of the curve, and explains less than 1% of the variation.

The Principal Components of the Forward Curve for Two Commodities

Finally, in Exhibits 14.12 and 14.13, we can show that 99% of the relationship between the natural gas (NG Contracts) and crude oil (CL contracts) curves can be explained with five principal components.

Four of these components should look familiar; they are the level, tilt, and curvature components that we saw in the natural gas and crude oil curves alone. However, we have added a new component, and it explains 23% of the variation of the two curves. The first principal component, the level component, explains much less variation when two commodities are considered. While different contracts of the same commodity may exhibit a greater tendency to move together; among different commodities it is less so. This second principal component reflects the tendency of natural gas and crude oil to move in opposite directions, or, for the natural gas/crude oil spread to change over time.

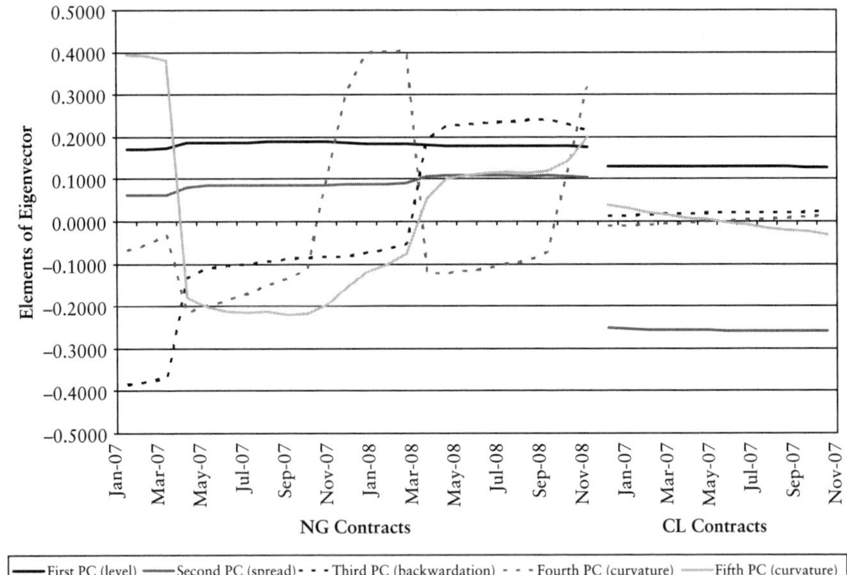

EXHIBIT 14.12 First Five Principal Components of the NG and CL Forward Curves

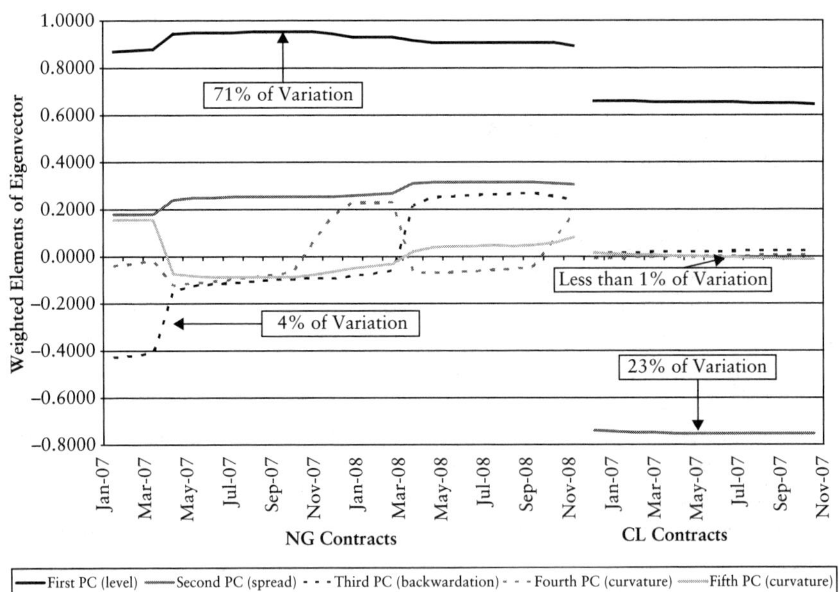

EXHIBIT 14.13 Weighted Principal Components of the NG and CL Forward Curves

A PRACTICAL HEDGING EXAMPLE

Hedging Considerations

But how does all of this work together? Let us consider a simple example of an electricity producer that owns natural gas and oil-fired generation. This entity hedges price exposure in the physical fuels markets with the purchase of crude oil and natural gas futures on the NYMEX. This hedging strategy itself is subject to the value at risk limits of the corporation, while the futures contracts are subject to exchange margin requirements. While considering a hedging strategy, then, this entity has to not only find one that mitigates price risk in the spot market, but can still be maintained while conforming to the organization's value at risk limits and margin requirements. These last two considerations are often overlooked. Even if you, as hedging specialist, devise the greatest hedging strategy in financial history, constraints outside of your immediate control can force premature liquidation of the portfolio, and no one would ever know how great your hedging strategy was.

Imagine that it is early December of 2004, and this entity has decided to purchase 50 natural gas contracts for each month of 2005, 25 natural gas contracts for each month of 2006, and five crude oil contracts for each month of 2005. This portfolio has a notional value of approximately $62 million. The salient questions for a hedging specialist are: Where are the risk limits, where are the stop limits, and how much capital is in reserve for possible margin calls?

Simulation of Forward Prices

We can use our volatility term structure model and the principal components of the correlation matrix to simulate natural gas and crude oil curves. Five such natural gas price curves may look like Exhibit 14.14. And five simulated crude oil curves may look something like Exhibit 14.15.

After simulating 1,000 curves for five days, the confidence bands for the natural gas and crude oil forward curves as of mid-December 2004 look like Exhibit 14.16 and Exhibit 14.17.

Note the considerably wider confidence bands for the front months of the simulated natural gas curves. The crude oil curves, with their greater tendency to move together, do not exhibit this behavior to the same degree. We can then use these 1,000 simulated curves and the composition of the test portfolio to calculate 1,000 daily mark to market values. The confidence bands for these mark to market values look like Exhibit 14.18.

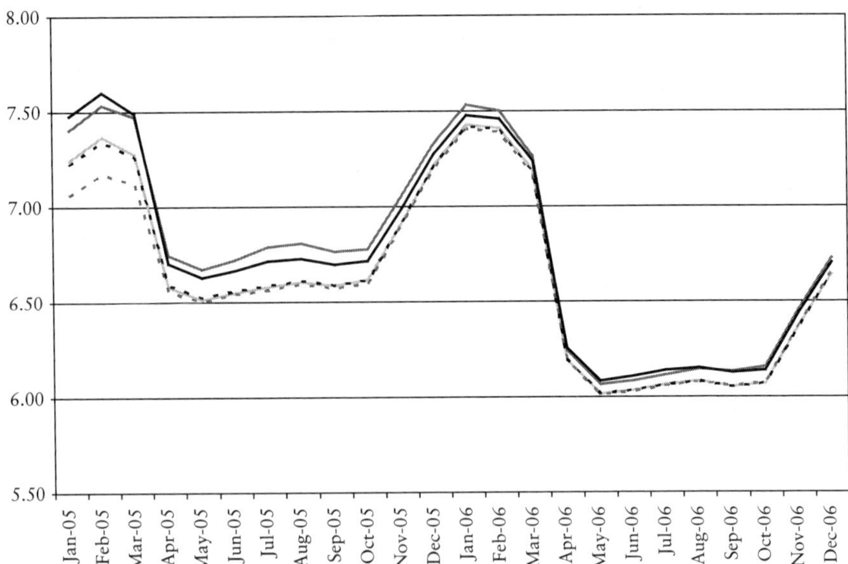

EXHIBIT 14.14 Five Sample Simulated Natural Gas Forward Curves

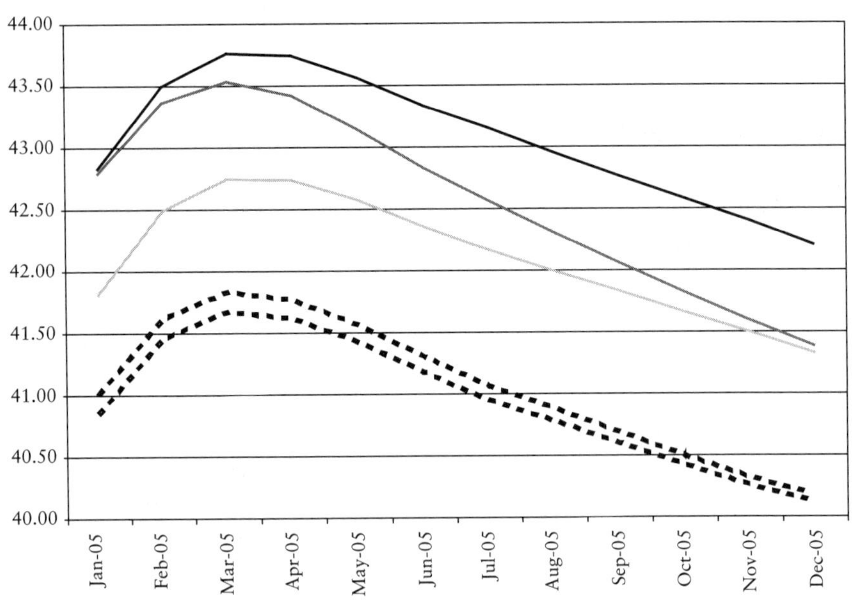

EXHIBIT 14.15 Five Sample Simulated Crude Oil Forward Curves

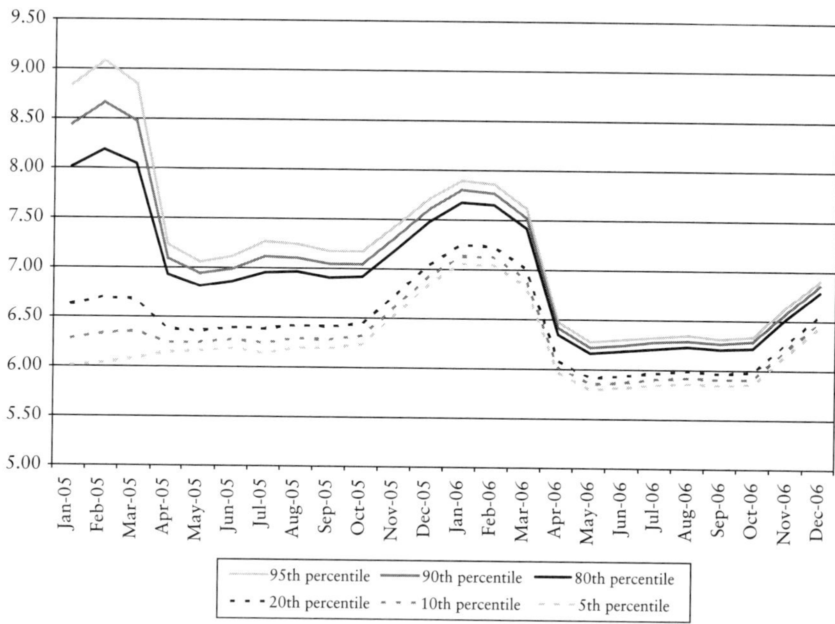

EXHIBIT 14.16 Confidence Bands for NG Forward Curves After Five Simulated Days

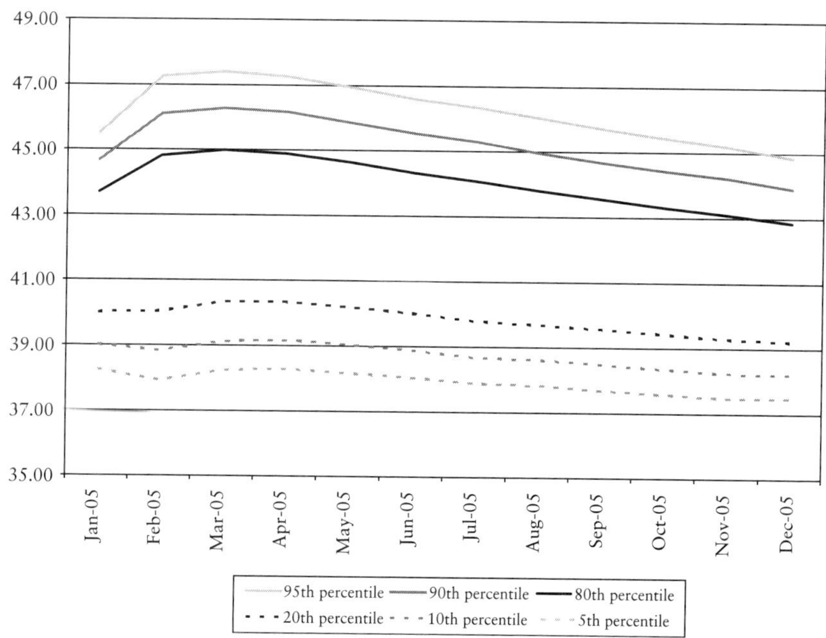

EXHIBIT 14.17 Confidence Bands for CL Forward Curves After Five Simulated Days

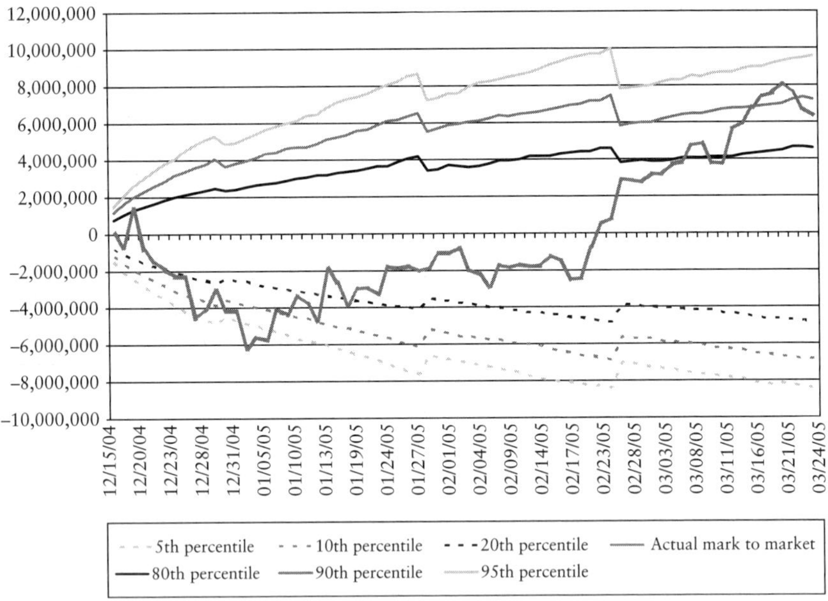

EXHIBIT 14.18 Time Series of Portfolio Mark to Market Values

Application of Simulated Portfolio Values

The jumps in the bands are the days that the natural gas positions expire. There are similar jumps in the middle of the months when the crude oil contracts expire, but they are a relatively small component of the overall portfolio and therefore do not stand out. The broken gray line is the actual mark to market of the portfolio through the first quarter of 2005. During this time span, 41% of the actual values fell outside the 60% confidence band, 18% fell outside the 80% confidence band, and 6% fell outside the 90% confidence band. This is consistent with our expectations, but a successful backtest is not the point of this exercise. When purchased, the notional value of this portfolio was about \$62 million, and if the entity was not internally prepared to suffer mark to market losses of \$6.3 million at some point (as actually happened in the middle of January), the positions would not be in the money as of the end of March, they would have been liquidated. The entity would have suffered losses of \$6.3 million in the futures market, and still paid higher fuel costs in the spot market. The entity would have been better off not hedging at all. If, however, the entity knows that the given hedging strategy is in danger of violating internal risk policy limits or cash reserves, then the volume of forward purchases can be reduced. A hedging strategy that provides some protection is better than one that cannot be maintained.

CONCLUSION

Many daily risk measurement and risk management applications rely on models of forward prices. With any process that is to be repeated often, it is helpful to use a model that reflects observed market behavior, is tractable, and is parsimonious. We have presented here a model of forward prices with time-varying volatility and time-varying correlation with all three attributes.

The model reflects the observed market behavior that forward price volatility tends to increases as the time to expiration of the forward contract decreases and that forward prices follow a random walk. Each individual contract follows its own volatility characteristics, thus preserving the effect of any fundamental differences between commodities on their forward prices.

The model is tractable and parsimonious, utilizing common nonlinear optimization techniques to fit the volatility function. The model also utilizes eigen decomposition of the correlation matrix to reflect the interaction between different contracts of the same commodity and across commodities.

This model will be useful for any application that requires an assessment of the risk inherent in the prices of forward contracts, and the evaluation of hedging strategies.

CHAPTER 15

Incorporating Futures in Commodity Price Forecasts

Chakriya Bowman, Ph.D.
Visiting Fellow
Australian National University

Aasim M. Husain, Ph.D.
Assistant Director, Middle East and Central Asia Department
International Monetary Fund

Although the share of primary commodities in global output and trade has declined over the past century, fluctuations in commodity prices continue to affect global economic activity. For many countries, especially developing countries, primary commodities remain an important source of export earnings, and commodity price movements have a major impact on overall macroeconomic performance. Hence, commodity-price forecasts are a key input to macroeconomic policy planning and formulation.

The views expressed here are those of the authors and do not necessarily represent those of the International Monetary Fund or IMF policy.

This chapter is an updated and revised version at the author's earlier work, Chakriya Bowman and Aasim M. Husain, "Forecasting Commodity Prices: Future versus Judgment," International Monetary Fund Working Paper WP/04/41 (2004). The authors are grateful to Paul Cashin, David Hallam, Sam Ouliaris, and George Rapsomanikis for helpful comments on earlier versions of the paper.

Forecasting commodity prices with reasonable accuracy is complicated by their considerable variability. Even the long-run trend behavior of commodities prices has generated debate, as typified by the important work of Cuddington,[1] who found little evidence to support the widely held Prebisch and Singer[2] view that prices of primary commodities were on a declining path over the long term. Cashin and McDermott[3] find some support for small and variable long-run downward trends in commodity price data, although they also find that such trends are swamped by the consistently high volatility of commodity prices. More recently, the International Monetary Fund (IMF)[4] observed that commodity prices relative to manufactures have stabilized in the last decade as the globalization of manufacturing has subdued producer price inflation.

This chapter aims to assess the accuracy of alternative price forecasts for 15 primary commodities over the past decade. In view of the difficulties in accurately forecasting future price movements, the assessment of forecast performance has to be a relative one—measured by how certain types of forecasts perform in relation to others. For this purpose, three types of forecasts are considered: (1) judgmental forecasts, or those based on quantitative and qualitative analysis of a variety of factors—including, possibly, analysis of supply and demand fundamentals—thought to determine the price of the commodity in question; (2) forecasts based on statistical models relying exclusively on historical price information; and (3) forecasts based on models that purport to systematically incorporate all available information—as captured by commodity futures prices—at the time of the forecast, together with historical price data. A number of alternate

---

[1]John T. Cuddington, "Long-run Trends in 26 Primary Commodity Prices: A Disaggregated Look at the Prebisch-Singer Hypothesis," *Journal of Development Economics* 39, no. 2 (1992), pp. 207–227.

[2]Raul Prebisch, *The Economic Development of Latin America and its Principle Problems* (New York: United Nations, 1950); and Hans Singer, "The Distributions of Gains between Investing and Borrowing Countries," *American Economic Review* 40, no. 2 (1950), pp. 473–485. The theory articulated in these works, published on the same topic at a similar time, has become known as the Prebisch-Singer hypothesis.

[3]Paul Cashin and C. John McDermott (2002), "The Long-Run Behavior of Commodity Prices: Small Trends and Big Variability," *International Monetary Fund Staff Papers,* pp. 175–199.

[4]International Monetary Fund (2006), "The Boom in Non-Fuel Commodity Prices: Can It Last?," *World Economic Outlook,* September, pp. 139–169.

measures of forecast performance, having to do with statistical as well as directional accuracy, are employed.[5]

The analysis indicates that although judgmental forecasts tend to outperform the model-based forecasts over short horizons of one quarter for several commodities, models incorporating futures prices generally yield superior forecasts over horizons of one year or longer. Spot and futures prices were generally found to be nonstationary and, in most cases, spot and futures prices appear to be cointegrated. Although there is considerable comovement between spot and futures prices, futures prices tend to exhibit less variability than spot prices. Hence, futures prices tend to act as an anchor for spot prices, and error-correction models that exploit the long-run cointegrating relationship provide better forecasts of future spot-price developments.

COMMODITY PRICE DEVELOPMENTS: SOME FACTS

The analysis reported in the "Results" section later in this chapter covers 15 primary commodities that are part of the IMF's commodities price index and for which three-month (or longer horizon) futures price data were available for the past decade. The commodities include six industrial metals (aluminum, copper, lead, nickel, tin, and zinc) as well as nine agricultural items (wheat, maize, soybeans, soybean meal, soybean oil, sugar, cotton, and coffee, both other milds and robusta).

Real prices of each of these commodities declined considerably between 1970 and 2003. During this time, the average quarterly change in the real price of each commodity was negative (Exhibit 15.1). On a cumulative basis, the real decline for coffee, copper, and tin was especially large—about 70% or more—while sugar (U.S. market), wheat, and zinc prices declined by 23% to 27%. Some reversal has been evident since 2003, with surging global demand for metals pushing prices higher—most notably nickel, copper, and zinc, which were all at real highs in Q4 2006, and lead was near highs last seen in 1979. Agricultural commodities, however, are far less sensitive to business cycle dynamics than nonfood commodities—particularly

[5]The ability of a forecasting methodology to predict adverse movements is perhaps a more relevant measure of accuracy in the context of commodity forecasts. Granger and Pesaran note that the literature on forecast evaluation has been biased toward statistical accuracy measures while neglecting measures of the economic importance of forecasts. See Clive W. J. Granger and M. Hashem Pesaran, Economic and Statistical Measures of Forecast Accuracy, DAE Working Paper 9910, University of Cambridge, 1999.

EXHIBIT 15.1 Select Commodities Spot and Futures Price Variability

Commodity	Real Price Decline Since 1970 (percent)	Standard Deviation[a]		Futures Position	Start Period[b]
		Spot	Futures		
Aluminum	39.3	0.096	0.082	3-months forward	87: Q2
Coffee: other milds	68.0	0.164	0.140	6-months forward	87: Q1
Coffee: robusta	79.6	0.155	0.171	6-months forward	91: Q3
Copper	69.5	0.088	0.064	12-months forward	89: Q1
Cotton	56.0	0.112	0.071	6-months forward	86: Q3
Lead	58.9	0.095	0.091	3-months forward	87: Q1
Maize	53.1	0.106	0.078	3-months forward	72: Q2
Nickel	33.6	0.144	0.140	3-months forward	88: Q1
Soybean meal	52.8	0.085	0.066	9-months forward	82: Q4
Soybean oil	56.4	0.101	0.073	9-months forward	80: Q2
Soybeans[c]	49.5	0.063	0.054	9-months forward	75: Q1
Sugar, U.S.	23.0	0.036	0.023	6-months forward	88: Q1
Tin	69.5	0.070	0.070	3-months forward	89: Q3
Wheat	53.1	0.087	0.068	6-months forward	76: Q4
Zinc	27.3	0.093	0.080	3-months forward	89: Q1

Source: Exhibit created from data obtained from IMF Primary Commodity Prices Database and Bloomberg.
[a]Standard deviation of nominal dollar prices.
[b]All commodities series, with the exception of maize, end in the first quarter 2003. The maize series ends in the third quarter 2002.
[c]Outlier data point for the third quarter 1994 removed.

EXHIBIT 15.2 Correlation of Spot and Futures Prices, 1991Q3 to 2003Q1 (correlation of log first differences, in percent)

	Futures Horizon			
Commodity	3-month	6-month	9-month	12-month
Aluminum	95.44			
Coffee, other milds	93.22	91.70		
Coffee, robusta	94.18	93.20		
Copper	93.15			90.76
Cotton	62.73	74.07		
Lead	96.80			
Maize	79.70	81.80		
Nickel	94.97			
Soybean meal	76.78		69.96	
Soybean oil	74.54		61.07	
Soybeans[a]	85.75		83.24	
Sugar, U.S.	82.49	84.73		
Tin	93.48			
Wheat	70.82	79.23		
Zinc	93.03			

Source: Exhibit created from data obtained from IMF Primary Commodity Prices Database and Bloomberg.
[a]The reported correlation of nine-month soybeans futures with spot prices removes an outlier for first quarter 1994.

metals, which take time to bring increased supply on stream. As a result, agricultural commodity prices have been more subdued, although several (wheat, sugar, maize, and soybean oil) were above 36-year averages at the end of 2006.

Futures prices tend to fluctuate in step with spot prices (Exhibit 15.2), although the volatility of futures is markedly lower for virtually all commodities. Generally speaking, metals prices have tended to be less volatile than prices of agricultural commodities, which Isengildina, Irwin, and Good[6] attribute to a combination of inelastic demand for food coupled with production technology that is subject to natural interference, be that weather, disease, or pests. Exhibits 15.3 and 15.4, which illustrate movements in cotton and copper prices, capture the relatively lower variability of futures prices.

[6]Olga Isengildina, Scott H. Irwin, and Darrel L. Good, "Evaluation of USDA Interval Forecasts of Corn and Soybean Prices," *American Journal of Agricultural Economics* 86, no. 4 (2004), pp. 990–1004.

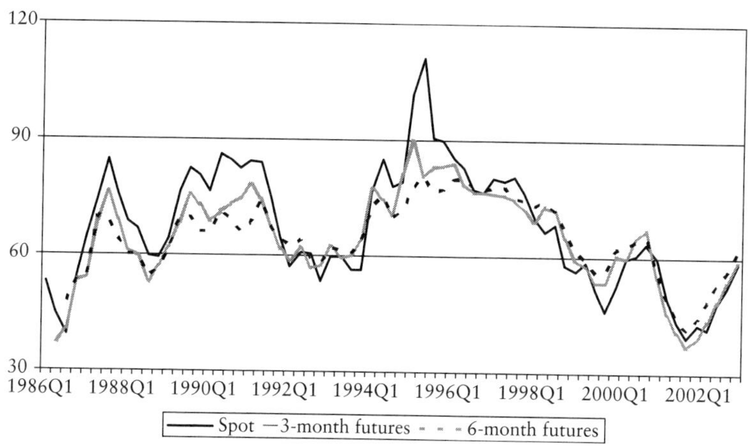

EXHIBIT 15.3 Cotton: Spot and Futures Prices, 1986–2003 (cents per pound)
Source: Exhibit created from data obtained from IMF Primary Commodity Prices Database.

Researchers have come to varying conclusions regarding the efficiency of commodity futures markets and whether futures prices are unbiased predictors of future spot prices. For example, Moosa and Al-Loughani[7] find evidence of a risk premium in crude oil futures markets and conclude that

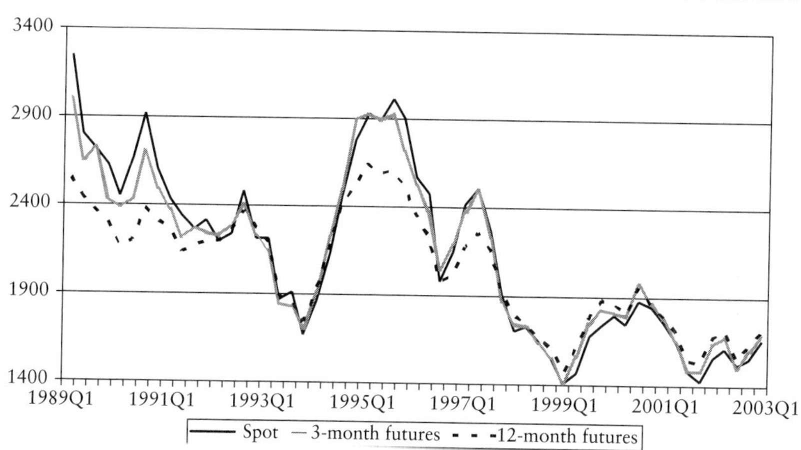

EXHIBIT 15.4 Copper: Spot and Futures Prices, 1989–2003 (dollars per metric ton)
Source: Exhibit created from data obtained from IMF Primary Commodity Prices Database and Bloomberg.

[7] Imad A. Moosa and Nabeel E. Al-Loughani, "Unbiasedness and Time-Varying Risk Premia in the Crude Oil Futures Market," *Energy Economics* 16, no. 2 (1994), pp. 99–105.

futures prices are not efficient forecasters of future spot prices. On the other hand, Kumar[8] presents evidence to support market efficiency and finds in favor of futures prices as unbiased forecasters of crude oil prices. This position is supported by recent evidence from Chinn, LeBlanc, and Coibion,[9] who find that futures predictions slightly outperform random walk and *autoregressive moving average* (ARMA) time-series models for four energy commodities (petroleum, natural gas, heating oil, and gasoline), and Abosedra,[10] who finds that forecasts from oil futures outperform a simple univariate spot-based pricing model. Brenner and Kroner[11] suggest that the inconsistencies observed between futures and spot prices may be the result of carrying costs rather than a failing of the efficient market hypothesis, while Avsar and Goss[12] observe that inefficiencies are likely to be exacerbated in relatively young and shallow futures markets such as the electricity market, where forecast errors may indicate a market still coming to terms with the true market model. Inefficiencies could also be exacerbated in markets with thin trading, or at time-to-maturity horizons that are relatively long, as market liquidity is also likely to affect risk premia.[13]

Rather than test for market efficiency directly, the objective here is to investigate simply whether futures prices can help predict developments in spot prices up to two years in the future. If spot and futures prices of a commodity are found to be nonstationary, and if there is evidence to suggest a cointegrating relationship between the two series, it would be expected that the addition of futures prices to a forecasting model will improve the performance of model forecasts. A related exercise was conducted by Kaminsky and Kumar,[14] who looked into the power of futures prices to forecast future spot prices for seven commodities at horizons of up to nine months,

[8]Manmohan S. Kumar, "The Forecasting Accuracy of Crude Oil Futures Prices," *International Monetary Fund Staff Papers* (1992), pp. 432–461.
[9]Menzie D. Chinn, Michael LeBlanc, and Olivier Coibion, "The Predictive Content of Energy Futures: An Update on Petroleum, Natural Gas, Heating Oil and Gasoline," National Bureau of Economic Research Working Paper no. 11033, January 2005.
[10]Salah Abosedra, "Futures versus Univariate Forecast of Crude Oil Prices," *OPEC Review* 29, no. 4 (2005), pp. 231–241.
[11]Robin J. Brenner and Kenneth F. Kroner, "Arbitrage, Cointegration and Testing the Unbiasedness Hypothesis in Financial Markets," *Journal of Financial and Quantitative Analysis* 30, no. 1 (1995), pp. 23–42.
[12]S. Gulay Avsar and Barry A. Goss, "Forecast Errors and Efficiency in the US Electricity Futures Market," *Australian Economic Papers* 40, no. 4 (2001), pp. 479–499.
[13]Graciela Kaminsky and Manmohan S. Kumar, "Time-Varying Risk Premia in Futures Markets," International Monetary Fund Working Paper WP/90/116, 1990.
[14]Graciela Kaminsky and Manmohan S. Kumar, "Efficiency in Commodity Futures Markets," *International Monetary Fund Staff Papers,* (1990), pp. 671–699.

although they did not exploit potential cointegrating relationships between spot and futures prices. Beck,[15] on the other hand, used cointegration techniques to test for market efficiency and the presence of risk premia in five commodity markets at the 8- and 24-week horizons. McKenzie and Holt[16] employed cointegration and error correction models to test market efficiency and unbiasedness in four agricultural commodity markets, finding that for two of the four commodities in their sample, statistical model-based forecasts outperformed futures in a statistical sense.

Previous studies examining the performance of forecasts implied by futures prices versus those generated by models or "expert" opinion (judgment) come to mixed conclusions about the performance of futures-based forecasts relative to judgmental or models-based forecasts. For example, Bessler and Brandt[17] found that their expert opinion livestock forecaster performed significantly better in a statistical sense at the one-quarter horizon than the futures market for cattle but not for hogs, while Irwin, Gerlow, and Liu[18] concluded that their expert opinion forecaster failed to perform significantly better than the futures market at the one- and two-quarter horizons, both for cattle and for hogs. It should be noted, however, that because of the time-restricted nature of futures contracts, futures prices have not been used to generate longer-term forecasts (one to five years). Hence, the performance of such forecasts, especially in relation to judgmental forecasts, has not been consistently examined at the longer horizons for a reasonably wide set of commodities. Moreover, these studies do not assess directional performance—the ability to predict turning points—across different types of forecasts.

STATIONARITY AND COINTEGRATION

Commodity prices have generally been found to be nonstationary, although the precise nature of the trend—deterministic, stochastic, or containing

[15]Stacie E. Beck, "Cointegration and Market Efficiency in Commodities Futures Markets," *Applied Econometrics* 26, no. 3 (1994), pp. 249–257.
[16]Andrew M. McKenzie and Matthew T. Holt, "Market Efficiency in Agricultural Futures Markets," *Applied Economics* 34, no. 12 (2002), pp. 1519–1532.
[17]David A. Bessler and Jon A. Brandt, "An Analysis of Forecasts of Livestock Prices," *Journal of Economic Behavior and Organizations* 18, no. 2 (1992), pp. 249–263.
[18]Scott H. Irwin, Mary E. Gerlow, and Te-Ru Liu, "The Forecasting Performance of Livestock Futures Prices: A Comparison to USDA Expert Predictions," *Journal of Futures Markets* 14, no. 7 (1994), pp. 861–875.

structural breaks—is open to debate.[19] The Prebisch-Singer hypothesis posits that there is a general downward trend in primary commodity prices, a thesis supported by many subsequent researchers[20]—with the important exception of Cuddington—who generally find a small but long-term negative deterministic trend in commodity price series,[21] and some cyclical movement.[22] This trend is typically augmented by long-lasting price shocks[23] and there is a significant degree of variability in the commodity prices that has increased over time.[24]

The overwhelming majority of commodity prices analyzed in this study were found to have nonstationary characteristics (Exhibits 15.5 and 15.6). The time series properties of commodity prices—spot and futures—were assessed by performing unit root tests. Rejection of the null hypothesis of a unit root under both the Augmented Dickey Fuller (ADF) test and the Phillips-Perron (PP) test was taken as evidence of stationarity. As the tables indicate, stationarity cannot be rejected only for soybean meal spot prices.

---

[19]Paul Cashin, Hong Liang and C. John McDermott, "How Persistent are Shocks to World Commodity Prices?," *IMF Staff Papers* (2000), pp. 177–217.

[20]See, for example, Matthias G. Lutz, "A General Test of the Prebisch-Singer Hypothesis," *Review of Development Economics* 3, no. 1 (1999), pp. 44–57; and Paul Cashin and C. John McDermott, "The Long-Run Behavior of Commodity Prices: Small Trends and Big Variability," *International Monetary Fund Staff Papers* (2002), pp. 175–199.

[21]See, for example, Rodolfo Helg, "A Note on the Stationarity of the Primary Commodities Relative Price Index," *Economics Letters* 36, no. 1 (1991), pp. 55–60; Javier León and Raimundo Soto, "Structural Breaks and Long-Run Trends in Commodity Prices," *Journal of International Development* 9, no. 3 (1997), pp. 347–366; and Paul Cashin and C. John McDermott, "The Long-Run Behavior of Commodity Prices: Small Trends and Big Variability," *International Monetary Fund Staff Papers* (2002), pp. 175–199.

[22]See, for example, Cashin and McDermott, "The Long-Run Behavior of Commodity Prices: Small Trends and Big Variability."

[23]See, for example, Rodolfo Helg, "A Note on the Stationarity of the Primary Commodities Relative Price Index," *Economics Letters* 36, no. 1 (1991), pp. 55–60; John T. Cuddington, "Long-run Trends in 26 Primary Commodity Prices: A Disaggregated Look at the Prebisch-Singer Hypothesis," *Journal of Development Economics* 39, no. 2 (1992), pp. 207–227; Javier León and Raimundo Soto, "Structural Breaks and Long-Run Trends in Commodity Prices," *Journal of International Development* 9, no. 3 (1997), pp. 347–366; and Paul Cashin, Hong Liang, and C. John McDermott, "How Persistent Are Shocks to World Commodity Prices?," *IMF Staff Papers* (2000), pp. 177–217.

[24]See Cashin and McDermott, "The Long-Run Behavior of Commodity Prices: Small Trends and Big Variability," *International Monetary Fund Staff Papers* (2000), pp. 175–199.

EXHIBIT 15.5 Unit Root Tests: Logged Spot Prices

Commodity	Augmented Dickey-Fuller[a] t-Statistic (p-value)	Sample Period (Lag Length)	Phillips-Perron[b] t-Statistic (p-value)	Sample Period (Bandwidth)
Aluminum	−4.9561[c] (0.00)	1970:1–2003:1 (1)	−2.4976 (0.33)	1970:1–2003:1 (4)
Copper	−3.2944 (0.07)	1970:1–2003:1 (0)	−3.0447 (0.12)	1970:1–2003:1 (3)
Lead	−2.6932 (0.24)	1970:1–2003:1 (1)	−2.4655 (0.35)	1970:1–2003:1 (2)
Nickel	−4.2437[c] (0.00)	1970:1–2003:1 (3)	−3.1011 (0.11)	1970:1–2003:1 (5)
Tin	−2.3549 (0.40)	1970:1–2003:1 (2)	−2.0096 (0.59)	1970:1–2003:1 (4)
Zinc	−3.5434[d] (0.04)	1970:1–2003:1 (1)	−2.8584 (0.18)	1970:1–2003:1 (6)
Wheat	−3.9887[d] (0.01)	1970:1–2003:1 (0)	−3.1688 (0.09)	1970:1–2003:1 (6)
Maize	−3.3869 (0.06)	1970:1–2003:1 (1)	−3.2192 (0.085)	1970:1–2003:1 (1)
Soybean	−3.8390[d] (0.02)	1970:1–2003:1 (1)	−3.4013 (0.06)	1970:1–2003:1 (7)
Soybean meal	−4.0548[c] (0.01)	1970:1–2003:1 (1)	−3.5545* (0.04)	1970:1–2003:1 (5)
Soybean oil	−4.1239[c] (0.01)	1970:1–2003:1 (3)	−3.3624 (0.06)	1970:1–2003:1 (5)
Sugar, U.S.	−4.0799[c] (0.01)	1970:1–2003:1 (1)	−3.2117 (0.09)	1970:1–2003:1 (10)
Cotton	−3.7001[d] (0.03)	1970:1–2003:1 (1)	−3.1343 (0.10)	1970:1–2003:1 (1)
Coffee, other milds	−2.5325 (0.31)	1970:1–2003:1 (1)	−2.2919 (0.43)	1970:1–2003:1 (0)
Coffee, robusta	−2.9624 (0.15)	1970:1–2003:1 (3)	−2.2449 (0.46)	1970:1–2003:1 (2)

Source: Exhibit created from data obtained from IMF Primary Commodity Prices Database and Bloomberg.

Note: Rejection of the null hypothesis by both tests is regarded as evidence of stationarity. The evidence suggests that soybean meal is $I(0)$. All tests include trend and intercept.

[a]The Augmented Dickey-Fuller statistic is used to test the null hypothesis of a unit root. Lag lengths were determined by minimizing the Schwarz information criteria.

[b]The Phillips-Perron statistic tests the null hypothesis of a unit root, and adjusts the standard Dickey-Fuller statistic for the presence of serial correlation using nonparametric procedures. Bartlett kernel estimation is used and bandwidth estimations made according to the Newey–West procedure.

[c]Indicates rejection of unit root hypothesis at 1%.

[d]Indicates rejection of unit root hypothesis at 5%.

EXHIBIT 15.6 Unit Root Tests: Logged Three-Month Futures Prices

Commodity	Augmented Dickey-Fuller[a] *t*-Statistic (*p*-value)	Sample Period (Lag Length)	Phillips-Perron[b] *t*-Statistic (*p*-value)	Sample Period (Bandwidth)
Aluminum[c]	−2.7701 (0.21)	1987:2–2003:1 (1)	−2.4970 (0.33)	1987:2–2003:1 (3)
Copper[d]	−3.0264 (0.13)	1989:1–2003:1 (1)	−2.4936 (0.33)	1989:1–2003:1 (1)
Lead[c]	−2.5875 (0.29)	1987:1–2003:1 (1)	−3.0222 (0.13)	1987:1–2003:1 (2)
Nickel[c]	−4.5162[h] (0.00)	1987:1–2003:1 (1)	−3.6610[i] (0.03)	1987:1–2003:1 (3)
Tin[c]	−18.4609[h] (0.00)	1989:2–2003:1 (0)	−11.8541[h] (0.00)	1989:2–2003:1 (4)
Zinc[c]	−2.8849 (0.17)	1989:1–2003:1 (1)	−2.8842 (0.17)	1989:1–2003:1 (0)
Wheat[e]	−4.3683[h] (0.00)	1972:1–2003:1 (4)	−4.4731[h] (0.00)	1972:1–2003:1 (7)
Maize[e]	−3.8003[i] (0.02)	1972:1–2003:1 (1)	−3.8555[i] (0.02)	1972:1–2003:1 (0)
Soybean[e]	−3.5232[i] (0.04)	1975:1–2003:1 (0)	−3.7568[i] (0.02)	1975:1–2003:1 (4)
Soybean meal[e]	−3.7646[i] (0.03)	1978:1–2003:1 (2)	−3.3851 (0.06)	1978:1–2003:1 (1)
Soybean oil[e]	−2.6274 (0.27)	1979:2–2003:1 (0)	−3.0474 (0.13)	1979:2–2003:1 (3)
Sugar, U.S.[f]	−3.5857[i] (0.04)	1988:1–2003:1 (1)	−2.6563 (0.26)	1988:1–2003:1 (0)

Cotton[f]	−3.6600	1986:2–2003:1	−3.3315	1986:2–2003:1
	(0.03)	(1)	(0.07)	(2)
Coffee: other milds[f]	−2.2277	1986:3–2003:1	−2.4779	1986:3–2003:1
	(0.47)	(0)	(0.34)	(2)
Coffee: robusta[g]	−3.0968	1991:3–2003:1	−1.7741	1991:3–2003:1
	(0.12)	(1)	(0.70)	(2)

Source: Exhibit created from data obtained from IMF Primary Commodity Prices Database and Bloomberg.

Note: Tests are for quarterly 3-month futures series. Rejection of the null hypothesis by both tests is regarded as evidence of stationarity. The evidence suggests that soybean, tin, wheat, nickel, and maize futures are $I(0)$. All tests include trend and intercept.

[a]The Augmented Dickey-Fuller statistic is used to test the null hypothesis of a unit root. Lag lengths were determined by minimizing the Schwarz information criteria.

[b]The Phillips-Perron statistic tests the null hypothesis of a unit root, and adjusts the standard Dickey-Fuller statistic for the presence of serial correlation using nonparametric procedures. Bartlett kernel estimation is used and bandwidth estimations made according to the Newey-West procedure.

[c]Contract is listed on the London Metals Exchange.

[d]Contract is listed on the New York Mercantile Exchange (NYMEX) or Commodity Exchange Inc. (COMEX).

[e]Contract is listed on the Chicago Board of Trade.

[f]Contract is listed on the New York Board of Trade Coffee, Sugar and Cocoa Exchange or Cotton Exchange.

[g]Contract is listed on the London International Financial Futures and Options Exchange.

[h]Indicates rejection of unit root hypothesis at 1%.

[i]Indicates rejection of unit root hypothesis at 5%.

Among three-month futures prices, soybean, tin, wheat, nickel, and maize prices appear to be stationary. As discussed previously, it can be anticipated that both commodity and futures prices are nonstationary, and that stationary results are period specific and may reflect the presence of structural breaks or other confounding features in the series. We proceed from an assumption of nonstationarity, recognizing that we may obtain spurious results if this is not the case. Most commodity prices appear to be cointegrated with at least their three-month or six-month futures price series. Results of cointegration testing using the Johansen test for cointegration are summarized in Exhibit 15.7.[25] In the cases where no evidence is found for cointegration with any of the relevant futures price series (lead and coffee, other milds), this may be due to structural breaks in the series, which would result in this form of the Johansen test becoming biased against the rejection of the null hypothesis of no cointegration. As the results presented below indicate, error correction models tend to perform relatively well for virtually all commodities, suggesting that spot and futures prices are of the same order of integration and are cointegrated.

FORECASTING MODELS

The simplest form of a forecasting model is the random walk model with trend and drift, which may be written as

$$S_t = \alpha + \beta S_{t-1} + \gamma T + e_t \tag{15.1}$$

where S_t is the natural logarithm of the commodity spot price at time t and T is a trend variable, with the model incorporating both a trend and a drift component. The error term, e_t, is assumed to be white noise. If the commodity price series contains a unit root, then a different stationary model could be used to model prices, otherwise the basic trend stationary model is appropriate. This simple model can serve as a useful benchmark for comparison of other, more sophisticated models.

An alternative forecasting model could be one that allows for an autoregressive process in the first difference of S_t and a moving average model for the errors. A suitable time series model of this form, the ARIMA model, may be written as

$$\Delta S_t = \alpha + \sum_{j=1}^{p} \beta_j \Delta S_{t-j} + u_t \tag{15.2}$$

[25]For each commodity, the appropriate lag length was determined by minimizing the Akaike information criteria for each set of spot and futures prices, with a maximum of six lags tested.

EXHIBIT 15.7 Johansen Cointegration Test Results

Commodity	Sample Period	Test Statistic $k=0$	Test Statistic $k \leq 1$	Lags[d]
Aluminum 3-month[a]	1987:2–2003:1	19.04[e]	0.27	6
Copper 3-month[a]	1989:1–2003:1	19.26[e]	0.74	6
Copper 6-month[b]	1989:1–2003:1	28.73[f]	5.50	6
Copper 9-month[b]	1989:1–2003:1	21.36	8.08	1
Copper 12-month[b]	1989:1–2003:1	22.99	8.53	1
Lead 3-month[b]	1987:1–2003:1	18.76	7.97	2
Nickel 3-month[b]	1987:1–2003:1	58.14[e]	10.84	6
Tin 3-month[a]	1989:2–2003:1	14.62[f]	0.87	2
Zinc 3-month[b]	1989:1–2003:1	18.71	5.61	6
Wheat 3-month[c]	1972:1–2003:1	21.20[f]	6.63	6
Wheat 6-month[b]	1976:4–2003:1	16.59	5.27	1
Maize 3-month[b]	1972:1–2003:1	29.34[f]	10.45	3
Maize 6-month[b]	1972:1–2003:1	30.05[f]	11.40	2
Soybean 3-month[c]	1975:1–2003:1	23.26[f]	5.12	5
Soybean 6-month[c]	1975:1–2003:1	22.18[f]	4.54	3
Soybean 9-month[a]	1989:2–2003:1	15.64[f]	0.09	1
Soybean meal 3-month[c]	1978:1–2003:1	25.19[e]	8.57	1
Soybean meal 9-month[c]	1982:3–2003:1	14.25	3.97	6
Soybean oil 3-month[c]	1979:2–2003:1	26.16[e]	8.24	1
Soybean oil 6-month[c]	1979:4–2003:1	21.23[f]	7.31	1
Soybean oil 9-month[c]	1980:2–2003:1	22.91[f]	8.14	2
Sugar, U.S. 3-month[b]	1988:1–2003:1	20.36	8.01	2
Sugar, U.S. 6-month[b]	1988:1–2003:1	19.32	5.81	2
Cotton 3-month[b]	1986:2–2003:1	16.14	3.30	4
Cotton 6-month[a]	1986:3–2003:1	14.48[f]	0.09	5
Coffee: other milds 3-month[b]	1986:3–2003:1	17.03	6.30	1
Coffee: other milds 6-month[b]	1987:1–2003:1	15.89	6.53	1
Coffee: robusta 3-month[a]	1991:3–2003:1	14.34[f]	0.48	1
Coffee: robusta 6-month[a]	1991:3–2003:1	11.33	0.48	1

[a]Results found no deterministic trend in the data, and no intercept or trend in the cointegrating equation.

[b]Results found a linear trend in the data, and both an intercept and a trend in the cointegrating equation.

[c]Results found no deterministic trend in the data, and an intercept but no trend in the cointegrating equation.

[d]Lag length determined by minimizing the Akaike information criteria for a maximum of 6 lags. Weak exogeneity was confirmed using restriction testing.

[e]Indicates rejection of unit root hypothesis at 1%.

[f]Indicates rejection of unit root hypothesis at 5%.

Source: Exhibit created from data obtained from IMF Primary Commodity Prices Database and Bloomberg.

Note: Evidence of cointegration between spot and futures prices was found for most commodities with 3-month futures and several with later-dated contracts. The exceptions were lead, zinc, sugar, and coffee: other milds, for which no evidence of cointegration was found. This may be due to a variety of factors, including the presence of structural breaks in the series. Contracts with evidence of cointegration are highlighted in bold.

with errors given by

$$u_t = \sum_{i=1}^{q} \gamma_i \varepsilon_{t-i} + \varepsilon_t$$

and where ε_t is white noise. Such a model may be particularly appropriate for commodities where prices are mean reverting.[26]

If markets are efficient, futures prices should be unbiased predictors of future spot prices and a simple prediction model should give superior results to those using alternative variables. The general futures forecast model is

$$S_t = \alpha + \beta F_{t|t-k} + e_t \quad (15.3)$$

where $F_{t|t-k}$ is the price for period t implied by futures markets in period $t-k$. Rather than testing market efficiency, which would imply $\alpha = 0$ and $\beta = 1$, the aim here is to examine whether futures prices can enhance the forecasting ability of simple models.[27] To that end, futures prices can be added to the random walk and ARIMA specifications in an effort to obtain more accurate forecasts.

Finally, if commodity spot and futures prices are cointegrated, an *error-correction model* (ECM) can be used to capitalize on this relationship. Engle and Granger[28] show that a system of two cointegrated series implies an error-correcting equation. Assuming futures prices are weakly exogenous,[29] the general form of the ECM is

$$\Delta S_t = \alpha + \beta_0 \varepsilon_{t-1} + \sum_{i=1}^{m} \beta_i F_{t-i|t-k} + \sum_{j=1}^{n} \gamma_j \Delta S_{t-j} + u_t \quad (15.4)$$

where ε_t are the residuals of the cointegrating equation given by equation (15.3). The ECM is used in this study as a contrast to the best forecast obtained from the random walk and ARIMA models (with and without futures), as well as judgmental forecasts.

[26]For a discussion see Scott H. Irwin, Carl R. Zulauf, and Thomas E. Jackson, "Monte Carlo Analysis of Mean Reversion in Commodity Futures Prices," *American Journal of Agricultural Economics* 78, no. 2 (1996), pp. 397–399.

[27]Efficiency tests would require careful matching of futures contract horizons and expiry dates with actual spot prices. As described below, the averaging of futures and spot prices in our data set does not permit such tests with reasonable accuracy.

[28]Robert F. Engle and Clive W. J. Granger, "Cointegration and Error Correction: Representation, Estimation and Testing," *Econometrica* 55, no. 2 (1987), pp. 251–276.

[29]This was verified during cointegration testing. Results are available on request.

More complex models may, of course, be developed, such as that of Heaney[30] which incorporates cost-of-carry into a forecasting model for lead prices and hence contains an interest rate component, or GARCH models[31] and probability-based forecast models.[32] However, for the purposes of this study, where the objective is to gauge whether the incorporation of futures prices potentially yields superior forecast performance, forecasts use only historical spot prices and futures prices in an effort to identify simple models which may be successfully applied to a wide range of commodities, rather than to specific commodities.

ASSESSING FORECAST PERFORMANCE

When evaluating the ex post effectiveness of forecasts, standard statistical measures are commonly used. Mean pricing error, mean absolute pricing error, *mean absolute relative pricing error* (MARPE), median absolute relative pricing error, and *root mean squared error* (RMSE) are typically calculated and the results used to generate conclusions about the accuracy of forecasts.[33] This research will focus primarily on RMSE, which gives a measure of the magnitude of the average forecast error, as an effectiveness measure. It may be noted, however, that the RMSE is a measure that is

[30]Richard Heaney, "Does Knowledge of the Cost of Carry Model Improve Commodity Futures Price Forecasting Ability? A Case Study Using the London Metal Exchange Lead Contract," *International Journal of Forecasting* 18, no. 1 (2002), pp. 45–65.

[31]Claudio Morana, "A Semiparametric Approach to Short-Term Oil Price Forecasting," *Energy Economics* 23, no. 3 (2001), pp. 325–338.

[32]Bruce Abramson and Albert Finizza, "Probabilistic Forecasts from Probabilistic Models: A Case Study in the Oil Market," *Journal of Forecasting* 11, no. 1 (1995), pp. 63–72.

[33]See, for example, Richard E. Just and Gordon C. Rausser, "Commodity Price Forecasting with Large-Scale Econometric Models and the Futures Market," *American Journal of Agricultural Economics* 63, no. 2 (1981), pp. 197–208; Gordon Leitch and J. Ernest Tanner, "Economic Forecast Evaluation: Profits Versus the Conventional Error Measures," *American Economic Review* 81, no. 3 (1991), pp. 580–590; David A. Bessler and Jon A. Brandt, "An Analysis of Forecasts of Livestock Prices," *Journal of Economic Behavior and Organizations* 18, no. 2 (1992), pp. 249–263; and Mary E. Gerlow, Scott H. Irwin, and Te-Ru Liu, "Economic Evaluation of Commodity Price Forecasting Models," *International Journal of Forecasting* 9, no. 3 (1993), pp. 387–397.

time series specific, and cannot be readily used for comparison across commodities.[34]

The RMSE may be defined as

$$RMSE = \sqrt{\frac{1}{n}\sum_{i=1}^{n}(S_i - FC_i)^2} \tag{15.5}$$

where S_i is the actual (spot) commodity price, and FC_i is the forecast price.

As the magnitude of the RMSE is specific to each price series, it can be difficult to quickly assess the performance of a model from this statistic. Hence, in this application, the RMSE result is displayed relative to the RMSE of either the random walk model or the judgmental forecast, to facilitate comparison between models. The base model (the judgmental forecast) will have a value of unity. If a comparison model has a relative RMSE value greater than unity, it may be considered to underperform the base model in terms of statistical accuracy. On the other hand, a relative RMSE value less than unity would indicate superior RMSE performance in relation to the base model.

Directional accuracy is also relevant to commodity forecasts, where the ability to identify future turning points is of particular importance. When assessing forecast performance, identification of directional changes may indeed be more important than the actual magnitude of error. Two methods are used to assess directional accuracy in this study. The first is the Harding and Pagan[35] test of concordance, which seeks to identify synchronicity in the turning points of two series. The Harding-Pagan test is a statistical measure that casts no preference on the ability of the model to predict "important" changes as opposed to small but directionally accurate changes. This measure is augmented by the Cumby-Modest[36] test, which weights the prediction of significant turning points more highly and therefore is often used as a measure of the profitability of a prediction.

A rough measure of directional accuracy can be obtained by simply counting the times that the forecast and actual prices move in the same

[34] *Theil's U* is an alternate measure that could be used to compare forecast errors across commodities, however as the focus of this chapter is on directional accuracy and turning points, this measure was omitted. Theil's U can be found in Henri Theil, *Economic Forecasts and Policy* (Amsterdam: North-Holland Publishing Company, 1958).

[35] Don Harding and Adrian Pagan, "Synchronisation of Cycles," *Journal of Econometrics* 127, no. 1, pp. 59–79.

[36] Robert E. Cumby and David M. Modest (1987), "Testing for Market Timing Ability: A Framework for Forecast Evaluation," *Journal of Financial Economics* 19, no. 1, pp. 169–189.

direction. From this, a percentage of accurate directional forecasts may be calculated for each model. On average, a random walk model should pick the direction successfully around 50% of the time, and that more accurate forecast models should improve on this. Harding and Pagan extend this concept of directional accuracy, creating a measure of synchronicity that may be used to determine whether forecasts are "in synch" with actual price movements, or whether the confluence of prediction and reality is simply luck. This test is generated by creating two series, X_F for the forecasted (or futures) series and X_S for the actual spot price series:

$$X_{F,t} = 0 \quad \text{if } F_{t+n|t} - S_t < 0$$

$$X_{F,t} = 1 \quad \text{if } F_{t+n|t} - S_t \geq 0$$

and

$$X_{S,t} = 0 \quad \text{if } S_{t+n} - S_t < 0$$

$$X_{S,t} = 1 \quad \text{if } S_{t+n} - S_t \geq 0,$$

where F and S are the futures and spot price series, respectively, and n is the forecast horizon.

The Concordance statistic, for a given forecast horizon, is determined by:

$$C_{S,F} = T^{-1}\left[\sum_{t=1}^{T}(X_{S,t}X_{F,t}) + \sum_{t=1}^{T}(1 - X_{S,t})(1 - X_{F,t})\right]. \tag{15.6}$$

Hence, this statistic measures how closely—in directional terms—prices implied by futures move with actual spot prices. As noted above, forecasts from a random walk model would be expected, on average, to yield Concordance statistics of about 0.5. To obtain a sense of the statistical significance of the synchronicity between the series, a regression of the form:

$$X_{S,t} = \alpha + \beta X_{F,t} + u_t \tag{15.7}$$

is run using Newey-West[37] heteroskedastic autocorrelated consistent standard errors. If the series are not synchronous, the Harding-Pagan statistic (β) will equal zero. Hence, the estimated t-statistic for the β coefficient can be considered to yield a measure of the statistical significance of the synchronicity.

---

[37]Whitney K. Newey and Kenneth D. West (1994), "Automatic Lag Selection in Covariance Matrix Estimation," *Review of Economic Studies* 61, no. 4 (2006), pp. 631–653.

Another test of the directional performance of forecast models is the Cumby and Modest test for market timing ability, which is an extension of the Merton[38] market timing test and was designed to use information about the magnitude of change as well as the direction of change to generate a performance statistic. The Cumby-Modest test is obtained from the estimated β coefficient from a regression of the form:

$$S_t = \alpha + \beta X_t + \varepsilon_t \tag{15.8}$$

where S is the (natural logarithm of the) actual spot price and X is a dummy variable that takes the value of zero if the forecast anticipates a price decline for period t, and a value of unity if the forecast anticipates a price increase (or no change) for period t.[39] In essence, this differs from the Harding-Pagan statistic in that the dependent variable incorporates both the magnitude as well as the direction of the change. Hence, the Cumby-Modest statistic gives extra weight to situations under which the forecast would have correctly predicted the direction of large actual changes in spot prices, and when a forecast misses a directional change in prices that is small in magnitude, it is not penalized as heavily by the Cumby-Modest statistic as it is by the Harding-Pagan statistic.

DATA

As noted thus far, the objective of this study is to compare the performance of three alternative types of commodity price forecasts: (1) Those based on judgment; (2) those relying on statistical models using only historical price data; and (3) those incorporating both futures prices as well as historical spot prices to yield statistical forecasts. Before turning to the assessment of the performance of the various forecasts, however, some explanation of how the forecasts were obtained and/or constructed is in order.

For the judgmental forecasts, commodity price projections prepared by the IMF, in collaboration with the World Bank, were used. These projections are prepared about once a quarter for each of the roughly 50 commodities in the IMF's primary commodity price index. The projections are for

[38]Robert C. Merton, "On Market Timing and Investment Performance, I. An Equilibrium Theory of Value for Market Forecasts," *Journal of Business* 54, no. 3 (1981), pp. 363–406.

[39]The estimates apply the White adjustment for heteroskedasticity. See Halbert White, "A Heteroskedasticity-Consistent Covariance Matrix Estimator and a Direct Test for Heteroskedasticity," *Econometrica* 48, no. 4 (1980), pp. 817–835.

quarterly average prices, typically for the subsequent five to eight quarters, and are available from the fourth quarter of 1993. To the extent that judgmental forecasts incorporate information contained in futures prices, albeit not in a systematic fashion, they may be expected to be at least as accurate as futures-based forecasts.

The statistical forecasts were generated using the models described in equations (15.1) and (15.2), both with and without futures prices.[40] The estimated equations were used to generate forecasts as of each quarter for one-, four-, and eight-quarter horizons. Of the four statistical forecasts for each commodity, the best performing model in terms of statistical as well as directional accuracy was selected as the "best model" for comparison against the judgmental forecasts and the ECM forecasts.

For 8 of the 15 commodities, the best model at the one-quarter horizon incorporated futures.[41] For most of the metals (copper, lead, nickel, and tin), as well as wheat and cotton, this took the form of a random walk with futures prices (i.e., equation (15.1) with an additional explanatory variable for futures prices), while for zinc and soybean oil the best model was an ARIMA model with futures (i.e., equation (15.2) with an additional explanatory variable for futures prices). At the four-quarter horizon, the best model for 6 of the 15 commodities (tin, zinc, wheat, maize, soybean meal, and soybean oil) included futures, in most cases in a random walk framework. At the eight-quarter horizon, the best model incorporated futures for 10 commodities (aluminum, copper, lead, nickel, tin, zinc, wheat, soybean oil, cotton, and robusta coffee).

Similarly, the quarterly ECM forecasts were generated at the one-, four-, and eight-quarter horizons using estimated versions of equation (15.4). Exhibits 15.8 and 15.9, which illustrate the judgment and ECM forecasts generated in the third quarter of 1994 against actual price developments, indicate reasonable convergence between the forecasts at the one-quarter horizon for aluminum but not for coffee–other milds. By eight quarters, however, the opposite holds. Judgmental and ECM forecasts for coffee appear to converge while the forecasts for aluminum seem to move apart. The next

[40]ARIMA (p,q) models were generated from an iterative test of the combination of p,q that yielded the lowest Schwarz criterion per Terence C. Mills, *The Econometric Modelling of Financial Time Series* (Cambridge: Cambridge University Press, 1999), with $\max(p, q) \leq 10$ for the standard series, and $\max(p, q) \leq 6$ for the futures series (due to limits on the size of most futures series). This test was run for a model that fit the full range of data (i.e., start date to 2003), and the parameters determined were then applied over the appropriate, out-of-sample testing and forecasting windows.

[41]Information on which the random walk/ARIMA model performs best for each commodity at each horizon is contained in Exhibits 15.2–15.12.

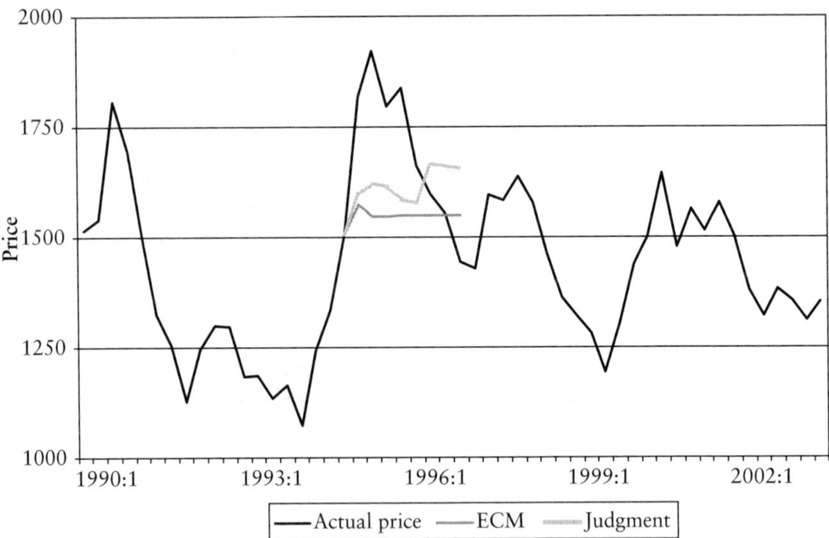

EXHIBIT 15.8 Aluminum: Judgmental and ECM Forecasts, 1994Q3
Source: Exhibit created from data obtained from IMF Primary Commodity Prices Database and Bloomberg.

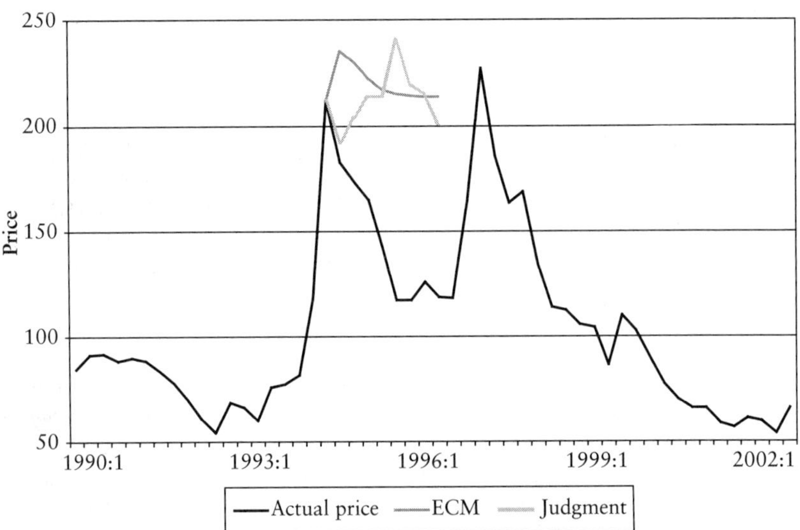

EXHIBIT 15.9 Coffee—Other Milds: Judgmental and ECM Forecasts, 1994Q3
Source: Exhibit created from data obtained from IMF Primary Commodity Prices Database and Bloomberg.

section describes the extent to which both types of forecasts, as well as the best random walk/ARIMA forecasts, deviate on average from actual price developments in directional and statistical accuracy terms.

Quarterly futures price series were constructed to facilitate comparability to the quarterly average price projections in the judgmental forecasts. Monthly futures price quotes from Bloomberg are available for contracts with maturity dates near the end of the subsequent one to five months for all 15 commodities in our sample. The one-quarter ahead price implied by futures was thus taken as the average of the prices prevailing at the end of each month in the current quarter of the contracts maturing in the next quarter. This procedure allowed the construction of one-quarter ahead prices for all 15 commodities. For wheat, maize, soybean oil, sugar, cotton, coffee—other milds, and robusta coffee, we were able to also construct two-quarter ahead futures prices. Up to three-quarter ahead prices were constructed for soybeans, soybean meal, and soybean oil, while up to four-quarter ahead futures were constructed for copper.[42]

In terms of market depth, most of the futures contracts used are liquid, with open interest of over 100,000 contracts and with over 15,000 contracts normally traded on any given day. The exceptions to this are sugar (U.S.), robusta coffee, and cotton, which usually have less than 10,000 trades on any given day.[43] The London Metals Exchange gives monthly volume figures for the metals forwards, with aluminum and zinc being the most heavily traded metals (over one million trades per month) and tin being the least traded (around 100,000 trades per month).

RESULTS

The various directional and statistical accuracy measures tend to favor forecasts incorporating futures prices, particularly at the four- and eight-quarter horizons. At the shorter horizon of one quarter ahead, however, futures price based models performed at least as well as the judgment based models only for six of the 15 commodities in the sample (Exhibit 15.10). For nickel and zinc, the ECM outperforms the judgmental and the best random walk/

[42]Futures prices that most closely matched the forecast horizon (one, four, or eight quarters) were used in the econometric models for the model-based forecasts.

[43]The coffee commodities and tin are the least traded contracts (about 8,000 to 10,000 trades per day), while wheat futures are traded somewhat more (about 24,000 trades per day) and maize futures are a liquid market (about 62,000 trades per day). It is therefore not surprising that wheat and maize futures tend to be part of the "best" model, while coffee futures do not.

EXHIBIT 15.10 Forecast Performance at One-Quarter Horizon

Commodity	RMSE Ratio (RMSE actual value)			Harding Pagan Statistic (β) (*t*-statistic) Concordance Statistic			Cumby-Modest Statistic (*t*-statistic)		
	Judgment	Best RW/ ARIMA	ECM	Judgment	Best RW/ ARIMA	ECM	Judgment	Best RW/ ARIMA	ECM
Aluminum[a]	1.00	1.31	1.15	0.36[e]	0.24	0.34[e]	0.07[f]	0.04*	0.07[f]
	(82.58)	(108.43)	(95.00)	(2.08)	(1.30)	(1.91)	(3.60)	(1.76)	(3.43)
				(0.68)	(0.62)	(0.68)			
Copper[b]	1.00	1.38	1.26	0.48[f]	0.30[f]	0.41[f]	0.09[f]	0.07[f]	0.07[f]
	(124.72)	(172.08)	(157.34)	(3.22)	(2.32)	(2.54)	(3.70)	(2.49)	(2.32)
				(0.73)	(0.65)	(0.70)			
Lead[b]	1.00	1.07	1.03	0.21	0.28[e]	0.19	0.03	0.02	0.03
	(36.78)	(39.24)	(37.91)	(1.37)	(2.02)	(1.10)	(1.16)	(0.75)	(1.19)
				(0.59)	(0.62)	(0.59)			
Nickel[b]	1.00	1.04	0.90	0.30	0.40[f]	0.47[f]	0.10[f]	0.09[f]	0.13[f]
	(670.36)	(697.62)	(603.99)	(1.62)	(2.27)	(3.05)	(2.60)	(2.29)	(4.41)
				(0.65)	(0.70)	(0.70)			
Tin[b]	1.00	3.31	3.28	0.89[f]	−0.36[f]	0.07	0.10[f]	−0.01	−0.00
	(99.66)	(329.64)	(327.22)	(11.87)	(−4.71)	(0.40)	(7.86)	(−0.76)	(−0.20)
				(0.95)	(0.62)	(0.46)			
Zinc[c]	1.00	1.32	1.24	0.19	0.34[f]	0.31[e]	0.07[f]	0.08**	0.08[f]
	(71.72)	(94.87)	(89.20)	(0.92)	(2.44)	(2.25)	(2.73)	(3.08)	(2.61)
				(0.59)	(0.68)	(0.62)			
Wheat[b]	1.00	1.54	1.48	0.42[f]	0.44[f]	0.42[e]	0.10[f]	0.07[e]	0.09[f]
	(11.38)	(17.47)	(16.80)	(2.51)	(3.94)	(2.13)	(3.13)	(2.14)	(2.51)
				(0.70)	(0.70)	(0.70)			
Maize[a]	1.00	1.26	1.17	0.44[f]	0.08	0.24[e]	0.09[f]	0.08[e]	0.06
	(11.11)	(13.95)	(13.00)	(2.44)	(0.61)	(1.92)	(2.35)	(1.92)	(1.48)
				(0.70)	(0.54)	(0.62)			

Soybean[d]	***1.00***	**1.08**	**1.16**	***0.56***[f]	**0.24**[e]	**0.29**[e]	***0.07***[f]	0.02	**0.05**[e]
	(14.71)	(15.86)	(16.99)	*(3.71)*	(1.77)	(1.89)	*(3.46)*	(1.12)	(2.19)
				(0.78)	(0.62)	(0.65)			
Soybean meal[a]	***1.00***	**1.00**	***1.01***	**0.32**[f]	**0.18**	*0.18*	***0.07***[f]	0.01	***0.09***[f]
	(18.01)	(17.96)	*(18.13)*	(2.58)	(1.27)	*(0.99)*	*(2.35)*	(0.36)	*(2.42)*
				(0.65)	(0.59)	*(0.59)*			
Soybean oil[c]	**1.00**	***1.13***	**1.01**	0.13	***0.32***[f]	−0.03	0.04	*0.01*	0.05
	(44.51)	*(50.10)*	(45.17)	(0.86)	*(2.64)*	(−0.18)	(1.44)	*(0.43)*	(1.47)
				(0.57)	*(0.68)*	(0.51)			
Sugar, U.S.[d]	***1.00***	**1.41**	**1.39**	***0.51***[f]	***0.31***[e]	0.26	***0.04***[f]	**0.03**[e]	**0.03**[e]
	(0.72)	(1.02)	(1.00)	*(4.15)*	(2.09)	(1.50)	*(3.02)*	(1.93)	(2.10)
				(0.76)	(0.62)	(0.62)			
Cotton[b]	***1.00***	***0.97***	***0.96***	***0.45***[f]	***0.34***[f]	***0.29***[f]	***0.11***[f]	***0.11***[f]	***0.10***[f]
	(5.81)	*(5.64)*	*(5.59)*	*(3.35)*	*(2.52)*	*(2.58)*	*(3.42)*	*(3.75)*	*(3.12)*
				(0.73)	*(0.68)*	*(0.65)*			
Coffee: other milds[d]	**1.00**	**1.43**	**1.38**	0.22	0.20	0.11	0.10	0.07	0.09
	(18.26)	(26.16)	(25.15)	(1.17)	(1.34)	(0.57)	(1.36)	(1.14)	(1.35)
				(0.68)	(0.59)	(0.59)			
Coffee: robusta[d]	***1.00***	**2.11**	**4.04**	***0.73***[f]	**0.29**[e]	0.19	***0.20***[f]	**0.13**[f]	0.08
	(7.97)	(16.82)	(32.20)	*(5.48)*	(1.71)	(1.05)	*(3.86)*	(2.49)	(1.64)
				(0.86)	(0.65)	(0.57)			

Source: Exhibit created from data obtained from IMF Primary Commodity Prices Database and Bloomberg.
Note: Significant statistics in bold and best forecasts in italics.
[a]Best RW/ARIMA model was a standard random walk model.
[b]Best RW/ARIMA model was a random walk model with lagged futures prices.
[c]Best RW/ARIMA model was an ARIMA (p,q) model with futures, with (p,q) equal to (1,2) for zinc and (3,3) for soybean oil.
[d]Best RW/ARIMA model was an ARIMA (p,q) model with (p,q) equal to (7,8) for soybeans; (2,5) for sugar; (1,1) for coffee–other milds; and (2,10) for robusta coffee.
[e]Denotes significance at 5%
[f]Denotes significance at 1%.

EXHIBIT 15.11 Forecast Performance at Four-Quarter Horizon

	RMSE Ratio (RMSE actual value)			Harding Pagan Statistic (β) (t-statistic) Concordance Statistic			Cumby-Modest Statistic (t-statistic)		
Commodity	Judgment	Best RW/ ARIMA	ECM	Judgment	Best RW/ ARIMA	ECM	Judgment	Best RW/ ARIMA	ECM
Aluminum[a]	1.00 (257.23)	1.18 (303.09)	0.94 (241.22)	0.30[e] (2.11) (0.61)	0.50[f] (2.97) (0.76)	0.63[f] (5.04) (0.76)	0.05 (0.92)	0.14[f] (2.43)	0.18[f] (4.22)
Copper[a]	1.00 (468.65)	1.08 (508.36)	1.18 (554.36)	0.34[e] (2.05) (0.70)	−0.10 (−0.49) (0.43)	0.12 (0.56) (0.54)	0.14[e] (2.29)	−0.06 (−0.90)	−0.01 (−0.10)
Lead[a]	1.00 (94.00)	1.14 (107.06)	1.02 (95.84)	0.15 (1.33) (0.52)	0.29[f] (2.78) (0.65)	−0.06 (−0.26) (0.43)	0.11[e] (2.03)	0.05 (0.99)	0.01 (0.16)
Nickel[a]	1.00 (2006.69)	0.85 (1703.79)	0.93 (1858.68)	0.38[e] (1.83) (0.73)	0.45[f] (2.41) (0.65)	0.52[f] (2.85) (0.62)	0.05 (0.37)	0.27[f] (2.90)	0.44[f] (7.24)
Tin[b]	1.00 (585.76)	1.13 (660.10)	1.16 (679.95)	0.26 (1.35) (0.67)	0.19 (0.91) (0.57)	0.35[e] (1.68) (0.65)	−0.01 (−0.26)	−0.00 (−0.09)	0.02 (0.51)
Zinc[c]	1.00 (185.69)	1.15 (213.09)	0.98 (181.40)	0.23 (1.31) (0.55)	−0.21 (−0.88) (0.54)	0.54[f] (4.17) (0.68)	0.16[e] (1.69)	−0.16[e] (−1.88)	0.22[f] (3.48)
Wheat[b]	1.00 (31.69)	1.28 (40.51)	0.93 (29.40)	0.24 (1.20) (0.61)	−0.35[f] (−2.42) (0.35)	0.21 (0.96) (0.59)	0.15[e] (1.73)	−0.21[f] (−3.31)	0.12 (1.51)
Maize[b]	1.00 (26.08)	1.06 (27.77)	0.93 (24.14)	0.30[e] (1.88) (0.58)	0.09 (0.57) (0.57)	0.27[e] (1.78) (0.62)	0.21[e] (1.87)	0.05 (0.69)	0.16[e] (1.79)
Soybean[d]	1.00 (29.36)	1.31 (38.48)	1.32 (38.65)	0.63[f] (5.05) (0.82)	0.12 (0.41) (0.49)	0.36[e] (1.90) (0.68)	0.19[f] (4.14)	−0.05[e] (−1.75)	0.08 (1.44)

Soybean meal[b]	1.00	1.03	1.01	0.51[f]	0.73[f]	0.53[f]	0.27[f]	0.33[f]	0.28[f]
	(38.09)	(39.16)	(38.47)	(3.29)	(6.96)	(3.21)	(2.78)	(4.72)	(3.30)
				(0.76)	(0.86)	(0.76)			
Soybean oil[c]	1.00	1.09	0.94	0.32[e]	−0.26	0.30	0.20[f]	−0.19[f]	0.16[e]
	(102.88)	(112.06)	(96.84)	(2.29)	(−1.08)	(1.13)	(2.61)	(−2.69)	(1.99)
				(0.67)	(0.38)	(0.68)			
Sugar, U.S.[a]	1.00	1.14	0.89	0.38[e]	0.45[f]	0.34[f]	0.01	0.07[e]	0.05
	(1.69)	(1.93)	(1.50)	(2.24)	(3.83)	(2.29)	(0.17)	(1.92)	(1.61)
				(0.70)	(0.54)	(0.65)			
Cotton[a]	1.00	1.08	1.25	0.36[e]	0.06	0.16	0.10	−0.04	−0.01
	(13.49)	(14.51)	(16.88)	(2.72)	(0.32)	(0.77)	(1.64)	(−0.52)	(−0.19)
				(0.58)	(0.51)	(0.59)			
Coffee, other milds[d]	1.00	1.21	0.96	−0.22	0.37[f]	−0.12	−0.06	0.22[e]	0.02
	(49.14)	(59.48)	(47.33)	(−1.23)	(2.39)	(−0.58)	(−0.54)	(2.02)	(0.21)
				(0.45)	(0.70)	(0.49)			
Coffee, robusta[a]	1.00	1.43	—[g]	0.06	0.42[f]	0.38[e]	−0.03	0.33[f]	—[h]
	(31.52)	(44.99)	—	(0.27)	(3.12)	(1.86)	(−0.29)	(3.43)	—
				(0.58)	(0.70)	(0.49)			

Source: Exhibit created from data obtained from IMF Primary Commodity Prices Database and Bloomberg.

Note: Significant statistics in bold and best forecasts in italics.

[a]Best RW/ARIMA model was an ARIMA (p,q) model with (p,q) equal to (1,1) for aluminum; (4,4) for copper; (2,6) for lead; (2,3) for nickel; (2,5) for sugar; (1,2) for cotton; and (2,10) for robusta coffee.

[b]Best RW/ARIMA model was an ARIMA (p,q) model with futures, with (p,q) equal to (4,4) for tin; (2,3) for wheat; (2,2) for maize; and (3,1) for soybean meal.

[c]Best RW/ARIMA model was a random walk model with lagged futures prices.

[d]Best RW/ARIMA model was a standard random walk model.

[e]Denotes significance at 5%.

[f]Denotes significance at 1%,

[g]Results were affected by a spike in the data; hence statistical results are grossly inaccurate. Direction statistics were unaffected.

[h]Results indicated a similar price movement over all estimation periods; hence it was not possible to calculate Cumby-Modest and/or Harding-Pagan statistics.

ARIMA forecasts in both directional and statistical terms. For soybean meal and cotton, the ECM forecast does at least as well as the other forecasts from either the statistical accuracy or the directional accuracy standpoint. For lead and soybean oil, the best random walk/ARIMA forecast, in both cases based on models incorporating futures data, outperforms other forecasts in terms of directional accuracy. Judgmental forecasts for the remaining eight commodity prices, however, outperform the models-based forecasts—with or without futures prices—at the one-quarter horizon.

At the four-quarter horizon, judgmental forecasts outperform the models-based forecasts for only 4 of the 15 commodities (Exhibit 15.11). Among the remainder, the ECM forecast does best for four commodities (aluminum, tin, zinc, and maize), while the best random walk/ARIMA model does best for coffee–other milds. For the remaining six commodities (lead, nickel, soybean meal, soybean oil, sugar, coffee–other milds, and robusta coffee), no single type of forecast consistently outperforms the others, although forecasts that incorporate futures either in the ECM or in the best random walk/ARIMA framework—do at least as well as other forecasts in five of these six cases.

The ECM forecasts outperform the other types of forecasts for 8 of the 15 commodities at the eight quarter horizon (Exhibit 15.12). In some of these cases, the ECM forecast performance is superior in both statistical and directional terms (wheat, soybeans, and soybean meal), although for several commodities the ECM yields significantly better directional accuracy at the expense of somewhat lower statistical accuracy (aluminum, lead, nickel, zinc, and maize). For another four commodities (tin, soybean oil, sugar, and cotton), the ECM performs about as well as judgment at the eight-quarter horizon, and both perform better than the best random walk/ARIMA forecasts. Of the remaining three commodities, the best random walk/ARIMA framework yields the best forecasts. In the case of robusta coffee, the model includes futures, while in the case of coffee–other milds it does not. Only for copper does judgment outperform the other forecasts by a sizable margin, although without significantly better directional accuracy. In sum, then, for 13 of the 15 commodity prices, models incorporating futures prices in either an error correction or random walk/ARIMA framework produce forecasts that are at least as good as—and in most cases better than—forecasts that do not explicitly incorporate futures, including judgmental forecasts, at the eight-quarter horizon.

It may be noted that the model forecasts for robusta coffee encounter problems due to a spike in futures prices. As a result, forecast prices increase rapidly and over longer horizons forecast errors become very large. This contributes to the very low statistical accuracy of the forecasts. From a practical perspective, therefore, futures- and model-based forecasts may

EXHIBIT 15.12 Forecast Performance at Eight-Quarter Horizon

Commodity	RMSE Ratio (RMSE actual value)			Harding Pagan Statistic (β) (t-statistic) Concordance Statistic			Cumby-Modest Statistic (t-statistic)		
	Judgment	Best RW/ ARIMA	ECM	Judgment	Best RW/ ARIMA	ECM	Judgment	Best RW/ ARIMA	ECM
Aluminum[a]	1.00	1.60	*1.04*	—[e]	−0.22	***0.35***[f]	—[e]	−0.05	***0.11***[f]
	(264.28)	(422.95)	*(275.69)*	—	(−0.15)	*(2.66)*	—	(−0.75)	*(2.74)*
				(0.43)	(0.62)	*(0.59)*			
Copper[b]	*1.00*	1.22	1.19	—[e]	−0.12	0.23	*0.08*	**−0.24**[f]	0.12
	(542.42)	(660.28)	(643.98)	—	(−0.86)	(1.14)	*(0.75)*	(−3.32)	(1.33)
				(0.86)	(0.62)	(0.62)			
Lead[b]	1.00	1.32	*1.04*	—[e]	0.11	*0.07*	0.21	−0.12	***0.18***[g]
	(126.12)	(167.09)	*(131.47)*	—	(0.40)	*(0.34)*	(1.97)	(−0.98)	*(2.24)*
				(0.71)	(0.70)	(0.54)			
Nickel[b]	1.00	1.37	*1.13*	0.50	−0.01	**0.44**[f]	0.20	−0.23	***0.24***[g]
	(1971.64)	(2710.85)	*(2221.59)*	(1.20)	(−0.03)	*(2.99)*	(0.50)	(−1.52)	*(2.28)*
				(0.86)	(0.51)	*(0.62)*			
Tin[a]	*1.00*	1.50	*1.11*	*0.50*	0.21	*0.17*	*0.20*	0.05	*−0.00*
	(733.11)	(1093.49)	*(810.76)*	*(1.20)*	(1.41)	*(1.08)*	*(1.53)*	(0.81)	*(−0.03)*
				(0.86)	(0.54)	(0.60)			
Zinc[a]	1.00	1.52	*1.35*	0.33	**−0.47**[f]	***0.68***[f]	**0.44**[f]	**−0.29**[f]	***0.29***[f]
	(174.64)	(264.90)	*(236.38)*	(1.04)	(−3.48)	*(5.36)*	(5.46)	(−4.85)	*(4.21)*
				(0.71)	(0.46)	*(0.81)*			

(Continued)

EXHIBIT 15.12 (Continued)

Judgment	Judgment	Best RW/ ARIMA	ECM	Judgment	Best RW/ ARIMA	ECM	Judgment	Best RW/ ARIMA	ECM
Wheat[b]	1.00	1.20	0.80	0.50	0.55[f]	0.56[f]	0.23	—[e]	0.38[f]
	(42.59)	(51.18)	(34.11)	(1.15)	(3.05)	(2.83)	(0.93)	—	(3.91)
				(0.83)	(0.65)	(0.78)			
Maize[e]	1.00	1.16	1.15	0.50	0.09	0.39[g]	0.08	0.10	0.32[f]
	(22.85)	(26.48)	(26.38)	(1.15)	(0.63)	(2.54)	(0.49)	(0.93)	(3.23)
				(0.83)	(0.62)	(0.70)			
Soybean[d]	1.00	1.16	0.91	−0.17	0.41[f]	0.31[g]	0.13	—[e]	0.21[f]
	(47.86)	(55.34)	(43.42)	(−0.91)	(2.72)	(1.67)	(1.07)	—	(2.94)
				(0.71)	(0.54)	(0.68)			
Soybean meal[d]	1.00	1.33	0.80	—[e]	0.27	0.67[g]	—[e]	−0.15	0.55[f]
	(56.66)	(75.24)	(45.14)	—	(1.15)	(4.17)	—	(−1.41)	(5.18)
				(0.00)	(0.59)	(0.84)			
Soybean oil[b]	1.00	1.65	1.25	0.80[f]	−0.15	0.58[f]	0.32	−0.31[f]	0.37[f]
	(101.56)	(167.92)	(126.81)	(3.66)	(−0.64)	(2.58)	(1.13)	(−2.68)	(3.11)
				(0.86)	(0.43)	(0.81)			
Sugar, U.S.[c]	1.00	1.54	1.01	—[e]	0.46[f]	0.59[f]	0.24[g]	—[h]	0.06
	(1.48)	(2.29)	(1.50)	—	(2.72)	(4.34)	(3.68)	—	(2.24)
				(1.00)	(0.59)	(0.81)			
Cotton[b]	1.00	1.28	1.00	—[e]	0.13	0.11	−0.15	0.05	0.06
	(18.98)	(24.35)	(18.93)	—	(1.41)	(0.92)	(−1.29)	(1.20)	(1.11)
				(0.57)	(0.46)	(0.68)			

Coffee: other milds[c]	**1.00**	***1.39***	**1.11**	−0.17	***0.32***[g]	−0.16	−0.62	***0.23***[g]	−0.14
	(50.20)	*(70.02)*	(55.93)	(−0.91)	*(2.15)*	(−1.00)	(−2.56)	*(2.06)*	(−1.15)
				(0.71)	*(0.59)*	(0.54)			
Coffee: robusta[a]	**1.00**	***1.91***	**1.61**	−0.17	***0.32***[f]	0.11	**−0.92**[g]	***0.44***[f]	—[e]
	(46.75)	*(89.28)*	(75.26)	(−0.91)	*(2.80)*	(0.99)	(−5.55)	*(3.54)*	—
				(0.71)	*(0.65)*	(0.39)			

Source: Exhibit created from data obtained from IMF Primary Commodity Prices Database and Bloomberg.
Note: Significant statistics in bold and best forecasts in italics.
[a]Best RW/ARIMA model was an ARIMA (p,q) model with futures, with (p,q) equal to (4,3) for aluminum; (4,4) for tin; (1,2) for zinc; and (2,2) for robusta coffee.
[b]Best RW/ARIMA model was a random walk model with lagged futures prices.
[c]Best RW/ARIMA model was an ARIMA (p,q) model with (p,q) equal to (6,10) for maize; (2,5) for sugar; and (1,1) for coffee–other milds.
[d]Best RW/ARIMA model was a standard random walk model.
[e]Results indicated a similar price movement over all estimation periods; hence it was not possible to calculate Cumby-Modest and/or Harding-Pagan statistics.
[f]Denotes significance at 1%.
[g]Denotes significance at 5%.
[h]Results demonstrated no heteroskedasticity; hence it was not possible to calculate statistics.

need to be "sanity checked" to ensure that short-term price panics do not create model forecasts that are unrealistic. Alternatively, discretionary inclusion of dummy variables in the estimated equations to adjust for such spikes may be appropriate in improving forecast accuracy.

CONCLUSION

The results suggest that futures prices can provide reasonable guidance about likely developments in spot prices over the longer term, at least in directional terms. For most of the commodities analyzed in this study, the incorporation of futures prices in an error-correction framework yields superior forecast performance at the two-year horizon. Since spot and futures prices are cointegrated for most commodities, and with futures prices exhibiting lower variability, longer-term spot price movements appear to be anchored by futures prices.

The generally superior performance of models with futures prices is somewhat surprising in light of the procedure employed to construct futures price series that were comparable to those forecasted by the judgmental approach, particularly in view of the potential incorporation of futures price information, albeit not systematically, in the judgmental forecasts. The averaging across various futures contracts and over various dates at which these contracts were priced may have resulted in a significant loss of information contained in the futures prices. Further research, which more fully exploits this information by matching the dates of futures contracts with forecast horizons, would clearly be desirable and may yield even stronger performance of futures-based models. Indeed, more careful date matching may well produce futures-based forecasts that more consistently outperform judgment at even the shorter horizons. The predictive capacity of the models may also be enhanced by incorporating variables capturing the demand for individual commodities, possibly via an economic activity variable, and perhaps by pooling forecasts generated by various alternative statistical models or by employing more sophisticated time series techniques—such as ARCH, GARCH, or those incorporating structural breaks—to generate the models-based forecasts. These also remain on the agenda for future work.

PART Four

Asset Allocation

CHAPTER 16

Commodity Trading Strategies: Examples of Trading Rules and Signals from the CTA Sector

François-Serge Lhabitant, Ph.D.
Chief Investment Officer
Kedge Capital
Professor of Finance
HEC Lausanne and EDHEC Business School

Professional asset managers, whose activity primarily focuses on trading futures on behalf of their clients, are known under the name of *commodity trading advisors* (CTAs). Some run managed accounts where they act as consultants while others operate through a fund. Collectively, commodity trading advisors manage more than $140 billion of assets and comprise the alternative investment area called managed futures. Unlike hedge funds, they are not regulated by the Securities and Exchange Commission (SEC), but are registered with the Commodity Futures Trading Commission (CFTC) through membership in the National Futures Association.

Today, commodity trading advisors pursue hundreds of different strategies and substrategies. Although each commodity trading advisor claims to be unique, the reality is that three major categories span the universe: systematic traders, discretionary traders, and hybrids. Systematic traders develop computer-based mathematical models to analyze historical data. Their goal is to identify patterns created by inefficient markets that can be used to forecast market movements and generate market-trading decisions. By contrast, discretionary traders rely on fundamental analysis of market conditions to determine their trading strategies. The hybrid traders attempt to get the best from both worlds by using a combination of systematic and discretionary approaches.

Not surprisingly, the increased availability of computing power and data in the last few years has dramatically increased the number of systematic traders, which now represents more than 80% of the commodity trading advisors universe. These traders have removed the human judgment or intervention in their decision-making process. Their computer models, which are often called *systems*," range from simple formulas on a spreadsheet to complicated proprietary software. They analyze market data such as prices and trading volume information and attempt to identify specific price patterns such as market trends or market reversals. Then, they generate buy and sell signals that should be followed to the letter. By construction, they are without emotion, opaque and obscure, and give no winks and nods—almost like a perfect girlfriend. The most sophisticated of them are designed to either "learn" like humans or to detect nonintuitive relationships among a sea of data that cannot be readily seen by humans. Ultimately, they should be better than humans because they can act faster, trade more cheaply, make decisions dispassionately, process more information, and see things humans simply cannot see due to the limits of their cerebral cortex.

However, the downside to these systems is their black box*ness*. While upon request, systematic traders will often provide some transparency on trades and positions, they are usually very secretive with regards to the trading rules that make their system. And requests for higher transparency will usually be handled as diligently as requests from a foreign tax authority to a Swiss Bank. As a result, systematic trading rules usually remain a mystery to the uninitiated. In this chapter, our goal is therefore to open the black box and provide an introduction to the basic trading rules and signals that are commonly used by commodity trading advisors. As we will see, many of these rules and signals are direct descendants of the diagrammatic analysis methods that were so popular in technical analysis.

TECHNICAL ANALYSIS

Technical analysis is based on the hypothesis that markets are driven more by psychological factors than fundamental values. Its proponents believe that commodity prices reflect not only the underlying "value" of the commodity but also the hopes and fears of market participants. If the emotional makeup of investors does not change, then in a certain set of circumstances, investors will react in a similar manner to how they did in the past, so that the resultant price moves are likely to be the same—that is, history tends to repeat itself.

Over the years, numerous empirical studies have investigated the profitability of technical analysis rules in a variety of markets. The first studies examined primarily simple rules such as filters,[1] stop-loss orders,[2] moving averages,[3] channels,[4] momentum oscillators[5] and relative strength.[6] Performance was usually disappointing on equity markets, but tests on foreign exchange markets and commodity futures markets often exhibited substantial net profits. However, most of these early studies did not conduct statistical tests of significance on technical trading returns, nor did they incorporate risk considerations in their performance assessment or pay serious attention to data snooping problems and out-of-sample verification. By contrast, recent studies attempt to provide a more comprehensive analysis.[7] They typically increase the number of trading systems tested,

---

[1]See for instance Sidney S. Alexander, "Price Movements in Speculative Markets: Trends or Random Walks," *Industrial Management Review* 2, no. 2 (1961), pp. 7–26; Sidney S. Alexander, "Price Movements in Speculative Markets: Trends or Random Walks," *Industrial Management Review* 5, no. 2 (1964), pp. 25–46; Eugene F. Fama and Marshall E. Blume, "Filter Rules and Stock Market Trading," *Journal of Business* 39, no. 1 (1966), pp. 226–241; or Richard J. Sweeney, "Some New Filter Rule Tests: Methods and Results," *Journal of Financial and Quantitative Analysis* 23, no. 2 (1986), pp. 285–300.

[2]See, for instance, Hendrik S. Houthakker, "Systematic and Random Elements in Short-Term Price Movements," *American Economic Review* 51 no. 1 (1986), pp. 164–172; or Roger W. Gray and Soren T. Nielsen, Rediscovery of Some Fundamental Price Behavior Characteristics, Paper presented at the meeting of the Econometric Society, Cleveland, Ohio, 1963.

[3]See, for example, Paul H. Cootner, "Stock Prices: Random vs. Systematic Changes," *Industrial Management Review* 3, no. 1 (1963), pp. 24–45; James C. Van Horne and George G. C. Parker, "The Random-Walk Theory: An Empirical Test," *Financial Analysts Journal* 23, no. 2 (1967), pp. 87–92; James C. Van Horne and George G. C. Parker, "Technical Trading Rules: A Comment," *Financial Analysts Journal* 24, no. 4 (1968), pp. 128–132; or Dale and Workman, "The Arc Sine Law and the Treasury Bill Futures Market," *Financial Analysts Journal* 36 no. 6 (1980), pp. 71–74.

[4]See, for example, Richard D. Donchian, "High Finance in Copper," *Financial Analysts Journal* 16, no. 6 (1960), pp. 133–142; Scott H. Irwin and J. William Uhrig, "Do Technical Analysts Have Holes in Their Shoes?," *Review of Research in Futures Markets* 3, no. 3 (1984), pp. 264–277.

[5]See Seymour Smidt, "A Test of Serial Independence of Price Changes in Soybean Futures," *Food Research Institute Studies* 5, no. 2 (1965), pp. 117–136.

[6]See, for instance, Robert A. Levy, "Relative Strength as a Criterion for Investment Selection," *Journal of Finance* 22, no. 4 (1967), pp. 595–610; or Michael C. Jensen and George A. Benington, "Random Walks and Technical Theories: Some Additional Evidence," *Journal of Finance* 25, no. 2 (1970), pp. 469–482.

[7]See, for example, Louis P. Lukac, B. Wade Brorsen, and Scott H. Irwin, "A Test of Futures Market Disequilibrium Using Twelve Different Technical Trading

assess the risk of their trading rules, perform statistical tests on their performance, and conduct parameter optimization and out-of-sample verification. But surprisingly, several of them still identify positive technical trading profits although these profits seem to gradually decrease over time. As an illustration, a recent literature survey[8] shows that among a total of 95 recent studies, 56 studies find profitability or predictability of technical trading strategies, while only 20 studies report negative results and 19 studies indicate mixed results. This seems to support the claim that technical analysis may be a useful tool for commodity trading advisors to capture sufficiently strong movements in commodity prices without necessarily knowing the economic forces behind them.

In the following, we are going to review some of the rules commonly used by commodity trading advisors. Needless to say, rather than being subjective and hence difficult to apply or examine empirically, these rules and signals have been adapted to enable the construction of a computerized algorithm. Nevertheless, to simplify the reading, we have divided the universe of commodity trading advisors into two categories, namely trend followers and nontrend followers.

TREND FOLLOWERS AND MOVING AVERAGES SIGNALS

Trend followers currently dominate the universe of systematic commodity trading advisors.[9] Simply stated, they attempt to capture the majority of a trend, up or down, for profit. As their name indicates, they normally wait for the trend to shift first, and then they follow it.

The easiest way to identify a trend on a commodity once it has started is by looking for some sort of lagging indicator and comparing it to the

Systems," *Applied Economics* 20, no. 5 (1988), pp. 623–639; Louis P. Lukac and B. Wade Brorsen, "A Comprehensive Test of Futures Market Disequilibrium," *Financial Review* 25, no. 4 (1990), pp. 593–622; Stephen J. Taylor, "Rewards Available to Currency Futures Speculators: Compensation for Risk or Evidence of Inefficient Pricing?," *Economic Record* 68, no. 2 (1992), pp. 105–116; Stephen J. Taylor, "Trading Futures Using a Channel Rule: A Study of The Predictive Power of Technical Analysis with Currency Examples," *Journal of Futures Markets* 14, no. 2 (1994), pp. 215–235; or Blake LeBaron, "Technical Trading Rule Profitability and Foreign Exchange Intervention," *Journal of International Economics* 49, no. 1 (1999), pp. 125–143.

[8] See Cheol-Ho Park and Scott H. Irwin, "What Do We Know about the Profitability of Technical Analysis?," *Journal of Economic Surveys* 21, no. 4 (2007), pp. 786–826.

[9] See William Fung and David A. Hsieh, "The Information Content of Performance Track Records: Investment Style and Survivorship Bias in the Historical Returns of Commodity Trading Advisors," *Journal of Portfolio Management* 24, no. 1 (1997), pp. 30–41.

present market level. Although it is difficult to make a strong theoretical case for any particular lagging indicator, moving averages rules seem to be very widely used by commodity trading advisors as they are relatively simple to understand and test. In addition, they are statistically well defined in the sense of being Markov-time; that is, they generate signals by using only information available to date.[10]

In its simplest form, a moving average is an average of past prices calculated over a given period of time. Mathematically, it is calculated as follows:

$$MA_N = \frac{1}{N} \sum_{t=k-N+1}^{k} P_t \tag{16.1}$$

where N is the number of periods included in the average, k is the relative position of the period currently being considered within the total number of periods, and P_t is the asset price at time t. Note that old prices are equally as relevant as more recent ones, as each price in the moving average is equally weighted irrespective of its relative position in the time series. Regarding N, any time span can be considered from minutes to years. For example, a 15-day moving average takes the last 15 closing prices, adds them up, and divides the result by 15. On the next day, the oldest price is dropped, the newest price is added, and the new sum of 15 prices is divided by 15 to obtain the new average. In this manner, the average "moves" each day.

By construction, moving averages work as a smoothing device—they take the "noise" out of price movements and reduce the effects of short-term volatility. For instance, if an upward-trending market suddenly has one day of lower prices, a moving average would factor that day's price in with several other days, thus lessening the impact of one single trading day on the moving average and facilitating the recognition of underlying trends.[11]

Lao Tzu, a philosopher from the 6th century BCE, said, "Those who have knowledge don't predict, and those who predict do not have

---

[10]Conversely, any trading rule that is not Markov-time would be anticipating the future. For an interesting discussion of this topic, we will refer the reader to Saher N. Neftci, "Naive Trading Rules in Financial Markets and Wiener–Kolmogorov Prediction Theory: A Study of Technical Analysis," *Journal of Business* 64, no. 4 (1991), pp. 549–571.

[11]Note that there also exist more complex weighting schemes. For instance, *linear weighted moving average* (LWMA) and *exponentially weighted moving average* (EWMA) weight each observation according to its relative position in the average, with generally more weight given to recent observations.

knowledge." At this stage, it is essential to understand that moving averages do not *predict* market trends, but rather systematically *lag* the current market price. This is easy to understand by plotting on the same graph the moving average and the current price (see Exhibit 16.1). The moving average captures well the trends but is smoother than the oil price curve. In a rising market, because of the lag, the moving average is below the current price line, whereas in a falling market it is above it. When the current price changes direction, the moving average and price lines cross. This happens by construction because the moving average, by nature of the lag, still reflects the "old" trend. The direction of the crossing therefore provides the basic systematic rules by which all moving average systems operate. Simply stated, one should (1) buy when the current price crosses the moving average from below; and (2) sell when the current price crosses the moving average from above.[12] In Exhibit 16.2, an up triangle, for instance, indicates a buy signal, where the current gold price crosses the moving average from below. In contrast, when the current gold price crosses the moving average from above, such a down triangle represents a sell signal.

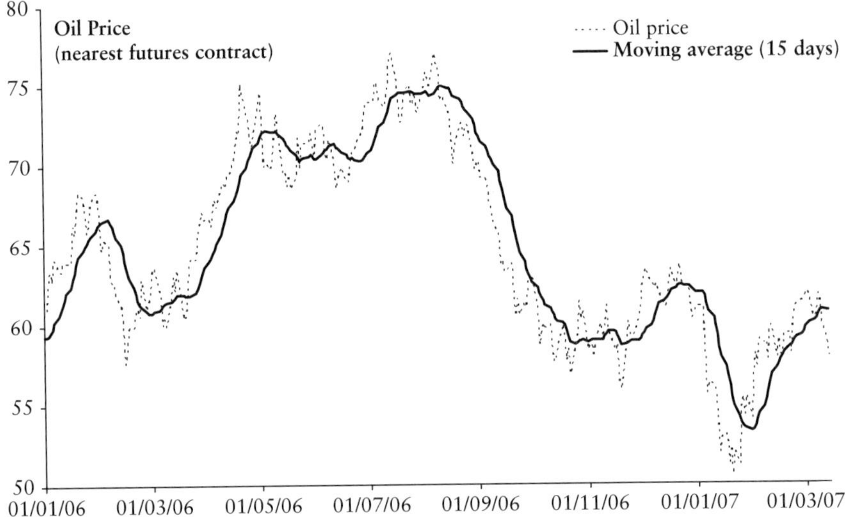

EXHIBIT 16.1 Comparison of Oil Prices (rolling nearest futures) with Its 15-Day Moving Average
Source: Exhibit created from data obtained from Bloomberg.

[12]Note that a possible variation of these rules consists in generating signals when the price differs from the moving average by a certain percentage.

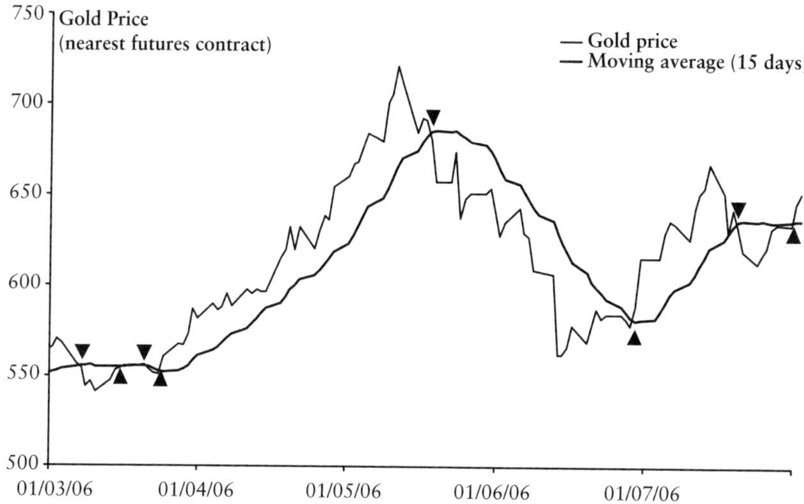

EXHIBIT 16.2 Fifteen-Day Moving Average to Generate Buy and Sell Signals for Gold Futures
Source: Exhibit created from data obtained from Bloomberg.

Of course, the number of days used to calculate the moving average window will dramatically impact its behavior. Shorter-length moving averages tend to follow changes in underlying asset prices more closely. They are very sensitive to trends, but are also prone to "whipsaw" losses, as small erratic price movements generate false trading signals. Using them systematically creates a high frequency of position changes, which results in high transactions costs and relatively many false signals. The later point is particularly disturbing in ranging markets, as short-term rules always buy late (after a rise in value) and sell late (after a fall in value). By contrast, longer-length moving averages alternatively desensitize asset price movements and highlight only major trends. Their drawback is that they generate fewer signals than a shorter-length average and may therefore miss some opportunities. Hence, using a longer-term moving average (60-day rather than 15-day) allows the system to capture well long term trends and reduces the number of trades (see Exhibit 16.3). When the market is trendless, however, the system still produces useless signals.

The objective is therefore to find a sufficiently sensitive average, which gives signals at the early stage of a new trend, but not so sensitive to be affected by market noises. Most major primary trends can usually be monitored with a 40-week (200-day) moving average, intermediate term trends with a 40-day moving average, and short-term trends by a 20-day (or less)

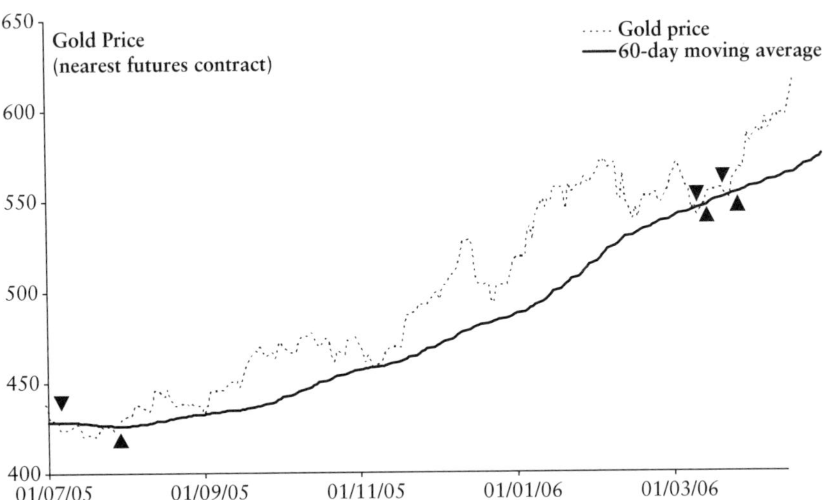

EXHIBIT 16.3 Longer-Term Moving Average (60-day rather than 15-day)
Source: Exhibit created from data obtained from Bloomberg.

moving average. However, the "optimal" length of a moving average should be determined on a case-by-case basis, as it depends on the market considered and its cyclicality. Besides the length of the moving average, one must also decide upon the types of prices used (closing, open, high, low, averages, etc.), as well as the threshold levels to signal a buy or a sell. Most of the time, the models used by managed futures are the result of hundreds of hours of development, testing, and fine-tuning. The basic rules that constitute them are remarkably simple, but the calibration of these rules to specific markets is not. Remember that once set up, a systematic trading system should operate alone and undisturbed, until or unless it no longer works properly. It is crucial to be confident in the system quality.

LIMITS OF MOVING-AVERAGE-BASED TREND-FOLLOWING SYSTEMS

Even when properly and regularly calibrated, trend-following systems based on moving average rules usually suffer from two drawbacks. First, they are slow. Because of the inherent lag of the moving average compared to market prices, they tend to enter late in a trend and exit late, that is, after the trend has reversed and losses have occurred. Investors in commodity trading advisors are familiar with this idea that they have to "give back" a significant portion of their gains at the end of a trend. As an illustration, consider the three signals observed in May, June, and July in Exhibit 16.2. All of them give correct information, but with a 10 to 15 day lag—approximately the length of the moving average.

The second drawback is that moving average rules are designed to exploit momentum in commodity prices. In order for them to be effective, commodity prices should diverge from a random walk in that their returns should exhibit significant positive autocorrelations. This is obviously the case in trending markets, but moving average rules tend to perform poorly in markets that evolve in a narrow range without any real trend. In this case, moving average rules tend to generate useless and costly signals; that is, they buy high (after the uptrend seems to have started) and sell low (after the decline has taken place).

Of course, CTAs are continuously working on their system, and attempt to find and test more sophisticated moving average rules. Let us just mention a few of them.

- *Variable length moving averages* (VMAs) rules are usually based on the comparison of two moving averages. One average would be the short term (strictly relative to the other moving average) and the other long term. Mathematically speaking, the long-term moving average will have a lower variance and will move in the same direction as the short-term moving average but at a different rate. The different rates of direction induce points where the values of the two moving averages may equal and or cross one another. These points are called the crossover points. A buy signal is generated when the short-term average crosses over the long-term average from below. Conversely, a sell signal is generated when the short-term average crosses the long-term average from above. Following a buy (sell) signal, the long (short) position is maintained until the opposite signal is received.
- *Fixed length moving averages* (FMAs) rules are similar to VMA rules except that the position established following a signal is only maintained for a fixed holding period. Commodity trading advisors using fixed length moving averages aim at avoiding the trend reversal.
- *Adaptive moving averages* (AMAs) are based on the premise that a short-length moving average will respond more quickly when market prices are trending, yet a long-length moving average will be preferred when markets are ranging. Consequently, AMAs systems seek to identify the current changing market conditions in order to adapt the length of the moving average that they use, as well as the minimum price movement that is required beyond crossing before a trade (buy or sell) is initiated.

- *High-low moving averages* (HLMAs) run two moving averages, one of high prices and another of the low prices, effectively creating a channel of prices. Generally, the high/low moving average is not a crossover system. Some traders use it as a measure of the market's support and resistance areas (at what price level do buyers enter the market and support prices, or at what price level do sellers take profits and pressure the market lower?). The moving average of the high could be the resistance area, while the moving average of the low is the support area. Some traders prefer to buy or sell breakouts above or below the resistance and support areas, respectively. Others use the resistance and support areas as zones to establish a market position in the direction of the dominant market trend.
- *Triple moving averages* (TMAs) rules use three moving averages at the same time. When the shorter moving average of a commodity's price crosses a medium moving average, and the medium crosses a longer moving average, a bullish or bearish signal is generated depending on the direction of the crossovers.

Unfortunately, most of these advanced moving average rules will still perform poorly—or at least not make money—in a market without trend. Surprising? Not really. Remember that we were looking at trend followers. If we want to see commodity trading advisors that are profitable during range trading periods, we have to look at another category, namely the nontrend followers.

NONTREND FOLLOWERS AND TRADING RANGE SIGNALS

Nontrend-following commodity trading advisors have a completely different and complementary approach. Although the rules they use are also directly inherited from technical analysis and Chartism, they aim at capturing opportunities when markets trade in a narrow range. To illustrate how these rules operate, let us mention two of them, namely the *relative strength index* and the *stochastic oscillator*.

The *relative strength index* (RSI) is a counter-trend indicator that measures the ratio of the upward trends (gains) in a market compared to its downward trends (losses) and standardizes the calculation so that the index is expressed by a figure between 1 and 100. The RSI is calculated as follows:

$$RSI = 100 - \left(\frac{100}{1 + RS}\right) \tag{16.2}$$

where RS is the ratio of total number of days with a higher close over the past N days over the total number of days with a lower close over the past N days, and N days is the number of days that one wants to consider.[13] RSI levels of 70% and 30% (sometimes 80% and 20%) are known as overbought/oversold levels. A buy signal is generated when the market is oversold, and a sell signal is generated when the market is overbought. In practical terms, an N-day criterion means that a sustained move in one direction that exceeds N days will retain a very high RSI value and may result in losses if a short position was entered. However, as many other signals, the RSI usually works well inside range-trading phases, but produces losses during trend phase.

The *stochastic oscillator* indicates the conditions of overbought/oversold on a scale from 0% to 100% by comparing a closing price for a market to its price range over a given time period. It is based on the observation that when a market is going to turn, say from up to down, its highs are higher, but the closing price often settles within the previous range.

The original stochastic oscillator, developed by George Lane,[14] is plotted as two lines called $\%K$, a fast line and $\%D$, a slow line. The formula for $\%K$ is

$$\%K = 100 \times \left(\frac{\text{Closing price} - \text{Lowest low}_N}{\text{Highest low}_N - \text{Lowest low}_N}\right) \tag{16.3}$$

where Lowest low_N represents the lowest low level reached over the past N periods, and Highest low_N represents the highest low level reached over the past N periods. The formula for $\%D$ is a simple moving average of $\%K$ over some period of time, which needs to be specified.

Although this sounds complex, it is similar to the plotting of moving averages—simply think of $\%K$ as a fast moving average and $\%D$ as a slow moving average. Then, a stochastic oscillator generates signals in three main ways:

- Extreme values: The first rule is usually to buy when the stochastic ($\%H$ or $\%K$) falls below 20% and then rises above that level. The second

[13]Traders often use $N = 14$ days because it represents one half of a natural cycle. But N can in fact be chosen arbitrarily. Note that the RSI is also sometimes calculated by summing up the total price gains on up days and dividing by how many total price changes you are examining for the up average. For the down average, one adds up the absolute value of the changes on the days prices fell and then divides that figure by the number of price changes. The result compares the magnitude of recent gains to recent losses.

[14]See George C. Lane, "Lane's Stochastics," *Technical Analysis of Stocks and Commodities* 2 (May–June 1984), pp. 87–90.

rule is usually to sell when the stochastic rises above 80% and then falls below that level.[15]

- Crossovers between the %*D* and %*K* lines: This is very similar to moving averages rules; that is, buy when the %*K* line rises above the %*D* line and sell when the %*K* line falls below the %*D* line.
- Divergences between the stochastic and the underlying price. For example, if prices are making a series of new highs and the stochastic is trending lower, this is usually a warning signal of weakness in the market.

Stochastic oscillators are very effective in trading ranges, but not during trending markets. In a trading range, as the price moves back and forth in a narrow range, the oscillator should indicate an oversold condition at the lower side of the range and an overbought situation at the upper side of the range. In contrast, during an upward or a downward trend, the stochastic oscillator will prematurely indicate an extreme in price, positioning the trader against the prevailing trend.

BACK-TESTING AND CALIBRATION

Before putting a new trading rule into action, both trend followers and non-trend followers have to test how well this rule would have performed in the past using historical data. The rationale for back-testing is that, if a trading rule did not do well in the past, the chance that it will work in the future is slim. As we all know, reality is that past performance is not necessarily a forecast of future performance, but most people will nevertheless want to see the successful back-testing of a trading rule before accepting it.

Most of the time, the trading rules used by commodity trading advisors often appear to work remarkably well once they have been back-tested. But this may hide several biases.

- *Pretest bias.* Trading rules typically derive from personal experience or the observation of past market movements. In either case, the formulation of the trading rule is heavily influenced by history, so that the back test of its performance using the very same historical period is likely to be attractive.

[15]Some systems also use more complex rules that analyze the pattern of the stochastic. For instance, when it stays below 40% to 50% for a period and then swings above, the market is shifting from overbought and offering a buy signal and vice versa when it stays above 50% to 60% for a period of time.

- *Data mining.* In the most extreme form, one could start with thousands of possible trading rules and test them all over some historical period. Some would appear to work simply because of chance.
- *Trading cost bias.* Many back-tests ignore the implicit and explicit trading costs that one has to pay to execute a trade such as bid-ask spreads, commissions, margin deposits, and the like. Failure to account for these trading costs will overstate the performance of a trading rule, especially for one that requires frequent trading and involves less liquid or more volatile markets.
- *Slippage control.* Many back-tests assume that they can buy and sell at the closing prices. In reality, there are slippage effects; that is, differences between the price that triggers a buy or a sell order and the price at which the order has been executed. For commodity trading advisors, slippage may be a significant cost of doing business and is therefore more important than saving a few cents on commissions. To ensure best execution and to limit slippage, most commodity trading advisors analyse as follows: the types of orders they place, the time they place them, the manner they place them, and the people that they place them with. But this is rarely analyzed in back tests.
- *Look ahead bias.* During their back-testing, some trading rules use information that would not yet be available at the time of the trade, e.g. information which is published only a few hours or a few days after the closing of the market. Failure to exclude this future information in the back-testing period tends to significantly overstate the historical performance of a trading rule.

All of these biases can cause spurious profits in the back-testing period and as a result past performance does not always foretell future performance. It is therefore essential to assess the robustness of the performance of any trading rule over different subperiods and different market conditions before validating it. It is quite common to observe that trend followers tend to underestimate the volatility of commodity prices, causing them to see patterns in randomness.[16] And not surprisingly, they also tend to be overconfident about their forecasting ability. Interestingly, Griffin and Tversky found that it is when predictability is low that they usually become more overconfident.[17]

---

[16]See David A. Hirshleifer, "Investor Psychology and Asset Pricing," *Journal of Finance* 56, no. 4 (2001), pp. 1533–1597.

[17]See Dale Griffin and Amos Tversky, "The Weighing of Evidence and the Determinants of Confidence," *Cognitive Psychology* 24, no. 3 (1992), pp. 411–435.

PORTFOLIO CONSTRUCTION

The majority of commodity trading advisors build their portfolio using *several trading rules* applied *simultaneously* on a *large number* of futures markets. These rules may use different types of analysis or cover different sources of returns (trends or nontrends) and different time frames. This allows capturing returns from different origins and diversifying away the risks inherent to each individual futures position. In particular, the losses that usually occur at the end of a trend on a given market may easily be compensated by the gains linked to a starting or ongoing trend in another market.

An essential point when analyzing managed futures is the portfolio construction rules used by the fund manager. One of the key advantages of trading futures contracts rather than their underlying assets is that they require a relatively small amount of margin. Consequently, managers have a lot of flexibility in designing their investment programs, based on the return, risk, and correlation expectations of their client base.

The simplest approach is to systematically place identical size orders in terms of notional amounts invested (long or short) or in terms of margins. But the danger of that approach is that the risk of each position is not really taken into consideration, as some commodities are much more volatile than others. A better solution is to think in terms of capital at risk and allocate the same amount of *risk capital* to each position in the portfolio, for instance using stop losses to limit the downside risk. Consider a managed futures fund with \$200,000 of equity capital. Say we have a buy signal on gold with a futures price at \$400 per ounce, and the manager wants to risk an initial 1% of its capital to each trade. Buying one future and setting a stop-loss at \$390 results in a \$1,000 risk per contract ((400 – 390)× \$100/point). If the manager agrees to risk 1% of its capital on each trade (i.e., \$2,000 as of this writing), he should buy two contracts. Note that the position needs to be continuously reassessed as prices are changing. For instance, if gold price increases, the manager has the choice between maintaining the position and adjusting the stop loss upward, or maintaining the stop loss at \$390 but reducing the number of contracts—as the spread between the futures price and the stop loss price widens, the capital at risk increases. Some managers go even one step further and take into account the diversification benefits of their various positions when calculating the capital at risk. That is, they do not consider the total risk of each position, but the risk that each position effectively contributes to the portfolio.[18] This allows them to split evenly the risk of their portfolio across all positions.

[18]See François-Serge Lhabitant, *Hedge Funds: Quantitative Insights* (London: John Wiley & Sons, 2004), pp. 315–319.

CONCLUSION

In this chapter, we have provided a brief overview of the some of the tools used by the systems of commodity trading advisors to run their futures portfolios. While most commodity trading advisors regard their trading system as proprietary complex tools, reality is that most systems are conceptually rather simple—they use rules that are often directly inherited from the good old days of technical analysis and aim at providing entry and exit points on various commodity markets. The value added is therefore often not in the system itself but more in its constant calibration to current market conditions and in the development of new rules in response to changes in market conditions as soon as they occur. Indeed, it would be naive to believe that a fixed, time-invariant set of given rules will perform consistently well across different commodities and time periods. Flexible systems are the key to success in any technical trading program in the commodity futures market.

CHAPTER 17

How to Design a Commodity Futures Trading Program

Hilary Till
Principal
Premia Capital Management, LLC

Joseph Eagleeye
Principal
Premia Capital Management, LLC

We provide a step-by-step primer on how to design a commodity futures trading program. A prospective commodity manager not only must discover trading strategies that are expected to be generally profitable, but also must be careful regarding each strategy's correlation properties during different times of the year and during eventful periods. He or she also must ensure that the resulting product has a unique enough return stream that it can be expected to provide diversification benefits to an investor's overall portfolio.

When designing a commodity futures trading program, a commodity manager needs to create an investment process that addresses these steps:

1. Trade discovery
2. Trade construction
3. Portfolio construction
4. Risk management
5. Leverage level
6. How the program will make a unique contribution to the investor's overall portfolio

---

This chapter is taken from Greg N. Gregoriou, Vassilios Karavas, François-Serge Lhabitant, and Fabrice Douglas Rouah (eds.), *Commodity Trading Advisors: Risk, Performance Analysis,* and Selection, John Wiley and Sons. Inc., 2004.

This chapter covers each of these subjects in succession.

TRADE DISCOVERY

The first step is to discover a number of trades in which it is plausible that the investor has an "edge" or advantage. Although a number of futures trading strategies are well known and publicized, commodity managers continue to apply them. Three examples of such strategies follow.

Grain Example

In discussing consistently profitable grain futures trades, Cootner stated that the fact that they "persist in the face of such knowledge indicates that the risks involved in taking advantage of them outweigh the gain involved. This is further evidence that . . . [commercial participants do] not act on the basis of expected values; that . . . [these participants are] willing to pay premiums to avoid risk."[1] Cootner's article discussed detectable periods of concentrated hedging pressure by agricultural market participants that lead to "the existence of . . . predictable trends in future prices." It provided several empirical examples of this occurrence, including "the effect of occasional long hedging in the July wheat contract." Noting the tendency of the prices of futures contracts to "fall on average after the peak of net long hedging," Cootner stated that the July wheat contract should "decline relative to contract months later in the crop year which are less likely to be marked by long hedging." Exhibit 17.1 summarizes Cootner's empirical study on a wheat futures spread. The spread on average declined by about 2.5 cents over the period. The significant issue for us is that this phenomenon, which is linked to hedging activity, was

EXHIBIT 17.1 Cootner's Empirical Study on the July versus December Wheat Futures Spread

1948 to 1966 Average of July Versus December Wheat Futures Price on the Indicated Dates	
January 31	−5.10 cents
February 28	−5.35 cents
March 31	−5.62 cents
April 30	−5.69 cents
May 31	−6.55 cents
June 30	−7.55 cents

Source: Paul Cootner, "Speculation and Hedging," 100.

[1]Paul Cootner, "Speculation and Hedging," Food Research Studies, Supplement 7 (1967), p. 98

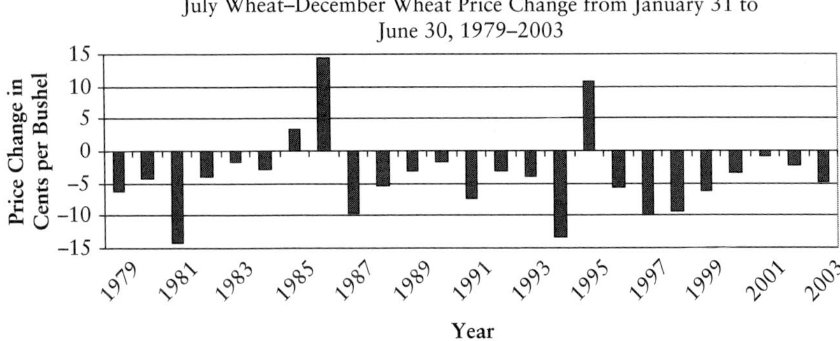

EXHIBIT 17.2 Cootner's Example Out of Sample
Source: Premia Capital Management, LLC.

published in 1967. Does this price pressure effect still exist for the present? The answer appears to be yes.

From 1979 to 2003, on average, this spread declined by 3.8 cents with a Z-statistic of –3.01. Exhibit 17.2 illustrates the yearly performance of this spread.

This trade is obviously not riskless. To profit from this trade, a manager generally would short the spread, so it is the positive numbers in Exhibit 17.2 that would represent losses. Note from the figure the magnitude of potential losses that this trade has incurred over the past 25 years. That said, Cootner's original point that a profitable trade can persist in the face of knowledge of its existence seems to be borne out 36 years later.

Exhibit 17.3 summarizes the information in Exhibit 17.2 differently to emphasize the "tail risk" of a July to December wheat spread strategy. If a manager took a short position in this spread, the possible outcomes incorporate losses that are several times the size of the average profit. Again, in a short position, the manager wants the price change to be negative, so the historical losses on this trade are represented by the positive numbers in Exhibit 17.3. A

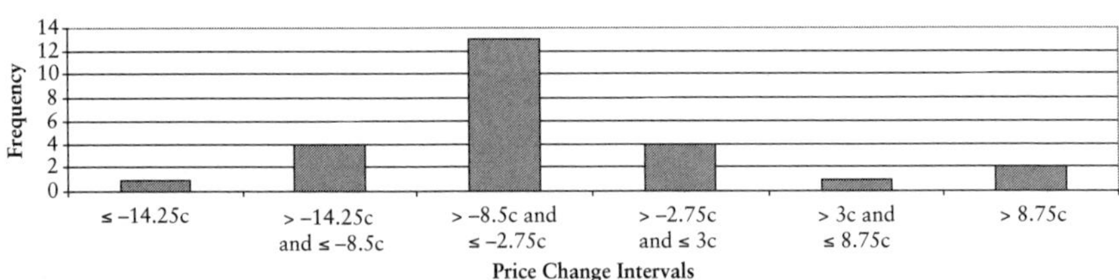

EXHIBIT 17.3 Histogram of the Frequency Distribution for the July Wheat–December Wheat Price Changes, 1979–2003
Source: Premia Capital Management, LLC.

manager might conclude that this trade can continue to exist because of the unpleasant tail risk that must be assumed when putting on this trade.

Petroleum Complex Example

Are there any persistent price tendencies that can be linked to structural aspects of the petroleum market? After examining the activity of commercial participants in the petroleum futures markets, it appears that their hedging activity is bunched up within certain time frames. These same time frames also seem to have detectable price trends, reflecting this commercial hedging pressure.

Like other commodities, the consumption and production of petroleum products are concentrated during certain times of the year, as illustrated in Exhibit 17.4. This is the underlying reason why commercial hedging pressure also is highly concentrated during certain times of the year.

The predictable price trends that result from concentrated hedge pressure may be thought of as a type of premium the commercial market participants are willing to pay. That commercial participants will engage in hedging during predictable time frames and thus will pay a premium to do so may be compared to individuals willing to pay higher hotel costs to visit popular locations during high season. They are paying for this timing convenience.

Corn Example

Corn provides another example of a persistent price pressure effect. The futures prices of some commodity contracts, including corn, sometimes

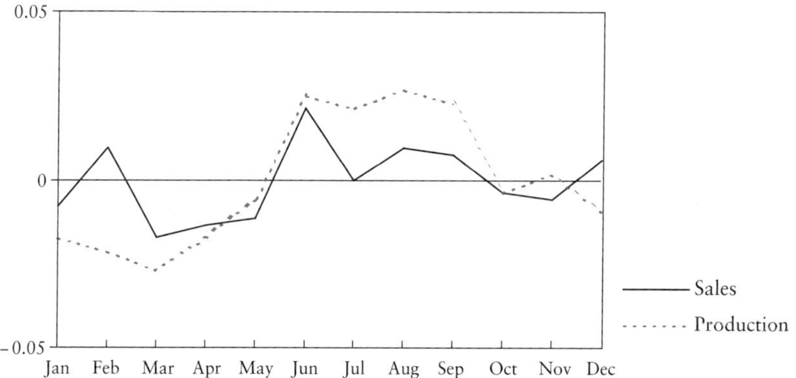

EXHIBIT 17.4 Petroleum Seasonal Sales and Production Patterns
Source: Jeffrey Miron, *The Economics of Seasonal Cycles* (Cambridge, MA: MIT Press, 1996), p. 118.
Note: The seasonal coefficient plotted for each month is the average percentage difference for that month from a logarithmic time trend.

embed a fear premium due to upcoming, meaningful weather events. According to a Refco commentary: "The grain markets will always assume the worst when it comes to real or perceived threats to the food supply."[2] As a result, coming into the U.S. growing season, grain futures prices seem to systematically have a premium added into the fair value price of the contract. The fact that this premium can be easily washed out if no adverse weather occurs is well known by the trade. A Salomon Smith Barney commentary notes: "The bottom line is: any threat of ridging this summer will spur concerns of yield penalties. That means the market is likely to keep some 'weather premium' built into the price of key markets. The higher the markets go near term, the more risk there will be to the downside if and when good rains fall."[3] By the end of July, the weather conditions that are critical for corn yield prospects will have already occurred. At that point, if weather conditions have not been adverse, the weather premium in corn futures prices will no longer be needed. According to the Pool Commodity Trading Service: "In any weather market there remains the potential for a shift in weather forecasts to immediately shift trends, but it appears as though grains are headed for further losses before the end of the week. With 75% of the corn silking, the market can begin to get comfortable taking some weather premium out."[4] Again, this example shows that the commercial trade can be well aware of a commodity futures price reflecting a biased estimate of future valuation, and yet the effect still persisting.

TRADE CONSTRUCTION

Experience in commodity futures trading shows that a trader can have a correct commodity view, but how he or she constructs the trade to express the view can make a large difference in profitability.

Outright futures contracts, options, or spreads on futures contracts can be used to express a commodity view.

At times, futures spreads are more analytically tractable than trading outright. Some economic boundary constraint usually links related commodities, which can (but not always) limit the risk in position taking. Also, a trader hedges out a lot of first-order, exogenous risk by trading spreads. For example, with a heating oil versus crude oil futures spread, each leg of the trade is

[2]Refco, Daily Grain Commentary (May 2, 2000), Report, Chicago.
[3]Salomon Smith Barney, Daily Grain Commentary (May 2, 2000), Report, New York.
[4]Pool Commodity Training Service. Daily Market Commentary (July 29, 1999), Internal Report, Winnipeg, Manitoba.

equally affected by unpredictable OPEC shocks. What typically affects the spread instead is second-order risk factors such as timing differences in inventory changes among the two commodities. It is sometimes easier to make predictions regarding these second-order risk factors than the first-order ones.

PORTFOLIO CONSTRUCTION

Once an investor has discovered a set of trading strategies that are expected to have positive returns over time, the next step is to combine the trades into a portfolio of diversified strategies. The goal is to combine strategies that are uncorrelated with each other to end up with a dampened-risk portfolio.

Diversification

Exhibit 17.5 illustrates a commodity futures portfolio from June 2000, which combines hedge-pressure trades with weather-fear-premium trades. The figure shows the effect of incrementally adding unrelated trades on portfolio volatility.

Inadvertent Concentration Risk

A key concern for all types of leveraged investing is inadvertent concentration risk. In leveraged commodity futures investing, one must be careful

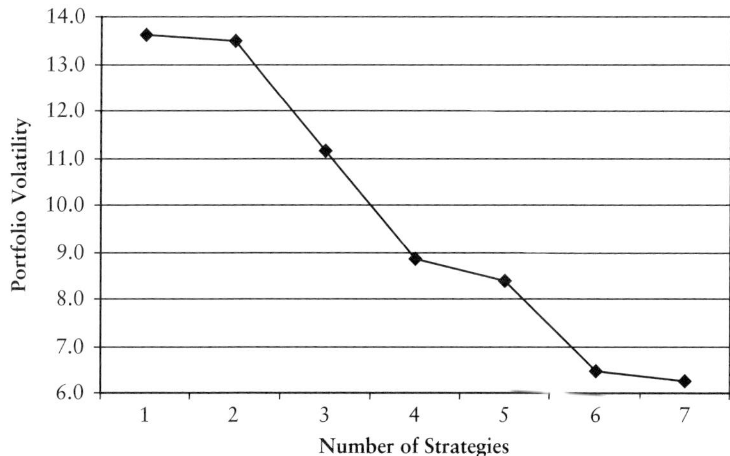

EXHIBIT 17.5 Annualized Portfolio Volatility versus Number of Commodity Investment Strategies, June 2000
Source: Hilary Till, "Passive Strategies in the Commodity Futures Markets," *Derivatives Quarterly* (2000), Exhibit 5. Copyright © Institutional Investor, Inc.

with commodity correlation properties. Seemingly unrelated commodity markets can become temporarily highly correlated. This becomes problematic if a commodity manager is designing a portfolio so that only a certain amount of risk is allocated per strategy. The portfolio manager may be inadvertently doubling up on risk if two strategies are unexpectedly correlated.

Exhibits 17.6 and 17.7 provide examples from the summer of 1999 that show how seemingly unrelated markets can temporarily become quite related.

Normally natural gas and corn prices are unrelated, as shown in Exhibit 17.6. But during July, they can become highly correlated. During a three-week period in July 1999, the correlation between natural gas and corn price changes was 0.85, as illustrated in Exhibit 17.7.

Both the July corn and natural gas futures contracts are heavily dependent on the outcome of weather in the U.S. Midwest. And in July 1999, the Midwest had blistering temperatures (which even led to some power outages). During that time, both corn and natural gas futures prices responded in nearly identical fashions to weather forecasts and realizations.

If a commodity portfolio manager had included both natural gas and corn futures trades in a portfolio during this time frame, then that investor would have inadvertently doubled up on risk.

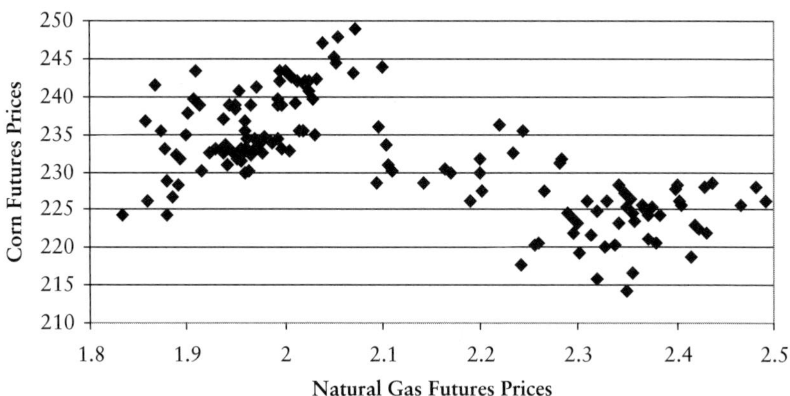

EXHIBIT 17.6 September Corn Futures Prices versus September Natural Gas Future Prices, November 30, 1998 to June 28, 1999
Source: Hilary Till, "Taking Full Advantage of the Statistical Properties of Commodity Investments," *Journal of Alternative Investments* (2001), Exhibit 3. Copyright © Institutional Investor, Inc.
Note: Using a sampling period of every three days, the correlation of the percent change in corn prices versus the percent change in natural gas prices is 0.12.

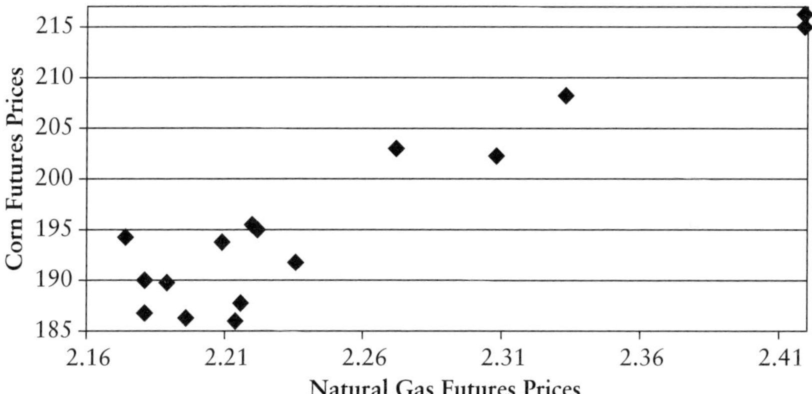

EXHIBIT 17.7 September Corn Futures Prices versus September Natural Gas Prices, June 29, 1999 to July 26, 1999
Source: Hilary Till, "Taking Full Advantage of the Statistical Properties of Commodity Investments," *Journal of Alternative Investments* (2000), Exhibit 4. Copyright © Institutional Investor, Inc.
Note: Using a sampling period of every three days, the correlation of the percent change in corn prices versus the percent change in natural gas prices is 0.85.

To avoid inadvertent correlations, it is not enough to measure historical correlations. Using the data in Exhibit 17.6, an investor would have concluded that corn and natural gas price changes are only weakly related. An investor needs, however, to have an economic understanding of why a trade works in order to best be able to appreciate whether an additional trade will act as a portfolio diversifier. In that way, the investor will avoid doubling up on the risks that Exhibit 17.7 illustrates.

RISK MANAGEMENT

The fourth step in designing a commodity futures trading program is risk management, because the portfolio manager needs to ensure that during both normal and eventful times, the program's losses do not exceed a client's comfort level.

Risk Measures

On a per-strategy basis, it is useful to examine each strategy's:

- Value-at-Risk (VaR) based on recent volatilities and correlations.
- Worst-case loss during normal times.

- Worst-case loss during well-defined eventful periods.
- Incremental contribution to portfolio value at risk.
- Incremental contribution to worst-case portfolio event risk.

The last two measures give an indication if the strategy is a risk reducer or risk enhancer. On a portfolio-wide basis, it is useful to examine the portfolio's:

- VaR at risk based on recent volatilities and correlations.
- Worst-case loss during normal times.
- Worst-case loss during well-defined eventful periods.

Each measure should be compared to some limit, which has been determined based on the design of the futures product. So, for example, if clients expect the program to lose no more than, say, 7% from peak-to-trough, then the three portfolio measures should be constrained to not exceed 7%. If the product should not perform too poorly during, say, financial shocks, then the worst-case loss during well-defined eventful periods should be constrained to a relatively small number. If that worst-case loss exceeds the limit, then the manager can devise macroportfolio hedges accordingly, as will be discussed later.

For the purposes of extraordinary stress testing, we would recommend examining how a portfolio would have performed during the four eventful periods listed in Exhibit 17.8.

A commodity portfolio that would do poorly during these time frames may be unacceptable to clients who are investing in a nontraditional investment for diversification benefits. Therefore, in addition to examining a portfolio's risk based on recent fluctuations using value at risk measures, a manager also should examine how the portfolio would have performed during the eventful times listed in Exhibit 17.8.

Exhibits 17.9 and 17.10 provide examples of the recommended risk measures for a particular commodity futures portfolio. Note, for example, the properties of the soybean crush spread. It is a portfolio event-risk reducer, but it also adds to the volatility of the portfolio. An incremental

EXHIBIT 17.8 Meaningful Eventful Periods

October 1987 stock market crash
1990 Gulf War
Fall 1998 bond market debacle
Aftermath of 9/11/01 terrorist attacks

EXHIBIT 17.9 Strategy-Level Risk Measures

Strategy	Value-at-Risk	Worst-Case Loss during Normal Times	Worst-Case Loss during Eventful Period
Deferred reverse soybean crush spread	2.78%	−1.09%	−1.42%
Long-deferred natural gas outright	0.66%	−0.18%	−0.39%
Short-deferred wheat spread	0.56%	−0.80%	−0.19%
Long-deferred gasoline outright	2.16%	−0.94%	−0.95%
Long-deferred gasoline vs. heating oil spread	2.15%	−1.04%	−2.22%
Long-deferred hog spread	0.90%	−1.21%	−0.65%
Portfolio	3.01%	−2.05%	−2.90%

Source: Hilary Till, "Risk Management Lessons in Leveraged Commodity Futures Trading," *Commodities Now* (September 2002).

EXHIBIT 17.10 Portfolio-Effect Risk Measures

Strategy	Incremental Contribution to Portfolio Value at Risk[a]	Incremental Contribution to Worst-Case Portfolio Event Risk[a]
Deferred reverse soybean crush spread	0.08%	−0.24%
Long-deferred natural gas outright	0.17%	0.19%
Short-deferred wheat spread	0.04%	0.02%
Long-deferred gasoline outright	0.33%	0.81%
Long-deferred gasoline vs. heating oil spread	0.93%	2.04%
Long-deferred hog spread	0.07%	−0.19%

Source: Hilary Till, "Risk Management Lessons in Leveraged Commodity Futures Trading," *Commodities Now* (September 2002).
[a]A positive contribution means that the strategy adds to risk while a negative contribution means the strategy reduces risk.

contribution to risk measure based solely on recent volatilities and correlations does not give complete enough information about whether a trade is a risk reducer or risk enhancer.

Macroportfolio Hedging

Understanding a portfolio's exposure to certain financial or economic shocks can help in designing macroportfolio hedges that would limit exposure to these events. For example, a commodity portfolio from the summer of 2002 consisted of these positions: outright long wheat, a long gasoline calendar spread, and short outright silver. When carrying out an event-risk analysis on the portfolio, one finds that the worst-case scenario was a 9/11 scenario. This is because the portfolio was long economically sensitive commodities and short an instrument that does well during time of flights to quality. Normally, though, these positions are unrelated to each other. Given that the scenario that would most negatively impact the portfolio was a sharp shock to business confidence, one candidate for macroportfolio insurance was short-term gasoline puts to hedge against this scenario.

LEVERAGE LEVEL

Another consideration in designing a commodity futures program is how much leverage to use. Futures trading requires a relatively small amount of margin. Trade-sizing is mainly a matter of how much risk one wants to assume. An investor is not very constrained by the amount of initial capital committed to trading.

What leverage level is chosen for a program is a product design issue. The manager needs to determine how the program will be marketed and what the client's expectations will be.

According to *Barclay Managed Funds Report* for 2001, a number of top *commodity trading advisors* (CTAs) have had losses in excess of –40 percent, which have been acceptable to their clients since these investment programs sometimes produce 100+ percent annual returns. Investors know up front the sort of swings in profits and losses to expect from such managers.[5]

Choosing the leverage level for a futures program is a crucial issue because it appears that the edge that successful futures traders are able to

[5]Barclay, *Barclay Managed Funds Report* (2001), p. 7.

EXHIBIT 17.11 Levered and Delevered Returns by Hedge Fund Strategy, 1997 to 2001

Style	Average Levered Return (%)[a]	Average Delevered Return (%)[a]
Short Biased	13.7	9.3
Global Macro	16.8	8.9
Emerging Markets	16.9	8.8
Event Driven	14.7	8.3
Merger Arbitrage	14.7	7.0
Long/Short Equity	14.0	6.3
Fixed Income	9.6	4.8
Convertible Arbitrage	10.6	4.2
Managed Futures	10.5	4.2
Distressed Securities	n/a	n/a

Source: Altvest, CSFB/Tremont, EACM, HFR, *Institutional Investor* (June 2002), and CMRA, in Leslie Rahl, "Hedge Fund Transparency: Unraveling the Complex and Controversial Debate," RiskInvest 2002, Boston, December 10, 2002, Slide 52.
[a]Leverage analysis was done for funds with five-year historical leverage and performance data.

exploit is small. Only with leverage do their returns become attractive. Exhibit 17.11 shows how the returns to futures programs, here labeled "managed futures," become competitive only after applying the most amount of leverage of any hedge fund strategy.

In Patel, Bruce Cleland of Campbell and Company, a pioneer of futures investing, discusses how essential leverage is to his firm's success:

> *"Campbell's long-term average rate of return compounded over 31 years is over 17.6 percent net [of fees]. No market-place is going to be so inefficient as to allow any kind of systematic strategy to prevail over that period of time, to that extent. 'Our true edge is actually only around 4 percent per year, but through leverage of between 4-1 and 5-1 you are able to get a much more attractive return,' Cleland says."*[6]

This quote from the president of Campbell is very instructive for neophyte futures traders who must determine how much leverage to use in delivering their clients an attractive set of returns.

---

[6]Navroz Patel "Its All in the Technique," *Risk*, (2002, July) no. 49.

UNIQUE CONTRIBUTION TO THE INVESTOR'S OVERALL PORTFOLIO

A final consideration in creating a futures trading program is to understand how the program will fit into an investor's overall portfolio. For investors to be interested in a new investment, that investment must have a unique return stream: one that is not already obtained through their other investments. More formally, the new investment must be a diversifier, either during normal times or eventful times.

It is up to investors to determine how a new investment should fit into their portfolios. A futures trading program may be evaluated on how well it diversifies an equity portfolio. Or it may be judged based on how well it diversifies a basket of veteran CTAs. Finally, a new futures trading program may be evaluated on how well it improves a fund of hedge fund's risk-adjusted returns. Examples of each kind of evaluation follow.

Equity Diversification Example

One potential commodity futures investment is based on the Goldman Sachs Commodity Index (GSCI). One way to evaluate its potential benefits for an international equity portfolio is to use a portfolio optimizer to create the portfolio's efficient frontier both with and without an investment in the GSCI. Exhibit 17.12 from Satyanarayan and Varangis[7] illustrates this approach. The efficient frontier with commodity assets lies everywhere higher than the portfolio without commodity assets, implying that for the same levels of return (risk), the portfolio with commodity assets provides lesser (higher) risk (return). This would be regarded as attractive provided that the historical returns, volatilities, and correlations used in the optimizer are expected to be representative of future results.

CTA Diversification Example

A futures program that invests solely in commodities has a natural advantage in claiming diversification benefits for a portfolio of CTAs. As Exhibit 17.13 illustrates, an index of managed futures returns is most strongly related to investment strategies focused on currencies, interest rates, and stocks. Commodities are in fourth place.

---

[7]Sudhakar Satyanarayan and Panos Varangis, An Efficient Frontier for International Portfolios with Commodity Assets, Policy Research Working Paper 1266, The World Bank, March 1994.

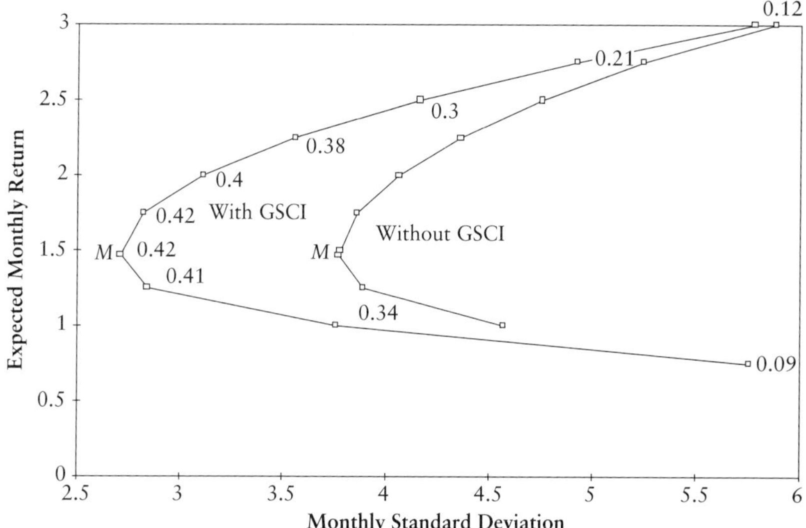

EXHIBIT 17.12 Optimal International Portfolios with and without Commodity Assets

Source: Sudhakar Satyanarayan and Panos Varangis, An Efficient Frontier for International Portfolios with Commodity Assets, *Policy Research Working Paper* 1266, The World Bank, March 1994, p. 19.

Note: The numbers on the mean-standard deviation frontier refer to the percentage of the portfolio invested in commodity assets. M = minimum-risk portfolio.

EXHIBIT 17.13 Regression of Managed Futures Returns on Passive Indexes and Economic Variables, 1996 to 2000

	Coefficient	Standard Error	*t*-Statistic
Intercept	0.00	0.00	0.01
S&P 500	0.00	0.07	0.05
Lehman U.S.	0.29	0.39	0.76
Change in credit spread	0.00	0.01	0.30
Change in term spread	0.00	0.00	0.18
MFSB/interest rates	1.27	0.24	5.24
MFSB/currency	1.37	0.25	5.48
MFSB/physical commodities	0.27	0.15	1.79
MFSB/stock Indexes	0.36	0.11	3.17
R-squared	0.70		

Source: Center for International Securities and Derivatives Markets (CISDM), 2nd Annual Chicago Research Conference, May 22, 2002. Slide 48.

Note: The Managed Futures Securities Based (MFSB) Indexes are designed to mimic the performance of CTAs who employ trend-following or countertrend strategies.

EXHIBIT 17.14 Example of How the Sharpe Ratio of CTA Indexes Changes with the Addition of a Particular Commodity Futures Program, September 1999 to March 2003

	Index Alone			With 10% GA[b] Component		
Index	CARR[a]	Vol %	Sharpe Ratio	CARR	Vol %	Sharpe Ratio
Stark Fund Index	6.80%	13.60%	0.50	7.80%	11.80%	0.66
Stark 300 CTA Index	8.70%	10.80%	0.80	09.40%	9.60%	0.98
Stark Diversified CTA	9.50%	11.60%	0.82	10.10%	10.30%	0.98

Source: "The Case for Commodities," *Global Advisors* (June 2003). Copyright © Daniel B. Stark & Company.
[a]Compounded annualized rate of return.
[b]Global Advisors Discretionary Program, a futures trading program.

One way of demonstrating that a commodity investment strategy is of benefit to a diversified portfolio of CTAs is to calculate how the Sharpe ratio (excess return divided by standard deviation) would change once the new investment is added to the portfolio. Exhibit 17.14 shows how the addition of a particular commodity manager to three diversified portfolios increases the Sharpe ratio of each portfolio. The three diversified portfolios are represented by CTA indexes provided by Daniel B. Stark & Co.

Exhibit 17.15 illustrates another way of confirming that a futures trading program would be a diversifier for an existing investment in a basket of futures traders. Exhibit 17.15 shows that the Stark Diversified CTA index alone has a Sharpe ratio of about 0.72. If 60 percent is allocated to the Stark index and 40 percent to a specific advisor's program, the Sharpe ratio rises to 1.0 even though the specific advisor's program alone has a Sharpe ratio of below 1.0.

Fund of Hedge Fund Diversification Example

Similarly, if the futures program is expected to be a diversifier for a fund of hedge funds portfolio, whether the Sharpe ratio of the enhanced portfolio improves as well must be verified. This is illustrated in Exhibit 17.16.

CONCLUSION

This chapter has outlined the considerations involved in creating a commodity futures trading program. Commodity managers need to be aware that trading strategies can exhibit periods of high correlation, which can

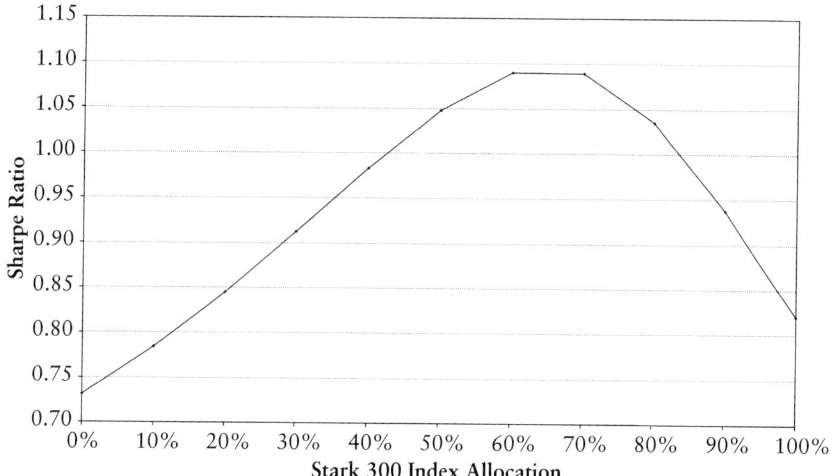

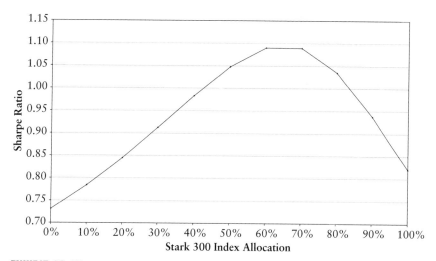

EXHIBIT 17.15 Efficient Portfolio GALP[a] + Stark Diversified CTA Index, September 1999 to March 2003
Source: "The Case for Commodities," *Global Advisors* (June 2003), Chart 1. Copyright © Daniel B. Stark & Company.
Note: The vertical axis is the Sharpe ratio. The horizontal axis is the amount allocated to the Stark Index; the balance is allocated to the GALP trading program.
[a]Global Advisors LP.

EXHIBIT 17.16 Example of How the Sharpe Ratio of a Fund of Hedge Funds Changes with the Addition of a Particular Commodity Futures Program, September 1999 to March 2003

	Index Alone			With 10% GA[a] Component		
Index	CARR[b]	Vol%	Sharpe Ratio	CARR	Vol%	Sharpe Ratio
Model Fund of Funds Portfolio[c]	7.80%	5.00%	1.56	8.50%	5.00%	1.7

Source: "The Case for Commodities," *Global Advisors* (June 2003).
[a]Global Advisors Discretionary Program, a futures trading program.
[b]Compounded annualized rate of return.
[c]The model fund of funds portfolio comprises Edhec Business School indexes in the following weights: 40% Long/Short Equity, 10% Convertible Arbitrage, 10% Global Macro, 10% Managed Futures, 5% Equity Market Neutral, 5% Fixed Income Arbitrage, 5% Distressed Securities, 5% Emerging Markets, 5% Merger Arbitrage, and 5% Event Driven.

lead to doubling risk. We showed that adding commodity futures to a portfolio can potentially reduce overall portfolio risk. We also showed that futures programs must employ leverage in order for their returns to be competitive. To provide diversification benefits to investors, commodity managers must produce return streams that are sufficiently unrelated to those of other manager strategies as well as to traditional investments.

CHAPTER 18

Sources of Alpha in Commodity Investing

Markus Mezger
Managing Partner
Tiberius Asset Management

Commodity futures are one of the oldest asset classes. Today, commodity futures represent opportunities for active management because of two reasons. First, as we show in this chapter, commodity markets are heterogeneous and cover a broad range of different returns. Therefore, the potential for alpha returns of an actively managed commodity portfolio is comparatively high. *Alpha* is defined as the uncorrelated excess return of an actively managed commodity portfolio to a commodity index, which serves as a benchmark. The return of an actively managed commodity portfolio can be split into a (1) beta component, which represents the benchmark correlated returns; and (2) an independent residual return, which consists of the alpha return and of a random component.[1]

Second, commodity futures as an asset class are predominantly represented by passive commodity index investments. The volume invested in long-only commodity index vehicles is estimated to have risen from $40 billion in 2002 to more than $120 billion at the beginning of 2007. However, commodity indexes suffer some serious shortcomings. The initial weights of the index constituents mostly depend on the monetary value of supply, demand, and liquidity. The yearly changes of these weights are often minor and cannot be considered to comprise changing relative performance trends. Furthermore the commodity indexes are restricted to the nearby contracts. As a consequence of the massive inflows into passive investments,

[1]See Richard C. Grinold and Ronald N. Kahn, *Active Portfolio Management* (New York: McGraw-Hill, 2000), p. 111.

especially the front months of the forward structure are often priced relatively unattractive in comparison to the longer dated contracts. And finally, commodity indexes are per definition fully invested. Since commodity prices are very cyclical by nature, severe drawdowns in a passive investment have to be expected.

This chapter is divided into two parts. The first section describes the return composition and the risk return profile of a broad spectrum of commodity futures. The second section contains three different starting points for alpha generation: commodity weighting, contract selection, and market timing. It is the aim of this chapter to show that active management is capable to add value on all of these three decision levels.

COMMODITY FUTURES AS AN ASSET CLASS

Due to its long history, there has been done a lot of empirical research on the return characteristics of commodity futures.[2] However, with regard to the boom in bonds and equities between 1982 and 2000, only a few practitioners promoted the attractive risk-return profile of the asset class at the beginning of this century.[3] From 2005 onward, the academic world has rediscovered commodities as an asset class. Four papers clearly stand out.

Gorton and Rouwenhorst showed that an equally weighted portfolio of 36 commodity futures offered a similar total return[4] and a similar Sharpe ratio in comparison to the U.S. stock market in the period between 1959 and 2004. Furthermore, they found that, due to different behavior over the business cycle, commodity futures returns are negatively correlated with equity and bond returns and therefore suited as a risk diversifier.[5]

---

[2]See, for example, Katherine Dusak, "Futures Trading and Investor Returns. An Investigation of Commodity Market Risk Premiums," *Journal of Political Economy* 81, no. 6 (1973), pp. 1387–1406; Zvi Body and Viktor I. Rosansky, "Risk and Return in Commodity Futures," *Financial Analysts Journal* 36, no. 3 (1980), pp. 27–39; and Robert W. Kolb, "Is Normal Backwardation Normal?" *Journal of Futures Markets* 12, no. 1 (1992), pp. 75–91.

[3]See, for example, Robert J. Greer, "The Nature of Commodity Index Returns," *Journal of Alternative Investments* 3, no. 1 (2000), pp. 45–52; and Hilary Till, "Two Types of Systematic Returns Available in the Commodity Futures Markets," *Commodities Now* (September 2000), pp. 1–5.

[4]The total return of commodity futures includes the spot return, the roll return, which is positive when the futures price is below the spot price (backwardation), and the yield earned on the collateral of futures investment.

[5]Gary B. Gorton and K. Geert Rouwenhorst, "Facts and Fantasies about Commodity Futures," *Financial Analysts Journal* 62, no. 2 (2006), pp. 47–68.

Contrary to Gorton and Rouwenhorst, Erb and Harvey presented a portfolio of 12 commodity futures, which on average did not exhibit a positive excess return and risk premium from 1982 to 2004. Erb and Harvey pointed out that the returns of commodity futures vary strongly across the different commodity sectors and that the correlation of their returns is very low.[6] They show that the different roll returns are the main driver for excess returns and that the term structure is a strong explanatory for the return characteristics of the individual commodities.

Kat and Oomen came to similar conclusions. Across a sample of 27 commodities they found that, "with the notable exception of energy, commodity futures do not appear to generate a consistent risk premium" between 1987 and 2005.[7] Like Erb and Harvey, they detected the roll returns to be the primary driver for futures returns. They suggest that the shape of the forward curve is one important determinant of futures returns. Kat and Oomen worked out that especially commodity spot returns are positively linked with unexpected inflation and are therefore uncorrelated with the returns of stocks and bonds.[8]

Markert analyzed a sample of 28 commodity futures from 1986 to 2003.[9] She showed that significant positive excess returns are concentrated in the energy and the livestock sector, whereas especially among the soft commodities coffee and cocoa a negative risk premium occurred. Furthermore, she came to the result that the a priori convenience yields, which are defined as the relation between the deferred contracts against the nearby contract less the risk free rate, are significantly positive for those commodities, offering the strongest futures returns. Nevertheless Markert concluded that "in line with the market efficiency hypothesis, there is no evidence for a relationship between convenience yields and successive futures returns."[10]

The empirical studies thus far mentioned have clearly elaborated the extraordinary heterogeneity of commodity futures, but suffer from some

---

[6]Claude B. Erb and Campbell R. Harvey, "The Strategic and Tactical Value of Commodity Futures," *Financial Analysts Journal* 62, no. 2 (2006), pp. 69–97.

[7]Harry M. Kat and Roel C. A. Oomen, "What Every Investor should know about Commodities Part I: Univariate Return Analysis," *Journal of Investment Management* 5, no. 1 (2007), pp. 1–25.

[8]Harry M. Kat and Roel C. A. Oomen, "What Every Investor Should Know About Commodities, Part II: Multivariate Return Analysis," *Journal of Investment Management* 5, no. 3 (2007), pp. 1–25.

[9]Viola Markert, Commodities as Assets and Consumption Goods: Implications for the Valuation of Commodity Futures, Ph.D. Thesis, University of St. Gallen, May 2005.

[10]Markert, Commodities as Assets and Consumption Goods: Implications for the Valuation of Commodity Futures.

common shortcomings. First, it should be kept in mind that the period from 1980 to 2004 is not representative for the average long-term spot returns of commodities. As will be shown in the subsection on commodity market timing, the great commodity bull markets were before and after this time span.

Second, some of the empirical studies cannot be considered to capture the asset class entirely. Except for the Gorton and Rouwenhorst study, the studies cited are missing the base metals, which were—leaving energy aside—the star performer in the commercial commodity futures indexes. Base metals have had superior spot and roll returns over the last 15 years.[11] With regard to these facts, one has to reject the argumentation of Erb and Harvey and Kat and Oomen that commodity futures on average offer no positive risk premium. Even if we adjust for the "hindsight bias" of the commercial indexes—GSCI, Dow Jones AIG Commodity Index (DJAIG), Rogers International Index (RICI), and Deutsche Bank Liquid Commodity Index (DBLCI)[12]—the equally weighted Gorton and Rouwenhorst portfolio returned significantly more than the risk-free rate. On the other hand, the Gorton and Rouwenhorst study does not split the total return series per commodity into their components spot yield, roll yield, and collateral yield. The performance results are calculated over the lifetime of the singular commodity contracts, which means that an annualized total return of 12.16% of the COMEX copper contract (introduced in 1959) compares to an annualized total return of 1.7% from the NYMEX natural gas contract (introduced in 1990).

RETURN STATISTICS OF COMMODITY FUTURES

We use daily price data prepared by the Commodity Research Bureau (CRB). For the LME contracts we refer to data distributed by Datastream and Bloomberg. Since the notice and delivery period begins well in advance of the last trading day, at least in the case of the COMEX-traded metals and

[11]Base metals are traded as forwards on the London Metal Exchange (LME) and refer to a fixed time to maturity instead of a fixed maturity date. Liquid contracts are the cash and three-month forward contract for all six base metals traded on the LME. In the case of copper, aluminum, nickel, and zinc, there are liquid 15 and 27 month contracts as well. Price history goes back at least to the year 1989; nickel, lead, and zinc prices are available at least from 1979 onward. LME Base Metals are included in the GSCI and DJAIG since January 1991. Spot and roll returns can be calculated with buying the three-month forward and rolling the position after three months, when the bought three-month forward becomes the cash contract.

[12]For a comparison of commodity indexes see Chapter 7.

most agricultural commodities, we roll every futures position approximately 10 days before the first notice day/last trading day (depending on which comes first). For contracts where all calendar months are traded (we roll 12 times per year), the roll frequency for the precious metals and agricultural commodities is determined by the existing liquid contract months per year (as a rule of thumb: four to six).[13] The returns are calculated as geometrical averages of daily returns. The roll return equals the arithmetical difference between excess and spot return.

Return Composition

Exhibit 18.1 proves that commodities indeed cannot be treated as a homogenous asset class. Over all analyzed time frames the level and the composition of returns differ wildly among and within the different commodity groups. Those with the longest history—grains and soft commodities—mostly delivered negative roll and excess returns, which have been more pronounced in the last 20 years. However, the soybean complex managed to generate positive roll and excess returns on average at the same time when the other grains suffered from huge roll losses. The livestock sector stands out with significantly positive roll and excess returns for both periods. With comparatively low volatility, cattle futures especially offered a very similar Sharpe ratio as the U.S. stock market. From the second half of the 1980s the commodity futures world was clearly dominated by the energy and base metals markets. Both sectors enjoyed high roll yields, which led to mostly double digit excess returns per annum. Even after the huge bull run of energy since 2003 the spot yields make up the smaller part of the impressive excess returns. The exception is natural gas, yielding the highest spot returns within the energy group since 2000. However, these gains were absorbed by negative roll returns of more than 30% per annum.

The energy and livestock markets were the only ones with time in backwardation in excess of 50%. This finding is especially pronounced for the one year deferred contracts of WTI crude oil and NYMEX gasoline. In times of backwardation the average annualized premium of the nearby over the one-year deferred contract is lower than the premium between first and second nearby; that is, the term structure curve is steeper for the front months. Again natural gas stands out. The time in backwardation (nearby to second nearby) was only 24%, but at a time when the annualized

[13]The starting point for the excess returns, the roll date, defined in days before the last trading day and contract months can be taken from Exhibit A18.1 in this chapter's appendix.

EXHIBIT 18.1 Return Statistics for Selected Commodity Futures until December 2006

				Lifetime[a] Backwardation (BW) Nearby (NB)					1970–2006			1992–2006		
				1. NB/2. NB		1 Year								
	Commodity	Exchange	Ticker	Start	Avg BW	Days BW (%)	Avg BW	Days BW (%)	Volatility	Spot	Roll	Excess	Spot	Roll	Excess
Energy	Brent	IPE	LCO	1989	20.6%	56.1%	12.0%	49.6%	33.4%				8.4%	5.5%	13.8%
	Crude oil WTI	NYMEX	CL	1983	22.8%	57.3%	11.9%	67.5%	33.7%				7.8%	1.3%	9.1%
	Gasoline	NYMEX	RB/HU	1984	36.3%	58.1%	12.4%	75.3%	34.3%				7.1%	5.2%	12.2%
	Natural gas	NYMEX	NG	1990	57.6%	24.0%	13.5%	47.6%	49.8%				11.0%	−21.4%	−10.4%
	Heating oil	NYMEX	HO	1978	37.5%	35.4%	10.7%	58.2%	32.8%				8.1%	−0.4%	7.8%
	Gas oil	IPE	LGO	1986	27.2%	46.5%	12.3%	54.7%	33.2%				8.0%	2.9%	10.9%
Base Metals	Aluminum	LME	MAL	1980	7.1%	18.3%	2.8%	42.8%	20.6%				6.3%	−6.1%	0.3%
	Nickel	LME	MNI	1979	11.7%	46.0%	9.0%	72.8%	43.9%				11.0%	0.6%	11.6%
	Copper	COMEX	HG	1959	19.8%	44.1%	11.8%	47.4%	24.7%	3.8%	0.4%	4.2%	7.7%	1.2%	8.8%
	Copper	LME	MCU	1991	12.7%	36.7%	10.6%	37.5%	21.8%				7.4%	3.3%	10.7%
	Lead	LME	MPB	1979	14.0%	33.3%	9.0%	36.9%	25.0%				8.3%	−4.2%	4.1%
	Zinc	LME	MZN	1988	7.7%	12.4%	5.1%	26.8%	21.5%				9.0%	−5.7%	3.3%
	Tin	LME	MSN	1989	6.5%	32.9%	3.6%	46.3%	18.5%				5.1%	−2.0%	3.1%
Precious Metals	Gold	COMEX	GC	1974	5.1%	0.2%			19.2%				4.0%	−3.7%	0.4%
	Silver	COMEX	SI	1963	4.6%	0.8%	1.3%	0.9%	27.1%	5.3%	−7.3%	−2.0%	8.2%	−4.4%	3.8%
	Palladium	NYMEX	PA	1977	6.0%	31.8%	3.0%	17.5%	31.6%				9.8%	0.3%	10.1%
	Platinum	NYMEX	PL	1968	6.4%	28.6%	7.2%	14.2%	26.4%	5.3%	−3.2%	2.0%	8.3%	1.7%	10.0%
Livestock	Lean hogs	CME	LH	1966	39.8%	52.2%	14.0%	64.0%	23.0%	1.3%	6.1%	7.4%	1.1%	−3.5%	−2.4%
	Feeder cattle	CME	FC	1971	14.4%	61.2%			15.2%				1.6%	4.6%	6.2%
	Live cattle	CME	LC	1964	20.7%	53.8%	5.1%	46.1%	16.0%	3.1%	2.3%	5.5%	1.6%	1.6%	3.3%
	Pork bellies	CME	PB	1961	20.2%	55.1%	11.9%	42.6%	31.7%	1.9%	−5.9%	−4.0%	6.5%	−1.0%	5.5%

Grains	Corn	CBOT	C	1959	19.6%	20.2%	8.1%	25.1%	19.0%	3.2%	−8.2%	−4.9%	3.0%	−11.9%	−8.9%
	Wheat	CBOT	W	1959	25.5%	26.1%	7.0%	37.1%	21.7%	3.4%	−6.8%	−3.3%	1.5%	−10.1%	−8.5%
	Wheat	KCBOT	KW	1970	18.8%	38.6%	8.2%	39.1%	21.2%				1.7%	−1.9%	−0.2%
	Soybeans	CBOT	S	1959	22.1%	27.7%	9.0%	35.4%	21.4%	2.8%	−2.9%	−0.1%	1.5%	0.4%	2.0%
	Soybean oil	CBOT	BO	1959	26.1%	34.0%	9.6%	35.3%	25.0%	3.4%	0.2%	3.6%	3.1%	−5.3%	−2.2%
	Soybean meal	CBOT	SM	1959	23.0%	41.3%	10.9%	45.7%	25.0%	2.6%	−0.6%	2.0%	0.9%	6.1%	6.9%
	Oats	CBOT	O	1959	23.6%	33.3%	19.1%	21.1%	26.0%	4.0%	−8.5%	−4.5%	4.9%	−5.9%	−1.1%
	Rice	CBOT	RR	1986	29.9%	15.5%	17.2%	13.1%	23.4%				1.5%	−11.9%	−10.3%
Softs	Orange, juice	NYBOT	OJ	1967	20.6%	36.8%	8.7%	36.7%	28.1%	4.0%	−3.7%	0.3%	1.5%	−8.9%	−7.3%
	Coffee, arabica	NYBOT	KC	1972	23.7%	34.3%	12.2%	38.8%	34.7%				3.1%	−8.1%	−4.9%
	Coffee, robusta	LIFFE	LKD	1991	27.5%	31.3%	7.5%	27.0%	32.8%				3.6%	−1.5%	2.0%
	Sugar No. 11	NYBOT	SB	1961	17.4%	38.3%	12.4%	46.3%	43.8%	3.8%	−5.4%	−1.6%	2.2%	1.9%	4.1%
	White Sugar	LIFFE	LSU	1990	21.1%	67.3%	8.4%	71.8%	19.7%				1.6%	9.2%	10.8%
	Cocoa	NYBOT	CC	1959	21.8%	25.1%	14.2%	22.6%	28.4%	2.0%	−2.5%	−0.5%	1.8%	−9.6%	−7.8%
	Cotton	NYBOT	CT	1959	20.8%	29.1%	10.1%	45.9%	20.3%	2.2%	−2.7%	−0.6%	−0.3%	−8.2%	−8.5%
Exotics	Lumber	CME	LB	1969	25.2%	38.6%	9.9%	22.1%	26.2%	3.2%	−6.8%	−3.6%	1.8%	−5.5%	−3.7%
	Barley	WCE	AB	1989	16.3%	21.4%	11.9%	39.1%	17.1%				5.0%	−3.7%	1.3%
	Canola	WCE	RS	1974	32.5%	24.3%	7.9%	51.4%	20.2%				2.5%	−3.0%	−0.5%
	Wool	SFE	YGS	1995	13.4%	29.7%	5.9%	21.8%	18.3%						

Source: Exhibit created from data obtained from the Commodity Research Bureau.
[a]Term structure for LME metals available since 1997.

premium of the nearby averaged an astonishing 57.6%. A steeper backwardation of the front months in comparison to the one year deferred contract was also observable for all agricultural commodities. This emphasizes the strong seasonal pricing influences in this sector.

An annualized negative roll yield of more than 20% in the case of natural gas clearly demonstrates that, unlike financial futures, arbitrage does not work between commodity spot and futures prices. In the case of a contango above financing and storage costs, theory suggests to sell the future and to buy the physical commodity. However, this opportunity can be assessed only by the owners of suitable underground caverns, where natural gas can be stored. The availability of storage capacity for financial investors is limited nearly in all commodity sectors with the exception of metals. In the same way a backwardated commodity contract could not be arbitraged, because short selling spot and buying the long-dated futures requires liquid leasing markets. This is given only for the gold and silver market. Both metals are held as financial and monetary assets and therefore a large pool of above-ground stocks exists. In contrast to the erratic nature of the lease rates of the more "industrialized" precious metals platinum, palladium, and silver, the gold lease rate is depressed by central bank lending (the one year lease rate yields have remained below an annualized 0.5% for 18 months now). The key to a backwardated gold market is an abrupt attitude change of central banks. Despite the negative roll yields of a future position, holding the physical commodity yielded lower returns than the gold future, because contrary to the latter, no collateral yield could be earned.[14]

Theory of Backwardation

The absence of arbitrage is a technical precondition for backwardated commodity markets. But what are the economic reasons behind the high roll yields of the energy, base metals, and livestock sector? The oldest explanation is the Theory of Normal Backwardation by Lord Keynes.[15] According to his theory, producers of nonstorable or perishable commodities feel much stronger hedging pressures than the consumer of these commodities.

---

[14]Due to the collateral yield the total return of the gold future was about 1.5% higher than the return of physical gold. See Christoph Eibl and Markus Mezger, "The Precious Commodity," *The Alchemist* (April 2005).

[15]John Maynard Keynes, *A Treatise on Money*, vol. 2 (London, 1930), pp. 127–129; and John R. Hicks, *Value and Capital: An Inquiry into Some Fundamental Principles of Economic Theory*, 2nd ed. (Oxford: Oxford University Press, 1946), pp. 135–139.

Speculators are willing to step into these markets if there is a positive premium for alleviating the hedgers of their risk. There has been a lot of empirical research to test normal backwardation in commodity markets. It seems that the markets for livestock are, in respect to the time in backwardation and future price appreciation, most commonly subject to normal backwardation.[16] The negative roll returns of pork bellies over the longer term fits into this concept, since the underlying of the future can be stored frozen, whereas the contract specifications of lean hogs, feeder cattle, and live cattle refer to living animals, where the pressures to market the "commodity" in a defined time window and at a given weight are felt much more strongly.

Hedging pressures can hardly be an explanation for backwardation when a net short position of producers is empirical not observable. The Commitments of Traders data for the COMEX copper contract reveal no consistent commercial net short position since 2005, although long-only investors earned substantial roll yields and excess returns. This explanatory gap has been filled by the Theory of Storage and the concept of convenience yield developed by Working, Telser, and Brennan.[17] The convenience yield captures a liquidity premium for immediately available consumer stocks. Especially the commodities processed in industry applications exhibit a relatively inelastic demand. In case of supply disruptions and low available stock, consumers are bidding up spot prices far above future levels until the excess demand is crowded out. Indeed there is a strong link between stock levels and term structure for a wide variety of commodities. We will investigate this question in more detail in the section on contract selection models.

Both theories cannot account entirely for the high roll yields in the energy sector. There is some evidence that the irrational price skepticism of oil producers and analysts kept the crude oil markets in backwardation from 2002 to 2005.[18]

[16]See Thomas Benedix, Cross-Examining Backwardation. An Investigation into the Term Structure of Commodity Futures, Master Thesis of Economics of the University Ulm, August 2005, pp. 31–39 and 78–89.

[17]Holbrook Working, "The Theory of Price of Storage," *American Economic Review* 39, no. 6 (1949), pp. 1254–1262; Lester G. Telser, "Futures Trading and the Storage of Cotton and Wheat," *Journal of Political Economy* 66, no. 3 (1958), pp. 233–255; and Michael J. Brennan, "The Supply of Storage," *American Economic Review* 48, no. 1 (1958), pp. 50–72.

[18]Consequently, the backwardation in the WTI crude oil contract disappeared exactly at the time, when spot price targets of 100 US-Dollar per barrel crude oil spread among the investment community.

ALPHA STRATEGIES IN COMMODITY MARKETS

Commodity Selection Models

Commodity futures offer a variety of starting points for commodity selection strategies ranging from the exploitation of hedging pressures to weather fear premia.[19] However, in this section we will focus on momentum strategies, which are often implied by Commodity Trading Advisors (CTA) and Hedge Funds, and on scarcity models, which use the shape of the forward curve as the main weighting factor.

Technical Strategies and Manager Selection Akey promoted an indirect alpha approach to the commodity futures markets. He argues that Commodity Trading Advisors (CTA) are best suited to exploit short-term, tactical price movements.[20] He created a benchmark of CTAs who trade exclusively in nonfinancial futures. From January 1991 until December 2004 the CTA portfolio gave an annual return of 15.9% with a standard deviation of 7.6%, whereas the passive index investments delivered annual returns between 3% and 10% with a standard deviation on average of 14%.[21] This finding is in line with our research. We constructed a multistrategy portfolio out of a sample of 30 CTAs. From January 2001 to December 2006, the portfolio had a total annualized return of 15.7% with a standard deviation of 8.4% (see Exhibit 18.2).

Miffre and Rallis elaborated that momentum strategies contributed to alpha in commodity markets.[22] Whereas contrarian strategies did not prove profitable, momentum strategies earned 9.38% a year at the same time when an equally weighted long-only portfolio lost 2.64% per annum. The performance results "indicate that the momentum strategies buy backwardated contracts with high volatility, sell contangoed contracts with high volatility and ignore contracts with low volatility."[23]

Scarcity Models Based on Backwardation A strong correlation between the time in backwardation and the annualized excess return is obvious in

---

[19]An overview is given by Hilary Till and Joseph Eagleeye, "Commodities: Active Strategies for Enhanced Return," Robert Greer (ed.), *The Handbook of Inflation Hedging Investments* (McGraw-Hill companies, 2006), pp. 127ff.

[20]Rian P. Akey, Commodities: A Case for Active Management, Cole Partners White Paper, May 2005.

[21]Akey, Commodities: A Case for Active Management.

[22]Joelle Miffre and Georgios Rallis, Momentum in Commodity Futures Markets, Cass Business School Working Paper, April 2006.

[23]Miffre and Rallis, Momentum in Commodity Futures Markets.

EXHIBIT 18.2 Return Statistics CTA Portfolio, January 2001 to December 2006

Year	Jan	Feb	Mar	Apr	May	June	July	Aug	Sep	Oct	Nov	Dec	Year
2001	−0.50%	0.84%	5.78%	−1.18%	−4.08%	9.52%	8.01%	−2.33%	0.31%	1.20%	2.74%	−1.21%	19.76%
2002	0.09%	0.30%	3.06%	−1.66%	4.69%	2.70%	2.93%	3.23%	−0.61%	0.19%	0.81%	−0.78%	15.77%
2003	1.90%	2.49%	−4.01%	−1.17%	3.62%	1.13%	3.37%	0.15%	0.89%	4.61%	−1.30%	2.09%	14.30%
2004	0.98%	4.70%	0.29%	1.38%	−0.25%	−1.19%	3.30%	−0.82%	2.51%	−0.12%	0.94%	−0.66%	11.45%
2005	−0.92%	2.52%	1.63%	−0.16%	1.10%	0.79%	1.76%	0.19%	2.52%	0.08%	1.37%	2.95%	14.65%
2006	5.62%	−0.04%	4.42%	4.45%	1.42%	−0.59%	−2.19%	−0.71%	0.33%	2.26%	1.85%	0.56%	18.48%

Source: Exhibit created from data obtained from Tiberius Asset Management.

Exhibit 18.2.[24] From an ex post perspective the trading rule "buy backwardated sell contangoed commodities" can easily be drawn. However, does the term structure of futures prices really contain predictive power for futures returns, therefore contradicting the theory of efficient markets?

Humphreys and Shimko developed a trading model where the investment weights depend on the degree of backwardation in energy futures markets.[25] They showed that from 1984 to 1994 an excess return of more than 20% per year could have been achieved. Gorton and Rouwenhorst divided all commodities in their sample into bimonthly rebalanced and equally weighted portfolios.[26] The high basis portfolio contained the commodities with above average backwardation between the nearby and second nearby contract leaving the low basis portfolio with the remaining commodities. On average, the high basis portfolio was able to outperform the low basis portfolio by a margin of approximately 10 percent per annum. Feldman and Till demonstrated a rising correlation between the percentage of days in backwardation and excess returns with a rising investment horizon for soybeans, corn, and wheat.[27]

Mezger and Eibl showed that a commodity portfolio based on the term structure would have significantly outperformed the major commodity indexes.[28] We elaborate on this approach further, providing evidence that the forward curve does indeed possess strong forecasting power for the future performance of the vast majority of commodities.

Using the term structure as a standardized selection parameter involves several practical difficulties. First, the time difference between the nearby and second nearby may vary considerably. For example, the time difference between nearby and second nearby of the NYBOT sugar contract amounts to five months in December but only to two months in January of any given year. Thus, the expected roll yield has to be annualized using two different time factors. Second, the structure is heavily influenced by the seasonality of spot prices. Agricultural prices especially, are seasonal because different

[24]The coherence between backwardation and excess return was emphasized first by Daniel J. Nash, "Long Term Investing in Commodities," *Global Pensions Quarterly* (January 2001).

[25]H. Brett Humphreys and David Shimko, Beating the JPMCI Energy Index, Working Paper, JP Morgan, August 1995.

[26]Gorton and Rouwenhorst, "Facts and Fantasies about Commodity Futures."

[27]Barry Feldman and Hilary Till, Separating the Wheat from the Chaff: Backwardation as the Long-Term Driver of Commodity Futures Performance; Evidence from Soy, Corn and Wheat Futures from 1950 to 2004, White Paper, Premia Capital and Prism Analytics, revised version, November 2006.

[28]Markus Mezger and Christoph Eibl, "Gewinne mit Rohstoffen, [Profits with commodity futures]," *Die Bank* 51, no. 7 (2006), pp. 20–26.

contract maturities may relate to different crop years.[29] Another typical example of seasonal price behavior is the natural gas contract traded on the NYMEX. Due to seasonal heating demand, underground stocks of natural gas tend to decline in the winter months. The forward prices of the latter, therefore, usually reflect a premium against the deferred spring months. Third, the limitation to the nearby contracts misses information about the shape and different roll yields in the latter part of the term structure. As will be shown in the section about contract selection, the front months can display a large contango at the same time when the long-dated contracts are in backwardation in relation to the immediately preceding contract months.

In order to meet these challenges, we constructed an indicator with the nearby contract as the starting point and the exactly one-year deferred contract as the termination point. The slope of a straight line between these two points reflects the average roll yield per month. As both contracts apply to the same calendar month, seasonal influences can be disregarded. The shape and convexity of the term structure can be measured with the differences between the real term structure and the straight line (see Exhibit 18.3). As will be shown in the section on contract maturity selection, physical

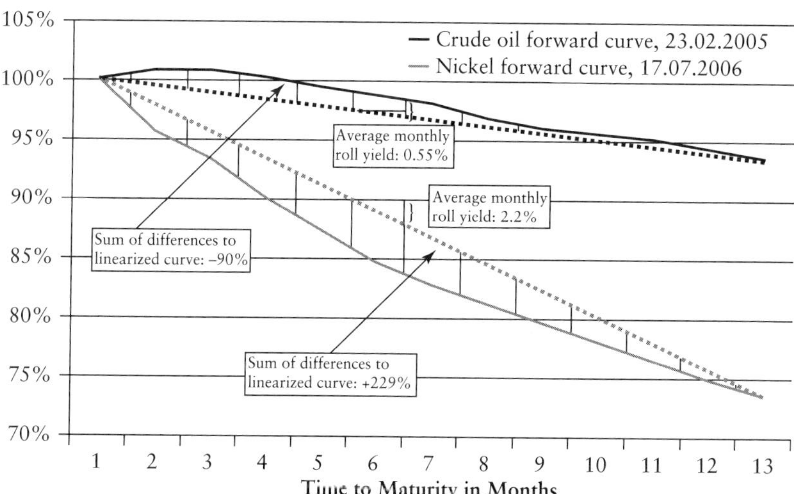

EXHIBIT 18.3 Selection Indicator Based on the Relative Term Structures
Source: Exhibit created from data obtained from Reuters.

[29]Eugene Fama and Kenneth French, "Commodity Futures Prices: Some Evidence on Forecast Power, Premiums, and the Theory of Storage," *Journal of Business* 60, no. 1 (1987), pp. 55–73.

tightness and low stock levels are positively correlated with the steepness of the term structure. An upward bias in the front months and a flattening out of the roll yields in the back months are a clear sign of drastic physical scarcity and below-average stock levels. Therefore, we interpret all prices beneath the linear approximation as positive and all prices above as negative values. The sum of the differences makes up our shape indicator of the term structure.

In Exhibit 18.3, the forward curves of crude oil and nickel are displayed. Both curves exhibit a negative slope with nickel being much more in backwardation (average monthly roll yield = 2.20%) than crude oil (average monthly roll yield = 0.55%). Considering this indicator in isolation, one would conclude to overweight nickel at the expense of crude oil, if both curves were relating to the same date. The shape indicator is pointing in the same direction. The nickel curve is convex, the crude oil curve is concave. The sum of differences between the linear and the real curve delivers a positive value of 229% for the 13 months in the nickel contract, whereas for crude oil a negative value is reached, as all data points lie above the linearized term structure.

We tested a combination of both signals in a long-only approach against the commodity indexes GSCI, DJAIG, RICI, and DBLCI (see Exhibit 18.4). We restricted our backtesting portfolios to the commodity contracts that are part of the corresponding index. The maximum over- and underweight was defined with plus/minus 10% for every commodity. Any commodity, where no term structure signal could be detected, was weighted neutral. If an underweight signal for a commodity could not be fully implemented because the index weight was too small, the portfolio weight of this commodity was set to zero and the portfolio weights of the remaining commodities were adjusted correspondingly, to obtain again 100% portfolio weights. The portfolios were rebalanced with two frequencies: monthly at the first business day and daily.[30] The monthly rebalancing was done in two different ways. Our initial methodology employed monthly average weights for our term structure signals and index weightings. Thus, the information content of the term structure at the end of a month was incorporated into the average weight of that month. The second way was fixing the term structure at the end of every month and applying the obtained signal to the initial portfolio weight of the following month. Between two rebalancing

[30] A monthly history of index weightings at the first business day of every month was available for the GSCI since January 1982, for the DJAIG since January 1991. We calculated daily index weights for the DJAIG with the excess returns, available on the DJAIG web site. For the DBLCI daily weights were available since January 1988 and for the RICI since July 1998.

EXHIBIT 15.4 Annualized Arithmetical Outperformance of the Term Structure Indicator per Commodity

			Nearby/Second Nearby			Term Structure Indicator Slope and Shape First 13 months										
			Daily			Daily			Monthly (old)				Monthly (new)			
	Commodity	Exchange	DJAIG	RICI	DBLCI	DJAIG	RICI	DBLCI	DJAIG	GSCI	RICI	DBLCI	DJAIG	GSCI	RICI	DBLCI
Energy	Brent	IPE		3.5%			1.9%			0.5%	0.8%			0.0%	0.7%	
	Crude oil WTI	NYMEX	0.6%	−1.0%	0.7%	0.3%	−0.1%	0.4%	0.8%	0.3%	0.2%	0.4%	0.1%	0.0%	−0.3%	0.3%
	Gasoline	NYMEX	0.2%	0.2%		0.3%	0.6%		0.8%	0.4%	1.1%		−0.1%	−0.2%	−0.1%	
	Natural gas	NYMEX	−0.4%	0.3%		−0.4%	−0.6%		0.8%	0.9%	0.6%		−0.8%	−0.6%	−0.6%	
	Heating oil	NYMEX	0.5%	0.6%	0.6%	−0.1%	0.2%	0.1%	0.4%	0.2%	0.6%	0.3%	0.0%	0.0%	0.4%	0.1%
	Gas oil	IPE		−0.5%			0.4%			0.4%	0.3%			0.1%	0.0%	
Base Metals	Aluminum	LME	0.0%	0.0%	−1.1%	0.0%	0.0%	−1.0%	0.1%	0.1%	0.2%	0.1%	0.0%	0.0%	0.0%	0.0%
	Nickel	LME	0.7%	1.1%		0.5%	0.9%		0.6%	0.0%	0.9%		0.4%	−0.1%	0.7%	
	Copper	COMEX	4.7%	0.8%		3.5%	0.6%		3.8%	0.6%	0.7%		3.1%	0.2%	0.5%	
	Copper	LME	0.3%													
	Lead	LME		1.1%			0.4%			0.3%	0.7%			0.1%	0.3%	
	Zinc	LME	0.3%	0.7%		0.2%	0.5%		0.3%	0.1%	0.6%		0.2%	0.0%	0.3%	
	Tin	LME		0.3%			0.0%			0.2%	0.0%			0.0%	−0.1%	
Precious Metals	Gold	COMEX	0.2%	0.1%	0.5%	0.1%	0.0%	0.3%	0.2%	0.2%	0.1%	0.1%	0.1%	0.2%	0.0%	0.2%
	Silver	COMEX	0.2%	0.0%		0.1%	−0.1%		0.2%	0.1%	0.0%		0.0%	0.0%	−0.1%	
	Palladium	NYMEX		0.2%			0.2%				0.1%				−0.1%	
	Platinum	NYMEX		0.4%			0.1%			0.2%	0.1%			0.2%	0.2%	
Livestock	Lean hogs	CME	0.5%	0.2%		−0.2%	−0.3%		0.2%	0.3%	0.1%		−0.1%	−0.3%	−0.4%	
	Feeder cattle	CME								0.6%				0.4%		
	Live cattle	CME	−0.8%	−1.1%		−0.3%	−0.6%		0.0%	0.1%	−0.3%		−0.2%	−0.1%	−0.4%	
	Pork bellies	CME														
Grains	Corn	CBOT	0.3%	0.8%	0.0%	0.4%	0.8%	0.2%	0.5%	0.3%	0.7%	0.6%	0.3%	0.2%	0.7%	0.1%
	Wheat	CBOT	0.2%	1.1%	0.8%	0.2%	0.9%	0.4%	0.4%	0.6%	1.1%	0.6%	0.3%	0.4%	0.9%	0.5%
	Wheat	KCBOT								0.3%				0.1%		
	Soybeans	CBOT	0.3%	0.1%		0.1%	0.0%		0.2%	0.1%	0.1%		0.0%	−0.1%	−0.1%	

(Continued)

EXHIBIT 18.4 (Continued)

	Commodity	Exchange	Nearby/Second Nearby Daily DJAIG	Nearby/Second Nearby Daily RICI	Nearby/Second Nearby Daily DBLCI	Term Structure Indicator Slope and Shape First 13 months Daily DJAIG	Daily RICI	Daily DBLCI	Monthly (old) DJAIG	Monthly (old) GSCI	Monthly (old) RICI	Monthly (old) DBLCI	Monthly (new) DJAIG	Monthly (new) GSCI	Monthly (new) RICI	Monthly (new) DBLCI
	Soybean oil	CBOT	0.1%	−0.1%		0.0%	−0.2%		0.1%		−0.1%		−0.1%		−0.3%	
Grains (continued)	Soybean meal	CBOT		−0.7%			−0.4%				−0.2%				−0.5%	
	Oats	CBOT		0.6%			0.2%				0.6%				−0.1%	
	Rice	CBOT		−0.1%			−0.2%				0.0%				0.0%	
	Orange juice	NYBOT		−0.3%			−0.2%			−0.2%	0.0%			−0.5%	−0.2%	
	Coffee, arabica	NYBOT	0.7%	0.5%		0.7%	0.3%		0.9%	0.6%	0.4%		0.6%	0.3%	0.3%	
Softs	Coffee, robusta	LIFFE														
	Sugar No. 11	NYBOT	−0.5%	−0.3%		−0.4%	−0.2%		0.0%	0.0%	0.0%		−0.2%	−0.2%	0.0%	
	White sugar	LIFFE														
	Cocoa	NYBOT	0.2%	−0.1%		0.2%	0.1%		0.3%	0.1%	0.3%		0.1%	0.0%	0.1%	
Exotics	Cotton	NYBOT	0.1%	0.5%		0.4%	0.3%		0.4%	0.3%	0.4%		0.2%	0.0%	0.3%	
	Lumber	CME		−0.6%			0.0%				0.0%				0.0%	
	Barley	WCE		0.3%			0.0%				0.0%				0.0%	
	Canola	WCE		−0.2%			0.0%				0.0%				0.0%	
	Wool	SFE		0.3%			0.1%				0.4%				0.0%	
	Rubber	TOCOM		−0.7%			0.0%				0.0%				0.0%	
	Azuki beans	TGE		−1.6%			0.0%				0.0%				0.0%	
	Flaxseed	WCE		0.0%			0.0%				0.0%				0.0%	
	Raw Silk	YCE		0.0%			0.0%				0.0%				0.0%	
	Yearly Outperformance		8.6%	6.4%	1.4%	5.5%	5.5%	0.5%	11.1%	7.7%	10.6%	2.2%	4.1%	0.2%	2.0%	1.2%

GSCI February 1983–March 2006
DJAIG January 1991–December 2006
DBLCI December 1988–December 2006
RICI July 1998–December 2006

dates dynamic weights for the portfolio or the index were not calculated. The results are positive for the majority of commodities in all indexes. The base metals especially contributed to the outperformance. However, the results for the average signals are clearly better than the end of preceding month signals. This suggests that spot prices and backwardation move for a good part in tandem. The scarcity signal of the term structure could not be fully exploited if the adjustment time to a steepening forward curve is weeks or even longer. Consequently, we reduced the reaction time to a daily rebalancing.[31] The results clearly improved, but nevertheless for some of the commodities the performance contribution stays negative. This is especially true for natural gas, where the one year term structure is a good contraindicator of future returns.

In light of the good performance results of other studies, based on the backwardation between first and second nearby, we tested to what extent a standardized signal of these two contracts could enhance the results. Indeed, there is an improvement from 5.5% annual outperformance for the RICI and DJAIG indexes to 6.4% and 8.5%, respectively. This clearly demonstrates that even if the relation between nearby and second nearby is distorted by seasonal influences, scarcity has to be indicated in the front months. The results can be enhanced further if the restriction to use only commodities which are index members and the maximum over- or underweight restrictions are dropped. We constructed an outright portfolio where only the above average commodities are weighted accordingly to their term structure signals. First results indicate that the outperformance more than doubles on an index level.[32]

Selection of Contract Maturities and Calendar Spreads

After the commodity selection, the next step of the asset allocation process is to identify the most promising contract maturities. As shown in the previous section, forward curves rarely display a linear structure. Even when the straight line between nearby and deferred contracts exhibits a large contango, positive roll yields can be earned. A typical example was the crude oil curve in spring 2006 (see Exhibit 18.5). The first 12 months showed negative roll yields in relation to the preceding months, whereas the long-dated contracts at the end of the curve were less expensive than their predecessors.

---

[31]Direct transaction costs vary between 0.004% and 0.008% per future round turn and are therefore disregarded.

[32]A comparison between the performances of outright and index portfolios can be found in Mezger and Eibl, "Gewinne mit Rohstoffen, [Profits with commodity futures]," p. 23.

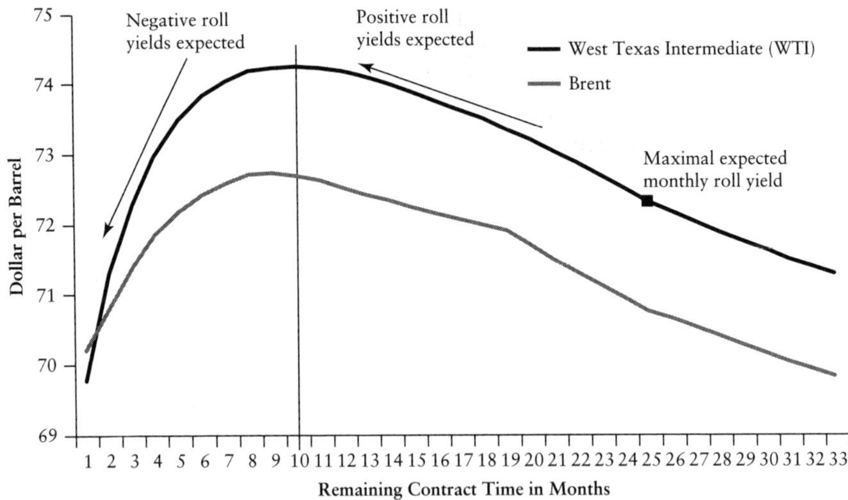

EXHIBIT 18.5 Forward Structure of NYMEX Crude Oil, May 2006
Source: Exhibit created from data obtained from Reuters.

With an unchanged term structure a substantial roll premium could be expected by selling the 10 month maturity and buying the 18 month contract.

The key questions here are, whether the term structure will remain unchanged and which factors are driving the turns in the shape of the forward curve? Pursuant to the Theory of Storage, convenience yields reflect scarcity and physical tightness of the underlying commodity. Therefore, it is obvious to assume a link between the change of stock levels and the change of convenience yields.[33] Due to a lack of representative and reliable stock data, there is only little empirical research on the relation between stock data and forward curves. Boesch argued that the relationship between the spot price of crude oil and U.S. crude oil inventories broke down after 2003.[34] Instead, a robust relationship between the spread of nearby to second nearby emerged. Therefore, he suggests applying the concept of mean reversion not to spot prices but to the contract spreads of the term structure. Heaney analyzed the relation between LME warehouse stocks and the interest rate adjusted convenience yield between three-month forwards and cash prices for copper, lead, and zinc from November 1964 to December 2003.[35]

[33]We define *convenience yields* as the percentage premium of the nearby contract to a deferred contract plus the risk free rate.
[34]Rick Boesch, Is Mean Reversion Dead in the Crude Oil and Natural Gas Markets, 2006 Sungard Kiodex White Paper.
[35]Richard Heaney, Pricing LME Commodity Futures Contracts, Working Paper, RMIT University Australia, May 2004.

His statistical analysis supported the existence of convenience yields as a decreasing, nonlinear function of stocks.

Dincerler, Khokher, and Simin provide a good overview on academic convenience yield models.[36] They found that the convenience yield increases nonlinearly in the spot price and that this convenience yield–spot price correlation is negative and significantly related to stock levels. They suggested that the rate of mean reversion varies over time and is highest, when stock levels are low. Across a sample of weekly and daily, seasonally adjusted stock data for the four commodities crude oil, natural gas, copper, and gold they found a significant negative correlation with convenience yields for crude oil, natural gas, and copper. Feldman and Till plotted a chart of the average monthly backwardation of soybeans and the stocks-to-use ratio. They found that a negative relationship is "plainly visible."[37]

In Exhibit 18.6, we analyzed the correlation between inventory levels and convenience yield for three different groups: energy, base metals, and grains. Weekly data was available from the reports published by the Department of Energy and the LME warehouses. For some metals, we had monthly updated global stock estimates by international research companies. For the grain markets, the United States Department of Agriculture (USDA) releases a monthly report with estimates for the global ending stocks of the different marketing years (September to August). For our backtesting, we used the average of the next two consecutive marketing years. Stock data of energy and grains exhibited a strong seasonal pattern. In the case of energy, we adjusted the data, calculating the excess stocks in comparison to the five year average of every week. Since the grain estimates always refer to the end of the marketing year, a seasonal adjustment was not necessary. For some of the commodities we examined whether the application of stocks-to-use improves the predication of the absolute stock data.

The strongest relationship between stocks and convenience yields is given for the base metals, with a Pearson correlation measure well above 0.6 for lead, copper, aluminum, and tin. The term structure on the LME seems to mirror the LME warehouse developments and not the monthly global stock estimates of Metal consultancies. The same is true for oil stocks, where the figures for the United States exhibit a better correlation with convenience yields than the broader measure of stocks in the OECD

[36]Cantekin Dincerler, Zeigham Khokher, and Timothy Simin, "An Empirical Analysis of Commodity Convenience Yields," *Risk Management Abstract s*6, no. 11 (2006).

[37]Feldman and Till, Separating the Wheat from the Chaff: Backwardation as the Long-Term Driver of Commodity Futures Performance; Evidence from Soy, Corn and Wheat Futures from 1950 to 2004, p. 23.

EXHIBIT 18.6 Correlation of Inventory Levels and One-Year Convenience Yields

Commodity	Inventory description	Source	start	freqency	comment	Linear Function: slope	Linear Function: Axis intercept	Linear Function: Pearsson (R^2)	Parabolic Function Pearsson (R^2)
Crude Oil	US commercial stocks	DOE/EIA	1984	weekly		−2.5480E−06	0.9184	0.291	0.351
	US commercial stocks	DOE/EIA	1989	weekly	seas. adj.	−1.2977E+00	1.3912	0.587	0.612
	OECD stocks		1984	monthly		−2.9945E−04	1.2631	0.139	0.158
Heating Oil	US commercial stocks	DOE/EIA	2001	weekly		−3.5090E−03	0.5220	0.197	0.351
	US commercial stocks	DOE/EIA	1993	weekly		−5.0248E−06	0.3531	0.302	0.399
	US commercial stocks	DOE/EIA	1998	weekly	seas. adj.	−6.2999E−01	0.6775	0.589	0.602
	US commercial stocks	DOE/EIA	1993	weekly	stocks to use	−1.6600E−02	0.3683	0.289	0.291
Natural Gas	US commercial stocks		1993	weekly		−6.9952E−05	0.1955	0.084	0.086
	US commercial stocks		1998	weekly	seas. adj.	−6.9952E−05	−0.5864	**0.417**	**0.422**
Aluminum	LME warehouse stocks	LME	1997	weekly		−6.4671E−01	0.7002	**0.645**	0.632
	Global stocks	WBMS	1997	monthly		−1.6834E−04	−0.4881	0.319	0.328
Copper	LME warehouse stocks	LME	1997	weekly		−2.4278E−07	0.1726	**0.743**	**0.870**
	Total stocks	ICSG	1997	monthly		−2.0158E−04	0.2854	**0.715**	**0.840**
	Global stocks	WBMS	1997	monthly		−7.7222E−08	0.1094	0.481	0.528
Nickel	LME warehouse stocks	LME	1997	weekly		−2.4793E−06	0.1680	0.310	0.323
	Global stocks	WBMS	1997	monthly		−1.7591E−06	0.2890	0.194	0.234
Lead	LME warehouse stocks	LME	1997	weekly		−1.2478E−06	0.1867	**0.701**	**0.870**
	Global stocks	WBMS	1998	monthly		9.0140E−05	0.0477	0.039	0.230
	Total stocks	ILZSG	1995	monthly		9.1002E−05	0.2453	0.077	0.104
Zinc	LME warehouse stocks	LME	1997	weekly		−2.1261E−07	0.1189	0.356	0.445
	Total stocks	ILZSG	1995	monthly		2.0000E−04	0.2453	0.448	0.500
Tin	LME warehouse stocks	LME	1997	weekly		−3.4295E−06	0.0903	**0.597**	**0.647**
Wheat	Global Stocks Estimates	USDA	1995	monthly		−2.2427E−03	0.2730	0.120	0.328
	Global Stocks Estimates	USDA	1995	monthly	stocks to use	−9.2590E−01	0.1852	0.047	0.140

Corn	Global Stocks Estimates	USDA	1995	monthly		−3.7686E−03	0.3272	**0.536**	**0.635**
	Global Stocks Estimates	USDA	1995	monthly	stocks to use	−2.2600E+00	0.3184	0.414	0.462
Cotton	Global Stocks Estimates	USDA	1995	monthly		−1.0207E−02	0.3844	0.331	0.534
Soybeans	Global Stocks Estimates	USDA	1995	monthly		1.1400E−03	0.0839	0.022	0.022

DOE/EIA Department of Energy/Energy Information Administration
LME London Metal Exchange
USDA United States Department of Agriculture
WBMS World Bureau of Metal Statistics
ICSG International Copper Study Group
ILZSG International Lead and Zinc Study Group

Source: Exhibit created from data obtained from Department of Energy/Energy Information Administration, London Metal Exchange, United States Department of Agriculture, World Bureau of Metal Statistics, International Copper Study Group, and International Lead and Zinc Study Group.

countries. The seasonal adjustment of stocks clearly improves the correlation for crude oil, heating oil, and notably natural gas. Among the grains only the pricing of the corn term structure seems to be partly determined by the development of stocks. The stocks-to-use data does not deliver better results for heating oil, corn, and wheat. For the base metals it is evident that the pricing function of the term structure is nonlinear to the stocks data, when certain stock thresholds are breached. The parabolic character is more pronounced at the lower end of the stock data. Thus, the assumption of the Theory of Storage that the convenience yield on inventory falls at a decreasing rate as inventory increases, can be affirmed.

All in all, we conclude that stock developments and the term structure are synchronized in energy and base metals markets. Interestingly, the pricing looks more oriented toward the local data than to global stock developments. The key question is to what extent the changes in stocks and hence the changes in the term structure can be anticipated? Good chances for alpha might arise when a mismatch between local and global stock data occurs. For example, in January 2007, the LME copper contract was a good example (see Exhibit 18.7). The LME copper warehouses denoted huge inflows of 85,000 tonnes in the preceding six months. Consequently, the term structure flattened out. The one-year convenience yield fell from 18% to 6%. However, the increase in LME inventory most likely does not reflect an underlying surplus in the refined copper market, but rather a movement

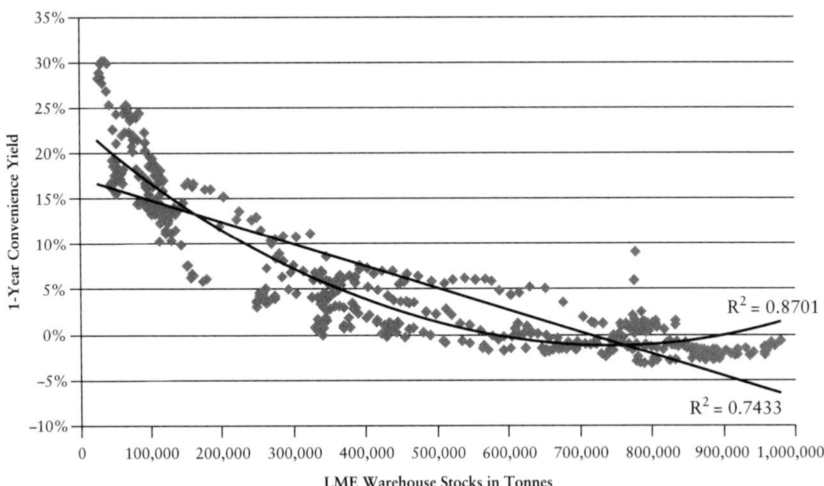

EXHIBIT 18.7 Correlation of One-Year LME Convenience Yield and Warehouse Stocks of Copper, July 1997 to December 2006
Source: Exhibit created from data obtained from Datastream and Reuters.

from unreported to reported stocks. The true alpha comes from a correct estimate of the following determinants of the term structure:

- Expected roll yield of the contract maturity in relation to the preceding maturities.
- Expected seasonal price behavior.
- Expected change of stocks as a consequence of global market balances.
- Mean reversion of the front to the back months.

Commodity Cycles and Market Timing

Commodity prices swing in long cycles. Bannister and Forward detected three commodity cycles between 1870 and 2002, ranging from 16 to 22 years duration.[38] They demonstrated that the energy markets, the metals, and the farm products moved in tandem. The authors suggest that a fourth commodity cycle began in 2002 and will last until 2015. Bannister and Forward expected a relatively small price appreciation of 130% compared to the previous upswings (219% for cycle 1, 167% for cycle 2, and 204% for cycle 3).

We came to similar conclusions, constructing an equally weighted monthly cash index of commodity prices, taken from the National Bureau of Economic Research (NBER) and the Commodity Research Bureau (CRB).[39] In Exhibit 18.8, four cycles, consisting of a consolidation and a price appreciation phase, could be clearly identified. The first one was the longest. The consolidation phase covers the gold standard when restricted money supply prevented commodity and consumer price inflation. The bull market began in the pre-war period when monetary discipline started to abate and culminated during the commodity shortage after World War I. The second bull market was prepared by the expansionary policy stimulus of the New Deal following the Great Depression. The economic crisis of the 1930s marks the only downward sloped consolidation phase. At the end of the sixties it was again a monetary regime which laid the foundation for the bull market of the seventies. This time it was a huge mismatch between the U.S. money growth and the fixed parities of the U.S. currency against gold

---

[38]Barry B. Bannister and Paul Forward, The Inflation Cycle of 2002 to 2015, Legg Mason Equity Research Report, April 2002.

[39]A list of index participants, the starting point of prices, and the sources can be found in Exhibit A18.2 in this chapter's appendix.

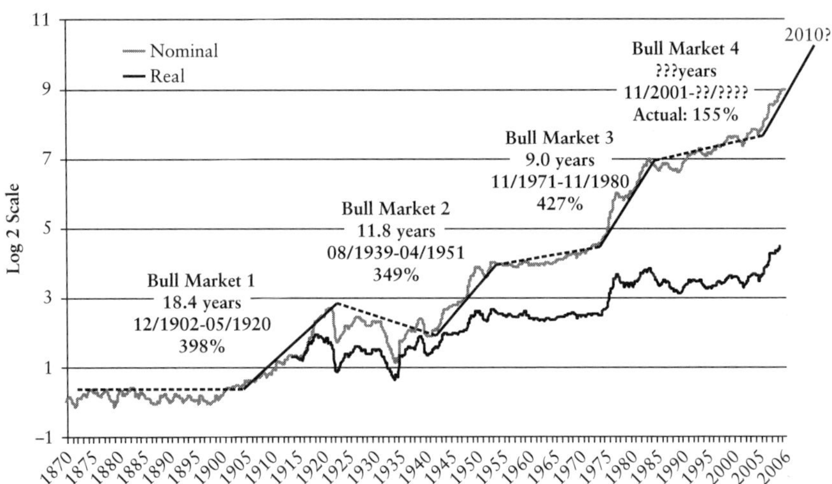

EXHIBIT 18.8 Long Term Cycles of Commodity Cash Prices, January 1870 to October 2006
Source: Exhibit created from data obtained from the Commodity Research Bureau and various sources (see Appendix Exhibit A18.2).

and the other world currencies. As early as 1970 the commodity markets started anticipating the blow-off of the Bretton Woods system in 1973. The bull market we are in today began in November 2001, triggered by the threat of war and an acceleration of money supply in the key regions of world economy.

From a technical point of view the bull market has some more years to go. If we take the seventies as a guide, the year 2010 could mark the end of the current commodity boom. But as in the seventies (1975 to 1976), a setback of commodity prices in real terms is not unlikely. Thus, medium-term timing techniques have to complement the strategic case.

Within this time pattern, commodity prices seem to be influenced by the business cycles. Gorton and Rouwenhorst studied the performance of commodity future returns from 1959 until 2004 during the business phases defined by the NBER. Not surprisingly commodities rallied when business activity and demand were high. The return during early and late expansion (6.76% and 16.71%) was substantially higher than during early and late recession (3.74% and −1.63%).[40] Kat and Oomen verified that monetary conditions play an important role as well. Some of the commodities,

[40]Gorton and Rouwenhorst, "Facts and Fantasies about Commodity Futures."

including the energy sector and industrial metals, performed particularly well during restrictive monetary policy regimes.[41] Since most of the prices of the industrial commodities are an important input factor for consumer price inflation, this finding fits the observation of a strong commodity performance during late expansion, when monetary policy often feel obliged to a restrictive regime.

Vrugt and Bauer combined business cycle and monetary environment indicators as well as investor sentiment measures.[42] From August 1992 to December 2003 their timing approach attained an annualized mean excess return of 2.9% after and 11.8% before transaction costs with a comparable standard deviation as the passive investment. The active strategy did particularly well during the severe commodity downturn of 1998. In our model for the medium-term economic commodity cycles we focused on the leading indicators for industrial activity in the key commodity consuming regions of the world, for instance, the purchasing manager index of the Institute for Supply Management (ISM) for the manufacturing sector in the United States. We standardized and translated the results in nonleveraged long and short signals for the commodity futures indexes. From 1970 to 1990 we were long/short of the GSCI, which was replaced with the DJAIG index at the beginning of the year 1991.[43] The model in Exhibit 18.9 displays only modest but stable excess returns over money market of 1.83% per annum.

The actual model recommendation is a moderate long signal, since most of the leading indicators held up well and are forecasting robust growth of the world industrial production at least for the next six to nine months. On the other hand, the supply reaction should prove limited in the short term and the stock-to-use levels are well below their historic average for most of the commodities after four years' economic boom. Furthermore, the restrictive attitude of monetary policy in the United States and Japan in the last 18 months matches the observation of a late expansion phase with high commodity returns. As demonstrated above, the term structure of commodity prices is considered to be a good predictor of future returns. It is self-evident to apply this indicator to the timing of commodity indexes/portfolios. Till and Eagleeye compared a passive investment in the GSCI

---

[41]Kat and Oomen "What Every Investor Should Know about Commodities, Part I: Univariate Return Analysis."

[42]Evert Vrugt, Rob Bauer, Roderick Molenaar, and Tom Steenkamp, "Dynamic Commodity Timing Strategies," Limburg Institute of Financial Economics Working Paper 04–012, July 2004.

[43]The DJAIG Index offered a better Sharpe ratio than the GSCI from 1991 to 2006.

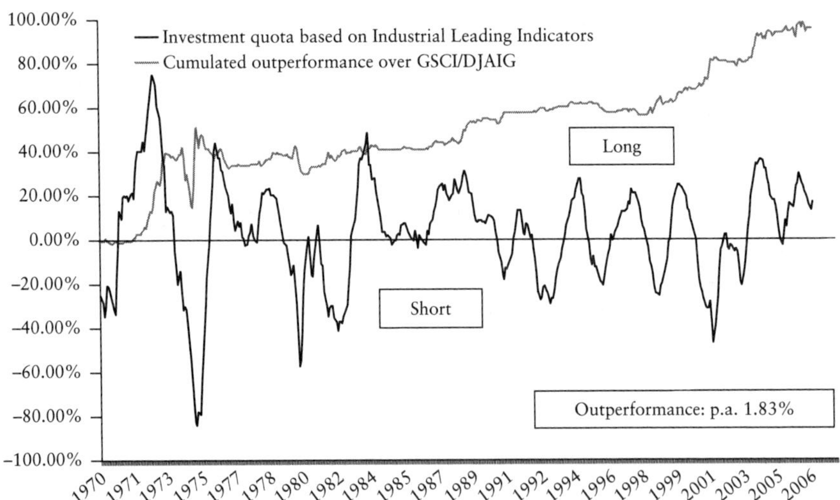

EXHIBIT 18.9 Economic Cycles and Medium-Term Market Timing
Source: Exhibit created from data obtained from Datastream and Bloomberg.

with two different investment policies.[44] The first one was only to invest in the GSCI, when the future curve is in backwardation; the second one was just the opposite with an investment in the GSCI, when the index was in contango. From 1992 to 2000, the backwardation investment conditional yielded 39.1% whereas the contango investment conditional ended up with a loss of −25.3%. Similar results were found from 2000 to 2003. Erb and Harvey added to this approach a fourth alternative: long if GSCI backwardated, short if contangoed.[45] From July 1992 until May 2004 the returns of the long/short portfolio were 8.1%, far above the passive index investment (2.7%) and the contango investment conditional (−5.0%), but below the backwardation investment conditional (11.3%).We took a weekly, equally weighted average of all available term structures, for which the prices of the nearby and the exactly one year deferred contract were given (see Exhibit 18.10).[46] The signals were translated into a net long investment quota between 30% and 175% and backtested against the GSCI

[44]Hilary Till and Joseph Eagleeye, "Timing is Everything, Especially with a Commodity Index," *Futures Magazine* (August 2003), pp. 46–48; and Hilary Till and Joseph Eagleeye, "Trading Scarcity," *Futures Magazine* (October 2000), p. 50.
[45]Erb and Harvey, "The Strategic and Tactical Value of Commodity Futures."
[46]See the discussion of commodity selection models in this chapter.

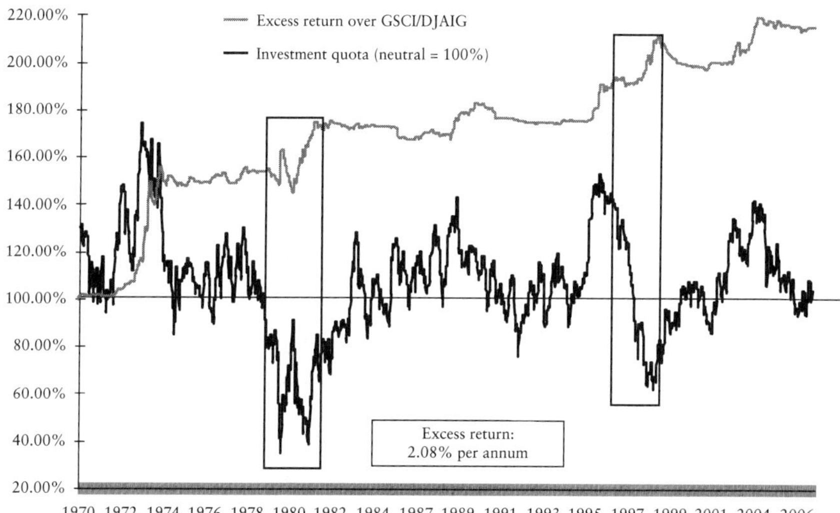

EXHIBIT 18.10 Average Term Structure Timing Indicator, January 1970 to December 2006
Source: Exhibit created from data obtained from the Commodity Research Bureau and Bloomberg.

(1970–1990) and the DJAIG (1991–2006). The result is an annualized excess return of 2.1%. This looks small in relation to the results above, but the excess return was achieved with a comparatively small tracking error and could easily be leveraged. The term structure gave clear warning signs just before the severe sell offs at the beginning of the eighties and during the Asian crisis.

At the beginning of 2007, the situation looks more dangerous than three years earlier because the forward curves of the energy contracts have turned from backwardation to contango. On the other hand, the huge contango in the grain markets has disappeared in the last two years. Due to rapidly dwindling world stocks, the one year deferred contracts of corn and wheat fell again into backwardation. With rising investment flows to commodities, investors supposedly will bid up the prices of backwardated contracts. In the last few years the quadrupling of investors' funds pouring into the commodity sector could be felt in the relatively unattractive pricing of the front months, which are part of commercial commodity indexes. At present, an exuberant investor appetite and a further deterioration of forward curves is not in sight. Thus a short of the commodity markets could prove to be far too early.

CONCLUSION

Diversified commodity futures portfolios represented by the commodity indexes delivered a substantial risk premium to the risk free return in the last decades. Nevertheless huge performance spreads occurred between the star performing sectors energy and base metals and the underperforming agricultural sector. The main driver in commodity returns appeared to be the roll returns. Therefore, it is not surprising that a good part of the described alpha strategies is based on the structure of the forward curve, which reflects the expected roll yields, as the main indicator to forecast commodity returns. Despite seasonal distortions, the spread between the nearby and the second nearby contract contained more information about future price developments than the spread between the nearby and longer dated contracts.

In line with the theory of storage, stock level developments seemed to be the main factor behind the changes of the forward price structure. The link between stock levels held and convenience yields was especially accentuated for base metals traded at the London Metal Exchange (LME). Interestingly, the LME stocks, which cannot be considered to mirror the developments of global market balances perfectly, showed a stronger correlation to convenience yields than the global stock estimates of international metal consulting firms.

It has been demonstrated that alpha strategies were able to generate excess returns in comparison to the commodity indexes on all three levels—commodity selection, contract selection, and market timing—of the commodity asset allocation process. Therefore, we expect a rising trend from passive to actively managed commodity portfolios.

EXHIBIT A18.1 Commodity Contract Months

Contract	Exchange	Reuters Ticker	Roll Date[a]	Data since	Contract Months	Comment
1. Energy						
Crude oil brent	IPE	LCO	10	24.07.1989	F,G,H,J,K,M,N, Q,U,V,X,Z	
Crude oil WTI	NYMEX	CL	10	30.03.1983	F,G,H,J,K,M,N, Q,U,V,X,Z	
Gasoline	NYMEX	HU/RB	10	03.12.1984	F,G,H,J,K,M,N, Q,U,V,X,Z	
Natural gas	NYMEX	NG	10	04.04.1990	F,G,H,J,K,M,N, Q,U,V,X,Z	
Gas oil	IPE	LGO	10	03.06.1986	F,G,H,J,K,M,N, Q,U,V,X,Z	
Heating oil	NYMEX	HO	10	14.11.1978	F,G,H,J,K,M,N, Q,U,V,X,Z	
2. Base Metals						
Aluminum	LME	MAL	10	02.01.1980	Cash-, 3M-, 15M-Forwards	All months since 1997
Nickel	LME	MNI	10	23.07.1979	F,G,H,J,K,M,N, Q,U,V,X,Z	All months since 1997
High-grade copper	COMEX	HG	40	01.07.1959	F,H,K,U,V,Z	
Primary copper	LME	MCU	10	09.05.1991	Cash-, 3M-, 15M-Forwards	All months since 1997
Lead	LME	MPB	10	02.01.1979	Cash-, 3M-Forwards	All months since 1997
Zinc	LME	MZN	10	29.11.1988	Cash-, 3M-, 15M-Forwards	All months since 1997
Tin	LME	MSN	10	29.06.1989	Cash-, 3M-Forwards	All months since 1997
3. Precious Metals						
Gold	COMEX	GC	40	31.12.1974	G,J,M,Q,V,Z	
Silver	COMEX	SI	40	12.06.1963	F,H,K,N,U,Z	
Palladium	COMEX	PA	40	03.01.1977	H,M,U,Z	
Platinum	COMEX	PL	40	04.03.1968	F,J,N,V	
4. Livestock						
Lean hogs	CME	LH	10	28.02.1966	G,J,M,N,Q,V,Z	
Feeder cattle	CME	FC	10	30.11.1971	F*,H,J,K,Q,U,V,Z	* Since 1978
Live cattle	CME	LC	35	30.11.1964	G,J,M,Q,V,Z	
Pork bellies	CME	PB	30	18.09.1961	G,H,K,M,N,Q	

(Continued)

EXHIBIT A18.1 (Continued)

Contract	Exchange	Reuters Ticker	Roll Date[a]	Data since	Contract Months	Comment
5. Grains						
Corn	CBOT	C–	25	01.07.1959	H,K,N,U,Z	
Kansas wheat	KCBOT	KW	25	05.01.1970	H,K,N,U,Z	
Wheat	CBOT	W–	25	01.07.1959	H,K,N,U,Z	
Soybeans	CBOT	S–	25	01.07.1959	F,H,K,N,Q,U,X	
Soybean oil	CBOT	BO	25	01.07.1959	F,H,K,N,Q,U,V,Z	
Soybean meal	CBOT	SM	25	01.07.1959	F,H,K,N,U,V,Z	
Oats	CBOT	O–	25	01.07.1959	H,K,N,U,Z	
Rice	CBOT	RR	35	20.08.1986	F,H,K,N,U,X	
6. Softs						
Orange juice	NYBOT	OJ	20	01.02.1967	F,H,K,N,U,Z	
Coffee Robusta	LIFFE	LKD	40	01.03.1991	F,H,K,N,U,X	
Coffee Arabica	NYBOT	KC	40	16.08.1972	H,K,N,U,Z	
Sugar	NYBOT	SB	10	03.01.1961		
White sugar	LIFFE	LSU	10	11.04.1990	H,K,Q,V,Z	
Cocoa	NYBOT	CC	40	01.07.1959	H,K,N,U,Z	
Cotton	NYBOT	CT	25	01.07.1959	H,K,N,V,Z	
7. Exotics						
Lumber	CME	LB	10	01.10.1969	F,H,K,N,U,Z	
Barley	WCE	AB	25	24.05.1989	$G^{*},K^{*},Q^{**},X^{**}$,H,K,N,V,Z	** Until 96
Canola	WCE	RS	25	03.09.1974	$F^{2},H^{2},K^{3},M^{3},N^{2}$,U,X	^{2}Since 97. ^{3}Until 96.
Wool	SFE	GW	15	18.04.1995	G,J,M,Q,V,Z	

[a]Roll date in days before last trading day:

F	January	J	April	N	July	V	October
G	February	K	May	Q	August	X	November
H	March	M	June	U	September	Z	December

EXHIBIT A18.2 Data Sources for Cash Price Index, 1870–2006

Commodities	Start	Freq.	Data Sources
1. Agricultural Commodities			
Weizen, Winter, Chicago	1841	M	1841–1870: Newspapers, 1871–1922: CBOT, 1922–2006: CRB
Coffee, Rio #7, New York	1890	M	1890–1940: BLS Records, 1940–2006: CRB
Corn, No. 2, Chicago	1860	M	1860–1951: Wallace, Bressman, 1951–2006: CRB
Oats No. 2, Chicago	1890	M	1890–1952: BLS Bulletin, 1952–2006: CRB
Beanoil, New York	1911	M	CRB
Cotton, New York	1870	M	1890–1928: USDA, 1929–1945: BLS, 1945–2006: CRB
Lumber	1959	M	CRB
Rice	1914	M	CRB
Soybean meal	1929	M	CRB
Soybeans	1890	M	CRB
Sugar, granulated, New York	1890	M	1890–1945: BLS Bulletin, 1945–2006: CRB
2. Livestock			
Cattle, Gr. 4-A1, Chicago	1858	M	1858–1900: CBOT Records, 1900–1940: USDA, 1940–2006: CRB
Hogs, Grade H.P., Chicago	1858	M	1858–1859: USDA, 1860–1920: Wallace, 1920–1940: CBOT, 1940–2006: CRB
Pork bellies	1914	M	CRB
3. Metals			
Aluminum, 98–99%, NY	1913	M	1913–1933 BLS Records, 1934–2006: CRB
Copper, electrol, New York	1860	M	1860–1891: "Min. Industry," 1892–1955: "Min. Journal," 1956–2006: CRB
Tin, New York	1889	M	1889–1955: Iron Age, 1955-2006: CRB
Lead	1860	M	1860-1891: "Min. Industry," 1892–1955: "Mining Journal," 1956–2006: CRB
Ironsteel	1929	M	CRB
Zinc, New York	1910	M	"Mineral Industry," "Engineering and Mining Journal," 1955–2006: CRB
Gold	1941	M	CRB
Silver	1910	M	CRB
Platinum	1910	M	CRB
4. Energy			
Natural gas	1976	M	CRB
Crude oil, at wells	1890	M	1890–1955: BLS Bulletin, 1955–2006: CRB
Gasoline	1976	M	CRB
Heating oil	1966	M	CRB

CHAPTER 19

Efficient Frontier of Commodity Portfolios

Juliane Proelss
Research Assistant
European Business School
International University Schloss Reichartshausen

Denis Schweizer
Research Assistant
European Business School
International University Schloss Reichartshausen

We have known since Markowitz's seminal paper on portfolio theory that diversification can increase portfolio expected returns while reducing volatility.[1] However, investors should not blindly add another diversifier[2] to their portfolios without careful consideration of its properties in the context of the portfolio. Otherwise, the diversifier may not improve the risk-return profile of the portfolio, and may even worsen it. This raises the question of whether commodities really improve the performance of a (mixed) portfolio.

Before examining this question further, we define which assets are considered commodities. Normally there are two types that can be included in a portfolio: (1) "hard" commodities, nonperishable real assets such as energy (e.g., oil), industrial metals (e.g., aluminum), precious metals (e.g., gold), and timber, and (2) "soft" commodities, perishable and consumable

[1]Harry M. Markowitz, "Portfolio Selection," *Journal of Finance* 7, no. 1 (1952), pp. 77–91.

[2]We define a diversifier as another asset added to an already existing portfolio to reduce risk and/or enhance portfolio returns. However, not all assets are "good" investments or "real" diversifiers. Many assets do not satisfy the demand for higher portfolio returns and/or lower portfolio risk.

real assets such as agricultural products (e.g., wheat) and livestock (e.g., live cattle).[3] Using commodities as a financial investment opens up a whole new universe of potential assets. But what makes a new asset or asset class a good investment and a "real" portfolio diversifier?

WHAT TO LOOK OUT FOR

Investors should consider carefully certain aspects of the asset such as the risk premium, the returns distribution (or, more precisely, the second to fourth moments), the correlation to other assets in the portfolio, the correlation of the diversifier with inflation, and finally liquidity, the fungibility of the asset or asset class.[4] For example, if an asset offers a high positive risk premium, it is considered a good "standalone" investment. As for the probability of possible returns, the higher the second moment, the wider the distribution of the returns. The probability of more extreme returns decreases as the third moment increases. And the probability of extreme returns increases with the fourth moment.

Correlation describes an asset's behavior in a portfolio. The risk-return profile of a portfolio may improve if correlation among assets is low or negative. Furthermore, the more positively an asset is correlated with inflation, the more the asset's performance will improve during times of inflation. Finally, the higher the liquidity of an asset, the faster an investor will be able to sell the asset.

We next assess the characteristics of commodities in regard to these points.

The Case of the Risk Premium

While the existence of a risk premium can be easily ascertained for stocks, it is less obvious for commodities. The question of whether a risk premium exists for commodities can be traced back to the 1930s, and it is still widely discussed in the literature. Among the contemporary and oft-cited works on this topic is the study by Erb and Harvey who researched the strategic and tactical value of commodities.[5] They find that the geometric average return of single-commodity futures, the basic components of a commodity portfolio, have historically been close to zero. This implies that most single commodities do not exhibit trends over longer periods, but rather follow a mean

[3]Thomas M. Idzorek, "Strategic Asset Allocation and Commodities," PIMCO, 2006.
[4]Harry M. Kat, "How to Evaluate a New Diversifier with 10 Simple Questions," *Journal of Wealth Management* 9, no, 4 (2007), pp. 29–36.
[5]Claude B. Erb and Campbell R. Harvey, "The Strategic and Tactical Value of Commodity Futures," *Financial Analysts Journal* 62, no. 2 (2006), pp. 69–97.

reversion process.[6] Given convincing evidence that commodity portfolios have historically exhibited stock-like returns, there must be different sources of portfolio returns than the returns of the single components.[7]

Erb and Harvey analyzed different possibilities and conclude that the sole reliable source of portfolio returns is portfolio diversification. They note it may be possible to earn equity-like returns with a portfolio containing commodity futures that show positive roll or spot returns over a longer period. However, the authors reason that past positive roll or spot returns do not necessarily correspond with future returns.

Other researchers, such as Kat and Oomen,[8] also found no evidence of a consistent risk premium, except for energy commodities.[9] They note that their results should be taken with caution because of the presence of atypical returns distributions. They argue that the existence of a bubble in commodity prices is possible because of rising commodity demand from the so-called BRIC countries (Brazil, Russia, India, and China)

Other renowned researchers who have examined the subject of commodities disagree, however. Gorton and Rouwenhorst find statistically significant average returns that are comparable to equity returns for a periodically rebalanced equally weighted commodity portfolio.[10] They explain this via a commodity risk premium that follows Keynes' theory of normal backwardation.[11] Gorton and Rouwenhorst believe that the existence of hedgers, who are willing to pay a premium to avoid price risks, implies the existence of a commodity risk premium.

---

[6]The problem goes back to whether one believes in economic cycles (and many distinguished economists do). If one does, evidence for the existence of trends in commodity prices can be found (for example, the upward trend in energy prices since around 2002). See Hélyette Geman, "Stochastic Modeling of Commodity Price Processes," Chapter 3 in *Commodities and Commodity Derivatives* (Chichester: John Wiley & Sons, 2005).

[7]Zvi Bodie and Victor I. Rosansky, "Risk and Returns in Commodity Future," *Financial Analysts Journal* 36, no. 3 (1980), pp. 27–39.

[8]Harry M. Kat and Roel C. A. Oomen, "What Every Investor Should Know About Commodities, Part I: Univariate Return Analysis," *Journal of Investment Management* 7, no. 1 (2007), pp. 1–25.

[9]Energy is considered a subgroup of commodities, which normally include only natural gas, crude oils, unleaded gasoline, and heating oil.

[10]Gary Gorton and Geert K. Rouwenhorst, "Facts and Fantasies about Commodity Futures," *Financial Analysts Journal* 62, no. 2 (2006), pp. 47–68.

[11]"The spot price must exceed the forward price by the amount which the producer is ready to sacrifice in order to hedge himself. Thus in normal conditions the spot price exceeds the forward price, i.e., there is a backwardation."—John M. Keynes, *The Applied Theory of Money* (London: Macmillan, 1930).

Others, such as Greer,[12] believe in the existence of natural returns, namely the *commodity strategy premium* caused by the inherent returns from investing in a fully collateralized commodity index.

To summarize these arguments, the existence of a risk premium for commodities is still a contentious issue. Nevertheless, we conclude that structuring a commodity portfolio will gain in importance for investors, for a simple reason: Even if there is no risk premium for single commodities, a well diversified portfolio of commodities still offers a reliable source of returns. We next focus on the other characteristics of commodities in order to evaluate their strategic value in a portfolio.

The Matter of Higher Moments

Unlike the risk premium discussion, the literature is consistent about higher moments of commodities. In addition to the researchers already mentioned, Geman[13] and Till and Eagleeye[14] come to the same conclusions about the characteristics of higher moments. All use historical evidence from work such as Fama and French[15] and Bodie and Rosansky.[16] The following sections are based on their results.

Variance or Second Central Moment

The variance is one the most widespread risk measures in portfolio theory. It is calculated as follows:

$$\sigma^2 = \sum_{i=1}^{n} (r_i - \bar{r})^2 / n$$

Contrary to public perception, commodity returns do not show significantly different standard deviations from those of large U.S. stocks.

---

[12]Robert Greer, "Commodities—Commodity Indexes for Real Return and Diversification," in *The Handbook of Inflation Hedging Investments*, edited by Robert Greer (New York: McGraw-Hill, 2005).

[13]Geman, "Stochastic Modeling of Commodity Price Processes."

[14]Hilary Till and Joseph Eagleeye, "Commodities: Active Strategies for Enhanced Return," *Journal of Wealth Management*, 8, no. 2 (2005), pp. 42–61.

[15]Eugene F. Fama and Kenneth R. French, "Commodity Futures Prices: Some Evidence on Forecast Power, Premiums, and the Theory of Storage," *Journal of Business* 59, no. 4 (1987), pp. 55–73.

[16]Bodie and Rosansky, "Risk and Returns in Commodity Futures."

Next to mean and variance, skewness and kurtosis are two measures which contain additional information about the shape of the *probability density function* (PDF) and, therefore, additional information about the risk and return characteristics of a return distribution of an asset or portfolio. If a return distribution does show skewness and kurtosis significantly different from a normal distribution then variance as a risk measure does not grasp the risk characteristics of the respective return distribution function correctly. In order to understand the risks involved given a not normal return distribution, we look closer at how to calculate and interpret the so-called "higher moments" namely skewness and kurtosis.

Skewness or Third Central Moment The skewness describes the asymmetry of a probability distribution. If the distribution has a longer tail on the right (left) side then the distribution is referred to as positively (negatively) skewed (see Exhibit 19.1). The skewness of a symmetrical probability distribution is equal to zero. Skewness S is calculated as follows:

$$\text{Skewness } (S) = \left[\frac{1}{n}\sum_{i=1}^{n}(r_i - \bar{r})^3\right] \Big/ \sigma^3$$

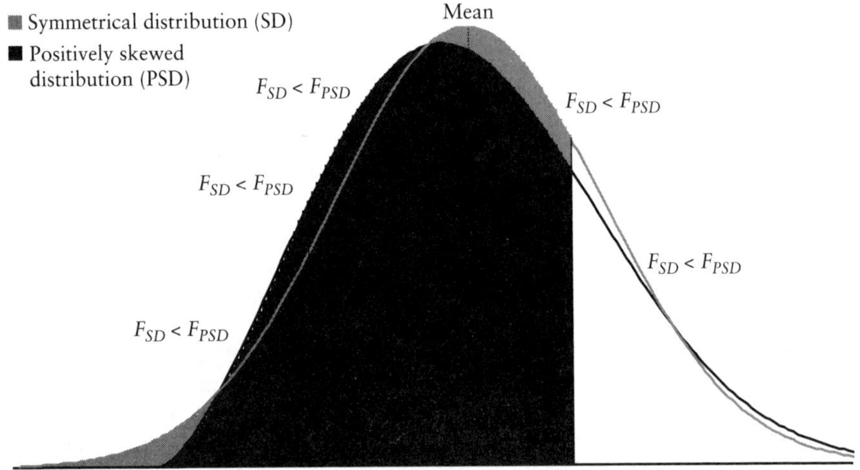

EXHIBIT 19.1 Symmetric versus Skewed Distribution
Source: Authors.

Based on research periods from 25 to 40 years, analysis of the third moment of monthly commodity returns conclude that most commodity return distributions are positively skewed. Unlike normally distributed returns, where the median equals the modus equals the mean of the returns, positively skewed distributions have a mean greater than the modus and greater than the median.

Exhibit 19.1 compares a symmetric return distribution with a positively skewed distribution, with identical means and standard deviations. Note that the symmetric distribution exhibits more returns on the left tail than the positively skewed distribution. If the value of the distribution function of symmetric distribution F_{SD} is equal to the value of positively skewed distribution function F_{PSD} (the vertical black lines in Exhibit 19.1), then there are just as many returns below the line for both distributions. This means there are more returns between the two lines for the positively skewed distribution.

Furthermore, the positively skewed distribution has more returns below the mean. This indicates investors will earn on average smaller returns while still avoiding extreme losses. As compensation, the probability of earning larger positive returns is higher for a positively skewed return distribution than for a comparable symmetric distribution. Risk-averse investors generally prefer positively skewed return distributions so they can avoid extreme losses.[17]

Kurtosis or Fourth Central Moment Kurtosis describes whether a probability distribution is more acute or wider in comparison to a normal distribution, which has a kurtosis of three. If a probability distribution is more acute (wider) and has more (less) returns at the tails then a normal distribution then the distribution is referred to as leptocurtic (platycurtic). Kurtosis K is calculated as follows:

$$\text{Kurtosis}\,(K) = \left[\frac{1}{n}\sum_{i=1}^{n}(r_i - \bar{r})^4\right] \Big/ \sigma^4$$

Financial theory often refers to excess kurtosis. The excess kurtosis is the deviation of the kurtosis of a probability distribution in comparison to the kurtosis of the normal distribution. The excess kurtosis equals the kurtosis minus three.

---

[17]Fred D. Arditti, "Risk and the Required Return on Equity," *Journal of Finance* 22, no. 1 (1967), pp. 19–36.

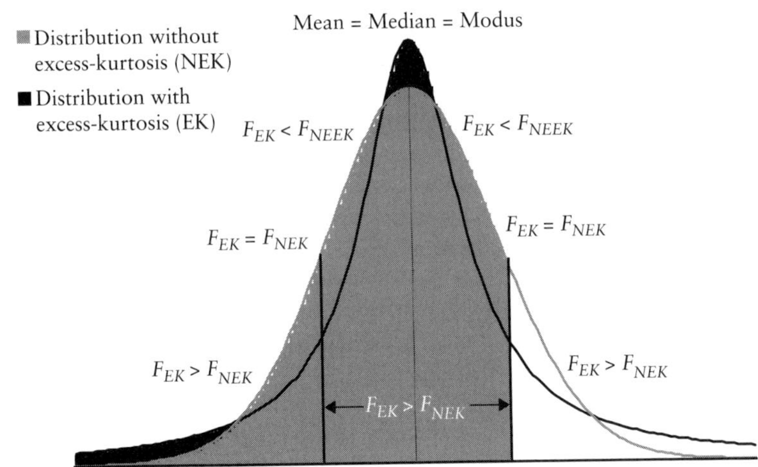

EXHIBIT 19.2 Distributions with and without Excess Kurtosis
Source: Authors.

Unlike stocks, commodity return distributions often exhibit a kurtosis greater than three or a positive excess kurtosis, Exhibit 19.2 shows two symmetric return distributions with identical means, one with kurtosis and the other without. Note that return distributions with excess kurtosis generally exhibit higher and more frequent extreme returns. Thus, when we analyze the distributions below where F_{EK} equals F_{NEK} (the left vertical line), the mean average loss is higher for distributions with excess kurtosis. These distributions often exhibit a higher or more acute peak than distributions without excess kurtosis. Thus most returns lie within the immediate vicinity of the mean.

Risk-averse investors who wish to avoid extreme losses may choose to invest in assets with return distribution without excess kurtosis. However, this "insurance" comes with a higher volatility of the returns around the mean—in the positive as well as the negative case.

The Matter of Correlation

Because of the heterogeneity of commodities, we need to distinguish between correlations among different commodities, and correlations between commodities and other asset classes like stocks and bonds.

Correlations between Commodities Correlations between nonrelated commodities like soybeans and oil are low or even negative. They may vary from approximately −0.3 to 0.3.[18] In practice, closely related commodities like heating oil, crude oil, and gasoline, or wheat and soybeans, are often sorted into a commodity grouping or subindex.

Nonrelated commodity groupings like "energy" and "soft" commodities, or "energy" and "grains," also generally exhibit low or negative correlations. Closely related commodities such as silver and gold, or commodity groupings like "energy" and "petroleum," generally have high correlations and vary from approximately 0.5 to 0.95.[19] Generally, the effect of diversification increases as correlation decreases, making nonrelated commodities good diversifiers for each other.

Correlations between Commodities and Other Asset Classes The correlation between commodity indexes such as the GSCI, the Dow Jones-AIG Commodity Index, and the Deutsche Bank Commodity Index with stocks, bonds, and real estate investment trusts (REITs) is small or negative.[20] The correlation of commodities with other alternative investments, such as hedge funds, private equity, and real estate, is a special case. The heterogeneity of those asset classes makes assessing their correlations more complicated and for this reason has not been researched entirely.

Commodities and Inflation

Generally, stocks and bonds are negatively correlated with inflation, which makes their returns vulnerable to inflation. Commodities, however, exhibit the opposite effect. They are positively correlated with inflation, unexpected inflation, and changes in the inflation rate.[21] That makes commodities a generally good investment during periods of high inflation.

However, it is important to note that not all commodities provide an adequate hedge against inflation. Wheat and silver do not exhibit exceptionally high correlations with inflation because their prices do not rise as prices increase. Energy or livestock are better choices. However, investors should remember that historically positive correlations with inflation are no guarantee of future positive correlations.[22]

---

[18]Dow Jones Indexes, *Dow Jones AIG Commodity Indexes: Performance Summary* (2006).

[19]Dow Jones Indexes, *Dow Jones AIG Commodity Indexes: Performance Summary* (2006).

[20]Thomas E. Toth, "Commodity Index Comparison," White Paper, 2005.

[21]Zvi Bodie, "Commodity Futures as a Hedge Against Inflation," *Journal of Portfolio Management* 9, no. 3 (1983), pp. 12–17.

[22]Erb and Harvey, "The Strategic and Tactical Value of Commodity Futures."

Nevertheless, commodities remain a historically good investment during periods of high inflation, particularly over bonds. And during low-inflation periods, commodities show at least bond-like returns.[23]

What Does the Market Say?

Despite the favorable characteristics of commodities, there are many reasons why they are still rarely used to diversify portfolios. There are few regulatory obstacles for institutional investors like pension funds, but also many arguments against commodity investing. We summarize the most important next.

The lack of familiarity with this asset class and the issue of how best to gain exposure are surely among the most important.[24] Many large investors like pension funds, high-net worth individuals, insurance companies, and trusts do not have experience with commodity funds or index trackers. This asset class is still young, and thus time series are short, especially for commodity funds. Commodity indexes, in fact, are often backfilled.

Furthermore, institutional investors usually want to avoid physical delivery, so they may not be allowed to invest in such assets. Finally, commodity investments do not usually offer dividends, which may be important for nonprofits and trusts.

However, since 2003 commodity markets have shown a significant upward trend, illustrated by a significant increase in the amount of money invested in commodity indexes. The GSCI commodity index, for example, has quintupled in size since 2002 to $60 billion. Goldman Sachs in a 2006 report estimated that about $90 billion is currently invested in commodity indexes, almost seven times the amount invested in 2002.

The long price run-up in commodity sectors like energy has played a large part in this surge. But increasing global demand for commodities from Asia, India, and China is also responsible. Other triggers for investment in commodities include decreasing investment in production and manufacturing, and inflation concerns.

Commodities as an Investment and Potential Portfolio Diversifier

To summarize the arguments so far expressed, we find no convincing evidence for the existence of a risk premium in a commodity portfolio. However, efficient and well diversified commodity portfolios are a reliable

[23]Kenneth A. Froot, "Hedging Portfolios with Real Assets," *Journal of Portfolio Management* 21, no. 4 (1995), pp. 60–77.

[24]See Mark J. P. Anson, Chapter 14, Commodity Futures in a Portfolio Context, in *Handbook of Alternative Assets* (Hoboken, NJ: John Wiley & Sons, Inc., 2006).

source of returns. The third moment of commodity return distributions is considered beneficial for risk-averse investors since most commodity returns are positively skewed. The fourth moment, often found to be larger than three, is considered less beneficial for risk-averse investors.

In contrast, the correlations between commodities themselves, and between commodities and stocks, bonds, and REITs, are low, meaning commodities are a good portfolio diversifier. As we noted earlier, commodities perform well during high-inflation periods, and provide bond-like returns during low-inflation periods. Commodities are also likely to perform well during adverse economic surprises, times during which stock and bond returns are likely to drop significantly.[25]

Along with the classical exposure to commodities through physical purchases, commodity futures or options, and related stocks, the number of potential commodity investment vehicles has been growing steadily. Commodity-related funds, commodity indexes and index trackers, and commodity-related notes all enhance market liquidity.

Considering all of these points, we would argue that commodities are a basic part of our economy and a unique asset class. We believe a basket of commodities is a sensible portfolio diversifier and an improvement over strategic asset allocation, making it possible to reach a superior efficient frontier.[26]

EXPOSURE TO COMMODITIES

Because of their increasing popularity and amount invested, the relevance of commodity investment vehicles like commodity indexes or index tracker has increased. We know that not all single commodities are equally good investments, so it would be useful to establish an efficient commodity allocation to use as a "real" diversifier. In the course of this chapter, we examine how to obtain an efficient frontier of commodity portfolios. We also determine which commodities are important in efficient portfolios, and where the risks lie.

To answer these questions, however, we need to solve the problem of how best to gain exposure to different commodities first. We mentioned previously

[25]Franklin R. Edwards and Mustafa O. Caglayan, "Hedge Fund and Commodity Fund Investment Styles in Bull and Bear Markets," *Journal of Portfolio Management* 27, no. 4 (2001), pp. 97–108.

[26]Geman, Chapter 14, Commodities as a New Asset Class, in *Commodities and Commodity Derivatives: Modeling and Pricing for Agriculturals, Metals and Energy*; Theo E. Nijman and Laurens P. Swinkels, Strategic and Tactical Allocation to Commodities for Retirement, Working Paper, 2003; and Robert Gordon, "Commodities in an Asset Allocation Context," *Journal of Taxation of Investment* 23, no. 2 (2006), pp. 101–189.

that it is almost impossible to invest directly in commodities. Investors may gain exposure to commodities through commodity-related stocks. They may also choose an exposure through commodity futures, or through indexes based on commodity futures or spots. Among these alternatives, commodity indexes are an easy way to gain the desired direct exposure to commodities and their return characteristics without the problem of physical delivery.

Spot, Excess Return, and Total Return Indexes

Three basic types of commodity indexes are offered by different providers: spot indexes, excess return indexes, and total return indexes. A spot index tracks the prices of nearby futures contracts (not the returns, as with commodity indexes). An excess return index measures returns from investing in commodity futures rolling over shortly expiring contracts in the next corresponding contract. A total return index measures the returns of a fully collateralized commodity futures investment that is also rolled regularly to avoid physical delivery. In this option, three-month Treasury bills (T-bills) add an interest component to the futures investment.

Because of different tracking methods, none of these indexes is directly comparable with another. It is theoretically possible to add T-bills to an excess return index. However, the results would not be the same, for two reasons: (1) the impact of reinvesting the interest on the collateral into commodity futures would be ignored; and (2) the gains (or losses) of the commodity futures could not be reinvested into T-bills.

While an excess return index resembles a leveraged futures investment, a total return index is significantly different from a direct physical commodity investment. Because of the collateral interest yield, it can earn positive returns even if commodity prices decline.[27] To present the characteristics of commodities in as clear a way as possible, we focus on the exposure to commodities gained by an excess return commodity index.

Commodity Index Provider and Commodity Index Characteristics

Having chosen the index, we still need to choose the index provider. Currently, there are five large commodity indexes offered by different providers: Commodity Research Bureau Index (CRB), Goldman Sachs Commodity Index (GSCI), Dow Jones-American International Group Commodity Index (DJ-AIGCI), Standard & Poor's Commodity Index (SPCI),

---

[27] Idzorek, Strategic Asset Allocation and Commodities.

and Deutsche Bank Commodity Index (DBLCI).[28] At first glance, investors have a wide choice of options to fill their needs. But how to choose among these different options? Commodity indexes often exhibit differing risk-return characteristics. Consequently, monthly correlations range from about 0.65 (CRB and GSCI) to 0.96 (DBLCI and GSCI).[29]

These results emphasize how important it is to choose the right index and index provider if considering an investment in a mixed commodity index.[30] Investors especially face the difficulty of knowing the risk-return profile of the respective index, and how to determine whether it is efficient and appropriate for their investment purposes. In the analysis following, we attempt to close this gap. The efficient commodity portfolios we estimate are based on the single commodities underlying the above indexes. This enables direct investment into the efficient portfolio with the most desired risk-return profile.

Data Underlying the Efficient Frontier

The choice of the right index is essential to avoid biases in the analysis. Characteristics of a good index are on the one hand that the index mirrors the development of the respective sector, and on the other hand that the index is accepted in public and by financial investors. Both criteria are met by the Dow Jones-American International Group and its commodity indexes.[31] The following analysis uses 20 commodity indexes from the Dow Jones index classification. The commodities represented through the indexes are widely distinguished, and are therefore a good representation of the investment universe.

---

[28]See Geman, Chapter 14, Commodities as a New Asset Class, in *Commodities and Commodity Derivatives: Modeling and Pricing for Agriculturals, Metals and Energy*.

[29]Thomas E. Toth, "Commodity Index Comparison," White Paper, 2005.

[30]Using different data sets might have caused the contradicting results for the existence of a commodity risk premium. Erb and Harvey, for example, use commodity data without any bias toward a single commodity, while Gorton and Rouwenhorst use energy-weighted commodity data.

[31]The aim of the Dow Jones-American International Group is to provide a continuous, liquid, and well-diversified commodity benchmark for institutional investors. This index was created in 1998, with a backfilled history until January 1991, for a data set of about 190 monthly returns for each single commodity. The commodity indexes track the hypothetical long investments in futures contracts on physical commodities. Except for some metals (aluminium, lead, tin, nickel, and zinc), which are traded at the London Metals Exchange, all futures contracts are traded on a U.S. exchange. See DJ-AIGCI^{SM}, the *Dow Jones-AIG Commodity Index*^{SM} *Handbook* (2006).

Single-Commodity Return Characteristics

To provide an overview of the return characteristics and to better interpret the results later, we calculate the first four moments, derive the minimum and maximum monthly returns and the maximum drawdown of the different commodity returns, and, finally, test for normally distributed returns. We use returns derived from the excess price indexes from February 1991 through November 2006. Antecedent the interpretation of the return characteristics of the single commodity indexes shown later we will have a closer look at the maximum drawdown as an important risk measure.

Maximum Drawdown Earlier, we described the importance of the first four moments and how to interpret them. To better understand the risks any investor faces when considering a commodity investment, we derive the minimum and the *maximum drawdown* (MaxDD) for each commodity index. The MaxDD is particularly useful because it numbers the maximum absolute loss of the sample period.

Exhibit 19.3 illustrates how to calculate the MaxDD. It is measured from the last peak price (marked by the left, upper dot) to the all-time low

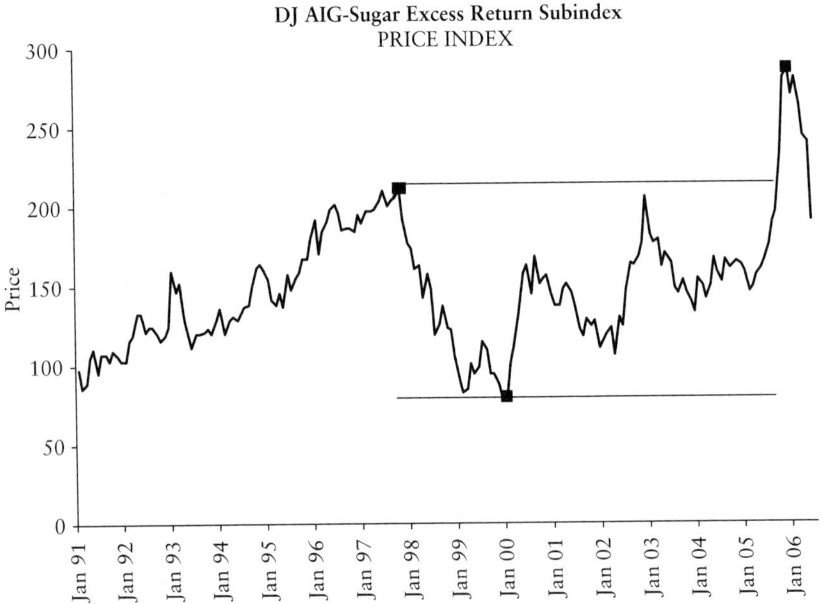

EXHIBIT 19.3 Maximum Drawdown (MaxDD)
Source: Exhibit created from data obtained from Dow Jones.

(marked by the lower vertical line, and the middle, lower dot), until a new price transcends the former peak price (marked by the upper vertical line and the right, upper dot):

$$\text{MaxDD} = \left[\text{Min}\left(\frac{\text{Price}_{t+1}}{\text{Price}_t}\right) - 1\right] \cdot 100$$

Price_t is equal to the peak price with $t = 1, \ldots, n$, where 1 marks the start of the research period and n the end. Price_{t+1} is a price lower or equal to Price_t. As soon as Price_{t+1} is larger than the former peak price, Price_{t+1} becomes the new peak price.

Analyzing our data set, we find five commodities with high negative average monthly returns. All are agricultural products or livestock. Approximately half the analyzed commodities show average monthly returns of more than 0.30%; all are metals or fossil fuels. However, a high average monthly return is no guarantee that the maximum monthly return will be above the average of the maximum monthly returns of the single commodities considered. Coffee, for example, has a low positive average monthly return and a very high maximum monthly return.

High average monthly returns are also no insurance against low minimum monthly returns or a high MaxDD. More than half the commodities with average monthly returns greater than 0.50% show a MaxDD greater than −80%. Except for cotton, the MaxDD for commodities with negative average returns did not exceed −60%.

Normally or Nonnormally Distributed Monthly Returns Consistent with the literature, we find only two out of 20 monthly commodity index return distributions that are not positively skewed (see Exhibit 19.4).[32] Furthermore, 12 of the 20 have excess kurtosis of more than 3.80. Those two measures taken together are a good indication that most of the monthly commodity index return distributions appear to have nonnormal distributions. We would mention in this context coffee and gold, which have exceptionally high positive skewness and excess kurtosis.

In order to verify this assumption, we calculate the Jarque-Bera (JB) test statistic, which tests the hypotheses of a normal return distribution.[33] The

[32]Gorton and Rouwenhorst, "Facts and Fantasies about Commodity Futures."

[33]The JB test statistic is based on skewness (S) and kurtosis (K), and is defined as: $JB = n(S^2/6 + (K-3)^2/24)$, where n is the number of observations. See Anil K. Bera and Carlos M. Jarque, "Efficient Tests for Normality, Homoscedasticity and Serial Independence of Regression Residuals," *Economics Letters* 6, no. 3 (1980), pp. 255–253.

EXHIBIT 19.4 Moment Statistics, Maximum and Minimum Returns, and Jarque-Bera Statistics Based on Monthly Excess Return Data, February 1991 to November 2006

	Mean	Maximum	Minimum	MaxDD	Std. Dev.	Skewness	Kurtosis	JB
DJ AIG–Aluminum Index	0.00%	13.51%	−12.03%	−61.9%	4.80%	0.16	2.87	1.02
DJ AIG–Cocoa Index	−0.51%	28.46%	−19.90%	−59.2%	7.69%	0.69	4.30	25.70[a]
DJ AIG–Coffee Index	0.06%	67.27%	−19.68%	−87.7%	12.01%	1.74	9.56	402.77[a]
DJ AIG–Copper Index	0.93%	25.93%	−16.55%	−86.7%	6.44%	0.54	4.03	15.80[a]
DJ AIG–Corn Index	−0.66%	25.60%	−18.26%	−55.5%	6.15%	0.45	4.75	27.26[a]
DJ AIG–Cotton Index	−0.59%	19.38%	−14.98%	−89.2%	6.40%	0.41	3.05	5.19
DJ AIG–Crude Oil Index	1.25%	27.79%	−25.22%	−87.6%	8.76%	−0.05	3.01	0.10
DJ AIG–Gold Index	0.04%	20.13%	−12.60%	−66.0%	3.89%	1.10	6.96	148.50[a]
DJ AIG–Heating Oil Index	0.87%	28.17%	−18.51%	−72.0%	8.55%	0.27	3.06	2.29
DJ AIG–Lean Hogs Index	−0.39%	36.26%	−24.33%	−51.5%	7.10%	0.25	6.78	103.18[a]
DJ AIG–Live Cattle Index	0.07%	9.98%	−12.10%	−79.6%	3.49%	−0.24	3.64	4.20
DJ AIG–Natural Gas Index	0.34%	44.34%	−33.01%	−55.4%	13.72%	0.42	3.30	5.69
DJ AIG–Nickel Index	0.99%	30.93%	−22.67%	−84.2%	8.47%	0.55	3.98	15.57[a]
DJ AIG–Silver Index	0.48%	21.08%	−16.99%	−47.5%	6.53%	0.30	3.88	7.61[b]
DJ AIG–Soybean Oil Index	−0.08%	17.23%	−18.85%	−61.2%	5.86%	0.29	3.69	5.55
DJ AIG–Soybean Index	0.20%	20.42%	−16.09%	−69.3%	5.96%	0.39	3.99	11.10[a]
DJ AIG–Sugar Index	0.63%	29.16%	−20.44%	−49.5%	8.51%	0.51	3.80	11.93[a]
DJ AIG–Unleaded Gas Index	1.11%	26.56%	−22.37%	−62.8%	8.90%	0.09	3.31	0.65
DJ AIG–Wheat Index	−0.38%	26.22%	−16.59%	−59.3%	6.89%	0.77	4.14	26.72[a]
DJ AIG–Zinc Index	0.51%	25.38%	−17.94%	−89.7%	6.03%	0.67	5.08	43.75[a]

Source: Exhibit created from data obtained from Dow Jones.

[a]Denotes that the null hypothesis of normality is rejected at the 1% level if JB is higher than 9.21.

[b]Denotes that the null hypothesis of normality is rejected at the 5% level if JB is higher than 5.99.

statistics follow an asymptotic chi-squared distribution, with two degrees of freedom.

The hypothesis of normality is rejected at the 5% (1%) level if the JB test statistic is greater than 5.99 (9.21). For commodities labeled with "a", the hypothesis of normality can be rejected at the 5% confidence level; for commodities labeled with "b", it is rejected at the 1% level.

We find that the hypothesis of normal return distributions is rejected for eleven commodities at the 1% level, and for one (silver) at the 5% level (see Exhibit 19.4). As a result, in general portfolios consisting of different commodities, which use only variance as a risk measure, underestimates risk and must be suboptimal, since risk is only expressed by variance. Higher moments must be taken into account if we face nonnormal return distributions.

Correlation

In order to analyze the potential of single commodities to diversify each other in a portfolio consisting solely of commodities, we calculate a correlation matrix among the 20 commodities we study here. The results are shown in Exhibit 19.5.

Consistent with the earlier descriptions of commodity characteristics, we find the correlation among nonrelated commodities to be small or zero, and the correlation among related commodities to be high. A good example is cocoa, a commodity unrelated to any of the others. It has no correlation greater than 0.17 with any commodity shown in Exhibit 19.5. Crude oil exhibits the opposite. It is closely related to heating oil and unleaded gas, and has a correlation of about 0.9 with them. Its correlation with the other commodities is lower than 0.18, except for natural gas, with which it has a correlation of about 0.32.

DERIVING EFFICIENT COMMODITY PORTFOLIOS

To summarize the characteristics of single commodities, we find it cannot be assumed that all single commodities have normally distributed monthly returns. We also note that single commodity returns are often skewed, exhibit fat tails, and show large MaxDDs.

We conclude that the assumption of normally distributed returns, one of Markowitz's basic assumptions of portfolio theory, is violated for many single commodities. As a result, standard deviation (or variance) is not an adequate risk measure for the characteristics of single commodity returns. There is a widespread discussion in the literature about the limitations of

EXHIBIT 19.5 Correlation of Commodity Indexes Based on Monthly Excess Return Data, February 1991 to November 2006

	Aluminum	Cocoa	Coffee	Copper	Corn	Cotton	Crude Oil	Gold	Heating Oil	Lean Hogs	Live Cattle	Natural Gas	Nickel	Silver	Soybean Oil	Soybean	Sugar	Unleaded Gas	Wheat	Zinc
Aluminum	1.00	0.08	0.18	0.58	0.03	0.05	0.13	0.17	0.11	−0.09	0.05	0.05	0.50	0.22	0.07	0.06	0.07	0.13	0.05	0.52
Cocoa		1.00	0.14	0.08	0.10	0.01	0.10	0.10	0.02	−0.12	−0.06	−0.02	0.03	0.06	0.06	0.12	0.17	0.12	0.15	0.05
Coffee			1.00	0.16	−0.07	−0.01	0.02	0.11	−0.02	0.01	−0.04	−0.10	0.15	0.21	−0.03	0.00	0.08	−0.02	0.03	0.16
Copper				1.00	0.01	0.08	0.16	0.27	0.14	0.00	−0.11	0.07	0.50	0.28	0.21	0.16	0.07	0.12	0.05	0.52
Corn					1.00	0.12	0.00	0.11	−0.02	0.06	−0.06	0.02	0.11	0.13	0.49	0.65	−0.01	0.00	0.61	0.05
Cotton						1.00	0.10	−0.07	0.10	0.05	0.10	0.05	0.08	−0.04	0.19	0.24	−0.04	0.07	0.00	0.09
Crude oil							1.00	0.15	0.91	−0.05	0.02	0.32	0.18	0.11	−0.07	0.00	0.05	0.89	0.01	0.14
Gold								1.00	0.15	0.00	0.02	0.09	0.30	0.54	0.12	0.16	0.11	0.14	0.16	0.22
Heating oil									1.00	−0.03	0.04	0.44	0.16	0.09	−0.06	0.02	0.08	0.88	0.01	0.11
Lean hogs										1.00	0.32	0.07	−0.03	−0.04	0.13	0.08	0.02	−0.05	0.02	−0.04
Live cattle											1.00	0.04	0.04	−0.14	−0.03	0.03	0.07	0.01	0.03	−0.03
Natural gas												1.00	0.03	0.04	0.01	0.09	0.06	0.32	−0.01	0.04
Nickel													1.00	0.28	0.10	0.12	0.00	0.13	0.10	0.47
Silver														1.00	0.14	0.18	0.12	0.10	0.05	0.26
Soybean oil															1.00	0.73	0.00	−0.07	0.32	0.05
Soybean																1.00	0.05	−0.03	0.40	0.03
Sugar																	1.00	0.04	0.11	0.11
Unleaded gas																		1.00	0.03	0.15
Wheat																			1.00	0.00
Zinc																				1.00

Source: Exhibit created from data obtained from Dow Jones.

Markowitz's mean-variance analysis. Possible solutions and suggested frameworks abound. We are searching for a risk measure to account for the high risks involved in a commodity investment, namely the fat tails and the high MaxDD. We believe the *conditional Value-at-Risk* (CVaR) measure meets these requirements.

Conditional Value-at-Risk as a Risk Measure

The possible use of CVaR as a criterion for optimal portfolio selection has attracted the attention of researchers such as Artzner et al.[34]; Rockafellar and Uryasev[35]; and Embrechts, Kaplanski, and Kroll.[36] But what makes the CVaR a good risk measure? In the following section, we take a closer look at CVaR and compare it to the popular Value-at-Risk (VaR) risk measure.

CVaR versus VaR Exhibit 19.6 gives an example of a random nonnormal return distribution. The downside risk of this distribution can be measured by the quantiles of the distribution. The alpha quantile is defined as the cut-

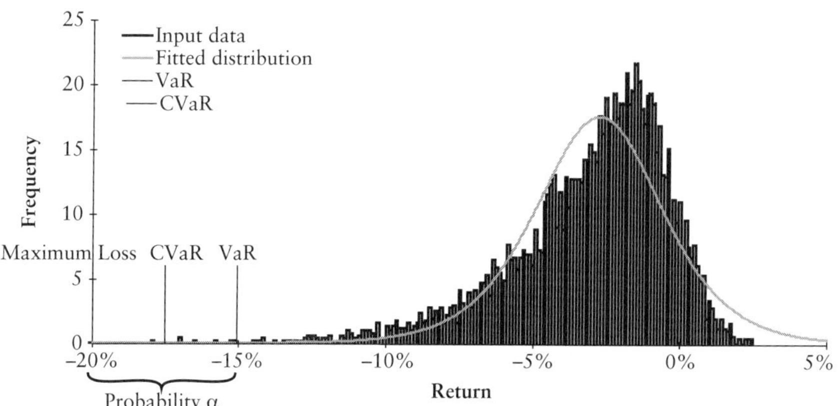

EXHIBIT 19.6 VaR versus CVaR as Risk Measure of Choice
Source: Authors.

[34]Philippe Artzner, Freddy Delbaen, Jean-Marc Eber, and David Heath, "Coherent Measures of Risk," *Mathematical Finance* 9, no. 3 (1999), pp. 203–228.
[35]Tyrrell R. Rockafellar and Stanislav Uryasev, "Optimization of Conditional Value-at-Risk," *Journal of Risk* 2, no. 3 (2000), pp. 21–41.
[36]Paul Embrechts, Claudia Klüppelberg, and Thomas Mikosch, *Modelling Extremal Events for Insurance and Finance* (Heidelberg: Springer, 2003).

off return, so that lower returns only appear alpha percent of the time. Alpha is a real number between 0 (no case of the return distribution) and 1 (all cases of the return distribution).

Consider where the alpha quantile is 5% in Exhibit 19.6. The VaR is calculated at −15%, meaning 95% of the returns will be greater than −15% (or only 5% of the returns will be below −15%). For normal return distributions, VaR is a good risk measure because the losses beyond the alpha quantile or the tail of the distribution decrease very quickly. However, as Exhibit 19.6 shows, VaR is not adequate for heavily negative skewed and/or fat-tailed return distributions, because 5% of the losses are so great as to be virtually unacceptable. The VaR basically truncates the distribution at the 5% level, blissfully ignorant of what lays beyond.[37]

CVaR is the risk measure that we need: A risk measure that can also account for the losses beyond the alpha quantile. CVaR can consider the amount of losses beyond the −15% cutoff return, defined as the expected loss if VaR is exceeded at the alpha quantile. In our example, CVaR would equal about −17%.

Drawbacks of VaR As demonstrated and illustrated in Exhibit 19.6, VaR has several properties that can be problematic in the context of a commodity portfolio optimization and in typical financial applications. Next, we give a short summary of the reasons against VaR.

Given rational utility functions, one possible outcome when using VaR is an inconsistent ranking in the risk-return framework. VaR can cause the elimination of desirable protections against rare but high-loss events. This argument is most relevant in the context of commodity investments because of the possibility of high monthly losses (e.g., from energy commodities), and high maximum drawdowns (e.g., from coffee and cotton).[38]

As Exhibit 19.6 already demonstrated, losses beyond the threshold amount of probability remain outside further consideration. Consequently, CVaR and VaR risk-return optimal portfolios may be quite different for heavily skewed distributions. By calculating an optimal portfolio by minimizing the VaR, one neglects all distribution properties beyond the alpha quantile. This makes it theoretically possible to stretch the tail and the losses exceeding the VaR ad infinitum without altering the results of the optimization.[39]

---

[37]The VaR and CVaR calculations are based on the fitted distribution.

[38]Suleyman Basak and Alex Shapiro, "Value-at-Risk Based Risk Management: Optimal Policies and Asset Prices," *Review of Financial Studies* 14, no. 2 (2001), pp. 371–405.

[39]Alexei A. Gaivoronski and Georg Pflug, "Value-at-Risk in Portfolio Optimization: Properties and Computational Approach," *Journal of Risk* 7, no. 2 (2005), pp. 1–31.

Another drawback of the estimation of a commodity portfolio frontier using VaR as a risk measure is its determinability: If the returns are not normally distributed, the estimation of mean-VaR-efficient portfolios may be very difficult, especially if the return distribution is discrete. In this case, the frontier estimated by the VaR dependent on the portfolio weights is nonconvex, nonsmooth, and has multiple local extrema.[40]

To summarize, VaR has some undesirable characteristics. Unlike CVaR, it is not a coherent risk measure according to Artzner et al.[41] For a more detailed discussion of risk measures see also Ortobelli et al.[42] and Wu and Xiao.[43] The disadvantages of VaR in the context of evaluating risky alternatives of nonnormal return distributions have led to the development of CVaR as a coherent and superior risk measure.

In line with Kaplanski and Kroll,[44] we believe CVaR is more adequate for modelling the properties of commodity return distributions. Thus we estimate the efficient frontier for a portfolio consisting of different commodities by using the mean-conditional Value-at-Risk (mean-CVaR) approach.

TECHNICAL IMPLEMENTATION OF THE MEAN-CVaR APPROACH

To implement this approach, we consider the 20 (n) previously described commodities. Formally, for each point in time, we have a vector $\rho = (\rho_1, \rho_2, \ldots, \rho_n)$ of commodity returns, which measure the relative price changes during the period. The returns are not known at the time of the allocation of the commodity portfolio and are thus considered random variables.

Investors are free to choose the fraction they want to invest in each commodity, described by the portfolio vector $x = (x_1, x_2, \ldots, x_n)$, allowing for budget constraints, short-selling restrictions, and the constraint to a

---

[40]Pavlo Krokhmal, Jonas Palmquist, and Stanislav Uryasev, "Portfolio Optimization with Conditional Value-at-Risk Objective and Constraints," *Journal of Risk* 4, no. 2 (2001), pp. 43–68.

[41]Artzner, Delbaen, Eber, and Heath, "Coherent Measures of Risk."

[42]Sergio Ortobelli, Svetlozar T. Rachev, Stoyan Stoyanov, Frank J. Fabozzi, and Almira Biglova, "The Proper Use of Risk Measures in Portfolio Theory," *International Journal of Theoretical and Applied Finance* 8, no. 8 (2005), pp. 1–27.

[43]Guojun Wu and Zhijie Xiao, "An Analysis of Risk Measures," *Journal of Risk* 4, no. 4 (2002), pp. 53–75.

[44]Guy Kaplanski, and Yoram Kroll, "VaR Risk Measures versus Traditional Risk Measures: An Analysis and Survey," *Journal of Risk* 4, no. 3 (2002).

minimum demand for diversification. Mathematically, this means the portfolio weights must sum to 1, cannot be negative, and must have an upper bound of 30%. These are standard assumptions in finance theory except for the constraint on the diversification demand. We impose this restriction to avoid the portfolio being dominated by a single commodity.

The portfolio return at the end of the period is equal to $\theta = \sum_{i=1}^{n} x_i \rho_i$. Assume we have a given minimal expected return $\overline{\mu}$, and the investor uses CVaR. We need to solve the following optimization problem:

$$\min_{x} CVaR(\Theta)_{\alpha} = \left(\int_{0}^{\alpha} VaR_{\Theta} d\Theta \right) \Big/ \alpha$$

Subject to

$$\theta = \sum_{i=1}^{n} x_i \rho_i \geq \overline{\mu},$$

$$1 = \sum_{i=1}^{n} x_i,$$

$$30\% \geq x_i > 0, \qquad \forall i = 1, \ldots, n$$

The curve representing the dependence of the optimal value of this problem on the parameter $\overline{\mu}$ is the boundary of the feasible set of mean-CVaR return pairs. A subset of this boundary forms the CVaR-efficient frontier, where investors do not receive more expected return for a given level of risk, and cannot reduce the risk for a chosen expected return. This is a generalization of the well-known calculation of the Markowitz mean-variance efficient frontier.

THE EFFICIENT FRONTIER OF COMMODITY PORTFOLIOS

According to this procedure, we estimate the mean-CVaR efficient frontier. We first calculate the frontier including all 20 commodities. Next, we discard energy commodities (crude oil, heating oil, natural gas, and unleaded gas) because investors are either afraid to invest in those more risky assets,[45]

[45]The risk is measured by MaxDD, standard deviation, and minimum monthly return. Energy commodities on average have a higher risk measured by those criteria.

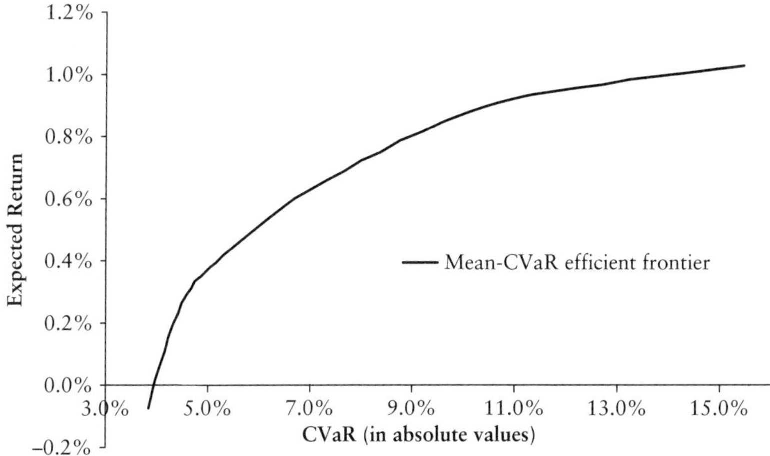

EXHIBIT 19.7 Mean-CVaR Efficient Frontiers for Commodity Portfolios
Source: Exhibit created from data obtained from Dow Jones.

or they already have sufficient exposure through other assets such as energy-related equities. Issuers of investable commodity indexes, such as Goldman Sachs, also offer an index without energy-related commodities.

Exhibits 19.7 and 19.8 show the efficient frontiers for commodity portfolios with and without energy commodities. On the ordinate, we show the

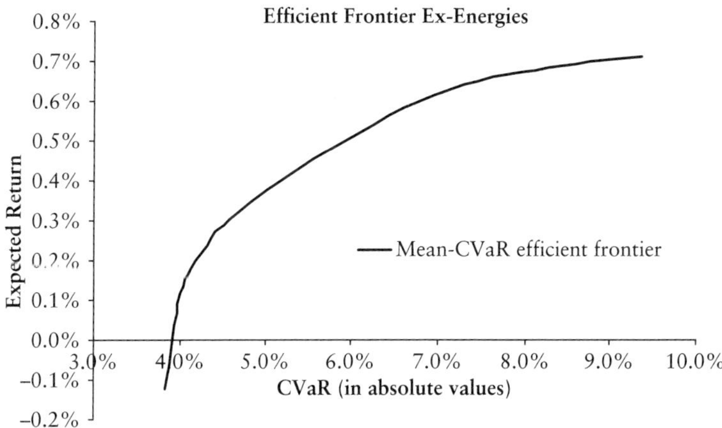

EXHIBIT 19.8 Mean-CVaR Efficient Frontiers for Commodity Portfolios Ex-Energies
Source: Exhibit created from data obtained from Dow Jones.

expected return of the efficient portfolios; the abscissas shows the risk of the respective portfolio measured by the CVaR (or rather the mean average loss below the 5% alpha quantile). Note that the value for CVaR is always positive. In financial analysis, the loss is often shown in absolute values. Thus we take −1 times CVaR to better illustrate the efficient frontier, which is the locus of all efficient risk-return combinations.

Note also from the two exhibits that the minimum-risk portfolios have negative expected monthly returns whether energies are included or not. Analyzing the components of the minimum-risk portfolios, we find live cattle and gold make up the highest proportion. Their portfolio weights including all commodities are about 29% for live cattle and 30% for gold. In the optimization without energy, the weights are about 25% for live cattle and 25% for gold. Both commodities have a lower maximum loss and a lower standard deviation than the others.

For the optimization using all commodities, the weights of live cattle drop as portfolio risk and expected return increase, until they vanish from the portfolio completely. For the optimization excluding energy, the portfolio weights for live cattle initially increase with expected return, until the minimum 30% diversification constraint is reached. For efficient commodity portfolios with expected CVaRs greater than 5%, the weights decrease until they completely vanish. The weight of gold drops for both portfolios as risk and expected return increase. One reason for this may be that the two commodities are acting as risk buffers to the portfolios as shown in Exhibits 19.9 and 19.10.

If investors impose high constraints on portfolio risk, they will be willing to include most commodities considered here in their portfolios. For all commodities in the optimization, ten of 20 commodities would be included in the efficient portfolio; for the optimization without energy, nine out of 16 are still found to be an efficient combination. This is consistent with our finding that nonrelated commodities exhibit low correlations with each other and therefore are good diversifiers for each other (see Exhibit 19.5).

As the riskiness of the efficient commodity portfolios increases (measured by CVaR), the number of commodities decreases, until only four are left (those with the highest expected returns) (see Exhibit 19.10). Those are unleaded gas, heating oil, and crude oil, each with a weight of 30%, and nickel, with a weight of 10%. Because of high expected returns, energy commodities are virtually the only ones included (see Exhibit 19.10).

In the optimization without energy, those commodities are replaced by zinc, nickel, and copper, with weights of about 30% each, and silver with 10% (see Exhibit 19.10). In this case, precious metals and industrial metals take the place of energy commodities in the overall optimization.

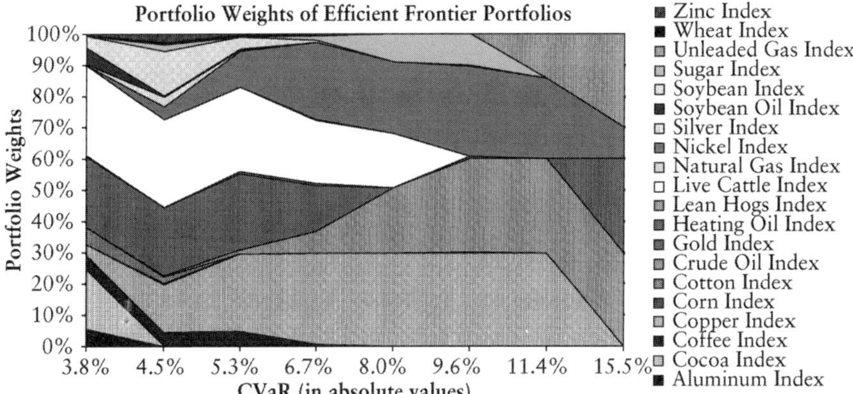

EXHIBIT 19.9 Development of Commodity Weights with Increasing Expected Return on the Efficient Frontier
Source: Exhibit created from data obtained from Dow Jones.
Note: This Exhibit shows the weights of the single commodities for portfolios with different levels of riskiness expressed through CVaR. The wider the area, the larger the weight or share of the single commodity in the portfolio. Note that for low levels of CVaR, the diversification is high. This means no single commodity dominates the portfolio. The higher the riskiness, the lower the diversification, and single commodities start to dominate until they reach the demand for minimum diversification restriction.

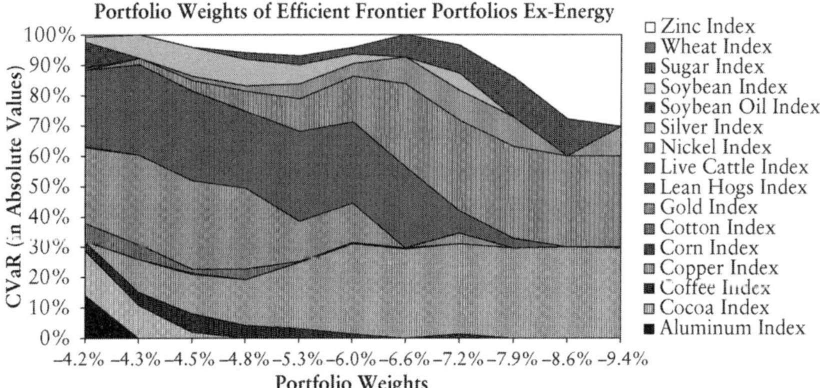

EXHIBIT 19.10 Development of Commodity Weights Excluding Energy with Increasing Expected Returns on the Efficient Frontier
Source: Exhibit created from data obtained from Dow Jones.

CONCLUSION

We find it important to first analyze the return distribution characteristics of single commodities before considering those as a diversifier to a portfolio. In doing so, we find that most returns of single commodities, the components of a commodity portfolio, have historically been close to zero. However, a portfolio of single commodities has historically offered investors equity like returns. This emphasizes the importance of the right commodity portfolio composition.

If choosing to invest in commodities, an investor additionally has to pay attention to the higher moments. Whereas the monthly volatility of most single commodities is not significantly different from large stocks, monthly return distributions of single commodities are positively skewed and often exhibit leptokurtosis. Furthermore nonrelated single commodities show a low correlation among each other and to stocks, bonds, and REITs making them good portfolio diversifiers. Among the positive characteristics of single commodities is surely also the high correlation with inflation. However, we find that not every single commodity is a good investment.

We find that single commodities can exhibit very different return characteristics. If a commodity has a positive average return over our sample period, it does not necessarily have a low MaxDD or low standard deviation. In fact, it is often the contrary. Several commodities did show a negative average monthly return, but they exhibited on average lower MaxDD and reasonable maximum monthly returns. Combined with a low correlation with other commodities, they might be effective portfolio diversifiers.

For the above characteristics, especially high MaxDDs, we do not find single commodities are a good standalone investment. As noted by Erb and Harvey in their study, single commodities may not offer a positive risk premium, which makes it even more important to carefully structure an efficient commodity portfolio. Such work will be rewarded, because commodities have a low correlation with each other and are thus good diversifiers for each other.

It is thus possible to structure efficient commodity portfolios with reduced risk and enhanced returns in comparison to a single-commodity investment. Furthermore, it is possible to earn high expected monthly returns, but these may depend heavily on the amount of risk investors are willing to accept. Ultimately, we find that an efficient mixed commodity portfolio can be a promising investment, not only on its own but as a good portfolio diversifier.

CHAPTER 20

Active Management of Commodity Investments: The Role of CTAs and Hedge Funds

R. McFall Lamm, Jr., Ph.D.
Chief Investment Strategist
Global Investment Management
Deutsche Bank

Commodity investment has moved to the forefront of portfolio management over the past few years, largely in response to strong outperformance versus stocks and bonds. Supporters promote commodities as a new asset class, which they believe should further reward investors in the future as a new "super cycle" unfolds. In contrast, skeptics argue that commodity prices have a tendency to mean-revert and are wary of committing at what may be the late phase of the current cyclical upturn.

Regardless of one's view about the immediate future of commodities, most practitioners now acknowledge that there are circumstances when tactical commodity allocations make a great deal of sense. In this chapter, I presume the commodity investment decision has been made to the affirmative and focus on the mechanics of position implementation. While my major concern is the efficacy of active commodity-specialist managers, this necessarily requires considering benchmarks since the active/passive manager split is interdependent.

Because increased interest in commodity investing is a recent phenomenon, the population of active commodity managers competing against benchmarks is sparse. Consequently, in keeping with prior research, I define *active commodity management* to include *commodity trading advisors* (CTAs) and hedge funds that specialize in trading physical commodities. The first section of the chapter provides a brief background on commodity investing. The general framework used for evaluating active commodity managers is then discussed, while the subsequent sections review the performance characteristics of commodity-specialist CTAs and hedge funds. Throughout, I emphasize distinguishing between alpha and the implicit commodity beta exposure provided by the typical manager. Lastly, I discuss the portfolio ramifications of various passive/active commodity allocations.

The key conclusions are that active commodity managers offer distinctive advantages over passive indexing. The reason is that the investment techniques of commodity-specialist active managers differ substantially from stock and bond managers in that they exhibit beta switching and do not employ benchmarks. In this regard, they appear on the surface to be pure alpha generators. Consequently, adding active commodity managers not only imparts portfolio diversification benefits but also provides a convenient hedge if one's return forecasts turn out to be incorrect.

BACKGROUND

Commodity Investing: A Very Brief History

Investing in commodities is hardly a new development. Indeed, during the high inflation era of the 1970s to the early 1980s, many investors made substantial allocations to hard assets—including both commodities and property—as they sought refuge from depreciating paper assets. As a result, commodity futures trading exploded and the property sector boomed, providing extraordinary returns to investors and an effective shield against ravaging inflation. Simultaneously, stock and bond investors experienced a lost decade with essentially zero real return. Few questioned whether commodities were a legitimate asset class at the time.

Unfortunately, the 1970s commodity boom was followed by a prolonged performance drought, which persisted through the end of the century. The turning point came in 1980 with a crash in precious metals prices following the Hunt Brothers' failed attempt to corner the silver market. However, the overall experience was not a massive commodity bubble burst replete with cross-market contagion. Rather, there was a 20-year interval of jagged sideways price movement around a very gradual modest downtrend as periodic rallies were consistently followed by relapses. This is illustrated in Exhibit 20.1, which shows the Commodity Research Bureau *commodity price index* (CRY) compared with the *producer price index* (PPI) for crude materials and the *consumer price index* (CPI).

Although some critics believe that supply fundamentals were the major force underlying the protracted stagnation in commodity prices in the 1980s

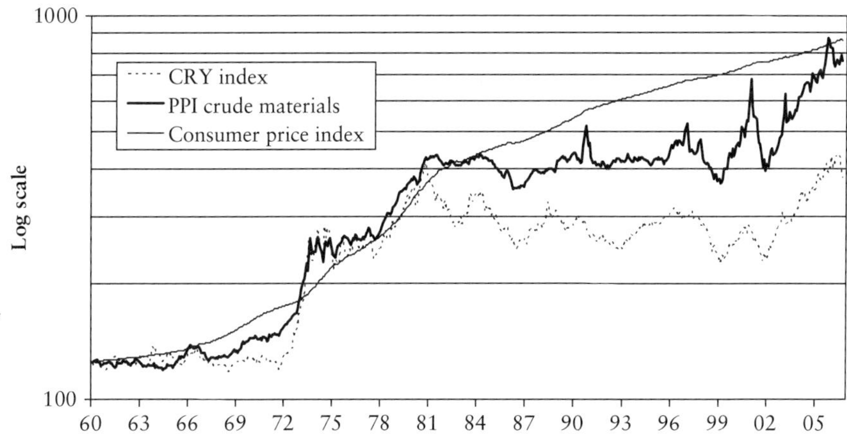

EXHIBIT 20.1 The Super Cycle: Commodities vs. Consumer Prices

and 1990s, reinvigorated central bank discipline also played a critical role. As tighter monetary policy forced down inflation, the need for hedging against paper asset depreciation gradually faded. Furthermore, declining inflation pulled down interest rates, making stock and bond ownership attractive once again. In response, investment demand for commodities ebbed, leading to a downsizing of commodity trading desks and adjunct services.

The final nail in the coffin for commodities appeared to be the introduction of U.S. *inflation-protected securities* (TIPS) in 1997. These securities provided a near-perfect hedge against inflation, rendering moot the conceptual appeal of commodities as a shield against debased currency.[1]

Evolution of Active Commodity Managers

The 1970s commodity boom produced a cadre of successful traders who by the early 1980s had evolved into full-fledged investment enterprises, which we now know as the CTA-managed futures industry. When commodity prices stagnated, CTAs responded by migrating to trading financial instruments such as currencies, equities, and interest-rate derivatives. This was a natural development stimulated largely by the introduction of financial futures contracts by commodity exchanges at the time and the fact that commodity trading techniques were generally applicable in other markets. The

[1]I discussed the importance of TIPS as a hedge against inflation in R. McFall Lamm, Jr., "Asset Allocation Implications of Inflation Protection Securities: Adding 'Real' Class to Portfolios," *Journal of Portfolio Management* (Summer 1998), pp. 93–100.

CTA industry consequently thrived in the 1980s and 1990s—during the woes of the commodity price recession—essentially by following the mainstream investment community rotation from commodities to financial assets.[2]

Now, with a new century bull market in energy, metals, and other physicals, investment demand for commodities is resurrected in another cyclical upswing. The rationale for commodity investing has changed a little—with commodities viewed not so much as an inflation hedge but rather as a low-correlation asset that produces attractive returns. However, there is a dilemma—investors confront a situation where many commodity-specialist CTAs have long since moved on to the greener pastures of financial futures and options. Moreover, over the two-decade bear market in commodities, investment in intellectual capital lagged. This left the sector with a deficit of active managers, an absence of generally accepted benchmarks, and a shortfall of suitable liquid investment vehicles.

THE ROLE OF COMMODITIES IN INVESTMENT PORTFOLIOS

Asset Allocation to Commodities

The traditional approach used by most investors in building investment portfolios is to apply mean-variance optimization or other techniques to a predefined investable asset domain. Returns and covariances are forecast and the optimal portfolio derived mathematically given the investor's volatility target, sometimes subject to various constraints. For much of the 1980s and 1990s, and until recently, most investors only included stocks and bonds in this process. Little thought was given to nontraditional assets, especially when equity markets were delivering strong returns.

Of course, there were a few rebels who advocated commodity investing. For example, Goldman Sachs recommended a modest commodity allocation for years following the 1992 introduction of the Goldman Sachs Commodity Index (GSCI). In addition, I encouraged investors to include passive commodities—as well as other nontraditional assets such as CTAs—to improve portfolio performance. Froot, Greer, and Till also recognized the

[2] I note that to a considerable extent the hedge fund industry was spawned from CTAs in the 1990s as many managers grew large and sought additional liquidity available in public equities and OTC product markets.

portfolio diversification benefits of commodities.[3] However, most research explicitly omitted commodities from consideration.

Interestingly, CTAs did receive a great deal of attention in asset allocation studies during the 1990s. However, CTAs were viewed generally as an independent asset class void of any major dependence on commodity markets.[4] This delinking of CTA performance from commodity markets was reasonable since, as already noted, by the 1990s much of their performance was attributable to active trading of financial market derivatives.

Recently, Rian Akey argued that the commodity allocation in portfolios should be separated into two components. The first consists of passive commodity exposure, which is implemented by investing in index replication instruments. The second is an active allocation to commodity-specialist CTAs and hedge funds. Akey specifically suggests using the GSCI and the AIG Commodity Index to capture passive exposure, while drawing from a

---

[3]See R. McFall Lamm, Jr., "The Exotica Portfolio," Chapter 9, in *Insurance and Weather Derivatives*, edited by Helyette Geman (Somerset, U.K.: Financial Engineering Ltd., 1999); R. McFall Lamm, Jr., "Asset Allocation Applications in Financial Management," Chapter 18, in *Handbook of Industrial Engineering*, edited by Gaviel Salvendy (New York: John Wiley & Sons, 2001); Kenneth Froot, "Hedging Portfolios with Real Assets," *Journal of Portfolio Management* (Summer 1995), pp. 60–77; Robert Greer, "The Nature of Commodity Index Returns," *Journal of Alternative Investments* (Summer 2000), pp. 45–52; Hilary Till, "Passive Strategies in the Commodity Futures Market," *Derivatives Quarterly* (Fall 2000), pp. 49–54; and Hilary Till, "Taking Full Advantage of the Statistical Properties of Commodity Investments," *Journal of Alternative Investing* (Summer 2001), pp. 63–66.

[4]See, for example, E. Elton, M. Gruber, and J. Rentzler, "Professionally Managed, Publicly Traded Commodity Funds," *Journal of Business* (April 1987), pp. 175–199; E. Elton, M. Gruber and J. Rentzler, "The Performance of Publicly Offered Commodity Funds," *Financial Analysts Journal* (July–August 1990), pp. 23–30; F. R. Edwards and J. M. Park "Do Managed Futures Make Good Investments?" *Journal of Futures Markets* (August 1996), pp. 475–517; Randall S. Billingsley and Don M. Chance, "Benefits and Limitations of Diversification Among Commodity Trading Advisors," *Journal of Portfolio Management* (Fall 1996), pp. 65–80; F. R. Edwards and J. Liew, "Hedge Funds versus Managed Futures as Asset Classes," *Journal of Derivatives* (Summer 1999), pp. 45–64; Thomas Schneeweis, Richard Spurgin, and David McCarthy, "Survivor Bias in Commodity Trading Advisor Performance," *Journal of Futures Markets* (October 1996), pp. 757–772; and Thomas Schneeweis, "The Benefits of Managed Futures," Chapter 6, in, edited by Thomas Schneeweis and Joseph F. Pescatore. The Handbook of Alternative Investment Strategies, (New York: Institutional Investor, 1999).

proprietary sample of commodity-specialist CTAs and hedge funds to construct a portfolio of active managers.[5]

Akey's conceptual approach is commendable and takes us one step forward toward a more sophisticated asset allocation process for commodity investing. That said, Akey employs a small sample in constructing his active manager performance record (for example, only one manager is used to represent performance from 1982 to 1984). In addition, the data used is proprietary and outside the public domain. Furthermore, there is a need to address a more critical question in portfolio construction when active commodity managers are used. This is how much pure commodity exposure (if any) is actually embedded in the performance of generalist CTAs, commodity-specialist CTAs, and commodity-centric hedge funds?

Framework for Evaluating Commodity Investments

The issue of the extent to which active managers carry identifiable and persistent beta exposure to commodities is more transparent if one considers commodities as one of many classes in the standard asset allocation problem. In this regard, like stocks and bonds, commodity investments can be made either passively via index replication, or one can pursue "beta plus" via active management. In either case, following the standard approach, manager performance can be represented as

$$r_{it} = \sum \beta_j r_{jbt} + (\alpha + \varepsilon_t) \qquad t \subset T \tag{20.1}$$

where r_{it} is return for the ith manager in period t, r_{jbt} is benchmark return, β_j are the exposures to the $j = 1, \ldots, J$ benchmarks, and the expression in parentheses is manager alpha, which consists of skill and a random element. For passive investment in a single index, $\beta_j = 1$ and $r_{it} = r_{bt}$. Investing in an active manager with a mandate to outperform a single index gives $r_t = \beta_0 r_{bt} + (\alpha_0 + \varepsilon_t)$. Furthermore, in situations where active managers trade commodities and other assets (that is, they employ different styles to outperform), adding the constraints that $\sum \beta_j = 1$ and $\beta_j \geq 0 \ \forall \ j$, and estimating via restricted least squares provides the standard Sharpe style analysis, which allows exposures to be quantified.

[5]See Rian P. Akey, "Commodities: A Case for Active Management," *Journal of Alternative Investments* (Fall 2005), pp. 8–30, and Rian P. Akey, "Alpha, Beta and Commodities: Can a Commodities Investment be Both a High Risk-Adjusted Return Source, and a Portfolio Hedge?" *Journal of Wealth Management* (Fall 2006), pp. 63–84.

One complicating factor is that, in the case of CTAs, it is well known that managers engage in beta-switching behavior. That is, over time managers flip from long to short positions or vice versa depending on market conditions. For example, in the simple case of one factor exposure over two sequential time periods we have

$$r_t = \beta_1 r_{bt} + (\alpha_1 + \varepsilon_t) \qquad t \subset T_1 \tag{20.2}$$

and

$$r_t = \beta_2 r_{bt} + (\alpha_2 + \varepsilon_t) \qquad t \subset T_2 \tag{20.3}$$

Analysts sometimes calculate beta exposure over a long horizon and estimate $r_t = \beta_0 r_{bt} + (\alpha_0 + \varepsilon_t)\ t \subset T$. This is a misrepresentation unless $\beta_1 = \beta_2$ since the true model from combining (20.2) and (20.3) is:

$$r_t = [\alpha_1 + (\alpha_2 - \alpha_1)x_t] + \beta_1 r_{bt} + (\beta_2 - \beta_1) r_{bt} x_t + \varepsilon_t \qquad t \subset T \tag{20.4}$$

where x_t is binary with zero values for $t \subset T_1$ and unit values for $t \subset T_2$. Neglecting CTA beta switching would likely be a significant issue when β_1 and β_2 have large values with opposite signs. In this instance, regressing total sample returns on the benchmark might show no significant beta and embed beta switching in alpha.

From a passive/active asset allocation perspective, there are three issues that need to be considered in commodity investing. First, which passive index is appropriate as the asset class benchmark? Second, to what extent (if any) is commodity factor exposure hidden in CTA and hedge fund allocations? Third, when commodity-specialist CTAs and hedge funds are employed as active managers, how much beta exposure to commodities does the investor really receive? I consider each of these in turn.

PASSIVE COMMODITY INVESTING

Benchmarks

Before exploring the performance of active commodity managers in depth, benchmarks are required for analytical purposes since benchmark selection defines the asset class in a behavioral context. Furthermore, benchmark selection influences the choice of active managers because the allocation decision is based on relative active versus passive performance. This same question must be addressed for any asset class. However, because the performance of various commodity indexes can differ dramatically depending on weighting scheme and constituents, commodity benchmark selection is more imperative than in the case of stocks and bonds where indexes generally exhibit similar returns and risk.[6]

In decades past, the Commodity Research Bureau CRY index—which originated in 1959—was generally deemed the "flagship" indicator of commodity returns. Designed as an objective index of broad commodity price movements, it is a simple geometric average of near futures prices for the major traded commodities. However, the index does not reflect the true performance of commodities since it neglects financial returns accruing from interest on marginable funds.

The GSCI total return index was introduced in 1992 to rectify deficiencies in the CRY index. This was followed by the introduction of the Dow Jones-AIG and the Rogers International Commodity Index (RICI) in 1998, the S&P Commodity Total Return Index in 2001, and more recently, the CRB Total Return Index, which was an effort to translate the CRY index into its total return equivalent. While total return indexes are clearly more suitable as investment performance indicators when compared with spot or near-spot market price indexes, they are potentially fallacious. For example, other than the CRB, the available total return indexes were designed "after the fact" with arbitrary weighting schemes and constituents. As a result, they are subject to design bias in that weights and commodities may have been selected to present performance in a better light.

While some indexes such as the GSCI have a sufficient live track record to allay such anxieties, the others do not. This is illustrated in Exhibit 20.2, which displays historical returns for various spot and total return commodity indexes from January 1995 to August 2006.[7] While the various measures are fairly highly correlated, cumulative performance differs dramatically. The first part of Exhibit 20.3 highlights the extent of these differences by presenting descriptive statistics for the CRY and *Journal of Commerce* commodity price indexes and the CRB, GSCI, and AIG total return indexes.

---

[6]The different properties of commodity indices have been a longstanding concern. For example, see Nathan Ranga, "A Review of Commodity Indexes," *Journal of Indexes* (October 2004), pp. 30–35; Gerald R. Jensen, Robert R. Johnson, and Jeffrey M. Mercer, "Tactical Asset Allocation and Commodity Futures," *Journal of Portfolio Management* (Summer 2002), pp. 100–111; and David J. Nash, "Long-Term Investing in Commodities," *Global Pensions Quarterly* (January 2001), pp. 25–31.

[7]The 1995 to 2005 sample period is selected so as to incorporate both a period of relatively weak commodity performance (the late 1990s) and one of robust returns (since that time). This period also represents the one with the greatest commonality in data series coverage.

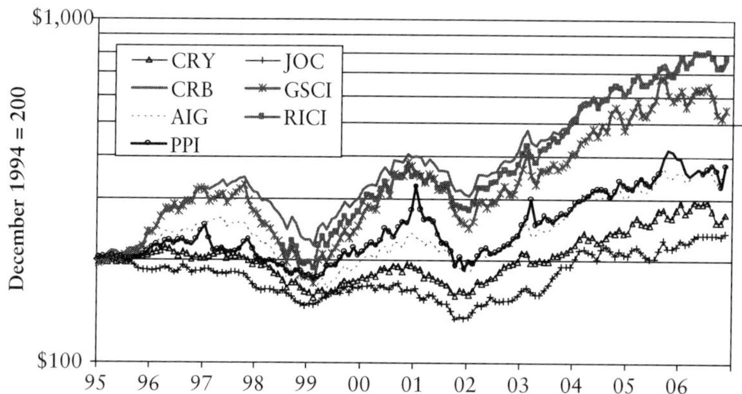

EXHIBIT 20.2 Selected Commodity Price and Total Return Indexes, 1995–2006

The total return indexes clearly outperform the spot or near spot indexes, but at the same time they show considerable disparity with average annual returns of 12.1%, 9.5%, and 5.0%, respectively, for the CRB, GSCI, and AIG indexes. Volatility ranges from 13.4% for the AIG total return index to 20.6% for the GSCI. Combining risk and reward produces a Sharpe ratio for the CRB that is twice that of the AIG index. These are strikingly large variances and, therefore, confirm that commodity benchmark selection makes a big difference.

As for which index is in some sense "best," I leave that decision to the reader since we are early in the evolution of commodities investing and there is no consensus as of yet. Certainly, the CRB Total Return Index has great intellectual appeal since it can be matched to a price index that was designed a priori and not based on "look back" design. Furthermore, the CRB index extends backward over a sufficiently long period to reflect the ups and downs of commodity cycles that—as already described—can endure for decades. Nonetheless, the CRB is not easily investable, while one can readily purchase GSCI or AIG futures or *exchange-traded funds* (ETFs).

How Much Commodity Exposure Do CTAs Offer?

The CTA industry is extremely well studied due to its longevity. The general conclusions from most research are that (1) CTA returns are uncorrelated with stocks, bonds, and other traditional assets; (2) returns have been high historically (although there has been some decay in 2004 to 2006); and (3) CTAs generally exhibit positive asymmetry unlike stocks which have

EXHIBIT 20.3 Performance Statistics: Commodity Prices vs. Passive and Active Manager Total Returns, January 1995 to August 2006

	Spot Indexes		Total Return Indexes			Active Managers (CTAs/hedge funds)					
Metric	CRY	JOC	CRB	GSCI	AIG	SYS	CTA	PHY	AGR	BTU	S&P
Annualized:											
Return	2.9%	1.4%	12.1%	9.7%	5.0%	6.6%	8.8%	8.0%	2.9%	18.9%	9.4%
Volatility	9.8%	8.9%	14.0%	20.6%	13.4%	9.9%	8.7%	7.6%	8.8%	18.4%	14.7%
Skew	−0.03	0.25	0.06	0.06	0.05	0.24	0.38	0.06	0.08	0.06	−0.62
Kurt	−0.23	−0.01	0.09	−0.01	−0.31	0.12	0.02	0.37	0.71	0.81	0.78
JB test	0.31	1.46	0.14	0.08	0.62	1.47	3.39	0.42	3.05	3.94	12.51
Sharpe ratio	−0.11	−0.11	0.65	0.47	0.37	0.67	1.01	0.74	0.33	1.03	0.44
Correlations:											
CRY	1	0.57	0.84	0.72	0.85	0.13	0.13	0.12	0.02	0.34	0.15
JOC		1	0.54	0.44	0.55	0.05	0.05	0.24	0.01	0.28	0.04
CRB			1	0.93	0.94	0.18	0.17	0.24	0.07	0.50	0.09
GSCI				1	0.90	0.21	0.19	0.29	0.14	0.48	0.00
AIG					1	0.24	0.24	0.28	0.11	0.48	0.10
SYS						1	0.97	0.48	0.07	0.14	−0.09
CTA							1	0.49	0.10	0.16	−0.10
PHY								1	0.49	0.05	0.01
AGR									1	0.00	−0.04
BTU										1	−0.04

Note: Calculations based on 140 months of data from January 1995 to August 2006, except for PHY which begins in January 2001.

greater downside than upside risk.[8] Because CTA correlations with other asset markets are generally very low, CTAs are typically viewed as pure alpha producers with returns generated primarily by actively trading currency, fixed income, equities, and commodities.

A natural question is whether allocating to CTAs as a standalone investment provides implicit exposure to commodities. In this regard, the correlation coefficients presented in Exhibit 20.3 offer some insight. For example, the Barclay Systematic and CISDM CTA indexes (SYS and CTA) show approximately a 0.2 correlation with the CRB, GSCI, and AIG total return indexes over the January 1995 to August 2006 period.[9] While this is not high, it does suggest a portion of CTA returns may be coming from commodity exposure. In addition, beta switching might mask a stronger relationship than appears to be the case from a simple correlation analysis.

Note that there is a substantial amount of research on CTA returns and their link to factor markets—characterized importantly by the work of Fung and Hsieh—that finds a weak association between CTA and commodity returns.[10] However, this research is dated and the conclusions rely on the presumption of static beta exposure over fairly extended time periods. In reality, CTA behavior is more likely to fall into the time-varying parameter or beta-switching category. Because beta switching may be obscured in estimates based on lengthy horizons, the Fung and Hsieh conclusions are not surprising.

To explore the possibility of time-varying beta, I estimate rolling 24-month regressions of the Barclays SYS index on returns for commodities, equities, currency, and fixed income securities. The SYS index is fairly comprehensive having originated in 1980 and included 439 funds as of 2006. Its

---

[8]For example, see R. McFall Lamm, Jr., "The Answer to Your Dreams? Investment Implications of Positive Asymmetry in CTA Returns," *Journal of Alternative Investments* (Spring 2005), pp. 22-32; R. McFall Lamm, Jr., "Asymmetric Returns and Optimal Hedge Fund Portfolios," *Journal of Alternative Investments* (Fall 2003), pp. 9–21; and Chris Brooks and Harry M. Kat, "The Statistical Properties of Hedge Fund Return Index Returns and Their Implications for Investors," *Journal of Alternative Investments* (Fall 2002), pp. 26–44.

[9]One reason for low correlations might be that the returns are not normally distributed and correlation coefficients are biased. In addition, autocorrelation can lead to lower correlation coefficients.

[10]See William Fung and David A. Hsieh, "Empirical Characteristics of Dynamic Trading Strategies: The Case of Hedge Funds," *Review of Financial Studies* (Summer 1997), pp. 275–302; Fung and Hsieh "Survivor Bias and Investment Style in the Returns of CTAs," *Journal of Portfolio Management* (Fall 1997), pp. 30–41; and Fung and Hsieh "Risk in Hedge Fund Strategies: Theory and Evidence from Trend Followers," *Review of Financial Studies* (Summer 2001), pp. 313–341.

correlation with the CISDM CTA index is 0.97 over the January 1995 to August 2006 period—so it probably makes little difference which is used. I define commodity exposure as the combined beta on CRY and near futures on WTI crude oil to reflect the fact that energy is more important than the equal weighting implied in the CRY index. *Bonds* are defined as the return on the Merrill Lynch Treasury Master Index, *equity* as the S&P 500 return, and *currency* as the return on the FINEX dollar index (DXY). Although this is a very crude approach, it nonetheless should provide a rough indication of the amount of commodity exposure carried by CTAs.

The results indicate that from 1995 to 2006, average CTA commodity exposure was approximately 13% long (see Exhibit 20.4). This represents a little less than a quarter of the average 62% net long exposure to all markets and is consistent with the commonly held view that the bulk of CTA exposure and returns come primarily from fixed income, currency, and equity derivatives. However, the evolution of exposures over time is striking. For example, commodity exposure ranges from 58% long in July 1996 to 24% short in July 2002 (when the 11% long energy position is included). Bond, equity, and currency average exposures exhibit similar variability.

The quick conclusion is that CTAs appear to carry nontrivial commodity positions. However, these exposures are highly time variant and investors have no assurance that a commitment on any date will provide any commodity beta whatsoever. This indicates that if one possesses substantial CTA allocations in their portfolios, there may occasionally be hidden

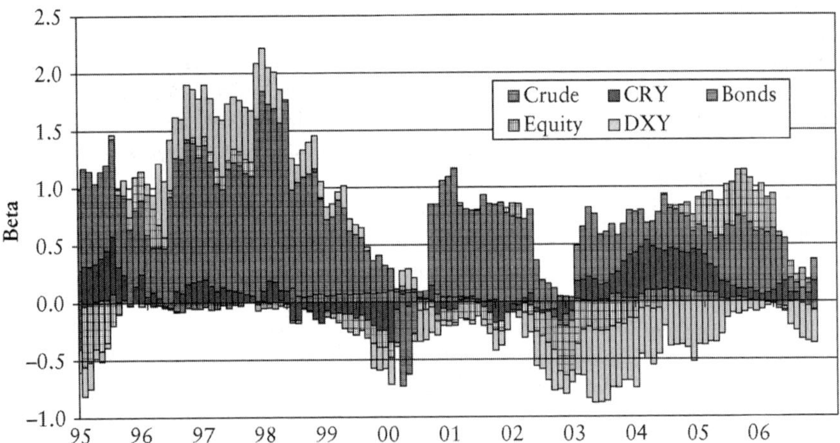

EXHIBIT 20.4 CTA Market Factor Exposures
Note: Based on trailing 24-month regression.

commodity beta but it is not persistent. For this reason, viewing overall portfolio CTA and commodity allocations as essentially independent would appear to be a reasonable premise.

ACTIVE COMMODITY INVESTING VIA SPECIALIST CTAs AND HEDGE FUNDS

Performance Overview

I now turn to the more pertinent question of the degree of commodity exposure carried by commodity specialist CTAs and hedge funds. If such managers carry no systematic commodity beta and only deliver alpha, can they realistically be classified as "active commodity managers"? Otherwise they might more correctly be viewed as an independent pool of alpha generators and a distinct asset class in the overall portfolio allocation problem.

In contrast to Akey—who builds up a portfolio of commodity specialist CTAs and hedge funds from scratch—I elect to employ publicly available information. The available data pool includes returns from (1) CISDM, which maintains a performance index for CTAs that trade physicals including energy, agriculture, and metals; (2) Barclays, which publishes returns for CTAs specializing in agricultural commodities; and (3) Hedge Fund Net (HFN), which compiles returns for hedge funds specializing in the energy sector. While this sample excludes some commodity groups, it nonetheless provides an objective basis for deriving embedded beta for active commodity managers.

The CISDM physicals index (PHY) originates in January 2001 and consequently is relatively short lived. However, it is the broadest available measure encompassing CTAs that trade all of the basic commodity sectors. The Barclays Agricultural Traders Index (AGR) is equally weighted and originated in 1987. It included 15 funds in 2006. Managers specialize in trading specific groups within the agricultural complex or across sectors. These include crops (corn, wheat, soybeans, etc.), meats (live cattle, feeder cattle, hogs, pork bellies, etc.), tropicals (sugar, coffee, cocoa), and fibers (cotton).

The HFN energy hedge fund index (BTU) includes funds that invest in energy-related equities, commodity futures, or derivatives. While most energy hedge funds specialize in trading energy company stocks, many also make long/short directional bets on crude oil, natural gas, heating oil, gasoline, and other energy commodities, as well as trade energy spreads. The index originates in October 1992 and included 67 funds as of September 2006.

As for the relative performance of these three manager samples, Exhibit 20.3 indicates that energy hedge funds as measured by BTU outperformed the spot commodity and total return indexes both in annual returns and Sharpe ratios over the 1995 to 2006 period. In contrast, agricultural CTAs—as measured by AGR—produced a muted 2.9% annual return and a correspondingly low Sharpe ratio. CTAs specializing in physicals (PHY) performed more or less in line with broad-based CTAs over the 2001 to 2006 period. Of course, these results are highly conditional on prevailing market conditions during a period when the energy sector boomed and agricultural prices generally meandered.

The information in Exhibit 20.3 also suggests that active managers carry some embedded long commodity exposure. For example, the correlations between PHY, AGR, and BTU versus the CRB, GSCI, and AIG total return indexes are all positive and statistically significant. BTU exhibits the highest correlation with the three total return indexes—near 0.5—while AGR shows the lowest. This may be spurious or it could simply be attributable to the larger relative size of the energy sector versus agriculture. Nonetheless, the implication is that energy hedge funds possess substantial implicit beta.

CTA Specialists in Physicals

To explore commodity-specialist beta dependence in depth, I follow the procedure described in the previous section for generalist CTAs. I first estimate embedded commodity exposure in the CISDM physicals index by running 24-month regressions of PHY returns on changes in commodity near-futures prices. The commodity groups consist of energy (NYMEX WTI crude, gasoline, heating oil, and natural gas); industrial metals (COMEX copper, LME aluminium, and nickel); precious metals (COMEX gold and silver, plus NYMEX platinum); agriculture (CME and CBOT corn, wheat, soybeans, and meats); and tropicals (CSCE sugar, coffee, cocoa, and frozen orange juice concentrate).

As with the rolling regressions for general CTA returns, this methodology is approximate for several reasons. First, a 24-month window is arbitrary and extracts exposures carried over monthly intervals. In reality, CTAs trade intermittently, sometimes terminating new positions within days or weeks. Therefore, actual positions could swing more dramatically than estimated.

Second, one can argue whether using sequential *ordinary least squares* (OLS) is the appropriate estimation technique. Alternative models could be applied—including ones with other explanatory factors such as commodity volatility, return-to-risk ratios, or option proxies as suggested by Fung and

Hsieh. Autocorrelation-correction models might also be appropriate.[11] Instead, one might use other estimation techniques such as restricted least squares in a pure Sharpe-type style approach.

A third issue is that total returns on the underlying futures price contracts are not taken into account, so using price performance may be somewhat misleading. Lastly, there is the possibility that survivor or other types of bias are present in the PHY return series as researchers such as Spurgin, Diz, and others have discovered.[12] Despite these caveats, the purpose of the analysis is simply to determine whether CTAs that trade physicals appear to carry persistent commodity beta exposure. Therefore, rather than argue technicalities—which may not alter the conclusions—I employ sequential OLS as described, recognizing its inexact nature.[13]

The results are shown in Exhibits 20.5 and 20.6. Indications are that physical commodity traders do in fact tend to carry substantial commodity exposure. However, long exposure is more or less offset by short positions, so average net exposure from 2001 to 2006 is not significantly different from zero. The estimates also reveal that beta exposure exhibits substantial variance over time. For example, PHY managers were generally long agricultural commodities from 2001 to 2004. However, over the past few years they rotated more to long energy and metals positions while going short agriculture and tropicals. The average explanatory power of the estimated equations is fairly high with R^2 and adjusted R^2 values of 0.70 and 0.37, respectively. The intercept—a crude estimate of alpha—is generally positive and statistically significant although small.

CTAs Specializing in Agricultural Commodities

Moving to CTAs specializing in agricultural commodities, I estimate running regressions using the AGR series with four groups of commodities as

[11] For example, see Mila Getmansky, Andrew W. Lo, Igor Makarov, "An Econometric Model of Serial Correlation in Hedge Fund Returns," *Journal of Financial Economics* (December 2004), pp. 529–609.

[12] See Richard Spurgin, "A Study of Survival: Commodity Trading Advisors, 1988–1996," *Journal of Alternative Investments* (Winter 1999), pp.16–22; Fernando Diz, "CTA Survivor and Nonsurvivor: An Analysis of Relative Performance," *Journal of Alternative Investments* (Summer 1999), pp. 57–71; and Gaurav S. Amin and Harry M. Kat, "Welcome to the Dark Side: Hedge Fund Attrition and Survivorship Bias over the Period 1994–2001," *Journal of Alternative Investments* (Summer 2003), pp. 57–73.

[13] I did explore a myriad of more technically complex approaches in additional work, the results of which I do not report. However, by and large, the essence of the conclusions presented is not substantially altered.

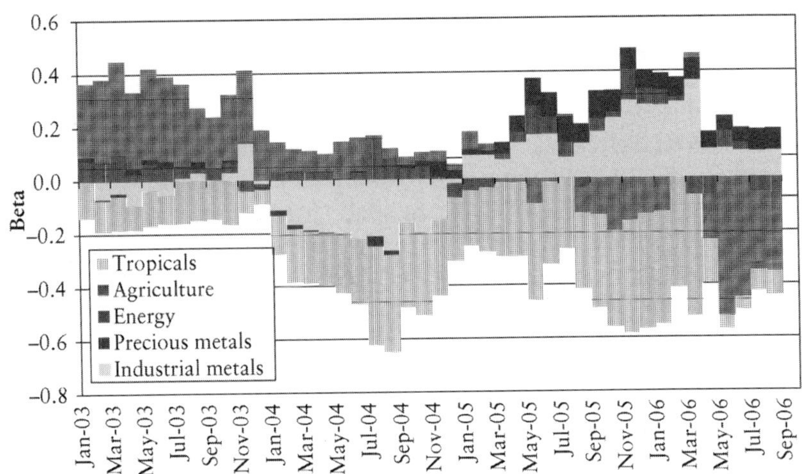

EXHIBIT 20.5 CTI "Physicals" Market Factor Exposure

explanatory factors. These include crops (corn, wheat, and soybeans), meats (cattle and hogs), tropicals (sugar, coffee, and cocoa), and industrials (cotton and limber). As before, I employ near-futures prices and an equally weighted grouping scheme.

Note that there may be some information loss in aggregation because the structure of the agricultural commodity market is particularly complex. Not only is seasonality very important—with crops typically showing contango until harvest due to storage costs, followed by a reset at lower prices when new supply enters the market—but meat and crops exhibit convoluted dynamics since feedgrains are ingredients in the production process. Therefore, even before beginning, one would imagine beta extraction might be difficult.

This is confirmed by the estimates shown in Exhibits 20.6 and 20.7. Indications are that agriculture-specialist CTAs display substantial beta rotation. But this averages out to virtually zero net exposure over the 1995 to 2006 time horizon. Furthermore, in contrast to PHY, the average R^2 values are fairly low (average of 0.31). Therefore, we can attribute only a much smaller portion of returns for agriculture specialists to monthly commodity price variation.

Hedge Funds Specializing in Energy

Turning to hedge funds specializing in the energy sector, I again apply the same running regression technique already described to the BTU return series. For explanatory factors, I include crude oil, heating oil, gasoline, and

EXHIBIT 20.6 Estimates of Commodity Exposure Embedded in Commodity Specialist CTAs and Hedge Funds

		CTA Physicals			CTA Agricultural			Energy Hedge Funds		
Commodity Group	Subcategory	Mean	Min	Max	Mean	Min	Max	Mean	Min	Max
Agriculture	All	0.03	−0.32	0.52	—	—	—	—	—	—
	Crops	—	—	—	0.09	−0.13	0.47	—	—	—
	Meats	—	—	—	−0.04	−0.40	0.26	—	—	—
	Tropical	−0.22	−0.45	−0.04	−0.08	−0.29	0.17	—	—	—
	Industrial	—	—	—	0.01	−0.15	0.30	—	—	—
Energy	All	0.04	−0.04	0.10	—	—	—	—	—	—
	Crude	—	—	—	—	—	—	0.13	−0.19	0.77
	Gasoline	—	—	—	—	—	—	0.12	−0.14	0.41
	Heating oil	—	—	—	—	—	—	−0.03	−0.33	0.29
	Natural gas	—	—	—	—	—	—	0.07	−0.03	0.23
Metals	Precious	0.03	−0.07	0.15	—	—	—	—	—	—
	Industrial	0.02	−0.27	0.36	—	—	—	—	—	—
Equity	S&P	—	—	—	—	—	—	0.42	−0.09	1.09
Intercept		0.006	−0.003	0.015	0.002	−0.010	0.014	0.009	−0.013	0.029
Avg. R^2		0.70	0.43	0.84	0.31	0.15	0.56	0.52	0.31	0.73
Avg. adj. R^2		0.37	−0.18	0.66	0.17	−0.05	0.47	0.38	0.14	0.66

Note: Based on rolling 24-month regressions: January 1995 to August 2006, for AGR and BTU, and January 2001 to August 2006 for PHY.

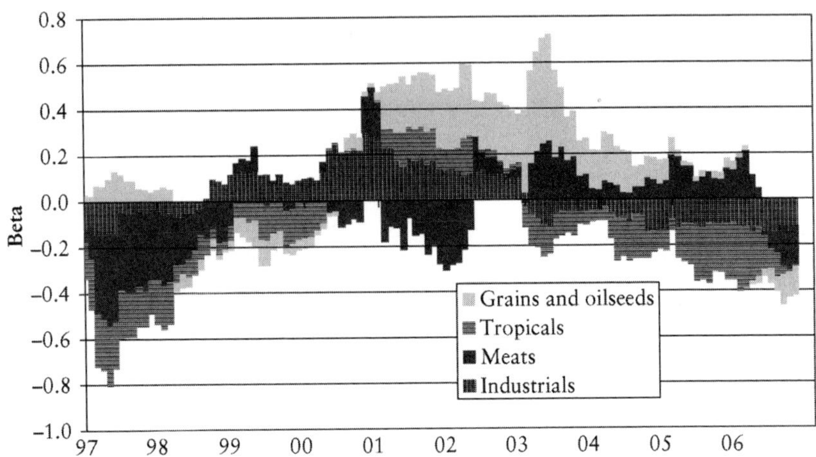

EXHIBIT 20.7 Agricultural CTAs Market Factor Exposure

natural gas near futures prices. In addition, I add S&P returns to capture stock market effects since energy hedge funds often concentrate on trading energy stocks with naked energy positions being a tangential concern.

Since the BTU series is longer than PHY, the results offer more insight into the extent of beta rotation over time. The findings presented in Exhibits 20.6 and 20.8 are similar to those reported for CTAs that trade physical commodities—namely that managers exhibit significant beta rotation over time. In this regard, managers were long crude and gasoline in the late 1990s—offset by short heating oil positions. However, this exposure reversed in recent years as managers went long heating oil.

More important is the fact that energy hedge funds beta exposure to stock market returns is very high. Indeed, average S&P beta is slightly more than 0.4 over the sample, indicating that equity market performance is an important contributor to BTU performance. This may explain in part why energy hedge fund returns exceed those of CTAs over the sample.[14]

[14] I also note that traditional investors often argue that another method for obtaining commodity exposure is to simply invest in resource stocks. For example, if one desires precious metals exposure, then the appropriate strategy is to purchase gold, silver, and platinum mining companies or the XAU index. Similarly, if one desires exposure to energy commodities, then the solution is to buy the oil producing majors, oil service companies, or the XOI index. While this approach has merit, resource stocks have even higher beta exposure to equity markets than do energy hedge funds. For this reason, I view allocations to commodity-related stocks to be sector choices by equity portfolio managers.

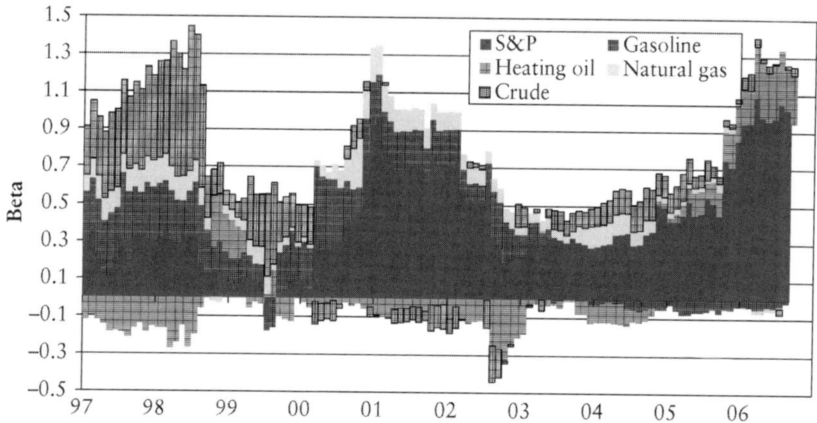

EXHIBIT 20.8 Energy Hedge Funds Market Factor Exposure

PORTFOLIO IMPLICATIONS

Commodity Specialists as Active Managers

The findings reported so far indicate that commodity-specialist CTAs carry little net commodity exposure. In this sense, they can be regarded as alpha generators—whether "alpha" is generated via time-varying beta or otherwise. However, energy specialist hedge funds also carry long net equity exposure. This is not surprising because, as already noted, many energy hedge funds focus on stock trading. Moreover, this is consistent with past research that shows equity long/short hedge funds generally carry substantial net long equity exposure.

This implies that breaking the commodity allocation into two components—a passive index allocation and one to active commodity specialists—is radically different from the normal situation for most asset classes. Investing in CTAs that specialize in physicals, agriculture-specialist CTAs, and energy-specialist hedge funds, does not involve making bets on commodity market performance. Such managers do not trade against benchmarks and are therefore not obliged to carry any systematic benchmark exposure whatsoever.

Why then should one employ commodity specialists in lieu of alpha generators that extract returns from any market? The answer is that if one is correctly bullish (or bearish) on commodity prices, then commodity specialists should benefit since they would be expected to rotate beta to take advantage of return opportunities—after all, this is the source of their identifiable skill. This is confirmed by the statistical analysis presented in the prior sections where on two-year windows, statistically significant beta rotation is observed over time.

The Passive/Active Allocation

Turning to the passive/active allocation question, one could forecast benchmark and active manager expected returns, and then apply the usual portfolio optimization regimen. However, subjective return forecasting typically produces extreme portfolio allocations and one is left to agree or disagree with the results depending on whether one believes the forecasts. Accordingly, I evade this dilemma by examining the implied returns embedded in various arbitrary passive/active allocations that investors might employ.

I proceed as follows. First, I regard the commodity allocation as predetermined and presume one is faced with subdividing the investment among passive and active managers. I use weighting schemes that range from zero to 100% passive allocations to the CRB, the GSCI, and the AIG indexes, matched with various combinations of allocations to PHY, AGR, and BTU that range from all exposure in one type of active manager to others where the active manager allocation is divided equally.

Second, I then reengineer implied returns of these allocations to assess what expectations are required to justify the splits. I presume that investors expect a 3% commodity benchmark return above a 5% risk-free rate and presuppose that the trailing covariance matrix holds in the future. This establishes a neutral starting point. Third, I then examine the portfolio characteristics for the various allocation splits and also estimate the implicit beta on stocks accounted for by the energy hedge fund allocation.

Implied manager returns are presented in Exhibit 20.9. Indications are that the required returns for active managers to enter the portfolio are in most cases several percentage points lower than for benchmarks. The reason for this is simply that the passive benchmarks generally exhibit higher volatility than combinations of active managers. Therefore, investors allocating higher proportions to commodity specialists expect this to have a return and risk dampening impact on the overall portfolio. Thus, the commodity allocation split decision essentially becomes one of how much return investors are prepared to sacrifice for lower risk—not how much return enhancement is expected for greater risk.

This is clear if one examines overall commodity portfolio characteristics (see Exhibits 20.10 and 20.11). Importantly, indications are that diversifying across active managers only modestly reduces the implied portfolio expected return while significantly damping risk. This is particularly the

EXHIBIT 20.9 Implied Returns for Selected Passive and Active Commodity Allocations (percent)

Portfolio	1	2	3	4	5	6	7	8	9	10	11	12	13	14
Allocation Mix														
Passive index		25	25	25	25	50	50	50	50	75	75	75	75	100
CTA physicals	33	25	75			17	50			8	25			
CTA agricultural	33	25		75		17		50		8		25		
Energy hedge funds	33	25			75	17			50	8			25	
Implied Returns														
CRB benchmark	8.0	8.0	8.0	8.0	8.0	8.0	8.0	8.0	8.0	8.0	8.0	8.0	8.0	8.0
CTA physicals	7.4	6.1	7.1	6.5	5.3	5.7	6.1	5.8	5.3	5.5	5.6	5.5	5.4	5.4
CTA agricultural	7.6	6.1	6.1	8.0	5.0	5.6	5.5	6.2	5.1	5.3	5.3	5.5	5.1	5.1
Energy hedge funds	8.5	7.0	6.0	5.8	8.3	6.6	6.1	6.1	7.3	6.3	6.2	6.1	6.6	6.2
GSCI benchmark	8.0	8.0	8.0	8.0	8.0	8.0	8.0	8.0	8.0	8.0	8.0	8.0	8.0	8.0
CTA physicals	6.5	5.6	6.0	5.8	5.2	5.4	5.6	5.5	5.3	5.4	5.4	5.4	5.3	5.3
CTA agricultural	6.7	5.6	5.6	6.4	5.0	5.3	5.3	5.6	5.1	5.2	5.2	5.3	5.1	5.2
Energy hedge funds	7.3	6.1	5.6	5.5	6.9	5.8	5.6	5.6	6.3	5.7	5.6	5.6	5.9	5.7
AIG benchmark	8.0	8.0	8.0	8.0	8.0	8.0	8.0	8.0	8.0	8.0	8.0	8.0	8.0	8.0
CTA physicals	7.3	6.2	7.1	6.6	5.3	5.8	6.2	5.9	5.4	5.6	5.7	5.6	5.4	5.5
CTA agricultural	7.5	6.1	6.2	8.1	5.0	5.6	5.6	6.3	5.1	5.4	5.4	5.6	5.2	5.2
Energy hedge funds	8.4	7.1	6.0	5.8	8.5	6.6	6.1	6.1	7.4	6.4	6.2	6.2	6.7	6.2

EXHIBIT 20.10 Portfolio Characteristics for Selected Passive and Active Commodity Allocations (percent)

Portfolio	1	2	3	4	5	6	7	8	9	10	11	12	13	14
Allocation Mix														
Passive index	—	25	25	25	25	50	50	50	50	75	75	75	75	100
CTA physicals	33	25	75	—	—	17	50	—	—	8	25	—	—	—
CTA agricultural	33	25	—	75	—	17	—	50	—	8	—	25	—	—
Energy hedge funds	33	25	—	—	75	17	—	—	50	8	—	—	25	—
CRB as Benchmark														
Implied return	7.8	6.8	7.3	8.0	8.2	7.0	7.0	7.1	7.6	7.4	7.4	7.4	7.7	8.0
Portfolio risk	6.1	6.9	7.4	7.7	10.9	8.9	8.8	8.6	11.2	11.4	11.3	11.0	12.3	14.2
Equity exposure	8.9	5.2	2.5	2.1	8.4	4.0	2.8	2.7	5.8	3.4	3.0	2.9	4.2	—
Lambda	7.7	3.8	4.3	5.1	2.7	2.5	2.6	2.8	2.1	1.9	1.9	2.0	1.8	1.5
GSCI as Benchmark														
Implied return	6.8	6.3	6.5	6.8	7.2	6.7	6.8	6.8	7.1	7.4	7.3	7.3	7.5	8.0
Portfolio risk	6.1	8.5	8.9	9.0	12.1	12.6	12.6	12.3	14.4	17.2	17.1	16.8	17.8	21.9
Equity exposure	5.8	2.8	1.4	1.3	4.9	2.1	1.6	1.6	3.2	1.9	1.6	1.6	2.3	—
Lambda	5.0	1.8	1.9	2.2	1.5	1.1	1.2	1.2	1.0	0.8	0.8	0.8	0.8	0.6
AIG as Benchmark														
Implied return	7.7	6.9	7.3	8.1	8.4	7.0	7.1	7.2	7.7	7.5	7.4	7.4	7.7	8.0
Portfolio risk	6.1	6.9	7.4	7.7	10.9	8.7	8.7	8.5	11.0	11.1	11.0	10.8	12.0	13.7
Equity exposure	8.6	5.3	2.5	2.1	8.9	4.1	2.9	2.8	6.2	3.6	3.0	3.1	4.4	—
Lambda	7.4	3.9	4.3	5.2	2.9	2.6	2.8	3.0	2.3	2.0	2.0	2.1	1.9	1.6

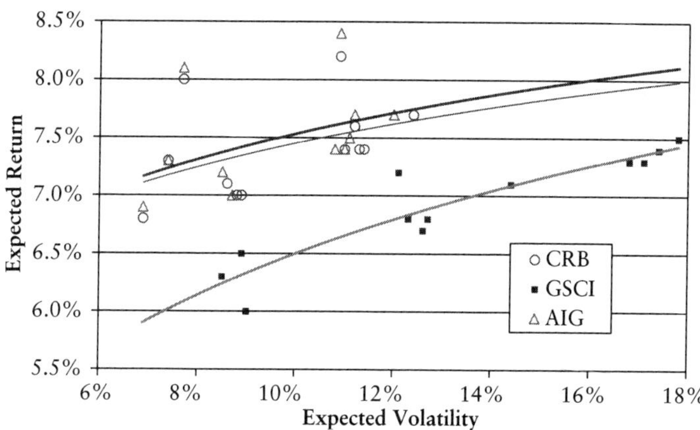

EXHIBIT 20.11 Implied Return and Risk from Various Commodity Weighting Schemes

case if one is employing the energy-intensive GSCI as a benchmark, which exhibits high standalone volatility. As a result, it appears that risk-averse investors are well advised to allocate more to active managers and less to passive indexing.

One further issue is that the active/passive commodity split will likely have some effect on allocations to other assets in the portfolio. This is particularly likely if one can invest in other alpha generators such as various hedge fund strategies. Although I do not evaluate the extent of such effects—the focus here is just on the active/passive commodity allocation—it may affect the overall portfolio composition with higher or lower commodity exposure.

MACRO FUNDAMENTALS AND ACTIVE MANAGERS AS A HEDGE

Commodity prices are particularly difficult to predict for a number of reasons. First, most commodities are traded in dollars; therefore, there is an implicit currency linkage. For example, it is no accident that the commodity price surge of the past few years occurred simultaneously with a sharp fall in the value of the dollar. Indeed, the correlation between the trade-weighted value of the dollar and the CRB index over the past decade is close to 0.7. Consequently, to a considerable extent a commodity bull is a dollar bear.

Second, commodity prices eventually mean-revert to their cost of production. This is a simple response to economic dynamics—higher prices encourage capacity investment that eventually stimulates supply as firms seek to maximize profits. The problem is that the reaction can sometimes take years since resource discovery and infrastructure expansion are often required. Therefore, predicting when new supply flows will drive down commodity prices is difficult—even though one knows it is coming.

Third, commodity prices are significantly influenced by investment demand. In this regard, there has been a huge build in net long speculative open interest in the past few years. Of course, this comes after a long period in the 1980s and 1990s when investment demand was virtually negligible. Can such pressure continue and is there a chance for a reversal as has occurred in the past?

Of course, if we are entering an era of extended dollar weakness, an ongoing build in economic and investment demand, and a very long supply response, then commodity prices could continue to move up for a long time. Indeed, global growth appears skewed to the positive at the moment thanks to industrial revolutions underway in China, India, and other emerging markets. Even agricultural commodities have reacted to surging protein demand in emerging markets and increased needs for biofuels. In addition, supply response may be curbed by resource depletion with energy bulls arguing that peak production—the point where consumption exceeds reserve additions—has been reached. Furthermore, production costs have increased in part due to more stringent environmental controls.

The counterargument is that commodity demand growth might slow in future years as the global economy mean-reverts to more normal growth levels, that commodity supply may increase as new investment projects bear fruit, and dollar adjustment is eventually concluded—thereby creating a negative environment for further commodity price increases. Clearly, the best time to invest in commodities is early in the global expansionary cycle when demand is booming; after a period of underinvestment when costs are rising due to events such as environmental regulation; and when the dollar is falling and other currencies are appreciating.

There is a point to what may appear to be a curious digression—forecast uncertainty is exceptionally high in the case of commodities. This applies both to the direction of prices as well as to roll yield, where the recent reversal from backwardation to contango in oil futures was largely unanticipated. In this respect, if one is uncertain about the future of commodities, the solution may be a larger allocation to active commodity managers. The reason is that if one's return forecast turns out to be substantially off target—or more tragically, has the wrong sign—then active commodity managers could provide protection since they have no persistent beta exposure. In this regard, active managers serve as a hedge against forecast error while preserving the attractive low-correlation properties of the commodity asset class.

CONCLUSIONS

Allocating to commodities is not a new development—they were a frontline investment during the high inflation 1970s until the market peak in 1980. The subsequent fade in investment demand occurred primarily due to weak performance relative to stocks and bonds. Certainly, commodities no longer offer the effective inflation hedge they once did—having been supplanted to a considerable degree by TIPS—but commodities have very long cycles and prices can move up much faster than inflation for extended periods. This tendency supports longer term tactical allocations when market conditions are favorable.

Of course, commodity investing presents unusual challenges when compared with other assets. There is no agreement on benchmarks. The usual approach of choosing active managers who strive to deliver beta-plus is not applicable. Nor can one presume that investing in broad-based CTAs will provide commodity exposure.

The opportunity for astute investors is therefore in creative benchmark selection and pairing this with investments in commodity specialist CTAs. A particular advantage of the latter is that active managers pursue alpha without regard to benchmarks. This provides an unusual hedge against forecast error while still providing some directional access to commodity price movements. Investing in a combination of passive indexes and active managers would appear to be the best approach.

CHAPTER 21

Introducing Alternative Investments in a Traditional Portfolio: The Case of Commodities, Hedge Funds, and Managed Futures

Mark S. Shore
Head of Risk
Octane Research, Inc.

While recent years have seen an increased demand for commodity investments, especially from institutional investors, there has also been an increase in the development of new commodity indexes. This increased demand was the motivational factor in asking three very simple, but key questions that led to this chapter: (1) What is the performance result of allocating to commodities as a method of diversification and risk management in a traditional portfolio? (2) Relative to other alternative investments such as hedge funds and managed futures, are commodities more or less efficient as a diversifier with traditional investments? And (3) can commodities complement other alternative investments in the portfolio? While the first question has been discussed by many commentators over the years, we believe that the relationship of commodities to other alternative investments as found in the second and third questions has been less frequently discussed. As alternative investments become more popular, the importance of this discussion increases.

The author would like to thank Joel L. Franks, Fabrice Rouah, Paul Gomm, and Elissa Bloom for their support in this chapter.

In our discussion in this chapter, the Goldman Sachs Commodity Index (GSCI) is used as our sample commodity index because it makes up the majority of tradable commodity indexes. The GSCI is parsed into three indexes: the Spot Index, Excess Index, and Total Return Index. In this chapter all three are tested and compared.

Equity indexes are embedded with a growth component and, for this reason, investors seek higher net asset values over time due to economies expanding and businesses growing. Commodities by their very nature are mean-reverting markets and, in the truest sense, the prices reflect the constant exchange between supply and demand. Therefore, one must realize commodities may rally for a few months or possibly even several years as demand exceeds supply. Once production bottlenecks are resolved or the substitution effect occurs, supply usually converges toward demand, prices converge toward equilibrium, and the markets are more likely to emerge into a sideways or downward trading pattern.[1]

Examples of the substitution effect may include the development of alternative fuels when crude oil prices become relatively expensive. In the grain markets, there is a common ratio between corn and wheat as both are used for feed grain; but wheat contains greater protein than corn. As corn becomes more expensive, farmers are more likely to choose wheat and as corn becomes cheaper relative to wheat, farmers are more likely to choose corn.

COMMODITIES AS AN INFLATION HEDGE

Because commodity indexes are a long only strategy, they are often viewed as a gauge of inflation rather than an investment vehicle with a long-term growth component. One must also realize the history of commodities is often plagued by booms, busts, seasonal volatility, political issues, transportation issues, weather issues, and the occasional speculator attempting to corner the market. For example, in 1973, the Hunt brothers of Texas began accumulating silver as a hedge against inflation (it was illegal for private citizens to hold gold at that time). By 1979, they held 200 million ounces of silver estimated to be 50% of the global deliverable supply. At the beginning of 1979 the price of silver was $5 per ounce, by the beginning of 1980, the price hit $49. The COMEX reduced the speculator's position limit and increased the margin on silver causing liquidation of long positions for traders with large positions and traders unable to provide margin, thus causing

[1]*Substitution effect* is defined as end users substituting other commodities that can perform the same function, but at a relatively cheaper price.

prices to fall. On March 27, 1980 ("Silver Thursday"), the price fell from $21.62 to $10.80. The Hunt brothers were ultimately convicted of manipulating the market in 1988

Cashin, McDermott, and Scott discussed their findings of testing commodity data from January 1957 to August 1998, as a longer average duration of downward, or "slumping" markets than upward or "booming" markets.[2] As well, they found the magnitude of falling prices slightly larger than rising prices. The Federal Reserve Act, as amended in 1977, designated the Fed to utilize monetary policies for pursuing maximum employment and price stability. The Fed studies commodity indexes as a metric of inflation along with a number of other inflation gauges such as the Consumer Price Index and the Personal Expenditures Index.[3] In so doing, they are indirectly attempting to keep the value of commodities relatively stable. Thus, it may beg the question, why invest in a commodity index?

As we demonstrate in this chapter, commodity indexes have a low correlation to traditional assets as well as to alternatives. Low correlation or noncorrelation to a portfolio is a sought-after factor for diversification, but it's not the only factor. As an inflation barometer, commodities can assist a portfolio when the returns are reduced by unforeseen inflation. As Greer points out, it is not so much the level of inflation that causes damage to stocks and bonds, it is more of the unforeseen change in inflation that may impair the returns of stocks and bonds.[4] If the inflation rate assumes 5% acceleration and then changes to 7%, the markets and economy should not find too much concern. However, if inflation moves from a 5% expected rate to an unforeseen 10% or 15%, this could cause at least an immediate shock to the markets and economy. Gorton and Rouwenhorst derived the same conclusion when examining an equally weighted commodity index from 1959 to 2004.[5] It is this sort of regime shift that commodity-related investments may prove their added value of diversification, that is, their low levels of correlation. Various articles have revealed commodities to have a positive correlation to inflation over the longer term. This chapter

---

[2]Paul Cashin, C. John McDermott, and Alasdair Scott, Booms and Slumps in World Commodity Prices, IMF Working Paper No. 99/155, November 1999.

[3]Anthanasios Orphandies, "The Road to Price Stability," Finance and Economics Discussion Series, Divisions of Research & Statistics and Monetary Affairs, Federal Reserve Board, Washington, D.C. (2006), pp. 1–11.

[4]Robert J. Greer, "Commodity Indexes for Real Return," Chapter 1 in *The Handbook of Inflation Hedging Investments,* edited by Robert J. Greer (New York: McGraw-Hill, 2006), pp. 114–115.

[5]Gary Gorton and K. Geert Rouwenhorst, "Facts and Fantasies about Commodity Futures," *Financial Analyst Journal* 62, no. 2 (2006), pp. 47–68.

demonstrates the effect of commodity allocations from 5% of the portfolio to 15% and what other alternative investments may best compliment commodities. One could think of commodities as a quasi-form of inflation insurance.

DISTRIBUTIONAL CHARACTERISTICS OF COMMODITIES

Embedded into the question of added value is the focus on the distribution of returns via skewness, kurtosis, and volatility of downside risk. Skewness describes the symmetrical behavior of the return distribution. The shift toward the right (left) equals positive (negative) skewness creating asymmetrical returns. Therefore, considering the tail risk affects of coskewness is a critical aspect when considering portfolio components. As skewness references the return distribution of an investment, coskewness references the relative skewness of the investment components and their aggregated affect to the portfolio. Will the addition of negatively skewed components decay or improve the skewness of the portfolio? Kurtosis relates to the return distribution's tail fatness via its peakedness or flatness. The greater the peakedness of a return distribution, the higher is the excess kurtosis of the distribution. Bacmann and Scholz illustrate a greater probability of extreme returns for any investment as the kurtosis increases.[6] It would be ideal for an investment to have positive skewness coupled with high kurtosis so that it has a greater potential for positive extreme returns than negative extreme returns.

When discussing return distributions, we need to also mention shortfall risk. Shortfall risk relates to the magnitude and frequency of negative returns or returns below a stated target. An investment with a relatively low downside frequency, but greater downside deviation and negative skewness could be considered riskier. Shortfall risk is often viewed by pension funds and endowments as their target returns of assets are needed to meet their liabilities. Shortfall risk is calculated on the probability of a specified amount to be lost.[7]

---

[6] Jean-Francois Bacmann and Stefan Scholz, "Alternative Performance Measures for Hedge Funds," *Alternative Investment Management Association Journal* (June 2003).

[7] Brian M. Rom and Kathleen W. Ferguson, "A Software Developer's View: Using Post-Modern Portfolio Theory to Improve Investment Performance Measurement," in *Managing Downside Risk in Financial Markets*, edited by Frank Sortino and Stephen Satchell (Oxford: Butterworth-Heinemann, 2001), pp. 62–71.

Shore studied negative tail risk with the standard deviation ratio or *S*-ratio = (Upside deviation/Downside deviation).[8] By parsing the upside deviation from the downside deviation, one can better understand where volatility or inherent risk is derived. If the *S*-ratio >1, more volatility is derived in the positive months. Therefore, a high standard deviation may imply more about the potential for positive skewness than its implication for risk. The *S*-ratio can be argued to have a general positive or directional correlation to skewness.

Often investments with high standard deviations are considered risky, and tend to be penalized via the Sharpe ratio or other metrics as a result of portfolio theory, which assumes a normal distribution. However, most asset classes are asymmetrical as demonstrated in this chapter. The use of the Sortinoratio=[(Return−minimumacceptablereturn)/Semideviation][9] inspects downside risk only and offers more efficient results of what investors perceive as risk opposed to standard deviation.[10] Some examples why a standard deviation could be low and thus potentially misleading include low leverage, smoothness of returns due to stale pricing, *S*-ratio <1, and negative skewness.

Payne discusses the tendency for some investors to use skewness when mean and variance are controlled, as positive skewness may be perceived as more risky than negative skewness because the returns of positive skewness may not be as consistent as those investments with negative skewness.[11] Cremers, Kritzman, and Page find investors with an S-shaped utility curve prefer kurtosis and negative skewness as it implies more consistent returns due to the high kurtosis.[12] Higher moments and the *S*-ratio may offer greater understanding toward arguing the flaw of this decision making

[8]Mark S. Shore, "Skewing Your Diversification," in *Hedge Funds: Insights in Performance Measurement, Risk Analysis, and Portfolio Allocation,* edited by Greg N. Gregoriou, Georges Hubner, Nicolas Papageorgiou, and Fabrice Rouah (Hoboken: John Wiley & Sons, 2005), pp. 515–525.

[9]*Minimum acceptable return* (MAR) is the minimum an investor will accept based on their investment structure in contrast to the Sharpe ratio which uses the risk-free rate. In this chapter, we assume MAR is equal to 0%.

[10]Rom and Ferguson, "A Software Developer's View: Using Post-Modern Portfolio Theory to Improve Investment Performance Measurement."

[11]John W. Payne, "Alternative Approaches to Decision Making Under Risk: Moments Versus Risk Dimensions," *Psychological Bulletin* 80 no. 6 (1973), pp.439–453.

[12]Jan-Heim Cremers, Mark Kritzman, and Sebastien Page, "Optimal Hedge Fund Allocations: Do Higher Moments Matter?" *Journal of Portfolio Management* 31, no. 3 (2005), pp. 70–81.

behavior.[13] Investments with high kurtosis and negative skewness may show steady returns and relatively lower standard deviation, but may also contain greater tail risk (short optionality) relative to an investment with positive skewness (long optionality). Harvey, Liechty, Liechty, and Muller note a utility function condition combining mean, variance, and skewness will not obtain an optimal result when applied to the mean-variance efficient portfolio of Markowitz also explained in 1952.[14] Because investors want to maximize returns and minimize their loss, but they also want a higher probability of a maximum gain than of a maximum loss, thus introducing the idea of higher moments.

INDEXES USED IN THE OPTIMIZATION

The GSCI Commodity Indexes

How does the GSCI perform as a spot index, excess return index and total return index? Are there differences to their return distributions, volatility and how does it affect a traditional portfolio?

First let us define each of the GSCI commodity indexes. Twenty four commodity futures markets comprise the components of the indexes. The sectors include energy, industrial metals, precious metals, agricultural, and livestock products. All of the GSCI indexes are long only commodity indexes and are world production-weighted and potentially reallocated each year. Meaning, the quantity of each component is based on the five-year production average and then annually reweighted to be in line with the five-year average.

Historically, the energy markets, especially crude oil have held the greatest allocation for the GSCI. According to Goldman Sachs, the index gave WTI Crude Oil and Brent Crude Oil a 46% allocation. Keep in mind that crude oil historically has maintained backwardation, thus allowing the roll yields (convenience yields) to add positive returns to the excess and total return indexes. One could argue this is the major factor for the indexes to maintain positive performance. In 2006, crude oil had been in contango causing the roll yields to negatively impact the excess and total return

[13]Daniel Kahneman and Amos Tversky, "Prospect Theory: An Analysis of Decision Risk," *Econometrica* 47, no. 2 (1979), pp. 263–293.
[14]Harvey, Liechty, Liechty, and Muller, "Portfolio Selection With Higher Moments."

indexes.[15] This is demonstrated when comparing the spot index to the other two indexes in 2005 and 2006.

In this chapter, we differentiate between the three following index types:

- *GSCI Spot Index.* Total value of the components in the index with regard to their respective weightings within the index based on nearby futures contracts.
- *GSCI Excess Return Index.* Derives the return from the nearby contracts along with the positive or negative returns derived from the roll yield based on markets being in backwardation or contango. Because of the futures component, this index is considered leveraged.
- *GSCI Total Return Index.* Computes the interest received from fully collateralizing the theoretical position during the holding period, thus making it an unleveraged investment. The equation for the Total Return Index derives the effect from reinvesting Treasury bill (T-bill) returns into futures contracts and the gains and losses from futures contracts into and out of T-bill returns.[16] The index also accounts for roll yields.

From January 1970 to December 1972, the GSCI Spot Index rallied 47.1%. From January 1973 to December 1999, the GSCI Spot Index mostly traded sideways and returned 32.2%. When the roll yield is introduced into the returns of the index, the *net asset value* (NAV) of the GSCI Excess Return Index grows gradually, but with some volatility. From January 1973 to December 1999 the GSCI Excess Return Index returned 108.3% and the GSCI Total Return Index returned 1,295.5%. The NAV of the GSCI Total Return Index shows a strong growth component, thus deriving its largest source of returns from T-bills. If one extracts the roll yield and T-bill returns, then the GSCI has not performed well as a standalone investment based on absolute returns, but has shown promise as a diversifier. When the roll yield and T-bill returns are included, the GSCI demonstrates promise against other benchmarks.

---

[15] *Backwardation* is when the front month trades at a premium to the back months, often due to supply shortages. Thus allowing rolls to purchase the back month at a discount to the front month and creating a positive return from the roll yield. In essence, the discount is the risk premium that the buyer can expect for assuming the risk. *Contango* (also known as a *normal market*) is when the front month trades at a discount to the back months due to carrying charges. Rolling long positions in a contango market creates negative roll yields.

[16] The source for the returns is GSCI Manual, January 2006.

From January 1990 to December 2000, the GSCI spot, excess, and total return indexes traded sideways with a downward bias (upward bias for the Total Return Index), as noted in Exhibit 21.4 and returned 19%, 26%, and 119% respectively. From January 1990 to June 2006, the return of the Spot Index was 133.86% versus 85.21% of the Excess Index demonstrating the roll yield from August 2005 to June 2006 had a negative impact on the return of the index as noted in Exhibits 21.2 and 21.4. From 1990 to 2006 the Total Return Index returned 269% demonstrating the T-bill returns had an enormous impact on its returns as seen in Exhibit 21.2.

One could argue the lower returns of the Excess and Total Return indexes relative to the Spot Index from 2000 to 2006 would be due to negative returns of the rolls as crude oil moved from a backwardation market to a contango market. Therefore, the T-bill return of the GSCI Total Return Index offset the negative roll yields.

From 1969 to 2006 each index (especially the Total Return Index) had very positive returns as found in Exhibit 21.1. Between the three indexes, the metrics are very similar with the exception of their respective total return, average monthly return, and annual return. The Total Return Index has roughly twice as much an annualized return as the other indexes. All indexes have positive skewness and *S*-ratios greater than 1. Till points out the rebalancing of the portfolio may also add a source of returns to the index that may not be found when the weights are stationary.[17] Exhibit 21.1 displays various metrics of the three GSCI indexes.

In Exhibit 21.1, most of the metrics are similar with the exception of the return related metrics. The difference in returns can be attributed to roll yields and T-bill returns.

Exhibit 21.2 demonstrates the GSCI Excess index underperformed the other indexes from 1990 to 2006 basis the returns. However, the various downside metrics show the GSCI Excess Index to be roughly equivalent to the other indexes.

Even with the T-bill returns, the Total Return Index underperformed the Spot Index from 2000 to 2006 (Exhibit 21.3), implying the roll yields created a negative impact on the index due to crude oil moving from a backwardation market to a contango market. Drilling deeper we found from September 2005 to June 2006, the Spot Index returned 3.22%, Excess Index returned −9.65% and the Total Return Index returned a −6.64%. During this period, all indexes contained negative skewness and *S*-ratios around 1.

[17]Hilary Till, Structural Sources of Return and Risk in Commodity Futures Investments, White Paper, EDHEC Risk and Asset Management Research Centre, Nice, France, 2006, p. 4.

EXHIBIT 21.1 Metrics of the GSCI Indexes, January 1969 to June 2006

	GSCI Spot	GSCI Excess	GSCI Total Return
Average monthly return	0.51%	0.60%	1.12%
Monthly standard deviation	5.45%	5.39%	5.40%
Annual return	6.08%	7.20%	13.40%
Annual standard deviation	18.89%	18.65%	18.71%
Total return	384.68%	639.99%	6753.97%
Skewness	0.50	0.46	0.47
Kurtosis	2.03	2.21	2.29
Monthly maximum	26.19%	24.89%	25.77%
Monthly minimum	–16.62%	–16.11%	–15.63%
Sharpe ratio	0.06	0.12	0.45
Sortino ratio	0.55	0.65	1.21
Average monthly "+"	4.28%	4.20%	4.44%
Average monthly "–"	–3.82%	–3.77%	–3.56%
Standard deviation months "+"	4.03%	3.96%	4.00%
Standard deviation months "–a"	3.18%	3.22%	3.20%
S-ratio	1.27	1.23	1.25

Source: Exhibit created from data obtained from Bloomberg.

EXHIBIT 21.2 Metrics of the GSCI Indexes, January 1990 to June 2006

	GSCI Spot	GSCI Excess	GSCI Total Return
Average monthly return	0.58%	0.47%	0.82%
Monthly standard deviation	5.60%	5.63%	5.65%
Annual return	7.00%	5.60%	9.80%
Annual standard deviation	19.39%	19.51%	19.57%
Total return	133.86%	85.21%	268.78%
Skewness	0.38	0.45	0.46
Kurtosis	1.01	1.17	1.26
Monthly maximum	19.84%	22.23%	22.94%
Monthly minimum	–16.62%	–14.49%	–14.41%
Sharpe ratio	0.10	0.03	0.25
Sortino ratio	0.64	0.51	0.89
Average monthly "+"	4.51%	4.47%	4.57%
Average monthly "–"	–3.99%	–4.01%	–3.92%
Standard deviation months "+"	4.07%	4.16%	4.20%
Standard deviation months "–"	3.15%	3.19%	3.17%
S-ratio	1.29	1.30	1.33

Source: Exhibit created from data obtained from Bloomberg.

EXHIBIT 21.3 Metrics of GSCI Indexes, January 2000 to June 2006

	GSCI Spot	GSCI Excess	GSCI Total Return
Average monthly return	1.16%	0.74%	0.94%
Monthly standard deviation	6.38%	6.31%	6.30%
Annual return	13.87%	8.88%	11.32%
Annual standard deviation	22.10%	21.87%	21.83%
Total return	89.04%	43.79%	64.71%
Skewness	−0.18	−0.10	−0.10
Kurtosis	0.01	−0.28	−0.26
Monthly maximum	15.71%	14.78%	15.14%
Monthly minimum	−16.62%	−14.49%	−14.41%
Sharpe ratio	0.40	0.18	0.29
Sortino ratio	1.03	0.70	0.91
Average monthly "+"	5.61%	5.18%	5.10%
Average monthly "–"	−4.68%	−5.08%	−5.21%
Standard deviation months "+"	3.77%	3.76%	3.84%
Standard deviation months "–a"	3.88%	3.68%	3.58%
S-ratio	0.97	1.02	1.07

Source: Exhibit created from data obtained from Bloomberg.

Exhibit 21.4 represents the NAV of the GSCI Spot Return, Excess Return, and Total Return indexes from January 1990 to June 2006. One can see how the GSCI Excess Return Index either equaled or outperformed the GSCI Spot index until 2005 when crude oil became a contango market.

Bond, Equity, Hedge Fund, and Managed Futures Indexes

In this section, we examine all of the indexes that are tested components of our studied portfolios. The indexes include the S&P 500 Total Return Index, Citigroup Corporate Bond Index, HFRI (Hedge Funds Research Institute) Fund of Fund Index,[18] CISDM (Center for International Securities and

[18]HFRI Fund of Fund Index contains: 800 U.S. and offshore fund of funds, equal weighted index, and all funds are reported net of fees.

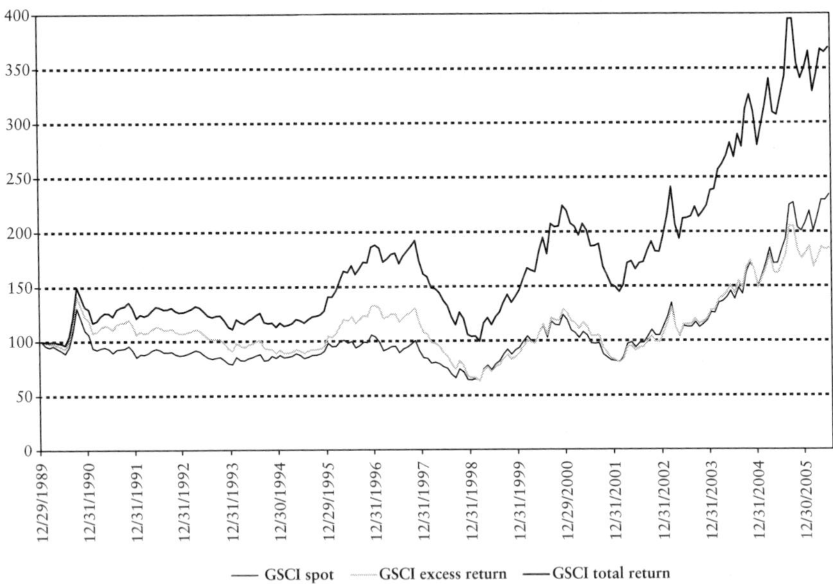

EXHIBIT 21.4 NAV of the GSCI Indexes from January 1990 to June 2006
Source: Exhibit created from data obtained from Bloomberg.

Derivatives Markets) Public CPO Asset Weighted Index,[19] and the GSCI Total Return Index (GSCI TR).[20]

In a direct comparison between U.S. equities and the GSCI, we find some of the metrics to be similar from 1990 to 2006. The GSCI TR index demonstrates slightly greater returns and standard deviation. But when parsing the standard deviation of the GSCI TR, more volatility is derived from the upside as viewed with positive skewness, an *S*-ratio greater than 1, a monthly maximum return greater than the S&P 500s, and a monthly minimum return about the same. This implies the potential for less tail risk in the GSCI. Gorton and Rouwenhorst show their fully collateralized index of commodities from 1954 to 2004 also demonstrated commodities to have

[19]CISDM Public CPO Asset Weighted Index contains: Commodity pool operators with at least $500,000 assets under management and at least a 12-month track record. All funds are reported net of fees.

[20]The GSCI futures contract is similar to the GSCI Spot Index and began trading as a futures contract in July 1992. According to the CME, the first nine months of 2006 realized an increase of trading by 22%. The Excess Return Index began trading as a futures contract March 2006. The Total Return Index began trading as an exchange traded note in June 2006.

EXHIBIT 21.5 Metrics of Each Index, January 1990 to June 2006*

	S&P 500	Citigroup Corp	HFRI	CISDM	GSCI TR
Monthly average return	0.73%	0.63%	0.80%	0.54%	0.82%
Monthly standard deviation	4.07%	1.35%	1.60%	3.66%	5.65%
Annual return	8.78%	7.53%	9.65%	6.46%	9.80%
Annual standard deviation	14.09%	4.66%	5.54%	12.66%	19.57%
Total returns	259.57%	239.27%	376.34%	154.64%	268.78%
Skewness	−0.45	−0.30	−0.26	0.46	0.47
Kurtosis	0.80	0.80	4.16	1.13	1.26
Monthly maximum	11.16%	4.70%	6.85%	15.72%	22.94%
Monthly minimum	−14.58%	−4.42%	−7.47%	−9.60%	−14.41%
Sharpe ratio	0.27	0.54	0.84	0.12	0.25
Sortino ratio	0.91	2.60	2.39	0.98	0.89
Average months "+"	3.17%	1.31%	1.48%	3.15%	4.53%
Average months "−"	−3.35%	−1.02%	−1.05%	−2.49%	−3.92%
Standard deviation months "+"	2.42%	0.88%	1.15%	2.67%	4.20%
Standard deviation months "−"	2.80%	0.84%	1.16%	1.90%	3.17%
S-ratio	0.86	1.05	0.99	1.41	1.33

Source: S&P 500 Total Return Index, Citigroup Corporate Bond Index, HFRI Fund of Fund Index and CISDM Public CPO Asset Weighted Index are provided by Strategic Financial Solutions, LLC, Memphis, TN. Goldman Sachs Commodity Indicies provided by Bloomberg.

Note: The statistical results of the employed indexes are intended to represent the respective asset class. Results may vary with individual funds and/or trading strategies.

similar metrics relative to U.S. equities.[21] If tested only for the Sharpe ratio, then corporate bonds and hedge funds would be the preference of choice.

The indexes in Exhibit 21.5 cover U.S. equities, corporate bonds, hedge funds, managed futures, and commodities. Only the CISDM Public CPO Asset Weighted Index and GSCI TR have positive skewness, the largest monthly maximum returns, and the smallest Sharpe ratios. As Greer notes about commodities, "So if supply shocks are more likely than demand shocks, then surprises should tend to be to the upside, which creates positive skew—certainly better than volatility to the downside."[22] Investments with positive skewness especially when coupled with lower kurtosis may result in less consistent returns, thus higher standard deviation. Conventional

[21]Gorton and Rouwenhorst, "Facts and Fantasies about Commodity Futures."
[22]Greer, "Commodity Indexes for Real Return."

thinking of the Sharpe ratio states low Sharpe ratios are not in the best interest of the portfolio; however, a low Sharpe ratio may be indicative of larger upside potential than downside, assuming a constant risk-free rate. Sharpe points out an investment with a low correlation to the other components of the portfolio and a low Sharpe ratio may prove added value to a portfolio.[23] The CISDM and GSCI indexes fill these requirements.

In Exhibit 21.5, the HFRI index has the largest total return followed by the GSCI TR index. The HFRI index also has the largest kurtosis accompanied with negative skewness, implying greater potential for steadier returns and tail risk opposed to the other alternative indexes we studied. Kat and Lu studied a number of hedge fund subsectors and found the standard deviation does not sufficiently explain the risk of the average hedge fund.[24] Most subsectors have a low standard deviation, negative skewness, and high kurtosis. Thus implying a "free lunch" is not available to the investor. This concept can easily be extended to any investment with the same attributes.

The *S*-ratio as noted in Exhibit 21.5, reveals the S&P 500 to be below 1 and the bond index and HFRI index hovering around 1. Shore demonstrates the validity of the *S*-ratio as a metric to determine if the volatility is derived from the positive or negative monthly returns.[25] This is an important concept to understand as the standard deviation only implies total movement and does not take into consideration the skewness of the monthly distribution of returns. An investment with a high standard deviation, positive skewness, and a low Sharpe ratio may be avoided by many investors if they use the traditional method of portfolio theory because the positive skewness may increase the standard deviation. Keep in mind how each of these indexes affect the coskewness and other metrics of the various portfolios of Exhibit 21.7.

Messina states the standard deviation is not what most investors perceive as risk.[26] Downside frequency and the magnitude of a potential loss have a much greater relevancy to an investor's concept of risk than upside volatility or positive skewness. When *minimum acceptable returns* (MAR) are included into the equation, as applied in the Sortino ratio, the mean-variance model offers suboptimal choices.

---

[23]William F. Sharpe, "The Sharpe Ratio," *Journal of Portfolio Management* 21, no. 1 (1994), pp. 49–58.

[24]Harry M. Kat and Sa Lu, An Excursion into the Statistical Properties of Hedge Fund Returns, Working Paper, 2002, p. 9.

[25]Shore, "Skewing Your Diversification." *S*-ratio > 1 implies more upside volatility and has a general correlation to skewness of the monthly distribution.

[26]Joseph Messina, "An Evaluation of Value at Risk and the Information Ratio (for Investors Concerned with Downside Risk)," Chapter 6, in *Managing Downside Risk in Financial Markets,* edited by Frank Sortino and Stephen Satchell (Oxford: Butterworth-Heinemann, 2001), p. 85.

EXHIBIT 21.6 Correlations of the Tested Benchmarks, January 1990 to June 2006

	S&P 500	Citigroup	HFRI	CISDM	GSCI TR
S&P500	1	0.24	0.44	–0.09	–0.07
Citigroup		1	0.18	0.25	0.01
HFRI			1	0.19	0.19
CISDM				1	0.14
GSCI TR					1

Source: Exhibit created from data obtained from Bloomberg.

The results reported in this chapter demonstrate (Exhibit 21.6) that the GSCI TR has a low correlation to other asset classes, thus offering a potential for diversification via improved skewness, and reduced tail risk. As Schneeweis and Spurgin stated, the standalone returns of an investment are not as important as the net effect of the portfolio from the addition of that investment.[27]

The correlation between the GSCI and the CISDM are low, but, in certain moments, may find some tendencies to be more positively correlated. For example, some CTAs only trade commodities, but many trade both commodity and financial futures. When commodities, especially energy futures are rallying, the source of returns may be similar between the GSCI and CTAs. However, CTAs may also be holding short positions in commodities as well as long and short positions in financial futures.

THE EFFECT OF ALTERNATIVE INVESTMENTS ON TRADITIONAL PORTFOLIOS

We tested eight portfolio allocations for various metric effects and complimentary attributes to the following portfolios:[28]

- 100% stocks
- 60% stocks, 40% bonds
- 55% stocks, 30% bonds, 15% hedge funds
- 55% stocks, 30% bonds, 15% managed futures

[27]Thomas Schneeweis and Richard Spurgin, Hedge Funds: Portfolio Risk Diversifiers, Return Enhancers or Both? Working Paper, CISDM, University of Massachusetts, 2000, p. 2.

[28]Portfolios were also tested as 60% stocks, 25% bonds, and 15% alternatives; 60% stocks, 30% bonds, and 10% alternatives with results similar to what we report in this chapter.

- 55% stocks, 30% bonds, 15% GSCI Total Return
- 55% stocks, 30% bonds, 7.5% hedge funds, 7.5% GSCI Total Return
- 55% stocks, 30% bonds, 7.5% managed futures, 7.5% GSCI Total Return
- 55% stocks, 30% bonds, 5% hedge funds, 5% managed futures, 5% GSCI Total Return

Overall, the metrics in Exhibit 21.7 demonstrate the use of alternatives may reduce some downside risk to a traditional portfolio. Total returns do not change much with each portfolio; however, the distribution of monthly returns does change, thus implying a changing tail risk. Portfolio #2 shows an improvement of the skewness relative to portfolio #1. When allocation is given to hedge funds and/or commodities, the skewness decays with the exception of portfolio #7 and #8 as managed futures are allocated into these two portfolios. It is interesting to note portfolio #3 (stocks, bonds, and hedge funds) have very similar results as portfolio #5 (stocks, bonds, and commodities). The skewness and *S*-ratio of portfolio #5 finds some improvement over portfolio #3. With regard to the tails of the portfolios, #5 has a reduced maximum monthly return and an improved minimum monthly return than #3. The results are demonstrating a slight to moderate benefit to allocate to commodities instead of hedge funds due to the negative skewness and an *S*-ratio <1 of hedge funds and positive skewness and an *S*-ratio >1 for commodities.

More detailed research is needed, but when comparing the GSCI to the HFRI Index, Exhibit 21.7 suggests a larger allocation preference to commodity indexes over hedge funds. It also implies a heavier allocation to managed futures over commodities. This logic is consistent with Shore[29] and Kat[30] studies of managed futures to have greater efficiency of reducing portfolio tail risk than hedge funds. Kat stated further that at least 45% to 50% of the allocation should be given to managed futures when choosing allocations among hedge funds and managed futures.

As shown in Exhibit 21.8, most of the returns of the portfolios are very similar, with the difference in the skewness. Portfolio #4 definitely shows an improved skewness with allocations to stocks, bonds, and managed futures. If an allocation is made to commodities, then portfolio #7 shows the most improved skewness. It also implies the ability to reach the skewness levels of portfolio #4 and #7, managed futures-like attributes must be employed as well. If you want only alternative allocation to commodities then one must

[29]Shore, "Skewing Your Diversification."

[30]Harry M. Kat, "Managed Futures and Hedge Funds: A Match Made in Heaven," *Journal of Investment Management* 2, no. 1 (2004), pp. 1–9.

EXHIBIT 21.7 Metrics of the Portfolios Tested from January 1990 to June 2006

	Portfolio #1 S&P 500	Portfolio #2 S&B	Portfolio #3 S, B, & HFRI	Portfolio #4 S, B, & CISDM	Portfolio #5 S, B, & GSCITR	Portfolio #6 S, B, HFRI & GSCITR	Portfolio #7 S, B, CISDM & GSCITR	Portfolio #8 S, B, HFRI, CISDM & GSCITR
Monthly average return	0.73%	0.69%	0.71%	0.67%	0.71%	0.71%	0.69%	0.70%
Monthly standard deviation	4.07%	2.62%	2.48%	2.40%	2.46%	2.43%	2.39%	2.40%
Annual return	8.78%	8.28%	8.53%	8.06%	8.56%	8.55%	8.31%	8.38%
Annual standard deviation	14.09%	9.08%	8.59%	8.33%	8.52%	8.43%	8.26%	8.33%
Total returns	259.57%	264.81%	283.02%	255.61%	284.90%	284.61%	270.76%	275.03%
Skewness	−0.45	−0.36	−0.46	−0.07	−0.40	−0.46	−0.26	−0.33
Kurtosis	0.80	0.52	0.85	0.51	0.71	0.79	0.46	0.58
Monthly maximum	11.16%	7.94%	7.74%	9.43%	6.04%	6.87%	7.72%	7.73%
Monthly minimum	−14.58%	−8.67%	−9.08%	−6.79%	−8.84%	−8.96%	−7.82%	−8.24%
Sharpe ratio	0.27	0.36	0.41	0.37	0.42	0.42	0.40	0.41
Sortino ratio	0.91	1.40	1.47	1.67	1.53	1.53	1.62	1.60
Average months "+"	3.17%	2.19%	2.13%	2.03%	2.10%	2.09%	2.05%	2.05%
Average months "−"	−3.35%	−2.11%	−1.94%	−1.93%	−1.94%	−1.93%	−1.90%	−1.94%
Standard deviation months "+"	2.42%	1.60%	1.47%	1.55%	1.49%	1.45%	1.48%	1.47%
Standard deviation months "−"	2.80%	1.71%	1.67%	1.39%	1.61%	1.62%	1.46%	1.51%
S-ratio	0.86	0.93	0.88	1.11	0.92	0.90	1.01	0.97

Source: S&P 500 Total Return Index, Citigroup Corporate Bond Index, HFRI Fund of Fund Index and CISDM Public CPO Asset Weighted Index are provided by Strategic Financial Solutions, LLC, Memphis, TN. Goldman Sachs Commodity Indicies provided by Bloomberg.

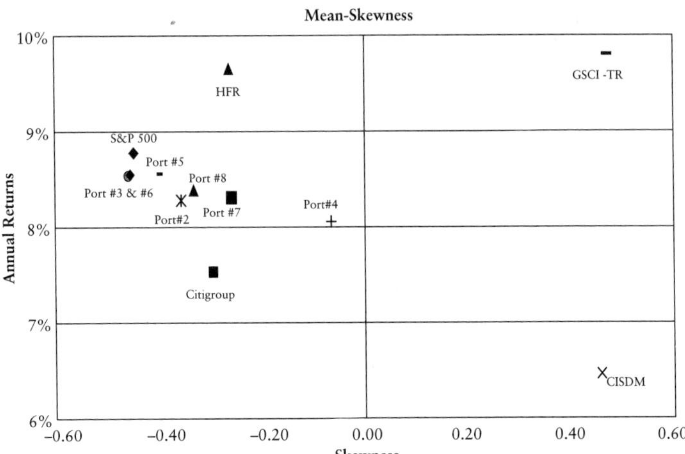

EXHIBIT 21.8 Mean-Skewness Chart of Tested Indexes and Portfolios
Source: S&P 500 Total Return Index, Citigroup Corporate Bond Index, HFRI Fund of Fund Index and CISDM Public CPO Asset Weighted Index are provided by Strategic Financial Solutions, LLC, Memphis, TN. Goldman Sachs Commodity Indicies provided by Bloomberg.

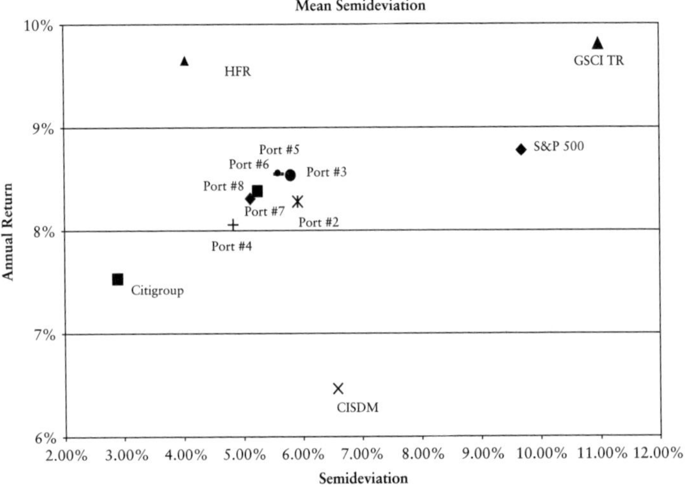

EXHIBIT 21.9 Mean Semideviation Model of Indexes and Portfolios Tested
Source: S&P 500 Total Return Index, Citigroup Corporate Bond Index, HFRI Fund of Fund Index and CISDM Public CPO Asset Weighted Index are provided by Strategic Financial Solutions, LLC, Memphis, TN. Goldman Sachs Commodity Indicies provided by Bloomberg.

look at portfolio #5 with its higher return and greater potential for tail risk than portfolio #7.

When looking at these portfolios in a mean semideviation model (Exhibit 21.9) you will see the portfolios have very similar returns, therefore it's the downside risk that becomes a priority to view and it should, as this is the real risk we discussed earlier. Portfolio #4 performed with the greatest efficiency in our test. Where the GSCI has an allocation, portfolio #7, followed by #8, also performed well. These results are consistent with the mean skewness results and reinforce the positive effects of adding commodity investment vehicles to a portfolio.

CONCLUSION

Commodity investment vehicles, such as the GSCI Total Return Index may offer diversification and reduced tail risk to a portfolio of traditional and alternative investments via exposure to commodities and T-bill returns combined; low correlation to other asset classes, positive skewness, and lower downside deviation.

Difference of returns among the GSCI Spot, GSCI Excess, and GSCI Total return indexes may be attributed to roll yields and T-bill returns. Performance metrics of the GSCI Total Return are similar to the performance metrics of the S&P 500, but with positive skewness and an *S*-ratio greater than 1 for the GSCI Total Return.

The results demonstrate a slight to moderate benefit of allocating to commodities, but more effective allocation may be obtained when commodities are combined with managed futures. As an inflation barometer, commodities may assist a portfolio when the returns of the portfolio are reduced by unforeseen inflation.

CHAPTER 22

Strategic and Tactical Allocation to Commodities for Retirement Savings Schemes

Theo E. Nijman, Ph.D.
F. Van Lanschot Bankiers Professor of Investment Theory
Tilburg University
Board of Scientific Directors
Network on Savings, Pensions, Aging & Retirement

Laurens A. P. Swinkels, Ph.D.
Senior Quantitative Researcher
Robeco Asset Management
Assistant Professor in Finance
Erasmus University Rotterdam

Institutions such as insurance companies and pension funds are investigating the benefits of investing part of their assets in alternative asset classes such as commodities. For example, the Dutch pension fund for civil servants ABP allocates 2.5% to commodities (€5 billion) and the pension fund for health care employees PGGM 5.0% (€4 billion). Also, the U.K. pension scheme of British Telecom allocated 3% (£1 billion) to commodities in 2006 and the California Public Employees' Retirement System (CalPERS) announced in December 2006 that it will start a pilot program on commodity investing worth $500 million. The trade-off between risk and return in

We would like to thank Renée Bies, Frans de Roon, Betrand Melenberg, Roderick Molenaar, Tom Steenkamp, and Bas Werker for their helpful comments. A large part of this research was conducted when Laurens Swinkels was affiliated with ABP Investments and the CentER Graduate School at Tilburg University.

this relatively new asset class and the portfolio implications of investing in commodities are considered in this chapter. More specifically, we aim to shed further light on the benefits of investing in commodities for investors with a liability structure sensitive to the nominal or real interest rate and inflation, respectively.

The interest in commodity investments dates at least back to Bodie,[1] who points out the potential benefits of commodities for pension funds. Froot[2] suggests that commodities are better portfolio diversifiers than, for example, real estate and equity of commodity-related companies because correlations with traditional asset classes are generally lower. Chow et al.[3] indicate that commodities can be particularly valuable diversifiers in adverse economic circumstances, when other alternative assets tend to correlate more with traditional assets. More recently, Erb and Harvey[4] as well as Gorton and Rouwenhorst[5] investigated the potential benefits of investing in commodity futures. Both of these papers find that commodity futures have substantial diversification benefits for investors with traditional balanced portfolios of equities and bonds. These studies focus on asset returns and find that the benefits of investing in (derivatives on) commodities are most pronounced for investors with high risk aversion. However, for many institutional investors the optimal portfolio is determined by the risk and return of the surplus of assets and liabilities rather than assets only. Depending on the nature of these liabilities commodities could be more or less attractive depending on their liability hedging properties. Hoevenaars, Molenaar, Schotman, and Steenkamp[6] indicate that commodities are attractive risk diversifiers in an asset liability context and can be used to hedge inflation risk, a claim that is also supported by Erb and Harvey and Gorton and Rouwenhorst.

---

[1]Zvi Bodie, "An Innovation for Stable Real Retirement Income," *Journal of Portfolio Management* (Fall 1980), pp. 5–13.

[2]Kenneth A. Froot, "Hedging Portfolios with Real Assets," *Journal of Portfolio Management* (Summer 1995), pp. 60–77.

[3]George Chow, Eric Jacquier, Mark Kritzman, and Kenneth Lowry, "Optimal Portfolios in Good Times and Bad," *Financial Analysts Journal* (May–June 1999), pp. 65–74

[4]Claude B. Erb and Campbell R. Harvey, "The Tactical and Strategic Value of Commodity Futures," *Financial Analysts Journal* (March–April 2006), pp. 69–97.

[5]Gary Gorton and K. Geert Rouwenhorst, "Facts and Fantasies about Commodity Futures," *Financial Analysts Journal* (March–April 2006), pp. 47–68.

[6]Roy P. M. M. Hoevenaars, Roderick D. J. Molenaar, Peter C. Schotman, and Tom Steenkamp, Strategic Asset Allocation with Liabilities: Beyond Stocks and Bonds, (February 2007).

The first contribution of this chapter is our examination of the benefits of investing in commodities for investors with financial liabilities. This is an extension to the asset-only approach that has thus far been used in the commodities literature. When taking correlations between the returns on assets and liabilities into account, the optimal portfolio weights might substantially change. We consider two types of pension schemes: one with purely nominal liabilities (as is often the case for U.S. defined-benefit pension plans) and one with inflation-protected liabilities (sometimes referred to as cost-of-living-adjusted pension plans that are more popular in Europe). Our second contribution is that we use the framework from Huberman and Kandel[7] to also include *statistical* evidence on the benefits of commodity investing in addition to the *economic* evidence that is usually reported in the literature. The third and final contribution is that we investigate multiple investment horizons, where buy-and-hold horizons ranging from three years to three months are distinguished. The former are labeled strategic and the latter tactical. Since there is some evidence that expected returns and correlations change over time, we also examine whether the current economic state is informative about the optimal level of commodity investments. This way we can also investigate whether active commodity timing strategies improve the strategic asset allocation.

Our results indicate that the value of commodities is limited for nominal pension schemes, while for inflation-protected pension schemes they reduce the volatility of the surplus both from an economic and statistical perspective. For investors with a quarterly investment horizon the conclusion is different. We document that for certain economic situations, allocations to commodities can also be valuable for pension schemes with nominal liabilities. Finally, our empirical results also suggest that timing strategies on commodity investing is improving the strategic mean-variance efficient frontier beyond that of fixed allocations to commodities. Hence, active tactical trading strategies can improve upon fixed strategic asset allocations to commodities.

STRATEGIC ASSET ALLOCATION

Pension funds have assets that should be allocated in such a way that pensions can be paid when its participants retire. Financial regulation and accounting standards increasingly make use of mark-to-market of pension liabilities. In Denmark, for example, market valuation of pension liabilities

[7]Gur Huberman and Shmuel Kandel, "Mean-Variance Spanning," *Journal of Finance* 42, no. 4 (1987), pp. 873–888.

started with the introduction of the traffic light model in 2001, and more recently the United Kingdom, Sweden, and the Netherlands followed similar approaches. Moreover, pension accounting standards in the United States and Europe also move toward market valuation of liabilities. This means that funding ratios and risk-based solvency requirements become more important in these countries and that liability driven investing has gained popularity.

Sharpe and Tint[8] use surplus optimization as a method to reflect the presence of liabilities and its effect on optimal portfolio choice. The surplus at time t is a function of $\tilde{k}$, a parameter that measures the importance that the pension fund management attaches to the value of the liabilities,

$$S_t\left(\tilde{k}\right) = A_t - \tilde{k} \times L_t \tag{22.1}$$

with A_t the value of the assets and L_t the value of the pension liabilities at time t. Linking the change in surplus by the value of the assets at the end of the previous period A_{t-1} gives

$$R_t^S\left(\tilde{k}\right) = \frac{S_t\left(\tilde{k}\right) - S_{t-1}\left(\tilde{k}\right)}{A_{t-1}} = \frac{A_t - A_{t-1}}{A_{t-1}} - \tilde{k} \times \frac{1}{FR_{t-1}} \times \frac{L_t - L_{t-1}}{L_{t-1}} \tag{22.2}$$

$$R_t^S(k) = R_t^A - k \times R_t^L$$

with FR_{t-1} the funding ratio at time $t-1$, and R_t^S, R_t^A, and R_t^L the return on the surplus, the assets, and the liabilities, respectively. In equation (22.2), the parameter k is defined as the importance parameter $\tilde{k}$ times the inverse of the funding ratio at the end of the previous period. This implies that the actual importance of the liabilities reduces when the assets exceed the pension liabilities. Note that for a pension fund with $k = 1$ equation (22.2) simplifies to

$$R_t^S = R_t^A - R_t^L \tag{22.3}$$

Thus, equation (22.3) is closely related to the concept of the funding ratio return, which is introduced by Leibowitz, Kogelman, and Bader.[9]

---

[8]William F. Sharpe and Lawrence G. Tint, "Liabilities—A New Approach," *Journal of Portfolio Management* (Spring 1990), pp. 5–10.

[9]Martin L. Leibowitz, Stanley Kogelman, and Lawrence N. Bader, "Funding Ratio Return," *Journal of Portfolio Management* (Fall 1994), pp. 39–47.

We assume that the pension fund has a mean-variance utility function in the return on the surplus

$$U\left(R_t^S\right) = E\left\{R_t^S\right\} - \gamma \times Var\left\{R_t^S\right\} \tag{22.4}$$

with $U(.)$ the utility function and γ the risk aversion coefficient. The optimal portfolio weights w^* can straightforwardly be derived (see Appendix A to this chapter) to equal

$$w^* = 1/\gamma \times \Sigma^{-1}(\mu - \eta \times \iota) + k \times \Sigma^{-1}\Sigma_L \tag{22.5}$$

with Σ the covariance matrix of the asset returns, Σ_L the vector of covariances between assets and liabilities and μ the expected return on the assets and ι a vector of ones. The zero-beta return is denoted by η and has a direct relation with risk aversion coefficient γ and the importance parameter k

$$\eta = \frac{\mu'\Sigma^{-1}\iota + \gamma \times k \times \Sigma_L'\Sigma^{-1}\iota - \gamma}{\iota'\Sigma^{-1}\iota} \tag{22.6}$$

The first term in equation (22.5) is the vector of asset-only optimal portfolio weights. The second term accounts for the covariance between the returns on the assets and liabilities. When these returns are independent, the optimal portfolio from funding ratio return optimizing is the same as optimizing the asset-only portfolio. A positive relation between an asset and the liability will increase the portfolio weight relative to the asset-only case, because the volatility of the funding ratio is decreased by investing additionally in this asset (see, for example, Blake).[10]

Empirical Investigation on the Benefits of Commodity Investing

Two types of pension schemes are examined in this chapter. The first pension scheme is required to pay nominal pensions to its participants, whereas the second pension scheme is required to make cost-of-living adjustments, which means that the liabilities are protected against price inflation. This type of pension scheme is more in line with the actual practice in the United Kingdom and the Netherlands, although in the latter country most pension

[10] David Blake, "UK Pension Fund Management after Myners: The Hunt for Correlation Begins," *Journal of Asset Management* 3 (June 2003), pp. 32–72.

funds formally have nominal liabilities but a strong ambition to compensate retirees for inflation. The value of pension liabilities is in general not easy to determine since there is no liquid market in which these claims are traded. We use mark-to-model liability valuation by using nominal and real interest rates and do not take into account actuarial risks such as changes in the mortality rate.

For the return on nominal liabilities we make use of the long-term U.S. government bond returns from the Ibbotson Associates.[11] We use the long-term government bond series because pension liabilities tend to have a higher duration than the overall government bond market. The return on the inflation-protected liabilities is more cumbersome, since the U.S. Treasury started issuing inflation-protected securities just in 1997. We make use of a returns series from Bridgewater, which modeled U.S. inflation expectations going back to 1970.[12] We use the Lehman U.S. Treasury Inflation Notes (5+ Years) index since its launch in January 1999.

The basic assets available to the pension fund are bonds, equities, and real estate. These total returns for intermediate-term bonds and stocks are taken from the Ibbotson Associates and updated until December 2006.[13] For the returns on listed real estate, we use the NAREIT index on real estate investment trusts.[14] For commodities, we take the GSCI Total Return Series. The GSCI is a fully cash-collateralized index consisting of a variety of commodity futures, with weights that reflect world-production of the commodity (see Ankrim and Hensel[15]).

Exhibit 22.1 contains the average annualized returns and volatilities of the base assets, commodities, and two types of liabilities over the sample period January 1970 to December 2006, based on a three-year holding period. We observe that equities and listed real estate had similar returns of 14% per annum. Commodities had the highest return (16.6%) and volatility (35.0%) and real estate the worst three-year return (−25.2%). We observe that traditional bond portfolios had a 1.1% per annum lower return

---

[11]Roger Ibbotson, *Stocks, Bonds, Bills, and Inflation Yearbook* (Chicago: Ibbotson Associates, 2005).

[12]See http://www.bwater.com/ for more information.

[13]The series are updated using the Lehman U.S. Intermediate Treasury Index and the Standard & Poor's 500 Composite Index.

[14]The NAREIT series starts only in January 1972. Therefore, we use the equity return as a proxy for the return on listed real estate over the period January 1970 to December 1971.

[15]Ernest M. Ankrim and Chris R. Hensel, "Commodities in Asset Allocation: A Real-Asset Alternative to Real Estate?" *Financial Analysts Journal* (May–June 1993), pp. 20–29.

EXHIBIT 22.1 Descriptive Statistics Based on a Three-Year Holding Period, 1970–2006

3 year 1970–2006	Average	Volatility	Minimum	Maximum
Government bonds	9.1	8.1	6.1	58.1
Equity	14.3	20.8	−37.6	125.6
Real estate	14.5	24.8	−53.3	141.8
Commodities	16.6	35.0	−26.1	247.9
Liabilities nominal	10.2	11.6	−6.3	88.4
Liabilities inflation	10.4	6.4	6.5	52.2

Note: Calculations based on 35 three-year periods, starting each calendar year; arithmetic average return and volatility are annualized; minimum and maximum are three-year returns based on the sample of 35 overlapping returns.

than the nominal pension liabilities and due to the higher duration the nominal pension liabilities also have a higher volatility. The average return for both types of liabilities is almost the same, but the inflation-indexed pensions have a much lower volatility than the nominal pensions.

In Exhibit 22.2 we display the correlation matrix between the liabilities, basic and alternative assets. These correlations are calculated by assuming a quarterly three-year investment horizon. In order to obtain more estimates, we make use of overlapping annual periods to estimate the correlation matrix.

Exhibit 22.2 gives three insights that drive the results throughout this section. First, the correlation between nominal and real liabilities is negative, indicating that when nominal bond returns are higher than the

EXHIBIT 22.2 Correlation Matrix Based on a Three-Year Holding Period, 1970–2006

Three years: 1970–2006	Government bonds	Equity	Real Estate	Commodity	Liab Nominal	Liab Inflation
Government bonds	1					
Equity	0.19	1				
Real estate	0.07	0.21	1			
Commodities	−0.27	−0.38	−0.52	1		
Liabilities nominal	0.85	0.30	0.10	−0.32	1	
Liabilities inflation	0.01	−0.60	−0.16	0.48	−0.24	1

Note: Correlation coefficients are calculated between the 35 overlapping three-year returns of the assets and nominal and inflation-protected pension liabilities.

historical average, inflation-linked bonds have lower returns than their historical average on the strategic horizon of three years. A second observation is that commodities are the only assets that have a positive correlation with real liabilities (while they have a negative correlation with nominal liabilities). Hence, inclusion of commodities in the asset portfolio is a hedge against risks in the inflation-protected liabilities. Note that our fully cash-collateralized commodity index consists of a cash and a commodity futures component. The correlation between cash and inflation-protected liabilities is 30%, so only cash also hedges against inflation risk. The correlation between the excess return on our commodity index and inflation-protected liabilities is 42%. This is slightly smaller than the 48% reported in Exhibit 22.2, but shows that our results are driven by commodity futures returns and not by the choice of collateralization. The finding that commodities are a hedge against inflation risk is in line with the observations of Erb and Harvey.[16] Third, the correlation between bonds, equity, and real estate with commodities is negative, suggesting that diversification benefits from commodity investing can be substantial. These observations are in line with those resulting from the equally weighted commodity index constructed by Gorton and Rouwenhorst[17] over the period 1952–2004.

We start our analysis with the traditional asset-only analysis, which is a special case of our setup with the importance parameter $k = 0$ in equation (22.2). The mean-variance frontiers with and without the opportunity to invest in commodities, based on the entire sample period is shown in Exhibit 22.3. The opportunity to invest in commodities creates more efficient portfolios, as can be seen from the frontier with commodities that is shifted to the left. This means that for the same level of return, the risk can be reduced by investing in commodities. For example, a required expected return of 13% corresponds to a minimum portfolio volatility of 13.5% when there is no opportunity to invest in commodities, while the minimum volatility is 7.2% by investing 22% in commodities.

We plot the mean-variance frontiers for surplus of the nominal and inflation-protected pension scheme in Exhibits 22.4 and 22.5, both with and without the opportunity to invest in commodities. In order to generate these statistics, we assume that the initial funding rate is 100% so that $k = 1$ in equation (22.2).

For the calculation of Exhibit 22.4, we replaced the government bond portfolio with a liability matching portfolio. The latter can be seen as a risk-free investment for a pension fund. This risk-free alternative results in a straight mean-variance efficient frontier. The optimal portfolio now

[16]Erb and Harvey, "The Tactical and Strategic Value of Commodity Futures."
[17]Gorton and Rouwenhorst, "Facts and Fantasies about Commodity Futures."

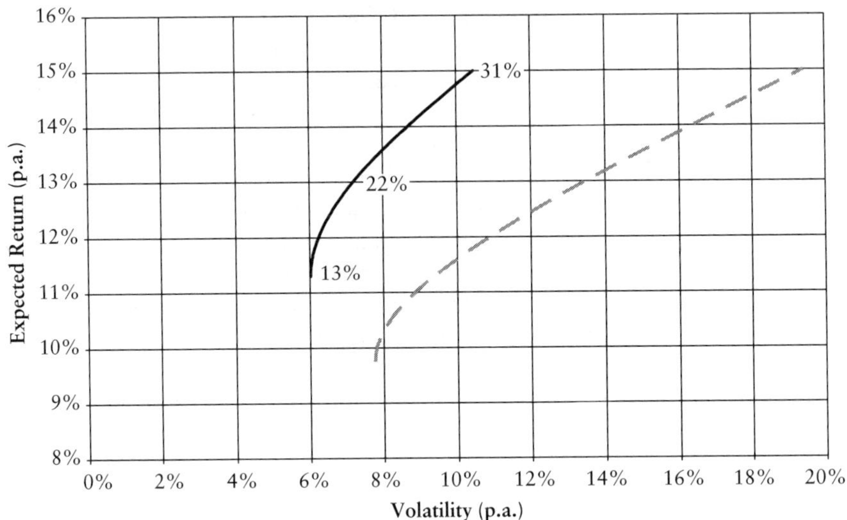

EXHIBIT 22.3 Asset-Only Mean-Variance Frontier with a Three-Year Investment Horizon

Note: The dotted mean-variance frontier is constructed using as basic assets intermediate-term government bonds, equities, and listed real estate. The solid mean-variance frontier contains these basic assets and commodities. The percentages near the solid line denote the portfolio weight in commodities.

consists of an investment in the liability matching portfolio, and in the risky portfolio. The composition of the risky portfolio itself remains the same for all investors. The risky portfolio consists of 26% of commodities. A 4% surplus return can be achieved with 22% investment in commodities and only 15% in the liability matching portfolio. This portfolio has a surplus volatility of 13%. A pension fund with very high risk aversion would choose a fully liability-matched portfolio and refrain from commodity investing.

In Exhibit 22.5 it is clear we assumed that inflation-protected bonds (the riskless asset) are not available to the investor. Although for a large part of our sample no inflation-protected bonds have been available; one could argue that this is not a relevant situation today. However, also at this stage the inflation-protected bond market with maturity over five years is about $250 billion in size, only a fraction of the total bond market and not nearly enough to match all U.S. pension liabilities.

Exhibit 22.5 shows that the minimum-risk portfolio still implies a volatility of the funding ratio of 10% when commodity investing is not allowed. This portfolio is mainly invested in traditional bonds and, since there is a

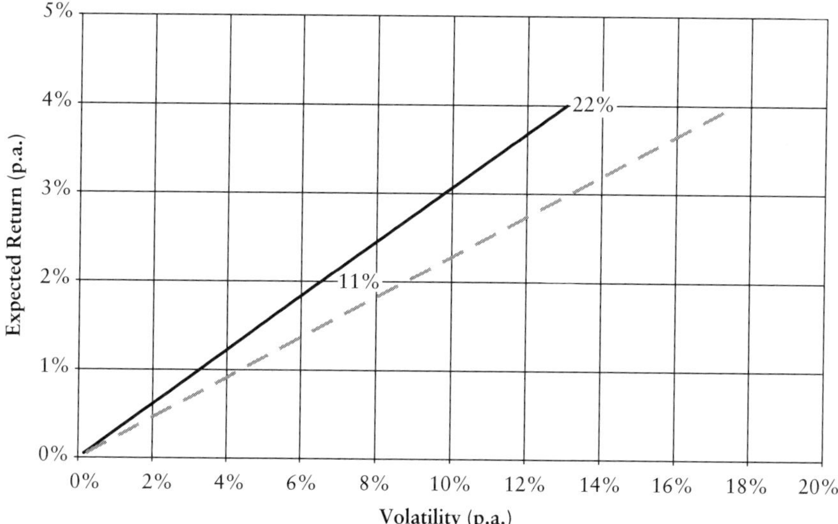

EXHIBIT 22.4 Mean-Variance Frontier for an Investor with Nominal Liabilities
Note: The dotted mean-variance frontier is constructed using as basic assets long-term government bonds, equities, and listed real estate. The solid mean-variance frontier contains these basic assets and commodities. The percentages near the solid line denote the portfolio weight in commodities.

term premium in our sample, this results in a negative surplus return. When we allow for commodity investments, the frontier shifts to the left, indicating that the most risk-averse pension fund would benefit from investing 20% in commodities. This increases to 36% for a less risk-averse investor with a 4% surplus return.[18]

The optimal strategic portfolio is, according to equation (22.5), a combination between the optimal asset-only portfolio and a liability hedging portfolio. For the nominal pension liabilities, we already saw that the liability hedging portfolio is the matching bond portfolio. The liability hedging portfolio is, in the case of inflation-protected liabilities, a combination of the available assets that mimics the return of the liabilities as closely as possible. This liability hedging portfolio composition without commodities is 10.7% long in intermediate bonds, 19.0% short in equities, and 1.1% short in listed real estate. When commodities are allowed, this portfolio changes to 17.1% long in intermediate bonds, 15.8% short in equities, 3.9% long in

[18]We performed a robustness analysis for expected returns lower than the historical averages, which still indicates that commodity investment can be valuable, see Appendix B to this chapter.

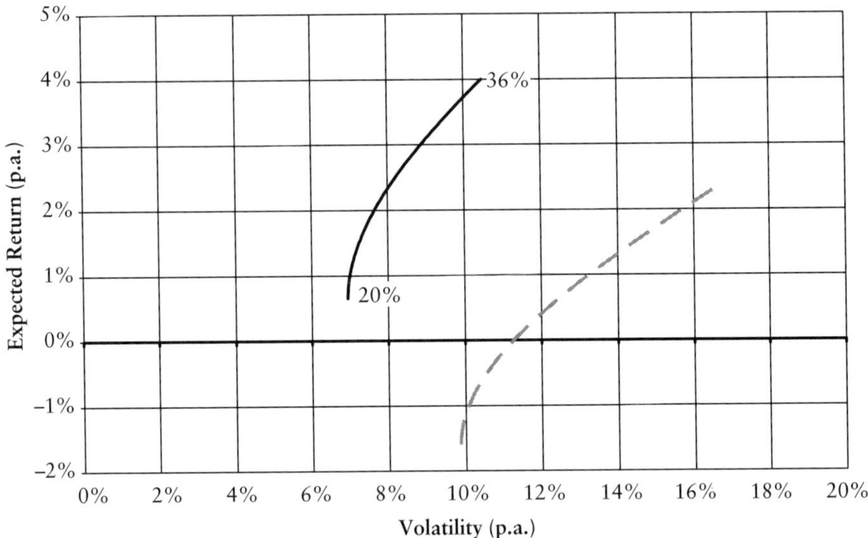

EXHIBIT 22.5 Mean-Variance Frontier for an Investor with Inflation-Protected Liabilities

Note: The dotted mean-variance frontier is constructed using as basic assets intermediate-term government bonds, equities, and listed real estate. The solid mean-variance frontier contains these basic assets and commodities. The percentages near the solid line denote the portfolio weight in commodities.

real estate, and 7.7% long in commodities. Hence, relative to an asset-only investor, a pension fund with inflation-protected liabilities will have a 7.7% higher allocation to commodities in its portfolio. This can be seen when we look at, for example, the portfolio weights in the minimum risk portfolios of Exhibits 22.3 and 22.5. For the asset-only investor the optimal strategic allocation to commodities is 13%, while this is 20% for the investor with inflation-protected pension liabilities.

So far, we only investigated optimal portfolios for asset-only investors ($k = 0$) and pension funds with full surplus optimization ($k = 1$). In Exhibit 22.6 we show the optimal portfolio weights for intermediate values of k, which can be relevant when the value of assets is exceeding the value of the pension liabilities. Exhibit 22.6 shows that an asset-only investor with high risk aversion allocates 13% to commodities, and a pension fund with high risk aversion that fully optimizes against its inflation-protected liabilities 20%. The allocation to commodities for different values of k is also displayed, for different risk aversions. A higher risk tolerance implies higher allocation to commodities, as does a higher importance to the inflation-protected liabilities.

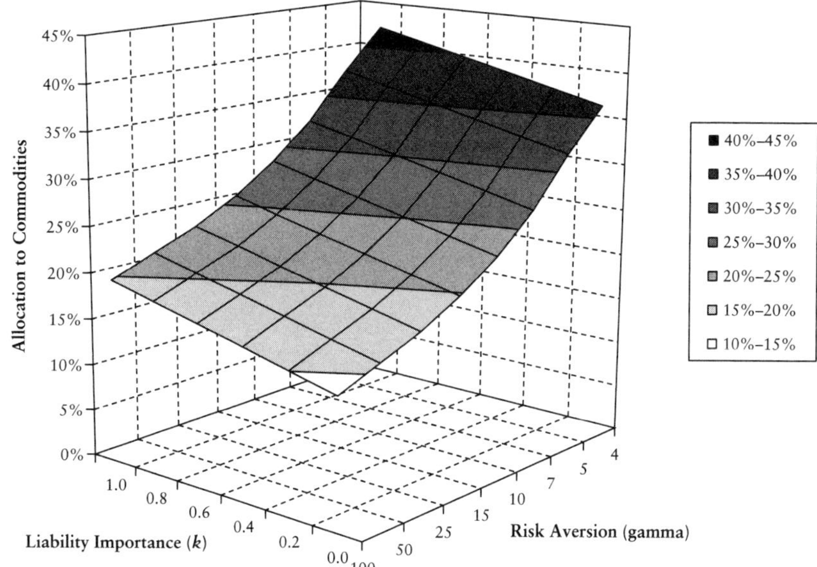

EXHIBIT 22.6 Optimal Strategic Allocation to Commodities for Inflation-Protected Liabilities
Note: The optimal strategic allocation to commodities for a pension fund with inflation-protected liabilities for different values of liability importance parameter k is calculated according to equation (22.5). The value $k = 0$ corresponds to an asset-only investor and $k = 1$ to an investor with full surplus optimization.

STATISTICAL SIGNIFICANCE OF THE PORTFOLIO IMPROVEMENT

The mere observation that adding a new asset class shifts the efficient mean-variance frontier to the left should not be surprising, as an investor can only gain when more opportunities are available. While the analyses above suggest that a pension fund with inflation-protected liabilities should invest a significant amount in commodities, we have not tested our results for statistical significance. Without such test the resulting allocations could be based on statistical coincidences in our data set. We test for statistical significance using the method of Huberman and Kandel.[19] This test is equivalent with testing whether the optimal portfolio weight is *significantly* positive. In an

[19]Huberman and Kandel, "Mean-Variance Spanning."

asset-only context without a risk-free asset, the regression equation that can be used is

$$R_t^{com} = \alpha + \beta_1 R_{1,t} + \beta_2 R_{2,t} + \cdots + \beta_K R_{K,t} + \varepsilon_t \tag{22.7}$$

with R_t^{com} the return on commodities, $R_{k,t}$ the return on the basic assets, and K the number of basic assets in the portfolio. The hypothesis of mean-variance spanning, that is that the two efficient frontiers are statistically identical, can be formulated as

$$\text{spanning } H_0 : \alpha = 0 \quad \text{and} \quad \sum_{k=1}^{K} \beta_k = 1 \tag{22.8}$$

When a risk-free asset is available, equation (22.7) is stated in excess returns relative to the risk-free return, and the spanning regression reduces to a test for the significance of α. In a similar fashion, De Roon and Nijman[20] show how this test can be modified when the investor faces nontradable liabilities. The regression equation (22.7) is changed and now is relative to the return of these non-traded liabilities

$$R_t^{com} - R_t^L = \alpha + \beta_1 \left(R_{1,t} - R_t^L\right) + \ldots + \beta_K \left(R_{K,t} - R_t^L\right) + \varepsilon_t \tag{22.9}$$

but the spanning test remains as in equation (22.8). Note that for each pension fund with a different liability structure the added value of an alternative asset class can be different. Extensions of portfolio tests to the case where assets cannot be shorted are provided in De Roon, Nijman, and Werker.[21]

We test for significance of the commodity weight in each of the three cases that we have shown in the figures above. The testing results are displayed in the three panels in Exhibit 22.7. We test for mean-variance spanning for an asset-only investor over the full sample period and for the post-1984 subsample. In both cases, mean-variance spanning is rejected, implying that the optimal portfolio weights for commodities obtained above are

---

[20]Frans A. De Roon and Theo E. Nijman, "Testing for Mean-Variance Spanning: A Survey," *Journal of Empirical Finance* 8, no. 2 (2001), pp. 111–155.

[21]Frans A. De Roon, Theo E. Nijman, and Bas J. M. Werker, "Testing for Mean-Variance Spanning with Short-Sales Constraints and Transactions Costs: The Case of Emerging Markets," *Journal of Finance* 56 (2001), pp. 723–744.

EXHIBIT 22.7 Statistical Significance of Strategic Allocation to Commodities

Asset-Only Commodities	1970–2006			1984–2006		
	Coefficient	*t*-Value	*p*-Value	Coefficient	*t*-Value	*p*-Value
Alpha	1.18	4.10	0.000	0.64	1.90	0.058
Government bonds	−0.83	−1.66	0.096	−0.30	−0.50	0.616
Equity	−0.41	−1.30	0.195	−0.17	−0.78	0.438
Real estate	−0.64	−2.37	0.018	−0.21	−0.48	0.634
Spanning (F-stat)		23.73	0.000		6.50	0.038

Nominal Liabilities Commodities	1970–2006			1984–2006		
	Coefficient	*t*-Value	*p*-Value	Coefficient	*t*-Value	*p*-Value
Alpha	0.24	1.19	0.232	0.02	0.11	0.912
Equity	−0.10	−0.24	0.809	0.02	0.07	0.941
Real estate	−0.30	−0.83	0.406	0.14	0.40	0.689
Spanning (F-stat)		1.43	0.232		0.01	0.912

Inflation-Protected Commodities	1970–2006			1984–2006		
	Coefficient	*t*-Value	*p*-Value	Coefficient	*t*-Value	*p*-Value
Alpha	0.21	2.02	0.044	0.15	1.36	0.174
Government bonds	−1.03	−2.28	0.023	−2.04	−2.53	0.012
Equity	0.08	0.36	0.718	0.27	1.04	0.300
Real estate	−0.61	−2.70	0.007	−0.45	−1.38	0.168
Spanning (F-stat)		34.49	0.000		13.18	0.001

Note: For the asset-only investor equation (22.7) is estimated using ordinary least squares regression and for pension funds with liabilities equation (22.9) is estimated, where L refers to nominal liabilities or inflation-protected liabilities, respectively. The reported t-values correspond to the null hypothesis that the estimated parameter equals zero. The spanning F-test can be found in equation (22.8). Estimations are based on 35 three-year returns for the period 1970–2006 and 21 three-year returns for the period 1984–2006. Newey and West standard errors are used to correct for the overlapping three-year returns that are used in this analysis.

statistically significant.[22] We do the same, but now for the pension fund with nominal liabilities. Since we allow the pension fund to match its nominal

[22]Note that our observations are at the annual frequency, but have a three year investment horizon. Applying the usual test statistics would overestimate the significance because our observations are overlapping. We make use of the covariance

liabilities, we left the intermediate government bond investments out of the analysis. The test for mean-variance spanning is now on the intercept alone, which is insignificant with a *p*-value of 23.2%. Thus, the improvement of the efficient mean-variance frontier is not statistically significant for the pension fund with nominal pension liabilities. Finally, we replace the nominal with inflation-indexed pension liabilities. The low *p*-values in both the full sample and subsample indicate that mean-variance spanning is rejected, just as in the asset-only context. The conclusion from this analysis is that a strategic allocation to commodities for retirement schemes with inflation-protected pension liabilities improves portfolio efficiency, but for nominal schemes this seems not to be the case.

TACTICAL ASSET ALLOCATION

In this section we shorten the three-year buy-and-hold investment horizon of the previous section and investigate the short-term benefits of investing in commodities. We start this section with a myopic analysis with a quarterly investment horizon. Next, we investigate whether information about the state of the economy improves the conditional mean-variance efficient frontier, by allowing expected asset returns and covariances to change depending on economic variables. Lastly, we determine whether tactical investment strategies to commodities improve the strategic mean-variance efficient frontier. The last section answers the question whether tactical timing strategies are valuable in addition to strategic asset allocation.

Short-Term Allocations to Commodities

Although pension schemes in principle have a long-term objective, their performance is evaluated at shorter horizons, too. The short-term perspective becomes more important through increased regulation in the pension industry. For example, large pension funds in the Netherlands have to report at a quarterly frequency to the regulator about their funded status. Moreover, they are required to assess their solvency-at-risk each quarter. The results

---

matrix of Newey and West with lag two to correct for this potential problem of autocorrelation and heteroskedasticity. See Whitney K. Newey and Kenneth D. West, "A Simple, Positive Semi-Definite, Heteroskedasticity and Autocorrelation Consistent Covariance Matrix," *Econometrica* 55 (1987), pp. 703–708.

EXHIBIT 22.8 Descriptive Statistics Based on a Quarterly Holding Period, (1970–2006)

Quarterly 1970–2006	Average	Volatility	Minimum	Maximum
Government bonds	8.1	6.5	−6.4	16.6
Equity	12.2	16.5	−25.2	22.9
Real estate	12.1	17.2	−24.8	36.0
Commodities	12.9	20.0	−20.2	55.2
Liabilities nominal	9.2	11.4	−14.5	24.4
Liabilities inflation	9.0	4.3	−3.9	11.0

Note: We make use of 148 quarterly returns. The arithmetic average return and volatility are annualized. The minimum and maximum are quarterly returns.

from the strategic mean-variance spanning analysis in the previous section can be different from a short-term analysis due to a changing covariance structure at different horizons.[23]

Exhibits 22.8 and 22.9 contain the descriptive statistics and correlation matrices for the quarterly investment horizon. The average returns based on a quarterly horizon in Exhibit 22.8 are slightly lower to those based on the three-year horizon mentioned in Exhibit 22.1, because we display arithmetic averages. The correlations between the inflation-protected pension liabilities and the other asset classes have changed substantially compared to the

EXHIBIT 22.9 Correlation Matrix Based on a Quarterly Holding Period, (1970–2006)

Quarterly 1970–2006	Gov. Bonds	Equity	Real Estate	Commodity	Liab. Nom.	Liab. Infl.
Government bonds	1					
Equity	0.15	1				
Real estate	0.31	0.62	1			
Commodities	−0.09	−0.28	−0.22	1		
Liabilities nominal	0.93	0.23	0.33	−0.14	1	
Liabilities inflation	0.70	−0.06	0.14	0.08	0.71	1

Note: Correlation coefficients are calculated between the 148 quarterly returns of the assets and nominal and inflation-protected pension liabilities.

[23]Hoevenaars et al. estimate a vector-autoregressive model to capture the covariance dynamics of asset and liabilities on the long run. See Hoevenaars et al., "Strategic Asset Allocation with Liabilities: Beyond Stocks and Bonds."

strategic three year horizon discussed above. For example, government bonds seem to be a reasonable hedge for inflation-risk on the short-run, with a correlation of 70% compared to 1% before. The correlation with equities is substantially less negative with −6% compared to −60% before. Commodities are less suitable to hedge inflation-protected liabilities on the quarterly horizon, as its correlation dropped from 48% to 8%.

Based on these quarterly returns, we perform the mean-variance spanning tests from equation (22.8) and display the results in Exhibit 22.10. The conclusions are qualitatively the same as in the case with the strategic investment horizon. Asset-only investors and inflation-protected pension schemes can significantly improve portfolio efficiency by investing in commodities, but for nominal schemes this is not the case.

Tactical Allocations to Commodities

So far, we have analyzed the unconditional mean-variance efficient frontiers, which implies that the portfolio weights are fixed and are not allowed to change over time depending on the macroeconomic situation. There is a large body of academic literature claiming that asset returns are predictable up to a certain degree; see Campbell[24] for an overview. Moreover, covariances of asset returns might depend on economic circumstances. In this study, we allow expected asset returns and covariances to vary depending on the economic situation as in Shanken,[25] and test whether efficient investment strategies can exploit this time-variation.

The conditioning information we use to characterize the economic situation are based on Ferson and Schadt:[26] (1) the government bond yield, (2) the term spread, (3) the default spread, and (4) the inflation rate. For the government bond yield we take the yield on a constant maturity 10-year government bond. The term spread is defined as the yield of a 10-year minus a 1-year government bond. The default spread is the difference between the Moody's seasoned Baa corporate bond yield and the Moody's seasoned Aaa corporate bond yield. These variables are obtained from the Federal Reserve Bank of St. Louis. Inflation has been lagged one quarter to avoid a look-ahead bias from the publication lag in these figures.

[24]John Y. Campbell, "Asset Pricing at the Millennium," *Journal of Finance* 55 (2000), pp. 1515–1568.

[25]Jay Shanken, "Intertemporal Asset Pricing: An Empirical Investigation," *Journal of Econometrics* 45 (1990), pp. 99–120.

[26]Wayne E. Ferson and Rudi Schadt, "Measuring Fund Strategy and Performance in Changing Economic Conditions," *Journal of Finance* 51 (1996), pp. 425–461.

EXHIBIT 22.10 Statistical Significance of Myopic Short-Term Allocation to Commodities

Asset-Only Commodities	1970–2006			1984–2006		
	Coefficient	*t*-Value	*p*-Value	Coefficient	*t*-Value	*p*-Value
Alpha	0.05	4.22	0.000	0.05	3.00	0.003
Government bonds	−0.11	−0.42	0.675	−0.59	−2.47	0.014
Equity	−0.29	−1.98	0.047	−0.30	−1.65	0.100
Real estate	−0.07	−0.50	0.616	−0.08	−0.34	0.734
Spanning (F-stat)		28.65	0.000		29.23	0.000

Nominal Liabilities Commodities	1970–2006			1984–2006		
	Coefficient	*t*-Value	*p*-Value	Coefficient	*t*-Value	*p*-Value
Alpha	0.01	0.82	0.411	0.00	−0.06	0.953
Equity	0.06	0.41	0.685	0.07	0.47	0.642
Real estate	0.03	0.22	0.830	0.26	1.19	0.233
Spanning (F-stat)		0.68	0.411		0.00	0.953

Inflation-Protected Commodities	1970–2006			1984–2006		
	Coefficient	*t*-Value	*p*-Value	Coefficient	*t*-Value	*p*-Value
Alpha	0.01	1.35	0.176	0.01	1.12	0.263
Government bonds	−0.68	−1.95	0.052	−1.50	−3.03	0.003
Equity	−0.15	−1.05	0.296	−0.09	−0.53	0.597
Real estate	−0.10	−0.82	0.410	−0.18	−0.84	0.403
Spanning (F-stat)		31.22	0.000		22.06	0.000

Note: For the asset-only investor equation (22.7) is estimated using ordinary least squares regression and for pension funds with liabilities Equation (22.9) is estimated, where L refers to nominal liabilities or inflation-protected liabilities, respectively. The reported t-values correspond to the null hypothesis that the estimated parameter equals zero. The spanning F-test can be found in equation (22.8). Estimations are based on 148 quarterly returns for the period 1970–2006 and 92 quarterly returns for the period 1984–2006.

The conditioning data is displayed in Exhibit 22.11. We observe that since 1985 inflation has been modest and that bond yields have come down since then. The term spread has been quite volatile in the late 1970s and early 1980s, but has generally been positive since 1983. The default spread has been relatively constant at around 1% for most of the sample.

We can test for conditional spanning, which means that we investigate whether, given the current economic situation, commodities have a

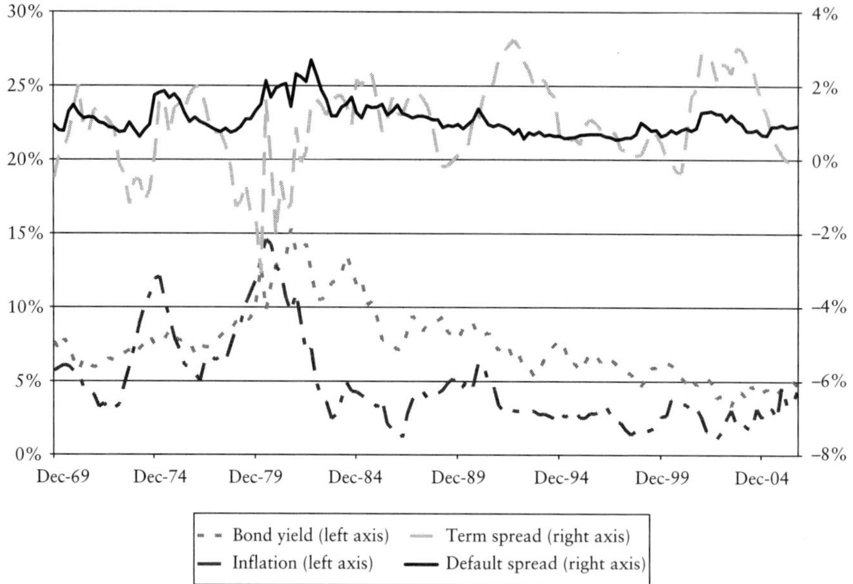

EXHIBIT 22.11 Graphical Description of Macroeconomic Conditioning Variables
Note: Raw time-series of the following four economic conditioning variables are displayed: the 10-year bond yield, the 10 – 1 year term spread, the Baa–Aaa credit spread, and the annual inflation.

significantly positive or negative weight in the efficient asset allocation. The regression equation that can be used for conditional spanning is

$$R_t^{com} = \alpha_0 + \alpha_1' Z_{t-1} + \beta_0' R_t^{basic} + \beta_1' \left(Z_{t-1}' \otimes R_t^{basic} \right) + \varepsilon_t \qquad (22.10)$$

where Z_{t-1} is a L-dimensional vector of macroeconomic variables known at the end of period $t-1$ and β_1 a $K \times L$ dimensional vector of cross-products of the returns on the basic assets and the macroeconomic variables. When we want to test for spanning given the current economic situation captured by Z_{t-1} we need to test

$$H_0 : \alpha_0 + \sum\nolimits_{l=1}^{L} \alpha_{1,l} Z_{l,t-1} = 0 \ \text{ and } \ \sum\nolimits_{k=1}^{K} \left(\beta_{0,k} + \sum\nolimits_{l=1}^{L} \beta_{1,k,l} Z_{l,t-1} \right) = 1 \qquad (22.11)$$

If we would like to test whether the basic assets span the alternative for all economic situations, the test expands to

$$\begin{aligned} H_0 : \alpha_0 = 0 \ \text{ and } \ \alpha_{1,l} = 0 \text{ and} \\ \sum\nolimits_{k=1}^{K} \beta_{0,k} = 1 \ \text{ and } \ \beta_{1,k,l} = 0 \ \forall \, l, k \end{aligned} \qquad (22.12)$$

Both conditional spanning tests are performed on our data and for each of the liability types. For an asset-only investor and the pension fund with inflation-protected liabilities, the conditional spanning hypothesis is rejected for each quarter in our sample period, suggesting that no matter the economic situation, commodities for them always add value. For pension funds with nominal pension liabilities, the situation is different. Testing the hypothesis in equation (22.12) gives a p-value of 15.7%, confirming that commodities *in general* do not add value. However, in Exhibit 22.12 we plot the p-values from the tests in equation (22.11) that investigate whether for a specific economic situation we have mean-variance spanning. Most of the time we find that the p-value is above 5%, but for certain periods we observe that the p-value is below 5%, suggesting that in these economic situations commodities are also attractive for pension funds with nominal liabilities. We see that this is the case in short periods starting in 1974, 1984, and 2005. These have been periods with historically low interest rates in combination with low term and credit spreads (1974, 2005) and high interest rates in combination with high term and credit spreads (1984). In the latter case it would be attractive to have a short position in commodities, while in the former cases this would be a long position.

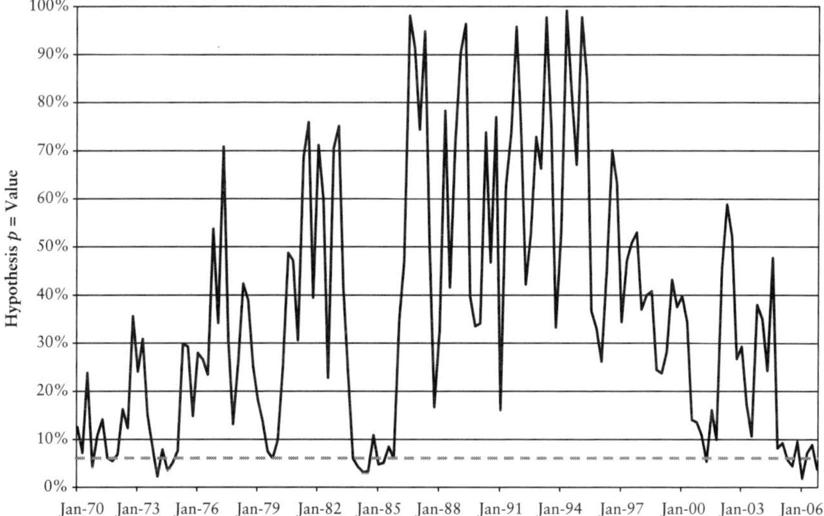

EXHIBIT 22.12 Conditional Mean-Variance Spanning Test for Nominal Pension Liabilities

Note: The p-value of the conditional spanning hypothesis from equation (22.11), based on regression equation (22.10) for each quarter, are displayed. The basic assets are long-term government bonds, equities, and listed real estate. The alternative asset is commodities. The following four conditioning variables are included: bond yield, term spread, credit spread, and inflation.

Do Tactical Timing Strategies Expand the Strategic Mean-Variance Efficient Frontier?

In this subsection we examine whether active tactical commodity timing strategies add value for a pension fund with a strategic investment horizon of three years. These dynamic tactical allocation strategies (or managed portfolios) are interpreted as new asset classes in which the pension scheme can decide to invest. We use the same four variables as before to investigate the effects of timing between commodities and equities. We normalize the macroeconomic variables for ease of interpretation, such that the return on the trading strategy becomes

$$\frac{Z_{l,t-1} - Z_l}{\sigma\{Z_l\}} \times \left(R_t^{com} - R_t^{cash}\right) \tag{22.13}$$

A positive signal implies that a long position is taken in the commodities market by shorting cash. We evaluate the trading strategies based on the individual macroeconomic variables and the combined trading strategy. Note that we already take into account that the pension fund has a fixed strategic allocation to commodities. Similar active trading strategies have been investigated by De Roon, Nijman, and Werker[27] for currency markets. In this case the spanning hypothesis changes because the timing strategy between commodities and stocks is an excess return or overlay strategy.

$$\text{Spanning}\, H_0 : \alpha = 0 \quad \text{and} \quad \sum\nolimits_{k=1}^{K} \beta_k = 0 \tag{22.14}$$

We test this restriction for each of the four trading strategies already mentioned for the asset-only case this time with nominal and inflation-protected liabilities.

The results are displayed in Exhibit 22.13. We see that the strategy based on the 10-year yield and inflation rate have low p-values, while the term spread is not significant. Most likely, more sophisticated tactical trading strategies, such as for example mentioned in Vrugt, Bauer, Molenaar, and Steenkamp[28] might improve the mean-variance frontier for each of the investor types even further. In addition, Erb and Harvey[29] find that conditioning on past 12-month performance and using information on the

[27]Frans A. De Roon, Theo E. Nijman, and Bas J. M. Werker, "Currency Hedging for International Stock Portfolios: The Usefulness of Mean-Variance Analysis," *Journal of Banking and Finance* 27 (2003), pp. 327–349.

[28]Evert B. Vrugt, Rob Bauer, Roderick Molenaar, and Tom Steenkamp, "Dynamic Commodity Timing Strategies," in *Intelligent Commodity Investing*, edited by Hillary Till and Joseph J. Eagleeye (London: Risk Books, 2007).

[29]Erb and Harvey, "The Tactical and Strategic Value of Commodity Futures."

EXHIBIT 22.13 Spanning of Tactical Commodity Timing Strategies on a Three-Year Horizon

p-Values	Asset-Only	Nominal	Inflation-Protected
10-year yield	0.071	0.122	0.025
Term spread	0.789	0.894	0.117
Credit spread	0.107	0.028	0.541
Inflation	0.032	0.017	0.021

Note: Using the hypothesis in equation (22.14), it is testing whether tactical commodity timing strategies based on macroeconomic variables are spanned by passive portfolios. Each managed portfolio is based on one macroeconomic variable as in equation (22.13) and tested against the passive basic assets bonds, equities, listed real estate, and commodities.

term structure of futures prices (backwardation or contango) yields potential timing returns. Moreover, these strategies can also be used to time *between* constituents of the commodity index and thus select the most attractive commodities at each point in time.

These tests indicate that quarterly timing strategies based on macroeconomic information are beneficial for investors with a strategic investment horizon because their returns cannot be captured by a fixed-combination of the base assets in which commodities are already represented. This holds especially for inflation, for which *p*-values are below 0.05 for the case of asset-only, nominal, and inflation-protected pension schemes. The term spread is the only variable that does not seem to add value from a tactical timing perspective, because its *p*-values are above 0.05.

CONCLUSION

We analyzed the benefits of having the opportunity to invest in commodities for retirement savings schemes. We left the traditional asset-only framework and incorporated marked-to-market returns for both nominal and inflation-protected pension liabilities. Our results indicate that for nominal pension schemes the value of commodities is limited, while for inflation-protected pension schemes they reduce the volatility of the surplus both from an economic and statistical perspective.

We also considered a quarterly investment horizon. While our unconditional results are similar on the short horizon, that is, commodities are mainly interesting for inflation-protected retirement schemes, we document different insights when conditioning on the economic situation. In some economic situations, investing in commodities can be attractive for nominal pension schemes as well.

Finally, our empirical results also suggest that timing strategies on commodity investing is improving the strategic mean-variance efficient frontier beyond that of fixed allocations to commodities. Hence, active tactical trading strategies can improve upon fixed strategic asset allocations to commodities.

APPENDIX A: THE OPTIMAL MEAN-VARIANCE PORTFOLIO WITH PENSION LIABILITIES

The mean-variance optimization problem is stated as follows:

$$\max_{w} E\left\{R_t^S\right\} - \gamma \times \sigma^2\left\{R_t^S\right\} s.t.\, w'\iota = 1 \tag{A22.1}$$

The corresponding objective function L can then be defined as

$$L(w,\eta) = E\left\{R_t^A - k \times R_t^L\right\} - \gamma \times \sigma^2\left\{R_t^A - k \times R_t^L\right\} - \eta \times (w'\iota - 1) \tag{A22.2}$$

with $R_t^A = w'R_t$ and R the vector with returns on assets with $E\{R_t\} = \mu$ and

$$\begin{aligned}\sigma^2\left\{R_t^A - k \times R_t^L\right\} &= \sigma^2\{R_t^A\} + \sigma^2\{-k \times R_t^L\} + 2 \times cov\{R_t^A, -k \times R_t^L\} \\ &= w'\Sigma w + k^2 \times \sigma_L^2 - 2 \times k \times w'\Sigma_L\end{aligned} \tag{A22.3}$$

with Σ the covariance matrix of the returns of the assets and Σ_L the vector with covariances between the assets and liabilities.

Maximizing the objective function L leads to the following first order conditions

$$\begin{aligned}\partial/\partial w L(w,\eta) &= \mu - \gamma \times \Sigma w + \gamma \times k - \eta \times \iota = 0 \\ \partial/\partial \eta L(w,\eta) &= w'\iota - 1 = 0\end{aligned} \tag{A22.4}$$

Solving equation (22.18) yields the optimal portfolio weights w and an expression for the zero-beta return η

$$\begin{aligned}w^* &= 1/\gamma \times \Sigma^{-1}(\mu - \eta \times \iota) + k \times \Sigma^{-1}\Sigma_L \\ \eta &= \frac{\mu'\Sigma^{-1}\iota + \gamma \times k \times \Sigma_L'\Sigma^{-1}\iota - \gamma}{\iota'\Sigma^{-1}\iota}\end{aligned} \tag{A22.5}$$

Equation (A22.5) contains equations (22.5) and (22.6) from the main text.

APPENDIX B: ROBUSTNESS ANALYSIS: DIFFERENT EXPECTED RETURNS

Erb and Harvey[30] point out that extrapolation of past returns can be dangerous for forward-looking investment decisions. Since historical average commodity future returns are largely attributed to roll returns, they claim that forward-looking returns will be lower once more investors provide commodity price hedging opportunities for commodity producers. We appreciate this view and also investigate the optimal portfolio with perhaps more realistic expected future returns, which are especially conservative on commodities. We display the assumed expected returns in Exhibit B22.1. The expected returns are set equal to the maximum expected returns that are allowed by the Dutch pensions regulator, which are displayed in the last column. Note that each of the expected returns are equal to the maximum, except commodities, which is set to return a conservative 4%, which is 1% below bond returns.

EXHIBIT B22.1 Robustness Analysis on Expected Returns

	Returns		
Robustness	Historical	Expected	Dutch Regulator
Government bonds	9.1%	5.0%	5.0%
Equity	14.3%	8.0%	8.0%
Real estate	14.5%	8.0%	8.0%
Commodities	16.6%	4.0%	6.5%
Liabilities nominal	10.2%	—	—
Liabilities inflation	10.4%	—	—

Note: The first column contains the historical returns over the period 1970–2006 taken from Exhibit 22.1 in the main text. The expected future returns are listed in the second column. These two return series were compared to the final column, which are the maximum expected returns allowed by the Dutch pensions regulator.

[30] Erb and Harvey, "The Tactical and Strategic Value of Commodity Futures."

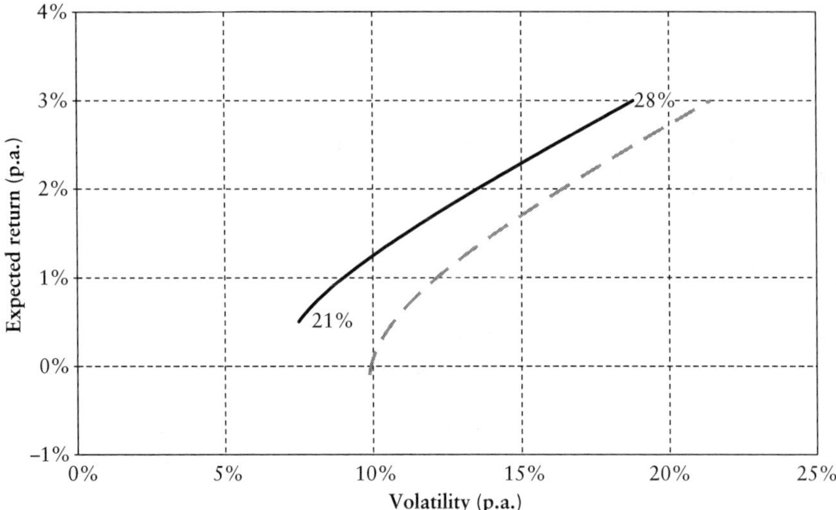

EXHIBIT B22.2 Mean-Variance Frontier for an Investor with Inflation-Protected Liabilities

Note: The dotted mean-variance frontier is constructed using as basic assets intermediate-term government bonds, equities, and listed real estate. The solid mean-variance frontier contains these basic assets and commodities. The percentages near the solid line denote the portfolio weight in commodities. The assumptions on the expected returns are taken from Exhibit B22.1.

Exhibit B22.2 shows the mean-variance frontiers for a pension fund with inflation-protected liabilities in an environment with expected returns as in Exhibit B22.1 and risks and correlations as in Exhibit 22.1. This exhibit shows that commodities are also an attractive asset class with these conservative assumptions, with the optimal investment weight ranging from 21% to 28%.

PART Five

Commodity Products

CHAPTER 23

Types of Commodity Investments

Lynne Engelke
Director, Performance Analysis and Risk Management
Hedge Fund Management Group
Citi Alternative Investments

Jack C. Yuen
Vice President/Analyst
Hedge Fund Management Group
Citi Alternative Investments

Commodities can provide benefits as a source of absolute return, a hedge against inflation, and a diversifying asset, uncorrelated to a traditional portfolio of stocks and bonds. However, commodities have not historically been a part of most investors' portfolios. Many institutional investors have little or no experience in direct commodity investing and many are specifically excluded from the market by policy or statute. High net worth individuals and retail investors historically have been limited in their direct investments to mostly precious metals in the form of coins or bullion.

The growing popularity of commodity investing has in part been fueled in recent years by a proliferation of new investment vehicles that have made commodity investing available to a wider audience. Investors, based on their risk-return criteria and individual requirements, may select from a broad range of financial instruments and investment vehicles. These

We have benefited, in the preparation of this Chapter, from conversations with our colleagues at Citi Alternative Investments (CAI), David Vogel, Jerry Pascucci, and Daryl Dewbrey.

investment vehicles take advantage of the ability to indirectly invest in commodities through financial instruments such as futures, options, and commodity-related equities. There are various types of investment vehicles, including mutual funds, *exchange-traded funds* (ETFs), managed futures and hedge funds, through which one may access these classes of investments and which can provide either passive or actively managed exposure. This chapter explores various methods and types of investment vehicles available to investors for gaining commodity exposure and highlights the advantages and disadvantages of each.

DIRECT CASH INVESTMENT

Direct purchase of commodities is an obvious method, although an approach that has a number of disadvantages. Purchasing can be problematic due to the variability in asset quality. Storage charges, insurance expenses, cash opportunity costs, assay and valuation expenses increase the cost and complexity of holding commodities. In addition, when holding physical commodities no current income is earned. Returns are only obtained when the commodity is sold. During the period of ownership, the above-mentioned costs constantly erode the value of the investment.

Some high-profile investors have turned to the purchase of hard, non-perishable commodity assets such as timber-growing properties and water resources. These assets are only for the most sophisticated investors who can manage the ownership of such properties and have longer-term investment objectives. There is difficulty valuing these assets, which is a problem if interim pricing and mark-to-market are important to the investor.

Forward Contracts

One may enter into an agreement with a seller to deliver a specific cash commodity for a specified price at a specified date in the future. Such forward contracts are privately negotiated. The buyer may be required to put up collateral by the selling party; otherwise there is little initial outlay required. The price set will be dependent on several factors: the anticipated supply/demand situation at the forward date (which may be a function of weather, seasonal, economic, or political factors), the current spot price and the cost of carry, the sum of the risk-free rate of return, and all costs associated with the purchase and holding of the commodity. For nonperishable commodities, we normally find that the longer the term of the contract, the greater the cost will be. This time based term structure, in which the price rises along with the amount of time remaining until delivery, is known as *contango*.

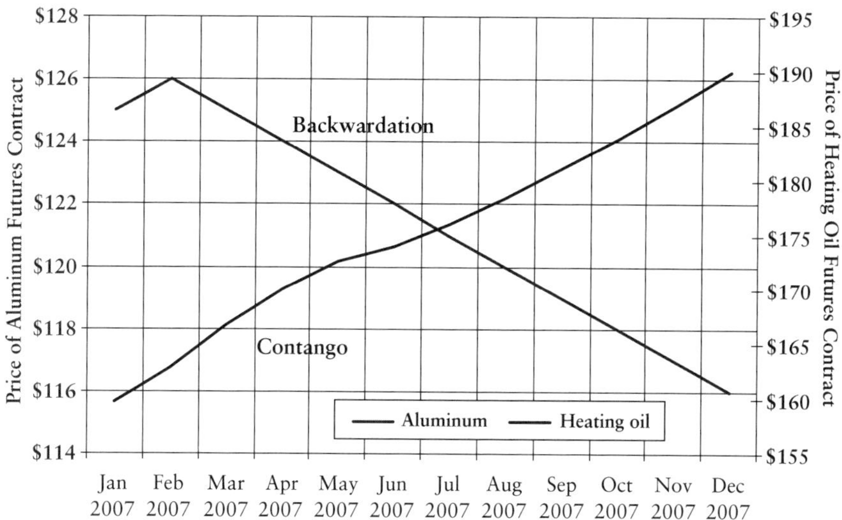

EXHIBIT 23.1 Backwardation versus Contango
Source: Data from Bloomberg Financial Markets.

The market is fairly efficient at arbitraging the cost structure and spot prices to appropriately value forward prices. One exception is when markets move into a cost structure called *backwardation*, in which short-term usable supply is not ample to meet short-term needs (See Exhibit 23.1). This occurs occasionally and, in recent years, has happened primarily in the petroleum and natural gas markets.

The two parties are also subject to counterparty credit risk. This is the risk that one of the parties may default on the agreement—they may be negotiating in bad faith or lack sufficient funds, or unforeseen events could prevent one of the parties from fulfilling the terms of the contract at the time it comes due. This risk premium will also be incorporated into the price of the contract. The lack of standardization in forward contract agreements allows for an individual investor's specific needs and time frame, but is ill-suited to the growth of a secondary market.

Futures

A futures contract is a standardized legal agreement that confers the obligation to buy (or sell) the commodity at a specified future date and price. The price of a futures contract is determined through an auction-like process, on the floor of an organized futures exchange, or in an electronic marketplace.

EXHIBIT 23.2 Some Major World Commodities Futures Exchanges

Exchange	Products Traded
United States	
Chicago Board of Trade (CBOT)	Grains, metals
Chicago Mercantile Exchange (CME)	Agricultural, livestock
New York Board of Trade (NYBOT)	Softs
New York Mercantile Exchange (NYMEX)	Energy, metals
Europe	
London Metal Exchange (LME)	Industrial metals
ICE Futures (IPE/ICE)	Energy
EURONEXT LIFFE	Softs
EURONEXT PARIS	Grains
Asia	
Tokyo Commodity Exchange (TOCOM)	Metals, energy, rubber
Tokyo Grain Exchange (TGE)	Grains, softs

Exhibit 23.2 lists some of the major world commodities futures exchanges and the products traded on each. The exchange functions as a clearinghouse. Standing as a third party between buyers and sellers, the clearinghouse replaces the direct link between a single buyer and seller so that each is free to buy and sell independently. The clearinghouse guarantees every trade, thus removing counterparty risk.

Another way to physically own commodities is to purchase contracts on a futures exchange for future delivery and, at contract expiry, take delivery, not of the physical goods themselves, but of warehouse receipts that guarantee the availability of a given quantity and quality of the commodity in storage at a specific delivery point. These receipts are fungible and can later be retendered for delivery against a short position and transferred to a new owner. This reduces the complexity of quality control involved with buying and selling physical commodities because the exchange sets the quality standards for delivery.

However, in each of these methods, the investor incurs the risk of concentration in one particular market and a single bet on price movement. Multiple physical purchases increase the complication and can usually only be handled by institutions employing professional staff with expertise in the buying and selling of individual commodity groups.

In summary, while direct purchase and ownership is the most straightforward way to capture a commodity's return and appreciation, it is impractical for most investors.

INDIRECT INVESTMENT

To avoid many of the drawbacks of outright purchase, investors can participate in the price changes of commodities via financial instruments linked to the hard commodity.

Futures Trading

Because futures contracts are standardized, a secondary market is possible. Sellers and buyers may exchange one contract for another and offset their obligation to take delivery (or deliver) the actual commodity. This approach allows investors to manage a portfolio of commodities futures contracts, without needing to take delivery and store the commodities themselves. Before the date upon which delivery of the physical commodity would occur, the investor "rolls" the contracts, selling the expiring contracts and simultaneously purchasing contracts for later delivery, thus maintaining exposure to the commodity without taking actual delivery. The current futures price reflects the expected value of the spot price at the time of expiration. As discussed, the price of a futures contract will differ from the physical commodity spot price because the futures contract price takes into account the carrying costs incurred during the contract holding period and the expected supply/demand at the time of expiration. As carrying costs are generally time sensitive, a longer-term futures contract should cost more than a nearer-term contract, reflecting the additional costs incurred during the longer holding period (i.e., contango). As a result, simply investing and rolling forward is normally a losing situation. However, the nearby contract may in some circumstances cost more than the farther-delivery contract (i.e., backwardation), implying an availability premium. Oil, for example, is frequently in backwardation, reflecting the difficulty of holding inventory and supply concerns from weather, geopolitical risks and other factors. Rolling forward in backwardated markets will therefore generate an additional source of return (See Exhibit 23.3).

Typically, futures markets participants are required to post margin, a good faith security deposit meant to be sufficient to cover any daily fluctuation in the value of the position and adjusted daily to account for gains or losses. Margin is determined on the basis of market risk and helps to ensure the financial soundness of futures exchanges, while requiring a minimum tie-up of capital. Margins run from about 5% to 20% of the value of the commodity represented by the contract, allowing the investor use of most of his capital for the duration of the contract. However, this same advantage is also a source of risk. The leveraged nature of the investment will increase volatility and amplify the effect of price fluctuations, creating profits

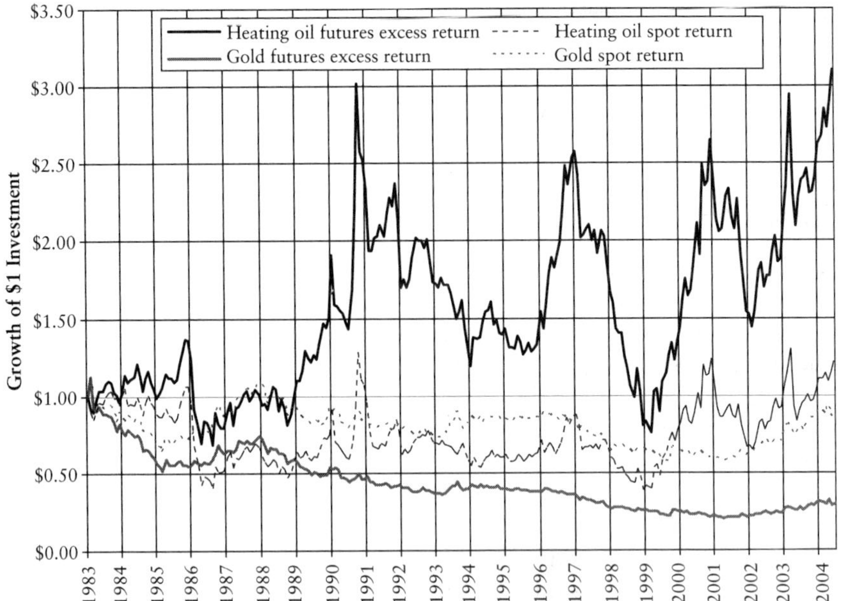

EXHIBIT 23.3 Average Spot Return of Several Commodities
Sources: Data from GSCI subindexes for gold and heating oil; excess return and spot return are taken from Claude B. Erb and Campbell R. Harvey, The Tactical and Strategic Value of Commodity Futures, January 12, 2006.
Note: Over a long period (12/82–5/04), the average spot returns of heating oil (a market mostly in backwardation) and gold (in contango) are close to zero. Positive roll return from the backwardated heating oil market results in a positive futures excess return, while negative roll return from the contangoed gold market reduces the futures excess return.

and losses that are greater, as a percentage of the actual amount invested, than is usual in more common forms of investment. Inexperienced investors, who may be tempted to take larger positions because of the low initial outlays of capital, may incur larger losses than acceptable because of the inherent leverage of the position.

Options on Futures

Rather than trading futures, an investor may elect to invest in options on futures. Options can be used to protect against adverse price movements in the underlying futures market, or as a standalone means to gain exposure in commodities. An option confers the right, but not the obligation, to buy (call) or sell (put) a particular futures contract at a specific price (the strike price, set by the exchange, at an amount above or below the current futures price) within a certain time frame (expiration date). For this right, the option buyer pays a premium to the option seller. The risk of the investment is limited to this defined, upfront payment. An investor can exercise his option at any time within the period, buying or selling the underlying futures contract. If the option is never exercised, it will expire worthless, and the investor will have lost only the amount of the original premium. One can also take advantage of price moves in the futures market, without actually having a futures position by offsetting the options contract in the market before expiration, as long as they have value. The price of the option is dependent on the volatility of the underlying futures market, the nearness of the strike price to the underlying futures price, and the time remaining until the option expires. As the price of the underlying futures contract changes, the option price will also change. The sensitivity of a particular option to its underlying futures contract is called its delta, which approaches 1 as the strike price approaches the futures price.

An experienced futures trader may take advantage of the term structure of the futures curve and the minimal tie-up of capital, as well as anticipated price movements. With an understanding of options, an investor could hedge, or limit the risk of loss on his futures position, or even gain exposure solely through options. However, because of the volatility of commodities and their dependence on seasonal, weather, and economic factors, and the complexity of option pricing, investing in these instruments requires considerable market expertise. For this reason, most investors look for a means of investing that has been packaged by professional managers.

Passive (Long-Only) Investing: Investable Commodity Indexes

A commodity index offers broad exposure to commodity assets or subsectors through futures markets and is constructed based on mechanical rules. Institutions often find these passive, long-only indexes attractive because many are limited to benchmarkable, replicable investments. Goldman Sachs estimates approximately $110 billion is invested in funds tracking the main commodity indexes as of January 2007, an enormous increase from the $12 billion invested in these indexes in 2002.[1] There are several major investable indexes, with a range of compositions and methods of construction. Exhibit 23.4 lists five popular investable commodity indexes.

While the indexes provide passive, long-only commodities exposure, reliance on price appreciation as a major source of inherent return has not been a

[1]Bill Barnhart, "Commodities Drawing Interest in Spite of Risks," *Chicago Tribune* 10 (November 2006), p. 5.

EXHIBIT 23.4 Five Popular Investable Commodity Indexes

- *Goldman Sachs Commodity Index* (GSCI). 24 commodities, world-production weighted and therefore dominated by an energy weighting of 75%. The GSCI has the largest market share of its index peers. Goldman Sachs estimates $60 billion is invested in the GSCI.
- *Dow Jones-AIG Commodity Index*. 19 commodities, limits weight of individual commodity sectors and thus considerably lower weight in energy than GSCI at around 30%. Currently there is about $30 billion invested in financial products tracking the DJ-AIG Index
- *S&P Commodity Index*. 17 commodities, six sectors, constant dollar exposure across underlying commodities. Weights determined using the dollar value of commercial open interest in futures markets.
- *Deutsche Bank Liquid Commodity Index*. Selects the most liquid market from each of six sectors—crude, heating oil, gold, aluminum, corn, and wheat. Weighting factors include world production, usage, and stocks.
- *Reuters/Jefferies CRB*. 19 commodities from a broadly diversified basket, weighted by liquidity and "significance" (as of 2005).

successful strategy over the long term. Commodities have historically gone through cycles of bull and bear markets; however, prices tend to mean-revert to the cost of production, which has been gradually falling over the long term. In fact, some studies have shown that the average long-term appreciation in real commodity prices is near zero.[2] For this reason, collateral return (interest component), roll return (in backwardated contracts), and in some cases, rebalancing return, become substantial sources of return for commodity indexes.

Commodity indexes typically include a rate of return on the underlying collateral that is approximately equivalent to money market rates. During periods of backwardation, positive return from rolling forward will result in a return greater than the appreciation of the commodity. Conversely, when in contango, rolling will create a drag on performance. For much of the past several years, the energy markets have been backwardated. The impact of roll return can be seen in the out performance

[2]Paul Anthony Cashin and C. John McDermott, The Long-Run Behavior of Commodity Prices: Small Trends and Big Variability, IMF Working Paper No. 01/68, May 2001; Enzo Grilli and M. C. Yang, and the Terms of Trade of Developing Countries: What the Long Run Shows, "Primary Commodity Prices, Manufactured Goods Prices," *World Bank Economic Review* 2, no. 1 (1988), pp. 1–47; K. Geert Rouwenhorst and Gary B. Gorton, "Facts and Fantasies about Commodity Futures," *Financial Analysts Journal* (April 2006), pp. 47–68.

of the GSCI, which is overweighted in energy, during this period. For much of 2005 and 2006, however, the energy complex went into contango. Investors should be aware that long-term passive investing exposes them to short-term volatility and risks of losses during commodity price downturns, little appreciation in spot prices over the long term, and if the term structures of the futures curves remain in contango for extended periods, to built-in losses during systematic monthly rolls. Indexes employ various mechanical rules to determine roll procedures and weightings. The DBLCI rolls monthly for energy contracts and yearly for the remaining contracts, attempting to take advantage of the generally backwardated markets in energy and minimizing roll losses in the contango markets that comprise the index. Rebalancing policies also vary, and can impact the return. GSCI and DJ-AIG recalibrate yearly, CRB rebalances monthly, and DB has also launched a second version of the DBLCI, the DBLCI Mean-Reversion (MR), which over- or underweights its commodities to take advantage of the mean reverting nature of commodity prices. During rebalancing, appreciating commodities that have increased their weighting are sold to bring their weighting back to the target level. Since commodity prices are often cyclical, rebalancing in effect books profit and locks in some extra return. Diversification and composition should be carefully considered when selecting a commodity index. Timing the investment is also key. Investors often wait for evidence of a price trend before investing, and by the time they do, the asset may no longer be cheap.

There are several points of access for investors seeking exposure to these benchmarks. Most of the indexes have publicly traded commodity futures index contracts, which can be purchased and rolled. One may also enter into an over-the-counter (OTC) swap with a counterparty to gain direct participation in these indexes. There are also mutual fund managers who offer funds tied to various indexes by investing in structured notes or swaps that receive the index total return in exchange for paying the Treasury bill component of the index plus fees. The PIMCO Commodity Real Return fund tracks the Dow Jones/AIG Commodity Index through swaps, while Oppenheimer Real Asset fund invests in notes tied to the GSCI.

Active Investing: Managed Futures

Because of the low average long-term return of commodities, active trading—which can take advantage of short-term cycles and trending markets—may be preferable to a passive investment approach. Ideally, an actively managed portfolio can benefit from these upward (or downward) price movements by being long (or short) the underlying contracts as commodities appreciate (or depreciate) in value. In reality, however, prices can sometimes remain in a narrow trading range, creating a harsh market condition for an active manager as small losses accumulate.

Managed Futures is an asset class that allocates funds to money managers called *commodity trading advisors* (CTAs). CTAs typically trade a diversified basket of futures contracts, including those in the financial and commodity markets, though some take a sector focus approach. Managed futures is an active strategy that uses either systematic or fundamental techniques to evaluate and take long or short positions in futures markets. According to Barclay Trading Group, Ltd., as of September 2006, the managed futures industry managed assets of over $156 billion.[3]

Access to a professional manager who will actively manage a portfolio allows the investor to potentially profit in down markets as well as in appreciating markets. An actively managed portfolio should be less subject to commodity market downturns, and therefore offers the potential for a better risk-adjusted return. With a diversified portfolio of commodities, an active manager can opportunistically allocate assets to those sectors or markets that offer the best risk/reward scenario, which should ultimately result in a higher risk-adjusted return than that of a passive, statically weighted portfolio. As an example, examine the long-term performance of the passive GSCI index versus the CISDM[4] actively managed index of managed futures traders (see Exhibit 23.5). The GSCI's average annual return of 6.8% is less than the CISDM's 9.9%, while its volatility is much higher, annualized at approximately 20% versus 10% for the active index. The drawdown (percentage decline from a previous high) is likewise much more severe, at 48% for the GSCI compared to the CISDM index's 11%. However, unlike the GSCI, the CISDM is a noninvestable index. The index reflects the average asset-weighted return for CTAs voluntarily reporting to the CISDM database and may also be distorted by *survivorship bias*. Survivorship bias can arise when failing CTAs discontinue providing their monthly performance information to the database prior to closing down. The average, excluding these nonreporting CTAs, is calculated on the performance of the "survivors," and

---

[3]Barclay Trading Group, Ltd. http://www.barclaygrp.com/indexes/cta/Money_Under_Management.html (January 5, 2007).

[4]The CISDM CTA Assets Weighted Index (Managed Futures) is a dollar-weighted index of over 300 commodity trading advisors published by the Center for International Securities and Derivatives Markets, which is affiliated with the Isenberg School of Management at the University of Massachusetts–Amherst. To qualify for the index, a trading advisor must have at least $500,000 under management and 12 months of track record. The underlying CTA performance is net of fees and expenses.

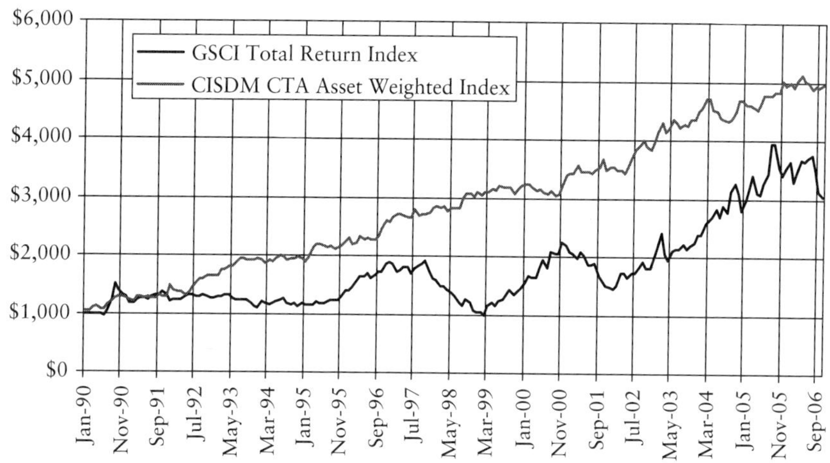

	CISDM CTA	GSCI TR
Annual ROR	9.99%	6.28%
Annualized Std Dev	9.63%	19.70%
Worst Drawdown	−10.69%	−48.26%
Sharpe Ratio	0.61	0.22

EXHIBIT 23.5 Active versus Passive CISDM CTA Index versus GSCI Total Return Value of a Hypothetical $1,000 Investment, January 1990 to October 2006
Source: Data from Bloomberg Financial Markets.

thus tends to be inflated. Investors in managed futures programs may receive returns significantly different than that of the index.

The ability of active managers to profit in market downturns is reflected in their tendency to be positively correlated with market prices in upturns, but negatively correlated in down markets. Statistics drawn between the GSCI Agricultural Sub-Index (a passive portfolio) and Barclay Agricultural Traders Index[5] (an active portfolio), show that in a declining market environment in corn, sugar, and wheat, the Agricultural Sub-Index is positively correlated with each of these markets and therefore losing value, while the actively managed Traders Index has a positive return. As an example, Exhibit 23.6 displays the correlation between the passive portfolio and the active portfolio, respectively, with the corn market.

[5]The Barclay Agricultural Traders Index is an equal weighted composite of managed programs that trade agricultural markets, such as grains, meats, and foods. In 2007, 20 agricultural programs were included in the index. In order for a managed program to be included in the index, the program's trader must have at least 12 months prior performance history and extracted performance is not acceptable.

a. **GSCI Agricultural Sub-Index.** The passive portfolio displays positive correlation in both up and down markets. Investors lose value in down markets.

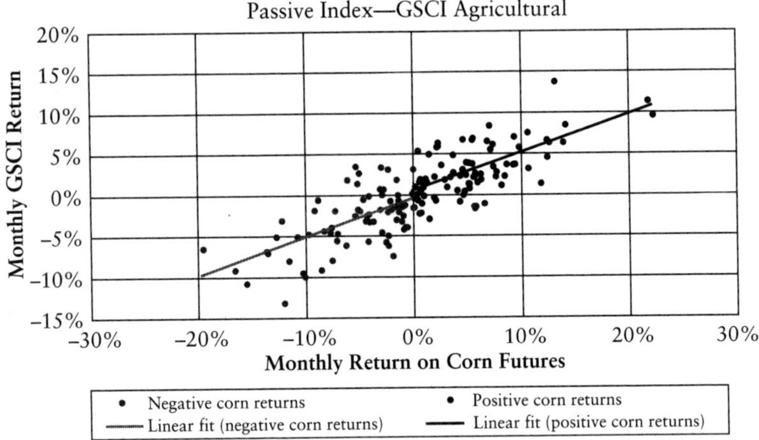

b. **Barclays Agricultural Trader Index.** The active portfolio displays negative correlation in down markets and positive correlation in up markets. Investors may profit in both up and down markets.

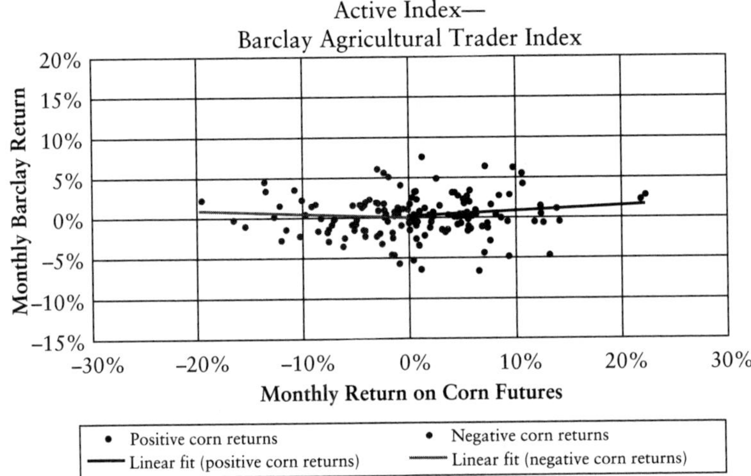

EXHIBIT 23.6 Correlation in Up and Down Markets, March 1994 to December 2006
Source: Data from Bloomberg Financial Markets.

Another advantage of an actively managed program employing the futures markets is the implicit use of leverage. As only a small percent of the total notional value of a contract is required to be put up as margin, a manager has the ability to leverage his trading, while the remaining assets continue to earn interest, adding an interest-income component to the strategy's total return, just as in collateralized commodity index investments.

However, there is no assurance that a managed futures program will capture all or even part of an appreciation in a commodity. For various reasons, managers may enter a price move late, or not at all. Choppy markets without sustained directional moves may result in "whip saws" as managers trade in and out of positions, generating losses through trading costs, as well as inopportune entries and exits. Leverage, sector exposure, strategies, and expertise vary widely among managers. Investing in a managed futures program will introduce manager risk as well as commodity risk. In addition, a single manager managed futures fund can have significantly higher risks than the CISDM CTA Asset Weighted Index as volatility and drawdowns are usually amplified by the lack of manager diversification. Investors or their advisors must carefully assess the manager's trading strategy and risk management before investing.

Managed futures offers the advantage of being highly regulated. CTAs must be registered in the United States with the CFTC, and are subject to periodic audits. Most trading takes place on regulated futures exchanges in the United States and abroad, offering access to global markets with price transparency and liquidity. Clearing firm and clearing house mechanisms minimize counterparty risk and provide additional financial strength.

Managed futures trading programs may be accessed through individual managed accounts, set up with each CTA, or in pooled investments. Commodity futures limited partnership fund structures provide added benefits of limited liability and are often overseen by risk management and asset allocation professionals who select and monitor a portfolio of one or more active managers, mitigating some of the manager risk.

Commodity-Based Equities

One of the most common, but more indirect, ways investors participate in commodity markets is by purchasing stock in companies whose businesses are related to or dependent on various commodities. There are a number of factors to consider before investing in equities, such as which commodity sectors or markets to focus on, where to invest along the value chain and the company's geographic domicile and capitalization. For example, in the oil and gas sector, an investor would have to consider whether to invest in companies involved in exploration, drilling, refining, transportation, or distribution. An investor might also consider the risk-return trade-offs between a domestic large-cap company and a small-cap or startup company, or country risk inherent in the purchase of foreign, locally listed securities.

However, investing indirectly through equities introduces additional sources of risk beyond that of the underlying commodity market: company specific risk and equity market risk.

When purchasing equity shares in commodity related companies, the investor assumes the idiosyncratic risk associated with a specific company (earnings, corporate management risk, etc.). Such company risk can be substantial, as is demonstrated in the case of Enron, which was viewed by many investors as a proxy for the burgeoning energy sector.

Secondly, an investment in commodity-based equities is also subject to the systematic risk of the overall equity market. Many companies may have greater correlation to the stock market in general than to the commodity market itself. Commodity-based companies often hedge their exposure to the raw materials they produce or depend on to protect themselves from significant price shocks, which also tends to dissociate stock price from the underlying commodity price.

As Exhibit 23.7 illustrates, the correlation of equities and commodity prices has not been high or stable. The relationship between company shares and underlying commodities can vary dramatically.

In addition to investing in a commodities-related equity portfolio on ones own, there exist various vehicles, run by professional managers, through which an investor can participate in the commodities markets.

Passive (Long-Only) Investing: Mutual Funds

Certain suitable investors could enter into equity total return swaps or equity derivatives on customized baskets of shares with counter parties to build diversified portfolios and lower idiosyncratic risk. Access to this market is limited and requires an understanding of the mechanics and costs associated with specialized products. By far, the simplest and most common means of accessing a portfolio of commodity-linked equities is provided by mutual funds. The mutual fund industry manages over $10 trillion in combined assets, with more than half in stock funds and nearly half of all U.S. households own investments in mutual funds.[6] Low barriers to entry have attracted large numbers of fund sponsors to the marketplace, and the

[6]ICI statistics and research (*Investment Company Factbook 2006*). Investment Company Institute (ICI) is the national association of U.S. investment companies, with members representing 95% of the total investment company industry's assets, and publishes statistical data on the industry.

EXHIBIT 23.7 Correlation of Commodities and Equity Prices 360-Day Rolling Correlation, October 2000 to December 2006

			Crude Oil	Natural Gas	Copper	Aluminum	Gold	Soybean	CRB Index	GSCI Total Return	GSCI Energy Subindex	GSCI Industrial Metals Subindex
Top Five Positions in ishares DJ Energy Index	Exxon Mobil	Min	(0.04)	(0.01)	(0.03)	0.01	(0.21)	(0.12)	0.02	0.00	(0.00)	(0.03)
	Exxon Mobil	Max	0.49	0.30	0.23	0.22	0.27	0.17	0.49	0.50	0.50	0.19
	Exxon Mobil	Avg	0.24	0.15	0.14	0.13	0.01	0.05	0.21	0.25	0.25	0.07
	Chevron Corp	Min	(0.00)	0.09	0.07	0.03	(0.19)	(0.02)	0.05	0.05	0.05	0.05
	Chevron Corp	Max	0.52	0.35	0.28	0.25	0.31	0.13	0.52	0.54	0.53	0.22
	Chevron Corp	Avg	0.30	0.21	0.19	0.16	0.06	0.04	0.26	0.32	0.31	0.13
	ConocoPhillips	Min	0.04	0.05	0.03	0.02	(0.17)	(0.05)	0.05	0.09	0.09	0.02
	ConocoPhillips	Max	0.56	0.36	0.30	0.26	0.32	0.16	0.56	0.57	0.56	0.25
	ConocoPhillips	Avg	0.34	0.21	0.19	0.16	0.08	0.06	0.30	0.36	0.35	0.11
	Schlumberger	Min	0.04	0.17	0.09	0.05	(0.08)	(0.05)	0.16	0.16	0.14	(0.03)
	Schlumberger	Max	0.53	0.37	0.23	0.22	0.31	0.17	0.54	0.55	0.54	0.23
	Schlumberger	Avg	0.33	0.25	0.17	0.14	0.09	0.06	0.29	0.36	0.35	0.11
	Occidental Petroleum	Min	0.01	0.12	0.06	0.07	(0.09)	(0.02)	0.15	0.18	0.17	0.04
	Occidental Petroleum	Max	0.58	0.36	0.26	0.28	0.31	0.19	0.55	0.60	0.58	0.23
	Occidental Petroleum	Avg	0.36	0.22	0.17	0.18	0.10	0.07	0.33	0.39	0.37	0.13

(Continued)

EXHIBIT 23.7 (Continued)

Top Five Positions in ishares DJ U.S. Basic Materials Index		Crude Oil	Natural Gas	Copper	Aluminum	Gold	Soybean	CRB Index	GSCI Total Return	GSCI Energy Subindex	GSCI Industrial Metals Subindex
EI Du Pont de Nemours	Min	(0.26)	(0.01)	0.05	0.07	(0.31)	(0.04)	(0.11)	(0.23)	(0.26)	0.04
EI Du Pont de Nemours	Max	0.05	0.07	0.26	0.21	0.09	0.12	0.11	0.09	0.08	0.19
EI Du Pont de Nemours	Avg	(0.09)	(0.03)	0.16	0.15	(0.01)	0.05	(0.01)	(0.07)	(0.08)	0.13
Dow Chemical	Min	(0.20)	(0.15)	0.02	0.02	(0.26)	(0.06)	(0.08)	(0.19)	(0.21)	(0.06)
Dow Chemical	Max	0.02	0.07	0.25	0.22	0.13	0.11	0.09	0.04	0.02	0.17
Dow Chemical	Avg	(0.09)	(0.03)	0.17	0.13	(0.06)	0.03	(0.00)	(0.06)	(0.08)	0.01
Alcoa	Min	(0.13)	(0.06)	0.16	0.09	(0.32)	(0.01)	(0.03)	(0.09)	(0.13)	0.08
Alcoa	Max	0.19	0.12	0.35	0.38	0.27	0.13	0.29	0.22	0.17	0.31
Alcoa	Avg	0.02	0.05	0.27	0.24	0.00	0.07	0.01	0.05	0.03	0.21
Newmont Mining	Min	0.06	(0.06)	0.00	(0.05)	0.47	(0.00)	0.15	0.06	0.04	(0.03)
Newmont Mining	Max	0.36	0.23	0.40	0.40	0.69	0.19	0.50	0.40	0.35	0.36
Newmont Mining	Avg	0.15	0.01	0.20	0.18	0.60	0.06	0.30	0.18	0.15	0.18
Monsanto	Min	(0.19)	(0.09)	0.04	0.01	(0.15)	(0.07)	(0.14)	(0.17)	(0.18)	0.00
Monsanto	Max	0.04	0.09	0.19	0.16	0.15	0.01	0.08	0.05	0.06	0.16
Monsanto	Avg	(0.06)	(0.02)	0.10	0.08	(0.00)	0.02	(0.03)	(0.05)	(0.06)	0.08

resulting highly competitive, but highly regulated environment has encouraged the growth of a great variety of offerings.

A wide-ranging array of natural resource or other commodity-focused mutual funds exist, offered by many well-known fund families, including Fidelity, Vanguard, and Franklin Templeton. Natural resource funds tend to invest in a variety of energy, mining, chemical, paper or forest products, and other natural resource-based stocks. Sector funds also exist, offering exposure to energy, precious metals, or basic materials. More narrowly based subsector funds focus on individual commodities like natural gas, gold, and oil, or points along the value chain, such as gas exploration companies, or oil equipment and distribution companies. These funds entail risks similar to the risks involved in stock purchases but provide greater levels of diversification and the comfort of professional due diligence and oversight to mitigate company risk. However, as in commodity index investing, mutual fund investors will face the added constraints of long-only investing as well as cost considerations.

Exchange-Traded Funds

For retail investors, *exchange-traded funds* (ETFs) could possibly be the landmark invention of the 1990s. Since the creation of the Standard & Poor's Depositary Receipt (SPDR) in January 1993, ETFs have matured significantly. While ETFs were initially created for institutional investors[7] as a hedging instrument, retail investors now comprise a significant portion of the overall ETF market.[8] The American Stock Exchange (AMEX) offers over 200 different ETFs, including broad-based indexes, international equities, and sector specific funds. As of November 2006, of $397 billion of combined assets in U.S. ETFs, $44.8 billion were devoted to domestic U.S. sector or industry specific ETFs.[9] One of the most important benefits of an ETF is to provide investors with opportunities to capture the potential appreciation in value of a particular market segment, including commodities or regional economic trends without the risk of single-stock exposure. The implicit diversification benefits, lower cost structures versus similar mutual funds, and the tax benefits of a passively managed portfolio, make ETFs effective and flexible instruments for investors.

[7]"The Genesis Shows the Genius: ETFs and Nate Most," *Bloomberg Wealth Manager*, September 1, 2004, p. 113.

[8]Ian Salisbury, "ETF Appeal Shifts to Main Street," *Wall Street Jounal,* August 1, 2006.

[9]ICI statistics and research. Trust-issued receipts are not included in this figure.

EXHIBIT 23.8 Some of the More Popular Commodities-Related Exchange-Traded Funds (assets as of January 5, 2007)

- DJ Energy Sector Fund (IYE) $847.1 million
- S&P Global Energy Sector Inx (IXC) $653.5 million
- Goldman Sachs Natural Resources Fund (IGE) $1,556 million
- SPDR Energy (XLE) $3,077.48 million
- SPDR Materials (XLB) $932.69 million
- Powershares Water Resources (PHO) $1,299.60 million
- iShares US Basic Materials Sector Index (IYM) $490.51 million

Source: Data from Bloomberg Financial Markets.

Commodities-Related ETFs In recent years there has been a proliferation of ETFs with commodity-related themes such as energy, natural resources, and basic materials that invest in stocks of companies involved in the production, processing, and distribution of certain commodities (See Exhibit 23.8).

Investing indirectly through equities via ETFs once again introduces additional sources of risk beyond that of the underlying commodity, namely corporate management risk and general market risk. In fact, commodities-linked equities tend to have as strong or a stronger correlation with the S&P than with the underlying commodities themselves. For example, based on daily returns data since its inception (12/22/98–12/29/06), the Energy Select Sector SPDR fund has exhibited a 0.23 correlation to the GSCI Energy Sub-Index, versus a correlation of 0.43 to the S&P 500.

Commodities-Linked ETFs A new, fast-growing segment of the ETF industry provides exposure to commodities themselves, rather than related equities, through either holding the physical commodity itself, or futures contracts. *Exchange-traded notes* (ETNs) have also recently been introduced, which are similar to ETFs, and are traded on major stock exchanges. Currently, there are specialized commodity-linked ETFs for gold, silver, and crude oil. The commodity-specific ETFs are limited and nondiversified, but the sector is expanding rapidly, and may soon include others. An investor may access commodity indexes through new ETF and ETNs as well, providing another point of access to passive long-only commodity indexes. A selection of offerings is briefly outlined in Exhibit 23.9.

The ease of trading and low transaction costs associated with ETFs can tempt an investor to trade in and out of these instruments to capture short-term price movements. However, once again, such trading requires expertise and experience to make this a successful strategy over the long term. Many ETF investors are tempted to follow the hot sector because they have

EXHIBIT 23.9 An Outline of Commodities-Linked, Exchange-Traded Funds: Assets as of January 5, 2007

- Gold ETFs
  - **Barclays Global Investors iShares COMEX Gold Trust (IAU)** (started 1/21/05). Seeks to correspond to the day-to-day movement of the price of gold bullion. The objective of the Gold Trust is to reflect the price of gold owned by the Gold Trust at that time, less the expenses and liabilities of the Trust. (Assets: $864 million)
  - **State Street, StreetTracks Gold (GLD)** (started 11/04). Holds physically allocated gold bullion with the objective of reflecting the performance of the price of gold bullion less expenses. (Assets: $8,799.31 million)
- **Barclays Global Investors iShares Silver Trust (SLV)** (started 4/28/06). The assets of the trust consist primarily of silver held by the custodian on behalf of the trust. The objective of the trust is for the shares to reflect the price of silver owned by the trust, less the trust's expenses and liabilities. (Assets: $1,482.13 million)
- **U.S. Oil Fund (USOF)** (started 4/06). The USOF is a commodity pool that invests in oil futures contracts and other oil interests to track the performance of West Texas intermediate light, sweet crude oil and other types of crude oil, heating oil, gasoline, natural gas, and petroleum based fuels futures. The fund issues units that may be purchased on the AMEX. (Assets: $744.5 million)
- **Deutsche Bank Commodity Index Tracking fund (DBC)** (started 2/06). Attempts to mirror the DB Commodity index by investing in exchange-traded futures on the commodities comprising the index. (Assets: $666.42 million)
- **iPath Dow Jones-AIG Commodity Index Total Return ETN (DJP)** (started 6/06). Reflects returns potentially available to an unleveraged investment in futures contracts on the commodities comprising the DJ-AIG index, plus the rate of interest that could be earned on cash collateral invested in Treasury bills, less expenses. (Assets: $837.03 million)

Source: Data from Bloomberg Financial Markets.

the power to effortlessly move in and out of any fund. Consequently, they could easily suffer losses from inopportune entries and exits as the prevailing trends reverse.

Active Investing: Hedge Funds Exposure to commodity-based equities and futures can also be gained through an investment in a natural resources-focused or diversified directional long-short equity hedge fund. Hedge funds are actively managed, highly leveraged portfolios of investments that use various investment strategies, based on discretion or quantitative rules, and various investment instruments such as equities, futures, derivatives, or other financial structures, to take long or short positions in global and domestic markets. According to Hedge Fund Research, Inc., as of September 2006, there were more than 9,000 hedge funds, managing assets of over $1 trillion in total, and about $67 billion in sector focused funds.[10]

Because of the complexity of hedge fund strategies and the lack of disclosure and transparency that often characterizes these funds, investors may find it difficult to assess manager skill or the models behind the quantitative strategies used. Once an investment is made, it may not be possible to track ones exposure to commodities.

As interest in commodities has grown, more hedge funds have focused on this area, or added commodities strategies to diversify their portfolios. In 2006, an estimated $60 billion was invested in energy markets by 140 dedicated commodity-trading hedge funds.[11]

Though the addition of commodities can benefit a portfolio, it also poses risks. Nominally diversified hedge funds may be tempted to shift too much risk into volatile commodities, without appropriate risk management or disclosure to clients. The recent collapse of several well-known hedge funds due to losses in energy trading, notably Amaranth in September 2006, illustrates the dangers that even sophisticated traders may encounter in overweighting their portfolios' exposures to a single commodity.

Hedge funds are largely unregulated, and cater to sophisticated investors that meet accreditation rules based on income and net worth. They usually require very large minimum investment and because of the illiquidity of many of the investments, often require investors to commit their funds for a period known as a lock-up, which can be as much as a year or more, and subject the investor to large penalties for early redemption.

Funds of hedge funds can mitigate manager risk through diversification among many funds, and offer fund selection, oversight, and risk monitoring by experienced professional staff. Liquidity terms may also be more favorable. Some funds of hedge funds elect to register with the SEC. These funds must provide investors with a prospectus and must file certain reports regularly with the SEC. Many registered funds of hedge funds require a much lower minimum investment than individual hedge funds.

CONCLUSION

Commodities can provide benefits as a source of absolute return, as a hedge against inflation, and as a diversifying, noncorrelated asset in a traditional portfolio of stocks and bonds. Beyond direct investments, which are

[10]HFR Industry Report Q3 2006 © HFR Inc., 2006, www.hedgefundresearch.com.

[11]Peter C. Fusaro and Gary M. Vasey, "Energy & Environmental Funds: Continuing to Offer Superior Opportunities," *Commodities Now*, 2005.

impractical for most investors, recent innovations in capital markets have resulted in more varied avenues for investment in this asset class. Futures- and options-based investments offer the most direct link to underlying commodities, but exposure may also be obtained through commodity-related equities. The investor may choose between focused, undiversified investments, and broader-based commodity exposure, as well as between passive investment and actively traded portfolios. Various investment vehicles, including futures funds, mutual funds, exchange-traded funds, and hedge funds provide access to these investments. Ultimately, each investor must choose which method of accessing the market is most suitable, based on his or her risk appetite and sophistication.

CHAPTER 24

Commodity Options

Carol Alexander
Chair of Risk Management and Director of Research
ICMA Centre
University of Reading

Aanand Venkatramanan
Doctoral Researcher
ICMA Centre
University of Reading

There are three reasons to trade commodity options: diversification, hedging, and speculation. Options are included in investment portfolios because they have a limited upside or downside, compared with futures. Commodity options provide diversification because they have low correlations with equities and bonds. For that reason it is optimal to diversify by adding commodity options to standard portfolios despite their being risky instruments.

Risk managers use commodity options to hedge price risk. For instance, calendar spreads can be used to protect producers in a market that tends to swing between backwardation and contango. Average price options (where the payoff depends on the difference between some average of underlying prices and the option strike) are also popular for risk management because they are much cheaper than standard options—yet they still allow the purchaser to secure supplies at a fixed price.

Speculators use options as highly leveraged bets on price direction. For instance, a U.S. calendar spread call on the difference between the one-month futures price and the three-month futures price is a bet that futures will move to stronger backwardation at some time before the option's expiry. At exercise the purchaser receives a long position on the one-month futures and a short position on the three-month futures, at their prevailing market prices.

To buy an option is to be long volatility. Hence commodity options can also be used to speculate on volatility and to hedge volatility risk. All commodity prices are volatile, some more than others. Agriculturals tend to have the lowest volatilities, generally only around 30% to 50% but metals and energy have much higher volatility. For instance, the volatility of on-peak spot electricity prices in the United States was almost 200% in 2005.

This chapter provides a survey of the market for commodity options, the products that are commonly traded and the models that we can use to price and hedge commodity options.

COMMODITY OPTIONS MARKETS

The volume of exchange-traded options on commodities has grown steadily since the first contracts were introduced in the late 1980s. NYMEX and COMEX are the most active platforms for trading, mostly in different types of U.S. options on energy and metals futures. In 2006 a total of 60 million commodity options contracts were traded on the Nymex and Comex exchanges, over 25% of the total volume traded on commodity futures contracts (see Exhibit 24.1).

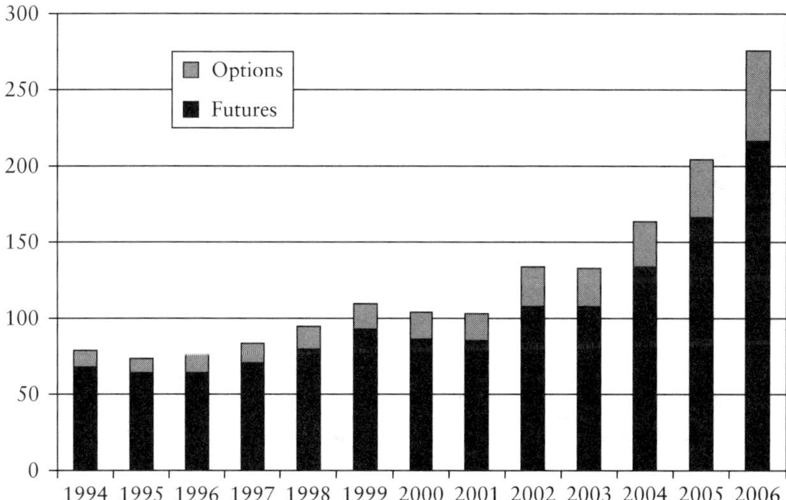

EXHIBIT 24.1 NYMEX Futures and Options Trading Volume

There is much more exchange trading on energy options than on metal options. Exhibit 24.2 shows that the most liquid energy options on NYMEX are American options on crude oil and natural gas. American crack spread options have traded for many years but trading volume remains low. American calendar spread options and average price options have grown more popular during the last few years (see Exhibit 24.3). Calendar spreads and average price options provide flexibility for the risk management of commodity futures and, since they are cheaper than standard options, increase the potential for speculation.

The more liquid energy contracts also have cash-settled European-style options contracts that are traded on exchanges: daily options available solely for clearing and inventory options that help manage exposure to the impact of reported inventories. The strike units of inventory options are the potential difference in inventory from the previous week's report, the change in the inventories determine which options are in-the-money and which are out-of-the-money, and the premium collected from those holding out-of-the-money options is paid to those holding in-the-money options. As well as vanilla options, digital inventory options pay a fixed amount for in-the-money contracts.

Exhibit 24.4 shows that most of the options traded on COMEX are standard American gold and silver futures options, although average daily volumes on copper futures options are also significant.

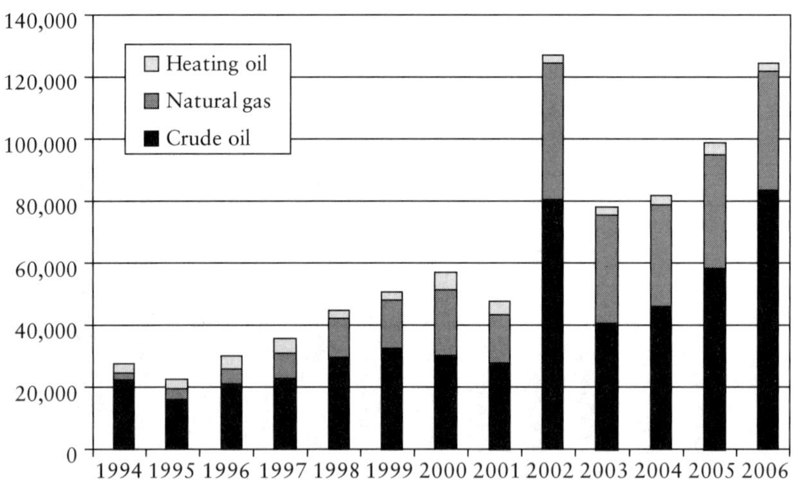

EXHIBIT 24.2 NYMEX Energy Options Trading Volume

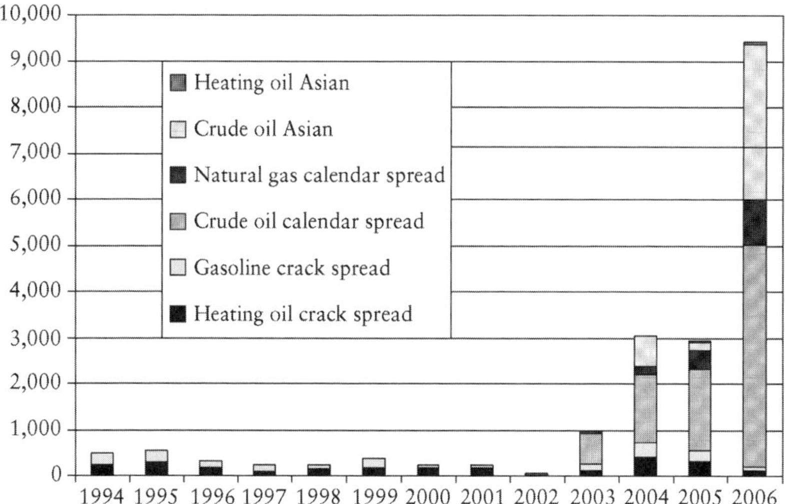

EXHIBIT 24.3 Energy Spread Options Trading Volume

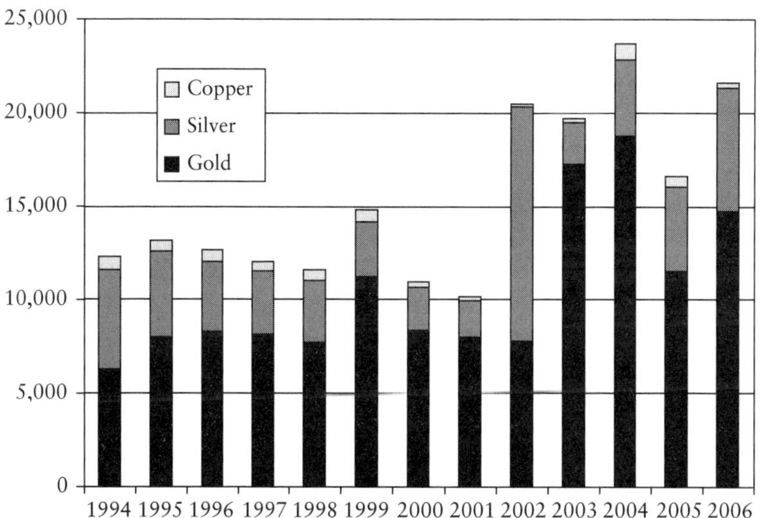

EXHIBIT 24.4 COMEX Metal Options Trading Volume

Two other large exchanges specialize in options on futures of agriculturals such as dairy products, cocoa, coffee, sugar, soybean products, corn, wheat, live cattle, and lean hogs. These are the CME group (created by the merger of Chicago Mercantile Exchange (CME) and the Chicago Board of Trade (CBOT)) and the main commodity options exchange outside the U.S., Euronext.Liffe.

Hence the major commodities exchanges all trade in options on futures of the same maturity as the option, and not in options on spot prices. There are two good reasons for this. First, the no-arbitrage argument that gives the option price has to be based on the possibility of hedging with a liquid asset, and the futures are usually far more liquid than the spot. Secondly, spot prices are more difficult to model than futures prices because they display mean reversion that is related to seasonally and long-term economic equilibria that equate supply and demand. (For instance, if a Chinese car manufacturer dramatically increases production of inexpensive cars, the price of gasoline will increase in the short term but over the longer term more refineries would be built to meet the demand for gasoline.) In contrast, a fixed-term futures contract is a martingale under the risk neutral measure.

A variety of commodity options are traded *over-the-counter* (OTC) and for these the underlying can be the spot price rather than the futures price. Common products include caps (which provide upside protection), floors (which provide downside protection), and collars (which provide both). Path dependent options such as average price options and barriers, which are cheaper than standard options, are also traded OTC.

A particularly risky OTC option is the *floating strike option*. The holder of a floating strike European call contract has the right, but not the obligation, to buy the commodity at the strike price every day during the exercise month. The strike price is based on the previous end-of-month price. The price of the commodity could change considerably during the exercise month, hence the writers of such options face huge risks. These products are also difficult to hedge and so are rather expensive. Nevertheless, the demand for such products is considerable and even more complex and risky products such as have recently become popular.

HISTORICAL PRICE BEHAVIOR

This section examines the behavior of daily spot and futures prices during 2005 and 2006 in five different commodities that have actively traded futures options on U.S. exchanges. These are corn, lean hogs, silver, natural gas, and electricity. They have been chosen to represent the three main classes of commodities: agriculturals, metals, and energy. We demonstrate

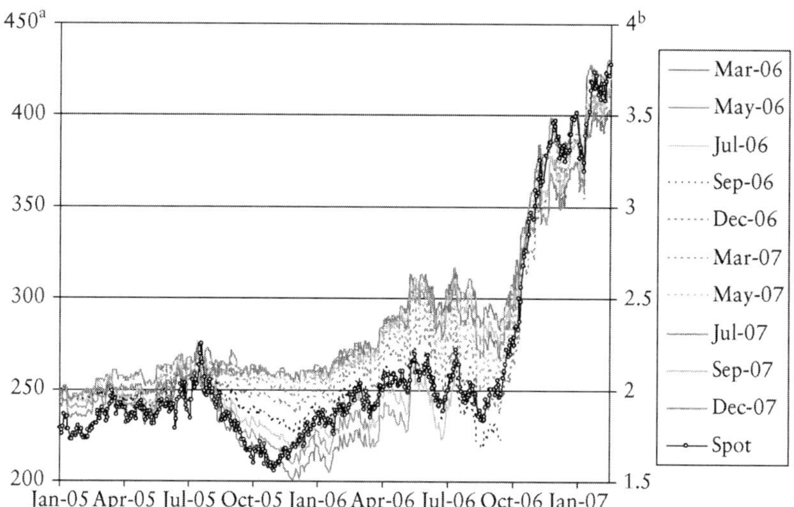

EXHIBIT 24.5 Corn Futures and Spot Prices
Source: Data from Bloomberg.
[a]USDA Illinois Northern No. 2 Yellow Corn Spot Price (USD/bushel).
[b]CBOT No. 2 Yellow Corn Futures Price (cents/bushel).

that the price processes for these five different commodities are remarkably different.

Corn

Exhibit 24.5 depicts the spot price on the right hand scale and several futures prices on the left hand scale. Throughout most of 2005 and 2006, the market was in contango and futures of different maturities are highly correlated with each other and with the spot price. Prices can jump at the time of the U.S. Department of Agriculture crop production forecasts and in response to news announcements. A recent example of this was the reaction to President Bush's announcement of plans to increase ethanol production, clearly visible in January 2007.

Lean Hogs

Exhibit 24.6 shows the spot and futures prices of lean hogs. Futures prices display low correlation across different maturities with winter futures prices being noticeably lower than summer futures prices. The market is

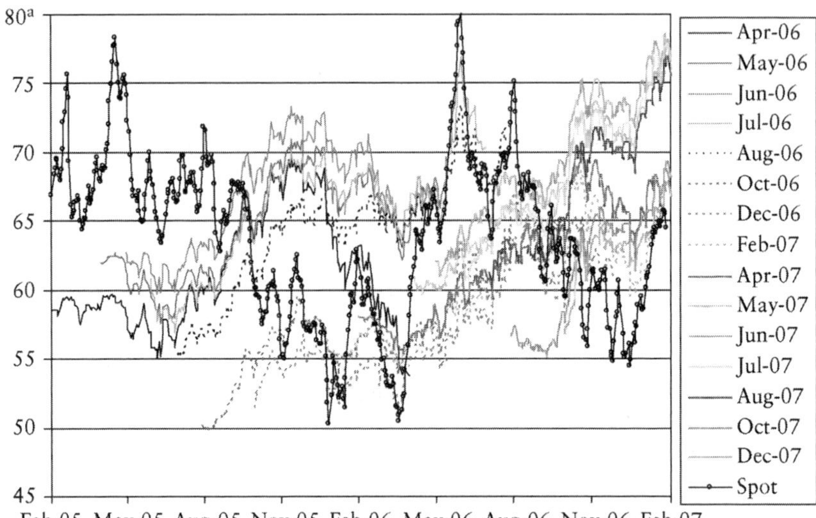

EXHIBIT 24.6 Lean Hogs Futures and Spot Prices
Source: Data from Bloomberg.
[a]USDA National Markets 51% to 52% Lean Hogs Weighted Spot Price and CME Lean Hogs Futures Price (USD/lb).

characterized by a relatively flat demand and an inelastic supply that is set by the farmer's decision to breed 10-months previously. High prices induce producers to retain more sows for breeding. This pushes the price even higher—and prices tend to peak in the summer months when supply of live hogs is usually at its lowest. Price jumps may correspond to the U.S. Department of Agriculture official "hogs and pigs" report on the size of the breeding herd.

Silver

Exhibit 24.7 shows the spot and futures prices of silver. Silver futures contracts are actively traded on NYMEX for every month and only a selection of months is shown in Exhibit 24.7. The market is narrower than the gold market because there are less reserves of silver. On the demand side, silver is used in industrial processes (e.g, silver plating and electronics); but there is no inherent seasonality in these. Hence, the term structure is very highly correlated indeed, basis risk is small, and prices display no seasonality. The frequent spikes and jumps are the result of speculative trading.

EXHIBIT 24.7 Silver Futures and Spot Prices
Source: Data from Bloomberg.
[a]Comex Silver Spot and Comex Silver Futures (USD/Troy ounce).

Natural Gas

Exhibit 24.8 shows the spot and futures prices of natural gas. Natural gas futures are less highly correlated than oil futures prices, and swings between backwardation and contango are seasonal. Backwardation tends to occur during winter months when short-term futures prices can jump upward. Contango is more likely during summer months. There is a large basis risk with spot price spikes arising during unexpected cold snaps. Down spikes may also occur in the summer when storage is full to capacity.

Electricity

Exhibit 24.9 illustrates the prices of PJM spot electricity and associated futures contracts (data were only available for 2005). Since electricity cannot be stored, spot prices are excessively variable and rapidly mean reverting, especially during summer months when the air conditioning required during heat waves increases demand. The term structure on six different days during the sample period is shown in Exhibit 24.10. This is very different to the term structure of other commodity futures prices. The general level of futures prices is lowest in the spring (March to May) and highest in the winter

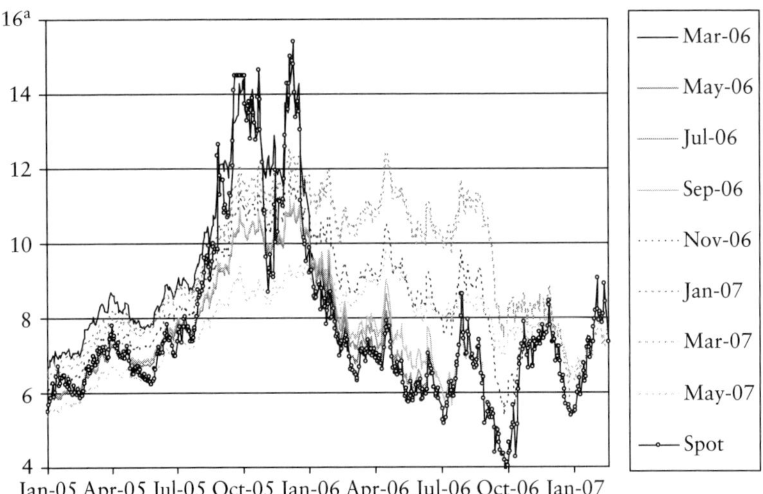

EXHIBIT 24.8 Natural Gas Futures and Spot Prices
Source: Data from Bloomberg.
[a]Henry Hub Natural Gas Spot and Henry Hub Natural Gas Futures prices (USD/MMBtu).

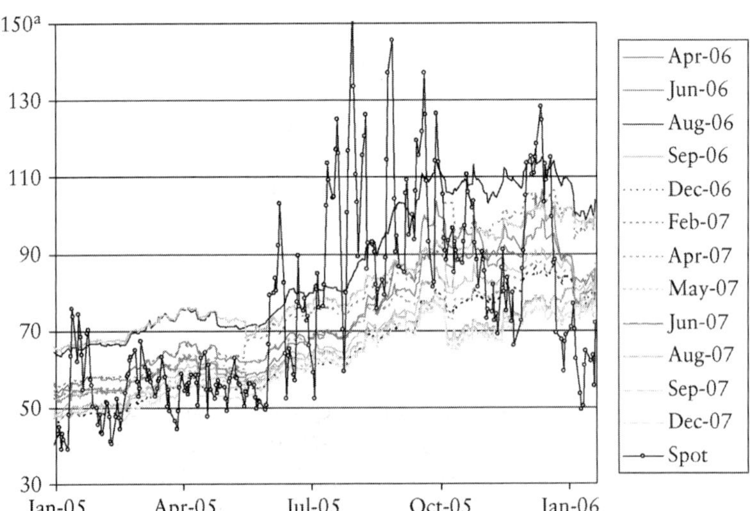

EXHIBIT 24.9 Electricity Futures and Spot Prices
Source: Data from Bloomberg.
[a]Real Time LMP Electricity Spot Price Western P-J-M and P-J-M Electricity Futures (USD/MwH).

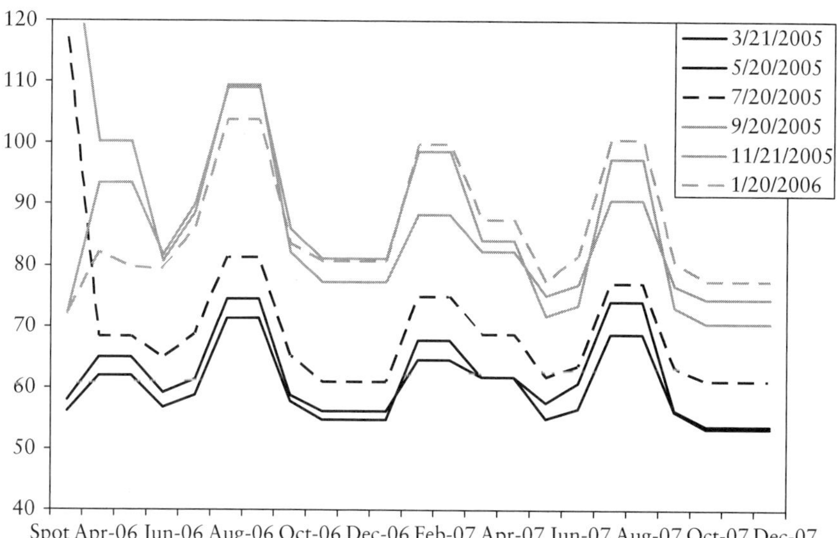

EXHIBIT 24.10 Electricity Futures Term Structure
Source: Data from Bloomberg.

(November to January) and the futures that expire in July, August, January, and February have the highest prices.

STOCHASTIC PROCESSES

The prices of liquid exchange-traded commodity options will be set by market makers responding to demand and supply. However, some exchange-traded commodity options are highly illiquid (e.g., aluminum futures options on NYMEX). Also, many commodity options trades are over the counter. To price such options traders need to specify a stochastic process for the underlying (spot or futures) price.

Option pricing models have parameters that should be calibrated to liquid market prices of associated options, such as exchange-traded standard call and put options. This is to avoid arbitraging a trader's price by replicating its payoff using the liquid options. For instance the price of a calendar spread option on crude oil futures should be consistent with the market prices of the American crude oil futures options in the two legs of the spread.

The stochastic process should provide a tractable solution for the prices of vanilla options, as this considerably simplifies the calibration to market data. Often approximate analytic prices of American and European vanilla options are available, but if not, at least these models are amenable to numerical methods of resolution.[1]

Comparison of Processes for Spot and Futures Prices

Seasonal patterns and mean reversion are often evident in spot prices and can give rise to term structures of futures that fluctuate between backwardation and contango. But it is important to note that there is no seasonality or mean reversion in the price of any given fixed term futures.

Indeed, every fixed term futures price is a martingale, irrespective of whether the commodity is an investment asset or a consumable asset. Since the contract is virtually costless to trade, its risk-neutral expected value tomorrow should be its value today. Otherwise, all investors could expect to profit from buying the futures (if the expectation is for the price to rise) or from selling the futures (if the expectation is for the price to fall).

Most traded commodity options are options on futures. Moreover, the price of any option on a spot price can be obtained from the futures price process, provided only that the payoff is path independent. At expiry, the spot and futures prices are equal, so they have the same distribution. But the price of a path independent option depends only on the underlying price distribution at expiry. Hence, it makes no difference whether we use the spot price or the futures price to value such an option. We conclude that it is only in the special case of an OTC path dependent option on the spot that we need to specify the spot price process. In the vast majority of cases, therefore, the option price can be based on a martingale process for the futures.

Geometric Brownian Motion

Geometric Brownian motion (GBM) models are widely used due to their simplicity and flexibility. Under GBM the price has a lognormal distribution, or equivalently the log returns are normally distributed. The GBM for the price at time t of a futures contract with maturity T, denoted $F_{t,T}$, is the martingale process, under the risk neutral probability measure $\mathbb{Q}$:

$$dF_{t,T} = \sigma F_{t,T} dW_t \tag{24.1}$$

[1]Peter James, *Option Theory* (New York: John Wiley & Sons, 2003); and Helyette Geman, *Commodities and Commodity Derivatives: Modelling and Pricing for Agriculturals, Metals, and Energy* (Hoboken, NJ: John Wiley & Sons, 2005).

where the volatility σ is constant and W is a Wiener process. Application of Ito's lemma to the no-arbitrage relationship between spot and futures prices provides the following representation for the spot price S_t:[2]

$$dS_t = (r - y)S_t dt + \sigma S_t dW_t \tag{24.2}$$

where r is the carry cost (including financing, transportation, storage, insurance, etc.) and y is the convenience yield.

It is important to note that equations (24.1) and (24.2) will only be equivalent processes for the market prices of the spot and futures if the futures is fairly priced; that is, $F^*_{t,T} = F_{t,T}$. But commodity futures can fall far below their fair price relative to the spot market price because only a one-way arbitrage is possible (spot commodities cannot be sold short). The deviation of the market price of the futures from its fair price relative to the spot is attributed to the convenience yield, and this is very uncertain.

Therefore, the equations (24.1) and (24.2) are generally driven by different Wiener processes because the uncertainty in the basis appears the spot price, but this never changes the fact that the futures price must be a martingale under the risk-neutral measure.

Spot Price Processes

Spot prices can exhibit mean-reversion and seasonality, and their uncertainty includes uncertainty about the basis. This section explains how to extend the process (24.2) to allow for these.

Gibson and Schwartz[3] introduced the following two-factor process with stochastic convenience yield:

$$\begin{aligned} dS_t &= (r - y)S_t dt + \sigma_1 S_t dW_{1,t} \\ dy &= (\kappa(\alpha - y) - \lambda)dt + \sigma_2 dW_{2,t} \text{ and } \left(dW_{1,t}, dW_{2,t}\right) = \rho dt \end{aligned} \tag{24.3}$$

where κ is the rate of mean reversion for the convenience yield, α is the mean convenience yield, and λ is the convenience yield risk premium.[4]

[2] The No-Arbitrage Condition for the Fair Price $F^*_{t,T}$ of The Future is $F^*_{t,T} = S_t e^{(r-y)(T-t)}$.

[3] Rajna Gibson and Eduardo S. Schwartz, "Stochastic Convenience Yield and the Pricing of Oil Contingent Claims," *Journal of Finance* 45, no. 3 (1990), pp. 959–976.

[4] This allows for risk adjusted drift as convenience yield risk cannot be completely hedged.

The fair value relationship between spot and futures under these processes is given by[5]

$$F_{t,T} = S_t \exp\left(-y\frac{1-e^{\kappa(T-t)}}{\kappa} + A_{t,T}\right) \tag{24.4}$$

where

$$\begin{aligned} A_{t,T} = {} & \left(r - \alpha + \frac{\lambda}{\kappa} + \frac{1}{2}\frac{\sigma_2^2}{\kappa^2} - \frac{\sigma_1\sigma_2\rho}{\kappa}\right)(T-t) + \frac{1}{4}\sigma_2^2\frac{1-e^{-2\kappa(T-t)}}{\kappa^3} \\ & + \left(\left(\alpha - \frac{\lambda}{\kappa}\right)\kappa + \sigma_1\sigma_2\rho - \frac{\sigma_2^2}{\kappa^2}\right)\frac{1-e^{-\kappa(T-t)}}{\kappa^2} \end{aligned}$$

An alternative to modeling mean reversion in a stochastic convenience yield is to apply a mean reverting stochastic process to the spot price itself, such as the one-factor Pilipovic model:[6]

$$dS_t = \kappa(X - S_t)dt + \sigma S_t^{\gamma} dZ_t \tag{24.5}$$

where κ is the speed of mean reversion, X is the equilibrium price, and γ any positive real number. Beyond this we have multifactor mean reverting models that assume a stochastic, mean-reverting equilibrium price.[7]

These models are useful for pricing path dependent options on spot prices where the processes display mean-reversion linked, for example, to seasonal patterns.

Jump Diffusion

One of the main limitations of GBM is that the underlying price has a lognormal distribution, yet this is rarely borne out in practice. Traders

[5]Petter Bjerksund, "Contingent Claims Evaluation when the Convenience Yield is Stochastic: Analytical Results," Norwegian School of Economics and Business Administration. Department of Finance and Management Science, 1991.

[6]Dragana Pilipovic, *Energy Risk: Valuing and Managing Energy Derivatives* (McGraw-Hill), 1997.

[7]See Eduardo S. Schwartz, "The Stochastic Behavior of Commodity Prices: Implications for Valuation and Hedging," *Journal of Finance* 52, no. 3 (1997), pp. 923–973; and David Beaglehole and Alain Chebanier, "A Two-Factor Mean-Reverting Model," *Risk*, 15, no. 7 (2002), pp. 65–69.

know that asset returns have skewed and heavy-tailed distributions and this is the reason why we observe a volatility smile and skew in the market prices of plain European options. Heavy tails are a common feature in commodity returns distributions, particularly in energy and power markets where price spikes and jumps are frequent.[8]

To capture such behavior a *jump diffusion* (JD) process is necessary. Taking the martingale process in equation (24.1) and adding a Poisson distributed random jump variable gives

$$dF_{t,T} = F_{t,T}(-\lambda k dt + \sigma dW_t + Y_t dq_t) \tag{24.6}$$

where q_t is a Poisson process, λ is the jump risk premium, k is the jump intensity, and Y_t is the magnitude of the jump, being a random variable with some specific distribution. A popular choice is to assume that Y_t is lognormally distributed, following Merton,[9] because it gives an analytic formula for the option price. But lognormality implies that price jumps can only be positive, which is not a suitable assumption for energy and power markets where prices spike and can jump down as well as up. For such markets, double-jump processes are more realistic.

Jump diffusion models have theoretical and practical disadvantages. The inability to hedge all sources of risks means that we have an incomplete markets setting, and calibration of these models is very difficult.

Stochastic Volatility

In a general stochastic volatility framework, the underlying price and its variance follow correlated processes:

$$\begin{aligned} dF_{t,T} &= \sqrt{V_t} F_{t,T} dW_{1,t} \\ dV_t &= \alpha dt + \beta V_t^{\gamma} dW_{2,t} \\ \text{with} < dW_1, dW_2 > &= \rho dt \end{aligned} \tag{24.7}$$

The parameters α and β can depend on $F_{t,T}$ and V_t, but then numerical methods must be used to obtain the price of even standard European options.

[8]Jumps can occur in futures prices as well as spot prices so in the following, since most commodity options are on futures, we describe the futures price process leaving readers to infer the associated spot price process themselves.

[9]Robert C. Merton, "Theory of Rational Option Pricing," *Bell Journal of Economics and Management Science* 4, no. 1 (1973), pp. 141–183.

One of the few stochastic volatility models with a (quasi) analytic solution for standard European options is Heston's model.[10] In this model α is a mean reversion term with a volatility risk premium in the mean reversion rate, β is constant, and $\gamma = 0.5$. Its popularity rests on the fact that it is relatively easy to calibrate.[11]

The Heston model also has nonzero price-volatility correlation and this is essential if the model is to capture the skewed and leptokurtic price densities of commodity futures. With a zero correlation between the price and volatility, as for instance in the Hull and White model,[12] the price density is leptokurtic but not skewed. The model-implied volatilities therefore must have symmetric smiles. This is unrealistic for almost all markets.

Recent additions to the family of stochastic volatility models are the stochastic-implied volatility model of Ledoit and Santa-Clara and Schonbucher[13] and the stochastic local volatility model of Alexander and Nogueira.[14] Stochastic implied volatility assumes a different, correlated stochastic process for each implied volatility and stochastic local volatility assumes the parameters of a deterministic volatility function are stochastic. Alexander and Nogueira prove that the two approaches are equivalent. They give identical option prices and hedge ratios, but stochastic local volatility models are easier to calibrate.

Local Volatility

The concept of local volatility was first introduced by Dupire[15] and Derman.[16] *Local volatility* $\sigma(F_{t,T}, t)$, also known as *forward volatility*, is the future volatility locked in by the prices of traded options, just as forward

[10] Steven L. Heston, "A Closed-Form Solution for Options with Stochastic Volatility with Applications to Bond and Currency Options," *The Review of Financial Studies* 6, no. 2 (1993), pp. 327–343.

[11] See Darrell Duffie, Jun Pan and Kenneth J. Singleton, "Transform Analysis and Option Pricing for Affine Jump-Diffusions," *Econometrica* 68, no. 6 (2000), pp. 1343–1376.

[12] John Hull and Alan White, "The Pricing of Options on Assets with Stochastic Volatilities," *Journal of Finance* 42, (1987), pp. 281–300.

[13] See Olivier Ledoit and Pedro Santa-Clara, Relative Option Pricing with Stochastic Volatility, Technical Report, UCLA, 1998; and Philipp J. Schonbucher, "A Market Model for Stochastic Implied Volatility," Technical Report, Department of Statistics, Bonn University, 1999.

[14] Carol Alexander and Leonardo M. Nogueira, "Hedging with Stochastic Local Volatility," SSRN eLibrary, 2004.

[15] Bruno Dupire, "Pricing with a Smile" *Risk* 7, no. 1 (1994), pp. 18–20.

[16] Emanuel Derman, "Volatility Regimes," *Risk* 12, no. 4 (1999), pp. 55–59.

interest rates are locked in by the prices of traded bonds. Since volatility is deterministic, markets are arbitrage free and we can find a unique local volatility surface that is consistent with any implied volatility surface.

Local volatility is a way to avoid complete specification of the price process and preserve the simplicity of Black-Scholes framework. There is only one source of risk, the markets are complete, and preference free option valuation is possible. Dupire derived a celebrated equation for the local volatility function:

$$\sigma(F_{t,T}, t) | (F_{t,T} = K, t = T) = 2 \frac{\frac{\partial f_{K,T}}{\partial T}}{K^2 \frac{\partial^2 f_{K,T}}{\partial K^2}} \tag{24.8}$$

where $f_{K,T}$ is the market price of an option with strike K and maturity T.

Local volatility implies that the martingale process for the futures price has nonconstant volatility. The local volatility $\sigma(F_{t,T}, t)$ is a deterministic function of the underlying price and time. The difficulty lies in extracting a local volatility function from the market data that is stable over time. For this reason many practitioners now use the term *local volatility* to refer to any processes with a nonconstant but deterministic volatility. Many different parametric forms have been proposed, amongst the most popular being the lognormal mixture diffusion of Brigo and Mercurio[17] where the price density is assumed to be a mixture of two or more lognormal densities. The lognormal mixture approach has two great advantages: It captures the skewness and leptokurtosis observed in price densities and it retains the tractability of lognormal models. In particular, the price of a European option is just a weighted sum of Black-Scholes option prices based on different volatilities.

GARCH

Market prices of options are always not easy to find. For instance there are no exchange traded options on electric power. Hence to price an OTC contract for an option on power futures, or for any other options where market data are not available, we may consider calibrating the option pricing model using historical data and adjusting the drift for risk neutrality.

It is possible to formulate discrete time versions of any of the continuous time processes described above and many of these will be equivalent to

[17]Damiano Brigo and Fabio Mercurio, "Lognormal-Mixture Dynamics and Calibration to Market Volatility Smiles," *International Journal of Theoretical and Applied Finance* 5, no. 4 (2002), pp. 427–446.

a GARCH process. GARCH—for *generalized autoregressive conditional heteroscedasticity*—is the standard framework for modeling time varying volatility in discrete time and was introduced by Engle[18] and Bollerslev.[19] By now there are numerous different GARCH models and a vast literature on the comparative quality of their fit to historical data on returns. A survey of this is provided by Alexander and Lazar[20] who demonstrate the advantages of using a GARCH model where the conditional returns distribution is a mixture of two normal distributions.

From this vast literature the consensus option is that an asymmetric GARCH model with any skewed and leptokurtic conditional returns distribution fits most financial returns far better than the plain vanilla symmetric normal GARCH (1,1) model:

$$\sigma_t^2 = \omega + \alpha\epsilon_{t-1}^2 + \beta\sigma_{t-1}^2 \tag{24.9}$$

where $\omega > 0$ is a constant, $\alpha \geq 0$ is the error coefficient, and $\beta \geq 0$ lag coefficient.

It can be proved that the continuous limit of these models is a continuous time stochastic volatility model. Therefore, estimating GARCH model parameters using a series of historical returns allows one to infer option prices in a stochastic volatility framework. Nelson[21] proved that the standard normal GARCH (1,1) model converges to a stochastic volatility model with zero price-volatility correlation. This is unfortunate since such models are of limited use. However, the assumptions made by Nelson were questioned by Corradi,[22] and later work by Alexander and Lazar[23] has not only shown that Nelson's conclusion should be questioned, but that an assumption-free

[18]Robert F. Engle, "Autoregressive Conditional Heteroscedasticity with Estimates of the Variance of United Kingdom Inflation," *Econometrica* 50, no. 4 (1982), pp. 987–1008.

[19]Tim Bollerslev, "Generalized Autoregressive Conditional Heteroskedasticity," *Journal of Econometrics* 31, no. 3 (1986), pp. 307–327.

[20]Carol Alexander and Emese Lazar, On the Continuous Limit of GARCH, ICMA Centre Discussion Papers in Finance 2005-13, 2005.

[21]Daniel B. Nelson, "ARCH Models as Diffusion Approximations," *Journal of Econometrics* 45, (1990), pp. 7–38.

[22]Valentina Corradi, "Reconsidering the Continuous Time Limit of the GARCH (1,1) Process," *Journal of Econometrics* 96, (2000), pp. 145–153.

[23]Alexander and Lazar, "On The Continuous Limit of GARCH."

continuous limit of (weak) GARCH is actually a wonderful stochastic volatility model! It takes the form:

$$\begin{aligned} dF_{t,T} &= \sqrt{V}F_{t,T}dW_{1,t} \\ dV_t &= (\omega - \theta V)dt + \sqrt{\eta - 1}\alpha V_t dW_{2,t} \\ < dW_{1,t}, dW_{2,t} > &= \rho dt \\ \rho &= \frac{\tau}{\sqrt{\eta - 1}} \end{aligned} \tag{24.10}$$

The nonzero correlation ρ between the price process and the volatility captures a proper volatility skew, and the correlation is related to the skewness τ and kurtosis η of returns, which is very intuitive.

Forward Curve Models

The single-factor models of futures prices that we have considered so far ignore any relationship between futures of different maturities. Yet term structures of commodity futures are very highly correlated and options that depend on more than one futures price, such as the calendar spread energy options that are actively traded on NYMEX, need to account for this correlation. The general forward curve model for commodities is similar to the HJM model for interest rates:[24]

$$dF_{t,T} = \sum_{i=1}^{m} \sigma_i(t, T, F_{t,T}) F_{t,T} dZ_{i,t} \tag{24.11}$$

where m is the number of uncorrelated common factors. These models are difficult to calibrate due to the large number of parameters and prices are often computed using Monte Carlo simulation.[25]

PRICING OPTIONS

In this section we describe some common types of commodity options and, where possible, state their prices under different assumptions about the stochastic process governing the underlying price dynamics.

[24]David Heath, Robert Jarrow, and Andrew Morton, "Bond Pricing and The Term Structure of Interest Rates: A New Methodology for Contingent Claims Valuation," *Econometrica* 60, no. 1 (1992), pp. 77–105.

[25]See Carol O. Alexander, "Correlation and Cointegration in Energy Markets," *Managing Energy Price Risk* 3, (2004).

Standard European Options

Under the assumption that the futures price follows the zero-drift geometric Brownian motion in equation (24.1), Black and Scholes[26] derived the following analytic formula for the price at time t of a standard European option on $F_{t,\,T}$ with strike K and maturity T:

$$f_t^{K,T} = \omega e^{-r(T-t)}\left(F_t\Phi\left(\omega d_{1,t}\right) - K\Phi\left(\omega d_{2,t}\right)\right) \tag{24.12}$$

where Φ is the standard normal distribution function, $\omega = 1$ for a call and $\omega = -1$ for a put and

$$d_{1,t} = \frac{ln\left(\frac{F_{t,T}}{K}\right)}{\sigma\sqrt{T-t}} + \frac{1}{2}\sigma\sqrt{T-t} \qquad d_{2,t} = _{1,t} - \sigma\sqrt{T-t} \tag{24.13}$$

The associated formula for a European option on the spot price with GBM dynamics, equation (24.2) is the celebrated Black-Scholes formula:

$$f_t^{K,T} = \omega\left(S_t e^{-y(T-t)}\Phi\left(\omega d_{1,t}\right) - Ke^{-r(T-t)}\Phi\left(\omega d_{2,t}\right)\right) \tag{24.14}$$

Under the lognormal jump diffusion model of Merton[27] the price of a standard European option is a Poisson distributed sum of Black or Black-Scholes prices with adjusted drift and volatility to compensate for the effect of the jumps. Specifically, in equation (24.7), suppose $\log(Y_t)$ has a normal distribution with mean α and standard deviation β, that is, $\log(Y_t) \sim N(\alpha, \beta)$. Then the price of a standard European option under the jump diffusion process is

$$f_t^{K,T} = \sum_{n=0}^{\infty} \frac{e^{-\lambda\Delta t}(\lambda\Delta t)^n}{n!} f_t^{BS}\left(S, K, T, r - Ak + \frac{n\lambda}{T}, \sqrt{\sigma^2 + \frac{n\beta^2}{T}}, \omega\right) \tag{24.15}$$

where $A = \lambda, \omega = 1$ for calls, $A = \alpha, \omega = -1$ for puts, and $f_t^{BS}(S, K, T, r, \sigma, \omega)$ is the Black-Scholes price as in equation (24.14).

[26]Fischer Black and Myron Scholes, "The Pricing of Options and Corporate Liabilities," *Journal of Political Economy* 81, no. 3 (1973), pp. 637–654.
[27]Merton, *Theory of Rational Option Pricing*.

American Options

Before expiry, the possibility of early exercise means that the price of an American option is always greater than or equal to the price of its European counterpart. Since no traded options are perpetual the expiry date forces the price of an American option to converge to the European price.

The majority of exchange-traded commodity options are standard American options on futures. For a standard American call or put on a futures contract, and under the assumption that the premium is paid at expiry, it can be shown that the early exercise premium will not affect the price of the option.[28] But of course option premiums are payable up front, so this theoretical result does not hold exactly in practice. The possibility of early exercise implies standard American options on futures may have prices above those of the corresponding European option, but the effect is quite small.

More generally, and for path dependent options such as the Asian options we discuss next, the price of an American-style option is determined by the type of the underlying asset, the prevailing discount rate, and if the option is on the spot price, also the convenience yield.

American options can be priced using the free boundary pricing methods of McKean,[29] Kim,[30] Carr et al.,[31] Jacka,[32] and others. For instance, the price of a standard American option with payoff max $\{\omega(S_t - K), 0\}$ on a commodity with spot price process (24.2) is given by

$$\begin{aligned} P(S_t, t, \omega) = P^E(S_t, T, \omega) &+ \omega \int_t^T yS_t e^{-y(s-t)} \Phi(\omega\, d_1(S_t, B_t, s-t))\, ds \\ &- \omega \int_t^T rKe^{-r(s-t)} \Phi(\omega\, d_2(S_t, B_t, s-t))\, ds \end{aligned} \tag{24.16}$$

where $\omega = 1$ for a call and -1 for a put and B_t is the early exercise boundary. That is, an American call option price is the price of its European

[28] See James, *Option Theory*.

[29] Henry P. McKean, "Appendix: A free boundary problem for the heat equation arising from a problem in mathematical economics", *Industrial Management Review* 6(2):32–39, 1965.

[30] I. N. Kim, "The Analytic Valuation of American Options, *Review of Financial Studies*," 1990.

[31] Peter Carr, Robert A. Jarrow, and Ravi Myneni, Alternative Characterizations of American Put Options, Cornell University, Johnson Graduate School of Management, 1989.

[32] S. D. Jacka, "Optimal Stopping and the American Put", *Mathematical Finance* 1, no. 1 (1991), pp. 1–14.

counterpart plus the income from dividends (after exercise) minus the risk-free interest lost due to the payment of the strike price. At the boundary (optimal exercise), the price of the American option is its intrinsic value; that is, $\omega(S_t - K)$, and the slope of the price function is one. These are called value-match and high-contact conditions respectively. B_t is often estimated numerically using a gradient algorithm.[33]

Asian Options

An Asian option reduces the risk faced by the writer and allows the holder to secure his supplies at a cheaper price at the same time. For commodities that are prone to frequent spikes or jumps, Asian options considerably reduce the calendar basis risk. As the volatility of the average price is less than the price itself these options are cheaper than their standard counterparts.

There are two types of Asian options: average price options and average strike options. The payoff to these is given by

$$\begin{aligned} V_{Average\ Price} &= max\left(\overline{S}_{t_0,t_n} - K, 0\right) \\ V_{Average\ Strike} &= max\left(\overline{S}_T - \overline{S}_{t_0,t_n}, 0\right) \end{aligned} \tag{24.17}$$

where

$$\overline{S}_{t_0,t_n} = \frac{\sum_{t_i=t_0}^{t_n} S_{t_i}}{t_n - t_0}, \quad 0 \leq t_0 < T; \quad t_n = T$$

The averaging period can start right on day zero or at a forward date. Contracts which involve trades with different volumes over a period of time might use (volume) weighted averages.

Asian options are widely traded OTC and in recent years options on futures have been introduced in exchanges worldwide. Exhibit 24.2 shows the dramatic increase in the volumes of Asian options, particularly crude oil, traded in the last two years. Exchange-traded contracts are primarily financially settled while an OTC contract might involve physical delivery.

The most widely used techniques to price Asian options assume a process of the form (24.2). But pricing under this assumption is not easy as the

---

[33]For example, see Giovanni Barone-Adesi and Robert E. Whaley, "Efficient Analytic Approximation of American Option Values," *Journal of Finance* 42, no. 2 (1987), pp. 301–320.

average of the prices is not lognormal. There is no closed form solution and the prices are often computed numerically or using analytic approximations. Few methods assume that average price is lognormally distributed but the results are not accurate.[34]

An approximation by Vorst[35] uses the difference between the arithmetic and geometric averages to compute the price of the option. The advantage of using geometric averages is the fact that a product of lognormal variables remains lognormal. For example, for an Asian option on the spot we have,

$$f_t^G \leq f_t^A \leq f_t^G + e^{-r(T-t)}\left(\mathrm{E}\left[\bar{S}_A\right] - \mathrm{E}\left[\bar{S}_G\right]\right) \tag{24.18}$$

The approximate price is given by

$$\begin{aligned}
\hat{f}_t &= \omega e^{-r(T-t)}\left(S^*\Phi\left(\omega d_1^*\right) - K^*\Phi\left(\omega d_2^*\right)\right) \\
S^* &= \mathbb{E}\left[\bar{S}_G\right] = e^{\mu_G + \frac{1}{2}\sigma_G^2} \\
K^* &= K - \left(\mathbb{E}[\mathrm{S_A}] - \mathbb{E}\left[\bar{\mathrm{S}}_\mathrm{G}\right]\right) \\
d_1^* &= \frac{\ln\left(\frac{\bar{S}^*}{K^*}\right) + \frac{1}{2}\sigma_G^2}{\sigma G} \\
d_2^* &= d_1^* - \sigma_G
\end{aligned} \tag{24.19}$$

where $\ln\left(\bar{S}_G\right) \sim N\left(\mu_G, \sigma_G^2\right)$.[36]

Spread Options

A standard spread option is just like a plain vanilla option but it is written on the spread between two futures prices (or, less commonly, on the spread

[34]See Edmond Levy, "Pricing European Average Rate Currency Options," *Journal of International Money and Finance* 11, no. 5 (1992), pp. 474–491; and Stuart M. Turnbull and Lee MacDonald Wakeman, "A Quick Algorithm for Pricing European Average Options," *Journal of Financial and Quantitative Analysis* 26, no. 3 (1991), pp. 377–389.

[35]Ton Vorst, Prices and Hedge Ratios of Average Exchange Rate Options White Paper, Econometric Institute, Erasmus University Rotterdam, 1990.

[36]For a similar (and better) analytic approximation see Michael Curran, "Beyond Average Intelligence," *Risk* 5, no. 10 (1992), p. 60.

between two spot prices). Spread options comprise a diverse range of products that are used to hedge a variety of risks, correlation and lock in revenues. A few examples are options on intercommodity spreads (cracks and sparks), intracommodity spreads (quality), calendar spreads, and locational spreads.

The most basic approach to pricing a spread option would be to assume the spread follows an arithmetic Brownian motion. But this ignores the correlation between the two price processes and would lead to inaccurate results. Ravindran Transpose,[37] Shimko,[38] Kirk[39] and others assume the two prices follow correlated geometric Brownian motions (2GBM). Pricing European spread options in this framework is difficult because a linear combination of lognormal processes is not lognormal.

The analytic approximation to the price of a European spread option on futures was given by Kirk.

$$P_t = \omega e^{-r(T-t)}\left(F_{1,t}\Phi\left(\omega d_1^*\right) - \left(K + F_{2,t}\right)\Phi\left(\omega d_2^*\right)\right) \tag{24.20}$$

The problem with approximations such as Kirk's is that it is only valid for spread options with very low strikes. As soon as the option strike rises even to the at-the-money (ATM) level, the approximation is inaccurate. A much better approximation to the price of a spread option, one that is accurate for all strikes, has been developed by Alexander and Venkatramanan.[40] They represent the price of spread option as the sum of prices of two compound exchange options and then apply the exchange option price derived by Margrabe.[41] The exchange options are: to exchange a call on one asset with a call on the other asset, and to exchange a put on one asset with a put on the other asset. The risk neutral price of the spread option at time t is given by

$$\begin{aligned} f_t &= e^{-r(T-t)}\mathbb{E}_{\mathbb{Q}}\left\{\left[\omega\left(U_{1,T} - U_{2,T}\right)\right]^+\right\} \\ &\quad + e^{-r(T-t)}\mathbb{E}_{\mathbb{Q}}\left\{\left[\omega\left(V_{2,T} - V_{1,T}\right)\right]^+\right\} \end{aligned} \tag{24.21}$$

[37]K. Ravindran, "Low-Fat Spreads," *Risk* 6, no. 10 (1993), pp. 56–57.

[38]David C. Shimko, "Options on Futures Spreads: Hedging, Speculation and Valuation," *Journal of Futures Markets* 14, no. 2 (1994), pp. 183–213.

[39]Ewan Kirk, "Correlation in Energy Markets," *Managing Energy Price Risk*, 1996.

[40]Carol Alexander and Aanand Venkatramanan, "Analytic Approximations For Spread Option," ICMA Centre Discussion Papers 2007–11, 2007.

[41]William Margrabe, "The Value of an Option to Exchange One Asset for Another," *The Journal of Finance* 33, no. 1 (1978), pp. 177–186.

where $U_{1,T}$, $V_{1,T}$ are payoffs to European call and put options on asset 1 with strike mK and $U_{2,T}$, $V_{2,T}$ on asset 2 with strike $(m-1)K$, respectively. $\mathbb{E}_{\mathbb{Q}}$ is the expectation under the risk neutral measure and $\omega = 1$ for calls, -1 for puts.

Because the payoff to a spread option decreases with correlation, "frowns" in the correlation implied from market prices of spread options of different strikes are evident. Market prices of out-of-the-money (OTM) call and put spread options are higher than the standard 2GBM model prices based on the ATM implied correlation, because traders recognize the skewed and leptokurtic nature of commodity price returns. Hence the implied correlations that are backed-out from OTM options in the 2GBM model are lower than the ATM implied correlation.

A model that captures this feature is the stochastic volatility jump diffusion of Carmona and Durrleman.[42] However, pricing and hedging in this model necessitates a computationally intensive numerical resolution method such as a fast Fourier transforms. An alternative is to use the bivariate normal mixture approach of Alexander and Scourse,[43] which provides an analytic approximation to the price of a spread option that is accurate, consistent with implied volatility skews, and also consistent with correlation frowns in spread option market prices.

SWING OPTIONS

Swing options are volumetric contracts that are mainly traded in markets which require a high degree of flexibility in the delivery of the physical asset. For instance, in natural gas markets, since storage capacities are limited, the distributor might require variable supplies due to sudden changes in demand from the end user. In a typical contract, the holder of the option agrees to buy a fixed amount of gas (base amount) and has an option to raise or decrease his required quantity (swing) within a prespecified limit for the agreed strike price.

A swing contract with N days to expiry would allow the holder to exercise $n \leq N$ swings at a rate of one per day. When $n = N$ the pricing problem reduces to pricing a strip of n European options with corresponding strikes and maturities. When $n < N$ then the problem becomes that of optimal exercises equivalent to pricing n early exercise options. When $n = 1$ then the

[42]Rene Carmona and Valdo Durrleman, "Pricing and Hedging Spread Options in a Log-Normal Model," Technical Report, 2003.

[43]Carol Alexander and Andrew Scourse, "Bivariate Normal Mixture Spread Option Valuation," *Quantitative Finance* 4, no. 6 (2004), pp. 637–648.

price is that of a single American option. This gives us a range of prices between which the swing option price must lie:

$$P^{n=N}_{European} \leq P^{0<n\leq N}_{Swing} \leq P^{n=1}_{American}$$

Swing options can be priced dynamically using K simultaneous 2-D trees in a similar fashion as the American options.[44]

CONCLUSION

Commodity options are traded for portfolio diversification, speculative, and risk management purposes. Most of the activity is on the U.S. exchanges where options on energy futures, metals futures, and agricultural futures are traded. The majority of these options are standard American calls and puts; but the market for calendar spreads and average price options has been growing during the last few years.

The historical characteristics of commodity prices are specific to the commodity type. We have examined five representative commodities:

- *Corn*. Where the market is now usually contango and price jumps are associated with news.
- *Live hogs*. Where futures prices are not highly correlated and seasonal price peaks occur in summer months.
- *Silver*. Where the term structure is almost flat, there is no seasonality and prices jump with speculative trading.
- *Natural gas*. Where the term structure swings between backwardation in winter and contango in summer, and prices can spike up during winter cold snaps and down in the summer when storage is full to capacity.
- *Electricity*. Where spot prices are excessively volatile in the summer, futures prices are highest in the winter and the term structure has jump for futures expiring in winter and spring.

Almost all commodity options prices can be based on a martingale process for the futures, possibly with jumps. The only exception is path

[44]For a detailed discussion on this, see Patrick Jaillet, Ehud I. Ronn, and Stathis Tompaidis, "Valuation of Commodity-Based Swing Options," *Management Science* 50, no. 7 (2004), pp. 909–921.

dependent options on the spot price, for which a spot price process with mean reversion, jumps, and possibly a stochastic convenience yield could be used.

American options on futures have prices that are either equal to or very close to those of the equivalent European options when the premium from the discount rate is very small. Analytic formulas or approximations have been given for standard options, average price options, and spread options and these are the options that are most actively traded.

CHAPTER 25

The Pricing of Electricity Forwards

Dr. Matthias Muck
Professor of Finance
University of Bamberg

Markus Rudolf, Ph.D.
Professor of Finance
WHU–Otto Beisheim School of Management

The turnover in electricity markets has become increasingly important. According to the European Federation of Energy Traders (EFET) in Germany, it has been more than 2,500 TWh in 2004. This equals five times the German consumption of electricity and corresponds to approximately €75 billion. The turnover in Great Britain has been slightly below 2,500 TWh; in the Scandinavian countries it was 2,000 TWh in 2004. The leading exchange in Europe alone, the Leipzig based energy exchange EEX, exhibited a 2005 turnover of 602 TWh which implies an increase of 52% compared to the year before. In addition to the EEX, other important energy exchanges in Europe are the French Powernext, the Italian IPEX, the Dutch APX, the Austrian EXAA, the Polish PolPX, the Scandinavian Nordpool, the Slowenian Borzen, the Spanish OMEL, and the British UKPX. In January 2006, there were 133 companies from 17 countries trading energy on the EEX.

Typically, electricity prices are very volatile during the day. At night, prices usually are only half of the daytime's price. Price peaks can be observed especially between 10 A.M. and 1 P.M. as well as between 5 P.M. through

We thank Jan Marckhoff for helpful comments.

9 P.M. This curiosity is due to the nonstorability of electricity. It has to be consumed immediately. Therefore, peak prices are observed when the usage of electricity is especially high in the households. Energy exchanges therefore offer different contracts for peak load (8 hours to 20 hours) and base load (0 to 24 hours).

The growing importance of energy exchanges and energy-related products is also reflected by a growing literature on the matter. Since energy is not storable, the applicability of traditional valuation models for commodity futures such as that proposed by Gibson and Schwartz[1] and Schwartz[2] is limited. Recently, several new approaches for modeling electricity were proposed in the literature.[3] In particular, the model formulated by Bessembinder and Lemmon[4] has received much attention in the literature. It derives a testable pricing equation for electricity forward contracts that must hold in economic equilibrium. Therefore, we focus on this model. After an introduction of the traditional approach of forward pricing, the pricing of electricity forwards is discussed and subsequently illustrated by a numerical implementation.

---

[1]Rajina Gibson and Eduardo S. Schwartz, "Stochastic Convenience Yield and the Pricing of Oil Contingent Claims," *Journal of Finance* 45, no. 3 (1990), pp. 959–976.

[2]Eduardo S. Schwartz, "The Stochastic Behavior of Commodity Prices: Implications for Valuation and Hedging," *Journal of Finance* 52, no. 3 (1997), pp. 923–973.

[3]Examples are Martin T. Barlow, "A Diffusion Model for Electricity Prices," *Mathematical Finance* 12, no. 4 (2002), pp. 287–298; Francis A. Longstaff and Ashley W. Wang, "Electricity Forward Prices: A High-Frequency Empirical Analysis," *Journal of Finance* 49, no. 4 (2004), pp. 1877–1900; Julio J. Lucia and Eduardo S. Schwartz, "Electricity Prices and Power Derivatives: Evidence from the Nordic Power Exchange," *Review of Derivatives Research* 5, no. 1 (2002), pp. 5–50; Hendrik Bessembinder and Michael L. Lemmon, "Equilibrium Pricing and Optimal Hedging in Electricity Forward Markets," *Journal of Finance* 57, no. 3 (2002), pp. 1347–1382; Fred E. Benth, Lars Ekeland, Ragnar Hauge, and Bjoern F. Nielsen, "A Note on Arbitrage-Free Pricing of Forward Contracts in Energy Markets," *Applied Mathematical Finance* 10, no. 4 (2003), pp. 325–336; Shi-Jie Deng and Shmuel S. Oren, "Electricity Derivatives and Risk Management," *Energy* 31, no. 6–7 (2006), pp. 940–953; and Sascha Wilkens and Josef Wimschulte, "The Pricing of Electricity Futures: Evidence from the European Exchange," *Journal of Futures Markets* 27, no. 4 (2007), pp. 387–410.

[4]Bessembinder and Lemmon, "Equilibrium Pricing and Optimal Hedging in Electricity Forward Markets."

TRADITIONAL FORWARD PRICING

The traditional way of pricing derivatives contracts is the no-arbitrage pricing approach.[5] Consider a forward contract. In such a contract, two parties agree to buy/sell a particular good at a future point of time. The price which must be paid in exchange for the good is fixed today. The contract is a binding commitment. The seller must deliver the product and the buyer must pay the negotiated forward price regardless of the future market conditions.

To see how forwards work, consider the example of a forward on the European stock market index EURO STOXX 50. The EURO STOXX 50 can be seen as a basket consisting of the 50 largest European companies. Of course, the EURO STOXX 50 cannot be bought or sold directly but we may assume that we can easily replicate it by direct investments in the relevant stocks. Exhibit 25.1 illustrates that the forward price which should be negotiated between our two parties follows from no-arbitrage considerations. The example reflects the market data observed on February 27, 2007. The EURO STOXX 50 is 4,157 points and the annual interest rate 4%. Let us assume that the settlement of the forward contract is on September 21, 2007 (0.5644 years from now) and that the forward price is 4,500.

Such a situation establishes an arbitrage opportunity. How can we see this? Put yourself in the shoes of the seller of the forward contract. She may buy the EURO STOXX 50 at a price of €4,157 today. In order to finance the transaction, she may borrow the same amount at the risk-free rate of interest (4%) from a bank. Hence, on September 21, 2007, she can deliver the EURO STOXX 50 in exchange for €4,500. However, she has to pay back the bank debt which totals up to

$$\text{Bank debt} = 4{,}157 \cdot 1.04^{0.5644} = 4{,}250$$

EXHIBIT 25.1 Pricing a Futures Contract on the EURO STOXX 50 on February 27, 2007

	February 27, 2007	September 21, 2007
Buy EURO STOXX 50	−4157	???
Borrow	4157	−4250
Forward	0	4500
Cash Flow	0	250

Note: EURO STOXX 50: 4,157; Risk-free interest rate: 4% per annum; Maturity: September 21, 2007 (206 days), Futures price: 4,500.

[5] See, for instance, John C. Hull, *Options, Futures, and Other Derivatives: 6th Edition* (Upper Saddle River, NJ: Pearson Prentice Hall, 2006).

She may then keep the difference of €4, 500 − €4, 250 = €250. Note that no initial investment was necessary in order to generate this (risk-free) cashflow. In other words the €250 were generated "from thin air." Obviously such a situation cannot be persistent in a well-functioning capital market: Everybody would like to be the seller in such a "too good to be true" deal. As a consequence the forward price would decrease (everybody sells) until it is equal to 4,250.

In a similar fashion we can show that the forward contract cannot be less than €4,250. In other words, the forward price is linked to the spot price by no-arbitrage considerations. It must be equal to the spot price compounded to the settlement date. However, note that this no-arbitrage argument works only because the seller in this case can buy the EURO STOXX 50 today and store it. Therefore, we can be sure that we can apply the model to most physical goods. Sometimes the computations must be adjusted a little bit when, for example, storage costs are involved. Nevertheless, the general considerations remain unchanged.

The forward described in the example is a very simple contract. For ease of exposition, we assume that there is no credit risk involved; that is, there is no uncertainty that the seller and the buyer will deliver the EURO STOXX 50 and the money. In reality things are not so simple. This is one reason why market participants frequently trade derivatives on exchanges such as the EUREX. The EUREX takes the counterparty risk. Market participants do not have to worry about getting their contracts settled. Instead of forwards, so-called "futures contracts" are traded on derivatives exchanges. The setup of a futures contract is slightly different from a forward contract but economically both are very similar.[6] For instance, under the simplifying assumption that interest rates are constant, the futures price is identical to the forward price. This relationship is guaranteed by no-arbitrage considerations similar to those stated above.

ELECTRICITY FORWARD PRICING

As previously stated, electricity cannot physically be stored. An alternative approach must be developed in order to price forward contracts on electricity. The approach by Bessembinder and Lemmon explicitly models supply

[6]In a futures contract, two parties agree to buy/sell at the market price on the delivery day. The exchange foresees a daily settlement of the contracts. Each day futures prices are quoted by market participants at which they want to enter into futures contracts. The buyer of the futures price receives the difference between today's and yesterday's futures price (or pays it if the amount is negative). The opposite is true for the seller. On the delivery day the futures price is equal to the spot market price.

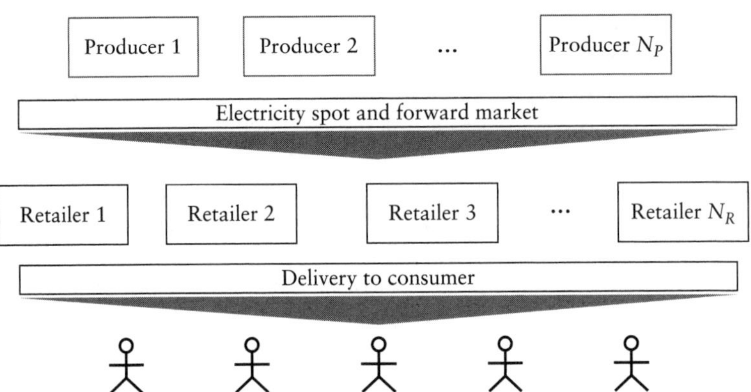

EXHIBIT 25.2 Assumptions about the Market for Electricity

and demand for forward contracts. The general setup of the model is summarized in Exhibit 25.2. The market consists of N_P electricity producers and N_R retailers in the electricity market. The producers produce electricity that they can sell to retailers on the wholesale market. There is no regulation on this market and the price is negotiated independently between producers and retailers. The retailers themselves enter into contracts with final consumers. The Bessembinder-Lemmon model assumes a two-period model. Today, retailers and consumers agree on a fixed price P_R at which consumers can consume as much energy as they like. The total amount of energy to be consumed in the next period is stochastic. For instance, if the next period is the summer we do not know whether the weather is hot or cold. If we have a hot summer, then consumers turn on their air conditioners and consume a lot of energy. If the summer is cold and rainy, then the opposite applies.

Retailers face uncertainty. They do not know the total consumer's demand at the next period. Since electricity is not storable it must be produced at the same moment when it is consumed. A higher consumer demand Q^D must therefore lead to a higher demand on the wholesale market. This, in turn, should result in a higher price P_W. The trading margin per unit of electricity is the difference between the price on the wholesale market P_W (stochastic) at which electricity is bought from producers and P_R at which electricity is sold to consumers. An increase in demand by consumers is hence ambiguous. A retailer sells more electricity to consumers. This has a positive effect if the trading margin is positive. On the other hand, the price on the wholesale market increases and the trading margin becomes smaller.

In a similar fashion, producers face uncertainty: They are also affected by the risk associated with demand by consumers. However, they do not fear price increases on the wholesale spot market. Price and demand increases both result in higher sales for producers.

In order to hedge price risks, producers and retailers may enter into forward contracts on electricity; that is, they may negotiate a price today at which they are willing to trade electricity on the wholesale market in the next period. As we shall see later, they choose the forward price such that both producers and retailers optimize their risk/expected return profiles.

To sum up, we will distinguish the following variables:

1. The quantity $Q_{P_i}^W$ of electricity produced for the wholesale market by producer $i(1 \leq i \leq N_P)$ in the next period.
2. The quantity Q_{R_j} sold by retailer $j(1 \leq j \leq N_R)$ to consumers in the next period.
3. The quantity $Q_{P_i}^F$ of electricity sold forward by producer $i(1 \leq i \leq N_P)$. The quantity is fixed today and delivered in the next period. If producer i buys forward then $Q_{P_i}^F$ has a negative sign.
4. The quantity $Q_{R_j}^F$ of electricity sold forward by retailer $j(1 \leq j \leq N_R)$. The quantity is fixed today and delivered in the next period. If retailer j buys forward then $Q_{R_j}^F$ has a negative sign.
5. The wholesale price P_W is stochastic and applies to electricity traded between retailers and producers in the next period.
6. The forward price P_F is the price which applies on the forward market, that is, it is negotiated today and applies to all forward contracts.
7. The retail price P_R is already fixed today. It applies to electricity delivered from retailers to consumers in the next period. The quantity which consumers can consume is not fixed. Please note that P_R is specified exogenously. As such it is given and cannot be "optimized" by retailers today.

The ultimate goal is to determine the forward price today. Therefore, we must analyze the next period first in order to establish a relationship between total consumer demand and wholesale (spot) price. In a second step we can compute the forward price as market clearing price when both producers and retailers optimize their risk/expected profit profiles.

Determination of the Wholesale Price in the Second Period

The starting point is the total cost function TC_i for producer i. The total cost depends on the quantity sold on the spot wholesale market and through forward contracts entered before. Let us assume that it is given by

$$TC_i = F + \frac{a}{c} \cdot \left(Q_{P_i}^W + Q_{P_i}^F\right)^c \tag{25.1}$$

where F is the fixed cost and a and c are variable cost parameters ($c \geq 2$). Exhibit 25.3 shows the shape of the total cost function. Energy is produced with increasing marginal cost.

The profit π_{P_i} of producer i equals the total revenues TR_i from wholesale and the forward transactions minus total costs

$$\pi_{P_i} = TR_i - TC_i = P_W \cdot Q_{P_i}^W + P_F \cdot Q_{P_i}^F - TC_i \tag{25.2}$$

From standard microeconomic theory, we know how to determine the optimal quantity that producer should supply given a certain spot wholesale price P_W. All we have to do is set $d\pi_{P_i}/dQ_{P_i}^W = 0$. After a few calculations we get

$$Q_{P_i}^W = \left(\frac{P_W}{a}\right)^x - Q_{P_i}^F \quad x \equiv \frac{1}{c-1} \tag{25.3}$$

In order to determine the optimum wholesale price, the supply Q^S and demand Q^D for electricity have to be equal in equilibrium. The electricity

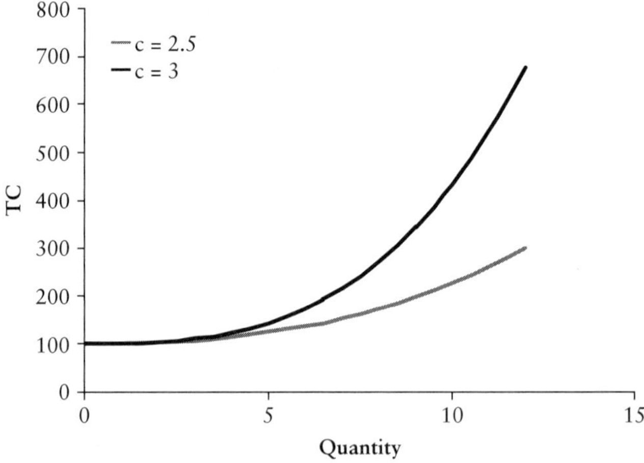

EXHIBIT 25.3 Total Costs Functions

supply is $Q_{P_i} \equiv Q_{P_i}^W + Q_{P_i}^F$ of all N_P producers of both spot and forward market transactions

$$Q^S = \sum_{i=1}^{N_P} Q_{P_i} = \sum_{i=1}^{N_P} \left(Q_{P_i}^W + Q_{P_i}^F \right) = Q^D \tag{25.4}$$

Substituting this for $Q_{P_i}^W$ in equation (25.3) delivers the wholesale price in equilibrium

$$P_W = a \cdot \left(\frac{Q^D}{N_P} \right)^{c-1} \tag{25.5}$$

Intuitively, this is the price that provides an incentive for producers to supply the necessary amount of electricity to meet consumers' demand. The relationship is consistent with economic intuition: The higher consumers' demand the higher is the price on the wholesale spot market.

Determination of the Forward Price in the First Period

In the following, we assume that both producers and retailers are risk averse. More precisely we define the objective function for producers as

$$\max_{Q_{P_i}^F} Z^W = E(\pi_{P_i}) - \frac{A}{2} \cdot Var(\pi_{P_i}) \tag{25.6}$$

Intuitively, producers like higher expected profits because they increase the objective function. In contrast, they dislike uncertainty characterized by the variance profits. Their aversion is higher the higher coefficient A is. Thus, with A we can control the risk aversion of the market participants. Substituting the cost function (25.1), the optimum wholesale quantity (25.3), and the wholesale price (25.5) into the profit function (25.2) refines the expected profit

$$\begin{aligned} E(\pi_{P_i}) &= E\left(P_W \cdot \frac{Q^D}{N_P} - F - \frac{a}{c} \cdot \left(\frac{Q^D}{N_P} \right)^c + Q_{P_i}^F \cdot (P_F - P_W) \right) \\ &\equiv E\left(\rho_{P_i} + Q_{P_i}^F \cdot (P_F - P_W) \right) \\ &= E(\rho_{P_i}) + Q_{P_i}^F \cdot (P_F - E(P_W)) \end{aligned} \tag{25.7}$$

where

$$\rho_{P_i} = P_W\left(\frac{Q^D}{N_P}\right) - F - \frac{a}{c}\left(\frac{Q^D}{N_P}\right)^c$$

represents the profit of the wholesale spot transaction and $Q^F_{P_i} \cdot (P_F - P_W)$ the profit from the forward transaction. $Var(\pi_{P_i})$ can be calculated when the covariance between the two stochastic quantities P_W and ρ_{P_i} in (25.7) is considered. More precisely the variance turns out to be

$$Var(\pi_{P_i}) = Var(\rho_{P_i}) - 2 \cdot Q^F_{P_i} \cdot Cov(\rho_{P_i}, P_W) + \left(Q^F_{P_i}\right)^2 \cdot Var(P_W) \quad (25.8)$$

Finally, the covariance between the two random variables can be determined by using the definition of ρ_{P_i}

$$\begin{aligned} Cov(\rho_{P_i}, P_W) &= Cov\left(P_W \cdot \frac{Q^D}{N_P} - F - \frac{a}{c} \cdot \left(\frac{Q^D}{N_P}\right)^c, P_W\right) \\ &= \frac{1 - 1/c}{a^x} \cdot Cov\left((P_W)^{x+1}, P_W\right) \end{aligned} \quad (25.9)$$

Using these intermediate results we can maximize the objective function of the producer. Therefore, we compute the first derivative of the objective function with respect to $Q^F_{P_i}$ and set it equal to zero. Taking into account (25.8) and (25.9) we can determine the optimal quantity to be sold forward by producers given a market forward price P_F. For producer i it turns out to be

$$\begin{aligned} Q^F_{P_i} &= \frac{P_F - E(P_W)}{A \cdot Var(P_W)} + \frac{Cov(\rho_{P_i}, P_W)}{Var(P_W)} \\ &= \frac{P_F - E(P_W)}{A \cdot Var(P_W)} + \frac{1 - 1/c}{a^x} \cdot \frac{Cov\left((P_W)^{x+1}, P_W\right)}{Var(P_W)} \end{aligned} \quad (25.10)$$

Intuitively, this is the quantity that producer i should sell forward today given the forward price P_F in order to maximize her risk/expected return profile.

Next we can compute the optimal quantity to be sold forward by retailer j. We assume the same objective function as for the producer. That is,

$$\max_{Q^F_{R_j}} Z^R = E\left(\pi_{R_j}\right) - \frac{A}{2} \cdot Var(\pi_{R_i}) \quad (25.11)$$

Similar calculations as for the producer show that the optimal quantity to be sold forward today given the market forward price P_F is

$$Q_{R_j}^F = \frac{P_F - E(P_W)}{A \cdot Var(P_W)} + \frac{Cov\left(\rho_{R_j}, P_W\right)}{Var(P_W)} \tag{25.12}$$

This quantity guarantees that retailers optimize their risk/expected return profile. In (25.12), the profit of the retailer's spot transaction ρ_{R_j} results from the difference between the selling price P_R and the buying price P_W; that is,

$$\rho_{R_j} = Q_{R_j} \cdot (P_R - P_W) \tag{25.13}$$

This allows us to rearrange (25.12) to

$$Q_{R_j}^F = \frac{P_F - E(P_W)}{A \cdot Var(P_W)} + \frac{P_R \cdot Cov\left(Q_{R_j}, P_W\right) - Cov\left(P_W \cdot Q_{R_j}, P_W\right)}{Var(P_W)} \tag{25.14}$$

Equations (25.10) and (25.14) are very important results. They show the quantities sold forward by producers and retailers given a particular forward price P_F. In equilibrium we should have a situation of zero net supply for forward contracts (i.e., for each seller in a forward contract we should find a buyer). Mathematically this means that the sum over all quantities sold forward must be equal to zero. Hence, we obtain the equilibrium condition

$$\sum_{i=1}^{N_P} Q_{P_i}^F + \sum_{j=1}^{N_R} Q_{P_j}^F = 0 \tag{25.15}$$

Using equations (25.10) and (25.14) and making some algebraic transformations as shown in Appendix A to this chapter yields the desired forward price in equilibrium

$$P_F = E(P_W) - \frac{N_P}{c \cdot a^x \cdot N} \cdot \left(c \cdot P_R \cdot Cov(P_W^x, P_W) - Cov\left(P_W^{x+1}, P_W\right)\right)$$
$$N \equiv \frac{N_P + N_R}{A} \tag{25.16}$$

The equilibrium forward price for electricity hence depends on the expected wholesale price and on the two covariance expressions.

Unfortunately, especially the covariances in equation (25.16) are difficult to deal with. Appendix B to this chapter contains further simplifications of the two covariance expressions in (25.16). They lead to a very tractable approximation of the forward price

$$P_F \approx E(P_W) + \alpha \cdot Var(P_W) + \gamma \cdot Skew(P_W) \tag{25.17}$$

where $Var(P_W)$ and $Skew\ (P_W)$ are defined in Appendix B. Thus, the forward price can easily be approximated by the first three moments of the distribution of the wholesale market spot price. This is a convenient property which enhances the models applicability in practice.

A NUMERICAL APPLICATION

In order to investigate the relationship between consumers' demand, wholesale market prices, and forward prices in greater detail we now turn to a numerical implementation of the model. The model parameters are given in Exhibit 25.4. The choice for the parameter values is similar to that used by Lemmon and Bessembinder. Since the fixed cost parameter F in (25.1) does not affect the wholesale quantity $Q_{P_i}^W$ and the further results, we do not

EXHIBIT 25.4 Input Parameters for the Numerical Example

Parameter		According to . . .
Demand quantity Q^D	100	
Cost parameter		
a	0.3	
c	3	
x	0.5	Equation (25.3)
Retailers and wholesalers		
N_P	10	
N_R	10	
Risk aversion parameter A	0.1111	
N	180	Equation (25.16)
Demand quantity Q^D		
$E(Q^D)$	100	
$VAR(Q^D)$	20	

have to make any assumptions about it at the moment. Consumers' demand is normally distributed with mean 100 and variance 20. Furthermore, we assume that retailers set the spot price equal to

$$P_R = 1.2 \cdot E[P_W] \tag{25.18}$$

Thus, intuitively retailers price with a security buffer of 20% above the expected wholesale price. The number of retailers is equal to the number of suppliers (= 10) in this example.

For the first step, we must determine the distribution of the wholesale prices in the next period. Therefore, we run a Monte Carlo simulation in which we consider 1,000 random scenarios of future consumers' demand according to the normal probability distribution. Once we know the consumer demand, we can compute the wholesale price immediately according to equation (25.5).

Exhibit 25.5 shows the first 18 simulated consumer demands and the corresponding wholesale prices. For instance, the first wholesale price is simply given by considering the demand of 128.97

$$P_W = 0.3 \cdot \left(\frac{128.97}{10}\right)^{3-1} = 49.90$$

EXHIBIT 25.5 18 Simulations of Demand Quantities Q^D

Q^D (simulated)	P_W
128.97	49.90
92.88	25.88
131.59	51.95
68.54	14.09
71.10	15.17
105.73	33.54
111.65	37.40
87.91	23.18
93.04	25.97
84.79	21.57
104.98	33.06
67.82	13.80
77.00	17.79
103.31	32.02
123.06	45.43
114.47	39.31
154.09	71.24
62.53	11.73

In a similar fashion, we can proceed for all other simulations. Altogether we get 1,000 scenarios of future wholesale market spot prices. From these scenarios, we can compute the arithmetic average, the variance, and the skewness in order to estimate the mean, variance, and skewness of the distribution of wholesale prices. They turn out to be

$$\begin{aligned} \mathrm{E}(P_W) &= €31.09/\mathrm{MWh} \\ \mathrm{Var}(P_W) &= 142.54 \\ \mathrm{Skew}(P_W) &= 0.57 \end{aligned}$$

According to the pricing strategy stated above, the retail price is

$$P_R = 1.2 \cdot 31.09 = 37.31.$$

Substituting the results into the pricing equation (25.17) yields

$$\begin{aligned} \alpha &= -0.0566 \\ \gamma &= 0.005 \\ P_F &\approx 31.09 - 0.0566 \cdot 142.54 + 0.57 \cdot 0.0050 = 23.03 \end{aligned}$$

The forward price is more than €8 below the spot price. Such relationships are frequently observed in markets for other commodity forwards and futures. This phenomenon, when forward prices are below expected spot prices, is called *backwardation*. Backwardation situations are often observed when the underlying products are expensive to store.[7] Oil causes significant storage costs as soon as it has been pumped out of the ground.

However, in the case of electricity forwards, we cannot link this discount to storage costs. Instead, the discount is mainly due to the variance of the wholesale prices. Obviously, it is connected to the hedging demand of producers and retailers. In general, both profit from increases of wholesale market prices (although, as discussed above, the effect is less clear cut for retailers since their trading margin shrinks). Thus, both are interested in selling forward, which leads to a discount of forward prices. In contrast, price spikes are bad for retailers as they then would sell

[7]This was analyzed in detail by Markus Rudolf, Heinz Zimmermann, and Claudia Zogg-Wetter, "Anlage und Portfolioeigenschaften von Commodities am Beispiel des GSCI," *Financial Markets and Portfolio Management* 7, no. 3 (1993), pp. 339–359; and Schwartz, "The Stochastic Behavior of Commodity Prices: Implications for Valuation and Hedging."

electricity to consumers at a price below their production cost. This creates hedging demand in the opposite direction (that is, induces forward purchases). Therefore, the relationship between forward prices and skewness is positive.

CONCLUSION

The usual approach for the valuation of forward contracts is the no-arbitrage approach. This approach cannot be applied to nonstorable goods as it is the case for electricity. Electricity forwards have to be priced with different models. The Bessembinder-Lemmon model is an equilibrium model. In that model, both supply and demand on the spot forward market for electricity are equalized. This allows Bessembinder and Lemmon to derive an equilibrium forward price. The equilibrium price can be approximated by the first three moments of the distribution of the wholesale price.

This chapter shows that electricity forwards may be biased downward compared to expected wholesale prices. This is due to hedging demand. In the example considered forward prices react negatively on the variance of the wholesale prices and positively on their skewness.

APPENDIX A

Derivation of equation (25.16)—the equilibrium forward price:

First we note that

$$\sum_j \frac{P_R COV\left[Q_{R_j}, P_W\right] - COV\left[P_W Q_{R_j}, P_W\right]}{VAR[P_W]}$$

$$= \frac{P_R COV[Q^D, P_W] - COV[P_W Q^D, P_W]}{VAR[P_W]}$$

$$= \frac{N_P}{a^x} \frac{P_R COV[P_W^x, P_W] - COV[P_W^{x+1}, P_W]}{VAR[P_W]}$$

The equilibrium condition is

$$\sum_i Q_{Pi}^F + \sum_j Q_{Rj}^F = 0$$

Using (25.10) and (25.14), we get

$$\sum_i \frac{P_F - E[P_W]}{A \cdot VAR[P_W]} + \frac{1}{a^x}\left(1 - \frac{1}{c}\right)\frac{COV\left[(P_W)^{x+1}, P_W\right]}{VAR[P_W]}$$
$$+ \sum_i \frac{P_F - E[P_W]}{A \cdot VAR[P_W]} + \frac{P_R COV[Q_{Rj}, P_W] - COV[P_W Q_{Rj}, P_W]}{VAR[P_W]} = 0$$

From this follows

$$P_F \frac{N_P + N_R}{A \cdot VAR[P_W]} - \frac{E[P_W](N_P + N_R)}{A \cdot VAR[P_W]} + \frac{N_P}{a^x}\left(1 - \frac{1}{c}\right)\frac{COV[P_W^{x+1}, P_W]}{VAR[P_W]}$$
$$+ \frac{N_P}{a^x}\frac{P_R COV[P_W^x, P_W] - COV[P_W^{x+1}, P_W]}{VAR[P_W]} = 0$$

$$\Leftrightarrow P_F \frac{N_P + N_R}{A \cdot VAR[P_W]} - \frac{E[P_W](N_P + N_R)}{A \cdot VAR[P_W]} =$$

$$\frac{N_P}{a^x}\frac{COV[P_W^{x+1}, P_W] - P_R COV[P_W^x, P_W]}{VAR[P_W]} - \frac{N_P}{a^x}\left(1 - \frac{1}{c}\right)\frac{COV[P_W^{x+1}, P_W]}{VAR[P_W]} =$$

$$\frac{N_P}{ca^x}\frac{COV[P_W^{x+1}, P_W]}{VAR[P_W]} - \frac{N_P}{a^x}\frac{P_R COV[P_W^x, P_W]}{VAR[P_W]}$$

This leads to (25.16).

APPENDIX B

The variance of P_W is given by

$$Var(P_W) = E\left[(P_W - E(P_W))^2\right] = E\left[P_W^2\right] - E^2[P_W]$$

Skewness can be calculated as

$$Skew(P_W) = E\left[(P_W - E(P_W))^3\right]$$
$$= E\left[P_W^3 - 3 \cdot P_W^2 \cdot E(P_W) + 3 \cdot P_W \cdot E^2(P_W) - E^3(P_W)\right]$$
$$= E\left[P_W^3\right] - 3 \cdot E\left[P_W^2\right] \cdot E[P_W] + 2 \cdot E^3[P_W]$$

A Taylor series expansion of the function P^z around y yields

$$P^z \approx y^z + zy^{z-1}(P-y) + \frac{1}{2}z(z-1)y^{z-2}(P-y)^2$$
$$= y^z\left(1 - z + \frac{1}{2}z(z-1)\right) + y^{z-1}z(2-z)P + \frac{1}{2}z(z-1)y^{z-2}P^2$$

The three equations above are used to derive the simplifying equation (25.17) for the equilibrium forward price. It is based on a Taylor series expansion of the first of the three equations above with $y = E(P) = \mu$. Then we have

$$COV[P^z, P]$$
$$\approx E\left[\begin{pmatrix} \mu^{z-1}z(2-z)P + \frac{1}{2}z(z-1)\mu^{z-2}P^2 - \mu^{z-1}\mu z(z-2) \\ -\frac{1}{2}z(z-1)\mu^{z-2}E\left[P^2\right] \end{pmatrix}(P-\mu)\right]$$
$$= \mu^{z-1}z(2-z)\underbrace{E\left[(P-\mu)^2\right]}_{VAR[P]} + \frac{1}{2}z(z-1)\mu^{z-2}E\left[\left(P^2 - E\left[P^2\right]\right)(P-\mu)\right]$$
$$= \mu^{z-1}z(2-z)VAR[P] + \frac{1}{2}z(z-1)\mu^{z-2}E\left[\left(P^3 - PE\left[P^2\right] - P^2\mu + E\left[P^2\right]\mu\right)\right]$$
$$= \mu^{z-1}z(2-z)VAR[P] + \frac{1}{2}z(z-1)\mu^{z-2}\underbrace{\left\{E\left[P^3\right] - \mu E\left[P^2\right]\right\}}_{=SKEW[P] + \underbrace{2\mu E[P^2] - 2\mu^3}_{=2VAR[P]\mu}}$$
$$= VAR[P]\left(\mu^{z-1}z(2-z) + z(z-1)\mu^{z-1}\right) + \frac{1}{2}z(z-1)\mu^{z-2}SKEW[P]$$
$$= z\mu^{z-1}VAR[P] + \frac{1}{2}z(z-1)\mu^{z-2}SKEW[P]$$

It follows then that

$$COV\left[P_W^x, P_W\right] \approx xE[P_W]^{x-1}VAR[P_W] + \frac{1}{2}x(x-1)E[P_W]^{x-2}SKEW[P_W]$$

$$COV\left[P_W^{x+1}, P_W\right] \approx (x+1)E[P_W]^{x}VAR[P_W] + \frac{1}{2}x(x+1)E[P_W]^{x-1}SKEW[P_W]$$

This yields the following approximation of the forward price:

$$P_F \approx E[P_W] - \frac{N_P}{ca^x N}\begin{pmatrix} cP_R x E[P_W]^{x-1} VAR[P_W] \\ +\frac{1}{2} cP_R x(x-1)E[P_W]^{x-2} SKEW[P_W] \\ -(x+1)E[P_W]^x VAR[P_W] \\ -\frac{1}{2} x(x+1)E[P_W]^{x-1} SKEW[P_W] \end{pmatrix}$$

$$E[P_W] + \underbrace{\frac{N_P}{ca^x N}(x+1)\left[E[P_W]^x - P_R E[P_W]^{x-1}\right]}_{\equiv\alpha} VAR[P_W]$$

$$+\underbrace{\frac{N_P}{2ca^x N}(x+1)\left[xE[P_W]^{x-1} - P_R(x-1)E[P_W]^{x-2}\right]}_{\equiv\gamma} SKEW[P_W]$$

CHAPTER 26

Securitization of Commodity Price Risk

Paul U. Ali
Associate Professor
Melbourne University Law School

Securitization typically involves removing selected income-producing assets, such as mortgages, trade receivables, and corporate loans, from the balance sheet of a corporation or financial institution and repackaging those assets into securities that can readily be sold to investors in the capital markets. The investors are exposed to the risks of the assets, not to the risks associated with the corporation or financial institution, and, in this manner, the corporation or financial institution is able to raise funds more cheaply than if it had raised funds directly on the strength of its own balance sheet.[1]

Over the last decade, securitization has evolved from being primarily a fund-raising instrument to also encompassing the issue of securities principally for hedging purposes. The latter involves the unbundling of risks with investors being given exposure only to specific risks, ranging from risks that attach to individual assets or business lines to enterprise-wide risks, in contrast to having exposure to the entirety of the risks associated with particular assets. In theory, any risk that is capable of being quantified can be individually securitized employing this newer form of securitization. Credit risk, catastrophic risk, and mortality risk are

[1]Steven L. Schwarcz, *Structured Finance*, 3rd ed. (New York: Practising Law Institute, 2002), §1:1.

The author wishes to acknowledge the assistance of Jan Job de Vries Robbe, Structured Finance Counsel, FMO, The Hague.

among the specific risks that have been successfully transferred to investors using such securitizations.[2]

The structures employed to securitize these individual risks have now been adapted to transfer separately the price risk of various commodities, including precious metals, base metals, oil, and natural gas, to investors.[3] These *collateralized commodity obligations* (CCOs), which form the subject of this chapter, have been described as "the world's first rated credit instrument that provides fixed income investors with access to commodities as an asset class."[4] The market for CCOs is still in its early stages. As at the end of 2006, an estimated $900 million securities had been issued to investors through two publicly rated CCO structures.[5] This figure does not, however, take into account CCOs that have been placed privately with investors.[6] Moreover, prospects for the CCO market appear bright due to the interest of institutional investors and the fact that CCOs adhere to the credit securitization structures with which those investors have a high degree of familiarity.[7]

CCOs, however, differ markedly from other securities—commodity-linked notes—that also deliver investors exposure to commodities. Commodity-linked notes are primarily fund-raising instruments which, depending upon how they have been structured, may also combine fund-raising with hedging. The structures employed can be categorized as forward-linked or option-linked.[8]

---

[2]This form of securitization has primarily been used by banks to hedge the credit risk of their loan portfolios and insurers/reinsurers to hedge the catastrophic and mortality risks of their insurance policies. As regards the limited use of such instruments by corporations, see Charles Smithson and David Mengle, "The Promise of Credit Derivatives in Nonfinancial Corporations (and Why It's Failed to Materialize)," *Journal of Applied Corporate Finance* (Fall 2006), pp. 54–60.

[3]The first CCO was launched in December 2004. See Deborah Kimbell, "Barclays Pioneers a Commodity Vehicle," *Euromoney* (January 2005).

[4]Saskia Scholtes, "Introducing CCOs," *Credit* (February 2005), 26–27.

[5]"Barclays Breaks CDO Mould with Commodity Price Bond," *Euroweek*, December 2004, p. 61; and "Barcap Brings Managed Commodity CCO—Because It's There," *Euroweek*, June 9, 2006, p. 68.

[6]Fitch Ratings, "Considerations for Rating Commodities-Linked Credit Obligations (CCOs)," *Structured Credit Global Special Report*, November 14, 2006.

[7]"First Managed CCO Comes to Market," *Asset Securitization Report*, June 12, 2006, pp. 1 and 13.

[8]Satyajit Das, *Structured Products and Hybrid Securities*, 2nd ed. (Singapore: John Wiley & Sons, 2001), pp. 339–350; and Calum G. Turvey, "Managing Food Industry Business and Financial Risks with Commodity-Linked Credit Instruments," *Agribusiness* (Autumn 2006), pp. 523–545.

In forward-linked structures, the issuer's principal and/or interest payments are calculated by reference to the price of a designated commodity, basket of commodities, or commodity index (for example, the Goldman Sachs Commodity Index). The issuer is protected against a fall in the reference price through the debt raised being less costly to repay. By linking its cost of borrowing to commodity prices, the issuer can better match the burden of servicing the funds raised to its own cash flow situation and reduce the risk of bankruptcy or default, as its payment obligations will rise or fall in line with changes in commodity prices and thus changes in the cash flows it derives from those commodities.[9]

Option-linked structures also facilitate fund raising. The securities issued carry principal and interest payments like a conventional debt security but, on maturity, the investor is entitled to exercise an option to buy or sell a fixed quantity of a reference commodity at a fixed price.[10] The value to the investors of the embedded option means that the issuer is able to raise funds more cheaply than if it had issued conventional debt securities.[11]

CCOs, in contrast to commodity-linked notes, irrespective of whether a forward-linked or option-linked structure has been used for the latter, are not fund-raising instruments but are, instead, primarily hedging instruments. In a CCO, the issuer is a conduit for commodity price risk. Securities are issued for the purpose of passing on to investors the exposure to commodity prices that has been assumed by the issuer under its own hedging obligations to one or more third parties. A CCO thus, in effect, represents a back-to-back hedge of the issuer's own hedging obligations, with the

---

[9]John D. Finnerty, "An Overview of Corporate Securities Innovation," *Journal of Applied Corporate Finance* (Winter 1992), pp. 23–39; Aswath Damodaran, "Financing Innovations and Capital Structure Choices," *Journal of Applied Corporate Finance* (Spring 1999), pp. 28–39; N. K. Chidambaran, Chitru S. Fernando, and Paul A. Spindt, "Credit Enhancement through Financial Engineering: Freeport McMoRan's Gold-Denominated Depositary Shares," *Journal of Financial Economics* (May 2001), pp. 487–528; and Joel S. Telpner, "A Survey of Structured Notes," *Journal of Structured and Project Finance* (Winter 2004), pp. 6–19.

[10]Turvey, "Managing Food Industry Business and Financial Risks with Commodity-Linked Credit Instruments." This option may be physically or cash-settled.

[11]Robert J. Myers, "Incomplete Markets and Commodity Linked Finance in Developing Countries," *World Bank Research Observer* (January 1992), pp. 79–94. Alternatively, option-linked structures may also incorporate a hedge against an adverse movement in commodity prices with the embedded option being sold by the investors: Das, *Structured Products and Hybrid Securities*; Turvey, "Managing Food Industry Business and Financial Risks with Commodity-Linked Credit Instruments." The investors are compensated for this assumption of risk by the payment of an option premium in the form of an enhanced coupon on the securities.

proceeds from the issue of securities being held by the issuer to cover those hedging obligations. From the investors' perspective, they are purchasing exposure to commodity price risk for a fee in the form of interest rate payments on their securities.

This chapter provides an overview of the motivations of the participants in CCOs and the legal structure of a generic CCO, making reference to the first CCO, Apollo, launched in December 2004 by Barclays Capital.[12] The chapter also examines the key legal risks—concerning compliance with the prudent investor rule and recharacterization by a court or regulator of the derivatives underpinning a CCO as unauthorized insurance products—confronting the participants in CCOs.

DRIVERS FOR COLLATERALIZED COMMODITY OBLIGATIONS

Issuers and Originators

A CCO issuer is merely a conduit for the transmission of commodity price risk to the investors in the securities issued by it. The issue of securities, as already noted, completes the implementation by the issuer of a back-to-back hedge of commodity price risk. Thus, in order to understand the motivation for CCOs, it is necessary to inquire into the motivation of the party—the originator—to whom the issuer, itself, is exposed in terms of the securitized commodity price risk.

As is the case with commodity-linked notes, the originator may be a corporation that is exposed to the risk of adverse movements in commodity prices as part of the ordinary course of its business. For example, a mining corporation will suffer a fall into its revenues and also its profits if prices fall for the metals that it produces. Equally, an agricultural corporation will suffer if the prices of its farm products fall. However, in practice, the originators in CCOs are typically financial institutions, which are not themselves directly exposed to the commodity price risks to which the CCOs relate.

The hedge against commodity price risk provided by CCOs to these originators operates, instead, as a substitute for a hedge against credit risk, with commodity price risk being used as a proxy for credit risk. For instance, a decline in commodity prices that leads to reduced revenues for a borrower may impair the borrower's creditworthiness and thus increase the credit risk of the obligations owed by that borrower to the originator. It is possible for the originator to create a hedge against that credit risk by using

[12] Kimbell, "Barclays Pioneers a Commodity Vehicle."

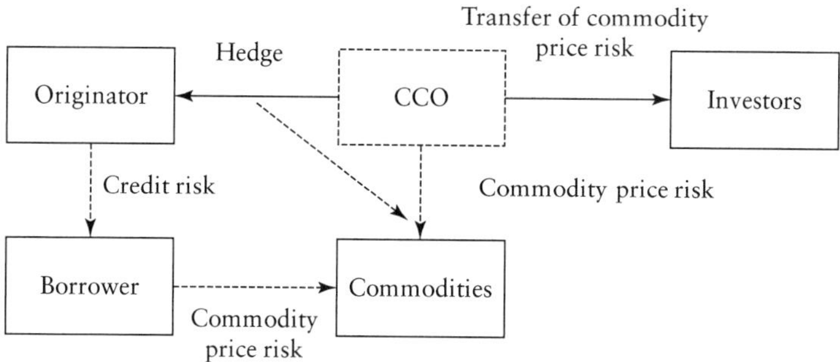

EXHIBIT 26.1 Commodity Price Risk as a Proxy for Credit Risk

a CCO to hedge the commodity price risk to which the borrower's own business is exposed. The use of commodity price risk as a proxy for credit risk is illustrated in Exhibit 26.1

Given the large number of businesses whose revenues (and thus creditworthiness) are correlated to commodity prices, CCOs have the potential to enable originators to hedge the credit risk of a far greater number of corporations and other reference entities than is now possible through the use of credit derivatives and securitized credit derivatives. A key advantage of CCOs—and what has proved to be the major driver for their use—is their capacity to address the relatively small number of liquid reference entities traded in the global credit markets.[13] While thousands of corporate and other entities have been referenced by credit derivatives, only about 650 entities are referenced on a regular basis.[14]

Investors and the Prudent Investor Rule

The main investors in CCO securities, in common with investors in other securitizations, are institutional investors, including pension funds, hedge

[13]This relative lack of liquid reference entities in the global credit markets has also provided the impetus for the securitization of equity price risk in the form of *equity collateralized obligations* (ECOs), the precursor of CCOs. See Michael J. Logie and John-Peter Castagnino, "Equity Default Swaps and the Securitisation of Risk," Chapter 4, in *Innovations in Securitisation* edited by Jan Job de Vries Robbe and Paul U. Ali (The Hague: Kluwer Law International, 2006), p. 51.

[14]Fitch Ratings, "CDS Roundup: Volumes Expand across Most Sectors while Spreads Ratchet Higher," *Special Report*, November 17, 2006.

funds, and mutual funds.[15] These investors, however, do not invest for their own account but for the benefit of third parties who have entrusted the management of their assets to these investors (by contributing to a pension fund, or investing in a hedge fund or mutual fund). Unlike individual investors who invest only their own personal funds and, accordingly, are legally unconstrained in their choice of investments, institutional investors are constrained by their legal duties to their own investors.

The critical duty here is the duty of prudence that applies when selecting investments and which is an important source of legal risk for institutional investors in CCO securities (and other complex financial products). Failure to discharge this duty will render an institutional investor personally liable for any losses or underperformance attributable to the selection of the noncomplying investment.

This duty of prudence—referred to as the *prudent investor rule*—requires persons who invest on behalf of others to ensure that the investments selected are both suitable (as regards the pension fund, hedge fund, or mutual fund's investment strategy and objectives, the expected return contribution of the investment to the fund, and the requirements of the fund for liquidity, regularity, and stability of income, and the preservation or appreciation of capital) and contribute positively to portfolio diversification.[16] Whether CCO securities or other instruments should be included in a portfolio must therefore be determined by examining whether investing in such instruments is consistent with the strategy and objectives of the fund, including the fund's risk and return parameters, the impact of the investment on the overall return and riskiness of the fund's portfolio, and the investment's contribution to portfolio diversification.

This whole-of-portfolio approach to investment selection does not automatically exclude complex or risky instruments but it means that an

[15]"First Managed CCO Comes to Market," pp. 1 and 13. This is both a function of investor demand and the fact that most securitizations do not involve public offerings of securities in order to take advantage of the regulatory safe harbors applicable to offerings limited to sophisticated, high net worth individuals and entities.

[16]Paul U. Ali, Geof Stapledon, and Martin Gold, *Corporate Governance and Investment Fiduciaries* (Sydney: Thomson Legal & Regulatory, 2003), pp. 76–78. The prudent investor rule, in the terms framed in this chapter, applies in the United States and the United Kingdom as well as Australia, Canada, and the major off-shore common law jurisdictions, including the Bahamas, Bermuda, the British Virgin Islands, and the Cayman Islands.

institutional investor considering allocating the funds under its management to an investment in CCO securities must at least:

1. Understand the legal structure of the CCO, including the mechanism by which the investor is exposed to commodity price risk, the priority ranking of the investor's claims against the issuer for principal and interest, and the fact that the securities issued in a CCO are limited recourse securities.
2. Understand the risk and return attributes of the CCO securities, in particular whether the coupon carried by the securities is sufficient compensation for the exposure of the investor's principal to risk of loss.
3. Understand the situations in which the investor's claims for principal will be impaired by an adverse movement in commodity prices.
4. Assess the liquidity of the CCO securities.

For investors, the attraction of CCOs lies in the enhanced coupon carried by the securities compared to conventional debt instruments of equivalent creditworthiness and the diversification benefits of exposure to the commodities referenced in a CCO.[17] Commodity prices, in general, display only low correlations with the returns on shares and conventional bonds, and thus their inclusion in portfolios of shares and bonds should assist the optimization of portfolio returns.[18] Those generalized characteristics are useful in making a case for the inclusion of CCO securities in a portfolio but are not, on their own, sufficient to ensure compliance with the prudent investor rule. The investors in a CCO are effectively purchasing commodity price risk for a fee and placing their principal at risk. Accordingly, an institutional investor must ensure the coupon on the particular CCO securities sufficiently compensates it for the assumption of commodity price risk and that these putative diversification benefits are actually present as regards the investor's own portfolio.

[17]Turvey, "Managing Food Industry Business and Financial Risks with Commodity-Linked Credit Instruments."

[18]Ernest M. Ankrim and Chris R. Hensel, "Commodities in Asset Allocation: A Real Alternative to Real Estate?" *Financial Analysts Journal* (May–June 1993), pp. 20–29; Kenneth A. Froot, "Hedging Portfolios with Real Assets," *Journal of Portfolio Management* (Summer 1995), pp. 60–77; and Georgi Georgiev, "The Benefits of Commodity Investment: 2006 Update," Center for International Securities and Derivatives Markets, Working Paper, May 2006.

LEGAL STRUCTURE OF A GENERIC CCO

Securitization of Commodity Derivatives

CCOs utilize the same structures that are now routinely employed by banks to securitize credit derivatives.[19]

These securitizations, in their simplest form, involve a bank establishing a *special purpose vehicle* (SPV) to hedge the credit risk of a portfolio of corporate loans, bonds or other debt obligations held by the bank. The transfer of credit risk to the SPV is effected via a credit derivative and the SPV funds that transfer by issuing securities to investors in the capital markets. This credit derivative typically provides for the SPV to make predetermined payments to the bank on the occurrence of certain events representing an increase in credit risk of the portfolio. These events include the bankruptcy or default of the borrowers or other obligors in respect of the debt obligations in the portfolio. Should an event occur that triggers a payment under the credit derivative, that payment will be made by the SPV out of the proceeds generated from the issue of securities. Such a payment will lead to a corresponding loss of principal on the part of the investors, as payments to the bank will diminish the assets of the SPV which support principal and interest payments on the investors' securities. If, however, no such event occurs, the principal amount of the securities will be repaid in full to the investors on the maturity of the securities.

The use of securitization to transfer credit risk to investors is illustrated in Exhibit 26.2.

Similarly, in a CCO, the price risk in relation to a pool of commodities is transferred by the originator to an SPV and that risk is, in turn, transferred to investors in the capital markets through the issue of securities to them. The structural overview of CCOs that follows draws upon the legal structure of the first-ever CCO, Apollo.[20]

The initial transfer of commodity price risk from the originator to the SPV is effected by the SPV transacting a commodity trigger swap that references the commodities in the pool, with the SPV assuming the sold position under the swap. That risk is passed on to the investors by linking the

[19]Fitch Ratings, "CDO Structures and Definitions," *CDOs/Global Special Report*, July 19, 2006.

[20]Standard & Poor's, "Belo PLC," *Synthetic CDO of Commodities Presale Report*, November 5, 2004; Turvey, "Managing Food Industry Business and Financial Risks with Commodity-Linked Credit Instruments"; Jan Job de Vries Robbe, "That's One Small Step for Man . . . Securitising Commodity Risk Through Apollo," Chapter 5, in *Innovations in Securitisation* edited by Jan Job de Vries Robbe and Paul U. Ali (The Hague: Kluwer Law International, 2006), pp. 77–78.

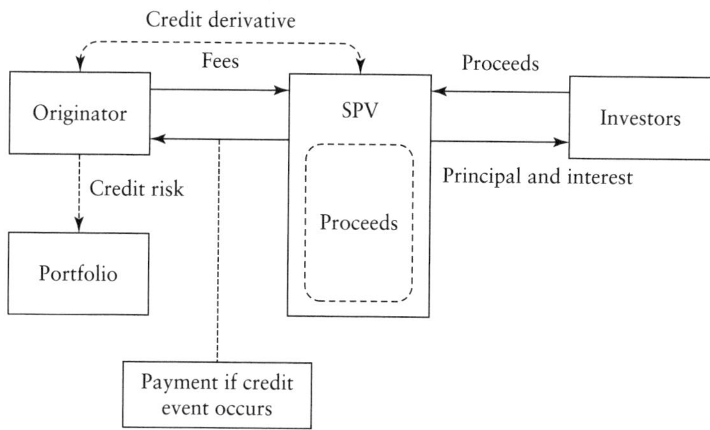

EXHIBIT 26.2 Securitization of Credit Risk

securities held by them to the SPV's exposure under the commodity trigger swap and thus to the price performance of the reference commodities.

The proceeds from the issue of the securities are used by the SPV to acquire interest-bearing investments (typically, highly rated, highly liquid, fixed income securities). Those investments support or "collateralize" the SPV's obligations to the originator under the swap, and the cash flows generated by the investments are used by the SPV to service principal and interest payments on the investors' securities. The SPV's obligations to the originator are senior to the SPV's obligations to the investors. Thus, the SPV's obligation to repay the principal amount of the securities is subject to the SPV not suffering a loss under the swap, due to an adverse movement in the prices of the reference commodities.

As is made clear in Exhibit 26.3, CCOs are structurally similar to securitizations of credit risk.

If the SPV does suffer such a loss, that loss will be made good out of the interest-bearing investments held by the SPV, leading to a depletion of the assets of the SPV that are available to meet the investors' claims for principal on the maturity of the securities. As the securities are limited recourse obligations of the SPV, a loss on the swap necessarily translates into an equivalent reduction in the SPV's obligation to repay principal. If, on the other hand, the SPV does not suffer a loss on the swaps during the term of the securities, the principal amount of the securities will be repaid in full on the maturity of the securities.

To compensate the investors for the risks to which their principal and possibly also interest payments are exposed, the securities carry an enhanced coupon relative to comparably credit-rated conventional debt

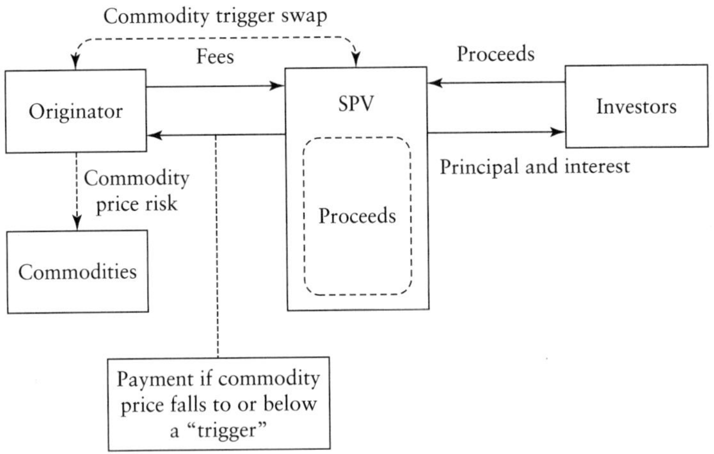

EXHIBIT 26.3 CCO

securities. These risks, in common with other securities, include the credit risk of the issuer and liquidity risk in relation to the CCO securities. However, the coupon on the CCO securities is chiefly compensation for commodity price risk, that is, uncertainty as to the likelihood of the commodity price falling and the severity of the losses to the investors of such a fall in price.[21] An examination of similar securities to those issued in CCOs has also shown that an enhanced coupon is necessary to address investor concerns about the complexity of the transaction structure, the risk aversion displayed by investors in such securities (which leads investors to overestimate the likelihood of the SPV suffering a loss on the swap), and investors' anxiety about losing their entire principal.[22]

The coupon on the securities is a combination of the interest paid on the interest-bearing investments held by the SPV and the fees received from the originator as consideration for the SPV assuming a sold position under the commodity trigger swap. In contrast to principal, the coupon on the securities is not usually exposed to commodity price risk. In the CCOs that have been brought to market, losses on the swap only reduce the principal on maturity, and so for the term of the securities the investors will continue to receive interest calculated on the full principal amount of the securities.[23]

[21]de Vries Robbe, "That's One Small Step for Man . . . Securitising Commodity Risk Through Apollo."
[22]Vivek J. Bantwal and Howard C. Kunreuther, "A Cat Bond Premium Puzzle?" *Journal of Psychology and Financial Markets* (Spring 2000), pp. 76–91.
[23]Standard & Poor's, "Belo PLC."

Commodity Trigger Swaps

A commodity trigger swap, like the credit default swaps on which it is modeled, provides for the SPV, in exchange for payment of fees by the originator, to pay a fixed sum to the originator if the price of a commodity falls below a certain threshold ("trigger").[24] Should this trigger be breached, the SPV will, as noted above, satisfy its payment obligations under the swap out of the assets that have been purchased by it with the proceeds from the issue of securities.

A trigger usually ranges from 20% to 80% of the price of the commodity at the time the CCO is implemented.[25] The particular trigger selected will, where the CCO is being used by the originator to hedge credit risk, be designed to mimic the occurrence of an event of default under the debt obligations to which that credit risk relates. Accordingly, a fall in the commodity price to or below the trigger should equate to a material deterioration in the creditworthiness of the borrower or other obligor in respect of those debt obligations.

The exposure of a borrower to commodity price risk thus permits commodity trigger swaps—and CCOs—to be used as substitutes for credit default swaps as regards the hedging of the credit risk of such borrowers. In addition to the potentially greater number of entities whose credit risk can be traded via a commodity trigger swap or CCO, commodity trigger swaps possess the attraction of being more transparent than credit default swaps. The determination of a credit event under a credit default swap depends upon the quality of publicly available information in relation to the borrower and, in particular for small-to-medium enterprises and unlisted entities, the quality of the monitoring of the borrower. In addition, the scope of "restructuring" as a credit event remains a matter of contention for market participants, which may make it difficult to ascertain whether a credit event has in fact occurred in respect of the borrower.[26] In contrast, the fall of a commodity price below a stipulated trigger can be readily determined by reference to spot prices or futures contract prices for the commodity.

---

[24]de Vries Robbe, "That's One Small Step for Man . . . Securitising Commodity Risk Through Apollo." A commodity trigger swap may reference several commodities in which case different triggers and payouts may be selected for each commodity.

[25]Fitch Ratings, "Considerations for Rating Commodities-Linked Credit Obligations (CCOs)."

[26]Jan Job de Vries Robbe and Paul U. Ali, *Opportunities in Credit Derivatives and Synthetic Securitisation* (London: Thomson Financial, 2005), p. 52.

Commodity Trigger Swaps and Recharacterization Risk

The parties to commodity trigger swaps and similar derivatives—as well as the participants in securitizations of those derivatives—face the legal risk that a regulator or court will treat the derivatives as disguised insurance products. This recharacterization risk is due to the superficial similarities between the transfer of risk under commodity trigger swaps (and also credit default swaps on which the former are modeled) and insurance.

Although the market consensus has long been that such derivatives do not constitute insurance, the risk of recharacterization is not a trivial one. This is well borne out by the unexpected attempt, in 2003, of the Property and Casualty Insurance Committee of the National Association of Insurance Commissioners to classify weather derivatives (which are used to hedge the risk of an adverse change in weather) as insurance products. The committee only pulled back from that view following intensive lobbying by the International Swaps and Derivatives Association and other financial markets associations.[27]

If a regulator or court were to treat commodity trigger swaps as insurance products, a number of undesirable consequences will follow. The SPV, as the party that has assumed risk under the swap, will be treated as carrying on an insurance business and should the SPV not hold the requisite regulatory authority to carry on that business, it and its officers will be exposed to criminal liability. It is unlikely that an SPV in a CCO would be so authorized or that the SPV would have the benefit of exemptions from the insurance laws that are available in the majority of U.S. states and many offshore jurisdictions for securitizations of insured risks.[28] In addition, the swap may be rendered unenforceable at law.

The status of a commodity trigger swap as insurance or noninsurance depends upon the nature of the payout under the swap.[29] Such swaps clearly possess the first of the two commonly accepted attributes of insurance, which is that the payout must be conditional upon some uncertain, future event occurring (commodity prices falling to or below a trigger). Accordingly, the status of the swap will be determined by whether it possesses the second of these attributes, namely whether the payout under the swap compensates or indemnifies the payee for losses caused by the occurrence of that event.

---

[27]International Swaps and Derivatives Association, Member Update, March 24, 2004.

[28]Tamar Frankel and Joseph W. LaPlume, "Securitizing Insurance Risks," *Annual Review of Banking Law* (2000), pp. 203–226.

[29]Paul U. Ali, "The Legal Characterization of Weather Derivatives," *Journal of Alternative Investments* (Fall 2004), pp. 75–79.

Commodity trigger swaps are unlikely to possess this second attribute.

There is no requirement for the originator to have an existing exposure to commodity price risk or for the originator to suffer actual losses as a result of a fall in commodity prices. In fact, the originator's sole exposure to commodity prices can be the risk created by the swap itself, namely the risk of not receiving the payout provided for in the swap due to commodity prices not falling to or below the trigger.

In addition, commodity trigger swaps are typically used by originators not to hedge commodity price risk but to create a hedge against credit risk. The payout under the swap is designed not to compensate or indemnify the originator for losses incurred as a result of a fall in commodity prices but to protect it against an increase in the credit risk of a borrower or other obligor that is exposed to commodity price risk. The fact that a payment under the swap may allow the originator to recoup losses attributable to the default or bankruptcy of the borrower is, however, merely coincidental. Neither the risk transferred under the swap to the SPV nor the payout provided for in the swap concerns credit risk, and that risk continues to reside with the originator.

CONCLUSION

CCOs are yet another example of the high degree of innovation that characterizes the global securitization markets. For financial institutions, CCOs offer a new means of hedging or trading credit risk, and one which possesses the advantages of greater coverage of borrowers and transparency than securitizations involving credit derivatives. For investors, CCOs offer exposure to commodity prices in the form of debt securities that can be readily traded in the secondary market. This, and the ability to create CCOs that reference diversified pools of commodities, are likely to make CCOs an attractive alternative to institutional investors to direct investments in commodities and commodity futures.

In addition, the CCOs that have been brought to market to date have referenced either static or lightly managed pools of commodities. It is likely that these CCOs represent only the early stages of the CCO market. Looking at the securitizations of credit derivatives on which CCOs have been modeled, it is likely to be only a matter of time before the next generation of CCOs arrives, in particular CCOs involving actively managed pools of commodities where the SPV is able to buy and sell commodity trigger swaps (rather than being confined to sold positions as is the case with the current generation of CCOs).[30]

[30]de Vries Robbe, "That's One Small Step for Man . . . Securitising Commodity Risk Through Apollo."

CHAPTER 27

Commodity Trading Advisors: A Review of Historical Performance

Martin Eling, Ph.D.
Institute of Insurance Economics
University of St. Gallen

In recent years, alternative investments have gained widespread acceptance owing to their interesting risk-return characteristics and their low correlations to traditional asset classes. In this chapter we focus on the alternative asset class called *managed futures*, which refers to professional money managers known as *commodity trading advisors* (CTAs). These managers trade a wide variety of *over-the-counter* (OTC) and exchange-traded forwards, futures, and options in different markets based on a wide variety of trading models.

CTAs have been active in the capital market since 1948, but until the 1970s they represented only a very small market segment.[1] However, with the increasing market for derivatives and short selling, there has been growth within the CTA market. Today, CTAs have approximately $135

[1]See Harry M. Kat, "Managed Futures and Hedge Funds: A Match Made in Heaven," in *Commodity Trading Advisors*, edited by Greg N. Gregoriou, Vassilios N. Karavas, François-Serge Lhabitant, and Fabrice Rouah, (Hoboken, NJ: John Wiley & Sons, 2004), pp. 5–17.

I am grateful to Thomas Parnitzke, Hato Schmeiser, and Denis Toplek for valuable suggestions and comments.

billion in assets under management,[2] making them an important part of the alternative investment industry.

Since the mid-1990s, CTAs have been the subject of much academic research. In the academic literature and in practice the performance of alternative investments is often evaluated by Markowitz's portfolio selection theory and by classical performance measures such as the Sharpe ratio.[3] Especially due to the low correlations with traditional investments such as stocks and bonds, managed futures appear very attractive in this model framework.

However, recent literature points out problems in connection with the returns of alternative investments, which casts doubt on the suitability of classical performance analysis for the evaluation of alternative investments.[4] In particular, the estimation of the input parameters for the performance measurement proves to be critical because some studies show that these parameters are not stable over time or across different market environments. Fung and Hsieh analyze the empirical characteristics of CTAs and show, on the basis of different market conditions, that the risk-return profiles of some CTAs are similar to those of options.[5] Hübner and Papageorgiou analyze the performance of CTAs in different market environments and under extreme events and find that traditional multifactor, as well as multimoment, asset pricing models do not adequately describe the CTA returns within the subperiods.[6] Gregoriou and Chen find that CTA returns are nonlinear due to long/short positions as well as derivatives, and

---

[2]See CISDM Research Department, The Benefits of Managed Futures: 2006 Update, Center for International Securities and Derivatives Markets, May 2006. The number of CTAs is about 650.

[3]See Scott H. Irwin, Terry R. Krukemyer, and Carl R. Zulauf, "Investment Performance of Public Commodity Pools: 1979–1990," *Journal of Futures Markets* 13, no. 7 (1993), pp. 799–820; and Franklin R. Edwards and Jimmy Liew, "Hedge Funds versus Managed Futures as Asset Classes," *Journal of Derivatives* 6, no. 4 (1999), pp. 45–64.

[4]See, for example, Clifford Asness, Robert Krail, and John Liew, "Do Hedge Funds Hedge?" *Journal of Portfolio Management* 28, no. 1 (2001), pp. 6–19.

[5]See William Fung and David A. Hsieh, "Survivorship Bias and Investment Style in the Returns of CTAs," *Journal of Portfolio Management* 24, no. 1 (1997), pp. 30–41.

[6]See Georges Hübner and Nicolas Papageorgiou, "The Performance of CTAs in Changing Market Conditions," in *Commodity Trading Advisors,* edited by Greg N. Gregoriou, Vassilios N. Karavas, François-Serge Lhabitant, and Fabrice Rouah (Hoboken, NJ: John Wiley & Sons, 2004), pp. 105–128.

use data envelopment analysis to overcome problems with classic performance measurement.[7]

In this chapter, we study monthly returns of the Center for International Securities and Derivatives Markets (CISDM) CTA indexes in order to analyze their stability over time and in different market conditions. Our goal is to bring together the results of different literature contributions to time and market phase stability and to point out their implications for the performance measurement of CTAs. The analysis shows that the attractiveness of CTA investments depends on time period and market phase. However, this is particularly due to the large variations in performance measurement results found for traditional investments, whereas CTA returns and performance numbers are relatively stable. Therefore, we advise caution in interpreting the results of classical performance measures.

The uncertainty of input parameters is a general problem in performance measurement and is often discussed in literature. More than a half century ago, Markowitz discussed the problem that the input parameters necessary for portfolio selection cannot be observed.[8] Several researchers try to integrate this estimation risk as a further source of risk into performance measurement.[9] Other researchers try to improve the parameter estimation procedure in performance measurement.[10]

In this chapter, we focus on CTAs because the estimation problem is especially relevant in connection with two frequently cited arguments in favor of investing in CTAs and other alternative investments. First, we analyze whether CTAs exhibit attractive combinations of risk and return that lead to a high risk-adjusted performance (despite the described estimation problems). Second, we question whether the correlations of the CTA returns are

---

[7]See Greg N. Gregoriou and Yao Chen, "Evaluation of Commodity Trading Advisors Using Fixed and Variable and Benchmark Models,"*Annals of Operations Research* 145, no. 1 (2006), pp. 183–200.

[8]See Harry M. Markowitz, "Portfolio Selection," *Journal of Finance* 7, no. 1 (1952), pp. 77–91.

[9]See, for example, Christopher B. Barry, "Portfolio Analysis under Uncertain Means, Variances, and Covariances," *Journal of Finance* 29, no. 2 (1974), pp. 515–522.

[10]See, for example, Peter A. Frost and James E. Savarino, "An Empirical Bayes Approach to Efficient Portfolio Selection," *Journal of Financial and Quantitative Analysis* 21, no. 3 (1986), pp. 293–305.

really low in relation to the returns of traditional investments (taking into consideration the parameter estimation problems).

THE CISDM CTA INDEXES

In the empirical investigation, we examine monthly returns of the CISDM CTA indexes over the period from January 1996 to December 2005. Six CTA strategies are reflected in the indexes: Currency, Discretionary, Diversified, Financials, Equity, and Systematic. Furthermore, there are two aggregated indexes that represent a diversified investment in all CTA reporting to the database, with the first one being asset weighted and the second one equally weighted.[11]

The CTA indexes are compared with five market indexes that measure the performance of stocks, bonds, the money market, real estate, and commodities. The Morgan Stanley Capital International (MSCI) World is used as an equity index and the JPMorgan (JPM) Global Government Bond as a bond index. To illustrate the money market, we use the JPM U.S. Cash 3 Month, while development of the asset class covering real estate is illustrated by the Global Property Research (GPR) General Property Share index (PSI). The commodity market is represented by the Goldman Sachs (GS) Commodity Index Total Return.

All indexes were calculated on a US$ basis. Thus, we model the perspective of a U.S. investor. The returns were calculated at the end of each month. To measure returns from price changes and dividends, we consider performance indexes. The data on the market indexes were collected from the Datastream database.

[11]For details on these strategies, indexes, and data, see www.cisdm.org. Note that these indexes are not investable. There are also investable indexes available, for example, the Standard & Poors Managed Futures Index. However, due to the long time series and the broad basis of different CTA strategies, we chose the CISDM indexes that contain both closed and open funds. Furthermore, it must be noted that the database of CTAs exhibits different biases, which can affect the measurement result in the sense that index returns are too high. See William Fung and David A. Hsieh, "Survivorship Bias and Investment Style in the Returns of CTAs," *Journal of Portfolio Management* 24, no. 1 (1997), pp. 30–41; and William Fung and David A. Hsieh, "Performance Characteristics of Hedge Funds and Commodity Funds: Natural vs. Spurious Biases," *Journal of Financial and Quantitative Analysis* 35, no. 3 (2000), pp. 291–307.

PERFORMANCE ANALYSIS OF CTA RETURNS

There are two often-mentioned advantages of CTAs:[12] (1) CTAs exhibit attractive combinations of risk and return, which lead to a high risk-adjusted performance and (2) the low correlations of the CTA returns to the returns of traditional investments makes them appear to be very attractive diversification elements in a portfolio of traditional investments.

To investigate these two statements, our performance analysis is centered on four groups of financial ratios. First, the arithmetic mean of the historical monthly returns is analyzed as a return measure. Second, the standard deviation of the returns is considered as a risk measure. Third, we look at four risk-adjusted performance measures (Sharpe ratio, Omega measure, Sortino ratio, Calmar ratio) and, finally, the Bravais Pearson coefficient is used to measure the correlation between the returns of the investments.

In the performance analysis we consider the mean of the historical returns. It makes a difference whether this average return is computed arithmetically or geometrically. The arithmetic case assumes withdrawal of gains; the geometric case assumes reinvestment of gains. Since CTAs are usually analyzed in combination with an existing investment portfolio, the arithmetic method seems adequate for our purpose.[13] If T stands for the number of months being investigated and if the time-discrete return of security i in the month $t(t = 1, \ldots, T)$ is r_{it}, then the average return r_i^d is:

$$r_i^d = \frac{1}{T}\sum_{t=1}^{T} r_{it}. \tag{27.1}$$

The mean return is an indicator for the location of the return distribution; the standard deviation indicates the dispersion of the return distribution. The standard deviation accounts for both the positive and the negative deviations from the average value and is thus a measure for the total risk of an

[12]See Franklin R. Edwards and James M. Park, "Do Managed Futures Make Good Investments?" *Journal of Futures Markets* 16, no. 5 (1996), pp. 475–517; and Franklin R. Edwards and Jimmy Liew, "Hedge Funds versus Managed Futures as Asset Classes," *Journal of Derivatives* 6, no. 4 (1999), pp. 45–64.

[13]Arithmetic returns are used in the context of portfolio selection theory; see, for example, Roger G. Ibbotson and Peng Chen, "Long-Run Stock Returns: Participating in the Real Economy Stocks," *Financial Analysts Journal* 59, no. 1 (2003), pp. 88–98.

investment. The standard deviation σ_i of the security i is estimated as

$$\sigma_i = \sqrt{\frac{1}{T-1}\sum_{t=1}^{T}\left(r_{it} - r_i^d\right)^2}. \tag{27.2}$$

In investment performance analysis, risk-adjusted performance measures are generally used. With these measures, the return is set into relation with a suitable risk measure. The most widely known performance measure is the Sharpe ratio, which considers the relationship between the risk premium and the standard deviation of the returns generated by a fund.[14] The risk premium is the excess of the obtained return over the risk-free interest rate r_f. The Sharpe ratio (SR_i) is thus given by:

$$\mathrm{SR}_i = \frac{r_i^d - r_f}{\sigma_i}. \tag{27.3}$$

In addition to the Sharpe ratio, we analyze three other risk-adjusted performance measures that are particularly popular in CTA analysis: The Omega measure (O_i) considers the excess of the fund return over a minimal acceptable return τ in relation to the lower partial moments of order 1, the Sortino ratio (SOR_i) computes the excess of the fund return over τ in relation to the lower partial moments of order 2, and the Calmar ratio (CR_i) is the excess of the fund return over r_f divided by the maximum drawdown:[15]

$$\mathrm{O}_i = \frac{r_i^d - \tau}{\mathrm{LPM}_{1i}(\tau)} + 1 \tag{27.4}$$

$$\mathrm{SOR}_i = \frac{r_i^d - \tau}{\sqrt[2]{\mathrm{LPM}_{2i}(\tau)}} \tag{27.5}$$

$$\mathrm{CR}_i = \frac{r_i^d - r_f}{\mathrm{MD}_i} \tag{27.6}$$

Finally, we need the return correlations of the individual securities. The Bravais Pearson correlation coefficient gives the linear relationship between

[14]See William F. Sharpe, "Mutual Fund Performance," *Journal of Business* 39, no. 1 (1966), pp. 119–138.

[15]Note that τ is set to r_f in the following calculations. For more details on the performance measures, see Martin Eling and Frank Schuhmacher, "Does the Choice of Performance Measure Influence the Evaluation of Hedge Funds?" *Journal of Banking and Finance* 31, no. 9 (2007), pp. 2632–2647.

the returns of two securities. We calculate Bravais Pearson correlation coefficient $k_{i,j}$ of the securities i and j as

$$k_{i,j} = \left(\sum_{t=1}^{T}(r_{it} - r_i^d)(r_{jt} - r_j^d)\right) \Big/ \sqrt{\sum_{t=1}^{T}(r_{it} - r_i^d)^2 \sum_{t=1}^{T}(r_{jt} - r_j^d)^2}. \quad (27.7)$$

HISTORICAL CTA RETURNS

Analysis from 1996 to 2005

In this section, we analyze the financial ratios presented in the last section for the entire investigation period. We can thus clarify the two classical arguments in favor of investing in CTAs that were set out at the beginning of the last section. The results for the entire investigation period are also used as a benchmark for the following analysis of different time horizons and market conditions.

Exhibit 27.1 shows the mean return, the standard deviation, the four risk-adjusted performance measures, and the correlation with regard to different market indexes for the entire investigation period of January 1996 through December 2005 (we use the mean return of the JPM U.S. Cash 3 Month (0.30% per month) as the risk-free interest rate; note that the Calmar ratio cannot be calculated for the JPM U.S. Cash 3 Month because all returns of this index are positive).

The first argument in favor of CTA investment was that CTAs provide an attractive combination of risk and return, which leads to a high risk-adjusted performance. The results presented in Exhibit 27.1 support this argument: CTAs exhibit a much better performance than traditional investments. For example, the Sharpe ratio of the aggregated CTA indexes (0.16 for both indexes) exceeds the Sharpe ratio of the traditional investments and even lies above their maximum (i.e., 0.15 with the GPR General PSI Global). Four of the eight CTA indexes offer a higher performance than stocks, bonds, the money market, or real estate, with the CTA Asset Weighted Discretionary Index offering the highest performance of 0.30. Although most CTAs offer relatively high returns, the standard deviation of most of the CTA returns is between those of stocks and bonds. Based on the Sharpe ratio, we can thus conclude that many CTAs offer better combinations of risk and return than traditional investments do. These findings are confirmed by the other risk-adjusted performance measures.[16]

[16]Note that all figures are based on indexes and that the results of individual funds can differ substantially from these values.

EXHIBIT 27.1 Analysis of Total Investigation Period

Index	CTA Asset Weighted Index	CTA Equal Weighted Index	CTA Asset Weighted Currency Index	CTA Asset Weighted Discretionary Index	CTA Asset Weighted Diversified Index	CTA Asset Weighted Financials Index	CTA Asset Weighted Equity Index	CTA Asset Weighted Systematic Index	Stocks — MSCI World	Bonds — JPM Global Government Bond	Money — JPM US Cash 3 Month	Real Estate — GPR General PSI Global	Commodities — GS Commodity Index
Mean (%)	0.69	0.70	0.47	0.75	0.66	0.91	0.49	0.59	0.72	0.51	0.30	0.79	0.95
Standard deviation (%)	2.41	2.57	1.74	1.51	2.90	3.31	2.32	2.44	4.18	1.82	0.09	3.36	6.17
Sharpe ratio	0.16	0.16	0.10	0.30	0.12	0.18	0.08	0.12	0.10	0.11	0.00	0.15	0.11
Omega	1.52	1.49	1.30	2.30	1.38	1.63	1.27	1.37	1.29	1.35	1.00	1.44	1.30
Sortino ratio	0.27	0.27	0.16	0.66	0.21	0.33	0.12	0.20	0.14	0.19	0.00	0.21	0.17
Calmar ratio	0.05	0.05	0.02	0.10	0.03	0.04	0.01	0.04	0.01	0.03	Div/0	0.02	0.01
Correlation stocks	−0.05	−0.11	0.16	0.18	−0.09	−0.13	0.06	−0.04	1.00	0.01	−0.13	0.58	0.03
Correlation bonds	0.32	0.33	−0.01	0.15	0.30	0.35	0.11	0.31	0.01	1.00	0.01	0.10	0.13
Correlation money market	0.16	0.19	0.05	0.13	0.19	0.09	0.04	0.14	−0.13	0.01	1.00	−0.10	−0.16
Correlation real estate	0.09	0.09	0.15	0.17	0.08	0.04	0.09	0.10	0.58	0.10	−0.10	1.00	0.08
Correlation commodities	0.18	0.19	−0.06	0.11	0.19	0.16	−0.10	0.17	0.03	0.13	−0.16	0.08	1.00

Source: Exhibit created from data obtained from CISDM and Datastream.

The second argument in favor of CTA investment is that CTA returns exhibit low correlations to the returns of traditional investments. The results in Exhibit 27.1 are again supportive: Most CTAs show small correlations with stock markets, which is also true of the correlations with bonds, the money market, and real estate. For example, the correlation of the CTA Asset Weighted Index is –0.05 with stocks (MSCI World), 0.32 with bonds (JPM Global Government Bond), 0.16 with the money market (JPM U.S. Cash 3 Month), and 0.09 with real estate (GPR General PSI Global). The correlations of the CTA returns are also low with regard to commodities. For example, the correlation of the CTA Asset Weighted Index is 0.18 with the GS Commodity Index. Due to these low correlations, integrating CTAs into a portfolio of traditional investments seems promising within this model framework.

The analysis of the CTA indexes for the entire investigation period is very supportive of the classical arguments in favor of alternative investments. CTAs appear to be attractive investments both on a stand-alone basis and as elements of traditional investment portfolios. Will these results hold true when the investigation period is varied or if different market conditions are considered?

Analysis of Different Time Periods

To analyze the time stability of the results, the total investigation period of 10 years (120 monthly returns) is divided into four subperiods of equal length (i.e., 30 monthly returns each). Subsequently, all financial ratios (mean, standard deviation, Sharpe, Omega, Sortino, Calmar, and correlation) are determined for each subperiod. Exhibit 27.2 shows the results.

Exhibit 27.2 shows that for all financial ratios there is a strong variation of results for different time periods. For example, the returns of the CTA Asset Weighted Diversified Index vary between 0.26% per month (from July 2003 to December 2005) and 0.97% per month (from July 1998 to December 2000). However, we find that these variations in returns are much larger for traditional investments. For example, the returns of the MSCI World vary between –0.82% and 1.55% per month, and those of the GPR General PSI Global between 0.23% and 1.96% per month. Moreover, we notice that all CTA returns are positive for all time horizons, whereas in the case of traditional investments, there are also negative returns. Therefore, it seems that CTAs offer relatively stable returns compared to traditional investments.

The relative comparison of the returns of the various investments provides further interesting insights. In the period from January 2001 to June 2003, there are three CTA indexes offering higher returns than any of the

EXHIBIT 27.2 Analysis of Time Stability: Mean, Standard Deviation, Sharpe Ratio

Index		CTA Asset Weighted Index	CTA Equal Weighted Index	CTA Asset Weighted Currency Index	CTA Asset Weighted Discretionary Index	CTA Asset Weighted Diversified Index	CTA Asset Weighted Financials Index	CTA Asset Weighted Equity Index	CTA Asset Weighted Systematic Index	Stocks — MSCI World	Bonds — JPM Global Government Bond	Money — JPM US Cash 3 Month	Real Estate — GPR General PSI Global	Commodities — GS Commodity Index
Mean (%)	Total	0.69	0.70	0.47	0.75	0.66	0.91	0.49	0.59	0.72	0.51	0.30	0.79	0.95
	01.96–06.98	0.80	0.81	0.81	0.78	0.59	1.07	0.20	0.74	1.52	0.30	0.37	0.23	−0.11
	07.98–12.00	0.66	0.78	0.29	0.77	0.97	0.60	0.24	0.54	0.63	0.29	0.32	0.56	1.94
	01.01–06.03	0.81	0.81	0.48	0.75	0.82	1.08	0.84	0.63	−0.82	0.81	0.32	0.41	0.11
	07.03–12.05	0.48	0.39	0.32	0.70	0.26	0.86	0.68	0.46	1.55	0.62	0.18	1.96	1.86
Standard deviation(%)	Total	2.41	2.57	1.74	1.51	2.90	3.31	2.32	2.44	4.18	1.82	0.09	3.36	6.17
	01.96–06.98	2.69	2.65	1.91	1.70	3.23	3.79	1.80	3.01	3.19	1.18	0.05	4.01	4.47
	07.98–12.00	2.25	2.69	1.16	1.50	3.05	3.49	3.30	2.53	4.90	2.02	0.07	3.87	7.11
	01.01–06.03	2.67	2.94	1.86	0.88	2.86	3.51	2.59	2.47	5.28	2.05	0.07	2.63	6.62
	07.03–12.05	2.07	2.03	1.94	1.87	2.52	2.43	1.01	1.67	2.42	1.92	0.02	2.51	6.19
Sharpe ratio	Total	0.16	0.16	0.10	0.30	0.12	0.18	0.08	0.12	0.10	0.11	0.00	0.15	0.11
	01.96–06.98	0.16	0.16	0.23	0.24	0.07	0.18	−0.10	0.12	0.36	−0.06	0.00	−0.04	−0.11
	07.98–12.00	0.15	0.17	−0.02	0.30	0.21	0.08	−0.02	0.09	0.06	−0.01	0.00	0.06	0.23
	01.01–06.03	0.18	0.17	0.09	0.49	0.17	0.22	0.20	0.13	−0.22	0.24	0.00	0.03	−0.03
	07.03–12.05	0.14	0.11	0.07	0.28	0.03	0.28	0.49	0.17	0.57	0.23	0.00	0.71	0.27

(Continued)

EXHIBIT 27.2 (Continued)

Index		CTA Asset Weighted Index	CTA Equal Weighted Index	CTA Asset Weighted Currency Index	CTA Asset Weighted Discretionary Index	CTA Asset Weighted Diversified Index	CTA Asset Weighted Financials Index	CTA Asset Weighted Equity Index	CTA Asset Weighted Systematic Index	Stocks — MSCI World	Bonds — JPM Global Government Bond	Money — JPM US Cash 3 Month	Real Estate — GPR General PSI Global	Commodities — GS Commodity Index
Omega	Total	1.52	1.49	1.30	2.30	1.38	1.63	1.27	1.37	1.29	1.35	1.00	1.44	1.30
	01.96–06.98	1.87	1.89	2.02	2.01	1.38	2.27	0.63	1.68	3.43	0.83	1.00	0.78	0.39
	07.98–12.00	1.84	2.07	0.93	2.38	2.53	1.55	0.86	1.49	1.45	0.94	1.00	1.40	3.08
	01.01–06.03	2.09	2.01	1.41	2.57	2.05	2.51	2.26	1.71	−0.24	2.32	1.00	1.18	0.77
	07.03–12.05	2.00	1.68	1.43	3.17	1.22	3.40	3.84	2.06	6.38	2.72	1.00	7.86	3.90
Sortino ratio	Total	0.27	0.27	0.16	0.66	0.21	0.33	0.12	0.20	0.14	0.19	0.00	0.21	0.17
	01.96–06.98	0.49	0.53	0.69	0.79	0.19	0.66	−0.21	0.36	1.14	−0.13	0.00	−0.09	−0.27
	07.98–12.00	0.53	0.66	−0.05	1.01	0.93	0.29	−0.06	0.29	0.18	−0.04	0.00	0.18	0.83
	01.01–06.03	0.56	0.52	0.25	1.30	0.52	0.71	0.65	0.38	−0.52	0.85	0.00	0.09	−0.09
	07.03–12.05	0.48	0.33	0.21	1.26	0.10	1.05	2.02	0.54	2.51	0.76	0.00	2.33	0.92
Calmar ratio	Total	0.05	0.05	0.02	0.10	0.03	0.04	0.01	0.04	0.01	0.03	Div/0	0.02	0.01
	01.96–06.98	0.09	0.11	0.12	0.14	0.04	0.12	−0.03	0.07	0.17	−0.01	Div/0	−0.01	−0.02
	07.98–12.00	0.06	0.08	−0.01	0.10	0.12	0.02	0.00	0.03	0.02	0.00	Div/0	0.02	0.07
	01.01–06.03	0.08	0.07	0.02	0.39	0.08	0.07	0.05	0.05	−0.03	0.09	Div/0	0.01	−0.01
	07.03–12.05	0.04	0.02	0.02	0.14	0.01	0.11	0.33	0.05	0.37	0.10	Div/0	0.26	0.12

Source: Exhibit created from data obtained from CISDM and Datastream.

traditional indexes. However, in the period from January 1996 to June 1998 and in the period from July 2003 to December 2005, not a single CTA index offers a higher return compared to the traditional indexes. It thus seems that the relative evaluation of the different investments is vulnerable to change over time.

We also find large variations over time regarding the standard deviation of returns. For example, the standard deviation for the CTA Asset Weighted Equity Index varies between 2.43% and 3.79% per month. There is an even wider range of variation in the standard deviation of the CTA Asset Weighted Equity Index—from 1.01% to 3.30% per month. CTA Asset Weighted Equity thus appears to be very safe in the first investigation period but quite risky in the second investigation period.

Finally, we also observe large fluctuations in the risk-adjusted performance measures across the four subperiods. For example, the Sharpe ratio of the CTA Asset Weighted Equity Index runs between −0.02 and 0.49. However, once again, traditional investments show even larger fluctuations: the Sharpe ratio of the MSCI World varies between −0.22 and 0.57 and that of the GPR General PSI Global between −0.04 and 0.71. We thus conclude that CTAs have relatively stable performance compared to traditional investments. These findings are again confirmed by the other risk-adjusted performance measures. For example, the Omega of the CTA Asset Weighted Equity Index runs between 0.63 and 3.84, but that of the MSCI World between −0.24 and 6.38.

The relative evaluation of the Sharpe ratios produces results very similar to those found with the CTA returns. In the period from July 1998 to December 2000, there are six CTA indexes among the best seven indexes based on a Sharpe ratio ranking. However, in the period from January 1996 to June 1998 and in the period from July 2003 to December 2005, not a single CTA index offers a higher Sharpe ratio compared to traditional investments. Thus, it once again appears that CTA performance can vary widely over time. Based on the results shown in Exhibit 27.2, we do not find much support for the first argument in favor of CTA investment, which is that CTAs always offer attractive combinations of risk and return. However, it must be emphasized that this result is mostly due to the variations found for traditional investments because CTAs do provide quite stable positive returns independent of the time period considered. This is certainly an attractive feature for most investors.

Exhibit 27.3 shows the Bravais Pearson coefficients of correlation of the CTA returns with stocks, bonds, the money market, and real estate returns for the four subperiods.

According to the results set out in Exhibit 27.3, the correlations are also subject to strong fluctuations over time. For example, the correlations for

EXHIBIT 27.3 Analysis of Time Stability: Correlation

Index		CTA Asset Weighted Index	CTA Equal Weighted Index	CTA Asset Weighted Currency Index	CTA Asset Weighted Discretionary Index	CTA Asset Weighted Diversified Index	CTA Asset Weighted Financials Index	CTA Asset Weighted Equity Index	CTA Asset Weighted Systematic Index	Stocks — MSCI World	Bonds — JPM Global Government Bond	Money — JPM US Cash 3 Month	Real Estate — GPR General PSI Global	Commodities — GS Commodity Index
Correlation	Total	−0.05	−0.11	0.16	0.18	−0.09	−0.13	0.06	−0.04	1.00	0.01	−0.13	0.58	0.03
Stocks	01.96–06.98	0.38	0.41	0.03	0.26	0.41	0.32	0.46	0.41	1.00	0.09	0.07	0.76	0.01
	07.98–12.00	−0.25	−0.32	−0.12	0.26	−0.31	−0.37	0.16	−0.35	1.00	0.13	0.01	0.53	0.07
	01.01–06.03	−0.40	−0.45	0.33	−0.29	−0.48	−0.39	−0.25	−0.28	1.00	−0.18	−0.38	0.64	0.01
	07.03–12.05	0.63	0.62	0.43	0.58	0.65	0.42	0.46	0.54	1.00	0.27	0.08	0.54	−0.05
Correlation	Total	0.32	0.33	−0.01	0.15	0.30	0.35	0.11	0.31	0.01	1.00	0.01	0.10	0.13
Bonds	01.96–06.98	−0.08	−0.12	−0.38	−0.12	−0.04	−0.03	0.07	−0.10	0.09	1.00	−0.20	−0.04	0.10
	07.98–12.00	0.37	0.34	−0.08	0.07	0.36	0.45	0.18	0.37	0.13	1.00	0.33	0.08	0.16
	01.01–06.03	0.46	0.51	−0.14	0.36	0.44	0.53	0.04	0.46	−0.18	1.00	−0.10	−0.03	0.37
	07.03–12.05	0.44	0.48	0.41	0.33	0.39	0.34	0.05	0.54	0.27	1.00	0.56	0.44	−0.15
Correlation	Total	0.16	0.19	0.05	0.13	0.19	0.09	0.04	0.14	−0.13	0.01	1.00	−0.10	−0.16
Money Market	01.96–06.98	0.24	0.21	0.28	0.19	0.25	0.17	−0.19	0.25	0.07	−0.20	1.00	0.22	0.05
	07.98–12.00	0.34	0.31	0.20	0.25	0.29	0.22	0.18	0.27	0.01	0.33	1.00	0.23	−0.10
	01.01–06.03	0.09	0.16	−0.40	0.29	0.20	0.05	0.26	0.03	−0.38	−0.10	1.00	−0.30	−0.30
	07.03–12.05	0.04	0.16	−0.05	0.10	0.04	0.01	−0.06	0.06	0.08	0.56	1.00	0.35	0.01
Correlation	Total	0.09	0.09	0.15	0.17	0.08	0.04	0.09	0.10	0.58	0.10	−0.10	1.00	0.08
Real Estate	01.96–06.98	0.34	0.37	0.02	0.22	0.41	0.27	0.21	0.35	0.76	−0.04	0.22	1.00	0.14

	07.98–12.00	–0.04	–0.03	0.14	0.08	–0.14	–0.06	0.05	–0.08	0.53	0.08	0.23	1.00	0.11
	01.01–06.03	–0.32	–0.31	0.38	–0.17	–0.37	–0.39	–0.11	–0.19	0.64	–0.03	–0.30	1.00	0.18
	07.03–12.05	0.45	0.45	0.26	0.44	0.43	0.39	0.43	0.34	0.54	0.44	0.35	1.00	–0.24
Correlation	Total	0.18	0.19	–0.06	0.11	0.19	0.16	–0.10	0.17	0.03	0.13	–0.16	0.08	1.00
Commodities	01.96–06.98	0.10	0.10	–0.10	0.16	0.10	0.15	0.09	0.08	0.01	0.10	0.05	0.14	1.00
	07.98–12.00	0.19	0.16	0.08	0.15	0.12	0.22	–0.13	0.16	0.07	0.16	–0.10	0.11	1.00
	01.01–06.03	0.39	0.35	0.14	0.23	0.37	0.37	–0.17	0.44	0.01	0.37	–0.30	0.18	1.00
	07.03–12.05	0.04	0.12	–0.29	0.01	0.18	–0.13	–0.05	0.00	–0.05	–0.15	0.01	–0.24	1.00

Source: Exhibit created from data obtained from CISDM and Datastream.

the CTA Asset Weighted Diversified Index and the MSCI World vary between −0.48 (from January 2001 to June 2003) and 0.65 (from July 2003 to December 2005). Comparable changes can be found for other CTA indexes, for example, the CTA Asset Weighted Index (from −0.40 to 0.63 with stocks) and the CTA Asset Weighted Currency Index (from −0.38 to 0.40 with bonds). Therefore, the second argument in favor of CTA investment (CTA returns exhibit low correlations with the returns of traditional investments) also seems open to criticism, since the input parameters are not too stable over time.

Analysis of Different Market Environments

We now analyze different market environments and their effect on the financial ratios. Therefore, all 120 monthly returns are arranged according to size and divided into four groups. Market environment "—"covers the 30 smallest returns of the traditional market index and thus represents a very bad market condition. Market environment "−" contains the 30 following returns and illustrates a bad market condition. In similar style, "+" and "++" stand for a good and a very good market environment, respectively.[17] Exhibit 27.4 shows the market environment analysis for the MSCI World index.[18]

Comparing the four market environments, we find that most CTA strategies achieve positive returns independent of the market environment. For example, the returns of the CTA Asset Weighted Index are relatively high both in a very bad (i.e., —) and a very good (++) market environment. Furthermore, this index exhibits its highest returns in a good (+) market environment and its lowest returns in a bad market environment (−). The returns of the CTA Asset Weighted Index are also displayed in Exhibit 27.5, together with those of the CTA Asset Weighted Currency Index, the CTA Asset Weighted Discretionary Index, and the MSCI World.

The return profiles of the CTA Asset Weighted Currency Index and the CTA Asset Weighted Discretionary Index are very different from that of the MSCI World. Both indexes provide returns near zero in a negative market environment and positive returns in a positive market environment. Comparable results can be found for other CTA indexes. In the literature, the return profile of these indexes is compared with those of options because it

[17]See Magnus Könberg and Martin Lindberg, "Hedge Funds: A Review of Historical Performance," *Journal of Alternative Investments* 4, no. 1 (2001), pp. 21–31.

[18]Note that we cannot analyze the Calmar ratio in different market environments, because calculation of this measure requires a time series analysis over a certain investment period.

EXHIBIT 27.4 Analysis of Market Environments: Mean, Standard Deviation, Sharpe Ratio

Index		CTA Asset Weighted Index	CTA Equal Weighted Index	CTA Asset Weighted Currency Index	CTA Asset Weighted Discretionary Index	CTA Asset Weighted Diversified Index	CTA Asset Weighted Financials Index	CTA Asset Weighted Equity Index	CTA Asset Weighted Systematic Index	Stocks — MSCI World	Bonds — JPM Global Government Bond	Money — JPM US Cash 3 Month	Real Estate — GPR General PSI Global	Commodities — GS Commodity Index
Mean (%)	Total	0.69	0.70	0.47	0.75	0.66	0.91	0.49	0.59	0.72	0.51	0.30	0.79	0.95
	—	0.71	0.94	0.07	0.19	0.73	1.38	0.16	0.52	−4.88	0.33	0.31	−1.49	0.29
	-	0.01	−0.08	0.45	0.42	−0.28	−0.02	0.24	0.13	−0.09	0.64	0.29	−0.34	0.85
	+	1.25	1.30	0.72	1.39	1.42	1.45	0.74	1.13	2.20	0.31	0.30	1.83	1.97
	++	0.77	0.63	0.66	1.00	0.78	0.82	0.82	0.60	5.64	0.74	0.29	3.16	0.69
Standard deviation(%)	Total	2.41	2.57	1.74	1.51	2.90	3.31	2.32	2.44	4.18	1.82	0.09	3.36	6.17
	—	2.58	2.92	1.56	1.19	3.38	3.49	3.40	2.59	2.84	2.34	0.08	3.86	6.53
	-	2.10	2.25	1.92	1.09	2.61	2.74	1.90	2.32	0.90	1.63	0.09	2.56	5.79
	+	2.18	2.32	1.59	1.50	2.62	3.09	1.47	2.39	0.61	1.65	0.12	2.23	5.72
	++	2.68	2.66	1.86	1.90	2.81	3.78	2.11	2.48	1.47	1.60	0.08	2.48	6.77
Sharpe ratio	Total	0.16	0.16	0.10	0.30	0.12	0.18	0.08	0.12	0.10	0.11	0.00	0.15	0.11
	—	0.16	0.22	−0.15	−0.10	0.12	0.31	−0.05	0.08	−1.83	0.01	0.00	−0.47	0.00
	-	−0.14	−0.16	0.08	0.12	−0.22	−0.11	−0.03	−0.07	−0.43	0.22	0.00	−0.25	0.10
	—	0.44	0.43	0.27	0.72	0.43	0.37	0.30	0.35	3.15	0.01	0.00	0.69	0.29
	++	0.18	0.13	0.20	0.37	0.17	0.14	0.25	0.12	3.63	0.28	0.00	1.16	0.06

(Continued)

EXHIBIT 27.4 (Continued)

Index		CTA Asset Weighted Index	CTA Equal Weighted Index	CTA Asset Weighted Currency Index	CTA Asset Weighted Discretionary Index	CTA Asset Weighted Diversified Index	CTA Asset Weighted Financials Index	CTA Asset Weighted Equity Index	CTA Asset Weighted Systematic Index	Stocks — MSCI World	Bonds — JPM Global Government Bond	Money — JPM US Cash 3 Month	Real Estate — GPR General PSI Global	Commodities — GS Commodity Index
Omega	Total	1.52	1.49	1.30	2.30	1.38	1.63	1.27	1.37	1.29	1.35	1.00	1.44	1.30
	—	1.92	2.37	0.42	0.67	1.82	3.35	0.72	1.45	–2.39	1.05	1.00	–1.13	0.98
	–	0.36	0.22	1.40	1.43	–0.07	0.36	0.87	0.63	–0.05	2.09	1.00	–0.11	1.79
	+	3.86	3.97	2.28	5.19	4.20	3.99	2.43	3.41	9.62	1.03	1.00	5.79	3.89
	++	2.10	1.77	2.00	3.30	2.10	2.01	2.50	1.69	25.35	2.39	1.00	11.70	1.46
Sortino ratio	Total	0.27	0.27	0.16	0.66	0.21	0.33	0.12	0.20	0.14	0.19	0.00	0.21	0.17
	—	0.52	0.82	–0.34	–0.22	0.44	1.22	–0.12	0.25	–1.75	0.03	0.00	–0.89	–0.01
	–	–0.34	–0.42	0.25	0.33	–0.50	–0.32	–0.06	–0.19	–0.75	0.70	0.00	–0.56	0.29
	+	1.81	1.92	0.77	3.26	1.88	1.61	0.82	1.49	7.47	0.02	0.00	2.59	1.11
	++	0.57	0.38	0.64	1.67	0.54	0.45	0.80	0.37	21.08	1.04	0.00	7.17	0.19

Source: Exhibit created from data obtained from CISDM and Datastream.

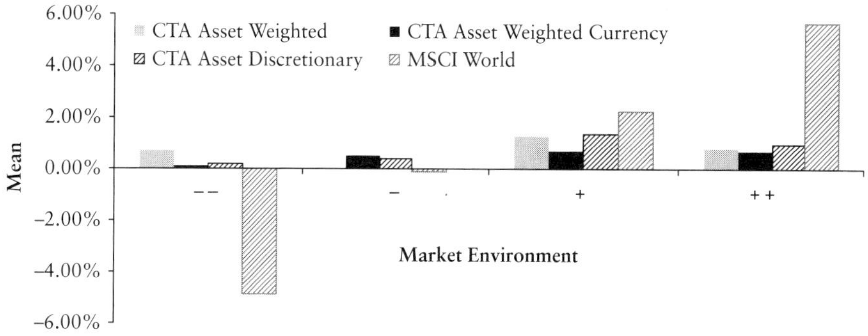

EXHIBIT 27.5 Analysis of Market Environments
Source: Exhibit created from data obtained from CISDM and Datastream.

is similar to a call option on the MSCI World.[19] Investors should take note of the fact that they could be creating an option-like risk-return profile by adding managed futures to their portfolios.

Moreover, Exhibit 27.4 again shows that the results of classical performance measurement are unstable. For example, the standard deviation of the returns of the CTA Asset Weighted Equity Index varies from 1.47% to 3.40% per month. Again, this index seems to be very safe in the first market condition and quite risky in the second market condition. The Sharpe ratio of the CTA Asset Weighted Discretionary Index is between −0.10 and 0.72. CTAs offer a higher Sharpe ratio than traditional investments only in one of the four market environments (i.e., the very bad market environment "—"). It thus seems that the first argument in favor of CTA investment (attractive risk-return combinations, high performance) does not hold true for all market environments. But again the performance numbers of CTAs are more stable than those of traditional investments.

There is empirical evidence that the correlations of hedge fund returns compared to the returns of traditional investments are relatively high if the market environment is very bad.[20] This characteristic might displease investors who are seeking stable portfolio returns in falling stock markets. Does this result also hold for CTAs? Exhibit 27.6 shows the Bravais Pearson coefficients of correlation of the CTA returns with stocks, bonds, the money market, real estate, and commodities across different market environments.

[19]See Fung and Hsieh, "Survivorship Bias and Investment Style in the Returns of CTAs."
[20]See, for example, Könberg and Lindberg, "Hedge Funds: A Review of Historical Performance."

EXHIBIT 27.6 Analysis of Market Environments: Correlation

Index		CTA Asset Weighted Index	CTA Equal Weighted Index	CTA Asset Weighted Currency Index	CTA Asset Weighted Discretionary Index	CTA Asset Weighted Diversified Index	CTA Asset Weighted Financials Index	CTA Asset Weighted Equity Index	CTA Asset Weighted Systematic Index	Stocks — MSCI World	Bonds — JPM Global Government Bond	Money — JPM US Cash 3 Month	Real Estate — GPR General PSI Global	Commodities — GS Commodity Index
Correlation Stocks	Total	−0.05	−0.11	0.16	0.18	−0.09	−0.13	0.06	−0.04	1.00	0.01	−0.13	0.58	0.03
	—	−0.40	−0.48	0.29	−0.32	−0.56	−0.40	−0.18	−0.35	1.00	−0.29	−0.42	0.42	0.09
	–	0.21	0.21	0.14	0.38	0.15	0.18	0.00	0.20	1.00	0.06	−0.07	0.39	−0.13
	+	−0.25	−0.14	−0.19	−0.10	−0.20	−0.30	0.30	−0.21	1.00	−0.07	−0.03	−0.14	0.24
	++	−0.27	−0.28	−0.04	−0.13	−0.25	−0.29	−0.15	−0.29	1.00	0.20	0.10	0.02	−0.26
Correlation Bonds	Total	0.32	0.33	−0.01	0.15	0.30	0.35	0.11	0.31	0.01	1.00	0.01	0.10	0.13
	—	0.49	0.44	−0.08	0.41	0.45	0.54	0.28	0.42	−0.29	1.00	0.29	−0.05	0.28
	–	0.02	0.02	−0.10	0.16	0.01	0.10	0.03	0.10	0.06	1.00	−0.34	0.15	−0.04
	+	0.40	0.45	0.02	0.05	0.38	0.50	−0.35	0.37	−0.07	1.00	0.05	0.16	0.22
	++	0.34	0.44	0.13	0.07	0.36	0.25	0.13	0.35	0.20	1.00	−0.03	0.29	0.01
Correlation Money Market	Total	0.16	0.19	0.05	0.13	0.19	0.09	0.04	0.14	−0.13	0.01	1.00	−0.10	−0.16
	—	0.25	0.25	−0.19	0.50	0.31	0.15	0.24	0.10	−0.42	0.29	1.00	−0.08	−0.10
	–	0.18	0.19	0.28	0.22	0.15	0.07	−0.08	0.03	−0.07	−0.34	1.00	−0.11	−0.28
	+	0.37	0.39	0.36	0.39	0.40	0.19	−0.14	0.45	−0.03	0.05	1.00	−0.13	−0.23
	++	−0.18	−0.16	−0.36	−0.38	−0.22	−0.09	0.03	−0.16	0.10	−0.03	1.00	−0.01	−0.03

Correlation Real Estate	Total	0.09	0.09	0.15	0.17	0.08	0.04	0.09	0.10	0.58	0.10	–0.10	1.00	0.08
	—	–0.07	–0.14	0.28	0.09	–0.14	–0.19	–0.17	–0.02	0.42	–0.05	–0.08	1.00	–0.01
	–	0.10	0.18	–0.05	0.18	0.11	0.18	0.28	0.11	0.39	0.15	–0.11	1.00	–0.10
	+	0.15	0.19	0.11	–0.18	0.07	0.29	–0.20	0.09	–0.14	0.16	–0.13	1.00	0.29
	++	0.15	0.28	–0.01	0.05	0.24	0.10	0.43	0.19	0.02	0.29	–0.01	1.00	0.15
Correlation Commodities	Total	0.18	0.19	–0.06	0.11	0.19	0.16	–0.10	0.17	0.03	0.13	–0.16	0.08	1.00
	—	0.26	0.22	0.18	0.19	0.16	0.20	–0.06	0.26	0.09	0.28	–0.10	–0.01	1.00
	–	–0.02	–0.05	–0.42	–0.24	0.05	–0.01	–0.12	0.03	–0.13	–0.04	–0.28	–0.10	1.00
	+	0.02	0.17	–0.18	0.01	0.17	–0.05	–0.31	–0.04	0.24	0.22	–0.23	0.29	1.00
	++	0.34	0.33	0.11	0.24	0.31	0.39	–0.07	0.35	–0.26	0.01	–0.03	0.15	1.00

Source: Exhibit created from data obtained from CISDM and Datastream.

We cannot confirm the above-mentioned findings for CTAs since the correlations in the bad market environment are, in general, not higher than in a good market environment. For example, the correlation of the CTA Asset Weighted Index with stocks is −0.27 in a very good market environment and −0.40 in a very bad market environment. Comparable results can be found with the other traditional indexes; e.g., the correlation of the CTA Asset Weighted Index with commodities is 0.34 if the market is very good and 0.26 if the market is very bad.

CTAs thus prove to be good portfolio diversifiers in all market environments. It also seems that CTAs are better portfolio diversifiers than hedge funds because they do not show the unattractive high correlations in bad market environments that have been documented in the hedge fund literature.[21]

CONCLUSION

CTAs are often analyzed using classical performance measures (e.g., Sharpe ratio) or the classical Markowitz portfolio selection model. Due to their specific risk-return profile and their small correlation with traditional investments, CTAs are very attractive investments within this model framework. We confirm this finding on the basis of the Center for International Securities and Derivatives Markets (CISDM) CTA indexes in the period from 1996 to 2005.

However, we also found that the attractiveness of CTA investments can vary depending on what time period or market environment is looked at. For some time periods, almost all CTA indexes offered a better performance than traditional market indexes, but in other time periods, there is hardly any index that exceeds the performance of traditional investments. However, it must be emphasized that the largest variations in performance measurement results were not found for CTAs but for traditional investments. Compared to traditional investments, CTAs provide quite stable positive returns independent of the time period considered. Additionally, we found that CTAs differ from hedge funds in that in a bad market environment, their return correlation with traditional investments is not particularly high, as is the case with hedge funds. It thus seems that CTAs are better portfolio diversifiers than hedge funds.

[21]See, for example, Könberg and Lindberg, "Hedge Funds: A Review of Historical Performance."

Classical performance analysis is based on input parameters that are unstable over time and across different market environments. This fact has a large impact on the evaluation of CTAs by means of classical performance measures because, depending on the time period or the market environment, CTAs can look like either very attractive or very unattractive investments. We thus recommend caution in interpreting the results of classical performance measures.

CHAPTER 28

Catching Future Stars Among Micro-CTAs

Greg N. Gregoriou, Ph.D.
Professor of Finance
State University of New York (Plattsburgh)

Fabrice Douglas Rouah, Ph.D.
Vice President
State Street Corporation

When it comes to investing in *commodity trading advisors* (CTAs), institutional investors often prefer funds with higher assets under management as microsized CTAs suffer from high mortality rates and often display returns that are very volatile. Some microsized CTAs, however, have the potential to evolve into future stars that post superior performance and survive a long time. The desire to identify these potential stars must be balanced with the need to avoid funds that die off prematurely. While some microsized CTAs become stars, they arise from a pool of funds that are at very high risk of death. This high risk of death, however, does not necessarily extend to all micro-CTAs. This chapter investigates the potential of microsized CTAs to evolve into future stars.

CTAs AND THEIR ASSETS

When investors decide to select a CTA for inclusion in their portfolio, their first inclination is typically to select according to performance and size.

The views expressed in this chapter are those of the authors and not necessarily those of the State Street Corporation.

Small funds are often discarded, out of fear that these CTAs may not thrive in the long run. Investors view small funds as potential failures, especially if these funds have not performed up to par. Moreover, small funds tend to have higher volatility than large funds, which again may ward off potential investors. On the other hand, small CTAs may be eager to develop a good reputation and therefore may be more aggressive than larger CTAs, more nimble, less passive in their investment strategies and less risk averse, and their small size may allow them to execute trades more efficiently. Hence, their potential for good returns may make them attractive investments. Some CTAs, however, start out very large. These funds are typically created by well-known individuals that have been trading managed futures for many years, and eventually decide to strike out on their own. Because of their reputation, these individuals are able to attract large amounts of capital, often from existing clients, and launch their funds with a large initial capital base.

Small CTAs can usually raise enough money to reach a critical mass, whereby their operating expenses are guaranteed to be covered by their management fee, especially during bad times when their performance fee is not being earned.[1] Small CTAs that do not reach critical mass have a tendency to underperform large CTAs because of the high expense ratios that erode their returns. Institutional investors, pension funds, and endowment funds typically require a three- to five-year track record before allocating any assets to a CTA. They prefer large funds over small funds because large funds tend to have longer track records and a broader client base. CTAs that fail to attract a large amount of capital in order to meet operating expenses may face a rapid death. The results of this chapter show that this can be the case. Nonetheless, some very small CTAs tend to perform well and stay in operation a long time. Investors may wish to invest in a small CTA in the hope that the CTA will develop into a future star, and before the CTA refuses new capital because of capacity constraints. CTAs often define a targeted asset size when launching their fund. Once that size is reached, they refuse new money because if they grow too large, they cannot move in and out of positions as quickly as smaller funds can. This is especially true for CTAs that operate in illiquid markets.

The number of micro-CTAs—which we define as those with less than $10 million under management during their first two years of operation—has grown at an exponential rate since the mid 1990s, according to the Barclay Trading Group database (www.barclaygrp.com). Some micro-CTAs reach critical mass and continue to gather momentum and attract capital, but in this chapter we find that more than 70% of CTAs with less than $10

[1]The median management and incentive fees for live and dead micro- and large CTAs are 2% and 20%, respectively.

million in assets are dead. Hence, investors wishing to invest in CTAs during the early phases of a CTA's operation are faced with a dilemma. On one hand, they would like to select future stars, but on the other hand, they are selecting from a pool for which the attrition rate is very high. A high attrition rate[2] implies that over a given period, many funds in a pool of CTAs will die before the end of the period. Since funds usually die with poor returns, holding a portfolio of funds that are subject to a high attrition rate will lead to erosion in performance.

In this chapter, we show how survival analysis can be a useful tool for screening and selection of these CTAs, and help rationalize the trade-off between the need to select future winners, and the very risky pool of CTAs from which these future winners eventually emerge.

MORTALITY AND SURVIVORSHIP BIAS OF CTAS

A number of studies have shown that the mortality of CTAs is usually high. Brown, Goetzmann, and Park estimated the median survival time of CTAs at 24 months, and found a yearly attrition rate of 20%, even higher for young funds.[3] Diz observed nearly one half of CTAs in his sample to die over the 1989 to 1995 period.[4] Spurgin found a yearly attrition of 22% in 1994 to 1995, with a vast majority of smaller CTAs dying.[5] The results of Fung and Hsieh are comparable. They found an average annualized attrition rate of 19.0% during 1989 to 1995, with a high of 25% in 1995, and an overall mortality rate of 52% over the 1989 to 1994 period.[6] Gregoriou, Hübner, Papageorgiou, and Rouah[7] estimate the median survival time of CTAs at 4.42 years, using the Barclay database from 1990 to 2003. They

[2]Attrition rates are usually calculated annually, as a proportion. For example, if a portfolio consists of 100 funds at the beginning of the year, and if five funds die before the end of the year, then the annual attrition rate is 5%.

[3]Stephen J. Brown, William N. Goetzmann, and James T. Park, "Careers and Survival: Competition and Risk in the Hedge Fund and CTA Industry," *Journal of Finance* (October 2001), pp. 1869–1886.

[4]Fernando Diz, "Is Performance Related to Survival?" Working Paper, The Barclay Group, 1996.

[5]Richard Spurgin, "A Study of Survival: Commodity Trading Advisors, 1988–1996," *Journal of Alternative Investments* (Winter 1999), pp. 16–22.

[6]William Fung and David A. Hsieh, "Survivorship Bias and Investment Style in the Returns of CTAs," *Journal of Portfolio Management* (Fall 1997), pp. 30–42.

[7]Greg N. Gregoriou, Georges Hübner, Nicolas Papageorgiou, and Fabrice Rouah, "Survival of Commodity Trading Advisors: 1990–2003," *Journal of Futures Markets* 25, no. 8 (2005), pp. 795–816.

find that large CTAs with good performance and low margin-to-equity ratios live longer, on average, reflecting the superior performance of CTAs when liquidity constraints do not affect their trading strategies.

Other studies have shown that, in general, live CTAs post better significant performance than dead CTAs. Ths implies that the survivorship bias[8] in CTA databases is likely to be a problem. Fung and Hsieh found an average monthly return of 0.81% and 1.61% for dead and live CTAs, respectively, over the 1989 to 1995 period, comparable to those found by Billingsley and Chance.[9] According to Diz[10] the annual difference between live and dead CTAs is approximately 9%, while Fung and Hsieh,[11] find approximately 3.5%. Diz[12] estimates the survivorship bias of randomly selected portfolios at roughly 4.5% per year.

In this chapter, we take a slightly different approach and examine the performance and life cycle of micro-CTAs exclusively, over a substantially longer time horizon than in previous studies. We show that some micro-CTAs are able to grow in size and produce future returns that are above those of most CTAs, so that future stars are more likely to emerge from CTAs that start out microsized than from CTAs that start out large. We also show that the life expectancy of micro-CTAs depends on a number of predictor variables representing performance, size, fees, and classification, and that future stars survive substantially longer than other micro-CTAs.

DATA AND METHODOLOGY

The data set consists of 546 live and 965 defunct CTAs reporting monthly returns net of management and performance fees to the Barclay Group database during the January 1988 to December 2005 time frame, a total of 216 months. Among these CTAs, 344 live and 829 dead funds managed less than $10 million during their first two years of existence, and are thus classified as micro-CTAs. Exhibit 28.1 presents statistics on the micro-CTAs in our sample, classified by survival status (live or dead), and in increments of

[8]Survivorship bias is introduced when historical returns are calculated using live funds only, and omitting dead funds. Since dead funds usually have poor returns, ignoring survivorship bias leads to overestimates of historical performance.

[9]Randall Billingsley and Donald M. Chance, "Benefits and Limitations of Diversification among Commodity Trading Advisors," *Journal of Portfolio Management* (Fall 1996), pp. 65–80.

[10]Diz, "Is Performance Related to Survival?"

[11]Fung and Hsieh, "Survivorship Bias and Investment Style in the Returns of CTAs."

[12]Diz, "Is Performance Related to Survival?"

EXHIBIT 28.1 Statistics of Live and Dead CTAs by Size

	Live CTAs			Dead CTAs		
Size Classification	Number	Mean Return	S.D.[a]	Number	Mean Return	S.D.[a]
\$0M–\$0.5M	73 (20%)	2.28	11.07	294 (80%)	1.77	12.23
\$0.5M–\$1M	40 (24%)	1.91	7.83	126 (76%)	1.75	10.21
\$1M–\$2M	62 (32%)	1.77	7.13	133 (68%)	1.79	9.17
\$2M–\$3M	38 (34%)	1.84	7.39	75 (66%)	1.44	7.67
\$3M–\$4M	34 (39%)	1.48	5.52	53 (61%)	1.84	7.41
\$4M–\$5M	24 (36%)	1.39	5.70	42 (64%)	1.52	7.64
\$5M–\$10M	73 (41%)	1.55	6.80	106 (59%)	1.63	7.28
Total \$0M–\$10M	344 (29%)	1.82	8.09	829 (71%)	1.72	10.13
> \$10M	202 (60%)	1.11	5.25	136 (40%)	1.17	7.19
All CTAs	546 (36%)	1.16	6.46	965 (64%)	1.07	8.84

[a]Monthly standard deviation.

the average assets under management during their first two years of life. In the Barclay database, all CTAs stay alive until they stop reporting their net monthly returns for three consecutive months, at which time they are deemed dead and are transferred to the dead group. However, they may subsequently reenter the database at any time and their returns at that point will be backfilled.

The CTA classifications that we use in this chapter are presented in Exhibit 28.2. Discretionary and Systematic are trading styles and are not examined, whereas others classifications are usually considered as portfolios of options and futures.

EXHIBIT 28.2 Definition of CTA Classifications

Classification	Definition
Agricultural	Traders who trade exclusively agricultural and meat markets
Currency	Traders who trade currencies exclusively
Diversified	Traders who trade a diversified portfolio including most of the major sectors
Energy	Traders who trade exclusively in energy markets
Financial/Metals	Traders who trade at least two of the following: currencies, interest rates, stock indexes, precious metals
Interest Rates	Traders who trade futures contracts whereby the underlying asset is in the form of a debt obligation.

Source: The Barclay Group.

We use the Kaplan-Meier (KM) estimator to estimate the survival function defined as $S(t) = \Pr(T > t)$, which is the probability that a CTA will survive past time t. With the KM estimator $\hat{S}(t)$ we obtain the median survival time, defined as the age at which one half of the funds die, as well as the mean survival time, obtained by integrating $\hat{S}(t)$ over all values of t. We use the actuarial estimator to estimate the hazard function and produce hazard plots. Finally, we use the *accelerated failure time* (AFT) survival model to investigate the dependency of micro-CTA survival time on predictor variables. This model assumes that the survival time T has the log-linear form

$$\log(T) = \alpha + \beta^T X + \sigma\varepsilon$$

where α is the intercept, X and β are vectors of predictor variables and coefficients, ε is a random disturbance. We select the generalized gamma distribution for T, since we find this distribution to produce a better fit to the micro-CTA survival times than other distributions we attempted, such as the Weibull distribution.[13]

EMPIRICAL RESULTS

Size, Survival, and Returns

As shown in Exhibit 28.1, there exists a positive relationship between survival and size. In particular, among CTAs with less than \$0.5 million in assets during their first two years of existence, 80% die before the end of the observation period. Among funds with more than \$10 million, however, 40% die. The mortality rate for the entire cohort of micro-CTAs (0 to \$10 million) is high, as more than 70% die. However, Exhibit 28.1 shows that the performance of micro-CTAs can be very good. Indeed, the smallest live CTAs post the largest mean monthly return during the first two years of existence, 2.28%. With a monthly standard deviation of 11.07%, however, these CTAs are quite volatile. Nonetheless, Exhibit 28.1 shows a tendency for small CTAs to post good performance, even among those that eventually die. The performance of dead micro-CTAs (1.72%) is even higher than that of live CTAs with more than \$10 million in assets (1.11%). These results present the first evidence that despite their high mortality rate, there are good investment opportunities among the micro-CTAs that eventually survive.

[13]Jack D. Kalbfleisch and Ross L. Prentice, *The Statistical Analysis of Failure Time Data* (New York: John Wiley & Sons, 2002).

EXHIBIT 28.3 Survival Time of CTAs, by Size Classification

Size Classification (in millions)	Median Survival Time (year)	95% Confidence Interval (year)	Mean Survival Time (year)	Standard Error (year)
\$0m–\$0.5m	3.7	(3.3, 4.2)	4.7	0.2
\$0.5m–\$1m	3.9	(3.5, 4.4)	5.1	0.3
\$1m–\$2m	4.7	(4.1, 5.1)	5.5	0.2
\$2m–\$3m	4.9	(4.3, 5.8)	6.3	0.5
\$3m–\$4m	4.4	(3.4, 5.5)	6.2	0.5
\$4m–\$5m	5.5	(3.9, 6.8)	6.3	0.5
\$5m–\$10m	5.2	(4.6, 6.2)	6.6	0.4
Total \$0m–\$10m	4.3	(4.0, 4.6)	5.6	0.1
> \$10m	6.8	(6.2, 7.9)	8.4	0.3
All CTAs	4.7	(4.4, 4.9)	6.1	0.1

Exhibit 28.3 presents estimates of how long micro-CTAs can be expected to survive. It presents estimates of the median survival time and 95% confidence interval, and of the mean survival time and its standard error. Similar to Exhibit 28.1, it shows an increasing pattern of longevity with size. The median survival time of the smallest group of CTAs is only 3.7 years, but for those in the \$5 million to \$10 million category, the median survival time is 5.2 years and for the large CTAs (with more than \$10 million in average assets) it nearly doubles, to 6.8 years. Exhibit 28.1 has shown that despite their good returns, the mortality of micro-CTAs is high. In addition, Exhibit 28.3 indicates that, unfortunately, those that avoid mortality do so for a short time only, roughly 4.3 years. The median survival time of all CTAs is 4.7 years, close to the value of 4.42 years obtained by Gregoriou et al.[14]

To investigate the risk of death of micro-CTAs more closely, in Exhibit 28.4 we plot the hazard function estimated from the actuarial estimator for $S(t)$, for CTAs with \$0 to \$5 millions in assets during the first two years of life (solid line), for CTAs with \$5 millions to \$10 millions (dashed line), and for CTAs with more than \$10 millions (dotted line). The hazards are roughly proportional to one another, although the hazard decreases with size, which reflects the findings of Exhibits 28.1 and 28.3 that small funds are at increased risk of death relative to larger ones. Note that in all three categories, the hazard is not constant. It starts out small, rises

[14]Gregoriou, Hübner, Papageorgiou, and Rouah, "Survival of Commodity Trading Advisors: 1990–2003."

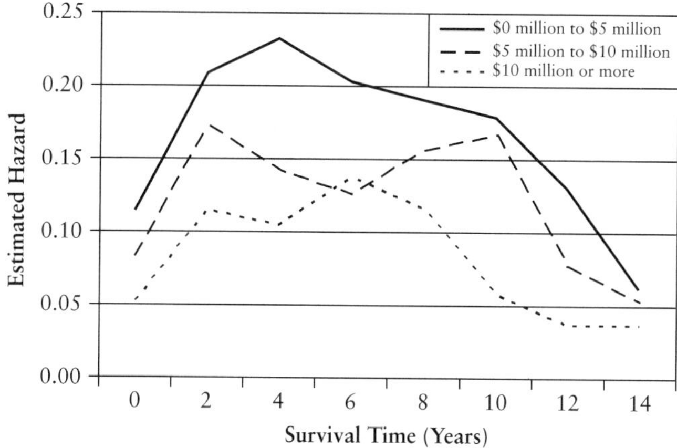

EXHIBIT 28.4 Estimated Hazard Functions

dramatically during the first years of life to peak at year 4 or 5 approximately, and decreases thereafter. This could reflect the fact that CTAs will struggle during their first years if they cannot produce good returns and attract enough capital to meet their overhead costs. If they can endure their initial formative years and establish themselves, however, their long-term outlook becomes increasingly favorable.

Identifying Future Stars

Given these results, investors might be willing to endure the high mortality and short lifetimes that micro-CTAs experience, in the hope that some CTAs in their start up phase might evolve into future stars. To investigate this possibility, for micro-CTAs in each category we calculate the monthly return, monthly standard deviation, and size during their first two years of existence (the "early" period), and after two years (the "late" period). We then calculate the proportion of live and dead CTAs that produce late returns that beat the mean return of all CTAs in the entire sample of live and dead funds, regardless of size, namely 1.159% per month for live funds and 1.071 for dead funds. Exhibit 28.5 shows that more stars emerge among micro-CTAs than among large CTAs, especially among live CTAs. For example, among the smallest live micro-CTAs (less than $0.5 million), 49% produce late returns that are above those of the entire sample, while among all live micro-CTAs (less than $10 million), 38% do so. Among large live CTAs (greater than $10 million), however, only 17% produce late returns that beat the sample. In general, future stars are more prevalent among the

EXHIBIT 28.5 Future Stars in Returns, Size, and Volatility

	Live Funds			Dead Funds		
Size Classification (million)	Percent Increase Returns	Percent Increase Size and Returns	Percent Increase Returns and Decrease Volatility	Percent Increase Returns	Percent Increase Size and Returns	Percent Increase Returns and Decrease Volatility
\$0m–\$0.5m	49	44	20	22	20	10
\$0.5m–\$1m	39	32	24	23	18	6
\$1m–\$2m	32	30	23	14	11	7
\$2m–\$3m	33	30	21	19	14	8
\$3m–\$4m	29	29	7	20	16	14
\$4m–\$5m	37	30	26	15	9	4
\$5m–\$10m	34	31	19	17	11	9
Total \$0m–\$10m	38	34	21	20	16	8
> \$10m	17	13	9	14	9	6
All CTAs	30	28	16	19	15	8

smaller micro-CTA classes. The proportion of stars that emerge from each dead category, however, is less than half that in the corresponding live category.

To investigate how small CTAs are able to grow and produce superior returns after two years, in each category of CTAs we calculate the proportion of CTAs that produce returns that beat the sample and that grow larger. CTAs are observed to grow larger if their average size after the first two years of life is larger than during the first two years of life. Stars are defined as those that grow large and produce returns that beat the sample. In this sense, Exhibit 28.5 again shows that micro-CTAs produce more stars than large CTAs. For example, among the smallest live CTAs, 44% emerge as stars, while among the largest CTAs (greater than \$10 million), only 13% do so. Again, most of the stars arise from CTAs that survive, and few from CTAs that eventually die off. However, some micro-CTAs grow in size simply because among these CTAs there is more room to grow before capacity constraints close the fund to new capital.

As noted by Brown, Goetzmann, and Park,[15] stars might emerge simply because they increase their volatility in an attempt to bolster future returns. To correct for this possibility, in each size category, we calculate the

[15]Brown, Goetzmann, and Park, "Careers and Survival: Competition and Risk in the Hedge Fund and CTA Industry."

proportion of CTAs that produce returns after two years that are above that of the sample, and reduce their volatility relative to the first two years. CTAs that are able to accomplish both are defined as stars. Exhibit 28.5 shows that, again, more stars evolve from smaller CTAs, but the pattern is less evident. In particular, among the smallest live CTAs, 20% become stars, close to that produced by the entire cohort of micro-CTAs (21%). Among large live CTAs, only 9% become future stars.

Survival Times of Micro-CTAs

Given the short survival times among micro-CTAs, it is important to identify features related to longevity, since stars should not only produce superior returns and grow in size, but should also be able to survive a long time. We fit the AFT model to all micro-CTAs and present the results in Exhibit 28.6. We find strong evidence that future stars—defined as micro-CTAs that increase both returns and size after two years, as enumerated in columns 3 and 6 of Exhibit 28.5—have increased longevity. Exhibit 28.6 also shows returns and assets during the first two years of life to be strong predictors of survival time. Volatility during the first two years of life decreases survival time, but this effect is not significant at the 10% level. The management fee significantly decreases survival time, but the incentive fee is not a significant predictor. We find no evidence that the CTA classification, treated as a categorical variable, affects survival. In our model, the energy classification is

EXHIBIT 28.6 Survival Prediction of Micro-CTAs

Variable	β Coefficient	Standard Error	*p*-value
Intercept	1.8161	0.1806	0.0001
Future star	0.3888	0.0581	0.0001
First 24 months return	0.0455	0.0118	0.0001
First 24 months STD	−0.0070	0.0045	0.1212
First 24 months AUM	0.0203	0.0085	0.0165
Diversified	0.1039	0.1172	0.3757
Financials/Metals	0.1102	0.1205	0.3603
Currency	0.1389	0.1255	0.2682
Agriculture	−0.1445	0.1436	0.3143
Energy	—	—	—
Incentive fee	−0.0004	0.0050	0.9414
Management fee	−0.0407	0.0153	0.0077
Scale parameter (σ)	0.5742	0.0172	—
Shape parameter (δ)	−0.5800	0.1534	—

chosen as the baseline category. Because of the small number of CTAs in the interest rate category, these have been removed.

To illustrate how the effect of these predictor variables affects the percentage change in survival time, consider two CTAs with survival times T_1 and T_2, and with identical values of all predictor variables except that one is a future star and the other is not. This implies that $T_1/T_2 = \exp(\beta_{FS})$, where $\beta_{FS} = 0.3888$ from Exhibit 28.6 is the coefficient for the dummy variable corresponding to whether or not a micro-CTA is a future star. Hence, future stars have survival times that are increased by $[\exp(0.3888) - 1] \times 100\%$, or nearly 50%, compared to CTAs that do not evolve into future stars. The effect of control variables can be similarly quantified. For example, an increase of 1% in monthly returns leads to an increase in survival time of $[\exp(0.0455) - 1] \times 100\%$, or roughly 5%. Similarly, a \$10 millions increase in initial assets leads to an increase of $[\exp(0.0203) - 1] \times 100\%$, or slightly over 23%, while an increase of 1% in the management fee can be expected to reduce the lifetime by $[\exp(-0.0407) - 1] \times 100\%$, or approximately 4%. Finally, the 95% confidence intervals for the scale and shape parameters are (0.5414, 0.6090) and (−0.8806, −0.2794) respectively, neither of which include the null value of 1. Exhibit 28.7 presents a probability plot of the micro-CTA data, based on our survival model that uses the generalized gamma distribution. The plot is approximately a

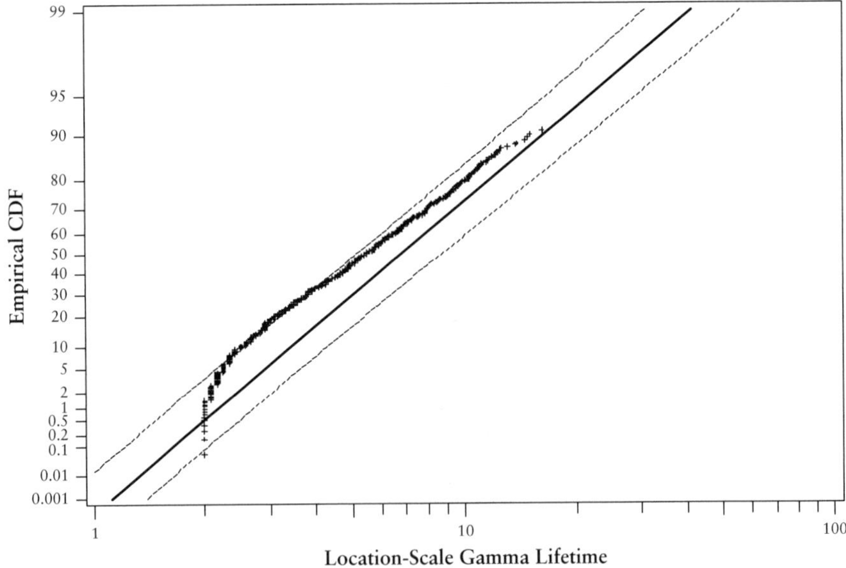

EXHIBIT 28.7 Probability Plot

straight line, which indicates a good visual assessment of goodness-of-fit. Most of the points lie within the confidence bands, which appear as dashed lines in Exhibit 28.7.[16]

CONCLUSION

This chapter investigates the performance and survival of micro-CTAs over the 1988 to 2005 period. Our findings suggest that micro-CTAs are at high risk of death, but that these CTAs can nonetheless be attractive investments since they have the potential to produce future stars. We find that identifying stars is heavily dependent upon survival because the majority of stars emerge from the pool of CTAs that do not die off prematurely. Hence, future stars are also those micro-CTAs that show good potential for long survival.

It is difficult to perform survival analysis on CTAs, since data on defunct CTAs must be requested separately from the database vendor. Furthermore, the defunct label in the database equates with having stopped reporting, owing not only to operational failure or shutdown, but also to diverse reasons such as a streak of poor performance, merging with another fund, or the unwillingness to attract new capital because of capacity constraints. Hence, as pointed out by Fung and Hsieh[17] and Liang[18] many of the CTAs counted as dead in databases are not defunct, and some have very good returns. However, micro-CTAs are more likely than large CTAs to stop reporting because they have actually closed and shut down, and are not likely to stop reporting because of capacity constraints.

Investors often dislike small CTAs, since it can be difficult for these CTAs to thrive and remain in operation a long time. They are perceived as too risky and not to be taken seriously. The results of this chapter, however, suggest that some future stars start out microsized and develop good long-term survival prospects. By ignoring micro-CTAs, investors miss out on the opportunity to invest in future stars at their start-up phase, when investor potential for negotiating management and incentive fees is highest, and before the CTA closes to new investors.

---

[16]Exhibit 28.7 presents a *probability plot* (PP), constructed by plotting the empirical *cumulative distribution function* (CDF) for the observed lifetimes (vertical axis) against the CDF for the logarithm of the lifetimes fitted to the generalized gamma distribution (horizontal axis).

[17]Fung and Hsieh, "Survivorship Bias and Investment Style in the Returns of CTAs."

[18]Bing Liang, "Alternative Investments: CTAs, Hedge Funds, and Funds-of-Funds," *Journal of Investment Management* 3, no. 4 (2004), pp. 76–93.

CHAPTER 29

A Primer on Energy Hedge Funds

Oliver Engelen
Risk Analyst
Benchmark Capital Management GmbH

Dieter G. Kaiser, Ph.D.
Director Alternative Investments
Feri Institutional Advisors GmbH
Research Fellow
Centre for Practical Quantitative Finance
Frankfurt School of Finance and Management

The number and diversity of energy hedge funds increased dramatically from 2004 to 2006, from about 20 at the end of 2003 to over 500 as of May 2006.[1] From a hedge fund viewpoint, the energy markets and the commodity trading segment are a young, early-stage market.

According to HedgeFund.net, assets under management in the energy hedge fund sector have grown concurrently, from US$19.37 billion in 2003 to US$79.26 billion in 2006.

The primary reasons for this remarkable increase are (1) supply and demand dynamics across energy commodities; (2) the opportunity to earn better returns; and (3) the influx of skilled and experienced energy traders from the collapsed merchant segment (see Fusaro and Vasey[2]). The dynamics

[1]Energy Hedge Fund Center. Directory of Energy Hedge Funds, November 2006.
[2]Peter C. Fusaro and Gary M. Vasey *Energy and Environmental Hedge Funds: The New Investment Paradigm* (Hoboken, NJ: John Wiley & Sons, 2006).

We would like to thank Joel Schwab and Peter Laurelli at Channel Capital Group for providing the data on the energy hedge funds from the HedgeFund.net Database.

across energy commodities have driven commodity prices to record highs. As a result, volatility, the main source of arbitrage opportunities for hedge funds, has also increased.

Because of the early-stage character of this segment of hedge funds and the high degree of passive or index product types, energy-focused strategies can provide opportunities for active investment. However, according to a study by the New York Mercantile Exchange (NYMEX), the volatility energy is negatively correlated with the number of funds; that is, the higher the number of actively trading energy hedge funds, the lower the price volatility.[3]

TYPES OF COMMODITY HEDGE FUNDS

Many hedge funds trade commodities. Some focus on only one sector (e.g., base metals); others trade several commodities (e.g., energy, grains, and precious metals). Some use a discretionary approach; others use technical signals or a combination of both. The majority of commodity hedge funds can be classified as either green hedge funds or energy hedge funds, and we describe these two in more detail next.

Green Hedge Funds

An alternative energy ("green") fund specializes in environmental investment strategies. It may focus on equities, commodities, or both, but its environmental mission revolves around the energy industry (e.g., emissions, renewable energy, energy efficiency, etc.). According to Ali, environmental hedge funds face one issue not commonly encountered by their hedge fund counterparts: They "need to address the potential tension between the financial criteria for investment as expressed in the prudent investor rule and the non-financial environmental objectives or philosophy that drives environmental hedge funds."[4]

Another type of energy hedge fund targets the water industry, either through equities or other investments like water rights. And an energy distressed debt and assets fund specializes in distressed assets in energy and other industries, as well as in corporate and debt restructuring.

[3]NYMEX, A Review of Recent Hedge Fund Participation in NYMEX Natural Gas and Crude Oil Futures Markets, Working Paper, 2005, p. 10.

[4]Paul Ali, "Investing in the Environment: Some Thoughts on the New Breed of Green Hedge Funds," *Journal of Derivatives and Hedge Funds* 12, no. 4 (2007), pp. 351–357.

Energy Hedge Funds

According to Fusaro and Vasey, there are several types of energy hedge funds. One distinction can be made between specialist energy funds that invest solely in the energy industry or in energy-related investments, and energy-oriented funds that have only a proportion (more than 20%) of assets exposed to various energy investments. Hedge funds with more than a 20% energy exposure are commonly defined as energy hedge funds.[5]

Exhibit 29.1 shows how dedicated energy hedge funds are classified. A fund that invests in energy company equities (public or private), other securities, and options is defined as an energy equity fund. It will often use energy *exchange-traded funds* (ETFs) or other instruments for hedging purposes, too. We can distinguish between energy equity long/short funds, and energy equity long-only funds.

Energy equity funds have relatively low price volatility compared to other energy hedge fund types. A diversified energy equity fund is defined as a predominantly energy equity fund that invests up to 20% of its assets in energy commodities through either exchange-traded futures and options, or through, for example, oil and gas reserves in the ground. This fund's exposure to commodities can provide arbitrage against equities.

The most risky strategy for hedge funds is commodity trading, followed by the energy sector commodity funds. The commodities traded may be exchange-traded futures and options through over-the-counter transactions or passive indexes. The funds can also trade financial and/or physical energy

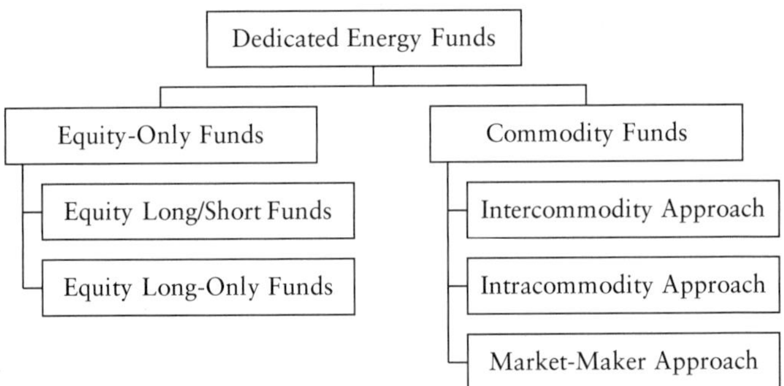

EXHIBIT 29.1 Classification of Dedicated Energy Hedge Funds
Source: Authors.

[5]Fusaro and Vasey, *Energy and Environmental Hedge Funds: The New Investment Paradigm*, pp. 21–25.

and any set of energy or energy-related commodities (e.g., weather, sugar, and uranium).

According to Hilpold, there are three main trading strategies for this type of fund: intercommodity, intracommodity, and market maker.[6] In the intercommodity approach, profits come mainly from arbitrage opportunities. Investors interested in this approach are seeking short-term supply/demand dynamics across energy commodity prices.[7] Intracommodity managers invest in options, futures, or forward contracts of the same commodity with different durations to profit from changes in the price structure curve.[8] The market maker substrategy brings liquidity to the markets by providing continuous offer prices, where the profit is the difference between future and spot prices.

Energy Funds of Hedge Funds

A fund that invests in more than one energy hedge fund for diversification is defined as an *energy fund of hedge fund.* The aim of these fund of funds

[6]Claus Hilpold, "Hedgefonds im Rohstoff-Bereich: Relative Value Commodities," in *Handbuch Alternative Investments,* vol. 2, edited by Michael Busack and Dieter G. Kaiser (Wiesbaden: Gabler, 2006), pp. 393–412.

[7]Some of the typical trading strategies are (1) *heat rates,* which focus on trading electricity in highly correlated electricity markets, and natural gas in regions with a high percentage of natural gas energy production; (2) *crack spreads,* which focus on correlations between crude oil, heating oil, and gasoline, and are characterized by movements of the historical price structure; (3) *spark spreads,* which focus on the correlation between electricity and gas; (4) *frac spreads,* which focus on the correlation between natural gas and propane; (5) *energy securities,* the holding of long and short positions in equities of energy sector companies; and (6) *weather,* which focuses on mispricings between weather risks and energy markets, and between electricity and gas. While the weather is the leading factor that influences the short-term development of energy contract prices, there are sometimes arbitrage opportunities when the weather market is incorrectly priced relative to energy prices.

[8]Examples of intracommodity trading strategies are (1) *regional spreads,* which focus on trading in highly correlated and physically connected regional electricity markets; (2) *natural gas time spreads,* which focus on trading in calendar spreads, that is, spreads between two months; (3) *regional gas spreads,* which focus on trading in specific gas regions set at Henry Hub; (4) *day ahead versus real time,* which focuses on the difference between the daily market clearing prices and anticipated real-time closing prices; and (5) *crude oil and refinery product time spreads,* which include trades along the forward curve. As an example, consider the gas market, which is usually in contango during the summer because of a decline in demand. In 2006, the summer was in backwardation with high volatility.

is to limit the idiosyncratic and operational risk of individual commodity managers, and to minimize market risk by diversifying investment strategies.[9] This class has become quite attractive. During 2005 and 2006, more than 25 energy and natural resources funds of hedge funds entered the energy area.[10] By investing in a portfolio of energy managers, investors are exposed to a much wider range of energy opportunities. However, because it is difficult to assess the risks and general volatility of the energy sector, the individual hedge fund manager must be cautiously selected. The fund of hedge fund management must be especially knowledgeable about the many facets of the energy sector.

RISKS ASSOCIATED WITH ENERGY HEDGE FUNDS

According to Till and Gunzberg, there are two main types of risks associated with commodity investments: idiosyncratic and macro.[11] The idiosyncratic risks are linked to one specific commodity market, while macrorisks include those that result in unplanned correlations. As Khoja shows in his case study of three energy sector commodity funds, the main risk these funds face is event risk.[12] But the definition of event risk can vary substantially between funds. Event risks may arise from (1) extraordinary events, such as a US$30 dollar change in the prompt crude contract; (2) unusually high levels of intermonth volatility; and/or (3) unexpected correlation changes.[13]

Fusaro and Vasey also note that in addition to price risks, volume risks are a key concern in energy markets. Volume risk arises from the requirements of physical commodity delivery, and is interrelated with many other risk factors. In the physically oriented energy business, there are almost unlimited risks, for instance, political risk, event risk, weather risk, legal risk,

[9]Rian Akey, Hilary Till, and Aleks Kins, "Natural Resources Funds of Funds: Active Management, Risk Management, and Due Dilligence," in *Funds of Hedge Funds,* edited by Greg N. Gregoriou (Oxford: Elsevier, 2006), pp. 383–399.

[10]Fusaro and Vasey, *Energy and Environmental Hedge Funds: The New Investment Paradigm*, pp. 21–25.

[11]Hilary Till and Jodie Gunzberg, "Absolute Returns in Commodity (Natural Resource) Futures Investments," in *Hedge Fund & Investment Management,* edited by Izzy Nelken (Oxford: Elsevier, 2006), pp. 25–42.

[12]Moazzam Khoja, Risk Management Practices within Three Leading Commodity Hedge Funds, Working Paper, SunGard Kiodex, 2006.

[13]Khoja, "Risk Management Practices within Three Leading Commodity Hedge Funds."

tax risk, and the like. The cases of Amaranth[14] and MotherRock[15] provide cautionary tales of the riskiness of trading energy commodities.

Besides investment risk, investors should also be aware of the operational risks associated with hedge fund exposures. Empirical research has shown that operational issues are the primary source of hedge fund failures.[16] Operational risks are more pronounced in the alternative asset world than in the more traditional asset management world, because hedge funds can trade complex instruments that are difficult to value properly. Hedge funds also tend to be very small, entrepreneurial firms with heterogeneous infrastructures, organizations, and operational quality.

Moix and Bachmann outline two ways of combating these operational risks.[17] *Basic* operational risk management approaches identify and assess controls that can mitigate the risks at an investor's governance level; *fundamental* operational risk management approaches focus on the investment strategies, and use applied risk management techniques to identify the operational risks. Aldrich highlights five key operational questions for hedge funds to keep in mind:[18]

- What is the experience level of operations personnel?
- Are compliance policies clearly stated and understood? Are they being consistently monitored and enforced?

[14]After a decline in natural gas futures in the beginning of September 2006, Amaranth, a multistrategy fund that specialized in energy trading, lost 65% of its assets betting on natural gas prices. Amaranth apparently held short summer/long winter natural gas spreads and long March/short April natural gas spreads. The fund's strategy, which usually profited from weather shock situations, experienced serious liquidation pressures because the invested sum was far too high in relation to the fund's capital basis. See Hilary Till, EDHEC Comments on the Amaranth Case: Early Lessons from the Debacle, Working Paper, 2006.

[15]The natural gas-focused fund MotherRock was established by ex-NYMEX president Robert Collins. The fund lost \$300 million in August 2006 and collapsed. The fund's short position of a September versus October natural gas (NG U-V) spread (i.e., holding long October and short September positions) also experienced liquidation pressures. See Till, EDHEC Comments on the Amaranth Case: Early Lessons from the Debacle.

[16]Christopher Kundro and Stuart Feffer, "Valuation Issues and Operational Risk in Hedge Funds," *Journal of Financial Transformation* 10 (2004), pp. 41–47.

[17]Pierre-Yves Moixand Bernard Bachmann, "Operational Risk Management Approaches and Concepts: Lessons Drawn from a Fund of Hedge Funds Provider," in *Hedge Funds and Managed Futures: A Handbook for Institutional Investors,* edited by Greg N. Gregoriou and Dieter G. Kaiser (London: Risk Books, 2006), pp. 175–196.

[18]David Aldrich, Hedge Fund Operational Risk: Meeting the Demand for Higher Transparency and Best Practices, Working Paper, The Bank of New York, 2006.

- Are there sufficient strategic internal controls and procedures?
- Are portfolio valuations transparent, consistent, and independent?
- Is there a high quality of service providers (prime brokers, administrators)?

FUND CHARACTERISTICS

The data we use to describe the energy hedge fund characteristics are obtained from the HedgeFund.net (HFN) database,[19] which includes 695 commodity-related hedge funds. Our sample consists of 158 energy sector single-hedge funds.[20] Except for two of the funds, we classify them as energy equity funds. We used several criteria to analyze them over the January 1991 to December 2006 time period.[21]

The dominant region of origin of our sample is North America, with 104 of the funds (65.82%) located either in the United States (56.33%), Canada (5.06%), the Bahamas (1.27%), or Bermuda (1.90%). Almost one-third (30.38%) were established in Europe. Most of the European funds are located in the United Kingdom (19.62%), followed by Norway (3.80%), and Switzerland (3.16%). The EMU countries France, Ireland, and Spain have one fund each.

Moreover, 18 of the funds in our sample (11.39%) were launched using the euro currency (EUR). The currencies of the non-EMU European countries, such as the U.K. pound (1.90%), the Norwegian krone (1.27%), and the Swiss franc (0.00%), are used by few or no funds as the base currency. The dominant currency of hedge funds in our sample is the U.S. dollar, with 127 (80.38%) launched using it.

Examining *assets under management* (AuM) of the energy hedge funds illustrates large differences between the minimum value of US$510,000 and the maximum value of US$5 billion. The median is US$53 million, with a *standard deviation* (SD) of US$498.26 million (Exhibit 29.2).

We also notice a mixed picture from examining energy hedge fund age. We define fund age here as the number of return reporting months from

[19]The HedgeFund.net database includes returns documentation for 3,900 funds starting in 1976. From these data, we construct five aggregate indexes and 33 single strategy indexes.

[20]Besides the energy sector, the HFN database lists 241 commodity-specific funds and 296 CTA/managed futures specializing in energy.

[21]Hedge fund data are provided by Channel Capital Group Inc. and its affiliates, and the aforementioned firms and each of their respective shareholders, employees, directors, and agents have not independently verified the hedge fund data, do not represent it as accurate, true, or complete, make no warranty, express or implied, regarding it, and shall not be liable for any losses, damages, or expenses relating to its adequacy, accuracy, truth, or completeness.

EXHIBIT 29.2 Different Characteristics of the Single Hedge Funds (a)

	n/a	No	Yes	Min	Max	Diff	SD	Median	Ø
AuM (in US$ mil.)	9	0	149	0.51	5500.00	5499.49	498.26	53.00	189.11
Fund age (in months)[a]	0	0	158	1.00	192.00	191.00	48.88	53.00	66.08
Minimum investment (US$ thousands)	0	5	153	25.00	20000.00	19975.00	1733.92	500.00	747.06
Subscription terms (days)	0	2	156	1.00	180.00	179.00	28.83	30.00	36.60
Redemption terms (days)	0	2	156	1.00	360.00	359.00	70.63	30.00	73.01
Lockup period (months)	5	75	78	1.00	36.00	35.00	5.08	12.00	12.05
Management fee (p.a.)	0	6	152	0.75%	3.00%	2.25	0.41%	1.50%	1.50%
Performance fee (p.a.)	0	6	152	7.50%	25.00%	17.50	2.12%	20.00%	19.59%

Source: Exhibit created from data obtained from Channel Capital Group.

Note: N/A means that no information was provided at all for this number of funds; No means that the criteria are not met by this number of funds; Yes means that the criteria are met for this number of funds (e.g., in row 1, nine funds) reported no AuM information; 0 funds did not meet the AuM criteria, and 149 funds did meet the AuM criteria.

[a]The number of return reporting months during the time period January 1997–December 2006.

EXHIBIT 29.3 Different Characteristics of the Single Hedge Funds (b)

	Yes	No	n/a	Total	Yes	No	n/a
Fund status (open)	145	13	0	158	91.77%	8.23%	0.00%
"Dead funds"[a]	7	151	0	158	4.43%	95.57%	0.00%
High watermark	152	6	0	158	96.20%	3.80%	0.00%
Hurdle rate	17	139	2	158	10.76%	87.97%	1.27%

Source: Exhibit created from data obtained from Channel Capital Group.
Note: "N/A means that no information was provided at all for this number of funds; No means that the criteria were not met by this number of funds; Yes means that the criteria were met for this number of funds.
[a]In this context, *dead funds* are those that stopped reporting returns before the end of our observation period (December 2006).

January 1991 until December 2006 (for our sample it varies between 1 and 192 months). The median age is 4.5 years, and only 4.43% stopped reporting returns before December 2006.

The vast majority of energy hedge funds (91.77%) are open (i.e., currently accepting investments). About 8.23% have reached their maximum investment capacity and are not accepting any further investments. The minimum investment is on average US$500,000 (Exhibit 29.3). The notice periods for subscription and redemption have the same thirty-day median, but the latter has a higher deviation. Almost half the energy hedge funds have a lockup period (12 months on average).

The median management fee and performance fee are 1.50% and 20.00%, respectively. The vast majority of the funds in our sample (96.20%) charge a performance fee only on new profits (high watermark). A minority (10.76%) set up a minimum performance limit that must be achieved before a performance fee is charged (hurdle rate).

RISK AND RETURN CHARACTERISTICS

In this section, we use several indexes to study the risk and return characteristics of energy hedge funds in more detail. We choose the HedgeFund.net Energy Sector Average Index (HNES) as our benchmark for energy hedge funds. We compare this index to the Standard and Poor's 500 (S&P 500), the MSCI World (MSCW), the JPMorgan Global Government Bond Index (JPGB), the Credit Suisse Hedge Fund Composite Index (CSHF),[22] the Goldman Sachs Commodity Spot Index (GSCS), the Goldman Sachs

[22]The CSHF that is based on TASS and the Tremont database is an asset-weighted index; that is, it is calculated according to the net asset values of the funds. The CSHF applies as an industry standard in the hedge fund industry.

Commodity Spot Energy Index (GSEN),[23] the Barclay CTA Index (BARC),[24] and the Dow Jones-AIG Commodity Index (DJAC)[25] for January 1997 to December 2006. All calculations are based on monthly rates of return.

We first take the "index perspective" to show the basic risk and return features of a portfolio of energy hedge funds versus traditional and alternative market benchmarks. Next, we take the "fund perspective" to demonstrate the dispersion investors face if they decide to go the energy hedge fund way with individual fund allocations.

The Index Perspective

Exhibit 29.4 shows the heterogeneous characteristics of the indexes. As the results show, the highest returns are achieved by the HNES, with a 1.11% average monthly rate of return and a 14.13% average annualized rate of return. The worst annualized rate of return is generated by the JPGB (5.32%). This leads to an 8.81 difference[26] for annualized rates of return. The second highest return is generated by the CSHF.[27]

---

[23]The Goldman Sachs Commodity Spot Return Index is based on the price levels of the contracts included in the Goldman Sachs Commodity Index (GSCI). The GSCI is calculated using futures contracts on a world production-weighted basis. The Goldman Sachs Commodity Spot Return Energy Index is a subindex of the GSCI that represents parts of the Goldman Sachs Commodity Spot Return Index.

[24]The BARC is an equally weighted index that currently includes 428 programs of commodity trading advisors and is the leading industry benchmark.

[25]The DJAC is calculated using futures contracts on 23 physical commodities. The DJAC is based on rolling futures positions (i.e., for the index construction), it assumes that nearby contracts are sold and contracts that have not yet reached the delivery period are purchased.

[26]The difference is defined as the maximum value minus the minimum value.

[27]However, in this context it is important to note that the benchmarks we use for hedge funds and CTAs (HNES, CSHF, and BARC) are noninvestable indexes. Due to their construction methodologies, these indexes are also subject to several distortions that might overestimate their performance (e.g., survivorship bias, reporting bias, etc.). For more information about these biases, see Mark J. P. Anson, *Handbook of Alternative Assets,* 2nd ed. (Hoboken, NJ: John Wiley & Sons, 2006), pp. 180–186; William Fung and David A. Hsieh, "Benchmarks of Hedge Fund Performance: Information Content and Measurement Biases," *Financial Analysts Journal* 58, no. 1 (2002), pp. 22–34; Thomas Heidorn, Christian Hoppe, and Dieter G. Kaiser, "Construction Methods, Heterogeneity and Information Ratios of Hedge Fund Indices," in *Hedge Funds and Managed Futures: A Handbook for Institutional Investors,* edited by Greg N. Gregoriou and Dieter G. Kaiser (London: Risk Books, 2006), pp. 3–30; and François-Serge Lhabitant, *The Handbook of Hedge Funds* (Hoboken, NJ: John Wiley & Sons, 2007), pp. 479–511.

EXHIBIT 29.4 Different Risk and Return Characteristics, January 1997 to December 2006

	HNES	SP500	MSCW	JPGB	CSHF	BARC	GSCS	GSEN	DJAC
Monthly rate of return (RoR)	1.11%	0.54%	0.49%	0.43%	0.83%	0.44%	0.59%	0.76%	0.65%
Annualized RoR	14.13%	6.71%	6.10%	5.32%	10.48%	5.43%	7.26%	9.47%	8.08%
SD	5.38%	4.42%	4.17%	1.90%	2.08%	2.25%	6.34%	9.59%	4.22%
Volatility	18.64%	15.33%	14.45%	6.58%	7.22%	7.80%	21.96%	33.21%	14.61%
Semi-SD	3.76%	3.31%	3.19%	1.27%	1.42%	1.52%	4.41%	6.49%	2.88%
Sharpe ratio (2%)	0.65	0.31	0.28	0.50	1.17	0.44	0.24	0.22	0.42
Sharpe ratio (4%)	0.54	0.18	0.15	0.20	0.90	0.18	0.15	0.16	0.28
Sortino ratio (2%)	1.09	0.44	0.40	0.87	2.19	0.73	0.37	0.37	0.69
Sortino ratio (4%)	0.89	0.25	0.20	0.32	1.59	0.29	0.23	0.26	0.44
Calmar ratio	0.33	0.12	0.11	0.09	0.32	0.10	0.11	0.13	0.14
Sterling ratio	0.35	0.03	0.05	0.01	0.07	0.01	0.08	0.11	0.07
Omega (2%)	1.73	1.31	1.28	1.46	2.65	1.41	1.27	1.31	1.41
Omega (4%)	1.60	1.20	1.17	1.17	2.11	1.17	1.19	1.26	1.28
Skew	0.13	−0.54	−0.64	0.33	0.18	0.25	0.11	0.38	0.18
Excess kurtosis	0.95	0.53	0.62	0.10	3.94	0.21	−0.13	0.65	−0.45
Jarque-Bera	4.84	7.16	10.26	2.24	78.12	1.43	0.35	4.98	1.67
Maximum drawdown	−43.02%	−54.26%	−57.29%	−56.96%	−32.53%	−56.10%	−64.82%	−70.64%	−59.00%
Average positive	4.09%	3.42%	3.19%	1.79%	1.70%	2.00%	5.50%	8.07%	3.60%
Average negative	−4.02%	−3.68%	−3.61%	−1.18%	−1.28%	−1.47%	−4.79%	−7.19%	−3.01%
Positive months	65.00%	60.83%	61.67%	55.00%	71.67%	55.83%	54.17%	55.00%	56.67%
Autocorrelation	0.22	−0.01	0.05	0.14	0.11	−0.05	0.01	0.01	0.03
VaR (0.99)	−12.52%	−10.29%	−9.71%	−4.42%	−4.85%	−5.24%	−14.75%	−22.30%	−9.81%

Source: Exhibit created from data obtained from Channel Capital Group and Bloomberg.

The high performance level of the HNES is associated with high standard deviation (5.38%) and high volatility (18.64%); only the CSCS and the GSEN have higher values, with standard deviations of 6.34% and 9.59%, respectively, and volatilities of 21.96% and 33.21%, respectively.

The risk-adjusted performance measures, the Sharpe ratio, the Sortino ratio, and the Omega of the HNES are also relatively high. The most attractive Sharpe, Sortino, and omega ratios are seen in the CSHF. The HNES has the highest Calmar (0.33) and Sterling (0.35) ratios.

The maximum drawdown of the HNES is −43.02%, which is relatively low, although the value-at-risk (VaR) is comparatively high. The GSCS and GSCE have the highest maximum drawdown and value-at-risk, and the lowest risk-adjusted performance ratios. In particular, the GSEN shows poor risk and return characteristics. Very high differences are noted in connection with VaR (17.88).

During our sample time period, the HNES achieved positive returns in 65.00% of the months, and also obtained the highest autocorrelation (0.22). Only the CSHF obtained a higher degree of positive returns. The BARC obtained the worst autocorrelation (−0.05), and the GSCS had the worst percentage of positive months (54.17%).

The HNES shows a right-skewed and leptokurtic return distribution, in contrast to the GSCS and DJAC commodity indexes. The Jarque-Bera test, which is based on a combination of skewness and excess kurtosis and formulates the null hypothesis of normal distribution, confirms these results, with values below 5.991 at a 95% significance level. We express the Jarque-Bera test as follows:

$$JB = \frac{n}{6} \times \left[S^2 + \frac{1}{4} \times (K-3)^2 \right] \tag{29.1}$$

where n is the sample size; S is the skewness of the fund returns; and K is the excess kurtosis of the fund returns.

Exhibit 29.5 examines more closely the trailing 12-month risk and return ("snail trail"), and compares investments in energy hedge funds with those in U.S. stocks and global hedge funds. The exhibit should be interpreted as follows: Investors are seeking investments that have low risk (left corner), high returns (upper bounds), and where the risks and returns do not offer too many surprises (low variance). The exhibit shows that the HNES returns are representative of higher volatility and variance when compared to the SP500 and CSHF, although some of the returns have lower volatility. The CSHF returns have the best risk/rewards.

Exhibit 29.6 shows the evolution of the 12-month rolling Sharpe ratio, assuming a 2% risk-free rate between the commodity-related indexes

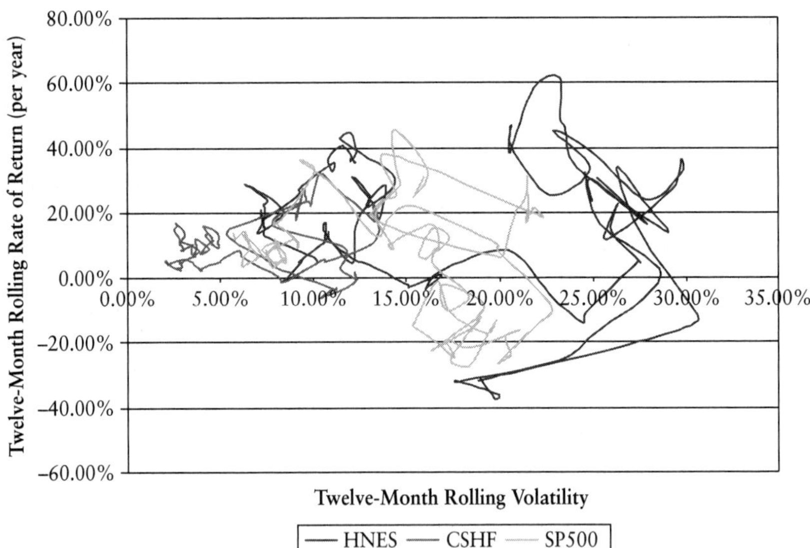

EXHIBIT 29.5 Snail Trail of the HNES, the SP500, and the CSHF
Source: Exhibit created from data obtained from Channel Capital Group and Bloomberg.

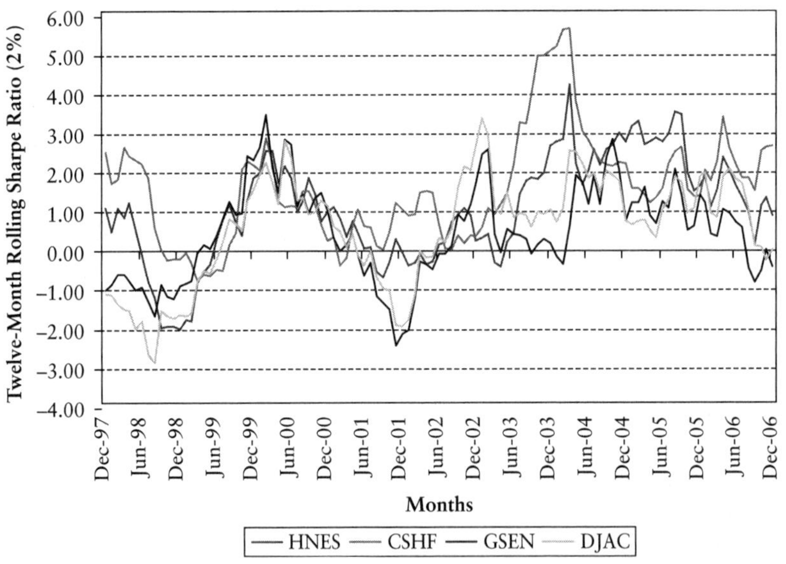

EXHIBIT 29.6 Twelve-Month Rolling Sharpe Ratio (2%) between Several Indexes
Source: Exhibit created from data obtained from Channel Capital Group and Bloomberg.

HNES, GSEN, DJAC, and CSHF. The highest Sharpe ratio (5.71) on a rolling basis was generated by the CSHF; the DJAC has the lowest, at −2.85.

In contrast to the acute differences of the risk-adjusted performance ratios, the HNES is highly correlated with the GSCS. Furthermore, the correlation between positive returns and the GSCS and GSEN (upside correlation) is higher than that between negative returns (downside correlation) and the GSCS (Exhibit 29.7). The HNES is positively correlated with the broad market indexes SP500 (0.30) and MSCW (0.33).

A closer look at the downside and upside correlation shows that the HNES is negatively correlated with "bear" markets, and positively correlated with "bull" markets (see Exhibit 29.8). Thus a diversification effect exists.

Note also that the correlations with the GSEN, as well as with the commodity-related indexes (BARC, DJAC) and the CSHF, seem to increase over our sample time period (Exhibit 29.8). There is also a high level of correlation with the noncommodity-related CSHF.

The returns of the HNES offer the highest persistence on a monthly basis between past and future positive returns (PP), but relatively low performance persistence between past and future negative returns (NN).[28] Contrary to the benchmark indexes, the HNES does not show an increase of performance persistence between past and future positive returns when quarterly versus monthly returns are used (Exhibit 29.9).

The Fund Perspective

In this section, we calculate different performance measures for the 158 energy hedge funds in our database to assess the dispersion between index performance and individual funds.[29] We observe dramatic differences in regard to the risk and return characteristics. As the results in Exhibit 29.10 show, the energy hedge funds achieved a 0.88% monthly median rate of return, and an 11.06% annualized median rate of return. The −1.53% minimum annualized rate of return and the 63.95% maximum value lead to a difference of 65.48.

A similarly heterogeneous picture is seen upon examining the risk measures. The standard deviation, with a median of 2.26%, and the volatility, with a median of 7.82%, show differences of 14.74 and 49.32, respectively.

[28]The returns were classified according to past and future returns: Positive returns follow positive returns (PP), negative returns follow positive returns (PN), positive returns follow negative returns (NP), and negative returns follow negative returns (NN).

[29]In order to calculate the different performance measures, we deleted from our sample any funds that had less than 12 reporting months during our sample time period and any double funds.

EXHIBIT 29.7 Correlations, January 1997 to December 2006

	HNES	SP500	MSCW	JPGB	CSHF	BARC	GSCS	GSEN	DJAC
Correlation (SP500)	0.30	~	0.95	−0.07	0.49	−0.15	−0.03	−0.05	0.08
Correlation (MSCW)	0.33	0.95	~	0.02	0.52	−0.13	0.03	0.00	0.14
Correlation (JPGB)	0.13	−0.07	0.02	~	−0.06	0.32	0.17	0.18	0.16
Correlation (CSHF)	0.31	0.49	0.52	−0.06	~	0.16	0.12	0.11	0.14
Correlation (BARC)	0.09	−0.15	−0.13	0.32	0.16	~	0.21	0.19	0.24
Correlation (GSCS)	0.45	−0.03	0.03	0.17	0.12	0.21	~	0.97	0.82
Correlation (GSEN)	0.47	−0.05	0.00	0.18	0.11	0.19	0.97	~	0.76
Correlation (DJAC)	0.42	0.08	0.14	0.16	0.14	0.24	0.82	0.76	~
Pos. correlation (SP500)	0.27	~	0.81	0.26	0.41	0.12	0.01	0.17	−0.07
Pos. correlation (MSCW)	0.23	0.81	~	0.05	0.28	−0.07	−0.16	−0.01	−0.08
Pos. correlation (JPGB)	0.09	0.26	0.05	~	0.25	0.54	0.02	−0.01	−0.10
Pos. correlation (CSHF)	0.40	0.41	0.28	0.25	~	0.19	−0.10	−0.07	−0.21
Pos. correlation (BARC)	0.21	0.12	−0.07	0.54	0.19	~	0.15	0.15	0.02
Pos. correlation (GSCS)	0.32	0.01	−0.16	0.02	−0.10	0.15	~	0.95	0.75
Pos. correlation (GSEN)	0.39	0.17	−0.01	−0.01	−0.07	0.15	0.95	~	0.62
Pos. correlation (DJAC)	0.23	−0.07	−0.08	−0.10	−0.21	0.02	0.75	0.62	~
Neg. correlation (SP500)	−0.14	~	0.93	−0.05	0.52	0.16	0.05	−0.18	0.01
Neg. correlation (MSCW)	−0.04	0.93	~	0.11	0.54	0.07	−0.12	−0.28	−0.15
Neg. correlation (JPGB)	−0.16	−0.05	0.11	~	0.33	0.06	−0.40	−0.39	−0.08
Neg. correlation (CSHF)	−0.10	0.52	0.54	0.33	~	−0.12	0.00	0.04	0.07
Neg. correlation (BARC)	−0.11	0.16	0.07	0.06	−0.12	~	0.07	0.14	−0.14
Neg. correlation (GSCS)	0.05	0.05	−0.12	−0.40	0.00	0.07	~	0.92	0.60
Neg. correlation (GSEN)	0.27	−0.18	−0.28	−0.39	0.04	0.14	0.92	~	0.38
Neg. correlation (DJAC)	0.12	0.01	−0.15	−0.08	0.07	−0.14	0.60	0.38	~

Source: Exhibit created from data obtained from Channel Capital Group and Bloomberg.

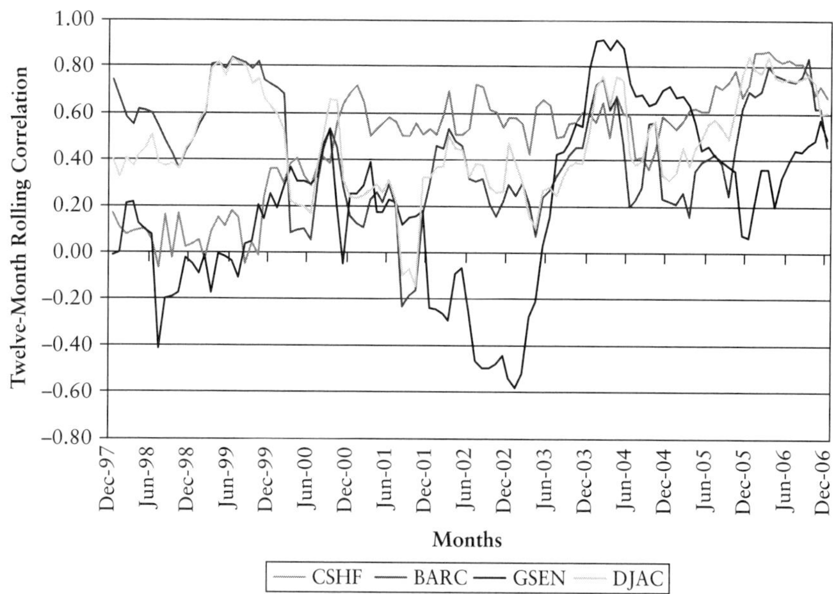

EXHIBIT 29.8 Twelve-Month Rolling Correlations between the HNES and Several Indexes
Source: Exhibit created from data obtained from Channel Capital Group and Bloomberg.

Accordingly, the risk-adjusted performance ratios are vastly different (the Sharpe Ratio, Sortino ratio, Calmar ratio, Sterling ratio, and Omega).

The returns of the single-energy hedge funds in our sample are normally distributed according to the average skew. The vast majority of funds (75%) have positive excess kurtosis and therefore show leptokurtic return distribution characteristics. These results are confirmed by a low level of the Jarque-Bera test.

A closer look at the maximum drawdown shows a heterogeneous picture. The minimum value of −0.7% and the maximum value of −90.3% lead to a difference of 89.6. Large differences also exist for the VaR values. The single-energy hedge funds here present a positive average correlation of 0.38 to the S&P 500, but correlate slightly with the GSCS (0.11) and the GSEN (0.08) on average.

Exhibit 29.11 shows graphically the dispersion of the annualized *rate of return* (RoR), the *volatility* (VOL), the *maximum drawdown* (MD), and the VaR between the database (indexed with a *d*) and the index (indexed with an *i*), on a 12-month rolling basis for our time period. All four measures are significantly higher on the database level than on the index level. This may be

EXHIBIT 29.9 Performance Persistence, January 1997 to December 2006

Monthly Returns	HNES	SP500	MSCW	JPGB	CSHF	BARC	GSCS	GSEN	DJAC
PP	46.22%	34.45%	45.38%	32.77%	25.21%	26.89%	31.09%	30.25%	31.09%
PN	19.33%	24.37%	21.01%	19.33%	29.41%	28.57%	23.53%	25.21%	25.21%
NP	18.49%	23.53%	20.17%	22.69%	28.57%	28.57%	23.53%	25.21%	25.21%
NN	15.97%	17.65%	13.45%	25.21%	16.81%	15.97%	21.85%	19.33%	18.49%

Quarterly Returns	HNES	SP500	MSCW	JPGB	CSHF	BARC	GSCS	GSEN	DJAC
PP	42.50%	40.00%	60.00%	40.00%	30.00%	32.50%	40.00%	45.00%	37.50%
PN	22.50%	25.00%	20.00%	20.00%	30.00%	30.00%	22.50%	17.50%	20.00%
NP	22.50%	25.00%	17.50%	22.50%	27.50%	27.50%	22.50%	20.00%	20.00%
NN	12.50%	10.00%	2.50%	17.50%	12.50%	10.00%	15.00%	17.50%	22.50%

Source: Exhibit created from data obtained from Channel Capital Group and Bloomberg.

EXHIBIT 29.10 Different Risk and Return Characteristics of the Single-Energy Hedge Funds, January 1997 to December 2006

	Min	Max	Diff	Mean	Median
Monthly rate of return (RoR)	−0.13%	4.21%	4.33	1.00%	0.88%
Annualized RoR (ann)	−1.53%	63.95%	65.48	12.92%	11.06%
SD	0.11%	14.35%	14.24	2.72%	2.26%
Volatility	0.39%	49.71%	49.32	9.43%	7.82%
Semi-SD	0.07%	10.32%	10.25	1.87%	1.48%
Sharpe ratio (2%)	−0.68	8.64	9.32	1.49	1.25
Sharpe ratio (4%)	−1.49	6.86	8.35	1.11	0.94
Sortino ratio (2%)	−8.98	18476.07	18485.05	215.57	29.45
Sortino ratio (4%)	−65.73	39.48	105.21	13.08	13.40
Calmar ratio	−0.10	16.52	16.63	2.28	1.49
Sterling ratio	−0.13	2.45	2.58	0.65	0.56
Omega (2%)	0.55	2280.00	2279.45	24.45	2.58
Omega (4%)	0.26	152.93	152.67	4.63	2.13
Skew	−3.93	5.25	9.18	0.01	−0.04
Excess kurtosis	−0.98	31.37	32.36	2.40	1.14
Jarque-Bera	0.00	5280.87	5280.86	167.97	4.99
Maximum drawdown	−90.27%	−0.71%	89.56	−13.70%	−8.03%
Average positive	0.36%	11.62%	11.25	2.41%	1.99%
Average negative	−9.56%	−0.26%	9.30	−1.93%	−1.34%
Positive months	50.48%	100.00%	49.52	71.36%	69.54%
Autocorrelation	−0.46	0.68	1.15	0.16	0.16
VaR (0.99)	−33.38%	−0.26%	33.12	−6.33%	−5.25%
Correlation (SP500)	−0.69	0.94	1.63	0.34	0.38
Correlation (GSCS)	−0.30	0.78	1.08	0.12	0.11
Correlation (GSEN)	−0.29	0.73	1.02	0.09	0.08

Source: Exhibit created from data obtained from Channel Capital Group.

interpreted as selection bias if we assume investors choose energy hedge funds solely for reasons of benchmarking with energy hedge fund indexes (where the return series are smoothed), instead of looking at the individual funds.

CONCLUSION

The single-energy hedge funds we investigate here show heterogeneous characteristics in regard to assets under management, fund age, and minimum investment. Although the short average subscription and redemption terms seem to constitute a flexible investment environment, a relatively high number of funds have lockup periods, usually for 12 months. The risk and return characteristics show that the HedgeFund.net Energy Sector Average

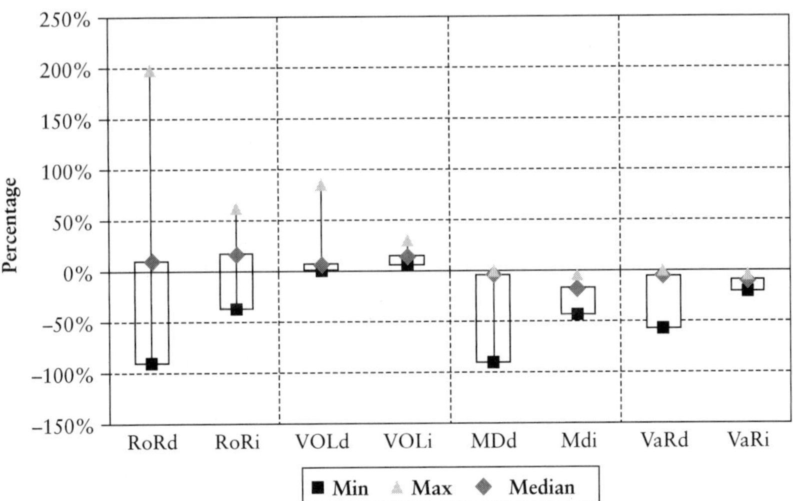

EXHIBIT 29.11 Dispersion of Risk and Return Characteristics
Source: Exhibit created from data obtained from Channel Capital Group.

has a high performance level, even though this is normally associated with high risk-adjusted performance ratios. Only the Credit Suisse Hedge Fund Composite Index offers higher risk-adjusted returns for our time period.

The HedgeFund.net Energy Sector Average shows the following risk and return characteristics: (1) a high percentage of positive returns; (2) positive performance persistence; (3) low maximum drawdowns; (4) a positive correlation with the Dow Jones-AIG Commodity Index; (5) a negative correlation with "bear" equity markets; (6) a positive correlation with "bull" equity markets; and (7) a high long-term positive correlation with the Goldman Sachs Energy Spot Return Index that, on a rolling 12-month basis, can also become significantly negative.

From the single-energy hedge fund perspective, these risk and return characteristics offer a heterogeneous picture. The risk-adjusted performance ratios are relatively high on average. The majority of funds (75%) show leptokurtic return distribution characteristics. Contrary to the HedgeFund.net energy sector average, the single-energy hedge funds have a low correlation with the Goldman Sachs Commodity Spot Return Index and the Goldman Sachs Commodity Spot Energy Index, but they have a noticeable correlation with the broad equity market.

We conclude that investors can use energy hedge funds as either diversification instruments for a traditional portfolio, or as a substitute for hedge fund, commodity, or even equity exposures. Energy funds of hedge funds can also be considered for further diversification benefits.

PART Six

Special Classes

CHAPTER 30

An Overview of Commodity Sectors

Roland Eller
Managing Director
Roland Eller Consulting GmbH

Christian Sagerer
Structured Products Sales Manager
JPMorgan Chase Bank

The late 1980s through early 1990s were huge years for equities and favorable interest rates. Since then, the commodities asset class has taken a backseat as an investment class.

As shown in Exhibit 30.1, commodities can basically be categorized in two ways: *hard* and *soft*. Hard commodities can further be subdivided into energy and metals, while soft commodities are based on three subsegments: comestible goods, industrial agrarian goods, and animal products. In the energy subcategory, we can differentiate between fossil and alternative substrates. In the metal subcategory, we can differentiate between precious, industrial, and ferrous metals. Within the soft commodities, only the subsegment "comestible goods" can be further broken down among corn, oils, and consumer products.

HARD COMMODITIES: ENERGY

Energy includes fossil and alternative energy. We describe both in this section.

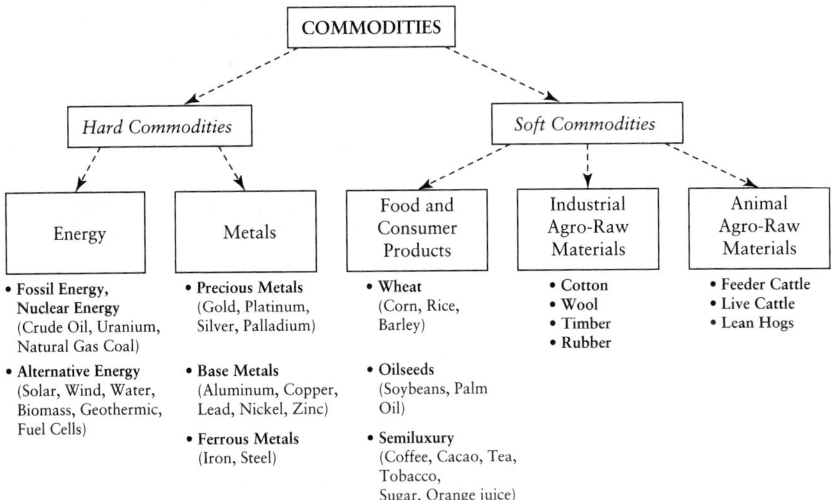

EXHIBIT 30.1 Classification of Asset Class Commodities
Source: Authors.

Fossil Energies

The energy supply has always been of primary importance to mankind. Energy is the solution to our most basic needs: It provides light, protection against cold or heat, and makes modern technology and transportation possible. But due to the limitations of "fossil resources," energy politics is starting to increase its focus on alternative energies.

Crude Oil *Crude oil* makes up the largest portion of fossil energy raw materials worldwide, at almost 45% as of 2005. This raw material is our most significant energy source, followed by coal and natural gas.

The raw material for crude oil arose from the remnants of algae and plankton deposited on underwater seabeds as they died. Over millions of years, deoxygenation occurred, and combined with water pressure, what is referred to as host rock arose. From that organic material, at depths of 1,500 meters and temperatures of 100°C to 150°C, were the components of today's oil deposits. The light components of oil advanced up the earth's surface, and formed oil slate and oil sand. Above these reservoirs, natural gas chambers also often formed.

There are about 250 different types of crude oil worldwide, with varying degrees of quality and sulphur content. Oil is not therefore a homogeneous product, and cannot be used in its natural form without being modified in refineries.

Oil is one of the youngest raw materials, dating back just 150 years. In the middle of the 19th century, Americans searching for new sources of lamp oil accidentally discovered liquid petroleum. With the use of sulphuric acid in 1855, science succeeded in making petroleum into an energy source.

Today, gasoline is considered the most important raw energy material. Ironically, gasoline was once considered just an annoying byproduct of crude oil. With the invention of the automobile, however, and then mass production in 1905 by Henry Ford, the rise of crude oil could not be stopped.

Crude oil is geologically widespread. In fact, over 43,000 oil fields are known worldwide as of 2007. Of those, the 10 biggest oil fields contain about 12% of all the oil in the world. The biggest oil field is Ghawar in Saudi Arabia, which produces 5 million barrels of crude oil per day. Five countries in the Middle East (Saudi Arabia, Iraq, Iran, United Arab Emirates, and Kuwait) have almost two-thirds of the crude oil reserves that is relatively easy to extract.

For about 20 years, discoveries of new crude oil fields have fallen far short of the increases in annual consumption. Currently, only one new barrel is discovered for every four consumed. The Association for the Study of Peak Oil (ASPO), a group of former oil geologists in the service of crude oil company groups, estimates that modern seismic methods have already discovered approximately 95% of all existing reserves. They believe crude oil production will soon decrease worldwide, even as demand continues to grow. This is expected to lead to strong price reactions and macroeconomic disturbances.

Unlike other important raw materials, a partial monopoly exists for crude oil on the *supply* side in the form of the OPEC cartel (the Organization of Petroleum Exporting Countries). This organization was founded in 1960 by six countries: Iran, Iraq, Kuwait, Saudi Arabia, and Venezuela. Six more countries have since joined: Qatar (1961), Indonesia (1962), Libya (1962), United Arab Emirates (1967), Algeria (1969), and Nigeria (1971).

Since 1965, OPEC has been based in Vienna and is responsible today for almost 40% of worldwide oil production. OPEC has a coordinated policy that controls the delivery amount of each OPEC member to protect themselves against a price collapse. Thus they exert enormous influence over prices and production of crude oil. The types of oil produced by OPEC members are: *Saharan Blend* from Algeria, *Minas* from Indonesia, *Iran Heavy* from Iran, *Basra Light* from Iraq, *Export Kuwait* from Kuwait, *Es Sider* from Libya, *Bonny Light* from Nigeria, *Qatar Marine* from Qatar, *Arab Light* from Saudi Arabia, *Murban* from the United Arab Emirates, and *BCF 17* from Venezuela.

Enormous imbalances also exist on the *demand* side for oil, however. The 10 largest countries currently use almost 60% of the available crude oil. The main consumer is the United States, with 25% alone. World crude oil demand is currently about 85 million barrels per day (1 barrel = 159 liters). But daily demand has risen more than 20% (1.2% per annum) over the time period from 1980 to 2006.

While demand from OECD countries has risen only slightly, consumption in China and India has increased dramatically and has played an especially large role in total oil demand during the last few years. For example, China was the second-largest oil consumer in the world in 2006. But average Chinese per capita oil consumption is only 6% of that in the United States where about 800 of every 1,000 people have a car; in China the ratio is just 18 of every 1,000.

India is the fifth-largest oil consumer. Per capita oil consumption there is only 3% of that in the United States. But as the Chinese and Indian economies have grown, car sales have soared. Today, crude oil demand in these two countries has already reached the point where they cannot satisfy it themselves. Thus we can assume that they will continue to show huge increases in demand.

Next to the basic supply and demand considerations, which are the long-term basis for pricing decisions, speculation plays an important short-term role. Although crude oil is the most traded raw material worldwide, only a very small part is sold on the spot market (Rotterdam and New York). The daily volume sold on the over-the-counter markets (New York, London, Singapore, and Tokyo) is higher than worldwide production by a multiple of 1. For example, every day on the over-the-counter market, several hundred millions of barrels of American WTI light sweet crude oil is sold. But actual production is under 1 million barrels per day.

After the huge increases of the 1970s, crude oil prices started an 18-year slide, which from a peak of U.S. $40 per barrel in 1980 plummeted to $10 per barrel in December 1998. Since then, crude oil prices have been trending upward, as proven by the recent historic highs.

Upon closer examination of the seasonal cycle of crude oil, the months of March and April and from July to September appear to be favorable for taking a tactical long position in oil.

Nowadays, we no longer question whether worldwide crude oil reserves will be exhausted, but when it will happen. Natural sources of crude oil are not expected to grow significantly, thus crude oil prices will continue to rise.

Natural Gas The development of natural gas was similar to the development of crude oil. Natural gas developed above crude oil deposits, and its composition also differs depending on geographic position. The main component of all natural gas is methane. Ethane, propane, and butane are other common components, as well as hydrosulphide, which is not used to generate energy. Natural gas is a nontoxic and burnable gas, without color or smell. It is lighter than air and has an ignition temperature of 600°C.

An even more complex transportation infrastructure is needed to obtain natural gas. Therefore, distribution only began during the 1960s, much later than crude oil. However, it is possible to change the condition of natural gas, or aggregate it, to simplify transportation. Technical methods used include:

- Compression in pressure tanks, which results in compressed natural gas (CNG).
- Liquefaction via compression and cooling, which results in liquefied natural gas (LNG), usually transported by ship.
- Conversion into liquid hydrocarbon, or *gas-to-liquids.*

Liquefied natural gas at 160°C will reduce the volume to two-tenths of 1% of its original volume. It is important that the tank of the transportation ship remain at a constant temperature, however, to keep the low volume of gas at a constant level. About 190 LNG ships are currently in use. This figure is expected to rise to 300 by 2010.

In 2004, worldwide production of natural gas was 2.7 trillion cubic meters. The main producers are Russia, with 22%, and the United States with 20%. About 36% of natural gas deposits are found in the gulf region, 31% are found in Western Siberia, and 20% are in North Africa and Europe.

Similarly to crude oil, the supply of natural gas seems to be limited. The development of new natural gas resources has also not kept pace with demand. Studies have projected that the crude oil supply will last for the next 43 years. Natural gas is projected to last for about 65 years.

Natural gas and crude oil have a strongly positive correlation. Natural gas reached its historic low at around the same time as crude oil, at US$2 in 1998–1999. Since a price correction in 2001, natural gas has been trending upward again.

Coal Among fossil energies worldwide, only coal appears to be plentiful enough to satisfy demand for the foreseeable future. The biggest reserves of coal are near those for crude oil in the Middle East. But the main coal stockyards are in Europe, North America, and Australasia.

Coal, which is black or brownish-black rock, arose through carbonization of shives. Dead plants sank to the bottom of swamps, and then turned into peat due to oxygen loss. Over time, the peat was covered with sediment, and increasing water pressure created carbonization, which resulted in the formation of brown coal. Wherever the earth experienced plate shifting, brown coal formed. Where pressure was strongest, more water was squeezed out, and anthracite coal formed. Therefore, the quality of coal increases with the depth of the deposit.

The higher moisture level of brown coal leads to inferior quality. It is mainly produced through open pit mining and used almost exclusively for electric power production. Among the types of brown coal, we can differentiate among shiny, matte, and soft brown coal.

Black coal, on the other hand, has a higher gross calorific value than brown coal. And anthracite coal is considered among the best types. It is especially hard and used almost exclusively for heating. It burns with a very short and hot blue flame, giving off very little soot.

Coal today is used for more than 25% of world energy demand. The largest coal producers are Australia, South Africa, Indonesia, the United States, and China. It is presently estimated that worldwide reserves will last for about 200 years. Coal has experienced a significant price increase over the last few years, caused by its relative scarcity due to the boom of the steel industry. Worldwide coal reserves have been at a low point for about five years.

Uranium Uranium is a silver-white, shiny, and soft radioactive heavy metal. When it meets air, it begins to oxidate in a yellowish way. Uranium was discovered in 1789 by German chemistry professor Martin Klaproth and named after the planet Uranus.

While Klaproth identified the element, Frenchman Eugene Peligot succeeded in 1841 in extracting pure uranic metal. The radioactivity of uranium was discovered in 1896 by Henri Becquerel. In 1938, Otto Hahn and Fritz Strassmann succeeded in producing the first atomic split through the neutron bombardment of uranium. In 1942, the first nuclear reactor opened in Chicago, and under J. R. Oppenheimer, Project Manhattan constructed the first atomic bomb only a year later. This was ignited on July 16, 1945 in New Mexico. The second atomic bomb was ignited during World War II on August 6, 1945 above Hiroshima, Japan. More than 90,000 people died, and large regions became contaminated from radioactivity.

Uranium ore does not occur in nature as pure metal, but as uranic connections. The most significant uranic minerals are pitchblende and coffinite, followed by uranocircite, uranic ocher, and torbernite. Uranium is not a stable element, and continuously short-lived daughter nuclides may arise. The most common is radon. Other less mobile ones include thorium, radium, polonium, and lead. The uranic mining industry can pose great dangers to humans and the environment.

The most important uranic reserves lie in the United States, Australia, South Africa, Niger, Canada, Kazakhstan, Brazil, Russia, Ukraine, and Uzbekistan. Only ten countries produce about 95% of worldwide uranium, and 442 nuclear power plants are currently in operation, accounting for 16% of the current supply.

The International Atomic Energy Organization (IAEO) expects that global consumption of atomic and nuclear power will increase by 2.5 times by 2030. Nuclear power plants currently consume 66,000 tons of uranium annually. Nuclear energy is also projected to gain in importance in the future, despite the daunting and unresolved problems of how to dispose of the final radioactive waste products.

In 2004, the biggest energy consumer was by far the United States. However, China was the biggest consumer of coal. Energy consumption of coal is still higher in China than crude oil. Next to China, only India consumes more coal than crude oil.

Alternative Energy

The expected shortage of traditional energy sources in the long term, and the increasing global demand for energy, make it urgent that we begin to consider alternative energy sources. In addition to price factors, including alternative fuels can improve the competitiveness of the fossil raw material sector.

The expansion of alternative energies is especially important from an environmental standpoint, for example, within the framework of the Kyoto Protocol for climate protection. The Kyoto Protocol was ratified on February 16, 2005 by 55 nations (that were together responsible for 55% of worldwide emissions in 1990). Nations that signed the Kyoto Protocol pledged to reduce their output of greenhouse gases by 5.2% by 2012. Greenhouse gases, which emanate from burning fossil fuel, are widely believed to be responsible for the rise of global warming.

Switzerland and the European Union further committed themselves to a reduction of 8%. The United States, the highest carbon dioxide emitter, refused ratification. Nevertheless, Kyoto succeeded in achieving the necessary rate reduction with Russia's ratification. The rapid growth of a pollutant-free energy stream, via wind, solar, or geothermal installations, is attributed to the OECD countries accepting the Kyoto Protocol, in addition to dramatic price increases of fossil fuels.

Europe takes the expansion of alternative energies very seriously. In 2004, Germany adopted the Renewable Energy Sources Act—known by its German abbreviation, EEG—which mandates that Germany increase its usage of alternative energies to at least 12.5% by 2010, and 20% by 2020. In 2000, the European Union presented a "green book" as a strategic basis for further development of renewable energies. The European Union expects renewable energy to make up 21% of its total power consumption by the end of this decade.

Solar Power Solar energy, which can be either thermal or photovoltaic, comes from the tiny amount of solar radiation that hits the earth's surface. This is in the range of 25,000 times total worldwide energy consumption. The sun emits over 20 days energy equal to 4,000 megawatts. Thus it is not surprising that solar power has become an increasingly important part of our energy supply equation.

Thermal Use: Solar Heat Installations Thermal solar power is obtained from solar thermal collectors and is used primarily for industrial water warming. Efficacy is about 85%. To convert thermal power, flat or vacuum tube commentators are used. A metal absorber passes the radiation onto the water circulating in the tubes. The tubes are contained in an isolated case, under a high-transparent glass or plastic covering. Within the vacuum tube commentator, the absorber faces are contained in evacuated glass tubes, which are more efficient than the flat plate collector method. Because of the increased flexibility of single tubes, tube commentators can be mounted on curved areas or less sunny areas.

A fundamental problem with thermal heat, however, lies in the chronic discrepancies between supply and demand. During the winter, the supply of energy is at its lowest point, but demand is at its highest level, and vice versa. Solar heating systems are therefore dependent on large heat accumulators.

Photovoltaic: Electric Power Production The photovoltaic effect was discovered in 1839 by the French physicist Edmond Becquerel. Albert Einstein first unraveled the interaction between light and electrons when he discovered the quantum nature of lights in 1905. The first photoelectric cell was developed in 1883 by the American Charles Fritts. It had an efficacy of 1% to 2%.

In 1954, a team of researchers at Bell Telephone Laboratories laid the foundation for present-day photovoltaics. They constructed a cell based on the element silicon. This raw material is widely and cheaply available and is commonly used in electronic semiconductors. A solar cell consists of two crystalline, positive and/or negative shifts of ultrapure silicon. Boron is used for the positive endowment, and phosphorus for the negative. There is a so-called "p-n crossing" between the positively and negatively loaded shifts. If the sunlight encounters the silicon shifts, electrons are released in the form of high-energy photons. This allows electrostatic strengths to enter the n-Zone, causing a hole to develop in the p-Zone. This photovoltaic effect produces an electricity stream.

Within photovoltaics, we can differentiate between *island installations* and *net-linked installations*. The island system is used mostly in remote situations, such as during camping. The direct current from sunlight can be stored through either an island installation (no connection to the public electricity network), or through batteries, and be usable from there for direct consumption. Alternatively, it can be converted into alternating currents through an inverted rectifier, so that it can enter the public electricity network in the form of a net-coupled installation.

The EEG mandated that stream delivery in Germany become available from network carriers. The solar stream must be produced for twenty years with a minimum amount of 45.7 cents compensated per kilowatt-hour (as of December 31, 2004).

Photovoltaic modules can be installed on almost all styles of roofs and facades, and usually do not require any special planning or building permissions. After installation costs, solar stream installations are almost maintenance-free, thus costs are very low.

Passive Use of Solar Power Solar architecture has revealed new possibilities for optimizing the energy supply. So-called intelligent design creates buildings that use significantly less energy without higher additional costs, by incorporating, for example, larger windows or conservatory ventilating systems, which warm the air in a conservatory and then distribute it evenly through the whole house. Comfort ventilations are also becoming more common. They ensure consistently good air quality and reduce energy typically lost through windows in the winter.

Transparent thermal insulation (TWD) is another possibility for passive solar use. This consists of small, transparent plastic structures that insulate the internal surface from the external. Such thermal insulation can exist, for example, between two panes of glass. It can also be mounted as wall heating onto an absorbent external wall.

Wind Energy Wind power arises indirectly as a result of solar power. Solar radiation warms up the earth's surface to varying degrees, according to geographic placement. Above more strongly warmed regions, air rises, creating low-pressure areas. In cooler regions, higher-pressure areas exist. The air flows from high- to low-pressure areas, creating wind. The relative amount of wind depends on geography: Higher wind velocities are reached above water surfaces and lowlands than in inland areas. Also, wind speed increases as height increases.

Wind energy is one of the most important and oldest available energy sources. The first windmills operated in Europe in the 12th century. During the 18th century, the Netherlands built about 9,000 windmills, which greatly stimulated the Dutch economy.

However, modern wind energy use began in 1891 in Denmark, when rural regions were supplied with a direct current. The first industrial mass production of wind energy occurred in the United States at the end of the 19th century for groundwater. The worldwide decrease in wind energy use began with the advent of the steam engine and cheap oil. However, it tended to regain popularity during inflationary phases and during times of high energy prices—for example, during World War I and World War II, as well as during the oil price shocks of the 1970s. In Denmark especially, the country that originated modern wind energy, the wind industry developed exports during 1973 and 1979.

Wind parks are a way to take advantage of having several wind energy installations in one place, which reduces the concurrent infrastructure and maintenance costs. Wind parks are preferable in windy coastal regions, directly in the sea (as offshore installations), or on free field face constructs. Offshore installations are actually more economical in spite of higher installation costs because the wind is so much higher out on the open sea. Offshore installations need at least a wind force of three to produce energy. When wind force reaches 10, the installations turn off automatically.

Water Energy In the same way as wind, water power arises as a result of solar power. Solar radiation causes water to vaporize and rise. It then flows down again, and its potential energy can be harnessed. Water is one of the oldest sources of energy. Energy from dams or waterwheels has been used by the Chinese since the year 3 BCE.

Since the beginning of the 20th century, water energy has been used for electric power production. Today, about 17% of the electric energy worldwide is achieved through water power. Thus this alternative form of energy has nearly reached the level of nuclear power.

The advantages of water energy include high efficiency and low pollution and heat runoff to the surroundings. Disadvantages, however, include damage to the ecological balance of waters. Limiting the size of water power installations, and thus limiting the potential damage to natural resources, is the best solution for satisfying both sides.

Biomass Energy Biomass refers to the entire organic substance of plants, animals, and people. It represents an alternative source of energy that is continuously available regardless of season and weather. With reference to biomass, we can differentiate among:

- Solids (for example, wood and straw)
- Liquids (vegetable oil, biofuel, and bioethanol)
- Gases (for example, biogas)

To use biomass as a means of energy production, carbon dioxide circulation must stay largely constant. The carbon dioxide released during biomass combustion is absorbed by plants. The energy balance of the biomass is positive, because energy used for the production is smaller than the amount that is released.

Solid Biomass: Wood The oldest and best-known biomass energy producer is the burning of wood and waste woods. This type of heating is the most effective and most compatible with the environment. The carbon bound in the biomass attaches itself to oxygen in the air and the resulting chemical reaction (combustion) releases heat. In this case, wood is climate-neutral during combustion, because as much carbon dioxide is released during as before.

Wood pellets are an especially efficient method of heating with wood. The scales and energy content of high-quality wood pellets are defined as DIN 51731 (norm) and the OENORM M7135 (norm) and standards are:

- Diameter of six millimeters
- Length of ten to thirty millimeters
- Calorific value of 4.9 to 5.0 kilowatt-hours per kilogram

Wood pellets made it possible to create a fully automatic heating system with wood. The pellets are carried above the oven by an integrated transportation channel into the combustion chamber and ignited automatically. Through use of a thermostat and timer, fully automatic pellet heaters offer the same comfort as oil and gas central heaters at up to 95% efficacy.

Nowadays, wood pellet heating systems are even more expensive to install than those that use fossil fuels. But since fossil energy prices are expected to increase so dramatically, these additional expenditures will easily pay for themselves.

Liquid Biomass: Bioethanol as a Gasoline Substitute Bioethanol is obtained via a specific fermenting and distillation procedure of biomass involving types of alcohol (e.g., ethyl alcohol). The procedure is similar to the way liquor is distilled. The gasoline substitute ethanol can be obtained from almost all organic substances, including sugar cane, grains, shives, or waste woods. Even the organic part of household waste can be used for alcohol production.

The simplest way, however, involves extracting bioethanol from sugarcane or sugar beets. Their glucose is tied by yeast mushrooms or bacteria directly to alcohol, which is then distilled and drained. During the more extensive grain ethanol production, enzymes first convert the seeds into glucose before fermentation takes place. The ecological advantage of biogasoline is the considerably better carbon dioxide balance. The plants from which ethanol is made use photosynthesis to absorb the majority of the carbon dioxide that is released.

Bioethanol can now be added to traditional gasoline in amounts up to 10% without making any changes to the engine. Performance and noise are almost identical to gasoline. In addition, biofuels are subject to tax rebates in many countries.

As the biggest sugar producer in the world, Brazil is also a leading producer and consumer of ethanol fuel. In 2005, for the first time, Brazil sold more FFV vehicles than traditional gasoline-powered vehicles. And today about half their sugar production is processed into ethanol. In fact, even as far back as the oil crisis of the 1970s, Brazil used about one-third of their sugar for biogasoline.

In July 2005, a new kind of biogasoline, *G8-peak*, was introduced by the Canadian company Logen Corporation. G8-peak uses cellulose ethanol, which, unlike traditional bioethanol, is made from straw, not from grain, sugar beets, or sugarcane. Enzymes divide the straw into a sugary liquid, which is distilled into alcohol and a waste product that can be used as a combustible. Logen is the first enterprise to offer cellulose for commercial use, in partnership with the two oil companies Royal Dutch and Petro-Canada, and the Canadian government.

Again, because of the finite nature of fossil energy sources, biogasoline, bioethanol, and biofuel are expected to gain in importance in the coming decades.

Gaseous Biomass: Biogas The main component of biogas is methane hydrocarbon as a natural gas. The biogas arises through the microbial breakdowns of organic substances. The energy contained in the biomass is based on photosynthesis—plants convert the energy of the sun into biochemical energy. Biogas thus represents an indirect use of the sun as a renewable energy carrier.

In biogas plants, conversion machines are used to produce biogas in a four-stage process, which involves diverse organisms. When the organic biomass is decomposed, a mixture results made up of water, organic substance that is not decomposed (cellulose), as well as inorganic substances (minerals).

The first stage of the conversion is hydrolysis, where high-molecular organic substances are split by bacteria into smaller units. In the second stage, the smaller units are broken down further into simpler molecular organic acids. The third stage is acidification, where the simpler molecular organic acids and alcohols are decomposed into acetic acid, carbon dioxide, and hydrogen. Methanogenesis is the fourth and last stage. In this closing phase, the acetic acid, carbon dioxide, and hydrogen are transformed into methane by bacteria. Carbon dioxide is the surplus, and it remains at rest in the gas mixture.

Biogas is made up of the following materials. Weighting depends on the substrates used for the conversion: Methane (45% to 75%), Carbon dioxide (25% to 55%), Vapor (0% to 10%), Nitrogen (0% to 5%), Oxygen (0% to 2%), Hydrogen (0% to 1%), Ammonia (0% to 1%), and Hydrogen sulphide, 0% to 1%.

The use of biogas furthers the ecological rule of using agricultural waste. It also offers another means of profit to agriculture. Biogas is used today primarily in electric engines that produce energy above a generator. Furthermore, the gas extracted from biomass is burned in block heating plants, where the heat used and produced also enters the electricity stream. About 30% of the resultant heat is required for the biogas production itself. The surplus is used for home heating, to dry agricultural products, and for external customer supply. In Europe, Denmark and Germany are the leading consumers of biogas, which is used primarily for generating electricity and for the disposal of agricultural residues.

Geothermic Geothermal heat is one of the most productive renewable sources of energy. Heat is stored in the earth's upper crust at depths up to ten kilometers. Geothermic energy can be used directly for heat production and also indirectly for power generation.

On the one hand, the origin of geothermal energy is the origin of the earth itself. On the other hand, there has been considerably more thermo development generated by the radioactive decay process in the earth's crust. This process began millions of years ago, and continues today. The temperature of the earth's core increases about 3°C per one hundred meters depth. Within the magma of the internal core, temperatures reach between 4,000°C and 5,000°C. Geothermal heat is thus the only form of renewable energy that is neither directly nor indirectly related to solar radiation.

Geothermal energy can be used for generating heat and electricity. We distinguish according to usage between:

- Surface-near geothermic (to about 500 meters of depth)
- Deep geothermic (1,000 to 6,000 meters)

For direct heat use, earth-coupled heat pumps are used for the surface-near geothermic. For the deep geothermic, warm water is pumped up from the depths to the surface, where the heat obtained is entered into a district heating system. That heat can be further differentiated, according to drilling depth and procedure, between hydrothermal (1,500 to 3,000 meters) and hot-dry skirt geothermic (3,000 to 6,000 meters). The available thermal stores of water are tapped with hydrothermal systems, but hot-dry skirt systems work with water artificially brought in through cracks and fissures in the hot rock formations.

Geothermic heat is always available, independent of weather, day, or time of year. It can be used in the winter for heating and in the summer for cooling. It represents an inexhaustible source of energy and has been in use for millennia in the form of geothermal water warmed up for cooking, bathing, and heating. Early applications are found, for example, in the baths of the Roman Empire and in the Middle kingdom of the Chinese.

In 2005, worldwide installations capable of producing about 28 gigawatts of geothermic heat were installed. Sweden and Iceland are the leaders of producing geothermic heat. Both countries have been pioneers in this field through widespread use of this method.

Fuel Cell Technology Fuel cell technology is not, strictly speaking, a renewable energy, it is an alternative form of energy. In fuel cell technology, reactive power from combustible hydrogen and the oxidizing agent oxygen is converted chemically into electricity. The principle of the hydrogen oxygen fuel cell was discovered in the middle of the 19th century by Christian Friedrich Schönbein. Hydrogen is a secondary energy carrier, because production presupposes the use of fossil or renewable energy carriers. In contrast, oxygen is naturally found in the earth's atmosphere.

A fuel cell basically consists of two electrodes with a membrane between them that act as ionic conductors. While the anode (negative pole) is surrounded by the oxidizing combustible (hydrogen), the reduced oxidizing agent (oxygen) surrounds the cathode (positive pole). The combustible is then converted to hydrogen ions, through delivery of electrons to the anode. These corpuscles overflow through an electrical conductor to the cathode. Here the oxygen becomes anions. The oxygen ions react with the loose hydrogen ions via water. Since the only byproduct of burning hydrogen with oxygen is water, fuel cell technology is actually an emission-free energy source.

Until recently, fuel cell technology has been used solely for space travel and in submarines. But the portable fuel cell industry (portable electric appliances) is reaching maturity. Mobile fuel cells for the automotive industry are being tested for the first time by DaimlerChrysler in Chinese city buses.

The greatest problem with mobile hydrogen fuel cells is storage of the high-fleeting hydrogen. There are three traditional alternatives for storage: a pressure bottle, liquid hydrogen, or metal hydride. An additional storage possibility for the future may be silicon. Since silicon is made of arenaceous quartz, it could probably be used to store and transport energy fairly easily.

This would also greatly reduce the potential dangers of storing and transporting hydrogen.

Due to the limitations of oil and gas resources, as well as the increasing global environmental problems, the future of fossil fuels within the general energy mix will be reduced. We believe a global mass market awaits the producers of renewable and alternative energies.

HARD COMMODITIES: METALS

Metal include precious metals, base metals, and ferrous metal. Each is described in this section.

Precious Metals

Metals in general are the largest group of chemical elements. They are characterized by metallic shine, opaqueness, and good malleability. Metals are consistent, homogeneous, and easily broken down and mixed together. Metals are also transportable in every size. We can differentiate between heavy- and light-density metals, and we can also differentiate, according to reactivity, between precious and base metals.

Gold, silver, and platinum are referred to as *precious metals*. Platinum, palladium, rhodium, iridium, ruthenium, and osmium are referred to as the platinum metals. The major feature of precious metals is their permanence. They exhibit high resistance against corrosion and oxidation. Their shine comes from the reaction between light and free electrons: the brighter the source of light, the stronger the shine.

Precious metals have many commercial forms:

- *Bullion* can be poured or shaped into a plate or bar form. Both are used in capital investment and in industrial processing.
- *Granules* are irregular grains that arise through immersing liquid precious metal in a water bath. The grains are used in industrial processing and in the jewelry industry.
- *Coins* are a means of payment governed by individual countries. Coins are available only for capital investment.
- *Medals* have no nominal value, unlike coins. They are manufactured today mostly by private companies and often bought by collectors. There is not much of a market for medals, and they therefore trade at face value.
- *A delivery claim* is an account balance for a certain amount of precious metal. This trading form was the precursor of the banking business.

- A *co-ownership* is a claim to a physical safe, a deposit, or an inventory of precious metals.
- *Physical precious metal* can be borrowed against an agreed interest as a credit.

Every bank sets precious metal prices for wholesale at their own discretion. But competition can lead to price approximations. The total weight of a coin is its gross or raw weight, which consists of the precious metal weight and the weight of base additions needed for the hardening of the coin. The net weight represents the pure precious metal weight.

The fineness of precious metals results from the amount of any alloy. In coinage, the specification occurs per 1,000 parts, but jewelers usually specify in carats. Note that carats referring to precious metal fineness should not be confused with carats referring to precious stone weight (1 carat corresponds to 0.2 grams). Fineness is distinguished in seven gradations:

- 24 carats has a proportion of 999 to 1,000
- 22 carats has a proportion of 917 to 1,000
- 18 carats has a proportion of 750 to 1,000
- 14 carats has a proportion of 585 to 1,000
- 10 carats has a proportion of 416 to 1,000
- 9 carats has a proportion of 375 to 1,000
- 8 carats has a proportion of 333 to 1,000

Gold The precious metal gold (its elemental name, Au, comes from the Latin, Roman word *aurum*) has always fascinated people. Its metallic yellow color inspired the pharaohs to compare it with the sun. The Romans and the Incas called gold the metal of the gods.

Gold is often regarded as a measurement of richness and power. The name appears to have come from the Indo-European word "ghel," meaning shining or gleaming. Although gold is considered a rare precious metal, it is actually found almost everywhere in the world. However, since it is not worthwhile to mine for less than 2.5 grams per ton of soil concentration, today's procedures actually remove only a small part of the gold available.

The use of gold in jewelry production can be traced to the 4th millennium BCE. However, gold was not used as money until the 6th century BCE. Legend says that Croesus, the king of Libya, used gold for the first time to emboss coins with his coat of arms, which became an official means of payment.

Gold has all seven money properties:

- It is a *luxury good*, valued by most people.
- It is *dividable* in almost any denomination.

- It is *easy to transport.*
- It remains completely *stable* over time.
- It can be *weighed* exactly.
- It is *not easy to forge* or artificially producible.
- It *cannot be multiplied.*

Gold can thus fulfill the three money functions: It can be used as a means of exchange or means of payment, it comes in an arithmetic unit, and its purchasing power does not diminish over time.

Gold is found in nature mainly as either high-quality free gold (lumps or grains), or as finely distributed minerals mixed with silver, copper, or mercury. Mixing gold with silver gives it a whiter appearance. Mixing it with copper gives it a pinkish hue.

There are two main types of gold: primary mountain gold, which is found underground in quartz, and secondary soap gold, which is the by-product of the decomposition of primary gold. Mountain gold still exists in its initial (primary) deposits, but it is usually accompanied by sulfides. Soap gold is found where gravel was washed away in creeks or rivers (secondary deposits) through climate changes.

The simplest form of gold production is through mining for gold by washing and shaking gold-bearing earth until the heavy gold separates from the rock. Besides this simple scrubbing procedure, cyanide leaching, a chemical procedure, can also be used to separate gold from rock through sodium and calcium cyanide dilution. Significant amounts of gold are also extracted during the electrolytic cleaning of copper.

Today, primary mountain gold mines are only run by mine companies (industrial mining), usually at depths of 3,000 to 4,000 meters. The price of gold is not expected to rise significantly unless new deposits are located. But in general, for the last seven years, new discoveries have lagged development. The relatively low gold prices of the last 15 years have led to less exploration, which in turn has led to a significant decrease in price. Today, worldwide gold reserves are estimated at approximately 100,000 tons in about 900 mines.

Unlike other raw consumer materials, almost 90% of mined gold is still in circulation. Demand per year is estimated at 4,000 tons, while supply is currently only 2,500 tons. Central bank gold sales and old gold recycling make up this supply deficit.

To trade physical gold, it is poured into metal bullion. A gold standard bar weighs about 400 ounces or about 12.5 kilograms (an ounce equals 31.1035 grams). The manufacturer name, the fineness of the gold, and the barrier number are punched onto the bar. Fineness must be at least 995. Barrier numbers are used for identification.

Next to standard gold bars, there are also smaller bars, smaller plates for coining, and granular materials for the jewelry industry. The most important commercial centers for physical gold are London (the London Bullion Market Association), Zurich, and Tokyo. Gold futures contracts are traded in New York at the Commodity Exchange (COMEX).

On the supply side, the mining companies and central bank sales are the major suppliers. South Africa is the leader with 15%, followed by the United States with 11%, Australia with 9%, China with 8%, Russia and Peru with 7% each, Indonesia with 6%, and Canada with 5%. The production of all other countries amounts to less than 5%.

After mining, the gold reserves of central banks have the next largest supply. These gold supplies date from the time of the gold standard, when national currencies had to be coated with gold. The U.S. central bank currently has 8,135 tons of gold, followed by Germany with 3,440 tons, the International Monetary Fund (IMF) with 3,217 tons, France with 3,025 tons, Italy with 2,452, Switzerland with 1,666, the Netherlands with 801, the ECB with 767, Japan with 765, and China with 600 tons. There are thus about 32,000 tons of gold in central banks worldwide.

Demand comes primarily from the jewelry industry, the manufacturing and dental industries, and private investment in gold. The jewelry industry accounts for more than 80%; investing in gold is about 2%, the smallest part of the demand.

After the enormous price increases of the 1970s, gold began a 19-year bearish trend in 1980. The price peaked at U.S. $850 per barrel, and bottomed out in September 1999 at U.S. $252 per barrel. Since then, the price of gold has again been trending upward.

Examining the seasonal cycle of gold prices, it appears that the months of May and September, as well as December through February, are favorable for taking a long position in gold.

Silver Silver (element Ag, from the Latin *argentum*) is the most common precious metal. It occurs about 15 to 20 times more often than gold. Silver almost never occurs in mines in pure form. About 60% is extracted as a secondary metal during copper, zinc, or lead production, 15% comes from gold production, and only 25% comes from pure silver mines.

The name silver originates from the Norse, and means light, white, or bright. Similarly to gold, silver has been used since the 4th millennium before Christ, as both jewelry and money. In ancient times, silver was actually thought to be more valuable than gold by the Egyptians, the Greeks, and the Romans.

As a precious metal, silver has outstanding firmness (it is softer than copper, but harder than gold), durability, and malleability. It also has the best electric and thermal conductivity of all metals, as well as the best reflectivity and light absorption. In addition to the electric industry, colloidal silver is used in photography and in medicine. But long before industrial applications became common, silver had been used as money. It also fulfills the three money functions excellently.

During the Middle Ages and in modern times, silver has maintained its purchasing power and price relative to gold remarkably well. From the year 1600 BCE, a fixed gold-silver price relationship was decreed as 13:33. In the 19th century, there was one bimetal money standard by which gold and silver in a ratio of 1:15 were equal. All money in circulation had a corresponding cover in either gold or silver. After the bimetal standard was abolished, and the pure gold standard was established at the end the 19th century, silver languished until it ceased to play any monetary role, and came to exist primarily as currency reserve in central banks.

On the supply side, mining is currently the sole means of production because central banks no longer hold silver. Total annual production of silver is 630 million ounces, and 90% of that comes from 10 countries: Mexico and Peru lead with 16% and 15%, respectively, followed by Australia with 11%, China with 10%, Poland and Chile with 7% each, Canada, the United States, and Russia with 6% each, and Kazakhstan with just 3%.

On the demand side, the jewelry industry, the manufacturing and photo industries, and private investors account for most of the demand. The manufacturing industry is the largest customer, with about 43%, followed by the jewelry industry with 30%, and the photo industry with 22%. Private investment in silver stands at about 4%, and is the smallest part of demand.

Similarly to gold, silver also had an enormous increase in value during the 1970s that ended in January 1980 at $50 per ounce. Silver then began a downward trend, ending in 1992 at $3.55. After a very long phase of low prices, silver also began to trend upward, along with gold, in 2001.

Examining the seasonal cycle of silver prices, we see that the months of July and September, as well as December through February, are favorable for taking a long position in silver.

Silver is highly correlated with gold. Physical demand for silver exceeds supply even more than for gold. Although silver price increases have been larger than gold, the relationship between their prices is still about 1:60 (for an ounce of gold you can acquire sixty of silver), which is historically very high. The historical means is near 1:15, the historical low is 1:3, and the high is more than 1:100. In addition, silver is the only metal that has such a high discrepancy between its current market value and its historic high. While many industrial metals and platinum are reaching new historic peaks, silver is still 80% below its high of $50.

Warren Buffett, the CEO of Berkshire Hathaway and one of the most successful investors of all time, bought 129 million ounces of silver between July 1997 and January 1998. He publicized his purchase on February 3, 1998, which caused the price of silver to jump. In addition to Warren Buffett, the hedge fund legend George Soros, and Microsoft's founder Bill Gates also invested significantly in silver and/or silver stocks (Apex Silver and Pan American Silver). Thus, for smart investors, silver appears to be an interesting alternative to gold.

Platinum Unlike gold and silver, platinum (Pt) was discovered later, in 1750 by the Briton William Watson. Spanish gold detectors had found platinum much earlier in the South American Andes, but thought this unknown metal was worthless. They called it *platina*, meaning small silver.

In the 19th century, scientists discovered that other metals exist within platinum that today are referred to as *platinum group metals* (PGM), for example, palladium, rhodium, iridium, ruthenium, and osmium. Rhodium is currently the most expensive precious metal, followed by rhodium. Platinum and its group metals are naturally very high quality, and they occur with the same frequency as gold. In pure form, platinum is very soft, which is why it needs group metals to gain its extreme firmness. Platinum is primarily generated as a byproduct of copper and nickel production.

On the supply side, annual worldwide production of platinum is about 200 tons. From that, about 75% comes from South Africa, where 90% of the known reserves are located, 15% comes from Russia, the second largest producer, and the rest comes mainly from North America.

In South Africa and the United States, the production of the platinum metals is itself a major industry, but in Russia and Canada these metals are primarily produced as a byproduct of nickel production. The geography of the deposits causes varying degrees of each platinum group metal to be present in relation to platinum. For example, South African platinum has a higher platinum content, while Russia and American platinum contains more palladium.

On the demand side, the automotive industry (for catalysts) accounts for about 43% of the platinum supply, and the jewelry industry is about 35%. The rest is distributed within the electronics, glass, chemistry, and petrochemistry industries. Platinum is suitable for use in automotive catalytic converters because of its excellent chemical ability. It keeps hydrogen, oxygen, and other gases in an active state. Platinum also plays an important role within the automotive fuel cell technology industry. Within the jewelry industry, a real piece of platinum jewelry bears the stamp "950 Pt."

Along with gold and silver, platinum prices reached a historic high in January 1980. Prices peaked at $1,050 per ounce, and then began a downward trend that ended in 1998 at $340 per ounce. Since then, platinum has also started to trend upward again, similarly to gold and silver.

Because of the recent high platinum prices, palladium has increasingly been used as a replacement within the automotive and jewelry industries.

Palladium Palladium (Pd), the lightest platinum group metal, was discovered in 1803 by the Briton William Wollaston during a platinum exploration in South America. The name palladium came from the planetoid Pallas, which had been discovered in 1802.

Within nature, palladium almost always occurs with the other platinum metals. Its most important attributes are its ability to absorb hydrogen and its high responsiveness. It has become especially important to the automotive industry in catalytic converter production. Engines are now developed so that exhaust systems can use either platinum or palladium, depending on which is cheaper at any given time.

On the supply side, annual worldwide production of palladium is about 200 tons. From that, about 46% comes from Russia, 36% from South Africa, and 14% from North America. Palladium is also a byproduct of nickel, copper, lead, gold, silver, and platinum production. In the future, recycling used palladium (e.g., from old catalytic converters) is expected to become an increasingly important industry, similarly to the recycling of platinum.

On the demand side, the automotive industry dominates with about 50% of the demand. Next is the electronics industry with 15%, the dental industry with 14%, the jewelry industry with 12%, and the chemical industry with about 6%. In the jewelry industry, palladium is used to turn gold into white gold. A pure palladium piece of jewelry bears the stamp "950 Pd."

As with all the other precious metals, palladium's price peaked in January 1980. Prices then began to trend downward, ending in 1992 at U.S. $80. After a longer period of low prices, palladium again began an upward trend in 1997.

Base Metals

Industrial metals (base metals) are used mainly in the building industry. Therefore, demand depends highly on worldwide economic development. Due to enormous current demand from China—which currently absorbs more than 20% of worldwide base metal production—there is increasing concern about shortages of these metals.

Aluminum Aluminum (Al) is the most significant raw base metal, and the metal that occurs most frequently in the earth's crust. This silvery gray light metal is not naturally very high quality, but is improved using chemical connections. It is primarily extracted from bauxite, which is found around the equator. Bauxite is related to alumina, iron oxide, silicon monoxide, and water.

A disadvantage of aluminum production is its high cost, which is due to the high amounts of energy released during the melting procedure, when alumina is melted with cryolite. This can be up to 50% of the production costs. Therefore, aluminum is highly correlated with oil price development. Aluminum processing happens mostly via casting procedures. Next to the production of bauxite, the recycling of items like soda cans also became an important source of this raw material. Aluminum's light weight, corrosion resistance, and very good malleability make it indispensable for the vehicle, airplane, and construction industries.

On the supply side, annual worldwide production of aluminum is about 30 million tons. Of that, 20% comes from China, 13% from Russia, and 10% from the United States.

On the demand side, the automotive industry dominates, with about 26% of the supply, followed by the packaging and building industries with 22% each. On a country level, the biggest demand comes from the United States and Europe.

Similarly to all the other metals, aluminum reached its historic high in 1980. The price then began to trend downward, and ended in 1993 at $1,020. Aluminum prices again began to trend upward in 1999.

Copper Copper (Cu), an alloy component of bronze, is one of the oldest metals and has been used since the Bronze Age. Copper occurs as a heavy metal in nature and is naturally of very high quality. Its Latin name, *cuprum*, comes from the island of Cyprus (*aes cyprium*: ore of the cyprus). Due to its excellent ability to transport heat, as well as its transforming abilities and high corrosion resistance, copper is, next to aluminum, one of the most commonly used industrial metals. Copper is also used for the production of brass (a copper/zinc alloy), and bronze (a copper/tin alloy). Both alloys are harder than copper itself.

The raw material of copper is made up of 60% ore concentrates and 40% old copper (copper scrap). In this case, copper has gone through several stages. The ores of copper condensate are produced by the copper mines. This concentrate of copper, iron, and sulfur, which is similar to powder, is melted down in the refineries into blister and anode. The anodes are then run through an electrolytic refining process and become high-grade copper, so-called "copper cathodes." The final products are copper sheets, which are used for roofs, installation conduits, and electric cable, because of their excellent conductivity. To be considered tradable on the stock exchange, copper cathodes must be 99.99% pure.

On the supply side, annual worldwide production of copper is 16 million tons. From that, about 35% comes from Chile, 9% from Indonesia, and 8% from the United States; 10% comes from copper scrap.

On the demand side, the building industry (for copper sheets) dominates, with about 37%, followed by electronics (for twisted-pair cables) with 26%, the manufacturing systems engineering industry with 15%, and the transportation and consumer goods industries with 11% each. In 2003, China replaced the United States for the first time ever as the leading copper consumer.

Copper reached its historic high in 1980. It then began a downward trend, ending similarly to gold in 1999 at $1,320. After a second historic low in 2001, copper prices began trending upward again.

Nickel Nickel (Ni) has been in use for about 5,000 years. However, this was only by mistake as an unmeltable component of copper ore (white copper). Because it complicated the production of pure copper ore, it was called the "metal of the devils" (during the Middle Ages). An independent metal nickel industry first arose in the middle of the 18th century through the efforts of Baron Cronstedt.

Nickel is a magnetic metal of the iron group, and is commonly used in more than 300,000 different products. It is a very hard conductive metal, and has a strong silvery color. More than 60% of the nickel produced worldwide is for the production of high-grade steel and other unoxidizable alloys. Small alloy components of nickel promote firmness and anticorrosion properties of steel very well. Although it occurs in small amounts as a trace element in human beings, nickel is actually toxic to humans in amounts of more than 50 milligrams. Allergic reactions from skin contact are also known to occur.

On the supply side, annual worldwide production of nickel is 1.2 million tons. From that, 24% comes from Russia, 16% comes from the United States, and 13% from Canada. The recycling of old nickel is gaining in importance, however, as about 20% of worldwide output now comes from nickel scrap.

On the demand side, the building industry is the main consumer, followed by the automotive industry. The high-grade steel generated by nickel is especially suitable for the construction industry. About 40% of the nickel produced worldwide goes to Europe, followed by Asia and America.

Coin prices also reached historic highs in 1980. The bearish market ended in 1998, at $3,725, when coin prices again began trending upward.

Zinc Zinc (Zn) is the third most commonly used industrial metal after aluminum and copper. Zinc is a bluish-white metal that is often used for the protection of other metals, for example, in the bodies of cars to protect against corrosion. The electronic procedure, which uses about 50% of zinc production, is called galvanization. Zinc forms a weather-resistant protective coating in the air called zinc carbonate. Furthermore, zinc is also used in combination with copper to produce brass. At 20%, brass production is the second highest use for zinc.

Zinc does not occur in pure form in nature. Sphalerite (a zinc/sulphur combination that is about 65% zinc) and smithsonite (a zinc carbonate that is about 50% zinc) are extracted from the two zinc ores. Sphalerite is converted in a melting furnace and smithsonite in a toploader kiln to create zinc oxide, which is then mixed with coal and reduced in a muffle furnace to vaporous raw zinc (98%). High-quality zinc (99.99%) is extracted by repeatedly remelting via an electrolysis procedure.

On the supply side, annual worldwide production of zinc is 10 million tons. China and Australia are the two biggest zinc producers, with 20% each, followed by Canada and Peru, with a total of about 25% each.

On the demand side, the building industry is the main consumer of zinc, followed by the automotive industry. Besides those industries, dovetailed steel is commonly used in both machine building and in household appliances.

Zinc reached its historic high in 1980. It then began a downward trend, which ended in 2001 at $737. Since then, zinc prices have been trending upward again.

Lead The heavy metal lead (Pb) occurs in nature primarily in combination with copper, zinc, or silver. Its name is Indo-Germanic, and means glimmering, radiant, or shining. From the early Bronze Age, lead was used, among other things, for bronze production. The best known type of lead is galena, made of 87% lead, lead ore, and lead vitriol.

Lead is corrosion-resistant, very soft, and slightly malleable. It was therefore an early choice during Roman times for pipeline construction. Due to its toxicity, however, it has not been used in most developed countries for pipeline construction since 1970. The use of lead in dinner plates is likewise prohibited today. Small amounts, taken over a long period, are stored in the body and can produce a chronic lead poisoning, characterized by headache, fatigue, and muscle reduction. Plastic, aluminum, zinc, and iron are common substitutes for lead.

Lead nowadays is used mainly for car batteries, standby units, and for blasting shield uses. As with other industrial metals, lead is run through two production stages, promotion and smelter, and more than half the lead currently in circulation has been recycled from car batteries. The most important smelters are in industrialized nations, but disassembly mainly takes place in developing countries.

On the supply side, annual worldwide production of lead is 7 million tons. From that, 22% comes from the United States, 20% from China, and 6% from Germany. On the demand side, the production of car batteries accounts for more than 75%, followed by the production of standby units with 15%. Safety devices are another area where lead can be useful to protect against radiation, for example, lead aprons in medicine or in transportation appliances for "KASTOR" transportation of radioactive waste.

Again similarly to all other industrial metals, lead reached its historic high in 1980. After that peak, prices began a downward trend, which ended relatively late, in 2001, when the market for lead began to trend upward. Since then, lead prices have been on an upward trend.

Precious and industrial metals do not contain any iron, and are referred to as *nonferrous* metals (NE metals). Industrial metals can technically be divided into heavy metals (with a density above 4.5 grams per cubic centimeter), and light metals (a density under 4.5 grams per cubic centimeter). While aluminum is a light metal, copper, nickel, zinc, and lead are heavy metals.

Iron The oldest objects made of iron (Fe) are about 6,000 years old and come from Egypt and the ancient civilization of Sumer (in present day Iraq). In Europe, the Celts began to treat iron in charcoal fires about 700 years before Christ. Its name comes from the Indo-Germanic word *eison*, meaning shining. With more than 6%, iron is the fourth most common element in the earth's crust.

Iron is a soft, silver-white metal that is related to the base metals. It is almost never found in nature alone. Rocks that contain more than 20% iron are referred to as iron ores. These are decomposed in surface mining and mining, nowadays mainly in South America. Brazil is the biggest worldwide iron ore producer, followed by Australia, Canada, China, and Eastern Europe. The original largest iron ore producers were France, Sweden, and Germany, but they do not play a role in iron ore production nowadays. The last German iron ore pit was in the upper Palatinate Auerbach, and closed in 1987.

Liquid iron comes from the initial ore through a chemical reduction created by use of a blast furnace heated to 2,000°C. The byproducts from iron fusion are slag and blast furnace gas. Slag is used as fertilizer and in street building materials; blast furnace gas is used for firing coke ovens.

Steel Under the heading of steel, we can characterize all plastically malleable, metallic alloys whose main component is iron. In this case, carbon is removed from the pig iron until it accounts for less than 2%. Brittle iron is thus transformed into malleable steel. If the percentage of carbon is higher than 2%, we refer to it as cast iron.

Steel is the most frequently used metallic material. Next to pig iron, steel scrap also plays an important role in steel production. During the classic oxygen blast furnace process, steel scrap usage is nearly 20%. The properties of high-grade steel are improved by suballoys of a suitable steel refiner, such as chrome or nickel. These are mostly used in construction or to make tools. The most significant steel-producing countries are China, Japan, and the United States. In Europe, the most important steel manufacturers are Russia, Germany, and Italy.

Steel developed from iron is an ideal ecological material because it is recyclable for an almost unlimited time period, with no loss of quality.

SOFT COMMODITIES

While most hard commodities have reached historically high levels over the last few months, prices for the primary soft commodities also remain strong. However, due to inflation, agricultural raw material prices are ironically near their all-time lows despite increased demand from worldwide industrialization. Especially because of the increasing prosperity of Asian national economies such as China and India, the amount of food consumed has increased dramatically.

Eating habits have also changed as prosperity has increased, meaning more meat and fruit consumption, and increased consumption of products such as pasta. The use of grains and sugar as fuel are likely to increase further because of the increasing fossil fuel prices worldwide. Thus, it may be only a matter of time before increasing demand results in significant price increases.

Food and Consumer Products

Wheat Wheat is among the most significant agro-raw materials in the world. More than one-fifth of worldwide calorie need is fulfilled through this grain. Flour is the main product made from wheat, but it is also used in the production of alcoholic drinks such as beer and whiskey, as well as ethanol and within the cattle industry. We can distinguish between different types of wheat according to the time the crop is planted, as well as the climatic conditions of the grain. The two most important types are Chicago wheat (soft red winter wheat) and Kansas wheat (hard red winter wheat). While the name winter refers to a point in time when the grain is planted, the characterizations hard and/or soft refer to the climatic relationships under which the wheat is grown.

On the supply side, annual worldwide production of wheat is about 560 million tons. From that, 18% comes from the European Union, 16%

comes from China, and 13% from India. Russia and the United States harvest 9% and 8%, respectively. On the demand side, China and the European Union dominate the market, with 17% and 16% of the supply, respectively. Russia follows with 7% and the United States with 5%. Only one-fifth of worldwide wheat production makes it onto the international market, however. The rest is consumed by the producing countries themselves.

Corn After wheat, corn is another of the most important grains in the world. Corn is an extremely hardy plant, and can be grown almost anywhere. It is commonly used as animal feed, but it is also used in the production of food (for example, for alcohol, margarine, and sweeteners). Similarly to wheat, it can be used to produce ethanol.

On the supply side, annual worldwide production of corn is 600 million tons. From that, 38% comes from the United States, 20% from China, 8% from Brazil, and 7% from the European Union. On the demand side, the United States and China dominate the market, with 32% and 20%, respectively. Brazil and Mexico follow, with 6% and 4%, respectively. Since the biggest producers are also the biggest consumers, only a small part of the supply makes it onto the international market.

Soybeans After wheat and corn, soybeans are the next most important farm product. Due to their 40% protein content, they have been used in many diverse ways. In addition to food production (20%), they are also commonly used in baby food, diet foods, noodles, margarine, tofu, and soy milk. However, the biggest part of the soy harvest, 80%, is used as animal feed in the form of soy meal. Another product is soybean oil, which is obtained through the pressing of the beans.

In addition, soy products have become more frequently used in industrial applications, such as varnishes, colors, soaps, adhesives, inks, and even biofuels. Again due to the increasing energy problems, the production of biofuel has attracted a great deal of attention.

On the supply side, annual worldwide production of soybeans is 210 million tons. About 90% comes from the United States, Brazil, and Argentina. On the demand side, the European Union leads with almost 50%, followed by China. Grain and soy are the most important soft commodity groups when measured in world production, and their weighting in raw material indexes is higher than that of gender, agro-industry, and animal raw materials by more than double.

Coffee The coffee bean had its origin in Ethiopia, where it was roasted for the first time in the 14th century and then brewed into coffee. Today coffee has become one of the most important international agro-raw materials. Worldwide there are two main coffee types grown in about eighty subtropical and tropical countries over 11 million hectares. The higher-quality Arabica beans (traded in New York) come mainly from the western hemisphere, while the stronger Robusta beans (traded in London) grow in the tropical regions of Asia and Africa.

The coffee bean is regarded as especially precious among useful plants, because few plants are as weather-sensitive. A small ground frost in the morning can destroy millions of coffee trees. In addition, it takes three to four years from planting until the first harvest, which leads to a long amortization of costs. Since the trend in Asian regions has been to plant less tea crops and more coffee crops, demand for this agro-sector is only expected to increase in the future.

On the supply side, worldwide annual production of coffee is 115 million bags (60 kilograms). From that, 35% comes from Brazil, followed by 10% from Vietnam, and 9% from Colombia. On the demand side, the European Union dominates with about 34%, followed by the United States. In Europe, Germany is the leading coffee consumer, with 8% of world demand. Additional demand has been coming from the producer countries. For example, Brazil now uses up to 40% of their harvest themselves.

Cocoa Cocoa is an especially temperamental plant and it can only be grown in the warmest zones. The cacao tree yields its first orange-brown or yellow-green beans after three to five years. The very sensitive cacao tree can then be harvested twice a year. While the main harvest (80%) occurs during the winter months, the additional harvest (20%) can occur during the summer. The typical cocoa flavor occurs after fermentation of the bean semen.

On the supply side, annual worldwide production of cocoa is 3.5 million tons. From that, about 70% comes from West Africa (40% of that from the Ivory Coast), 17% from Southeast Asia, and 13% from Central and South America. On the demand side, the Netherlands leads with 13% of the demand, followed by Germany, which has the highest per capita chocolate consumption in the world. The sweets industry in general accounts for more than 90% of the world harvest. The rest is used in cosmetics and the pharmaceuticals industry.

Sugar The agro-raw material sugar is manufactured from sugarcane and from sugar beets. Sugarcane is grown in tropical regions such as Brazil, India, and Cuba; sugar beets come from moderate climates, such as in Europe, Australia, and China. The ratio of sugarcane crops to sugar beet crops is about 60:40.

Sugar is used to improve flavor and preserve foods, but it has also been used increasingly as a gasoline competitor in the form of ethanol fuel. Brazil, the biggest sugar producer in the world, is also the leading producer and consumer of ethanol. Brazil produces 15 million cubic meters of ethanol per year, and that amount is increasing. Half the Brazilian sugar harvest is currently processed into biofuel. In 2005, for the first time, more Brazilians bought ethanol-powered vehicles (which can operate using either gasoline or ethanol) than bought traditional gasoline-powered models.

However, as progressively more sugar is used for ethanol, there is less available for Brazil to export, which may eventually lead to supply problems. If the supply problems of crude oil intensify, such alternatives would most likely continue to gain in popularity, for both economic and ecological reasons.

In the 18th century, the English sweetened their tea with crystals obtained from sugarcane (*saccharum*) from the colonies. In 1747, the German pharmacist and chemist Andreas Marggraf discovered that the same sweet material (sucrose) that came from sugarcane could also be obtained from the root of a goosefoot plant, the sugar beet. Sugar has been an energy source ever since for both humans, and now machines.

While sugar consumption approaches 23 kilograms per person per year on average worldwide, China uses only 11 kilograms per person per year. There is a positive correlation between increasing prosperity and sugar consumption, and China may end up playing a decisive role in sugar prices, as it has for most other raw materials.

Sugar is currently subsidized in both the United States and in Europe. About 5,000 American sugar farmers receive subsidies of $5 billion annually, while about 6,000 EU sugar beet farmers receive €3 billion per year in subsidies.

On the supply side, annual worldwide production of sugar is 150 million tons. The largest producers are Brazil with 20%, followed by the European Union with 15%, India with 10%, China with 7%, and the United States with 5%.

On the demand side, India leads with 13%, followed by the European Union with 12%, Eastern Europe and Latin America with 11% each, Africa with 10%, China with 8%, and the United States with 7%.

Industrial Agro-Raw Materials

Cotton Cotton has been in use for more than 5,000 years in India. In China, Egypt, and the United States, it has also been in use for 1,000 years. Today, cotton is grown in more than 70 countries worldwide, of which China and the United States are the most important producers. Cotton requires a subtropical climate with a lot of sun and moisture. During planting, usually from April to May, cotton plants react extremely sensitively to overly hot or wet climates. In the harvest period, from September until December, as dry a climate as possible is needed. After the harvest, the cotton is dried, cleaned, and packed into bales. Cotton fibers are then used in the textile industry. On the supply side, about 25% of worldwide cotton production comes from China, followed by the United States with 20%, and India with 14%. On the demand side, China and Indonesia are the biggest importers.

Timber The agro-raw material wood is subdivided into hard and soft woods. Soft woods make up about 85% of total wood consumption. Around one third of the earth's surface is covered with woods, which is similar to 4 billion hectare. Tropical rain forests represent only seven percent of the earth's surface. These woods protect us against erosions, avalanches, and flooding and in addition these woods save half of the carbon worldwide.

Every year around 6 million hectares are cutover worldwide. This cutover has been reduced within the last couple of years, since the cutover in 1980 till 1990 reached its peak at 15 million hectares.

Animal Agro-Raw Materials

Feeder Cattle The term *feeder cattle* describes young animals, mostly castrated bulls, that are being raised to slaughter weight. After six to eight months of feeding, the animals weigh between 600 and 800 pounds. The young animals are then classified as live cattle.

Live Cattle The term *live cattle* describes cattle that are ready for slaughter, and weigh an average of 1,200 pounds. After attaining their target weight, the cattle are sold to slaughterhouses. On the supply side, annual worldwide production is 50 million tons of cattle beef. From that, about 25% comes from the United States, 16% comes from Brazil, 15% from the European Union, and 12% from China. The demand side is dominated by the United States, with 26%, followed by the European Union with 15%, Brazil with 13%, and China with 12%.

Lean Hogs The term *lean hogs* describes slaughter-ready pigs, which are about six months old. Unlike cattle, pigs generally remain on the same farm until they are ready for market. Pigs reach optimal slaughter weight at 250 pounds. From that, 90 pounds of meat are reserved for the market, with the rest processed as ham.

On the supply side, annual worldwide production is 90 million tons of pork. From that, about 50% comes from China, followed by 20% from the European Union, and 10% from the United States. On the demand side, China is the leading consumer, followed by the European Union and the United States. Since China is simultaneously the biggest producer and a big consumer, the European Union represents the biggest exporter of pork worldwide.

Note that the energy balance during animal product production is relevant: In order to produce one calorie of meat, 10 vegetable calories must be expended.

CONCLUSION

There is one main difference within the commodity categories. Fossil resources are limited in quantity and cannot (or only under high expenditure) be reproduced (e.g., crude oil). Soft commodities are not limited in quantity (e.g., coffee) and are relatively easy to reproduce. Both categories are essential resources for human beings.

The market value of fossil resources is influenced by demand, supply, and worldwide known deposit volume; renewable resources are only valued by supply and demand.

Market values of most of the hard commodities are still below their historic highs. The prices of these commodities have been in a bullish market cycle for several years. One reason is the faster usage of the known remaining resources as well as political issues. Since demand has already exceeded supply, and no further large increases on the supply side are expected, the market values for these commodities are expected to continue to rise.

Soft commodities such food and consumer products, animal agro-raw materials, and industrial agro-raw materials are all renewable resources, which have an overall increase in demand. Corn, wheat, and sugar are fundamental components of the daily meals of most people. Consumer products like coffee and cacao are also considered a part of our daily life. All these products are renewable, but may still be influenced by different external factors (e.g., weather). These factors influence supply and thus indirectly the value of these products as well.

CHAPTER 31

A Practical Guide to Gold as an Investment Asset

Charlie X. Cai, Ph.D.
Lecturer
Leeds University Business School
The University of Leeds

Iain Clacher, Ph.D.
Lecturer
Leeds University Business School
The University of Leeds

Robert Faff, Ph.D.
Professor of Finance
Department of Accounting and Finance
Monash University and Principal Research Fellow
Leeds University Business School
The University of Leeds

David Hillier, Ph.D.
Professor of Finance
Leeds University Business School
The University of Leeds

As a precious metal, gold is synonymous with both wealth and power. For thousands of years, society has placed a great importance on the acquisition and ownership of gold. In ancient civilizations such as the Roman and the Byzantine, gold was used as a (direct) form of currency as well as a symbol of luxury through ornamentation and decoration in jewelry. Today gold is still a measure of wealth and luxury, and as recently as the 1970s it was the base measure of national currency value. Gold also forms the basis for a monetary standard used by the International Monetary Fund (IMF) and the Bank for International Settlements (BIS). In addition to the above, with the advancement of technology, gold is now used frequently in modern industrial activities such as dentistry and electronics.

The objective of this chapter therefore is twofold. First, we provide an overview of gold investments and the operation of gold markets. Second, the chapter provides a survey of the latest developments in gold research. We begin with a review of the uses of gold.

USES OF GOLD

One of the unique characteristics of gold is that it preserves wealth and provides liquidity to both individuals and institutions. As a result, since the late nineteenth century, gold has played a key role as a central bank reserve asset. Since it is essentially homogenous and distinguished only by purity, it serves as a comparable measure of currency value across countries. There have been a number of agreements, known as gold standards, in history between nations that valued a sovereign nation's currency in relation to their gold reserves.

Gold as a Monetary Standard

Under a gold standard, the notes issued by the central bank are a guarantee to the bearer of the note(s) that, on demand from the central bank, they will receive a fixed amount of gold in exchange for the bank note(s). In an international context this essentially fixes the exchange rate (known as *specie* points) between currencies. For central banks, the result is that balance of payment accounts are settled in gold. If there is a balance of payments surplus, the central bank would receive an inflow of gold to its gold reserves. This would allow the central bank to increase money supply, resulting in a possible increase in prices, which in turn, should increase the demand for exports. Balance of payments deficits would have the opposite effect.

The last international gold standard was the Bretton-Woods system. It was established in July 1944 to introduce a framework for rebuilding international trade once World War II ended. The system had a number of important features, and led to the establishment of two significant international banking institutions, namely the International Bank for Reconstruction and Development (IBRD), which is now part of the World Bank, and the IMF. One of the key features, in terms of monetary policy, was that central banks had to peg their currency to within 1% of the U.S. dollar which was fixed at $35 per troy ounce. However, the system failed in

1971, as the requirement to stay within the 1% band put a significant amount of pressure on the global economy, which resulted in the suspension of all conversion rights from U.S. dollar to gold.

Gold as a Reserve Asset

Despite the absence of these pegged arrangements since the collapse of Bretton-Woods, gold was, and still is, held as a reserve asset. The rationale is perhaps not as compelling now as it was in the past, but in times of crisis and strain on central banks it is a very useful tool. One recent example of the benefits of gold to a central bank occurred during the Asian financial crisis in 1997. Due to the devaluation of its local currency against the U.S. dollar, South Korea was unable to service its external debt. The Government of South Korea embarked upon a mass purchase of private gold stocks from its citizens in exchange for local currency debt instruments. The Korean government raised over 5 million ounces of gold from this exercise, which it then sold for U.S. dollars. As a result it was able to service its external debt and prevent default. This gives credence to the view that gold is, as stated by Alan Greenspan, then-chairman of the Board of Governors of the Federal Reserve, in testimony before the U.S. Congress in 1999, the "ultimate means of payment and is perceived to be an element of stability in the currency and is the ultimate value of the currency."

Despite a number of upward revisions of the fixed gold price by 1973, all major currencies floated against the dollar price of gold. The result was that gold transformed from being solely a reserve asset to become an investment commodity. In 1971, the price of gold was $35 per troy ounce under the old gold standard, but, by the end of 1973 the London Gold Fixing price had risen to $120 per troy ounce. This rapid gold price hike was a major factor in the New York Commodities Exchange (COMEX) offering the first gold futures instrument in 1975. Investment demand for gold increased significantly over the ensuing few years, peaking in 1980 when gold prices reached the unprecedented level to over $700 per troy ounce.[1]

Since the collapse of the Bretton-Woods system, and the gradual deregulation of financial markets all over the world, the demand for gold and gold derivatives for investment purposes has remained strong. This has occurred for a number of reasons. First, gold is largely uncorrelated with other financial assets and therefore offers many diversification opportunities in investment portfolios. Second, these low correlations make gold a good

[1]It should be noted that the price escalation to the peak of 1980 was unlikely to have been caused solely by demand—for example, high oil prices and a weaker dollar will have been contributory factors. Demand will however, have been a very significant factor in the price increase.

hedging instrument for investors, and last, gold investment is desirable as it offers liquidity in portfolios in times of financial constraint.

GOLDEN FUNDAMENTALS

To evaluate the role of gold, and derivatives of gold, as an investment asset, it is important to understand the unique dynamics of the forces underlying its supply and demand. Gold supply comes from two sources: aboveground gold supply (i.e., the gold that is already in circulation) and newly mined gold. The demand for gold comes from three main sources: industry, the luxury goods market, and investors.

In terms of supply, according to the World Gold Council (WGC), the supply of gold in 2005 consisted of 61% from mined production (70% of which comes from South Africa), 17% from official sales, and 22% from recycled gold. Paradoxically, although the largest component of gold supply is mined production, the gold price is not particularly sensitive to changes in the level of mined production.[2] The explanation is quite straightforward: the other two sources of supply, namely, official sales and recycled gold, constitute the "actual" supply of gold.

Theoretically, all the gold in central banks and all privately owned sources of gold could be supplied to the market. It is estimated that the total volume of gold that has already been extracted is approximately 155,500 tonnes. In contrast, a typical annual flow of newly mined gold is estimated to be only about 2,400 tonnes, which represents an addition of about 2% per annum to the existing gold pool according to a 2006 report by the World Gold Council. This percentage is far less than for any other commodity and especially oil. As such, this is one of the features which differentiates gold from almost all other commodities. Most commodities are consumed on extraction or converted into other materials and processes. Gold, however, is acquired and held by banks and individuals. This vast (potential) gold supply forms a buffer to absorb any supply shocks that may occur.

Central banks and supranational organizations, such as the IMF and the World Bank, play a significant role in the supply side of the international gold market, since they hold around one fifth of all global aboveground stocks of gold as reserve assets. In addition to buying and selling gold in the open market, central banks also affect the gold price through their lending, swaps, and other derivative activities. In addition, they are the biggest supplier of leased gold to the market.

---

[2]This is in contrast to the acute price sensitivity of oil or copper to changes in the level of their extraction.

The demand for gold can be classified into three categories: jewelry and fashion, industry, and investment. Jewelry consistently accounts for the largest share of final demand in actual gold at around 75% of total demand.[3] Trends in the jewelry sector are therefore extremely important to the overall performance of the gold market.

One important feature of jewelry demand is its seasonal nature. The fourth quarter of the year is the strongest due to the occurrence of several end-of-year celebrations and festivals including the Hindu festival of Diwali and Christmas, when jewelry gifts are common. The first quarter is normally the second strongest as a result of the Chinese New Year, the Indian wedding season, and, to a lesser extent, St. Valentine's Day. The second and third quarters usually experience lower demand with a relative absence of major gold-giving occasions.

Another factor, which is important in the seasonality of jewelry and induces increased gold demand, is economic development in countries such as India and China. In India, for example, it is estimated that the middle class has grown to around 200 million people. With this economic prosperity, individuals with higher disposable incomes are spending more on the gifts they give for Diwali for example, and so economic development in these countries is contributing to both the seasonal changes and increasing demand for gold.

Industrial and medical uses of gold represent 11% of demand globally, constituting approximately 400 tonnes per annum.[4] Gold also has a number of industrial and decorative purposes such as gold plating, coating, and gold thread. Overall, these uses of gold account for 2% to 3% of total demand. Notably, they yield very little gold which can be recycled and, thus in general, industrial and medical uses of gold result in the holding of larger stocks.

As a precious metal, gold is an attractive constituent in an investment portfolio because of its ability to preserve wealth, as well as its diversification properties. The investment demand for gold, reported by the World Gold Council (WGC), is relatively small at about 4% per annum. However, this seemingly low figure reflects the fact that the WGC only counts physical investment in coins and small bars and other identifiable forms of retail investment such as investment in listed exchange-traded gold funds. As such, this ignores the significant level of investment in gold through indirect means.

---

[3]According to the WGC, this was the average annual demand between 2001 and 2005.

[4]According to the WGC, this was the average annual demand between 2001 and 2005.

GOLD INVESTMENT PRODUCTS

Forwards

Forward contracts in gold are the same as any other forward contract, such as forward interest rates or forward exchange rates. They are an agreement to buy or sell, in this case gold, at some point in the future based upon an agreed price today.

Futures

Gold futures are essentially exchange-traded standardized forward contracts. In theory, they are a contract for delivery of a specified quantity and quality of gold at a set price on a specific date. In practice, physical delivery will not take place and the contracts are settled based upon gains or losses in relation to the price of gold. The gold futures price is determined by a number of factors and essentially reflects the market's estimate of the cost of carrying gold. That is, the interest cost on gold borrowing, insurance, storage, and delivery costs.

To invest in gold futures, a margin account is set up with a broker and money is placed into this account to provide some security to the exchange and liquidity for the position taken. The initial margin for NYMEX members of the exchange is $2,500 per contract, and for nonmembers this is $3,375 per contract.

The merit of the significant growth in the gold derivatives market and its potential impact on the spot price of gold is an issue which is contested. The main criticism of the significant growth in the derivatives market is the fall in the dollar spot price of gold which has been observed over the same period. Contrary to this however is the view that the growth of the derivatives market has improved liquidity in the gold market, and increased the risk management and hedging opportunities that gold provides.

What is without question is the positive impact that the derivatives market has had on participants in the gold market. Central banks have been able to generate an income on their reserve holdings. Those who hold large inventories of gold have the ability to hedge their risk from falling gold prices. Gold manufacturers and producers can also use the derivatives market to hedge gold prices. This ability to hedge has also enabled producers to develop new mines using project finance.

Options

Gold options give the holder the right but not the obligation to buy (*call option*) or sell (*put option*) a specified quantity of gold at a predetermined price by an agreed date. The price of a gold option depends on a number of underlying factors. These are the spot price of gold, the exercise price, the rate of interest, the estimated volatility of the gold price, and the time left until the option expires.

Warrants

During the 1980s gold warrants were used to finance mining projects. A gold warrant has many of the features of a gold option—the investor buys the warrant and the warrant allows the buyer the right to buy gold on a specified date for a specific price.

Gold Account and Gold Accumulation Plans

Gold Accumulation Plans (GAPs) were first introduced in Japan in the 1980s. In Japan these schemes are popular with major Japanese banks and it is estimated that GAPs now hold around 200 tonnes of gold. GAPs are similar to conventional savings plans. However, where a savings account receives interest on the amount deposited, the monthly payments to a GAP are invested in gold. As a form of investment in gold these schemes are very useful as they allow exposure to gold for even the smallest investor. The fixed monthly payment into the account can be as small as an individual desires, this also removes the risk to small investors of wrongly investing large amounts since the investment is long-term in nature. As a result of the indirect investment in gold, the premium and cost of investing in physical gold such as coins is also avoided.

Gold Certificates

Gold certificates originated in the United States at the time of the Civil War and were used as part of the gold standard. They were essentially bank notes issued by the treasury and could be redeemed for the equivalent value in gold. The U.S. Department of the Treasury stopped issuing gold certificates in 1933 and they are no longer in general circulation. The certificates are actually much sought-after collectables.

Gold certificates are now issued by investment banks. They are a way for investors to hold gold without physical delivery. These certificates are common in both Switzerland and Germany. Because banks hold the certificates in trust, the investor owns the gold but does not have to deal with storage, security, or insurance. Further to this, if the owner of the certificate holder needs to sell some or all of their holdings then this can be done at any time.

Exchange-Traded Funds

Another form of securitized gold investment is exchange-traded gold funds. Exchange-traded funds (ETFs) are regulated financial products and, unlike most derivative products, they closely track the gold price. One reason for this is that ETFs are 100% backed by physical gold; as a result, they are also described as exchange-traded gold. Some of the largest ETFs are LyxOR Gold Bullion Securities, Gold Bullion Securities (Australia), streetTRACKS Gold Shares, NewGold Gold Debentures, iShares Comex Gold Trust, Zürcher Kantonalbank Gold ETF, Istanbul Gold ETF, and Central Fund of Canada and Central Gold Trust.

Mining Stocks and Funds

There are many forms of collective investment schemes for investing in gold mining shares. They include mutual funds, open-ended investment companies, closed-end funds and unit trusts. These funds are traded in many countries all over the world and are generally regulated financial products. The range of investments across funds can be quite significant and some of these funds will invest solely in gold mining stocks but more generally they will invest in mining companies. In certain funds, there may also be an exposure to the gold price through the use of derivatives or direct investment in gold.

Gold-Linked Bonds and Structured Notes

Gold-linked bonds are issued by some of the world's largest gold dealers and investment banks. These investments are also useful as they provide some exposure to changes in the gold price, a yield, and varying degrees of principal protection. Structured notes can be issued depending on whether or not the investor is bullish about the gold price or bearish about the price of gold. Depending on this view, some of the investment will be placed into put or call options. The remainder of the investment is then placed into the money market to generate a yield from the investment. These products can also provide capital protection depending on the design of the product and this will be dependent on the expectation and risk profile of the investor.

GOLD MARKET INVESTMENT AND GOLD INSTRUMENTS

Markets and Exchanges

Gold like other investments is traded in a number of markets around the world. The main exchanges for the physical trading of gold are London and New York. There are, however, a number of emerging exchanges that are developing rapidly such as Shanghai and Dubai. Furthermore, there rise also a range of gold derivatives that are traded around the world including over-the-counter forwards, exchanges traded futures, and options.

Gold Exchanges The main physical exchanges in the gold market are the London over-the-counter (OTC) market, New York Mercantile Exchange

(NYMEX), and the COMEX being a division of the NYMEX. However, worldwide, there are a number of other physical exchanges. The Chinese Gold and Silver Exchange Society was registered with the British government in 1918 and the Tokyo Commodities Exchange (TOCOM) started trading in 1982. Other established exchanges include the Istanbul Gold Exchange, which is primarily aimed at the jewelry market, and the Shanghai Gold Exchange.

Trades on the Shanghai market can take place in quantities of either 1 kg or 3 kg, with purities of 99.99% and 99.95%, and are quoted in yuan per gram. Similar to the Istanbul market, Shanghai largely serves the jewelry industry, and the physical turnover in 2006 was approximately twice the national jewelry demand. The Shanghai market will be interesting to watch over the coming years for a range of reasons including: the ongoing program of liberalization in China and the fact that the three members of the exchange have been given permission to trade in derivative products.

The Indian exchanges represent another area of keen interest in coming years. Their electronic platforms started in 2003 and trade through the Multi Commodity Exchange of India (MCX) and the National Commodity and Derivative Exchange (NCDEX). Both MCX and NCDEX trade other commodities in addition to gold and NCDEX offers contracts on many precious metals. MCX has also set up strategic alliances with other commodity exchanges as well as the Bombay Bullion Association. Trading volumes in both exchanges have been encouraging since trading started.

The most recent development in gold trading is the opening in 2005 of the Dubai Gold and Commodity Exchange (DGCX). Dubai already has an important role as a physical trading center with much of gold trading being in the Middle East and India. Notably, 20% of the world's physical trade in gold goes through Dubai.[5] Another significant development in Dubai is the establishment of the Dubai Good Delivery Standard by the Dubai Metals and Commodities Centre. The Dubai Standard means that bars traded through the exchange must be between 100 g and 1 kg, with a minimum purity of 99.5%. The standard is also complimentary to the established London Large Bar Delivery Standard and the small bars all follow the London standard in terms of shape, appearance, and markings.

Over-the-Counter Market The global trade in gold consists of OTC transactions in the gold spot market, gold forwards and options, exchange-traded

[5]See World Gold Council, London, http://www.gold.org/value/markets/supply_demand/.

futures and options as well as other more complex derivatives such as swaps. OTC transactions take place directly between individuals rather than through exchanges. This is because OTC trades incorporate trade specific terms and conditions. In this respect individuals also manage the counterparty risk and credit arrangements for each transaction. As a result, these transactions offer a high degree of flexibility and account for the majority of global gold trading.

The OTC market operates on a 24-hour basis around the world. The main centers for OTC dealings are London, New York, and Zurich, which are all wholesale markets. Although these markets are more flexible due to their OTC status, their accessibility is constrained by the fact that the lowest transaction size is typically not less than 1,000 ounces. It is also important to note that intraday liquidity within the wholesale market will vary depending on the time of day, as the main OTC markets are in different time zones.

London and New York are the main trading centers for mining companies and central banks. The New York market also handles trades from the jewelry sector, industrial transactions, as well as investment and speculative trades. Zurich specializes in physical gold delivery to manufacturers of both jewelry and industrial products. There are also a number of smaller OTC centers in Dubai and in the Far East that deal mainly with the jewelry sector and private investment, which is usually in small bars of less than 1 kg.

Gold investment security trading is usually done over the phone through an electronic dealer system. One important feature in these markets is the *London fix*—twice daily (morning and afternoon), during London trading hours there is a "fix" which offers reference prices for that day's trading. This fix is then used as the basis for the pricing of long-term contracts and other contract valuations over the trading day.

The London afternoon fix is particularly important as it is used as the reference price for all gold transactions around the world. The afternoon fixing takes place when most of the markets around the world are trading, including the U.S., European, Middle East, and African exchanges. As a result, this period tends to be the most liquid period during the trading day. The fix is set by the five market maker members of the London Bullion Market Association who are also members of the London Fixing. Currently the five market makers are Deutsche Bank, Société Générale, HSBC, Scotia Mocatta, and Barclays Capital. Any trades on the fix are executed through one of these five dealers.

The fixing process is essentially an open auction with offers and bids netted out throughout the market before the final bidding process is conducted during the fix itself. The fix is executed on a single price. Clients place orders with their counterparties, who will either be one of the four fixing members themselves, or another bullion dealer who will be in touch with a fixing member (and with the client) while the fixing proceeds. The fixing members net out all orders before communicating their individual net interest at the fixing. The fix begins with the chairman suggesting a "trying price," reflecting the market price prevailing at the opening of the fix. The fixing members then relay this to their dealing rooms who are themselves in touch with all interested parties. Market participants may enter the fixing process at any time, or adjust or withdraw his order according to his view of the price as relayed to him. The gold price is adjusted up or down until all the buy and sell orders are matched and the price is declared fixed. Very occasionally, if it is impossible to strike a balance, the price will be fixed at the discretion of the chairman, an event known as *fixing on discretion*. All fixing orders are transacted on the basis of this fixed price. These fixing prices are quoted immediately through the various wiring channels, as well as numerous gold information web sites. The fix is therefore a full and fair representation of all market interest at the time according to the London Bullion Market Association.

GOLD PRICING DYNAMICS

After considering the fundamentals of the gold market and the different types of investment that can be undertaken, we now consider the role of gold in financial markets. First, we review the performance and properties of the gold price return.

Properties of Gold Price and Return

Exhibit 31.1 shows the London afternoon fix gold price from 1971 to 2006. After the breakdown of the Bretton Woods system in 1973, the gold price was allowed to float freely. Subsequently, the price of gold doubled by 1975 and peaked at an all time high in 1980. Between 1980 and 2000, due to the strength of the U.S. dollar and low inflation levels, the gold price did not perform well and reached a 20-year low in 1999. However, the gold price has more than doubled since then. A number of factors have been cited as drivers for this recovery. One often cited factor is the increase in the uncertainty of global security which is consistent with the view that gold is a "safe haven."[6] Other factors that have been cited include rising energy prices, rising oil prices, and a weak U.S. dollar exchange rate.

[6]David Hillier, Robert Faff, and Paul Draper, "Do Precious Metals Shine? An Investment Perspective," *Financial Analyst Journal* 62, 2 (2006), pp. 98–106.

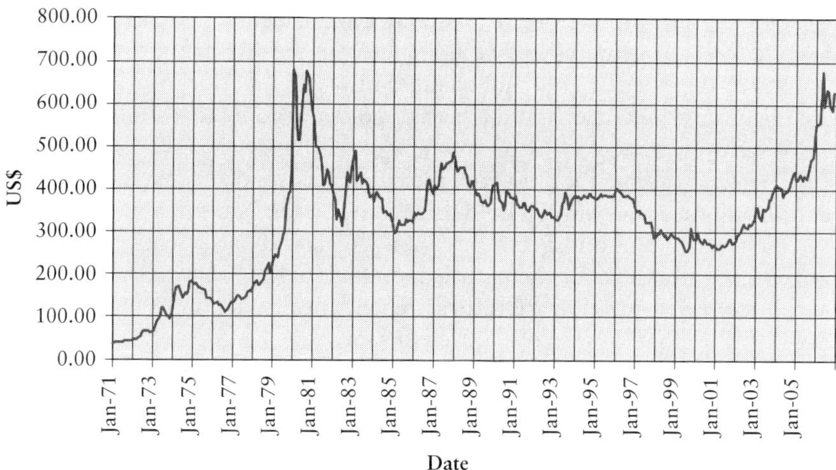

EXHIBIT 31.1 London PM Dollar Fixing Price, 1971–2006
Source: Data from London Bullion Market Association.

This raises questions on what are the underlying determinants of the gold price. There are a large number of studies that have attempted to statistically model the long-term and short-term dynamics of the price of gold and these can be summarized into three categories.

The first approach examines gold as a hedge against inflation.[7]

The general findings confirm that gold is a long-term hedge against inflation. For every one percentage point increase in the U.S. price index there is a corresponding increase in the gold price. Furthermore, when there are deviations from this long-run relationship, there is a slow mean reversion in gold prices.

In terms of short-run price fluctuations, gold is positively related to U.S. inflation, U.S. inflation volatility, and credit risk, while there is a significant

[7]David Chappell and Kevin Dowd, "A Simple Model of the Gold Standard," *Journal of Money, Credit and Banking* 29, 1 (1997), pp. 94–105; Dipak Ghosh, Eric J. Levin, Peter Macmillan, and Robert E. Wright, "Gold as an Inflation Hedge?" *Studies in Economics and Finance* 22, 1 (2004), pp. 1–25; Bahrat R. Kolluri, "Gold as a Hedge against Inflation: An Empirical Investigation," *Quarterly Review of Economics and Business* 21, 4 (1981), pp. 13–24; Saeid Mahdavi and Su Zhou, "Gold and Commodity Prices as Leading Indicators of Inflation: Tests of Long-Run Relationship and Predictive Performance," *Journal of Economics and Business* 49, 5 (1997), pp. 475–489; David Ranson, *Why Gold, Not Oil, Is the Superior Predictor of Inflation* (London: World Gold Council, 2005); and David Ranson, *Inflation Protection: Why Gold Works Better Than "Linkers"* (London: World Gold Council, 2005).

negative relationship with the U.S. dollar trade-weighted exchange rate and the gold lease rate. Interestingly there appears to be no relationship between changes in the price of gold and changes in world inflation, world inflation volatility, world income, and the beta of gold according to a study by Levin and Wright.[8]

The second branch of research into gold focuses on the impact of speculation and the rationality of gold price movements.[9]

Tschoegl,[10] Solt and Swanson,[11] and Aggarwal and Soenen[12] have explored various aspects of the nature and efficiency of the U.S. gold market. Despite some suggestion of return dependence and nonnormality, they broadly agree that these markets are efficient.

Smith[13] tests the random walk hypothesis for London morning and afternoon fixings and the closing price. He finds that autocorrelations exist in both the morning and afternoon fixing prices while the closing price follows a random walk. He argues that the closing price is more efficient because it is determined by additional information during the day and involves many more market participants.

The third category of research studying gold prices is focused on gold derivative contracts. Lucey and Tully[14] examine seasonality in the conditional and unconditional mean and variance of daily gold and silver contracts in the COMEX cash and futures market between 1982 and 2002. They find that there is a negative Monday effect in both gold and silver across cash and futures markets.

---

[8]Eric J. Levin and Robert E Wright, *Short-Run and Long-Run Determinants of the Price of Gold* (London: World Gold Council, June 2006).

[9]Jess Chua, Gordon Sick, and Richard Woodword, "Diversifying with Gold Stocks," *Financial Analysts Journal* 46, 4 (1990), pp. 76–79; Anna Koutsoyiannis, "A Short-Run Pricing Model for a Speculative Asset, Tested with Data from the Gold Bullion Market," *Applied Economics* 15, 5 (1983), pp. 563–581; Robert S. Pindyck, "The Present Value Model of Rational Commodity Pricing," *Economic Journal* 103, 418 (1993), pp. 511–530.

[10]Adrian Tschoegl, "Efficiency in the Gold Market—A Note," *Journal of Banking and Finance* 4, 4 (1980), pp. 371–379.

[11]Michael Solt and Paul Swanson, "On the Efficiency of the Markets for Gold and Silver," *Journal of Business* 54, 3 (1981), pp. 453–478.

[12]Raj Aggarwal and Luc Soenen, "The Nature and Efficiency of the Gold Market," *Journal of Portfolio Management* 14, 3 (1988), pp. 18–21.

[13]Graham Smith, "Tests of the Random Walk Hypothesis for London Gold Prices," *Applied Economics Letters* 9, 10 (2002), pp. 671–674.

[14]Brian M. Lucey and Edel Tully, "Seasonality, Risk and Return in Daily COMEX Gold and Silver Data 1982–2002," *Applied Financial Economics* 16, 4 (2006), pp. 319–333.

At the intraday level, Cai, Cheung, and Wong[15] provide a detailed characterization of the return volatility in gold futures contracts traded on the COMEX. They show a distinctive U-shaped pattern in the intraday volatility corresponding to the opening and closing of daily trading sessions. The strong intraday periodicity in turn gives rise to an equally strong and regular pattern in the autocorrelation of absolute returns. In studying the effect of the U.S. macroeconomic announcements, they find that employment reports, gross domestic product, consumer price index, and personal income have the greatest impact on gold volatility. Finally, examining the 25 largest five-minute absolute returns during 1983 to 1997, they find most of these returns are linked to the following events: sales of gold reserves by central banks, concerns about consumer demand for gold, interest rates, oil prices, inflation rates, U.S. unemployment rates, the Asian financial crisis, and political tension in South Africa.

Gold as Tactical Plays of Strategic Assets

Hillier, Draper, and Faff[16] show that the idea of a purely tactical role for precious metals may not fully reflect the potential long-term benefits they can offer in investment portfolios. The findings of the paper show that the passive long-term approach of a buy and hold strategy is clearly superior to an active short-term switching strategy of including gold in a broad-based asset portfolio. The results also show that over the 28-year period from January 1976 to December 2004, the optimal weight of gold in a broad-based international equity portfolio would have been approximately 9.5%.

The case for gold as a long-term or strategic investment is further examined by Michaud, Michaud, and Pulvermacher.[17] They show that

> *gold may be a valuable tactical asset. Gold is highly susceptible to geopolitical factors. During times of relative stability a small positive allocation may be useful. During time periods of abnormally positive economic activity gold returns may reflect multiplier effects associated with cultural issues. During periods of fiscal or monetary mismanagement, crises of various kinds or fundamental changes in the dominant currency, gold may be a very useful asset for hedging risk. (p. 26)*

Conversely, they find that gold has a comparable portfolio weight to asset classes such as small-cap and emerging market stocks due to its value

---

[15] Jun Cai, Yan-Leung Cheung, and Michael C. S. Wong, "What Moves The Gold Market?" *Journal of Futures Markets* 21, 3 (2001), pp. 257–278.

[16] Hillier, Draper, and Faff, "Do Precious Metals Shine?"

[17] Richard Michaud, Robert Michaud, and Katharine Pulvermacher, *Gold as a Strategic Asset* (London: World Gold Council, September 2006).

as a diversifying asset. The level of the strategic allocation to gold is, however, dependent upon the level of portfolio risk. Their findings showed that a small allocation to gold, in the order of 1% to 2%, is a significant and useful component of low risk portfolios, while an allocation of 2% to 4% is found to be a significant component of balanced portfolios.

Gold as a Potential Hedging Instrument

For centuries, gold has been used as money either directly as coinage or indirectly under the different gold standards that existed. Unlike other commodities, its primary function throughout history has been as a liquid store of wealth, not as an industrial input or for consumption. The gold price is therefore subject to less change over the business cycle. Changes in the gold price of a currency tend to reflect changes in the market's evaluation of currencies. Gold is often regarded as a safe haven against the debasement of paper money. One of the main reasons for this is that the purchasing power of gold is quite stable over long periods of time. For example, in 1833 the price of gold was $20.65 per ounce, which is about $415 in 2005 prices, while in 2005 the actual price of gold was $445. This is only a very small change in the real price of gold over a period of 172 years according to Levin and Wright.[18]

The "safe haven" characteristics of gold and its high liquidity make it an attractive commodity to institutional investors such as pension funds.

Gold as a Hedging Proxy for Uncertainties in State Variables

Merton's[19] *intertemporal capital asset pricing model* (ICAPM) assumes that investors can construct portfolios to hedge against uncertainties in state variables. Since the ICAPM is theoretically silent on the identity of such factors, it becomes an empirical problem to identify appropriate factors. Merton proposed that interest rates represent one such state variable, and Rubio,[20] Shanken,[21] and Scruggs,[22] among others, have investigated this possibility.

[18]Levin and Wright, Short-Run and Long-Run Determinants of the Price of Gold.

[19]Robert Merton, "An Intertemporal Capital Asset Pricing Model," *Econometrica* 41, 5 (1973), pp. 867–887.

[20]Gonzalo Rubio, "An Empirical Evaluation of the Intertemporal Capital Asset Pricing Model: The Stock Market in Spain," *Journal of Business Finance and Accounting* 16, 5 (1989), pp. 729–743.

[21]Jay Shanken, "Intertemporal Asset Pricing: An Empirical Investigation," *Journal of Econometrics* 45, 1–2 (1990), pp. 99–120.

[22]John T. Scruggs, "Resolving the Puzzling Intertemporal Relation between the Market Risk Premium and Conditional Market Variance: A Two-Factor Approach," *Journal of Finance* 53, 2 (1998), pp. 575–603.

Davidson, Faff, and Hillier,[23] considered gold as an alternative hedging factor. Using 34 global industry indexes from 1975 to 1994, they examined the role of gold in an international ICAPM setting. Despite a negative real gold premium (since the early 1980s), they found many industries have a significant gold price exposure. Generally, their international ICAPM with the inclusion of gold finds support from the data and, in particular, gold does seem to act as a reasonable hedging proxy. In Michaud, Michaud, and Pulvermacher,[24] gold is also found to provide stability to long-term institutional strategic investors in poor markets and economic climates, adding further strength to support the notion that gold could be a state variable within the ICAPM.

Gold as a Currency Hedge

When considering the effectiveness of gold as a currency hedge, it is important to take into account the difference between hedging against internal domestic price changes and against the purchasing power of a currency itself.

Gold, like other commodities, is denominated in U.S. dollars. Holding other things constant, a weakness in the U.S. dollar would increase the gold price. This has partly accounted for the strength of the gold price in recent years. Given this, separating the effect of changes in the U.S. dollar exchange rate from other factors on the gold price return will indicate how effective gold will be as a hedge against fluctuations in the U.S. currency. This becomes more important when we consider the effect of diversification using gold and other assets which are also denominated in U.S. dollars.

Capie, Mills, and Wood[25] investigated the relationship between gold and the exchange rate of various currencies against the U.S. dollar from 1971 to June 2002. They conclude that despite the large volatility in the gold price during this period, gold can be considered as an asset which provides good protection against dollar exchange rate fluctuations. Kavalis[26] also showed that gold is superior to other commodities as a hedge against

[23]Sinclair Davidson, Robert Faff, and David Hillier, "Gold Factor Exposures in International Asset Pricing," *Journal of International Financial Markets, Institutions and Money* 13, 3 (2003), pp. 271–289.

[24]Michaud, Michaud, and Pulvermacher, *Gold as a Strategic Asset.*

[25]Forrest Capie, Terence C. Mills, and Goeffrey Wood, *Gold as a Hedge against the U.S. Dollar* (London: World Gold Council, 2004).

[26]Nikos Kavalis, *Commodity Prices and the Influence of the U.S. Dollar* (London: World Gold Council, 2006).

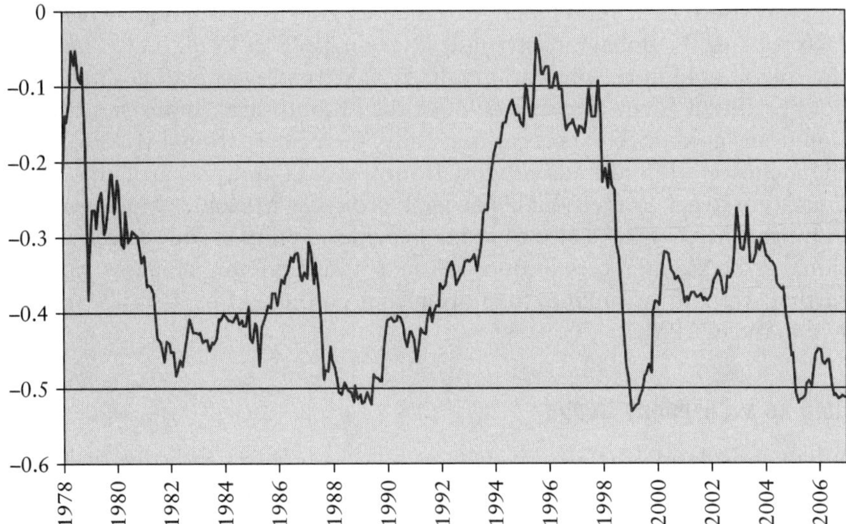

EXHIBIT 31.2 60-Month Rolling Correlation between Returns to the U.S. Dollar Gold Price and the Returns to the Trade-Weighted Dollar, 1978–2006
Source: Data from LBMA and Federal Reserve Bank of St. Louis.

the dollar. Given this, gold can therefore be viewed as a standalone and distinct investment from other commodities.

An examination of Exhibit 31.2 illustrates the time-varying nature of gold price correlation with the trade weighted dollar since 1978. It can be seen that over the period 1978–2006, gold-dollar correlations were consistently negative, and in some periods reached significant lows of −0.6.

Gold as Inflation Hedge

Jastram[27] demonstrated that gold kept its purchasing power over very long periods in both inflationary and deflationary times. In updating Jastram's research, Harmston[28] finds that despite the price fluctuations in gold, it has consistently reverted to historic purchasing power parity against both currencies and other commodities. This gives support to those who believe that holding gold can preserve wealth over time, overchanging economic circumstances, and business cycle fluctuations. The findings of Harmston also

[27]Roy W. Jastram, *The Golden Constant: The English and American Experience 1560–1976* (New York: John Wiley & Sons, 1977).

[28]Stephen Harmston, *Gold as a Store of Value* (London: World Gold Council, 1998).

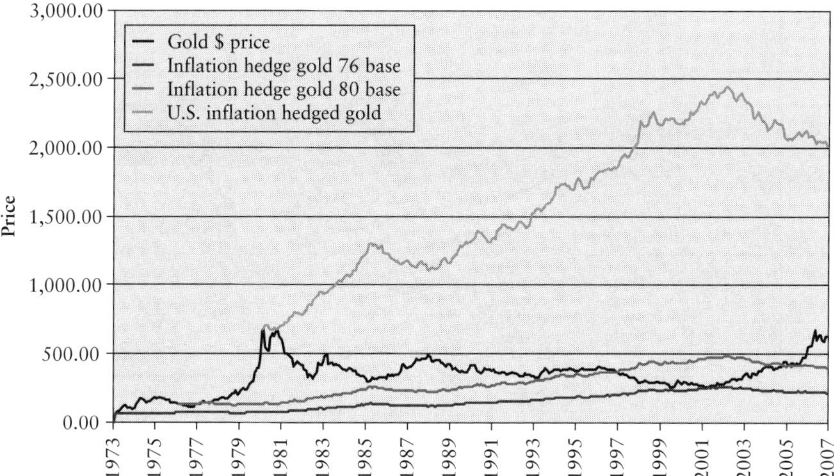

EXHIBIT 31.3 U.S. Dollar Price of Gold required for Gold to be an Inflation Hedge, January 1973 to December 2006

show that long-term investment in gold appears to be a very effective long-run inflation hedge not just in the United States but also in the United Kingdom, France, Germany, and Japan.

Further to the evidence that gold is a good hedging instrument against inflation, recent work by Ranson[29] shows that gold can be used as a superior predictor of inflation when compared with other measures such as the Consumer Price Index (CPI) and oil. This provides strong support for the view that gold is a hedge against extreme events and adverse economic conditions, including inflationary shocks.

Exhibit 31.3 shows the propensity for gold to act as an inflation hedge in the United States from January 1973 to 2007. The return from holding gold is sensitive to the choice of the start date. For investors who bought gold in the early 1970s when gold was below fair value, gold price increases are above inflation for the whole sample. However, investors purchasing gold in the early 1980s would have experienced losses relative to inflation. For example, if gold was purchased at the gold price peak in 1980, the price of gold would need to have risen to $2,016 per ounce by December 2006 in order to have been an effective inflation hedge.

[29]See Ranson, *Why Gold, Not Oil, Is the Superior Predictor of Inflation* and *Inflation Protection: Why Gold Works Better Than "Linkers."*

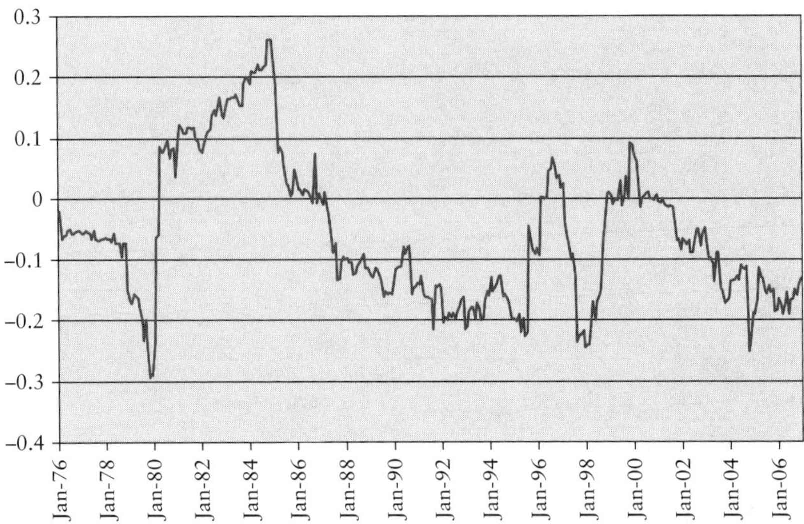

EXHIBIT 31.4 60-Month Rolling Correlation between Returns of Gold and S&P 500 Index, January 1976 to December 2006
Source: Data from LBMA and DataStream.

Investment and Diversification Properties

One of the important reasons to invest in gold is its ability to act as a good diversification asset. Gold return tends to move independently of other investments and key economic indicators. As shown in the rolling correlations in Exhibits 31.2 and 31.4, the effectiveness of gold in reducing portfolio risk is time varying. Gold, in general, is a very good diversification asset in a portfolio with stocks. Only in the 1980s did the correlation move above 0.1, peaking at around 0.25 in 1984.

Jaffe[30] argues the case for gold and gold stocks as a suitable investment for institutional portfolios by showing that the addition of gold increases average return to the portfolio while reducing standard deviation of the returns. Portfolios that contain gold are generally more robust and better able to cope with market uncertainties.

An interesting research question related to the diversification benefits of gold is why there is a lack of correlation between returns on gold and those of other commodities and financial assets. Lawrence[31] studies the correlations

[30]Jeffrey F. Jaffe, "Gold and Gold Stocks as Investments for Institutional Portfolios," *Financial Analysts Journal* 50, 5 (1989), pp. 53–59.
[31]Colin Lawrence, *Why is Gold Different From Other Assets? An Empirical Investigation* (London: World Gold Council, 2003).

of gold returns with other assets and finds that the low correlation can be attributed to the existence of accessible aboveground stocks of gold. This pool of gold acts as a strong buffer for different stages of the economic cycle, making it a useful asset to include in a portfolio for diversification purposes.

Gold or Gold Producing Stocks?

Several researchers have asked the interesting question of whether or not the diversification benefits of gold can be achieved simply by including gold producing stocks. Since many gold-exporting countries are emerging economies with the concomitant political and economic risks associated with such regions, it is often more convenient to invest domestically in cross-listed or foreign gold producing stocks.

Jaffe suggests that because the liquidity, consumption, and the convenience values of gold is high, the expected return on gold may be less than for a capital asset of comparable risk. It would therefore be better for investors who want to gain exposure to gold to invest in financial assets that mirror gold's performance, without having its high liquidity, consumption, and convenience value. One obvious choice for such an investment alternative is gold mining stocks. However, Jaffe also notes one of the major differences that the inclusion of gold producing stocks in a portfolio produces, rather than gold, is that the stocks will provide a smaller reduction in the combined portfolio's standard deviation.

McQueen[32] presents additional support for the diversification benefit of gold stocks in a portfolio. He shows that although gold stocks should not have as strong a diversification effect as bullion, their ability to diversify a common stock portfolio should be greater than that of a typical common stock.

Another interesting facet of the gold market was considered in McQueen and Thorley.[33] In 1979, David Fitzpatrick, a gold analyst interviewed for a story in the August 27, 1979 issue of the *Wall Street Journal* discussed how mining industry indexes were leading indicators of the gold price in the late 1970s. In support, McQueen and Thorley show that monthly gold returns are positively correlated with the previous month's returns on a portfolio of gold mining stocks. They also find that this anomaly diminished after its publication in the *Wall Street Journal*.

[32]Grant McQueen, Diversifying with Gold Bullion and Gold Stocks, Working Paper, Brigham Young University, 1991.

[33]Grant McQueen and Steven Thorley, "Do Investors Learn? Evidence From a Gold Market Anomaly," *Financial Review* 32, 3 (1997), pp. 501–525.

For those who invest in gold mining stocks however, there is another concern. The investment in gold mining stocks is often not a "pure play"—for example, the stock is essentially a leveraged investment for gold mining companies with debt on their balance sheets. Consequently, if all other factors are held constant, a rise or fall in the gold price should result in a rise or fall in the share price that is greater than the change in the gold price. That is to say, the gold price elasticity of such a gold mining stock should be greater than 1. Blose and Shieh[34] present a theoretical model and empirical evidence showing that for a company whose primary business is gold mining, the gold price elasticity of the company's stock is indeed greater than gold. Blose[35] in another study further shows that this relationship also holds for mutual funds investing in gold mining companies. However, gold return is by no means the sole determinant of gold mining stock returns. Blose and Shieh show that the value of gold is also affected by production costs, the level of gold reserves, and the proportion of assets unrelated to gold price risk. This highlights the fact that mutual funds and mining stocks have very different characteristics from gold itself as a diversifying asset in investment portfolios.

Gold and Commodity Futures Indexes

An alternative means by which investors can gain exposure to the benefits of gold and other commodity investments, without the inconvenience of taking delivery of the underlying products, is to invest in diversified baskets of commodity futures contracts. Typically these products are based on commodity indexes.

Several popular commodity indexes exist, including the Goldman Sachs Commodity Index, the Reuters/Jefferies CRB, the Dow Jones-AIG Commodity Index and the Rogers International Commodities Index.

In these commodity futures indexes, gold holds a low allocation of between 1.5% to 6% and so gold exposure gained is minimal.[36] Michaud, Michaud, and Pulvermacher consider the relative gains from directly investing in gold over a well diversified basket of commodities. They show returns of commodity futures are irrelevant for understanding gold price return and

---

[34]Laurence E. Blose and Joseph C. P. Shieh, "The Impact of Gold Price on the Value of Gold Mining Stock," *Review of Financial Economics* 4, 2 (1995), pp. 125–140.

[35]Laurence E. Blose, "Gold Price Risk and the Returns on Gold Mutual Funds," *Journal of Economics and Business* 48, 5 (1996), pp. 499–514.

[36]For more discussion on the composition of commodity indexes, see Gillian Moncuicle, *Indexes Enticing Investors* (London: World Gold Council, September 2005).

suggest that the gold price return index can be a more transparent and direct measure.

Research Summary

The gold market itself is relatively efficient. In addition, gold offers potential diversification opportunities, with most studies finding some support for the long-term inclusion of gold in an investment portfolio. Interestingly, the inclusion of mining stocks does not have the same effect as direct investment in gold since the inclusion of some mining stocks in a portfolio was shown to have a different diversification effect. Gold is also shown to be a good hedging instrument, and against currency movements the gold price, despite its volatility, is found to be effective against a range of currencies. However, as an inflationary hedge, the effectiveness of the hedge is time dependent.

One fruitful area of future research would be to apply more sophisticated empirical techniques, compared to the previous studies which only consider linear relationships. It is plausible to assume that there will be a number of nonlinear interactions that will impact upon the price of gold. If these relationships could be examined, then the effectiveness of gold as a hedge, or as an asset for diversification in investment portfolios, may be enhanced.

The Future of Gold

The past 30 years of gold investment and the way in which the gold price dynamics have changed would have been extremely difficult to predict—even in general terms. Thus, what lies in the future for gold is a hazardous question to answer. With caution, our approach is to consider the main areas of gold use, first as a central bank reserve asset, second as an industrial commodity, and last as an investment.

As a central bank asset, the role of gold is changing. In 1999 European Central Banks signed up to the Central Bank Gold Agreement (CBGA). The CBGA essentially capped the amount of gold that could be sold by central banks over the next five years to 2,000 tons. This was a significant move as the need to cap the sales shows that there are a number of central banks who no longer desire to hold large amounts of gold in reserve. The main sellers of gold over the subsequent period were the United Kingdom and Switzerland. By the end of 2002, the total reserves held by the European Central banks had fallen to 14,289 tonnes from 16,128 tonnes in 1999. Prior to the agreement Belgium sold 299 tonnes thereby halving their reserves, the United Kingdom intended to sell half of their reserves as did the Swiss.

These sales therefore show that the use of gold as a reserve asset is in decline.

The main reason for the United Kingdom wishing to sell was that in early 1999, its foreign currency net reserves stood at around $13 billion. Of this, gold accounted for just under $6.5 billion or 50%. An analysis of past volatilities of returns on the assets held in the net reserves and the correlations between the returns on different asset classes suggested that market risk on the net reserves could be reduced if the level of gold holdings was decreased to between 0 and 20%, depending on the sample period used.[37] Based upon this, the U.K. Treasury decided to halve the U.K. gold holdings over the medium-term. Holding a balanced/well diversified reserve portfolio is a different strategy to that which was previously followed by central banks and gives further credence to the view that gold is no longer the reserve asset of choice, but merely another asset in a portfolio of reserve assets.

In jewelry, there is significant scope for increased demand. Given that much of the jewelry demand across the world is closely linked to religious festivals, then economic development could have an impact on the demand for gold. As economies prosper and individuals attain greater wealth and disposable income, it is logical to predict that there will be greater demand for gold around these festivals. This is a trend which is already occurring in India and in China.

As for future industrial applications, research over the last decade has uncovered a number of new practical uses, some of which are under development and would markedly increase the industrial use of gold. These include catalysts in fuel cells, chemical processing, pollution control, and nanotechnology. The use of gold in coated superconductors could also create significant new industrial demand for gold. In addition, there are many new medical techniques being developed which utilize gold, such as anticancer treatments and X-ray technology.

As an investment, gold has evolved into a readily investable commodity. Through the derivative products on offer, it is now possible for all investors to have an exposure to gold in their portfolio whether for speculative, hedging, or diversification purposes. Furthermore, it is likely that demand for these products will remain high as the demand for gold as an investment or as an industrial commodity is unlikely to fall.

[37]H.M. Treasury, Review of the Sale of Part of the UK Gold Reserves, October 2002.

CONCLUSION

The renewal of investment interest in gold is rooted in a range of factors including concerns about dollar volatility, inflationary expectations, continuing high levels of geopolitical uncertainty, and increased acceptance of the role that gold can play as a portfolio diversifier.

The trends that are currently appearing in the gold market would suggest that the role of gold is changing, with increasing demand for gold in jewelry and industry concomitant with less demand for gold as a reserve asset. What is not in doubt is the demand for gold as an investment asset. Regardless of whether this is for physical investment in coins and bars or whether this is for hedging or diversification, gold as an asset performs very well.

The role of gold in portfolios is also unlikely to diminish; the potential for increased demand from industry and the jewelry sector and the need to hedge and offset adverse movements in the gold price means that the demand for gold derivative products will remain strong. In addition, the increasing evidence of the diversification benefits of holding gold in investment portfolios means that the future demand for gold will remain strong.

CHAPTER 32

The Effect of Gold in a Traditional Portfolio

Thomas Heidorn, Ph.D.
Professor of Finance
Frankfurt School of Finance and Management

Nadeshda Demidova-Menzel
Equity Analyst
Equinet AG (ESN)

The price of gold has risen dramatically since 2000, making gold an interesting addition to a portfolio. One significant influence on the price of gold has been the decision that 15 European central banks made in 2004 to limit their gold sales over the next five years. Another influence may be the underperformance of many asset classes, which has forced portfolio managers to seek new investment ideas.

This chapter first outlines the main drivers of the price of gold, and examines both short- and long-term effects. We discuss gold's correlation with inflation, and with the U.S. dollar and Euro exchange rate. Building on these elements, we examine the contribution of gold to a traditional portfolio.

From a return and diversification standpoint, gold had a positive impact on euro (EUR) and U.S. dollar (USD) portfolios between 2000 and 2006 because of its high returns and low correlation with other assets. However, this time period is the exception. During most other periods, correlation with equity and bonds was low, but returns were small, overriding the positive diversification effect.

FACTORS DRIVING GOLD PRICES

Similarly to other markets, the price-determining mechanism in the gold market is supply and demand. More precisely, we mean "real" supply and demand, which does not include central bank gold sales and purchases, or old gold scrap, which is a kind of "recycling" of aboveground stocks. Oversupply from central bank sales caused the price of gold to trend downward for many years prior to 2000, despite a long-term excess of demand from the global gold market.

However, in September 2004, 15 European central banks agreed to limit their annual sales of gold over the next five years to 500 tons, with total gold sales over that period to reach no more than 2,500 tons each. This agreement, as well as a persistently low gold price that had forced many gold mines to close, caused a shortage in the gold supply (see Exhibit 32.1).

As gold prices began to rise, a supply deficit arose. The time lag between gold exploration and production meant that mining companies could not keep up with demand. The real supply obtained from gold mining is also limited by available underground resources. It is estimated that approximately 100,000 tons of gold are available underground, but only half can be obtained at a reasonable cost.

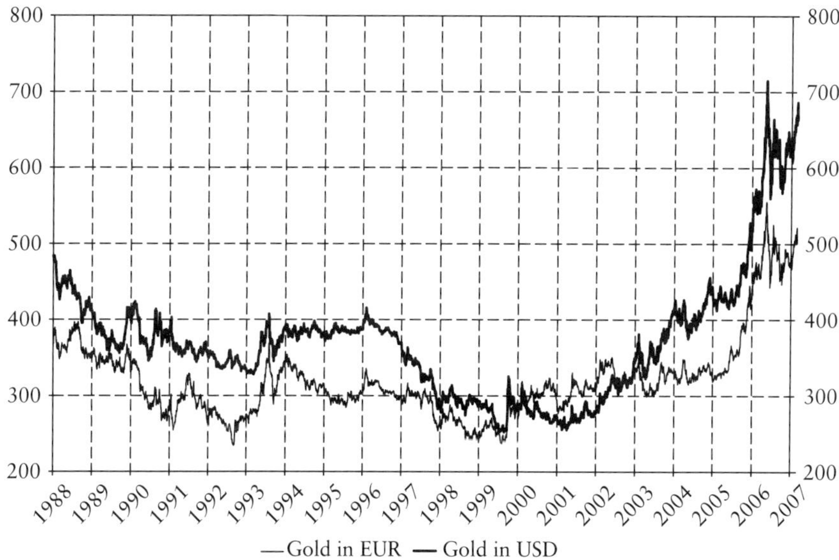

EXHIBIT 32.1 Gold Prices in Euros (EUR) and U.S. Dollars (USD), January 1988 to January 2007
Source: Exhibit created from data obtained from Bloomberg.

Gold mining has also become extremely expensive, due to increasing energy and transportation prices and stricter environmental regulations. Political uncertainty in many gold-mining regions (Africa, Latin America, Asia) and unclear owners' rights in Russia[1] are further risk factors that can cause a sudden supply reduction, and contribute to an increase in gold price volatility.

At the same time, on the *demand side*, there was an increase in gold's popularity. There are two components of the demand for gold: the "use" demand (e.g., jewelry, industry), and the "asset" demand (e.g., investments). On the one hand, gold is a "real" commodity used for consumption and production. But it is also a financial or reserve asset. About 15% of annual gold production is held by investors in physical form.[2] Because of its negative correlation with the U.S. dollar, gold provides a natural hedge against currency weakness.[3]

The "use" demand for gold is a negative function of its price (price elasticity), and a positive function of income (income elasticity). Therefore, demand for jewelry is affected by price (volatility), and positively influenced by an increase of available income. The best example is the continuous growth of wealth in Asian countries such as India and China, where gold jewelry has traditionally been very popular. Demand from the jewelry sector accounted for 71% of worldwide gold production in 2005, a 12% increase from 2004.

India accounted for 22% of worldwide gold jewelry demand in 2005, a 17% increase from 2004. India is thought to hold close to 15,000 tons, or 10% of the world's entire aboveground gold stock. China's demand also showed an upward trend: Its gold trading volume (together with net retail investment in the form of coins and bars) increased by 36% in 2005).[4]

The "asset" demand for gold is based on a number of factors, including the real interest rate, dollar exchange rate expectations, inflationary expectations, "fear" due to political turmoil, returns on other assets, and the lack of correlation with other assets. Investing in gold can be an excellent way to reduce portfolio volatility, because events that cause a collapse of stock prices often tend to raise the price of gold.

In addition to these factors, we should also consider purchases of physical gold by central banks of countries that hold high foreign exchange

[1]In Russia, only minor ownership in mining companies is allowed. This regulation is a clear disadvantage for gold-mining stocks.

[2]According to statistics from the World Gold Council, as of December 2005, central banks worldwide held 30,988.3 tons of gold. Of that, approximately 26% is held by the Federal Reserve Bank.

[3]Nikos Kavalis, *Commodity Prices and the Influence of the US Dollar* (London: World Gold Council, 2006).

[4]According to the World Gold Council, http://www.gold.org/value.

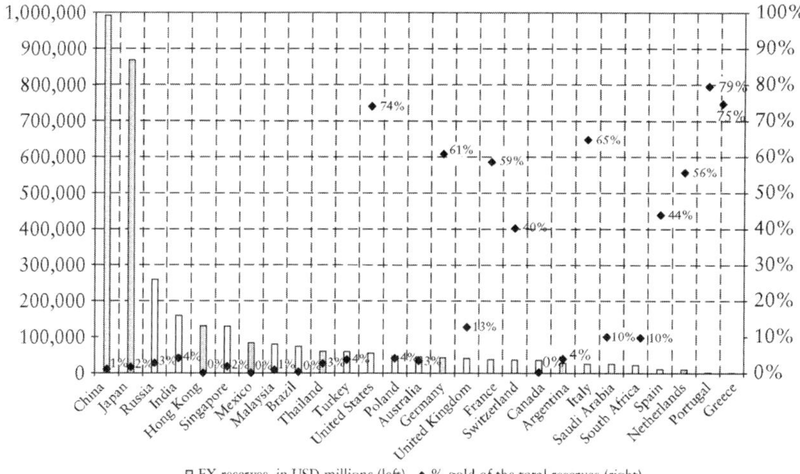

EXHIBIT 32.2 Foreign Exchange and Gold Reserves, Third Quarter 2006
Source: Exhibit created from data obtained from World Gold Council.

reserves for diversification purposes (e.g., China, Japan, Russia, and India). This can also potentially cause a surge in gold prices (see Exhibit 32.2).

Note that these countries hold less than 5% of their total reserves in gold. As a comparison, the international average is about 10.5% at current market prices, while it is over 40% for the European Union (EU), and about 70% for the United States.

To consider gold price development in more detail, it is important to differentiate between *short-* and *long-run determinants* of gold prices. The *long-run* price of gold is expected to rise in concert with inflation. It thus acts as an *inflation hedge*, because the long-run price of gold is related to the marginal cost of gold extraction. Assuming a close relationship between production cost and inflation, the price of gold will rise with an increase in production costs and with inflation. However, this effect is not as substantial as the theory proposes, and it is not true for Europe.

Over the *short run*, the price of gold is very volatile. As we noted earlier, it is determined by supply and demand, and fluctuates considerably around this so-called *inflation hedge price*.[5] These short-run movements of the price of gold occur in response to factors that alter the supply and/or demand.

[5]Eruic J. Levin and Robert E. Wright, "Short-Run and Long-Run Determinants of the Price of Gold." World Gold Council, Research Study, no. 32, June 2006. The *inflation hedge price* is the mean reversion price.

Short-Run Price Determinants

Factors that influence the *short-run supply of gold* are the current and lagged gold price, the gold lease rate in the previous and current period (the physical interest rate and the proxy for the real interest rate), convenience yield and default risk, and the previous period quantity of leased gold to be repaid at the previous gold lease rate. The *short-run demand for gold* is described as a function of the price of gold, the available income per capita, the U.S. dollar/world exchange rate, the gold lease rate, gold's beta, U.S. inflation, credit risk, and political uncertainty.

Short-Run Gold Supply Higher current gold prices motivate gold producers to make supply available by either extracting more from mines, or by leasing it from central bank gold reserves. There is usually a substantial time lag, however, before mines can react to a price change and begin to actually extract gold, so there is a positive relationship between the quantity of gold supplied from extraction and the price of gold in an earlier period (the *lagged gold price*).

The level of the *gold lease rate* determines the amount of gold leased. If the gold lease rate is lower than marginal extraction costs, gold producers will decide to satisfy short-run gold demand by leasing from a central bank. At the same time, producers incur a repayment commitment in the following period. Hence, the quantity of gold supplied from extraction is negatively related to the amount of leased gold in the previous period that must be repaid to the central bank in the current period. It is also negatively related to the gold lease rate in the previous period.

The *gold lease rate* represents the physical interest rate, and we use it here as a proxy for the real interest rate. The term "gold lease rate" is linked to the terms *convenience yield* and *default risk premium*. The *default risk premium* is a measure of financial credit risk that depends on the credit quality of the borrower. Credit default risk is also associated with financial shocks and structural changes in the international economy. It is assumed that, during periods of financial turmoil, demand for gold (and, therefore, its price) will be higher. This premium varies, and may include a surcharge during periods of political uncertainty.

The *convenience yield* is the benefit obtained from physically holding gold. Central banks lease gold at a physical interest rate (the gold lease rate), which is in equilibrium equal to the convenience yield plus default risk. Central banks determine the amount of gold supplied by adjusting their gold lending to the point where the physical rate of interest is equal to the convenience yield plus default risk. This explains why central banks reduce the quantity of gold leased to the industry during periods of political or financial turmoil. It causes a rise in default risk or a rise in convenience yield, and therefore an increase in the gold lease rate.

Short-Run Gold Demand The short-run "use" demand for gold is a negative function of its price and a positive function of available income per capita. Exhibit 32.3 uses worldwide *gross domestic product* (GDP) per capita as a proxy for the income variable. Exhibit 32.4 plots total world GDP, which also follows an upward trend.

Exhibits 32.3 and 32.4 show that an increase in world income (and consequently in income per capita) might affect the long-run price of gold by increasing demand for jewelry and for gold as an investment (this is supported by a correlation coefficient of more than 0.50). However, it is difficult to interpret this relationship precisely, because both income and gold prices rose over time with the general price level, and it is necessary to separate these two effects.

The short-term "asset demand" is based on a number of factors, including dollar exchange rate expectations, inflationary expectations, the gold lease rate, returns on other assets, and the lack of correlation with other assets. Exhibits 32.5 through 32.9 show the individual relationships between the nominal price of gold (denominated in U.S. dollars) with each of the explanatory variables.

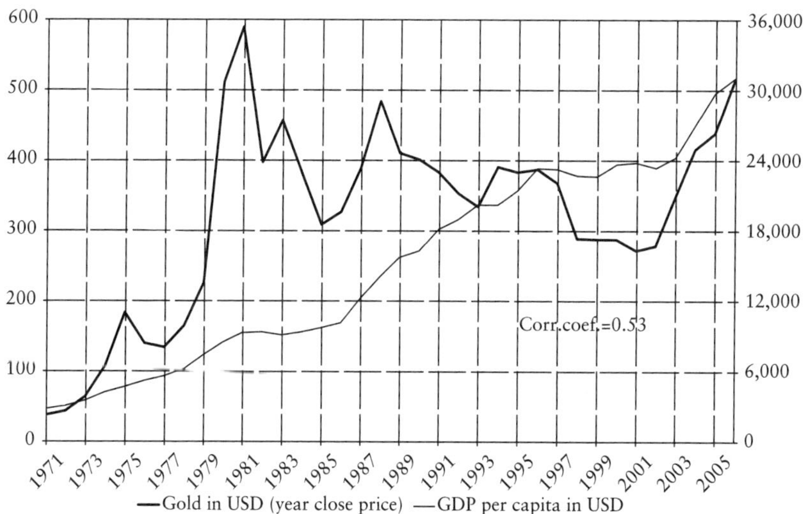

EXHIBIT 32.3 Gold Prices and World GDP per Capita in U.S. Dollars, 1971 to Third Quarter 2006
Source: Exhibit created from data obtained from OECD.

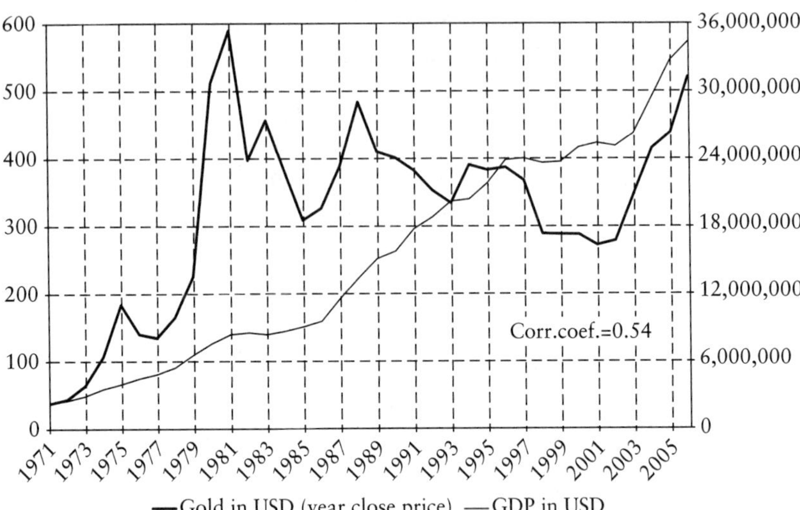

EXHIBIT 32.4 Gold Prices and World GDP in U.S. Dollars, 1971 to Third Quarter 2006
Source: Exhibit created from data obtained from OECD.

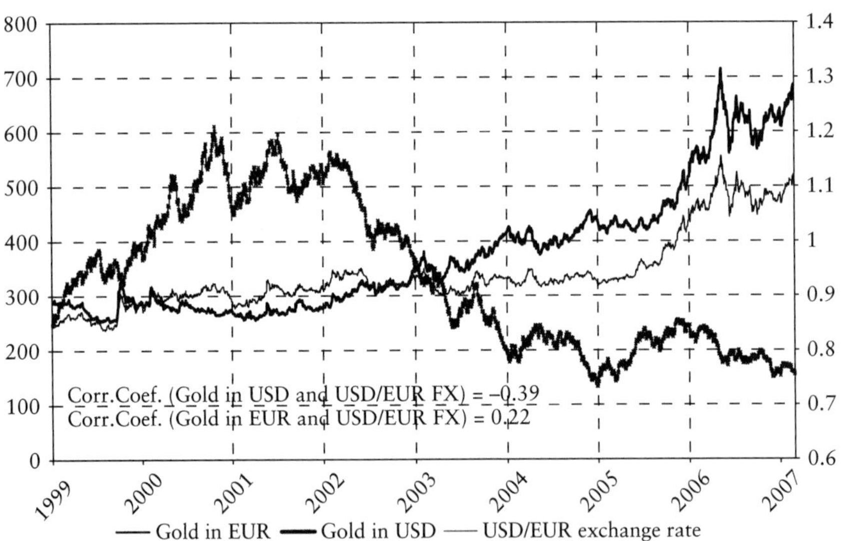

EXHIBIT 32.5 Gold Prices and USD/EUR Exchange Rate, January 1999 to January 2007
Source: Exhibit created from data obtained from Bloomberg.

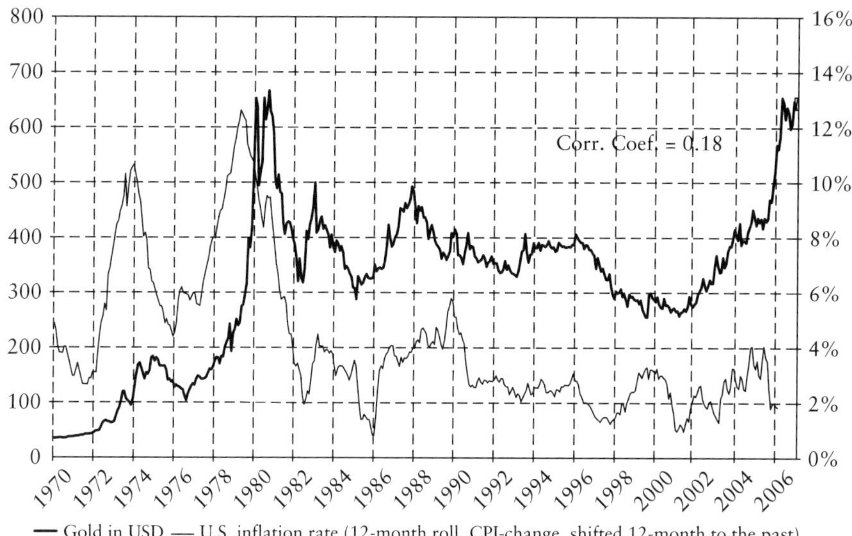

EXHIBIT 32.6 Gold Prices and the U.S. Inflation Rate, January 1970 to January 2007
Source: Exhibit created from data obtained from Bloomberg.

Exhibit 32.5 shows a clear negative relationship between the price of gold and the USD/EUR exchange rate. If the USD exchange rate rises, gold becomes more expensive for investors outside the dollar area. This, in turn, reduces demand for gold, which lowers the price.

Two important conclusions can be reached from Exhibit 32.5. If the U.S. dollar weakens, the price of gold denominated in U.S. dollars will rise. At the same time, the price of gold denominated in euros will fall (i.e., gold denominated in euros will get cheaper, which will boost the demand for gold, and cause gold prices to trend upward).

Exhibit 32.6 calculates the U.S. inflation rate on a twelve-month basis, and then graphically shifts it twelve months into the past. A positive relationship between the shifted U.S. inflation rate and gold prices is obvious, especially during the years 1973–1974 and 1978–1979.

Exhibit 32.7 shows the relationship between gold prices and the *gold lease rate*. We calculate this by subtracting the three-month gold forward rate from the three-month LIBOR dollar interest rate.[6] As we mentioned, the gold lease rate is used as an empirical proxy for the *real interest rate*

[6]Gold was not leased every day in the early years. Thus we averaged gold prices and lease rates over the month for the entire sample period.

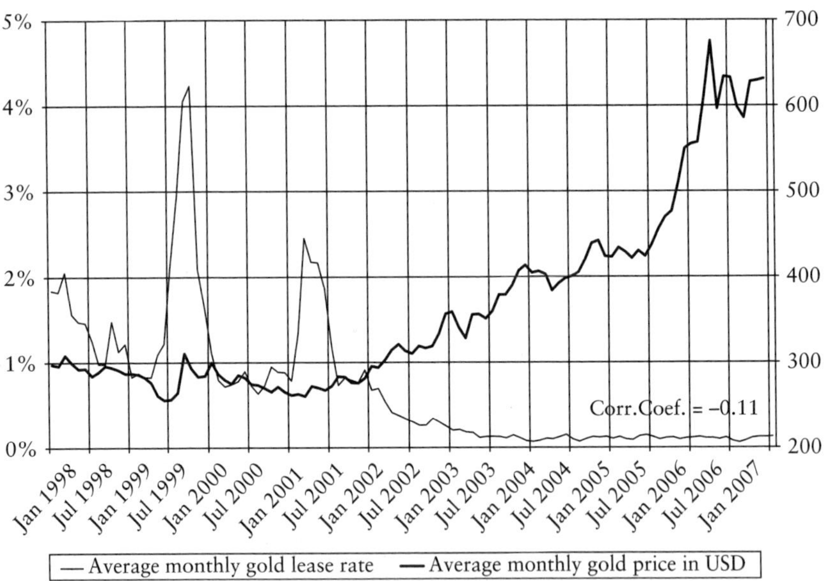

EXHIBIT 32.7 Gold Prices and the Gold Lease Rate, January 1998 to January 2007
Source: Exhibit created from data obtained from Bloomberg and LBMA.

because in market equilibrium there is an arbitrage relationship that drives the *physical interest rate* (the gold lease rate) into equality with the real interest rate.

Theoretically, in equilibrium, a mine is indifferent between (1) extracting gold now and selling it now, or (2) leasing gold now, selling it now, investing the sell price in a bond, selling the bond in one year, and using the bond sell price plus interest to pay for extracting the gold to be paid back plus the physical interest rate. If the costs of extraction rise along with the general inflation rate, the gold lease rate is equal to the real interest rate.[7]

It can now be assumed that the asset demand for gold will fluctuate in response to changes in the real interest rate, and there is an assumption that gold prices move inversely with interest rates (see Exhibit 32.7). The real interest rate represents the opportunity cost of holding gold in the form of foregone yield, instead of holding an alternative interest-bearing asset. In the case of a low gold lease rate, investors would prefer gold instead of low interest-bearing assets, and the resultant rising "asset demand" would drive gold prices upward.

[7]Eric J. Levin and Robert E. Wright, "Short-Run and Long-Run Determinants of the Price of Gold," World Gold Council, Research Study, No. 32, June. 2006.

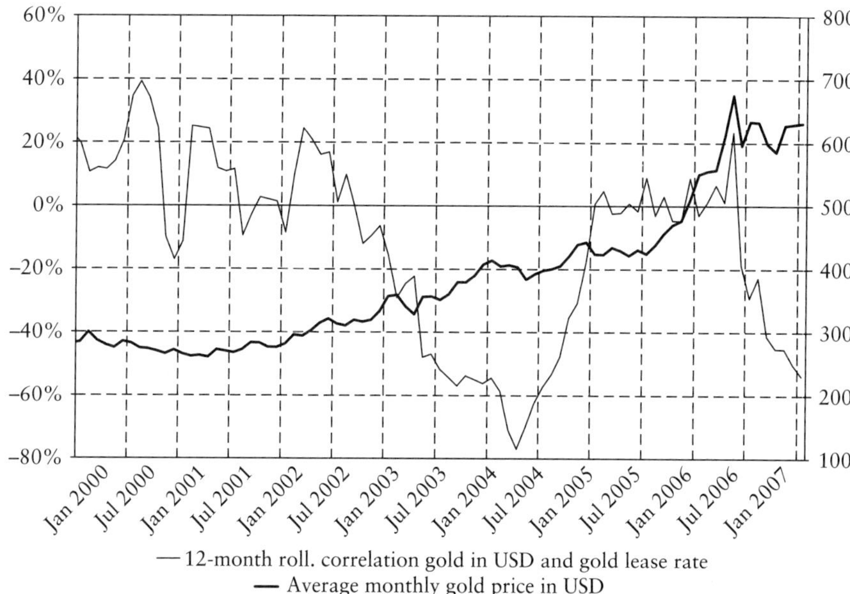

EXHIBIT 32.8 Rolling Correlations between Gold Prices and the Gold Lease Rate, January 2000 to January 2007
Source: Exhibit created from data obtained from Bloomberg and LBMA.

Hence, the real price of gold moves in the opposite direction from the lease rate. But there are periods where this relationship is not that obvious, and the correlation coefficient lies in the positive area (see Exhibit 32.8).

Moreover, if rising interest rates reflect inflation or U.S. dollar exchange rate concerns, gold prices and interest rates will move together (both will rise). The relationship between interest rates and the price of gold depends on a clear distinction between real and nominal interest rates and the precise cause of the rise in interest rates. When the nominal interest rate (the Fed funds rate) increases more slowly than inflation (which causes a negative real interest rate), an increase in the gold price can be observed (see Exhibit 32.9).

The correlation with other assets, especially the stock market, is represented by gold's beta. Gold's beta influences investor demand for gold in accordance with gold's ability to reduce portfolio volatility. The effectiveness of gold investment in reducing portfolio risk is inversely related to beta, which measures the extent to which the price of gold moves in the opposite direction from the stock market. It is believed that gold has a low beta in relationship to the stock market.

Exhibit 32.10 calculates beta by regressing the monthly gold return on the monthly return of the Standard & Poor's 500 (Total Return) Index, based on information from the previous 36 months.

Empirical evidence shows no correlation on average (gold has a very low beta of near zero in Exhibit 32.10).[8] If, however, the beta for gold rises for a period of time, portfolio demand for gold will fall during that period. Negative beta makes gold an attractive ingredient for investor portfolios because the diversification effect reduces risk. Therefore, demand for gold as an investment is negatively related to beta.

That was not the case in 2006, however, when demand for gold was driven mainly by professional investors like hedge funds. Exhibit 32.10 indicates a positive relationship between gold's beta and the price of gold between 1980 and 1986, and in 2006, and a negative relationship for most of the remaining periods. It seems investors would need perfect foresight to opt for an exposure to gold only during the periods it has a negative beta to the stock market.

The correlation between the returns from holding gold and stock market returns also became negative for periods when the stock market

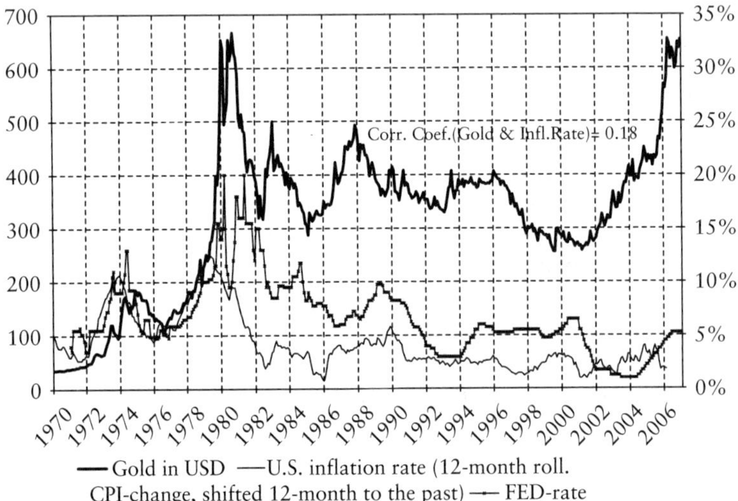

EXHIBIT 32.9 Inflation, the Fed Rate, and Gold Prices, 1970 to January 2007
Source: Exhibit created from data obtained from Bloomberg.

[8]Colin Lawrence, *Why Is Gold Different from Other Assets? An Empirical Investigation*, (London: World Gold Council, 2003); Rhona O'Connell, *What Sets the Precious Metals Apart from Other Commodities?* (London: World Gold Council, 2005); and Katherine Pulvermacher, *Investing in Commodities: A Risky Business?* (London: World Gold Council, 2005).

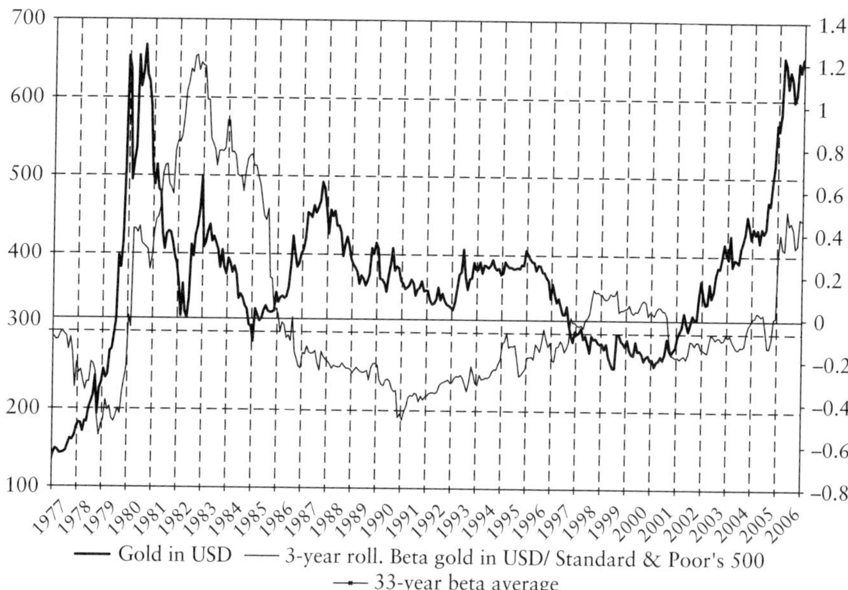

EXHIBIT 32.10 Gold Prices and Correlations with the Stock Market, 1977–2006
Source: Exhibit created from data obtained from Bloomberg.

exhibited significant underperformance. This relationship is very obvious in the years 2001 to 2002.

Long-Run Price Determinants

Short-run fluctuations in the price of gold are expected to result from political and financial turmoil, changes in inflation and exchange rates, real interest rates, and the beta for gold. But a number of macroeconomic factors also play a critical role in the development of the price of gold over the long run. Fear of inflation would play an essential role in increasing investor interest in gold because physical gold has always been used to hedge against currency weakness. Investors' increasing interest in using gold as a hedge against the weakness of the U.S. dollar has also driven gold prices up in 2006. In the long run, however, gold has maintained its real purchasing power because it is a *real* asset.

The long-run price of gold is expected to move with general price levels (the consumer price index) to act as a hedge against inflation. This occurs because it is related to the marginal costs of extraction, which rise with the inflation rate. Note that this conclusion is not affected by whether gold producers decide to supply customers by leasing from central banks or by extracting gold from mines. Because this leased gold must be repaid, it affects supply only in the short term.

Profit-maximizing behavior by gold producers ensures that the cost of gold from leasing is equal to the cost of gold from extraction. We use the general price level in the United States as an explanatory variable to test the hypothesis that the price of gold moves with the general price level. Exhibit 32.11 gives the results of our empirical analysis for the U.S. price index.

The upward trends shown in Exhibit 32.11 are consistent with the view that a long-run relationship between the price of gold and the general price level is likely, and that gold can be a long-run hedge against inflation. However, there are significant deviations between movements in the price of gold and the general price level in the short run. It is obvious that gold is not a short-run hedge against inflation.

If we transform the consumer price index into inflation rates, we see a link between the price of gold and U.S. inflation in Exhibit 32.11. Including the U.S. inflation rate suggests that the price of gold is higher during periods of high inflation because the demand for gold as an inflation hedge rises

EXHIBIT 32.11 Gold Prices and U.S. CPI, January 1970 to January 2007
Source: Exhibit created from data obtained from Bloomberg.

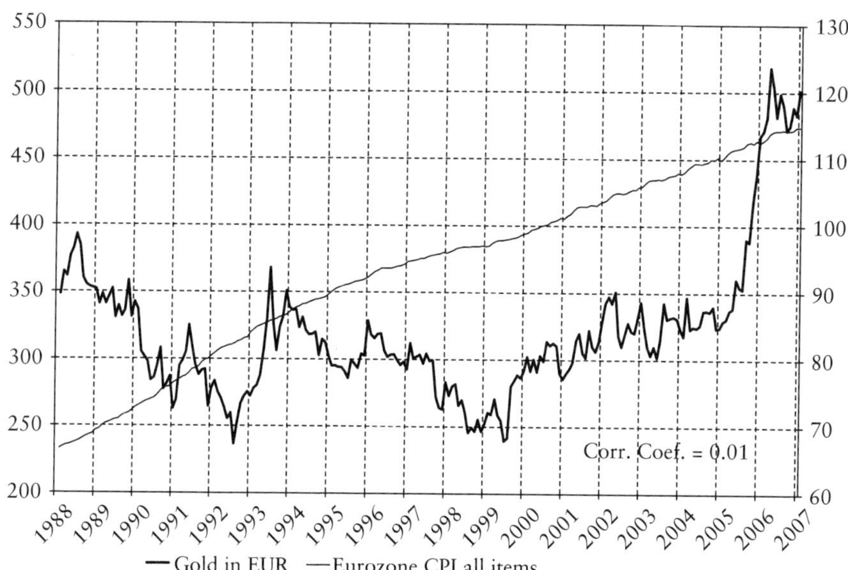

EXHIBIT 32.12 Gold Prices in Euros and Eurozone CPI, 1988–2007
Source: Exhibit created from data obtained from OECD.

during such periods. This can be seen for 1972–1974, 1978–1980, and 1986–1987. However, the relationship does not appear to hold for 2002–2005.

In the Eurozone, however, there is absolutely no relationship between the price of gold denominated in euros and the CPI (or, rather, the inflation rate) (see Exhibits 32.12 and 32.13). In Exhibit 32.12, a convergence of the gold price to the so-called *inflation hedge price* can be seen in 2007. This means that the current gold price is very close to the long-run inflationary hedge price.

For countries other than the United States, the question of whether gold can be considered as a long-run inflation hedge depends on the country's currency strength against the U.S. dollar. It is important to note that (1) exchange rates between the U.S. dollar and other currencies fluctuate over time; (2) inflation rates vary among countries and over time; and, (3) gold is denominated in U.S. dollars. Thus, if it is considered an inflation hedge for the United States, holding gold will be profitable for investors in countries whose currencies depreciate against the U.S. dollar more than is necessary to compensate for inflation rate differences between the two countries.

It is thus no coincidence that the major gold-consuming countries are overrepresented among those who have profited from holding gold. As the

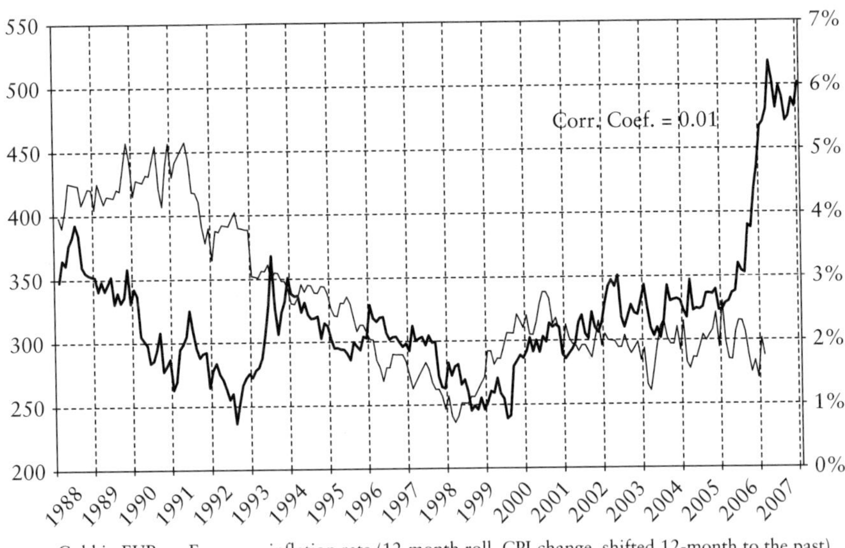

EXHIBIT 32.13 Gold Prices in Euros and Eurozone Inflation, 1988–2007
Source: Exhibit created from data obtained from OECD.

euro appreciates against the U.S. dollar, this favorable investment effect of gold currently does not exist in the Eurozone.[9]

Specific Attributes of Gold

Gold possesses three distinct attributes that make it unique in the commodities universe: (1) it is fungible, (2) it is indestructible and storable, and (3) it is characterized by massive aboveground stocks that are enormous relative to the supply flow.[10] This last attribute means that a sudden increase in gold demand can be quickly and easily met through sales of existing holdings of

[9]Some researchers consider gold to be a better inflation predictor than the consumer price index or the bond market. That means the causality is exchanged; that is, it is not that inflation influences the price of gold, but it is possible to predict inflation from the development of the gold price. See David Ranson, *Why Gold, Not Oil, Is the Superior Predictor of Inflation* (London: World Gold Council, 2005).

[10]Current aboveground gold stocks total 150,000 tons. The supply contribution from gold production amounted to approximately 2,500 tons in 2005; total supply (including central bank sales, scrap recycling, and short positions) amounted to approximately 3,700 tons in 2005.

gold jewelry, or by increasing the amount of gold recovered from scrap. It can also be met through the mechanism of the gold leasing market.

Gold is also different from other commodities because it has the potential to be highly liquid and to have a high price elasticity. Another crucial characteristic is that the gold market is always in contango,[11] which is a function of the storability of gold and its large aboveground stocks. These attributes also explain why the future price of gold is always higher than its spot price:

$$\text{Forward price} = \text{Spot price} + \text{Interest costs}(= \text{Gold lease rate}) + \text{Storage/Insurance costs}$$

The existence of storage acts as a damper on price volatility because it balances supply and demand, but it also causes additional costs. The convenience yield is the benefit from owning physical gold, which means being able to avoid production disruptions or to provide investors with peace of mind. The convenience yield is included in the gold lease rate, along with the credit risk premium.

GOLD AS A PORTFOLIO CONSTITUENT

Gold has good diversification properties in a portfolio because its price behaves in a completely different way than the prices of stocks or bonds. It is therefore worth examining gold's contribution to the overall portfolio risk-return relationship.

First, possible returns from any gold investment should be considered, and it is necessary to distinguish between expected returns in U.S. dollars and those in Euros. Exhibit 32.14 gives our calculation results. It is obvious that the return in Euros is lower than the U.S. dollar returns. Additionally, gains in U.S. dollar gold prices are often translated into losses in Euros, as the price increase of gold denominated in dollars often coincides with a weaker U.S. dollar against the Euro.

As Exhibit 32.14 shows, gold experienced negative returns for substantially long periods. It was not an attractive portfolio asset until about 2002, except for during 1993 and 1999, which were relatively good years for gold. In 1999, however, U.S. dollar movements turned the gain to a loss for a

[11]The market is said to be in contango when spot prices are below forward prices. Contango is the opposite of backwardation, when spot prices are higher than forward prices.

EXHIBIT 32.14 Gold Returns in Euros and U.S. Dollar (percent)

	Compound Annual Returns									
	1 Year		3 Years		5 Years		10 Years		15 Years	
To the End of the Year	in EUR	in USD	in EUR	in USD	in EUR	in USD	in EUR	in USD	in EUR	in USD
1987										
1988	−4.31	−15.26								
1989	−15.70	−9.84								
1990	−3.41	3.49	−7.98	−7.53						
1991	−7.74	−7.75	−9.10	−4.87						
1992	4.04	−5.28	−5.93	−5.88	−5.64	−7.13				
1993	27.32	16.80	6.91	0.68	−0.10	−0.97				
1994	−10.91	−1.92	5.68	2.76	−1.14	−0.92				
1995	−3.12	1.02	3.19	4.99	1.07	0.22				
1996	−1.55	−5.01	−5.28	−2.00	2.39	0.81				
1997	−11.79	−21.39	−5.60	−8.97	−0.93	−2.88	−3.32	−5.03		
1998	−6.32	−0.28	−6.65	−9.36	−6.83	−5.90	−3.52	−3.47		
1999	16.25	−0.09	−1.33	−7.82	−1.73	−5.55	−1.44	−3.26		
2000	1.18	−5.47	3.29	−1.98	−0.88	−6.80	0.09	−3.35		
2001	8.13	2.46	8.34	−1.09	1.00	−5.37	1.69	−2.33		
2002	5.75	24.77	4.98	6.52	4.73	3.78	1.86	0.40	−2.18	−0.71
2003	0.81	21.72	4.50	15.13	6.06	7.58	−0.59	0.62	0.08	−0.43
2004	−2.18	5.54	1.07	16.27	2.46	8.77	0.34	1.36	0.59	−0.16
2005	35.08	17.92	9.66	14.10	8.56	13.69	3.73	2.94	2.02	2.84
2006	10.49	23.15	13.44	15.29	4.29	10.37	4.94	5.64	4.01	4.08

Source: Exhibit created from data obtained from Bloomberg.

euro investor. As Exhibit 32.14 shows, gold has been less attractive overall for a euro investor.

Eurozone

Exhibit 32.15 shows the three-year rolling correlations between monthly changes in gold prices denominated in Euros with the German stock and bond markets. There is an especially low correlation with the REXP (the German government bond index), as well as with the DAX (the German share index). The low correlation of gold compared to other financial assets leads to a better diversified portfolio. Exhibit 32.16 summarizes the performance of gold, stocks, and bond investments for various periods.

Because the REXP data only begin in 1988, we examine the period from 1988 through 2006. Gold denominated in euros had a very low correlation with bonds, which was true for all subperiods. Because of the low returns of gold before 1990, we looked at a period of high share returns (1990–1999), and at a period of negative equity returns (2000–2006).

Markowitz's portfolio theory introduced the idea of efficient portfolios, showing the optimal risk-return combination in a μ,σ-diagram. If an additional asset is moving the portfolio line in the direction to the top left, it is

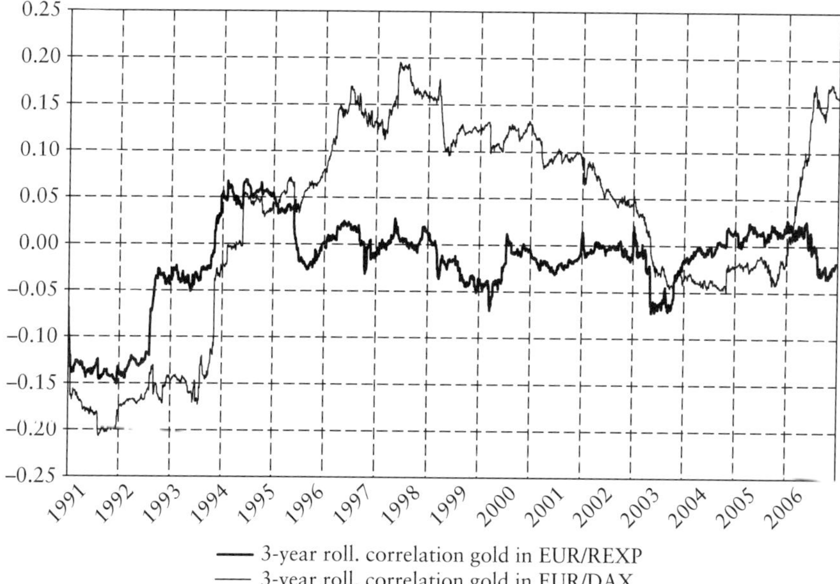

EXHIBIT 32.15 Rolling Correlations between Gold and the Bond/Equity Markets: Eurozone, January 1991 to December 2006
Source: Exhibit created from data obtained from Bloomberg.

EXHIBIT 32.16 Returns, Correlation, and Volatility in the Gold, Bond, and Equity Markets: Eurozone

1988–2006					
Correlation	Gold in EUR	Gold in USD	REX	DAX	EuroStoxx 50
Gold in EUR	1.00	0.67	−0.02	0.02	0.13
REX			1.00	0.08	−0.01
DAX				1.00	0.45
EuroStoxx 50					1.00
Compound annual return	1.43%	1.45%	5.88%	10.44%	14.09%
Annual					
Performance (average return)	1.37%	1.39%	5.52%	9.59%	12.74%
Volatility	14.83%	13.80%	3.35%	21.87%	30.11%
1990–1999					
Gold in EUR	1.00	0.57	−0.02	0.00	0.14
REX			1.00	0.25	0.06
DAX				1.00	0.27
EuroStoxx 50					1.00
Compound annual return	−1.44%	−3.26%	7.62%	14.54%	31.36%
Annual					
Performance (average return)	−1.40%	−3.20%	7.09%	13.11%	26.33%
Volatility	14.86%	12.22%	3.11%	19.40%	36.20%
2000–2006					
Gold in EUR	1.00	0.80	−0.01	0.04	0.07
REX			1.00	−0.16	−0.18
DAX				1.00	0.91
EuroStoxx 50					1.00
Compound annual return	7.91%	11.95%	5.24%	−0.33%	−0.35%
Annual					
Performance (average return)	7.21%	10.95%	4.90%	−0.74%	−0.49%
Volatility	14.93%	16.14%	3.00%	25.43%	23.31%

Source: Exhibit created from data obtained from Bloomberg.

considered attractive for an investor because these portfolios offer higher returns with less risk.

Exhibits 32.17 through 32.19 show the effect of adding gold to an investment portfolio over various periods. Exhibit 32.17 shows the overall period

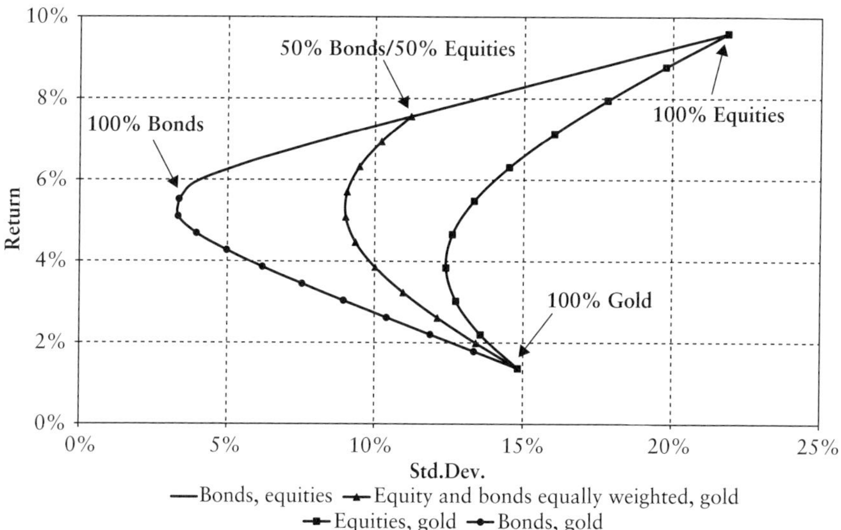

EXHIBIT 32.17 Eurozone: Yearly Returns, 1988–2006
Source: Exhibit created from data obtained from Bloomberg.

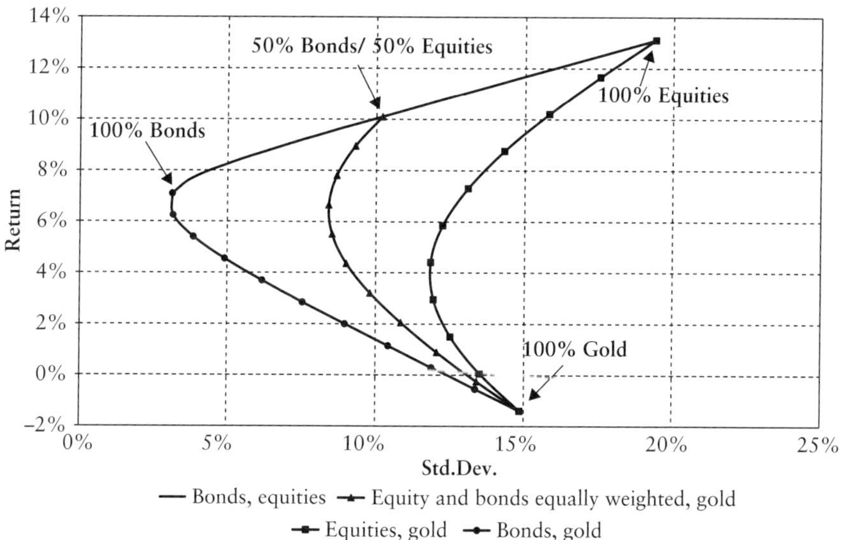

EXHIBIT 32.18 Eurozone: Yearly Returns, 1990–1999
Source: Exhibit created from data obtained from Bloomberg.

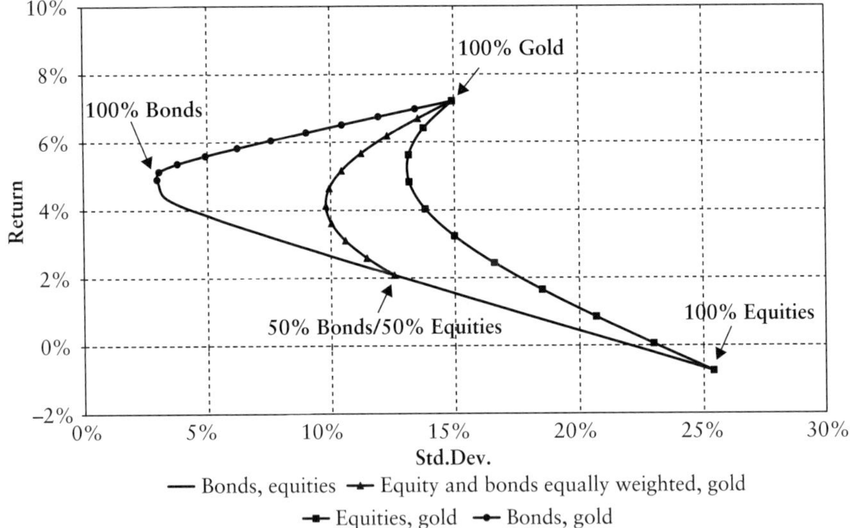

EXHIBIT 32.19 Eurozone: Yearly Returns, 2000–2006
Source: Exhibit created from data obtained from Bloomberg.

from 1988 through 2006. It is evident that gold makes no reasonable risk-adjusted performance contribution to the total portfolio. Despite its low correlation, a return of below 2% and volatility almost four times higher than bonds ultimately made gold unattractive. A combination of just bonds and equity performed better. This is true for almost all subperiods before 2000.

Consider the period 1990–1999, which is characterized by extraordinary equity returns (see Exhibit 32.18). Gold has a negative return during these years, so investors would obtain less performance with higher risk by adding gold to the portfolio. A combination of bonds and equity is more sensible.

Exhibit 32.19 emphasizes the risk-reducing ability of gold during 2000–2006. The efficient line is moved to the left in the area of lower volatility and higher returns. Because its performance was above 7%, gold was attractive compared to the very low returns in the equity sector (but, again, this was a change from most other periods).

United States

The fact that gold returns are generally higher when measured in U.S. dollars suggests that a closer look at this currency is warranted. Exhibit 32.20 summarizes the performance of gold, stocks, and bond investments for various periods. The data are available from 1974.

In U.S. dollars, we find a very low correlation with gold. The annual USD returns of gold are considerably higher than gold returns denominated

EXHIBIT 32.20 Returns, Correlations, and Volatility in the Gold, Bond, and Equity Markets: United States

1974–2006			
Correlation	**Gold in USD**	**Lehman U.S. Treasury**	**S&P 500**
Gold in USD	1.00	0.00	−0.01
Lehman U.S. Treasury		1.00	0.18
S&P 500			1.00
Compound annual return	5.56%	8.34%	8.45%
Annual			
Performance (average return)	7.33%	8.19%	9.31%
Volatility	19.79%	5.48%	15.27%
1974–1979			
Gold in USD	1.00	0.01	−0.11
Lehman U.S. Treasury		1.00	0.32
S&P 500			1.00
Compound annual return	25.80%	6.05%	1.87%
Annual			
Performance (average return)	29.96%	6.08%	3.09%
Volatility	27.32%	3.85%	16.98%
1980–1989			
Gold in USD	1.00	0.01	0.17
Lehman U.S. Treasury		1.00	0.25
S&P 500			1.00
Compound annual return	−4.75%	12.35%	11.96%
Annual			
Performance (average return)	0.14%	11.81%	13.28%
Volatility	22.95%	7.40%	16.38%
1990–1999			
Gold in USD	1.00	−0.04	−0.13
Lehman U.S. Treasury		1.00	0.35
S&P 500			1.00
Compound annual return	−3.59%	7.60%	16.14%
Annual			
Performance (average return)	−2.58%	7.29%	15.23%
Volatility	12.24%	4.27%	13.42%
2000–2006			
Gold in USD	1.00	0.09	−0.01
Lehman U.S. Treasury		1.00	−0.34
S&P 500			1.00
Compound annual return	12.25%	6.12%	0.24%
Annual			
Performance (average return)	12.35%	6.11%	0.51%
Volatility	14.07%	4.81%	14.28%

Source: Exhibit created from data obtained from Bloomberg.

in euros. Unfortunately, the higher returns come with a very high volatility, although gold returns outperformed in 1974–1979 and 2000–2006. We also consider 1980–1989 and 1990–1999, which had negative gold returns, but lower gold volatility during the second period.

Exhibit 32.21 shows the three-year rolling correlation between monthly changes in gold prices denominated in U.S. dollars and the U.S. stock and bond markets. Gold is shown here to be a substantial asset for portfolio diversification.

Exhibits 32.22 through 32.26 show the effect of adding gold to the U.S. dollar investment portfolio. Even though gold returns were higher compared to the Euro, gold was often an undesirable asset in the portfolio due to its high volatility. Exhibit 32.22 shows that combining bonds and equity during 1974 to 2006 was more efficient.

Exhibit 32.23 shows that gold improved total portfolio returns during 1974 to 1979, a time of high inflation and low equity returns. Even though gold's volatility and therefore risk were high during this period, its very high returns above 25% made it attractive.

However, this was not true for the following years until 1999. Exhibit 32.24 shows that gold destroyed value for the period 1980–1989 due to negative returns and high volatility.

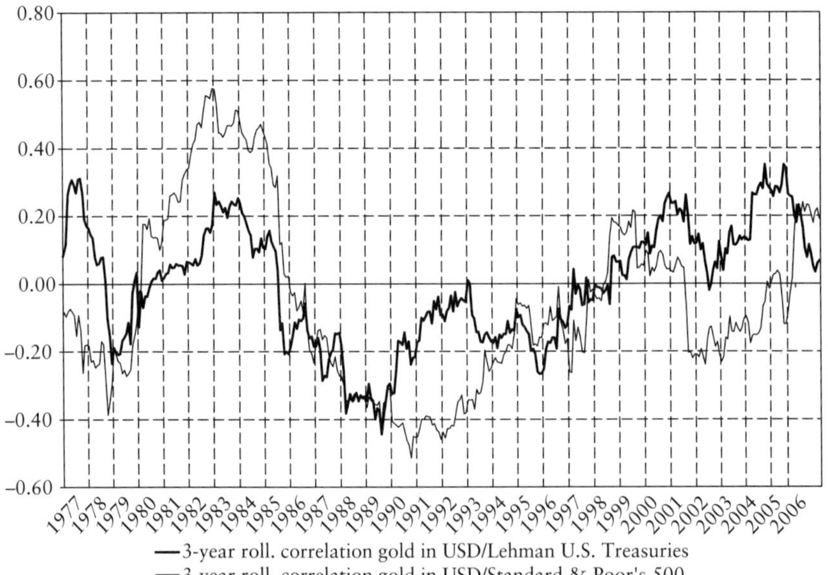

EXHIBIT 32.21 Rolling Correlations between Gold and the Bond/Equity Markets: U.S. Monthly Returns, January 1977 to December 2006
Source: Exhibit created from data obtained from Bloomberg.

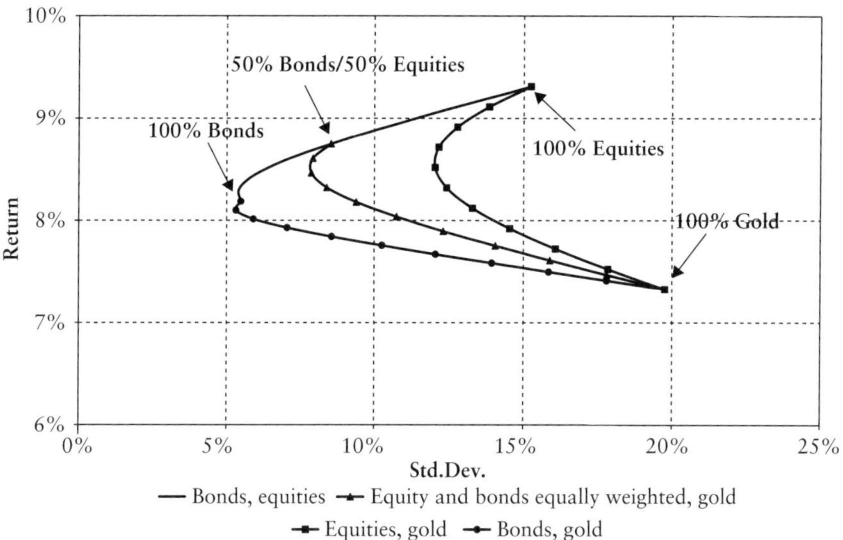

EXHIBIT 32.22 United States: Yearly Returns, 1974–2006
Source: Exhibit created from data obtained from Bloomberg.

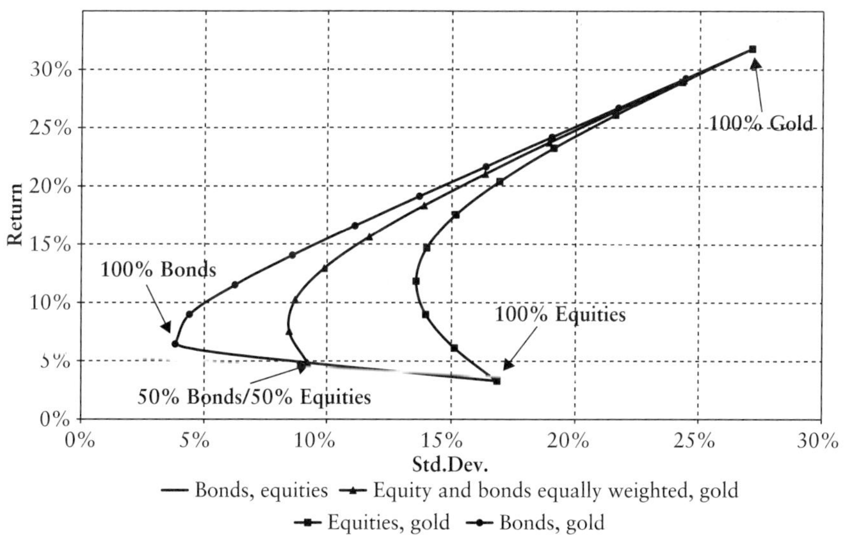

EXHIBIT 32.23 United States Yearly Returns, 1974–1979
Source: Exhibit created from data obtained from Bloomberg.

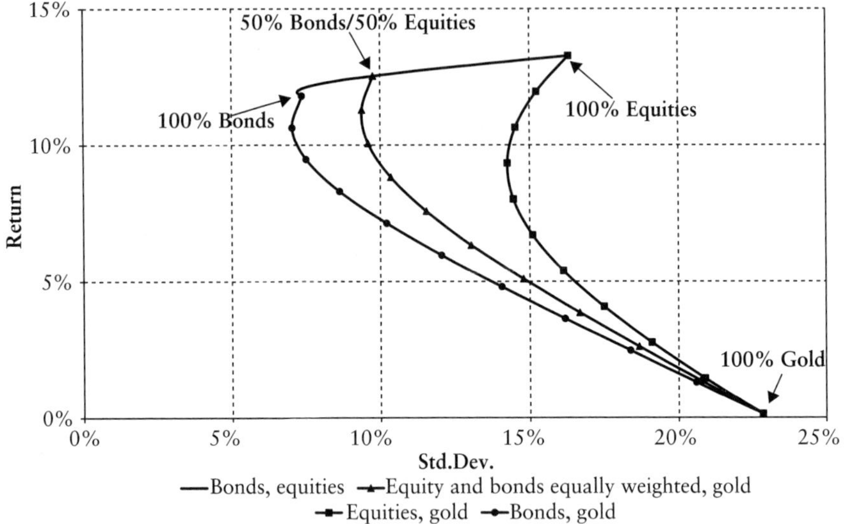

EXHIBIT 32.24 United States Yearly Returns, 1980–1989
Source: Exhibit created from data obtained from Bloomberg.

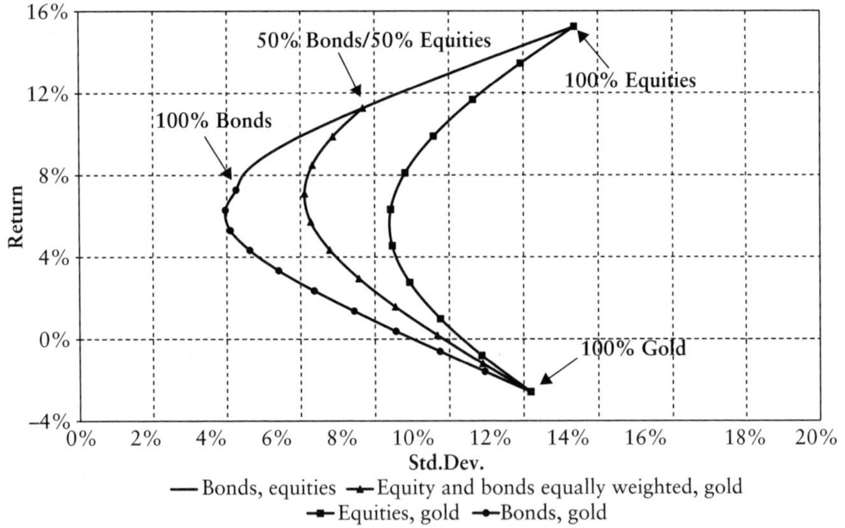

EXHIBIT 32.25 United States Yearly Returns, 1990–1999
Source: Exhibit created from data obtained from Bloomberg.

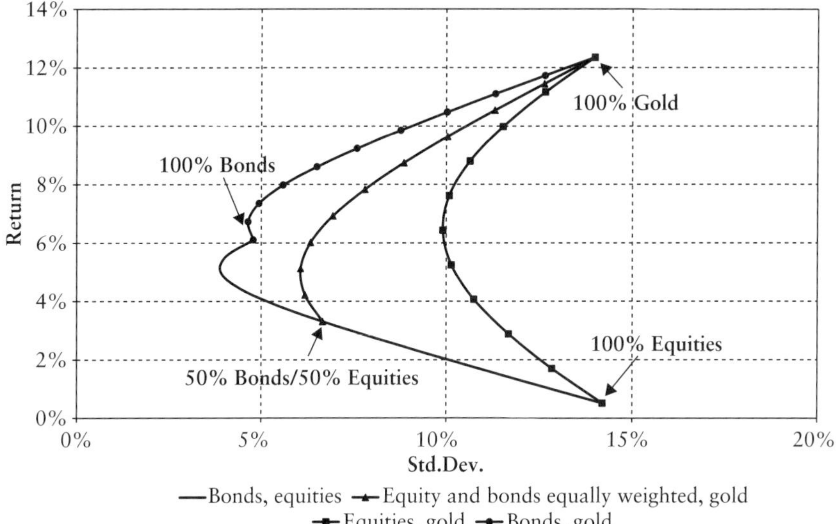

EXHIBIT 32.26 United States Yearly Returns, 2000–2006
Source: Exhibit created from data obtained from Bloomberg.

From 1990 to 1999, gold's volatility fell by almost half compared to the prior period. Nevertheless, due to negative returns, gold was still not considered a sensible asset in the portfolio, as Exhibit 32.25 shows. From 1980 to 1999, equities were more attractive. They exhibited higher returns and similar or lower volatility.

Exhibit 32.26 emphasizes the risk-reducing and return-increasing ability of gold during the last six years. During this time period, equity returns were almost zero, while gold returns were above 12%. From 2000 to 2006, combining gold with bonds shifted the efficient line considerably to the left. Therefore, portfolio managers now tend to consider gold an attractive supplement.

CONCLUSION

Over the last 30 years or so, gold had extremely low returns for long subperiods. Prior to 2000 in the United States, gold was only an attractive long-term investment during 1974–1979. Despite the fact that gold exhibited a low correlation with bonds and equity for almost all subperiods, this diversification effect did not compensate for negative returns in the United States and small returns of under 1.5% in euros.

Development of the price of gold changed after central banks decided to limit their gold sales in 2004. Since then, supply and demand has been less dependent on central banks' gold selling policies. This has resulted in a supply shortage, and a substantial increase in price.

Because the price of gold had already begun to rise in 2002, we find an annual euro performance of almost 8% and 12%+ for the U.S. dollar between 2000 and 2006. Correlation with other financial assets remains low, and the return variability of gold is currently comparable to equity return volatility.

We believe future investment in gold will depend on how central banks deal with their gold reserves. If they continue the current policy, we might see further positive effects on gold prices caused by higher demand, especially from India and China. Gold can help diversify a portfolio, but in the past this quality was only attractive during periods of low-performing equity markets.

The empirical evidence for gold as an inflation hedge is small for the United States and nonexistent for the Eurozone. Gold may be considered a hedge against the USD exchange rate for "soft" currencies, but not for the euro. Because the correlation and volatility of gold appear to remain low, future investments in gold will depend critically on investor price expectations.

CHAPTER 33

Fundamental Analysis of the World Silver Market

Jeffrey M. Christian
Managing Director
CPM Group

Silver is a rather unique commodity in that it straddles both the financial markets and the commodities markets. It trades like a financial asset, but also is an industrial commodity the bulk of which is used in a wide range of fabricated products.

In some ways, silver shares further characteristics with gold. Nevertheless, there are important differences between silver and gold. Silver has much more of an industrial base to its fabrication demand than gold does. Almost all of the gold absorbed each year in the world either goes into investor inventories of gold bullion, or it is used in jewelry. Gold jewelry has a quasi-investment nature to it, being used as a form of investment and a form of savings in many cultures and countries. Less than 10% of annual gold use goes into nonjewelry fabricated products. In contrast to this, most silver is used in fabricated products that have nothing to do with silver's other roles as an investment product and a form of savings. Silver is purchased as an investment and as a form of savings, but in the silver market these purchases represent a much smaller portion of annual total demand. Typically less than one-third of total silver demand goes into investment and jewelry products. Thus silver's price is determined by a more diverse mix of factors

---

For a more detailed discussion, see Jeffrey M. Christian's *Commodities Rising* (Hoboken, NJ: John Wiley & Sons, 2006) and *The CPM Silver Yearbook* (Hoboken, NJ: John Wiley & Sons, 2007).

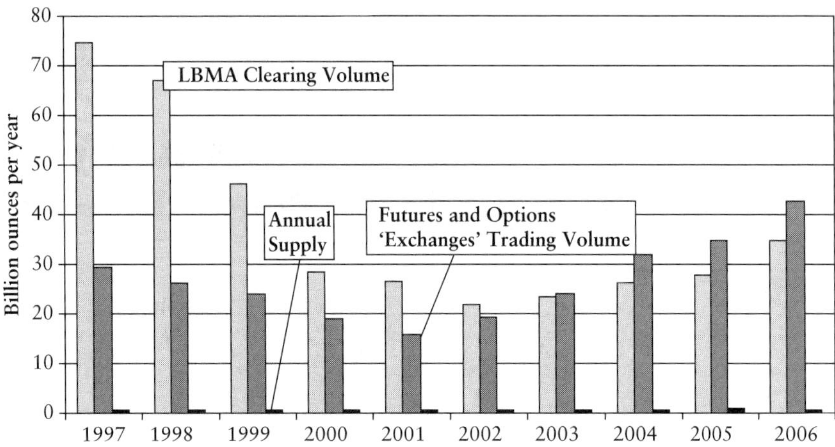

EXHIBIT 33.1 The Silver Market
Source: Exhibit created from data obtained from New York Commodities Exchange, London Bullion Market Association, Chicago Board of Trade, Tokyo Commodity Exchange, Multi Commodity Exchange, and CPM Group.

than is the price of gold, which is largely driven by investment demand patterns. (See Exhibit 33.1.)

On the other hand, silver shares many characteristics with gold. Like its more expensive cousin, silver was used as a form of money for much of the past five millennia. Because of this, there are vast amounts of silver that have been mined and saved over the centuries. Inventories of silver are measured in the hundreds of millions of ounces in bullion form, and in the tens of billions of ounces in the forms of jewelry, decorative objects, religious objects, and other fabricated products with recoverable, recyclable silver. The amount of silver estimated to exist in these forms represents decades' worth of silver fabrication demand. In this way, it is quite different from base metals that do not have millennial monetary heritages. Base metals such as copper, aluminum, lead, and zinc have inventory levels that are measured in terms of weeks' worth of consumption, that is, the size of the market inventories that are known to exist. Gold and silver have inventories that are measured in years and decades because there is so much of these two metals around. These are metals with millennia of use as stores of value. People, and governments, have not thrown silver and gold away, at least not lightly. These metals, unlike more industrial commodities, do not normally end in garbage dumps and landfills at the end of product cycles. They are coveted and hoarded, and have been for millennia. They also do not rust or deteriorate like base metals.

Interestingly, but not surprisingly, a much larger portion of the amount of silver mined throughout history is estimated to have been lost and not be recoverable than is the case with gold. Around 4.6 billion ounces of gold are estimated to have been mined since antiquity. Of this, roughly 90% is believed to still exist in more or less identifiable and recoverable form, in bullion held by private individuals and central banks, and in gold jewelry, decorative objects, and religious items. In contrast, more than half of the 42.6 billion ounces of silver estimated to have been mined since the beginning of mining is estimated to be lost and not recoverable. This makes intuitive sense, given the greater value and less widespread use of gold. People have tended not to lose gold, in coin or jewelry form, whereas they are less careful with their silver.

THE PRICE OF SILVER

Silver, like gold, also behaves more like a financial asset than it does a commodity (see Exhibit 33.2). There is a tremendous amount of silver that trades every day, far in excess of what one would expect based on fundamentals of supply and demand. Silver trading in the London interbank market totals around 25 to 30 billion ounces per year, or 50 to 150 million ounces per day, as of the middle of the 2000s. Another 30 billion ounces of silver are traded across the New York COMEX in terms of silver futures and options contracts each year. These volumes compare to annual new supply and fabrication demand of less than one billion ounces per year. These numbers, as astounding as they are, are way off from the late 1990s.

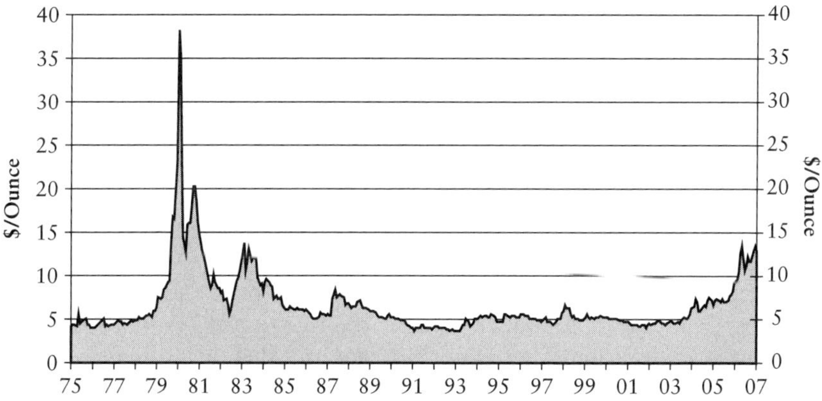

EXHIBIT 33.2 The Price of Silver
Source: Exhibit created from data obtained from New York Commodities Exchange and CPM Group.

When the London Bullion Market Association began publishing its clearing volumes in late 1996 and early 1997, more than 74 billion ounces per year were cleared through London banks.

These volumes are characteristic of a financial asset and not an industrial commodity. Such volumes cannot represent the normal flow of an industrial commodity from producer to semifabricator to fabricator, with banks and dealers serving as middlemen. Similar ratios of derivatives to underlying physical trade volumes are not readily available for other commodities, but market estimates are that the ratios probably range from around 5:1 derivatives to physicals for more traditional commodities such as corn, to around 20:1 for commodities like petroleum. Silver, with a ratio close to 60:1, down from 100:1, is far larger, as is gold. Ratios such as those in the gold and silver markets are found in financial markets, such as U.S. Treasury bonds and bills, and currencies, calculated based on the volumes of debt securities and currencies traded in both the international dealer market and on organized futures and options exchanges.

The price of silver is extremely volatile compared to other commodities and other financial assets over time. While some observers believe that part of silver's interest to investors is that it has a lower dollar per ounce price than gold, allowing people to buy more volume for equal values, it seems that many investors actually invest in silver in order to diversify their precious metals portfolios and because of silver's greater price volatility. They seek greater returns based on a perception that silver's price tends to outpace gold in percentage terms.

That said, the two metals' prices move only partially in tandem with each other. Another perception about silver and gold is that the prices always move in close concert. In fact, the prices often vary quite greatly. The gold-to-silver ratio has ranged from 16:1 to 100:1 over the past three decades, since gold and silver prices were freed from governments setting their levels in the 1960s.

Some market participants base their investment and trading decisions on the gold-silver ratio. The gold-silver ratio is an excellent barometer of the relative value of each metal one against the other, but there is no law of physics, chemistry, nature, or man that says the ratio ought to be anything in particular. In contrast, some investors and traders, as well as the newsletter writers who service them, look at the average price ratio of these two metals, and assume that sooner or later the ratio must revert toward its long-term average value. That is not the case and there is no reason to believe this. There are no economic theories, physical properties, or other demonstrable rationales for believing that any such financial ratio must revert to its mean at some point in the future. Market conditions change, and with them the intermarket relationships. Fortunes have been lost by people waiting for one asset to regain its former glory relative to other assets, only to find that, like cordage in the early age of steamships, sometimes the fundamental and economic bases for the value of assets change permanently.

Like gold, silver has a lot of true believers who think they understand this market, vest all sorts of unattainable attributes to silver, and then say there must be a conspiracy to control silver prices when silver does not live up to their sometimes unreasonable and irrational expectations. Yes, there are silver market conspiracy theories.

World Silver Production

The vast majority of the mine production of silver since the dawn of man has been mined in the past century. About six billion of this 42 billion ounces has been mined in the past 15 years alone (see Exhibit 33.3).

Of this total, perhaps 21 billion ounces can be identified. Around half a billion ounces is in bullion bar form. Another half billion ounces exists in coin form. Around 20 billion ounces are in the form of jewelry, silverware, sterling objects, religious objects, and art. The remaining 21 billion ounces has been used in products from which it had not been reclaimed or otherwise lost. Since silver traditionally is less valuable than gold, there is a lower intensity of recycling of silver than there is of gold. Much silver is recovered, recycled, and reused every year, and has been for centuries. However, in many manufactured products, the silver is not heavily recovered. Over the past several decades most of the silver refined from old scrap has been from spent photographic materials: old films, papers, and developing solutions. That said, and even though there are regulations against discharging silver-bearing spent photographic developing solutions in many parts of the world, it is obvious that enormous volumes of these solutions are simply flushed into waste water systems.

The silver market has been susceptible to large investors making significant price impacts. This reflects the relatively small size of the silver market. The dollar value of the silver market is much smaller than that of the gold market, and is utterly dwarfed by the size of overall financial markets. In the middle of the 1990s, Berkshire Hathaway studied the silver market and concluded it would be a good place in which to invest. Berkshire Hathaway is an equity- and bond-oriented company and does not typically invest in commodities. At the time, 1996–1997, it had around $35 billion under management, so, to be significant enough to its portfolio, a silver position would have needed to be around $700 million, or around 2% of its overall portfolio. That was larger than the market capitalization of all silver mining companies then in existence in the world. In other words, for Berkshire Hathaway to have been able to build a silver equity position large enough

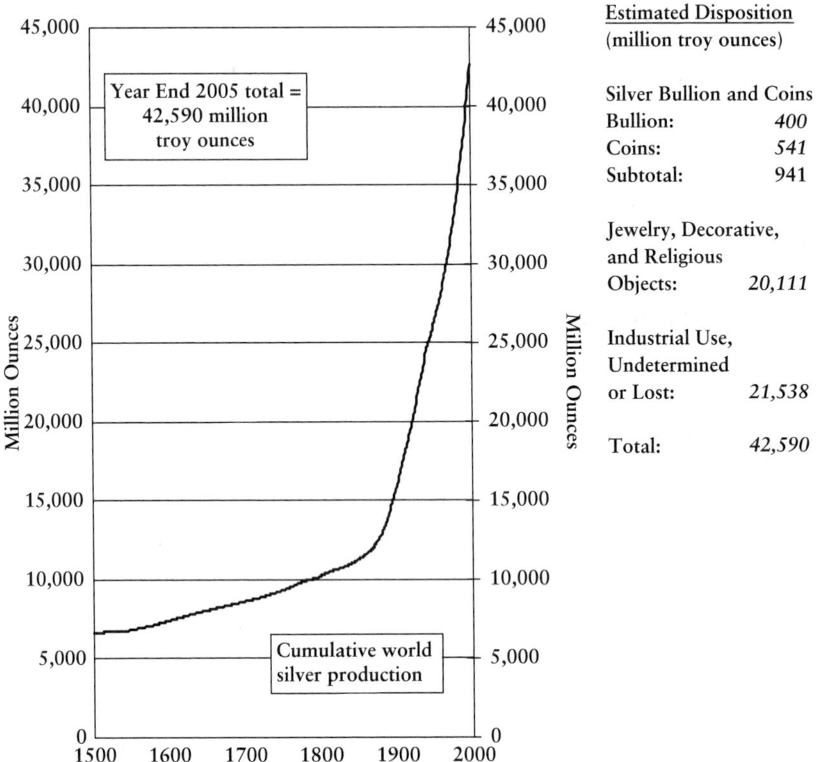

EXHIBIT 33.3 Cumulative World Silver Production and Distribution
Source: Exhibit created from data obtained from Australian Minerals Economics Pty. Ltd., Schmitz, Metschaft, United Nations, Handy and Harman, Ministry of Natural Resources Ontario, Dr. Adolph Soetbeer 1493–1850, USGS, and CPM Group.
Note: Total disposition may not equal cumulative production due to rounding and other discrepancies in the historical data. The distribution of 6,681 million ounces of pre-1493 production is not able to be discerned. Silver in product form includes jewelry, art, sterlingware, religious objects, museum pieces, and other silver-bearing objects. Historical information on the production and consumption of silver over the past five millennia necessarily has a high degree of potential error. Some estimates of cumulative production vary by a couple of billion ounces from the sources used here.

to matter to it, it would have had to buy every share of every silver mining company, obviously an untenable approach. Intrigued by silver, the company decided to buy silver bullion. It further decided to buy the silver, take delivery of it, and hold it away from the major market participants in allocated deposits. By not allowing the metal to be held in unallocated or pool accounts by bullion banks, Berkshire Hathaway denied the bullion banks the ability to use such deposits as collateral against which to lend silver to others and to short the market. In 2006, Berkshire Hathaway announced that it had disposed of its silver, having reached its price objectives. The price of silver had risen from levels below $5.00 per ounce when Berkshire Hathaway was buying its silver, in 1997–1998, to levels around $8 to $9 per ounce.

Berkshire Hathaway was only the most recent, and one of the most prominent silver investors. The silver market also saw the Hunt brothers invest in silver in the late 1970s. Others were involved in other periods as well. Several prominent investors have built sizable silver market positions at times.

One of the myths that has been accepted as bible truth in the silver market is that the Hunt brothers, Nelson and Herbert, tried to corner the silver market in the 1970s. I had some contact with them at that time and was plugged into other parts of the silver market at that time. I never saw the Hunts try to corner the silver market and am willing to bet that is not what they were trying to do. What I saw was the Hunts buying a lot of silver. They seemed to think that the silver market was ready to see a sharp increase in prices and wanted to ride that wave. At some point, they had a really nice position established. They started telling everyone, from wealthy Arab sheiks and Brazilian magnates to brokers that dealt with smaller investors, what a great investment silver was. Silver prices were destined to rise, they told everyone: "We have loaded up on silver, and so should you." The basic story they had about silver, that supply and demand imbalances were likely to drive prices sharply higher, was based on an accurate and honest analysis of silver's fundamentals, and the macroeconomic environment as it stimulates investor interest in silver and other commodities. I am convinced, from what they said at the time and from everything that I saw, that the Hunts intended to establish a large silver position and then ride a wave. They may have helped heighten the wave's intensity, but it was coming regardless of anything they would do or say.

A study conducted by economists after the fact concluded that the Hunt's silver buying activity added very little to the price of silver, suggesting that silver prices' increase from around $5 to $50 in late 1979 and early 1980 was due to other factors, coming as it did at the same time oil prices quadrupled, gold rose from $200 to $850, and platinum went from $340 to $1,040. This econometric study concluded that the Hunts had not done much to the price of silver.[1]

[1]L. C. G. Rogers and Surbjeet Singh, "Modelling Liquidity and List Effect on Price," Working Paper, University of Cambridge, 2006.

This actually makes intuitive sense: Prices of a wide range of commodities were rising at the time, and not just the silver. It was a dreadful time, with 13% inflation, 21% interest rates, U.S. hostages in Iran, Soviet troops in Afghanistan, and Iranian and Soviet assets were frozen worldwide. There was a wide range of ugly economic, financial market, and political problems. The stock market was on its back in most countries, and bond yields had been lower than inflation rates for most of the past decade. Oil prices had quadrupled. There were no easy ways for most investors around the world to hedge their exposure to stocks, bonds, and currencies. There were no currency options at the time, and no stock index options or futures. The only two readily available ways to protect oneself financially from all of this was to buy gold or silver.

THE SUPPLY OF SILVER

Silver is mined in dozens of countries worldwide. Much of the silver mined in the world is produced in polymetallic mines, along with lead, zinc, copper, gold, and sometimes all sorts of other metals from bismuth and cadmium to tellurium and selenium. Around four-fifths of the silver mined in the world comes from mines at which silver is not the primary product.

Mexico traditionally has been the largest silver mining country. It has been producing close to 100 million ounces of silver per year since 2001. Peru has been an important producer for centuries, but as recently as the late 1990s was producing around 60 million ounces per year. Peruvian output has risen sharply since then, however, and by the middle of the 2000s was producing roughly as much silver each year as was Mexico. Other large silver mining countries include the United States, Canada, and Australia.

In total, around 530 million ounces of silver is produced annually at mines in the market economy nations at present. China, Kazakhstan, and other countries also produce silver, but getting accurate counts of production has been slower to occur. Chinese mine production is rising rapidly during the 2000s, and could surpass both Mexico and Peru in the coming decade as the largest silver mining country.

China also has become a major refiner of silver, both from domestic ores and from mining concentrates imported for their lead, zinc, and copper content. As China has developed economically over the past decade, it has taken a major role in the world as a refiner of these base metals. Much of the base metal concentrates that China today imports from Indonesia, Peru, Mexico, Canada, and other countries has byproduct gold and silver in it. Since China has more gold and silver than its domestic fabricators and investors want, after the concentrates are refined into their constituent metals the gold and silver has been exported and sold in Zurich, London, Saudi Arabia, India, and other countries. Additional amounts of silver have come from scrap, including old silver jewelry and foreign silver coins that were used as currency prior to the Communist revolution in 1949. Some people have misidentified these silver exports as coming from government stocks. Others have double counted the metal, measuring silver content in mine production in various countries, and then adding silver exports from China onto these totals to come up with estimates of how much silver is coming into the market.

In addition to the 530 million ounces being refined from mine production, another 230 million ounces are refined from scrapped fabricated products each year at present. Some of this is jewelry and silverware, especially in India, Pakistan, and other Asian nations. The largest portion, however, is from spent photographic materials. As mentioned already, a lot of spent photographic developer solutions are believed to be illegally flushed into sewer systems. Even so, a tremendous amount of silver is recovered from photographic papers, films, and solutions. As much as 80% of the 230 million ounces of silver that is refined from scrap each year may come from photographic materials. There also are several million ounces of silver recovered from old electronics each year. A lot of other silver products do not get recycled, or get reprocessed in closed-loops by the consuming companies. For example, silver is used as a catalyst in the manufacture of ethylene oxide, a basic plastic feedstock. These catalysts get recycled every so often, but the ownership of the silver does not change hands.

The sources of silver scrap are shifting during the first decade of this century. Until recently most of the silver that was recovered from secondary sources came from spent photographic materials. The photo industry is using significantly less silver each year, as the silver-halide technology used in photography has been losing market share to digital imaging. As this technological shift has been occurring, the amount of silver available for recovery from spent photographic papers, films, and solutions is decreasing in direct proportion to the decline in the amount of silver being used in these materials. Silver-bearing photographic materials tend to have relatively short product lives, being used and recycled within one year of being used. This source of silver scrap is declining worldwide.

This decline is being offset, at least temporarily, by two other emerging trends. One is the increased use of silver in electronic equipment and batteries, with increased silver recycling from these products. The other has been an increase in the sale of silver jewelry and decorative objects in the middle of this decade in response to the sharp rise in silver prices. As the price of silver has risen, investors holding silver jewelry, statuary, and decorative objects have been selling these products for their silver content. This tendency is particularly common in India and the Middle East.

THE DEMAND FOR SILVER

Around 800 million ounces of silver is used in fabricated products each year at present.

While many observers and investors have expressed concern that the demise of silver's use in photography represents a negative trend for silver's potential price appreciation, the negative consequences for total demand, the balance between silver supply and demand, and the price of silver have been overstated by some observers who failed to take into account the decline in silver supply from recycled photographic products that is occurring concomitantly with the decline in silver use in these products. The net effect on the silver market is significantly less dramatic than the gross reduction in demand only. Whereas silver use in photography, at its peak, was 267.2 million ounces at its peak in 1999, spent photographic products supplied an estimated 140 million ounces of silver in that year, so that the "net demand" from this industry was closer to 127 million ounces, or less than half of the gross volumes being used by photographic material manufacturers.

Silver use in jewelry and silverware has supplanted photography as the major end use and its combined use about 246 million ounces of silver in 2005. This was down from 294 million ounces in 1997, but the pace of decline in silver use in these products has not been as drastic as it has been in photography. Silver also is used in a wide range of manufactured products. Most people know that silver is used as backing in mirrors. Some know that silver is used in batteries for hearing aids, cameras, calculators, and other small electronic products. It also is used in larger batteries used in torpedoes and other military applications. It is used in brazing alloys and solders, in electronics, in biocides, and in ethylene oxide, and other chemical process catalysts.

Silver use appeared to be growing as a sheathing in superconductive wire earlier in the 2000s decade. The industry was very secretive about its silver usage and requirements, however, and did not disclose much information about the volumes being used. Market observers developed estimates of how much silver was being used by this emerging industry based on tradeflow studies and other market research. After a few years, it appeared that further technological developments in superconductive wires led to a sharp reduction in the amount of silver being used in this application. Silver use also is growing in biocides, being used on everything from bandages and socks to industrial coatings on ships and seaside buildings. There has been talk about silver chemicals replacing chromated copper arsenate as a wood preservative, but this does not appear likely to happen. There are more efficient and lower-priced, copper-based chemicals that do a better job in replacing this chemical, which environmental authorities in various countries around the world are trying to phase out for health reasons.

MARKET BALANCE

One of the intriguing aspects of the silver market over the past 15 years has been the extended period of market deficits. The silver market's supply and demand tend to shift slowly. Partly this reflects low price sensitivity on both the supply and demand sides of the market.

Much of silver supply comes as byproduct of other metals, or from scrap with very low operating costs. As a result, silver supply does not respond quickly or forcefully to changes in silver prices.

On the demand side of the market, much of silver's fabricated usage is highly price insensitive. A one-dollar increase in silver prices raises the price of taking a photograph only about one cent. The substitution that has occurred in photography has not been a function of the price or cost of using silver, but rather of technological change. The same is true in many other industrial applications, from silver use in batteries, electronic components and connectors, brazing alloys, and solders to silver use in bearings, ethylene oxide catalysts, and mirrors. The one place where price sensitivity is readily visible in the fabrication demand is in silver jewelry and silverware, especially in countries in South Asia and the Middle East where these products sometimes are forms of silver investments and savings. This reflects the fact that in many fabricated products only a small portion of the product's value is silver, whereas in jewelry or silverware the value of the silver content is greater as a percentage of the value of the product.

The other factor that comes into play in the silver price's slow response to market balances is the fact of those 5,000 years of silver inventories. When the silver market moved into a deficit in 1990, at least 2.4 billion ounces of silver were lying around in bullion bar form. Several hundred million ounces of silver were around in coin form, and some of the billions of ounces of silver held in jewelry and silverware form also were available to the market should prices start to rise.

As a result of these large inventories, the silver market was able to sustain a current account deficit of newly refined metal entering the market relative to fabrication demand for a long period of time without there being a price response so dramatic as to be noticeable to many in the market. This effect of large inventories is visible in other markets, but the period of time is shorter because the inventory levels are smaller. People tend not to hoard copper, lead, coffee, or cocoa the way they do gold and silver. There are not centuries' worth of copper or coffee in bank vaults and private safes. With silver, and gold, you do. So the market was able to move into a deficit in 1990, and the price took nearly 14 years to show any major response. That is an oversimplification, and there were indications as early as 1994 that these inventories were being drawn down. Prices bottomed out at $3.51 in 1991 and $3.52 in 1993, and then rose into a range roughly of $4.40 to $5.80 for many years while stocks were absorbed. The stocks were disappearing. Banks that had run vaulting businesses started getting out of that business by the late 1990s, because the silver inventories had dwindled to the point where the vaulting operations no longer were profitable. The forward carry in silver contracted sharply during this time, and the market saw a few spikes in prices when suddenly someone needed or wanted physical silver and adequate supplies were not there. So there were indications that the market indeed was operating in a current account deficit, and that stocks were falling steadily. It took until late 2003 for these bullion inventories to drop to levels low enough that prices started to more fully respond to tight silver supplies.

One reason for the weak silver price in the late 1980s was the oversupply in the market. Another was that investors had stopped buying large volumes of silver and were beginning to dispose of silver bought earlier. The third was that no one was marketing silver to investors.

The 1980s witnessed a long and persistent period of large surpluses of newly refined silver entering the market relative to the amount of silver being bought by fabricators to manufacture into products. Investors had been buying this silver, lured into the market by the rise from $5 to $50 at the start of the decade, but by 1988 investors as a group had grown cautious of silver and were selling stocks bought earlier.

HOW TO INVEST IN SILVER

Silver is a major investment product. There are physical silver investment products, including 1,000 ounce bars and 100 ounce bars. Some refiners also produce 1 ounce and 10 ounce silver bars and medallions for investors. There also are silver bullion coins minted by the U.S. Mint, the Silver Eagle; and the Royal Canadian Mint, the Maple Leaf.

Silver futures and options are traded on the New York COMEX. They also are traded, to a lesser extent, on the Tokyo Commodities Exchange (TOCOM) and the Chicago Board of Trade (CBOT). The Multi Commodities Exchange in Mumbai (MCX) began trading silver, and gold, futures in 2004. By 2006, the MCX had surpassed the TOCOM and CBOT in terms of the number of ounces trading on its contracts, becoming the second largest exchange for silver trading after the New York COMEX.

Silver equities are a common way for investors to buy exposure to silver prices. There are several major silver producing companies, including Hecla Mining, Coeur d'Alenes Mines, and Pan American Silver. There are companies developing silver mines, including Apex Silver and Silver Standard. There are exploration companies and companies in the predevelopment phase, such as MacMin Silver and Mines Management. There are larger Mexican producers, including Industrias Penoles.

A silver exchange-traded fund was launched in April 2006 by Barclays Global Investors in the United States. By the end of the year 2006 the silver ETF had around 120 million ounces of silver in its assets, held for it in allocated accounts at the London vaults of JPMorgan Chase.

Investors buy silver using any number of methodologies and strategies. Their investment horizons stretch from intraday and daily positions to multiyear positions. Some investors will have a core position of physical silver and silver equities, which they hold as long-term investments, while also taking shorter-term positions to seek to capture shorter-term price moves.

CONCLUSION

Silver along with gold is one of the oldest investment vehicles and stores of value known to mankind. Some observers write about a fundamental, inexorable allure of silver to investors. Others see it as one of two investments that will stand the test of time, along with gold. Others cite religious scriptures as reasons for investing in silver. Stepping away from all of these belief systems, it is clear that silver does offer investors an interesting investment, both on its own and as part of a diversified investment portfolio. Silver prices are more volatile than those of many other assets. This attracts some investors, as they see the potential returns being worth the increased risk.

CHAPTER 34

Investing in Base Metals

Michael Killick, M. Eng.
Managing Director
Lincoln Vale

On September 29, 1980 two men entered into a famous wager. Julian Simon, an economist, believed that technological development can and will solve our exhaustible resource problem. Paul Ehrlich, a biologist, believed that overpopulation was depleting the world's resources at a disastrous rate and this process would drive up prices for all commodities. Simon bet Ehrlich that the price of any nongovernment-controlled raw material would be less in ten years time. In consultation with two Berkeley physicists, Ehrlich chose not oil or gas or lumber, but five metal prices as the subject of the wager. Ehrlich could not have chosen better. Base metals are the quintessential exhaustible resource. Just like land and oil and other natural resources, the mineral deposits from which we obtain base metals are not renewable. There are renewable energy sources, but so far no way to synthesize metal. Ehrlich lost. Each of the five metals was cheaper on September 29, 1990 than they had been ten years earlier. In each case, a technological advance either introduced a substitute or enabled an increase in supply. In this chapter, we tour the base metals industry from the investor's standpoint. While one has to concede the longer-term trend in their prices is very likely up, we must also concede their prices are extremely volatile as demonstrated in the above wager and the reader will find in this chapter investment advice for helping to cope with this price volatility. The reader interested in the debate about technological innovation and its efficacy in mitigating resource depletion should note that such debate rages on.[1]

[1]Howard Petith, "The Possibility of Continuous Growth with Exhaustible Resources," *Natural Resource Modeling* 16, no. 2 (Summer 2003), pp. 161–174.

I thank Chris Harris for his invaluable advice and perspective.

WHAT ARE BASE METALS?

Base metals are loosely defined in the chemical sense as being of medium reactivity somewhere between the very reactive *alkali metals* (such as potassium and sodium) and the unreactive *precious metals* (such as gold and platinum). In the commodities markets the term base metals refers to that group of industrial metals that are of medium liquidity somewhere between occasional, like cobalt and liquid, like gold. They are copper, aluminum, nickel, zinc, lead, and tin.

Humans have been extracting metal from ores for thousands of years.[2] The fruits of this extraction technology were so critical to our ancient ancestors' advancement that two of the three Prehistoric Ages, the Bronze Age and the Iron Age, were named for metals. The bronze of the Bronze Age was a mixture (called an *alloy*) of copper and tin, two metals that are still part of our everyday lives. The importance of these metals has graduated from the tools and weapons of antiquity to being vital input materials used in a multitude of different ways to create today's complex goods from refrigerators to computers.[3]

WHERE DO BASE METALS COME FROM?

The investment fundamentals of base metal economics are, in essence, the fundamentals of the metal mining industry. While recycling of base metals is an important source of metal in developed economies, any global marginal expansion of metal consumption must be met by new mine output rather than increased yield from recyclables. This is because consumption growth is taking place in developing economies where recycling is a smaller source of material. So where do base metals come from?

Rocks are aggregates of minerals. Minerals are basic solid matter (otherwise known as *dirt*) that was created when the earth was formed. Where minerals are found and what they are composed of are the words and letters of the written history of the earth's formation. It is critical to realize that the forces that created the Earth's crust are gone (hopefully), but consequently, minerals are essentially not being created anymore (unfortunately). Base metal elements are all found combined with other elements as compounds left to us in mineral form. These compounds are formed when a metal bonds with oxygen, silicon, sulfur, carbon, and occasionally fluorine and chlorine. A rock formation that contains metal compounds can be referred

[2]Arthur Wilson, *The Living Rock: The Story of Metals Since Earliest Times And Their Impact On Civilization* (Cambridge: Woodhead Publishing, 1994).
[3]Martin Lynch, *Mining in World History* (London: Reaktion Books, 2003).

to as a *mineral deposit* or *ore body*. The business of getting nearly pure metal back out of an ore body involves two distinct kinds of actions: (1) physical such as digging the rocks from the ground; or (2) chemical—separating the metal from the other elements in the chemical compound. The actions are broadly called *mining* and *extraction*.

Getting the rocks out of the ground is similar for all kinds of mining tasks. Clearly the economics of the mining operation are driven by (1) the location of the ore body physically, environmentally, and geopolitically and (2) the nature of the rocks.

The physical location of the ore body is significant because of the requirement for labor, power, water, and basic infrastructure for civilization, necessary to do anything pertaining to any ore body. Environmental and geopolitical concerns are important because one needs to know if an ore body mine is in a beautiful state park or a war zone. The nature of the geology (rocks) is significant because different geological formations cause different mining engineering challenges. A few mining challenges include the ease with which the ore can be mined (how much digging do you have to do), the richness or *grade* of the ore deposit (how much can I get by digging it up), and its locations in relation to the surface (is this going to be an open pit mine or a deep shaft mine). Typically, the deepest mines are only economically viable for highly rich deposits of precious stones and metals like diamonds and gold.

The economics of undoing the chemical bond between the metal and the other atoms in the mineral compound is driven by:

1. *The type of compound in the ore body*. For example, oxides of copper are generally cheaper and easier to extract than sulfides.
2. *The choice of metallurgical process to separate the metal*. By heat (*pyrometallurgy*), which includes techniques such as roasting (sulphide ores), smelting, and converting; or by solvents (*hydrometallurgy*), which includes techniques such as leaching, heap leaching, and pressure reduction.
3. *The choice of refining process to purify the metal*. By *electro-winning* (low-temperature electrolysis of metal solution in water, metal deposited at the cathode); or *electrolysis* (high-temperature electrolysis of a molten metal compound; metal deposited at the cathode).
4. *The price and availability of fuel, electricity, and reducing agents*. To implement metal extraction and refining choices.
5. *The environment*. The cost of treating/recycling toxic agents/reagents and byproducts. The cost of reclaiming disrupted countryside.

Exhibit 34.1 shows the quantity in tonnes of mine output that came from six regions of the globe. Asia (China, Kazakhstan, etc.) is the world's

EXHIBIT 34.1 2006 Geographic Distribution of Major Base Metal Global Production in Tonnes

	Copper	Nickel	Aluminum	Zinc
North America	2,024,000	162,000	5,271,000	1,104,000
Latin America	4,367,000	180,000	2,496,000	810,000
Africa	695,000	54,000	1,715,000	276,000
Australia	449,000	161,000	2,277,000	475,000
Asia	7,146,000	298,000	12,864,000	5,614,000
Eurasia	1,671,000	296,000	4,658,000	550,000
Europe	2,047,000	190,000	4,164,000	1,997,000

Source: Reuters.

largest source of base metals. Chile, in Latin America, is home to some of the world's biggest mining operations. The Escondida Mine, high in the Atamaca Desert in the Andes Mountains of Chile, is responsible for 8% of the world's copper mine output on its own.[4]

The extraction processes are distinctly different for aluminum than for the other metals. Aluminum is extracted from bauxite, the principle aluminum ore, in two stages that require a lot of electric power: 79 kWh of power for every kilogram of aluminum produced.[5] That power consumption is nearly double the amount required to extract the same mass of copper and four times as much to extract a kilogram of zinc. It is not surprising, therefore, that aluminum refiners are often located close to or owned by hydroelectric power generators. It is also important to note that the location of mining is not necessarily the location of extraction because of the necessary extraction energy requirement.

The extraction processes for the other base metals in the group are typically the same. The ore is concentrated by a froth-floatation process in which the same rocks are ground into fine particles; the dust is added to a bubbly water bath in which special reagents are introduced to preferentially attach only the desirable particles to the air bubbles in the solution that carry the particles to the top of the bath. The top is then skimmed off and dried. The result is known as *concentrate*, which can have 40% to 70% metal by weight.

[4]Helmut Waszkis, *Mining in the Americas: Stories and History* (Cambridge: Woodhead Publishing, 1993).

[5]First, it is converted into alumina (aluminum oxide) by the Bayer process, which is a low temperature (200°C) solvent extraction. This is followed by a high temperature baking stage. Aluminum is extracted from alumina by the Hall Heroult process, which is a high temperature electrolytic process using an electric current of 150,000 amps and 3 volt to 5 volt potential difference.

Further metal extraction is achieved in a variety of ways. Some concentrates lend themselves to low temperature chemical reactions such as leaching and other forms of solvent extractions. These are usually concentrates of oxide ores. Sulfide ores usually require smelting with various reducing agents such as carbon, silica, or limestone, either by roasting or electrolytic heating.

BASE METAL INDUSTRY

Base Metal Production

Mining companies are naturally undergoing a consolidation because of economic, environmental, and regulatory forces. It is notable that integration is occurring both vertically in terms of companies moving into multiple aspects of a particular metals mining, extraction, and fabrication as well as horizontally, such as companies moving into mining for multiple commodities.[6] Exhibit 34.2 shows the scale of the base metals industry by presenting metal production in tonnes.

Mining output of all the base metals is dominated by large multinational and, in most cases, diversified mining companies. Typically, 30% to 40% of mining output is accounted for by the top five producers in any given base metal market. In any climate of low risk premiums in the credit markets (cheap debt) and high base metal prices (healthy producer cash flows) such as 2005 to 2007, the large diversified companies swallow up the smaller

EXHIBIT 34.2 Annual Global Base Metal Production in Tonnes

	Copper	Nickel	Aluminum	Zinc	Lead	Tin
2006	18,399,000	1,340,000	33,445,000	10,825,000	8,051	280
2005	17,270,000	1,309,000	31,149,000	9,924,000	7,579	274
2004	16,147,000	1,274,000	29,751,000	10,181,000	6,951	262
2003	15,420,000	1,213,000	27,880,000	9,957,000	6,764	263
2002	15,669,000	1,186,000	26,256,000	9,741,000	6,670	268

Source: Reuters.

[6] Alcoa Inc., the world's largest aluminum company, mines bauxite, makes aluminum commodity feedstock (sheets, foil, wire, cable), and parts for doors, windows, and cars. Alcoa Inc. has integrated vertically. BHP Billiton, the world's largest mining company by market capitalization, currently compromises about 16% of the Bloomberg World Mining Index. In addition to its commanding presence in mining aluminum, it is also a major miner and refiner of iron, diamonds, coal, and copper. BHP Billiton has integrated horizontally.

specialized companies. Witness Xstrata's takeover of Falconbridge and the interest of Companhia Vale do Rio Doce (CVRD) in acquiring INCO as two examples of this consolidation. As we noted in the previous section, mining and extraction are distinct parts of the metal production industry. Some smaller companies own and operate either the mine or the refinery. Given the tightening global regulatory environment for environmental protection, it becomes harder than it was for these smaller, nondiversified companies to maintain cost-effective production in the future. Exhibit 34.3 is a list of the top 10 global mining companies drawn from the Bloomberg Mining Index.

Exhibit 34.4, shows the marginal cash cost of mining/refining a marginal quantity of metal. The curve has three identifying segments. First, a limited amount of metal is relatively easy to access. Secondly, there is a middle section which serves to show that there is a large quantity of material that is readily available given current known locations and development of existing ore bodies. Finally, the third section shows the rapidly escalating costs of: mining lower grade ores, digging deeper to reach new ore bodies, and extracting metal from compounds that are more difficult to process chemically.

Labor costs are an input cost to the cash cost of production. Labor costs are the subject of recurring union contract negotiations and other political concerns. These mines are often in developing countries and mining companies must be sensitive to the economic needs of the local populace.

Ultimately, by considering the economics of chasing a dwindling resource, it is easy to see why the marginal cost curve is shaped the way it is. Producers always seem to find innovative technological means to exploit ore bodies more efficiently than they originally anticipated. It is inevitable, however, that one day we will begin to truly exhaust our mineral resources.

EXHIBIT 34.3 Top Mining Companies Worldwide as a Percentage of the Bloomberg Mining Index

BHP Billiton	15.8%
Rio Tinto	10.9%
Anglo American PLC	9.5%
CVRD	6.7%
MMC Norilsk	4.5%
Xstrata PLC	4.0%
Anglo Platinum Ltd	3.7%
Alcoa Inc	3.7%
Phelps Dodge Corp	3.3%
Alcan Inc	2.5%

Source: Bloomberg Mining Index.

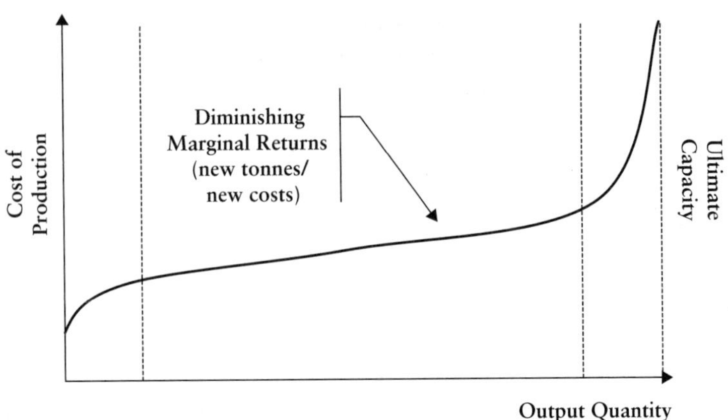

EXHIBIT 34.4 Typical Cash Cost (Supply) Curve for Global Production

Base Metal Consumption

Base metal producers have to be very good at gauging demand for their products and as a consequence are also good at producing just enough material each year for which there is a buyer. As a result, just about all material that is produced is consumed. Exhibit 34.5 shows where each metal finds its application in the world.

Base metals' physical properties promote various specific applications in the economy today; they are malleable and ductile, meaning that they can be drawn into pipes and wire and hammered into complex shapes that they will maintain.

Copper is a great conductor of electricity and easily extruded into pipes, which is why 50% of copper consumption goes into residential and commercial construction wiring and plumbing. Just about every motor and generator in the world uses copper wiring in the core. Copper is also a great conductor of heat, which is why it finds application as a material to fabricate heat exchangers used for cooling chipsets in computers, electronics, air conditioners and refrigerators.

Aluminum has a high strength-to-weight ratio and is used in making airplane frames and skins as well as high-end automobiles. It is also a good conductor of electricity. However, being lighter than copper, it is used for high tension wires in electrical distribution for the most part. Aluminum is highly resistant to corrosion and is used in a variety of packaging applications, most notably beverage cans.

Nickel is used primarily to make stainless steel. Nickel is also used in the production of coins and magnets.

Zinc is used in the construction industry as a protective layer over iron and steel components to prevent rusting. Zinc is used in vehicles for

EXHIBIT 34.5 Applications of Base Metals as a Percentage of Use

	Copper	Zinc	Lead	Nickel	Aluminum	Tin
Alloy						19.0%
Ammunition			6.0%			
Batteries			71.0%			
Cable sheathing			3.0%			
Packaging					16.0%	
Chemicals	12.5%					
Construction	50.0%	48.0%			18.0%	
Consumer product	12.5%	10.0%			7.0%	
Electronics	12.5%	9.0%			8.0%	28.0%
Machinery		10.0%			8.0%	
Other				23.0%	12.0%	15.0%
Pigment			12.0%			
Plating				10.0%		38.0%
Rolled extrusions			8.0%			
Steel making				67.0%		
Transport	12.5%	23.0%			31.0%	

Source: Goldman Sachs, JBWere, Lehman Brothers.

the same reason. It is also a constituent of soft solder used in electronics assembly.

Seventy-one percent of lead production is used in lead-acid batteries. In the health care industry lead is used as a protective shield against X-ray radiation. Most bullet ammunition is made from lead. Lead is also used as a coolant in nuclear power generating plants.

Exhibit 34.6 shows how the consumption of copper in China and India has grown since 1990. Industrially developing countries such as Brazil, India, Russia, and China, have high single-digit or low double-digit GDP growth. Increasingly, companies from these countries are stepping into the market to buy base metals for use in their developing economies. In fact, per capita consumption of copper and aluminum in China is one third and one quarter, respectively, of what it is in the United States. There is plenty of room for base metal demand growth in these economies.[7]

[7]See the following resources for further information on the base metals industry James F King, *The Aluminum Industry* (Cambridge: Woodhead, 2001); Nnamdi Anyadike, *Copper: A Material For The New Millenium* (Cambridge: Woodhead, 2002); Simon Clow, *International Nickel Trade* (Cambridge: Woodhead, 1992); Nnamdi Anyadike, *Lead and Zinc: Threats and Opportunities In The Years Ahead* (Cambridge: Woodhead, 2002); and Peter Roddy, *The International Tin Trade* (Cambridge: Woodhead, 1995).

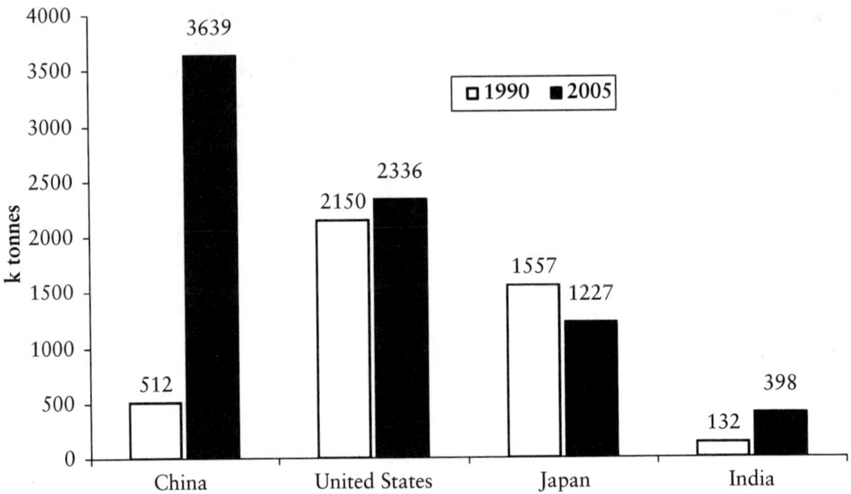

EXHIBIT 34.6 Copper Consumption in China, the United States, Japan, and India, 1990 and 2005

MARKET STRUCTURE

It is no great surprise that the futures market began in commodities. Unless you actually want the physical delivery of 25 tonnes of copper cathode it is probably better to buy and sell commodities on paper. What better way than to trade metals for delivery dates in the future? For those who actually have or need physical metal, the cushion of time between transaction and delivery gives buyers and sellers plenty of time to finalize their needs for a particular upcoming day.

Exchanges

The London Metal Exchange On the London Metal Exchange (LME) metals are traded in tonnes. A tonne is a metric unit equivalent to 2204.0623 pounds (as distinct from a ton which is equivalent to 2240 pounds). The distinguishing feature of the LME metals is that the most liquid contract for each metal is traded for a rolling three-calendar month delivery date (i.e., *prompt dates* on the LME) adjusted for weekends and holidays. There are three other constant maturity dates: 2-day delivery, 15-month delivery, and 63-month delivery. In addition to these four constant maturity contracts, there are a string of fixed settlement dates in customary futures fashion. In the case of the LME the maturity string is:

- Every day up to the three month date.
- Every Wednesday from the three month date to the sixth month.
- Every third Wednesday of the calendar month up to 63 months.

Copper, aluminum, zinc, and lead futures contracts are for delivery of 25 tonnes of metals each, nickel is 6 tonnes, and tin is 5 tonnes per contract.

The London Metal Exchange Index (LMEX) is an index of six metals averaged over three settlement dates. These six metals are the six primary base metals (copper, aluminum, tin, lead, zinc, and nickel) and the dates are the third Wednesday(s) of the first three calendar months being currently traded. Trade in the longer range maturity dates rarely takes place in individual months but instead usually takes place in the form of averages. The longer the maturity dates the longer the averaging period. In addition, the LME is now offering futures in 5 tonne contracts on copper, aluminum, and zinc, which are cash settled to the parent (physically settled) contract called LME Minis.

Though LME contracts are called futures, it is important to note that they are really forwards, which are distinguished from futures in that the cash flows generated by price fluctuations do not settle until the settlement date of the contract.

The LME is the most important and liquid source of base metal prices in the world today. Exhibit 34.7 lists total futures and options volumes for the last few years.

The LME warehouse network is global. There are warehouses in every major port in the world. The investor can track the quantity of metal on warrant at these locations just as they can track 3 million metal prices using Reuters, Bloomberg, or Basemetals.com as the interface to the exchange's data. Great resources for the workings of the LME are to be found in the literature.[8]

EXHIBIT 34.7 LME Futures and Options Volumes in Millions of Contracts

	2003		2004		2005		2006	
	Futures	Options	Futures	Options	Futures	Options	Futures	Options
Aluminum	26.95	1.76	26.95	2.27	30.43	4.62	36.42	4.79
Copper	19.44	1.33	18.17	1.76	19.23	2.18	18.86	1.90
Lead	4.50	0.10	3.79	0.09	4.06	0.14	4.57	0.17
Nickel	4.22	0.15	3.18	0.12	3.48	0.20	4.18	0.17
Tin	1.45	0.01	0.97	0.00	1.10	0.01	1.28	0.02
Zinc	10.47	0.40	10.21	0.48	10.62	1.02	11.71	1.36

Source: London Metal Exchange.

[8]Paddy Crabbe, *Metals Trading Handbook* (Cambridge: Woodhead, 1999).

Commodity Exchange of New York

The Commodity Exchange of New York (COMEX), a division of the New York Mercantile Exchange (NYMEX), offers base metal futures and options contracts on copper (25,000 lbs) and aluminum (44,000 lbs). These are conventional futures in which the cash flows thrown off by the contract's price fluctuations are settled the day after the price fluctuation (as opposed to the contract settlement date on the LME). In the base metals markets, COMEX is best known for its copper contract. Metals futures dates are fixed in the normal way. Delivery of metal is at the seller's option any time in the delivery month. Unlike the LME, as of 2006 COMEX warehouses are located only in the United States. Exhibit 34.8 lists the total futures and options volume for copper and futures volume for aluminum traded on COMEX in recent years.

Trading is conducted by open outcry and electronically through the GLOBEX system. It is now possible to trade COMEX copper and aluminum futures through any number of retail electronic brokers who are plugged into GLOBEX.

COMEX base metal options are American and can be exercised into the futures contract at any time up to the fourth last day in the month prior to the delivery month of the underlying futures contract.

Shanghai Futures Exchange

The Shanghai Futures Exchange (SHFE) trades copper and aluminum futures and options. At the moment, trading on the exchange is only open to domestic individuals and companies, although non-Chinese companies can enter into joint ventures with a Chinese company. The futures contracts are

EXHIBIT 34.8 COMEX Copper Futures, Options, and Aluminum Futures Volumes in Millions of Contracts

	Copper		Aluminum
	Futures	Options	Futures
2006	3.28	0.08	0.01
2005	3.95	0.14	0.03
2004	3.19	0.22	0.07
2003	3.09	0.05	0.11
2002	2.81	0.03	0.07
2001	2.86	0.02	0.04
2000	2.78	0.07	0.05

Source: NYMEX.

EXHIBIT 34.9 Shanghai Futures Exchange Volume in Millions of Contracts

	2003	2004	2005	2006
Copper	22.3	42.5	24.7	10.8
Aluminum	4.3	13.7	4.3	27.9

Source: Reuters, SHFE Annual report, and Calyon Financial.

for 5 tonnes for both copper and aluminum. The contracts are for physical metal delivery anytime in the delivery month at the seller's option. The SHFE warehouse network is entirely based in China. The futures prices are denominated in Renminbi. Exhibit 34.9 shows the total futures volume from 2003 to 2006.

Price Discovery Process

There are two basic attributes of a commodity that heavily influence the nature of price discovery: (1) the economics of storage and transportation for the commodity and (2) the economics of production.

Consumers' Point of View

The distinguishing nature of commodities is that a commodity ready for use when and where it is needed is wholly a different asset from the same substance either somewhere else and/or at some other time. A further consideration to the commodity consumer is the quality or specification of the material (think brackish water when you need mountain spring water). A good part of commodity price volatility can be explained by the fact that the material in question is either very expensive to store (time) and/or very expensive to transport (location). The ability to store a base metal means that metal available for use today at a given location is a close substitute for metal for use next week but it is important to realize that the reverse is not nearly as true. Metal 1,000 miles away is also a pretty close substitute for metal where you want it. One last point, even though a commodity can be stored a consumer would rather not pay for it until they actually need it. The concept of just-in-time (JIT) inventory is based on maximizing earnings while using minimum balance sheet; that is, avoid carrying material that you do not need.

Producers' Point of View

The considerable time and expense it takes to mine and extract metal from ore provide incentives for the producer to bring to market only what metal can be expected to meet demand. It takes months to turn ore in the ground into metal in a warehouse. In fact the producer's problem is even worse than that. It takes several years to identify and begin to develop an ore body.

Producers are trying to gauge demand several quarters in advance. The consumers we talk about are themselves manufacturing value-added goods to market to their customers. So there is a lot of uncertainty in the demand for raw base metals. This uncertainty leads to base metal price fluctuations. It is possible for a mine to start operations when the metal price is above its break even price and have the price fluctuate to a level that is not profitable for that operation. What then if a mining project is viable only if the metal can be sold at $1,000 a tonne and the price falls halfway through the life of the mine? There are two sides to the desirability of whether or not a mining project should welcome exposure to the underlying metal price. First, the stockholders of a mining company may want to be exposed to the commodity price because they believe metal prices are going to rise, especially if we are at the beginning of a commodity supercycle. In contrast the bondholders or bankers of the mining project—who do not benefit from the increased price of the commodity—would rather have the security of being certain of the project's revenue streams and therefore would prefer the mining company to hedge the value of its income stream by selling the future production of the mine in the open market today. The ideal situation from the producer's standpoint would be one where the producer controls the supply of material to the consumer to always just match consumption demand less a bit for good measure. This ability to keep prices both stable and high would satisfy bondholders and the stockholders simultaneously. The fact that there is more than one producer makes it difficult for the producers as a group to control supply at any given price. However, there are incentives for producers to follow the same course of action (be less aggressive toward each other) when commodity prices are low and incentives to follow different courses of action (be more aggressive toward each other) when prices are high. In fact, this oscillation in behavior of the producer group accounts for the natural cap and floor on metal prices during the course of past business cycles.

Base Metal Term Structure

There is no simple functional relationship between what a scarce metal will cost from one day to the next in an undersupplied market: A survey of price movement models in the academic literature revealed that there is no consensus.[9] We shall proceed intuitively. The governing economic principle at

[9]Clinton Watkins and Michael McAleer, "Econometric Modeling of Non-Ferrous Metals Prices," *Journal of Economic Surveys* 18, no. 5 (2004), pp. 651–701.

work here is that "today is a close substitute for tomorrow but tomorrow is not necessarily a close substitute for today." This asymmetry in the possible change in value of a base metal from one day to the next is a key concept in the understanding the shape of base metal forward curves. In practice, there can be from time to time an incentive for a consumer to buy more metal earlier than their anticipated needs because of a perceived shortage. Consumers can be persuaded to abandon their just-in-time inventory management if there is a whiff of supply interruption in the air. This "hoarding" tendency in consumer behavior only tends to drive up shorter dated prices relative to longer dated prices because it is rational to think that the shortage will last only for a finite time. Unlike a store of value such as money or gold (which cannot exhibit negative interest rates in an efficient market),[10] there is only a one-sided boundary condition on the evolution of a commodity forward curve and that is the cash-and-carry arbitrage. Like all other commodities, base metals forward curves have the following boundary condition: The rate of change in a base metal price as a function of time is capped by the opportunity cost of buying and storing the metal.[11] Thus, the cash and carry rate can be formulated as

$$\text{Cash and carry rate} = \text{Cost of borrowing money to buy the metal} + \text{Cost of storage} \tag{34.1}$$

Storage costs include the cost of renting the warehouse space and insuring the contents. Differences in commodity prices in time are colloquially called spreads and are expressed as price differences (either dollars/tonne or cents/lb).

$$\text{Cash and carry spread} = \text{Cash and carry rate} \times \text{Purchase price of the metal} \tag{34.2}$$

Exhibit 34.10 is a simplified illustration of a typical steady state in a base metals curve. The front end of the curve is most susceptible to spiking due to supply disruptions while the long end is more placidly associated with the full finance curve of an imaginary long-term mean price for the metal.

---

[10]Chris Harris, "Structure of Metal Markets and Metal Prices," in *Commodities and Commodity Derivatives Modeling,* edited by Helyette Geman (Chichester: Wiley, 2005).

[11]Harold Hotelling, "The Economics of Exhaustible Resources," *Journal of Political Economy* 39, no. 2 (1931), pp. 137–175.

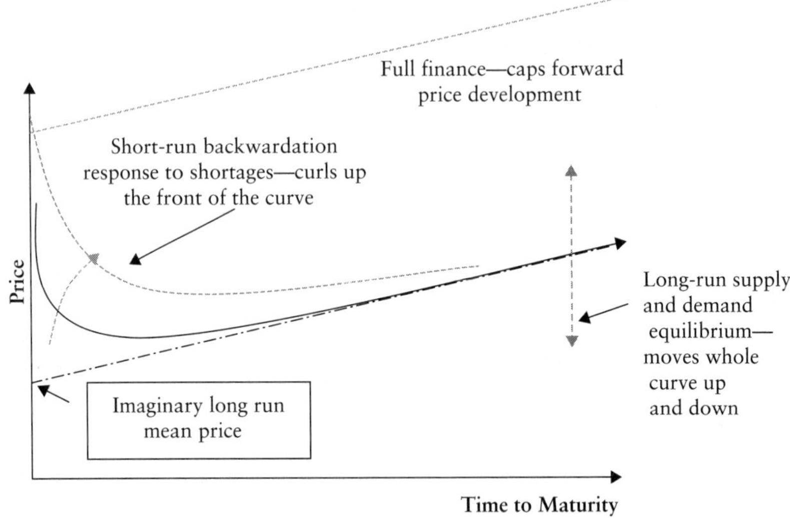

EXHIBIT 34.10 The Base Metal Forward Curve

The state of a commodity spread where the longer dated future is higher priced than the near one is described as *contango*, whereas a situation where the contangoed spread is equal to the cash and carry spread is called *full finance*. Of course, for a metal to be in a full-finance condition, it must be sufficiently abundant that buying the metal and storing it does not alter the supply/demand balance. Consequently true full finance is the exception rather than the rule.

When there is a genuine or perceived shortage of metal, readily available metal commands a premium over metal deliverable in the future.

Base metals traders closely watch the level of metal sitting in warehouses. Some of the worlds available warehousing is registered with the metal trading exchanges. The level of metal inventory in these registered warehouse spaces is made public and is updated frequently, daily in the case of the LME and COMEX and weekly in the case of SHFE. Hence, when market participants, for example, see these inventory numbers or stocks falling, there is a tendency to plan for an upcoming shortage and vice versa. Exhibit 34.11 illustrates quite clearly the inverse relationship between price and stock levels in copper over the period 1995 to 2006. This cause and effect response is not binary either, in fact there is a point of dynamic equilibrium reached between the consumer and the producer and the location and quantity of available metal. Normally, given that consumers operate in a just-in-time world, market participants perceive serious shortage as an

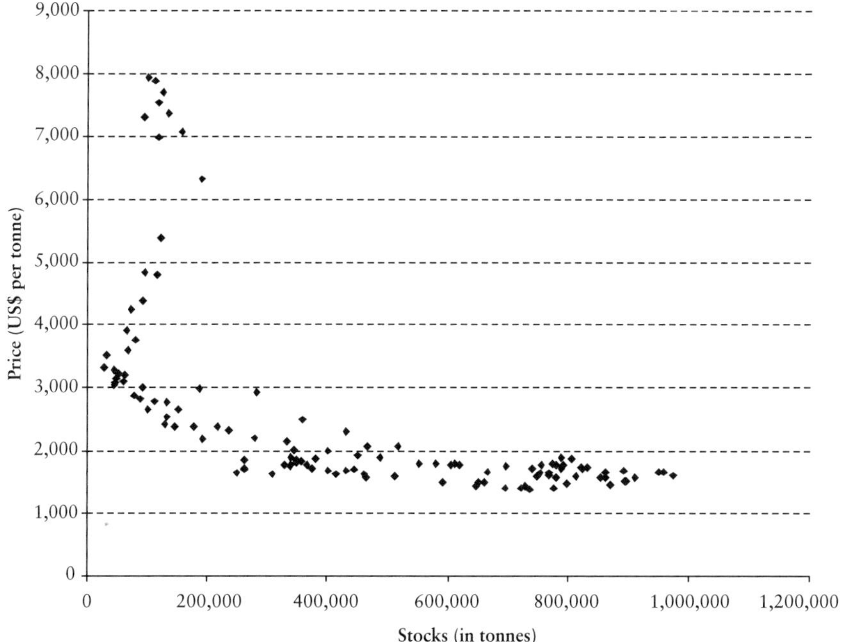

EXHIBIT 34.11 Scatter Graph of Stocks versus Price for Copper, 1995 to 2006
Source: Data from Reuters.

imminent risk. The development of the consumer's response to the apparent shortage is expressed by buying futures with maturities that are further and further away from today. A measure of the depth and severity of the perceived shortage is how far out in time the shortage premium extends and size of the premium of one day's supply of metal over the next. The state of a base metal spread where the near term contract price is higher than the far term contract price is described as backwardation.

Many companies specialize in trading physical metal and these market participants have the best knowledge regarding the location of official warehouse stocks and so-called "free metal"; that is, metal that is available but its whereabouts only located by searching through the network of physical metal dealers (or metal merchants as they are known in LME circles). In addition to "free metal," the industry upstream of the refineries keeps inventory in the form of partly processed metal such as copper concentrate or alumina. Thus it is wise to look beyond official exchange warehouse stocks to gauge the condition of the supply-demand balance. This extra inventory information may only be in the hands of industry insiders who have no obligation to make it public.

Following the logic of the preceding paragraphs, it would be reasonable to deduce that falling stocks lead to climbing prices and an inversion or backwardation in the futures term structure. This effect is part of conventional wisdom but has been somewhat interfered with in recent years due to the effect of rolling large passive index investments in base metals futures. In other words, a tightening in physical metal supply would, all other things being equal, drive a metal curve into backwardation. In a fully backwardated market rolling a long futures position from short maturity date to a longer maturity date lends metal to the starved market and has the effect of ameliorating the backwardation.

INVESTMENT STRATEGIES

There are many ways to invest in base metals that can be grouped into three broad classes: (1) direct exposure to metal prices; (2) exposure to metal prices through equity in base metal companies; and (3) risk arbitrage and relative value.

Direct Exposure to Metal Prices

In the early part of this century, we find there is enormous scope for demand increases in raw materials the growth of industrial production in rapidly developing economies such as Brazil, Russia, India, and China, referred to as the BRIC countries. Given finite mineral resources and the scope for future demand growth, metals prices ought to be going up in the long run. For this reason, there has been a flood of money pouring into passive commodity indexes and commodity-based hedge funds from 2002 to 2007. By the end of 2005, there was an estimated $80 billion of Commodity Index investment. The biggest market share goes to the Goldman Sachs Commodity Index, which has attracted an estimated $50 billion investment of which approximately 10% goes into base metals direct price investment (approximately 3% each into copper and aluminum) and nearly all of this investment has taken place from 1995 onward. Exhibit 34.12 shows the effect of this investment supercycle on the price of copper.

Metal futures traders often have an apocalyptic view of the world and this view does not always accompany rising prices and falling stocks. In previous decades industrial metal prices have been assumed to be cyclical as demand has been cyclical. Furthermore, there is competitive downward pressure on demand coming from close substitutes such as plastics and composites and ultimately yet to be invented technological advances. Given these huge speculative forces on the base metals group, it is not surprising

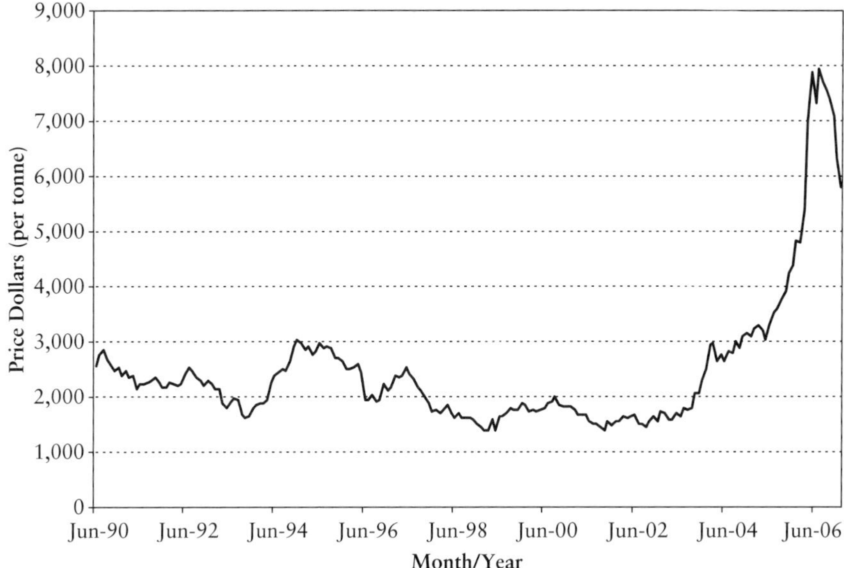

EXHIBIT 34.12 Copper Price Since 1990
Source: Data from Reuters.

that base metals prices are very volatile (see Exhibit 34.13) for a comparison of the volatility of the various base metals.

Exhibit 34.14 shows how base metal prices have behaved from April 1995 to March 2006. In Exhibit 34.14, prices have been indexed to 100 for April, 1995 so that the reader can more easily compare each base metal's relative performance over time. The first two thirds of the exhibit follow a cyclical pattern with metal prices snaking between index values of 50 to 150. The last third of the exhibit illustrates the investment supercycle. Nickel is the best performer and aluminum is the worst performer. There is a good degree of association in the price fluctuations. Pairwise correlation averages 52% and has an annual standard deviation of 17%, all based on monthly samples.

Where we really start to get a good picture of what direct investment in individual base metal really means is when we study the Sharpe ratio over the last decade. From the summary statistics of Exhibit 34.15, for the whole metal group, an investor would have made 0.15 standard deviations a year over the whole period based on daily data. From the beginning of 2002 to the end of 2006, the same statistic is a much improved 1.10 which for passive investment is an acceptable level of risk reward and over this period the average return has been 23% per annum. If there is a continuation of the

EXHIBIT 34.13 Annualized Metal Volatility Based on Daily Data

	Tin	Nickel	Copper	Zinc	Aluminum	Lead
1995	15%	17%	14%	7%	14%	22%
1996	11%	29%	42%	7%	19%	20%
1997	10%	32%	39%	32%	8%	25%
1998	13%	48%	20%	21%	21%	22%
1999	19%	81%	38%	29%	37%	12%
2000	11%	46%	15%	14%	14%	19%
2001	45%	46%	30%	38%	25%	13%
2002	17%	27%	15%	12%	10%	20%
2003	37%	77%	39%	32%	18%	55%
2004	38%	38%	24%	24%	18%	30%
2005	38%	34%	42%	46%	28%	22%
2006	44%	108%	64%	75%	17%	60%

Source: Reuters.

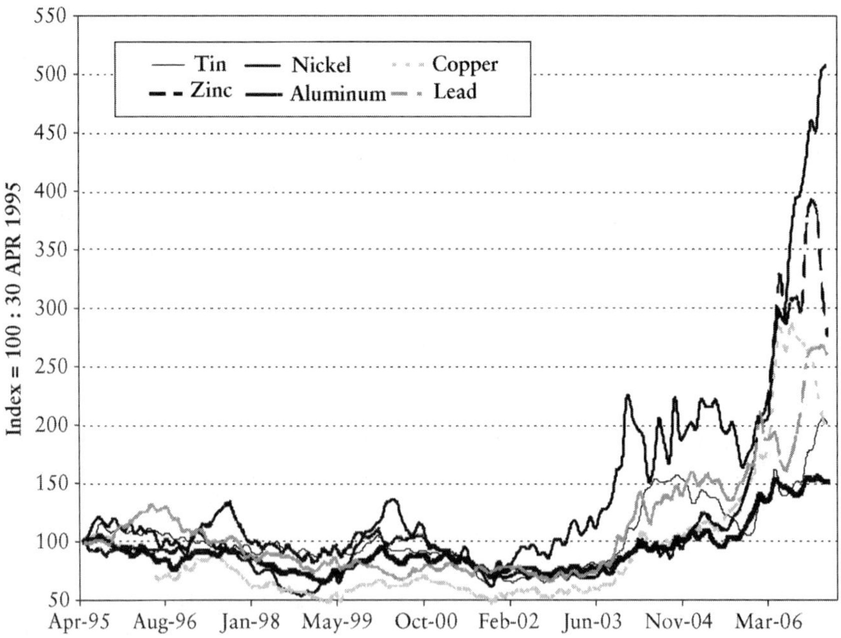

EXHIBIT 34.14 Base Metal Prices Index, 1995 to 2006

EXHIBIT 34.15 Sharpe Ratio Direct Investment in Base Metal, Annual Return/Annual Volatility

	Tin	Nickel	Copper	Zinc	Aluminum	Lead
1996	(0.80)	(0.92)	(0.81)	0.35	(0.63)	(0.14)
1997	(0.98)	(0.23)	(1.14)	0.20	0.04	(1.50)
1998	(0.41)	(2.07)	(1.10)	(1.12)	(2.84)	(1.30)
1999	1.43	2.08	0.82	1.27	1.52	0.25
2000	(1.76)	(0.72)	(0.23)	(1.18)	(0.34)	(0.18)
2001	(2.14)	(0.69)	(2.48)	(4.26)	(1.17)	0.18
2002	0.45	1.01	0.27	(0.20)	(0.04)	(1.00)
2003	4.21	2.64	1.68	1.36	1.16	2.12
2004	0.83	(0.18)	1.14	0.75	1.72	1.07
2005	(1.33)	(0.39)	2.22	2.47	0.83	0.26
2006	1.72	3.02	1.04	2.00	1.05	1.14

Source: Reuters.

supercycle investment phenomena, these kinds of numbers will most likely be repeated, which is a relatively attractive proposition.

One can achieve direct metal investment in a number of ways: (1) Buy and store the metal in a warehouse; (2) buy and roll a futures position; (3) invest in a structured note; and (4) buy an OTC swap. Furthermore, all of the above can be entered into for a single metal or for basket of two or more metals. The basket weights can be defined in constant metal or in constant dollar. In order to decide which of these very different routes to take, the investor must make several decisions. First, the initial margin on the futures position is much less than the total value of the metal underlying the futures contract and this implied leverage is an extra risk that has to be managed. Simply put, if the initial margin is 20% of the value of the contract then a "real money" investment would require the other 80% of the initial value of the contract to be sitting in a bank account somewhere and available for variation margin against the long futures position (the position is said to be fully collateralized).

To create 2 times leverage using the futures position, then the investor keeps 30% of the initial value of the contract in the bank account as well as the 20% initial margin. The same collateralization issues apply to the OTC swap. Secondly, the futures position has to be rolled, which is another risk that has to be managed. In the case of rollover cost and in addition to the bids and offers, consider the following: Absent transaction costs and in an efficient market, rolling a futures position is always going to be the same price or cheaper than buying and storing the metal. There are two rollover cases to think about: (1) rolling a position in full finance where buying the longer dated contract and selling the shorter dated contract has the same economics as buying and storing the metal, as dictated by the cash-and-carry arbitrage; and (2) rolling a futures position in a contango where the market contango is less than the full finance or even better in a backwardation. In these latter cases, the shape of the forward curve is a benefit to the investor because the investor is being rewarded for effectively lending metal into a starved market.

This extra risk can be a hazard or a benefit, but here are some starting guidelines: If the metal forward curve is in full finance all the way down the forward curve when you enter into the front futures position, then the only rollover risk that you have is (apart from transaction costs) market efficiency. (In a state of inefficiency, the cash-and-carry arbitrage constraint could disappear and the roll would cost more than full finance would imply). If the metal curve is flat or in backwardation, then the investor bears the risk that the hoarding fear may end and the curve readjusts back to full finance shape—and the roll would cost more than implied in the initial curve shape. To avoid this risk, one could simply buy the futures contract with a maturity equal to one's investment horizon. In other words, the metal you are investing in is for delivery at the end of the investment period and the interim curve shape becomes irrelevant.

In the end, if the metal price is going up, the shape of the curve will be a secondary issue. As for buying and storing the metal in a warehouse, that is an easy task to accomplish because the metal is already there sitting in the warehouse. The investor merely needs to let a long futures position go into delivery and the seller will have to hand over a warrant that gives the investor the title to a pallet or two of actual metal in an actual warehouse. This warrant can be delivered back to a maturing short futures position. Investors be aware that the futures long position has no control over the location of the metal being delivered and warrants carry a rent payment, some rents being higher than others. Suffice to say this is not an activity to be entered into casually.

A basket or (sub) index investment has several advantages over an individual metal: (1) it is diversified and therefore less volatile than a single metal; and (2) the constant-dollar-weighted version has the added bonus of converting some volatility into return. The LME has an index future called the LMEX, which is an investor-friendly, off-the-shelf basket. Exhibit 34.16 shows the average pairwise correlation of three-month base metal over time.

If it is your view that base metals prices are going up and that they will go up en masse, then one strategy to consider is to use a constant dollar portfolio weighting. The strategy is to buy a portfolio of metals with an initial weighting according to your preferences, let us say equally weighted for the sake of argument. The portfolio is periodically rebalanced throughout the life of the portfolio so that all the metals have the original equal

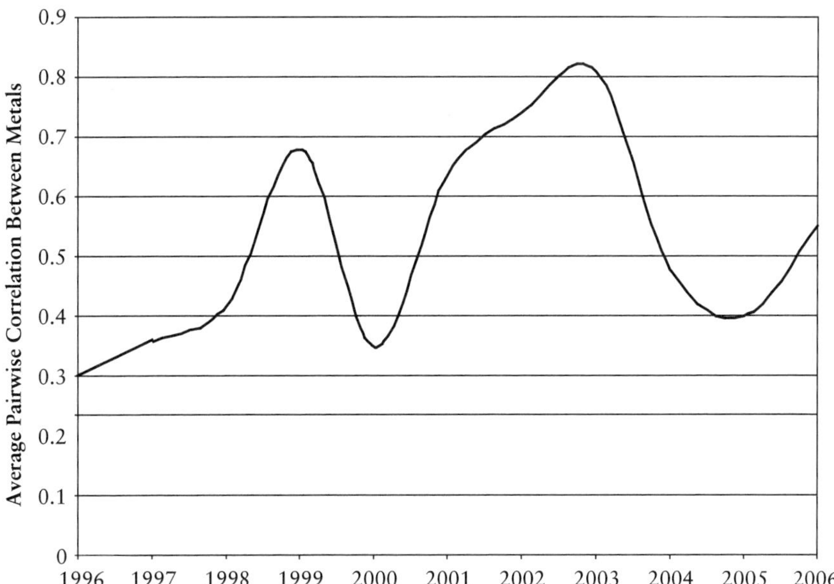

EXHIBIT 34.16 Average Pairwise Correlation of Base Metals to Each Other

dollar-weighting. As time goes by the prices begin to fluctuate and at the end of the rebalancing period the weightings are adjusted. For metals that have appreciated in value we will need to sell some futures contracts and for those that have depreciated in value we will need to buy some contracts. In fact, the appreciation and depreciation is relative so that supposing all the metals go up in value, we will still be selling the best performing and buying the worst performing. However, since your view is that pairwise correlation will be mean reverting that on average the pairwise movements will be in the same direction. This alone is no guarantee that the returns will be better than the flat constant tonnes index as correlation is scaled and the strong trending metals may have returns that are multiples of the weak trending metal. However, visual inspection of Exhibit 34.4 shows that there is also a central tendency to the mass of the group in price return terms. The key to success here is choosing the optimal rebalancing frequency. Too short and you miss the performance of the relatively strong performers, too long and you miss the recovery of the relatively bad performers.

Investing in Base Metal Equities

Investors should take note that there are many sensible reasons for investing in the common stock of companies in the metals and mining industry sector.

A key research objective would be to find companies who are on record as saying they will not hedge or only partly hedge their base metal production and use their shares to gain exposure to the underlying metal price. A word of caution: If a producer is hedging/partly hedging of has entered into a fixed price, long term contract with a consumer, then the company will not have metal price exposure. Care must be taken to avoid cases where the metal price hedger has cash collateralized long term sales of metal in which case the company may have negative exposure to the metal price.

Risk Arbitrage/Relative Value

There is so much volatility and kurtosis in the distribution of returns from base metals that second order risky variables are not just interesting but actually attractive. These kinds of risks can be exploited by trading price differences and ratios both between metals and along the curve in the same metal.

In the search for pairs of base metal prices that are less volatile than their constituents we have to remember the following guidelines. Adding random variables together reduces risk if the correlation is less than 1. Subtracting random variables from each other reduces the risk if the correlation is greater than 0. Yet (and this is the peril of spread trading) you want your selected long/short pair to be sufficiently uncorrelated so that you can make money yet this is going to happen when your trade is most risky. Diversification is a much more appealing principle because it is easier to find unrelated things and put them together for the purpose of reducing risk than it is to find related things and try to profit from their differences. Considering Exhibit 14, observe the precipitous rise of nickel versus the leisurely gains of aluminum. Over this period, being long aluminum and short nickel as a spread trade because their correlations are mean reverting would have been a disaster. The bottom line is you have been short nickel and the fact that you have an aluminum position (long or short) had nothing to do with this calamitous decision to be short nickel because it turned out they were uncorrelated. However, being long both aluminum and nickel was extremely profitable even though it was a much less risky trade than the previous example.

Just as one might expect, steep yield curves, strong currency, and a rising stock market to go hand in hand, one can expect dwindling metal inventories, rising metal prices, and steepening backwardation to go hand in hand. These tuples are about as common as each other but it is a good place to start the discussion. It is all too easy to predicate a spread trade on an assumed process. For example, it might be rational to say that if copper and aluminum can both be used for electrical wiring and if copper is getting extremely expensive because it is scarce that the price differential between them ought to have a natural cap in that consumers would stop buying copper and start buying aluminum at some price differential between the two. The utility of this assumption depends on how completely true it is. There may be other uses for each metal that are more important and that would drive the prices away from each other.

Exhibit 34.17 shows a period of divergence and recovery between aluminum and copper. In this exhibit the ratio and price differential have both been indexed to 100 at the beginning of the period. There is a huge difference between being long short a tonne (difference) and being long short a dollar (ratio). This is because the (1) volatility of copper in the period was higher than the volatility of aluminum and (2) the copper contract was worth more to begin with. Bearing in mind that the goal of the spread is to profit from the relative outperformance of one metal over another, then it is important to eliminate the other embedded risks in the spread trade. There are three components of the risk in trading a pair of assets against each other: their weightings (contract value), their respective volatilities, and their relative performance (return). The least aggressive spread trade is to go long

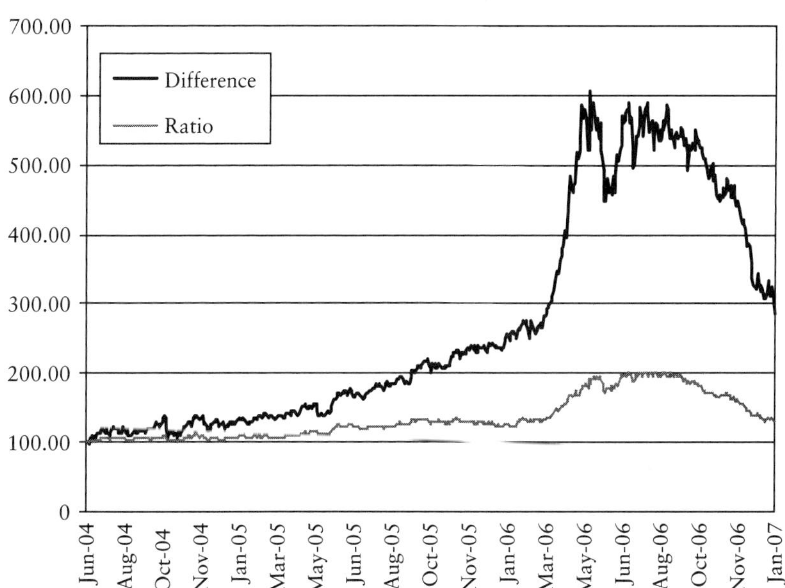

EXHIBIT 34.17 Copper-Aluminum Spread and Ratio

short a pair with an initial equal dollar amount adjusted for relative volatility. Going long short an equal number of tonnes seems simpler, but has the extra weighting risk embedded in it.

Borrowing and lending metal is the equivalent of curve steepeners and flatteners in the fixed income markets. One borrows a metal when going long the shorter dated delivery and lends the metal when going short the shorter dated delivery. The motivation for borrowing a metal is to benefit from a tightening in supply between the two delivery dates. Such calendar spreads are much more volatile in the shorter dated maturities than the longer dated maturities because the tightness in supply is quintessentially only relevant in the short term.

These short-term spreads are volatile and liquid enough to be tradable in their own right. The tightening of the spread was accompanied by rising copper prices and the easing of the spread was accompanied by falling copper prices. That is true of both the cash to 3's spread in Exhibit 34.18 and the 3's to 15 spread in Exhibit 34.19.

Exhibit 34.20 shows the short term spread (cash to 3's) plotted against the long term spread (3's to 15) both being expressed as a percentage of the 3 month price. This relationship has just the right kind of degree of association. Sufficiently well associated to limit spread trade (long one short the other) and not so well associated that there is no opportunity to trade.

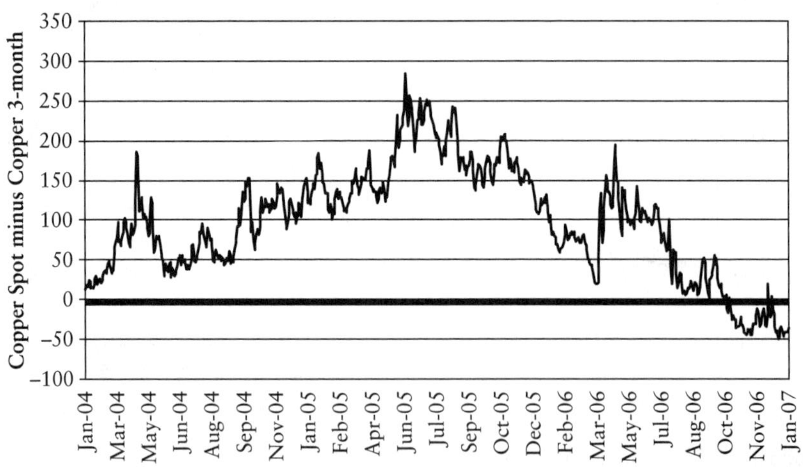

EXHIBIT 34.18 Spread of Spot Copper over Cash Copper (cash minus 3-month)

EXHIBIT 34.19 Spread of 3-Month Copper Price over the 15-Month Copper Price (3-month minus 15-month)

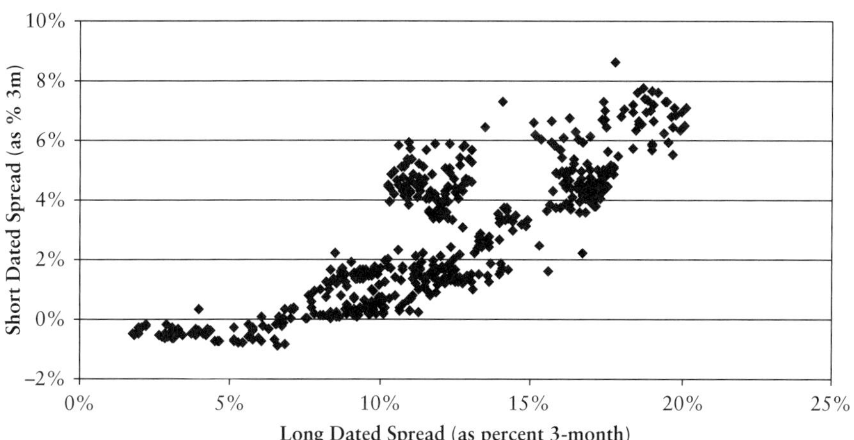

EXHIBIT 34.20 Scatter Plot of Short-Term Spread against Long-Term Spread

CONCLUSION

When formulating an investment strategy it is vital to carefully consider the factors facilitating and disrupting base metal supply and demand. The critical macro factor for the future is whether or not technology and innovation will slow down the rate of mineral resource depletion. In turn a key factor in this macroeconomic development is whether or not abundant capital resource is used efficiently and properly to mitigate the scarcity of the natural resource. In the environment of low long-term interest rates that exists at the time of this writing, high metals prices and low credit spreads seem to be enabling the opposite scenario for the future: one of producer consolidation, oligopoly, and therefore higher metals prices. That situation may in turn depend on the political climate in key metals producing states.

No wonder then that it is important to cope with outright metal price volatility by using opportunities presented by the shape of metals forward price curves for example, or investing in the stock of mining companies.

Readers who like to look back a long way in time should note that the copper price spiked to $4.00 a pound (in 1997 dollars) once before in 1917.[12]

[12]Daniel E. Sullivan, John L. Sznopek, and Laurie A. Wagner, "20th Century US Mineral Prices Decline in Constant Dollars," U.S. Department of the Interior, U.S. Geological Survey, Open File Report 00-389.

CHAPTER 35

Electricity Trading in the European Union

Stefan Ulreich, Ph.D.
Generation/Upstream
E.ON AG

The electricity markets in Germany, the Netherlands, and the United Kingdom have been liberalized and have developed into very important marketplaces—especially due to the high relevance of electricity for different consumer groups. Similarly, other European countries have developed their electricity markets as a consequence of the European Union (EU)-wide liberalization, leading to a continuous growth of international electricity trading. The integration of new EU-member states will enhance the development of a European energy market.

The trading volumes for electricity and gas in Europe are still increasing. Estimates of the trading volume in 2005 by the European Federation of Energy Traders (EFET)[1] for the German power market were over 2,500 TWh[2], that is, roughly five times the consumption of electricity in Germany. Volumes in the United Kingdom for the same year were also 2,500 TWh and in the Scandinavian region about 2,000 TWh. EFET estimates that the total European electricity and gas turnover for the year 2004 was about €600 billion. The sector inquiry of the EU showed a further increase of trading activity: In Germany over 650% of the annual national consumption was traded and in the Nordic Region over 550% of the annual consumption. At the European Energy Exchange (EEX), based in Leipzig and viewed as a Central European benchmark exchange for electricity, the turnover in 2006 was almost 1,100 TWh compared to 602 TWh in 2005 and 397 TWh in

[1]For more information about EFET, see http://www.efet.org.
[2]1 TWh = 1 million MWh, 1 MWh = 1,000 kWh.

2004. These figures demonstrate that the market still has an enormous growth potential.

Electricity shows one peculiarity as a commodity: It cannot be stored, but has to be consumed at the moment of production. Storing of electricity is only possible to a limited extent, for example, by pump hydroelectricity. In power stations based on this technology, water is pumped into a reservoir and can be used to produce large amounts of electricity over a short period of time. The efficiency of this technology, however, limits the economic use. Pump hydroelectricity is mainly used for the delivery of electricity in peak hours (e.g., around lunch time). As a result, the missing storage opportunity of electricity leads to the fact that electricity has a different market price for each hour of a day. Furthermore, this leads to a fundamental different market in comparison to the storable commodities crude oil and natural gas. Storing allows for the latter two commodities to smooth out seasonal effects, for example, the higher demand for oil and gas during the heating period.

MARKETPLACES FOR ELECTRICITY IN EUROPE

Electricity is traded both *over-the-counter* (OTC) and on exchanges in Europe. In an OTC trade the parties are dealing directly with each other, perhaps brought into contact with the help of a broker. Deals are performed via phone and in the last several years increasingly via electronic internet platforms. These platforms are run by the large broker houses. By *click-and-trade*, standardized electricity can be bought and sold. The electricity market has thus imitated the development of longer-existing markets for bonds and stocks where electronic trading is now common.

The market participants are, of course, the usual suspects: Both large and small companies that produce and consume electricity. The direction of delivery is however not generic, as one might think. Large electricity producers act also as buyers on the market, for example, in case power plants of competitors produce electricity cheaper than their own generation fleet. Consumers on the other hand perform revisions of their plants from time to time—planned and unplanned—and can then sell the excess electricity on the market. Furthermore, there is a large number of industrial consumers running their own power plants. The management of these companies face the daily make-or-buy decision: Do we produce electricity with our own power plant or is the market price cheaper so that we should buy? Additionally, more and more speculative traders having neither a production nor a consumption facility take part in this marketplace. In particular, investment banks with a strong background in commodity trading have become increasingly active in the electricity markets. For these firms, financial trading is the main focus, of course, not the physical delivery of electricity.

Often underestimated is the international nature of the wholesale market for electricity. Naively, one would assume that the local electricity production would set the market price and the electricity trade would happen between the local power plant operators and the local consumers in a region. However, due to the presence of a European-wide high-voltage grid, this is not the case and there are links between the national markets in Europe. Germany, for example, is connected with Denmark, the Netherlands, France, Switzerland, and Austria. Also the new EU-member states, Czech Republic and Poland, can deliver electricity to Germany or import electricity from Germany. What may be surprising to some is that there is even a subsea connection of the German electricity grid to the Swedish one. This leads to international competition at the level of electricity generation. Price differences between the different regions in Europe, however, still exist, since the European high-voltage grid still shows some bottlenecks. Some countries have a rather close connection by huge transport capacities (e.g., Germany with France), so wholesale market prices do not show large differences. Between other countries the transport capacities are limited. An example is Germany and the Netherlands. Since the Dutch wholesale market usually has a higher price level, the transport is usually unidirectional from Germany to the Netherlands. The transport capacities in Europe are enhanced continuously. For example, the connection between Switzerland and Italy has been improved in the last few years and a new project is the subsea connection between the Netherlands and Norway. New transport capacities will lead to an equalization of the wholesale market prices (see Exhibit 35.1).

The direct access to the OTC market or to an electricity exchange makes sense only for those parties with a reasonably sufficient turnover. Smaller consumers or producers, however, are not excluded from the market, since there are intermediaries offering market access as a service. This is similar to the financial markets, where banks or brokers offer their clients access to stock exchanges.

Electricity Exchanges

Comparable to other commodities or financial securities, first an OTC-market is established and then exchanges emerge. A short time after the liberalization in Europe, the first exchanges were created in the EU. They primarily reduced counterparty credit risk. Usually the exchange is the trading partner for the seller and for the buyer. Each of them needs a margin account at the exchange. The exchange guarantees the delivery of goods by

EXHIBIT 35.1 Average Hourly Total Import Capacity NTC Related to Installed Generation Capacity for Selected Countries in 2004

Country	Percent
United Kingdom	2%
Italy	6%
Spain	6%
Greece	12%
Netherlands	17%
Belgium	25%
Hungary	38%
Denmark	50%
Slovenia	68%
Luxembourg	90%

Source: Exhibit created from data obtained from sector inquiry of the EU (final report as of January 10, 2007).

the seller and the payment by the buyer. This service is financed by exchange fees. An additional service is the clearing of OTC trades. This service, for example, is provided by the Nordpool, the EEX or Powernext.

Moreover, exchanges fulfill a central role by publishing prices and volumes of the traded products. Thus all market participants receive information that is provided by a neutral source. Similarly, brokers offer information about the liquidity and the wholesale prices, for example, via emails. In Europe, a number of electricity exchanges are now active, the most important of which are listed in Exhibit 35.2.

The participants in these exchanges are from different countries. The EEX has participants from 19 countries, the APX from 14 countries, and the Nordpool market (the oldest electricity exchange in Europe) from 20 countries. Furthermore, the exchanges have also begun trading international products. For example, the EEX not only trades German power, but French and Swiss power as well.

OTC Market

Necessary for performing deals via phone or an electronic platform is a master agreement between the two parties. This master agreement defines the relevant details such as delivery location for physical delivery and payment and delivery dates. Furthermore, *force majeure* is defined when a

EXHIBIT 35.2 European Electricity Exchanges

Name of the Exchange	Internet Address	Based in:
EEX	www.eex.com	Germany
Powernext	www.powernext.fr	France
IPEX	www.mercatoelettrico.org	Italy
APX	www.apx.nl	The Netherlands
EXAA	www.exaa.at	Austria
PolPX	www.polpx.pl	Poland
Nordpool	www.nordpool.com	Denmark, Finland, Norway, Sweden
Borzen	www.borzen.sl	Slovenia
OMEL	www.omel.es	Spain
UKPX	www.ukpx.co.uk	United Kingdom

Source: Author.

delivery cannot be performed due to grid problems. In continental Europe, the EFET master agreement is widely used.[3]

A crucial point for OTC deals is credit risk. Since deals are done bilaterally, the electricity seller needs some information about the credit risk of the buyer company. For some companies the credit rating assigned by rating agencies (e.g., Moody's, Fitch Rating, or Standard & Poor's) can be used. Nonrated companies can either be rated by an internal rating system or by using bank guarantees. The case of Enron[4] a few years ago led to greater awareness of credit issues also in Europe since Enron was a major player in the European electricity markets. Similarly, the buyer of electricity needs the guarantee that the electricity bought will be delivered. This guarantee can also be translated into financial terms, since the nondelivery of electricity can be cured by using other electricity buyers. In cases like this, a financial compensation is necessary.

Most market participants do trades both on exchanges and on the OTC-market. Others take a close look at the transaction costs and compare the advantages and disadvantages of trading locations and then decide in which of these two marketplaces to trade. For the wholesale market prices, there is no difference, however. The liquidity in both market segments and

[3]The most actual version of the EFET master agreement can be downloaded from http://www.efet.org.

[4]The bankruptcy of the trading house Enron caused some turmoil in the electricity market since the delivery and the financial settlement of outstanding contracts was not possible respectively.

the existence of arbitrageurs ensure that the price differences lie within the bid-ask-spread.

SPOT AND FORWARD MARKETS FOR ELECTRICITY

In this section, our focus is on the exchanges, although the OTC markets operate in an analogous way. Price formation on the spot market is driven by the competition between demand and supply, typically the physical delivery of electricity is most relevant. In contrast, deals on the futures market can have a physical background, but this is not necessarily the case. The liquidity of the market also allows participants to use futures and forwards for pure financial trading since open positions can be closed every day. The peculiarities for the physical delivery of electricity (e.g., contracts needed with grid operators) will not be considered here because they are not important for price formation.

Spot Market

As already noted, electricity cannot be stored. Thus the spot market is not dealing with the actual consumption at the moment of trading—this is done on the market for balancing energy—but with the day-ahead consumption. Furthermore, the price of electricity depends on the exact time of consumption. As a consequence, the standard products on the spot market are delivery for each of the 24 hours of the next day.[5] If the trading day is a Friday, on the spot market the hours of Saturday, Sunday, and Monday are traded. If the next day is a holiday, the day following the holiday is also included in the bidding process on the spot market.

To make trading more convenient and enhance liquidity, there are usually two additional products on the spot market available: The base block and the peak block. The *base block* covers all 24 hours of the next day; the *peak block* covers only the hours with high demand. The definition of peak block depends largely on the national market. In Germany, peak is defined as the hours 08:00 to 20:00 (i.e., 8:00 A.M. to 8:00 P.M.) of a working day (Saturday excluded); that is, delivery is between 07:00 in the morning until 20:00 in the evening (i.e., 7:00 A.M. to 8:00 P.M.). In the Netherlands, peak is defined as the hours 7:00 till 23:00 (i.e., 7:00 A.M. to 11:00 P.M.).[6]

[5]When the switching due to daylight savings occurs, there are 23 hours respectively, 25 hours traded for the next day.

[6]An exception to this rule is the Nordpool market. Since this market is dominated by large hydroelectric power plants, where the production of electricity can be controlled very easily, there is no need for defining peak products.

Typical minimum size for block products and for hour products are 5 MW (i.e., 5,000,000 W). In comparison, typical light bulbs have a demand of 100 W. That is, a spot transaction corresponds to 50,000 light bulbs!

Base and peak for day-ahead delivery are traded continuously. The prices for single hours, however, are determined via an auction process on the exchange. Every market participant sends a bid curve to the exchange (in most cases electronically). This curve has to be sent to the exchange until a certain moment in time (e.g., at noon). For each hour, the bid curve consists of a value for demanded or supplied electricity and a price at which the party is willing to buy or sell electricity. Naturally, with higher price the offers in the bid curve rise and the buying interest declines. All bid curves are now used by the exchange to calculate the price, where the highest trading turnover for electricity takes place: This price is then the market price. All sellers or producers that bid this price must then deliver electricity for this hour on the next day; all buyers or consumers who were willing to pay at least this price will receive the electricity for this hour.[7]

As an example, in Exhibit 35.3, we consider an auction result on the EEX. One recognizes that the electricity demand in the peak hours is higher and, as a consequence, the price level is higher compared to off-peak hours. The most expensive hour is usually the hour 12:00 (11:00 to 12:00, i.e., 11:00 A.M. to 12:00 noon) because this is when lunch is prepared. During the evening hours, there is often also a second peak when electric lights are used and televisions are operating. During the night hours, however, demand for electricity is low since neither private nor industrials use electricity in this time to a large extent. Thus the price of electricity is also low. Of course, there are exceptions to this typical auction result such as on New Year's Day. Since on this special day social life concentrates on the early night hours and is very quiet during the day, we see a completely different demand pattern (see Exhibit 35.4).[8]

The property of electricity to be used at the moment of production leads to rather high volatilities in the spot market. This volatility is furthermore driven by other volatile factors that affect the price of electricity, leading to sometimes very drastic prices in a few hours.

Especially unexpected weather changes can induce huge price movements. An example is a period of extreme cold temperatures or a heat wave such as Europe experienced in 2003. In the latter case, low availability of

---

[7]Using forward products, one can also use the spot market for financial deals, for example, by selling to the spot market from a long position in a forward.

[8]Furthermore, industrial demand is generally low on a holiday—the price level is much lower: The most expensive hour of New Year's Day 2003 was cheaper by a factor of 3 in comparison to the typical work day in May 2003.

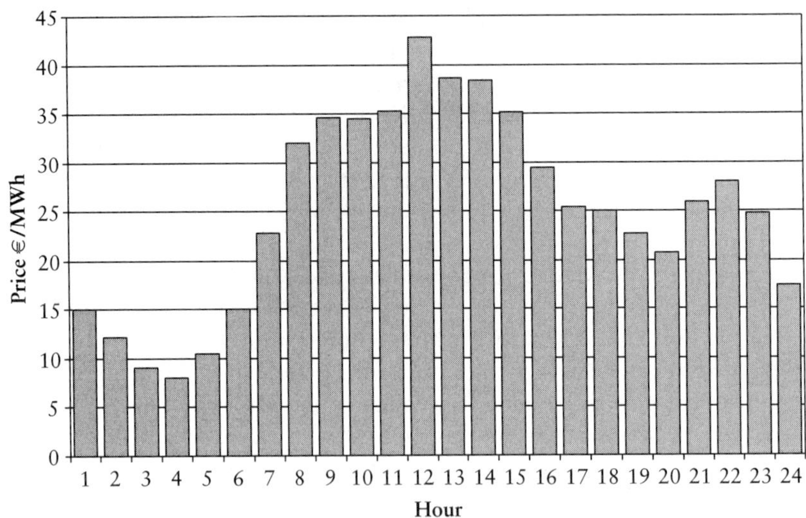

EXHIBIT 35.3 Result of Spot Auctions of EEX, Tuesday, May 6, 2003
Source: Exhibit created from data obtained from EEX.

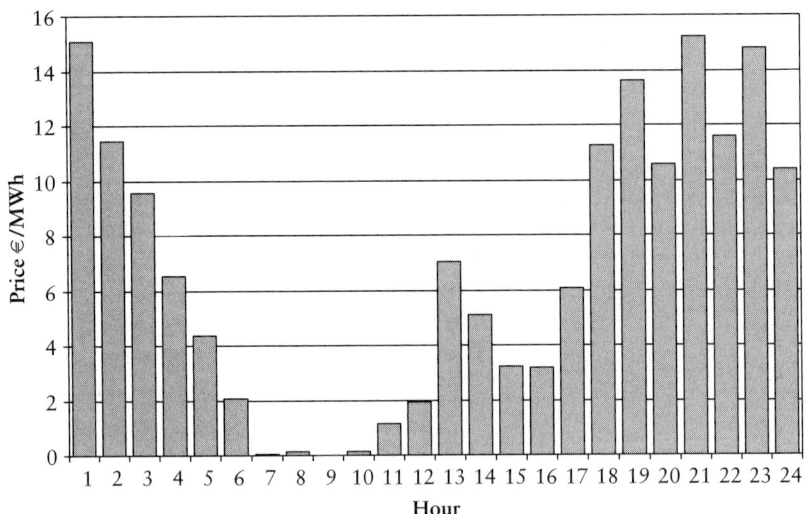

EXHIBIT 35.4 Result of Spot Auctions of EEX, January 1, 2003
Source: Exhibit created from data obtained from EEX.

hydroelectric production met with high demand for electricity due to the use of air conditioning. However, only a few hours show these extreme high prices. Furthermore, with reasonable hedging on the futures and forward markets the financial risk due to these events can to a large extent be minimized.

Forward Market

Similar to the spot market, there are base and peak products on the forward market. The products are deliveries of electricity for the coming months, quarters, and years. The German EEX, for example, offers trading for contracts for the next six months, the next seven quarters, and the next six years. Exhibit 35.5 lists the contracts available for trading on February 5, 2007.

Trading on the futures market and on the forward market is continuous. Typically the product with the nearest time to delivery is the most liquid one, and the base is traded more actively than peak. The more liquid a product, the narrower is the bid-ask-spread. For the benchmark base delivery the usual bid-ask-spread is about €0.10/MWh.

The benchmark contract of the exchange and of the OTC market in continental Europe is the base delivery for the next year. In the previous EEX

EXHIBIT 35.5 Futures Traded on the EEX, February 5, 2007

Month	Base March 2007	Peak March 2007
	Base April 2007	Peak April 2007
	Base May 2007	Peak May 2007
	Base June 2007	Peak June 2007
	Base July 2007	Peak July 2007
	Base August 2007	Peak August 2007
Quarter	Base 2nd Quarter 2007	Peak 2nd Quarter 2007
	Base 3rd Quarter 2007	Peak 3rd Quarter 2007
	Base 4th Quarter 2007	Peak 4th Quarter 2007
	Base 1st Quarter 2008	Peak 1st Quarter 2008
	Base 2nd Quarter 2008	Peak 2nd Quarter 2008
	Base 3rd Quarter 2008	Peak 3rd Quarter 2008
Year	Base 2008	Peak 2008
	Base 2009	Peak 2009
	Base 2010	Peak 2010
	Base 2011	Peak 2011
	Base 2012	Peak 2012
	Base 2013	Peak 2013

Source: Exhibit created from data obtained from EEX.

example, the base is 2008. Since 2008 is a leap year, delivery is for 366 days (i.e., 366 days $\times$ 24 hours/day $=$ 8.784 hours). The typical size of a base delivery is 25 MW, the base band for the year 2008 corresponds to electric energy of 219,600 MWh. Assuming that the yearly consumption of a household with three people lies roughly near 3.5 MWh, the base contract is the amount of electricity consumed by more than 60,000 households annually.[9]

Traded futures offer no opportunity for arbitrage; that is, the market price of a quarter delivery has to be the same within the bid-ask-spread in comparison with the market price for delivery in the months of the corresponding quarter. Contracts coming closer to their delivery are cascaded. For instance, a quarter delivery will cascade into three-month contracts, a year contract will cascade into three-month contracts and three-quarter contracts. The month contract that enters delivery can be monetized by using the spot market as an index.

To see the relevant order of magnitudes, we consider the base delivery 2007 (Exhibit 35.6) in more detail. With a market price of €55.33/MWh, the contract value is 219,000 MWh $\times$ €55.33/MWh $=$ €12,117,270, slightly more than €12 million. A change in market price of €0.10/MWh leads to a change in the contract value by €.21,900. On the OTC market, smaller sizes are also traded; for example, 5 MW deliveries and intermediaries also offer access to the market at lower sizes.

Using the example in Exhibit 35.6 we can also try to find out whether the market is free of arbitrage. Using the four quarters of the year 2007 to calculate the market price for a base delivery in 2007, we find

$$(2{,}160 \times 62.48 + 2{,}184 \times 49.61 + 2{,}208 \times 51.14 + 2{,}208 \times €58.18) \\ /8{,}760\,\text{h} = €55.33/\text{MWh}$$

This is the same price.

The different prices for the month contracts (Exhibit 35.7) result from the expectations for the weather situation, the number of holidays, and, of course, primarily the fuel markets. We will discuss this in more detail later.

In Exhibit 35.8, the quarter contracts reveal the seasonality of the electricity market. Note that the winter contracts are more expensive than summer contracts, due to the higher demand.

During most of 2006, the forward curve for the year contracts were in backwardation (i.e., the contracts with later delivery were cheaper). This is uncommon in the electricity market, but reflected the view prevailing in the

[9]For a nonleap year, the base contract means a delivery over 8.760 hours and corresponds to an energy of 219,000 MWh.

EXHIBIT 35.6 Future Prices of the EEX, February 10, 2006

Delivery period	Number of hours	Base in €/MWh	Peak in €/MWh
March 2006	744	62.75	87.40
April 2006	720	54.50	78.50
May 2006	744	50.90	69.84
June 2006	720	54.94	79.20
July 2006	744	55.15	79.23
August 2006	744	55.40	79.20
2nd Quarter 2006	2.184	53.42	75.67
3rd Quarter 2006	2.208	55.88	80.50
4th Quarter 2006	2.208	61.48	89.66
1st Quarter 2007	2.160	62.48	89.86
2nd Quarter 2007	2.184	49.61	68.39
3rd Quarter 2007	2.208	51.14	69.86
4th Quarter 2007	2.208	58.18	81.81
Year 2007	8.760	55.33	77.50
Year 2008	8.784	54.30	76.14
Year 2009	8.760	53.60	74.18
Year 2010	8.760	53.00	73.75
Year 2011	8.760	52.33	73.35
Year 2012	8.784	52.28	73.25

Source: Exhibit created from data obtained from EEX.

market at that time especially with respect to fuel markets and the emission trading market (Exhibit 35.9).

Schedule

Almost no consumer can procure their demand for electricity just by using base and peak products, since they have a different demand during the 24 hours of the day. For this reason, in the OTC market schedules are traded. For a certain delivery period (e.g., three months), each hour of this period is equipped with a different demand or supply for electricity. The price of a schedule is determined with the help of a forward curve for every hour. This curve must reproduce the given forward prices for standard products at the exchange.

The mathematics underlying this curve is more or less based on empirical facts (e.g., the history of spot market prices on the exchanges). However, this also means that it is not really exact calculus.[10]

[10]Further markets not considered in detail are the market for balancing energy (needed to match the actual demand with the actual production) and cross-border auctions for grid capacities.

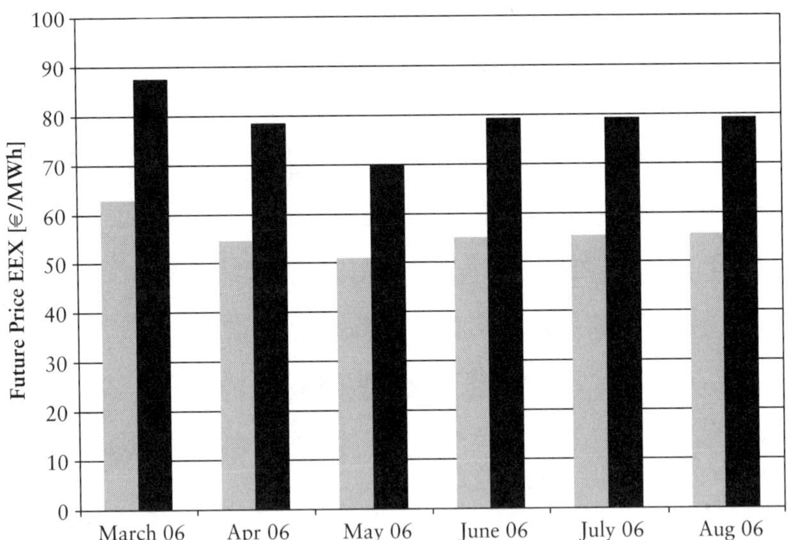

EXHIBIT 35.7 Future Price of the Month Contracts (base gray, peak black)
Source: Exhibit created from data obtained from EEX.

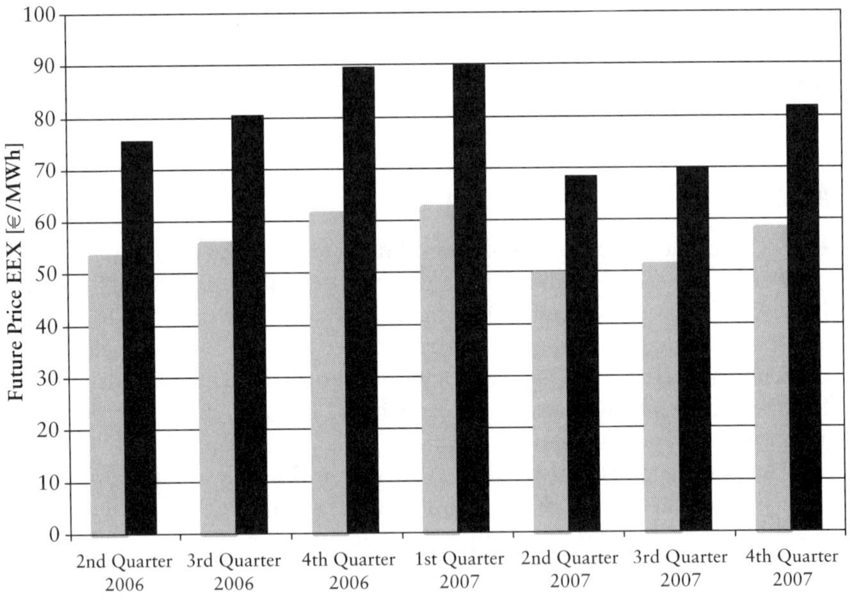

EXHIBIT 35.8 Future Price of the Quarter Contracts (base gray, peak black)
Source: Exhibit created from data obtained from EEX.

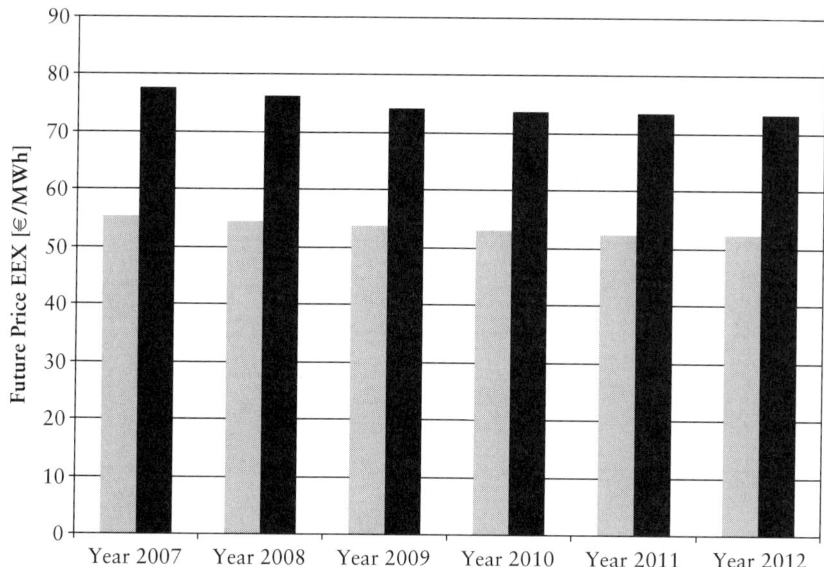

EXHIBIT 35.9 Future Price of the Year Contracts (base gray, peak black)
Source: Exhibit created from data obtained from EEX.

INFLUENCE FACTORS ON MARKET PRICE

Of course, the sum of all influence factors together with market psychology is driving prices. This means that a decreasing hard coal price might not be enough to bring electricity prices down when other influence factors give bullish signals to the market.

A trivial driver of the electricity price is economic growth. An increase in economic output is closely connected to the use of more energy. The correlation decreased in the last decades, especially since periods of high energy prices led to higher energy efficiency. Furthermore, structural changes helped to decouple the economic growth from the higher use of energy because some of the energy-intensive business in Europe has been replaced by other business segments with lower energy use. Additionally, there are some special influence factors operating in the electricity market.

Is There a Maximum Price for Electricity?

The spot market can show extreme price spikes when several negative influence factors are occurring. Incidents like this are rare. To illustrate, look at

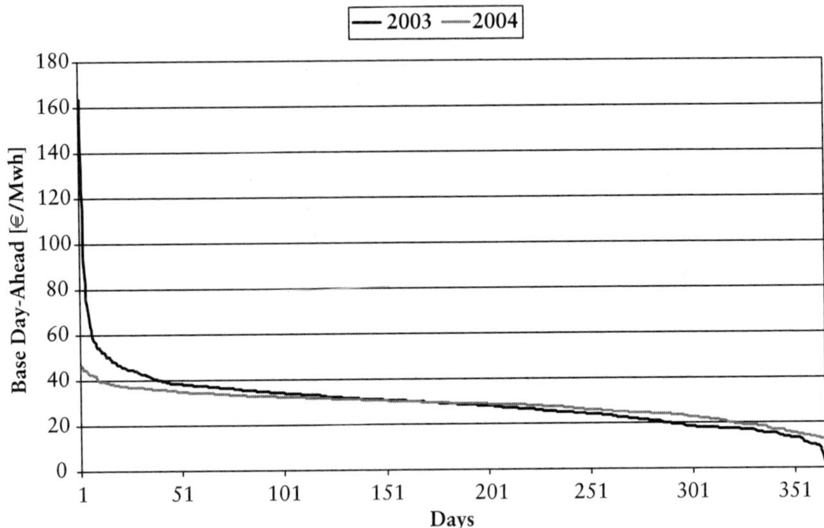

EXHIBIT 35.10 Daily Spot Prices EEX Base Day-Ahead for 2003 and 2004 (sorted in ascending order of market price)
Source: Exhibit created from data obtained from EEX.

the spot market for base load traded at the EEX in 2003 and 2004. In Exhibit 35.10, the prices are shown in the following way: The highest price is shown first, followed by the second highest and so on. In 2003, the heat wave in Europe led to high electricity prices especially in Italy and France and affected the German market as well. In contrast, 2004 was relatively calm and no special events happened. So the electricity prices in the spot market showed only little variation.[11]

On the forward market, these price spikes have a rather low influence. Since forward market products consist of several days of delivery, single events have only a minor influence.

The mid-term price expectation for long-running forward products, however, is given by the costs for a new production facility as on every other commodity market. This is a simple consequence of the marginal cost approach. In times of high forward prices there is an interest to build new power plants—these additional production capacities lead in the midterm to a price dampening. The costs for a new power plant are driven by the forward prices for fuels and therefore follow the forward curves for coal, gas,

[11]Special events can be forecasted on a short-term basis. For example, the weather forecast for the next day can be used. Midterm or long-term weather forecasts are not reliable enough to be useful for forecast models.

and oil—and since 2005 also the price for CO_2-allowances. Whereas the spot market can show extreme high prices, this is not the case for the forward market. Here the costs for new power plants are setting an upper price level. Only for short times will the market price be higher than this level.[12]

Seasonality

Electricity prices follow a seasonal pattern. The reason is that there are typical values for average temperatures during a year and the daylight patterns, as well as seasonal patterns on the fuel market (especially natural gas). In central Europe, the demand for electricity is higher in winter than in summer. As a consequence, the market prices in winter are on a higher level than in summer. Typically for the winter period there is the occurrence of a second price spike during a day. Apart from noon, in the evening the demand is also high because electric lights are switched on. In other countries, such as Italy or the United States, the summer prices for electricity are on a comparable level to the winter prices due to air conditioning.

The forward markets also show a seasonal pattern. This does not play a role in the year contracts since they average over the whole year. Month and quarter contracts show the seasonal effects. Therefore the contracts covering a colder period such as December or the first quarter, show higher prices than contracts with an expected higher temperature. The summer quarters and the winter quarters also show slight differences between each other. Generally, the first quarter of a year is more expensive than the fourth quarter since more cold months are present in the former period. The general seasonality can be seen in Exhibit 39.8.

Weekends and Holidays

Since most companies do not operate during the weekends, on Saturdays and Sundays electricity demand is lower than during the work week. Therefore, Saturdays and Sundays have lower spot prices than week days. Furthermore, Sundays are lower in price than Saturdays because many shops are open on Saturdays but not on Sundays. Similar considerations hold true for the vacation season.

---

[12]Most models used in the electricity industry for spot or forward forecasting are rather complicated numerical simulations based on the assumed marginal costs for the electricity production. The forward models also use price forecasts for gas and coal; furthermore, they have to anticipate the change of the overall power plant portfolio and the grid connections between different countries or grid regions.

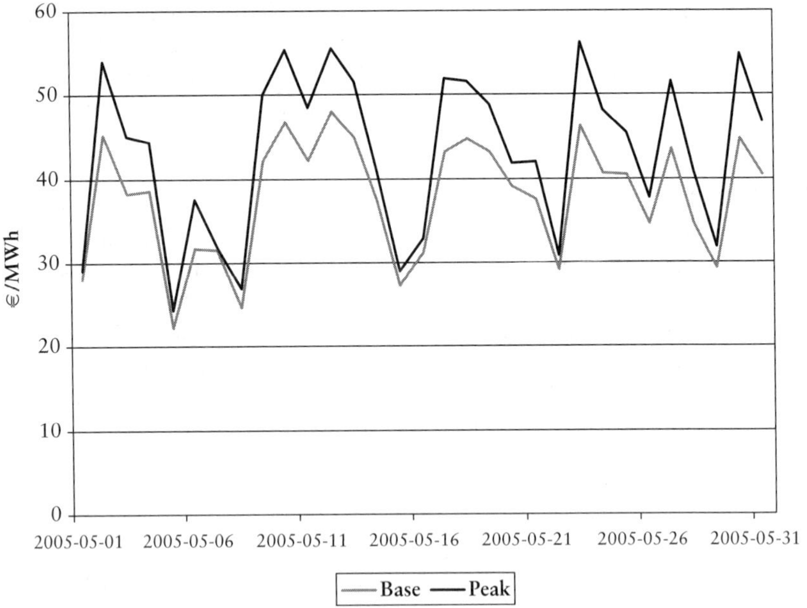

EXHIBIT 35.11 Spot Market Prices of the EEX, May 2005
Source: Exhibit created from data obtained from EEX.

In Exhibit 35.11 one can see the weekends as price dips. Base and peak in this case are calculated using the hour prices of the daily auction. The holidays Ascension on May 5, Pentecost Monday on May 16, and Corpus Christi on May 26 also show lower prices than usual workdays. Since Ascension and Corpus Christi are always on a Thursday, business activities are low on the following Friday due to the fact that many people take a long weekend. The mentioned holidays are at least in the Catholic parts of Europe, so the situation is similar.

The growing international exchange of electricity also has some impact: holidays in neighboring countries affect the price of electricity. Holidays in France, Austria, and Switzerland open the opportunity to export electricity to Belgium, Germany, or the Netherlands and lead to some price dampening. The same is true for a nationwide holiday season as is the case in France after that country's National Holiday. This is again a consequence of the fact that electricity cannot be stored.

Weather

Weather influences both the demand side and the supply side. Aside from the previously discussed seasonality, precipitation plays a major role. Rain and snow fill the reservoirs of the hydroelectric power stations, snow of course with a certain time lag given by its melting. The snow melting crucially depends on the average temperatures in the spring, and is therefore dependent on another weather variable. The development of wind power sites in the last few years across Europe also brought a new dependency of electricity production on the wind situation (i.e., wind force and also wind direction). Consequently, the weather forecast for the next day, especially the prediction for each of its 24 hours, plays a crucial role for the spot market of electricity.

As previously mentioned, rainfalls give bearish signals to the spot market since more production by river run hydroelectric and by dam hydroelectric is the consequence. This influence is, of course, higher if the share of hydroelectric production is rather high. Examples of this in Europe are the Nordic countries and Austria and Switzerland in the Alps. Since precipitation usually has a rather high volatility, these markets tend to have rather volatile spot markets—damped the more dam hydroelectric is present because of its storage capacity. Additionally, these countries are connected to the more fossil or nuclear fueled power plant portfolios of France, Italy, Germany, Denmark, and Finland. This helps to decrease the spot volatility or in the view of the electricity industry, to increase security of supply.

As a result, this interdependency makes regional weather effects important for all of Europe. During 2005, there was a massive drought in Spain, leading to lower hydroelectric production than the long-term average. This resulted in an increase in electricity imports from France. France, however, imported more from Germany. The usual direction of electricity delivery from France to Germany changed.

Snowfalls in the Alps or in Scandinavia also affect the forward market, especially for the spring month contracts and the contracts for the first two quarters. In the first place, the amount of fallen snow is important. During the melting of the snow, the reservoirs are filled. The exact time when melting commences, however, is not so easy to predict. Depending on the average temperatures, melting starts can vary by several months.

The increasing share of wind energy in Europe influences the spot market for electricity since the past few years. On windy days, this renewable way to produce electricity replaces the production of conventional power plants, especially since in most countries the laws guarantee a privileged feed-in for renewable energy. The forecast tools for wind energy have been developed in the last few years. Whereas nowadays the prediction of the wind strength is already quite successful, but still subject to considerable forecasting error; forecasting when the wind will blow is still difficult of course.

As of this writing, photovoltaic as another renewable energy source is experiencing a massive extension. Still the share of production is small, although this may change in the future. This will lead to a stronger dependency of the spot market prices on sunshine. This also means that the effects of clouds can start to play a crucial role.

Most of the renewable energy sources (i.e., hydroelectric, wind, and solar) will increase the weather dependency on electricity production. This dependency can only be compensated for if there are enough backup power plants present that will run in case the renewable production cannot produce (e.g., in a dark windless night of a rather dry period). Relying solely on renewable production will only be possible when the technology is developed that will allow storing of electricity in an economic way.

Fuel Markets

Fossil-fueled power plants need hard coal, lignite, or gas to produce electricity. Nuclear power plants rely on uranium. Consequently, the market prices for coal, gas, and uranium affect the costs of electricity production and thus the market price.

Uranium prices have only a minor impact. The most important cost factor for a nuclear power plant is the fixed cost due to construction. The cost of operation is not so important. Uranium is a tradable quantity and experienced a price increase in the last few years.[13] This price increase is on the supply side due to the fact that the conversion of old nuclear weapons already took place and new uranium has now to be taken from mines. But also the demand side showed an increased interest in uranium due to new constructions in China, India, Finland, France, and other countries. Market participants, however, do not consider the uranium price as crucial for forward prices of electricity.

More important is the hard coal price, especially for base load. Coal power plants are mainly used to cover the base and mid load. In contrast, gas prices have an effect on the peak load prices because gas plants are primarily used for this purpose. This is due to not only technology since gas plants can be switched on or off faster, but also due to economics since in most countries coal is less expensive than gas. In contrast to hard coal, there is no trading for lignite. Lignite mines are usually closely located to lignite power plants. The energy content of lignite is too low, so transport over long distance is not economic. Lignite is a backbone of the electricity system in Central European countries such as Germany, Romania, Czech Republic, and Poland.

[13]More information about the uranium market can be found at http://www.uxc.com.

Oil power plants do not play a major role in Europe, with the exception of Italy. Nevertheless, in all electricity markets the oil price has a hidden influence. Imports of coal are usually done by ships, linked with demand for ship diesel. This adds to the freight costs, so the coal price for power plants has in fact a component depending on the crude oil price. The huge economic growth China is facing currently led to an enormous increase of oil prices as well as of freight rates. The latter was mainly driven by the delivery of iron ore from Brazil to China. Also China and India drove up the international prices for coal due to their own increased demand. These reasons were among the most important drivers of electricity prices in Europe in the last few years. Obviously, the European market is not decoupled from global energy markets.

During 2005, the gas market experienced an impressive price hike. This was attributable to increasing oil prices. Additionally in United Kingdom the awareness rose that the country's North Sea gas fields will run dry in a few years giving another psychological bullish signal to the market. This development led to a huge rise in U.K. electricity market prices. The less severe winter 2006 greatly relaxed gas prices. Though the fundamental situation of gas supply has definitely not changed in the United Kingdom, the market psychology is reacting calmer regarding it.

Coal and crude oil are usually traded in U.S. dollars, so these markets have a foreign exchange risk for traders in Eurozone countries. Similar foreign exchange risks exist with respect to the U.K. market and the Scandinavian markets with Norwegian, Swedish, and Danish krone. This means, that the foreign exchange markets also enter as a factor affecting the price of electricity.

HEDGING

From our closer examination of the price formation and the price swings in the electricity market, the question arises as to how to hedge the financial risks in this market. For end consumers, this definitely means that they must have a sound knowledge about their own electricity demand to implement sufficiently precise prediction and control tools. However, transaction costs should also be taken into consideration. Total electricity costs only play a minor role in a company, the usual full supply contract being a convenient and sufficient solution. The more important a company's electricity costs are, the more a company should be interested in a structured procurement of its electricity. Specialists should then be responsible for decisions that affect an energy portfolio. For pure financial players, the following considerations may help in understanding some fundamental factors of the market better. In the case of analysts, these fundamental factors may aid in better understanding whether a company is well prepared for the electricity market.

The starting point for a company is the expected demand. Ideally this should have the form of hourly data. Analyzing this information can provide valuable information as to whether base and peak contracts for certain months, quarters, and years could make sense. Together with a view on the further development of the market prices, the decision will generally have the following outcomes: Expecting price increases, the procurement would slightly exceed the demand in order to have selling opportunities. The reverse is also true: Expecting lower prices, the procurement would be below expected demand in order to buy later. Of course, the overall strategy has to fit into the risk framework of a company. For instance, a complete procurement via the spot market is generally possible; however, the company is now completely affected by price movements. Usually a company tries to reduce its market risks to an acceptable level. As a consequence, a company will definitely procure reasonable amounts on the forward market.

Apart from financial aspects of electricity procurement, technical optimization also has to be considered. Can a company stabilize its power demand and get rid of demand peaks? Can a company transfer some demand from expensive hours to inexpensive hours? Electricity procurement is not merely a problem with price risk, but also with volume risk. In the case of other commodities such as gas and oil, volume risk can be handled with storage facilities. This is not the case for electricity, urging the need for detailed analysis during the procurement.[14]

Forward Curve for Electricity

The forecasted demand curve can now be evaluated for given market prices. Since most exchanges offer future prices at most with monthly quotes, some extra work is necessary to calculate a forward curve with hour prices. The simple solution would involve using for each hour in a month or of a quarter the price for the month or quarter contract. This can be a valid approximation, especially when the load curve only shows little variation. If this is not the case, as usual, one cannot avoid using an hourly forward curve. This curve has to reproduce the given prices for forward contracts in order to satisfy the no-arbitrage condition. Furthermore the seasonality of the market should be visible.

---

[14]More details about hedging issues can be found in Vincent Kaminski (ed.), *Managing Energy Price Risk* (London: Risk Books, 2005).

One of the many different ways to produce such a curve will be roughly sketched here. The starting point is the stepwise increase of the time resolution. In this first step, a forward curve for months will be created. Month quotes by the exchange can be used directly; for others the quarter or year quotes will be used.

The calculation of a month value is extremely simple in the case where a quarter price and two market quotes for this quarter are given. In Exhibit 35.6, we see the prices for base second quarter 2006 and the prices for base April and base May 2006. Using the arbitrage relationship, the following equation must hold:

$$720 \times 54.50 + 744 \times 50.90 + 720 \times \text{June base} = 2184 \times 53.42$$

Hence the price for electricity delivered in June 2006 is €54.94/—exactly the quote on the exchange.

With only the quarter price available, additional assumptions are needed in order to calculate the month price. Usually it is assumed that the ratio between the months has a certain and fixed value that is calculated via a statistical analysis of price histories.[15] With the curve of month quotes the forward curve for daily quotes can be constructed[16].

Options

On most exchanges in Europe, options on electricity futures are also traded. Underlying are base contracts for years and quarters. The contracts on years show more liquidity than the quarter contracts. This is expected because the annual contracts are also more actively traded on the forward market.

Exhibit 35.12 shows the quotes that were given for options on base delivery 2007 on February 10, 2006. The risk analysis of options is usually done using the well-known Black-Scholes formula. Though using the formula has also led to critics in other markets,[17] most market participants use it as a standard tool.

---

[15]For example, one can assume that April and June have the same weight of 1, whereas May has a smaller weight of 0.85 due to the holiday effects. In this case, the price for June would be the price for the second quarter divided by 2.85.

[16]For a more detailed discussion, see Les Clewlow and Chris Strickland, *Energy Derivatives* (London: Lacima Publications, 2000).

[17]Marek Musiela and Marek Rutkowski, *Martingale Methods in Financial Modelling* (Berlin: Springer Verlag, 1997).

EXHIBIT 35.12 Quotes for Options on Base Delivery in 2007

Option: Type and Strike	Quote
Call €44/MWh	11.581
Call €45/MWh	10.758
Call €48/MWh	8.500
Call €49/MWh	7.831
Call €60/MWh	3.256
Call €61/MWh	3.033
Put €39/MWh	0.106
Put €49/MWh	1.644

Source: Exhibit created from data obtained from EEX.

Swing Options

Swing options are rather unusual for financial markets, but more or less the general situation for electricity markets. Every reader uses a swing option, although you might not be aware of it. In every household, the lights are turned on and off without giving a notice to the electricity supplier upfront. The consumer has in this case the right to use at an arbitrary point in time an arbitrary amount of electricity, only restricted by technical limits. Options of this kind are called *swing options* and are very complex to value.[18] The evaluation of swing options involves rather complex numerical calculations, using binomial or even trinomial trees. Since many different decisions happen on each node of the tree, the calculations are also time-consuming.

CONCLUSION

The electricity markets in Europe offer interesting opportunities for traders since new accession countries to the EU have increased participation in the market and some member states are still on their way toward liberalization. As a result, the growth of trading turnover will continue. The huge number of producers and consumers, as well as the very different influence factors on market prices, also contributes to a vibrant marketplace. Electricity prices are influenced by movements on the fuel markets—by weather incidents, political decisions, and the general economic situation. Depending on the market situation, one of these factors will dominate. Thus a close look at the market is inevitable to derive one's own view of the market.

[18]Clewlow and Strickland, *Energy Derivatives.*

CHAPTER 36

The Natural Gas Market in the United Kingdom

Chris Harris, Ph.D.
Head of Industry, Networks and Agreements
RWE npower

This chapter describes the natural gas market in the United Kingdom from the perspective of gaining an understanding of the drivers of the principal traded commodity, which is physical and financial gas at the *national balancing point* (NBP). We pay particular attention to the relationship between the fundamentals of production, transportation and consumption, and the market and institutional arrangements. We find that while gas consumption has high weather sensitivity and potentially high elasticity, prevailing arrangements greatly reduce this elasticity, with a consequential elevation of price volatility. Efforts to improve demand side management are likely to change the demand fundamentals, and the related industry changes may increase the basis risk at the NBP. We also examine the high level relationships between gas and other commodities such as coal, oil, and carbon dioxide. These relationships are accessible in economic terms, but econometric analysis is challenging, as the relationships are periodic and variable as well as complex.

BASICS

To understand the movement of prices, we need to understand the basics of physical operations, the market mechanisms, and the elements of supply and demand. We do this here.

Physical

Production Natural gas is mainly methane with some higher hydrocarbons. It is formed through anaerobic decay of organic matter. Fossil gas is trapped in geological formations, with oil (associated gas) and without (dry wells). Gas is processed—to pipeline dry-gas quality at gas processing plants—by removing oil, condensates, water, natural gas liquids, sulphur, and carbon dioxide.

Gas composition from the different sources varies, with delivered Norwegian gas and *liquified natural gas* (LNG)[1] having a calorific "Wobbe" index that is relatively high with respect to the U.K. range, Dutch gas having a low index, and Russian gas being a good blending gas due principally to its high methane content.

Gas demand, at around 100 bcm/year[2] accounts for around 40%[3] of U.K. primary energy demand, and is rising by around 2% per year. More than 90% is currently sourced from U.K. fields, but due to depletion this is expected to fall below 20% by 2020.

Pipelines and Networks Gas from the United Kingdom and Norwegian continental shelves lands at St Fergus in Scotland, and (further southwards) Teesside, Easington, and Theddlethorpe. The pipeline to Theddlethorpe from the Ormen Lange Field is the world's longest underwater pipeline. Bacton has pipes from Balgzand in the Netherlands and to/from Zeebrugge in Belgium. Gas into Bacton comes ultimately from the Netherlands, Russia (different routes, with more planned), and North Africa (via Sicily).

Gas from the Northwest coast lands at Barrow, and two pipes from Scotland feed Ireland and Northern Ireland to support the limited consented production there. There is one LNG import facility (Isle of Grain on the Thames), with Teesport, Milford Haven, and several more planned.

Gas is transported around country through 275,000 km of iron, steel, and polyethylene mains pipeline. The high pressure transmission system operates at pressures of up to 85 bar[4] and consists of over 6,400 km of high quality welded steel pipeline.

Storage Gas can be stored in salt caverns, depleted gas fields, LNG terminals, and other voids and structures. Storage levels in the United Kingdom

[1]Stored below -160°C to reduce its volume by a factor of 600.

[2]Natural gas is measured in bcm—billion cubic meters. 1-bcm = 10.9TWh (terawatt hours). All figures should be regarded as indicative due to the high degree of variation.

[3]Gas volume figures have been subject to substantial change.

[4]1 bar is atmospheric pressure.

are low compared to, for example, Germany, and currently dominated by two installations—Rough (an offshore, depleted gas field, which can provide 10% of peak daily demand and 8% of all winter demand) and Hornsea (salt caverns). Under current proposals, storage levels are expected to more than double over the period 2007–2017.

Injection and withdrawal rates are limited and the lead times can be some hours. For example, the 30 TWh at Rough can only be released at 455 GWh/day, or around 1.5%. This limits the ability of storage to alleviate demand spikes and the associated price spikes.

There is a degree of tolerance for the pressure in the gas pipes. High pressure increases leakage in the distribution system and low pressure increases safety risk through loss of flame. The storage capability is called *linepack* and is managed separately in the transmission (96 GWh linepack) and distribution (290 GWh) systems. Under normal pressures, gas moves at around 25 mph through the pipes, a speed which limits the release and replenishment rate of linepack.

The Industry and Its Arrangements

Industry Restructure The gas industry in the United Kingdom has unbundled over the last few years. British Gas was privatized in 1986 and subsequently divided into production, transportation, and supply. Wholesale gas was deregulated in 1996, full competition came in 1998 and the final stage of domestic price deregulation was completed in 2002. The International Petroleum Exchange (IPE) contract at the national balancing point began in 1997 and was the first gas futures contract in Europe. The New Gas Trading Arrangements were implemented in 1999. Transportation was bought by National Grid, the electricity system owner/operator, who retained the (high pressure) *national transmission system* (NTS) and later sold 8 of the 13 (low pressure) Local Distribution Zone (LDZ) franchises, grouped into four distribution networks (DNs), to 3 different companies. Transmission and distribution are both regulated industries that are subject to 5-year price/revenue controls by the regulator. The trend in the United Kingdom is to continue the process of unbundling and deregulating the industry sectors (for example meter provision and management).

Market Structure and Players Shippers bring gas onshore to the NBP, trade gas and capacity, and charge gas to suppliers at the meter points. It is the suppliers who have the licences to engage with consumers. Producers, traders, and suppliers generally have shipper licences. Traders buy and sell principally at the NBP.

National Grid is responsible for the operation and maintenance of the National Transmission System as well as the management of gas through it. It plays a major role in the reporting on the long-term status of the gas system. The distribution network operators are responsible for the operation of the local distribution systems, including pressure and flow management. Xoserve, which is majority owned by National Grid companies and minority owned by distribution networks, is responsible for the financial arrangements, and manages meter point registrations and settlements. Ofgem, the gas and power regulator oversees the overall governance of the wholesale and retail market.

The key market is pure bilateral trading, directly or via brokers. The International Commodity Exchange (ICE, which bought the International Petroleum Exchange) acts as the main exchange for NBP gas and effectively acts as shipping counterparty. The London Clearing House/Clearnet clears for ICE. The imbalance between gas consumed/produced (strictly speaking the settlement volume associated with this) and the nominated volume arising from trades, is cashed out by Xoserve. Self balancing is facilitated by the *on-the-day commodity market* (OCM).

Landing Gas at the Beach Entry points to the transmission system are termed the "beach." While gas can be traded bilaterally at the beach or any point upstream, there is no active market at the beach points. Shippers engage in System Entry Capacity Auctions to gain the rights to take gas from the beach to the NBP. Commodity charges are paid to get gas to the NBP, but other than a small adjustment for shrinkage losses (from leaks and gas used for compression motors), there is no volume adjustment. There is a small volume of entry directly into the distribution system.

The National Balancing Point NBP is the principal traded location for gas in the United Kingdom. It does not have a specific location and gas is neither produced nor consumed at the NBP. The balancing period is currently one day beginning at 06:00 (i.e., 6:00 A.M.), so the daily shipper account is calculated according to gas settlement volume over the day, regardless of in day profile. There are proposals for higher balancing resolution, with a four hourly period being possible.

The On-the-Day Commodity Market The OCM is an anonymous screen based market upon which shippers can post bids and offers for gas deliveries. National Grid accepts bids and offers in order to balance the system, and the accepted bids and offers are used to calculate the cashout prices SMP Buy and SMP Sell. The OCM is governed by the rules laid down in the Uniform Network Code and operates up to two hours before the end of the gas day.

Imbalance Shippers buy/sell gas and nominate the net volume to Xoserve. If the production/consumption settlement volume differs from the nomination, the difference is cashed out at the System Buy/Sell Price. Since combined cycle gas turbines (CCGTs) require gas to enable them to participate in electricity balancing in under one hour, there is pressure to shorten the gas balancing period.

Networks Broadly speaking, the network operators charge to shippers an annual capacity fee that is actually or nominally (derived from settlement volumes by an algorithm) related to maximum flows, and a per unit commodity fee that is related to volume throughput. While network operator costs are around 90% fixed, the regulated charges have a much lower percentage of capacity charge relative to commodity charge, due principally to the difficulty of relating the charge to the incremental system expansion caused by particular consumers. Market development for network charging is subject to competing pressures. On the one hand, transportation companies prefer to lock in their revenues after agreeing their cost of capital, by loading the capacity charges (which are fixed per meter a year in advance) relative to the commodity charges (which depend on the energy that actually flows). On the other hand, the need to incentivize demand management and minimize waste in capacity overbuild drives toward a higher percentage of charge relating to the maximum consumption rate of the consumer, or the consumption rate on the day of maximum system demand.

Under exit reform, it is possible that each offtaker from the NTS may in future have to buy exit capacity from the 116 NTS-to-LDZ exit points[5] and other exit points, with capacity rights being defined in terms of maximum hourly flow.

Institutional Arrangements for Supply Shippers "sell" to suppliers at the consumer meter points and pay for transmission and distribution from the NBP according to settlement volumes for each meter point.[6] Settlement volumes and profiles are determined from metered volumes by *supplier volume allocation*,[7] which is managed by Xoserve and different for each consumer sector as described next.

[5]There are 64 "direct connects" to large consumers, power stations, and interconnectors.

[6]The actual arrangements are somewhat involved. The best economic view of the arrangement is that shippers sell to suppliers at NBP, and that suppliers pay all costs downstream of the NBP.

[7]This is actually an electricity term but best describes the process.

Consumption

Power Station Consumption Power generation accounts for 30% of gas demand, and 34% of power generation output is fueled by gas in CCGTs. Combined heat and power accounts for around 5GW[8] of production, with the government intention to double by 2010, and the great majority of this being large stations. The last oil, nuclear, and coal plants were built in 1981, 1995, and 1974 respectively and since then virtually all new generation has been gas-fired. The relative amount of gas-fired generation in future will depend on CO_2 prices and regimes, nuclear power, restrictions on build (restrictions on section 36 consents, or repeat of an outright moratorium), subsidies for combined heat and power, and concerns about gas concentration for geopolitical and electrical system stability reasons.

Industrial and Commercial Consumption Industrial consumption follows diurnal, working day, and seasonal cycles but is not particularly weather sensitive. Supplier volume allocation for all large consumers is on a daily metered basis. Those that are connected directly to the NTS do not pay distribution charges.

For smaller industrial and commercial consumers, the supplier volume allocation arrangement is that the system operator assumes consumption according to the *annual quantity* (AQ, determined from meter reading history) and an assumed profile. Meter readings are subsequently used to scale up/back the settled quantity while retaining the profile assumption. Network costs are not retrospectively scaled.

Experience to date has shown limited ability or willingness to manage demand in relation to prices, even when wholesale price rises are very high. Historically, the great majority of industrial and commercial supply contracts have a degree of "swing"—so the consumer can deviate from his contractual profile to a limited degree, without variation to the contract rate. While making contracts simpler, this reduces the incentive to demand manage.

In the event of local or national gas supply emergency, power stations and large users are required to self interrupt. Some enter voluntary arrangements to do this, in return for lower charges.

Domestic Consumption Gas is consumed in domestic premises for space heating, with some cooking, and accounts for 35% of all gas demand. Gas

[8]*Gigawatts*. Power trades in MW. 1MWh = 3.6GJ (Gigajoules). For comparison, transmission, connected power station capacity is around 80GW.

accounts for 70% of U.K. domestic energy consumption. U.K. demand is very sensitive to weather,[9] and domestic demand variation dominates gas demand variation. There is high sensitivity in the "shoulder" periods at the beginning and end of winter, when consumers turn their heating systems on for the winter and then off. There is a theoretical maximum demand when heating systems run flat out all day and night. This causes a negative curvature of the demand/temperature curve at very cold temperatures, but no observed maximum. There is also a time lag of a day or so between the temperature change and the domestic response.

Domestic consumers currently pay a fixed rate to their suppliers for gas over an average period between meter readings and tariff changes, and there is therefore currently no price signal to encourage short-term demand management. This makes domestic consumption both inelastic in the short term, and exogenously determined by weather. Tariff innovation is increasing, but at this point tariffs to support demand side management are not supported by adequate metering and supplier volume allocation arrangements.

The settlement account for the shipper for a domestic meter point is equal to the AQ from the meter reading, with a profile assumption that is weather corrected related to *seasonal normal demand* (SND), and is unrelated to actual consumption. This is an important fact in the consideration of demand management. Actual consumption does however adjust the AQ for the following year.

Domestic gas consumption is extremely important from a practical and policy perspective. The seasonal variation in mortality and morbidity ensures an important welfare element to home heating, with *fuel poverty* defined as existing when over 10% of household income is spent on fuel. This limits the use of pure price as a demand side management tool, without additional arrangements such as direct government subsidy, support with heat efficiency measures, and tools and education for demand side management.

[9]There are many studies on the relationship between consumption and weather. For example, Timothy J. Considene, "The Impacts of Weather Variations on Energy Demand and Emissions," *Resource and Energy Economics* 22, no. 4 (2000), pp. 295–314. There are less studies on price impacts and this is much affected by storage information. See, for example, Xiaoyi Mu, "Weather, Storage and Natural Gas Dynamics: Fundamentals and Volatility," *Energy Economics* 29, no. 1 (2007), pp. 46–63.

The gas account of the system operator is made up by the domestic sector using the *reconciliation by difference* (RBD) method. This causes the metered consumption for the domestic sector to be scaled up[10] for settlement purposes.

Due principally to the lack of relevant safety mechanisms in domestic cookers, resupply after domestic isolation is a laborious process, and for this reason, domestic gas supply is prioritized over all other supplies of gas and power in a security of supply event. This has a significant effect on gas and power management during gas shortage, and on market structures and peak prices.

Demand Trends There are several factors causing long-term trends in demand. Recent winters have been warm relative to the 70-year average, and continued urbanization further increases the average domestic winter temperature. The persistence of the recent warmth may be associated with climate change. Energy intensity (consumption divided by gross domestic product) in the United Kingdom is falling, but GDP per capita and population are both growing slowly, and the proportion of gas of total consumption is increasing due principally to increase in CCGT percentage in generation, and increasing percentage of the population connected to the gas network. Ongoing increase in the average quality of home insulation will offset this in the future. It is believed that *demand destruction* has occurred as a result of recent rises in retail prices, but there are not yet enough data to confirm this.[11]

COMMODITY RELATIONSHIPS

Oil

Gas is commonly associated with oil underground. There are similarities between gas and oil in property rights, politics, exploration production, and processing techniques, and somewhat lesser similarities in logistics and downstream markets (this connection is enhanced by LNG and nongas

[10]This is up on average, due to theft and other unregistered consumption, and shrinkage changes. RBD absorbs the forecasting errors of the system operator's profiling and other assumptions. Financial losses to the system operator arising from default are paid by the whole sector on a pro rata basis by settled quantity, using the "neutrality" mechanism, rather than RBD.

[11]For example, around 3% reduction is factored into the National Grid forecast.

heating). Largely for this reason there is much commonality between oil and gas in the major global players.

The commonality of life cycle and players creates a price association[12] between oil and gas. This is much increased by long-term gas contracts. Due to the need for dedicated pipeline infrastructure, gas supply contracts have commonly been long term. To improve hedgeability, cost reflectivity, and reduce contract frustration risk, these are commonly indexed to oil prices.

This indexation has two effects. The first effect is to raise the short- and long-tenor volatility of gas prices from a "natural" commodity level, to the OPEC driven long-term volatility of oil prices. The second effect is to create a partial vertical integration.

Long-term contracts can have the effect of raising entry barriers and reducing competition and there is regulatory pressure to reduce them, which in turn reduces the oil indexation of gas.

Research on the American markets reveals evidence of mutual transmission between oil and gas market volatilities, with gas volatility persistence to market shocks being somewhat higher.[13]

Electricity[14]

The market price at *gate closure* (one hour ahead of delivery) for electricity is related to the cost of the marginal plant.[15] Gas and power prices are closely related when gas plant is at the margin. Depending on demand levels, carbon dioxide prices, and other fuel prices, gas-fired generation in the United Kingdom has been at the margin at different times.

Due to the high seasonality of gas prices and near absence of seasonality in coal prices (due to global movement and ease of storage), gas-fired generation commonly runs ahead of coal in the summer and behind in the winter, although this relationship does vary and is additionally dependent on CO_2 prices.

---

[12]Oil prices drive gas prices, but less vice versa. See Frank Asche, Petter Osmundsen, and Maria Sandsmark, "The UK Market for Natural Gas, Oil and Electricity: Are the Prices Decoupled?" *Energy Journal* 27, no. 2 (2006), pp. 27–40.

[13]Bradley T. Ewing, Farooq Malik, and Ozkan Ozfidan, "Volatility Transmission in The Oil and Natural Gas Markets," *Energy Economics* 24, no. 6 (2002), pp. 525–538.

[14]For details on the electricity market, see Chris Harris, *Electricity Markets: Pricing, Structures, Economics* (Chichester: John Wiley & Sons, 2006).

[15]Generators factor in the cycle costs and the efficiency costs for running at minimum stable generation, to their marginal costs.

The medium long-term (from about four years out) relationship is different. From the early 1980s to 2007 and beyond, new entrant generation has been dominated by CCGT and most plant has been designed and intended to run baseload. Therefore the long-term baseload power price has been set by gas. It is possible that power prices play a role in setting gas prices, but this is limited by the long nature of gas supply contracts, which partially decouples production elasticity from short-term price.

It is theoretically possible that the long-term baseload[16] price could be set by renewables instead of gas. This would be enhanced by a high *renewables obligation*[17] (RO), absence of banding[18] in the recycling of renewables buyout, high carbon dioxide prices, and limitations on gas build. In the long-term, clean coal and ultimately nuclear may set the long-term baseload price.

Carbon Dioxide

Power prices in the United Kingdom are closely connected to European Trading Scheme (ETS) CO_2 prices. Gas throughput variation has only a minimal effect on ETS prices, but ETS prices can effect the marginal generation.

For medium CO_2 prices, increase in CO_2 price improves the short-term competitiveness of CCGT compared to coal, but for very high CO_2 prices, increase in CO_2 price reduces long-term competitiveness of CCGT relative to renewable and nuclear power. Both gas and coal plant can be made (nearly) emission free, but this has high capital and running/consumable/efficiency costs and there are currently no Zero Emission Plants in the United Kingdom.

For very high CO_2 prices, the flow through to power prices would cause demand side management, which could in turn affect gas prices. CO_2 prices do not directly affect consumer take, because domestic production of CO_2 from gas is not taxed directly or indirectly.

CO_2 price dependence is also dependent on a number of ETS specifics, such as the evolution of banking and borrowing arrangements, CO_2 cap

[16]Baseload plant runs all day every day, except on maintenance.

[17]In 2006–2007, suppliers must supply 6.7% (rising to an intended 20% in 2020) of their power from renewables sources (demonstrated by RO certificates) or pay the buyout price, currently £33.24. This revenue was intended to go entirely to renewable generators.

[18]Currently all renewables generators receive one certificate per MWh of production. Under banding, different technologies may receive different amounts of certificate.

allocation to new plant, and classification of emissions under the ETS and Kyoto.

Coal

The head on competition between coal and gas is very limited in world terms and hence there is little mutual global price influence. However there can be fairly high medium-term correlation[19] of annual contract prices due to their dependence on oil prices.

Coal prices do have a short-term local impact on gas prices where gas and coal compete. This is affected by CO_2 prices. CCGTs are on average more efficient than coal and nuclear (55% versus 35%). Due to this and the higher hydrogen content in gas, in the UK 1MWh of power generated from gas produces only around 40% of the CO_2 generated from coal.

The recent relationship between power, gas, coal, and CO_2 prices is shown in Exhibit 36.1. While we can clearly see both short-term relationships in movements and long-term relationships in prices, the divergence can be significant and sustained.

Distillate

After market tightness in the winter of 2005–2006 and subsequent concerns over security of supply, a number of CCGTs (rising from the current 23% of installed capacity) are now capable of running on distillate oil. This in theory has the effect of capping the short-term gas price. There has however been little evidence of this to date.

Continental Gas

The interconnector creates a strong connection between the United Kingdom and continental prices, but this is limited by short-term transportation costs, long-term transportation cost recovery, pipeline limits,[20] liquidity

[19]Correlation is perhaps too formal a term for a price association. Intercommodity relationships are often more accessible to traders than econometricians, as they are fleeting and dependent on the prevailing price structures. For inter- and intra-commodity market integration analysis in the United States, see Lance J. Bachmeier and James M. Griffin, "Testing for Market Integration, Crude Oil, Coal and Natural Gas," *Energy Journal* 27, no. 2 (2006), pp. 55–71.

[20]For a study on the relationship between pipeline capacity utilization and price connection, see Augusto Rupérez Micola and Derek W. Bunn, "Two Markets and a Weak Link," *Energy Economics* 29, no. 1 (2007), pp. 79–93.

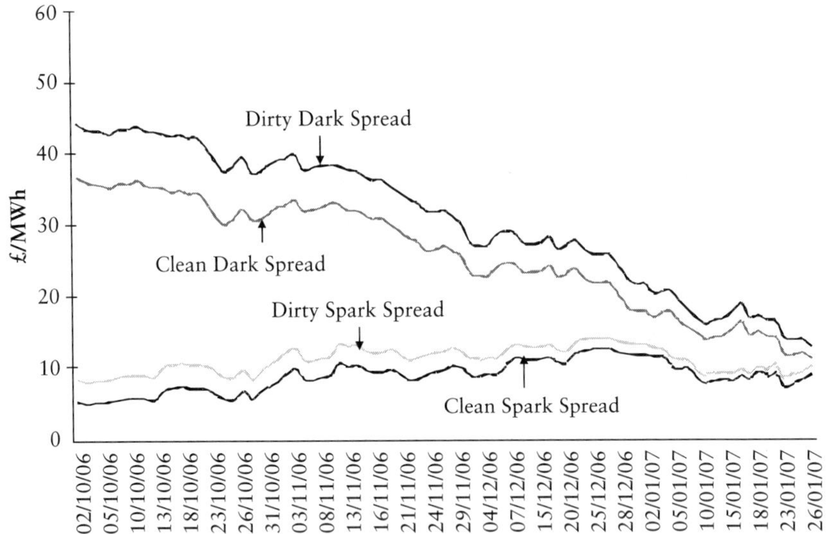

EXHIBIT 36.1 Convergence of Diverged Power-Gas (Spark) and Power-Coal (Dark) Spreads
Source: RWE npower.
Note: *Clean* denotes with carbon dioxide cost, and *dirty* is without. Contract month February 2007.

and logistics[21] of continental markets, market power at either end, and ultimately on national security of supply[22] policies that limit gas export at certain times.

Indexes

A number of indexes are directly relevant to gas, and have different degrees of liquidity. These are principally oil, temperature (at airports), composite weather variable (a better demand indicator than temperature), daily NTS

[21]For relatively low relationships between European hubs, see, for example, Anne Neumann, Boriss Siliverstovs, and Christian von Hirschhausen, "Convergence of European Spot Market Prices for Natural Gas? A Real-Time Analysis Using the Kalman Filter," *Applied Economics Letters* 13, no. 11 (2006), pp. 727–732.
[22]There is a degree of political risk priced into long-term contracts. See Frank Asche, Petter Osmundsen, and Ragnar Tveterås, "European Market Integration for Gas? Volume Flexibility and Political Risk," *Energy Economics* 24, no. 3 (2002), pp. 249–265.

exit volume, retail price index (regulated revenues are usually indexed to the retail price index), and electricity (currently the day ahead price as estimated by brokers).

PRICE STRUCTURES

Cross-Commodity Correlation

The cross-commodity relationships (particularly oil, coal, carbon dioxide and power) have diurnal/holiday/seasonal structures, are different across tenors, and are highly variable. Correlations are also strongly nonlinear (they change across different price levels).

Approximate correlation limits can be estimated by constructing a correlation matrix across all commodities and testing it for consistency (positive semidefiniteness[23]). For example, suppose that we have observed a 0.70 long-term correlation between gas and power (probably driven by oil as the exogenous variable), and that we reason that rising carbon dioxide prices will have a depressing effect on coal prices (say −0.20 correlation) and an indeterminate effect on gas prices due to opposed effects of generation substitution for coal, but overall demand reduction (try 0.00 correlation). The result from these estimates is shown in Exhibit 36.2.

Exhibit 36.3 shows the strong correlation in daily returns in practice. Note that these are both seasonal, and have an intraday structure.

It is important to note that the arbitrage relationships between commodities means that we should always examine cointegration (which is driven by absolute prices) as well as correlation (usually measured by price changes). As with correlations of returns, over a period we also witness

EXHIBIT 36.2 Self Consistent Correlation Matrix Constructed from First Estimate

	Coal	Gas	CO_2
Coal	100%	52%	−10%
Gas	52%	100%	−3%
CO_2	−10%	−3%	100%

[23]For a method of making the best self consistent matrix from an initial guess see Peter Jäckel and Riccardo Rebonato, "The Most General Methodology for Creating a Valid Correlation Matrix for Risk Management and Option Pricing Purposes," *Journal of Risk* 2, no. 2 (1999), pp. 17–24. This method is used in Exhibit NG.2.

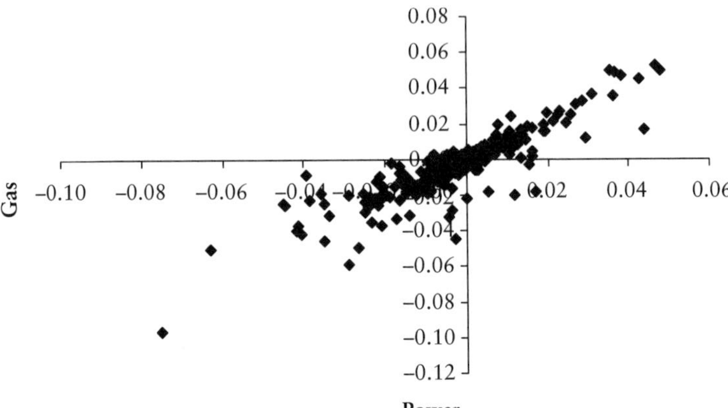

EXHIBIT 36.3 Correlation of Daily Gas and Power Returns
Source: Power data from RWE npower. Gas data from Spectron.
Note: February 2007 contract measured from May 2004 to February 2007.

relationships between prices, which have a seasonal and intraday structure. (See Exhibit 36.4.)

Forward Prices

The height and width of the winter peak is dependent on storage (volumes, injection and withdrawal rates, costs), domestic demand and demand management, general demand management, and CCGT running and flexibility.

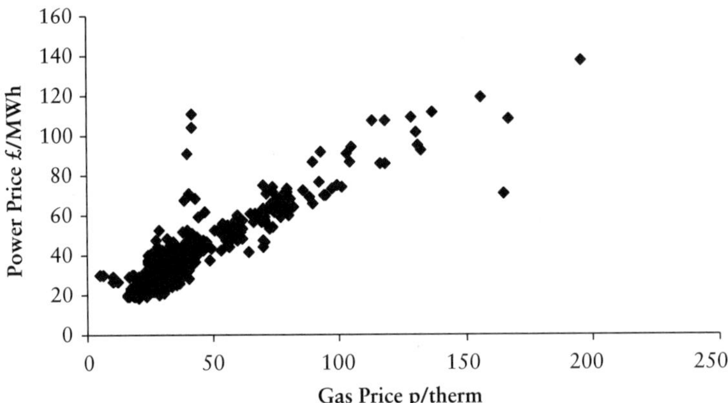

EXHIBIT 36.4 Relationship Between Day-Ahead Gas and Power Prices
Source: Power data from RWE npower. Gas data from Spectron.
Note: Period May 2004 to February 2007.

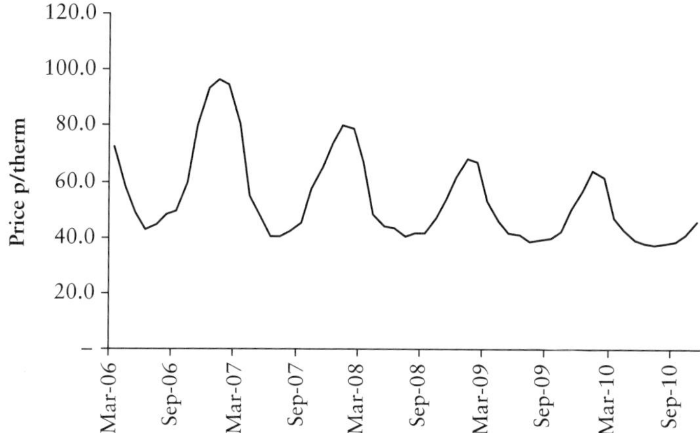

EXHIBIT 36.5 Seasonality of Gas Forward Price
Source: RWE npower.

The peakiness of the forward curve could be greatly affected by altered arrangements for charging for capacity, particularly in the networks and pipelines. The current seasonal structure is shown in Exhibit 36.5.

Volatility

The common volatility formula that works relatively well for gas is $\sigma_\tau = (a + b\tau)e^{-c\tau} + d$, where σ_τ is the instantaneous volatility,[24] and τ is the contract horizon. The *Samuelson effect* often referred to by economists, is associated with a positive a, and b serves to tilt the short to medium term volatility curve to improve the empirical fit to the prices of traded options. The "c" represents the speed to which resources can be mobilized or consumption can be changed to respond to price changes. Spot volatility ($a + d$) is commonly around 200%. Long-term volatility d[25] is dependent

[24]The average (option) volatility is found by integrating the square of this over the time period in question. This is a commonly used empirical formula without a perfect association to a price process. For further explanation on local volatility, see Riccardo Rebonato, *Volatility and Correlation* (New York: John Wiley & Sons, 1999).

[25]The parameter d can be estimated in a number of ways. For example, the decay of the persistence of shocks with contract tenor may be nonexponential. For a study of persistence of Henry Hub gas on NYMEX (but with an opening assumption of $d = 0$ and which we infer from the term structure of persistence) see Donald Lien and Thomas H. Root, "Convergence to Long-Run Equilibrium: The Case of Natural Gas Markets," *Energy Economics* 21, no. 2 (1999), pp. 95–110.

on calibration choices, and 10% is a workable figure. It is raised by the connection to oil, and currency fluctuations.

Volatility exhibits seasonality with observation time and also with contract delivery date, and because of the storage arbitrage (which raises the correlation between contracts of different tenors—the so-called "decorrelation[26] curve").

The absolute level and the term structure of volatility will be much affected by infrastructure build, demand management, and charging methodologies for capacity.

Over the long run, gas appears to have followed oil in having an approximately stationary (constant) volatility term structure prior to 1973, and then again after 1973 but at a higher level,[27] and a relatively increased elasticity, reflecting a flexible response to increased intensity of gas usage.

Swing

Before the growth of terminal markets, gas was traditionally supplied through long-term "take or pay" contracts. In these contracts, the buyer could vary the daily and annual take at the contract price, between certain limits. These had the convenience of guaranteeing a certain level of revenue for the producer (corresponding to the minimum annual take) while providing consumer flexibility up to a degree (with infrastructure requirement determined by the maximum take). For power stations, these were commonly *burner tip*, meaning that the gas had to be consumed if taken, and could not be on-sold. Increasingly, these contracts are becoming market contracts not dedicated to consumption, and can be provided from any player to any other in the form of *swing* contracts.

Swing contract valuation has enjoyed a great deal of academic attention due to the practical requirement for valuation and the ability to apply standard derivative techniques under some (rather limiting) assumptions

[26]For further information on price relationships, including correlation, see Alexander Eydeland and Krzysztof Wolyniec, *Energy and Power Risk Management: New Developments in Modeling, Pricing and Hedging* (New York: John Wiley & Sons, 2002).
[27]See Noureddine Krichene, "World Crude Oil and Natural Gas: A Demand and Supply Model," *Energy Economics* 24, no. 6 (2002), pp. 557–576. Alternatively, a principal components analysis can be done. See Boriss Siliverstovs, Guillaume L'Hégaret, Anne Neumann, and Christian von Hirschhausen, "International Market Integration for Natural Gas?: A Co-integration Analysis of Prices in Europe, North America and Japan," *Energy Economics* 27, no. 4 (2005), pp. 603–615.

(particularly the assumptions relating to long tenor and seasonality of volatility).

Cost of Risk

Most produced commodities have a positive cost of risk for long-term contracts (so the forward price is below the expectation of outturn), because producer costs are locked in before consumer requirements are known. However, oil is a possible exception because equity markets have a strongly positive cost of risk and stock basket prices are negatively correlated to oil prices. There is no general agreement on the net effect for gas. Most researchers believe that short-term cost of risk is negative (players avoid being short). This is because gas prices are limited on the downside but practically unlimited on the upside.

Distribution Shape

There are several problems with modeling distribution shapes in gas. The general lack of econometric consistency affords us less opportunity to observe distribution shape, and the periodicity and impacts of storage and changes in demand management make distribution shapes periodic and variable. Gas does exhibit price spikes[28] (about four per year of double the prevailing price) but their height and width depend on specifics and are hard to characterize. Negative prices are rare and transient, but they have occurred during interconnector commissioning. In general, the structure is similar to other commodities (lognormal with fat tails), with the fat tail driven largely by the temperature dependence of demand and the effect of the failures of large elements of the infrastructure (such as the Rough field). With a relative absence of demand management, there remains uncertainty about government intervention in relation to security of supply, which has an effect on prices during shortage events. We can clearly see the fat tail in the actual evolution of prices, as shown in Exhibit 36.6.

There is no price cap or regulatory value of lost load (VOLL) in the U.K. gas market. It is important to note that while power experiences strongly heterogeneous uses which cause an economic value of lost load about 1,000 times the baseload price, gas is mainly used for heating. Heat stores relatively well and the marginal economic VOLL of heat is relatively

[28]For further information on commodity price development, see Hélyette Geman, *Commodities and Commodity Derivatives* (Hoboken, NJ: John Wiley & Sons, 2005).

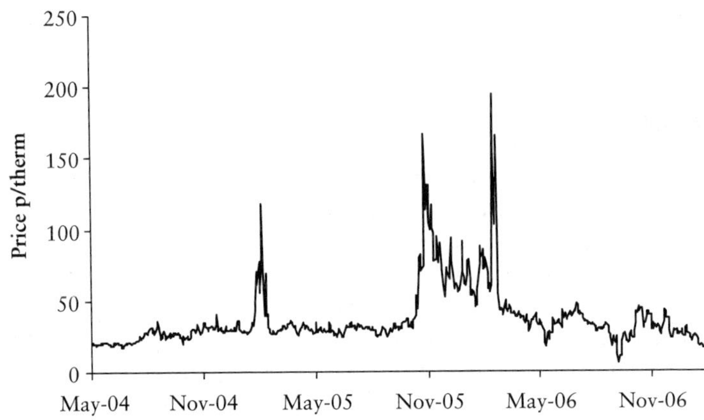

EXHIBIT 36.6 Gas Day Ahead Price Development
Source: Gas data from Spectron.

low. Studies[29] to date have indicated an economic VOLL of £5–£25/therm,[30] with energy intensive users being in the middle of this range.

Chaotic behavior of gas prices in the United Kingdom would indicate a trading opportunity. One study[31] of gas prices on the New York Mercantile Exchange (NYMEX) indicates no sign of chaotic behavior.

CONCLUSION

Natural gas at the national balancing point in the United Kingdom is a mature and liquid market. The overall trend of the forward price, its periodicity, its volatility and related behavior, and its term structure correlation are driven by production fundamentals and relationships, demand, demand elasticity, storage and information about storage. The relationships between gas and power, coal, oil and carbon dioxide are complex, periodic and variable. These are accessible from an economic standpoint but less so from an econometric standpoint, due to the transient nature of many relationships. The degree of demand elasticity is a key driver of volatility, and we have

29For example, see *Economic Implications of a Gas Supply Interruption to UK Industry*, ILEX Energy Consulting Ltd (2006).
30The market trades in therms. 1 therm = 0.0293MWh (megawatt hours). The price as of mid-2007 was around £0.4/therm.
31Victor Chwee "Chaos in Natural Gas Futures?" *Energy Journal* 19, no. 2 (1998), pp. 149–164.

seen that while the residential sector accounts for the greatest variation in demand, and has the potential to be the most elastic, it is in practice inelastic. Institutional changes to improve demand management may change volatility, price and price relationship structures substantially, and some of these changes may affect the relative price of NBP gas to upstream and downstream gas. The related issue of security of supply has significant political impact and there exists the possibility of significant government intervention in the gas system. Storage plays a key role in smoothing gas inflow to the system and price volatility, and the rapid development of storage projects could have a significant affect on price seasonality, short-term volatility, and term structure correlation. The connection to continental gas is dependent both on current interconnector utilization, and pipeline capacity management on the continent.

CHAPTER 37

Emissions Trading in the European Union

Stefan Ulreich, Ph.D.
Generation/Upstream
E.ON AG

Since January 1, 2005, an emissions trading system has started in the European Union (i.e., the EU-25, hereafter simply EU) established to provide an economic efficient tool for the abatement of greenhouse gas emissions. The purpose of the emissions trading system is to allow companies to find the cheapest possible CO_2-abatement options. A market for CO_2-allowances has emerged and developed into a vivid trading place throughout the EU. During the Bali conference in December 2007, the newly elected Australian government ratified the Kyoto Protocol. Other countries such as Norway, Canada, and Japan are considering a similar trading scheme in 2008. Countries such as the United States, which do not consider greenhouse gas abatement as necessary, have not ratified the Kyoto Protocol. However, in the United States, some regional activities have begun, the Regional Greenhouse Gas Initiative (RGGI) for example.[1]

Exhibit 1 shows the distribution of the emissions over various countries. Due to the economic growth, especially in China and India, the total emissions will increase in the future. China is expected to become the biggest emitter in a few years.[2]

BACKGROUND

The Kyoto Protocol

The background for the EU Emissions Trading System is the Kyoto Protocol. The signatories of the Kyoto Protocol have committed themselves to reduce

[1]For more information about RGGI, please refer to http://www.rggi.org.
[2]See UNFCCC, http://ghg.unfccc.int.

EXHIBIT 37.1 Global CO_2 Emissions, 2003 (26.1 billion tonnes)[a]

Country	Share of Global CO_2 Emissions
U.S.	21.7%
EU-25	14.8%
China	14.2%
Russia	5.8%
Other Asian countries	4.9%
Japan	4.7%
India	4.2%
Near East	4.2%
South America	3.2%
Africa	3%
Canada	2.1%
South Korea	1.7%
Australia	1.3%
Other countries	14.2%

[a]In contrast, global emissions in 1990 were 21.9 billion tonnes.
Source: Exhibit created from data obtained from UNFCCC.

the output of greenhouse gases to the atmosphere. Since the majority of scientists are viewing greenhouse gases as responsible for global warming, the Kyoto Protocol is viewed as the first global step against anthropogenic-induced (i.e., man-made) climate change. The protocol defines goals for the years 2008 until 2012. Since the EU wants to be on the forefront of climate protection, the EU emissions trading scheme started with a test phase for the period from 2005 until 2007. The test phase, however, is a somewhat misleading notion: The trading system is fully operational and obligatory for installations falling under the EU directive. Covered activities are, for example, emissions of electricity generation, steel production, and paper industry.

The basic idea is simple. Governments allocate allowances for a trading period to those companies who are obliged to take part in the emissions trading scheme. The allocation is done by a *national allocation plan* (NAP). Once a year, each installation covered by the emissions trading scheme has to meet its obligations by redeeming an amount of allowances corresponding to the emissions of the installation. Once the national allocation plan is settled, each company knows its amount of allowances and can decide whether to buy allowances on the market or to abate CO_2 emissions by technical measures and investments in their installation. A company that cannot meet its obligations has to pay a fine—and additionally to buy the missing amount of allowances on the market. The fine is €40 per ton for the trading period 2005 to 2007 and €100 per ton for the trading period 2008 to 2012. This mechanism guarantees that the environmental goals are fulfilled. The EU-installations will not emit more CO_2 to the atmosphere than the overall allocation of the EU national allocation plans.

As an example, consider a steel producing company that has been allocated with 1 million emission allowances. These allowances are generated in the electronic registry and were calculated based on the historical output data of the company. To fulfill environmental goals, the allocation is less than the historical output. The company now has the following choices:

- Produce less steel than before, and sell the unneeded allowances.
- Produce more steel than before, and buy the needed allowances.
- Identify abatement options that allow for more steel production with less emission.

In all cases, the emission allowance price is now an additional driver of the economic decision. In the case of high emission allowance prices, it might be attractive to invest in an abatement measure or to produce less.

Emission Allowances

To fulfill environmental goals and to establish a market, the total allocation is below the expected emissions of a business as usual scenario. The scarcity guarantees demand for emission allowances. The most relevant greenhouse gas is carbon dioxide CO_2—and the EU concentrated in the first two trading periods on this greenhouse gas.

The allowances are valid only in their trading period; that is, an allowance allocated in the year 2005 can be used to fulfill obligations for the year 2005, 2006, and 2007. Since banking of allowances is not possible, it cannot be used for the obligations in the year 2008. Similarly an allowance allocated in the period 2008 to 2012 is valid for the obligation in 2008 to 2012. As the annual allocation will take place before the obligation has to be fulfilled, it is rather unlikely that a plant operator will be short in the first years.

Whereas the NAPs for the first trading period are implemented, except for some legal disputes, the NAPs for the second trading period are only drafts in some cases. While EU commission wanted to receive all NAP drafts until June 30, 2006, only four member states delivered by that time. Nevertheless, the market is actively trading the allowances of the Kyoto period, but the risk of political decisions is considered by participants.

Emission allowances only exist virtually in electronic registries. Each EU member state has one registry in place. Transfers between the registries are done electronically in order to establish a European market. Each plant is equipped with an account where the emission allowances are allocated. Similar to electronic banking, transfers to other accounts on any other European registry can be done. To fulfill the obligations due to the Emissions Trading Directive, the allowances can be canceled. The registries offer access via the internet (see Exhibit 37.2). Opening an account is not restricted to plant operators—any individual can establish a private account in a registry and take part in emissions trading.

Predecessors of the EU emission trading scheme are the NO_x and SO_2 trading systems in some regions of the United States. Until there are regulations developed, emissions are a free good and their costs remain a burden to society as a whole. Thus no emission reductions will take place. A trading

EXHIBIT 37.2 Internet Links to the European Registries[a]

Registry	Web Site
Austria	http://www.emissionshandelsregister.at
Belgium	http://www.climateregistry.be
Czech Republic	http://www.ote-cr.cz
Denmark	http://www.kvoteregister.dk
Estonia	http://khgregister.envir.ee
Finland	http://www.paastokaupparekisteri.fi
France	https://www.seringas.caissedesdepots.fr
Germany	https://www.register.dehst.de/
Greece	http://WWW.EKPAA.GR
Hungary	www.hunetr.hu
Ireland	http://www.etr.ie/
Italy	http://www.greta-public.sinanet.apat.it/
Latvia	http://etrlv.lvgma.gov.lv/
Lithuania	http://etr.am.lt
Netherlands	http://www.nederlandse-emissieautoriteit.nl
Portugal	https://rple.iambiente.pt
Slovakia	http://co2.dexia.sk
Slovenia	http://rte.arso.gov.si
Spain	http://www.renade.es
Sweden	http://www.utslappshandel.se/
United Kingdom	http://emissionsregistry.gov.uk
Europe	http://ec.europa.eu/environment/ets/

[a]As of February 2007.
Source: Exhibit created from data obtained from EU communications.

system for CO_2, SO_2, or NO_x internalizes the costs by the "polluters pay" principle.[3]

Each market participant should be aware of the strong political influence on this market. Liquid trading will only occur after the regulatory framework is set and the market participants can rely on it. Changes to the framework during an allocation period should not occur, since they can have a dramatic influence on price formation and can lead to erratic price jumps.

OPERATIONAL TRADING OF EU ALLOWANCES

Operational Trading

Operational trading of emission allowances started long before the EU directive on emissions trading passed the EU parliament and before the 25 national allocation plans were approved by the EU commission. Of course, trading turnover initially was rather low due to the lack of knowledge about the details of the national allocation plans. Yet, this period was important not only because of the price signals in the market it provided, but due to valuable infrastructure for emission trading that was developed.

The necessary preparations required by a company for operational emissions trading are often underestimated. There are, for example, activities such as the development of a master agreement. Deals are usually done via telephone or via electronic platforms. To make these deals legally binding, but also to allow the traders to concentrate on the essential data (i.e., traded commodity, price, and volume), master agreements are used. This legally binding document defines details such as delivery location and delivery date, payment schedules, and specifies certain rules for dealing with credit and delivery risk. Spot market trades with only a few days between delivery and payment need less strict rules than forward market trades. For the latter, delivery and payment dates may occur in some years. Thus master agreements for forward deals are more complex. *Force majeure* was a long-discussed topic during the time before the allowance registries were in place—since the delivery of the allowances needs both an account for the seller and an account for the buyer in the electronic registry. So what to do in instances where the registry is not yet in place and delivery cannot be executed had to be defined legally. This is a common problem in commodity

[3]Cyriel de Jong, André Oosterom, and Kasper Walet, "Dealing with Emissions," Chapter 10 in *Managing Energy Price Risk,* edited by Vincent Kaminski (London: Risk Books, 2004), pp. 373–393.

markets. Based on the long-term experience in European electricity trading, the European Federation of Energy Traders (EFET) developed a master agreement for emissions trading that is used to a large extent in European emissions trading.[4] One of the most important purposes of the first emissions trading deals was to conduct a thorough testing of the master agreements using lawyers of several companies of different sectors. This helped considerably to create one commonly accepted master agreement.

Apart from this legal aspect, which is generally addressed by market participants themselves, there are further overarching issues faced by market participants such as taxes, the legal framework of trading in general, and the integration of emission allowances into the balance sheet of a company. By doing first trades, personnel in a company responsible for these issues became aware of the problems and developed solutions for their companies in preparation for trading. Unfortunately, some of these issues cannot be answered by companies on their own. Instead, companies have to wait for decisions on taxation from national tax authorities or for a clear description of accounting rules as set forth by the International Accounting Standards Board. Though these issues to a varying degree exist as of this writing, they are not viewed as a serious impediment to trading.

Companies with a high degree of active risk management were naturally among the leaders in the European emissions trading scheme, especially the international companies in the oil, gas, and electricity sectors. These companies are accustomed to commodity trading and already have the necessary infrastructure. By modifying their well-established trading and back-office processes, these companies could integrate operational trading with emission allowances quite easily. Companies with a less intense trading experience in commodity trading had to use consultants to a large extent in order to build up their trading infrastructure. Some of them were not ready for trading when the EU scheme started in 2005. For smaller participants, however, it made sense to outsource their trading activities. Due to transaction costs, for these participants a market approach via an intermediary is more cost efficient than building their own trading infrastructure with in-house trading expertise.

Currently the trading with allowances happens predominantly in the *over-the-counter* (OTC) market where market participants meet bilaterally, often with the help of a broker. Exchanges are becoming gradually more important as the market matures; their market share is expected to increase further in the next few years, following the general experience in other commodity or financial markets. The one major advantage exchanges offer is

---

[4]The latest version of the master agreement for electricity and the annex for emissions trading can be found on the EFET web site at http://www.efet.org.

that they can eliminate credit risk (i.e., counterparty risk). In a market with participants from 25 EU countries, most of the potential sellers and buyers never transacted before. For example, an electricity producer in Finland has usually never been in contact with a cement producing company in Portugal. Thus, most of the participants cannot assess the credit risk of all the other trading partners. Exchanges can resolve this difficulty. Furthermore, exchanges are useful as reliable sources for market prices, especially for smaller and medium sized companies because they can also offer easy access to the market. So far there are seven allowance exchanges in Europe:

- EEX (Germany)
- Nordpool (Scandinavia and Finland)
- EXAA (Austria)
- Powernext (France)
- ECX (Netherlands)
- NewValues (Netherlands)
- SendeCO_2 (Spain)

Currently under development are allowance exchanges in Poland and Italy. Every exchange is open to participants from the 27 EU member states as well as to non-EU members. It should be understood that a concentration of trading will start quite soon, since the allowance market will not be big enough to allow for so many exchanges. An exchange needs some critical trading activity in order to operate profitably. Some experts think that two or three allowance exchanges will survive in the end.[5]

Apart from brokers active on the emissions markets such as Spectron, TFS, and ICAP, the exchanges publish information for both market prices for EU allowances and daily turnover.[6] This increases the transparency of the market and as a result confidence in the market price by participants will grow. Another reason for confidence in the market price is that due to arbitrage the price differences between the OTC market and the exchanges are usually within the bid-ask-spread. The market is now liquid enough that arbitrageurs would make use of wider price differences and immediately

[5]Peter Koster [of ECX] and Patrick Weber [of Dresdner Kleinwort Wasserstein], "What Will Drive Survival in the Consolidation of Exchanges?" Presentation, Carbon Expo 2006, Cologne.

[6]The German EEX is publishing the spot and the future quotes of EU allowances on its web site at http://www.eex.de. Since the EEX—for European Electricity Exchange—is primarily an electricity exchange, prices for the electricity market are shown there as well.

buy in the cheaper marketplace in order to sell at the more expensive. This mechanism is so efficient now that price differences practically do not occur.[7] Most markets are organized by continuous trading, however, some exchanges still offer auctions. Like in other markets, exchange and broker quotes are collected and made available for the public together with comments on the market. While this is done by established news providers such as Dow Jones, Reuters, and Argus, there are also specialized companies such as the Norwegian PointCarbon that provide this service.

Price History and Price Formation

Since 2000, deals with EU emission allowances are done on a forward basis. The price of the EU allowances was assessed by the knowledge and opinion of buyer and seller on the details of the allocation in the current status of political discussion. So a high degree of uncertainty was present. In markets, uncertainty leads to a wide bid-ask-spread. By learning more about the details of the EU directive, the general framework of emissions trading, and the national allocation plans, the bid-ask-spread narrowed, signalizing the increasing certainty. For example, in February 2003 buyers offered €3.50/tonne, whereas sellers asked for €7.50/tonne. So the average market price was at €5.50/tonne with a spread of €4.00/tonne. By mid-2007, this spread narrowed to €0.10/tonne, sometimes even to €0.05/tonne.

The relationship between the spot and the forward prices of the same trading period is given by the interest rate prevailing between the two dates of delivery. That is,

$$\begin{aligned}\text{Forward price} = \ & \text{Spot price} \times \exp(\text{Interest rate} \\ & \times \text{Time difference between deliveries})\end{aligned}$$

Due to the banking options, any changes on the spot market (or the forward market) immediately affect the forward market (or the spot market). In this respect, emission allowances can be seen as zero-coupon bonds.

The market price of about €5.00/tonne mentioned already existed for a long time on the market due to the situation outlined above. Deviations from this market price started in the middle of 2003, as can be seen in Exhibit 37.3. These changes were mainly induced by political decisions.

[7]The data provider PointCarbon shows the daily settlement prices in its *Carbon Market Daily*. Using PointCarbon and Spectron data, on January 12, 2007, the spot price on the EXAA was €3.94/tonne; on the EEX €3.99/tonne; on the ECX €3.95/tonne; on the Nordpool €4.00/tonne; and on the Powernext €3.98/tonne. The OTC settlement price for this date by the broker Spectron was €4.00/tonne.

EXHIBIT 37.3 Price Quotes for EU Emission Allowances (euros/tonne)
Source: Exhibit created from data obtained from OTC Market data collected by the author.

The approval of the emissions trading directive by the EU, for example, led to an increase in market prices. By then it was clear that the commodity traded so far will have a market value on January 1, 2005. A price increase of €13.00/tonne was the result. The first drafts of the NAPs had a price dampening influence due to the generous allocation announced in these plans. These drafts have been criticized by the EU Commission as being out of line with the climate goals. As a consequence, the market reacted by firmer prices. In the second half of 2004, market prices moved in a narrow band around €9/tonne. Interestingly enough, by this time the market started to be driven more by fundamental factors rather than political influences. With the final approval of the 27 national allocation plans of the EU, the political framework was set. The EU Commission cut the NAP drafts by 290 million allowances, thus ending with a total EU allocation of 2.184 million allowances. Some NAPs were still under discussion during 2005 (e.g., the revision of the UK NAP). Nevertheless, the market followed most of the time fundamental factors.

In the beginning of 2005, mild temperatures, the low demand for electricity due to the holiday season, and an above-average power production by wind in Scandinavia and in Northern Germany led to softer prices of emission allowances. However, by the end of January 2005 the scenario changed completely and prices climbed to a level that had not been expected by most market participants. The main reason was the development of market prices for natural gas. The price changes in the gas market were immediately translated into a change for allowance prices since power plants are usually driven by the price difference between production costs (i.e., fuel and allowance prices to the market prices for electricity).

Fundamental Drivers of the Carbon Market

Weather is a major influence on the price formation on the spot market for electricity, affecting both the demand and the supply sides. Higher demand for electricity is usually satisfied by fossil-fueled power plants, since nuclear and hydroelectric facilities are covering the base load. As a consequence, the higher demand for electricity leads to increasing CO_2 output. Generically, above-average temperature in winter leads to a lower demand for electricity, while above-average temperature in summer leads to a higher demand. This is due to the fact that air conditioning is used to a much greater extent. This effect was clearly seen in the summer of 2005 in Southern and Western Europe (i.e., Spain, Portugal, southern France, and Italy). Furthermore, high temperatures in the summer can lead to cooling water problems in some areas of Europe and so the nuclear electricity production will be lowered. This happened in 2005 in France, for example.

Precipitation is the main influence factor for hydroelectric production. Annual hydroelectric production by country is shown in Exhibit 37.4. The more CO_2-free hydroelectric power available, the less fossil-fueled power plants have to run and vice versa. The drought in Southwestern

EXHIBIT 37.4 Annual Hydroelectric Production (in TWh)

Country	1980	1990	2000	2004
Austria	28.9	32.3	43.3	38.7
Germany	18.0	21.0	28.9	27.5
Spain	30.4	26.2	31.4	34.1
France	69.8	57.2	71.0	63.8
Italy	46.4	34.6	50.2	49.3
Portugal	7.9	9.1	11.6	10.0
Sweden	58.1	71.4	77.8	60.1
Norway	83.1	120.3	141.1	108.5

Source: Exhibit created from data obtained from EURELECTRIC.

Europe in 2005 led to an enormous reduction of the power produced by hydroelectric plants, especially Spain which had to use much more fossil power plants than anticipated. The deviations of the annual hydroelectric production in most European countries are in the magnitude of order of some TWhs; that is, the resulting deviations in the CO_2-inventory have the magnitude of order of some million tonnes.[8]

The dominating influence for the price of EU allowances in 2005 came from the primary fuel markets for coal, gas, and crude oil. The fuel switch from coal to gas is one of the rare fast options to abate CO_2 immediately and without any lengthy preparation time. It depends, however, on whether the power plant portfolio can realize the switch, that is, sufficient capacities of coal and gas plants have to be available. In Europe, mainly the United Kingdom and the Netherlands, fulfill this prerequisite. The decision to run a coal plant or a gas plant can then be done on a daily basis. This decision will be based on the fuel prices for gas and coal, on the market price for electricity, and the EU allowance price. With the price hike of natural gas that occurred in 2005, gas plants became much more expensive than coal plants. Just with an allowance price high enough, the use of gas plants could be justified on an economic basis. This, however, is precisely the goal of the emissions trading scheme—first to incorporate the carbon price in decisions and second to give incentives toward less carbon-intensive production. Consequently, the natural gas price increase together with more or less stable coal prices led to the price increase of emission allowances. Since the power plants in the rest of Europe also took the carbon price in their daily operating decisions into account, the effect of the higher carbon prices spread over Europe. Apart from this, the high electricity prices in the United Kingdom also led to greater exports from France into the United Kingdom via the so-called "interconnector"[9] and thus the electricity price in France increased, leading in turn to more imports of France from the neighboring countries.

The fact that the fuel switch is more or less the only option to abate CO_2 is not enough to explain why the switch from coal to gas is dominating the markets. The other factor is, that power producers in the United Kingdom were allocated with rather tight emission rights, thus having almost the entire burden of that national's abatement goals. In contrast, industrial

[8]As a rule of thumb, one can use for a rough estimate 1 kg/kWh CO_2 output for a coal plant and 0.5 kg/kWh for a gas plant. Modern plants have better values such as hard coal plants with 0.75 kg/kWh. However, for the purpose of estimating the magnitude of order the factor 1 kg/kWh (or 1 million tonnes/TWh) is more convenient.

[9]The interconnector is a DC connection between France and United Kingdom through the English Channel with a capacity of 1.000 MW.

plants in the United Kingdom received an allocation almost perfectly matching its demand. The tight allocation led to a risk-averse strategy; that is, electricity sold on the forward market was immediately hedged on the allowance market. To this end, the emission allowances needed for the production of the sold electricity were bought on the market. Consequently, the demand for allowances was quite high and failed to correspond to an increase on the supply side, for example, due to selling activities by industrial plants.

A fundamental price driver for all sectors covered by the emissions trading scheme is economic growth. A higher industrial output results in higher CO_2 emissions, leading to a growth in the demand for emission allowances. It is expected that this dependence will weaken in the future due to the interest of the industry and the electricity companies to reduce their CO_2 output. This is comparable to the situation in the 1970s with the crude oil price hike. Higher energy efficiency was induced by a dramatic oil price increase, and similarly the climate goals will set further incentives for a more efficient use of energy. In the literature, models for the carbon market basically rely on the marginal cost curve for abatements. Changes in supply and demand lead to modifications of this curve and thus to different market prices.[10]

Obviously, apart from the price drivers connected with political and regulatory issues, we mentioned factors purely in relation with electricity and heat generation. To some extent it is surprising because in Europe 57% of the allowances were allocated to the power and heat sector, whereas a share of 43% was given to industrial installations. Nevertheless, industry has not been an active player in the emissions market so far for several reasons.

First, the industrial sector has a rather high share of small installations with rather low total emissions per year. For example, in Germany there are 1,278 installations with annual emissions less than 50,000 tonnes per year. The total emissions of all these plants are less than 4% of the total allocated amount of the German installations falling under the Emissions Trading Scheme. These companies just use the market for meeting their obligations and do not actively trade. Furthermore, for most companies in the industrial sector the activity of trading is itself a challenge. Most companies still struggle with implementing the infrastructure needed for trading or are looking for external portfolio managers. Additionally, some of these companies are

---

[10] Bo Nelson and Clas Ekström, Influence of the future oil price on CO_2-abatement costs, the energy system and climate policy (29th IAEE International Conference, Cleveland (Ohio), 2006) pp. 1–2, Per-Anders Enkvist, Thomas Nauclér, and Jerker Rosander, A cost curve for greenhouse gas reduction (The McKinsey Quarterly 2007, Number 1) pp. 35–45.

still expecting (or sometimes hoping) for economic growth. This leads to the fear that the allocation might be insufficient. Companies that routinely trade do not share these thoughts because they just think in terms of risk management and would buy the needed amount and sell the surplus depending on their view on the price.

Publication of Emission Inventory

The most dramatic price effect in 2006 was due to the information policy of the EU registries in that year. In April and May 2006, the data of the emission inventories of the EU member states for 2005 was published. Since this happened in a rather uncoordinated way, most of the member states information was provided at a single moment to the market. Instead, each state published the data on its own. There were major news items: (1) the allocation was much higher than the total emissions of 2005; and (2) the allocation of the energy sector was short, whereas the industrial plants possessed the whole length of the market (see Exhibit 37.5). The length was even larger than the shortage; however, since the length could not enter the market because risk-averse participants did not sell their oversupply, market prices for emission allowances are still positive.

The EU representatives are now aware of the market influence that news on emission inventories have and they promised a better solution in 2007 when the publication of the data for the year 2006 will take place.

In the end, the fact that the market is virtually long led to a huge price drop: in mid-April 2006 the quotes for emission allowances exceeded €30.00/tonne, the low in mid-May was less than €9.00/tonne. After these events, prices stabilized for a few months around €15.00/tonne. Since more and more participants having an oversupply of allowances felt some selling pressure, prices since then gradually started going down to a level below €3.00/tonne as of the end of January 2007.

EXHIBIT 37.5 Allocation Information: EU Trading Sectors

Sector	Share on Total Allocation in EU	Length (+)/Shortage (−) of Allowances in Mt. for 2005
Electricity and Heat	59%	−35 Mt
Cement. Lime and Glass	11%	+17,2 Mt
Oil and Gas	8%	+13,1 Mt
Metal	11%	+35,1 Mt
Pulp and Paper	2%	+9,9 Mt
Others	11%	+26,6 Mt

Source: Exhibit created from data obtained from CITL.

Products in the Allowance Market

Spot and Forward Products So far the trading products have not been specified in detail. Emission allowances are traded in a spot and in a forward market. Within the spot market, delivery, and payment are done within a few business days. This is comparable to a stock market. Delivery happens via an electronic transfer in the registry. On the forward market, December 1 was established as the delivery date. This is due to the fact that late in the year the companies know their annual emissions quite well and so they face less price risk, but more volume risk. Volume risk in commodity markets, however, is preferably hedged on the spot market to keep the delivery risk as low as possible. So far there are two delivery dates in the EU, December 1, 2005 and December 1, 2006. For both dates, no problems with delivery was observed. As one would expect, the closer the time to delivery, the more liquid the product. Volatility, however, operates in parallel and depends on the forward market not largely on the time to delivery. Basically, the banking mechanism is responsible for this. As long as the interest rate between two relevant delivery dates does not show tremendous volatility, the price movement is parallel. For example, in January 2007, the traded products have delivery in December 2007, December 2008, and December 2009. Since the spot product is in the same trading period as the December 2007 forward, there is a risk-free arbitrage opportunity and thus the price difference between spot and 2007-forward is defined by the relevant money market interest rate. As allowances of the first trading period 2005 to 2007 lose their validity in the trading period 2008 to 2012,[11] there is no arbitrage relationship between the allowances for these two periods. It is generally assumed that after 2012 banking will be possible without any restrictions.

The typical size of OTC and exchange deals is 10,000 allowances, corresponding to the emission to 10,000 tonnes CO_2. With the already mentioned market price prevailing in the beginning of January 2007, these standard deals have a size of €40,000.

In contrast to other markets, there is one special rule concerning the registries: The allowance account shall never contain a negative number of allowances, that is, one cannot go short. Thus the forward market is also a vehicle to go short.

---

[11]In fact, some countries like France and Poland allow for banking of 2005–2007 allowances to the period 2008–2012. However, these amounts are tied to the condition that a real abatement project took place successfully and are furthermore restricted to plants in the mentioned countries. Thus the volume of bankable allowances is quite small and cannot lead to a reasonable arbitrage between the two trading periods.

As already mentioned, direct access to the market is also possible for individuals in the OTC market as well as to the exchanges. Additionally, there are intermediaries offering market access. Some banks have even developed certificates which are indexed to the price of emission allowances and are sold to their retail customers.

Option Market for Emission Allowances An option market for EU allowances has also emerged, but shows only limited liquidity. Whereas spot and forward prices are quoted regularly by brokers, this is not the case for options.[12] The value of an option is determined by the well-known Black-Scholes formula since emission allowances can be considered as shares without dividends. Some more complex models (e.g., GARCH) have already been used to study the price dynamics of EU allowances.[13] Due to the different phases of price and volatility behavior[14] in the returns (see Exhibit 37.6), these papers suggest the use of Markov switching and AR-GARCH models for stochastic modeling. The findings reported in the literature strongly support the adequacy of the models capturing characteristics such as skewness, excess kurtosis, and, in particular, different phases of volatility behavior in the returns.

Market participants expect the options market to become more vibrant in the Kyoto phase 2008 to 2012. Regulatory uncertainties should then be minimized and the spot and forward markets drive by fundamental factors.

The value of a deferral option (i.e., the decision to postpone a project) can be of particular interest for the decision-making process in companies, especially when considering a large number of projects. These considerations do not play a role in the current CO_2 market, but were shown to be important in the U.S. Acid Rain program.[15]

---

[12] A public available source for option prices on EU allowances is available from the European Climate Exchange ECX (http://www.ecxeurope.com). Volumes are still low.

[13] See Eva Benz and Stefan Trück, Modelling the Price Dynamics of CO_2 Emission Allowances, Working Paper, Graduate School of Economics Bonn, 2006; and George Daskalakis, Dimitris Psychoyios, and Raphael N. Markellos, Modelling CO_2 Emission Allowance Prices and Derivatives: Evidence from the European Trading Scheme, Working Paper, 2007.

[14] The different phases of price and volatility behavior are mainly a result of unexpected events due to regulatory uncertainties initially which in turn were due to unexpected weather situations or fuel market events.

[15] Hung-Po Chao and Robert Wilson, "Option Valuation of Emission Allowances," *Journal of Regulatory Economics* 5, no. 3 (1993), pp. 233–249.

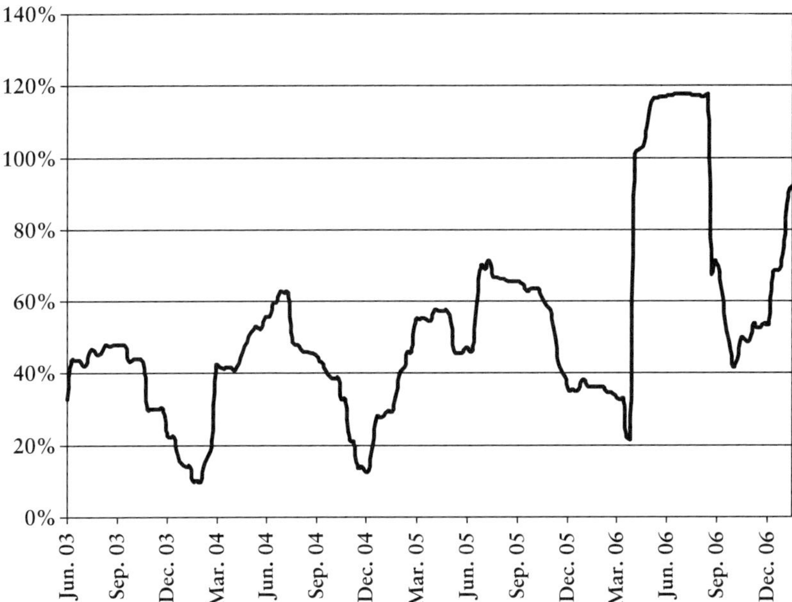

EXHIBIT 37.6 Historical Volatility: EU Allowances Calculated Using Spot Prices[a]
Source: Exhibit created from data obtained from OTC Market data collected by the author.
[a]For comparison, the implied volatility quoted by the ECX in January 2007 was 62%.

Project-Based Mechanisms Apart from emissions trading, there are two other flexible mechanisms mentioned in the Kyoto Protocol: joint implantation and clean development mechanism. With a *joint implantation* (JI) project an abatement project is done in another country with a Kyoto goal. The investor has to pay for the project, whereas the seller country has to subtract the abatement from its national abatements in order to avoid double counting. A *clean development mechanism* (CDM) project is done in a country without Kyoto goal, so the seller country has no further duties. However, all these projects have to follow certain rules and have to be validated, certified, and monitored by several independent authorities to ensure trust in these mechanisms. Project developers often hedge their delivery risk by using EU allowances. Exhibit 37.7 shows how different influence factors work on the emissions trading market. The hedging of project risks by using the forward market of allowances already plays a crucial role in the market. Furthermore the project based mechanisms also work on market sentiment—the expectation of more (less) supply by these projects induces bearish (bullish) market signals.

EXHIBIT 37.7 Influence Factors and Their Weights on Emission Allowance Market Prices Used by Société Générale in Its Weekly Research Papers.[a]

	Weight	15.1.	22.1.	29.1.
Market Fundamentals	**65%**	**2,2**	**2,9**	**2,6**
Demand	70%	2,2	3	2,4
Weather	40%	3	4	2
Power	40%	1	2	2
Industrial Activity	20%	3	3	4
Supply	30%	2,2	2,8	3,2
Gas versus coal	30%	2	4	2
CDM and JI hedging	50%	2	2	4
Industrial abatement	20%	3	3	3
Market Signals	**35%**	**2,9**	**2,6**	**2,6**
Market Momentum	20%	2,4	2,8	2
Traded volumes	40%	3	4	2
Technical Analysis	60%	2	2	2
Market Sentiment	80%	3	2,5	2,7
Oil prices	30%	2	3	3
Policy changes	50%	4	2	2
CDM and JI projects	20%	2	3	4
Total Trend		**2,4**	**2,8**	**2,6**

Source: Exhibit created from data obtained from Société Générale.
[a]Scoring: 1 = strongly bearish; 2 = bearish; 3 = neutral; 4 = bullish; and 5 = strongly bullish. The total trend in this model indicates a slightly bearish market movement.

Further Development of the Market: The Second Phase

In 2008, the second phase of the EU emissions trading scheme will start. So far the complete framework is not known in detail since most of the NAPs only exist as drafts—the emissions trading directive will not be changed. Active trading already takes place and the market for allowances of the second phase is firmer than for the 2007 allowances (see Exhibit 37.8). The basic reason is that everybody expects that the EU will cut the draft NAPs severely.

Nevertheless, in this phase some changes will occur. The EU plans to include a new participant: International air transport. Links to other schemes are considered, especially to Norway and to the Californian system. This can be seen as a first sign in extending the emissions trading scheme to a global one that is so necessary to combat climate change. For 70% of the global CO_2 emissions of 2003, the following countries or country bubbles were responsible: United States, European Union, China, India, Russia, Japan, Canada, South Korea, and Australia. In particular, China and India will

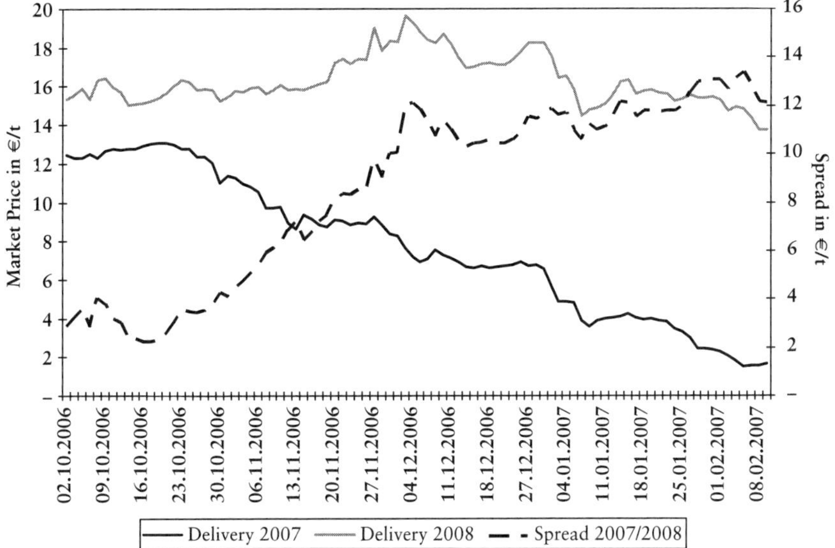

EXHIBIT 37.8 Price Quotes for EU Emission Allowances with Delivery in 2007 and 2008 and Its Spread (euro/tonnes)
Source: Exhibit created from data obtained from OTC Market data collected by the author.

experience massive increases in their annual emissions due to their tremendous economic growth and their hunger for energy.

As a consequence, this could lead to a real global market for a product with a pure environmental background. This will very likely not happen in the second phase, but will definitely take more time. However, there are now also initiatives driven by the industry with the vision of a global carbon market.[16] Within the EU it is very clear that emissions trading will also take place after 2013.

CONCLUSION

The market for emission allowances had some infant diseases but nevertheless still shows an increasing liquidity with potential for growth. Most market participants expect that allowance trading will realize enhanced liquidity in the next few years as regulatory issues are clarified. By linking

[16]One of them is the 3C Initiative. More information can be found at http://www.combatclimatechange.org.

schemes of other countries to the EU emissions trading scheme, the market has the potential to become a global one.

So far trading is mainly concentrated on the spot and forward markets. Due to the presence and strong trading activities of pure financial players, the further development of derivatives is very likely and the emergence of an options market is looming. There are several reasons for financial players to act in this market. First, emission allowances are a new asset class with interesting correlations to weather, fuel prices, and economic growth. As a result, some banks already have developed products for their retail customers based on allowance prices (e.g., index certificates). Second, it offers new opportunities for national and international project finance as well as the development of asset-backed securities. Finally, allowance prices have become an important issue for equity analysts to evaluate companies.

CHAPTER 38

The Fundamentals of Agricultural and Livestock Commodities

Ronald C. Spurga
Vice President
ABN AMRO Bank

Unlike the increased prices for commodities on energy and metals the market for agricultural products was not as profitable over the last years. After the consideration of inflation some agricultural commodities even showed a negative performance. Due to higher productivity in industrial and developing countries the supply was increasing and prices were under pressure. With increasing risks like global warming, illnesses/pandemics of plants or animals, higher prices of transportation, and problems of free trade and subsidies between developing countries and the two large free-trade regions, European Union (EU) and NAFTA, volatility of commodity prices could rise again. This chapter will provide an overview over the most important types of agricultural commodities and livestocks, namely grain, cattle, and hogs, as well as their fundamental influences.

GRAIN

The production, distribution, and processing of grain and oilseeds by U.S. firms represent a multibillion-dollar industry. This section focuses on the most important of these crops: wheat, corn, and soybeans. We will also briefly touch on lesser crops, such as barley, sorghum grain, oats, flaxseed, and rye. It should be noted, however, that many of the major grain companies also trade in these lesser crops.

Wheat

Wheat is divided into five classes: hard winter wheat, soft red winter wheat, hard spring wheat, durum, and white wheat.

Hard winter wheat represents the largest wheat class. It is grown in the Great Plains states of Colorado, Kansas, Nebraska, Oklahoma, and Texas. Kansas is by far the largest grower. This class of wheat has high protein content and is primarily used for bread and quality baking flour. It is deliverable on the Kansas City Board of Trade (KCBOT).

Soft red winter wheat is lower protein wheat, which is grown in the central and southern states. It is the second-largest wheat class in terms of production. It is primarily used in cookie and cake manufacturing. This class of wheat is deliverable on the Chicago Board of Trade (CBOT).

White wheat is similar to soft red winter wheat in protein and usage. It is grown in the Northwest and exported primarily out of the Pacific Coast.

Hard spring wheat is the highest protein wheat produced, which is used in quality breads. Produced in the north central states: Minnesota, North Dakota, South Dakota. This grade is deliverable on the Minneapolis Grain Exchange (MGEX).

Durum is used in producing semolina, which is used in the production of macaroni (pasta) products. It is grown in the same area as the hard spring wheat.

The winter wheats are planted in the fall and harvested in the summer, while the spring wheats are planted in the spring and harvested in late summer. The majority of domestic grain is either exported or milled into flour. The remainder of the usage is divided between feed and seed. The major exporters are the Russian Federation (and other countries of the former Soviet Union such as Ukraine), China, Japan, Eastern Europe, Brazil, Egypt, Iran, and South Korea. Other major exporting countries are Argentina, Canada, Australia, and the members of the European Union.

Corn

The two major classes of corn are yellow corn and white corn, with yellow being by far the predominant class. The major growing areas are the central states, that is, Iowa, Illinois, Minnesota, and Nebraska. Corn is planted in the spring and is harvested in the fall. Domestically, the primary use of corn is for feed, either directly to livestock or following a milling process. Processed corn is also used for human consumption and for the production of high-fructose corn syrup. Another potential market for corn is in the production of ethanol for gasohol. The major export markets for corn are Japan, Russia, Spain, West Germany, Italy, Poland, Taiwan, and Korea.

Soybeans

The classes of soybeans are yellow, green, brown, and black, with the predominant class being yellow. The major growing areas for soybeans are the midwestern and south central states, and the leading producers are Illinois and Iowa. Soybeans are planted in the late spring and harvested in late fall.

The soybean has little commercial use in itself; however, processing yields soybean meal and oil. Soybean meal is a high-protein livestock feed that is also being used increasingly as a protein and mineral fortifier in baking goods and sausage meats.

Soybean oil, after being refined, is added to vegetable shortenings, margarines, and salad oils. It also is used in oil paints and varnishes.

The major export markets for soybeans are Japan, the Netherlands, West Germany, and Spain. Brazil and Argentina are also major soybean producers.

The following represents an overview of the services provided by the elevator, merchandiser, and exporter and identifies certain common industry practices and risks. It must be pointed out that the industry is extremely complex and that the following represents a very general broad-brush approach.

Storage

Country Elevators Grain that moves into merchandising channels is normally first purchased from the producer or stored for the producer by a country elevator. The grain is usually brought to the elevator by truck. A sample is weighed and graded, and the grain is either purchased or stored by the elevator. If stored for the producer, the elevator issues a warehouse receipt. Normally, the weighing, sampling, and inspection at country elevators is not done by individuals employed by official agencies. The grading of the grain is critical as prices are based on the grade. Such things as test weight per bushel, damaged kernels, foreign material, moisture content, and so on, are considered when determining the appropriate grade.

In addition to grade, wheat is also classified by protein level, with the higher proteins usually being traded at premiums. Wheat and corn are graded from number 1 to number 5 plus a United States sample grade that does not meet the grades 1 through 5 requirements. Grade number 1 is the most favorable. Soybeans are classified by grades 1 through 4, with a United States sample grade for those that do not meet the grades 1 through 4 requirements. During the period of time that the grain is stored, it is important for the elevator to maintain the quality of the grain, as it is responsible for delivering to the receipt holder a specific amount and quality of grain.

In addition to grain storage, the country elevator provides drying, cleaning, scalping, and automatic sampling, for which fees are normally charged. The elevator also uses its drying and cleaning equipment to improve the grade of grain it purchases for its own account, which enables it to receive a better price on resale.

Two major risks that are associated with the storage of grain are quality deterioration and the possibility of the grain being destroyed, that is, through fire and elevator explosion. The maintenance of grain quality and condition is a function of warehouse management and proper equipment and is probably best evaluated by observing the experience of the warehouse and through checking with other firms in the industry. Deterioration of the grain through explosion, fire, and so on, can be covered by insurance and can also be reduced by proper operating procedures. Research is actively being done on the causes of grain explosions; and equipment is being designed to reduce the levels of grain dust, to better ventilate elevators, and to better measure concentration of gases and vapors. The insurance that is maintained should cover the value of both the real estate and grain, as well as the business interruption.

Terminal, Subterminal, and River Elevators The next step in the merchandising chain usually involves the grain moving directly into the processing industries; or being sold as feed; or being sold to terminal, subterminal, or river elevators. These elevators usually have a larger storage capacity and more efficient grain handling equipment than the country elevators and are situated on major transportation lines. These elevators serve the purpose of aggregating grain in convenient locations for bulk movement into export channels or domestic processing. Purchases are usually made from country elevators or merchandisers, and grain is stored for merchandisers and processors.

When the grain leaves the country elevator, it is weighed and graded before a bill of lading is issued by the carrier. If the elevator is not an official station, the grain is again weighed and graded en route at an official station. The official weight and grade are then sent along with a draft to the terminal elevators. The drafts are pro forma, calling for a 90% payment of the contract price. When the grain is received at the terminal elevator, it is again weighed and graded, and the remainder of the draft is paid. The drafts are normally documentary sight drafts and are collected through banking channels. The use of a negotiable bill of lading allows the grain to be traded frequently while en route.

The terminal elevators represent the major inland storage facilities, and certain elevators are designated as good for delivery on the grain exchanges. Grain can be received at these elevators by truck, rail, or barge; and one important factor in their success is the equipment and capacity they have to receive and load out grain. Normally at these elevators, grain is sampled, weighed, and graded by either employees of official agencies or by employees licensed under the United States Grain Standards Act. When these as well as other requirements are met, the weights and grades are considered official and are used in conducting trade. The terminal elevators provide the same services as country elevators, and the major risks associated with storage are the same.

Exchange Elevators Each one of the three-grain exchanges has designated elevators that are acceptable for delivery of the particular grain being traded. Before an elevator is declared "regular" for delivery on the CBOT, it must be inspected by the exchange. The CBOT may require that all grain in the elevator be removed and inspected and graded and that new receipts be issued. The elevator must also have appropriate rail facilities and must have adequate equipment for the receiving, handling, and shipping of grain in bulk. Appropriate bonds and insurance must be in place, and the warehouse must be in good financial standing. Records must be maintained of all grain received and delivered daily by grade and of grain remaining in store at the end of the week.

The warehouses are inspected at least twice a year by the exchange. The warehouses that are designated as "regular" for delivery of corn, wheat, and soybeans are located in switching districts in Chicago (47.3 million bushels), Toledo (45.4 million bushels), and St. Louis (16.9 million bushels) and are elevators of the major grain merchandisers and cooperatives. All warehouse receipts that are eligible for delivery on the CBOT must be registered with the exchange, and the exchange verifies signatures.

In order for a warehouse to be "regular" for delivery on the Kansas City Exchange, it must be licensed as a public warehouse by the federal government, or Kansas, or Missouri; and its capacity must be at least 100 bushels. The elevator must have appropriate facilities and rail connections and be of unquestioned financial standing. At a minimum, its net worth should be 15 cents per bushel, based on aggregate capacity. The elevator must be appropriately bonded and insured. The elevator's status as "regular" for delivery must be renewed annually. Total capacity for deliverable grain is 84.2 million bushels.

Export Elevators The main function of the export elevator is to move the grain from the inland transportation, that is, rail, barge, or truck, and place it on ships. A fee is charged for this service, which is known in the industry as "fobbing." The fee is a per-bushel charge; and, therefore, the elevator's capacity to unload and load the grain is crucial. To increase utilization, elevators will enter into throughput agreements with shippers, in which the shipper agrees to process a certain amount of grain through the elevator. Storage represents a minor portion of the operations of the export elevator as income to the export vessel. As the grain leaves the elevator and falls into the vessel, it is weighed and graded, based on a sample; and a mates receipt is issued. The mates receipt is the title document. The mates receipt is then exchanged for a bill of lading. Export elevators provide the same services as the terminal and country elevators.

Merchandising

An integral part of elevator operations is the merchandising of grain. The aim of the elevator is to use its capacity to the fullest extent. This is done by turning over the grain as quickly as possible and only storing grain when it is necessary from a marketing viewpoint or in order to use existing capacity. Ideally, the elevator, when purchasing grain, would like to immediately be able to sell the grain at a price that would cover its handling charges and provide a profit. This is not always possible, however, as the elevator must be able to service its customers and is, therefore, forced to buy when they are ready to sell. In this event, the elevator has the ability to hedge its purchase on one of the grain exchanges. Normally, elevators will be constantly in touch with other elevators and merchandisers, receiving bids for grain to be delivered at specific locations at specific times. The elevator can then discount transportation and interest charges and knows what to bid for grain. If there are no active buyers, the elevator can use the prices quoted on the grain exchanges as the base from which to discount transportation and interest costs. As the price of grain can be extremely volatile and as the elevators and merchandisers trade large amounts of grains in relation to their capital, their merchandising and hedging policies are of critical importance.

Merchandising Risk There appear to be three aspects to the merchandising risk: credit, contract cancellations, and transportation risks.

Credit

Generally speaking, supplier credit is not extended in the industry. Domestic sales are normally on sight draft against documents. The drafts are drawn for 90% of the contract value and are accompanied by bills of lading, weight certificate, certificate of grade, and other necessary shipping documents. These drafts are normally collected through bank channels; thus the seller does not release the title document (bill of lading) until the draft has been paid.

This drafting procedure reduces the credit risk associated with domestic transactions. The credit exposure taken by the seller is reduced to the 10% of the invoice price not covered by the draft. This 10% is paid by the buyer after weighing and sampling the grain. While in theory this 10% should be outstanding for a short period of time, transportation and paperwork delays may, according to industry sources, cause this payment to be deferred for a number of months.

Bulk shipments are normally made by rail or barge. A normal hopper carries 3,500 bushels, while a barge will carry 43,000 bushels. Rail shipments of 75 cars are now being made, due to transportation discounts; and multibarge shipments may be sold to substantial customers. The significance of this 10% exposure is obviously dependent upon the capital of the selling firm and the size of the transaction.

International transactions are normally shipped on confirmed or advised letters of credit (sight or time) or cash against documents. If time drafts under letters of credit are used, the drafts are normally discounted without recourse by a bank. Credit exposure is therefore limited to the instance in which the advising bank refuses to negotiate drafts although properly presented under a letter of credit. This exposure represents a sovereign and foreign bank risk that is similar to the risk when shipping CAD (cash against documents).

Contract Cancellations Grain companies commit themselves far in advance of shipment dates to purchase and sell grain. These commitments are normally either hedged or done on a back-to-back basis. Elevators may contract to purchase grain from producers in advance of the harvest or contract to purchase grain from the other elevators or merchandisers for deferred delivery.

In the event that the supplier of the grain defaults, the firm will have to either buy back its hedge or go into the open market and buy the grain. In a rising market, generally speaking, a loss will be sustained equal to the difference between the price at which the buyer contracted to purchase the grain and the open market price. In the event of a buyer's default, the firm could suffer a loss in a declining market.

Transportation

The ability to transport grain by the cheapest and most efficient manner is critical to a firm's profitability. The responsibility for providing transportation is dependent upon the terms of sales. The predominant modes of domestic transportation are barge and rail. Railroad hopper cars are the most frequently used to obtain transportation when needed. If the terms of sale require that the grain be in a railcar at a Gulf of Mexico port at a specific time, and due to a car shortage a timely delivery is not made, a default may exist. In order to reduce the risk of car shortages and also reduce rail charges, the large firms will lease or buy hopper cars.

The same situation exists with barge transportation, and the larger firms also maintain a fleet of barges. In addition to shortages of transportation, a risk that may be lessened by controlling railcars and barges, delays in the transportation system represent a separate risk. Barge transportation may be delayed due to low water levels or congestion on the rivers. Rail delays occur primarily when export elevators are unable to process the railcars quickly enough. The cars get backed up, and a rail embargo may be declared.

The inland transportation must also be coordinated with the arrival of the export vessel, as demurrage will be incurred if the grain is not in place when the vessel is in port and will also be incurred if the grain arrives early and the railcars or barge cannot be unloaded. Demurrage charges on large shipments can run up to $8 million to $10 million per day. In addition, the firm's capacity to load large quantities of grain at a given time will improve margins, as freight rates will be reduced.

As an example, railroads have recently introduced discounted rates for movement of grain in units of 75 cars. A firm that is able to take advantage of this discount can be more competitive than a smaller firm. The major grain firms have departments whose sole responsibility is coordinating transportation.

Summary of Major Risk

It appears that the major risks associated with elevator and merchandising operations are elevator explosion and fires, which are reduced by proper insurance coverage; grain deterioration, which can be controlled by adequate operating procedures; and inventory losses due to price fluctuations, which can be mitigated by a well-conceived hedging program. Contract defaults also represent a potential risk to a firm; however, defaults are reportedly rare in the industry.

The risk associated with receivables, which is common in any industry, is generally reduced to 10% of the invoice volume for domestic sales, due to their drafting procedure, and normally consists of a country and foreign bank exposure on foreign sales when unconfirmed letters of credit and CAD terms are used.

While the industry has developed methods of controlling their exposure to inventory price fluctuations and credit risks associated with their sales, such external factors as weather and transportation are out of its control.

Firms within the industry are therefore subject to reduced volume and lower margins due to a poor harvest or transportation delays. As the industry is very competitive, it is important that the grain delivery system be run in an efficient manner; or a firm may have the normally thin margins eliminated through excessive demurrage charges, grain deterioration during transportation, and so on.

As with any industry, the risk involved in this industry must be applied to individual firms; thus contract defaults or even the 10% credit exposure on receivables may be significant, depending on the size of the firm in relation to the contracts in which it deals.

Processors

The processing of grain is becoming concentrated to a greater degree with the large agribusiness firms. Discussions with firms in the industry indicate that the future of the industry lies with the larger firms and that the single processing firm is a dying breed.

Flour Milling The majority of wheat is milled for flour. Mills are normally established to process particular classes of wheat whose flour is used for different purposes. Hard winter and hard spring wheat produce a flour suitable for quality breads, due to its high protein content. Soft winter wheat is used to produce flour for baking and cookie and cracker manufacturers, while durum wheat produces semolina, which is used in the manufacture of pasta products. The extraction rate from the wheat is approximately 72%, with the remaining 28% classified as "millfeed," which is used in animal feed. The millers will purchase grain directly from farmers, elevators, or merchandisers and normally have elevator capacity at the mill to store the grain prior to processing. The grain is normally purchased on sight draft terms from the elevators and merchandisers. The flour is then sold to bakers or jobbers on draft or open-account terms of up to 60 days or, for the larger firms, retailed under their own name.

Milling firms used to book business out to 120 days, which did not include carrying charges to the buyer. In the recent environment of high interest rates, the free carrying charge period has been reduced to 60 days. The wheat futures markets are actively used by the firms to hedge inventory and purchase and sales commitments. While there is not a futures market for flour, there is an active physical market with prices quoted for the various types of flour. The price of flour is affected by the price of wheat as well as by the price of millfeed, which is also traded in physical markets. If the millfeed market is particularly strong, the miller may be able to reduce the price of flour in relation to the income being earned by millfeed sales. One other major factor in a mill's operation is transportation costs. The mill is affected by the cost of transporting grain to its facilities and also the cost of shipping the flour and millfeeds to its buyers. If the firm is able to take advantage of freight discounts through bulk loading, it will better be able to maintain its margin.

Corn Milling Two processing methods are used for corn: dry milling and wet milling. The dry milling process produces grits, cereal products, feed, meal, oil, and industrial products. The wet milling process produces, in addition to the products just mentioned, high-fructose corn syrup, which is used as a substitute for sugar. Corn will normally produce about 66% starch, which is used in making the syrup, 30% feed materials, and 3% oils. The feed products and high-fructose corn syrup, while not traded on a futures exchange, are traded actively in physical markets.

Soybean Processing The processing of soybeans results in soybean meal and soybean oil, both of which are traded on the Chicago Board of Trade. Trade standards are maintained for soybean meal according to the trading rules of the National Soybeans Processors Association (NSPA). The meal is used primarily as a livestock and poultry feed and is both consumed domestically and exported. The soybean oil that is initially extracted from the soybean must be degummed and refined before it is used for edible or industrial purposes. Grade and quality standards are established by the NSPA for crude soybean oil and crude degummed soybean oil. The refined oil is primarily used in food processing, although there are industrial uses in the production of soap, varnish, paint, and so on.

It is estimated that out of a 60-pound bushel of soybeans, the processor gets between 10 and 11 pounds of oil and between 47 and 48 pounds of meal. The basic profitability of a soybean processing operation is reflected in the price relationship between the bean and the meal and oil. This relationship is known as the "crushing margin." A wide crushing margin will result in a high utilization of crushing capacity, while a small margin will cause cutbacks in production. World markets determine the prices of the bean, oil, and meal; and it is, therefore, difficult for a company to control its margins. Due to the potential for sharp price swings in the bean, oil, and meal markets, firms normally hedge on the Chicago Board of Trade.

Risks

Some of the risks associated with the processors are similar to those identified with elevator operators. As both the price of the raw material (corn, wheat, and soybeans) and the end product can fluctuate widely, open positions represent a risk. It is therefore useful to understand the company's hedging policy with regard to its inventory and forward commitments. Loss through fire and explosion and deterioration of the grain or end product are risks that can be reduced by proper operating procedures and insurance coverage. Selling terms extended by the processor are generally more liberal than those extended by the grain merchandiser, as open account terms of up to 60 days may be granted to the baker, feed manufacturer, and so on, while the processor will purchase on sight draft terms. Transportation costs are also important; and normally, the greater its control over its transportation, the better the firm is able to maintain its margins.

Demand According to the U.S. Department of Agriculture (USDA) the world wheat consumption was 609.25 metric million tons in 2004. Consumption in key countries, such as India and Nigeria, is fueling the new high, as are record consumption levels in the countries of the former Soviet Union and in Europe.

The United States, according to the USDA, is the leading user of corn worldwide (228.23 million metric tons), followed by China (134.0 million metric tons), and the European Union-25 (EU) (50.6 million metric tons).

World soybean use climbed from 189.96 million metric tons in 2003–2004 to an estimated 205.65 metric tons in 2004–2005 (USDA).

South American exporters are expected to capture the biggest share of expanding global trade for soybeans and soybean products, much of which will be directed toward meeting China's skyrocketing demand. Led by Brazil, exports from South America have set record highs every year for nearly a decade, surpassing U.S. foreign trade for the first time in the marketing year 2002–2003 (USDA).

Even modest increases in domestic use will squeeze supplies available for export, however, with the result that larger price differences between the United States and foreign competitors could develop, driving down soybean exports to 1,040 million bushels by 2013–2014, compared with 1,060 million bushels in 2004–2005. And a strong expansion in foreign exports within the next 10 years could reduce the U.S. global soybean market share to 29%, compared with 45% in 2002–2003, according to the USDA Economic Research Service.

Supply The USDA estimates world wheat production at an estimated 627 million metric tons in 2004–2005. The following statistics are also from the USDA.

The EU leads wheat production worldwide with a production of 122.94 million metric tons in 2005–2006, followed by China (97 million metric tons), India (72 million metric tons), and the United States (57.28 million metric tons). Top exporters are the United States (27.22 metric million tons), Australia (16.5 metric million tons), and Canada (16.5 metric million tons).

In 2005–2006, the United States produced 57.3 million metric tons of wheat, compared with 58.7 million metric tons in 2004–2005, a decline of 2%. Exports were also lower due to smaller sales to China.

The USDA anticipates that hard wheat supplies should continue to tighten, with *hard red winter* (HRW) and *hard red spring* (HRS) wheat falling to 9- and 10-year winter lows, respectively. The tight supplies of HRW are the result of strong foreign demand, primarily in Nigeria and Iraq; and HRS tightening is due to lower production as well as to strong foreign demand. *Soft winter wheat* (SRW) exports could improve, on the other hand, due to higher SRW acreage and less competition in soft wheat.

Global corn production is estimated to total 708.38 metric million tons in 2004–2005 versus 623.04 metric million tons in 2003–2004. The United States, which dominates the global corn market, exported a total of 46.99 million metric tons in 2005–2006. The second-largest exporter, Argentina, provided 10 million metric tons in 2005–2006.

Worldwide soybean production has been on a steady climb, from 186.75 metric tons in 2003–2004 to an estimated 215.3 million metric tons in 2004–2005. Record Brazilian production and large newcrop supplies in the rest of South America are helping to pressure U.S. exports.

Trading

Whenever grain is purchased or sold, the firm is exposed to a price risk until the transaction is offset by either a physical purchase or a sale or is hedged on one of the futures exchanges. In assessing the risk associated in financing elevators or merchandisers, it is important to understand their hedging policy. Some aspects of a policy that should be addressed are the size of the net position that the firm is willing to maintain, the timing between taking a position and offsetting it with a physical or futures transaction, whether weekend positions are maintained, and the way physical trading is conducted after the exchanges close. While hedging reduces the price risk associated with carrying inventory, it does not eliminate it.

Once a transaction is hedged, the risk exists that the spread between the futures price and the price of the physical grain will move against the firm. This risk can be highlighted by the following example.

On April 2:
Firm purchases 5,000 bushels of wheat at $4.25/bushel
Firm sells 1 futures contract on the CBOT for May delivery for $4.35

On April 10:

Firm sells 5,000 bushels of wheat at \$4.35/bushel	\$0.10 profit
Firm buys back May future at \$4.46	–0.11 loss
Net	\$0.01 loss

If the pricing of the physical grain had increased more than the price of the May future, a profit would have been made on the hedge. The potential for disparity between price movements of the physical grain and the futures price is especially evident in the case of wheat, which has the three different classes traded primarily on three different exchanges. While soft winter wheat is primarily traded in Chicago, hard winter wheat in Kansas City, and hard spring wheat in Minneapolis, large transactions in all three classes are hedged in Chicago due to that exchange's larger volume. The prices of the three classes at times move independently, which increases the risk of hedging the hard wheats on CBOT. Prices demonstrate variation in the price movement. In connection with a firm's hedging philosophy, its policy toward hedges that are moving against it should also be discussed.

One other area that should be mentioned in conjunction with a position risk is basis pricing. Grain firms often enter into contracts to buy or sell at a specific spread over a specific contract month on one of the exchanges; for example, purchase of 40 cents over the May Chicago wheat, soft red wheat at the Gulf. Either buying or selling the May Chicago Wheat contract places the hedge. In the preceding examples, a hedge would be placed by selling the May contract. The firm would, therefore, be protected against price movements in the volatile futures market between the time the purchase commitment was made and the physical grain was sold. The price risk is reduced to a basis risk, which is less volatile. Thus, if at the time the grain was sold the basis dropped to 38 cents over the May future, a 2-cent loss would be incurred.

This example requires a thorough understanding of basis—the difference between the local cash price of a commodity and the price of a specific futures contract of the same commodity at any given point in time. In other words, Local cash price – Futures price = Basis.

Local cash price	\$2.00
December futures price	–2.20
Basis	–\$0.20 December

In this example, the cash price is 20 cents lower than the December futures price. In market "lingo," you'd say the basis is "20 under December." On the other hand, if the cash price was 20 cents higher than the December futures price, you'd say the basis is "20 over December."

Local cash price	\$2.20
December futures price	−2.00
Basis	+\$0.20 December

Basis, in a sense, is "localizing" a futures price, which represents the world price for grain, and is used as a benchmark in determining the value of grain at the local level. The fact that basis reflects local market conditions means it is influenced by a number of factors, including transportation costs, local supply and demand conditions, interest/storage costs, and handling costs and profit margins.

Paying attention to basis can help futures traders make informed decisions about whether to accept or reject a given price or a particular buyer or seller. Basis can also help clarify when to purchase, sell, or store a crop, depending on whether the current price is stronger or weaker than the average basis. And if basis improves or equals your estimated basis level, it could be a sign to close a hedge by purchasing or selling a commodity. Finally, a quoted basis from a deferred futures month that is more attractive than the nearby futures month could help determine whether, when, and in what delivery month to hedge.

The CBOT offers five characteristics of basis that futures traders need to keep in mind when timing purchases and sales:

- Basis tends to have a consistent historical pattern.
- Basis gives a good frame of reference for evaluating current prices.
- Basis usually weakens around harvest.
- Basis tends to strengthen after harvest.
- Basis tends to be consistent even as prices fluctuate.
- The CBOT offers the following two examples for a short and long hedger[1] of how to use basis to your advantage.

The first example is for a short hedger. Because there is a certain amount of "predictability" with basis, it is continually used by the grain industry to make buying and selling decisions. Let's say you have three years of basis history and know the local elevator's basis in early November averages 30 under (\$−0.30) the December futures contract. In the spring, you call your elevator and find out he's bidding \$1.95 a bushel for corn through a cash forward contract. Delivery is required by November 15. At the time, December corn futures are trading at \$2.35. You calculate the basis for early November delivery at 40 under December:[2]

[1]Data provided by the Chicago Board of Trade.
[2]Data provided by the Chicago Board of Trade.

Forward cash price November 15 delivery	$1.95
December futures price	−2.35
Basis	−$0.40 December

Would you take the forward bid? Because the basis is historically weak (−0.40 compared to −0.30) and there is potential for the basis to strengthen, you might consider passing on this bid. However, if you like the current futures price level, you could hedge your price risk using futures. Should the basis strengthen, you would unwind (offset) your futures hedge and sell corn through a forward contract or a spot cash sale.

If you hedge, the expected selling price is:

December futures price	$2.35
Expected basis early November delivery	+(−0.30)
Expected sale price	$2.05

The only factor that will affect the final sale price will be a change in basis from what is expected. If the basis is stronger than expected, you will receive more than $2.05 for your corn. If the basis is weaker than expected, you will receive less than $2.05. What if the cash forward bid was $2.15? With December futures at $2.35, this equates to a basis of −0.20:

Forward cash price November 15 delivery	$2.15
December futures price	−2.35
Basis	−$0.20 December

A basis of 20 under is significantly stronger than the historical average of 30 under, so you decide to sell a portion of your anticipated corn crop and take the cash forward bid of $2.15.

The second example is for the long hedger. Suppose that:[3]

Current cash offer for January delivery	$0.28
January futures contract	−0.25
Current basis	+$0.03

From your years of basis history, you determine that by January the basis is typically about 1/2 cent per pound, or 2½ cents weaker than the present basis. Given current fundamentals, you believe the basis will move toward the historical average. At this point, you can protect your buying price by hedging in the futures market-purchasing futures and later offsetting the futures position—or by entering a forward contract purchasing soybean

[3]Data provided by the Chicago Board of Trade.

EXHIBIT 38.1 Long Hedge

Local Cash Price	Futures Market Price	Basis
September		
Cash forward offer at \$0.280/lb	Buys CBOT January futures Contracts at \$0.250/lb	+\$0.030/lb
December		
Buys cash soybean oil at \$0.275/lb	Sells CBOT January futures contracts at \$0.270/lb	+\$0.005/lb
	\$0.020/lb gain	\$0.025/lb gain
Net Result		
Cash soybean oil	\$0.275/lb	
Futures gain (sells \$0.27 – buys \$0.25)	0.020/lb	
Net purchase price	\$0.255/lb	

Source: Exhibit created from data obtained from the Chicago Board of Trade.

oil for 28 cents per pound. If you establish a long hedge to protect your buying price level, the expected buying price can be calculated as follows:

Futures price + Expected basis = Expected buying price

Using this formula, you calculate your expected buying price:

\$0.25/lb + (+\$0.005) = \$0.255/lb

This is lower than the cash forward offer of 28 cents per pound. Since the expected buying price with futures is below the cash offer, due to an expected lower basis, you decide to initiate the long hedge and buy January soybean oil futures.

Assume in late December that the futures price has increased to 27 cents. Also, assume that the basis weakens from 3 cents to 1/2 cent. You purchase your January cash soybean oil requirements for 27 cents [(\$0.27 futures + (+\$0.005 basis) = \$0.275/lb)] from your supplier. At the same time, you unwind the hedge, or offset the futures position, by selling January futures for 27 cents. The results are shown in Exhibit 38.1.

CATTLE

Overview

Naturally bred herds consist on average of one mature bull per 23 cows. While natural breeding still dominates the cattle industry, artificial insemination has increased in recent years. Insemination allows a cattle producer to introduce additional genetic strains into a herd without having to bring in new bulls—strains that can improve the commercial value of the herd.

A cow's gestation period is nine months, and breeding generally takes place in the fall. This eliminates the risk of exposing the calves to cold winter weather and ensures an abundance of green pasture during the calves' first months. Cows that do not become pregnant are generally culled from the herd and replaced by new female calves. Each year, 16% to 18% of cows are culled from a herd on average. Other reasons for elimination include bad teeth, advanced age, drought, or high production costs.

Calves remain with their parent herd for the first six months of their lives. Their sole source of nutrition at birth is milk, a diet that is gradually supplemented with grass and grain. Calves are generally weaned from their mothers when they reach six to eight weeks of age.

A cattle-producing operation requires a certain amount of pasture acreage per cow-calf unit. This acreage, known as stocking, can vary widely, depending on levels of rainfall and on climate. In the Midwest and the East, for example, stockage is typically as low five acres per cow-calf unit, whereas in the West and Southwest, it can be 30 times higher.

Once a calf is weaned, it requires an increasing amount of stockage. A cattle producer may pay a stocker operator to provide calves with access to summer grass, winter wheat, or some type of harvest roughage. Or the producer may simply sell the calves outright to the stocker operator. Calves generally remain with a stocker until they achieve a weight of 600 to 800 pounds, at which point they move on to a feedlot.

Like stocker operations, the services of a feedlot can be purchased, or the feedlot can buy the calves outright. Many feedlots, called farmer feedlots, are extensions of a family (or neighborhood) cattle-producing operation and do not feed cattle from outside the local operation. These small feedlots represent the vast majority of feedlots in the United States, but they account for a relatively small portion of total cattle fed at U.S. feedlots.

Large commercial feedlots are defined as having the capacity to serve 1,000 or more head of cattle at one time. These lots are owned by large commercial enterprises for which feedlot care is the sole focus. These operations commonly have nutritionists and specialized equipment to closely monitor and prescribe feed regimens to meet a cow's dietary needs. This type of expertise allows these operations to customize and streamline the feedlot process, resulting in higher daily weight gains and lower feed conversions.

The menu at feedlots generally consists of grain (corn or wheat), protein supplements (soybeans, cottonseed, or linseed meal), and roughage (alfalfa, silage, or prairie hay). The feedlot phase of the cattle-production process continues until calves reach an optimum balance of weight, muscling, and fat, at which point the animal is considered ready for slaughter. According to the U.S. Department of Agriculture, the average live slaughter weight in the year 2000 was about 1,222 pounds, and the average carcass weight was 745 pounds.

Cattle producers sell market-ready cows at auction or directly to a packing operation. Packers slaughter the cattle, utilizing every portion of the animal in the fabrication process. Slaughtered cattle provide packers with two primary sources of revenue: the sale of meat and the sale of the remaining carcass parts (fat, bones, blood, glands, and hide).

Packers generally sell cow meat in packaged form. The major cuts are vacuum-packed and shipped to retailers in boxes, who finish fabricating them. Increasingly, however, the trend is for the packer to finish all the fabricating and to send meat-case-ready cuts to the retailer.

Packers utilize four different pricing methods in negotiating cattle purchases from feedlots. The first, called formula pricing, entails a mathematical formula using some other price as a reference, such as the average price of cattle purchased by the plant in the week preceding slaughter.

A second method, forward contracting, uses either a basis forward contract or a flat forward contract. In the case of a basis forward contract, a packer offers to buy cattle at a futures market basis for the month that the cattle are to be slaughtered; and the feeder who accepts the bid determines when to price the cattle. In the case of flat forward contracts, price is set at the time the contract is established.

Grid pricing establishes a baseline price, from which different contract attributes (e.g., quality, yield, grade, and carcass weight) command a specified discount premium. Packers use various techniques for arriving at a base price, including futures prices, boxed beef cutout value, and average price of cattle purchased by the plant in the week prior to the week of slaughter.

Finally, cattle can be sold on the cash market; that is, live cattle are sold at the current market price with no negotiations, contracts, or formulas. Auction sales and sales directly to packers at the spot bid (i.e., cash price) fall into this category.

Demand

Worldwide, beef accounts for 20% of consumers' meat protein intake and is the third most-consumed meat (excluding fish) on a per capita basis according to the USDA Economic Research Service. The *CRB Commodity Yearbook* for 2005 listed global consumption of beef and veal rose 0.4% to

49.2 million metric tons in 2004. It also reveals that the biggest consumers of beef and veal are the United States (12.58 million metric tons/2004), the European Union (8.175 million metric tons/2004), China (6.65 million metric tons), and Brazil (6.41 million metric tons).

In the United States, beef represented 56% of all red meats consumed in 2004 (USDA). Americans consume an average 67 pounds of beef per person per year, including 28 pounds of ground beef, 13 pounds of steaks, and 9 pounds of processed beef (USDA). The highest per capita consumption is in the Midwest (73 pounds), followed by the South and the West (65 pounds each), and the Northeast (63 pounds) (USDA). Low-income consumers tend to eat more beef than do individuals in other-income households (USDA). The USDA estimated that the United States consumed 27,757 million pounds of beef in 2005, or 65.4 pounds per person.

Supply

According to the *CRB Commodity Yearbook 2005*, world cattle and buffalo figures increased 0.5% in 2004 to 1.019 billion head. That total is only a slight advance over the 2003 total of 1.014 billion head, a four-decade low. Global production of beef and veal, on the other hand, climbed 1.2% to 50.66 million metric tons in 2004. The United States is the largest beef producer worldwide, with 11.206 million metric tons of production in 2004, followed by the European Union (8.035 million metric tons), Brazil (7.83 million metric tons), and China (6.683 million metric tons).

Trading[4]

Successful commodity trading requires the ability to estimate the quantity of a commodity at a future point in time based on observations during various points in the production cycle. This type of projection, called the pipeline approach to forecasting, views the life cycle of livestock animals in the food-production process as being in a "pipeline," which the animals enter at birth. It further assumes that, generally speaking, what goes into the pipeline will come out the other end.

Basic requirements for the pipeline approach to forecasting include estimates of current supplies at various points in the pipeline; average time required for a commodity to move from one stage in the pipeline to the next;

[4]This section adapted from *CME Livestock Futures and Options: Introduction to Underlying Futures and Options and Strategies for CME Livestock Futures and Options* (Chicago Mercantile Exchange Inc., 2005).

and information about significant influences on the pipeline flow (e.g., imports, animals diverted from slaughter back into the herd, and significant leakage due to death or exports). The U.S. Department of Agricultural offers much of this information over its web site.

The place to start compiling data for the pipeline approach to forecasting cattle supply is with the size of the cattle crop. The most accurate means of computing the size of a cattle crop is to count cattle placements (in feedlots) or marketings. Counting newborns is a less reliable method because an unknown number of newborns will die of disease or other causes before achieving market weight.

The USDA provides monthly estimates of the cattle placed on feed, as well as monthly estimates of cattle already on feed and cattle shipped out of feedlots to slaughter (marketings). Using this information, commodity traders can forecast total commercial slaughter and beef production 4 to 5 months in advance.

An inherent weakness in the pipeline approach to forecasting cattle slaughter is that it can be subject to under- or overforecasting, depending on the month in which placements occur. Extremes in weather, for example, can impede the ability of cattle to gain weight properly, thereby delaying their delivery to market and causing slaughter numbers to be lower than anticipated. Insights on weather disruptions as well as other forces that can impact supply (e.g., leakages and infusions) are available in *Livestock, Dairy, and Poultry Situation and Outlook* newsletter, published monthly by the USDA Economic Research Service and the *Red Meat Yearbook* data set files.

Commodity traders must also keep in mind when cattle imports and exports enter and exit the pipeline. Take, for example, total U.S. slaughter and production numbers, which represent total slaughter and production in the United States. Normally these totals would not be adjusted for exports because most U.S. beef exports are cattle that have been slaughtered in the United States and should therefore be included in total U.S. slaughter and production numbers. U.S. slaughter and production numbers need to be adjusted for exports of live animals; however, these animals are slaughtered outside the United States, which removes them from the U.S. production process.

Similarly, only imports of live cattle influence U.S. slaughter and production numbers, in that these animals are slaughtered in the United States, which adds them to the U.S. production process. Imports of slaughtered beef, on the other hand, do not impact U.S. production numbers because the animals were not slaughtered in the United States.

To arrive at a forecast of beef production, the trader multiplies the number of head to be slaughtered by the average weight per head (e.g., 745 pounds in 2000). Traders can reduce the margin of error in their estimates by using marketing rather than placements to compute production. Marketing is one stage further along the production pipeline than placements and thus avoids leakage due to death in the feedlot and uncertainties as to how long an animal remains in the feedlot. (Once marketed, the animal goes directly to slaughter.) Counting only marketings also reduces errors due to imports and exports, since cattle are no longer exported from (or imported into) the marketing stage.

HOGS

Overview

As with cattle, the hog-production cycle begins with the successful birth of pigs into a hog-producing operation. Boars are usually purchased by hog producers for reproduction purposes and have a work life of about two years. Sows are bred for two to three years before being sold for slaughter. Mating generally occurs twice a year to ensure a steady flow of new pigs for the production process.

The gestation period for a pig is approximately 110 days, and a sow has an average of 9 to 10 piglets in a litter. The piglets are weaned after three to four weeks, at which point the average litter size has declined to 8.7 piglets due to death from suffocation, disease, weather conditions, or other causes.

Young pigs are separated by sex after weaning in order to more efficiently deal with their differing nutritional requirements. The diet of young pigs is high in grains, generally a mix of corn, barley, milo, and oats. The pigs also receive protein in the form of oilseed mills and vitamin and mineral additives. In the last stages of the feeding process, the pigs generally convert three pounds of feed to one pound of weight, for a gain of about one and a half pounds per day.

Hogs are considered ready for market when they reach about 250 pounds, a process that requires about five months from the time the pig is weaned. The USDA reports that the average federally inspected slaughter weight was 262 pounds in 2000, while the carcass weight was 194 pounds.

There are three approaches to the hog-raising process. The first approach "farrow-to-wean operations" raises pigs from birth to three to four weeks, at which time the weaned pigs weigh about 10 to 15 pounds and are sold to a feeding operation. The second "farrow-to-nursery operations" raises pigs from birth to feeder weight (40 to 60 pounds), when the pigs are sent to finishing farms to complete their final weight gain. The last and increasingly popular approach "farrow-to-finish operations" keeps pigs in one place over the entire production process, from birth to slaughter. Pig producers like this vertically integrated approach because it gives them greater control over the quality of their product, that is, over the growth process of their pigs.

In addition to moving toward vertical integration, many hog producers are significantly expanding the size of their operations, which provide economies of scale that improve both feed efficiency and labor productivity. Industry analysts note that production costs decline sharply as marketings increase to 1,000 head and continue to drop, although at a slower rate, as marketings increase over 1,000 head. In 1978, about 67% of all marketings came from farms that sold fewer than 1,000 head, whereas in 2000, 78% of all marketings came from farms selling over 5,000 head.

The majority of hog-production operations, according to the USDA, are farrow-to-finish, and most are located in the Western Corn Belt (68% of the nearly 60 million U.S. hog herd) and the combined areas of Virginia and North Carolina (20% of the U.S. hog herd). New operations are also emerging in Oklahoma and Utah.

Producers sell their market-ready hogs to packers directly or through buying stations and auctions. Most transactions are nonspot transactions; less than a fifth of hog producers sell on the spot market.

Hogs are priced depending on how they are sold. Prices of hogs sold directly are determined relative to the actual percent lean of the hog carcasses (which determines the amount of meat the carcass will yield). Prices of hogs sold at auction, on the other hand, are based on expected percent lean of the hog carcasses.

Hog producers also use marketing contracts to sell their hogs. These contracts can be fixed price, fixed basis, formula basis, cost plus, ledger, price window, and price floor. The following is a quick overview.

Fixed price agreements, which set an actual price for future delivery, are commonly related to the futures price. They are usually short-term contracts that set the delivery date for one to two months out.

Fixed basis contracts are similar to fixed price agreements; but rather than setting the actual price, fixed basis contracts set the basis. And because basis agreements apply to a specific futures contract, these fixed basis contracts can last for more than a year.

Fundamental pricing is derived from a price-determining market. It may entail the addition or subtraction of a price differential due to location or overall quality of the hogs. Fundamental pricing is generally used when a producer forward contracts with a packer or another producer.

Cost-plus pricing derives from a formula that is generally based on feed costs. It normally sets a minimum price and has a balancing clause.

Ledger contracts typically last four to seven years and entail making payments to producers when market prices are below a contracted floor price. By the same token, when the contract base price rises above the floor price, producers must pay back money that was received when prices were low.

Price window agreements are cost-plus agreements with a twist. They generally set a price ceiling and floor between which hogs are exchanged at market price. When prices exceed these limits, however, the buyer and the seller split the difference between the market price and the ceiling or floor price.

Price floor agreements combine features of ledger and window contracts by setting both a floor price and a ceiling price. A producer places a portion of hog revenues received into a special account whenever hog prices rise above the ceiling price. The producer then draws on the account when prices drop below the floor price.

As with cattle, packers cut hog carcasses into wholesale cuts and ship them to retailers. The yield from a market hog with a live weight of 230 pounds is about 88 pounds of lean meat. Of this amount, 21% is ham, 20.3% is loin, 13.9% is belly (meat used for bacon), 3% is spareribs, 7.3% is Boston butt roast and blade steaks, and 10.3% is *picnic* (a ham-like cut from front leg of hog) (USDA averages). The remaining 24.2% goes to jowl, lean trim, fat, miscellaneous cuts, and trimmings.

Demand

World pork consumption rose 2.1% to 90.503 million metric tons in 2004 (*CRB Commodity Yearbook 2005*). The USDA estimated world pork consumption increased again in 2005, rising 0.8% to 91.197 million metric tons. The United States accounted for 9.9% of 2004 worldwide pork consumption, or 8.950 million metric tons (*CRB Commodity Yearbook 2005*), and the USDA estimated that U.S. consumption in 2005 increased by an additional 1% to 9.041 million metric tons.

Pork ranks number three in annual U.S. meat consumption behind beef and chicken. Americans consume an average of 51 pounds of pork per capita annually, most of it at home. The Midwest leads in pork consumption (58 pounds per capita) followed by the South (52 pounds), the Northeast (51 pounds), and the West (42 pounds).

Longer term, the Continuing Survey of Food Intakes by Individuals (CSFII) projects declines in per capita consumption of pork in the United States as Hispanics and the elderly—population groups that eat less pork than the national average—become an increasingly bigger share of the overall U.S. population. Total United States pork consumption should continue to expand, according to the USDA, however, due to overall growth in the U.S. population.

Supply

Global pork production rose 2.1% in 2004 to 90.858 million metric tons according to the *CRB Commodity Yearbook 2005*. The USDA estimated an additional 0.8% rise in worldwide consumption to 91.619 million metric tons in 2005. The *CRB Commodity Yearbook 2005* indicates that the world production leaders are China (52% of 2004 production), the European Union (23%), and the United States (10%).

Global exports of pork climbed 1.6% to 4.182 in 2004. The USDA estimated an additional increase in exports of 1.2% in 2005 to 4.223 million metric tons. The European Union dominates pork exports with 30% of the export total, followed by Canada (23%), the United States (22%), and Brazil (14%) (*CRB Commodity Yearbook 2005*).

The United States is the world's third-largest producer of pork, as well as the largest consumer, exporter, and importer of pork products (USDA). The United States exports about 6% of its domestic production, which rose 2.1% to 9.332 million metric tons in 2004. U.S. production was estimated to rise an additional 1.9% to 95.12 million metric tons in 2005.

According to the *CRB Commodity Yearbook 2005*, the number of animals in the U.S. hog herd rose 0.1% to 60.501 million in 2004 (January 1), its highest level since 1980. That compares with 466.017 million in China (January 1, 2004) and 152.569 million in Denmark (January 1, 2004), the world's other two largest herds. The total number of hogs worldwide in 2005 is estimated at 810.179 million (January 1).

Trading[5]

To apply the pipeline approach to forecasting hog production, traders need to begin with the size of the pig crop, data that is available from the USDA National Agricultural Statistics Service (NASS). Additional statistics are also available from the monthly Livestock Slaughter reports, also published by NASS, which provide statistics on total hog slaughter by head; average live and dressed weight in commercial plants by state and in the United States; and information about federally inspected hogs.

[5]This section adapted from *CME Livestock Futures and Options: Introduction to Underlying Futures and Options and Strategies for CME Livestock Futures and Options* (Chicago Mercantile Exchange Inc., 2005).

Information regarding leakages, infusions, and feedback loops is available from the USDA Economic Research Service (ERS), which provides data on imports and exports on a monthly basis. The ERS also publishes quarterly and yearly statistics (separated out by selected countries) on a carcass-weight and live-animal basis.

Data on animal retention for purposes of breeding can be found in the Hogs and Pigs report (see *Hogs Kept for Breeding* and *Monthly Sows and Gilts Bred*) published by the NASS. Traders, however, must be aware of variations in data related to whether the industry is in an expansion or a contraction phase.

All of these resources will help traders estimate hog production in a specified time period. For example, by multiplying the number of new pigs born in the United States during the first quarter 2006 by the average slaughter weight for hogs (250 pounds), traders will approximate the pork production total for third quarter 2006 (it takes about two quarters to bring a newborn pig to slaughter weight).

CONCLUSION

This chapter provided an overview of commodity market fundamentals for grain, cattle, and hogs. In doing so, we showed that the driving forces of agricultural commodity prices are characterized by supply, demand, seasonality, carry-over, and the stocks-to-use ratio. Additionally, while grain markets are predominantly for exports, livestock markets are much more domestic. In the past years, the prices of agricultural commodities were mainly driven by increased demand following the rapid growth of the economies of China and India, which has spurred their domestic food consumption. For example, today China is the world's leading soybean importer. However, investors should also be aware that changes in agricultural and trade policies in these countries could also influence these markets negatively in the near future.

CHAPTER 39

Fundamental Analysis of the World Sugar Market

Rohit Savant
Commodity Analyst
CPM Group

Sugar is one of the most widely consumed commodities in the world. Its use as a sweetener has existed for centuries. Today, with the world looking for renewable sources of energy such as ethanol, sugar's importance is growing in the energy complex. Sugar is widely used as feedstock for ethanol.

The market for sugar is complicated by several trade arrangements between various countries. Several governments, especially in developed countries, subsidize their domestic sugar production. Both trade agreements and subsidies greatly reduce the efficiency of the sugar market. While several trade distortions such as tariffs and quotas are being removed, there still are several that exist.

In the soft commodities complex, which includes cocoa, coffee, cotton, and orange juice, sugar is the largest market in terms of open interest on the Intercontinental Exchange (ICE). It is a market not covered and researched as much as other commodities such as gold, copper, or oil. The following chapter introduces the reader to an approach on forecasting sugar prices and analyzing the sugar market. The chapter discusses various factors and the degree to which they influence price.

PRICE FORECASTING

While conducting fundamental analysis to forecast sugar prices, the most important metric to forecast is carryover, or what is commonly known as ending stock. Calculating carryover captures various aspects of supply and demand. Estimated ending stock may be calculated using the following formula.

Estimated ending stock = Beginning stock
+ Estimated supply (Production)
– Estimated demand (Exports and consumption of domestic supplies)

Beginning stock is the carryover from the previous year. It is calculated using the same formula, except the components of the formula will be post data.

Estimating Supply

A beginning point for calculating the above equation is estimating supply or world production. Production of sugar for the coming year is largely dependent on weather conditions. Sugar being an agricultural commodity, unexpected poor weather can skew projections. For example, both sugar beet and sugarcane require cooler, drier weather with ample sunshine just prior to harvest.[1] In the absence of such weather, however, yield could decline, thus reducing supply. Output estimates therefore should be made under the assumption that average weather conditions will be experienced, at least, in the major producing nations of the world.

Assuming average weather conditions, the current price of sugar and the expected price of sugar can be used as one measure of estimating the amount of sugarcane or beet that will be planted in the following season. Price is used to compare profitability with competing crops such as soybean, wheat, and groundnuts. It is also used to determine if sugar itself can be grown profitably at those prices.

Prices can only partially answer questions regarding future supply, however. Several factors besides price influence the amount of sugar that a country may plant. For example in countries where governments provide support, through import tariffs or subsidized farm inputs, production can be maintained even at low market prices. For the period between 1960–1961 and 2005–2006, a correlation of 0.31 exists between prices in the current year and production in the next year.[2]

[1]Drier weather just prior to harvest helps boost sugar content in both the stem of the sugarcane and the root of the sugar beet.

[2]Data from the United States Department of Agriculture (USDA) and the ICE.

A gauge of future prices also could partially answer questions of profitably growing sugar in the next season. Attractive sugar prices in the future could encourage increased planting in the coming season. Flat or slightly reduced prices over the short term, into the future, may not necessarily reduce the area planted to sugar, however. This is especially true for cane sugar. Extended periods of low or declining prices could result in underinvestment in sugarcane plantations. Sugarcane is typically grown from a stub of cane left behind from the previous harvest. This method of cultivation called *ratooning* is economical for farmers and could result in switching costs. The method of cultivation can be repeated three to four times, depending upon soil quality, before farming costs exceed yield. The sugar yield, under the ratooning process, reduces with every progressing year. Farmers may reduce plantations based on market price only when the price falls below any savings they have from the ratooning process and any additional subsidies they may receive from the government.

The type of crop used for sugar production can increase the dynamic between sugar prices and production. If sugar beets are being used they are typically more sensitive to changes in price than sugarcane. This is because they have short crop cycles that permit sugar growers to respond quickly to rising prices. Sugar beets are harvested within six to eight months. Sugarcane, meanwhile, is relatively less responsive, especially to declining prices. The reason for this is the relatively longer crop cycle and the ratooning process used for growing sugarcane. A sugarcane cycle can take anywhere from 10 to 17 months to complete and typically averages 12 months. The cycle depends upon the variety of cane planted and the geographic location of growth. Cane grown closer to the equator has a shorter crop cycle. According to the Commodity Research Bureau approximately 75% of world sugar is produced from sugarcane.[3]

Nonetheless the sugar crop cycle is a lot shorter than some other crops such as cocoa which require approximately five years to bear fruit. Commodities in the metal and energy complex require far longer periods than sugar to respond to rising prices. This is primarily because of the longer gestation periods of mining and exploration projects. The ability of sugar to respond comparatively quickly to price can potentially reduce the duration of a sugar bull run compared to some of these other commodities. Extended periods of high prices in sugar may be experienced in the case of unfavorable weather conditions and/or depleted inventories.

---

[3]Commodity Research Bureau, "Sugar," *The CRB Commodity Yearbook 2006* (Hoboken, NJ: John Wiley & Sons, Inc., 2006).

Overview of World Sugar Production

The average compounded growth rate in global sugar supply over the long term (the long term being the past 47 years from 1959 to 2006) is 2.2%. The compounded growth rate in the most recent 10 years, beginning 1996–1997, has been only marginally lower at 1.7%. In some years, such as 1981–1982, production increased by as much as 13% over the previous year, while in other years, such as 1987–1988, it declined by as much as 9% over the previous year. Prices responded to these swings, declining approximately 56% in 1981–1982 and rising approximately 48% in 1987–1988.[4]

The production of sugarcane is relatively insensitive to price declines. Prices need to decline over extended periods for sugarcane production to be reduced. For this reason, prices have experienced significant increases or decreases in some years without much variability in sugar output. Increased production results in price declines, nonetheless. The two metrics have a negative correlation of approximately 0.23 for the period between 1960–1961 and 2005–2006.[5]

The largest producer of sugar today is Brazil. Over the decade beginning 1996–1997, Brazilian production has averaged approximately 21 million metric tons. Over the same period, Brazil accounted for an average 16% of world production. Its closest competitors, in terms of production over this period, were India and the European Union. Over the same period, India on average contributed 13% to world production, while the EU contributed roughly 14%.[6]

Brazil's role in world sugar markets is key because it is the single largest contributor to world production. What proportion of Brazil's sugarcane is being diverted toward ethanol production verses edible sugar is one of the most important factors to be considered while studying Brazilian production and its effect on sugar prices. An increase in the former reduces the total cane available for the latter. This results in lower sugar production and therefore higher prices. Furthermore, of the portion being processed into edible sugar, how much is being consumed domestically versus being exported is the second important metric. The amount of sugar that is being exported by Brazil, the world's largest exporter, is material to world sugar prices.

---

[4]Data from the United States Department of Agriculture and the Intercontinental Exchange.

[5]Data from the United States Department of Agriculture and the Intercontinental Exchange.

[6]Data from United States Department of Agriculture.

Since 1993–1994, the period for which data are available, on average 56% of Brazilian cane has been diverted toward ethanol with the remainder being diverted toward sugar production. In the current decade the ratio has been more or less 50:50.[7] Several factors affect the proportion of sugarcane diverted toward ethanol. Among these factors is the mandatory requirement by the government of Brazil to blend ethanol with gasoline, world crude oil prices, and the price of sugar itself.

In 1975, the Brazilian government initiated the Proalcool program. This program was an outcome of the first oil crisis of the 1970s, and its main objective was to reduce shocks from similar crises in the future. The government since then has required a mandatory blend of ethanol with all gasoline used by motor vehicles. As of December 2006, the Government of Brazil required a 23% blend of ethanol with gasoline. Brazil is the most efficient producer of sugar ethanol in the world and there is significant demand for its product globally.

The price for sugar also plays an important role in determining the amount of cane that would be diverted toward ethanol. Higher sugar prices tend to typically discourage diversion of sugarcane toward ethanol production.

Over the past 10 years, beginning 1996–1997, Brazilian exports have averaged approximately 12 million metric tons. Growth in domestic consumption in Brazil has been consistent, averaging approximately 3% annually. The long-term growth in sugar production has averaged approximately 5% per annum, while growth over the past 10 years has averaged 7.5%. This average growth in sugar production far outpaces the growth in domestic consumption, leaving a larger balance available for exports.[8]

India is the second largest producer of sugar in the world. The average sugar output in India over the past 10 years has been approximately 18 million metric tons. The long- term average growth rate of output in India has been 9.1%, which is comparable to that of Brazil (9.6%). Much of Brazil's current growth can be attributed to the recent past. Brazil's average growth rate of production over the past five years beginning 2001–2002 was 17.7%, while that of India over the same period was 13.1%.[9]

India is the largest consumer of sugar in the world and, therefore, a substantial portion of what it produces it consumes. Sugar production in India indirectly affects the world sugar market. Sugar production in India has one

[7]This was not the case in the 1990s, however. In 1994–1995 total sugarcane diverted toward ethanol stood at 65%, the highest level for the period under consideration (data from the Foreign Agricultural Services – Attaché Reports).

[8]Data from the United States Department of Agriculture.

[9]Data: United States Department of Agriculture.

important purpose, which is to satisfy domestic demand for the world's largest consumer rather than supply overseas demand. If there is a production shortfall in India, its demand would need to be satisfied by imports from other countries. This would suck up sugar from the world market and therefore affect prices positively (see Exhibit 39.1).

The European Union is among the top three sugar producers in the world. The inclusion of 10 East European countries in 2004 to the original 15 had further helped expand production capacity. The inclusion added approximately 4 million metric tons to total capacity.

This increase will be short-lived, however. In 2005, the World Trade Organization (WTO) passed a ruling in favor of Brazil, Thailand, and Australia, which had complained about the European Union's unfair trade practices. The WTO required that the EU limit its subsidized sugar exports to 1.3 million metric ton per year. Prior to the ruling the EU exported on average 5.5 million metric tons.[10]

Following the ruling, the European Union has embarked upon reforms to restructure the European sugar industry. The reforms are aimed at making the European sugar industry more competitive, reducing subsidized exports that adversely affect the global sugar market, and facilitating a smooth

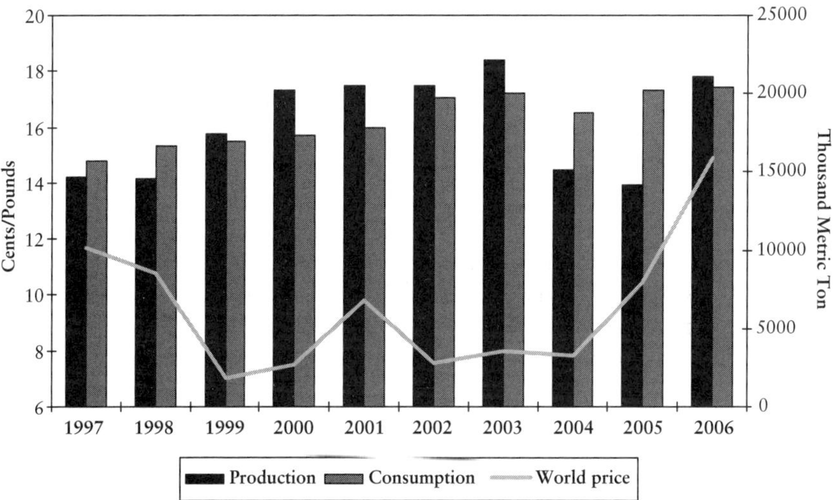

EXHIBIT 39.1 Indian Sugar Production: Consumption and World Sugar Prices
Source: Exhibit created from data obtained from the United States Department of Agriculture and the Intercontinental Exchange.

[10]Data from the United States Department of Agriculture.

transition. The reforms were put into effect July 1, 2006 and would include a 36% cut in the guaranteed minimum sugar price.[11] Previously prices were at 3 times world market prices. A restructuring fund has been put in place to encourage uncompetitive sugar producers to exit the market. Uncompetitive producers will be encouraged to exit the market by compensating them with €730 for every metric ton given up, for the first 2 years of the program. The amounts paid per metric ton will reduce as the years progress. The restructuring scheme ends in 2010. This payment structure has been set up in a way to encourage the most uncompetitive producers to bail out first, helping the union to reach its goal of making the European sugar industry more competitive. It is too early in the process to judge the eventual success of this scheme. The Union is targeting a reduction of 6 million metric tons of sugar by 2010. The United States Department of Agriculture (USDA) projects EU production in 2007 to total approximately 15 million metric tons. This is a decline of approximately 83% over the previous year.[12]

What would this development mean for the sugar industry going forward? The most apparent implication of this reduction in exports by the EU would be an increased importance of Brazil's role in the global sugar market. Sugar prices going forward would be more sensitive to changes in production and exports from Brazil. The WTO ruling on Europe's unfair trade practices, and similar rulings in the future on countries that heavily subsidize and protect their sugar industries, would be a reduction in price distortions. Subsidizing production encourages farmers to overproduce, increasing supply. Much of this excess supply is then dumped on the world markets, which depresses global sugar prices. End users in countries that subsidize pay a premium for the sugar.

Other important contributors to world supply are Thailand and Australia. Over the 10 years beginning in 1997, Thailand accounted for approximately 9% of total world exports, while Australia accounted for 10% of global exports. Australia on average exports 80% of its production, while Thailand on average exports approximately 65% of its produce.[13]

Australia's sugar industry has been in the doldrums in recent years due to a string of bad weather events, disease, reduced yields, and reduced acreage. Australia's ability to contain sugarcane smut, a fungal disease that reduces sugarcane yield, will play an important role in shaping Australia's role in the world sugar market going forward. The country's ability to fend

[11]Europa-Rapid-Press Releases, Common Agricultural Policy Reform, "CAP Reform: EU Agriculture Ministers Adopt Ground Breaking Sugar Reform," Reference IP/06/194, February 20, 2006.

[12]Data from Foreign Agricultural Services (FAS), November 1, 2006.

[13]Data from the United States Department of Agriculture.

off loss of acreage to other uses also will be an important factor. Loss of acreage will largely depend upon the price of sugar in the world market.

According to the USDA, Thailand is targeting an increase of its sugarcane production to a minimum of 72 million metric tons by 2010. The production target is being pursued to meet the government's plan of increasing ethanol production. The ideal level according to the USDA will be 80 million metric tons, however. At this level, there will be sufficient feedstock for ethanol as well as for sugar production. The USDA estimates 2005–2006 output at 46.7 million metric tons. The ethanol will be prepared from molasses, a sugar byproduct. According to the USDA, ethanol production in Thailand from sugarcane is currently not as cost effective as production from molasses, partially due to its availability for only four months during the year.[14]

The future developments in these two exporting markets will affect the total supply of sugar and therefore price. Any loss of output due to farming glitches or alternate uses of the crop will shrink world supply.

Estimating Demand The next component of our equation is demand or consumption. Income elasticity and price elasticity should be studied in examining demand. Income elasticity is measured as the percentage change in quantity of sugar demanded divided by the percentage change in real income. Income elasticity influences per capita consumption. The per capita consumption has been rising in developing countries such as India and China, which are experiencing significant growth in real gross domestic product. Per capita consumption in India for 2006 was approximately 41 pounds; this is an increase of 26% from 1995 levels. Meanwhile in China, per capita consumption rose 31% from 1995 levels to stand at 18.7 pounds in 2006.[15] The amount of sugar a person can consume is limited irrespective of a growth in his income. World per capita consumption between 1995 and 2006 has grown by approximately 8%.[16] Per capita consumption in developed nations has been steady to lower. This can essentially be attributed to changing dietary habits and a switch to non-fattening alternatives such as aspartame, a nonsugar sweetener.

The second factor to examine is price elasticity of sugar demand. Price elasticity is the sensitivity of demand to change in price. It is calculated as the percentage change in quantity of sugar demanded divided by the

---

[14]Ponnarong Prasertsri., "Thailand Sugar Semi-Annual 2006," USDA Foreign Agricultural Service, GAIN Report Number: TH6099, September 2006.

[15]Data: United Nations – Population Division, United States Department of Agriculture.

[16]Data from the United Nations – Population Division and United States Department of Agriculture.

percentage change in price over the same period. In the case of large consumers like soda or confectionery manufacturers, sugar forms a small portion of their total cost. If the price of sugar rises, this could impact their profits, albeit marginally. Meanwhile individual consumers, especially in developing nations, may be more sensitive to sugar's price than commercial consumers as a substantial increase in price could impact their budgets greatly.

Stock-to-Consumption Ratio

A very useful metric in forecasting price is the stock-to-consumption ratio. It captures the amount of stock (available inventory) for every unit of consumption (demand). Price typically has an inverse relation to this ratio. For the period between 1960–1961 and 2005–2006 the relationship between price and stock to consumption for sugar has a negative correlation of 0.63.[17] Given the strength of this correlation, a significant amount of weight should be given to this metric in forecasting price (see Exhibit 39.2).

Overview of World Sugar Consumption

Over the past 10 years, India accounted for 14% of total world consumption on average. It also is the second largest producer and usually self-sustaining. Production in India can be fairly volatile as it is susceptible to pest infestation and erratic weather conditions. Domestic consumption in India has exceeded domestic production in 18 of the past 47 years.[18] In times of tight supply and rising prices the government of India intervenes to curb the rise. Sugar is considered an essential commodity in India and forms a major percentage of the Indian Wholesale Price Index. Sugar accounts for 3.6% of this index.[19] A rise in price could significantly affect this index. If prices begin to rise the government could ban exports, allow duty free imports and loosen up stocks. A scheme commonly used by the government is the import of sugar under the Advance License Scheme (ALS). Under the ALS, the government permits Indian sugar mills to import raw sugar with zero duty. The mills are obligated, however, to re-export 1.0 metric tons of refined sugar for every 1.05 metric tons of raw sugar they import. The mills have to reexport the refined sugar within 24 months.

---

[17]Data from the United States Department of Agriculture and the Intercontinental Exchange.

[18]Data from the United States Department of Agriculture.

[19]Office of the Economic Adviser, to the Government of India, Ministry of Commerce and Industry.

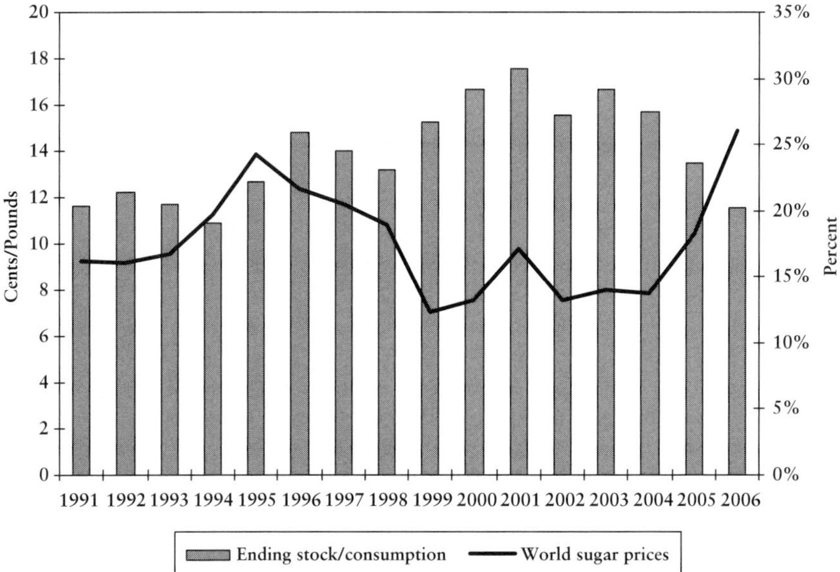

EXHIBIT 39.2 Stocks-to-Consumption Ratio and Annual Average Sugar Prices
Source: Exhibit created from data obtained from the United States Department of Agriculture and the Intercontinental Exchange.

Other large consuming nations include China, Brazil, and the United States. Each of these countries over the past 10 years starting 1997 have consumed on average 7.5%, 7.0%, and 6.5% of total world consumption, respectively.[20] On the other hand according to data provided by the USDA, countries such as Japan and Russia are experiencing on-average contracting demand of 1.5% and 0.5% per year[21].

Seasonality

Price seasonality for sugar is determined by the planting and harvest cycle. Prices typically fall during harvest and increase during the planting phase. Prices tend to rise during the planting phase because at this point in the crop's cycle there is significant uncertainty about the output; they weaken during harvest because by this time the market is fairly assured of the output and physical supplies are rising. Seasonality in sugar is not very explicit, however. This is largely because the two varieties of sugar

[20]Data from the United States Department of Agriculture.
[21]Data from the United States Department of Agriculture.

grow in different climatic conditions and therefore there always is sugar being harvested or planted in some part of the world all through the year.

SUGAR AS AN INVESTMENT

Sugar has a close to zero correlation with other soft commodities (see Exhibit 39.3). The weakest relation sugar has is with orange juice. The correlation between sugar and commodities in other complexes such as energy, grains, precious metals, and base metals also is very weak (see Exhibit 39.4).

Adding sugar to a portfolio containing these assets will therefore reduce the over all risk of such a commodity portfolio. Correlation among commodities in other groups is significantly stronger than that in the soft commodity group. That is, these commodities largely move together as a group as opposed to the soft commodities. This reduces their attractiveness as portfolio diversifiers.

Commodities in other groups have a higher correlation to each other for a couple of reasons. The way they are produced is one way—take, for example, the energy complex. Crude oil has a very strong correlation with heating oil and gasoline, both of which are distillates of crude oil. The supply of crude oil therefore affects the supply of the other two, which results in highly correlated prices. Similarly, in the case of base metals, one metal can be the byproduct of another in the mining process as they are found in the same ore body.[22] There is no such cohesiveness found in the supply or demand for soft commodities. They have little or no relation in the way that

EXHIBIT 39.3 Sugar's Correlation with Other Soft Commodities, January 1987 and January 2007

	Sugar	Cocoa	Cotton	Coffee	Orange Juice
Sugar	1				
Cocoa	0.068	1			
Cotton	0.063	0.036	1		
Coffee	0.049	0.113	0.027	1	
Orange Juice	0.005	0.033	0.027	0.046	1

Source: Exhibit created from data obtained from the Intercontinental Exchange.

[22]Demand for some of these products also is tightly related. China's push toward developing infrastructure and building new cities has increased the demand for everything from aluminum to zinc, which is used to galvanize steel. Similarly, investment in gold and silver could rise when markets are insecure or uncertain about the global economic environment.

EXHIBIT 39.4 Sugar's Correlation with Other Commodity Groups, January 1994 and September 2006

	Sugar
Energy Complex	
Crude oil	0.043
Heating oil	0.062
Unleaded gasoline	0.026
Natural gas	0.043
Grain Complex	
Corn	0.011
Wheat	0.014
Soybeans	0.029
Soybean Oil	0.045
Soybean Meal	0.015
Sugar	1
Precious Metals	
Gold	0.055
Silver	0.071
Platinum	0.048
Palladium	0.047
Base Metals	
Copper	0.033
Aluminum	0.020
Zinc	0.034
Lead	0.008
Nickel	0.015
Tin	−0.003

Source: Exhibit created from data obtained from Commodity Systems Inc.

they are produced and demand for one may have no significant impact on the other.

For the 10-year period between 1997 and 2006, the average total return on the nearby active sugar contract, returns based on capital appreciation only, exceeded all commodities in the soft commodities complex with the exception of orange juice (see Exhibit 39.5). Sugar's average stand-alone risk over the same period also was the highest, however. Risk is computed as the standard deviation of the return over any 12-month period. Over a longer period, between 1987 and 2006, sugar outperformed other commodities in its group providing average total returns, using prices on the nearby active contract, of approximately 9%. Meanwhile, average standalone risk moved lower, to third place.

EXHIBIT 39.5 Average Returns and Risk

	1997 – 2006			1987 – 1996			1987 – 2006		
	Average Return	Average Risk	Sharpe Ratio	Average Return	Average Risk	Sharpe Ratio	Average Return	Average Risk	Sharpe Ratio
Sugar	7.91%	21.05%	21.40%	10.48%	16.09%	31.00%	8.66%	17.51%	23.86%
Coffee	–1.04%	15.37%	–28.90%	8.32%	25.97%	10.89%	6.43%	22.23%	8.79%
Orange juice	13.67%	16.12%	63.68%	1.93%	21.52%	–16.56%	5.63%	19.49%	5.91%
Cotton	–0.05%	18.23%	–18.91%	3.68%	14.00%	–12.94%	1.37%	15.13%	20.53%
Cocoa	4.82%	18.47%	7.66%	–1.87%	13.96%	–52.72%	2.12%	15.37%	–15.32%
CRB	4.33%	7.56%	12.29%	1.43%	3.86%	–105.32%	2.61%	5.06%	–36.85%
Gold	7.88%	7.56%	59.28%	–1.09%	5.15%	–127.74%	2.45%	5.53%	–36.79%
Silver	12.13%	7.56%	115.57%	–1.88%	9.45%	–78.02%	4.57%	10.08%	0.93%
Platinum	14.38%	7.56%	145.28%	–3.13%	5.55%	–155.33%	5.25%	8.56%	9.03%
TW dollar	–1.58%	7.56%	–65.87%	–0.99%	3.76%	–172.37%	–0.80%	3.42%	–154.46%
DJIA	5.73%	7.56%	30.78%	11.67%	7.05%	87.58%	9.78%	7.31%	72.51%
S&P 500	6.15%	7.56%	36.36%	10.79%	8.03%	66.00%	9.59%	7.94%	64.35%
T–bills	3.40%	7.56%	3.40%	5.49%	0.40%	5.49%	4.48%	0.35%	4.48%
T–bonds	5.45%	7.56%	5.45%	7.93%	0.37%	7.93%	6.70%	0.33%	6.70%

Source: Exhibit created from data obtained from the Commodity Research Bureau, the Intercontinental Exchange, New York Mercantile Exchange, Federal Reserve Broad Trade Weighted Dollar Index, and Yahoo Finance.

The Sharpe ratio measures the risk-adjusted return and is an appropriate measure of return as opposed to total return, which does not consider risk. The higher this ratio, the more attractive the investment. For the period between 1997 and 2006, sugar's Sharpe ratio was again second only to orange juice in the soft commodity complex.

Studying sugar's performance over a longer period, between 1987 and 2006, shows that sugar's Sharpe ratio exceeded all the other soft commodities making it the most attractive investment in this complex. Sugar's Sharpe ratio over this period when compared to other assets, exceeded that of gold, silver, platinum, the U.S. dollar, and the CRB Index, a broad-based commodity index. Over the same period, on a return-risk basis, sugar underperformed compared to the broad equity indexes like the S&P 500 and the Dow Jones Industrial Average and underperformed when compared to U.S. Treasury securities. The underperformance when compared to U.S. Treasury securities can be explained by the significantly lower standard deviation of Treasury securities when compared to other assets. The underperformance when compared to the equity indexes can be explained by the diversification benefits of these indexes.

ETHANOL

In recent years, demand for ethanol has become an important metric for analyzing sugar prices. The increase in sugar prices experienced in late 2005 and early 2006 can largely be attributed to the growing importance of ethanol globally. Several countries are aiming to reduce their dependence on fossil fuels. There are two reasons why countries are taking ethanol seriously. One is most of the fossil fuels are sourced from politically unstable parts of the world. This makes prices of crude oil extremely sensitive to possible political disruptions in these (producing) countries. This price volatility negatively affects importing nations. The second reason is the reduction in greenhouse gases released while burning fossil fuels.

The two largest manufacturers of ethanol in the world today are the U.S. and Brazil. Brazil also is the largest exporter of ethanol. Both these countries use different feedstock to manufacture ethanol. Ethanol in the United States is manufactured using corn, while Brazil uses sugar. What must be noted is that both of these crops are essential foodstuffs. The rising demand for ethanol tightens the supply of these commodities for food. The effect of this will be further heightened in times of a poor crop yields.

In a push to reduce dependence on crude oil, countries are adding a certain percentage of ethanol to gasoline used in automobiles. Speculation of an increase in demand for ethanol as a fuel additive is especially

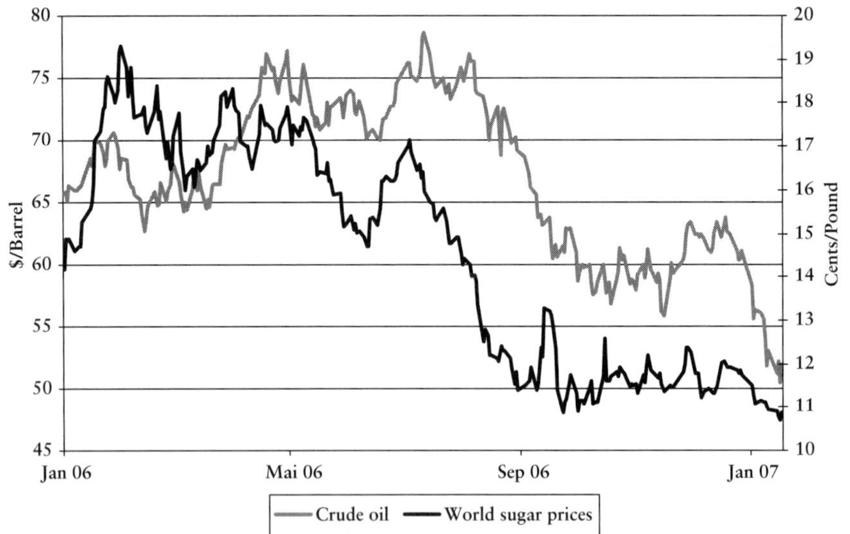

EXHIBIT 39.6 World Sugar Prices and Crude Oil Prices
Source: Exhibit created from data obtained from the Intercontinental Exchange and the New York Mercantile Exchange.

heightened in times of high crude oil prices. The reason is that a greater amount of ethanol will be demanded to offset the increase in oil prices. The increase in demand for ethanol in turn helps support sugar prices (see Exhibit 39.6). Brazil is a major consumer of sugar ethanol, as it requires a mandatory blend of ethanol with its gasoline. Several nations around the world do not have the capability to produce ethanol or are falling short of ethanol to meet their requirements. These countries typically import sugar-based ethanol from Brazil.

The United States, the world's largest consumer of gasoline, has an extremely ambitious ethanol program. President George W. Bush proposed an increase in the use of renewable fuels to 35 billion gallons by 2017. The law at the start of 2007 required blenders to use 7.5 billion gallons of ethanol by 2012. According to the Renewable Fuels Association (RFA), as of January 22, 2007, total capacity of 111 U.S. ethanol biorefineries stood at 5.4 billion gallons. The RFA projects ethanol production capacity in the United States to total 11.6 billion gallons by 2009. Of the total 194 refineries expected to come on stream by 2009, only nine refineries are using feedstock other than corn.

The price of corn could remain high as long as corn is the only feedstock used for ethanol production, in the United States. Currently research is being conducted on alternative methods of producing ethanol. With current technology and subsidies provided by the U.S. government corn is the only economical method for mass production available in the United States. Brazil on the other hand is the most efficient producer of sugar-based ethanol in the world. New methods for producing ethanol from non-food commodities, such as cellulosic ethanol, are being developed. This method of producing ethanol is currently uneconomical and could take several years before becoming viable for mass production. Until a new viable method is developed demand for sugar as a feedstock for ethanol will continue to grow.

Demand for gasoline in the United States typically picks up in the U.S. summer season, which could increase the demand for ethanol. The increase in demand for ethanol coupled with high feedstock cost for corn-based ethanol could cause ethanol prices to rise in peak driving seasons. This could indirectly affect demand for Brazilian sugar-based ethanol in times of tight supply in the U.S. market. In an effort to protect its ethanol industry the U.S. has imposed a 54-cent tariff on imported ethanol. The tariff to some extent is stifling for Brazilian exports. A significant portion of Brazilian ethanol makes its way into the United States through countries in Central America. These countries are covered under the Caribbean Basin Initiative. Ethanol imports under the Caribbean Basin Initiative are tariff free. This could support global sugar prices as demand for imported sugar-based ethanol rises.

The importance of ethanol is largely dependent on the price of crude oil. Higher crude oil prices raise the incentive for consumers to increase their consumption of ethanol. This is because it will help reduce their cost. If the price of crude declines, however, there is little or no incentive for consumers to demand ethanol. Ethanol is a comparatively less efficient fuel than gasoline. A gallon of E85, that is a blend of 85% ethanol and 15% gasoline, gives approximately 30% less mileage than a gallon of gasoline.[23] This further enhances the disincentive for consumers to demand ethanol at low gasoline prices. The threshold ratio for choosing between ethanol and gasoline will differ by country, depending upon the costs of these fuels in that country. Government incentives in the form of tax benefits to consumers, producers, or blenders could alter choices.

The only market where the demand for ethanol remains relatively insulated from declining gasoline prices is Brazil. In this country the gasoline is blended with a mandated amount of ethanol. If gasoline prices decline, *flex-fuel vehicle* (FFV) owners will shift from pure ethanol to gasoline. FFVs in Brazil can run on 100% ethanol or some combination of gasoline and

[23]U.S. Environmental Protection Agency, "Alternative Fuels: E85 and Flex Fuel Vehicles," October 2006.

ethanol. The gasoline, however, still contains at the least the government-mandated percentage of ethanol. Therefore every car consumes some proportion of ethanol.

For ethanol to have more sustainable demand (that is, even at lower oil prices) it would need to be produced more efficiently. Lower costs resulting from higher efficiency would reduce the threshold price at which consumers make a switch from ethanol to gasoline. This would protect ethanol from declining oil prices. To ensure higher efficiency new methods of production and new feedstock could be needed. This could create a paradigm shift in the ethanol industry when feedstocks other than sugar and corn would take center stage. Until more efficient methods of production are found and made economically viable, demand for sugar-based ethanol could continue to support sugar prices, more so in poor crop years.

HOW TO INVEST

Futures and options on sugar are traded on the Intercontinental Exchange (ICE) and the London International Financial Futures and Options Exchange (LIFFE). The ICE trades the raw sugar contract. Meanwhile LIFFE trades both the raw sugar contract as well as a white sugar contract. The raw sugar contract, traded in both London and New York, have similar contract specifications. Both the contracts have the same size—112,000 pounds or 50 long tons, the same delivery months – March, May, July, and October, similar quality requirements—raw sugar centrifugal cane sugar based on 96 degrees average polarization and the same price quotation, in cents per pound. The trading of identical raw sugar contracts on two major exchanges will offer traders arbitrage opportunities. Electronic trading increases volumes and liquidity, which could reduce spreads, however. The interplay between white sugar prices and raw sugar prices also presents an attractive trading opportunity (see Exhibit 39.7).

It is commonly observed that the U.S. dollar has an inverse relation with commodity prices.[24] This relation could be stronger for some commodities than for others. Cocoa for example reacts more strongly to movements in the U.S. dollar than does sugar. The movement in the U.S. dollar influences the price of all commodities nonetheless.

Sugar investments can be made indirectly via sugar equities. Equities of sugar mills typically rise when sugar prices rise. This is based on the assumption, however, that profits will increase as the value of the commodity

[24]Data from Commodity Research Bureau Index and the Federal Reserve Board Trade Weighted Dollar Index.

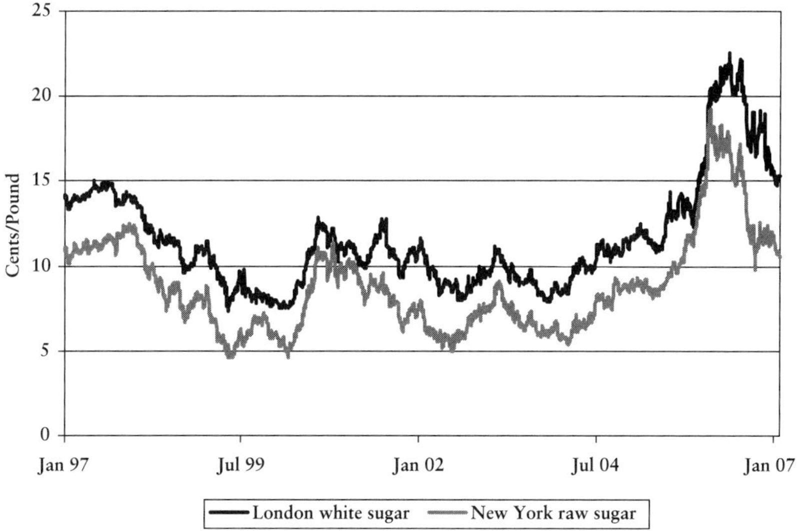

EXHIBIT 39.7 London White Sugar and New York Raw Sugar Price
Source: Exhibit created from data obtained from the Intercontinental Exchange and Bloomberg.

increases. Other factors such as the quality of management can distort this assumption. Poor management can increase costs due to poor financing decisions or increased operating costs. This could reduce any potential benefits that the company would have achieved from sugar price appreciation. Government policies in various countries can further stifle the sugar industry. The general sentiment in equity markets will also affect sugar equities, irrespective of whether sugar is selling at a good price. By investing in sugar equities an investor typically exposes himself to risks associated with the company.

CONCLUSION

In conclusion, the sugar market provides interesting investing opportunities. The phase-out of unfair trade practices, which has taken root in the WTO's ruling against the EU, is a step toward free market conditions. This will help align sugar's supply/demand fundamentals more closely with its price, making investments in sugar more favorable. It should be kept in mind that a complete removal of trade arrangements between countries is highly unlikely.

The trading of similar raw sugar contracts in both New York and London will give the market greater liquidity and depth, both highly desired attributes by investors. Developments in the ethanol market should be closely eyed. New production processes could have a dramatic impact on any ethanol related price premium factored into sugar prices. And lastly, this bears repeating, all forecasts should be made assuming average weather conditions.

PART Seven

Technical Analysis

CHAPTER 40

The Profitability of Technical Analysis in Commodity Markets

Cheol-Ho Park, Ph.D.
Economist
Korea Futures Association

Scott H. Irwin, Ph.D.
Laurence J. Norton Professor of Agricultural Marketing
University of Illinois Urbana-Champaign

Technical analysis is a method of forecasting price movements using past prices, volume, and/or open interest. Pring,[1] a leading technical analyst, provides a more specific definition:

> *The technical approach to investment is essentially a reflection of the idea that prices move in trends that are determined by the changing attitudes of investors toward a variety of economic, monetary, political, and psychological forces. The art of technical analysis, for it is an art, is to identify a trend reversal at a relatively early stage and ride on that trend until the weight of the evidence shows or proves that the trend has reversed. (p. 2)*

Technical analysis includes a variety of forecasting techniques such as chart analysis, cycle analysis, and computerized technical trading systems. Academic research on technical analysis generally is limited to techniques that can be expressed in mathematical form, namely technical trading

[1]Martin J. Pring, *Technical Analysis Explained* (New York: McGraw-Hill, 2002).

Substantial parts of this paper are reprinted, by permission, from the following article: Cheol-Ho Park and Scott H. Irwin, "What Do We Know about the Profitability of Technical Analysis?" *Journal of Economic Surveys* 21, no. 4 (September 2007), pp. 786–826.

systems, although some recent studies attempt to test visual chart patterns using pattern recognition algorithms. A technical trading system consists of a set of trading rules that generate trading signals (long, short, or out of the market) according to various parameter values. Popular technical trading systems include moving averages, channels, and momentum oscillators.

Technical analysis has a long history of widespread use by participants in commodity markets.[2] In pioneering work, Smidt[3] surveys amateur traders in U.S. commodity futures markets and finds that over half of the respondents use charts exclusively or moderately in order to identify trends. More recently, Billingsley and Chance[4] find that about 60% of *commodity trading advisors* (CTAs) rely heavily or exclusively on computer-guided technical trading systems. Fung and Hsieh[5] estimate style factors for CTAs and conclude that trend-following is the single dominant strategy.

In sharp contrast to the views of many practitioners, academics tend to be skeptical about technical analysis. The skepticism can be linked to: (1) acceptance of the efficient market hypothesis, which implies that it is futile to attempt to make profits by exploiting currently available information such as past price trends; and (2) negative empirical findings in several early and widely cited studies of technical analysis in the stock market, such as Fama and Blume,[6] Van Horne and Parker,[7] and Jensen and Benington.[8]

---

[2]The history of technical analysis dates back to at least the 18th century when the Japanese developed a form of technical analysis known as *candlestick charting*. This technique was not introduced to the West until the 1970s. (Steve Nison, *Japanese Candlestick Charting Techniques* (New York: New York Institute of Finance, 1991).)

[3]Seymour Smidt, *Amateur Speculators* (Ithaca, NY: Graduate School of Business and Public Administration, Cornell University, 1965).

[4]Randall S. Billingsley and Donald M. Chance, "Benefits and Limitations of Diversification among Commodity Trading Advisors," *Journal of Portfolio Management* 23, no. 1 (Fall 1996), pp. 65–80.

[5]William Fung and David A. Hsieh, "The Information Content of Performance Track Records: Investment Style and Survivorship Bias in the Historical Returns of Commodity Trading Advisors," *Journal of Portfolio Management* 24, no.1 (Fall 1997), pp. 30–41.

[6]Eugene F. Fama and Marshall E. Blume, "Filter Rules and Stock Market Trading," *Journal of Business* 39, no.1 (January 1966), pp. 226–241.

[7]James C. Van Horne and George G. C. Parker, "The Random-Walk Theory: An Empirical Test," *Financial Analysts Journal* 23, no. 6 (November-December 1967), pp. 87–92. James C. Van Horne and George G. C. Parker, "Technical Trading Rules: A Comment," *Financial Analysts Journal* 24, no. 4 (July–August 1968), pp. 128–132.

[8]Michael C. Jensen and George A. Benington, "Random Walks and Technical Theories: Some Additional Evidence," *Journal of Finance* 25, no. 2 (May 1970), pp. 469–482.

The controversy about the usefulness of technical analysis has led to a large literature on the subject. Empirical studies investigate the profitability of technical trading rules in a variety of markets for the purpose of either uncovering profitable trading rules or testing market efficiency, or both. Most studies concentrate on stock markets, both in and outside the U.S. and foreign exchange markets. A smaller number of studies analyze commodity markets.

The purpose of this chapter is to review the empirical literature on technical analysis in commodity markets and discuss the consistency and reliability of evidence on technical trading profits across markets and over time. Commodity markets for this review include agricultural, food, fiber, energy, and metals markets. The majority of the studies are collected from academic journals published from 1960 to the present and recent working papers. Only a few studies are obtained from books or magazines. Previous empirical studies are categorized into two groups, "early" studies and "modern" studies, based on an overall evaluation of each study in terms of the number of technical trading systems considered, treatment of transaction costs, risk, data-snooping problems, parameter optimization, out-of-sample verification, and statistical tests adopted. Empirical studies surveyed include those that test technical trading systems and trading rules formulated by genetic algorithms or some statistical models such as the *autoregressive integrated moving average* (ARIMA). Special attention is paid to testing procedures used in empirical studies and identification of their salient features and weaknesses. This will improve understanding of the profitability of technical trading strategies and suggest directions for future research.

THE EFFICIENT MARKET HYPOTHESIS

The efficient market hypothesis, long the dominant paradigm in describing the behavior of prices in speculative markets, provides the theoretical benchmark for most studies of technical analysis in commodity markets. Fama gives the textbook definition of an efficient market: "A market in which prices always 'fully reflect' available information is called *efficient*" (p. 383).[9] Jensen[10] develops a more detailed definition: "A market is efficient with respect to information set θ_t if it is impossible to make economic profits by trading on the basis of information set θ_t" (p. 96). Since the

[9]Eugene F. Fama, "Efficient Capital Markets: A Review of Theory and Empirical Work," *Journal of Finance* 25, no. 2 (May 1970), pp. 383–417.

[10]Michael C. Jensen, "Some Anomalous Evidence Regarding Market Efficiency," *Journal of Financial Economics* 6, nos. 2, 3 (June–September 1978), pp. 95–101.

economic profits are risk-adjusted returns after deducting transaction costs, Jensen's definition implies that market efficiency may be tested by considering the net profits and risk of trading strategies based on information set θ_t.

Jensen also subdivides the efficient market hypothesis into three types based on definitions of the information set θ_t:

1. Weak-form efficiency, where the information set θ_t is limited to the information contained in the past price history of the market as of time t.
2. Semistrong-form efficiency, where the information set θ_t is all information that is publicly available at time t. (This includes, of course, the past history of prices so the weak-form is just a restricted version of the semistrong-form.)
3. Strong-form efficiency, where the information set θ_t is all public and private information available at time t. (This includes the past history of prices and all other public information, so weak- and semistrong-forms are simply restricted versions of the strong-form.)

Timmermann and Granger[11] extend Jensen's definition by specifying how the information variables in θ_t are used to generate forecasts. In their definition, a market is efficient with respect to information set, θ_t, search technologies, S_t, and forecasting models, M_t if it is impossible to make economic profits by trading on the basis of signals produced from a forecasting model in M_t defined over predictor variables in the information set θ_t and selected using a search technology in S_t.

A key implication of the efficient market hypothesis is that any attempt to make profits by exploiting currently available information is futile. The market price already reflects all that can be known from available information. Therefore, the expected return for technical trading rules based only on the public record of past prices is zero. This logic is stated in colorful terms by Samuelson:[12]

> . . . *there is no way of making an expected profit by extrapolating past changes in the futures price, by chart or any other esoteric devices of magic or mathematics. The market quotation already contains in itself all that can be known about the future and in that sense has discounted future contingencies as much as is humanly possible. (p. 44)*

[11]Alan Timmermann and Clive W.J. Granger, "Efficient Market Hypothesis and Forecasting," *International Journal of Forecasting* 20, no. 1 (January-March 2004), pp. 15–27.

[12]Paul A. Samuelson, "Proof That Properly Anticipated Prices Fluctuate Randomly," *Industrial Management Review* 6, no. 2 (Spring 1965), pp. 41–49.

TECHNICAL TRADING SYSTEMS

Before surveying the empirical literature on the profitability of technical trading, it is useful to first introduce and explicitly define major types of technical trading systems. A technical trading system comprises a set of trading rules that can be used to generate trading signals. In general, a simple trading system has one or two parameters that determine the timing of trading signals. Each rule contained in a trading system is the result of a particular parameterization. For example, the Dual Moving Average Crossover system with two parameters (a short moving average and a long moving average) may be composed of hundreds of trading rules that can be generated by altering combinations of the two parameters. Among technical trading systems, the most well-known types of systems are moving averages, channels (support and resistance), momentum oscillators, and filters. These systems are widely used by academics, market participants, or both and, with the exception of filter rules, are featured prominently in well-known books on technical analysis, such as Schwager,[13] Kaufman,[14] and Pring.[15] Filter rules were exhaustively tested by academics for several decades (the early 1960s through the early 1990s) before moving average systems gained popularity in academic research. This section describes representative trading systems for each major category: Dual Moving Average Crossover, Outside Price Channel (Support and Resistance), Relative Strength Index, and Alexander's Filter Rule.

It is important to note that a very large number of technical trading systems have been proposed. For additional examples, readers should see Wilder[16] or other books on technical analysis. In addition, the above examples do not cover other forms of technical analysis such as charting. Most books on technical analysis explain a broad category of visual chart patterns, and some recent academic papers (e.g., Chang and Osler[17] and Lo, Mamaysky, and Wang[18]) investigate the forecasting ability of various chart patterns by developing pattern recognition algorithms.

---

[13]Jack D. Schwager, *Schwager on Futures: Technical Analysis* (New York: John Wiley & Sons, 1996).

[14]Perry J. Kaufman, *Trading Systems and Methods* (New York: John Wiley & Sons, 1998).

[15]Pring, *Technical Analysis Explained.*

[16]J. Welles Wilder Jr., *New Concepts in Technical Trading Systems* (Greensboro, NC: Hunter Publishing Company, 1978).

[17]P. H. Kevin Chang and Carol L. Osler, "Methodical Madness: Technical Analysis and the Irrationality of Exchange-Rate Forecasts," *Economic Journal* 109, no. 458 (October 1999), pp. 636–661.

[18]Andrew W. Lo, Harry Mamaysky, and Jiang Wang, "Foundations of Technical Analysis: Computational Algorithms, Statistical Inference, and Empirical Implementation," *Journal of Finance* 55, no. 4 (August 2000), pp. 1705–1765.

Dual Moving Average Crossover

Moving-average-based trading systems are the simplest and most popular trend-following systems among practitioners. According to Neftci,[19] the (dual) moving average method is one of the few technical trading procedures that is statistically well-defined. The Dual Moving Average Crossover system generates trading signals by identifying when the short-term trend rises above or below the long-term trend. Specifications of the system are as follows:

1. Definitions
   a. Shorter moving average (SMA) over s days at time t:

   $$(SMA_t) = \sum_{i=1}^{s} P^c_{t-i+1}/s,$$

   where P^c_t is the close at time t and $s < t$.

   a. Longer moving average (LMA) over l days at time t:

   $$(LMA_t) = \sum_{i=1}^{l} P^c_{t-i+1}/l,$$

   where $s < l \leq t$.
2. Trading rules
   a. Go long at P^o_{t+1} if $SMA_t > LMA_t$, where P^o_{t+1} is the open at time $t+1$.
   b. Go short at P^o_{t+1} if $SMA_t < LMA_t$.
3. Parameters: s, l.

Outside Price Channel

Price channels are another widely-used family of technical trading systems. The price channel is sometimes referred to as *trading range break-out* or *support and resistance*. The fundamental characteristic underlying price channel systems is that market movement to a new high or low suggests a continued trend in the direction established. Thus, all price channels generate trading signals based on a comparison between today's price with the price levels of some specified number of days in the past. The Outside Price

[19]Salih N. Neftci, "Naïve Trading Rules in Financial Markets and Wiener-Kolmogorov Prediction Theory: A Study of 'Technical Analysis'," *Journal of Business* 64, no. 4 (October 1991), pp. 549–571.

Channel system is analogous to a trading system introduced by Donchian,[20] who used only the two preceding calendar week's ranges as a channel length. More specifically, this system generates a buy signal anytime the closing price is outside (greater than) the highest price in a channel length (specified time interval), and generates a sell signal anytime the closing price breaks outside (lower than) the lowest price in the price channel. Specifications of the system are as follows:

1. Definitions
   a. Price channel = a time interval including today, n days in length.
   b. The highest high $(HH_t) = \max\{P^h_{t-1}, \ldots, P^h_{t-n+1}\}$, where P^h_{t-1} is the high at time $t-1$.
   c. The lowest low $(LL_t) = \min\{P^l_{t-1}, \ldots, P^l_{t-n+1}\}$, where P^l_{t-1} is the low at time $t-1$.
2. Trading rules
   a. Go long at P^c_t if $P^c_t > HH_t$, where P^c_t is the close at time t.
   b. Go short at P^c_t if $P^c_t < LL_t$.
3. Parameter: n.

Relative Strength Index

The Relative Strength Index, introduced by Wilder,[21] is one of the best-known momentum oscillator systems. Momentum oscillator techniques derive their name from the fact that trading signals are obtained from values that "oscillate" above and below a neutral point, usually given a zero value. In the simplest form, a momentum oscillator compares today's price with price of n-days ago. Wilder explains the momentum oscillator concept as follows:

> *The momentum oscillator measures the velocity of directional price movement. When the price moves up very rapidly, at some point it is considered to be overbought; when it moves down very rapidly, at some point it is considered to be oversold. In either case, a reaction or reversal is imminent. (p. 63)*

[20]Richard D. Donchian, "High Finance in Copper," *Financial Analysts Journal* 16, no. 6 (November–December 1960), pp. 133–142.
[21]Wilder, *New Concepts in Technical Trading Systems.*

Momentum values are similar to standard moving averages, in that they can be regarded as smoothed price movements. However, since the momentum values generally decrease before a reverse in trend takes place, momentum oscillators may identify a change in trend in advance, while moving averages usually cannot. The Relative Strength Index (RSI) is designed to overcome two problems encountered in developing meaningful momentum oscillators: (1) erroneous erratic movement, and (2) the need for an objective scale for the amplitude of oscillators. Specifications of the system are as follows:

1. Definitions
   a. Up closes (UC) at time t $(UC_t) = P_t^c - P_{t-1}^c$, if $P_t^c > P_{t-1}^c$. P_t^c is the close at time t.
   b. Down closes (DC) at time t $(DC_t) = -(P_t^c - P_{t-1}^c)$, if $P_t^c < P_{t-1}^c$.
   c. Average up closes (AUP_t) over n days at time $t, t+1, t+2, \ldots$:

$$AUC_t = \textstyle\sum_{i=1}^{n} UC_{t-i+1}/n,$$
$$AUC_{t+1} = (AUC_t \times (n-1) + UC_{t+1})/n,$$
$$AUC_{t+2} = (AUC_{t+1} \times (n-1) + UC_{t+2})/n, \ldots.$$

   d. Average down closes (ADC_t) over n days at time $t, t+1, t+2, \ldots$:

$$ADC_t = \textstyle\sum_{i=1}^{n} DC_{t-i+1}/n,$$
$$ADC_{t+1} = (ADC_t \times (n-1) + DC_{t+1})/n,$$
$$ADC_{t+2} = (ADC_{t+1} \times (n-1) + DC_{t+2})/n, \ldots.$$

   e. Relative strength (RS) at time t $(RS_t) = AUC_t/ADC_t$.
   f. Relative Strength Index at time t $(RSI_t) = 100 - (100/(1 + RS_t))$.
   g. Entry thresholds $(ET, 100 - ET)$: RSI values beyond which buy or sell signals are generated.
2. Trading rules
   a. Go long when RSI falls below ET and rises back above it.
   b. Go short when RSI rises above $100 - ET$ and falls back below it.
3. Parameters: n, ET.

Alexander's Filter Rule

This system was first introduced by Alexander[22] and exhaustively tested by numerous academics until the early 1990s. Since then, its popularity among

[22]Sidney S. Alexander, "Price Movements in Speculative Markets: Trends or Random Walks," *Industrial Management Review* 2, no. 2 (May 1961), pp. 7–26.

academics has been replaced by moving average methods. This system generates a buy (sell) signal when today's closing price rises (falls) by $x\%$ above (below) its most recent low (high). Moves less than $x\%$ in either direction are ignored. Thus, price movements smaller than a specified size are filtered out and the remaining movements are examined. Alexander argued that "If stock price movements were generated by a trend-less random walk, these filters could be expected to yield zero profits, or to vary from zero profits, both positively and negatively, in a random manner" (p. 23). Specifications of the system are as follows:

1. Definitions
   a. High extreme point (HEP) = the highest close obtained while in a long trade.
   b. Low extreme point (LEP) = the lowest close obtained while in a short trade.
   c. x = the percent filter size.
2. Trading rules
   a. Go long on the close, if today's close rises $x\%$ above the LEP.
   b. Go short on the close, if today's close falls $x\%$ below the HEP.
3. Parameter: x.

EMPIRICAL STUDIES

The earliest empirical study of technical trading profits included in this review is Donchian's[23] 1960 study. Although the boundary between early and modern studies is blurred, Lukac, Brorsen, and Irwin's[24] 1988 study is regarded here as the first modern study because it is among the first to substantially improve upon early studies in several important ways. This study considers 12 technical trading systems, conducts out-of-sample verification for optimized trading rules with a statistical significance test, and measures the performance of trading rules after adjusting for transaction costs and risk. Thus, early commodity market studies are assumed to commence with Donchian's 1960 study and include studies through 1987, while modern studies begin with Lukac, Brorsen, and Irwin's 1988 study and cover studies through July 2005.

[23]Donchian, "High Finance in Copper."

[24]Louis P. Lukac, B. Wade Brorsen and Scott H. Irwin, "A Test of Futures Market Disequilibrium Using Twelve Different Technical Trading Systems," *Applied Economics* 20, no. 5 (May 1988), pp. 623–639.

Early Studies (1960–1987)

Early studies investigate several technical trading systems, including filters, stop-loss orders, moving averages, channels, and momentum oscillators. Filter rules are the most popular trading system tested. A representative study in this regard is Stevenson and Bear.[25] In this study, three trading systems related to the filter technique—stop-loss orders attributed to Houthakker,[26] Alexander's filter rules, and combinations of both rules—are tested on July corn and soybean futures from 1957 through 1968. The stop-loss order works as follows: An investor buys a futures contract at the opening on the first day of trading and places a stop-loss order x% below the purchase price. If the order is not executed, the investor holds the contract until the last possible date prior to delivery. If the order is executed, no further position is assumed until the opening day of trading of the next contract. For each system, three filter sizes (1.5%, 3%, and 5%) are selected and a commission of 0.5 cents per bushel for both corn and soybeans is charged.

The results for soybeans indicate that the stop-loss order with a 5% filter outperforms a buy-and-hold (B&H) strategy by a large amount, while for corn it greatly reduces losses relative to the benchmark across all filters. The pure filter systems appear to have relatively poor performance. For corn, all filters generate negative net returns, although 3% and 5% filters perform better than the buy-and-hold strategy. For soybeans, 1.5% and 3% filters are inferior to the buy-and-hold strategy because they have losses, while a 5% filter rule outperforms the benchmark with positive net returns. The combination system is the best performer among systems. For soybeans, all filters beat the buy-and-hold strategy, and particularly 3% and 5% filters generate large net returns. The 3% and 5% filters also outperform the buy-and-hold strategy for corn. On the other hand, the combination system against market (countertrend system) indicates nearly opposite results. Overall, stop-loss orders and combination rules are profitable in an absolute sense, outperforming the buy-and-hold strategy. The results lead Stevenson and Bear to cast considerable doubt on the applicability of the random walk hypothesis to the price behavior of commodity futures markets.

As indicated by the summaries found in Exhibit 40.1, the majority of early technical trading studies in commodity markets find substantial net profits. These results suggest that commodity markets are not efficient

[25] Richard A. Stevenson and Robert M. Bear, "Commodity Futures: Trends or Random Walks?" *Journal of Finance* 25, no. 1 (March 1970), pp. 65–81.

[26] Hendrik S. Houthakker, "Systematic and Random Elements in Short-Term Price Movements," *American Economic Review* 51, no. 2 (May 1961), pp. 164–172.

Exhibit 40.1 Summary of Early Technical Analysis Studies in Commodities Markets, 1961–1987

Study	Markets Considered/ Frequency of Data	In-Sample Period (Out-of-Sample Period)	Technical Trading Systems	Benchmark Strategies/ Optimization	Transaction Costs	Conclusion
1. Donchian (1960)	Copper futures/ Daily	1959–1960	Channel	Not considered	$5.50 per round-trip	The current price is compared to the two preceding weeks' ranges. This trading rule generates net gains of $3,488 and $1,390, on margin of $1,000, for a single contract of the December 1959 delivery of copper and the December 1960 delivery, respectively.
2. Houthakker (1961)	Wheat and corn futures/Daily	1921–1939, 1947–1956	Stop-loss order (11 rules from 0% to 100%)	Buy & hold, Sell & hold	Not adjusted	Most stop-loss orders generate higher profits than the buy and hold (B&H) or a sell and hold strategy. Long transactions indicate better performance than short transactions.
3. Gray and Nielsen (1963)	Wheat futures/ Daily	1921–1943, 1949–1962	Top-loss order (10 rules from 1% to 100%)	Buy & hold, Sell & hold	Not adjusted	When applying stop-loss order rules to dominant contracts, there is little evidence of nonrandomness in wheat futures prices. They argue that Houthakker's results are biased because he used remote contracts and that postwar seasonality of wheat futures prices is induced by government loan programs.
4. Smidt (1965a)	May soybean futures contracts/ Daily	1952–1961	Momentum oscillator (40 rules)	Not considered	$0.36 per bushel per round-trip	About 70% of trading rules tested generate positive returns after commissions. Moreover, half of trading rules return 7.5% per year or more.
5. Stevenson and Bear (1970)	July corn and soybean futures/Daily	1957–1968	Stop-loss order, filter, and combination of both systems	Buy & hold	0.5 cents per bushel for both commodities	For all systems, a 5% filter rule works best as it generates larger net profits or greatly reduced losses relative to the B&H strategy. The filter rule also outperforms B&H for both corn and soybean futures.
6. Leuthold (1972)	30 live cattle futures contracts/Daily	1965–1970	Filter (1%, 2%, 3%, 4%, 5%, and 10%)	Not considered	Commissions of $36 per round-trip	Four of six filters are profitable after transaction costs. In particular, a 3% filter rule generates an annual net return of 115.8% during the sample period.
7. Martell and Philippatos (1974)	September wheat and September soybean futures contracts/Daily	1956–1969 (1958–1970)	Adaptive filter model and pure information model	Buy & hold/ Optimized trading rules	Adjusted but not specified	As an optimal filter size for period t, the adaptive model utilizes a filter size that yields the highest profits in $t - 1$, subject to some minimum value of the average relative information gain. The pure information model chooses as an optimal filter size in period t the one with the highest relative average information gain in period $t - 1$. Both models yield higher net returns than the B&H only for wheat futures. However, the variance in net profits is consistently smaller than that of the B&H in both markets.

(Continued)

Exhibit 40.1 (Continued)

Study	Markets Considered/ Frequency of Data	In-Sample Period (Out-of-Sample Period)	Technical Trading Systems	Benchmark Strategies/ Optimization	Transaction Costs	Conclusion
8. Praetz (1975)	Sydney wool futures/Daily	1965–1972	Filter (24 rules from 0.5% to 25%)	Buy & hold	Not adjusted	For 12 of 21 contracts of 18-month length and all three 8-year price series, the B&H strategy shows better performance than filter rules, with average differences of 0.1% and 2%, respectively. For the same data set, in 10 of 24 filters the B&H returns are greater than average filter returns. Thus, filter rules do not seem to outperform the B&H strategy consistently.
9. Martell (1976)	September wheat and September soybean futures contracts/Daily	1956–1969 (1958–1970)	Adaptive filter models and pure information model	Buy & hold/ Optimized trading rules	Adjusted but not specified	A new adaptive model is developed and applied to the same data set as that used in Martell and Philippatos (1974). The new model selects its optimal filter size for next period based on profitability (e.g., the highest cumulative net profits) and information gain. Although the model outperforms the previous adaptive model for around 80% of the sample period, it neither indicates any stability with respect to the information constraint nor beats the pure information model that allows a filter size in a particular period to reflect new information.
10. Solt and Swanson (1981)	Gold from London Gold Market and silver from Handy & Harman/ Weekly	1971–1979	Filter (0.5% to 50%) and moving average (26, 52, and 104 weeks with filters)	Buy & hold	1.0% per one-way transaction plus 0.5% annual fees	For gold, a 10% filter rule outperforms the B&H strategy after adjustment for transaction costs. However, none of the filter rules dominates the B&H strategy for either gold or silver. Moving average rules are not able to improve the returns for the filter rules as well.
11. Peterson and Leuthold (1982)	7 hog futures contracts from Chicago Mercantile Exchange (CME)/Daily	1973–1977	Filter (10 rules from 1% to 10% and additional 10 rules from $0.5 to $5)	Zero mean profit	Not adjusted	All 20 filter rules produce considerable mean gross profits. It seemes that these profit levels exceed any reasonable commission charges in most cases. In general, mean gross profits increase with larger filters, as do variance of profits.
12. Irwin and Uhrig (1984)	8 commodity futures: corn, cocoa, soy-beans, wheat, sugar, copper, live cattle, and live hogs/Daily	1960–1978 (1979–1981), 1960–1968 (1969–1972), 1973–1978 (1979–1981)	Channel, moving averages, momentum oscillator	Zero mean profit/ Optimized trading rules	Doubled commissions to capture bid-ask spread (not specified)	Trading rule profits during in-sample periods are substantial and similar across all four trading systems. Out-of-sample results for optimal trading rules also indicate that during the 1979–1981 period most trading systems are profitable in corn, cocoa, sugar, and soybean futures markets. The trading rule profits appear to be concentrated in the 1973–1981 period.

13. Neftci and Policano (1984)	4 futures: copper, gold, soybeans, and T-bills/Daily	1975–1980	Moving average (25, 50, and 100 days) and slope (trendline) method	Not considered	Not adjusted	Trading signals are incorporated as a dummy variable into a regression equation for the minimum mean square error prediction. Then the significance of the dummy variable is evaluated using F-tests. Overall, moving average rules indicated some predictive power for T-bills, gold, and soybeans, while the slope method shows mixed results.
14. Tomek and Querin (1984)	3 random price series (each series consists of 300 prices) generated from corn prices for each sample period/Daily	1975–1980, 1973–1974, 1980	Moving average (3/10 and 10/40 days)	Not considered	$50 per round-trip	From each of three random prices series, 20 sets of prices are replicated. The first 20 sets have moderate price variability, the second set large price variability, and the third set drift in prices. Both trading rules fail to generate positive average net profits for all three groups with an exception of the 10/40 rule for the relatively volatile price group. The results imply that technical trading rules may earn positive net returns by chance, although on average they cannot generate positive net profits.
15. Bird (1985)	Cash and forward contracts of copper, lead, tin, and zinc from London Metal Exchange (LME)/Daily	1972–1982	Filter: long positions (and cash profits) (25 rules from 1% to 25%)	Buy & hold	1% per round-trip	For cash and forward (futures) copper, over two-thirds of filter rules beat the B&H strategy. Similar results are obtained for lead and zinc but with weaker evidence. For tin, the results are inconsistent. Filter rules perform substantially better in the earlier period (1972–1977).
16. Taylor (1983, 1986)	London agricultural futures: cocoa, coffee, and sugar, Chicago IMM currency futures: sterling, mark, and Swiss franc/Daily	1971–1976 (1977–1981), 1961–1973 (1974–1981), 1974–1978 (1979–1981)	A statistical price-trend model	Buy & hold and interest rate for bank deposit/ Optimized trading rules	1% per round-trip for agricultural futures and 0.2% for currency futures	Taylor (1986) adds one more out-of-sample year (i.e., 1981) to the sample period in his 1983 work. For sugar, an average net return of the trading rule is higher than that of the B&H strategy by 27% per annum. For cocoa and coffee, returns from both the trading rule and the B&H are not much different. Trading gains for currencies during 1979–1980 are negligible, but in 1981 all currencies generate substantial gains of around 7% higher than the bank deposit rate.

(Continued)

Exhibit 40.1 (Continued)

Study	Markets Considered/ Frequency of Data	In-Sample Period (Out-of-Sample Period)	Technical Trading Systems	Benchmark Strategies/ Optimization	Transaction Costs	Conclusion
17. Thompson and Waller (1987)	Coffee and cocoa futures in the New York Coffee, Sugar, and Cocoa Exchange/6 weekly sets of transaction-to-transaction prices for each market	1981–1983	Filter (for coffee, 5¢ through 35¢ in multiples of 5¢ per 100 lb; for cocoa, $1 through $7 per metric ton)	Not considered	Estimated execution costs	For both nearby and distant coffee and cocoa contracts, filter rules generate average profits per trade per contract substantially lower than estimated execution costs per contract in all cases in which profits are statistically significantly greater than zero. The estimated execution costs per trade per contract are $32.25 (nearby) and $69.75 (distant) for coffee futures contracts and $12.60 (nearby) and $21.80 (distant) for cocoa futures contracts.

Notes: Full citations for the studies are as follows: (1) Richard D. Donchian, "High Finance in Copper," *Financial Analysts Journal* 16, no. 6 (November-December 1960), pp. 133–142. (2) Hendrik S. Houthakker, "Systematic and Random Elements in Short-Term Price Movements," *American Economic Review* 51, no. 2 (May 1961), pp. 164–172. (3) Roger W. Gray and Soren T. Nielsen, "Rediscovery of Some Fundamental Price Behavior Characteristics," paper presented at the meeting of the Econometric Society held in Cleveland, Ohio, September 1963. (4) Seymour Smidt, "A Test of the Serial Independence of Price Changes in Soybean Futures," *Food Research Institute Studies* 5, no. 2 (1965), pp. 117–136. (5) Richard A. Stevenson and Robert M. Bear, "Commodity Futures: Trends or Random Walks?" *Journal of Finance* 25, no. 1 (March 1970), pp. 65–81. (6) Raymond M. Leuthold, "Random Walk and Price Trends: The Live Cattle Futures Market," *Journal of Finance* 27, no. 4 (September 1972), pp. 879–889. (7) Terrence F. Martell and George C. Philippatos, "Adaptation, Information, and Dependence in Commodity Markets," *Journal of Finance* 29, no. 2 (May 1974), pp. 493–498. (8) Peter D. Praetz, "Testing the Efficient Markets Theory on the Sydney Wool Futures Exchange," *Australian Economic Papers* 14, no. 25 (December 1975), pp. 240–249. (9) Terrence F. Martell, "Adaptive Trading Rules for Commodity Futures," *Omega* 4, no. 14 (August 1976), pp. 407–416. (10) Michael E. Solt and Paul J. Swanson, "On the Efficiency of the Markets for Gold and Silver," *Journal of Business* 54, no. 3 (July 1981), pp. 453–478. (11) Paul E. Peterson and Raymond M. Leuthold, "Using Mechanical Trading Systems to Evaluate the Weak Form Efficiency of Futures Markets," *Southern Journal of Agricultural Economics* 14, no. 1 (July 1982), pp. 147–152. (12) Scott H. Irwin and J. William Uhrig, "Do Technical Analysts Have Holes in Their Shoes?" *Review of Futures Markets* 3, no. 3 (1984), pp. 264–277. (13) Salih N. Neftci and Andrew J. Policano, "Can Chartists Outperform the Market? Market Efficiency Tests for 'Technical Analysis'," *Journal of Futures Markets* 4, no. 4 (Winter 1984), pp. 465–478. (14) William G. Tomek and Scott F. Querin, "Random Processes in Prices and Technical Analysis," *Journal of Futures Markets* 4, no. 1 (Spring 1984), pp. 15–23. (15) Peter J. W. N. Bird, "The Weak Form Efficiency of the London Metal Exchange," *Applied Economics* 17, no. 4 (August 1985), pp. 571–587. (16a) Stephen J. Taylor, "Trading Rules for Investors in Apparently Inefficient Futures Markets," Chapter 8 in Manfred E. Streit (ed.), *Futures Markets – Modeling, Managing and Monitoring Futures Trading* (Oxford: Basil Blackwell, 1983). (16b) Stephen J. Taylor, *Modelling Financial Time Series* (Chichester: John Wiley & Sons, 1986). (17) Sarahelen R. Thompson and Mark L. Waller, "The Execution Cost of Trading in Commodity Futures Markets," *Food Research Institute Studies* 20, no. 2 (No. 2 1987), pp. 141–163.

before the mid-1980s. This conclusion should be tempered in light of several limitations in the testing procedures of early studies. First, early studies generally consider a small number of trading systems, typically investigating only one or two trading systems. Thus, even if some studies demonstrate that technical trading rules do not generate significant profits, it may be premature to dismiss technical trading strategies.

Second, most early studies do not conduct statistical tests of significance on technical trading returns. Although several studies measure statistical significance using *Z*- or *t*-tests under the assumption that trading rule returns are normally distributed, Taylor[27] notes that applying such conventional statistical tests to trading rule returns is likely invalid since distribution of the returns under the null hypothesis of an efficient market is not known. Furthermore, Lukac and Brorsen[28] report that technical trading returns are positively skewed and leptokurtic and thus argue that past applications of *t*-tests to technical trading returns may be biased.

Third, the riskiness of technical trading rules is ignored in early studies. If investors are risk-averse, they will consider the risk-return trade-off of trading rules. Thus, large trading returns do not necessarily refute market efficiency since the returns may be compensation for taking greater risks. For the same reason, when comparing trading rule and benchmark returns, it is necessary to make explicit allowance for the difference of returns due to different degrees of risk.

Fourth, the substantial technical trading profits found in early studies may be attributable to data-snooping (selection) biases. Since there is no structural form of a technical trading system that prespecifies parameters, technical trading studies inevitably tend to search over a large number of parameters. When a large number of technical trading rules are searched, profitable trading rules may be identified by pure luck, and thus mislead researchers into believing that the rules have genuine predictive power. Jensen[29] recognizes this problem and argues that:

> . . . *if we begin to test various mechanical trading rules on the data we can be virtually certain that if we try enough rules with enough variants we will eventually find one or more which would have yielded profits (even adjusted for any risk differentials) superior to a buy-and-hold policy. But, and this is the crucial question,*

[27]Stephen J. Taylor, "The Behaviour of Futures Prices over Time," *Applied Economics* 17, no. 4 (August 1985), pp. 713–734.
[28]Louis P. Lukac and B. Wade Brorsen, "A Comprehensive Test of Futures Market Disequilibrium," *Financial Review* 25, no. 4 (November 1990), pp. 593–622.
[29]Michael C. Jensen, "Random Walks: Reality or Myth—Comment," *Financial Analysts Journal* 23, no. 6 (November-December 1967), pp. 77–85.

> *does this mean the same trading rule will yield superior profits when actually put into practice? (p. 81)*

Along the same lines, Jensen and Benington[30] state that:

> *. . . given enough computer time, we are sure that we can find a mechanical trading rule which works on a table of random numbers—provided of course that we are allowed to test the rule on the same table of numbers which we used to discover the rule. We realize of course that the rule would prove useless on any other table of random numbers . . . (p. 470)*

Indeed, when Tomek and Querin[31] apply typical technical trading rules, such as filters and moving averages, to randomly generated price series, it turns out that the rules generate net profits for some of the random series by chance.

To deal with data-snooping problems, Jensen[32] proposes a validation procedure where the best-performing trading model or models are identified in the first half of the sample period, and then are validated on the rest of the sample period. Optimizing trading rules is important because actual traders are likely to choose the best-performing rules in advance. No early study in commodity markets follows an optimization and out-of-sample validation procedure, and only a few early studies optimize trading rules.

Modern Studies (1988–2007)

As noted previously, the first "modern" empirical study is assumed to be Lukac, Brorsen, and Irwin,[33] who provide a more comprehensive analysis than any early study. The authors simulate 12 technical trading systems on price series from 12 agricultural, metal, and financial futures markets over 1975–1984. Technical trading is simulated using a three-year re-optimization method in which parameters generating the largest profit over the previous three years are used for the next year's trading, and at the end of the next year, new parameters are again optimized, and so on. This procedure assures that optimal parameters are adaptive and the simulation results are

[30]Jensen and Benington, "Random Walks and Technical Theories: Some Additional Evidence."

[31]William G. Tomek and Scott F. Querin, "Random Processes in Prices and Technical Analysis," *Journal of Futures Markets* 4, no. 1 (Spring 1984), pp. 15–23.

[32]Jensen, "Random Walks: Reality or Myth—Comment."

[33]Lukac, Brorsen, and Irwin, "A Test of Futures Market Disequilibrium Using Twelve Different Technical Trading Systems."

out-of-sample. Two-tailed *t*-tests are performed to test the null hypothesis that gross returns generated from technical trading are zero, while one-tailed *t*-tests are conducted to test the statistical significance of net returns after transaction costs. Based on the assumption that the *capital asset pricing model* (CAPM) holds, Jensen's α is used to determine the significance of risk-adjusted returns.

Lukac, Brorsen, and Irwin find that four trading systems (dual moving average crossover, channel, MII price channel, and directional parabolic) yield statistically significant monthly portfolio net returns ranging from 1.89% to 2.78% after deducting transaction costs of $100 per contract per round-trip trade.[34] Technical trading systems generate significant net returns for five commodity contracts: (1) 5 out of 12 systems for corn; (2) two for lumber; (3) one for soybeans; (4) three for silver; and (5) five for sugar. Among commodity contracts, corn, silver, and sugar appear to be especially promising futures contracts since substantial net returns are observed across the various trading systems. Estimation results indicate that the same four trading systems have statistically significant Jensen's α intercepts, which implies that trading profits are not compensation for bearing systematic risk. Thus, Lukac, Brorsen, and Irwin conclude that some futures markets are indeed inefficient during their sample period.

Lukac, Brorsen, and Irwin's testing procedure alleviates data-snooping problems by considering a diverse set of technical trading systems and conducting parameter optimization and out-of-sample verification. However, their approach still has some limitations. First, the set of trading systems may not completely avoid data-snooping biases if the selected systems reflect "popular" systems known at the time of the study to have been profitable. Second, conventional *t*-tests may have reduced power if the return series are not normally distributed. Third, the CAPM may be an invalid pricing model for futures markets because the assumptions of the CAPM may not be consistent with the structure of futures markets (e.g., Stein[35]).

Lukac and Brorsen use similar procedures to those in Lukac, Brorsen, and Irwin[36] but consider more trading systems (23 systems) and futures

[34]These returns are based on the total investment method in which total investment is composed of a 30% initial investment in margins plus a 70% reserve for potential margin calls. The percentage returns can be converted into simple annual returns (about 3.8%–5.6%) by a straightforward arithmetic manipulation.

[35]Jerome L. Stein, *The Economics of Futures Markets* (New York: Basil Blackwell, 1987).

[36]Lukac and Brorsen, "A Comprehensive Test of Futures Market Disequilibrium." Lukac, Brorsen, and Irwin, "A Test of Futures Market Disequilibrium Using Twelve Different Technical Trading Systems."

contracts (30 contracts) and a slightly longer sample period (1975–1986). They find that 7 out of 23 trading systems generate statistically significant positive net returns after adjustment for transaction costs of $100 per contract. Twenty-three trading systems, on average, generate positive net returns for 18 out of 30 contracts. The monthly net return is more than 1% for the following contracts: corn, silver, platinum, gold, cotton, cocoa, sugar, mark, yen, and Swiss franc. In general, exchange rate futures earn the highest returns, while livestock futures have the lowest returns. These results are consistent with Lukac, Brorsen, and Irwin's original findings.

Lukac and Brorsen[37] evaluate a wide variety of ways of selecting parameters of technical trading systems. With 23 strategies (10 reoptimization strategies, one random strategy, and 12 fixed parameter strategies) to choose parameters, they simulate two trading systems, a channel and a directional movement system, on a portfolio of 15 futures contracts over 1965–1985. The portfolio includes nine agricultural, three metal, and three financial futures contracts. Results show that all the methods of selecting parameters but a five-day fixed parameter strategy for the channel system generate statistically significant mean net profits above zero. Moreover, except in a few cases, return differences between the parameter selection strategies are insignificant. Only returns from 5-day and 10-day strategies of the channel system are statistically lower than those from the majority of the other strategies. This would suggest that parameter optimization in simulating technical trading systems has little value.

Taylor and Tari[38] apply Taylor's[39] trading rule derived from a statistical price-trend model to cocoa, coffee, and sugar futures contracts traded in London over 1982–1985. The statistical model, similar to an ARIMA (1,1,1) model, is designed to capture both trends in prices and return volatility. The trading rule produces excess returns over a risk-free rate of 4.78% for cocoa, −4.16% for coffee, and 18.84% for sugar, after

[37]Louis P. Lukac and B. Wade Brorsen, "The Usefulness of Historical Data in Selecting Parameters for Technical Trading Systems," *Journal of Futures Markets* 9, no. 1 (February 9, no. 1 1989), pp. 55–65.

[38]Stephen J. Taylor and Abdelkamel Tari, "Further Evidence against the Efficiency of Futures Markets," in Rui M.C. Guimaraes, Brian G. Kingsman and Stephen J. Taylor (eds.), *A Reappraisal of the Efficiency of Financial Markets* (Berlin: Springer-Verlag, 1989), pp. 578–601.

[39]Stephen J. Taylor, "Trading Rules for Investors in Apparently Inefficient Futures Markets," Chapter 8 in Manfred E. Streit (ed.), *Futures Markets: Modeling, Managing and Monitoring Futures Trading* (Oxford: Basil Blackwell, 1983).

transaction costs of 1% of contract value per contract per round-trip. Trading rules based on the ARIMA-type model, therefore, appear to be profitable for cocoa and sugar contracts.

Silber[40] applies the moving average trading system to gold and silver contracts from the New York Commodity Exchange (COMEX, currently a division of NYMEX) and crude oil from the New York Mercantile Exchange (NYMEX) over 1980–1991. He investigates the profitability of 1,395 parameter combinations of moving averages using a similar parameter re-optimization procedure as in Lukac and Brorsen's 1990 study. During the out-of-sample period, optimized trading rules produce an annual mean net return of 16.7% and a Sharpe ratio of 0.40 for crude oil, but indicate negative performance for gold and silver. Since the moving average system generates substantial profits for foreign currencies and short-term interest rates over the same sample period, Silber concludes that government intervention such as central bank price-smoothing behavior may provide technical traders with the opportunity to earn abnormal returns.

Irwin et al.[41] compare the performance of the channel "break-out" trading system to ARIMA models in soybean-complex futures markets. A channel length of 40 days is used as a representative parameter of the channel system for all three soybean contracts, while an ARIMA (2,0,0) specification is applied to a soybean contract and an ARIMA (1,0,1) specification to soybean mean and oil contracts. During the out-of-sample period (1984–1988), the channel system generates statistically significant annual mean returns of 5.1% for soybeans, 26.6% for soybean meal, and 23.1% for soybean oil. The corresponding annual mean returns of the ARIMA models are −13.5%, 16.5%, and 5.0%. The channel rule dominates trading strategies based on the ARIMA models.

Hamm and Brorsen[42] develop a neural network trading model with lagged prices as inputs for hard red winter wheat and Deutsche mark futures during 1985–1992. Nonlinear models such as a feed-forward neural

[40]William L. Silber, "Technical Trading: When It Works and When It Doesn't," *Journal of Derivatives* 1, no. 3 (Spring 1994), pp. 39–44.

[41]Scott H. Irwin, Carl R. Zulauf, Mary E. Gerlow, and Jonathan N. Tinker, "A Performance Comparison of a Technical Trading System with ARIMA Models for Soybean Complex Prices," *Advances in Investment Analysis and Portfolio Management* 4 (November 1997), pp. 193–203.

[42]Lonnie Hamm and B. Wade Brorsen, "Trading Futures Markets Based on Signals from a Neural Network," *Applied Economics Letters* 7, no. 2 (February 2000), pp. 137–140.

network or a nearest neighbor regression are known to be capable of approximating nonlinear relationship in commodity prices, if any. Using the neural network trading model, Hamm and Brorsen estimate the number of hidden neurons that produces the highest mean net trading returns for the previous four testing periods, and then evaluate the optimal configuration on one-year out-of-sample testing periods starting in 1985. Statistical significance of trading returns is based on the model-based bootstrap methodology introduced by Brock, Lakonishok, and LeBaron.[43] In the bootstrap procedure, returns conditional on buy (or sell) signals from the original series are compared to the empirical distribution of conditional returns from simulated return series generated by widely used models for asset prices. The two null models are a random walk with drift and a GARCH (1,1). Results indicate that trading rules based on the neural network model generally fail to produce significant gross or net returns during the sample period. Neural networks generate significant profits only for the mark contract in 1989, while none of the sample periods indicate significant profits for the wheat contract.

Boswijk, Griffioen, and Hommes[44] test a large set of 5,350 trading rules for three popular trading systems (moving average, trading range break-out, and Alexander's filter rule) on the London International Financial Futures Exchange (LIFFE) and Coffee, Sugar and Cocoa Exchange (CSCE) cocoa futures prices over 1983–1997. For the LIFFE cocoa futures, 72% of the trading rules produce positive returns after accounting for transaction and borrowing costs. In particular, most returns from the LIFFE contract are obtained during the 1983–1987 period in which about 30% of all trading rules appear to possess statistically significant forecasting power, as measured with an EGARCH model. In contrast, only 18% of all the trading rules generate positive net excess returns for the CSCE cocoa futures. Boswijk, Griffioen, and Hommes attribute the substantial difference in the performance of technical trading rules between the LIFFE and CSCE cocoa futures markets to the pound-dollar exchange rate and differences in the fundamental demand and supply mechanisms between the two markets.

---

[43]William Brock, Josef Lakonishok, and Blake LeBaron, "Simple Technical Trading Rules and the Stochastic Properties of Stock Returns," *Journal of Finance* 47, no. 5 (December 1992), pp. 1731–1764.

[44]Peter Boswijk, Gerwin Griffioen, and Cars Hommes, "Success and Failure of Technical Trading Strategies in the Cocoa Futures Market," Tinbergen Institute Discussion Paper (September 2000).

Roberts[45] applies genetic programming to technical trading rules for 24 futures contracts over 1980–2000. The 24 markets consist of 19 commodity markets and five financial futures markets. *Genetic programming* is a numerical optimization procedure based on the Darwinian principle of survival of the fittest. In this procedure, a computer randomly generates a set of potential solutions for a specific problem and then allows evolution over many successive generations under a given fitness (performance) criterion. Solution candidates that satisfy the fitness criterion are likely to reproduce, while ones that fail to meet the criterion are likely to be replaced. When applied to technical trading rules, the building blocks of genetic algorithms consist of various functions of past prices, numerical and logical constants, and logical functions.

The aforementioned features of genetic programming may provide some advantages relative to traditional approaches for testing technical trading rules. The traditional approach investigates a predetermined parameter space of technical trading systems, while the genetic programming approach examines a search space composed of logical combinations of trading systems or rules. Thus, the fittest (or locally optimized) rules identified by genetic programming can be viewed as *ex ante* rules in the sense that their parameter values are not determined before the test. Since the procedure helps researchers avoid some of the arbitrariness involved in selecting parameters, it may reduce the risk of data-snooping biases. Of course, potential bias cannot be completely eliminated because the search domain of trading systems is still constrained to some degree in practice (Neely, Weller, and Dittmar[46]).

To avoid overfitting trading rules, Roberts uses two-year training and two-year selection periods beginning in 1980, with an out-of-sample period of 1984–2000. As an initial step, 20,000 random rules are generated and evolved based upon their fitness for a two-year trading period, and then the fittest rule is evaluated for another two-year selection period. If the fittest rule performs better than previously selected rules, it is saved for out-of-sample testing. Twenty optimizations are implemented over each set of training and selection periods to improve the quality of results, and the best rule from the 20 optimizations is evaluated in the out-of-sample test. The fitness criterion is the maximum net profit after subtracting transaction costs of

[45]Matthew C. Roberts, "Technical Analysis and Genetic Programming: Constructing and Testing a Commodity Portfolio," *Journal of Futures Markets* 25, no. 7 (May 2005), pp. 643–660.

[46]Christopher J. Neely, Paul A. Weller, and Rob Dittmar, "Is Technical Analysis Profitable in the Foreign Exchange Market? A Genetic Programming Approach," *Journal of Financial and Quantitative Analysis* 32, no. 4 (December 1997), pp. 405–426.

$100 per round-trip trade for training and selection, and $50 for out-of-sample tests. Results indicate that there is little evidence of profitability for genetically optimized trading rules in U.S. commodity futures markets. Trading rules generate statistically significant profits in only 2 of 24 markets when evaluated using data not available to the optimizing process. Returns are positive for only 7 of 13 agricultural futures contracts and just one contract, the pork belly futures contract, earns a statistically significant monthly mean net return. Among six metal and energy contracts, two have positive net returns but none of the average returns is statistically significant.

As summarized in Exhibit 40.2, six of nine modern studies find substantial evidence of technical trading profits in commodity markets. Given that a clear majority of studies report positive profits, it appears that commodity markets also are inefficient during the modern period (1988–2005). However, there is an interesting pattern in the results that should be considered before reaching a firm conclusion. Note that all studies with sample periods ending in the mid-1980s to the early 1990s, with the exception of Hamm and Brorsen, provide strong evidence of technical trading profits. In contrast, the two studies with samples ending in the late 1990s or 2000 show considerably less evidence of profits. Robert's results in this regard are particularly noteworthy. The pattern of results suggests that technical trading profits in commodity markets may have declined sharply during the 1990s. A similar pattern has been reported in recent studies of technical trading in stock and foreign exchange markets (Sullivan, Timmerman, and White[47] and Olson[48]).

EXPLANATIONS FOR TECHNICAL TRADING PROFITS

Previous empirical studies suggest that technical trading rules generate positive profits in at least some commodity markets. Various theoretical and empirical explanations have been proposed for observed technical trading profits. In theoretical models, technical trading profits may arise because of market "frictions," such as noise in current equilibrium prices, traders' sentiments, herding behavior, market power, or chaos. Empirical explanations focus on technical trading profits as a consequence of order flow, temporary market inefficiencies,

[47]Ryan Sullivan, Allan Timmermann, and Halbert White, "Data-Snooping, Technical Trading Rule Performance, and the Bootstrap," *Journal of Finance* 54, no. 5 (October 1999), pp. 1647–1691. Ryan Sullivan, Allan Timmermann, and Halbert White, "Forecast Evaluation with Shared Data Sets," *International Journal of Forecasting* 19, no. 2 (April 2003), pp. 217–227.

[48]Dennis Olson, "Have Trading Rule Profits in the Currency Markets Declined over Time?" *Journal of Banking and Finance* 28, no. 1 (January 2004), pp. 85–105.

Exhibit 40.2 Summary of Modern Technical Analysis Studies in Commodities Markets, 1988–2005

Study	Markets Considered/ Frequency of Data	In-Sample Period (Out-of-Sample Period)	Technical Trading Systems	Benchmark Strategies/ Optimization	Transaction Costs	Conclusion
1. Lukac, Brorsen, and Irwin (1988)	12 futures from various exchanges: agriculturals, metals, currencies, and interest rates/ Daily	1975–1983 (1978–1984)	12 systems (3 channels, 3 moving averages, 3 oscillators, 2 trailing stops, and a combination)	Zero mean profit/Optimized trading rules	\$50 and \$100 per round-trip	Out-of-sample results indicate that 4 of 12 systems generate significant aggregate portfolio net returns and 8 of the 12 commodities earn statistically significant net returns from more than one trading system. Mark, sugar, and corn markets appear to be most profitable during the sample period. In addition, Jensen test confirms that the same four trading systems having large net returns produce significant net returns above risk.
2. Lukac and Brorsen (1989)	15 futures from various exchanges: agricultural commodities, metals, currencies, and interest rates/ Daily	1965–1985 (various)	Channel and directional movement (both systems had 12 parameters ranging 5 days to 60 days in increments of 5)	Buy & hold/ Optimized trading rules	\$100 per round-trip	Technical trading rule profits are measured based on various optimization methods, which include 10 re-optimization strategies, one random strategy, and 12 fixed parameter strategies. The two trading systems generate portfolio mean net returns significantly greater than the B&H strategy. However, the trading systems yield similar profits across different optimization strategies and even different parameters. Thus, the parameter optimization appears to have little value.
3. Taylor and Tari (1989)	IMM currency futures: pound, mark, and Swiss franc; London agricultural futures: cocoa, coffee, and sugar/ Daily	1974–1978 (1979–1987); (1982–1985)	A statistical price-trend model	Buy & hold, Zero mean profit/Optimized trading rules	Currency futures: 0.2% per round-trip; Agricultural futures: 1%	During the out-of-sample period, 1979–1987, the trading rule earns aggregate mean net return of 4.3% per year for three currency futures. The mark is the most profitable contract (5.4% per year). From 1982–1985, the trading rule generates a mean net return of 4.8% for cocoa, –4.26% for coffee, and 18.8% for sugar, outperforming the B&H strategy for cocoa and sugar futures.

(Continued)

Exhibit 40.2 (Continued)

Study	Markets Considered/ Frequency of Data	In-Sample Period (Out-of-Sample Period)	Technical Trading Systems	Benchmark Strategies/ Optimization	Transaction Costs	Conclusion
4. Lukac and Brorsen (1990)	30 futures from various exchanges: agriculturals, metals, oils, currencies, interest rates, and S&P 500/ Daily	1975–1985 (1976–1986)	23 systems (channels, moving averages, oscillators, trailing stops, point and figure, a counter-trend, volatility, and combinations)	Zero mean profit/Optimized trading rules	\$50 and \$100 per round-trip	Only 3 of 23 trading systems have negative mean monthly portfolio net returns after transaction costs, and 7 of 23 systems generate net returns significantly above zero at 10% level. Most of the trading profits appear to be made over the 1979–1980 period. In the individual commodity markets, currency futures produce the highest returns, while livestock futures yield the lowest returns.
5. Silber (1994)	12 future markets: foreign currencies, short-term interest rates, metals, oil, and S&P 500/ Daily	1979 (1980–1991)	Moving average (short averages: 1 day to 15 days; long averages: 16 to 200 days)	Buy & hold (& roll over)/ Optimized trading rules	Bid-ask spread per round-trip (2 ticks for crude oil and gold; 1 tick for the rest of contracts)	After transaction costs, average annual net returns are positive for all contracts but gold, silver, and the S&P 500. In particular, most currency futures earn higher net profits (1.9%–9.8%). For those profitable markets, moving average rules beat the B&H strategy except for three-month Eurodollars. Test results using a Sharpe ratio criterion are similar. Hence, trading profits appear to be robust to transaction costs and risk. Central bank intervention is one of possible explanations for the trading profits.
6. Irwin, Zulauf, Gerlow, and Tinker (1997)	Futures contracts for soybean, soybean meal, and soybean oil/ Daily and Monthly	1974–1983 (1984–1988)	Channel (40 days), ARIMA (2,0,0) for soybean and ARIMA (1,0,1) for soybean mean and oil	Zero mean profits	Not adjusted	During the out-of-sample period, the channel system generates statistically significant mean returns ranging 5.1%–26.6% for all markets. The ARIMA models also produce statistically significantly positive returns (16.5%) for soybean meal, but significantly negative returns (−13.5.%) for soybeans. For every market, the channel system beats the ARIMA models.
7. Hamm and Brorsen (2000)	Futures contracts for Deutsche Mark and hard red winter wheat/Weekly	1981–1984 (1985–1992)	Trading rules based on feed forward neural network models	Optimized models	\$65 per round-trip	Trading rules based on the neural network model generally fail to produce significant gross or net returns during the out-of-sample period. Neural networks generate significant profits only for the mark contract in 1989, while none of the sample periods indicate significant profits for the wheat contract.

8. Boswijk, Griffioen, and Hommes (2000)	LIFFE and CSCE cocoa futures/ Daily	1983–1997	Moving average, channel, filter	Zero profits	0.1% per trade	A large set of 5,350 trading rules from the three popular trading systems are tested. For the LIFFE cocoa futures, 72% of the trading rules produce positive net excess returns. Most returns from the LIFFE contract are obtained during the 1983–1987 period in which about 30% of all trading rules appear to possess statistically significant forecasting power. In contrast, only 18% of all the trading rules generate positive net excess returns for the CSCE cocoa futures.
9. Roberts (2005)	24 U.S. futures markets/Daily	1980–1983 (1984–2000)	The best rule of the 20 rules optimized by genetic programming	Equity index returns/ Optimized trading rules	In-sample: $100 per round-trip; out-of-sample: $50	There is little evidence of profitability for genetically optimized trading rules in U.S. commodity futures markets. Seven of 13 agricultural markets have positive net returns, but only pork belly futures earn a statistically significant monthly mean net return. Among six metals and energies, two have positive net returns, but none are statistically significant.

Notes: Full citations for the studies are as follows: (1) Louis P. Lukac, B. Wade Brorsen, and Scott H. Irwin, "A Test of Futures Market Disequilibrium Using Twelve Different Technical Trading Systems," *Applied Economics* 20, no. 5 (May 1988), pp. 623–639. (2) Louis P. Lukac and B. Wade Brorsen, "The Usefulness of Historical Data in Selecting Parameters for Technical Trading Systems," *Journal of Futures Markets* 9, no. 1 (February 1989), pp. 55–65. (3) Stephen J. Taylor and Abdelkamel Tari, "Further Evidence against the Efficiency of Futures Markets," In Rui M.C. Guimaraes, Brian G. Kingsman and Stephen J. Taylor (eds.), *A Reappraisal of the Efficiency of Financial Markets* (Berlin: Springer-Verlag, 1989), pp. 578–601 (4) Louis P. Lukac and B. Wade Brorsen, "A Comprehensive Test of Futures Market Disequilibrium," *Financial Review* 25, no. 4 (November 1990), pp. 593–622. (5) William L. Silber, "Technical Trading: When It Works and When It Doesn't," *Journal of Derivatives* 1, no. 3 (Spring 1994), pp. 39–44. (6) Scott H. Irwin, Carl R. Zulauf, Mary E. Gerlow, and Jonathan N. Tinker, "A Performance Comparison of a Technical Trading System with ARIMA Models for Soybean Complex Prices," *Advances in Investment Analysis and Portfolio Management* 4 (November 1997), pp. 193–203. (7) Lonnie Hamm and B. Wade Brorsen, "Trading Futures Markets Based on Signals from a Neural Network," *Applied Economics Letters*, no. 2 (February 2000), pp. 137–140. (8) Peter Boswijk, Gerwin Griffioen, and Cars Hommes, "Success and Failure of Technical Trading Strategies in the Cocoa Futures Market," *Tinbergen Institute Discussion Paper* 7 (September 2000). (9) Matthew C. Roberts, "Technical Analysis and Genetic Programming: Constructing and Testing a Commodity Portfolio," *Journal of Futures Markets* 25, no. 7 (May 2005), pp. 643–660.

risk premiums, market microstructure deficiencies, or data-snooping. Although these issues are still controversial, a thorough discussion is necessary to better understand the current state of the literature on technical analysis.

Theoretical Explanations

Noisy Rational Expectations Models Under the standard model of market efficiency, the current equilibrium price fully reflects all available information and price adjusts instantaneously to new information. A basic assumption of the market efficiency model is that participants are rational and have homogeneous beliefs about information. Under a noisy rational expectations equilibrium, the current price does not fully reveal all available information because of noise (unobserved current supply of a risky asset or information quality) in the current equilibrium price. Thus, price shows a pattern of systematic slow adjustment to new information, thereby allowing the possibility of profitable trading opportunities.

Grossman and Stiglitz[49] represent the most influential work on noisy rational expectations equilibrium models. They demonstrate that no agent in a competitive market has an incentive to collect and analyze costly information if current price reflects all available information, and as a result the competitive market breaks down. However, Grossman and Stiglitz's model supports weak-form market efficiency in which no profits are made based on price history (i.e., technical analysis) because it is assumed that uninformed traders have rational expectations. In contrast, models developed by Hellwig,[50] Brown and Jennings,[51] Grundy and McNichols,[52] and Blume, Easley, and O'Hara[53] allow past prices to carry useful information for achieving positive profits in a speculative market.

---

[49]Sanford J. Grossman and Joseph E. Stiglitz, "Information and Competitive Price Systems," *American Economic Review* 66, no. 2 (May 1976), pp. 246–253; and Sanford J. Grossman and Joseph E. Stiglitz, "On the Impossibility of Informationally Efficient Markets," *American Economic Review* 70, no. 3 (June 1980), pp. 393–408.

[50]Martin Hellwig, "Rational Expectations Equilibrium with Conditioning on Past Prices: A Mean-Variance Example," *Journal of Economic Theory* 26, no. 2 (April 1982), pp. 279–312.

[51]David P. Brown and Robert H. Jennings, "On Technical Analysis," *Review of Financial Studies* 2, no. 4 (Winter 1989), pp. 527–551.

[52]Bruce D. Grundy and Maureen McNichols, "Trade and the Revelation of Information through Prices and Direct Disclosure," *Review of Financial Studies* 2, no. 4 (Winter 1989), pp. 495–526.

[53]Lawrence Blume, David Easley, and Maureen O'Hara, "Market Statistics and Technical Analysis: The Role of Volume," *Journal of Finance* 49, no. 1 (March 1994), pp. 153–181.

Brown and Jennings propose a two-period noisy rational expectations model in which the current price is dominated as an information source by a weighted average of past and current prices. More specifically, if the current price depends on noise (i.e., unobserved current supply of a risky asset) as well as private information of market participants, it cannot be a sufficient statistic for private information. Noise in the current equilibrium price does not allow full revelation of all publicly available information available in price histories. Therefore, past prices together with current prices enable investors to make more accurate inferences about past and present signals than do current prices alone.

As another example, Blume, Easley, and O'Hara propose an equilibrium model that emphasizes the informational role of volume. Unlike previous equilibrium models that consider the aggregate supply of a risky asset as the source of noise, their model assumes the source of noise is the quality of information. They show that volume provides information about the quality of traders' information that cannot be conveyed by prices, and thus, observing the price and the volume statistics together can be more informative than observing the price statistic alone. Technical analysis is valuable because current market statistics may be insufficient to reveal all information.

Behavioral Models In the early 1990s, financial economists began to develop the field of behavioral finance. There are two types of investors in a typical behavioral finance model: arbitrageurs (also called *sophisticated investors* or *smart money traders*) and noise traders (*feedback traders* or *liquidity traders*). Arbitrageurs are defined as investors who form fully rational expectations about security returns, while noise traders are investors who irrationally trade on noise as if it were information (Black[54]). Behavioral (or feedback) models are based on two key assumptions. First, noise traders' demand for risky assets is affected by irrational beliefs or sentiments that are not fully justified by news or fundamental factors. Second, arbitrage, defined as trading by fully rational investors not subject to sentiment, is risky and limited because arbitrageurs are likely to be risk-averse (Shleifer and Summers[55]).

Noise traders buy when prices rise and sell when prices fall, like technical traders or trend chasers. For example, when noise traders follow positive feedback strategies (buy when prices rise), this increases aggregate demand for an asset and results in a further price increase. Arbitrageurs may conclude that the asset is mis-priced and above its fundamental value, and

[54]Fisher Black, "Noise," *Journal of Finance* 41, no. 3 (July 1986), pp. 529–543.
[55]Andrei Shleifer and Lawrence H. Summers, "The Noise Trader Approach to Finance," *Journal of Economic Perspectives* 4, no. 2 (Spring 1990), pp. 19–33.

therefore sell it short. According to De Long et al.[56], however, this form of arbitrage is limited because it is always possible that the market will perform very well (fundamental risk) and that the asset will be even more overpriced by noise traders in the near future because they will become even more optimistic. As long as such risks are created by the unpredictability of noise traders' opinions, arbitrage by sophisticated investors will be reduced even in the absence of fundamental risk. A consequence is that sophisticated or rational investors do not fully counter the effects of the noise traders. Rather, it may be optimal for arbitrageurs to jump on the bandwagon themselves. Arbitrageurs optimally buy the asset that noise traders have purchased and sell much later when price rises even higher. Therefore, although arbitrageurs ultimately force prices to return to fundamental levels, in the short-run they amplify the effect of noise traders.

In feedback models, noise traders may be more aggressive than arbitrageurs due to overly optimistic (or overly pessimistic) views on markets, and thus bear more risk with associated higher expected returns. Despite excessive risk taking and consumption, noise traders may survive as a group in the long-run and dominate the market in terms of wealth. Hence, feedback models suggest that technical trading profits may be available even in the long-run if technical trading strategies (buy when prices rise and sell when prices fall) are based on noise or "popular models" and not on information such as news or fundamental factors.

Herding Models Froot, Scharfstein, and Stein[57] show that herding behavior of short-horizon traders can result in informational inefficiency. In their model, informed traders who want to buy or sell in the near future can benefit from their information only if it is subsequently impounded into the price by the trades of similarly informed speculators. Therefore, traders having short horizons will make profits when they can coordinate their trading based on the same or similar information. This kind of positive informational spillover can be so powerful that "herd" traders may even analyze information that is not closely related to the asset's long-run value. Technical analysis is one example.

[56]J. Bradford De Long, Andrei Shleifer, Lawrence H. Summers, and Robert J. Waldmann, "Noise Trader Risk in Financial Markets," *Journal of Political Economy* 98, no. 4 (August 1990), pp. 703–738; and J. Bradford De Long, Andrei Shleifer, Lawrence H. Summers, and Robert J. Waldmann, "Positive Feedback Investment Strategies and Destabilizing Rational Speculation," *Journal of Finance* 45, no. 2 (June 1990), pp. 379–395.

[57]Kenneth A. Froot, David S. Scharfstein, and Jeremy C. Stein, "Herd on the Street: Informational Inefficiencies in a Market with Short-Term Speculation," *Journal of Finance* 47, no. 4 (September 1992), pp. 1461–1484.

Froot, Scharfstein, and Stein (p. 1480) argue that, "the very fact that a large number of traders use chartist models may be enough to generate positive profits for those traders who already know how to chart. Even stronger, when such methods are popular, it is optimal for speculators to choose to chart."

Introducing a simple agent-based model for market price dynamics, Schmidt[58] shows that if technical traders are capable of affecting market liquidity, their concerted actions can move the market price in a direction favorable to their strategy. The model assumes a constant total number of traders consisting of "regular" traders and "technical" traders. Price moves linearly with excess demand, which in turn is proportional to the excess number of buyers drawn from both regular and technical traders. In the absence of technical traders, price dynamics form slowly decaying oscillations around an asymptotic value. However, inclusion of technical traders in the model increases the amplitude of price oscillations. The rationale behind this result is as follows: If technical traders believe price will fall, they sell, and thus, excess demand decreases. As a result, price decreases and the chartist component forces regular traders to sell. This leads price to decrease further until the fundamentalist priorities of regular traders become dominant again. The opposite situation occurs if technical traders make a buy decision based on their analysis.

Chaos Theory Clyde and Osier[59] provide another theoretical foundation for technical analysis by showing that charting methods may be equivalent to nonlinear forecasting methods for high dimension (or chaotic) systems. They tested this idea by applying the identification algorithm for a head-and-shoulders pattern to simulated high-dimension nonlinear price series. More specifically, the following two hypotheses were tested: (1) technical analysis has no more predictive power on nonlinear data than it does on random data; (2) when applied to nonlinear data, technical analysis earns no more hypothetical profits than those generated by a random trading rule. Results shows that hit ratios (proportion of positions with positive gross profits) exceed 0.50 in almost all cases. Moreover, profits of the head-and-shoulders pattern on the nonlinear data are higher than the median of those on the bootstrap simulated data in almost all cases. Thus, the first hypothesis is rejected. Hit ratio tests also reject the second hypothesis. Hence, technical analysis performs better on nonlinear data than on random data and generates more profits than a random trading rule.

---

[58]Anatoly B. Schmidt, "Why Technical Trading May Be Successful? A Lesson from the Agent-Based Modeling," *Physica A* 303, no. 1 (January 2002), pp. 185–188.

[59]William C. Clyde and Carol L. Osler, "Charting: Chaos Theory in Disguise?" *Journal of Futures Markets* 17, no. 5 (August 1997), pp. 489–514.

Empirical Explanations

Order Flow Osler[60] explains predictions of technical analysis in the foreign exchange market by order flows clustering at round numbers. Using stop-loss and take-profit orders placed at a large bank in three foreign exchange pairs (dollar-yen, dollar-U.K. pound, and eurodollar), two widely used predictions of technical analysis are examined: (1) downtrends (uptrends) tend to reverse course at predictable support (resistance) levels, which are often round numbers; and (2) trends tend to be unusually rapid after rates cross support and resistance levels that can be identified *ex ante*. Since others (e.g., Brock, Lakonishock, and LeBaron[61]) have shown that support and resistance levels (trading range break-out rules) possess predictive power in the stock market, these predictions may be applicable beyond the foreign exchange market.

Osler finds two critical asymmetries in the data that support the predictions of technical analysis. The first is that executed take-profit orders cluster more strongly at numbers ending in 00 than executed stop-loss orders. The second is that executed stop-loss buy (sell) orders are more strongly clustered just above (below) round numbers. According to Osler, clustering of order flows at round numbers is possible because (1) the use of round numbers reduces the time and errors incurred in the transaction process; (2) round numbers may be easier to remember and to manipulate mentally; and (3) people may simply prefer round numbers without any reasoning.

Kavajecz and Odders-White[62] provide a similar explanation for support and resistance levels by estimating limit order books in the stock market (i.e., NYSE) and analyzing the relation to support and resistance. Regression results show that support and resistance levels are positively and statistically significantly correlated with high cumulative depth, even after controlling for other current market conditions. In particular, technical indicator levels are statistically significant for 42% to 73% of the stocks when measures of cumulative depth in the limit order book such as mode and near-depth ratio are used as the dependent variable. Furthermore, the results of Granger causality tests and analyses on the flow of newly placed

[60]Carol L. Osler, "Currency Orders and Exchange Rate Dynamics: An Explanation for the Predictive Success of Technical Analysis," *Journal of Finance* 58, no. 5 (October 2003), pp. 1791–1819.

[61]Brock, Lakonishok, and LeBaron, "Simple Technical Trading Rules and the Stochastic Properties of Stock Returns."

[62]Kenneth A. Kavajecz and Elizabeth R. Odders-White, "Technical Analysis and Liquidity Provision," *Review of Financial Studies* 17, no. 4 (Winter 2004), pp. 1043–1071.

limit orders suggest that support and resistance levels tend to identify clusters of orders (high depth) already in place on the limit order book.

Kavajecz and Odders-White also show that buy (sell) signals of moving average rules, generated when the short moving average penetrates the long moving average from above (below), correspond to a shift in quoted prices toward sell-side (buy-side) liquidity levels and away from buy-side (sell-side) levels. That is, moving average signals appear to uncover information about the skewness of liquidity between the two sides of the limit order book. Hence, Kavajecz and Odders-White (p. 1066) conclude that, "the connection between technical analysis and limit order book depth is driven by technical analysis being able to identify prices with high cumulative depth already in place on the limit order book."

Temporary Market Inefficiencies Technical trading profits in commodity markets may be simply due to temporary market inefficiencies. There are two possible explanations for the temporary inefficiencies. The first is the self-destructive nature of technical trading rules. Timmermann and Granger[63] (p. 26) state that, "Ultimately, there are likely to be short-lived gains to the first users of new financial prediction methods. Once these methods become more widely used, their information may get incorporated into prices and they will cease to be successful." Several studies demonstrate that many of the well-known market anomalies in the stock market attenuate, disappear, or reverse after they are documented in the academic literature (e.g., Dimson and March,[64] Schwert,[65] and Marquering, Nisser, and Valla[66]). In the literature on technical trading rules, several prominent studies (e.g., Lukac, Brorsen, and Irwin[67] and Brock, Lakonishok, and LeBaron[68]), all of which document substantial technical

[63]Alan Timmermann and Clive W. J. Granger, "Efficient Market Hypothesis and Forecasting."

[64]Elroy Dimson and Paul Marsh, "Murphy's Law and Market Anomalies," *Journal of Portfolio Management* 25, no. 2 (Winter 1999), pp. 53–69.

[65]G. William Schwert, "Anomalies and Market Efficiency," Chapter 15 in George M. Constantinides, Milton Harris, and Rene M. Stulz (eds.), *Handbook of the Economics of Finance: Volume 1B, Financial Markets and Asset Pricing* (Amsterdam: North-Holland, 2003).

[66]Wessel Marquering, Johan Nisser, and Toni Valla, "Disappearing Anomalies: A Dynamic Analysis of the Persistence of Anomalies," *Applied Financial Economics* 16, no. 4 (February 2006), pp. 291–302.

[67]Lukac, Brorsen, and Irwin, "A Test of Futures Market Disequilibrium Using Twelve Different Technical Trading Systems."

[68]Brock, Lakonishok, and LeBaron, "Simple Technical Trading Rules and the Stochastic Properties of Stock Returns."

trading profits, were published during the mid-1980s and the early 1990s. In this context, an increase in the use of technical trading rules among investors and traders over the 1990s may have lowered or even eliminated profitable technical trading opportunities. The massive increase in hedge fund and CTA investment during the 1990s is consistent with this argument. Investment in CTAs (and other managed futures accounts) alone increased from about $7 billion at the beginning of the decade to over $40 billion at the end.[69]

The second possible explanation of temporary inefficiencies is structural change in markets. At a basic level, all technical trading rules depend on some form of sluggish reaction to new information as it enters the market. Structural changes in markets have the potential to alter the speed with which prices react to information and reach a new equilibrium. For example, cheaper computing power, the rise of electronic trading and advent of discount brokerage firms have probably lowered transaction costs and increased liquidity in many markets. These changes may have increased the speed of market price movements, and in turn, reduced the profitability of technical trading rules. Kidd and Brorsen[70] also argue that economy-wide changes such as freer trade, better economic predictions and fewer major shocks to the economy, lower price volatility, and the corresponding demand for technical speculators to move markets to equilibrium. In order to test this hypothesis, Kidd and Brorsen compute sample statistics for 17 futures markets across 1975–1990 and 1991–2001. Price volatility generally decreases across the two periods and kurtosis (extremeness) of price changes increases while markets are closed. The authors argue that both changes are consistent with a reduction in the profitability of technical analysis due to economy-wide structural changes.

Risk Premiums Positive technical trading profits may be compensation for bearing risk. Although a universally accepted model of risk is not available, the Sharpe ratio of excess returns to standard deviation has been widely used in studies of technical analysis as a risk-adjusted performance measure. To determine whether technical trading returns are abnormal on a

---

[69]The source for the data on CTA investment is the Barclay Group (http://www.barclaygrp.com/indices/cta/Money_Under_Management.html).

[70]Willis V. Kidd and B. Wade Brorsen, "Why Have the Returns to Technical Analysis Decreased?" *Journal of Economics and Business* 56, no. 3 (May-June 2004), pp. 159–176.

risk-adjusted basis, Sharpe ratios of technical trading rules are often compared to that of a benchmark strategy such as a buy-and-hold strategy. However, several studies find that technical trading rules generate higher Sharpe ratios than the benchmarks (e.g., Lukac and Brorsen[71]).

The *capital asset pricing model* (CAPM) provides another risk-adjusted performance measure. While most studies that have estimated risk-adjusted returns using the CAPM assume a constant risk premium over time, a few studies test whether technical trading returns can be explained by time-varying risk premiums. In the majority of studies, it turns out that a constant risk premium fails to explain technical trading returns. Results for time-varying premiums are mixed (e.g., Okunev and White[72] and Kho[73])

It should be noted that the above risk measures have several limitations. For example, the Sharpe ratio penalizes the variability of profitable returns exactly the same as the variability of losses, despite the fact that investors are more concerned about downside volatility in returns rather than total volatility, i.e., the standard deviation. The CAPM is also known to have a joint hypothesis problem. Namely, when abnormal returns (positive intercept) are found, researchers cannot differentiate whether markets are truly inefficient or the CAPM is misspecified.

Market Microstructure Deficiencies Technical trading rule profits can be exaggerated by using unrealistically low transaction costs and disregarding other market microstructure-related factors. Transaction costs generally consist of two components: (1) brokerage commissions and fees and (2) bid-ask spreads. Commissions and fees are readily observable, although they may vary according to investors (individuals, institutions, or market makers) and trade size. Data for bid-ask spreads (also known as execution costs, liquidity costs, or slippage costs), however, have not been widely available until recent years.

To account for the impact of the bid-ask spread on asset returns, various bid-ask spread estimators have been introduced by Roll,[74] Thompson

[71]Lukac and Brorsen, "A Comprehensive Test of Futures Market Disequilibrium."
[72]John Okunev and Derek White, "Do Momentum-Based Strategies Still Work in Foreign Exchange Markets?" *Journal of Financial and Quantitative Analysis* 38, no. 2 (June 2003), pp. 425–447.
[73]Bong-Chan Kho, "Time-Varying Risk Premia, Volatility, and Technical Trading Rule Profits: Evidence from Foreign Currency Futures Markets," *Journal of Financial Economics* 41, no. 2 (June 1996), pp. 249–290.
[74]Richard A. Roll, "Simple Implicit Measure of the Effective Bid-Ask Spread in an Efficient Market," *Journal of Finance* 39, no. 4 (September 1984), pp. 1127–1139.

and Waller,[75] and Smith and Whaley.[76] However, these estimators may not work particularly well in approximating actual bid-ask spreads if the assumptions underlying the estimators do not correspond to the actual market microstructure. Data on actual bid-ask spreads reflects true market-impact effects, or the effect of trade size on market price. Market-impact arises in the form of price concessions for large trades. The magnitude of market-impact depends on the liquidity and depth of a market. To date, only one study has directly estimated market impact (slippage) costs for technical traders. Greer, Brorsen, and Liu[77] examine the transactions of a commodity futures fund in the mid-1980s that uses trend-following technical systems to signal trades. They report that execution costs (slippage) average about $40 per trade, much larger than costs estimates based on statistical bid-ask estimators. In lieu of obtaining appropriate data sources regarding bid-ask spreads, plausible alternatives include the use of transaction costs greater than the actual historical commissions or assuming several possible scenarios for transaction costs.

Other market microstructure factors that may affect technical trading returns are non-synchronous trading and daily price limits. Technical trading studies typically assume that trades can be executed at closing prices on the day when trading signals are generated. However, Day and Wang[78] (p. 433) investigate the impact of non-synchronous trading on technical trading returns for the Dow Jones Industrial Average (DJIA) and argue that "if buy signals tend to occur when the closing level of the DJIA is less than the true index level, estimated profits will be overstated by the convergence of closing prices to their true values at the market open." This problem may be mitigated by using either the estimated "true" closing levels for asset prices or the next day's closing prices. In addition, price movements are occasionally locked at the daily allowable limits, particularly in futures

---

[75]Sarahelen R. Thompson and Mark L. Waller, "The Execution Cost of Trading in Commodity Futures Markets," *Food Research Institute Studies* 20, no. 2 (1987), pp. 141–163.

[76]Tom Smith and Robert E. Whaley, "Estimating the Effective Bid/Ask Spread from Time and Sales Data," *Journal of Futures Markets* 14, no. 4 (June 1994), pp. 437–455.

[77]Thomas V. Greer, B. Wade Brorsen, and Shi-Miin Liu, "Slippage Costs in Order Execution for a Public Futures Fund," *Review of Agricultural Economics* 14, no. 2 (July 1992), pp. 281–288.

[78]Theodore E. Day and Pingying Wang, "Dividends, Nonsynchronous Prices, and the Returns from Trading the Dow Jones Industrial Average," *Journal of Empirical Finance* 9, no. 4 (November 2002), pp. 431–454.

markets. Since trend-following trading rules typically generate buy (sell) signals in up (down) trends, the daily price limits generally imply that buy (sell) trades will be actually executed at higher (lower) prices than those at which trading signals were generated. This may result in seriously overstated trading returns if trades are assumed to be executed at the locked limit price levels.

Data-Snooping As noted earlier, studies that find positive technical trading returns have been challenged by subsequent studies because of apparent deficiencies in testing procedures. One of the most controversial issues is data-snooping. According to White[79] (p. 1097), "data-snooping occurs when a given set of data is used more than once for purposes of inference or model selection." When such data-snooping occurs, any successful results may be spurious because they could be obtained just by chance. More specifically, data-snooping results in overstated significance levels for conventional hypothesis tests, which can lead to incorrect statistical inference (e.g., Lovell,[80] Denton,[81] and Lo and MacKinlay[82]).

In testing technical trading rules, a fairly blatant form of data-snooping is an *ex post* and in-sample search for profitable trading rules, a distinctive feature of several early studies. Cooper and Gulen[83] suggest that more subtle forms of data-snooping arise when a set of data is repeatedly used to search for profitable choice variables, which in the present context include 'families' of trading systems, markets, in-sample estimation periods, out-of-sample periods, and trading model assumptions such as performance criteria and transaction costs. Therefore, even if a researcher optimizes trading rules in-sample and traces the out-of-sample performance of optimal rules, successful results may be obtained by deliberately investigating a number of combinations of in- and out-of-sample optimization periods and selecting the combination that provides the most favorable result. Prior selection of

[79]Halbert White, "A Reality Check for Data Snooping," *Econometrica* 68, no. 5 (September 2000), pp. 1097–1126.
[80]Michael C. Lovell, "Data Mining," *Review of Economics and Statistics* 65, no. 1 (February 1983), pp. 1–12.
[81]Frank T. Denton, "Data Mining as an Industry," *Review of Economics and Statistics* 67, no. 1 (February 1985), pp. 124–127.
[82]Andrew W. Lo and A. Craig MacKinlay, "Data Snooping Biases in Tests of Financial Asset Pricing Models," *Review of Financial Studies* 3, no. 3 (Fall 1990), pp. 431–467.
[83]Michael Cooper and Huseyin Gulen, "Is Time-Series Based Predictability Evidentin Real-Time?" *Journal of Business* 79, no. 3 (May 2006), pp. 1263–1292.

only one combination of in- and out-of-sample periods may be a safeguard, but this selection is also likely to be strongly affected by similar previous research.

A different form of data-snooping occurs when researchers consider only popular trading rules, as in Lukac, Brorsen, and Irwin.[84] Since Lukac, Brorsen, and Irwin's systems obtained their popularity over a long history they may be subject to survivorship bias. In other words, if a large number of trading rules have been investigated over time some rules may produce abnormal returns by chance even though they do not possess genuine forecasting power. Statistical inference based only on the surviving trading rules may cause a form of data-snooping bias because it does not account for the full set of initial trading rules, most of which are likely to have performed poorly (Sullivan, Timmerman, and White[85]).

Still another form of data-snooping is the application of a new search procedure, such as genetic programming or nearest neighbor neural networks, to sample periods before the development of the procedure. Cooper and Gulen argue that "it would be inappropriate to use a computer intensive genetic algorithm to uncover evidence of predictability before the algorithm or computer was available" (p. 7). Most genetic programming studies and non-linear optimization studies are subject to this problem.

CONCLUSION

A number of empirical studies examine the profitability of technical trading rules in commodity markets over the last four decades. In this survey, the empirical literature is categorized into two groups, early studies (1960–1987) and modern studies (1988–2005) depending on testing procedures. A majority of early technical trading studies in commodity markets find substantial net profits. However, early studies exhibit several limitations in their testing procedures. Only one or two trading systems are considered, risk of trading rules is often ignored, statistical tests of return significance generally are not conducted, parameter (trading rule) optimization and

[84]Lukac, Brorsen, and Irwin, "A Test of Futures Market Disequilibrium Using Twelve Different Technical Trading Systems."

[85]Sullivan, Timmermann, and White, "Data-Snooping, Technical Trading Rule Performance, and the Bootstrap"; Ryan Sullivan, Allan Timmermann, and Halbert White, "Dangers of Data Mining: The Case of Calendar Effects in Stock Returns," *Journal of Econometrics* 105, no. 1 (November 2001), pp. 249–286; and Sullivan, Timmermann, and White, "Forecast Evaluation with Shared Data Sets."

out-of-sample verification are not employed, and data-snooping problems are not given serious attention.

Modern studies improve upon the limitations of early studies and typically increase the number of trading systems tested, assess risks of trading rules, perform statistical tests with either conventional statistical tests or more sophisticated bootstrap methods, or both, and conduct parameter optimization and out-of-sample verification. Six of nine modern studies find substantial evidence of technical trading profits in commodity markets. There is a noteworthy pattern in the results of these studies. Nearly all of the studies with sample periods ending in the mid-1980s to the early 1990s provide strong evidence of technical trading profits. In contrast, the studies with samples ending in the late 1990s or 2000 show considerably less evidence of profits. This suggests that technical trading profits in commodity markets may have declined sharply during the 1990s. A similar pattern has been reported in recent studies of technical trading in stock and foreign exchange markets.

Positive technical trading profits can be explained by several theoretical models and/or empirical regularities. Noisy rational expectations equilibrium models, feedback models and herding models postulate that price adjusts sluggishly to new information due to noise in the market, traders' sentiments or herding behavior. Under chaos theory, technical analysis may be equivalent to a method for nonlinear prediction in a high dimension (or chaotic) system. Various empirical factors, such as clustering of order flows, temporary market inefficiencies, time-varying risk premiums, market micro-structure deficiencies, and data-snooping biases, have also been proposed as the source or explanation for technical trading profits.

Notwithstanding positive evidence about profitability, improved procedures for testing technical trading strategies, and plausible theoretical explanations, many academics still appear to be skeptical about technical trading rules. For example, in a textbook on asset pricing, Cochrane[86] argues that "Despite decades of dredging the data, and the popularity of media reports that purport to explain where markets are going, trading rules that reliably survive transactions costs and do not implicitly expose the investor to risk have not yet been reliably demonstrated" (p. 25). This statement suggests the skepticism is based on data-snooping problems and potentially insignificant economic profits after appropriate adjustment for transaction costs and risk.

[86]John H. Cochrane, *Asset Pricing* (Princeton, NJ: Princeton University Press, 2001).

There are two basic approaches to addressing the problem of data-snooping.[87] The first is to simply replicate a previous study on a new set of data. This approach is borrowed from the classical experimental approach to generating scientific evidence. That is, if similar results are found using new data and the same procedures as in the original study, more confidence can be placed in the original results.[88] For purposes of replication, the following three conditions should be satisfied: (1) the markets and trading systems tested in the original study should be comprehensive, in the sense that results can be considered broadly representative of the actual use of technical systems; (2) testing procedures must be carefully documented, so they can be "written in stone" at the point in time the study was published; and (3) the publication date of the original work should be sufficiently far in the past that a follow-up study can have a reasonable sample size. To date, no study has replicated earlier technical trading results in commodity markets on new data.

The second approach for dealing with data-snooping is White's bootstrap reality check methodology, which to date has not been applied in a study of technical trading in commodity markets. White's methodology provides "data-snooping adjusted" p-values for the best trading rule out of the full universe considered. Further research is needed using both the reality check and replication approaches in order to provide more conclusive evidence on the profitability of technical trading rules in commodity markets.

---

[87]Genetic programming can be considered a third approach to avoid data-snooping problems caused by *ex post* selection of technical trading rules, since genetic programming rules are chosen using price data available before the beginning of the test period. However, application of genetic programming to sample periods before the initial development of the procedure violates the market efficiency conditions proposed by Timmermann and Granger. That is, the set of forecasting models, estimation methods, and the search technology used to select the best (or a combination of best) forecasting model(s) at any point in time must have actually been available for use by market participants. In addition, trading rules formulated by genetic programming generally have a more complex structure than that of typical trading rules used by technical analysts. This suggests that the rules do not approximate real technical trading rules applied in practice.

[88]This statement strictly applies only to studies that replicate "old" results on "new" data for the same market(s). Numerous studies provide a form of replication by applying successful technical trading rules from one market to different markets over similar time periods. The independence of such results across studies is open to question because of the positive correlation of returns across many markets, i.e. U.S. and non-U.S. stock markets.

Treatment of risk and market microstructure issues also needs to be addressed in future studies. Risk is difficult to assess because each risk measure has its own limitations and all are subject to a joint hypothesis problem. The market microstructure issues of bid-ask spreads and non-synchronous trading need careful attention as well. The advent of large and detailed transactions databases should allow considerable progress to be made in addressing these problems. Future research should also incorporate accurate histories of daily price limits into technical trading models.

Finally, there remains a large and persistent gap between the views of many market participants and large numbers of academics about technical analysis. In their recent survey study, Gehrig and Menkhoff[89] (p. 3) state that, "According to our results, technical analysis dominates foreign exchange and most foreign exchange traders seem to be chartists now." Shiller[90] (p. 55) also recognized the gap in his early questionnaire survey work on the stock market crash of 1987, pointing out that, "Obviously, the popular models (the models that are used by the broad masses of economic actors to form their expectations) are not the same as those held by economists." He asserts that, "Once one accepts the difference, economic modeling cannot proceed without collecting data on the popular models themselves." While similar efforts have been made in several studies on the use of technical analysis in the foreign exchange market, few studies have directly surveyed technical traders in commodity markets. Moreover, popular models like technical analysis may differ across commodity markets and through time. Therefore, research is needed that directly elicits and analyzes the views and practices of technical traders in a broad cross-section of commodity markets. This would provide a much richer understanding of the actual use of technical trading strategies in real-world markets.

[89]Thomas Gehrig and Lukas Menkhoff, "Technical Analysis in Foreign Exchange—The Workhorse Gains Further Ground," Discussion Paper (University of Hannover, 2003).

[90]Robert J. Shiller, "Speculative Prices and Popular Models," *Journal of Economic Perspectives* 4, no. 2 (Spring 1990), pp. 55–65.

Index